THE

FOURTH ORD[illegible]

TRACTATES *SANHEDRIN*, *MA*[illegible]

AND *HORAIOT*

STUDIA JUDAICA

FORSCHUNGEN ZUR WISSENSCHAFT DES JUDENTUMS

BEGRÜNDET VON
E. L. EHRLICH

HERAUSGEGEBEN VON
G. STEMBERGER

BAND LI

DE GRUYTER

THE JERUSALEM TALMUD
תלמוד ירושלמי

FOURTH ORDER: NEZIQIN
סדר נזיקן
TRACTATES *SANHEDRIN*, *MAKKOT*,
AND *HORAIOT*
מסכתות סנהדרין מכות והוריות

EDITION, TRANSLATION, AND COMMENTARY

BY

HEINRICH W. GUGGENHEIMER

DE GRUYTER

ISBN 978-3-11-068070-6
e-ISBN (PDF) 978-3-11-021961-6

This volume is text- and page-identical with the hardback published in 2010.

Library of Congress Control Number: 2020942855

Bibliographic information published by the Deutsche Nationalbibliothek
The Deutsche Nationalbibliothek lists this publication in the
Deutsche Nationalbibliografie;
detailed bibliographic data are available on the Internet at http://dnb.dnb.de.

Printing and Binding: LSC Communications, United States

www.degruyter.com

Preface

The present volume is the twelfth in this series of the Jerusalem Talmud, the second in a three-volume edition, translation, and Commentary of the Fourth Order of this Talmud. The principles of the edition regarding text, vocalization, and Commentary have ben spelled out in detail in the Introduction to the first volume. The text in this volume is based on the manuscript text of the Yerushalmi edited by J. Sussman for the Academy of the Hebrew Language, Jerusalem 2001. The text essentially represents an outline, to be fleshed out by a teacher's explanation. The translation should mirror this slant; it should not endow the text with literary qualities which the original does not posses. In particular, the translation is not intended to stand separate from the Commentary.

The extensive Commentary is not based on emendations; where there is no evidence from manuscripts or early prints to correct evident scribal errors, the proposed correction is given in the Notes. As in the preceding volumes, for each paragraph the folio and line numbers of the Krotoschin edition are added. It should be remembered that these numbers may differ from the *editio princeps* by up to three lines. It seems to be important that a translation of the Yerushalmi be accompanied by the text, to enable the reader to compare the interpretation with other translations.

Unfortunately, the technical progress of computer systems combined with the ephemeral nature of magnetic storage media has made it impossible to continue using the multi-lingual word processor used for the previous volumes. The look of the pages therefore has changed. Since the new word processor allows for masoretic accents, biblical quotations are now given with the accents, except for words which differ (usually by *plene* spelling) from the masoretic texts. Since the quotes are part of oral tradition, the deviations in spelling are examples of substandard spelling, rather than changes in the text.

Again, I wish to thank my wife, Dr. Eva Guggenheimer, who acted as critic, style editor, proof reader, and expert on the Latin and Greek vocabulary. Her own notes on some possible Latin and Greek etymologies are identified by (E. G.).

I sincerely thank the staff of the Jewish Division of the New York Public Library for providing me with a copy of the Genizah text of Tractate *Makkot*.

Contents

Introduction to Tractates Sanhedrin and Makkot

The name *Sanhedrin* (Greek συνέδριον, "council") originally referred to the council of the High Priest as head of state. Talmudic tradition, which carefully obliterated all references to political institutions, turned the word into a name for the supreme judicial authority centered at the Temple. This reflects the reality of life under the last Hasmoneans, Herod and his successors, and the Roman governors before the Jewish revolt when the people essentially considered the political powers as alien forces irrelevant to private and religious lives. Whether this council, which for example set the calendar, was a generally accepted Jewish or a sectarian pharisaic institution is difficult to decide. By the time of the formulation of the Mishnah, under the Severan emperors, popular idealization of the past had turned the Synhedrion into a Supreme Court of 71 members, successor to Moses's Council[1], directing a full judicial system of courts of 23 members each, which eliminated the need for any political administration. In this popular remembrance, King David was imagined as head of the council, executing its decrees.

The greater part of Tractate *Sanhedrin* together with its appendix *Makkot* is devoted to the hypothetical construction of a system of criminal courts and rules of criminal justice. Neither the New Testament nor Josephus or any other contemporary ancient source give any indication that the full system ever was in actual use; the Ben Shetaḥ legend detailed in Chapter 6 indicates the same. The notice in the Talmudim that criminal jurisdiction was taken from the Jews 40 years before the destruction of the Temple refers to the jurisdiction of the political powers, not the pharisaic-rabbinic courts.

In the absence of a historical record, the theory is developed that procedural law may be disregarded in emergency situations[2], and only

1. *Num.* 11:16,17,245,25.
2. Cf. Chapter 6, Note 96.

emergency situations make it to the historical record. In addition, the Tractate institutes courts of three judges for civil matters. There one really considers two very different institutions: First, communal courts to adjudicate both matters of personal status and of civil disputes. These are considered only implicitly in the Tractate; their development is Babylonian, in particular from Gaonic Babylonia where each Jewish community had a court subject to the supervision of one of the great Yeshivot. We do not know the exact meaning of ordination and the title "Rebbi" expressing ordination in the 150 years between its introduction at Jabneh and the formulation of the Mishnah. But in Mishnaic and later Talmudic times, this title and the corresponding Babylonian title "Rav" designated a person competent to act as communal judge with powers of compelling attendance, in Palestine in matters of personal status and in Babylonia in all intra-communal matters[3].

While one may assume that these courts developed their own formal procedures, there is little evidence of their procedural law in any of the Talmudim. This makes it difficult for rabbinic courts to function in a modern world unless they develop their own written procedures as happened with the system of rabbinic courts in Israel. The other aspect, panels of arbitration, is more prominent and better developed, reflecting the actual situation in Mishnaic and Talmudic times, and is in continuous use since Talmudic times, amply documented in the Responsa literature.

The first Chapter mainly determines the competence of each court, whether of 3, 23, or 71 members. Since one of the competences of a court of three members is fixing the calendar (Halakhah 2), and this competence essentially determined the status of the Patriarch in Mishnaic times, the prerogative of the Patriarch's court and his power of ordination, i. e., appointing judges, are detailed in Halakhah 2. The later Halakhot clearly are an attempt to project the Mishnaic theory into the situation of the First Commonwealth.

The second Chapter discusses first the status of the High Priest as a consequence of the biblical restrictions imposed on him. This is followed by

3. Cf. *Gittin* 4:2 Note 17, the Introduction to Tractate *Neziqin* (pp. 4-5) and in the following, 3:10.

similar rules regarding the King. The first part of these rules clearly refers to the non-Davidic Kings of the Second Commonwealth who considered themselves to be above the law and who, therefore, are considered unfit to administer justice. Later Mishnaiot (5,6) and the corresponding Halakhot again are an attempt to describe First Commonwealth situations.

The first part of the third Chapter takes up the constitutions of panels of arbitration. These are supposed to render binding verdicts; committees to work out compromises may have an even number of members. The basic rule is that each party appoint one judge, subject to rules of eligibility. The two then together choose an independent third member. A party may also choose to bring the case before a local permanent rabbinic court. If one tries to bring the matter before a far-away court of higher standing, he can be forced to go before the local court who then has to present written protocols to the far-away authority for final determination. This rule turned out to be a very efficient way to guarantee the functioning of communal courts or panels of arbitration in the absence of any official courts of appeal but a general possibility of submitting a case to a recognized authority[4]. It has been suggested that the disappearance of government-sanctioned courts can be dated to the appearance of the ban (נִדּוּי, חֵרֶם) as a way of enforcing religious discipline, probably starting from the time of Simeon ben Šetaḥ. Therefore, the ban in its forms and rules is not treated in Sanhedrin.

Persons can be disqualified as judges or witnesses either because they are relatives of one of the parties (Halakhah 7), or because they are convicted felons (a biblical disqualification), or because their honesty is suspect since they earn their livelihood dishonestly (a rabbinic disqualification, Halakhah 6). This leads to a digression about the observance of the (today purely rabbinic) institution of the Sabbatical year and the parameters of the obligation to prefer martyrdom to breaking biblical law under Gentile oppression.

The second part of the Chapter discusses the interrogation of witnesses, mostly in criminal cases. The biblical decree that a verdict must be based on the testimony of two witnesses calls for rules about how two witnesses for the

4. Chapter 3, Note 13.

same circumstance are treated and how "same circumstance" is defined. In addition the Halakhah states that eavesdropping evidence in general is rejected (it is admitted as a great exception in a charge of missionary activity for idolatry.) The Chapter ends with the possibility of asking for a retrial in a civil suit if new evidence is uncovered. There is no provision for a superior appeals court.

The Fourth Chapter starts by emphasizing the differences between criminal and civil trials. Civil cases are decided by a simple majority of the judges; criminal convictions need a qualified majority. Since it is emphasized that criminal trials need a detailed written report of all proceedings, one may infer that such a report is not needed in civil cases. In criminal cases, the most junior judges are polled first about their verdict, to avoid them being influenced by the opinions of their senior colleagues.

The final part of the Chapter treats the interrogation of witnesses. Oaths are admitted in rabbinic courts only by parties to civil suits, either to deny or to affirm monetary claims. Witnesses testify without oaths; therefore, judicial admonitions about the importance of testimony and the severity of the crime of perjury are absolutely necessary.

Chapter five is devoted to the details of procedure in criminal cases; in particular the difference between facts that must be determined without ambiguity (the identity of persons, place, and date of the crime) and those where discrepancies between testimonies might be reconciled by judicial arguments. The main rule in such cases is that criminal intent can be proven only by testimony of two witnesses to the effect that the accused was warned not to commit the crime just before he actually committed it. This practically excludes convictions by biblical standards and turns the long list of death penalties in the Pentateuch into lists of sins which might deprive the unrepentant sinner of his part in the Future World.

Chapter six is devoted to the (hypothetical?) details of the stoning procedure, in particular the convict's confession before execution which assures him of being admitted to Paradise. This indicates that the Chapters to the end of the Tractate should be read as theological treatises and pleadings against the imposition of any death penalty. In addition, the Chapter contains the Simeon ben Šeṭah legend (which most historians accept at face value) and a shortened version of the Gibeonite story from *Qiddušin* 4:1.

Chapter seven starts with a systematic description of the death penalties prescribed in the biblical text: stoning, burning (which is explained as not burning), decapitation, and an unspecified death penalty which is identified as strangling. Just as a conviction needs two separate testimonies about warning and action, so a prohibition must be mentioned twice in the biblical text, once for the prohibition and once for determination of the penalty. This leads to a discussion of a number of hermeneutical principles needed for the understanding of the biblical text. The second part of the Chapter is devoted to discussion of crimes connected with idolatry, such as Moloch worship and sorcery.

Chapter eight is devoted to the rules of the deviant and rebellious son[5], a case which in the opinion of the Babli never happened in practice. On a more practical level, it also discusses the rules by which one may protect one's house by killing a stealthy intruder[6].

Chapter nine discusses the cases punishable by "burning", mostly of incest, and by decapitating, of murder. In addition, it is recognized that dangerous criminals who clearly cannot be sentenced to death by biblical standards must be kept in jail even though there is no biblical sanction for jail sentences.

The first part of Chapter ten (in most Babli sources Chapter eleven) asserts that all of Israel, including those who committed deadly sins, have part in the Future World. The Mishnah quotes exceptions to this rule; all of these are refuted in the Halakhah. The only persons excluded are those who deny the existence of a Future World and probably those who die unrepentant. Even people guilty of capital crimes have part in the Future World. This certainly holds for those executed for their crimes (Chapter 6:3) but also for those who confess on their death bed. This denies part in the Future World to evildoers who die suddenly and painlessly. Rabbinic Judaism (except for some Medieval aberrations) always rejected systematic theology. This Chapter is

5. *Deut.* 21:21.
6. *Ex.* 22:1.

the closest approximation one has to such a theology and its theodicy as fas as is possible in a world of thought based on aphorisms[7]. In this setting, Aramaic texts are sermon concepts, homiletics. Hebrew texts should be considered as serious theological arguments.

The second part of the Chapter deals with the detailed rules for destroying a town which publicly adopts idolatry[8], a case that in all likelihood never happened.

The eleventh Chapter returns to the topics of Chapters seven to nine in discussing the death penalty cases in which the biblical text does not specify the method of execution, which by rabbinic tradition means execution by strangulation. One topic is that of the lower court judge who disregards the decision of the High Court[9]. This does not establish the High Court as an appeals instance but requires that differences of opinions in lower courts, acting as judges and jury, be brought to the High Court *before* verdict is rendered[4].

The last Mishnah of the Chapter introduces the topic of the first Chapter of *Makkot*. In the Babli, the Savoraic introduction to *Makkot* clearly states that it is a separate Tractate following *Sanhedrin*. The Genizah text of *Makkot* and some ancient references treat *Makkot* as *Sanhedrin*, Chapters Twelve to Fourteen. Since it is good Mishnaic style to introduce a change of topic in the middle of a Chapter, the fact that the last Chapter of *Sanhedrin* in the Leiden ms. introduces the topic of the first Chapter of *Makkot* indicates that the separation of the text into two Tractates is due to the influence of the Babli.

Biblical law requires that a perjured witness be subject to the penalty which would have been imposed on the accused had his testimony been true[10]. But there are cases in which this cannot be done. The case treated in *Sanhedrin* is that of an adulterous daughter of a Cohen. The adulteress cannot be convicted unless the adulterer also be convicted. But the adulterer's penalty is strangulation while the adulteress's is burning which is more severe

7. Cf. H. Guggenheimer, *Die dialektische Philosophie im Thalmud*, Proceedings of the XIth International Congress of Philosophy, Bruxelles 1953, vol. XII, pp. 190-194.
8. *Deut.* 13:13-19
9. *Deut.* 17:8-12.
10. *Deut.* 19:18-21.

than strangulation. The perjured witness can be sentenced to the adulterer's penalty, but not the adulteress's.

The first Chapter of *Makkot* (*Sanhedrin* 12) deals with cases in which the prospective penalty awaiting the accused cannot be imposed on the perjured witness; then the perjurers are whipped. The main example are two witnesses who accuse a Cohen of being desecrated as son of a woman forbidden to his father. If the accusation stands, the man is stripped of his priestly status and all his descendants also are desecrated[11]. If the perjured accusers are not priests, they cannot be declared desecrated. But even if the accusers are priests, it is impossible to declare them desecrated since there is no reason to declare their children as desecrated but qualified priests cannot be children of disqualified ones. In all such cases, the perjured accusers are whipped.

Chapter two (Sanhedrin 13) treats the rules of exile for the homicide and the cities of refuge[12]. The treatment implies that actual vendetta killings for homicide were no longer considered real possibilities. What in the Bible is protection against clan vendetta becomes a very restricted form of punishment.

In the Leiden ms., Chapter Three (Sanhedrin 14) has only the Mishnah. The Genizah text has a theologically important homiletic Halakhah to the last Mishnah, the existence of which was deduced by S. Lieberman[13] from early Medieval quotes long before the Genizah text was identified.

---

11. Since his daughters may legally marry Israel husbands, their sons will be Israel without any disabilities; Mishnah *Qiddušin* 3:14.
12. *Num.* 35:9-34; *Deut.* 19:1-10.
13. *Tarbiz* 5 (5694), pp. 109-110.

דיני ממונות פרק ראשון

משנה א: דִּינֵי מָמוֹנוֹת בִּשְׁלֹשָׁה גְּזֵלוֹת וַחֲבָלוֹת בִּשְׁלֹשָׁה נֶזֶק וַחֲצִי נֶזֶק תַּשְׁלוּמֵי כֶפֶל וְתַשְׁלוּמֵי אַרְבָּעָה וַחֲמִשָּׁה. הָאוֹנֵס וְהַמְפַתֶּה וְהַמּוֹצִיא שֵׁם רַע בִּשְׁלֹשָׁה דִּבְרֵי רַבִּי מֵאִיר וַחֲכָמִים אוֹמְרִים הַמּוֹצִיא שֵׁם רַע בְּעֶשְׂרִים וּשְׁלֹשָׁה שֶׁיֵּשׁ בּוֹ דִינֵי נְפָשׁוֹת.

Mishnah 1: Money matters[1] are judged by three [judges]; robberies[2] and injuries[3] by three [judges], damages[4], half damages[5], double restitution[6] quadruple and quintuple restitution. The rapist[7], the seducer[8], and the calumniator[9] are judged by three [judges], the words of Rebbi Meïr; but the Sages say that the calumniator is judged by 23 because it might be a capital case[10].

1 Not only litigation involving loans, inheritances, gifts, or real estate, but also distribution of public funds (cf. Mishnah *Peah* 8:7).

2 Including fraud.

3 Inflicted on humans.

4 Caused on living or inanimate property.

5 Caused by somebody's animals (cf. Mishnaiot *Bava qamma* 1:4-5).

6 To be paid by the thief of inanimate objects, Mishnah *Bava qamma* 7:1. The thief of livestock pays quadruple or quintuple restitution.

7 Who has to pay under four different categories (Mishnah *Ketubot* 4:1).

8 Who has to pay under three different categories.

9 Who accuses his wife not to have been a virgin (*Deut.* 22:13-19).

10 Since the woman is stoned if the husband's accusation is proved correct (*Deut.* 22:20-21) and the biblical text implies that the court which might sentence the husband to a fine is the one which might pass a death sentence, the case has to be tried in a tribunal empowered to try capital cases.

According to rabbinic principles, *Deut.* 22:13-21 cannot refer to a husband accusing his wife of not being a virgin since 1° by marriage, the husband became his wife's relative and relatives are barred from appearing as witnesses; his case could not be heard. 2° there is no verse threatening a woman with death if she married when not a virgin. Therefore, the rabbinic interpretation of the paragraph is that the husband presents witnesses to the fact that his wife committed adultery while preliminarily married to him. A preliminarily married woman is married in respect to criminal but not civil law (cf. Introduction to Tractate *Qiddušin*).

Another aspect of criminal law in this case is the law of perjury, *Deut.* 19:18-19. Since the husband's witnesses intended to have the woman stoned, if they are shown to be perjured they themselves are stoned. Therefore, the case may be heard only in a court competent to impose death sentences.

(18a line 21) **הלכה א**: דִּינֵי מָמוֹנוֹת בִּשְׁלֹשָׁה כול'. מְנָן תֵּיתֵי לֵיהּ. וְהָיוּ אֵלֶּה לָכֶם לְחֻקַּת מִשְׁפָּט. הָיִיתִי אוֹמֵר. אֶחָד דִּינֵי מָמוֹנוֹת וְאֶחָד דִּינֵי נְפָשׁוֹת בִּדְרִישָׁה וּבַחֲקִירָה.

וּמְנַיִין לְדִינֵי מָמוֹנוֹת שֶׁהֵן בִּשְׁלֹשָׁה. וְנִקְרַב בַּעַל־הַבַּיִת אֶל־הָאֱלֹהִים רִיבָה בָהּ דַּיָּין אֶחָד. עַד הָאֱלֹהִים הֲרֵי שְׁנַיִם. אֲשֶׁר יַרְשִׁיעוּן אֱלֹהִים הֲרֵי כָּאן שְׁלֹשָׁה. דִּבְרֵי רִבִּי יֹאשִׁיָּה. רִבִּי יוֹנָתָן אָמַר. הָרִאשׁוֹן תְּחִלָּה נֶאֱמַר וְאֵין דּוֹרְשִׁין תְּחִילּוֹת. אֶלָּא עַד הָאֱלֹהִים הֲרֵי אֶחָד. אֲשֶׁר יַרְשִׁיעוּן אֱלֹהִים הֲרֵי שְׁנַיִם. אֵין בֵּית דִּין שָׁקוּל מוֹסִיפִין עֲלֵיהֶן עוֹד אֶחָד. הֲרֵי שְׁלֹשָׁה.

רִבִּי אוֹמֵר. בִּשְׁנַיִם הַכָּתוּב מְדַבֵּר. אַתָּה אוֹמֵר בִּשְׁנַיִם אוֹ אֵינוֹ אֶלָּא בְּאֶחָד. כְּשֶׁהוּא אוֹמֵר אֲשֶׁר יַרְשִׁיעֻן אֱלֹהִים אֵין כָּתוּב כָּאן אֶלָּא אֲשֶׁר יַרְשִׁיעוּן אֱלֹהִים. אֵין בֵּית דִּין שָׁקוּל מוֹסִיפִין עֲלֵיהֶן עוֹד אֶחָד. הֲרֵי שְׁלֹשָׁה.

Halakhah 1: "Money matters are judged by three [judges]," etc. From where comes this? *These shall be the laws of procedure to you,*[11] I would say that both civil cases and criminal cases are subject to the rules of verification and examination[12].

[13]From where that civil cases are heard by three [judges]? *The owner shall go to the judge,*[14] he added here one judge. *Before the judge,*[15] these are two. *Whom the judges will find guilty*, these are three[16], the words of Rebbi Joshia. Rebbi Jonathan said, the first mention introduces the subject; one does not infer anything from introductions[17]. But *before the judge,* there is one. *Whom the judges will find guilty,* there are two. No court may be even-numbered,[18] so one adds another one; this makes three.

Rebbi said, the verse speaks about two. You say about two, or maybe it is only about one? What He said, it is not written "whom the judge will find guilty" but *whom the judges will find guilty.*[19] No court may be even-numbered, so one adds another one; this makes three.

11 *Num.* 35:29. The chapter covers the rules of levitic cities, laws of property, and of the homicide, criminal law.

12 Mishnah 4:1. *Examination* refers to cross-examination relating to questions which answer to "who", "when", and "where". *Interrogation* refers to answers to

"how". The distinction between the two is in regard to rules about discrepancies in testimony between different witnesses, Mishnah 5:1. The verse makes it clear that the rules also apply to lawsuits about subjects not covered by the detailed list in the Mishnah.

13 Babli 3b.

14 *Ex.* 22:7.

15 *Ex.* 22:8.

16 Since the paragraph mentions *judge* three times.

17 This is a generally accepted principle (Babli *loc. cit.*). The expression which introduces a subject always is necessary and cannot be considered additional or extraneous to the subject at hand.

18 The duty of the court is to decide matters based on incomplete information. The possibility of a deadlock would defeat the purpose for which the court was convened. Therefore, no court may be even-numbered. If any of the judges did abstain from voting, the case would have to be tried anew with another judge substituting for the abstaining judge.

19 The plural in this sentence alone implies that at least two judges are involved.

(18a line 31) רִבִּי אַבָּהוּ בָּעֵי. וּכְרִבִּי דִּינֵי מָמוֹנוֹת בַּחֲמִשָּׁה וְשֶׁיִּגָּמֵר בְּכ"ג. אַשְׁכַּח תַּנֵּי רִבִּי חִזְקִיָּה. הוֹאִיל וְאָֽמְרָה תוֹרָה. הֲרוֹג עַל פִּי מַטִּים הֲרוֹג עַל פִּי עֵדִים. מַה עֵדִים שְׁנַיִם אַף מַטִּים שְׁנַיִם. אֵין בֵּית דִּין שָׁקוּל מוֹסִיפִין עֲלֵיהֶן אַחֵר. הֲרֵי חֲמִשָּׁה.

Rebbi Abbahu asked. According to Rebbi[20], should not civil suits be heard by five; should sentence not be passed by 23[21]? It was found stated by (Rebbi)[22] Ḥizqiah: Since the Torah said, kill by a vote of the majority[23], kill by the testimony of witnesses. Since witnesses must be two[24], a majority also must be two[25]. No court can be even-numbered; one adds another one. This makes five.

20 Who in Tosephta 1:1 requires five judges to hear civil cases.

21 Rebbi probably also will agree that common practice was to hear cases by a panel of three judges. If one already deviates from traditional practice, should not *Num.* 35:29 be interpreted as requiring identical procedural law for both civil and criminal cases?

22 Probably one should read דבי instead of (רבי) ר' and translate "the House of Ḥizqiah," referring to one of the twin sons of the Elder Rebbi Ḥiyya, known as the last person who formulated *baraitot.* The fourth generation *Rebbi* Ḥizqiah would be much too late. The *baraita* is found in both *Mekhiltot* (dR. Ismael, ed. Horovitz-Rabin p. 323, dR. Simeon ben Iohai ed. Epstein-Melamed p. 214.)

23 Majority rule for judicial sentences is introduced in *Ex.* 23:2: "to bend after the many." The same verse forbids a guilty verdict by a simple majority: "Do not follow the majority in bad things." Since the plural used for "many" implies at least two, it

follows that a guilty verdict by a majority of one is an acquittal, while by a majority of two it is a guilty verdict.

24 Since unanimity is not required, the court would have to be composed of at least 4, hence 5, members. The majority accepts this interpretation of *Ex.* 23:2 for criminal cases only.

(18a line 35) לֹא הֵן גְּזֵילוֹת הֵן חֲבָלוֹת. אַשְׁכָּח תַּנֵּי רִבִּי שִׁמְעוֹן בֶּן יוֹחַי. וְאֵ֫לֶּה הַמִּשְׁפָּטִים אֲשֶׁר תָּשִׂים לִפְנֵיהֶם. אֲתַא מֵימַר לָךְ כִּפְשׁוּטָהּ דִּקְרִייָא. וַתְיָיא כְּרִבִּי יוֹסֵי בַּר חֲלַפְתָּא.

רִבִּי יוֹסֵי בַּר חֲלַפְתָּא אֲתוֹן תְּרֵין בַּר נַשׁ מֵידוֹן קוֹמוֹי. אָמְרֵי לֵיהּ. עַל מְנָת שֶׁתְּדִינֵנוּ דִין תּוֹרָה. אֲמַר לוֹן. אֲנִי אֵינִי יוֹדֵעַ דִּין תּוֹרָה אֶלָּא הַיּוֹדֵעַ מַחֲשָׁבוֹת יִפְרַע מֵאוֹתָן הָאֲנָשִׁים. מְקַבְּלִין עֲלֵיכוֹן מַה דַּנָּא אֲמַר לְכוֹן.

רִבִּי עֲקִיבָה כַּד הֲוָה בַּר נַשׁ אֲזַל בָּעֵי מֵידוֹן קוֹמֵיהּ הֲוָה אֲמַר לֵיהּ. הֱווּ יוֹדְעִין לִפְנֵי מִי אַתֶּם עוֹמְדִין. לִפְנֵי מִי שֶׁאָמַר וְהָיָה הָעוֹלָם. שֶׁנֶּאֱמַר וְעָמְדוּ שְׁנֵי־הָאֲנָשִׁים אֲשֶׁר־לָהֶם הָרִיב לִפְנֵי יי. וְלֹא לִפְנֵי עֲקִיבָה בֶּן יוֹסֵף.

תַּנֵּי. קוֹדֶם לְאַרְבָּעִים שָׁנָה עַד שֶׁלֹּא חָרֵב הַבַּיִת נִיטְלוּ דִינֵי נְפָשׁוֹת וּבִימֵי שִׁמְעוֹן בֶּן שֶׁטַח נִיטְלוּ דִינֵי מָמוֹנוֹת. אָמַר רִבִּי שִׁמְעוֹן בֶּן יוֹחַי. בְּרִיךְ רַחֲמָנָא דְּלֵי נָא חֲכִים מֵידוֹן.

Do not robberies and injuries fall under the same rules[26]? It was found that Rebbi Simeon ben Iohai stated: *These are the procedures which you shall put before them.* It serves to explain to you the plain sense of the verse[27]. This follows Rebbi Yose bar Halaphta.

Rebbi Yose bar Halaphta, when two people came before him for judgment and told him, "on condition that you judge us by the law of the Torah," told them, "the law of the Torah I do not know[28], but He Who knows thoughts should collect from those people[29]. You have to accept what I shall tell you."

When a person came to Rebbi Aqiba to have a suit decided before him, he told him: "You should know before Whom you are standing, before Him Who commanded and the world came into existence, as it is said: *The two people who are quarrelling shall stand before the Eternal,*[30] not before Aqiba ben Joseph."

It was stated[31]: Forty years before the Temple was destroyed, criminal jurisdiction was removed from Israel[32], and in the days of Simeon ben (Šetah)[33] civil jurisdiction was removed. Rebbi Simeon ben Iohai said, praised be the Merciful[34], for I am not intelligent enough to judge [35].

26 The same question is asked in the Babli, 2b. In contrast to the Babli, here it is understood that torts do not necessarily follow the same rules as disputes over money, and it is not obvious that a panel of three judges would be sufficient for these.

27 *Ex.* 21:1. As in *Ex.* 21-23, pure money matters are treated first, then torts. The order of the Mishnah follows the order of topics in these chapters.

28 He knew the theoretical law of the Torah but not necessarily the application to the case before him, since that would have presumed perfect and complete information. But the judge, by biblical decree, is dependent on what is told him in court. The information given to him by necessity is incomplete.

29 Who either lie in court or withhold information.

30 *Deut.* 19:17. The verse continues: "before the priests and the judges."

31 The correct version of this *baraita* is in 7:2; the first part is also quoted in the Babli, *Šabbat* 15a. The second part never applied in Babylonia.

32 When Judea came under direct Roman rule.

33 One has to read with 7:2: Simeon ben Iohai, as confirmed by the next sentence. The removal of civil cases to Roman courts cannot be dated to the reign of Alexander Yannai, Simeon ben Shetah's brother-in-law, but to Hadrian, in the aftermath of the war of bar Kokhba.

34 For preventing me to have to act as a judge.

35 From his time on, rabbinic jurisdiction in Palestine was limited to courts of arbitration which are not representatives of God and therefore under less pressure to render absolutely correct judgment.

(18a line 46) שְׁמוּאֵל אָמַר. שְׁנַיִם שֶׁדָּנוּ דִּינֵיהֶן דִּין אֶלָּא שֶׁנִּקְרְאוּ בֵּית דִּין חָצוּף. רִבִּי יוֹחָנָן וְרֵישׁ לָקִישׁ תְּרֵיהוֹן מָרִין. אֲפִילוּ שְׁנַיִם שֶׁדָּנוּ אֵין דִּינֵיהֶן דִּין. תַּמָּן תַּנִּינָן. הָיָה דָן אֶת הַדִּין. זִיכֶּה אֶת הַחַיָּיב חִייֵב לַזַּכַּאי. טִמֵּא לַטָּהוֹר טִיהֵר לַטָּמֵא. מַה שֶׁעָשָׂה עָשׂוּי וִישַׁלֵּם מִבֵּיתוֹ. רִבִּי בָּא בְשֵׁם רִבִּי אַבָּהוּ. בְּשֶׁאָמְרוּ לוֹ. הֲרֵי אַתְּ מְקוּבָּל עָלֵינוּ כִשְׁנַיִם. מָה אֲנָן קַיָּימִין. אִם בְּשֶׁטָּעָה וְדָנָן מִשִּׁיקּוּל הַדַּעַת. בְּדָא מַה שֶׁעָשָׂה עָשׂוּי. אִם בְּשֶׁטָּעָה וְדָנָן דִּין תּוֹרָה. בְּדָא יְשַׁלֵּם מִבֵּיתוֹ. רִבִּי בָּא בְשֵׁם רִבִּי אַבָּהוּ. בְּשֶׁאָמְרוּ לוֹ. הֲרֵי אַתְּ מְקוּבָּל עָלֵינוּ כִשְׁלֹשָׁה עַל מְנָת שֶׁתְּדִינוּנוּ דִּין תּוֹרָה. וְטָעָה וְדָנָן מִשִּׁיקּוּל הַדַּעַת. מַה שֶׁעָשָׂה עָשׂוּי. מִפְּנֵי שֶׁטָּעָה וְדָנָן מִשִּׁיקּוּל הַדַּעַת. יְשַׁלֵּם מִבֵּיתוֹ. שֶׁהִגִּיס דַּעְתּוֹ לָדוּן יְחִידִי דִּין תּוֹרָה. דְּתַנִּינָן. אַל תְּהִי דָן יְחִידִי. שֶׁאֵין דָּן יָחִיד אֶלָּא אֶחָד.

Samuel said, if two men acted as judges, their judgment stands, but they are called an insolent court[36]. Rebbi Johanan and Rebbi Simeon ben Laqish both are instructing: Even[37] if two men acted as judges, their judgment is no judgment[38]. There, we have stated[39]: "If he rendered judgment, acquitted the guilty and condemned the innocent, declared the pure impure or the impure pure, what he did is done but he has to pay from his own pocket." Rebbi

Abba in the name of Rebbi Abbahu: if they told him, we accept you as if you were two[40]. What are we dealing with? If his error was that he judged them on his discretion[41], then what he did is done. If his error was that he judged them by Torah law[42], why should he pay from his own pocket? Rebbi Abba in the name of Rebbi Abbahu: if they told him, we accept you as if you were three on condition that you judge us by Torah law. He erred and judged them on his discretion. What he did is done, but since he erred and judged them on his discretion, he has to pay from his own pocket[43] because he was presumptuous to judge alone by Torah law, as we have stated[44]: "Do not judge sitting alone, for only One judges sitting alone."

36 Babli 3a,5b,30a,87b; *Ketubot* 22a. Cf. *Berakhot* 7:1, Note 18.

37 Even if the parties accepted them as judges.

38 In the Babli, this opinion is represented by Rava (5b) and R. Abbahu (87b), the student of R. Johanan and R. Simeon ben Laqish.

39 Mishnah *Bekhorot* 4:4. The Mishnah refers to a person who did not pass the required examinations and was not formally qualified as a judge.

40 Since R. Abbahu follows his teachers and holds that any judgment passed by a court of two judges is void, as well as from the following quote, it is clear that one has to read "three" in place of "two".

41 If there exists no clear precedent for the case; different schools promulgate different rules and he followed a minority opinion because it seemed to him to be the correct one, his judgment is valid but there is no reason why he should have to pay. The Babli, 33a, declares a judgment against a clear majority of opinions as an error in law.

42 If his judgment contradicted a Mishnah or a clear precedent, in Israel a judgment of the Patriarch's court or in Babylonia a concurrent judgment of both Yeshivot, his judgment is void (cf. *Ketubot* 9:2, Note 100). If any money changed hands as a consequence of the erroneous judgment, it has to be returned.

43 As a fine.

44 Mishnah *Avot* 4:8.

(18a line 56) אָמַר רִבִּי יְהוּדָה בֶּן פָּזִי. אַף הַקָּדוֹשׁ בָּרוּךְ הוּא אֵין דָּן יְחִידִי. שֶׁנֶּאֱמַר וְכָל־צְבָא הַשָּׁמַיִם עוֹמְדִים עָלָיו מִימִינוֹ וּמִשְּׂמאלוֹ. אֵילּוּ מַטִּין לְכַף זְכוּת וְאֵילּוּ מַטִּין לְכַף חוֹבָה. אַף עַל פִּי שֶׁאֵין דָּן יְחִידִי חוֹתֵם יְחִידִי. שֶׁנֶּאֱמַר אֲבָל אַגִּיד לְךָ אֶת־הָרָשׁוּם בִּכְתָב אֱמֶת. אָמַר רִבִּי יוֹחָנָן. לְעוֹלָם אֵין הַקָּדוֹשׁ בָּרוּךְ הוּא עוֹשֶׂה בְעוֹלָמוֹ דָּבָר עַד שֶׁנִּמְלַךְ בְּבֵית דִּין שֶׁלְּמַעְלָן. מַה טַעַם. וֶאֱמֶת הַדָּבָר וְצָבָא גָדוֹל. אֵימָתַי חוֹתָמוֹ שֶׁלְּהַקָּדוֹשׁ בָּרוּךְ הוּא אֱמֶת. בְּשָׁעָה שֶׁנִּמְלַךְ בְּבֵית דִּין

שֶׁלְּמַעֲלָן. אָמַר רִבִּי לְעָזָר. כָּל־מָקוֹם שֶׁנֶּאֱמַר יי אֱלֹהִים הוּא וּבֵית דִּינוֹ. וּבִנְיַין אָב שֶׁבְּכוּלָּם וַיי דִּבֶּר עָלָיו רָעָה.

מָהוּ חוֹתָמוֹ שֶׁלְהַקָּדוֹשׁ בָּרוּךְ הוּא. רִבִּי בֵּיבַי בְּשֵׁם רִבִּי רְאוּבֵן. אֱמֶת. מָהוּ אֱמֶת. אָמַר רִבִּי בּוּן. שֶׁהוּא אֱלֹהִים חַיִּים וּמֶלֶךְ עוֹלָם. אָמַר רֵישׁ לָקִישׁ. אָלֶ"ף רֵישֵׁיהּ דְּאַלְפָּה־בֵּיטָא. מֵ'ם בְּאֶמְצָעִיתָא. תָּי'ו בְּסוֹפָהּ. לוֹמַר אֲנִי יי רִאשׁוֹן שֶׁלֹּא קִיבַּלְתִּי מֵאַחֵר. וּמִבַּלְעָדַי אֵין אֱלֹהִים שֶׁאֵין לִי שׁוּתָף. וְאֶת־אַחֲרוֹנִים אֲנִי־הוּא. שֶׁאֵינִי עָתִיד לְמוֹסְרָהּ לְאַחֵר.

Rebbi Jehudah ben Pazi said, even the Holy One, praise to Him, does not judge alone, as it is said[45]: *all the hosts of Heaven were standing by Him, to His right side and to His left*. These vote to acquit, those to convict. Even though He does not judge alone, He signs alone, as it is said: *really I shall tell you what is noted in true writing.*[46]

Rebbi Johanan said, the Holy One, praise to Him, never does anything in His world unless He took counsel with the Heavenly Court[47]. What is the reason? *True is the statement and a large host.*[48] When is the seal of the Holy One, praise to Him, true? When He took counsel with the Heavenly Court. Rebbi Eleazar said, any place where it is said "the Eternal, Almighty,[49]" it is He and His Heavenly Court. The paradigm of all is: *and the Eternal spoke evil about him.*[50]

What is the seal of the Holy One, praise to Him? Rebbi Bevai in the name of Rebbi Reuben, "true.[51]" What means "true"? Rebbi Abun said, that He is a Living Power and the King of this World. Rebbi Simeon ben Laqish said, א is the start of the alphabet, מ the middle,[52] and ת the end. To say, *I, the Eternal, am First,*[53] I did not receive anything from another. *Besides Me there is no supreme power,*[54] for I have no co-owner. *And with the last, I shall be*,[53] I shall not in the future turn it over to anybody else.

45 *IK.* 22:19. In MT, "was standing."

46 *Dan.* 10:21.

47 Babli 38b.

48 *Dan.* 10:1.

49 In *Lev. rabba* 24(2) in the name of R. Eliezer, in *Num. rabba* 3(3) in the name of "the rabbis": Any place where it is said "*and* the Eternal." Since the verse quoted in support refers to this version, the editor of the Žitomir-Wilna edition changed the text here. It is more likely that the text originally read "the Eternal of hosts" and the proof text was *Jer.* 11:17.

50 *IK.* 22:23.

51 Babli *Šabbat* 55a, in the name of R. Hanina, a midrash on *IK.* 22:23.

52 Since the Hebrew alphabet has 22 letters, the middle is between the 11th (k) and the twelfth (l) letter.

53 *Is.* 41:4.

54 *Is.* 44:6. The verse probably should have been quoted three times.

(18a line 69) רִבִּי בָּא וְרִבִּי בִנְיָמִין בַּר יֶפֶת הֲווּ דַיְינִין קוֹמֵי רִבִּי יִצְחָק וּנְפַק דִּינָא עִם רִבִּי בִנְיָמִין. אֲתַא רִבִּי בָּא בָּעֵי מִיטְרוֹף. עָל רִבִּי אִמִּי וַאֲלַף. מוּמְחֶה שֶׁכָּפַף וְדָן דִּינוֹ דִּין.

רִבִּי אַבָּהוּ הֲוָה יְתִיב דַּיָּין בִּכְנִישְׁתָּא מְדַרְתָּא דְקֵיסָרִין לְגַרְמֵיהּ. אָמְרִין לֵיהּ תַּלְמִידוֹי. וְלָא כֵן אַלְפָּן רִבִּי. אַל תְּהִי דָן יְחִידִי. אֲמַר לוֹן. כֵּיוָן דְּאַתּוּן חֲמוּ לִי יְתִיב דַּיָּין לְגַרְמִי וְאַתּוּן לְגַבַּיי כְּמִי שֶׁקִּיבְּלוּ עֲלֵיהֶן. וְתַנֵּי כֵן. בַּמֶּה דְבָרִים אֲמוּרִים. בִּזְמַן שֶׁלֹּא קִיבְּלוּ עֲלֵיהֶן. אֲבָל אִם קִיבְּלוּ עֲלֵיהֶן דָּן אֲפִילוּ יְחִידִי.

Rebbi Abba and Rebbi Benjamin bar Jephet had a lawsuit before Rebbi Isaac; the judgment was for Rebbi Benjamin. Rebbi Abba wanted to complain[55]; Rebbi Immi came and taught: If an expert[56] forced his opinion as a judgment, his judgment stands.

Rebbi Abbahu was sitting as sole judge in the inclining[57] synagogue of Caesarea. His students said to him, did the rabbi not teach[44]: "Do not judge sitting alone"? He told them, since you see me sitting alone as a judge and they come to me, it is because they accepted this. It was stated thus[58]: "When was this said? If they did not accept it. But if they accepted it, he even judges as sole judge.[59]"

55 After the fact, he wanted to invalidate the judgment because R. Isaac sat as sole judge.

56 A person who passed the required examinations and was ordained as a judge, in Palestine by the Patriarch, in Babylonia by the Head of the Diaspora.

57 A synagogue built on an incline in his hometown of Caesarea Philippi on the slopes of the Golan Heights.

58 Babli 5a, *Rosh Haššanah* 25b.

59 Since he is acting as an arbitrator.

(18a line 76) רִבִּי יוֹחָנָן אֲזַל מֵידוֹן קוֹמֵי רִבִּי חִייָה רַבָּה. אַיְיתִיב גַּבֵּיהּ חַד תַּלְמִיד. וְלֹא כֵן תַּנֵּי. אָב וּבְנוֹ הָרַב וְתַלְמִידוֹ שְׁנֵיהֶן נִימְנִין אֶחָד. נֵימַר חָבֵר וְתַלְמִיד הָיָה. כְּרִבִּי לָעְזָר לְרִבִּי יוֹחָנָן.

גְּזַר דִּין נְפָקוּ מִן דְּרַב לְגַרְמֵיהּ. מִן דְּרִבִּי אָחָא לְגַרְמֵיהּ. מִן דְּרִבִּי יוֹנָה וְרִבִּי יוֹסֵי לְגַרְמֵיהוֹן.

Rebbi Johanan went with a lawsuit before the Elder Rebbi Ḥiyya. He took a student to sit with him. But did we not state: "A father and his son, a teacher and his student, the two are counted as one.[60]" Let us say that he was both student and colleague, like Rebbi Eleazar to Rebbi Johanan[61].

Judgments were rendered by Rav alone, by Rav Aha alone, by Rebbi Jonah and Rebbi Yose by themselves[62].

60 Tosephta 7:2; Babli 36a. The son or the student cannot be counted on for an independent opinion.

61 Where both Talmudim report many disagreements between them. At this stage, the former student will have independent opinions and, more importantly, will not be afraid publicly to state them.

62 The head of a Talmudic Academy everywhere is empowered to sit as sole judge.

(18b line 4) תַּמָּן תַּנִּינָן. הַנּוֹטֵל שְׂכָרוֹ לָדוּן דִּינָיו בְּטֵילִין. כֵּינִי מַתְנִיתָא. הֶחָשׁוּד לִיטּוֹל שְׂכָרוֹ וְדָן.

חַד בַּר נַשׁ אֲזַל מֵידוֹן קוֹמֵי רַב הוּנָא. אֲמַר לֵיהּ. אַייתִי לִי בַּר נַשׁ דִּיסוֹק תְּחוּתִי לְדִיקְלָא.

רַב הוּנָא הֲוָה רָעֵי תוֹרִין וַהֲוָה יְדַע שַׂהֲדוּ לְחַד בַּר נַשׁ. אֲמַר לֵיהּ. אַיְתָא שְׂהַד עָלַי. אֲמַר לֵיהּ. הַב לִי אַגְרִי. וְתַנֵּי כֵן. נוֹתְנִין לַדַּיָּין שְׂכַר בְּטֵילוֹ וְלָעֵד שְׂכַר עֵדוּתוֹ.

There, we have stated[63]: "If somebody takes a fee to judge, his judgments[64] are invalid." So is the Mishnah: "He who is suspected of taking a fee[65] but he judges."

A person brought a suit before Rav Huna[66], He told him, bring me a person who climbs the date palm instead of me.

Rav Huna was a cowherd when he knew testimony for a person, who told him, come and testify for me. He answered him, give me my wages. It was stated thus: "One pays the judge for his time and the witness for his testimony.

63 Mishnah *Bekhorot* 4:6, Babli *Bekhorot* 29a, *Ketubot* 105a, *Qiddušin* 58b.

64 The plural implies that all his judgments are invalid, even those for which he did not take money.

65 It takes an action of a supervising authority to invalidate his judgments.

66 Who started out poor as an agricultural worker and only became rich when middle aged. Babli *Ketubot* 105a.

(18b line 9) חַד בַּר נַשׁ סְאַב לְחַד כֹּהֵן. אֲתַא עוֹבְדָא קוֹמֵי רִבִּי יִצְחָק וְאוֹכְלֵיהּ חוּלִין. סֳבְרִין מֵימַר שֶׁיּוֹצְאִין לוֹ דְּמֵי תְרוּמָה מִתּוֹכָם.

A person made a Cohen impure[67]. The case came before Rebbi Isaac who made him eat profane food[68]. They wanted to say that one deducts the price of heave from the amount[69].

67 He made it impossible for him to eat heave, which must be eaten in purity. One has to assume that the impurity was that of corpses, which can be dissolved only by sprinkling with water containing the ashes of the red cow, which at that moment had become unavailable; cf. *Berakhot* 1:1, Note 3.

68 He forbade the Cohen to eat heave; this is a biblical rule agreed to by everybody. It is implied that he required the offending party to pay for the Cohen's food since heave, permitted only to Cohanim, is sold at a discount.

Impurity of persons and food is *invisible damage* which according to the Babli, *Gittin* 53a, can be punished only by a rabbinic fine. According to the Babli, *Sanhedrin* 8a, fines can be imposed only by a panel of three ordained judges. Since it is implied here that R. Isaac was sitting as sole judge, the Yerushalmi strongly disagrees with the Babli. (Cf. *Bava qamma* 9:2, Note 24.)

69 The guilty party only had to pay the difference between profane and sanctified food, i. e., the additional cost incurred by the victim.

(18b line 11) תַּנֵּי. רִבִּי אֱלִיעֶזֶר בֶּן רִבִּי יוֹסֵי הַגָּלִילִי אוֹמֵר. הַמְבַצֵּעַ חוֹטֵא וְהַמְבָרֵךְ אֶת הַמְבַצֵּעַ הֲרֵי זֶה כִּמְנָאֵץ לִפְנֵי הַמָּקוֹם. שֶׁנֶּאֱמַר וּבֹצֵעַ בֵּרֵךְ נִאֵץ יי. אֶלָּא יִקּוֹב הַדִּין אֶת הָהָר כְּשֶׁעָשָׂה מֹשֶׁה. אֲבָל אַהֲרֹן מֵשִׂים שָׁלוֹם. שֶׁנֶּאֱמַר בְּשָׁלוֹם וּבְמִישׁוֹר הָלַךְ אִתִּי.

It was stated[70]: Rebbi Eliezer ben Rebbi Yose the Galilean says, the person who arranges a compromise is sinning[71], and the one who praises a compromiser is like a blasphemer before the Omnipresent, as it is said[72]: *he who blesses a compromiser slanders the Eternal!* The law should pierce the mountain, as Moses did[73]. But Aaron promoted peace[74], as it is said[75], *in peace and straightness he went with Me.*

70 Tosephta 1:2, Babli 6b, *Yebamot* 92a.

71 It is clear from the following paragraphs and the parallels, that the statement is interpreted to apply to cases where either the trial already has started or where existing law allows a clear decision.

72 *Ps.* 10:3.

73 Who ordered all people with suits to appear before him for judgment (*Ex.* 18:16) and did not invite them to an arbitration panel.

74 The midrash (*Avot dR. Nathan* I 12, II 24) explains that he dissuaded people from going to court. This is preferable according to everybody.

75 *Mal.* 2:6.

(18b line 14) תַּנֵּי. רִבִּי לִיעֶזֶר בֶּן יַעֲקֹב אוֹמֵר. מַה תַלְמוּד לוֹמַר וּבֹצֵעַ בֵּרֵךְ נִאֵץ יי. מֶשְׁלוּ מָשָׁל לְמָה הַדָּבָר דוֹמֶה. לְאֶחָד שֶׁגָּנַב סְאָה חִיטִּין וְהוֹלִיכָהּ לַנַּחְתּוֹם וְהִפְרִישׁ חַלָּתָהּ וְהֶאֱכִילָהּ לְבָנָיו. הֲרֵי זֶה מְבָרֵךְ וְאֵינוֹ אֶלָּא מְנָאֵץ.

רִבִּי מֵאִיר אוֹמֵר. מַה תַלְמוּד לוֹמַר וּבֹצֵעַ בֵּרֵךְ נִאֵץ יי. אֵילוּ אֲחֵי יוֹסֵף. שֶׁנֶּאֱמַר מַה־בֶּצַע כִּי נַהֲרֹג אֶת־אָחִינוּ וגו'.

It was stated[70]: [76]"Rebbi Eliezer ben Jacob says, why does the verse say[72], *he who blesses unlawful gain slanders the Eternal*? They gave a parable, to what can this be compared? To one who stole a *se'ah* of wheat, brought it to the baker, separated its *ḥallah*[77], and fed it to his children. He pronounces blessings but it is blasphemy.

[78]Rebbi Meir says, why does the verse say[72], *he who blesses unlawful gain slanders the Eternal*? These are Joseph's brothers, as it is is said[79]: *What is the gain if we slay our brother,* etc."

76 Babli *Bava qamma* 94a. In other Yerushalmi sources (*Hallah* 1:9 Notes 218-221; *Šabbat* 13:3 14a l. 50) it is an Amoraic statement.

77 To avoid committing a deadly sin. If he recites the required blessing, he commits an intentional sin; if he induces the baker to recite the blessings, the baker commits an unintended sin and the thief violates the commandment not to put a stone in the way of a blind man.

78 In the Tosephta (1:3) an anonymous statement.

79 *Gen.* 37:26.

(18b line 19) רִבִּי יְהוֹשֻׁעַ בֶּן קָרְחָה אוֹמֵר. מִצְוָה לְבַצֵּעַ. שֶׁנֶּאֱמַר אֱמֶת וּמִשְׁפַּט שָׁלוֹם. כָּל־מָקוֹם שֶׁיֵּשׁ אֱמֶת אֵין מִשְׁפַּט שָׁלוֹם. יֵשׁ שָׁלוֹם אֵין מִשְׁפַּט אֱמֶת. וְאֵי זֶהוּ אֱמֶת שֶׁיֵּשׁ בּוֹ מִשְׁפַּט שָׁלוֹם. הֲוֵי אוֹמֵר. זֶה בִצּוּעַ.

דָּן אֵת הַדִּין זִיכֶּה אֶת הַזַּכַּיי חִייֵּב לַחַייָב. מַעֲלֶה עָלָיו הַכָּתוּב כִּילּוּ עָשָׂה צְדָקָה עִם הַזַּכַּיי וְכִילּוּ עָשָׂה צְדָקָה עִם הַחַייָב. צְדָקָה עִם הַזַּכַּיי. שֶׁהֶחֱזִיר לוֹ מָמוֹנוֹ. וְעִם הַחַייָב. שֶׁהוֹצִיא גְזֵילוֹ מִתַּחַת יָדוֹ. אָמַר רִבִּי אַבָּהוּ. מִשְׁפָּט מִשְׁפָּט אֲמוּרִין בַּפָּרָשָׁה. אֱמֶת וּמִשְׁפַּט שָׁלוֹם שִׁפְטוּ בְּשַׁעֲרֵיכֶם׃

[80]"Rebbi Joshua ben Qorḥa says, it is a good deed to mediate a compromise, as it is said[81]: *Truth and judgment of peace.* If there is truth, there is no judgment of peace. If there is peace, there is no judgment of truth.

What is truth containing a judgment of peace? I am saying, this is compromise."

[82]"If somebody judged correctly, absolved the innocent and condemned the guilty, the verse counts it as if he practiced kindness both towards the innocent and towards the guilty. Kindness towards the innocent, because he returned his money to him. And towards the guilty, for he removed the proceeds of robbery from his hands.[83]" Rebbi Abbahu said, *judgment* and *judgment* is written in the verse[81]: "Truth and judgment of peace judge in your gates."

80 Tosephta 1:3.

81 *Zach.* 8:16, cf. *Ta`aniot* 4:2 (68a l. 75), *Megillah* 3:7 (74b l. 48).

82 Tosephta 1:4, a statement of Rebbi; the same in the Babli 6b.

83 And therefore protects him from the judgment of Heaven.

84 Each referring to one aspect of the act of judging.

(18b line 26) רִבִּי זְכַרְיָה בָּעֵי קוֹמֵי רִבִּי אִמִּי. עָבְדִין עוֹבְדָא כְּהָהֵן תַּנָּייָא. תַּנֵּי. רִבִּי שִׁמְעוֹן בֶּן מְנַסְיָא אוֹמֵר. פְּעָמִים שֶׁאַתָּה רַשַּׁאי לְבַצֵּעַ. פְּעָמִים שֶׁאֵין אַתָּה רַשַּׁאי לְבַצֵּעַ. כֵּיצַד. שְׁנַיִם שֶׁבָּאוּ אֶל הַדַּייָן. עַד שֶׁלֹּא שָׁמַע דִּבְרֵיהֶן אוֹ מִשֶּׁשָּׁמַע דִּבְרֵיהֶן וְאֵינוֹ יוֹדֵעַ הֵיכָן הַדִּין נוֹטֶה רַשַּׁאי לוֹמַר לָהֶן. צְאוּ וּבִצְעוּ. מִשֶּׁתִּשְׁמַע דִּבְרֵיהֶן וְיוֹדֵעַ אַתָּה הֵיכָן הַדִּין נוֹטֶה אֵין אַתָּה רַשַּׁאי לְבְצוֹעַ. שֶׁנֶּאֱמַר פּוֹטֵר מַיִם רֵאשִׁית מָדוֹן וְלִפְנֵי הִתְגַּלַּע הָרִיב נְטוֹשׁ. עַד שֶׁלֹּא נִתְגַּלַּע הָרִיב אַתָּה רַשַּׁאי לְנוֹטְשׁוֹ. מִשֶּׁנִּתְגַּלַּע הָרִיב אֵין אַתָּה רַשַּׁאי לְנוֹטְשׁוֹ. אָמַר רִבִּי מַתַּנְיָה. אַף הפרשה[85] צְרִיכָה הֶכְרֵעַ הַדַּעַת.

Rebbi Zachariah asked before Rebbi Immi: Does one act following that Tanna, as it was stated: [86]"Rebbi Simeon ben Menassiah says, sometimes you are empowered to propose a compromise, sometimes you are not empowered to propose a compromise. How is this? Two come before a judge; before he heard their arguments, or after he heard their arguments but does not know how to correctly apply the law, he may tell them, go and work out a compromise. After you heard their arguments and know how to correctly apply the law, you may not propose a compromise, as it is said[87]: *One may remove the beginning of a quarrel like water; before it becomes manifest, the quarrel may be abandoned.* Before the quarrel became manifest, you are permitted to abandon it; after the quarrel became manifest, you are not permitted to abandon it." Rebbi Mattaniah said, even compromise needs intelligent decision[88].

85 Read with the parallel sources: הַפְּשָׁרָה.

86 Tosephta 1:6, Babli 6b.

87 *Prov.* 17:14.

88 He objects to the statement that the judge should send the parties away to work out a compromise on their own; he requires the judge to guide them towards a reasonable compromise.

(18b line 34) רִבִּי יְהוּדָה בֶּן לָקִישׁ אָמַר. שְׁנַיִם שֶׁבָּאוּ אֶל הַדַּיָּן אֶחָד רַךְ וְאֶחָד חָזָק. עַד שֶׁלֹּא שָׁמַע דִּבְרֵיהֶן רַשַּׁאי לוֹמַר לָהֶן. אֵינִי נִזְקָק לָכֶם. שֶׁמָּא יִתְחַייֵב הֶחָזָק וִיהֵא חָזָק אוֹיְבוֹ. מִשֶּׁשָּׁמַע דִּבְרֵיהֶן אֵין רַשַּׁאי לוֹמַר לָהֶן. אֵינִי נִזְקָק לָכֶם. שֶׁנֶּאֱמַר לֹא תָגוּרוּ מִפְּנֵי־אִישׁ.

רִבִּי יְהוֹשֻׁעַ בֶּן קָרְחָה אוֹמֵר. הֲרֵי שֶׁהָיָה יוֹשֵׁב אֵצֶל הַדַּייָן וְרָאָה זְכוּת לֶעָנִי וְחוֹבָה לֶעָשִׁיר. מְנַיִין שֶׁלֹּא יִשְׁתּוֹק. שֶׁנֶּאֱמַר לֹא תָגוּרוּ מִפְּנֵי־אִישׁ. אַל תַּכְנִיס דְּבָרֶיךָ מִפְּנֵי אִישׁ.

וִיהוּ הַדַּייָנִין יוֹדְעִין אֶת מִי הֵן דָּנִין וְלִפְנֵי מִי הֵן דָּנִין. וְיִהְיוּ הָעֵדִים יוֹדְעִין אֶת מִי מְעִידִין וְלִפְנֵי מִי מְעִידִין. לִפְנֵי מִי שֶׁאָמַר וְהָיָה הָעוֹלָם. שֶׁנֶּאֱמַר וְעָמְדוּ שְׁנֵי־הָאֲנָשִׁים אֲשֶׁר־לָהֶם הָרִיב לִפְנֵי יי וְאוֹמֵר אֱלֹהִים נִצָּב בַּעֲדַת־אֵל. וְכֵן יְהוֹשָׁפָט אוֹמֵר לַשּׁוֹפְטִים רְאוּ מָה־אַתֶּם עֹשִׂים כִּי לֹא לְאָדָם תִּשְׁפְּטוּ כִּי לַיי. וְכִי אֶיפְשַׁר לְבָשָׂר וָדָם לָדוּן אֶת בּוֹרְאוֹ. אֶלָּא אָמַר הַקָּדוֹשׁ בָּרוּךְ הוּא. אֲנָא אָמְרִית דִיהֵא לִרְאוּבֵן ק׳ דֵּינָרִים וּלְשִׁמְעוֹן וְלֹא כְלוּם. וְאַתְּ נוֹטְלָן מִזֶּה וְנוֹתְנָן לָזֶה. עָלַי לְשַׁלֵּם לוֹ וְלִפָּרַע מֵאוֹתוֹ הָאִישׁ.

תַּנֵּי. רַבָּן שִׁמְעוֹן בֶּן גַּמְלִיאֵל אוֹמֵר. הַדִּין בִּשְׁלֹשָׁה וּפְשָׁרָה בִשְׁנַיִם. יָפֶה כֹּחַ הַפְּשָׁרָה מִכֹּחַ הַדִּין. שֶׁשְּׁנַיִם שֶׁדָּנוּ יְכוֹלִין לַחֲזוֹר בָּהֶן וּשְׁנַיִם שֶׁפִּשְּׁרוּ אֵין יְכוֹלִין לַחֲזוֹר בָּהֶן.

[89]"Rebbi Jehudah ben Laqish said: If two people appeared before a judge, one decent and one agressive. Before he started to hear their arguments, he may tell them, I will not hear your case, lest the agressive one lose his case and become his enemy. After he started hearing their arguments, he may not tell them, I will not hear your case, for it is said,[90] *do not be afraid of anybody.*

[91]"Rebbi Joshua ben Qorha says, if somebody[92] was sitting next to a judge and saw a benefit for the poor and a detriment for the rich, from where that he should not keep silent? For it is said[90], *do not be afraid of anybody.*

[97]The judges have to know with Whom they judge, and the witnesses have to know before Whom they are testifying: before Him Who commanded and the world came into existence, as it is said[30], *the two people who are quarrelling shall stand before the Eternal,* and it is said[93], *the Almighty stands*

in the assembly of the judges. So Josaphat told the judges, *look what you are doing, for you do not judge for man, but for the Eternal*[94]. How is it possible for flesh and blood to judge his Creator? But the Holy One, praise to Him, said: I said that Reuben should have 100 denars and Simeon nothing. You take from one and give it to the other[95]. I have to repay it to him, and will Myself be paid by this man[96].

It was stated[97]: "Rabban Simeon ben Gamliel says, judgment is passed by three [judges], a compromise is made by two[98]. The compromise is stronger than the judgment in that two [judges] who judged can repeal their judgment[99] but two who negotiated a compromise cannot repeal[100].

89 Tosephta 1:7, *Tanhuma Mišpatim* 6, *Sheiltot Mišpatim* 58, and in all Medieval quotes; only in Babli 6b both in the Munich ms. and *editio princeps* incorrectly: R. Simeon ben Laqish.

90 *Deut*. 1:17.

91 Tosephta 1:8.

92 In a similar, anonymous, *baraita* in the Babli (*Ševuot* 31a): A student sitting before his teacher. This probably has to be understood here.

93 *Ps*. 82:1.

94 *2Chr*. 19:6.

95 Incorrectly.

96 The judge.

97 Tosephta 1:9.

98 This also is the text of the Babli, 5b. But in the Tosephta: Just as judgment is rendered by three [judges], so compromise is made before three [judges].

99 Since is was rendered in regular fashion.

100 From the moment a party acquired what was awarded to him by the compromise, since this is a monetary transaction following the rules of *Qiddušin* 1:4-6.

(18b line 50) הָאוֹנֵס וְהַמְפַתֶּה כול׳. רִבִּי מָנָא אָמַר. בְּנַעֲרָה מְאוֹרָסָה פְּלִיגֵי. רִבִּי מֵאִיר אוֹמֵר. מַפְסֶדֶת כְּתוּבָּתָהּ בִּשְׁלֹשָׁה וְנִסְקֶלֶת בְּעֶשְׂרִים וּשְׁלֹשָׁה. וַחֲכָמִים אוֹמְרִים. מָקוֹם שֶׁנִּסְקֶלֶת שָׁם מַפְסֶדֶת כְּתוּבָּתָהּ. אֲבָל בְּמוֹצִיא שֵׁם רַע כָּל־עַמָּא מוֹדוּ מָקוֹם שֶׁהָעֵדִים נִסְקָלִין שָׁם הַבַּעַל לוֹקֶה וְנוֹתֵן מֵאָה סֶלַע. אָמַר לֵיהּ רִבִּי יוֹסֵי בֵּירִבִּי בּוּן. הֵן תַּנִּינָתָהּ פְּלָגָה אַתְּ עֲבִיד פְּלֵגִיהּ. אֶלָּא בְּמוֹצִיא שֵׁם רַע פְּלִיגֵי. רִבִּי מֵאִיר אוֹמֵר. הַבַּעַל לוֹקֶה וְנוֹתֵן מֵאָה סֶלַע בִּשְׁלוֹשָׁה. וְהָעֵדִים נִסְקָלִין בְּעֶשְׂרִים וּשְׁלֹשָׁה. וְרַבָּנִין מָרִין. מָקוֹם שֶׁהָעֵדִים נִסְקָלִין שָׁם הַבַּעַל לוֹקֶה וְנוֹתֵן מֵאָה סֶלַע. אֲבָל בְּנַעֲרָה מְאוֹרָסָה כָּל־עַמָּא מוֹדוּ מָקוֹם שֶׁנִּסְקֶלֶת שָׁם מַפְסֶדֶת כְּתוּבָּתָהּ. וַתְיָיא דְּרִבִּי מָנָא כְּרִבִּי זְעִירָא וּדְרִבִּי יוֹסֵי בֵּירִבִּי בּוּן כְּרִבִּי אַבָּהוּ.

1 פליגי | כ פליגין 2 בעשרים ושלשה | כ בשלשה ועשרים 3 שם | כ שם היא הן תנינתה פלגה את עביד פלגיה | כ אין דלא תניתה פליגא[101] 5 פליגא | כ פליגין הבעל | כ - 6 מרין | כ אמ׳ 7 ותייא | כ ואתייא

"The rapist and the seducer," etc. [102]Rebbi Mana said, they disagree about the preliminarily married adolescent female. Rebbi Meïr says, she loses her *ketubah* in a court of three and is stoned in a court of 23; but the Sages say, at the same place which sentences her to be stoned she loses her *ketubah*. But in the case of the calumniator, everybody agrees that by the court in which the witnesses are stoned, the husband is flogged and pays 100 tetradrachmas. Rebbi Yose ben Rebbi Abun said to him, would they differ where it was not stated? But they differ about the calumniator! Rebbi Meïr says, he is flogged and pays 100 tetradrachmas by the judgment of three and the witnesses are stoned by the judgment of 23; but the rabbis say, by the court in which the witnesses are stoned, the husband is flogged and pays 100 tetradrachmas. But in the case of the preliminarily married adolescent female, everybody agrees that at the same place which sentences her to be stoned she loses her *ketubah*. It turns out that Rebbi Mana follows Rebbi Ze'ira and Rebbi Yose ben Rebbi Abun follows Rebbi Abbahu.

101 The *Ketubot* text is intelligible in contrast to the *Sanhedrin* text. The translation is taken from *Ketubot.*

102 This paragraph is from *Ketubot* 4:4, explained there in Notes 113-116. The *Ketubot* (כ) text is original since only there is the disagreement between Rebbis Ze'ira and Abbahu being explained.

(18b line 60) רִבִּי אַבָּהוּ שָׁאַל. שׁוֹר הַנִּסְקַל כְּרִבִּי מֵאִיר מָהוּ שֶׁיִּתֵּן הַכֶּסֶף בִּשְׁלֹשָׁה וְיִסָּקֵל בְּעֶשְׂרִים וּשְׁלֹשָׁה. אָמַר לֵיהּ רִבִּי יוֹסֵי בֵּירִבִּי בּוּן. שׁוֹר הַנִּסְקַל כּוּלּוֹ מָמוֹן הוּא וּגְזֵירַת הַכָּתוּב הוּא שֶׁיִּסָּקֵל.

[103]Rebbi Abbahu asked: Following Rebbi Meïr, should an ox which is stoned[104] have to pay damages[105] by a court of three and be stoned by 23? Rebbi Yose ben Rebbi Abun told him, the rules of an ox which is stoned are all about money[106]; it is a decision of the verse that it should be stoned.

103 The paragraph is repeated in Halakhah 4.

104 The animal which killed a human (*Ex.* 21:28).

105 Not the ox but its owner.

106 Since fines and corporal punishment are mutually exclusive (*Terumot* 7:1 Notes 19-70; *Giṭṭin* 5:5 Note 136), it is clear that stoning the ox is a fine imposed on its owner.

(fol. 17d) **משנה ב**: מַכּוֹת בִּשְׁלֹשָׁה מִשּׁוּם רַבִּי יִשְׁמָעֵאל אָמְרוּ בְּעֶשְׂרִים וּשְׁלֹשָׁה. עִבּוּר הַחֹדֶשׁ בִּשְׁלֹשָׁה עִבּוּר הַשָּׁנָה בִּשְׁלֹשָׁה דִּבְרֵי רַבִּי מֵאִיר. רַבָּן שִׁמְעוֹן בֶּן גַּמְלִיאֵל אוֹמֵר בִּשְׁלֹשָׁה מַתְחִילִין וּבַחֲמִשָּׁה נוֹשְׂאִין וְנוֹתְנִין וְגוֹמְרִין בְּשִׁבְעָה. וְאִם גָּמְרוּ בִשְׁלֹשָׁה מְעוּבֶּרֶת.

Mishnah 2: Whipping by three [judges]; in the name of Rebbi Ismael they said, by 23[107]. The lengthening of a month by three [judges][108], the intercalation of a year by three [judges][109], the words of Rebbi Meïr. Rabban Simeon ben Gamliel says, one starts with three, one discusses with five, and one votes with seven[110]. But if they voted with three, it is intercalated.

107 The imposition of corporal punishment needs an official court of duly ordained judges. The Mishnah is a reconstruction of what was assumed to be the historic procedure; R. Ismael lived about 70 years after the removal of criminal jurisdiction from Jewish courts and R. Meïr, represented by the anonymous opinion, more than 100 years afterwards. But the prescription of the Mishnah certainly was followed by the autonomous Jewish courts under the Parthians.

108 Whether a thirtieth day should be counted for the current month. Fixing the calendar was the sole privilege of a committee of the Patriarch's court as a successor to the Synhedrion. The current computed calendar was promulgated by such a court in the middle of the Fourth Century (*Eruvin* 3:11 21c l. 24).

109 In the current calendar, the addition of 30 days to the lunar year, labelled as "First Adar."

110 A committe of three has to decide whether the year be a candidate for intercalation; an enlarged committe of five has to do the detailed computations; a further enlarged committee of seven has to confirm the computations. Intercalated months in the lunar year are necessary to keep Passover in the "month of spring" as required by *Ex.* 13:4.

There is no basic disagreement between R. Meïr and Rabban Simeon, since the latter agrees that in an emergency situation, a duly empowered committee of three is competent. Since Rabban Simeon was the Patriarch of the restauration during the second half of the Second Century, his procedure was the one actually used.

(18b line 63) **הלכה ב**: מַכּוֹת בִּשְׁלֹשָׁה כול'. רִבִּי אַבָּהוּ בָּעֵי. מַכּוֹת בְּעֶשְׂרִים וּשְׁלֹשָׁה. פְּעָמִים שֶׁמֵּת מִמַּכּוֹתָיו וַהֲרֵי יֵשׁ בּוֹ דִּינֵי נְפָשׁוֹת.

Halakhah 2: "Whipping by three [judges]," etc. Rebbi Abbahu asked: Should not a sentence of whipping be passed by 23 [judges], since sometimes he might die from the whippings, so that it is a case of potential death sentence[111].

111 He holds that R. Ismael's position is the only reasonable one. But since the problem is purely theoretical (Note 32), it is not pursued further.

(18b line 65) בַּר קַפָּרָא שָׁמַע כּוּלְּהוֹן מֵהָדָא. יְבָרֶכְךָ יי וְיִשְׁמְרֶךָ׃ מִכָּן שֶׁמַּתְחִילִין בִּשְׁלֹשָׁה. יָאֵר יי פָּנָיו אֵלֶיךָ וִיחֻנֶּךָּ׃ מִכָּן שֶׁנּוֹשְׂאִין וְנוֹתְנִין בַּחֲמִשָּׁה. יִשָּׂא יי פָּנָיו אֵלֶיךָ וְיָשֵׂם לְךָ שָׁלוֹם. מִכָּן שֶׁגּוֹמְרִין בְּשִׁבְעָה.

רִבִּי יְהוֹשֻׁעַ בֶּן לֵוִי שָׁמַע כּוּלְּהוֹן מֵהָדָא. וַיִּקַּח רַב־טַבָּחִים אֶת־שְׁלֹשֶׁת שֹׁמְרֵי הַסַּף׃ מִכָּן שֶׁמַּתְחִילִין בִּשְׁלֹשָׁה. וַחֲמִשָּׁה אֲנָשִׁים מֵרֹאֵי פְנֵי־הַמֶּלֶךְ. מִכָּן שֶׁנּוֹשְׂאִין וְנוֹתְנִין בַּחֲמִשָּׁה. וְשִׁבְעָה אֲנָשִׁים מֵרֹאֵי פְנֵי־הַמֶּלֶךְ. מִכָּן שֶׁגּוֹמְרִין בְּשִׁבְעָה.

אָמַר רִבִּי יוֹנָתָן. מִיכָּן לְסַנְהֶדְרִין גְּדוֹלָה שֶׁלְּכָל־יִשְׂרָאֵל. וַיִּקַּח שַׂר הַטַּבָּחִים אֶת־שְׂרָיָה כֹּהֵן הָרֹאשׁ וְאֶת־צְפַנְיָה כֹּהֵן הֲרֵי שְׁנַיִם. וְשִׁבְעָה אֲנָשִׁים מֵרֹאֵי פְנֵי־הַמֶּלֶךְ הֲרֵי תִשְׁעָה. וְשִׁשִּׁים אִישׁ מֵעַם הָאָרֶץ הֲרֵי שִׁבְעִים חָסֵר אֶחָד. וּמִן־הָעִיר סָרִיס אֶחָד הֲרֵי שִׁבְעִים. אִית תַּנָּיֵי תַנֵּי. שִׁבְעִים וְאֶחָד. וַיִּקַּח רַב־הַטַּבָּחִים אֶת־שְׁלֹשֶׁת שֹׁמְרֵי הַסַּף וְשִׁבְעָה מֵרֹאֵי פְנֵי־הַמֶּלֶךְ וְשִׁשִּׁים אִישׁ מֵעַם הָאָרֶץ. וּמִן־הָעִיר לָקַח סָרִיס אֶחָד. הֲרֵי שִׁבְעִים וְאֶחָד. וְלָמָּה קוֹרֵיהוּ סָרִיס. שֶׁמְּסָרֵס אֶת הַהֲלָכָה.

כָּתוּב אֶחָד אוֹמֵר חֲמִשָּׁה וְכָתוּב אֶחָד אוֹמֵר שִׁבְעָה. לְהָבִיא שְׁנֵי סוֹפְרֵי הַדַּיָּינִים.

Bar Qappara understood everything from here: *May the Eternal bless you and preserve you*, from here that one starts with three. *May the Eternal illuminate His Presence for you and be gracious to you*, from here that one continues with five. *May the Eternal turn His Presence to you and give you peace,* from here that one finishes with seven[112].

Rebbi Joshua ben Levi understood everything from the following: *The chief executioner took . . . the three guards of the threshhold*[113], from here that one starts with three. *And five men from the king's entourage*[114], from here that one continues with five. *And seven men from the King's entourage*[115], from here that one finishes with seven[116].

Rebbi Jonathan said, from there the great Synhedrion of all of Israel. *The minister of the executioners took Seraiah the Chief Priest and Zephania the priest*[113], these are two. *And seven men from the king's entourage*[115], this makes nine. *And sixty men from the People of the Land*[117], this makes seventy minus one. *And from the city one eunuch*[115], this makes seventy. There are Tannaïm who state seventy-one: *The chief executioner took . . . the three guards of the threshhold, and seven men from the king's entourage, and sixty men from the People of the Land, and from the city he took one eunuch,* this makes seventy-one. And why is he called a eunuch? Because he transposes practice[118].

One verse says *five,* the other verse says *seven.* The latter includes the two clerks of court.

112 From the verses of the priestly blessings, *Num.* 6:24-26, which have 3, 5, and 7 words respectively, one may infer that proceeding by 3,5,7 will give a blessed result. In the Babli, 10b, this argument is attributed to early Amoraïm; in *Megillah* 23a it is applied to the number of people called to read from the Torah.

113 *Jer.* 52:24.

114 *2K.* 25:19.

115 *Jer.* 52:25.

116 Cf. Babli 10b. According to Rashi *ad loc.*, the verses describe the members of king Sedekia's court and therefore are appropriate to the determination of the calendar which is a governmental exercise.

117 *2K.* 25:19, *Jer.* 52:25.

118 In rabbinic Hebrew, סרס "to castrate" is also used in the sense of "to transpose words or letters". While in the verse he is described as minister of defense, he is taken here as president of the court who can transpose precedents to apply to other cases. Cf. Tosafot *Megillah* 21b, *s. v.* כנגד.

(18c line 3) לֵית כָּאן עִיבּוּר הַחוֹדֶשׁ אֶלָּא קִידּוּשׁ הַחוֹדֶשׁ. שְׁמוּאֵל אָמַר. אֵין קִידּוּשׁ הַחוֹדֶשׁ פָּחוּת מֵעֲשָׂרָה. חֲבֵירִים מָהוּ לִיכָּנֵס לְקִידּוּשׁ הַחוֹדֶשׁ. אָמַר רִבִּי הוֹשַׁעְיָה. חָבֵר הֲוֵינָא וְאַעֲלִי רִבִּי שְׁמוּאֵל בַּר רַב יִצְחָק לְקִידּוּשׁ הַחוֹדֶשׁ וְלֵי נָא יְדַע אִין סַלְקִית מִמְּנִייָנָא אִין לָא. פְּשִׁיטָא דְלָא סְלִיק. לָמָּה. בְּגִין דַּהֲוָה חַתְנֵיהּ. אוֹ מִשּׁוּם שֶׁאֵין חֲבֵירִין נִכְנָסִין לְקִידּוּשׁ הַחוֹדֶשׁ. אָמַר רִבִּי כַּהֲנָא. חָבֵר הֲוֵינָא וְאַעֲלִי רִבִּי תַּנְחוּם בַּר חִייָה לְקִידּוּשׁ הַחוֹדֶשׁ וְסַלְקִית מִמְּנִייָנָא. הָדָא אָמְרָה שֶׁחֲבֵירִים נִכְנָסִין לְקִידּוּשׁ הַחוֹדֶשׁ.

חֲבֵירִים מָהוּ לִיכָּנֵס לְעִיבּוּר שָׁנָה. נִישְׁמְעִינָהּ מֵהָדָא. מַעֲשֶׂה בְרַבָּן גַּמְלִיאֵל שֶׁאָמַר. יִקְרוּנִי שִׁבְעָה זְקֵינִים לָעֲלִייָה. וְנִכְנְסוּ שְׁמוֹנָה. אָמַר. מִי הוּא שֶׁנִּכְנַס שֶׁלֹּא בִרְשׁוּת. עָמַד שְׁמוּאֵל הַקָּטָן עַל רַגְלָיו וְאָמַר. אֲנִי עָלִיתִי שֶׁלֹּא בִרְשׁוּת. הֲלָכָה נִצְרְכָה לִי וְנִכְנַסְתִּי לִשְׁאוֹל עָלֶיהָ. אָמַר לוֹ רַבָּן גַּמְלִיאֵל. וּמָה אֶלְדָּד וּמֵידָד שֶׁכָּל־יִשְׂרָאֵל יוֹדְעִים שֶׁאֵילּוּ הֵן שְׁנַיִם אָמַרְתִּי שֶׁאַתָּה אֶחָד מֵהֶן. וַאֲפֵילוּ כֵן לֹא עִיבְּרוּהָ בְּהַהוּא יוֹמָא וְאַפְלִיגוּ בְמִילֵּי דְאוֹרַייָא וְעִיבְּרוּהָ בְיוֹמָא דְבַתְרָא.

There is no lengthening of the month, but sanctification of the month[119]. Samuel says, sanctification of the month needs no less than ten [participants][120]. Should Fellows [121] be able to enter for the sanctification of the month? Rebbi Hoshaia said, I was a Fellow and Rebbi Samuel bar Rav Isaac took me to the sanctification of the month, but I do not know whether I was counted or not. It is obvious that he was not counted[122], but why? Was it because he was his son-in-law[123], or because Fellows are nor able to enter for the sanctification of the month? Rebbi Cahana said, I was a Fellow when Rebbi Tanḥum bar Ḥiyya took me to the sanctification of the month and I was counted. This implies that Fellows enter for the sanctification of the month.

Are Fellows able to enter for the intercalation of the year? Let us hear from the following: [124]It happened that Rabban Gamliel said, call seven Elders to a meeting on the upper floor, but eight entered. He asked, who is the one who entered without permission? Samuel minor[125] stood up and said, I came up here without permission since I have a practical problem and I have to ask advice on it. Rabban Gamliel told him, you compare to Eldad and Medad; if I had said "two", you would have been one of them. Nevertheless, they did not intercalate on that day but talked about themes in the Torah and intercalated the next day[126].

119 Babli 10b. In the absence of a computed calendar, the lengthening of the month is automatic. If the Synhedrion does not declare the 30th of a month as the 1st of the next, the 31st automatically is the first of the next month since no lunar month has more than 30 days. Therefore, action by the Synhedrion is needed not to lengthen, but to shorten the month and to designate the 30th as a semi-holiday.

120 To make it a public event. In contrast to the intercalation of the year, the determination of the month has to be made public as soon as possible.

121 Members of the Academy who are pledged to follow the rules of fellowship (cf. Introduction to Tractate *Demay*) but have not yet reached the status of rabbi.

122 If the chair of the meeting had asked him for his opinion, he would have remembered.

123 Since relatives are barred from sitting together as judges and R. Hoshaia was R. Samuel's son-in-law, he could not participate even if qualified.

124 Babli 11a.

125 He is called "minor" because of all people called Samuel only the prophet of the same name reached a higher state of holiness.

126 To protect the secrecy of the algorithm with which the years of intercalation were computed. This supports the contention of the Yerushalmi Gaon Eviatar haCohen in his Epistle that during the entire time of the Second Temple the calendar was computed and testimony about the new moon was only used as confirmation of the computation (M. Gil, *Palestine during the first Moslem period*, vol. 2, Tel Aviv 1983).

(18c line 17) תַּנֵּי סַנְהֶדְרִין שֶׁרָאוּ אֶת הַהוֹרֵג. אִית תַּנָּיֵי תַנֵּי. שְׁנַיִם נַעֲשִׂין עֵדִים וּמְעִידִין בִּפְנֵי הַשְּׁאָר. אִית תַּנָּיֵי תַנֵּי. כּוּלָּן עֵדִים וּמְעִידִין בִּפְנֵי אֲחֵרִים. רִבִּי יְהוּדָה בַּר פָּזִי בְשֵׁם רִבִּי זְעִירָה. כְּשֵׁם שֶׁחוֹלְקִין כָּאן כָּךְ חוֹלְקִין בְּעֵדוּת הַחוֹדֶשׁ.

וִיקוּם חַד וִיתִיב חַד וִיקוּם חַד וִיתִיב חַד. שַׁנְיָיא הִיא שֶׁאֵין הָעֵד נַעֲשֶׂה דַיָּין. רַב הוּנָא הֲוָה יְדַע שַׂהֲדוּ לְחַד בַּר נַשׁ. אֲזַל בָּעֵי מֵידוֹן קוֹמֵיהּ וְכָפַר בֵּיהּ. אֲמַר רִבִּי שְׁמוּאֵל בַּר רַב יִצְחָק. בְּגִין דְּאַתְּ יְדַע דְּרִבִּי הוּנָא אִינְשָׁא רַבָּה אַתְּ כְּפַר בֵּיהּ. מָהוּ דְיֵיזִיל וְיִסְהוֹד עֲלָךְ קוֹמֵי בֵית דִּין חוֹרוֹן. אֲמַר לֵיהּ רַב הוּנָא. וְעָבְדִין כֵּן. אֲמַר לֵיהּ. אִין. וְשָׁרָא רַב הוּנָא גַרְמֵיהּ מִן הַהוּא דִינָא וַאֲזַל וְאַסְהִיד קוֹמֵי בֵית דִּין חוֹרוֹן.

1 רב הונא | **ר** כהדא רב חונה 2 קומיה | **ר** קומוי אמ' | **ר** אמ' ליה 3 דר' הונא אינשא רבא | **ר** דרב חונא בר נשא רבא מהו דייזיל | **ר** מה אילו ייזיל 3 ויסהוד | **ר** וישהד 4 הונא | **ר** חונה (פעמים) 5 ואסהיד | **ר** ואשהיד חורון | **ר** חורן

[127]It was stated: If the Synhedrion[128] saw the killer. Some Tannaïm state: two of them become witnesses and testify before the rest of them[129]. There are Tannaïm who state that they all are witnesses and have to go and testify before other [judges][130]. Rebbi Jehudah ben Pazi in the name of Rebbi Ze`ira: As they differ here, so they differ about testimony for the New Moon[131].

[132]Why cannot always one stand up and one sit down[133]? There is a difference because a witness cannot be a judge[134]. Rav Huna knew testimony for somebody. He[135] came and wanted to have the suit judged before Rav Huna, and denied all. Rebbi Samuel ben Rav Isaac told him, because you know that (Rebbi) [Rav][136] Huna is an important person[137] you deny everything. What if Rav Huna went and testified against you in another court? Rav Huna asked him, does one do that? He answered, yes. Rav Huna recused himself from that suit, went, and testified before another court[138].

127 This paragraph has parallels in *Roš Haššanah* 3:1, *Sotah* 9:1 (Notes 18-19). The two are copies of one another; the text here is a reformulation.

128 In the other sources, "a court". The text here is influenced by the sequel which deals with a court empowered to treat calendar matters, the Synhedrion.

129 After addition of another two judges to complete the required number of judges.

130 They hold that a witness is automatically disqualified as a judge since he has an opinion about the case before the start of the proceedings.

131 Whether members of the Synhedrion who saw the New Moon may act as witnesses before their colleagues.

132 This paragraph is a parallel to the text in *Roš Haššanah* 3:1 (58d l.2), noted **ר**.

133 This refers to Mishnah *Roš Haššanah* 3:1 which prescribes that if three members

of the Court saw the New Moon, one of them may sit with two others as a court and the other two who saw the New Moon appear as witnesses before them. The question arises, why does one have to call two others; would one not be sufficient if alternatingly one stands up as a witness and one sits down as a judge.

134 Even if one does not hold that a potential witness be automatically disqualified as a judge, he must hold that once a person acted as a witness he is disqualified as a judge.

135 Rav Huna knew testimony for a creditor. The debtor required that the suit be heard in Rav Huna's court. He knew that Rav Huna, as judge, could not act as witness and was prevented from using his knowledge in his judgment. He thought it was safe to deny any debt.

136 The correct title is in **ר**.

137 As Rav's successor, he was Chief Judge of all courts under the jurisdiction of the Academy of Sura. The debtor assumed that a Chief Judge could not appear in a lower court.

138 This decides practice. A judge who knows of the case has to disqualify himself and appear as a witness in another court. The Babli agrees, *Roš Haššanah* 25b, *Bava qamma* 90b.

(18c line 26) תַּנֵּי רִבִּי שִׁמְעוֹן בֶּן יוֹחַי. וְקִדַּשְׁתֶּם אֵת שְׁנַת הַחֲמִשִּׁים שָׁנָה. שָׁנִים אַתָּה מְקַדֵּשׁ וְלֹא חֳדָשִׁים. וְהָתַנִּינָן. רֹאשׁ בֵּית דִּין אוֹמֵר. מְקוּדָּשׁ. מָהוּ מְקוּדָּשׁ. מְקוּיָּם. תַּנֵּי. לְקִידּוּשׁ הַחוֹדֶשׁ מַתְחִילִין מִגָּדוֹל. אָמַר רִבִּי חִייָה בַּר אָדָא. מַתְנִיתָא אָמְרָה כֵן. רֹאשׁ בֵּית דִּין אוֹמֵר. מְקוּדָּשׁ. תַּנֵּי. לְעִיבּוּר הַחוֹדֶשׁ מַתְחִילִין מִן הַצַּד. אָמַר רִבִּי זְבִידָא. וְהָהֵן בֵּיתָא דִלְרַע לָא נְהִיגִין כֵּן. וְלָא שְׁמִעַ דָּמַר רִבִּי חִייָה נַּר מַרְיָיא וְרִבִּי יוֹנָה וְרִבִּי בָּא בַּר חִייָה בְּשֵׁם רִבִּי יוֹחָנָן. לְעִיבּוּר הַחוֹדֶשׁ מַתְחִילִין מִגָּדוֹל. לְעִיבּוּר שָׁנָה מַתְחִילִין מִן הַצַּד. וּכְבָר נִכְנַס רִבִּי יוֹחָנָן וְהָיָה קָטָן שֶׁבְּכוּלָּם. אָמְרוּ לוֹ. אֱמוֹר. הֲרֵי הַשָּׁנָה מְקוּדֶּשֶׁת בְּעִיבּוּרָהּ. אָמַר. הֲרֵי הַשָּׁנָה מְקוּדֶּשֶׁת בְּעִיבּוּרה. אָמַר רִבִּי יוֹנָתָן. רְאֵה לָשׁוֹן שֶׁלִּימְּדָנוּ בֶּן הַנַּפָּח. אִילּוּ אָמַר. בְּעִיבּוּרָהּ. הָיִיתִי אוֹמֵר. אֵילּוּ אַחַד עָשָׂר יוֹם שֶׁהַחַמָּה עוֹדֶפֶת עַל לְבָנָה. אֶלָּא בְעִיבּוּר. שֶׁהוֹסִיפוּ לָהּ חֲכָמִים שְׁלֹשִׁים יוֹם. רִבִּי יַעֲקוֹב בַּר אָחָא רִבִּי יַסָּא בְּשֵׁם רִבִּי יוֹחָנָן. לְעִיבּוּר הוֹלְכִין אַחַר הַמִּינּוּי. לְבֵית הַוַּעַד הוֹלְכִין אַחַר הָרֶגֶל. וְהוּא שֶׁיֵּשׁ כָּל־אֶחָד מְדַבֵּר בִּמְקוֹמוֹ וְחוֹתֵם. כְּגוֹן רִבִּי חֲנִינָה פָּתַח. רִבִּי יוֹחָנָן וְרֵישׁ לָקִישׁ חוֹתְמִין. רִבִּי בָּא בַּר זַבְדָּא פָּתַח. רִבִּי יַסָּא וְרִבִּי אִמִּי חָתְמִין. רִבִּי חַגַּיי פָּתַח. רִבִּי יוֹנָה וְרִבִּי יוֹסֵי חָתְמִין. רִבִּי כַהֲנָא אִימְנִי קוֹמֵי רִבִּי יַעֲקוֹב בַּר אָחָא וְעָל רִבִּי יַעֲקוֹב בַּר אָחָא קַמֵּיהּ מְנַיֵּיהּ לְעִיבּוּרָא. אָמַר. אָכֵן מָרָהּ דִּשְׁמַעְתָּא לָא מְקַיֵּים לָהּ.

1 יוחי | **ר** יוחי או' אתה מקדש | **ר** מקדשין 2 ולא | **ר** ואין מקדשין והתנינן | **ר** והא תנינן 3 מגדול | **ר** מן הגדול 4 החודש | **ר** השנה ביתא | **ר** בייתא 5 מרייא | **ר** מדייא ור' יונה | **ר** ר' יונה ר' בא בר חייה | **ר** ר' בא ר' חייה בשם ר' חייה 6 לעיבור | **ר** לקידוש שנה | **ר** השנה 7 והיה קטן שבכולם | **ר** והוא היה הקטן שבהן 8 בעיבורה | **ר** בעיבור 9 לבנה | **ר** הלבנה בכל שנה יום | **ר** יום ועיבורה 11 הרגל | **ר** הרגיל שיש | **ר** שיהא אחד | **ר** אחד ואחד וחותם | **ר** - וריש לקיש חותמין | **ר** ור' שמעון בן לקיש חתמין

12 ר' יסא ור' אמי | **ר** ר' חייה ור' אסי ור' אימי 13 יוסי | **ר** יסָא אימני | **ר** איתמני קומי | **ר** קדמיי מן ועל | **ר** אעל קמיה מנייה | **ר** קגמיי מיניה 14 אכן | **ר** הכין דשמעתא | **ר** דשמועתא

[138]Rebbi Simeon ben Iohai stated: *You shall sanctify the Fiftieth Year*[140]. You shall sanctify years but not months[141]. But did we not state[142]: "The president of the court says: sanctified"? What means sanctified? Confirmed[143]. It was stated: For sanctifying months one starts[144] with the most senior person. Rebbi Hiyya bar Ada said, the Mishnah says this: "The president of the court says: sanctified." It was stated, for intercalation of the (month) [year][145] one starts from the side[146]. Rebbi Zebida said, but this lower house[147] do not proceed in this way, for they did not hear what Rebbi Hiyya bar Marius[148] and Rebbi Jonah, Rebbi Abba bar Hiyya said in the name of Rebbi Johanan: For lengthening the month one starts with the most senior person, for intercalating the year one starts from the side. When Rebbi Johanan was participating as the most junior person, they told him, say: "this year is sanctified in its intercalation." He said, "this year is sanctified in intercalation." Rebbi Jonathan said, look at the language which the smith's son[149] taught us. If he had said, "in its intercalation," I would have said that this refers to the eleven days by which the solar year exceeds the lunar one, but [he said] "in intercalation", that the Sages added thirty days to it[150]. Rebbi Jacob bar Aha, Rebbi Yasa in the name of Rebbi Johanan: For intercalation one follows the date of ordination. In the Academy one follows usage; each one gives his opinion at his place and sums up. For example, Rebbi Hanina[151] started, Rebbi Johanan and Rebbi Simeon ben Laqisch summed up. Rebbi Abba bar Zavda started, Rebbi Yasa and Rebbi Immi[152] summed up. Rebbi Haggai started, Rebbi Jonah and Rebbi Yose summed up. Rebbi Cahana was ordained before Rebbi Jacob bar Aha, but Rebbi Rebbi Jacob bar Aha participated in intercalation before Rebbi Cahana was invited. He said, the person who formulated the tradition does not respect it for himself[153].

139 This and the following paragraphs are copied from *Roš Haššanah* 2:6 (ר), which is the original source.

140 *Lev.* 25:10.

141 The "sanctification of the month" (Note 119) really is a sanctification of the Day of the New Moon (*Num.* 28:11-15), not of the entire month. But the Jubilee year itself is holy.

In the Babli 10b, this is in the name of R. Eliezer or R. Eleazar; in *Roš Haššanah* 8b in the name of "the rabbis."

142 Mishnah *Roš Haššanah* 2:8.

143 The day is confirmed as one of additional religious services.

144 Polling the judges' opinions.

145 The text in brackets, from *Roš Haššanah*, is the correct one. The *Sanhedrin* text, in parentheses, is a scribal error.

146 The senior judge sat in the middle, the most junior judge sat on the last chair to his left or right. One starts polling the most junior judge.

147 The Patriarch's court, the only one empowered to determine the calendar, was held in low esteem by him.

148 It is impossible to determine whether מרייא or מדייא is the correct reading.

149 R. Johanan bar Nappaha, "son of the bellows-blower."

150 Any intercalary year has an additional month of 30 days; in the computed calendar this is Adar I.

151 He probably is R. Hinena, the student of R. Johanan in Tiberias, not R. Hanina, his teacher at Sepphoris

152 This is the correct text, not "R. Hiyya, R. Yasa, and R. Immi" as in *Roš Haššanah* since R. Hiyya (bar Abba), while also a student of R. Yasa, is not known to have participated in an Academy with him.

153 By his own teaching in the name of R. Johanan, he should have insisted that R. Cahana be invited first.

(18c line 44) רִבִּי חִיָּה בַּר וָוה הֲוָה קָאִים מַצְלֵי. אָעַל רַב כָּהֲנָא וְקָם לֵיהּ מִן חוֹרֵי מַצְלֵי. חֲסַל רִבִּי חִיָּה וִיתִיב לֵיהּ בְּגִין דְּלָא מֵיעֲבַר קוֹמוֹי. שָׁרֵי רַב כָּהֲנָא מַאֲרִיךְ בִּצְלוֹתֵיהּ. כֵּיוָן דַּחֲסַל אֲמַר. כֵּן אַתּוּן נְהִגִין לִצְעוּרֵי רַבְּכוֹן. אֲמַר לֵיהּ. אֲנָא מִבֵּית עֵלִי קָאֲתִינָא. דִּכְתִיב בְּהוֹ אִם־יִתְכַּפֵּר עֲוֹן בֵּית־עֵלִי בְּזֶבַח וּבְמִנְחָה. בְּזֶבַח וּבְמִנְחָה אֵין מִתְכַּפֵּר. אֲבָל מִתְכַּפֵּר בִּתְפִילָּה. וּצְלֵי עֲלוֹי וְזָכָה לְמֵיסַב עַד דְּאִיתְעַבְּדוֹן טוּפְרוֹי סוּמְקִין כְּהָדָא רַקִּקָה.

1 ווא | ר בא רב | ר ר' מן חורי מצלי | ר מצלי מן אחורויי חסל | ר מן דחסל 2 ר' חייה | ר ר' חייה בר בא מן צלותיה ויתיב | ר יתיב מיעבר | ר מיעבור שרי רב כהנא | ר ר' כהנא כיון | ר מן אמר | ר ר' כהנא אמ' ליה 3 כן | ר הכין נהגין לצעורי רבכון | ר נהיגין גביכון מצערין רברביכון ליה | ר ליה. ר'. מבית עלי קאתינא | ר מדבית עלי דבתיב בהו | ר וכתיב על בית עלי 4 ובמנחה | ר ובמנחה עד עולם מתכפר | ר מתכפר לו (2×) 5 טופרוי סומקין | ר טפרוי סומוקין רקקה | ר דקקה

[154]Rebbi Ḥiyya bar Abba was standing praying. Rav[155] Cahana came and stood behind him in prayer. When Rebbi Ḥiyya had finished, he sat down in order not to walk by him. Rav Cahana spent a long time praying. After he finished, he told him, is that your way to make your teacher suffer? He told him, I am a descendant of the House of Eli, of whom it is written[156]: *if the sin of the House of Eli would be atoned for by sacrifice and offering.* By sacrifice and offering it cannot be atoned for, but it can be atoned for by prayer[157]. He prayed for him, he reached old age while his fingernails remained red like those of a small child[158].

154 This paragraph is inserted only because R. Cahana, a very minor figure, was mentioned before and there was a story known about him. In the Babli, *Berakhot* 27a, it is told that R. Jeremiah bar Abba was praying behind Rav, and that Rav remained immovable until R. Jeremiah had finished praying, from which it is inferred that one may not walk by a person standing in silent prayer.

155 The person here must be *Rebbi* Cahana, as correctly identified in *Roš Haššanah*, not one of the *Rav* Cahanas mentioned in the Babli, one of which was a student (and possibly stepson) of Rav, one generation before R. Ḥiyya bar Abba, and the other a contemporary of Rav Ashi, five generations later. Nevertheless, this *Rebbi* Cahana is characterized as a Babylonian, first by his use of the prefix ק for the present participle and also because only Babylonian families of priests trace their family back to the priest Eli of Shiloh, whose male descendants are cursed to die young.

156 *1S.* 3:14.

157 In the Babli, *Roš Haššanah* 18a, the verse is applied to the family of Rabba bar Nahmani, who could prolong life by Torah study and charity work.

158 Translation of the text of **ר**, דקקה,rather than the text here, רקקה "exceedingly thin".

(18c line 50) רֵישׁ לָקִישׁ אַקְדְּמוֹן לֵיהּ חַד סָב בְּעִיבּוּר וְאַעֲלוּנֵיהּ מִן הַהוּא תַּרְעָא דִּלְהֹן. אָמַר. כֵּן יְהֵא בִשְׂכָרָן. וְלָא שְׁמִיעַ דָּמַר רִבִּי קְרִיסְפְּדָא בְשֵׁם רִבִּי יוֹחָנָן. מַעֲשֶׂה וְעִיבְּרוּ אֶת הַשָּׁנָה שְׁלֹשָׁה רוֹעֵי בָקָר. חַד אָמַר. בְּכִיר וְלָקִישׁ בְּאֲדָר מִינָץ. וְחַד אָמַר. תּוֹר בְּאֲדָר בְּעֶרְיָה יָמוּת וּבְטוּל תֵּינְתָא יִשְׁלַח מָשְׁכֵיהּ. וְחַד אָמַר. קָדוּם בְּאֲדָר פַּח בְּלוֹעַךְ יִפּוּק לְקִיבְלֵיהּ. וַנַּן חַמְיָין הָדֵין שַׁתָּא וְלֵית בָּהּ חַד מִינְּהוֹן. וְעִיבְּרוּ הַשָּׁנָה עַל פִּיהֶם. אָמַר רִבִּי חֶלְבּוֹ וּבֵית דִּין הִסְכִּים עִמָּהֶן. וְלֹא כֵן אָמַר רִבִּי זְעִירָא. וְהוּא שֶׁיְּהוּ הַכֹּל מוֹדִין מִצַּד אֶחָד. כֵּיוָן דְּאִילֵּין מוֹדִין לְאִילֵּין וְאִילֵּין לְאִילֵּין כְּמִי שֶׁכּוּלָּם מוֹדִין מִצַּד אֶחָד.

1 ריש | **ר** ר' שמעון בן בעיבור | **ר** לעיבורא דלהן | **ר** דלהל 2 דמר | **ר** דאמ' קריספדא | **ר** קריספא
ועיברו | **ר** שעיברו את | **ר** - 3 חד | ר חד מינון ולקיש | **ר** לקיש וחד | **ר** וחורנה 4-3 תור באֲדָר . . .
קדום באֲדָר | **ר** switched positions 3 בעריה | **ר** בעדרייה ובטול | **ר** ובטל ישלח משכיה | **ר** משכיה
ישלח פח בלועך | **ר** פוח לוחיך יפוק | **ר** ופוק לקיבליה | **ר** לקובליה ונן | **ר** ואנן הדין | **ר** - 5 ולית | **ר**
דלית השנה | **ר** את השנה ובית דין הסכים | **ר** והסכים בית דין ולא | **ר** לא 6 זעירא | **ר** זעורה והוא | **ר**
והן הכל מודין מצד | **ר** כולם מורין מטעם כיון | **ר** מכיון מודין | **ר** מורין לאילין | **ר** מודיי לאילין 7
שכולם מודין מצד | **ר** שכולן מורין מטעם

They preferred an old man to Rebbi Simeon ben Laqish for intercalation but had to remove him by the other door[159]. He said, this is their reward[160]. Did he not hear what Rebbi Crispus[161] said in the name of Rebbi Joḥanan: It happened that the year was intercalated by three cow hands. One said, in Adar, early and late grain[162] sprout together. One said, in Adar the ox will die naked[163] and try to strip off his hide under the fig tree. One said, if in Adar the East wind[164] blows, open your jaws and go towards it. And we see that this year nothing of these applies. They intercalated the year on their word. Rebbi Helbo said, because the Court agreed with them[165]. Rebbi Ze`ira said, but they all have to agree to the same reason[166]. But since they all agree with one another it was that they all agreed as to the reason[167].

159 He turned out not to have the required qualifications.

160 The embarassment of having to remove a member of the Court is deserved punishment for the powers-that-be who neglected R. Simeon ben Laqish.

161 The form קריספדא is Babylonian. The story is anonymous in Babli 18b.

162 Barley and wheat.

163 In *Roš Haššanah* בעדרייה "in its herd". In Adar (about March) sometimes it is cold and cattle might die; sometimes it is hot, cattle look for shade under trees and rub themselves against them as if they tried to remove their hides.

164 The start of the Hamsin season.

165 The cow hands might have provided the arguments but the action was the Court's; the story is irrelevant for R. Simeon ben Laqish's complaint.

166 How could they follow the cow hands if each of them gave a different reason?

167 All three of them agreed to all three reasons.

(18c line 59) וְרֵישׁ לָקִישׁ מַקְפִּיד עַל הָדָא מִילְּתָא. חָשַׁשׁ עַל מַה דָמַר רִבִּי לָעְזָר. דָּמַר רִבִּי לָעְזָר. וְהָיְתָה יָדִי עַל הַנְּבִיאִים הַחֹזִים שָׁוְא בְּסוֹד עַמִּי לֹא־יִהְיוּ זֶה עִיבּוּר וּבִכְתָב בֵּית־יִשְׂרָאֵל לֹא יִכָּתֵבוּ זֶה הַמִּינּוּי. וְאֶל־אַדְמַת יִשְׂרָאֵל לֹא יָבוֹאוּ זֶה אֶרֶץ יִשְׂרָאֵל. רִבִּי לָעְזָר כַּד סְלַק הָכָא אֲמַר. הָא גַבֵּיי חָדָא. כַּד מְנוּנֵיהּ אֲמַר. הָא גַבֵּיי תְּרֵי. כַּד אָעַל לְעִיבּוּרָא אֲמַר. הָא גַבֵּיי תְּלָת.

1 ריש | ר ר' שמעון בן מקפיד | ר מקפד על מה דמר | ר להיא דאמ' דמר | ר דאמ' 2 בסוד | ר וְהַקֹּסְמִים כָּזָב בְּסוֹד עיבור | ר סוד העיבור 3 ר' לעזר | ר ואמ' ר' לעזר סלק הכא אמ' | ר סלקית להכא אמרית 4 גביי | ר גבי מנוניה אמ' | ר מנונני אמרית גביי תרי | ר גבי תרתיי אעל | ר עלית אמ' | ר אמרית גביי תלת | ר תלתיהון גבי

Why was Rebbi Simeon ben Laqish offended by this? He was worried about what Rebbi Eleazar said, since Rebbi Eleazar said[168]: *My hand will be against the prophets who see . . . vain things, in my people's council*[169] *they shall not be;* that is [the secret of][170] intercalation; *in the documents of the House of Israel they will not be inscribed;* that is ordination; *and to the earth of Israel they shall not come;* that is the Land of Israel. When Rebbi Eleazar came here, he said, I have one. When they ordained him, he said, I have two.

When he was asked to participate in the intercalation, he said, I have all three [with me][170].

168 *Ez.* 13:9. In the Bali, *Ketubot* 112a.

169 Identifying biblical סוד "council" with rabbinic סוד "secret".

170 From the text in *Roš Haššanah*.

(18c line 64) רִבִּי בָּא בַּר זַבְדָּא בְשֵׁם רַב. טַעֲמָא דְּרִבִּי לָעְזָר בֵּירִבִּי צָדוֹק בְּשָׁעָה שֶׁרוֹאִין בֵּית דִּין שֶׁלְּמַעֲלָן דִּין שֶׁלְּמַטָּן שֶׁמְקַדְּשִׁין אוֹתוֹ גַּם הֵם מְקַדְּשִׁין אוֹתוֹ.

Rebbi Abba bar Zavda in the name of Rav: The reason of Rebbi Eleazar ben Rebbi Ṣadoq: When the Heavenly Court sees that the earthly Court sanctifies it, they also sanctify it[171].

171 This is a slightly garbled reformulation of the corresponding paragraph in *Roš Haššanah*; it has no relevance here. The reference is to Mishnah *Roš Haššanah* 2:8 where Rebbi Eleazar ben Rebbi Sadoq says that the New Moon after a month of 30 days does not need sanctification by the Court since it was sanctified by Heaven. In *Roš Haššanah* one reads: When the Heavenly court sees that the Earthly Court *did not* sanctify (the 30th day), they (automatically) sanctify (the 31st day.)

(18c line 66) רִבִּי לָעְזָר בְּשֵׁם רִבִּי חֲנִינָה. מַעֲשֶׂה בְּעֶשְׂרִים וְאַרְבַּע קְרִיּוֹת שֶׁלְּבֵית רִבִּי שֶׁנִּכְנְסוּ לְעַבֵּר שָׁנָה בְלוֹד וְנִכְנְסָה בָהֶן עַיִן רַע וָמֵתוּ כוּלָּם בְּפֶרֶק אֶחָד. מֵאוֹתָהּ שָׁעָה עֲקָרוּהָ מִיהוּדָה וּקְבָעוּהָ בַגָּלִיל. בְּעַיּוֹן מִיעֲקַר אַף אָהֵן סֵימָנָא. אֲמַר לוֹן רִבִּי סִימוֹן. אֵין אָנוּ מַנִּיחִין בִּיהוּדָה אֲפִילוּ זֶכֶר. וַהֲרֵי מָצִינוּ שֶׁקִּידְּשׁוּ אֶת הַשָּׁנָה בְּבַעֲלָת. הָדָא בַעֲלָת זִימְנִין מִיְּהוּדָה וְזִימְנִין מִדָּן. אֶלְתְּקֵה וְגִבְּתוֹן וּבַעֲלָת הֲרֵי הֵן מִיְּהוּדָה. בַּעֲלָה וְעִיִּים וָעֶצֶם הֲרֵי מִדָּן. וַהֲרֵי מָצִינוּ שֶׁקִּידְּשׁוּ אֶת הַשָּׁנָה בְּבַעֲלָת. מֵימַר. בָּתִּים מִיְּהוּדָה וְשָׂדוֹת מִדָּן. רִבִּי יִרְמְיָה בְעָא קוֹמֵי רִבִּי זְעִירָא. וְלוֹד לָאו מִיְּהוּדָה הִיא. אֲמַר לֵיהּ אִין. וּמִפְּנֵי מַה אֵין מְעַבְּרִין בָּהּ. אֲמַר לֵיהּ. שֶׁהֵן גַּסֵּי רוּחַ וּמְעוּטֵי תוֹרָה. הֲפִיךְ אַפּוֹי וַחֲמָא רִבִּי אָחָא וְרִבִּי יוּדָה בֶּן פָּזִי. אֲמַר לֵיהּ. אִיטָא עֲבַדְתָּנִי מְבַזֶּה רַבָּנָן.

Rebbi Eleazar in the name of Rebbi Ḥanina. It happened that 24 people appointed by the House of Rebbi entered to intercalate the year at Lydda when an evil eye entered with them and they all died at the same time. From that time on they removed it from Judea and established it in Galilee. They also wanted to remove the signal[172]. Rebbi Simon told them, do we not even want to leave a remembrance in Judea? But we find that they intercalated the year at Ba`alat. This Ba`alat is sometimes [mentioned as being] in Judea, sometimes in Dan. *Elteqe, and Gibbeton, and Ba`alat* are from Judea[173]. *Ba`alah, and Iyyim, and Asem*[174] are from Dan, and we find that they intercalated the year at Ba`alat. Let us say that the houses were in Judea and the fields in Dan. Rebbi Jeremiah asked before Rebbi Ze`ira: Is Lydda not in Judea[175]? He answered, yes. Then why does one not intercalate there? He told him, because they are coarse of spirit and have little learning[176]. He turned his face and saw Rebbi Aḥa and Rebbi Judah ben Pazi[177]. He said to him, presently[178] you made me insult rabbis.

172 They wanted to drop the condition of agriculture in Judea from consideration in deciding on intercalation, as described in the next paragraph.

173 *Jos*. 19:44, in the list of cities of *Dan*.

174 *Jos*. 15:29, in the list of cities of *Jehudah*. Probably the reference should have been to v. 24, mentioning the town of בְּעָלוֹת.

175 In post-biblical Judea; it was in biblical Benjamin (*1Chr*. 8:13).

176 While before the war of Bar Kokhba it was one of the main seats of learning.

177 Rabbis of Lydda.

178 Greek εἶτα. Since the word is also found in Syriac, it is not impossible that two native Babylonians used it when speaking to one another.

(18d line 1) עַל שְׁלֹשָׁה סֵימָנִין מְעַבְּרִין אֶת הַשָּׁנָה. עַל אָבִיב וְעַל הַתְּקוּפָה וְעַל פֵּירוֹת הָאִילָן. עַל שְׁנַיִם מְעַבְּרִין עַל אֶחָד אֵין מְעַבְּרִין. וְאִם עִיבְּרוּהָ הֲרֵי זֶה מְעוּבֶּרֶת. וּכְשֶׁהָיָה אָבִיב אֶחָד מֵהֶן הָיוּ שְׂמֵחִין. רַבָּן שִׁמְעוֹן בֶּן גַּמְלִיאֵל אוֹמֵר. אַף עַל הַתְּקוּפָה.

[179]"For three indications one intercalates a year: because of fresh grain[180], the equinox[181], and tree fruits[182]. One intercalates because of two of them, because of a single one does not intercalate; but if they intercalated, it is intercalated. If fresh grain was one of the reasons, everybody was happy[183]. Rabban Simeon ben Gamliel said, also[184] because of the equinox."

עַל שָׁלֹשׁ אֲרָצוֹת מְעַבְּרִין לַשָּׁנָה. עַל יְהוּדָה וְעַל עֵבֶר הַיַּרְדֵּן וְהַגָּלִיל. עַל שְׁתַּיִם מְעַבְּרִין עַל אַחַת אֵין מְעַבְּרִין. וְאִם עִיבְּרוּהָ אֵינָהּ מְעוּבֶּרֶת. וּכְשֶׁהָיְתָה יְהוּדָה אַחַת מֵהֶן הָיוּ שְׂמֵחִין מִפְּנֵי שֶׁהָעוֹמֶר בָּא מִמֶּנָּהּ.

"For three regions one intercalates a year, because of Judea, Transjordan, and Galilee[186]. One intercalates because of two of them, while because of one of them one does not intercalate; if they did intercalate it is not intercalated[187,188]. If Judea was one of the reasons, everybody[189] was happy since the `*Omer* was brought from there.

אֵין מְעַבְּרִין לֹא מִפְּנֵי הַצִּינָּה וְלֹא מִפְּנֵי הַגְּשָׁמִים. וְאִם עִיבְּרוּהָ אֵינָהּ מְעוּבֶּרֶת. אֵין מְעַבְּרִין לֹא מִפְּנֵי הַגְּדָיִים וְלֹא מִפְּנֵי הַגּוֹזָלִין וְלֹא מִפְּנֵי הֶחָלָב. וְכוּלָּם סַעַד לַשָּׁנָה. וְאִם עִיבְּרוּהָ מְעוּבֶּרֶת. רִבִּי יַנַּאי אָמַר מִשּׁוּם רַבָּן גַּמְלִיאֵל שֶׁהָיָה אוֹמֵר. אִימְּרַיָּא רַכִּיכִין וְגוֹזָלַיָּא דַקִּיקִין וּשְׁפַר בְּאַפּוֹי וּבְאַפֵּי חֲבֵירַיי מוֹסְפָא עַל שַׁתָּא דָא תַלְתִּין יוֹמִין.

[190]"One intercalates neither because of the cold, nor because of the rains[191]; if they did intercalate it is not intercalated[188]. One intercalates neither because of kid goats nor because of pigeon chicks, nor because of milk [lambs][192]; but all of them are ancillary reasons for the year. [193]Rebbi Yannai[194] said that Rabban Gamliel[195] used to say: The sheep are thin and the pigeon chicks small; it appears good in my eyes and in those of my colleagues to add thirty days to the year."

תַּנֵּי. אָמַר רִבִּי יוּדָן. מַעֲשֶׂה בְרַבָּן גַּמְלִיאֵל וּזְקֵינִים שֶׁהָיוּ יוֹשְׁבִין עַל גַּב מַעֲלָה בְהַר הַבַּיִת וְיוֹחָנָן סוֹפֵר הַלָּז יוֹשֵׁב לִפְנֵיהֶן. אָמַר לוֹ רַבָּן גַּמְלִיאֵל. כְּתוֹב. לַאֲחָנָא בְנֵי דְרוֹמָא עִילָּאָה לַאֲחָנָא בְנֵי דְרוֹמָא אַרְעַיָּא שְׁלַמְכוֹן יִסְגֵּא. מוֹדַעְנָא לְכוֹן דְּמָטָא זְמַן בִּיעוּרָא. לַאֲפוּקֵי מַעְשְׂרַיָּא מֵעוּמְרֵי שׁוּבְלַיָּא. וְלַאֲחָמָא בְנֵי גָלִילָא עִילָּאָה וּבְנֵי גָלִילָא אַרְעַיָּא שְׁלַמְכוֹן יִסְגֵּא. מוֹדַעְנָא לְכוֹן דְּמָטָא זְמַן בִּיעוּרָא. תַּפְקוּן מַעְשְׂרַיָּא מִמַּעְטָנֵי זֵיתַיָּא. לַאֲחָמָא בְנֵי גָלוּתָא דְבָבֶל בְּנֵי גָלוּתָא דְמָדַי בְּנֵי גָלוּתָא דְיָוָן וּשְׁאָר כָּל־גַּלְוָותָא דְיִשְׂרָאֵל שְׁלַמְכוֹן יִסְגֵּא. מוֹדַעְנָא לְכוֹן דְּאִימְּרַיָּא רַכִּיכִין וְגוֹזָלַיָּא דַקִּיקִין וְזִימְנָא דַאֲבִיבָא לָא מְטָא וּשְׁפַר מִילְּתָא בְּאַפַּיי וּבְאַנְפֵּי חֲבֵירַיי מוֹסְפָא עַל שַׁתָּא דָא תַלְתִּין יוֹמִין.

[196]"Rebbi Jehudah said: it happened that Rabban Gamliel and the Elders were sitting on stairs on the Temple Mount[197]; their scribe Joḥanan was sitting before them when Rabban Gamliel said to him, write: To our brothers in the Upper Southland and the Lower Southland[198], may you have much peace. We inform you that the time of liquidation has come, to deliver tithes from the sheaves of grain. To our brothers in the Upper Galilee and the Lower Galilee[199], may you have much peace. We inform you that the time of liquidation has come, to deliver tithes from the olive presses. To our brothers in the diaspora of Babylonia, the diaspora of Media, the diaspora of Greece, and all other diasporas of Israel, may you have much peace. We inform you that the sheep are thin, the pigeon chicks small, and springtime has not

arrived; it appears good in my eyes and those of my colleagues to add thirty days to this year."

אֵין מְעַבְּרִין אֶת הַשָּׁנָה אֶלָּא אִם כֵּן הָיְתָה חֲסֵירָה רוֹב הַחוֹדֶשׁ. וְכַמָּה רוֹב הַחוֹדֶשׁ. י"ו יוֹם. רִבִּי יְהוּדָה אוֹמֵר שְׁתֵּי יָדוֹת הַחוֹדֶשׁ כ"א יוֹם. אָמַר רִבִּי שְׁמוּאֵל בַּר נַחְמָן. וְהוּא שֶׁיִּקָּרֵב הָעוֹמֶר סוֹף נִיסָן שֶׁלַּתְּקוּפוֹת. אָמַר רִבִּי יוֹסֵי. עַד הַפֶּסַח. אָמַר רַב מַתַּנְיָה. וְהוּא שֶׁיִּטְּלוּ לוּלָב בְּסוֹף תִּשְׁרֵי שֶׁלַּתְּקוּפוֹת.

[200]"One does not intercalate a year unless it be missing most of a month. How much is most of a month? 16 days[201]. Rebbi Jehudah says two thirds of a month, 21 days." Rebbi Samuel bar Nahman said, only that the *`Omer* should be brought at the end of Nisan of equinoxes[202]. Rebbi Yose said, before Passover[203]. Rav Mattaniah said, only that *lulav* be taken at the end of Tishre of equinoxes[204].

אֵין מְעַבְּרִין לַשָּׁנָה לֹא פָּחוּת מֵחוֹדֶשׁ וְלֹא יוֹתֵר עַל חוֹדֶשׁ. וְאִם עִיבְּרוּהָ אֵינָהּ מְעוּבֶּרֶת.

[205]"One intercalates a year neither less than a month, nor more than a month; if it was intercalated[206], it is not intercalated."

179 The following paragraphs are all in the Tosephta, Chapter 2, 2-11. The present paragraph and the following also are in the Babli, 11b.

180 Since the celebration of the festival of unleavened bread requires the offering of fresh barley grain in the *`omer* ceremony (*Lev.* 23:9-14), the lunar year has to be adjusted so that Passover be celebrated in the "month of fresh grain" (*Ex.* 13:4-5).

181 As explained later, the verses *Ex.* 13:4-5 are interpreted to mean that the spring equinox must fall before Passover, but no more than 30 days earlier.

182 If it seems likely that the fruits will not be edible by Pentecost, the start of the season for First Fruits.

183 It is forbidden to eat from new grain before the *`omer* ceremony, *Lev.* 23:14. If the year was intercalated because new grain was not ready, it imposed no restrictions on people since new grain was not available anyhow.

184 Rashi in his Commentary wants to delete אַף "also", since it dos not make much sense in the context. But since the text is confirmed by three sources, it cannot be deleted.

185 The Babli is undecided as to whether Rabban Gamliel refers to the reasons for intercalations, that the date of the equinox is sufficient as single reason for intercalation, or to reasons for joy.

186 Since the *`omer* can be offered from any place in the Holy Land if barley is not ripe in Judea. Transjordan is defined as that part East of the Jordan which is included in the legal definition of the Land of Israel, cf. *Ševi`it* 6:1, Notes 32-51.

187 In the Tosephta: "it is intercalated." The sentence is missing in the Babli, which has to be read as tacit endorsement of the Tosephta (or better, the Tosephta has to be read as explaining the Babli's position.)

188 Since intercalation was the prerogative of the Synhedrion, the expression "it is not intercalated" can only mean that in this case the intercalation is revocable, in contrast to other cases where it is irrevocable once announced.

189 In Judea, where one could expect cheap new grain after Passover.

190 Babli 11a.

191 The convenience of travelers, pilgrims for the Passover festival, should not be a consideration.

192 Most private obligations of sacrifices are satisfied either with a couple of pigeons or with offerings of lambs and kid goats. It is desirable that there be an ample supply available for pilgrims at Passover time, but this is not an absolute necessity.

193 The text of the Babli makes clear that this sentence explains what is meant by "ancillary reasons for intercalation."

194 The Tanna.

195 In both Babylonian sources, Rabban Simeon ben Gamliel. The Yerushalmi version is preferable, as shown by the later text of Rabban Gamliel I's proclamations.

196 Babli 11b, Tosephta 2:6.

197 Since they assembled outside the Temple precinct, the procedure is to be dated to the time of the Roman procurators who had taken over criminal jurisdiction "40 years before the destruction of the Temple" (Note 31).

198 The grain growing areas South of Lydda, both in the hills (the Upper) and near the coast (the Lower). Heave and tithes, which have to be separated immediately after processing, have to be delivered before the holiday, and Second Tithe, in years 1,2,4,5 of the Sabbatical cycle, taken to Jerusalem for the holiday celebration.

199 For definition of these regions see *Ševi'it* 9:2, Notes 40-41.

200 Babli 13a, Tosephta 2:7.

201 The version of the Tosephta implies that a month has to be added if otherwise the Spring equinox would fall on the 17th of Nisan or later, for R. Jehudah on the 22nd or later.

202 "Nisan of the equinox" is the solar period 30 days from the equinox. He is more restrictive and holds that the equinox must fall on or before (but no more than 30 days before) the 15g of the lunar Nisan. "At the end" means "after the first." (Today's computed calendar sometimes violates this rule.)

203 Since the Passover day is the 14th of Nisan, he requires the Spring equinox not to fall after this date. He is reputed to be the editor of the computed calendar, which however has come to us only through the works of authors living several hundred years later.

204 He requires in addition that the fall equinox be no later than the 15th of Tishre. In our computed calendar, this rule is violated about once in a 19 year period.

205 Babli 11a, Tosephta 2:8. The Tosephta here follows the Yerushalmi text, which allows for a "month", i. e., either 29 or 30 days. The Babli prescribes 30 days; it notes 29 as permissible only for Rabban Simeon ben Gamliel (II). The computed calendar in this matter follows the Babli.

206 For a different number of days.

(18d line 28) אֵין מְעַבְּרִין לֹא בַשְּׁבִיעִית וְלֹא בְמוֹצָאֵי שְׁבִיעִית. וְאִם עִיבְּרוּהָ הֲרֵי זוֹ מְעוּבֶּרֶת. אֵימָתַי רְגִילִין לְעַבֵּר. בְּעַרְבֵי שְׁבִיעִיּוֹת. רִבִּי זְעִירָא בְשֵׁם רִבִּי אַבָּהוּ. הָדָא דְתֵימַר עַד שֶׁלֹּא הִתִּיר רִבִּי לִיקַּח יָרָק מֵחוּץ לָאָרֶץ לָאָרֶץ. אֲבָל מִשֶּׁהִתִּיר רִבִּי לִיקַּח יָרָק מֵחוּץ לָאָרֶץ לָאָרֶץ הִיא שְׁבִיעִית הִיא שְׁאָר שְׁנֵי שָׁבוּעַ.

[207]"One intercalates neither in a Sabbatical year nor the year following a Sabbatical; but if it was intercalated it is intercalated. When does one usually intercalate? The year preceding a Sabbatical." Rebbi Ze`ira said in the name of Rebbi Abbahu, that is before Rebbi permitted to import produce from outside the Land into the Land. But since Rebbi permitted to import produce from outside the Land into the Land, there is no difference between a Sabbatical and the remaining years of the Sabbatical cycle.

207 Babli 12a, Tosephta 2:9, *Nedarim* 6:13, *Šeqalim* 1:2 (46a l.51). The text from here to the end of the Halakhah is essentially copied in *Nedarim*, explained in Notes 83-141. The short parallel in *Šeqalim* belongs to a different tradition. The paragraphs are alternatingly shortened and extended; they cannot be considered exact copies of one another. The Notes to the text following are restricted to indicate deviations from the text in *Nedarim*.

(18d line 32) הָיָה רִבִּי מֵאִיר אוֹמֵר. הֲרֵי הוּא אוֹמֵר. וְאִישׁ בָּא מִבַּעַל שָׁלִשָׁה וַיָּבֵא לְאִישׁ הָאֱלֹהִים לֶחֶם בִּכּוּרִים עֶשְׂרִים־לֶחֶם וגו'. וְהוֹאִיל וְהָיְתָה הַשָּׁנָה צְרִיכָה לְהִתְעַבֵּר מִפְּנֵי מַה לֹא עִיבְּרָהּ אֱלִישָׁע. אֶלָּא מְלַמֵּד שֶׁהָיוּ שְׁנֵי רְעָבוֹן וְהָיוּ קוֹפְצִים לַגְּרָנוֹת.

[208]Rebbi Meïr used to say: it is said, *a man came from Baal Shalisha and brought to the Man of God first fruit bread, twenty loaves,* etc. Since the year should have been intercalated, why did Elisha not intercalate? This teaches that it was a year of famine and people were eager for threshing floors.

(18d line 36) אִית תַּנָּיֵי תַנֵּי. אֵין מְעַבְּרִין מִפְּנֵי הַטּוּמְאָה. רִבִּי יוֹסֵי אוֹמֵר מְעַבְּרִין. שֶׁכֵּן מָצִינוּ בְחִזְקִיָּה שֶׁעִיבֵּר מִפְּנֵי הַטּוּמְאָה. שֶׁנֶּאֱמַר כִּי מַרְבִּית הָעָם מֵאֶפְרַיִם וּמְנַשֶּׁה יִשָּׂשכָר וּזְבֻלוּן לֹא הִטֶּהָרוּ כִּי־אָכְלוּ אֶת־הַפֶּסַח בְּלֹא כַכָּתוּב כִּי הִתְפַּלֵּל יְחִזְקִיָּהוּ לֵאמֹר יְהֹוָה הַטּוֹב יְכַפֵּר בְּעַד. רִבִּי שִׁמְעוֹן אוֹמֵר. אַף עַל פִּי שֶׁעִיבְּרוּ נִיסָן אֵין מְעוּבָּר אֶלָּא אֲדָר. רִבִּי שִׁמְעוֹן בֶּן יְהוּדָה אוֹמֵר מִשּׁוּם רִבִּי שִׁמְעוֹן. עִישָּׂה יְחִזְקִיָּהוּ לְצִיבּוּר לַעֲשׂוֹת פֶּסַח שֵׁינִי.

Some Tannaïm state: "One does not intercalate because of impurity." Rebbi Yose[209] says, one intercalates, since we find that Hezekiah intercalated because of the impurity, as it is said: *For most of the people from Ephraim, Manasse, Issachar, and Zevulun had not been purified, for they ate the Passover contrary to what is written, for Hezekiah had prayed, saying, the Eternal, the Benevolent, will pardon this.* Rebbi Simeon says, even though he intercalated Nisan, it was Adar which was intercalated. Rebbi Simeon ben Jehudah said in the name of Rebbi Simeon: Hezekiah forced the community to celebrate the Second Passover."

(18d line 41) אִית תַּנָּיֵי תַנֵּי. מְעַבְּרִין מִפְּנֵי הַטּוּמְאָה. אִית תַּנָּיֵי תַנֵּי. אֵין מְעַבְּרִין. מָאן דְּאָמַר אֵין מְעַבְּרִין. מִינָהּ כִּי־אָֽכְלוּ אֶת־הַפֶּסַח בְּלֹא כַכָּתֽוּב. וּמָאן דָּמַר מְעַבְּרִין. מַה מְקַיֵּים בְּלֹא כַכָּתֽוּב. מִפְּנֵי שֶׁעִיבְּרוּ נִיסָן וְאֵין מְעַבְּרִין אֶלָּא אֲדָר. וַתְיָיא כַּיי דָּמַר רִבִּי סִימוֹן בַּר זְבִיד. גּוּלְגּוֹלֶת אָרְנָן הַיְבוּסִי מָֽצְאוּ תַּחַת הַמִּזְבֵּחַ.

Some Tannaïm state: One intercalates because of impurity. Some Tannaïm state: One does not intercalate. He who says, one does not intercalate, from the following: *for they ate the Passover contrary to what is written.* How does the one who says one does not intercalate, explain *contrary to what is written*? They intercalated in Nisan but one intercalates only in Adar. This follows what Rebbi Simon bar Zavdi said: they found the skull of Ornan the Yebusite under the altar.

(18d line 46) כְּתִיב כָּל־לְבָבוֹ הֵכִין לִדְרוֹשׁ הָֽאֱלֹהִים וְלַעֲשׂוֹת וּלְלַמֵּד בְּיִשְׂרָאֵל חֹק וּמִשְׁפָּט. רִבִּי סִימוֹן בַּר זְבִיד וְרִבִּי שְׁמוּאֵל בַּר נַחְמָן. חַד אָמַר. אֲפִילוּ כַמָּה עָשָׂה לְטָהֳרַת הַקּוֹדֶשׁ לֹא יָצָא יְדֵי טָהֳרַת הַקּוֹדֶשׁ. וְחַד אָמַר. אֲפִילוּ כָּל־מַעֲשִׂים טוֹבִים שֶׁעוֹשִׂין לְטָהֳרַת הַקּוֹדֶשׁ לֹא יָצָא יְדֵי טָהֳרַת הַקּוֹדֶשׁ. כְּתִיב וַיָּחֵילּוּ בְּאֶחָד לַחוֹדֶשׁ הָֽרִאשׁוֹן לְקַדֵּשׁ וּבְיוֹם שְׁמוֹנָה לַחוֹדֶשׁ בָּאוּ לְאוּלָם יי וַיְקַדְּשׁוּ אֶת־בֵּית־יי לְיָמִים שְׁלֹשָׁה וּבְיוֹם שִׁשָּׁה עָשָׂר לַחוֹדֶשׁ הָרִאשׁוֹן כִּילּוּ׃ וַהֲלֹא לְיוֹם אֶחָד הָיוּ יְכוֹלִין לְבָעֵר כָּל־עֲבוֹדָה זָרָה שֶׁהָיָה שָׁם. אָמַר רִבִּי אִידִי. מִפְּנֵי צַלְמֵי כַשְׂדִּים שֶׁהָיוּ חֲקוּקִים בַּשָּׁשֵׁר.

It is written[211]: *With all his heart he prepared himself to seek God,* to act, and to teach law and justice in Israel. Rebbi Simon bar Zavdi and Rebbi Samuel bar Naḥman. One said, with all he did for the purity of the Temple, he did not fully establish the purity of the Temple. One said, with all the good works he did, he did not fully do his duty for the purity of the Temple. It is written[212]: *They started on the first of the first month, and on the eighth day they entered the Eternal's Hall and sanctified the Eternal's House for* three *days; on the sixteenth of the month they finished.* Could they not have eliminated all idolatry from there in one day? Rebbi Idi said, because of Chaldean idols which were engraved in vermilion.

(18d line 49) שִׁשָּׁה דְבָרִים עָשָׂה חִזְקִיָּהוּ. עַל שְׁלֹשָׁה הוֹדוּ לוֹ וְעַל שְׁלֹשָׁה לֹא הוֹדוּ לוֹ. גִּירֵר עַצְמוֹת אָבִיו עַל מִיטַּת חֲבָלִים וְכִיתֵּת נְחַשׁ הַנְּחוֹשֶׁת וְגָנַז טַבְלָה שֶׁלְּרְפוּאוֹת. וְהוֹדוּ לוֹ. סָתַם מֵימֵי גִיחוֹן הָעֶלְיוֹן וְקִיצֵּץ דַּלְתוֹת הַהֵיכָל וְעִיבֵּר נִיסָן בְּנִיסָן. וְלֹא הוֹדוּ לוֹ.

Six things did Hezekiah do; with three they agreed, with three they did not agree. He dragged his father's bones on a bier of ropes, he smashed the bronze snake, and he hid the table of medicines; they agreed. He closed the upper Giḥon spring, and he cut down the Temple doors, and he intercalated Nisan in Nisan; they disagreed.

(18d line 57) אֵין מְעַבְּרִין קוֹדֶם רֹאשׁ הַשָּׁנָה וְאִם עִיבְּרוּהָ אֵינָהּ מְעוּבֶּרֶת. אֲבָל מִפְּנֵי הַדּוֹחַק מְעַבְּרִין אַחַר רֹאשׁ הַשָּׁנָה מִיָּד. אַף עַל פִּי כֵן אֵינוֹ מְעוּבָּר אֶלָּא אֲדָר. רִבִּי אוֹמֵר.נִיסָן לֹא נִתְעַבֵּר מִיָּמָיו. וְהָתַנִּינָן. אִם בָּא הַחוֹדֶשׁ בִּזְמַנּוֹ. אִם בָּא. לֹא בָא. רַב אָמַר. תִּשְׁרֵי לֹא נִתְעַבֵּר מִיָּמָיו. וְהָתַנִּינָן. אִם הָיָה הַחוֹדֶשׁ מְעוּבָּר. אִם הָיָה. לֹא הָיָה.

One does not intercalate before New Year's Day; if they did intercalate it would be invalid. But for an urgent need one may intercalate immediately after New Year's Day. Nevertheless, only Adar is intercalated.

[213]Rebbi says, Nisan was never lengthened. But did we not state: "If the New Moon appeared in time"? If it would appear; it did not appear. Rav said, Tishre was never lengthened. But did we not state: "If the month was long"? If it would be, it never was.

(18d line 62) וּכְשֶׁקִּידְּשׁוּ אֶת הַשָּׁנָה בְאוּשָׁה בַּיּוֹם הָרִאשׁוֹן עָבַר רִבִּי יִשְׁמָעֵאל בֶּן רִבִּי יוֹחָנָן בֶּן בְּרוֹקָה וְאָמַר כְּדִבְרֵי רִבִּי יוֹחָנָן בֶּן נוּרִי. אָמַר רַבָּן שִׁמְעוֹן בֶּן גַּמְלִיאֵל. לֹא הָיִינוּ נוֹהֲגִין כֵּן בְּיַבְנֶה. בַּיּוֹם הַשֵּׁינִי עָבַר רִבִּי חֲנַנְיָה בֶּן רִבִּי יוֹסֵי הַגְּלִילִי וְאָמַר כְּרִבִּי עֲקִיבָה. אָמַר רַבָּן שִׁמְעוֹן בֶּן

גַּמְלִיאֵל. כָּךְ הָיִינוּ נוֹהֲגִין בְּיַבְנֶה. וְהָתַנֵּי. קִידְּשׁוּהוּ בָּרִאשׁוֹן וּבַשֵּׁינִי. רִבִּי זְעִירָא בְּשֵׁם רַב חִסְדַּאי. אוֹתָהּ הַשָּׁנָה נִתְקַלְקְלָה. מַה בָּרִאשׁוֹן וּמָהוּ בַשֵּׁינִי. רַבָּא בְּשֵׁם רַב. שָׁנָה א' וְשָׁנָה ב'. וְהָתַנֵּי קִידְּשׁוּהוּ בַּיּוֹם הָרִאשׁוֹן וּבַיּוֹם הַשֵּׁינִי.

"When they sanctified the year at Usha, on the first day Rebbi Ismael, the son of Rebbi Johanan ben Beroqa, led and recited following the opinion of Rebbi Johanan ben Nuri. Rabban Simeon ben Gamliel said, we did not follow this at Jabneh. On the second day, Rebbi Hananiah, the son of Rebbi Yose the Galilean, led and recited following Rebbi Aqiba. Rabban Simeon ben Gamliel said, this we did follow at Jabneh." But does this not mean that they sanctified it on the first and the second day? Rebbi Ze`ira in the name of Rav Hisda: That year was disorganized. What is "on the first, on the second"? Rav Abba in the name of Rav: The first year, the second year! But was it not stated: the first day, the second day?

(18d line 64) קִידְּשׁוּהוּ קוֹדֶם זְמַנּוֹ אוֹ לְאַחַר עִיבּוּרוֹ יוֹם אֶחָד. יָכוֹל יְהֵא מְקוּדָּשׁ. תַּלְמוּד לוֹמַר אוֹתָם. אוֹתָם אֵלֶּא הֵם. אֵין אֵלֶּה הֵן מוֹעֲדָיי. קוֹדֶם לִזְמַנּוֹ כ"ט יוֹם. לְאַחַר עִיבּוּרוֹ ל"ב יוֹם. וּמְנַיִין שֶׁמְעַבְּרִין אֶת הַשָּׁנָה עַל הַגָּלִיּוֹת שֶׁגָּלוּ וַעֲדַיִין לֹא הִגִּיעוּ. תַּלְמוּד לוֹמַר בְּנֵי יִשְׂרָאֵל מוֹעֲדַי. עֲשֵׂה מוֹעֲדוֹת שֶׁיֵּעָשׂוּ כָל־יִשְׂרָאֵל. אָמַר רִבִּי שְׁמוּאֵל בַּר נַחְמָן. וְהֵן שֶׁהִגִּיעוּ לִנְהַר פְּרָת.

If they sanctified it before its time or after its lengthening, should I assume it was lengthened? The verse says, *them, them;* not *these are My holidays*? Before its time, the 29th day; after its lengthening, the 32nd day. From where that one intercalates for the year because of the diaspora[215] who set out but did not yet arrive? The verse says, *the Children of Israel.* Make the holidays so they can be observed by all of Israel. Rebbi Samuel bar Nahman said, only if they had reached the river Euphrates.

(18d line 75) אֵין מְעַבְּרִין אֶת הַשָּׁנָה אֶלָּא בִיהוּדָה. וְאִם עִיבְּרוּהָ בַגָּלִיל מְעוּבֶּרֶת. הֵעִיד חֲנִינָה אִישׁ אוֹנוֹ שֶׁאִם אֵינָהּ יְכוֹלָה לְהִתְעַבֵּר בִּיהוּדָה שֶׁמְעַבְּרִין אוֹתָהּ בַּגָּלִיל. אֵין מְעַבְּרִין אוֹתָהּ בְּחוּצָה לָאָרֶץ. וְאִם עִיבְּרוּהָ אֵינָהּ מְעוּבֶּרֶת. אַתְּ חֲמִי. בַּגָּלִיל אֵין מְעַבְּרִין בְּחוּצָה לָאָרֶץ מְעַבְּרִין. בַּגָּלִיל אֵין מְעַבְּרִין וְאִם עִיבְּרוּהָ מְעוּבֶּרֶת. בְּחוּצָה לָאָרֶץ אֵין מְעַבְּרִין וְאִם עִיבְּרוּהָ אֵינָהּ מְעוּבֶּרֶת. בִּיכוֹלִין לְעַבֵּר בְּאֶרֶץ יִשְׂרָאֵל. אֲבָל בְּשֶׁאֵינָן יְכוֹלִין לְעַבֵּר בְּאֶרֶץ יִשְׂרָאֵל שֶׁמְעַבְּרִין אוֹתָהּ בְּחוּצָה לָאָרֶץ.

"One intercalates a year only in Judea, but if it was intercalated in Galilee it is validly intercalated. Hanina from Ono testified that, if it cannot be intercalated in Judea, one intercalates in Galilee." One does not intercalate a year outside the Land; if it was intercalated, it is not validly intercalated. Look at it, one does not intercalate in Galilee; could one intercalate outside the Land[217]? One does not intercalate in Galilee; but if it was intercalated it is validly intercalated. One does not intercalate outside the Land; if it was intercalated it is not intercalated if it was possible to intercalate in the Land of Israel; but if one cannot intercalate in the Land of Israel, one intercalates it outside the Land.

(19a line 6) יִרְמְיָה עִיבֵּר בְּחוּצָה לָאָרֶץ. יְחֶזְקֵאל עִיבֵּר חוּצָה לָאָרֶץ. בָּרוּךְ בֶּן נֵרִיָּה עִיבֵּר בְּחוּצָה לָאָרֶץ. חֲנַנְיָה בֶּן אֲחִי רִבִּי יְהוֹשֻׁעַ עִיבֵּר בְּחוּצָה לָאָרֶץ. שָׁלַח לֵיהּ רִבִּי ג' אִיגְרִין גַּבֵּי רִבִּי יִצְחָק וְרִבִּי נָתָן. בְּחָדָא כָּתַב. לִקְדוּשַּׁת חֲנַנְיָה. וְחָדָא כָּתַב. גְּדָיִים שֶׁהִינַּחְתָּ נַעֲשׂוּ תַיָּשִׁים. וּבְחָדָא כָּתַב. אִם אֵין אַתְּ מְקַבֵּל עָלֶיךָ צֵא לָךְ לְמִדְבַּר הָאָטָד וּתְהִי שׁוֹחֵט וּנְחוּנְיוֹן זוֹרֵק. קְרָא קַדְמִייָתָא וְאוֹקְרוֹן. תִּנְייָתָא וְאוֹקְרוֹן. תְּלִיתָא בְּעָא מְבַסְרְתְּהוֹן. אָמְרִין לֵיהּ. לֵית אַתְּ יְכִיל דִּכְבָר אוֹקַרְתָּנִין. קָם רִבִּי יִצְחָק וְקָרָא בְאוֹרַיְתָא אֵלֶּא מוֹעֲדֵי חֲנַנְיָה בֶּן אֲחִי רִבִּי יְהוֹשֻׁעַ. אָמְרִין אֵלֶּה מוֹעֲדֵי יי. אֲמַר לוֹן. גַּבָּן. קָם רִבִּי נָתָן וְאַשְׁלִים. כִּי מִבָּבֶל תֵּצֵא תוֹרָה וּדְבַר־יְהֹוָה מִנְּהַר פְּקוֹד. אָמְרִין לֵיהּ. כִּי מִצִּיּוֹן תֵּצֵא תוֹרָה וּדְבַר־יי מִירוּשָׁלָם. אֲמַר לוֹן. גַּבָּן. אֲזַל קְבַל עֲלֵיהוֹן גַּבֵּי רִבִּי יְהוּדָה בֶּן בְּתֵירָה לִנְצִיבִין. אֲמַר לֵיהּ. אַחֲרֵיהֶם אַחֲרֵיהֶם. אֲמַר לֵיהּ. לֵי נָא יְדַע מַה תַּמָּן. מַה מוֹדַע לִי דְאִינּוּן חַכְמִין מְחַשְּׁבָה דִּכְוָותִי. מִכֵּיוָן דְּלָא יָדְעֵי מְחַשְּׁבָה דִּכְוָותֵיהּ יִשְׁמְעוּן לֵיהּ. וּמִכֵּיוָן דְּאִינּוּן חַכְמִין מְחַשְּׁבָה דִּכְוָותֵיהּ יִשְׁמַע לוֹן. קָם וּרְכַב סוּסְיָא. הֵן דִּמְטָא מְטָא הֵן דְּלָא מְטָא נְהַגִין בְּקִילְקוּל.

Jeremiah intercalated outside the Land. Ezechiel intercalated outside the Land. Baruch ben Neriah intercalated outside the Land. Hanania the nephew of Rebbi Joshua intercalated outside the Land. Rebbi sent him three letters through Rebbi Isaac and Rebbi Nathan. In one he wrote, to His holiness Hanania. And in one he wrote, the kid goats you left behind became rams. And in one he wrote, if you do not accept, go to the thistle desert, do the slaughtering and let Onias sprinkle. After the first [letter], he honored them. After the second, he honored them. After the third, he wanted to disgrace them. They said to him, you cannot do that since you already did honor us. Rebbi Isaac rose and read in the Torah: These are the holidays of Hanania the nephew of Rebbi Joshua. They said to him, *the holidays of the Eternal*. He told them, that is with us. Rebbi Nathan rose and concluded: For from Babylonia will Torah go forth and the Eternal's word from Nahar-Peqod. They said to him, *for from Zion will Torah go forth and the Eternal's word from Jerusalem.* He told them, that is with us. He went to complain about them to Rebbi Jehudah ben Bathyra at Nisibis. He said to him, follow them, follow them. He said to him, I do not know whom I left there. Who would tell me that they are knowledgeable in computations as I am? If they did not know the computations, they should listen to him. Since they are knowledgeable in computations as he is, he has to listen to them. He got up and rode on a horse. Where he reached, he reached. Where he did not reach, they continued to follow the corrupt [calendar].

(19a line 21) כְּתִיב אֶל־יֶתֶר זִקְנֵי הַגּוֹלָה. אָמַר הַקָּדוֹשׁ בָּרוּךְ הוּא. בְּיוֹתֵר הֵן עָלַי זִקְנֵי הַגּוֹלָה. חֲבִיבָה עָלַי כַּת קְטַנָּה שֶׁבְּאֶרֶץ יִשְׂרָאֵל מִסַּנְהֶדְרִין גְּדוֹלָה שֶׁבְּחוּצָה לָאָרֶץ. כְּתִיב הֶחָרָשׁ וְהַמַּסְגֵּר אֶלֶף. וְאַתְּ מַר הָכֵין. רִבִּי בֶּרֶכְיָה בְּשֵׁם רִבִּי חֶלְבּוֹ וְרַבָּנִן. הֶחָרָשׁ אֶלֶף וְהַמַּסְגֵּר אֶלֶף. וְרַבָּנִן אָמְרֵי. כּוּלְּהוֹן אֶלֶף. רִבִּי בֶּרֶכְיָה בְּשֵׁם רִבִּי. אֵילּוּ הַחֲבֵירִים. וְרַבָּנִן אָמְרִין. אֵילּוּ הַבּוּלְבּוּטִין.

It is written: *to the outstanding Elders in the diaspora.* The Holy One, praise to Him, said: The Elders of the diaspora are very dear to me. But more beloved by Me is a small group in the Land of Israel than a great Synhedrion outside the Land. It is written: *The craftsmen and the smiths one thousand,* and you say so? Rebbi Berekhiah in the name of Rebbi Ḥelbo and the rabbis. Rebbi Berekhiah said, one thousand craftsmen and one thousand smiths. But the rabbis say, together one thousand. Rebbi Berekhiah in the name of Rebbi [Ḥelbo said][218], these are the Fellows; but the rabbis say, these are the councilmen.

(19a line 27) רִבִּי הוֹשַׁעְיָה כַּד הֲוָה מְקַבֵּל שַׁהֲדַייָא בְּעֵינֵי טָב הֲוָה אֲמַר לוֹן. הֱיוּ יֶדְעִין כַּמָּה עֵדוּת יוֹצֵא מִפִּיכֶם. כַּמָּה שְׂכַר בָּתִּים יוֹצֵא מִפִּיכֶם. אָמַר רִבִּי אֲבוּנָא. וְאִין כֵּינִי אֲפִילוּ בְדִינֵי נְפָשׁוֹת. בַּת שָׁלֹשׁ שָׁנִים וְיוֹם אֶחָד בָּא עָלֶיהָ הֲרֵי זֶה בִסְקִילָה. נִמְלְכוּ בֵית דִּין לְעַבְּרוֹ וּבָא עָלֶיהָ אֵינוֹ בִסְקִילָה. אָמַר רִבִּי אָבִין. אֶקְרָא לֵאלֹהִים עֶלְיוֹן לָאֵל גֹּמֵר עָלָי. בַּת שָׁלֹשׁ שָׁנִים וְיוֹם אֶחָד נִמְלְכוּ בֵית דִּין לְעַבְּרוֹ אֵין הַבְּתוּלִין חוֹזְרִין. וְאִם לָאו הַבְּתוּלִין חוֹזְרִין.

Rebbi Hoshaia, when he received witnesses at Kallirhoë, used to say to them: you should know the importance of the testimony that comes from your mouths; how much rent money depends on your mouths. Rebbi Abuna said, if it is so, it is even a matter of criminal law. If somebody sleeps with a girl three years and one day old, he is stoned. The court decides to lengthen, if he sleeps with her he is not stoned. Rebbi Abun said, *I am calling to Almighty God, to the God Who decides with me.* If a girl is three years and one day old, if the court decides to lengthen her hymen does (not) repair itself, otherwise it does [not] repair itself[219].

208 This paragraph has been shortened and become incomprehensible. Cf. *Nedarim* 6:13, Notes 86-88. Both Talmudim always assume that a prophet by his office must have been a member of the High Court.

209 In *Nedarim*: R. Jehudah. This seems to be the correct quote.

210 *2Chr.* 30:18.

211 There is no such verse in the Bible. The text is a combination of *2Chr.* 30:19 and *Ezra* 7:10.

212 *2Chr.* 29:16.

213 This and the following paragraphs also are found in *Ševi`it* 10:2 (Notes 41-55) and *Roš Haššanah* 3:1 (58c l. 51).

214 *Lev.* 23:2. The verse which prescribes publication of the dates of festivals traditionally is spelled defectively אֹתָם "them" as if it were אַתֶּם "you", empowering the High Court to decree the times even in disagreement with the astronomical data.

215 The Babylonians who come to Jerusalem in caravans to celebrate Passover.

216 The full text of the verse, *Num.* 23:44, is quoted in the other sources, resulting in an intelligible argument.

217 Why has the prohibition of intercalation outside the Land to be mentioned at all? Could this prohibition not be inferred from the rule for Galilee?

218 Added from the consensus of the parallel texts, missing here.

219 The text here obviously is wrong, but is correct in the parallel texts. It is talmudic doctrine that a girl becomes nubile one day after her third birthday. If she should have been raped before that day, her hymen will regrow and she remains a virgin; after that day the deflowering is definitive. It is stated that her body will follow the calendar decreed by the court.

(fol. 17d) **משנה ג**: סְמִיכַת הַזְּקֵנִים וַעֲרִיפַת הָעֶגְלָה בִּשְׁלֹשָׁה דִּבְרֵי רִבִּי שִׁמְעוֹן. וְרִבִּי יְהוּדָה אוֹמֵר בַּחֲמִשָּׁה. הַחֲלִיצָה וְהַמֵּיאוּנִין, בִּשְׁלֹשָׁה. נֶטַע רְבִיעִי וּמַעֲשֵׂר שֵׁנִי שֶׁאֵין דָּמָיו יְדוּעִין בִּשְׁלֹשָׁה

וְהַהֶקְדֵּשׁוֹת בִּשְׁלֹשָׁה. וַעֲרָכִין הַמִּיטַּלְטְלִין בִּשְׁלֹשָׁה. רִבִּי יְהוּדָה אוֹמֵר אֶחָד מֵהֶן כֹּהֵן. וְהַקַּרְקָעוֹת תִּשְׁעָה וְכֹהֵן. וְאָדָם כַּיּוֹצֵא בָהֶן.

Mishnah 3: The leaning of Elders[220] and the breaking of the calf's neck[221] by three [judges], the words of Rebbi Simeon, but Rebbi Jehudah says, by five. *Halîṣah*[222] and repudiations[223] by three [judges], [redemption of] the growth of the fourth year[224] and Second Tithe[225] whose value is not known by three [appraisers], also of Temple dedications[226] by three. Estimations of movables[227] by three [appraisers], Rebbi Jehudah says that one of them must be a Cohen; of real estate[228] nine and a Cohen. The same holds for humans[229].

220 *Lev.* 4:15. If the High Court realized that they had erred in a ruling and permitted something which is biblically prohibited, they have to bring a purification sacrifice and a deputation of the Court has to lean with their hands on the head of the sacrificial animal while confessing their error, as detailed in Traxtate *Horaiot*.

221 The ritual of atonement for an unsolved murder, *Deut.* 21:1-9, *Soṭah* Chapter 9.

222 The ceremony by which the widow of a childless man is freed from levirate marriage, which requires involvement of "the Elders", *Deut.* 25:5-9.

223 The repudiation of a marriage by an underage girl, married off by her mother or brothers after her father's death and whose marriage during her minority is valid only rabbinically; cf. *Yebamot* Chapter 13.

224 The fruits of a tree in the fourth year after planting, the first year they are permitted as food, have to be eaten in holiness by the rules of Second Tithe (*Lev.* 19:24; *Ma`aser Šeni* Chapter 5). They may be redeemed under the rules of Second Tithe, the sanctity being transferred to the redemption money.

225 Cf. *Ma`aser Šeni* 4:2, Note 51. Second Tithe remains the farmer's property but must be eaten in purity at the site of the Temple. If there is any danger of spoilage in transport, the produce may be redeemed and the sanctity transferred to the redemption money, *Deut.* 14:22-26; cf. Introduction to Tractate *Ma`aser Šeni.*

226 Property donated to the Temple which will be sold by the Temple treasurer upon appraisal by a committee of three; *Lev.* 27:11.

227 If a person makes a vow to donate the estimated value of a person to the Temple, the amount payable is specified in *Lev.* 27:2-7 depending on age and sex. If the person wants to pay with movables in lieu of money, their value has to be determined by a committee of three. These rules are detailed in Tractate *`Arakhin.*

228 *Lev.* 27:14-25. In all verses speaking of redemption of property donated to the Temple, 'the Cohen" is mentioned in the singular.

229 Somebody promising to pay to the Temple the value a person would fetch if sold as a slave.

(19a line 33) **הלכה ג:** סְמִיכַת הַזְּקֵנִים וַעֲרִיפַת הָעֶגְלָה בִּשְׁלֹשָׁה דִּבְרֵי רִבִּי שִׁמְעוֹן. וְרִבִּי יְהוּדָה אוֹמֵר בַּחֲמִשָּׁה. מַה טַעֲמָא דְרִבִּי שִׁמְעוֹן. וְסָֽמְכוּ שְׁנַיִם. אֵין בֵּית דִּין שָׁקוּל מוֹסִיפִין עֲלֵיהֶן עוֹד אַחֵר הֲרֵי שְׁלֹשָׁה. מַה טַעֲמָא דְרִבִּי יְהוּדָה. וְסָֽמְכוּ שְׁנַיִם. זִקְנֵי שְׁנַיִם. אֵין בֵּית דִּין שָׁקוּל מוֹסִיפִין עֲלֵיהֶן עוֹד אֶחָד. הֲרֵי חֲמִשָּׁה. וּבְעֶגְלָה עֲרוּפָה מַה טַעֲמָא דְרִבִּי שִׁמְעוֹן. זְקֵנֶיךָ שְׁנַיִם. וְשֹׁפְטֶיךָ שְׁנַיִם. אֵין בֵּית דִּין שָׁקוּל מוֹסִיפִין עֲלֵיהֶן עוֹד אֶחָד הֲרֵי חֲמִשָּׁה. מַה טַעֲמָא דְרִבִּי יְהוּדָה. זְקֵנֶיךָ וְשׁוֹפְטֶיךָ שְׁנַיִם. אֵין בֵּית דִּין שָׁקוּל מוֹסִיפִין עֲלֵיהֶן עוֹד אַחֵר הֲרֵי שְׁלֹשָׁה. אָמַר רִבִּי. נִרְאִין דִּבְרֵי רִבִּי יְהוּדָה בָּעֲרוּפָה דְּלָא דְרִישׁ וְיָֽצְאוּ. וְנִרְאִין דִּבְרֵי רִבִּי שִׁמְעוֹן בִּסְמִיכָה דְּלָא דְרִישׁ וְסָֽמְכוּ. אִין תֵּימַר. נִרְאִין דִּבְרֵי רִבִּי יְהוּדָה בָּעֲרוּפָה כְּמוֹ דוּ דָרֵשׁ וְסָֽמְכוּ יִדְרוֹשׁ וְיָֽצְאוּ. אַשְׁכַּח תֵּימַר. וְיָֽצְאוּ שְׁנַיִם. זְקֵנֶיךָ שְׁנַיִם. וְשֹׁפְטֶיךָ שְׁנַיִם. אֵין בֵּית דִּין שָׁקוּל מוֹסִיפִין עֲלֵיהֶן עוֹד אֶחָד. הֲרֵי כָּאן שִׁבְעָה. מַה מְקַיֵּים רִבִּי שִׁמְעוֹן זְקֵנֶיךָ וְשֹׁפְטֶיךָ. זְקֵנֶיךָ שֶׁהֵן שׁוֹפְטֶיךָ. תַּנֵּי רִבִּי לִיעֶזֶר בֶּן יַעֲקֹב אוֹמֵר. זְקֵנֶיךָ. זֶה בֵּית דִּין הַגָּדוֹל. וְשֹׁפְטֶיךָ. זֶה מֶלֶךְ וְכֹהֵן גָּדוֹל.

Halakhah 3: "The leaning of Elders and the breaking of the calf's neck by three [judges], the words of Rebbi Simeon, but Rebbi Jehudah says, by five." [230]What is the reason of Rebbi Simeon? "[The Elders] shall lean," two. No court has an even number of members; one adds another one; that makes three. What is the reason of Rebbi Jehudah? "They shall lean," two. "The Elders," two. No court has an even number of members; one adds one; that makes five. And for the calf whose neck is broken, [231]what is the reason of Rebbi Simeon? "Your Elders," two, "and your judges," two. No court has an even number of members; one adds one; that makes five. What is the reason of Rebbi Jehudah? "Your elders, your judges," two. No court has an even number of members; one adds another one; that makes three. Rebbi said, the words of Rebbi Jehudah are reasonable for the breaking of the neck, for he does not refer to "they shall go out." The words of Rebbi Simeon are reasonable for the leaning of the hands, for he does not refer to "they shall lean." If you would say that the words of Rebbi Jehudah are reasonable for the calf whose neck is broken, if he refers to "they shall lean", he also should refer to "they shall go out." It turns out that you have to say "they shall go out" two, "your Elders" two, "and your judges" two. No court has an even number of members; one adds one more; that makes seven. How does Rebbi

Simeon explain "your Elders and your judges"? Your Elders who are your judges. It was stated: Rebbi Eliezer ben Jacob says "your Elders," that is the High Court; "and your judges," these are king and High Priest.

230 A very similar text is in *Sotah* 9:1. The commentary, Notes 32-45, also applies here. In the Babli, the parallels are *Sanhedrin* 13b, *Sotah* 44b.

231 The arguments of rabbis Simeon and Jehudah have to be switched; cf. *Sotah* 9:1 Note 33. The argument of R. Jehudah (attributed here to R. Simeon) is explicit in Mishnah *Sotah* 9:1. The corrected text, treating R. Jehudah's opinion before R. Simeon's, follows the Babli which as a matter of principle insists on strict chronological order.

(19a line 47) תַּנֵּי הַסְּמִיכוֹת בִּשְׁלֹשָׁה. לֹא סְמִיכָה הִיא סְמִיכוֹת. תַּמָּן קָרֵיי לְמְנוּיָּיה סְמִיכוּתָא. אָמַר רִבִּי בָּא. בָּרִאשׁוֹנָה הָיָה כָל־אֶחָד וְאֶחָד מְמַנֶּה אֶת תַּלְמִידָיו. כְּגוֹן רַבָּן יוֹחָנָן בֶּן זַכַּיי מִינָּה אֶת רִבִּי לִיעֶזֶר וְאֶת רִבִּי יְהוֹשֻׁעַ. וְרִבִּי יְהוֹשֻׁעַ אֶת רִבִּי עֲקִיבָה. וְרִבִּי עֲקִיבָה אֶת רִבִּי מֵאִיר וְאֶת רִבִּי שִׁמְעוֹן. אָמַר. יֵשֵׁב רִבִּי מֵאִיר תְּחִילָּה. נִתְכַּרְכְּמוּ פְנֵי רִבִּי שִׁמְעוֹן. אָמַר לוֹ רִבִּי עֲקִיבָה. דַּיֶּיךָ שֶׁאֲנִי וּבוֹרַאֲךָ מַכִּירִין כּוֹחֲךָ. חָזְרוּ וְחִלְקוּ כָבוֹד לַבַּיִת הַזֶּה. אָמְרוּ. בֵּית דִּין שֶׁמִּינָּה שֶׁלֹּא לְדַעַת הַנָּשִׂיא אֵין מִינּוּיוֹ מִינּוּי וְנָשִׂיא שֶׁמִּינָּה שֶׁלֹּא לְדַעַת בֵּית דִּין מִינּוּיוֹ מִינּוּי. חָזְרוּ וְהִתְקִינוּ שֶׁלֹּא יְהוּ בֵית דִּין מְמַנִּין אֶלָּא מִדַּעַת הַנָּשִׂיא וְשֶׁלֹּא יְהֵא הַנָּשִׂיא מְמַנֶּה אֶלָּא מִדַּעַת בֵּית דִּין.

It was stated: Leanings by three [judges]. Is not leaning the same as leanings[232]? There[233], they call ordination "leaning".

Rebbi Abba said, in earlier times[234], every one was ordinating his students; for example Rabban Joḥanan ben Zakkai ordained Rebbi Eliezer and Rebbi Joshua[235], Rebbi Joshua Rebbi Aqiba, and Rebbi Aqiba Rebbi Meïr and Rebbi Simeon[236]. He said, Rebbi Meïr shall preside; the face of Rebbi Simeon became yellow. Rebbi Aqiba told him, it is enough that I and your Creator recognize your power[237].

They changed and honored this dynasty[238], saying: If a court ordained without the consent of the Patriarch, their ordination is no ordination, but if the Patriarch ordained without consent of the court, his ordination is ordination. They changed again[239] and instituted that neither shall the Court ordain without consent of the Patriarch, nor the Patriarch without consent of the Court.

232 What does the *baraita* imply that is not implied by the Mishnah?

233 In Babylonia, ordination is called "leaning of the hands," in imitation of *Num.* 27:23. In the Babli, 13b, this usage is labelled as that of the Galilean R. Johanan. Modern usage naturally follows the Babli.

234 Before the war of Bar Kokhba.

235 Before his time, one finds neither formal ordination nor the title "Rebbi".

236 In the tradition of the Babli, both were ordained, together with three others, by R. Jehudah ben Bava. This tradition is questioned by the Babli itself, *loc. cit.;* its historical accuracy is in doubt since it counts among the five also R. Jehudah, who belongs to the school of R. Eliezer, not R. Joshua.

237 In the tradition of both Talmudim, R. Simeon is a higher authority than R. Meïr; cf. *Terumot* 3:1, Note 25.

238 In the time of the reconstruction after the war of Bar Kokhba, when the authority of the Patriarch became a political necessity. The dynasty is Hillel's family, reputed to be of Davidic descent.

239 Under Rebbi's successors, who had neither learning nor standing to act alone.

(19a line 56) תַּנֵּי. בָּרִאשׁוֹנָה הָיוּ כוֹתְבִין שְׁטָרֵי חֲלִיצָה. בְּמוֹתָב פְּלוֹנִי וּפְלוֹנִי חָלְצָה פְּלָנִית בַּת פְּלוֹנִי לִפְלוֹנִי בֶן פְּלוֹנִי בְּפָנֵינוּ. דְּקָרְבַת לְקַדְמָנָא וְשָׁרַת סְיָנֵיהּ מֵעִילּוֹי רִיגְלֵיהּ דִּימִינָא וְרָקַת קַדְמָנָא רוֹקָא דְּמִתְחֲזֵי לָנָא עַל אַרְעָא וְאָמְרַת כָּכָה יֵעָשֶׂה לָאִישׁ אֲשֶׁר לֹא־יִבְנֶה אֶת־בֵּית אָחִיו.

It was stated: From earlier times[240], one was writing documents of *halîṣah*[241]: Before X and V[242] did Z daughter of U perform *halîṣah* for V son of W, by coming before us, removing his shoe from his right foot, spitting before us visible spittle on the ground, and saying: *So shall be done to the man unwilling to build his brother's house*[243].

240 Meaning that the text is traditional; its first author is unknown. The parallel in *Mo`ed qatan* 3:5 (82a l. 48) does not have the introduction. [The text in *Mo`ed qatan* is somewhat shortened in the Leiden ms. and *editio princeps* but the full text is in the Ashkenazic fragments published by J. Sussman, *Kobez al Yad* 12(1994) p.70.] A somewhat enlarged text in the Babli, *Yebamot* 39b. is ascribed to R. Jehudah.

241 Needed by the widow to be able to remarry in another jurisdiction.

242 There should be three names mentioned here since the court must have three members.

243 *Deut.* 25:9.

(19a line 60) תַּנֵּי. בָּרִאשׁוֹנָה הָיוּ כוֹתְבִין שְׁטָרֵי מֵיאוּנִין. בְּמַעֲמַד פְּלוֹנִי וּפְלוֹנִי מֵיאֲנָה פְּלָנִית בַּת פְּלוֹנִי בִּפְלוֹנִי בַּר פְּלוֹנִי בְּפָנֵינוּ. לָא רְעִינָא בֵיהּ לָא שְׁוִייָהֲנָא לֵיהּ לָא צְבִינָא לְהִתְנַסְּבָא לֵיהּ.

It was stated: From earlier times[240] one was writing documents of repudiation[223]: Before X and Y[242] did Z daughter of U repudiate V son of W, by coming before us: I do not like him, I do not want to stay with him, I do not agree to be married to him[244].

244 In the Babli, *Yebamot* 107b, this is the required oral declaration of repudiation. The Babli has no document of repudiation; neither have medieval formularies.

(19a line 63) אָמַר רִבִּי יוֹחָנָן הֶקְדֵּשׁ שֶׁפְּדָייוֹ יוֹתֵר עַל דָּמָיו הֲרֵי זֶה פָּדוּי. וּמַעֲשֵׂר שֵׁינִי שֶׁפְּדָייוֹ יוֹתֵר עַל דָּמָיו הֲרֵי זֶה אֵינוֹ פָּדוּי. מַה בֵין הֶקְדֵּשׁ מַה בֵין מַעֲשֵׂר שֵׁינִי. אָמַר רִבִּי לָא. הֶקְדֵּשׁ יֵשׁ לוֹ תוֹבְעִין מַעֲשֵׂר שֵׁינִי אֵין לוֹ תוֹבְעִין. רִבִּי יוֹנָה בְעָא. כְּמָאן דָּמַר. אֵינוֹ כִנְכָסָיו. בְּרַם כְּמָאן דָּמַר. כִּנְכָסָיו הוּא. מַה בֵין הֶקְדֵּשׁ מַה בֵין מַעֲשֵׂר שֵׁינִי. אָמַר רִבִּי יוֹסֵי. וְלֹא כְבָר נֶאֱמַר טַעֲמָא. הֶקְדֵּשׁ יֵשׁ לוֹ תוֹבְעִין מַעֲשֵׂר שֵׁינִי אֵין לוֹ תוֹבְעִין.

רִבִּי זֵירָא בְּעָא קוֹמֵי רִבִּי אִמִּי. נִבְדַּק אוֹתוֹ הָאִישׁ וְאָמַר. לֹא נִתְכַּוונְתִּי. אָמַר לֵיהּ. לְכִי בָדֵק.

אָמַר רִבִּי יוֹחָנָן הֶקְדֵּשׁ שֶׁפְּדָייוֹ וְלֹא הוֹסִיף חוֹמֶשׁ הֲרֵי זֶה פָּדוּי. וּמַעֲשֵׂר שֵׁינִי שֶׁפְּדָייוֹ וְלֹא הוֹסִיף חוֹמֶשׁ אֵינוֹ פָּדוּי. מַה בֵין מַעֲשֵׂר שֵׁינִי לְהֶקְדֵּשׁ. אָמַר רִבִּי לָא. שֶׁכֵּן אָדָם מָצוּי לִהְיוֹת מַרְבֶּה בְהֶקְדֵּישׁוֹ. רִבִּי יוֹנָה בְעָא. כְּמָאן דָּמַר. אֵינוֹ כִנְכָסָיו. בְּרַם כְּמָאן דָּמַר. כִּנְכָסָיו. מַה בֵין הֶקְדֵּשׁ לְמַעֲשֵׂר שֵׁינִי. אָמַר רִבִּי יוֹסֵי. וְלֹא כְבָר אַתְּ אָמַרְתָּ טַעֲמָא. שֶׁאָדָם מָצוּי לְהַרְבּוֹת בְּהֶקְדֵּישׁוֹ.

[245]Rebbi Johanan said, if somebody redeemed Temple dedications for more than their worth, it is redeemed[246]. But if somebody redeemed Second Tithe for more than its worth, it is not redeemed. What is the difference between dedications and Second Tithe? [247,253]Rebbi La said, dedications have claimants, Second Tithe has no claimant. Rebbi Jonah asked, that is following him who says that it is not his property[249]. But for him who says it is his property, what is the difference between dedications and Second Tithe? Rebbi Yose said, the reason has already been explained: dedications have claimants, Second Tithe has no claimant.

[250]Rebbi Ze`ira asked before Rebbi Immi: If the person was checked and he said, that was not what I intended? He answered him, when he will be checked.

Rebbi Johanan said, if somebody redeemed Temple dedications without adding its fifth it is redeemed[251]. But if somebody redeemed Second Tithe dedications without adding its fifth, it is not redeemed[252]. What is the difference between dedications and Second Tithe? [248]Rebbi La said, because a person usually adds to his dedications. Rebbi Jonah asked, that is following him who says that it is not his property[249]. But for him who says it is his property, what is the difference between Second Tithe and dedications? Rebbi Yose said, did you not already give the reason? Because a person usually adds to his dedications.

245 This piece is a composite of two paragraphs in *Ma`aser Šeni* 4:3, Notes 63-68. In the order of subjects, the sources differ from one another.

246 These rules are purely rabbinical in character.

247 This is a *non sequitur.* The text in *Ma`aser Šeni* shows that the text is garbled; the text which belongs here is the other one starting with "R. La said," with Note 248.

248 If a person overpays for redemption of his Temple dedications, it is a natural thing to do. But if he overpays for Second Tithe, the amount set aside for consumption in Jerusalem would be a mixture of sacred and profane money.

249 This refers to R. Meïr's opinion regarding Second Tithe; cf. *Ma`aser Šeni* 4:3, Note 67.

250 This belongs after the text noted [248] and refers to the answer given in Note 248 (cf. *Ma`aser Šeni* 4:3 Note 66.)

251 Even though adding the fifth in general is a biblical obligation; *Lev.* 27:13,15,19.

252 Even though the obligation of adding a fifth to the redemption money (Mishnah *Ma`aser Šeni* 4:2) is not supported by a verse.

253 This is the appropriate answer to the question following Note 252. The Temple treasurer may attach the dedicator's property to collect the fifth; redemption of Second Tithe is a private matter.

(19a line 76) תַּנֵּי. הַהֶקְדֵּישׁוֹת בִּשְׁלֹשָׁה. הָדָא דְתֵימַר בְּמַקְדִּישׁ גּוּף הַשָּׂדֶה. אֲבָל אִם אָמַר. הֲרֵי עָלַי מְנָה לְהֶקְדֵּשׁ. נִישְׁמְעִינָהּ מֵהָדָא עֲרָכִים הַמִּיטַּלְטְלִין בִּג'. וְכִי יֵשׁ עֲרָכִים שֶׁאֵין מִיטַּלְטְלִין. רִבִּי יַעֲקֹב בַּר אָחָא רִבִּי שִׁמְעוֹן בַּר וָוא בְשֵׁם רִבִּי חֲנִינָה. הָאוֹמֵר. עֶרְכִּי עָלַי. וּבָא לְסַדְּרוֹ מִקַּרְקַע. שָׁמִין לוֹ בַעֲשָׂרָה. מִמִּטַּלְטְלִין בִּשְׁלֹשָׁה. הָאוֹמֵר עֶרְכִּי עָלַי. אֵינוֹ כָאוֹמֵר. דְּמֵי שָׂדִי עָלַי. אֲבָל אִם אָמַר. הֲרֵי עָלַי מְנָה לְהֶקְדֵּשׁ. שָׁמִין לוֹ בִּשְׁלֹשָׁה. לִכְשֶׁיַּעֲשִׁיר נִידּוֹן בְּהֶשֵּׂג יָד.

2 בג' | **מ** בשלשה וכי | **מ** - שאין | **מ** שאינן 3 ווא | **מ** בא האומ' | **מ** באומ' ערכי | **מ** הרי ערכי 4 מקרקע | **מ** מן הקרקע ממיטלטלין בשלשה | **מ** מן המיטלטלין שמין לו בשלשה ערכי | **מ** הרי ערכי 5 מנה | **מ** מאה מנה

It was stated: "Temple dedications by three [appraisers]." That is, if one dedicated the body of a field. But if he said, I am vowing a mina for the Temple, [254]let us hear from the following: "Appraisal of movables by three [appraisers]." Do there exist appraisals not of movables[255]? Rebbi Jacob bar Aḥa, Rebbi Simeon bar Abba in the name of Rebbi Ḥanina: If somebody says, I am vowing my appraisal, and comes to settle his debt by real estate, one appraises it by ten [people], by movables by three[257]. Is one who says, I am vowing my appraisal not like one who says, I am vowing my field's value[256]? But if he said, I am vowing a mina for the Temple, one appraises him by three [people]. Should he become rich, he will be judged by what he can afford[257].

254 From here to the end of the Halakhah there exists a copy in *Megillah* 4:4 (75b l. 16ff., **מ**).

255 By definition, "appraisals" refers to the sums of money detailed in *Lev.* 27:1-8. Money always is movable.

256 Since the rules of appraisal are the same in both categories.

257 This is difficult to understand; since the text is confirmed by two copies, it cannot be emended. By biblical law, a reduction of payments for the poor is mandated only for appraisals (*Lev.* 27:8), not for dedications of specified sums. The reduction, based on what he can afford, is determined by a committee of three which must include a Cohen. If the poor person paid only part of the reduced sum and then becomes rich, the original sum is reinstated as soon as he can afford it. If the poor person made his vow (in the *Megillah* version for 100 minas) in order to induce God to make him rich so he may fulfill his vow, it might be in the interest of the Temple to wait with the collection of the debt until the person became affluent.

(19b line 6) תַּנֵּי. הָעֲבָדִים וְהַשְּׁטָרוֹת וְהַמִּטַּלְטְלִין אֵין לָהֶן אִיגֶּרֶת בִּקּוֹרֶת. רִבִּי יוּדָן בַּר פָּזִי אָמַר. אַכְרָזָה. עוּלָּה בַּר יִשְׁמָעֵאל אָמַר. עֲבָדִים שֶׁלֹּא יִבְרְחוּ. הַשְּׁטָרוֹת וְהַמִּטַּלְטְלִין שֶׁלֹּא יִגָּנֵבוּ. רִבִּי בָּא בַּר כַּהֲנָא בְּעָא קוֹמֵי רִבִּי יוֹסֵי. לֵית הָדָא אָמְרָה שֶׁעֲבָדִים נִיפְדִּין בִּשְׁלֹשָׁה. אָמַר לֵיהּ. אִין. וְהָתַנִּינָן בַּקַּרְקָעוֹת תִּשְׁעָה וְכֹהֵן וְאָדָם כַּיּוֹצֵא בָהֶן. אָמַר לֵיהּ. אָכֵין. אָדָם דָּכָא בֶּן חוֹרִין הוּא. חֲנַנְיָה בֶּן שֶׁלֶמְיָה אָמַר בְּשֵׁם רַב. אֲתַא עוֹבְדָא קוֹמֵי רִבִּי וּבְעָא לְמֵיעֲבַד כְּרַבָּנָן. אֲמַר לֵיהּ רִבִּי לְעֶזָר בֶּן פְּרָטָא בֶּן בֶּן רִבִּי לְעֶזָר בֶּן פְּרָטָא. רִבִּי. לֹא כֵן לִימַּדְתָּנוּ מִשּׁוּם זְקֵינֶיךָ. אֶלָּא אִם עָשׂוּ אִיגֶּרֶת בִּקּוֹרֶת. אֲמַר לֵיהּ. אִין. וַחֲזַר וַעֲבַד כְּרַבָּן גַּמְלִיאֵל.

1 העבדים והשטרות והמטלטלין | **מ** עבדים ושפחות ומיטלטלין בקורת | **מ** ביקורת - | **כמ** מהו איגרת ביקורת בן | **כמ** בר 2 אמ' | **כ** אומ' השטרות והמטלטלין | **כ** ושטרות ומטלטלין **מ** שפחות ומיטלטלין יגנבו | **מ** ייגנבו 3 כהנא | **כמ** כהן יוסי | **מ** יוסה שעבדים נפדין | **כ** שהעבד נפדה 4 והתנינן | **מ** אמ' ליה. והא תנינן בקרקעות | **מ** ובקרקעות דכא | **כ** שכן **מ** דהכא 5 חנניה | **מ** חיננה בן | **כמ** בר אמ' | **מ** - למיעבד | **כמ** מיעבד 6 בן בן | **כמ** בן בנו של משום | **כמ** בשם אם | **מ** אם בן 7 אמ' ליה. אין | **כ** וקיבלה **מ** - וחזר | **מ** וחזר ביה גמליאל | **כמ** שמעון בן גמליאל

[258]It was stated: One does not make public tender for slaves, securities, and movables. [What is public tender?] Rebbi Jehudah ben Pazi said, announcement. Ulla bar Ismael said, slaves lest they flee, securities and

movables lest they be stolen. Rebbi Abba bar Cohen asked before Rebbi Yose: Does this not imply that a slave be redeemed in front of three people? He answered him, yes. But did we not state: "Real estate nine and a Cohen. The same holds for humans"? He answered him, but the human here is a free person.

Ḥanania bar Šelemiah in the name of Rav: A case came before Rebbi who wanted to act following the rabbis. Rebbi Eleazar ben Proteus, the grandson of Rebbi Eleazar ben Proteus, said to him: Rebbi, did you not teach us in your grandfather's name, "except if he offered public tender"? He answered, yes, changed his mind, and acted following Rabban Gamliel.

258 The origin of these paragraphs is in *Ketubot* 11:6 (כ), explained there in Notes 116-128. The final paragraph, while also found in *Megillah*, makes sense only in *Ketubot*. The sentence in brackets is not in the text here, it is from *Ketubot*, but is necessary to provide continuity of the text.

(fol. 17d) **משנה ד**: דִּינֵי נְפָשׁוֹת בְּעֶשְׂרִים וּשְׁלֹשָׁה. הָרוֹבֵעַ וְהַנִּרְבָּע בְּעֶשְׂרִים וּשְׁלֹשָׁה שֶׁנֶּאֱמַר וְהָרַגְתָּ אֶת־הָאִשָּׁה וְאֶת־הַבְּהֵמָה וְאוֹמֵר וְאֶת־הַבְּהֵמָה תַּהֲרֹגוּ. שׁוֹר הַנִּסְקָל בְּעֶשְׂרִים וּשְׁלֹשָׁה שֶׁנֶּאֱמַר הַשּׁוֹר יִסָּקֵל וְגַם־בְּעָלָיו יוּמָת כְּמִיתַת הַבְּעָלִים כָּךְ מִיתַת הַשּׁוֹר. הַזְּאֵב וְהָאֲרִי הַדּוֹב וְהַנָּמֵר וְהַבַּרְדְּלָס וְהַנָּחָשׁ מִיתָתָן בְּעֶשְׂרִים וּשְׁלֹשָׁה. רַבִּי לִיעֶזֶר אוֹמֵר כָּל הַקּוֹדֵם לְהָרְגָן זָכָה. רַבִּי עֲקִיבָה אוֹמֵר מִיתָתָן בְּעֶשְׂרִים וּשְׁלֹשָׁה.

Mishnah 4: Capital crimes [are judged] by 23. The participants in active or passive bestiality[259] [is judged] by 23, as it is said, *you shall slay the woman and the animal*[260], and it says, *and you shall slay the animal*[261]. The bull to be stoned[262] [is judged] by 23, as it is said, *the bull shall be stoned, also its owner shall die*[263]*;* like the owner's death sentence so is the ox's death sentence. The wolf and the lion, the bear, and the tiger, and the panther, and the snake are sentenced to death by 23[264]. Rebbi Eliezer says, anyone quick to kill them is meritorious[265]; Rebbi Aqiba says, they are sentenced by 23.

259 Whether human or animal; the additional statement is needed only for the animal.

260 *Lev.* 20:16. Since woman and animal are mentioned together, the animal can be condemned only by a court empowered to

judge the woman who had sex with the animal.

261 *Lev.* 20:15, about male bestiality.

262 Which had killed a human.

263 *Ex.* 21:29.

264 He does not need permission; it is no case for a court.

(19b line 15) **פסקא.** דִּינֵי נְפָשׁוֹת בְּעֶשְׂרִים וּשְׁלֹשָׁה. רִבִּי אַבָּהוּ שָׁאַל. שׁוֹר הַנִּסְקַל כְּרִבִּי מֵאִיר מָהוּ לִיתֵּן כֶּסֶף בִּשְׁלֹשָׁה וְיִסָּקֵל בְּעֶשְׂרִים וּשְׁלֹשָׁה. אָמַר לֵיהּ רִבִּי יוֹסֵי בֵּירִבִּי בּוּן. שׁוֹר הַנִּסְקַל כּוּלּוֹ מָמוֹן הוּא וּגְזֵירַת הַכָּתוּב שֶׁיִּסָּקֵל.

Paragraph. "Capital crimes [are judged] by 23." [265]Rebbi Abbahu asked: Following Rebbi Meïr, should an ox which is stoned have to pay damages by a court of three and be stoned by 23? Rebbi Yose ben Rebbi Abun told him, the rules of an ox which is stoned are all about money; it is a decision of the verse that it should be stoned.

265 End of Halakhah 1, Notes 103-106.

(19b line 18) אגנטוס הֶגֶמוֹן שָׁאַל לְרִבִּי יוֹחָנָן בֶּן זַכַּאי. הַשּׁוֹר יִסָּקֵל וְגַם־בְּעָלָיו יוּמָת. אָמַר לֵיהּ. שׁוּתָף לֵיסְטֵיס כְּלֵיסְטֵיס. וּכְשֶׁיָּצָא אָמְרוּ לוֹ תַלְמִידָיו. רִבִּי. לָזֶה דְחִיתָה בְקָנֶה. לָנוּ מָה אַתְּ מֵשִׁיב. אָמַר לָהֶן. כָּתוּב הַשּׁוֹר יִסָּקֵל וְגַם־בְּעָלָיו יוּמָת. כְּמִיתַת הַבְּעָלִים כָּךְ מִיתַת הַשּׁוֹר. הִקִּישׁ מִיתַת בְּעָלִים לְמִיתַת הַשּׁוֹר. מַה מִיתַת הַבְּעָלִים בִּדְרִישָׁה וַחֲקִירָה בְּעֶשְׂרִים וּשְׁלֹשָׁה. אַף מִיתַת הַשּׁוֹר בִּדְרִישָׁה וַחֲקִירָה בְּעֶשְׂרִים וּשְׁלֹשָׁה.

General[266] אגנטוס asked Rebbi[267] Johanan ben Zakkai: *the bull shall be stoned, also its owner shall die*[263]? He answered, the robber's[268] partner is like the robber. When he had left, his students asked him, rabbi, this one you pushed away with a cane[269]; what are you telling us? He said to them, it is written, *the bull shall be stoned, also its owner shall die,* like the owner's death sentence so is the ox's death sentence. Since the owner's death sentence would be by a court of 23, investigation[270] and cross-examination[271], so the ox's death sentence is by a court of 23, investigation and cross-examination[272].

266 Greek ἡγεμῶν "leader, commander." In 19c l. 61 (Note 366) his name is Antoninus, in 19d l. 4 (Note 373) Antigonos. The story has many parallels in which various forms of the name appear. Jastrow and Krauss think of Quietus, a general of Trajan not likely to have conversed with a person who died under Vespasian. A Genizah text shows that אגנטוס is the correct form. {Perhaps it is not

a name but a title, εὐγενής "noble, well-born."(E. G.)}

267 His title should be Rabban.

268 Greek, ληστής, ληϊστής.

269 Since the owner is not executed, the answer cannot be correct.

270 An exact investigation into the circumstances of the crime; the evaluation of the evidence is within the purview of the court.

271 The determination when, where, and how the crime was committed. Discrepancies in testimony about these questions make prosecution impossible; cf. Mishnah 5:1-2.

272 *Mekhilta dR. Simeon ben Iohai* 21:29.

(fol. 17d) **משנה ה**: אֵין דָּנִין לֹא אֶת הַשֵּׁבֶט וְלֹא אֶת נְבִיא הַשֶּׁקֶר וְלֹא אֶת כֹּהֵן הַגָּדוֹל אֶלָּא עַל פִּי בֵית דִּין שֶׁל שִׁבְעִים וְאֶחָד. וְאֵין מוֹצִיאִין לְמִלְחֶמֶת הָרְשׁוּת אֶלָּא עַל פִּי בֵית דִּין שֶׁל שִׁבְעִים וְאֶחָד. אֵין מוֹסִיפִין עַל הָעִיר וְעַל הָעֲזָרוֹת אֶלָּא עַל פִּי בֵית דִּין שֶׁל שִׁבְעִים וְאֶחָד. אֵין עוֹשִׂין סַנְהֶדְרָיוֹת לַשְּׁבָטִים אֶלָּא עַל פִּי בֵית דִּין שֶׁל שִׁבְעִים וְאֶחָד. אֵין עוֹשִׂין עִיר הַנִּדַּחַת אֶלָּא עַל פִּי בֵית דִּין שֶׁל שִׁבְעִים וְאֶחָד. וְאֵין עוֹשִׂין עִיר הַנִּדַּחַת בַּסְּפָר וְלֹא שָׁלֹשׁ אֲבָל עוֹשִׂין אַחַת אוֹ שְׁתַּיִם.

Mishnah 5: One judges neither a tribe[273], nor a false prophet[274], nor the High Priest[275], except by the court of 71 [judges]. One may start a war of choice[276] only by the court of 71 [judges][334]. One may add to the City[277] or to the Temple courtyards only by the court of 71 [judges]. One appoints high courts for the tribes[278] only by the court of 71 [judges]. One declares a town as deviant[279] only by the court of 71 [judges]; one does not declare a border town as deviant, nor three together, but one may declare one or two.

273 According to the Halakhah, either the head of the tribe or a case in which one of the parties is a tribe. The only court of 71 members was the Supreme Court, Mishnah 6.

274 *Deut.* 18:20.

275 Accused of a crime.

276 Any war except a defensive war started by an outside attacker.

277 The part of Jerusalem where sacrifices may legally be eaten. Cf. Mishnah *Ševuot* 2:2.

278 Required by *Deut.* 16:19.

279 A town collectively practicing idolatry, which must be destroyed, *Deut.* 13:13-19.

(19b line 24) **מתני'**. אֵין דָּנִין לֹא אֶת הַשֵּׁבֶט כול'. אִיתָא חֲמִי. שְׁנַיִם אֵין דָּנִים לֹא כָל־שֶׁכֵּן שֵׁבֶט. אָמַר רִבִּי מַתַּנְיָה. בִּנְשִׂיא שְׁבָטִים הִיא מַתְנִיתָא. אָמַר רִבִּי לִיעֶזֶר. בַּחוֹרֶשׁ שֶׁבֵּין שְׁנֵי שְׁבָטִים הִיא מַתְנִיתָא.

Mishnah: "One judges neither a tribe," etc. Come and look: One does not try two people together[280], so much less an entire tribe? Rebbi Mattaniah said, the Mishnah speaks of the head of the tribe[281]. Rebbi Eliezer[282] said, the Mishnah speaks about a forested area between two tribes[283].

280 Mishnah 6:8.

281 A criminal trial. In the Babli, 15b, this is reported in the name of a Rav Mattanah.

282 Read: R. Eleazar.

283 A border dispute.

(19b line 26) אָמַר רִבִּי זְעִירָא. נֶאֱמַר כָּאן זָדוֹן וְנֶאֱמַר לְהַלָּן זָדוֹן בְּזָדוֹן דִּבְּרוֹ הַנָּבִיא. מַה זָדוֹן שֶׁנֶּאֱמַר לְהַלָּן בִּנְבִיא הַשֶּׁקֶר הַכָּתוּב מְדַבֵּר. אַף זָדוֹן שֶׁנֶּאֱמַר כָּאן בִּנְבִיא הַשֶּׁקֶר הַכָּתוּב מְדַבֵּר. אָצַר רִבִּי חִזְקִיָּה . נֶאֱמַר כָּאן דִּיבֵּר וְנֶאֱמַר לְהַלָּן אֲשֶׁר יְדַבֵּר הַנָּבִיא בְּשֵׁם יי. מַה דִּיבֵּר שֶׁנֶּאֱמַר לְהַלָּן בִּנְבִיא הַשֶּׁקֶר הַכָּתוּב מְדַבֵּר. אַף דִּיבֵּר שֶׁנֶּאֱמַר כָּאן בִּנְבִיא הַשֶּׁקֶר הַכָּתוּב מְדַבֵּר.

Rebbi Ze`ira said, it says here "criminal" and it says there "criminal", *the prophet said it criminally*[284]. Since about "criminal" used there, the verse speaks about a false prophet, also about "criminal" used here, the verse speaks about a false prophet[285]. Rebbi Ḥizqiah said, it says here "spoke" and it says there, *that the prophet would speak in the Eternal's name*. Since about "spoke" used there, the verse speaks about a false prophet, also about "spoke" used here, the verse speaks about a false prophet.[286]

284 *Deut.* 18:22, the law of the false prophet. "Here" refers to the judge who refuses to obey the rulings of the Supreme Court, who acts criminally in his disobedience and is tried before the Supreme Court, *Deut.* 17:8-12.

285 The verse does not speak about a false prophet but about a lower court judge who refuses to accept the authority of the Supreme Court. What is meant is that the procedural details given for the treatment of the rebellious judge also apply to the treatment of the false prophet. The argument is known as הֶקֵּשׁ "trap". If the same word is used in two contexts, details found in one context and left indeterminate in the other can be transferred from one to the other. As a hermeneutic principle, *heqqeš* should be used only if the word in question is not loaded with additional meaning. But in *Sifry Deut.* 178, the expression "criminal" is interpreted to mean that the false prophet may be prosecuted

only if criminal intent can be shown, not if he acted in error.

In the Babli, 16a, the argument is in the name of R. Yose ben Hanina.

286 It seems that the *heqqeš* should not be about the verb דִּבֵּר but the noun דָּבָר "pronouncement", referring to the judgment of the Supreme Court in case of the rebellious judge, *Deut.* 17:10, and the false prophet who pronounces in the Eternal's name, *Deut.* 18:20.

(19b line 32) **מתני'.** אֵין מוֹצִיאִין לְמִלְחֶמֶת הָרְשׁוּת אֶלָּא עַל פִּי בֵית דִּין שֶׁל ע"א. רִבִּי יְהוּדָה אוֹמֵר. כַּתְּחִילָּה. וַיַּעַל דָּוִד בִּדְבַר גָּד זֶה מֶלֶךְ וְנָבִיא. וַיָּחֶל שְׁלֹמֹה לִבְנוֹת אֶת־בֵּית־יי אֱלֹהֵי יִשְׂרָאֵל בְּהַר הַמּוֹרִיָּה אֲשֶׁר נִרְאָה לוֹ אֵילּוּ אוּרִים וְתוּמִּים. לְדָוִיד אָבִיהוּ זֶה סַנְהֶדְרִין. שְׁאַל אָבִיךָ וְיַגֵּדְךָ זְקֵנֶיךָ וְיֹאמְרוּ לָךְ. הַשִּׁיר וַיֵּלֶךְ אַחֲרֵיהֶם הוֹשַׁעְיָה וַחֲצִי שָׂרֵי יְהוּדָה. תּוֹדוֹת וָאַעֲמִידָה שְׁתֵּי תוֹדוֹת גְּדוֹלוֹת וְתַהֲלוּכוֹת לַיָּמִין מֵעַל הַחוֹמָה לְשַׁעַר הָאַשְׁפֹּת. אָמַר רִבִּי שְׁמוּאֵל בַּר יוּדָן. מַה כָּתוּב מְהַלְּכוֹת לֹא תַהֲלוּחוֹת. אֶלָּא בְנִיטָּלוֹת עַל יְדֵי אַחֵר.

רַב הוּנָא בַּר חִייָה בְשֵׁם רַב מַייְתֵי לָהּ דְּבַר תּוֹרָה. כְּכֹל אֲשֶׁר אֲנִי מַרְאֶה אוֹתְךָ אֵת תַּבְנִית הַמִּשְׁכָּן וְאֵת... כָּל־כֵּלָיו וְכֵן תַּעֲשׂוּ׃ כֵּן תַּעֲשׂוּ לְדוֹרוֹת. מֹשֶׁה זֶה מֶלֶךְ וְנָבִיא. אַהֲרֹן אֵילּוּ אוּרִים וְתוּמִּים. אֶסְפָה־לִּי שִׁבְעִים אִישׁ מִזִּקְנֵי יִשְׂרָאֵל זֶה סַנְהֶדְרִין. שְׁאַל אָבִיךָ וְיַגֵּדְךָ וגו'. הַשִּׁיר וַיֵּלֶךְ אַחֲרֵיהֶם הוֹשַׁעְיָה וַחֲצִי שָׂרֵי יְהוּדָה. תּוֹדוֹת וָאַעֲמִידָה שְׁתֵּי תוֹדוֹת גְּדוֹלוֹת וְתַהֲלוּכוֹת לַיָּמִין מֵעַל הַחוֹמָה לְשַׁעַר הָאַשְׁפֹּת. אָמַר רִבִּי שְׁמוּאֵל בַּר יוּדָן. מַה כָּתוּב מְהַלְּכוֹת לֹא תַהֲלוּכוֹת. אֶלָּא בְנִיטָּלוֹת עַל יְדֵי אַחֵר.

Mishnah. "One may start a war of choice only by the court of 71 [judges][287]. [288]Rebbi Jehudah says, as at the start: [289]*David ascended following Gad's word*, that is king and prophet. [290]*Solomon started to build the Temple of the Eternal, Israel's God, on Mount Moriah where He had appeared to him*, there are Urim and Tummim. [290]*To his father David*, this is the Synhedrion, [291]*ask your father and he will tell you, your Elders and they will speak to you.* Song, *after them went Hoshaia and half the officers of Judea*[292]. Thanksgiving sacrifices, *I put up two large thanksgiving sacrifices being in procession going to their right on the wall going to the dung gate*[293]. Rebbi Samuel bar Yudan said, what is written, walking? No, being in procession, only being taken by others[294].

Rav Huna bar Hiyya[295] in the name of Rav quotes it from the words of the Torah. *As all that I am showing you, the shape of the building and the shape . . . of all its vessels, so you shall execute*[296]. So you shall execute in all generations. Moses is king and prophet. Aaron represents Urim and

Tummim. *Assemble for me seventy men from the Elders of Israel*[297], that is the Synhedrion; *ask your father and he will tell you,* etc. Song, *after them went Hoshaia and half the officers of Judea.* Thanksgiving sacrifices, *I put up two large thanksgiving sacrifices being in procession going to their right on the wall going to the dung gate.* Rebbi Samuel bar Yudan said, what is written, walking? No, being in procession, only being taken by others.

287 This probably should be deleted.

288 The following four paragraphs do not refer to the quote of the Mishnah but are a commentary to Mishnah *Ševuot* 2:2: "One only adds to the city and the Temple courtyards by king and prophet, Urim and Tummim, the Synhedrion of 71 members, two thanksgiving sacrifices, and song." Only the walled part of the city of Jerusalem counts as "before the Eternal", where family sacrifices may be consumed (*Deut.* 12:18,14:23); the suburbs are "countryside" which does not count for pilgrimage and sacrifice. Since there were no Urim and Tummim in the Second Temple, Pharisees did not consume sacrifices in the parts of Jerusalem which were added in Hasmonean and later times (Note 306).

In *Ševuot*, only beginning and end of the discussion here are quoted as a reference.

289 *2S.* 24:19, speaking of David going to buy the Temple area.

290 *2Chr.* 3:1. The verse is misquoted in several places.

291 *Deut.* 32:7. The persons one asks to get definitive answers to all questions of religion are the members of the High Court of 71 members.

292 *Neh.* 12:32. This refers to the members of the Synhedrion walking behind the thanksgiving sacrifices (*Ševuot* 15b); the musical part of the ceremony is described in verses 41,42.

293 *Neh.* 12:31.

294 In his opinion, the sacrifices were not walked on the wall but were carried. In the opinion of the Babli, *Ševuot* 15a and Tosephta *Sanhedrin* 3:4, not the animals were carried but the leavened bread required for a thanksgiving sacrifice (*Lev.* 7:13). It is possible that this is meant here.

295 In the Babli, *Sanhedrin* 16b, he is referred to as Rav Shimi bar Hiyya (in one ms. Shimi bar Ashi; this can be disregarded, replacing a *hapax* by a frequently quoted name).

296 *Ex.* 25:9. The final clause in the sentence seems to be redundant; it is explained as referring to future buildings.

297 *Num.* 11:16.

(19b line 46) כֵּיצַד הָיוּ מְהַלְּכוֹת. רִבִּי חִייָה רַבָּה וְרִבִּי שִׁמְעוֹן בְּרִבִּי. חַד אָמַר. זוֹ כְּנֶגֶד זוֹ. וְחָרָנָא אָמַר. זוֹ אַחַר זוֹ. וּשְׁנֵיהֶן מִקְרָא אֶחָד דּוֹרְשִׁין. וְהַתּוֹדָה הַשֵּׁנִית הַהוֹלֶכֶת לְמוֹל וַאֲנִי אַחֲרֶיהָ. מָאן דָּמַר. זוֹ כְּנֶגֶד זוֹ. וְהוּא יֹשֵׁב מִמֻּלָּי. וּמָאן דָּמַר. זוֹ אַחַר זוֹ. וּמָלַק אֶת־רֹאשׁוֹ מִמּוּל עָרְפּוֹ. וּמָאן דָּמַר. זוֹ כְּנֶגֶד זוֹ. נִמְצָא כָל־מָקוֹם וּמָקוֹם מִתְכַּפֵּר בְּתוֹדָה אַחַת. וּמָאן דָּמַר. זוֹ אַחַר זוֹ.נִמְצָא

כָּל־מָקוֹם וּמָקוֹם מִתְכַּפֵּר בִּשְׁתֵּי תוֹדוֹת. מָאן דָּמַר. זוֹ אַחַר זוֹ. יֵאוּת דְּתַנֵּינָן. הַפְּנִימִית נֶאֱכֶלֶת וְהַחִיצוֹנָה נִשְׂרֶפֶא. וּמָאן דָּמַר. זוֹ כְנֶגֶד זוֹ. אֵי זוֹ הִיא הַפְּנִימִית. זוֹ שֶׁסְּמוּכָה לַבַּיִת. רִבִּי יָסָא בְשֵׁם רִבִּי יוֹחָנָן. עַל פִּי נָבִיא נֶאֱכֶלֶת. אָמַר רִבִּי זֵירָא. תַּנֵּיי תַמָּן. נָבִיא יֵשׁ כָּאן אוּרִים וְתוּמִּים לָמָּה אֲנִי צָרִיךְ. אַשְׁכַּח תַּנֵּי. רִבִּי יְהוּדָה אוֹמֵר. צָרִיךְ אוּרִים וְתוּמִּים.

[298]How did the processions go? The elder Rebbi Ḥiyya and Rebbi Simeon ben Rebbi. One said, one opposite the other; the other said, one after the other; both are explaining the same verse: *The second thanksgiving sacrifice went* לְמוּל *and I after it*[299]. He who said, one opposite the other, *and he dwells opposite me*[300]. But he who said, one after the other, *he should break off its head behind its neck*[301]. For him who said, one opposite the other, it turns out that every place was purified by one thanksgiving sacrifice[302]; for him who said, one after the other, it turns out that every place was purified by two thanksgiving sacrifices[303]. For him who said, one after the other, this is correct following what he had stated: "the inner one is being eaten, the outer one is being burned.[304]" For him who said, one opposite the other, what is the inner one? The one closer to the Temple. Rebbi Yasa in the name of Rebbi Joḥanan: It was eaten on the instruction of a prophet[305]. Rebbi Ze`ira said, they state there: Since a prophet is there, for what do I need Urim and Tummim[306]? It was found stated: Rebbi Jehudah says, Urim and Tummim are needed[307].

298 *Ševuot* 15b, the entire paragraph.

299 *Neh.* 12:38, in MT למואל. According to Gesenius, one has to read מואל as contraction of מֵאֲוַל "not first, not with it". This justifies both meanings quoted here, "opposite" and "after".

300 *Num.* 22:5.

301 *Lev.* 5:8.

302 In principle, one sacrifice would suffice if the procession went around the entire wall.

303 Since we do not expect two sacrifices for the same purpose, one has to find differences of purpose for the two.

304 Tosephta 3:4, *Megillat Ta`anit* 6. The Babli, *loc. cit.* [299] suggests that the first makes sacrifices possible; therefore, it has to be burned outside the Temple. The second one then is a legitimate thanksgiving sacrifice, most of which has to be eaten by the priests as public well-being sacrifice (Mishnah *Zevahim* 5:5).

305 Who defined the meaning of "inner" and "outer"?

306 The nature of the Urim and Tummim oracle already was no longer known when the Second Temple was built; Nehemiah (7:65) uses the expression "the coming of a Cohen with Urim and Tummim" as

synonym with "the coming of the Messiah." The requirement of Urim and Tummim disqualifies all parts of Jerusalem not forming part of Solomon's city.

307 In the Babli, *Ševuot* 16a, it is a dispute among Babylonian Amoraïm whether Nehemiah's ceremony, without king and oracle, was a valid dedication of the rebuilt city of Jerusalem or whether it was a token ceremony to re-establish the intrinsic sanctity of Jerusalem created by Solomon's Temple. The quote here, from an otherwise unknown *baraita*, qualifies the second opinion as minority opinion of a Tanna.

(19b line 56) אָמַר רִבִּי אַבָּהוּ. אִתְפַּלְּגוּן רִבִּי יוֹחָנָן וְרֵישׁ לָקִישׁ. חַד אָמַר. בּוֹנִין וְאַחַר כָּךְ מַקְדִּישִׁין. וְחָרָנָה אָמַר. מַקְדִּישִׁין וְאַחַר כָּךְ בּוֹנִין. מָאן דָּמַר. בּוֹנִין וְאַחַר כָּךְ מַקְדִּישִׁין. אֵין רוֹאִין אֶת הַמְּחִיצוֹת כְּאִלּוּ הֵן עוֹלוֹת. בִּיקְּשׁוּ לְהוֹסִיף עַל הֵיכָל בַּמֶּה מוֹסִיפִין. בִּשְׁתֵּי הַלֶּחֶם. וּמַקְדִּישִׁין בְּיוֹם טוֹב. אֶלָּא בְלֶחֶם הַפָּנִים. וּמַקְדִּישִׁין בַּשַּׁבָּת. אֶלָּא בַלַּיְלָה. וּמַקְדִּישִׁין בַּלַּיְלָה. אָמַר רִבִּי יוֹסֵי בֵּירִבִּי בוּן. בְּמִנְחַת מַאֲפֶה. נִיחָה בַעֲלִייָתָן מִן הַגּוֹלָה שֶׁהִקְרִיבוּ וְאַחַר כָּךְ קִידְּשׁוּ. בְּהִכָּנְסָתָן לָאָרֶץ בַּמֶּה קִידְּשׁוּ. אָמַר רִבִּי יוֹסֵי בֵּירִבִּי בוּן. בִּשְׁתֵּי תוֹדוֹת הַבָּאוֹת מִנּוֹב וְגִבְעוֹן.

Rebbi Abbahu said, Rebbi Johanan and Rebbi Simeon ben Laqush disagreeed. One said, one builds and afterwards one dedicates[308]. The other one said, one dedicates and afterwards one builds[309]. For him who says, one builds and afterwards one dedicates, one does not say that the partitions are as if built up[310]. If one desires to add to the Temple Hall, by which means does one add[311]? By the two loaves[312]. Does one dedicate on a holiday[313]? Then by the Shew Bread. Does one dedicate on the Sabbath[314]? Then in the night[315]. Does one dedicate in the night[316]? Rebbi Yose ben Rebbi Abun said, with a baked flour offering[317]. One understands that on their return from the diaspora they sacrificed and then dedicated. When they entered the Land,[318] with what did they dedicate? Rebbi Yose ben Rebbi Abun said, with two thanksgiving sacrifices coming from Nob[319] and Gibeon.

308 One builds as if the buildings were profane. Only when the Temple enclosure is complete does one dedicate the Temple area, and when the walls of Jerusalem are rebuilt does one dedicate the city. During the building period one is not restricted by all the rules applying to the Temple area. This is possible since the dedication by Solomon was annulled by the destruction of the Temple. One has to assume that it is possible to dedicate the area of the altar and its enclosure without dedicating the Temple, as done in the time of the first return from Babylonia under Cyrus, *Ezra* 3:3,6.

309 He holds that the dedication by Solomon is permanent. Therefore, any

building must be done under restrictive rules (but it can be built in stages, cf. Mishnah *Idiut* 8:6). If the outline of the Temple enclosure or the original city walls was still visible in Zerubabel's time, no rebuilding was necessary in order to restore the service of the altar.

310 They actually have to be restored before Temple service can be resumed whole or in part.

311 In imitation of the rules given for dedication of the city of Jerusalem under Nehemiah, any dedication must involve a sacrifice. The Babli, *loc. cit.* [299], insists that the sacrifice be used in the place to be dedicated. This leads to a catch-22 situation since a sacrifice can be dedicated only after the dedication of the holy place. There is no reason to assume that the Yerushalmi accepts this reasoning.

312 The two loaves of leavened bread dedicated on Pentecost to permit use of new wheat, *Lev.* 23:17. This is in imitation of the leavened bread used for the dedication of the city, cf. [295]. A parallel discussion is in the Babli, *Ševuot* 15a/b.

313 Since the dedication has far-reaching legal consequences, it has the status of an acquisition, which is not acceptable on Sabbath or holiday, *Is.* 58:13. In addition, the Babli points out that the dedication of the leavened breads is the slaughter of the accompanying well-being sacrifice; then the dedication would not be by bread.

314 The Shew Bread is removed from the sanctuary on the Sabbath, *Lev.* 24:8. It becomes available for secondary use on the Sabbath, when it cannot be so used.

315 The following evening, after the end of the Sabbath.

316 *Ex.* 30:2 prescribes that the Tabernacle be erected during daytime. This rule then is extended to include all building activity of the Temple.

317 The daily flour offering of the High Priest, *Lev.* 6:12-16.

318 When they entered the Land, they had the Tabernacle which was dedicated in the desert. What one asks here is, how was Solomon's Temple dedicated?

319 The priests' settlement at Nob already was destroyed at the time when the priests from Nob resided at Anatot. The active place of worship was Gibeon, but "Nob and Gibeon" is used as a legal term to indicate the status of holy places after the destruction of Shiloh, before the building of the Temple; cf. Mishnah *Zevahim* 14:7.

(19b line 64) אַבָּא שָׁאוּל אוֹמֵר. שְׁנֵי בִּצִּים הָיוּ שָׁם. הַתַּחְתּוֹנָה וְהָעֶלְיוֹנָה אֵין קְדוּשָּׁתָהּ גְּמוּרָה. הַתַּחְתּוֹנָה נִתְקַדְּשָׁה בְכוּלָּן. וְהָעֶלְיוֹנָה בַּעֲלִייָתָן מִן הַגּוֹלָה לֹא בְמֶלֶךְ וְלֹא בְאוּרִים וְתוּמִּים. לְפִיכָךְ הַתַּחְתּוֹנָה עַם הָאָרֶץ אוֹכְלִין שָׁם קֳדָשִׁים קַלִּין וּמַעֲשֵׂר שֵׁינִי וַחֲבֵירִם אוֹכְלִין שָׁם קֳדָשִׁים קַלִּין אֲבָל לֹא מַעֲשֵׂר שֵׁינִי. וְהָעֶלְיוֹנָה עַם הָאָרֶץ אוֹכְלִין שָׁם קֳדָשִׁים קַלִּין אֲבָל לֹא מַעֲשֵׂר שֵׁינִי. וַחֲבֵירִם אוֹכְלִין שָׁם קֳדָשִׁים קַלִּין וּמַעֲשֵׂר שֵׁינִי. מִפְּנֵי מַה לֹא קִדְּשׁוּהָ. מִפְּנֵי שֶׁהָיְתָה תוֹרְפַּת יְרוּשָׁלַםִ שָׁם וְהָיְתָה יְכוֹלָה לִיכָּבֵשׁ מִשָּׁם.

[320]"Abba Shaul says, two subdivisions[321] were there, the lower and the upper, whose sanctification was not complete. The lower one was dedicated

with a full ceremony, but the upper one only when they came from the diaspora, without a king and without Urim and Tummim. Therefore, in the lower one the vulgar[322] eat family sacrifices and Second Tithe; Fellows eat there family sacrifices but not Second Tithe[323]. In the upper one, the vulgar eat family sacrifices but not Second Tithe[324]; Fellows eat there family sacrifices and Second Tithe[325]. Why did they not sanctify it? Because it was the vulnerable spot of Jerusalem; it could be conquered from there[326]."

320 This *baraita* exists in another three versions: Tosephta 3:4 (T), Babli *Ševuot* 15b (B), *Megillat Ta`anit* 6 (M). A detailed discussion of all four texts, to be used with due caution, is in Note 22 to volume 3 of H. Graetz's *Geschichte der Juden.*

321 ביצין corresponds to the readings of B,T, בצעין, ביצעין, ביצועין by degeneration of the guttural. One has to accept Graetz's derivation from בצע "to split" against Rashi's *marais* "marsh." M has "places on the Mount of Olives", an emendation by a person who did not understand the text.

322 For the notions of "vulgar" and "Fellow", cf. Introduction to Tractate *Demay*, p. 349.

323 Since family sacrifices have more holiness than Second Tithe, one has to accept the reading of M: "family sacrifices and certainly Second Tithe."

324 Because these were living quarters in the expanding city.

325 Read with B,T,M: "neither family sacrifices nor Second Tithe."

327 This defines the "upper subdivision" as the suburb between the second, Herodian wall and the incomplete third wall of Agrippas I. The lower subdivision then is the part of the old city between the Hasmonean and Herodian walls. Since the third wall could not be completed, the dedicated part of the city could not be expanded there. The subdivision is called *upper* because it slopes upwards from the Damascus gate to the North. The lower subdivision could have been dedicated by a ceremony imitating Nehemiah's.

(19b line 71) אֵין עוֹשִׂין סַנְהֶדְרָיוֹת לַשְּׁבָטִים. תַּלְמוּד לוֹמַר לִשְׁבָטֶיךָ וְשָׁפְטוּ אֶת־הָעָם.

אֵין עוֹשִׂין עִיר הַנִּדַּחַת. רִבִּי יוֹחָנָן בְּשֵׁם רִבִּי הוֹשַׁעְיָה. תְּלָתָא אֲמוֹרִין. חַד אָמַר. אַחַת עוֹשִׂין שְׁתַּיִם אֵין עוֹשִׂין. וְחָרָנָא אָמַר. הַסְּמוּכוֹת עוֹשִׂין הַמְפוּזָּרוֹת אין עוֹשִׂין. וְחָרָנָא אָמַר.מְפוּזָּרוֹת אֵין עוֹשִׂין כָּל־עִיקָּר שֶׁמָּא יָפוּצוּ גוֹיִים וְיָבוֹאוּ לְאֶרֶץ יִשְׂרָאֵל. וְאִית דְּבָעֵי מֵימַר. שֶׁמָּא יָפוּצוּ הָאוֹיְבִים וְיָבוֹאוּ לִידֵי קָרְחָה.

"One only appoints high courts for the tribes." The verse says[327], *for your tribes, they shall judge.*

"One only declares a town to be deviant." Rebbi Joḥanan in the name of Rebbi Hoshaia: [328]Three Amoraïm, one says, one makes[329] one but not two. The other said, clusters one makes[330], dispersed ones one does not make. The other said, dispersed[331] one does not make at all, lest Gentiles spread and come to the Land of Israel; some want to say that enemies should not spread and lay waste.

327 *Deut.* 16:18. For the argument behind the quote, cf. *Makkot* 1:17 (Note 74), Babli 16b.

328 In the Babli, 16b, the first opinion is attributed to Rav, the converse of the second to R. Simeon ben Laqish, the third opinion to R. Johanan.

329 No court is empowered to declare more than one town as deviant at the same time.

330 Two neighboring towns can be considered as one. There is no need to emend the Yerushalmi to follow the Babli.

332 This should read, or be interpreted as, "border town" as in the Mishnah.

(fol. 18a) **משנה ו:** סַנְהֶדְרִין גְּדוֹלָה הָיְתָה שֶׁל שִׁבְעִים וְאֶחָד וּקְטַנָּה שֶׁל עֶשְׂרִים וּשְׁלֹשָׁה. וּמְנַיִין לַגְּדוֹלָה שֶׁהִיא שֶׁל שִׁבְעִים וְאֶחָד. שֶׁנֶּאֱמַר אֶסְפָה לִּי שִׁבְעִים אִישׁ מִזִּקְנֵי יִשְׂרָאֵל וּמֹשֶׁה עַל גַּבֵּיהֶן הֲרֵי שִׁבְעִים וְאֶחָד. רִבִּי יְהוּדָה אוֹמֵר. שִׁבְעִים. וּמְנַיִין לַקְּטַנָּה שֶׁהִיא שֶׁל עֶשְׂרִים וּשְׁלֹשָׁה. שֶׁנֶּאֱמַר וְשָׁפְטוּ הָעֵדָה וְהִצִּילוּ הָעֵדָה עֵדָה שׁוֹפֶטֶת וְעֵדָה מַצֶּלֶת הֲרֵי כָאן עֶשְׂרִים. וּמְנַיִין לָעֵדָה שֶׁהִיא עֲשָׂרָה. שֶׁנֶּאֱמַר עַד מָתַי לָעֵדָה הָרָעָה הַזֹּאת יָצְאוּ יְהוֹשֻׁעַ וְכָלֵב.

Mishnah 6: The High Synhedrion[332] had 71 members and a lower one 23 members. From where that the High Court has 71 members? For it is said[333]: *Assemble for me 70 men of the Elders of Israel,* and Moses was presiding, that makes 71. Rebbi Jehudah says, 70[334]. From where that a lower court has 23 members? For it is said, *the congregation shall judge, the congregation shall save*[335]. One congregation judges, one congregation saves, this makes twenty. And from where that a congregation consists of ten persons? As it is said, *how long this evil congregation*[336], without Joshua and Caleb.

332 As usual in rabbinic sources, the political institution of the Synhedrion is identified with the juridical of the High Court, projecting Jabneh arrangements into Temple times.

333 *Num.* 11:16.

334 He is known for the correctness of his historical traditions. For the political functions of a Synhedrion, an even number of members is acceptable. The judicial functions were exercised by committees of 23 each.

335 *Num*. 35:24,25 speaking of the trial of the homicide; cf. *Sifry Num*. #160.

336 *Num*. 14:27, interpreted as speaking of the ten bad spies.

(19c line 2) **מתני'**. סַנְהֶדְרִין גְּדוֹלָה כול'. רִבִּי בָּא רִבִּי יָסָא בְשֵׁם רִבִּי יוֹחָנָן. נֶאֱמַר כָּאן עֵדָה וְנֶאֱמַר לְהַלָּן עַד־מָתַי לָעֵדָה הָרָעָה. מַה לָעֵדָה הָאֲמוּרָה לְהַלָּן עֲשָׂרָה אַף כָּאן עֲשָׂרָה. אָמַר רִבִּי סִימוֹן. נֶאֱמַר כָּאן תּוֹךְ וְנֶאֱמַר לְהַלָּן תּוֹךְ. מַה תּוֹךְ שֶׁנֶּאֱמַר לְהַלָּן עֲשָׂרָה אַף כָּאן עֲשָׂרָה. אָמַר לֵיהּ רִבִּי יוֹסֵא בֵּירִבִּי בּוּן. אִם מִתּוֹךְ אַתְּ יְלִיף לָהּ סַגִּין אִינּוּן. אֶלָּא נֶאֱמַר כָּאן בְּנֵי יִשְׂרָאֵל וְנֶאֱמַר לְהַלָּן בְּנֵי יִשְׂרָאֵל וַיָּבוֹאוּ בְּנֵי יִשְׂרָאֵל לִשְׁבֹּר. מַה בְּנֵי יִשְׂרָאֵל שֶׁנֶּאֱמַר לְהַלָּן עֲשָׂרָה אַף כָּאן עֲשָׂרָה.

Mishnah: "The High Synhedrion," etc. [337]Rebbi Abba, Rebbi Yasa in the name of Rebbi Johanan: It says here "congregation", and it says there "congregation", *how long the evil congregation*. Since "congregation" there means ten, so here also ten.

Rebbi Simon said, it is said here "amid", and it is said there "amid". Since "amid" there means ten, so here also ten. Rebbi Yose ben Rebbi Abun told him, if you want to infer from "amid", there are too many. But it is said here "the sons of Israel", and it is said there, "the sons of Israel", *the sons of Israel came to buy grain*. Since "the sons of Israel" there were ten, so here also ten.

337 This is not a repetition of the Mishnah. The paragraph really does not refer to the qualifications of a court but to the requirement of having 10 adult males in attendance for religious observations of a "congregation." The paragraph is an almost complete quote from *Berakhot* 7:3, Notes 106-108, is repeated in *Megillah* 4:4 (75b l. 7), Babli 23b, and is alluded to in *Sanhedrin* 4:10.

(fol. 18a) **משנה ז**: וּמְנַיִין לְהָבִיא עוֹד שְׁלֹשָׁה. מִמַּשְׁמַע שֶׁנֶּאֱמַר לֹא תִהְיֶה אַחֲרֵי רַבִּים לְרָעוֹת שׁוֹמֵעַ אֲנִי שֶׁאָמַר הֱיֵה עִמָּהֶם לְטוֹבָה. אִם כֵּן לָמָּה נֶאֱמַר אַחֲרֵי רַבִּים לְהַטּוֹת. לֹא כְהַטָּייָתְךָ לְטוֹבָה הַטָּייָתְךָ לְרָעָה. הַטָּייָתְךָ לְטוֹבָה עַל פִּי (עד) אֶחָד, הַטָּייָתְךָ לְרָעָה עַל פִּי שְׁנַיִם וְאֵין בֵּית דִּין שָׁקוּל מוֹסִיפִין עֲלֵיהֶן עוֹד אֶחָד הֲרֵי כָאן עֶשְׂרִים וּשְׁלֹשָׁה. וְכַמָּה יְהֵא בָעִיר וּתְהֵא רְאוּיָה לְסַנְהֶדְרִין מֵאָה וְעֶשְׂרִים. רִבִּי נְחֶמְיָה אוֹמֵר מָאתַיִם וּשְׁלֹשִׁים כְּדֵי שָׂרֵי עֲשָׂרוֹת.

Mishnah 7: From where that one adds another three[338]? From the interpretation of what is said[339], *do not follow the majority to be unfavorable*, I understand that He said, follow them to be favorable. Then why was it said, *to bend after the majority*? Your bending to be favorable is not equal to your bending to be unfavorable. Your bending to be favorable shall be by one [vote] (witness), your bending to be unfavorable shall be by two. Since no court may be even-numbered, one adds another one to obtain 23. How many people shall live in a town that it may have a criminal court? 120. Rebbi Nehemiah said 230, that they might be commanders over tens[340].

338 Since Mishnah 6 established that a criminal court must have 20 judges/jurors.

339 *Ex*. 23:2: *Do not follow the majority to do evil; do not testify in a quarrel, to bend, to twist after the majority*. This is read to mean that for acquittal one vote is enough but that for conviction one needs a qualified majority even without the one judge who is voting. Cf. *Mekhilta dR. Ismael Mišpaṭim* 20, *dR. Simeon ben Iohai* 23:2 (in the name of Rebbi.)

341 Since the verse requires that judges be outstanding personalities, *Ex*. 18:21, *Deut*. 1:15, each judge must be qualified at least to be the leader of ten men.

(19c line 9) **מתני'**. וּמְנַיִין לְהָבִיא עוֹד שְׁלֹשָׁה כול'. אָמַר רַבָּן שִׁמְעוֹן בֶּן גַּמְלִיאֵל. בָּרִאשׁוֹנָה לֹא הָיוּ חוֹתְמִין עַל כְּתוּבַּת נָשִׁים כְּשֵׁירוֹת אֶלָּא כֹהֲנִים לְוִיִּים וְיִשְׂרְאֵלִים מַשִּׂיאִין לַכְּהוּנָּה. אָמַר רִבִּי יוֹסֵי. בָּרִאשׁוֹנָה לֹא הָיְתָה מַחֲלוֹקֶת בְּיִשְׂרָאֵל אֶלָּא סַנְהֶדְרִין שֶׁלע"א הָיְתָה יוֹשֶׁבֶת בְּלִשְׁכַּת הַגָּזִית. וּשְׁנֵי בָּתֵּי דִינִין שֶׁל שְׁלֹשָׁה שְׁלֹשָׁה הָיוּ יוֹשְׁבִין אֶחָד בְּחֵיל וְאֶחָד בְּהַר הַבַּיִת. וּבָתֵּי דִינִין שֶׁלכ"ג הָיוּ יוֹשְׁבִין בְּכָל־עֲיָירוֹת אֶרֶץ יִשְׂרָאֵל. צָרַךְ אֶחָד מֵהֶן לִשְׁאוֹל דְּבַר הֲלָכָה הָיָה בָא וְשׁוֹאֲלָהּ בְּבֵית דִּין שֶׁבְּעִירוֹ. אִם שָׁמְעוּ אָמְרוּ לוֹ וְאִי לֹא הָיָה הוּא וּמוּפְלֵא שֶׁלָּהֶן בָּאִין וְשׁוֹאֲלִין אוֹתָהּ בְּבֵית דִּין הַסָּמוּךְ לְעִירוֹ. אִם שָׁמְעוּ אָמְרוּ לָהֶן וְאִי לֹא הָיָה הוּא וּמוּפְלֵא שֶׁלָּהֶן בָּאִין וְשׁוֹאֲלִין אוֹתָהּ בְּבֵית דִּין שֶׁבְּהַר הַבַּיִת. אִם שָׁמְעוּ אָמְרוּ לָהֶן וְאִי לֹא הָיָה הוּא וּמוּפְלֵא שֶׁלָּהֶן בָּאִין וְשׁוֹאֲלִין אוֹתָהּ בְּבֵית דִּין שֶׁבְּחֵיל. אִם שָׁמְעוּ אָמְרוּ לָהֶן וְאִם לָאו הָיוּ אֵילוּ וָאֵילוּ מִתְכַּנְּסִין לְבֵית דִּין הַגָּדוֹל שֶׁבְּלִשְׁכַּת הַגָּזִית שֶׁמִּשָּׁם תּוֹרָה יוֹצְאָה וְרוֹוַחַת לְכָל־יִשְׂרָאֵל. שֶׁנֶּאֱמַר מִן־הַמָּקוֹם הַהוּא אֲשֶׁר יִבְחַר יי וגו'. סַנְהֶדְרִין שֶׁבְּלִשְׁכַּת הַגָּזִית אַף עַל פִּי שֶׁהָיְתָה שֶׁלע"א לֹא הָיוּ פְּחוּתִין מִכ"ג. צָרַךְ אֶחָד מֵהֶן לָצֵאת הָיָה מִסְתַּכֵּל. אִם יֵשׁ שָׁם כ"ג הָיָה יוֹצֵא וְאִם לָאו לֹא הָיָה יוֹצֵא. וְהָיוּ יוֹשְׁבִין מִתָּמִיד שֶׁלְּשַׁחַר עַד תָּמִיד שֶׁלְּבֵין הָעַרְבַּיִם. וּבַשַּׁבָּתוֹת וּבְיָמִים טוֹבִים הָיוּ יוֹשְׁבִין בְּבֵית הַמִּדְרָשׁ שֶׁבְּהַר הַבַּיִת. נִשְׁאֲלָה הֲלָכָה. אִם שָׁמְעוּ אָמְרוּ לָהֶן וְאִי לֹא עוֹמְדִין עַל הַמִּנְיָין. רָבוּ הַמְזַכִּין זִיכּוּ. רָבוּ הַמְחַייְבִין חִייְבוּ. רָבוּ הַמְטַהֲרִין טִיהֲרוּ. רָבוּ הַמְטַמְּאִין טִימְּאוּ. שֶׁמִּשָּׁם תּוֹרָה יוֹצְאָה וְרוֹוַחַת לְכָל־יִשְׂרָאֵל. מִשֶּׁרָבוּ תַלְמִידֵי שַׁמַּי וְהִלֵּל שֶׁלֹּא שִׁימְּשׁוּ רַבֵּיהֶן כְּצוֹרְכָן רָבוּ

הַמַּחֲלוֹקוֹת בְּיִשְׂרָאֵל וְנַעֲשׂוּ שְׁתֵּי תוֹרוֹת. וּמִשָּׁם הָיוּ שׁוֹלְחִין בְּכָל־עֲייָרוֹת שֶׁבְּאֶרֶץ יִשְׂרָאֵל וְכָל־מִי שֶׁהָיוּ מוֹצְאִין אוֹתוֹ חָכָם עָנָיו שְׁפוּי עַיִן טוֹבָה נֶפֶשׁ שְׁפֵלָה רוּחַ נְמוּכָה לֵב טוֹב יֵצֶר טוֹב חֶלֶק טוֹב הָיוּ מוֹשִׁיבִין אוֹתוֹ בְּבֵית דִּין שֶׁבְּהַר הַבַּיִת וְאַחַר כָּךְ בְּבֵית דִּין שֶׁבְּחֵיל וְאַחַר כָּךְ בְּבֵית דִּין הַגָּדוֹל שֶׁבְּלִשְׁכַּת הַגָּזִית.

Mishnah: "From where that one adds another three, etc. It was stated: [341]Rabban Simeon ben Gamliel said, in earlier times the *ketubah* of qualified women[342] was signed only by priests, Levites, or Israel whose daughters were qualified to marry into the priesthood.

[343]Rebbi Yose said, in earlier times there was no disagreement in Israel[344] but the Synhedrion of 71 members were sitting in the free-stone hall[345]; two courts of three[346] members each were sitting, one in the glacis[347] and one on the Temple Mount[348]; and a court of 23 was sitting in every town of the Land of Israel. If somebody had a question of religious practice, he went and asked it from the court in his town. If they had heard [the answer], they told him; otherwise he and their distinguished member went and asked a court in their neighborhood. If these had heard [the answer], they told him; otherwise he and their distinguished member went and asked from the court on the Temple Mount. If these had heard [the answer], they told him; otherwise he and their distinguished member went and asked from the court on the glacis. If these had heard [the answer], they told him; otherwise they together entered the High Court in the free-stone hall since from there instruction came accepted in all of Israel, as it is said: *From this place which the Eternal will choose*[349]. Even though the Synhedrion in the free-stone hall had 71 members, those present never numbered less than 23. If one of them had to leave, he was looking around; if 23 others were present, he would leave, otherwise he would not leave[350]. They were in session from the daily morning sacrifice to the daily evening sacrifice. On Sabbaths and holidays, they were sitting in the study hall on the Temple Mount[348]. If a question of practice came up, if they had heard the answer, they told them; otherwise they prepared to vote. If a majority was for acquitting, they acquitted. If a majority[351] was for a guilty verdict, they rendered a verdict of guilty. If a majority was for declaring pure, they declared pure. If a majority was for declaring impure, they declared impure. From the time that there were many students of Shammai and Hillel

who did not study enough under their teachers, many disagreements arose and two doctrines developed[352]. From there[353], they were sending to all towns in the Land of Israel; any time they found a person who was wise, meek, even-tempered, benevolent, pleasing, humble, good-hearted, with good intentions, and well endowed, they were placing him on the court of the Temple Mount[354], from there to the court on the glacis, and from there to the High Court in the free-stone hall.

341 Tosephta 7:1, *Hagigah* 2:9.

342 Whose offspring were qualified to marry into the priesthood. In Temple times, this could serve as proof of qualification; cf. *Qiddušin* 4:4.

343 Most of the following text also is in the Babli, 88b. R. Yose, the collector of most of the material of *Seder `Olam*, represents a very idealized past.

345 A patently incorrect statement. The ancient rabbinic disagreement about the treatment of private sacrifices on holidays is the topic of *Ḥagigah* 2; the statement declares all non-rabbinic sects as non-Jewish.

345 Adjacent to the Temple, built into the Herodian Temple wall, constructed from large rectangular stones without mortar.

346 Read: 23. However, A. Weiss (לשאלת טיב בית דין של שבעים ואחד, ספר היובל לכ' לוי גינצבורג, ע' קץ-רטז New York 1946) insists that the only courts of 23 in Jerusalem were committees of the court of 71.

347 The space between the Temple wall and a smaller wall surrounding the Temple areas.

348 Outside any enclosure.

349 *Deut*. 17:10. Disobedience of a High Court ruling is only a capital crime if the ruling was delivered from "the place", from a court sitting in a room partially on Temple grounds. When the High Court lost its standing as court of criminal appeals (Note 31) and left the free-stone hall, it also lost its ability to prescribe practice *ex cathedra*.

350 Babli *Soṭah* 45a.

351 In his theory, on appeal only a simple majority is needed.

352 Babli *Soṭah* 47b.

353 The free-stone hall.

354 In all three Babylonian texts, the person is appointed judge in his town and the appeals courts replenished from sitting judges.

(19c line 36) סַנְהֶדְרִין הָיְתָה כַּחֲצִי גוֹרֶן עֲגוּלָה וְהַנָּשִׂיא יוֹשֵׁב בְּאֶמְצַע כְּדֵי שֶׁיְּהוּ רוֹאִין אוֹתוֹ וְשׁוֹמְעִין קוֹלוֹ. אָמַר רִבִּי לְעָזָר בֵּירִבִּי צָדוֹק. כְּשֶׁהָיָה רַבָּן גַּמְלִיאֵל יוֹשֵׁב בְּיַבְנֶה הָיָה אַבָּא וְאָחִיו יוֹשְׁבִין מִימִינוֹ וּזְקֵינִים מִשְּׂמֹאלוֹ מִפְּנֵי כְבוֹד הַזָּקֵן.

The Synhedrion was like a threshing floor in the shape of a semi-circle; the president sat in the middle so they might see him and hear his voice.

Rebbi Eleazar ben Rebbi Ṣadoq said, when Rabban Gamliel was sitting at Jabneh, my father and his brother were sitting to his right and the Elders to his left, to honor the old man[355].

355 The "old man" was R. Sadoq, a member already of Rabban Johanan ben Zakkai's school in pre-war Jerusalem.

(19c line 39) כַּמָּה הֵן שׁוֹפְטֵי יִשְׂרָאֵל. שֶׁבַע רִיבּוֹא וּשְׁמוֹנַת אֲלָפִים וְשֵׁשׁ מֵאוֹת. שָׂרֵי אֲלָפִים שֵׁשׁ מֵאוֹת. שָׂרֵי מֵאוֹת שֵׁשֶׁת אֲלָפִים. שָׂרֵי חֲמִשִּׁים י"ב אֶלֶף. שָׂרֵי עֲשָׂרוֹת ס' אֶלֶף. נִמְצְאוּ שׁוֹפְטֵי יִשְׂרָאֵל. ז' רִיבּוֹא וּשְׁמוֹנַת אֲלָפִים וְשֵׁשׁ מֵאוֹת.

מַה טַעֲמָא דְרִבִּי נְחֶמְיָה. וְהוּא שֶׁיְּהֵא שָׁם בֵּית דִּין שֶׁלְּכ"ג. וְהַנִּידּוֹנִין וְהָעֵדִים וְזוֹמְמֵיהֶן וְזוֹמְמֵי זוֹמְמֵיהֶן וְחַזָּן וְסוֹפְרֵיהֶן וְשַׁמָּשׁ. מַה טַעֲמָא דְרַבָּנִן. וְהוּא שֶׁיְּהֵא שָׁם י"ב סַנְהֶדְרִיּוֹת שֶׁל י"ב שְׁבָטִים.

[356]How many were the judges of Israel[357]? 78'600. Appointed over a thousand, 600. Appointed over a hundred, 6'000. Appointed over fifty, 12'000. Appointed over ten, 60'000. It turns out that the judges of Israel were 78'600.

[358]What is the reason of Rebbi Nehemiah? That there should be a court of 23, and the parties, and the witnesses, and the witnesses for perjury, and the witnesses for perjury of the witnesses for perjury, and the rabbi, and the clerks of court, and the beadle. What is the reason of the rabbis? That there might be twelve courts for the twelve tribes.

356 Halakhah 10:2 Note 214. Babli 18a, *Tanhuma Mišpaṭim* 6 (a *Šeïlta*).

357 Appointed by Moses. The numbers are inexact since in no census were there exactly 600'000 men.

358 This paragraph is thoroughly corrupt. In the Babli, 17b, a very forced count connects the 120 men required by the rabbis to a court of 23 acting as a law school to 3•23 = 69 students. Cf. also Tosephta 3:9. If one adds to the 35 people enumerated for R. Nehemiah the 69 law students mentioned in Mishnah 4:10, one arrives at a minimum number attributed in the Tosephta to R. Jehudah; but no emendation can be trusted.

(19c line 46) וּמֹשֶׁה עַל גַּבֵּיהֶן. דְּבַר תַּקָּנָה עָשָׂה מֹשֶׁה. בְּשָׁעָה שֶׁאָמַר לוֹ הַקָּדוֹשׁ בָּרוּךְ הוּא פְּקוֹד כָּל־בְּכֹר זָכָר֙ בִּבְנֵי יִשְׂרָאֵל אָמַר. אֵי זֶה מְקַבֵּל עָלָיו לִיתֵּן חֲמֵשֶׁת שְׁקָלִים לַגּוּלְגּוֹלֶת. מֶה עָשָׂה. נָטַל כ"ב אֶלֶף פִּיטְקִין וְכָתַב עֲלֵיהֶן בֶּן לֵוִי. וְרע"ג וְכָתַב עֲלֵיהֶן חֲמֵשֶׁת שְׁקָלִים. וְהִטִּילָן לְקַלְפֵּי. אָמַר לָהֶן. בּוֹאוּ וּטְלוּ פִּיטְקֵיכֶם. כָּל־מִי שֶׁעָלָה בְיָדוֹ בֶּן לֵוִי הָיָה אוֹמֵר לוֹ. כְּבָר פְּדָאֲךָ

בֶּן לֵוִי. וְכָל־מִי שֶׁעָלָה בְיָדוֹ חֲמֵשֶׁת שְׁקָלִים הָיָה אוֹמֵר לוֹ. מָה אֶעֱשֶׂה לָךְ מִן הַשָּׁמַיִם הוּא. רִבִּי יְהוּדָה וְרִבִּי נְחֶמְיָה מְתִיב תַּנַּייָא לַחֲבֵרַייָא. אִילּוּ כְתַבְתָּנִי לֵוִי סִילְקִית. אֶלָּא כָּךְ עָשָׂה. נָטַל כ"ב אֶלֶף פִּיטְקִין וְכָתַב לֵוִי וּמָאתַיִם וְשִׁבְעִים וּשְׁלֹשָׁה כָּתַב עֲלֵיהֶן חֲמֵשֶׁת שְׁקָלִים וְהִטִּילָן לְקַלְפֵּי. אָמַר לָהֶן. בּוֹאוּ וּטְלוּ פִיטְקֵיכֶם. כָּל־מִי שֶׁעָלָה בְיָדוֹ לֵוִי אָמַר לוֹ. כְּבָר פְּדָאֲךָ בֶּן לֵוִי. וְכָל־שֶׁעָלָה בְיָדוֹ חֲמֵשֶׁת שְׁקָלִים הָיָה אוֹמֵר לוֹ. מָה אֶעֱשֶׂה מִן הַשָּׁמַיִם הוּא. מְתִיב תַּנַּייָא לַחֲבֵרַייָא. הַגַּע עַצְמָךְ שֶׁעָלוּ כוּלָּם לֵוִי. אָמְרוּ לוֹ. מַעֲשֶׂה נֵס הָיָה וּמְסוּרָגִין עָלוּ. אָמַר רִבִּי שְׁמוּאֵל. עַל דַּעְתֵּיהּ דְּתַנַּייָא אֲחוֹרַייָא מַעֲשֶׂה נִיסִּין. עַל דַּעְתֵּיהּ דְּתַנַּייָא קַדְמִייָא אֵינוֹ מַעֲשֶׂה נִיסִּין. אָמְרוּ לֵיהּ. כּוּלְּהוֹן מַעֲשֶׂה נִיסִּין הָיוּ וּמְסוּרָגִין עָלוּ.

"And Moses was presiding." [359]Moses found a way to settle things. When the Holy One, praise to Him, told him, *count all male firstborns among the Children of Israel*[360], he said, who will consent voluntarily to give five sheqel per head? What did he do? He took 22'000 tickets[361] and wrote on them "Levite" and 273 on which he wrote "five sheqel" and put all of them in an urn[362]. He told them, come and take your ticket. To any one who drew a ticket saying "Levite" he said, a Levite already redeemed you. To anybody who drew a slip saying "five sheqel" he said, what can I do, it is from Heaven; Rebbi Jehudah[363]. But Rebbi Nehemiah the Tanna objected to the colleagues: If you had given me the possibility of a Levite, it would have come up for me.[364] But the following is what he did. He took 22'000 tickets[365] and wrote on them "Levite" and two hundred seventy three on which he wrote "five sheqel" and put all of them in an urn. He told them, come and take your ticket. To any one who drew a slip saying "Levite" he said, a Levite already redeemed you. The anybody who drew a ticket saying "five sheqel" he said, what can I do, it is from Heaven. The Tanna objected to the colleagues: Think of it, if all came up as "Levite"[366]? They told him, it was miraculous and they came up alternatingly. Rebbi Samuel said, in the opinion of the second Tanna, it was a miracle. In the opinion of the first Tanna, it was not a miracle[367]. They told him, it was a miracle in any case since they came up alternatingly.

359 *Tanhuma Bemidbar* 21, *Tanhuma Buber Bemidbar* 25, *Num. rabba* 4(9), shortened Babli 17a.

360 *Num.* 3:40. The reference should have been to vv. 46,47 where Moses was commanded to collect 5 *šeqel per person* from 273 of the 22'273 firstborn of the 11

tribes. The other 22'000 were redeemed by the service of 22'000 Levites. Since he was instructed to take the 5 *šeqel* from 273 persons, he could not simply collect 1'365 šeqel from 22'273 persons.

361 Greek πιττάκιον "ticket, label, etc."

362 Greek κάλπη, "urn".

363 The Midrash sources make it clear that the preceding was R. Jehudah's opinion; the following is R. Nehemiah's. The Babli only mentions R. Jehudah's opinion.

364 Since there were only 22'273 tickets, it was a mathematical necessity that 273 people would have to pay. The distribution of these was a pure matter of probabilities; there is no reason to invoke Heaven in the matter.

365 The parallel sources, and the paragraph after the next, make it clear that one has to read: 22'273 tickets reading "Levite".

366 Assuming that the tickets in the urn are well mixed and all tickets have the same probability to be drawn, the probability that in 22'273 drawings of 22'546 tickets no slip of "5 *šeqel*" or that all of the 273 extra tickets would be drawn is practically zero. (The first probability starts with a string of 117 zeroes after the decimal point, the second with 639.) If all 273 extra tickets were actually drawn, it was a clear sign from Heaven.

367 While in the first scenario by necessity 273 tickets of "5 *šeqel*" were drawn, these slips were drawn with approximately constant frequency, about 122.6 per 10'000 draws, against the probabilistic frequency of 121.1 per 10'000. One cannot say that alternatingly "Levite" and "5 *šeqel*" were drawn since then the drawing would have ended after 546 draws.

(19c line 61) אַנְטוֹנִינוּס הֵגֶמוֹן שָׁאַל אֶת רַבָּן יוֹחָנָן בֶּן זַכַּאי. בִּכְלָל חֲסֵירִין וּבִפְרָט יְתֵירִין. אָמַר לֵיהּ. אוֹתָן שְׁלֹשׁ מֵאוֹת יְתֵירִין בְּכוֹרֵי כְהוּנָּה הָיוּ וְאֵין קָדוֹשׁ מוֹצִיא קָדוֹשׁ.

[368]General Antoninus[369] asked Rabban Joḥanan ben Zakkai: The sum is deficient, the details are excessive. He told him, these 300 were firstborn of the priesthood; no holy one redeems a holy one[370].

368 Babli *Bekhorot* 5a, *Num. rabba* 4(7).

369 In *Bekhorot* קונטרוקוס, in *Num. rabba* הונגטיס; cf. Note 267.

370 In the census reported in *Num*. 3, the families of the Levites were reported as Gershon 7'500, Qehat 8'600, Merari 6'200, for a total of 22'300. But in the summation in v. 39 only 22'000 are reported and this number reappears as the number of Levites freeing firstborns from payment. Instead of "priesthood" one has to read "Levites".

(19c line 61) כְּיוֹצֵא בוֹ וַיֹּאמֶר יי אֶל־מֹשֶׁה אֶסְפָה־לִּי שִׁבְעִים אִישׁ מִזִּקְנֵי יִשְׂרָאֵל. אָמַר מֹשֶׁה. אִם אֶטּוֹל ו' מִכָּל־שֵׁבֶט הֲרֵי ע"ב. י' מִ' וּב' מֵה' אֵי זֶה שֵׁבֶט מְקַבֵּל עָלָיו לִהְיוֹת פָּגוּם. מֶה עָשָׂה. נָטַל שִׁבְעִים פִּיטְקִין וְכָתַב עֲלֵיהֶן זָקֵן וּב' חָלָק וְהִטִּילָן לְקַלְפֵּי. אָמַר לָהֶן. בּוֹאוּ וּטְלוּ פִיטְקֵיכֶם. כָּל־ שֶׁעָלָה בְיָדוֹ זָקֵן הָיָה אוֹמֵר לוֹ. מִינּוּךְ מִן הַשָּׁמַיִם. וְכָל־מִי שֶׁעָלָה בְיָדוֹ חָלָק הָיָה אוֹמֵר לוֹ.

מָה אֶעֱשֶׂה וּמִן הַשָּׁמַיִם הוּא.. רִבִּי יוּדָה וְרִבִּי נְחֶמְיָה מְתִיב תַּנַּיָּיא לַחֲבֵרַיָּא. אִילּוּ כְתַבְתָּנִי זָקֵן סַלְקִית. אֶלָּא כָּךְ עָשָׂה. נָטַל ע״ב פִּיטְקִין וְכָתַב עֲלֵיהֶן זָקֵן וּשְׁנַיִם חֲלָקִין וְהִטִּילָן לְקַלְפֵּי. אָמַר לָהֶן. בּוֹאוּ וּטְלוּ פִּיטְקֵיכֶם. מִי שֶׁעָלָה בְּיָדוֹ זָקֵן אוֹמֵר לוֹ. כְּבָר מִינּוּךְ מִן הַשָּׁמַיִם. וּמִי שֶׁעָלָה בְּיָדוֹ חָלָק הָיָה אוֹמֵר לוֹ. וּמָה אֶעֱשֶׂה וּמִן הַשָּׁמַיִם הוּא. מְתִיב תַּנַּיָּיא לַחֲבֵרַיָּא. הַגַּע עַצְמָךְ שֶׁעָלוּ כוּלָּם זָקֵן. אָמְרוּ לֵיהּ. מַעֲשֵׂה נִיסִּין הָיָה וּמְסוּרָגִין עָלוּ. אָמַר רִבִּי שְׁמוּאֵל. קַשִּׁיתֵיהּ קוֹמֵי רִבִּי אַבָּהוּ. עַל דַּעְתֵּיהּ דְּתַנַּיָּיא אֲחוֹרַיָּיא מַעֲשֵׂה נִיסִּים. עַל דַּעְתֵּיהּ דְּתַנַּיָּיא קַדְמִיָּיא אֵינוֹ מַעֲשֵׂה נִיסִּים. אֲמַר לֵיהּ. מַעֲשֵׂה נִיסִּין הָיוּ וּמְסוּרָגִין עָלוּ.

[371]Similarly. *the Eternal said to Moses, assemble for Me seventy men of the Elders of Israel*[334]. Moses said, if I am taking six per tribe, there will be 72, ten of six each and two of five, which tribe will agree to be discriminated against? What did he do? He took 70 tickets and wrote on them "Elder", two he left blank, and put them in an urn. He told them, come and take your ticket. To any one who drew a slip saying "Elder" he said, from Heaven they appointed you. To anybody who drew a blank slip he said, what can I do, it is from Heaven; Rebbi Jehudah[363]. But Rebbi Nehemiah the Tanna objected to the colleagues: If you had given me the possibility of an Elder, it would have come up for me.[364] But the following is what he did. He took 72 tickets and wrote on them "Elder" and two blank ones and put all of them in an urn. He told them, come and take your ticket. To any one who drew a slip saying "Elder" he said, from Heaven they appointed you. The anybody who drew a blank slip he said, what can I do, it is from Heaven. The Tanna objected to the colleagues: Think of it, if all came up as "Elder"? They told him, it was miraculous and they came up alternatingly[373]. Rebbi Samuel said, I objected before Rebbi Abbahu: in the opinion of the second Tanna, it was a miracle. In the opinion of the first Tanna, it was not a miracle. He told him, it was a miracle in any case since they came up alternatingly[374].

371 *Tanhuma Beha`alotekha* 11, *Tanhuma Buber Beha`alotekha* 22, *Sifry Num.* 95, *Num. rabba* 15(14), *Yalqut Šim`ony* 736, Babli 17a.

372 From here on there exists a Genizah fragment (L. Ginzberg, *Yerushalmi Fragments from the Genizah,* New York 1909, p. 256 ff.) where, however, few lines are complete. Its readings are noted G only in paragraphs where they are reasonably complete and mark a genuine difference in the text.

373 The probability of at least one of the blank tickets remaining in the urn, assuming uniform distribution (thorough mixing) of the tickets, was 0.14316.

374 I. e., about evenly spaced.

(19d line 3) שָׁאַל אַנְטִיגְנֹס הֶגֶמוֹן לְרַבָּן יוֹחָנָן בֶּן זַכַּאי. מֹשֶׁה רַבְּכֶם אוֹ גַנָּב הָיָה אוֹ לֹא הָיָה בָקִי בְחֶשְׁבּוֹן. דִּכְתִיב בֶּקַע לַגֻּלְגֹּלֶת. אִין תַּעֲבִיד קֵינְטֶרָא מְאָה לִיטְרִין חַד מִן אִישְׁתָּא גָנַב. וְאִין תַּעַבְדִּינֵיהּ שִׁיתִּין לִיטְרִין פַּלְגָּא גָנַב. אֲמַר לֵיהּ. מֹשֶׁה רַבָּן גִּזְבָּר נֶאֱמָן וּבָקִי בְחֶשְׁבּוֹן הָיָה. אֲמַר לֵיהּ. וְהָכְתִיב וּנְחוֹשֶׁת הַתְּנוּפָה עֶשְׂרִים כִּכָּר. וְהַיְידָא לוֹן סָלְקִין תִּשְׁעִין וְשִׁית לִיטְרִין וְאִית עֲבִיד לֵיהּ פְּרוֹטְרוֹט. אֲמַר לֵיהּ. מִשּׁוּם דְּלָא סָלִיק קֵינְטֵירָא. וְאִין תֵּימַר דִּסְלִיק קֵינְטֵירָא פַּלְגָּא גָנַב. אֲמַר לֵיהּ. וְהָכְתִיב וְאֶת־הָאֶלֶף וּשְׁבַע הַמֵּאוֹת וַחֲמִשָּׁה וְשִׁבְעִים. וְהַיְידָא לוֹן סָלְקִין שִׁבְעִים וְחַד לִיטְרִין וְאַתְּ עֲבִיד לֵיהּ פְּרוֹטְרוֹט. אֲמַר לֵיהּ. מִשּׁוּם דְּלָא סָלִיק קֵינְטֵירָא פַּלְגָּא גָנַב. אֲמַר לֵיהּ. וְהָכְתִיב וְהַשֶּׁקֶל עֶשְׂרִים גֵּרָה עֶשְׂרִים שְׁקָלִים חֲמִשָּׁה וְעֶשְׂרִים שְׁקָלִים עֲשָׂרָה וַחֲמִשָּׁה שְׁקָלִים הַמָּנֶה יִהְיֶה לָכֶם. כִּכָּרוֹ שֶׁל הַקָּדוֹשׁ בָּרוּךְ הוּא כָּפוּל הָיָה. אֲמַר לֵיהּ. גִּיזְבָּר נֶאֱמָן וּבָקִי בְחֶשְׁבּוֹן הָיָה.

1 שאל אנטיגנס הגמון לרבן | G אגנטס האגמון שאל את רבן לא | G שלא 2 בחשבון | G בחשבונות לגולגולת. אין תעביד קנטירא | G ואין תעביד קינטרא. 3 תעבדיניה שיתין | G תעבדינה אישתין נאמן | G נאמן היה 4 והכת' | G - עשרים ככר | G שבעים וגו' והיידא לון | G והיידילון ושית | G ושת 5 קינטרא | G קינטירא קינטרא | G קנטינר פלגא | G ופלגה 6 וחמשה ושבעים | G וגו' והיידא לון | G והיידילון שבעים וחד | G שובעין וחָדָה 6 ליה | G לה (twice) קינטרא פלגא | G קנטירא פלגא 9 כפול היה. אמ' ליה | G . . . כפול הוא אמר לה משה רבכון

[375]General Antigonos[376] asked Rabban Joḥanan ben Zakkai: Your teacher Moses either was a thief or he did not know how to compute, for it is written: *a beqa` per head*[377]. If you make the *centenarius* 100 pounds,[378] he stole one sixth. If you make it 60 pounds, he stole half. He answered him, our teacher Moses was a trustworthy treasurer expert in computations. He answered him, is it not written, *they contributed bronze twenty talents*[379]; for us that makes 96 pounds[380] and he mentions them in detail. He answered back, because it does not add up to a *centenarius*; if you would say that it added up to a *centenarius*, he would have stolen half. He told him, but it is written *1'775,* would that not make 71 pounds[381] and he mentions it in detail. He answered back, if you would say that it added up to a *centenarius*, he would have stolen half. He told him, but it is written, *the sheqel is 20 gera, twenty sheqel, twenty-five sheqel, twenty-five sheqel the maneh*[382] *shall be for you*[383]*;* the talent of the Holy One, praise to Him, was double. He answered back, he[384] was a trustworthy treasurer and expert in computations.

375 A different version is in the Babli, *Bekhorot* 5a.

376 In G, אגנטוס, cf. Note 267.

377 The discussion is about *Ex*. 38:25,26 (in the LXX, ed. A. Rahlfs, 39:2,3) where it is stated that the Temple tax of a *beqa`*, half a *šeqel*, paid by 603'550 men came to 100 *kikkar* 1775 *šeqel.* The LXX follows rabbinic tradition in identifying the *beqa`*, the Babylonian *zuz*, with the drachma, i. e., the *šeqel* with the *dupondius*, and the *kikkar* (Accadic *gaggarum* "disk") with the talent of 60 minas or 6'000 drachmas, i. e. 3'000 *šeqel* (cf. *Qiddušin* 1:1, Note 122.) But in *Qiddušin* 1:3 Note 339 it is declared that any *šeqel* mentioned in the Torah is a Roman tetradrachma. Then the silver contributed should have been twice the recorded amount, 201 talents 550 *šeqel.*

378 The *libra* weighing 100 *drachmae* is the natural weight equivalent of the Greek *mina* in coin. The *centenarius*, "hundredweight", 100 pounds, is taken as the equivalent of the talent. But if by *šeqel* a tetradrachma is meant, a talent should have been 120 *mina*, not 60 as usual, and not 100 as presumed here. Computed from above, one-sixth is missing in the latter, half in the former case.

379 A scribal error; in the verse (and G): 70 talents. The total recorded was 70 talents, 2'400 *šeqel.*

380 Since 25 *tetradrachma* make a *mina*, 2'400 *drachma* are 96 *mina.* Nevertheless, the verse mentions *šeqel*, not *mina.*

381 @ 25 *tetradrachma* each.

382 The Babylonian *mina.*

382 *Ez.* 45:12; the correct text, intended here, is: *20 šeqel, 25 šeqel, 15 šeqel make a maneh,* for a total of 60. Therefore, it is impossible to identify the Greek *mina* as 25 *šeqel.* Cf. *Qiddušin* 1:2 Note 204.

383 Read with G: "Your teacher Moses."

כהן גדול פרק שני

(fol. 19d) **משנה א**: כֹּהֵן גָּדוֹל דָּן וְדָנִין אוֹתוֹ מֵעִיד וּמְעִידִין אוֹתוֹ. חוֹלֵץ וְחוֹלְצִין לְאִשְׁתּוֹ וּמְיַבְּמִין לְאִשְׁתּוֹ. אֲבָל הוּא אֵינוֹ מְיַבֵּם מִפְּנֵי שֶׁהוּא אָסוּר בָּאַלְמָנָה. מֵת לוֹ מֵת אֵינוֹ יוֹצֵא אַחַר הַמִּטָּה אֶלָּא הֵן נִיכְסִין וְהוּא נִגְלֶה. הֵן נִיגְלִין וְהוּא נִכְסֶה. וְיוֹצֵא עִמָּהֶן עַד פֶּתַח הָעִיר דִּבְרֵי רַבִּי מֵאִיר. רַבִּי יְהוּדָה אוֹמֵר אֵינוֹ יוֹצֵא מִן הַמִּקְדָּשׁ שֶׁנֶּאֱמַר וּמִן הַמִּקְדָּשׁ לֹא יֵצֵא.

Mishnah 1: The High Priest judges and one judges him; he testifies and one testifies against him[1]. He gives *ḥalîṣah* and one gives *ḥalîṣah* to his wife, and one marries his wife in levirate marriage[2]. But he may not marry in levirate marriage since a widow is forbidden to him.[3] If a family member of his dies, he cannot follow the bier but if they[4] are unseen he can be seen; if they are seen he must be unseen. He leaves with them up to the city gate, the words of Rebbi Meïr; Rebbi Jehudah said, he does not leave the Temple since it is said: *The Sanctuary he shall not leave*[5].

1 These statements are only necessary as contrast to the rules for the king, to whom they do not apply (Mishnah 3).

2 If his brother dies childless, he gives *halîsah* to his sister-in-law, which will be allowed to marry anybody but a Cohen. If he dies childless, any brother not appointed High Priest in his stead may marry his widow.

3 *Lev*. 21:14.

4 The people carrying the bier. The High Priest may never be seen together with them.

5 *Lev*. 21:12.

(19d line 58) **הלכה א**: כֹּהֵן גָּדוֹל דָּן וְדָנִין אוֹתוֹ כול'. נִיחָא דָּן. דָּנִין אוֹתוֹ. וְיִמְנֶה לוֹ אֶנְטֶלָּר. הַגַּע עַצְמָךְ שֶׁנָּפְלָה לוֹ שְׁבוּעָה. וְאֶנְטֶלָּר בִּשְׁבוּעָה. דִּינֵי מָמוֹנוֹת שֶׁלּוֹ בְּכַמָּה. בְּכ"ג. נִישְׁמְעִינָהּ מֵהָדָא. אֵין מֶלֶךְ יוֹשֵׁב בַּסַּנְהֶדְרִין וְלֹא מֶלֶךְ וְכֹהֵן גָּדוֹל יוֹשְׁבִין בְּעִיבּוּר. רַבִּי חֲנִינָה וְרַבִּי מָנָא. חַד אָמַר. אֵין מֶלֶךְ יוֹשֵׁב בַּסַּנְהֶדְרִין מִפְּנֵי הֶחָשֵׁד. וְלֹא בְעִיבּוּר מִפְּנֵי הֶחָשֵׁד. וְלֹא מֶלֶךְ וְכֹהֵן גָּדוֹל יוֹשְׁבִין בְּעִיבּוּר. שֶׁאֵין כְּבוֹד הַמֶּלֶךְ לֵישֵׁב בְּשִׁבְעָה. תָּא חֲמִי. בְּשִׁבְעָה אֵין כְּבוֹדוֹ לֵישֵׁב לֹא כָל־שֶׁכֵּן ּשְׁלֹשָׁה. הָדָא אָמְרָה דִּינֵי מָמוֹנוֹת שֶׁלּוֹ בְּעֶשְׂרִים וּשְׁלֹשָׁה.

Halakhah 1: "The High Priest judges and one judges him," etc. One understands that he judges. Why does one judge him[6]? Can he not appoint a plenipotentiary[7]? Think of it, if an oath should be imposed on him, may a plenipotentiary take the oath?

His monetary suits are heard by how many? By 23, as we understand from the following[8]: "The king may not sit in the Synhedrion, neither king nor High Priest may participate in intercalations." Rebbi Ḥanina[9] and Rabbi Mana, one said the king does not sit in the Synhedrion because of suspicion[10]; he cannot participate in intercalations because of suspicion[11]. [12]Neither king nor High Priest may participate in intercalations since it is not to the king's honor to sit with seven, so much less with three. This implies that his monetary suits are heard by 23[13].

6 Why can he be compelled to appear in court in person?

7 In G אנטליר which S. Lieberman (*Greek and Hellenism in Jewish Palestine*, Jerusalem 1963, pp. 10-11) reads as *antellar* as a composite of Greek ἐντέλλω "enjoin, command, invest with legal powers" with Latin suffix *-arius* "belonging to, invested with," etc.

8 Tosephta 2:15.

9 In G correctly Hananiah, the contemporary of R. Mana II.

10 That the judges do not dare to voice an opinion contradicting the king.

11 Since the king can be expected to favor adding a 13th month every year so that all contracts for services which his government has concluded will be extended for another month without him having to pay for it.

12 The second opinion is missing here. In G it is extended for three lines but no intelligible text can be extracted from the few remaining words. G in all cases says "the king of Israel".

13 This is unknown to the Babli.

(19d line 66) אָמַר רִבִּי לָעְזָר. כֹּהֵן גָּדוֹל שֶׁחָטָא מַלְקִין אוֹתוֹ וְאֵין מַעֲבִירִין אוֹתוֹ מִגְּדוּלָּתוֹ. אָמַר רִבִּי מָנָא. כְּתִיב כִּ֣י נֵ֠זֶר שֶׁ֣מֶן מִשְׁחַ֧ת אֱלֹהָ֛יו עָלָ֖יו אֲנִ֥י יי. כִּבְיָכוֹל מָה אֲנִי בִקְדוּשָּׁתִי אַף אַהֲרוֹן בִּקְדוּשָּׁתוֹ. רִבִּי חֲנִינָה כְּתוֹבָא רִבִּי אָחָא בְשֵׁם רֵישׁ לָקִישׁ. כֹּהֵן גָּדוֹל שֶׁחָטָא מַלְקִין אוֹתוֹ. אֵין תֵּימַר בְּכ"ג. נִמְצֵאת עֲלִייָתוֹ יְרִידָתוֹ. וְרֵישׁ לָקִישׁ אָמַר. נָשִׂיא שֶׁחָטָא מַלְקִין אוֹתוֹ בְּבֵית דִּין שֶׁלִּשְׁלֹשָׁה. מַה מַחֲזִרִן לֵיהּ. אָמַר רִבִּי חַגַּיי. מֹשֶׁה. אֵין מַחֲזְרִין לֵיהּ דִּי קָטַל לוֹן. שָׁמַע רִבִּי יוּדָן נְשִׂייָא וְכָעַס. שָׁלַח גִּנְתּוֹן לְמִיתְפּוֹס לְרֵישׁ לָקִישׁ. טָרְפוֹן. עֲרַק לְדָא מוּגְדָּלָא. וְאִית דָּמְרִין לְהָדָא כְּפַר חִיטַּיָּא. לְמָחָר סְלַק רִבִּי יוֹחָנָן לְבֵית וַועֲדָא וּסְלַק רִבִּי יוּדָן נְשִׂייָא לְבֵית וַועֲדָא. אֲמַר לֵיהּ. לָמָּה לֵיה מָרִי אֲמַר לוֹן מִילָּה דְאוֹרַייָא. שְׁרֵי טְפַח בְּחָדָא יָדֵיהּ. אֲמַר לֵיהּ. וּבְחָדָא טַפְחִין.

אֶלָּא אֲמַר לֵיהּ. לֹא וְלֹא בֶן לָקִישׁ לֹא. אֲמַר לֵיהּ. אֶלָּא אֲנִי מְפַתְּחֵהּ. אֲמַר לֵיהּ. בְּהָדָא מַגְדְּלָא. אֲמַר לֵיהּ. לְמָחָר אֲנָא וְאַתְּ נִיפּוּק לְקַדְמֵיהּ. שְׁלַח רִבִּי יוֹחָנָן גַּבֵּי רֵישׁ לָקִישׁ. עֲתִיר לָךְ מִילָּה דְאוֹרַייָא דִנְשִׂייָא נְפִיק לְקַדְמָךְ. נְפַק לְקַדְמוֹן וָמַר. דֵּיגְמָא דִידְכוֹן דָּמְייָא לְבִירְיַיתְכוֹן. כַּד אֲתָא רַחֲמָנָא לְמִפְרוֹק יַת יִשְׂרָאֵל לֹא שְׁלַח לֹא שָׁלִיחַ וְלֹא מַלְאָךְ אֶלָּא הוּא בְעַצְמוֹ. דִּכְתִיב וְעָבַרְתִּי בְאֶרֶץ־מִצְרַיִם. הוּא וְכָל־דַּרְגּוֹן דִּידֵיהּ. אֲמַר לֵיהּ. וּמַה חֲמִית מֵימַר הָא מִילְּתָא. אֲמַר לוֹן. מָה אַתּוֹן סָבְרִין. מַה דְחִיל מִינְּכוֹן הֲוֵינָא מְנַע אוּלְפָּנֵיהּ דְּרַחֲמָנָא. דָּמַר רִבִּי שְׁמוּאֵל בַּר רַב יִצְחָק אַל בָּנַיי כִּי לוֹא־טוֹבָה הַשְּׁמוּעָה.

2 בקדושתי | **ה**G בגדולתי 3 בקדושתו | **ה**G בגדולתו - | **ה**G אמ' ר' אבון. קדוש יהיה לך. כביכול אני בקדושתי אף אהרן בקדושתו ריש | **ה**G ר' שמעון בן גדול | G משיח אותו | **ה**G אותן בבית דין **ה** שלשלשה G של שלשה 4 בכ"ג | **ה** בבית דין שלכ"ג G בבית דין שלעשרים . . . ירידתו | **ה**G ירידה לו וריש | **ה**G ר' שמעון בן 5 מחזרן | **ה**G מחזרין משה | **ה** מוטב דינון די קטל לון | **ה** גו קטלון ליה G דו קטילון 6 יודן נשייא | **ה** יודה נשיאה גנתון | **ה**G גותיין למיתפוס לריש לקיש | **ה** למיתפש ית ר' שמעון בן לקיש G למתפוס לר' שמעון בן לקיש טרפון | **ה** - ערק | **ה**G וערק לדא | G בהדה מוגדלא | **ה**G דמוגדלא דמרין להדא | **ה** דאמרין ברה G דמרין בהדה 7 חיטיא | G חטייה סלק | **ה**G סליק ווערא | G ווערה (2 times) וסלק ר' יודן נשייא | **ה** סליק ר' יודה נסייא 8 ליה | **ה**G לית דאורייא | G דאורייה בהגא | G בהדה ובחדא | G ובחדה - | G ידי 9 לא ולא | **ה** לאו. אין לא G לא ואין לוו אלא אני מפתחה | **ה** ואנו מפתחה G והנו מופתחה בהדא מגדלא | **ה** ברא דמוגדלא 10 ניפוק | **ה** נפיק ריש | **ה**G ר' שמעון בן 11 נשייא | G נסייא ומר | **ה** מר לביריתכון | **ה** לברייכון 12 למפרוק | **ה** למפרק ישראל | **ה**G ישראל ממצרים הוא | **ה** הקב"ה 13 דרגון | **ה** גורגון

[14]Rebbi Eleazar said, if a High Priest sinned, one whips him but does not remove him from his elevated status[13]. Rebbi Mana said, it is written[5]: *For the crown of his God's ointment is on him, I am the Eternal*; if one could compare it, just as I am in My Sanctity, so Aaron is in his sanctity[15]. Rebbi Ḥanina the scribe, Rebbi Aḥa in the name of Rebbi Simeon ben Laqish: if a High Priest sinned, one whips him[16]. If you would say by 23, his elevation would be his degradation[17]. And Rebbi Simeon ben Laqish said, if a patriarch sinned, one whips him by a court of three [judges]. Does one return him? Rebbi Ḥaggai said, by Moses, if one would return him, he would kill them. Rebbi Jehudah the Prince[18] heard this and became angry. He sent Goths[19] to catch Rebbi Simeon ben Laqish. They beat him. He fled to Magdala, some say to Kefar Ḥiṭṭim[20]. The next day, Rebbi Joḥanan went to the assembly hall, when Rebbi Jehudah the Prince also went to the assembly hall. He[21] said to him, why is the master not[22] telling us words of instruction? He[23] started clapping with one hand. He[21] asked, does one clap with one? He[23] answered

him, no, but without ben Laqish there is nothing[24]. He[21] told him, I shall free him. He[23] said to him, in Magdala. He[21] told him, tomorrow I and you will go out to meet him. Rebbi Johanan sent to Rebbi Simeon ben Laqish, prepare[25] for yourself some words of instruction since the Patriarch will go out to meet you. He went out to meet them and said, your example is similar to that of your Creator. For when the Merciful went to liberate Israel [from Egypt][26], He sent neither messenger nor angel but He went Himself, as is written: *I shall pass through the Land of Egypt*[27], He and all His Court[28]. He asked him, why did you say these things[29]? He told him, what are you thinking? That for fear of you I would refrain from the teachings of the Merciful? As Rebbi Samuel ben Rav Isaac said, *No my sons, because the reputation is not good*[30].

14 There exists a copy of this paragraph in *Horaiot* 3:2 (ה). It is missing in the Yerushalmi reproduced in the *editio princeps* of the Babli. A different version is in *Midrash Samuel* 7(5).

15 The two other sources read: I in My Greatness, also Aaron in his greatness. R. Abun said (*Lev*. 21:8), *holy he shall be to you*, if one could compare it, as I Am in My Holiness, so Aaron is in his holiness.

16 In the two other sources: by a court of three judges. The sequel requires this text.

17 Since so many people would sit in judgment over him.

18 R. Jehudah II.

19 Following the reading of the other two sources. Krauss conjectures that the inserted נ indicates nasal pronunciation, but by the evidence of the other two sources גנתון instead of גותיין seems to be a scribal error. [Instead of Goths they might have been *Gaetuli,* a people from Northwestern Africa (E. G.).]

20 Magdala is on Lake Genezareth, Kefar Hittim in the hills overlooking Tiberias.

21 R. Jehudah the Prince.

22 Translated following G.

23 R. Johanan.

14 Following the text of the other two sources. The text of the Leiden ms. is unintelligible.

25 Translated following G. The text of the other two sources, "get rich", does not make much sense.

26 Added from the other two sources.

27 *Ex*. 12:12.

28 Translated following Eliahu Fulda and H. L. Fleischer in Levy's Dictionary. A similar explanation of the verse is found in the Passover Haggadah (*Mekhilta dR.Ismael*, ed. Horovitz-Rabin, p. 23; cf. H. Guggenheimer, *The Scholar's Haggadah* pp. 298-299.)

Here ends the Geniza fragment. The text in *Horaiot* has additions both at this point and at the end of the paragraph which, while relevant, in the absence of a confirming Genizah text cannot be added here.

29 About whipping the Patriarch.

30 *IS.* 2:24. The explanation of the verse is missing; it is given in *Horaiot*. The verse about the misdeeds of Eli's sons ends, מַעֲבִירִים עַם יי [*the information*] *spread about by the Eternal's people*, which he interprets as *being removed by the Eternal's people*, implying that the High Priest has to be removed if he sins.

(20a line 9) רִבִּי לָעְזָר בְּשֵׁם כַּהֲנָא. לְמַעְלָן. לְמַעְלָן מִקָּנֶה שָׂפָה. לְמַטָּן. לְמַטָּן מִקָּנֶה שָׂפָה. רִבִּי יוֹחָנָן אָמַר. לְמַטָּן מַמָּשׁ. רִבִּי יוֹחָנָן סְלַק מְבַקְּרָה לְרִבִּי חֲנִינָה גּוֹ אִסְטְרָטָה. שְׁמַע דִּדְמָךְ. אָמַר. שְׁלַח וְאַייתִי לִי מָנוֹי טַבְיָיא דְשׁוּבְתָא וּבְזָעֵיהּ. רִבִּי יוֹחָנָן פְּלִיג עַל רִבִּי יוּדָן בְּתַרְתֵּי. וְאַתְיָיא דְרִבִּי לָעְזָר בְּשֵׁם כַּהֲנָא כְרִבִּי יוּדָה. וְאִי[31] כְרִבִּי יוּדָה לֹא יִפְרוֹס[32] כָּל־עִיקָּר. לָא אַתְיָיא דְלָא אֶלָּא עַל אָבִיו וְעַל אִמּוֹ כְרִבִּי מֵאִיר. דְּתַנֵּי. עַל כָּל־הַמֵּתִים אֵין מַבְדִּיל קָנֶה שָׂפָה אֶלָּא עַל אָבִיו וְעַל אִמּוֹ. דִּבְרֵי רִבִּי מֵאִיר. רִבִּי יוּדָן אוֹמֵר. כָּל־קֶרַע שֶׁאֵינוֹ מַבְדִּיל קָנֶה שָׂפָה הֲרֵי זֶה קֶרַע שֶׁלְּתִפְלוּת. מַאי כְדוֹן. חוֹמֶר הוּא בְכֹהֵן גָּדוֹל שֶׁיְּהֵא מַבְדִּיל קָנֶה שָׂפָה.

2 סלק | **ה** סליק מבקרה | **ה** למבקרא גו | **ה** כד הוה גו אמ' | **ה** - 3 ובזעיה | **ה** ובזען ר' יודן | **ה** דר' יודה בתרתי | **ה** תרתין 4 ואי | **ה** אין יפרוס | **ה** יפרום דלא | **ה** דא 5 כר' מאיר | **ה** כדברי ר' מאיר אין | **ה** אינו 6 דברי | **ה** כדברי 7 חומר | **ה** או'

[33]Rebbi Eleazar in the name of Cahana: On top, high starting with the seam[34], below, low starting with the seam. Rebbi Joḥanan said, really low[35]. Rebbi Joḥanan was going up the mountain[36] to visit Rebbi Ḥanina; on the road he heard that he had died. He sent, brought his good Sabbath garment, and tore it. Rebbi Joḥanan disagrees with Rebbi Jehudah in two things, but Rebbi Eleazar in the name of Cahana follows Rebbi Jehudah[37]. If following Rebbi Jehudah, he should not tear at all! This refers only to his father or mother, following Rebbi Meïr, as it was stated: One tears the seam for nobody who died except for father and mother, the words of Rebbi Meïr. Rebbi Jehudah says, any tear which does not completely sever the seam is a frivolous tear. How is that? It is a stringency for the High Priest that he shall sever the seam completely[38].

31 A Babylonism.

32 A scribal error, corrected in the parallel source.

33 This and the following paragraphs refer to Mishnah *Horaiot* 3:6; the origin is to be found there in Halakhah 3:6 (ה). The Yerushalmi printed in the Babli *editio princeps* from a ms. different from the Leiden one, only quotes the first sentence; it eliminated the remark "continue in Sanhedrin." The paragraph also appears in *Mo`ed qatan,* copied twice in the Leiden ms. The text there is a reformulation, not a copy.

Mishnah *Horaiot* 3:6 reads: "The High Priest tears his clothes below, the simple priest above. The High Priest officiates when he is a fresh mourner but may not eat; the simple priest neither officiates nor eats." The High Priest is forbidden to let his hair grow or tear his clothes (*Lev*. 21:10). R. Meïr interprets the verse to mean that in mourning he may not tear his garment in the way other people do [*Sifra Emor Parashah* 2(3)]. The Mishnah is R. Meïr's. It is obvious that one speaks here of the High Priest's personal belonging, not his robes of office, which may not be torn (*Ex*. 28:32,29:23).

34 He insists that a valid tear in mourning must sever the thread of the seam. If the cloth of the garment is folded over and then sewn, the tear must reach the place where the cloth is only a single layer.

In Babylonia, the Palestinian קָנֶה שָׂפָה was understood as קַמֵּי שָׂפָה "in front of the seam" (*Mo`ed qatan* 22b), correctly interpreted in the Rashi commentary edited by E. Kupfer (Jerusalem 1961). Cf. *Horaiot* 3:6, Note 201.

35 Without any minimal depth.

36 From Tiberias below Sea level to Sepphoris on a hilltop.

37 R. Jehudah does not require tearing one's clothing in mourning except for his parents, but if one tears he requires severing the seam.

38 This is the text here, in *Horaiot*, and in the first version of the Halakhah in *Mo`ed qatan* 3:8, but in the second version and in *editio princeps* one reads: "that he may not sever the seam completely." This seems to be the correct version. The point is made that *Lev*. 21:10 does not use the frequently used verb קרע "to tear" but the infrequent פרם "to tear in little pieces". The is interpreted in *Sifra Emor Parashah* 2(3) to mean that the High Priest is not totally forbidden to rend his garments, only he may not do what everybody does. If he rends it, it may only be at the bottom, where few people will notice, and it may not be deep.

(20a line 18) כֹּהֵן גָּדוֹל מַקְרִיב אוֹנֵן וְלֹא אוֹכֵל. דִּבְרֵי רִבִּי מֵאִיר. רִבִּי יְהוּדָה אוֹמֵר. כָּל־אוֹתוֹ הַיּוֹם. רִבִּי שִׁמְעוֹן אוֹמֵר. גּוֹמֵר כָּל־הָעֲבוֹדָה שֶׁיֵּשׁ בְּיָדוֹ וּבָא לוֹ. בֵּין רִבִּי מֵאִיר לְרִבִּי שִׁמְעוֹן חָדָא. בֵּין רִבִּי יוּדָה לְרִבִּי שִׁמְעוֹן חָדָא. בֵּין רִבִּי מֵאִיר לְרִבִּי יוּדָה הַכְנָסָה. רִבִּי יַעֲקֹב בֶּן דּוֹסַאי. מַפְסִיק בֵּינֵיהוֹן. רִבִּי מֵאִיר אוֹמֵר. הָיָה בִפְנִים הָיָה יוֹצֵא. הָיָה בַחוּץ הָיָה נִכְנָס. רִבִּי יְהוּדָה אוֹמֵר. הָיָה בִפְנִים הָיָה נִכְנָס. הָיָה בַחוּץ לֹא הָיָה נִכְנָס. רִבִּי שִׁמְעוֹן אוֹמֵר. גּוֹמֵר כָּל־הָעֲבוֹדָה שֶׁיֵּשׁ בְּיָדוֹ וּבָא לוֹ. רִבִּי יוֹסֵי בֵּירִבִּי בּוּן בְּשֵׁם רַב הוּנָא. מַתְנִיתָא לְרֵישׁ לָקִישׁ. וּמִן־הַמִּקְדָּשׁ לֹא יֵצֵא. עִמָּהֶן אֵין יֵצֵא. יוֹצֵא הוּא אַחֲרֵיהֶן. הֵן נִיכְסִין וְהוּא נִגְלֶה וְיוֹצֵא עִמָּהֶן עַד פֶּתַח הָעִיר. דִּבְרֵי רַבִּי מֵאִיר. רַבִּי יוּדָן אוֹמֵר. אֵינוֹ יוֹצֵא מִן הַמִּקְדָּשׁ. שֶׁנֶּאֱמַר וּמִן־הַמִּקְדָּשׁ לֹא יֵצֵא. יָצָא לֹא הָיָה חוֹזֵר.

1 יהודה | **ה** יודה 2 שיש בידו | **ה** שבידו 3 בן דוסאי | **ה** בר דסיי מפסיק | **ה** מפשק 4 היה נכנס | **ה** לא היה נכנס יהודה | **ה** יודה 5 נכנס | **ה** יוצא כל | **ה** את כל 6 הונא | **ה** חונא לריש לקיש | **ה** דר' שמעון 7 הן ניכסין | **ה** אלא הן נכנסין והוא יוצא. הן ניכסין 8 יודן | **ה** יודה שנא' | **ה** כת' יצא | **ה** למד אלא לא יצא. יצא

[39]"The High Priest sacrifices while in deep[40] sorrow but does not eat, the words of Rebbi Meïr; Rebbi Jehudah says, the entire day[41]. Rebbi Simeon says, he completely finishes the service he is engaged in and then leaves." Between Rebbi Meïr and Rebbi Simeon there is one [difference], between Rebbi Jehudah and Rebbi Simeon there is one [difference][42]. Between Rebbi Meïr and Rebbi Jehudah is entering[43]. Rebbi Jacob ben Dositheos: interruption is between them. Rebbi Meïr says, if he was inside, he leaves; if he was outside, he did [not][44] enter. Rebbi Jehudah says, if he was inside, he enters[45]; if he was outside, he did not enter. Rebbi Simeon says, he completely finishes the service he is engaged in and then leaves. Rebbi Yose ben Rebbi Abun in the name of Rav Huna: a *baraita* is from Rebbi Simeon ben Laqish[46]: [47]*The Sanctuary he shall not leave,* he may not leave with them, but he may leave after them. If they[4] are unseen he can be seen; he leaves with them up to the city gate, the words of Rebbi Meïr; Rebbi Jehudah said, he does not leave the Temple since it is said: *The Sanctuary he shall not leave*[5]. If he left, he may not return."

39 Tosephta *Zevahim* 11:3.

40 "Deep sorrow" is the period between the death of a close relative and his burial. This is a period of biblically mandated mourning in which consumption of sanctified food is forbidden, *Deut.* 26:14. A simple priest, who is required to defile himself for the burial of a close relative, automatically is barred from the holy precinct until he is purified from the impurity of the dead. The High Priest is prohibited from defiling himself and from leaving the holy precinct (*Lev.* 21:12). The question remains, what is his status on that day?

41 Everybody agrees that if a High Priest is engaged in Divine Service when he is informed of the death of a close relative, he finishes his task. R. Simeon requires that upon completion he leave immediately; if he was informed while idle he also must leave immediately. R. Meïr holds that if he was in the precinct, he can start sacrificing even after being informed but then has to leave; if he was outside he cannot enter. R. Jehudah does not require him to leave.

42 For R. Jehudah, he does not have to leave after finishing his task. In fact, there are two differences since for R. Jehudah he is permitted to start after being informed of the death, but not for R. Simeon.

43 Whether he has to leave after finishing. The verse seems to support R. Jehudah, *Lev.* 21:12: *The holy precinct he may not leave.*

44 Reading from *Horaiot.*

45 If he was in the Temple precinct, he may start serving; if he was outside, he may not enter, since *Lev.* 21:12 does not apply to his situation.

46 In *Horaiot*: R. Simeon. The name tradition here is quite corrupt. R. Yose bar Abun of the last generation of Galilean Amoraïm was a student of R. Jacob bar Dositheos. Also he cannot speak in the name of the second generation Babylonian Rav Huna; one has to read *Rebbi* Huna against both mss. sources. R. Simeon ben Laqish cannot formulate a *baraita*; neither *baraita* nor Mishnah address R. Simeon's opinion.

47 A similar text is in *Sifra Emor Parashah* 2(8).

(20a line 28) רִבִּי אַבָּהוּ בְּשֵׁם רִבִּי לְעָזָר. אֵין אֲנִינָה אֶלָּא לְמֵת בִּלְבַד. דִּכְתִיב וְאָנוּ וְאָבְלוּ פְּתָחֶיהָ. הָתִיב חִייָה בַּר אָדָא. וְהָכְתִיב וְאָנוּ הַדַּייָגִים. אָמַר רִבִּי חֲנִינָה. כֵּינִי מַתְנִיתָא. אֵין אֲנִינַת טוּמְאָה אֶלָּא לְמֵת בִּלְבַד. תַּנֵּי. אֵי זוֹ הִיא אֲנִינָה. מִשְּׁעַת מִיתָה עַד שְׁעַת קְבוּרָה. דִּבְרֵי רִבִּי. וַחֲכָמִים אוֹמְרִים. כָּל־אוֹתוֹ הַיּוֹם. אַשְׁכָּחַת מַר קוּלּוֹת וְחוּמְרוֹת עַל דַּעְתֵּיהּ דְּרִבִּי. קוּלּוֹת וְחוּמְרוֹת עַל דַּעְתְּהוֹן דְּרַבָּנִן. מַה מַפְקָה מִבֵּינֵיהוֹן. מֵת וְנִקְבַּר בְּשַׁעְתּוֹ. עַל דַּעְתְּהוֹן דְּרַבָּנִן אָסוּר כָּל־אוֹתוֹ הַיּוֹם. עַל דַּעְתֵּיהּ דְּרִבִּי אֵינוֹ אָסוּר אֶלָּא אוֹתָהּ שָׁעָה בִּלְבַד. מֵת וְנִקְבַּר לְאַחַר ג' יָמִים. עַל דַּעְתְּהוֹן דְּרַבָּנִן אָסוּר כָּל־אוֹתוֹ הַיּוֹם. עַל דַּעְתֵּיהּ דְּרִבִּי אָסוּר עַד שְׁלֹשָׁה יָמִים. אֲתַא רִבִּי אַבָּהוּ בְּשֵׁם רִבִּי יוֹחָנָן וְרַב חִסְדָּא תְּרֵוַיהוֹן מָרִין. מוֹדֶה רִבִּי לַחֲכָמִים שֶׁאֵין אָסוּר אֶלָּא אוֹתוֹ הַיּוֹם בִּלְבַד. כְּהָדָא דְתַנֵּי. רִבִּי אוֹמֵר. תֵּדַע לְךָ שֶׁאֵין אֲנִינוּת לַיְלָה תוֹרָה. שֶׁהֲרֵי אָמְרוּ. אוֹנֵן טוֹבֵל וְאוֹכֵל פִּסְחוֹ לָעֶרֶב. וַהֲרֵי אָמְרוּ אֲנִינוּת תּוֹרָה. רִבִּי יֹסֵא בְּרִבִּי בּוּן בְּשֵׁם רִבִּי חוּנָא. תִּיפְתָּר שֶׁנִּקְבַּר בְּדִמְדּוּמֵי חַמָּה.

2 חייה | **פה** ר' חייא הדייגים | **פה** הדייגים ואבלו כל משליכי חכה כיני | **ה** - 3 אנינת טומאה | **פה** אנינות טמאה תני | **ה** - 4 מר | **ה** אמר **פ** חמר על דעת' דר' | **פה** על דר' 5 על דעת' דרבנן | **פה** על דרבנן מת { **פ** קלת על דרבנן. מת 6 ג' { **ה** שלשה 7 שלשה | **ה** ג' 8 ורב { **ה** רב חסדא | **פ** חונא 10 אנינות תורה | **ה** אנינות היום תורה ר' חונא { **ה** רב הונא **פ** רב חסדא 11 בדמדומי חמה | **פה** עם דמדומי חמה. ולית מן שמע מינה כלום

[48]Rebbi Abbahu in the name of Rebbi Eleazar: "Deep sorrow"[49] is only for the dead, for it is written[50]: *Its gates are in deep sorrow and mourning.* Hiyya bar Ada objected: Is it not written[51]: *the fishermen are in deep sorrow*? Rebbi Hanina said, so is the *baraita*: there is no deep sorrow in impurity except for the dead. It was stated[52]: "What is deep sorrow? From the moment of death until the moment of burial, the word of Rebbi. Bur the Sages say, the entire day." It turns out that one describes leniencies and stringencies following Rebbi, leniencies and stringencies following the rabbis. What is the difference between them? If he died and was buried within the hour. Following the rabbis, he is forbidden the entire day; following Rebbi he is forbidden only that hour. If he died and was buried after three days.

Following the rabbis, he is forbidden the entire day; following Rebbi he is forbidden up to three days. There came Rebbi Abbahu in the name of Rebbi Joḥanan, and Rav Ḥisda, both of whom said that Rebbi agrees with the Sages that he is forbidden only during the first day, as it was stated[53]: Rebbi said, you know that deep mourning in the night is not biblical, since they said[54], "the deep mourner immerses himself and eats his Passover sacrifice in the evening." But they said, deep mourning [during daytime][55] is biblical. Rebbi Yose ben Rebbi Abun in the name of Rebbi Huna: Explain it[56] that he was buried close to sundown [and one cannot infer anything.[55]]

48 In addition to the parallel in *Horaiot,* there exists one in *Pesahim* 8:7 36a l. 76 ff. (פ).

49 In its legal implications, that the person not only be forbidden to eat sanctified food but also cannot be counted in a quorum for religious services; cf. *Berakhot* 3:1, Note 42.

50 *Is*. 3:26. The gates of Jerusalem are in sorrow because all its men are dead.

51 *Is*. 19:8. The fishermen are in *deep sorrow* (and they *mourn* as quoted in the two parallel texts) because the Nile dried up. This proves that both terms used for the religious obligations of a person whose close relative died are used in the Bible also to describe other situations.

52 *Babli Zevaḥim* 100b; a suspect text in *Semahot* 4:4.

53 *Babli Zevaḥim* 100b.

54 Mishnah *Pesahim* 8:8. This naturally presupposes that the person was not defiled by the impurity of the dead; otherwise, he would have to observe a seven day cleansing period. If he had no occasion to be near the corpse, the biblical prohibitions upon the deep mourner lapse at sundown.

55 Inserted from the parallel sources, necessary for understanding the text.

56 The Mishnah in *Pesahim* only refers to the unlikely case that the deep mourner was not defiled with the impurity of the dead in a case in which both Rebbi and the Sages will agree on the duration of the deep sorrow.

(fol. 19d) **משנה ב**: וּכְשֶׁהוּא מְנַחֵם אֶת אֲחֵרִים דֶּרֶךְ כָּל הָעָם עוֹבְרִין בְּזֶה אַחַר זֶה וְהַמְּמוּנֶּה מְמַצְּעוֹ בֵּינוֹ לְבֵין הָעָם. כְּשֶׁהוּא מִתְנַחֵם מֵאֲחֵרִים כָּל הָעָם אוֹמְרִים לוֹ אָנוּ כַּפָּרָתוֹ וְהוּא אוֹמֵר לָהֶן הִתְבָּרְכוּ מִן הַשָּׁמַיִם. וּכְשֶׁמַּבְרִין אוֹתוֹ כָּל הָעָם מְסוּבִּין עַל הָאָרֶץ וְהוּא מֵיסֵב עַל הַסַּפְסָל:

Mishnah 2: If he[57] consoles others, common behavior requires the people to come in single file and the executive officer[58] becomes a partition between himself and the people. If he is consoled by others, everybody tells him, we are his[59] atonement; he answers them, may you be blessed by Heaven. If one brings him the first meal[60], the people sit in a circle on the ground and he sits in their circle on a footstool[61].

57 The High Priest makes a visit of condolence.

58 The organizer of the Temple service walks to his left; all other people are required to make a single file to the organizer's left, to make sure that nobody touch the High Priest and defile him.

59 Meaning "your."

60 Mourners are not permitted to prepare their own first meal after the burial. The people who bring him the food are supposed to eat with him. This is an Amoraïc statement in the Babli (*Mo`ed qatan* 27b) but is implied as an ancient custom in *2S.* 3:35, *Ez.* 24:17.

61 Latin *subsellium*. Probably the vocalization should be סֶפְסֶל .

(20a line 41) **הלכה ב**: וּכְשֶׁהוּא מְנַחֵם אֶת אֲחֵרִים כול'. הָדָא אָמְרָה. סַפְסָל אֵין בּוֹ מִשּׁוּם כְּפִיַּית הַמִּיטָּה. כֹּהֵן גָּדוֹל חַיָּב בִּכְפִיַּית הַמִּיטָּה.

Halakhah 2: "If he consoles others," etc. This implies that a footstool is not meant by "overturning the couch." The High Priest is obligated to overturn his couch[62].

62 The mourner is not permitted to sit comfortably on a couch; cf. *Berakhot* 3:1, Notes 36-41. The prestige of the High Priest's office does not permit him to sit on the floor.

(20a line 43) תַּנֵּי אֵין מוֹצִיאִין אֶת הַמֵּת סָמוּךְ לִקְרִיַּית שְׁמַע אֶלָּא אִם כֵּן הִקְדִּימוּ שָׁעָה אַחַת אוֹ אִיחֲרוּ שָׁעָה אַחַת כְּדֵי שֶׁיִּקְרְאוּ וְיִתְפַּלְּלוּ. וְהָתַנִּינָן קָבְרוּ אֶת הַמֵּת וְחָזְרוּ. תִּיפְתָּר בְּאִינּוּן דַּהֲווֹן סָבְרִין דְּאִית בָּהּ עוֹנָה וְלֵית בָּהּ עוֹנָה.

[63]It is stated: "One does not take the dead for burial close to the recitation of the *Shema`* unless one do it one hour in advance or one hour afterwards, so that they may recite and pray." But did we not formulate: "When they buried the dead and returned"? Explain it for those who thought that they had a free period but they did not have a free period.

תַּנֵּי הַהֶסְפֵּד וְכָל־הָעוֹסְקִין בְּהֶסְפֵּד מַפְסִיקִין לִקְרִיַת שְׁמַע וְלֹא לִתְפִילָּה. מַעֲשֶׂה הָיָה וְהִפְסִיקוּ רַבּוֹתֵינוּ לִקְרִיַת שְׁמַע וְלִתְפִילָּה. וְהָתַנִּינָן אִם יְכוֹלִין לְהַתְחִיל וְלִגְמוֹר. מַתְנִיתָא בְּיוֹם רִאשׁוֹן. מַה דְתַנֵּי בְּיוֹם שֵׁינִי.

It is stated: The eulogizer and all who participate in a eulogy interrupt for the recitation of *Shema*` but do not interrupt for prayer. It happened that our teachers interrupted for the recitation of *Shema*` and prayer. Did we not state: "If they are able to start and finish"? Our Mishnah refers to the first day; that the Tanna stated for the second day.

אָמַר רִבִּי שְׁמוּאֵל בַּר אֶבְדַּימָא זֶה שֶׁנִּכְנַס לַכְּנֶסֶת וּמְצָאָן עוֹמְדִין לִתְפִילָּה. אִם יוֹדֵעַ שֶׁיָּכוֹל לִגְמוֹר עַד שֶׁלֹּא יַתְחִיל שְׁלִיחַ צִיבּוּר לַעֲנוֹת אָמֵן יִתְפַּלֵּל. וְאִם לָאו אַל יִתְפַּלֵּל. בְּאֵי זֶה אָמֵן אָמְרוּ. תְּרֵין אֲמוֹרִין. חַד אָמַר שֶׁלְהָאֵל הַקָּדוֹשׁ. וְ חַד אָמַר שֶׁלְשׁוֹמֵעַ תְּפִילָּה. בְּחוֹל.

Rebbi Samuel ben Eudaimon said: He who enters the synagogue and finds them standing and praying; if he knows that he could start and finish before the reader starts, so that he may answer "Amen", he may pray, otherwise he should not pray. About which "Amen" did the speak? Two Amoraïm, one says the Amen of "the Holy King", the other says the Amen of "Who listens to prayer." [64]On weekdays.

תַּנֵּי רִבִּי יְהוּדָה אוֹמֵר. הָיוּ כוּלָּן עוֹמְדִין בְּשׁוּרָה. מִשּׁוּם כָּבוֹד חַייָבִין. מִשּׁוּם אֵבֶל פְּטוּרִין. יָרְדוּ לִסְפֵּד. הָרוֹאִין פְּנִים פְּטוּרִין. וְשֶׁאֵין רוֹאִין פְּנִים חַייָבִין. וְהָדָא דְתַנִּינָן. כְּשֶׁמְּנַחֵם אֲחֵרִים כָּל הָעָם עוֹבְרִין בְּזֶה אַחַר זֶה וְהַמְּמוּנֶּה מְמַצְּעוֹ בֵּינוֹ לְבֵין הָעָם. כְּמִשְׁנָה הָרִאשׁוֹנָה. וְהָא דְתַנִּינָן. הַפְּנִימִין פְּטוּרִין וְהַחִיצוֹנִין חַייָבִין. כְּמִשְׁנָה הָרִאשׁוֹנָה. אָמַר רִבִּי חֲנִינָה. בָּרִאשׁוֹנָה הָיוּ מִשְׁפָּחוֹת עוֹמְדוֹת וְהָאֲבֵלִין עוֹבְרִין. מִשֶּׁרָבַת תַּחֲרוּת בְּצִיפּוֹרִין הִתְקִין רִבִּי יוֹסֵי שֶׁיְּהוּ מִשְׁפָּחוֹת עוֹבְרוֹת וְהָאֲבֵלִין עוֹמְדִין. אָמַר רִבִּי שְׁמוּאֵל דְּסוֹפְּפְתָּא. חָזְרוּ הַדְּבָרִים לְיוֹשְׁנָן.

It is stated: Rebbi Jehudah says, if they are all standing in one row, those who are standing because of honor are obligated, those because of mourning are exempt. When they descend for a eulogy, those who see inside are exempt, those who do not see inside are obligated. It would be what we stated: "If he consoles others, the people come in single file and the executive officer becomes a partition between himself and the people," the first teaching[65]. And what we stated: "the innermost are exempt and the outer ones obligated," is the first teaching.

Rebbi Ḥanina said: Originally, all families were standing still and the mourners passed between them. When competition increased in Sepphoris, Rebbi Yose ben Ḥalaphta instituted that the families should pass by and the mourners stand still. Rebbi Samuel Sofefta said: Matters returned to their original state.

63 From here to the end of the Halakhah, the text is from *Berakhot* 3:2, Notes 123-135. The last two paragraphs have been shortened to become partially unintelligible; they are intended to refer the student to the text in *Berakhot.*

64 A sentence has been omitted: R. Phineas said, the Amen of "the Holy King" refers to the Sabbath, that of "He Who listens to prayer" refers to *weekdays*. Only the last word was left.

65 Half a paragraph has been omitted (*Berakhot loc. cit.* Notes 132-133) that practice had changed in Mishnaic times. The practice of Temple times is not necessarily relevant for later generations.

(fol. 19d) **משנה ג**: מֶלֶךְ לֹא דָן וְלֹא דָנִין אוֹתוֹ לֹא מֵעִיד וְלֹא מְעִידִין אוֹתוֹ לֹא חוֹלֵץ וְלֹא חוֹלְצִין אֶת אִשְׁתּוֹ לֹא מְיַיבֵּם וְלֹא מְייַבְּמִין אֶת אִשְׁתּוֹ. רִבִּי יְהוּדָה אוֹמֵר אִם רָצָה לַחֲלוֹץ וּלְיַבֵּם זָכוּר לְטוֹב. אָמְרוּ לוֹ אִם רָצָה אֵין שׁוֹמְעִין לוֹ. וְאֵין נוֹשְׂאִין אֶת אַלְמְנָתוֹ. רִבִּי יְהוּדָה אוֹמֵר. נוֹשֵׂא הוּא הַמֶּלֶךְ אַלְמְנָתוֹ שֶׁל מֶלֶךְ. שֶׁכֵּן מָצִינוּ בְדָוִד שֶׁנָּשָׂא אַלְמְנָתוֹ שֶׁל שָׁאוּל שֶׁנֶּאֱמַר וָאֶתְּנָה לְךָ אֶת בֵּית אֲדֹנֶיךָ וְאֶת נְשֵׁי אֲדֹנֶךָ בְּחֵיקֶךָ:

Mishnah 3: The king does not judge[66], nor may one judge him;[67] he does not testify, nor may one testify against him; he does not give *ḥalîṣah*, nor does one give *ḥalîṣah* to his wife[68]. He does not marry in levirate, nor may one marry his wife in levirate. Rebbi Jehudah says, if he wants to give *ḥalîṣah* or marry in levirate, let his good deeds be remembered. They told him, even if he wants to, one does not listen to him[69]. One may not marry his widow; Rebbi Jehudah says, a king may marry a king's widow[70], since we find that David married Saul's widow, as it is said[71]: *I gave your master's house to you and your master's wives on your breast.*

66 In the theory of the Yerushalmi this is biblical law, even though historically the administration of justice was the hallmark of kingship. Historically, the explanation of the Babli (19a) has much to recommend it, that the Mishnaic theory of kingship, positing total separation of the executive from the judiciary, is a reaction to the

misrule of the later Hasmoneans and the Herodians.

67 This would be too dangerous for judges and witnesses.

68 The ceremony would not be consistent with the dignity of his office/

69 The king is obliged to sustain his dignity.

70 This seems to have been Solomon's interpretation when he ordered Adoniah killed for asking Avishag's hand (*1K.* 2:22).

71 *2S.* 12:8.

(20a line 60) **הלכה ג**: מֶלֶךְ לֹא דָן וְלֹא דָנִין אוֹתוֹ כול'. לֹא דָן. וְהָכְתִיב וַיְהִי דָוִד עֹשֶׂה מִשְׁפָּט וּצְדָקָה לְכָל־עַמּוֹ. וְתֵימַר הָכֵן. אֱמוֹר מֵעַתָּה. הָיָה דָן הַדִּין. זִיכָּה הַזַּכַּיי וְחִייֵב הַחַייָב. הָיָה הַחַייָב עָנִי נוֹתֵן לוֹ מִשֶּׁלּוֹ. נִמְצָא עוֹשֶׂה דִין לָזֶה וּצְדָקָה לָזֶה. רִבִּי אוֹמֵר. הָיָה דָן וְזִיכָּה הַזַּכַּיי וְחִייֵב הַחַייָב. מַעֲלֶה עָלָיו הַמָּקוֹם כִּילּוּ עָשָׂה צְדָקָה עִם הַחַייָב שֶׁהוֹצִיא גְזֵילָה מִיָּדוֹ.

Halakhah 3: "The king does not judge, nor may one judge him;" etc. But is it not written[72]: *David administered justice and charity for his entire people,* and you say so? One has to say that he judged by the law, cleared the innocent and condemned the guilty. [73]If a poor person was found liable, he paid from his own money; in that he was administering justice for one party and charity for the other. Rebbi said, if somebody judged, cleared the innocent and condemned the guilty, the Omnipresent will credit him with acting charitably with the guilty by taking the ill-gotten goods out of his hand[74].

72 *2S.* 8:15.

73 Babli 6b, the statements to the end of the paragraph. *Deut. rabba* 5(3).

74 Rebbi (in *Deut. rabba* Rav Nahman) objects to the first explanation since essentially it is a dishonest way of solving disputes. He declares correct judgment in money matters to be an exercise in charity. Cf. Chapter 1, Note 82.

(20a line 65) וְלֹא דָנִין אוֹתוֹ. עַל שֵׁם מִלְּפָנֶיךָ מִשְׁפָּטִי יֵצֵא. רִבִּי יִצְחָק בְּשֵׁם רִבִּי. הַמֶּלֶךְ וְהַצִּיבּוּר נִידּוֹנִין לְפָנָיו בְּכָל־יוֹם. שֶׁנֶּאֱמַר. לַעֲשׂוֹת | מִשְׁפַּט עַבְדּוֹ וּמִשְׁפַּט עַמּוֹ יִשְׂרָאֵל דְּבַר־יוֹם בְּיוֹמוֹ׃

"One may not judge him." Because *from You my judgment will come*[75]. Rebbi Isaac in the name of Rebbi: *To provide the judgment of His servant and the judgment of His people Israel day by day*[76].

75 *Ps.* 17:2. Only God judges the king.

76 *1K.* 8:59.

(20a line 68) רִבִּי יוּדָן אוֹמֵר אִם רָצָה לַחֲלוֹץ וּלְייַבֵּם זָכוּר לְטוֹב. אָמְרוּ לוֹ אִם אַתָּה אוֹמֵר כֵּן נִמְצֵאתָ פוֹגֵם כְּבוֹד הַמֶּלֶךְ.

אֵין נוֹשְׂאִין לֹא אַלְמָנָתוֹ וְלֹא גְרוּשָׁתוֹ שֶׁלְמֶּלֶךְ. עַל שֵׁם וַתִּהְיֶינָה צְרוּרוֹת עַד־יוֹם מוּתָן אַלְמְנוּת חַיּוּת: רִבִּי יוּדָה בַּר פָּזִי בְשֵׁם רִבִּי יוֹחָנָן. מְלַמֵּד שֶׁהָיָה דָוִד מְקַלְעָתָן וּמְקַשְׁטָתָן וּמַכְנִיתָן לְפָנָיו בְּכָל־יוֹם וְאוֹמֵר לְיִצְרוֹ הָרַע. תִּאַבְתָּה דָבָר הָאָסוּר לָךְ. חַיֶּיךָ שֶׁאֲנִי מַתְאִיבְךָ דָּבָר הַמּוּתָּר לָךְ. רַבָּנִין דְּקַיְסָרִין אָמְרִין. אֲסוּרוֹת מַמָּשׁ הָיוּ. וּמַה כְּלֵי הֶדְיוֹט שֶׁנִּשְׁתַּמֵּשׁ בָּהֶן הֶדְיוֹט אָסוּר לַמֶּלֶךְ לְהִשְׁתַּמֵּשׁ בּוֹ. כְּלֵי הַמֶּלֶךְ שֶׁנִּשְׁתַּמֵּשׁ בהֶן הֶדְיוֹט אֵינוֹ דִין שֶׁיְּהֵא הַמֶּלֶךְ אָסוּר לְשַׁמֵּשׁ בָּהֶן.

"Rebbi Jehudah says, if he wants to give *ḥalîṣah* or marry in levirate, let his good deeds be remembered." They told him, if you say so, you injure the king's prestige.

One marries neither the king's widow nor his divorcee, because *they were secluded to the day of their death, living in widowhood*[77]. Rebbi Jehudah bar Pazi in the name of Rebbi Johanan: This teaches[78] that David had them braided and adorned, and brought them before himself every day and told his evil inclination, you desire something which is forbidden to you;[79] by your life, I shall make you desire what is permitted to you. The rabbis of Caesarea said, they actually were forbidden to him. If a private person's vessel used by a private person is forbidden for the king's use[80], *a fortiori* the king is forbidden to use the king's vessels which were used by a private person.

77 *2S.* 20:3, speaking of David's concubines with whom Absalom had slept in public.

78 He reads צְרוּרוֹת not as "bound" but "tied, braided".

79 Since the concubines were not legally his wives, Absalom sinned by raping them, but they remained permitted to David by rabbinic rules. It was voluntarily that David refrained from sleeping with them.

80 Since the king is prohibited from marrying his childless brother's widow, it follows that the only women permitted to a king are either virgins or widows and divorcees of kings.

(20b line 1) רִבִּי יוּדָן אוֹמֵר. נוֹשֵׂא הוּא הַמֶּלֶךְ אַלְמְנַת הַמֶּלֶךְ. שֶׁמָּצִינוּ בְדָוִד שֶׁנָּשָׂא אַלְמְנַת שָׁאוּל. שֶׁנֶּאֱמַר. וָאֶתְּנָה לְךָ אֶת־בֵּית אֲדֹנֶיךָ וְאֶת־נְשֵׁי אֲדֹנֶיךָ בְּחֵיקֶךָ. זוֹ רִצְפָּה וַאֲבִיגַיִל וּבַת שֶׁבַע.

"Rebbi Jehudah says, a king may marry a king's widow, since we find that David married Saul's widow, as it is said: *I gave your master's house to you and your master's wives on your breast.*" This refers to Rispah[81], Abigail and Batseba[82].

81 Saul's concubine, cf. *Yebamot* 2:4, Note 116.

82 These two examples refer to the preceding paragraph and show that the argument of the rabbis of Caesarea is wrong. David married Abigail, Nabal's widow, when already he claimed kingship (in the interpretation of the next paragraphs) and Batseba, Uriah's widow, when actually he was king.

(20b line 4) שְׁלֹשָׁה בָנִים הָיוּ לְחֶצְרוֹן. דִּכְתִיב וּבְנֵי חֶצְרוֹן יְרַחְמְאֵל וְאֶת־רָם וְאֶת־כְּלוּבָי׃ הוּא יְרַחְמְאֵל קַדְמוֹי אֶלָּא שֶׁנָּשָׂא אִשָּׁה גּוֹיָה לְהִתְעַטֵּר בָּהּ. דִּכְתִיב וַתְּהִי אִשָּׁה אַחֶרֶת לִירַחְמְאֵל וּשְׁמָהּ עֲטָרָה הִיא אֵם אוֹנָם׃ שֶׁהִכְנִיסָה אֲנִינָה לְתוֹךְ בֵּיתוֹ. וְרָם הוֹלִיד אֶת־עַמִּינָדָב׃ וְעַמִּינָדָב הוֹלִיד אֶת־נַחְשׁוֹן וְנַחְשׁוֹן הוֹלִיד אֶת־שַׂלְמָה׃ וְשַׂלְמוֹן הוֹלִיד אֶת־בֹּעַז וּבֹעַז נָשָׂא אֶת רוּת.

[83]Hesron had three sons, as it is written[84]: *The sons of Hesron Yerahmeël, and Ram, and Kelubai*[85]. Yerahmeël should have been first,[86] but he married a Gentile woman to crown himself with her, as it is written[87]: *Yerahmeël had another*[88] *wife; her name was Crown, she is the mother of Onam*, for she brought deep sorrow to his house[89]. *And Ram fathered Amminadav, Amminadav fathered Nahshon, Nahshon fathered Salma, Salmon fathered Boaz*[90], and Boaz married Ruth.

83 This paragraph is inserted as preface to the story about Nabal and David, induced by the mention of Abigail in the preceding sentence.

84 A shortened quote from *1Chr.* 2:9.

85 He is Kaleb ben Hesron, presumed ancestor of Nabal.

86 As the firstborn, he should be first in the genealogical list, but his descendants are listed last, vv. 25 ff. The role of firstborn was taken over by Ram, the ancestor of David.

87 *1Chr.* 2:26.

88 Interpreting "another" as "foreign".

89 Deriving אוֹנָם from the root אנה "to be in deep sorrow".

90 *Ru.* 4:19-21, but probably *1Chr.* 2:10-11 was intended.

(20b line 14) הֵא נָבָל אֲתִי מִן דִּכְלוּבָי. אֲמַר נָבָל. לֵית בְּיִשְׂרָאֵל בַּר טָבִין סַגִּין מִינִּי. הָדָא הִיא דִכְתִיב וְאִישׁ בְּמָעוֹן וּמַעֲשֵׂהוּ בַכַּרְמֶל וְהָאִישׁ גָּדוֹל מְאֹד וְהוּא כָלִבִּי׃ דַּאֲתִי מִן כְּלוּבָי. וַיִּשְׁמַע דָּוִד בַּמִּדְבָּר כִּי־גֹזֵז נָבָל. וַאֲמַרְתֶּם כֹּה לֶחָי. לְקִיּוּמָא. וְאַתָּה שָׁלוֹם וגו'. אָמַר רִבִּי יוֹסְטָא בַּר שׁוּנֵם. נַעֲשׂוּ מַחֲנֶה. וַיַּעַן נָבָל אֶת־עַבְדֵי דָוִד וגו'. וּמְנַיִין לְדִינֵי נְפָשׁוֹת שֶׁמַּתְחִילִין מִן הַצַּד. תַּנָּא

שְׁמוּאֵל הַזָּקֵן קוֹמֵי רִבִּי אָחָא. וַיֹּאמֶר דָּוִד לַאֲנָשָׁיו וגו'. וַיָּעַט בָּהֶם. מָהוּ וַיָּעַט בָּהֶם. אַפְחִין בְּמִילִין. וְעַתָּה דְּעִי וּרְאִי מַה־תַּעֲשִׂי: וַתִּפְגּוֹשׁ אוֹתָם: גִּילַּת שׁוֹקָהּ וְהָלְכוּ לְאוֹרָהּ. וַתִּפְגּוֹשׁ אוֹתָם: הוּקְרוּ כוּלָּם. וחד אָמַר אַךְ לַשֶּׁקֶר שָׁמַרְתִּי וגו'. מַשְׁתִּין בְּקִיר: מָה עִיסְקֵיהּ דְּכַלְבָּא מַשְׁתִּין בְּכָתְלָא. אֲפִילוּ עַל כַּלְבָּא לֵי נָא חַיִיס. וַתֵּרֶא אֲבִיגַיִל אֶת־דָּוִד וגו'. אָמְרָה לֵיהּ. מָרִי דָּוִד. אֲנָא מָה עָבְדִית. בָּנַיי מָה עָבְדוּן. בְּעִירַיי מָה עֲבֵד. אָמַר לָהּ. מִפְּנֵי שֶׁקִּילֵּל מַלְכוּת דָּוִד. אָמְרָה לֵיהּ. וּמֶלֶךְ אַתָּה. אָמַר לָהּ. וְלֹא מְשָׁחַנִי שְׁמוּאֵל לְמֶלֶךְ. אָמְרָה לוֹ. עֲדַיִין מוֹנֵיטָא דְּמָרָן שָׁאוּל קַיָּם. וַאֲנִי אֲמָתְךָ. מְלַמֵּד שֶׁתְּבָעָהּ לְתַשְׁמִישׁ. מִיַּד הוֹצִיאָה כְתָמָהּ וְהֶרְאָת לוֹ. אָמַר לָהּ. וְכִי רוֹאִין כְּתָמִין בַּלַּיְלָה. אָמְרָה לֵיהּ. וְלֹא יִשְׁמְעוּ אָזְנֶיךָ מִי שֶׁפִּיךָ מְדַבֵּר. כְּתָמִין אֵין רוֹאִין בַּלַּיְלָה וְדִינֵי נְפָשׁוֹת דָּנִין בַּלַּיְלָה. אָמַר לָהּ. כְּבָר נִגְמַר דִּינוֹ מִבְּעוֹד יוֹם. אָמְרָה לוֹ. וְלֹא־תִהְיֶה זֹאת | לְךָ לְפוּקָה.

אָמַר רִבִּי לָעְזָר. פִּיקָפּוּקֵי דְּבָרִים הָיָה שָׁם. רִבִּי לֵוִי הֲוָה עֲבַר פַּרְשָׁתָא. וַהֲוָה רִבִּי זְעִירָא מְפַקֵּד לַחֲבֵרַיָּא. עֲלוֹן וְשָׁמְעוֹן קָלֵיהּ דְּרִבִּי לֵוִי דָּרַשׁ. דְּלֵית אֶיפְשַׁר לֵיהּ דְּהוּא מַפְקָא פַרְשָׁתָא דְּלָא רִיבָּווֹן. עֲעַל וַאֲמַר לוֹן. לָא. וּשְׁמַע רִבִּי זְעִירָא וָמַר. אוּף בְּאַגַּדְתָּא אִית רִיבּוֹון. לְפוּקָה. פִּיקָפּוּקֵי דְּבָרִים הָיָה שָׁם.

אָמְרָה לֵיהּ. כַּד תֵּיפּוּק פִּקְפּוּתָךְ יְהוּ אוֹמְרִים עָלֶיךָ. שׁוֹפֵךְ דָּמִים אַתְּ. וּלְמִכְשׁוֹל עָוֹן. אַתָּה עוֹמֵד לְהִיכָּשֵׁל בְּאֵשֶׁת אִישׁ. מוּטָּב אַחַת וְלֹא שְׁתַּיִם. עֲתִידָה רוֹבָה מִן הָדָה מֵיְיתֵי לֹא תֵהֵא דָא כְּדָא. וְלִשְׁפּוֹךְ דָּם. עוֹמֵד אַתָּה לִמְלוֹךְ עַל יִשְׂרָאֵל וְהֵן אוֹמְרִים עָלֶיךָ. שׁוֹפֵךְ דָּמִים הָיָה. וְהָדָא דְתֵימַר. כָּל־הַמְקַלֵּל מַלְכוּת בֵּית דָּוִד חַיָּב מִיתָה. אֲדַיִין מְחוּסַּר כִּסֵּא אַתְּ. וְזָכַרְתָּ אֶת־אֲמָתֶךָ: מְלַמֵּד שֶׁפָּקְרָה עַצְמָהּ. וְכֵיוָן שֶׁפָּקְרָה עַצְמָהּ פְּגָמָהּ הַכָּתוּב. בְּכָל־קִרְיָיא אַתְּ קָרֵי אֲבִיגַיִל בַּר מֵהָדֵין פְּסוּקָא וַיֹּאמֶר דָּוִד לַאֲבִיגַל בָּרוּךְ יי. מִבּוֹא בְדָמִים. דַּם נִידָּה וּשְׁפִיכוּת דָּמִים.

[91]This Nabal[92] was a descendant of Kelubai. Nabal said, nobody in Israel comes from a better family than I. That is what is written[93]: *A man from Ma`on had his business in Karmel; the man was exceedingly rich, a Kalebite,* a descendant of Kelubai. *David heard in the prairie that Nabal was shearing*[94]. *Tell him, to life*[95]*!* For long life. *Peace be with you*, etc. Rebbi Justus from Sunem said, they formed a camp[96]. *Nabal answered David's servants*[97], etc. From where that in criminal trials the voting starts from the side? Samuel the Elder stated before Rebbi Aḥa: *David told his men*[98], etc. *He flew at them*[99]. What means *he flew at them*? He made them fly with words[100]. *Now know this and consider what to do*[101]. *She fell in with them*[102], she bared her thigh and they walked by its light[103]. *She fell in with them*, they all were recognizable[104]. *[David] said, was it in vain that I watched*[105], etc.? *Pissing on a wall*[106]; why does he refer to the dog pissing on a wall? Even

with the dog I shall not have mercy. *Abigail saw David*[107],etc. She told him, my lord David, what did I do, what did my children do, what did my animals do? He answered her, because he insulted the kingdom of David. She asked him, are you a king? He told her, did not Samuel anoint me as king? She answered him, our Lord's Saul's coin[108] is still circulating. *And I am your servant*[109]; this proves that he asked her for sex[110]. Immediately, she brought out her stains[111] and showed him. He said, does one investigate stains in the night? She retorted, may your ears hear what your lips say! Stains one does not investigate in the night, does one judge capital cases in the night? He answered, his sentence was already passed in daytime. She retorted, *may this not be* פּוּקָה *for you*[112].

[113]Rebbi Eleazar said, matters of reproach are there. Rebbi Levi was reviewing the lesson, when Rebbi Ze`ira commanded the colleagues to come and hear the voice of Rebbi Levi sermonizing, for it was impossible that the lesson would be finished without new insight. He came and told them, *not be*; Rebbi Ze`ira heard it and said, even in his *aggadah* there is new insight. לְפוּקָה matters of reproach are there.

She told him, when you emerge from your tribulations, one will say of you that you that you are a murderer. *And a stumbling block for sin*[112,114]. You are set up to stumble over a married woman, better one than two. In the future it will be enough to bring one, and not to add *spilling blood.* Are you ready to rule over Israel when they will say about you that you were a spiller of blood? Even though anybody who curses the dynasty of David incurs the death penalty[115], still you are missing the throne. *But remember your servant*[112], this proves that she showed herself licentious[116]. Since she showed herself licentious, the verse damaged her. In all verses one reads Abigail, except for this verse[117]: *David said to Abigal, praised be the Eternal,* etc., *to come into blood guilts*, the blood of menstruation and the spilling of blood[118].

91 A Hebrew version of most of the story is in *Midrash Samuel* (ed. Buber) 25.

92 "Scoundrel". But the name seems to be Arabic نبل "possessed of superior qualities, generous, noble."

93 *1S.* 25:2.

94 *1S.* 25:4.

95 *1S.* 25:6.

97 This is a side remark; it is more explicit in *Erubin* 1, 19c l. 75. In v. 4, it is

stated that David sent 10 men to Nabal; in v. 6 it is stated *they encamped.* He concludes that the legal definition of a camp (for the religious obligations in wartime) refers to a minimum of 10 men.

97 *IS.* 25:10.

98 *IS.* 25:13. The argument is quoted in the Babli, 36a, in the name of R. Johanan. The verse explains that David told his men to gird their swords; he girded his sword last. This is read to mean that he first polled his men whether Nabal should be executed for the crime of lèse-majesty; he gave his vote last.

99 *IS.* 25:14.

100 Rashi quotes this in his Commentary to the verse.

101 *IS.* 25:17.

102 *IS.* 25:20.

103 Since in v. 3 she is described as a radiant beauty.

104 In the dark of the night.

105 *IS.* 25:21.

106 *IS.* 25:22.

107 *IS.* 25:23.

108 Latin *moneta.*

109 *IS.* 25:25.

110 Since in each sentence she repeats that she only is his servant, she has to emphasize that she is not going to be his companion.

111 Indicating that she was not available since she was menstruating, and treating him as a rabbi, competent to decide whether blood was menstrual or not (cf. Introduction to Tractate *Niddah.*)

112 *IS.* 25:31.

113 A paragraph inserted to discuss the meaning of the *hapax* פּוּקָה. It is assumed that the root פק is the same which appears reduplicated in the rabbinic Hebrew verb פקפק ("to doubt", Arabic "to dote"). In the Babli, a parallel argument is in *Megillah* 14b.

114 In the verse: *a stumbling block of my lord's heart.*

115 In imitation of Roman law; Babli *Megillah* 14a.

116 She indicated her desire to be his wife when she still was married to Nabal.

117 *IS.* 25:32.

118 *IS.* 25:33; explaining the plural "bloods" used in the verse. Babli *Megillah* 14b.

(fol. 19d) **משנה ד**: מֵת לוֹ מֵת אֵינוֹ יוֹצֵא מִפֶּתַח פַּלָטוֹרִין שֶׁלּוֹ. רַבִּי יְהוּדָה אוֹמֵר אִם רוֹצֶה לָצֵאת אַחַר הַמִּיטָּה יוֹצֵא שֶׁכֵּן מָצִינוּ בְדָוִד שֶׁיָּצָא אַחַר מִיטָּתוֹ שֶׁל אַבְנֵר שֶׁנֶּאֱמַר וְהַמֶּלֶךְ דָּוִד הֹלֵךְ אַחֲרֵי הַמִּיטָּה. אָמְרוּ לוֹ לֹא הָיָה הַדָּבָר אֶלָּא לְפַייֵס. וּכְשֶׁמַּבְרִין אוֹתוֹ, כָּל הָעָם מְסוּבִּין עַל הָאָרֶץ וְהוּא מֵיסֵב עַל הַדַּרְגֵּשׁ:

Mishnah 4: If a relative of his[119] died, he does not leave his palace[120]. Rebbi Jehudah says, if he wants to follow the bier, he may follow it, as we find that David followed Abner's bier, as it is said[121]: *King David followed* *the bier*. They told him, this was only to quiet[122]. When one brings him the first meal[60], the people sit in a circle on the floor and he sits in their circle on a couch[123].

119 The king's.

120 Latin *palatium*, "palace". The ending *-orium* may have been added in parallel to *praetorium* "official residence of the governor of a province".

121 *2S*. 3:31.

122 To quell rumors that the king was involved in Abner's murder.

123 For the particular kind of couch mentioned here; cf. *Berakhot* 3:1, Note 31.

(20b line 40) **הלכה ד**: מֵת לוֹ מֵת אֵינוֹ יוֹצֵא מִפֶּתַח פַּלָטוֹרִין שֶׁלּוֹ. הָדָא אָמְרָה. דַּרְגֵּשׁ יֵשׁ בּוֹ מִשּׁוּם כְּפִיַּית הַמִּיטָּה. הַמֶּלֶךְ אֵינוֹ חַייָב בִּכְפִיַּית הַמִּיטָּה.

Halakhah 4: "If a relative of his died, he does not leave his palace." This implies that a *dargesh* is included in overturning one's bed[124]. The king is not required to overturn his bed.

124 Since it is mentioned that the king is required to sit on a *dargesh* when receiving condolence visits, one implies that no other mourner may sit on this kind of couch since the king in mourning is not required to sit or sleep on an overturned coach. However, it is spelled out elsewhere (*Berakhot* 3:1 Note 31, *Mo`ed qaṭan* 5:1 83a l. 11, *Nedarim* 7:5 Note 49; Babli *Sanhedrin* 20a) that a *dargesh* is turned 90° in contrast to other couches which are turned upside down.

(20b line 42) אִית תַּנָּיֵי תַנֵּי. הַנָּשִׁים מְהַלְּכוֹת תְּחִילָּה וְהָאֲנָשִׁים אַחֲרֵיהֶם. וְאִית תַּנָּיֵי תַנֵּי. אֲנָשִׁים תְּחִילָּה וְהַנָּשִׁים אַחֲרֵיהֶם. מָאן דָּמַר הַנָּשִׁים תְּחִילָּה. שֶׁהֵן גָּֽרְמוּ מִיתָה לָעוֹלָם. מָאן דָּמַר הָאֲנָשִׁים תְּחִילָּה. מִפְּנֵי כְבוֹד בְּנוֹת יִשְׂרָאֵל שֶׁלֹּא יְהוּ מַבִּיטִין בַּנָּשִׁים. וְהָֽכְתִיב וְהַמֶּ֙לֶךְ דָּוִ֔ד הֹלֵ֖ךְ אַחֲרֵ֥י הַמִּטָּֽה׃ אָֽמְרוּ לֹא הָיָה הַדָּבָר אֶלָּא לְפַייֵס. מָאן דַּהֲוָה מְפַייֵס לִנְשַׁיָּא הֲוָה מְפַייֵס לְגוּבְרַיָּא וּמָאן דַּהֲוָה מְפַייֵס לְגוּבְרַיָּא הֲוָה מְפַייֵס לִנְשַׁיָּא.

Some Tannaïm state[125]: Women go first[126], after them men. But some Tannaïm state: Men first, women after them. He who says women first, since they caused death to the world. He who says men first, for the honor of the daughter of Israel, lest people[127] look at women. But was it not written: *King David followed the bier*[121,128]. They said, this was only to quiet. Whoever was calming the women was calming the men, and whoever was calming the men was calming the women.

125 *Gen. rabba* 17(13).

126 In a funeral procession, they precede the bier.

127 The onlookers.

128 In v. 32 it says that David cried at Abner's grave, and so did the entire people; *entire* includes women. But it still is undecided who went first. In the Babli, 20a, the verse is quoted as proof that the women must have preceded the bier since the king immediately followed it.

(20b line 48) כְּתִיב וַיִּסּוֹב דָּוִד וגו'. מָהוּ הָרֵיקִים. אָמַר רִבִּי בָּא בַּר כַּהֲנָא. הָרֵיקִים שֶׁבָּרֵיקִים זוֹ אַרְכֵסְטֵס. אָמְרָה לוֹ. הַיּוֹם נִגְלָה כְבוֹד בֵּית אַבָּא. אָמְרוּ עָלָיו עַל בֵּית שָׁאוּל שֶׁלֹּא רָאוּ אוֹתָן לֹא עָקֵב וְלֹא גוֹדֶל מִימֵיהֶן. הָדָא הוּא דִכְתִיב וַיָּבֹא אֶל־גִּדְרוֹת הַצֹּאן. רִבִּי בּוּן בֵּירִבִּי לָעְזָר. גָּדֵר לִפְנִים מִגָּדֵר הָיָה. וַיָּבֹא שָׁאוּל לְהָסֵךְ אֶת־רַגְלָיו. הֲוָה חֲמֵי לֵיהּ מְשַׁלְשֵׁל צִבְחַר וּמְסַלֵּיק צִבְחַר. אֲמַר. אָרוּר מַגַּע בְּהָדֵין צְנִיעָה. הָדָא דוּ מַר לֵיהּ. הִנֵּה הַיּוֹם הַזֶּה אֲשֶׁר רָאוּ עֵינֶיךָ וגו'. וָאָחוּס עָלֶיךָ אֵין כָּתוּב כָּאן אֶלָּא וַתָּחָס עָלֶיךָ. צְנִיעוּתָךְ הִיא חָסָה עָלֶיךָ. וַיֹּאמֶר דָּוִד אֶל־מִיכַל וגו'. וְעִם הָאֲמָהוֹת אֲשֶׁר אָמַרְתְּ עִמָּם אִכָּבֵדָה׃ שֶׁאֵינָן אֲמָהוֹת אֶלָּא אִימָּהוֹת. וּבַמֶּה נֶאֶנְשָׁה. וּלְמִיכַל בַּת־שָׁאוּל לֹא־הָיָה לָהּ וָלֶד. וְהָכְתִיב וְהַשִּׁשִּׁי יִתְרְעָם לְעֶגְלָה אֵשֶׁת. אֶלָּא שֶׁגָּעַת כְּעֶגְלָה וָמֵתָה.

[129]It is written: *David turned*[130]. Who are the "empty ones"[131]? Rebbi Abba bar Cahana said, the most empty one, that is the dancer[132]. She told him, today the honor of my father's house became obvious. One said about the family of Saul that one never saw a heel or a thumb of them. That is what is written: *He came to the sheep fences*[133]. Rebbi Abun ben Rebbi Eleazar: That was a fence inside a fence[134]. *Saul came to spread his feet*[133]. He saw him how he lifted a little and covered a little. He said, one who would touch such modesty would be cursed. That is what he told him, *behold, what your eyes saw today*[135], etc. Is it not written "I had mercy on you" but *it had mercy on you*[135], your modesty had mercy on you. *David told Michal*[136], etc. *With the servant girls you mentioned, with them I shall be honored*[137], for they are not servant girls but mothers. How was she punished? *Michal, Saul's daughter, had no child*[138]. But is it not written: *The sixth Yitre`am, of his wife Calf*[139]. She mood like a calf and died.

129 A somewhat more explicit version of this is in *Sukkah* 5:4 (55c l. 7); a different version of this and the following paragraphs is found in the last part of *Num. rabba* 4.

130 *1Chr.* 16:43. Probably what was intended was *2S.* 6:20 (correctly quoted in *Sukkah*), the end of the story of the transfer of the Ark to the City of David.

131 *2S.* 6:20, where Michal criticizes David for dancing in the street.

132 Greek ὀρχηστής, οῦ, ὁ.

133 *1S.* 24:3.

134 This explains the plural used in the verse and shows that Saul went to relieve himself in the cave guarded from the outside by a double fence. In the Babli, *Berakhot* 62b, this is quoted as tannaitic text.

135 *1S.* 24:10.

136 *2S.* 6:21.

137 *2S.* 6:22.

138 *2S.* 6:23. The verse ends: *up to the day of her death*, implying that she died in childbirth.

139 *2S.* 3:5. Only Michal is called "David's wife" (*1S.* 25:44). The problem that Yitre`am was born in Hebron is not addressed; it is discussed in the Babli, 21a.

(20b line 58) אֵין לְךָ אָדָם בְּיִשְׂרָאֵל שֶׁבִּיזָּה עַצְמוֹ עַל הַמִּצְוֹת יוֹתֵר מִדָּוִד. מִפְּנֵי מַה בִּיזָּה עַצְמוֹ עַל הַמִּצְוֹת. שֶׁהָיוּ מַבִּיטִין בָּאָרוֹן וּמֵתִים. דִּכְתִיב וַיַּךְ בְּאַנְשֵׁי בֵית־שֶׁמֶשׁ וגו'. רִבִּי חֲנִינָה וְרִבִּי מָנָא. חַד אָמַר. וַיַּךְ בָּעָם שִׁבְעִים אִישׁ זוֹ סַנְהֶדְרִין. וַחֲמִשִּׁים אֶלֶף שֶׁהָיוּ שְׁקוּלִין כְּנֶגֶד חֲמִשִּׁים אֶלֶף. וְחַד אָמַר. וַיַּךְ בָּעָם שִׁבְעִים אִישׁ זוֹ סַנְהֶדְרִין. וַחֲמִשִּׁים אֶלֶף מֵעַם הָאָרֶץ. כְּתִיב שִׁיר הַמַּעֲלוֹת לְדָוִד יי לֹא־גָבַהּ לִבִּי בְּשָׁעָה שֶׁמְּשָׁחַנִי שְׁמוּאֵל. וְלֹא־רָמוּ עֵינַיי בְּשָׁעָה שֶׁהָרַגְתִּי אֶת גּוֹלְיַת. וְלֹא־הִלַּכְתִּי | בִּגְדוֹלוֹת בְּשָׁעָה שֶׁהֶעֱלֵיתִי הָאָרוֹן. וּבְנִפְלָאוֹת מִמֶּנִּי בְּשָׁעָה שֶׁהֶחֱזִירוּנִי לְמַלְכוּתִי. אֶלָּא אִם־לֹא שִׁיוִּיתִי וְדוֹמַמְתִּי כְּגָמוּל עֲלֵי אִמּוֹ כַּגָּמוּל עָלַי נַפְשִׁי. כָּהֵן יְנוּקָא דִּנְחִית מִמְּעֵי אִמֵּיהּ כֵּן הֲוָת נַפְשִׁי עָלַי.

[140]No person in Israel was abasing himself before the Commandments more than David. Why was he abasing himself before the Commandments? Because people were looking at the Ark and dying, as it is written[141]: *He smote of the people of Bet Shemesh,* etc.

Rebbi Hanina and Rebbi Mana[142]. One said, *He smote among the people seventy men*, that is the Synhedrion. And *50'000 men*[143], for they were worth 50'000. The other said, *He smote among the people seventy men*, that is the Synhedrion. And *50'000 men* from the people of the Land.

It is written[143a]: *A song of ascent of David. O Eternal, my heart was not haughty* when Samuel anointed me; *my eyes were not overbearing* when I slew Goliath; *and I did not decide on matters too great* when I brought up the Ark; *and wonderful for me,* when He brought me back to my kingdom. But *rather I prayed, and silenced my soul like a baby by its mother, like a baby my soul is for me.* Like a baby delivered from his mother's womb is my soul for me.

140 Since the preceding paragraph speaks of the introduction of the Ark into Jerusalem, one continues with sermons about the Ark.

141 *IS.* 6:19. There, it is stated explicitly, *because they were staring at the Eternal's ark.*

143 A different interpretation is in the Babli, *Sotah* 35b, also by Galilean Amoraim.

143 The conjunction ו is not in the masoretic text. The quote is correct in the existing mss. (Munich and Rome) of Babli *Sotah*, incorrect in the Bomberg Babli of 1520-23.

143a *Ps.* 131.

(fol. 19d) **משנה ה**: וּמוֹצִיא לְמִלְחֶמֶת הָרְשׁוּת עַל פִּי בֵית דִּין שֶׁל שִׁבְעִים וְאֶחָד. וּפוֹרֵץ לַעֲשׂוֹת לוֹ דֶרֶךְ וְאֵין מְמַחִין בְּיָדוֹ. דֶּרֶךְ הַמֶּלֶךְ אֵין לוֹ שִׁיעוּר. וְכָל הָעָם בּוֹזְזִין וְנוֹתְנִין לְפָנָיו, וְהוּא נוֹטֵל חֵלֶק בָּרֹאשׁ.

Mishnah 5: He goes to a war of choice[144] by the word of the Court of 71[145]. He breaches fences on his way and one may not protest against him. The king's highway has no measure[146]. When all people plunder[147], it is put before him and he selects his part first.

144 Any war which is not purely defensive.

145 A misnomer for the Synhedrion, the High Priest's Council when the latter was head of the Commonwealth. The confusion in terminology was caused by the Court of Jabneh which took over the name of Synhedrion.

146 Cf. Mishnah *Bava batra* 6:7.

147 In war, if orders are given to plunder the enemy.

(20b line 69) **הלכה ה**: וּמוֹצִיא לְמִלְחֶמֶת הָרְשׁוּת כול׳. דִּכְתִיב עַל־פִּיו יֵצְאוּ וְעַל־פִּיו יָבוֹאוּ. וּפוֹרֵץ לַעֲשׂוֹת לוֹ דֶרֶךְ. דִּכְתִיב נָהֲגוּ לִפְנֵי הַמִּקְנֶה וַיֹּאמְרוּ זֶה שְׁלַל דָּוִד.

Halakhah 6: "He goes to a war of choice," etc. For it is written[148]: *on his saying they shall go out, on his saying they shall return.* "He breaches fences on his way," for it is written: *they drove before [this] flock and said, this is David's booty*[149].

148 *Num.* 27:21. The verse subordinates the political leader, Joshua, to the High Priest, Eleazar. It is presumed that the High Priest act on advice of his Council.

149 *IS.* 30:20. What the verse really proves is that the total booty is called "the king's booty", implying that he has the right to first select his share.

(20b line 71) הוּא־הָיָה עִם־דָּוִד בְּאֶפֶס דַּמִּים. רִבִּי יוֹחָנָן אָמַר. בַּחֲקַל סוּמַקְתָּה. וְרִבִּי שְׁמוּאֵל אָמַר. שֶׁמִּשָּׁם נִפְסְקוּ דָמִים. וּפְלִשְׁתִּים נֶאֶסְפִים וגו'. רִבִּי יַעֲקֹב דִּכְפַר חָנָן אָמַר. עֲדָשִׁין הָיוּ אֶלָּא שֶׁהָיְתָה עֲנָבָה שֶׁלָּהֶן יָפָה כְשֶׁלִּשְׂעוֹרִין. אָמַר רִבִּי לֵוִי. אֵילוּ הֵן הַפְּלִשְׁתִּים שֶׁהָיוּ בָאִין זְקוּפִין כִּשְׂעוֹרִין וְהָלְכוּ לָהֶן נְמוּכִין כָּעֲדָשִׁין. כָּתוּב אֶחָד אוֹמֵר. וַתְּהִי שָׁם חֶלְקַת הַשָּׂדֶה מְלֵיאָה שְׂעוֹרִים. וּכְתִיב מְלֵיאָה עֲדָשִׁים. רִבִּי שְׁמוּאֵל בַּר נַחְמָן אָמַר. שָׁנָה אַחַת הָיְתָה וּשְׁתֵּי שָׂדוֹת הָיוּ. אַחַת שְׂעוֹרִים וְאַחַת עֲדָשִׁים. פְּשִׁיטָא לֵיהּ לְאַבֵּיד וְלִיתֵּן דָּמִים. דִּילְמָא פְּשִׁיטָא לֵיהּ לְאַבֵּיד שֶׁלֹּא לִיתֵּן דָּמִים. אֵי זֶה מֵהֶן יְאַבֵּד וְאֵי זֶה מֵהֶן יִתֵּן דָּמִים. שֶׁלָּעֲדָשִׁין וְשֶׁלִּשְׂעוֹרִין. אֶלָּא שֶׁלָּעֲדָשִׁים מַאֲכַל אָדָם. וְשֶׁלִּשְׂעוֹרִין מַאֲכָל בְּהֵמָה. שֶׁלָּעֲדָשִׁים אֵינָהּ חַיֶּיבֶת בַּחַלָּה וְשֶׁלִּשְׂעוֹרִים חַיֶּיבֶת בַּחַלָּה. עֲדָשִׁין אֵין עוֹמֶר בָּא מִמֶּנָּהּ. שְׂעוֹרִים עוֹמֶר בָּא מִמֶּנָּהּ. וְרַבָּנִין אָמְרִין. שָׂדֶה אַחַת הוּשְׁתֵּי שָׁנִים הָיוּ. הָיָה לָמֵד מִשֶּׁלְּאֶשְׁתַּקַּד וְאֵין לְמֵידִין מִשָּׁנָה לַחֲבֵירָתָהּ. וַיִּתְיַצְּבוּ בְתוֹךְ־הַחֶלְקָה וַיַּצִּילוּהָ. כָּתוּב אֶחָד אוֹמֵר וַיַּצִּילוּהָ וְכָתוּב אֶחָד אוֹמֵר וַיַּצִּילָהּ. אֶלָּא מְלַמֵּד שֶׁהֶחֱזִירָהּ לִבְעָלֶיהָ וְהָיְתָה חֲבִיבָה עָלָיו כְשָׂדֶה מְלֵיאָה כַרְכּוֹם.

כְּתִיב וַיִּתְאַו דָּוִד וַיֹּאמַר מִי יַשְׁקֵנִי מַיִם מִבּוֹר בֵּית־לֶחֶם וגו'. רִבִּי חִיָּיה בַּר בָּא אָמַר. הֲלָכָה נִצְרְכָה לוֹ. וַיִּבְקְעוּ שְׁלֹשָׁה. וְלָמָּה שְׁלֹשָׁה. שֶׁאֵין הֲלָכָה מִתְבָּרֶרֶת פָּחוּת מִשְּׁלֹשָׁה. וְלֹא־אָבָה דָוִד לִשְׁתּוֹת. לֹא־אָבָה דָוִד שֶׁתִּיקָּבַע הֲלָכָה עַל שְׁמוֹ. וַיַּסֵּךְ אֹתָם לַיי. קְבָעָהּ מַסֶּכֶת לַדּוֹרוֹת. וּפוֹרֵץ לַעֲשׂוֹת לוֹ דֶרֶךְ.

בַּר קַפָּרָא אָמַר. חַג הָיָה וְנִיסּוּךְ הַמַּיִם הָיָה וְהֵיתֵר בָּמָה הָיָה. וַיִּבְקְעוּ שְׁלֹשָׁה. וְלָמָּה שְׁלֹשָׁה. אֶחָד הוֹרֵג וְאֶחָד מְפַנֶּה הֲרוּגִים וְאֶחָד מַכְנִיס צְלוֹחִית בְּטָהֳרָה.

כָּתוּב אֶחָד אוֹמֵר וַיְנַסֵּךְ אֹתָם לַיי. וְכָתוּב אֶחָד אוֹמֵר וַיַּסֵּךְ. מָאן דָּמַר וַיַּסֵּךְ מְסַייֵעַ לְרִבִּי חִיָּיה בַּר בָּא. מָאן דָּמַר וַיְנַסֵּךְ מְסַייֵעַ לְבַר קַפָּרָא. רִבִּי הוּנָא בְשֵׁם רִבִּי יוֹסֵי. הִילְכוֹת שְׁבוּיִים נִצְרְכָה לוֹ. רִבִּי שִׁמְעוֹן בֵּרִבִּי אוֹמֵר. בִּנְיַין בֵּית הַמִּקְדָּשׁ נִתְאַוָּה.

[150]*He was with David at Efes Dammim*[151]. Rebbi Joḥanan said, at the red field[152]. But Rebbi Samuel said, from there the money stopped.[153] *The Philistines assembled*[151,154], etc. Rebbi Jacob from Kefar Ḥanan said, they were lentils but a kernel was as good as a barley grain. Rebbi Levi said, this describes the Philistines who came straight as barley and went away low as lentils, as one verse says, *there was a field full of barley*[151], and one said, *full of lentils*[154]. Rebbi Samuel bar Naḥman said, it was one year but concerning two fields, one of barley and one of lentils. It was obvious to him that he might destroy it and pay for the damage. Perhaps it was obvious to him[155] that he might destroy it and not pay for the damage? Which one might he destroy

and for which one would he have to pay? For the one of lentils or the one of barley? For the one of lentils grows human food, the one of barley animal feed. The one of lentils will not be obligated for *ḥallah*[156], barley will be obligated for *ḥallah*. The *`omer* comes from barley[157]; *`omer* cannot be brought from lentils. But the rabbis said, it was one field and two years. Does one infer from last year, or does one not infer from one year to the next? *They stood up in the property and saved it*[158]. One verse says, *they saved it*, and one says, *he saved it*[159]. This shows that he returned it to its owner and it was dear to him as if it had been a field of saffron.

It is written: *David had a desire and said, who would give me to drink from the cistern of Bethlehem*[160], etc. Rebbi Ḥiyya bar Abba said, he questioned practice[161]. *Three broke through*. Why three? For no practice can be elucidated by less than three [opinions]. *But David refused to drink*. David did not want that the practice would be attached to his name[162]. *He poured it out for the Eternal,* he fixed it as a tractate for all generations, "he breaches fences on his way."

Bar Qappara said, it was the feast of Tabernacles, the time of water libations[163], and a time when private altars were permitted[164]. *Three broke through*. Why three? One was slaying, one was removing the corpses, and the third brought the flask in purity.

One verse says, *he made a libation for the Eternal*, but another verse says, *he covered*. He who says ויסך, supports Rebbi Ḥiyya bar Abba[165]. He who says, *he made a libation*, supports Bar Qappara. Rebbi Huna in the name of Rebbi Yose: He had a problem with the rules of captives[166]. Rebbi Simeon ben Rebbi said, he desired to build the Temple[167]

150 Parallel texts are in *Ruth rabba* 5(1), *Midrash Samuel* 10(1), *Yalqut Samuel* #165.

151 *1Chr*. 11:13. In the entire section, the verses are not quoted exactly.

152 He explains the reading of the masoretic text, פַּס דַּמִּים "a red strip."

153 He reads אֶפֶס דָּמִים "no money" in rabbinic Hebrew, to explain that the king does not pay for damage he inflicts on private property in the course of his activities on behalf of the people in war or peace. The storytelling is incidental to the attempt to find biblical justification for the rules of the Mishnah. There is no claim of historical validity.

154 *2S*. 23:11.

155 To David, who would be incapable of doing anything unlawful. The Mishnah does

not address the problem of indemnity for the exercise of the power of eminent domain.

156 The heave required to be taken from bread dough; cf. Introduction to Tractate *Hallah*.

157 The flour offering permitting the use of new grain, *Lev*. 23:9-14.

158 *1Chr*. 11:14.

159 *2S*. 23:12.

160 *2S*. 23:15-16; *1Chr*. 11:17-18.

161 One of the rules of the Mishnah, to ask the opinion of the Sages of a mythical Bethlehem. Rabbinic interpretation systematically reduces David to a rabbi, negates all qualities of a warrior, and tries to eliminate all memories of a warlike past.

162 Since the rules of the Mishnah are all anonymous.

163 The water libation at Tabernacles (Mishnah *Sukkah* 4:9), a purely pharisaic practice without biblical sanction, to ask for ample rains in the winter season. Cf. Note 161.

164 After the destruction of Shiloh, before the building of the Temple in Jerusalem, there was no central sanctuary which could claim exclusivity by deuteronomic rules. According to all opinions, private altars were biblically permitted in that period (Mishnah *Zevahim* 14:7). The pharisaic water libation was a public offering not appropriate for a private altar. It has to be assumed that in this interpretation David acted as king; his altar could represent the nation by public offerings.

165 He does not read the masoretic וַיַּסֵּךְ from the root נסך "to pour, offer a libation" but וַיָּסֶךְ, root סכך "to cover".

166 Probably what is the prerogative of the king in appropriating female prisoners of war. Rabbinic theory explains that Tamar was not David's daughter but the daughter of David's wife Ma`akha from the time before the latter was taken prisoner by David and forcibly converted by the rules of *Deut*. 21:10-14 (Babli 21a); therefore, she was unrelated to Amnon who could have married her under rabbinic rules.

167 It is unclear to what this may refer, but in any case it would be a case for the Sages of Bethlehem before the capture of Jerusalem.

(fol. 19d) **משנה ו**: לֹא יַרְבֶּה לּוֹ נָשִׁים אֶלָּא שְׁמוֹנֶה עֶשְׂרֵה. רִבִּי יְהוּדָה אוֹמֵר מַרְבֶּה הוּא לוֹ וּבִלְבַד שֶׁלֹּא יְהוּ מְסִירוֹת אֶת לִבּוֹ. רִבִּי שִׁמְעוֹן אוֹמֵר אֲפִילוּ אַחַת וּמְסִירָה אֶת לִבּוֹ הֲרֵי זֶה לֹא יִשָּׂאֶנָּה. אִם כֵּן לָמָּה נֶאֱמַר וְלֹא יַרְבֶּה לּוֹ נָשִׁים דַּאֲפִילוּ כַּאֲבִיגָיִל.

Mishnah 6: *He shall not add wives*[168], only eighteen[169]. Rebbi Jehudah says, he may have many on condition that they not deflect his mind[170]. Rebbi Simeon says, he should not marry even one if she deflects his mind[171]. Then why was it said, *he shall not add wives*? Even one like Abigail[172].

משנה ז: לֹא יַרְבֶּה לוֹ סוּסִים אֶלָּא כְדֵי מֶרְכַּבְתּוֹ. וְכֶסֶף וְזָהָב לֹא יַרְבֶּה לוֹ מְאֹד אֶלָּא כְדֵי לִיתֵּן אָפְּסָנְיָיא. וְכוֹתֵב לוֹ סֵפֶר תּוֹרָה לִשְׁמוֹ. יוֹצֵא לַמִּלְחָמָה וְהוּא עִמּוֹ נִכְנָס וְהוּא עִמּוֹ. יוֹשֵׁב בַּדִּין, הוּא אֶצְלוֹ. מֵסֵב וְהוּא כְנֶגְדּוֹ שֶׁנֶּאֱמַר וְהָיְתָה עִמּוֹ וְקָרָא בוֹ כָּל יְמֵי חַיָּיו.

Mishnah 7: *He shall not add horses*[173], over and above what he needs for his chariots. *And silver and gold he shall not add excessively*[168], over and above what he needs for his payroll[174]. *And he shall write a Torah scroll*[175] for himself. If he goes to war, it is with him; if he returns, it is with him; if he sits in court, it is with him; if he sits down for dinner, it is with him, as it is said: *It shall be with him, and he shall read in it all the days of his life*[176].

משנה ח: אֵין רוֹכְבִין עַל סוּסוֹ וְאֵין יוֹשְׁבִין עַל כִּסְאוֹ וְאֵין מִשְׁתַּמְּשִׁין בְּשַׁרְבִיטוֹ וְאֵין רוֹאִין אוֹתוֹ כְּשֶׁהוּא מִסְתַּפֵּר וְלֹא כְשֶׁהוּא עָרוֹם. וְלֹא בְבֵית הַמֶּרְחָץ שֶׁנֶּאֱמַר שׂוֹם תָּשִׂים עָלֶיךָ מֶלֶךְ שֶׁתְּהֵא אֵימָתוֹ עָלֶיךָ:

Mishnah 8: One does not ride on his horse, nor does one sit on his throne, nor does one use his scepter. One may not see him when he is barbered, nor when he is naked, nor when he is in the bath, as it is said[177]: *You certainly shall put a king over you*, that his fear be upon you.

168 *Deut.* 17:17.

169 This is the number of wives David could have had, as explained in the Halakhah.

170 *Deut.* 17:17 reads: *And he shall not add wives, lest his mind be deflected* (from his religious duties.) If the prohibition were absolute, it would not need a rationale.

171 R. Simeon in principle objects to R. Jehudah's argument. For him, every biblical commandment has a rationale indicated in the text, even if it is not explicit (Babli 21a). Therefore, *lest his mind be deflected* is a commandment in itself. Hence, 18 wives is the maximum permitted to a king under any circumstances.

172 Who prevented David from sinning, cf. Halakhah 3. Since she predicted that David would be king, she is counted as a prophetess (*Seder Olam* Chap. 2).

173 *Deut.* 17:16.

174 Greek ὀψώνιον, Latin *obsonium*, "victuals, allowance, gratuity", here taken as allowances for everybody on the king's payroll.

175 *Deut.* 17:18.

176 *Deut.* 17:19.

177 *Deut.* 17:15.

(20c line 22) **הלכה ו**: לֹא יַרְבֶּה לוֹ נָשִׁים כול'. רַב כַּהֲנָא אָמַר. עַל שֵׁם הַשִּׁשִּׁי יִתְרְעָם לְעֶגְלָה. וּמַה כְתִיב תַּמָּן. וְאִם־מְעָט וְאוֹסִפָה לְּךָ כָּהֵנָּה וְכָהֵנָּה:

Halakhah 6: “He shall not add wives,” etc. Rav Cahana said[178], because of *the sixth Yitream by Egla*[139]. What is written there? *At least, I shall give you twice as many*[179].

178 Babli 21a.

179 *2S.* 12:8. The verses *2S.* 3:2-5 prove that David had six wives in Hebron. The prophet Nathan then told David that God would have given him an addition of twice as many wives, for a total of 3×6=18, had he not sinned with Batseba. Therefore, 18 wives for a king have Divine sanction.

(20c line 24) לֹא יַרְבֶּה לּוֹ סוּסִים אֶלָּא כְדֵי מֶרְכַּבְתּוֹ. עַל שֵׁם וַיְעַקֵּר דָּוִד֙ אֶת־כָּל־הָרֶ֫כֶב וגו'. וְכֶסֶף וְזָהָב לֹא יַרְבֶּה לּוֹ מְאֹד אֶלָּא כְדֵי לִיתֵּן אַפְּסָנְיָא. רִבִּי יְהוֹשֻׁעַ בֶּן לֵוִי אָמַר. וּבִלְבַד אַפְּסָנְיָא שֶׁל שָׁנָה זוֹ בִלְבַד.

“*He shall not add horses* over and above what he needs for his chariots.” As in *David destroyed all the chariots*,[180] etc. “*And silver and gold he shall not add excessively* over and above what he needs for his payroll.” Rebbi Joshua ben Levi said, but only for this year’s payroll.

180 *2S.* 8:4. As usual, the argument is about the part of the verse which is not quoted: *but he reserved from them 100 chariots*. This shows that chariots and horses needed for the army are permitted.

(20c line 27) אָמַר רִבִּי אָחָא. אָמַר שְׁלֹמֹה. שְׁלֹשָׁה דְבָרִים שֶׁשִּׂחֲקָה עֲלֵיהֶן מִידַּת הַדִּין חִילַּלְתִּים. לֹא יַרְבֶּה לּוֹ נָשִׁים. וְכָתוּב וְהַמֶּ֣לֶךְ שְׁלֹמֹה אָהַ֞ב נָשִׁ֧ים נָכְרִיּ֛וֹת. רִבִּי שִׁמְעוֹן בֶּן יוֹחַי אָמַר. אָהַב מַמָּשׁ לִזְנוּת. חֲנַנְיָה בֶּן אֲחִי רִבִּי יְהוֹשֻׁעַ אוֹמֵר. עַל שֵׁם לֹא תִתְחַתֵּן בָּם. רִבִּי יוֹסֵי אוֹמֵר. לְמוֹשְׁכָן לְדִבְרֵי תוֹרָה וּלְקָרְבָן תַּחַת כַּנְפֵי הַשְּׁכִינָה. רִבִּי לִיעֶזֶר אוֹמֵר. עַל שֵׁם גַּם־אוֹת֣וֹ הֶחֱטִ֔יאוּ הַנָּשִׁ֖ים הַנָּכְרִיּֽוֹת׃ אַשְׁכַּח תֵּימַר. רִבִּי שִׁמְעוֹן בֶּן יוֹחַי וַחֲנַנְיָה וְרִבִּי לִיעֶזֶר חָדָא. וְרִבִּי יוֹסֵי פְּלִיג עַל תַּלְתֵּיהוֹן.

לֹא יַרְבֶּה לּוֹ סוּסִים. וְכָתוּב וַיְהִ֣י לִשְׁלֹמֹ֗ה אַרְבָּעִ֥ים אֶ֛לֶף אוּרְיוֹת סוּסִ֖ים לְמֶרְכָּב֑וֹ וּשְׁנֵים־עָשָׂ֥ר אֶ֖לֶף פָּֽרָשִׁים׃ בַּטְלָנִים הָיוּ. וְהַהֶדְיוֹט מוּתָּר בְּכוּלָּן.

וְכֶסֶף וְזָהָב לֹא יַרְבֶּה לּוֹ מְאֹד. וְכָתוּב וַיִּתֵּ֨ן הַמֶּ֧לֶךְ אֶת־הַכֶּ֛סֶף בִּירוּשָׁלִַ֖ם כָּאֲבָנִ֑ים. וְלֹא הָיוּ נִגְנָבוֹת. אָמַר רִבִּי יוֹסֵי בֶּן חֲנִינָה. אַבְנֵי עֶשֶׂר אַמּוֹת וּשְׁמוֹנֶה אַמּוֹת. תַּנֵּי רִבִּי שִׁמְעוֹן בֶּן יוֹחַי. אֲפִילוּ מִשְׁקָלוֹת שֶׁהָיוּ בִימֵי שְׁלֹמֹה לֹא הָיוּ שֶׁל כֶּסֶף אֶלָּא שֶׁלְּזָהָב. וּמַה טַעַם. אֵ֣ין כֶּ֔סֶף נֶחְשָׁ֖ב בִּימֵ֥י שְׁלֹמֹֽה.

Rebbi Aha said: Solomon said, three things I desecrated where I got the better of the law[181]. *He shall not add wives*, and it is written: *King Solomon loved foreign women*[182]. Rebbi Simeon ben Iohai said, he really made love to them immorally[183]. Hananiah, Rebbi Joshua's nephew, says, because *you shall not intermarry with them*[184]. Rebbi Yose said, to draw them to the words of the Torah and bring them under the Wings of the Divine Presence[185]. Rebbi Eliezer said, because *also the foreign wives made him sin*[186]. It turns out that one may say that Rebbi Simeon ben Iohai, Hananiah, and Rebbi Eliezer mean the same. Rebbi Yose disagrees with all three of them.

He shall not add horses, and it is written: *Solomon had 40'000 horse stables for his chariot, and 12'000 riders*[187]. They were idle[188]. A private person is permitted all of these[189].

And silver and gold he shall not add excessively, and it is written: *The king made silver in Jerusalem to be like stones*[190]. Were they not stolen? Rebbi Yose ben Hanina said, they were stones of ten cubits and eight cubits[191]. Rebbi Simeon ben Laqish stated: In Solomon's times, even weights were not of silver but of gold. Why? *Silver was not valuable in Solomon's times*[192].

181 *Eccl. r.* 2(3), *Tanhuma Ahare Mot* 1, *Tanhuma Buber Ahare Mot* 2, *Pesiqta dR. Cahana* (Buber) *Ahare Mot* 168b-168a.

Most of the verses quoted in these paragraphs are also quoted in the Babli, 21b. Cf. also *Cant. rabba* 1(10).

182 *1K.* 11:1.

183 He did not marry them but slept with them unmarried to increase his sexual enjoyment.

184 *Deut.* 7:3. He agrees with R. Simeon ben Iohai and notes that by behaving immorally he avoided violating the law. In *Num.* r. 10(8) only Hanania and R. Yose are mentioned.

185 He married all those women with good intentions but violated *Deut.* 17:17. The expression "to take shelter under the Wings of the Divine Presence" for "to convert to Judaism" is from *Ru.* 2:12.

186 *Neh.* 13:26. He violated Mishnah 7 according to all authorities quoted there.

187 *1K.*5:6.

188 If all of the chariots and horses had been for military purposes, it would not have been sinful. A Genizah fragment inserts a rhetorical question. Were the 40'000 stables not adequate since it also is written (*1K.* 4:20) that Israel were *many, like the sand at the seashore*? The answer is that the horses and carriages were sinful since the riders were idle most of the time.

189 Wives, horses, and money are limited only for a king.

190 *1K.* 10:27, *2Chr.* 1:15.

191 A silver block of 8 cubits side length would weigh 1.7 metric tons.

192 *1K.* 10:21, *2Chr.* 9:27.

(20c line 40) כָּתוּב לִשְׂחוֹק אָמַרְתִּי מְהוֹלָל. אָמַר הַקָּדוֹשׁ בָּרוּךְ הוּא לִשְׁלֹמֹה. מָה עֲטָרָה זוֹ בְרֹאשְׁךָ. רֵד מִכִּסְאִי. רִבִּי יוֹסֵי בֶן חֲנִינָה אוֹמֵר. בְּאוֹתָהּ שָׁעָה יָרַד מַלְאָךְ וְנִדְמֶה כִּדְמוּת שְׁלֹמֹה וְהֶעֱמִידוֹ מִכִּסְאוֹ וְיָשַׁב תַּחְתָּיו. וְהָיָה מְחַזֵּר עַל בָּתֵּי כְנֵסִיּוֹת וּבָתֵּי מִדְרָשׁוֹת וְאוֹמֵר אֲנִי קֹהֶלֶת הָיִיתִי מֶלֶךְ עַל־יִשְׂרָאֵל בִּירוּשָׁלָםִ׃ וַהֲווּ מָרִין לֵיהּ. מַלְכָּא יְתִיב עַל בְּסֵילְיוֹן דִּידֵיהּ וְתֵימַר אֲנִי קֹהֶלֶת. וְהָיוּ מַכִּין אוֹתוֹ בְקָנֶה וּמֵבִיאִין לְפָנָיו קְעָרַת גְּרִיסִין. בְּאוֹתָהּ שָׁעָה אָמַר וְזֶה־הָיָה חֶלְקִי. אִית דָּמְרִין. חוּטְרָא. וְאִית דָּמְרִין. קַנְיָא. וְאִית דָּמְרִין. קוֹשַׁרְתֵּיהּ. וּמִי קִיטְרְגוֹ. אָמַר רִבִּי יְהוֹשֻׁעַ בֶּן לֵוִי. יוֹ״ד שֶׁבְּיַרְבֶּה קִיטְרְגוֹ. תַּנֵּי רִבִּי שִׁמְעוֹן בֶּן יוֹחַי. עָלָה סֵפֶר מִשְׁנֶה תוֹרָה וְנִשְׁתַּטֵּחַ לִפְנֵי הַקָּדוֹשׁ בָּרוּךְ הוּא. אָמַר לְפָנָיו. רִבּוֹן הָעוֹלָם. כָּתַבְתָּה בְתוֹרָתָךְ. כָּל־דְּיַיתֵיקֵי שֶׁבָּטְלָה מִקְצָתָהּ בָּטְלָה כּוּלָּהּ. וַהֲרֵי שְׁלֹמֹה מְבַקֵּשׁ לַעֲקוֹר יוֹ״ד מִמֶּנִּי. אָמַר לָהּ הַקָּדוֹשׁ בָּרוּךְ הוּא. שְׁלֹמֹה וְאֶלֶף כְּיוֹצֵא בוֹ בְּטֵילִין וְדָבָר מִמֵּךְ אֵינוֹ בָטֵל.

רִבִּי הוּנָא בְשֵׁם רִבִּי אָחָא. יוֹ״ד שֶׁנָּטַל הַקָּדוֹשׁ בָּרוּךְ הוּא מֵאִמֵּנוּ שָׂרָה נִיתַּן חֶצְיוֹ עַל שָׂרָה וְחֶצְיוֹ עַל אַבְרָהָם. תַּנֵּי רִבִּי הוֹשַׁעְיָא. עָלָה יוֹ״ד וְנִשְׁתַּטֵּחַ לִפְנֵי הַקָּדוֹשׁ בָּרוּךְ הוּא וְאָמַר. רִבּוֹן הָעוֹלָמִים. עֲקַרְתָּנִי מִן הַצַּדֶּקֶת הַזֹּאת. אָמַר לוֹ הַקָּדוֹשׁ בָּרוּךְ הוּא. צֵא לָךְ. לְשֶׁעָבַר הָיִיתָ נָתוּן בְּשֵׁם נְקֵיבָה וּבְסוֹף תֵּיבָה. חַיֶּיךָ שֶׁאֲנִי נוֹתְנָךְ בְּשֵׁם זָכָר וּבְרֹאשׁ תֵּיבָה. הָדָא הוּא דִכְתִיב וַיִּקְרָ֥א מֹשֶׁ֛ה לְהוֹשֵׁ֥עַ בִּן־נ֖וּן יְהוֹשֻֽׁעַ׃

[181]It is written[193]: *To amusement I said, be praised.* The Holy One, praise to him, said to Solomon: What is this crown on your head? Descend from My throne! Rebbi Yose ben Ḥanina said, at that moment an angel came down looking like Solomon, removed him from his throne, and sat in his stead. He was going around in synagogues and houses of study, saying *I am Ecclesiastes, I used to be king over Israel in Jerusalem*[194]. They were telling him, the king sits on his chair of honor[195] and you say, *I am Ecclesiastes*? They hit him with a stick and brought a dish of split beans before him. At that moment, he said: *that is my part*[196]. Some say, a staff. Others say, a rod. Others say, with his belt. [197]Who had accused him? Rebbi Joshua ben Levi said, י in יַרְבֶּה[160] accused him. Rebbi Simeon ben Iohai stated: The book Deuteronomy ascended, bowed down before the Holy One, praise to Him, and said to Him: Master of the Universe, You wrote in Your Torah that any disposition[198] which is partially invalid is totally invalid, and now Solomon wants to uproot a י from me! The Holy One, praise to Him, said to it: Solomon and a thousand like him will disappear but nothing from you will disappear.

Rebbi Huna in the name of Rebbi Aḥa: The י which the Holy One, praise to Him, lifted from our mother Sarah was given half to Sarah and half to Abraham[199]. Rebbi Hoshaiah stated: The י ascended, bowed down before the Holy One, praise to Him, and said to Him: Master of the Universes, you uprooted me from this just woman[200]! The Holy One, praise to Him, said to him: leave. In the past you were the last letter of a woman's name. By your life, I shall make you the first letter of a man's name. That is what is written: *Moses called Hoshea bin Nun Yehoshua*[201].

193 *Eccl.* 2:2.
194 *Eccl.* 1:12.
195 Latin *bisellium*; cf. Löw in Krauss's *Lehnwörter*.
196 *Eccl.* 2:10.
197 *Cant. r. ad* 5:10, *Lev. r.* 19(2), *Ex. r.* 6(1). Solomon is accused of wanting to remove the imperative from *Deut.* 17:17.
198 Greek διαθήκη "will, disposition".

199 In the Alexandrian system, the numerical value of י is 10, that of ה is 5. Therefore, the *gematria* of the two former names אברם שרי of Abraham and Sarah is identical to that of the new names אברהם שרה.
200 By changing שָׂרַי into שָׂרָה.
201 *Num.* 13:16.

(20c line 58) וְכוֹתֵב לוֹ סֵפֶר תּוֹרָה לִשְׁמוֹ. שֶׁלֹּא יְהֵא נֵיאוֹת לֹא בְשֶׁלְּאָבִיו וְלֹא בְשֶׁלְּרַבּוֹ. וּמַגִּיהִין אוֹתוֹ מִסֵּפֶר עֲזָרָה עַל פִּי בֵּית דִּין שֶׁלע"א.

And he shall write a Torah scroll for himself. [202]That he should use neither his father's not his teacher's. One proofreads it from the Temple scroll under the supervision of the court of 71[203].

202 Babli 21b, Tosephta 4:7.
203 In the Tosephta: It is proofread first by priests, then by Levites, then by Israel whose daughters are qualified to marry priests.

(20c line 60) יוֹצֵא לַמִּלְחָמָה וְהִיא עִמּוֹ. שֶׁנֶּאֱמַר וְהָיְתָה עִמּוֹ וְקָרָא בוֹ כָּל־יְמֵי חַיָּיו. וַהֲרֵי הַדְּבָרִים קַל וָחוֹמֶר. וּמָה אִם מֶלֶךְ יִשְׂרָאֵל שֶׁהָיָה עָסוּק בְּצָרְכֵי יִשְׂרָאֵל נֶאֱמַר בּוֹ וְקָרָא בוֹ כָּל־יְמֵי חַיָּיו. הַהֶדְיוֹט עַל אַחַת כַּמָּה וְכַמָּה. כְּיוֹצֵא בוֹ נֶאֱמַר בִּיהוֹשֻׁעַ וְהָגִיתָ בּוֹ יוֹמָם וָלַיְלָה. וַהֲרֵי הַדְּבָרִים קַל וָחוֹמֶר. וּמָה אִם יְהוֹשֻׁעַ שֶׁעוֹסֵק בְּצָרְכֵי יִשְׂרָאֵל נֶאֱמַר בּוֹ וְהָגִיתָ בּוֹ יוֹמָם וָלַיְלָה. הֶדְיוֹט לֹא כָל־שֶׁכֵּן.

"If he goes to war, he carries it with him for it is said: *It shall be with him, and he shall read in it all the days of his life.* Is there not an inference *de minore ad majus*? Since for a king of Israel, who was occupied by the needs of Israel, is it said that *he shall read in it all the days of his life*, a private person so much more. Similarly, it was said to Joshua: *You shall meditate about it day and night*[204]. Is there not an inference *de minore ad majus*? Since for Joshua, who is occupied by the needs of Israel, it is said: *you shall meditate about it day and night*, then certainly a private person.

204 *Jos.* 1:8.

(20c line 65) מֶלֶךְ יִשְׂרָאֵל אֵין רוֹכְבִין עַל סוּסוֹ וְאֵין יוֹשְׁבִין עַל נִיסלוֹ וְאֵין מִשְׁתַּמְּשִׁין לֹא בְכִתְרוֹ וְלֹא בְשַׁרְבִיטוֹ וְלֹא בְאֶחָד מִכָּל־מְשַׁמְּשָׁיו. וּכְשֶׁמֵּת כּוּלָּן נִשְׂרָפִין לְפָנָיו. שֶׁנֶּאֱמַר בְּשָׁלוֹם תָּמוּת וּכְמִשְׂרְפוֹת אֲבוֹתֶיךָ יִשְׂרְפוּ עָלֶיךָ.

[205]One does not ride on a horse of a king of Israel, nor does one sit in his chair[195], nor does one use his crown or his scepter, or any of his personal utensils. When he dies, all these are burned before him, as it is said[206]: *You shall die in peace and like the burnings of your forefathers they will burn for you.*

205 An abbreviated version of Tosephta 4:2.

206 *Jer.* 34:5.

(20c line 68) וְאֵין רוֹאִין אוֹתוֹ עָרוֹם וְלֹא כְּשֶׁמִּסְתַּפֵּר וְלֹא בְבֵית הַמֶּרְחָץ. עַל שֵׁם מֶלֶךְ בְּיָפְיוֹ תֶּחֱזֶינָה עֵינֶיךָ. רִבִּי חֲנִינָה סְלַק גַּבֵּי רִבִּי יוּדָן נְשִׂיָּא. נְפַק לְגַבֵּיהּ לָבוּשׁ אוֹתָנִיתֵיהּ. אָמַר לֵיהּ. חֲזוֹר וּלְבוֹשׁ לָגִין דִּידָךְ. מִשּׁוּם מֶלֶךְ בְּיָפְיוֹ תֶּחֱזֶינָה עֵינֶיךָ. רִבִּי יוֹחָנָן סְלַק גַּבֵּי רִבִּי יוּדָן נְשִׂיָּא. נְפַק לְגַבֵּיהּ בַּחֲלוּקָא דְכִתְנָא. אָמַר לֵיהּ. חֲזוֹר וּלְבוֹשׁ חֲלוּקָךְ דְּעִימְרָא. מִשּׁוּם מֶלֶךְ בְּיָפְיוֹ וגו'. מִי נְפַק אֲמַר לֵיהּ. אַיְיתִי עטעמה. אֲמַר לֵיהּ. שְׁלַח וְאַיְיתִי לִי מְנַחֵם טַלְמָא. דִּכְתִיב וְתוֹרַת־חֶסֶד עַל־לְשׁוֹנָהּ׃ מִי נְפַק חֲמָא רִבִּי חֲנִינָה בַּר סִיסִי מְפַצֵּעַ קִיסִין. אֲמַר לֵיהּ. רִבִּי. לֵית הוּא כְבוֹדָךְ. אֲמַר לֵיהּ. וּמַה נִיעֲבִיד וְלֵית לִי מָאן דִּמְשַׁמְּשֵׁינִי. אֲמַר לֵיהּ. אִין לָא הֲוָה לָךְ מָאן דִּמְשַׁמְּשָׁךְ לָא מְקַבְּלָא עֲלָךְ מִתְמַנְיָיא.

One may not see him when naked, nor when he is being barbered, nor when he is in his bath, because *your eyes shall see the king in his beauty*[207]. Rebbi Hanina went to visit Rebbi Jehudah the Prince[208]. He came to meet him dressed in sail-cloth. He told him, go and wear your *lagin*[209], because of *your eyes shall see the king in his beauty*[210,211].

Rebbi Johanan went to visit Rebbi Jehudah the Prince. He came to meet him dressed in a linen gown. He told him, go and wear your woolen gown, because of *the king in his beauty*. When he left, he told him, bring עטעמה[212]. He answered, send and get Menahem Ptolemy, for it is written: *Graceful teaching is on her tongue*[213].

Leaving, he saw Rebbi Hanina bar Sisi splitting wood. He told him, Rebbi, that is not fitting for you. He answered, what can I do? I have nobody to serve me. He retorted, if you have nobody to serve you, you should not have accepted ordination[214].

207 *Is.* 33:17. The Babli, 22b, infers from the verse that a king has to get a haircut every day.

208 Rebbi's grandson.

209 Greek ὀθονή "sail-cloth".

210 Latin *lacinia, ae,* "edge, corner of garment, garment with fringes, ornament", generally "garment" (E. G.).

(In other occurrences the word לגין means "bottle", Greek λάγυνος, λάγηνος.)

211 The Patriarch, as member of the Davidic dynasty, should uphold the dignity of his family at all times.

212 The meaning and etymology of this word is totally unknown. The commentators see a connection with the word טעם "taste". It may have been a question about politics since the verse quoted is explained in *Midrash Prov.* as referring to good political advice. Menahem Ptolemy is only mentioned in *Eccl. r. ad* 5:10, in a discussion with R. Hanina, noting that good-looking food tastes better than undistinguished food, therefore it is possible to read the passage as an exhortation to the Patriarch to also show his status by his table.

213 *Pr.* 31:26.

214 An ordained rabbi should at all times uphold the dignity of the office. Similarly, the Babli (*Qiddušin* 70a) frowns upon an ordained rabbi engaged in bodily labor in public.

(20d line 2) תִּירְגֵּם יוֹסֵי מָעוֹנִי בִּכְנִישְׁתָּא בְטֵיבֵּרִיָּא. שִׁמְעוּ־זֹאת הַכֹּהֲנִים. לָמָּה לֵית אַתּוּן לָעֵין בְּאוּרַיְיתָא. לָא יְהָבִית לְכוֹן כ"ד מַתַּנְתָּא. אָמְרוּ לֵיהּ. לָא יְהָבִין לָן כְּלוּם. וְהַקְשִׁיבוּ | בֵּית יִשְׂרָאֵל. לָמָּה לֵית אַתּוּן יְהָבִין כ"ד מַתַּנְתָּא דִפְקִידִית יַתְכוֹן בְּסִינַי. אָמְרוּ לֵיהּ. מַלְכָּא נְסִיב כּוּלָּהּ. וּבֵית הַמֶּלֶךְ הַאֲזִינוּ כִּי לָכֶם הַמִּשְׁפָּט. לָכֶם אָמַרְתִּי וְזֶה מִשְׁפַּט הַכֹּהֲנִים. עָתִיד אֲנִי לֵישֵׁב עִמָּהֶן בַּדִּין וּלְפַסְקָן וּלְאַבְּדָן מִן הָעוֹלָם. שָׁמַע רִבִּי יוּדָן נְשִׂייָא וְכָעַס. דָּחַל וְעָרַק. סַלְקוֹן רִבִּי יוֹחָנָן וְרֵישׁ לָקִישׁ לְפַייֵס לֵיהּ. אָמְרוּ לֵיהּ. רִבִּי. גַּבְרָא רַבָּא הוּא. אָמַר לֵיהּ. אֶיפְשַׁר כָּל־מָאן דָּנָא שְׁאִיל הוּא מֵגִיב לִי. אָמְרוּ לֵיהּ. אִין. אָמַר לֵיהּ. מָהוּ דֵין דִּכְתִיב כִּי זָֽנְתָה אִמָּם. וְכִי שָׂרָה אִמֵּינוּ זוֹנָה

הָיְתָה. אָמַר לֵיהּ. כְּבַת כֵּן אִמָּהּ. כַּדּוֹר כֵּן הַנָּשִׂיא. כַּנָּשִׂיא כֵּן הַדּוֹר. כַּמִּזְבֵּחַ כֹּהֲנָיו. כַּהֲנָא אֲמַר כֵּן. כְּגִנְּתָא כֵּן גַּנָּנָהּ. אָמַר לֵיהּ. לָא טָב דִּקְלִיל לִי דְלָא בְאַפּוֹי חַד זְמַן. אֶלָּא בְאַפַּיי תְּלָתָא זִימְנִין. אָמַר לֵיהּ. מָהוּ דֵין דִּכְתִיב הִנֵּה֙ כָּל־הַמֹּשֵׁל עָלַ֫יִךְ יִמְשׁוֹל לֵאמֹר כְּאִמָּה֖ בִּתָּהּ. וְכִי אִימֵּינוּ לֵאָה זוֹנָה הָיְתָה. דִּכְתִיב וַתֵּצֵא דִינָה֙. אָמַר לֵיהּ. לְפוּם דִּכְתִיב וַתֵּצֵא לֵאָה לִקְרָאתוֹ. פָּשְׁטִין יְצִיאָה מִיצִיאָה.

[215]Yose from Maon interpreted[216] in the synagogue of Tiberias: *Listen to this, you priests*[217], why do you not study Torah? Did I not give you 24 gifts[218]? They told him, they do not give us anything. *And hearken, House of Israel,* why do you not give the 24 gifts which I commanded you at Sinai? They told him, the king[219] takes everything. *Listen, king's court, for yours are legal proceedings,* for you I did say, *these are the priests' legal rights*[220]; in the future I shall sit in judgment over you, to stop them and to eliminate them from the world. Rebbi Jehudah the Prince heard this and became angry. He[221] was afraid and fled. Rebbi Joḥanan and Rebbi Simeon ben Laqish went to appease him. They told him, Rabbi, he is a great man. He[222] asked them, would it be possible that he[221] could answer any question which I would ask him? They told him, yes. He asked him: What is that which is written[223]: *For their mother whored*? Was our mother Sarah a whore? He answered, like daughter like mother[224], *like mother like daughter*, like generation like the prince, like the prince like the generation, like the altar like its priests. Cahana used to say[224], like the garden like its gardener. He told them, not only did he curse me once in my absence, but he cursed me three times in my presence! He asked him, what is that which is written[225]: *Anybody wanting to formulate a simile about you will state as follows: like mother like daughter;* was our mother Leah a prostitute since it is written[226], *Dinah went out*? He told him, for it is written[227], *Leah went out towards him*. One identifies *going out* with *going out*.

215 A similar paragraph is in *Gen. r.* 80(1).

216 In the Talmudim, תרגם is only used for interpretation or translation of Scripture. One has to assume that Yose from Maon was reading *Hos.* 5 as *Haftara* to *Gen.* 34 in the Palestinian $3\frac{1}{2}$ year cycle of Torah reading (cf. J. Mann, *The Bible as Read and Preached in the Old Synagogue I*, Cincinnati 1940). One also has to assume that the Aramaic translator of the *Haftara* had the freedom to expound upon the verses read, similar to what is described in the New Testament (*Luke* 4:17-20).

217 *Hos.* 5:1.

218 The 24 emoluments of priesthood; cf. *Hallah* 4:11 (Note 146) and the sources quoted there.
219 The Patriarch was responsible for collecting the taxes due from the Jewish population in Palestine; there is an intentional ambiguity whether *king* refers to the Roman Emperor or the Davidic Patriarch.
220 *Deut*. 18:3.
221 Yose the Maonite.
222 The Patriarch.
223 *Hos*. 2:7.
224 The text is confirmed by a Genizah fragment (M. Sokoloff, *The Genizah Fragments of Bereshit Rabba*, Jerusalem 1982, p. 167.) The reading in the printed editions of *Gen. rabba* הָכָא אָמְרֵי "here, they say" has to be rejected as *lectio facilior*.
225 The Genizah fragment shows that instead of "like daughter like mother", the text read כְּבֵית כְּאוּמָּא "like dynasty like people, like generation like Prince" with the quote from the verse missing, a much more insulting formulation.
226 *Ez*. 16:44.
227 *Gen*. 34:1, the starting verse for the sermon. In both Galilean and Babylonian Aramaic is the prostitute called נָפְקַת בָּרָא "the one who goes out."
228 *Gen*. 30:16. Leah certainly went out to have sexual relations, with her husband.

(20d line 18) רִבִּי חִזְקִיָּה הֲוָה מְהַלֵּךְ בְּאוֹרְחָא. פָּגַע בּוֹ חַד כּוּתִי. אֲמַר לֵיהּ. רִבִּי. אַתְּ הוּא רַבְּהוֹן דִּיהוּדָאֵי. אֲמַר לֵיהּ. אִין. אֲמַר לֵיהּ. חֲמִי מַה כְתִיב שׂוֹם תָּשִׂים עָלֶיךָ מֶלֶךְ. אָשִׂים אֵין כְּתִיב אֶלָּא תָּשִׂים. דְּאַתְּ שָׁוֵי עֲלָךְ.

Rebbi Ḥizqiah was walking on a road when he met a Samaritan who asked him, Rabbi, are you not the head of the Jews? He answered him, yes. He said to him, look what is written: *You certainly shall put a king over yourself*[177]. It does not say "I shall put", but "you shall put", you appoint him over yourself[229].

229 For him the role of king and all appointed officers, including rabbis, is one of human convention, without religious meaning.

דיני ממונות פרק שלישי

(fol. 20d) **משנה א**: דִּינֵי מָמוֹנוֹת בִּג'. זֶה בּוֹרֵר לוֹ אֶחָד וְזֶה בּוֹרֵר לוֹ אֶחָד וּשְׁנֵיהֶן בּוֹרְרִין לָהֶן עוֹד אֶחָד דִּבְרֵי רַבִּי מֵאִיר. וַחֲכָמִים אוֹמְרִים שְׁנֵי הַדַּיָּינִים בּוֹרְרִין לָהֶן עוֹד אֶחָד.

Mishnah 1: Money matters by three [judges]. Each party selects one judge and both together select a third, the words of Rebbi Meïr[1]. But the Sages say, the two judges together select a third.

1 The "court" is a panel of arbitration. The parties have the option to go before the permanent court of the community but are not required to do so.

(21a line 5) **הלכה א**: דִּינֵי מָמוֹנוֹת בִּשְׁלֹשָׁה כול'. אָמַר רִבִּי זְעִירָא. שֶׁמִּתּוֹךְ שֶׁבֵּירְרוֹ מְרַדֵּף זְכוּתוֹ. מַאי טַעֲמָא דְרִבִּי מֵאִיר. כְּדֵי שֶׁיִּתְבָּרְרוּ שְׁלָשְׁתָּן מִדַּעַת אַחַת. וּמַאי טַעֲמוֹן דְּרַבָּנִן. לָאו כּוּלְּהּ מִינָּךְ מִיבְחַר וּמֵיסַב מַה דְאַתְּ בָּעֵי אֶלָּא אֲנָא וְאַתְּ מְבַחֲרִין וּמְסַבִּין מַה דְּנָן בְּעָיִן. וְקַשְׁיָא עַל דְּרַבָּנִן. מֵת אֶחָד לֹא נִמְצְאוּ שְׁלָשְׁתָּן מִתְבָּרְרִין מִדַּעַת אַחַת.

Halakhah 1: "Money matters by three," etc. Rebbi Ze\`ira said, because he selected him, he will take care of his interests[2]. What is Rebbi Meïr's reason? So that all three should be chosen unanimously. What is the rabbis' reason? "I do not trust you to select and let me sit with whom you want, but I and you shall select and empanel whom we want.[3]" It is difficult for the rabbis: If one of them[4] dies, will not all three have been chosen through the choice of one person?

2 The arbitration judgment will be acceptable to all parties since each party expects his point of view to be forcefully represented. The Babli, 23a, holds that the judgment will be just since each party is represented in the panel of arbitrators.

3 The judges cannot be forced to sit with a third judge who is not agreeable to them.

4 If one of the original judges dies after the third has been chosen, his replacement who is chosen by one party only and is forced upon the two judges already empaneled. The situation preferred by Rebbi Meïr may develop also if the rabbis are followed.

(fol. 20d) **משנה ב**: זֶה פוֹסֵל דַּיָּינוֹ שֶׁל זֶה וְזֶה פוֹסֵל דַּיָּינוֹ שֶׁל זֶה דִּבְרֵי רַבִּי מֵאִיר. וַחֲכָמִים אוֹמְרִים אֵימָתַי בִּזְמַן שֶׁהוּא מֵבִיא עֲלֵיהֶן רְאָיָה שֶׁהֵן קְרוֹבִין אוֹ פְסוּלִין אֲבָל אִם הָיוּ כְשֵׁרִים אוֹ מוּמְחִין מִפִּי בֵּית דִּין אֵינוֹ יָכוֹל לְפָסְלָן.

Mishnah 2: Each of them disqualifies the other's judge, the words of Rebbi Meïr. But the Sages say, when is this? If he brings proof that they are relatives[5] or disqualified[6]. But if they are unexceptionable or qualified by the court[7] he cannot disqualify them.

5 Anybody not acceptable as a witness in a case is unacceptable as a judge; cf. Mishnah 7.

6 A felon or a person disqualified under the rules of Mishnah 6.

7 He passed bar examinations.

(21a line 9) **הלכה ב**: זֶה פוֹסֵל דַּיָּינוֹ שֶׁלָּזֶה כול'. כֵּינִי מַתְנִיתא. זֶה פוֹסֵל דַּיָּינוֹ שֶׁלָּזֶה. הָא דַיָּינוֹ לֹא. רֵישׁ לָקִישׁ אָמַר. בְּאַרְכָאוֹת שֶׁבְּסוּרְיָא אָמְרוּ. הָא בְדִינֵי תוֹרָה לֹא. רִבִּי יוֹחָנָן אָמַר. אֲפִילוּ בְדִינֵי תוֹרָה. הֵיךְ אָמְרִין. תְּרֵין בְּנֵי נַשׁ הֲוָה לָן דִּין בְּאַנְטוֹכְיָא. אֲמַר חַד לְחַבְרֵיהּ. מַה דְרִבִּי יוֹחָנָן אָמַר מְקַבֵּל עָלַי. שָׁמַע רִבִּי יוֹחָנָן וָמַר. לֹא כָל־מִינֵּיהּ מִטְרְפָא בַעַל דִּינֵיהּ אֶלָּא שָׁמְעִין מִילֵּיהוֹן תַּמָּן וְאִין הֲוָת צוֹרְכָא כָּתְבִין וּמְשַׁלְּחִין עוּבְדָא לְרַבָּנִן. אָמַר רִבִּי לָעְזָר. זֶה אוֹמֵר. בְּטִיבֵּרְיָא. וְזֶה אוֹמֵר. בְּצִיפּוֹרִי. שׁוֹמְעִין לָזֶה שֶׁאָמַר. בְּטִיבֵּרְיָא.

וּלְעוֹלָם זֶה פוֹסֵל וְזֶה מֵבִיא. אָמַר רִבִּי זֵירָא. בִּטְפֵילָה שָׁנוּ. אָמַר רִבִּי לָא. וְהַאי דָּמַר רִבִּי לָעְזָר. זֶה אָמַר בְּטִיבֵּרְיָא. וְזֶה אָמַר בְּצִיפּוֹרִי. בְּאִינּוּן דַּהֲווֹן יְהִיבִין בְּחָדָא מִשְׁכְּנָא. מִן הָכָא לְהָכָא ז' מִילִין. מִן הָכָא לְהָכָא ט' מִילִין. אָמַר רִבִּי יוֹסֵי. וְאַתְּ שְׁמַע מִינָּהּ. תְּרֵין בְּנֵי נַשׁ הֲוָה לוֹן דִּין בְּטִיבֵּרְיָא. זֶה אוֹמֵר. בְּבֵית דִּין הַגָּדוֹל. וְזֶה אוֹמֵר. בְּבֵית דִּין הַקָּטָן. שׁוֹמְעִין לָזֶה שֶׁאָמַר. בְּבֵית דִּין הַגָּדוֹל.

Halakhah 2: "Each of them disqualifies the other's judge," etc. So is the Mishnah: Each of them disqualifies the *other's* judge, but not his own.

Rebbi Simeon ben Laqish said, they spoke about Syrian courts[8], but not about following Torah law[9]. Rebbi Joḥanan said, even following Torah law[10]. How was this said? Two people had a case in Antioch. One said to the other, I am accepting everything which Rebbi Joḥanan will decide[11]. Rebbi Joḥanan heard it and said, he is not empowered to tear apart his opponent[12], but they shall hear their arguments there and if need be they should write and send the case before the rabbis[13].

Rebbi Eleazar said, if one says in Tiberias, but the other said in Sepphoris, one listens to the one who says in Tiberias[14].

Can he forever disqualify and have the other appoint [a replacement][15]? Rebbi Ze`ira said, they taught this about subsidiaries[16].

Rebbi La said, what Rebbi Eleazar said about "one said in Tiberias, but the other said in Sepphoris," is about those who live at the same place[17], from where to [Sepphoris] it is seven *mil*, but from there to [Tiberias] it is nine *mil*[18]. Rebbi Yose said, one understands from this, that if two people had a case in Tiberias; one of them said in the permanent court, but the other said in an *ad hoc* court; one listens to the one who said in the permanent court[19].

8 Greek ἀρχεῖον, cf. *Giṭṭin* 1:5, Note 107.

9 *Ad hoc* courts formed by ignorant people.

10 In a court of arbitration it makes no difference whether a judge be learned in the law or not.

11 Implying that he wants the case to be tried before the permanent court of the Academy in Tiberias.

12 By forcing him to spend money and time in travelling from Antioch to Tiberias.

13 If one party wants to try a case out of town, the other party can appeal to the local permanent court to try the case in town, subject to submitting arguments in dispute to an out-of-town court of appeals; Babli 31b.

14 Between the court of the Academy in Tiberias and the local court in Sepphoris, precedence must be given to the court of the Academy.

15 According to R. Meïr, cannot one party endlessly drag out the case by objecting to the other's choice of judges?

16 R. Meïr permits rejections without cause only for judges not learned in the law. The other party can cut short the selection process either by appointing a judge learned in the law or by removing the case to the permanent local court.

17 And their village had no permanent local court.

18 A small inconvenience must be accepted in order to bring the case before the most competent court nearby.

19 Even though the Mishnah prescribes *ad hoc* courts of arbitration for monetary disputes, the party who wants to bring the case before the permanent rabbinic court of the community can force the opposing party to agree to his choice.

(fol. 20d) **משנה ג**: זֶה פּוֹסֵל עֵדָיו שֶׁל זֶה וְזֶה פּוֹסֵל עֵדָיו שֶׁל זֶה דִּבְרֵי רַבִּי מֵאִיר. וַחֲכָמִים אוֹמְרִים אֵימָתַי בִּזְמַן שֶׁהוּא מֵבִיא עֲלֵיהֶם רְאָיָה שֶׁהֵן קְרוֹבִים אוֹ פְּסוּלִין. אֲבָל אִם הָיוּ כְּשֵׁרִים אוֹ מוּמְחִין מִפִּי בֵית דִּין אֵינוֹ יָכוֹל לְפוֹסְלָן:

Mishnah 3: Each of them disqualifies the other's witnesses, the words of Rebbi Meïr. But the Sages say, when is this? If he brings proof that they are relatives[5] or disqualified[6]. But if they are unexceptionable or qualified by the court[7] he cannot disqualify them.

(21a line 22) **הלכה ג**: זֶה פּוֹסֵל עֵדָיו שֶׁלָּזֶה כול׳. רֵישׁ לָקִישׁ אָמַר. כֵּינִי מַתְנִיתָא. עֵדוֹ. הָא עֵידָיו לֹא. וְרִבִּי יוֹחָנָן אָמַר. אֲפִילוּ עֵדָיו. דְּתַנֵּי. לְעוֹלָם מוֹסִיפִין דַּיָּינִים עַד שֶׁיִּגָּמֵר הַדִּין וְהַדַּיָּינִין יְכוֹלִין לַחֲזוֹר בָּהֶן. נִגְמַר הַדִּין אֵין יְכוֹלִין לַחֲזוֹר בָּהֶן. מוֹדֶה רִבִּי יוֹחָנָן שֶׁאִם אֵין שָׁם אֶלָּא הֵן שֶׁאֵין יְכוֹלִין לְפוֹסְלָן. אָמַר זְעִירָה. וְהוּא וְאֶחָד מִן הַשּׁוּק מִצְטָרְפִין לִפְסוֹל עֵדוּת זֶה. רִבִּי חֲנִינָה בָּעֵי. וְאֵין עֵד אֶחָד זוֹקְקוֹ לִשְׁבוּעָה בְּכָל־מָקוֹם. אָמַר רִבִּי זְעִירָא. פָּסוּל צָרִיךְ לִיפָּסֵל בְּבֵית דִּין. קָרוֹב אֵין צָרִיךְ לִיפָּסֵל בְּבֵית דִּין. אָמַר רָבָא בַּר בִּינָא בְּשֵׁם רַב. שְׁלֹשָׁה כִגְמַר דִּין.

Halakhah 3: "Each of them disqualifies the other's witnesses," etc. Rebbi Simeon ben Laqish said, so is the Mishnah: "His witness," but not his witnesses[20]. But Rebbi Joḥanan said, even his witnesses[21], as it was stated[22]: "One always adds judges until judgment is rendered, and the judges may change their opinions. After judgment is rendered they may no longer change their opinions." Rebbi Joḥanan agrees, that if these were the only ones[23], he cannot disqualify them. Ze`ira said, he and a person from the street can team up to disqualify this testimony[24]. Rebbi Ḥanina asked, does not one witness force an oath everywhere[25]? Rebbi Ze`ira said, by disqualification one can only be disqualified by a court[26]. A relative does not have to be disqualified by the court[27]. Rava bar Binah said in the name of Rav: Three are like final judgment[28].

20 Since a single witness is never decisive, one of the parties can claim that a single witness appearing for one of the parties was unacceptable as a witness (Mishnah 6) without presenting formal proof. But if two witnesses are appearing together, only formal proof of ineligibility is admissible since "two or three witnesses are sufficient to confirm anything" (*Deut.* 19:15).

21 Even the credibility of a pair of witnesses can be attacked, under the conditions spelled out later in the Halakhah.

22 It seems that a text similar to Tosephta 6:4 is intended. That Tosephta states first that "One always may add judges until judgment is rendered." If after hearing the case, the arbitration panel is split, one judge voting for each side, but the third cannot decide how to vote, then each of the parties has to select an additional judge. In case of an evenly split court one always adds two new judges until a majority verdict is reached. After a lengthy discussion of the deadlines to be imposed for the presentation of witnesses, the Tosephta concludes: "Witnesses can always change their testimony before being cross-examined; after they were cross-examined they can no longer change their testimony; this is a matter of principle." R. Johanan holds that as long as witnesses may change their testimony, their credibility can be attacked.

23 If the other side's case depends on the testimony of one pair of witnesses, the other party has a monetary interest in seeing them disqualified. Therefore, the party to the dispute is barred from appearing as a witness against any of the witnesses since his testimony would be tainted (Babli 23b).

24 Ze`ira (in the Babli he is called *Ze`iri*) explains what it means that "a party to a suit may disqualify the other side's witness." He and another witness may appear before the permanent communal court as witnesses to ask for a judgment which will disqualify the witness for the other side. Even if the other side has alternative witnesses, one should disqualify the party as a tainted witness. He is admitted only because the opposing party, by presenting a multitude of witnesses, cast doubt on the reliability of their own witnesses.

25 Since *Deut.* 19:15 spells out that "a single witness is insufficient for any conviction," instead of saying that "a single witness is unacceptable," it follows that a single witness is acceptable for anything short of a conviction. In money matters this implies that a single witness to a claim can force a party to swear to dispute the claim (*Sifry Deut.* 188; Babli *Ketubot* 87b).

26 Only a permanent communal court is qualified to bar a person from being a witness, based on Mishnah 7.

27 A person can be an acceptable witness for anybody but his close relatives. This case of disability is a matter of showing facts; it does not need the formal proclamation of a court.

28 This has nothing to do with the Mishnah; it refers to the Tosephta quoted earlier, Note 22. As soon as a verdict is reached, one can no longer add judges. A verdict is rendered by three voting judges.

(fol. 20d) **משנה ד**: אָמַר לוֹ נֶאֱמָן עָלַי אַבָּא נֶאֱמָן עָלַי אָבִיךָ נֶאֱמָנִין עָלַי שְׁלֹשָׁה רוֹעֵי בָקָר רַבִּי מֵאִיר אוֹמֵר יָכוֹל לַחֲזוֹר בּוֹ. וַחֲכָמִים אוֹמְרִים אֵינוֹ יָכוֹל לַחֲזוֹר בּוֹ.

Mishnah 4: If somebody said, I am accepting my father; I am accepting your father[29]; I am accepting three cowboys[30]; Rebbi Meïr says, he may change his opinion, but the Sages say, he may not change his opinion.

29 These are disqualified by biblical law to serve as judges. They may be accepted on an arbitration panel as free choice of the parties.

30 They are illiterate and ignorant of the law.

(21 a line 30) **הלכה ד**: נֶאֱמָן עָלַי אַבָּא כול'. אָמַר לוֹ. נֶאֱמָן עָלַי אָבִיךָ. קִיבֵּל עָלָיו בִּפְנֵי שְׁנַיִם יָכוֹל הוּא לַחֲזוֹר בּוֹ. בִּפְנֵי שְׁלֹשָׁה אֵין יָכוֹל לַחֲזוֹר בּוֹ. שְׁמוּאֵל אָמַר. בְּשֶׁלֹּא נָטַל מִזֶּה וְנָתַן לָזֶה. אֲבָל נָטַל מִזֶּה וְנָתַן לָזֶה יָכוֹל הוּא לַחֲזוֹר בּוֹ. רִבִּי יוֹחָנָן וְרֵישׁ לָקִישׁ אָמְרֵי. אֲפִילוּ נָטַל מִזֶּה וְנָתַן לָזֶה יָכוֹל הוּא לַחֲזוֹר בּוֹ. קִיטה במקטיה דִּנְקוֹם. קִיבֵּל עֲלוֹי יָכוֹל לַחֲזוֹר בּוֹ.

Halakhah 4: "I am accepting my father," etc. If somebody said, I am accepting your father, [31]if he accepted in the presence of two others, he may retract[32]; in the presence of three[33], he may not retract. Samuel said, as long as he did not take from one and give to the other[35]; but if he took from one and gave to the other, he may retract. Rebbi Joḥanan and Rebbi Simeon ben Laqish say even if he took from one and gave to the other, he may retract[36]. [37]"If he hit him with a mace that he should agree; if he accepted he may renege."

31 The discussion is based on R. Meïr's point of view.

32 This is an agreement which according to R. Meïr can be rescinded.

33 If these three are persons qualified to act as judges, they act as a court and once a panel of arbitration is empanelled by a court it cannot be changed.

34 I. e., as long as judgment was not rendered.

35 The context requires that one read: "but if he took from one and gave to the other, he may *not* retract." This is Samuel's opinion in the Babli, 24b.

36 Their opinion is not mentioned in the Babli.

37 This sentence is corrupt, and probably belongs to the next Halakhah.

A similar text is in Tosephta 5:1: "If somebody became obligated to swear and the other party instead required him to make a vow for his life, or by קייטא ובמקייטא דנקיטי R. Meïr and the Sages disagree whether he may retract his agreement." D. Pardo declares the Tosephta text as unintelligible. *Arukh s.v.* קטו points to *Thr. r.* 1(30) *ad* 1:3 where קטו or קטיתא means "a bat". This would give as meaning of the Tosephta: "be exposed to *the mace and the bat* in my hands." The explanations in the standard commentaries are pure conjectures.

(fol. 20d) **משנה ה**: הָיָה חַיָּב לַחֲבֵרוֹ שְׁבוּעָה וְאוֹמֵר לוֹ דּוֹר לִי בְּחַיֵּי רֹאשָׁךְ רַבִּי מֵאִיר אוֹמֵר יָכוֹל לַחֲזוֹר בּוֹ. וַחֲכָמִים אוֹמְרִים אֵינוֹ יָכוֹל לַחֲזוֹר בּוֹ:

Mishnah 5: If one was obligated to swear to another, who asked him to make a vow "by his life"[38], Rebbi Meïr says, he may change his opinion[39], but the Sages say, he may not change his opinion.

38 He asked him to replace the oath by a vow not subject to dissolution. The claimant was afraid to be guilty of "putting a stumbling stone in the path of a blind man" if the other party was making a false oath because of him.

39 And require a formal oath.

(21a line 35) **הלכה ה**: הָיָה חַיָּב לַחֲבֵרוֹ שְׁבוּעָה כול'. רִבִּי חִייָה בַּר בָּא אָמַר. בְּשֶׁאָמַר לוֹ. יֹאמַר לִי אָבִיךָ וְאֵין לִי עִמָּךְ עֵסֶק. אֲבָל אִם אָמַר לוֹ. יֹאמַר אָבִיךָ וַאֲנִי מְקַבֵּל עָלַי. עִילָּא הָיָה רוֹצֶה לְהוֹדוֹת לוֹ. רִבִּי יוֹסֵי בֶּן חֲנִינָה אָמַר. וַאֲפִילוּ אָמַר לוֹ. יֹאמַר לִי אָבִיךָ וַאֲנִי מְקַבֵּל עָלַי. לֹא מָצִינוּ עֵדוּת יוֹצֵא מִפִּי קָרוֹב.

Halakhah 5: "If one was obligated to swear to another," etc. [40]Rebbi Ḥiyya bar Abba said, if he told him, let your father tell it to me, then I shall have no claim on you[41]. But if he told him: Let you father tell it, then I shall accept it; he seeks a pretext to confess to him[42]. Rebbi Yose ben Ḥanina said, even if he told him, let you father tell it to me, then I shall accept it. We never find that testimony be accepted from the mouth of a relative[43].

40 This paragraph refers to Mishnah 4.

41 The claimant tells the defendant that if the defendant's father states that his son owes nothing, he will retract his suit. R. Meïr lets him change his mind.

42 The defendant tells the claimant that if the claimant's father states that the sum is due to his son, the defendant will pay. R. Ḥiyya sees this as a confession cloaked in a face-saving device; R. Meïr will agree with the Sages that this is irrevocable.

43 While R. Ḥiyya bar Abba's argument may be correct, his conclusion is not, since as a matter of principle we never accept a relative's testimony to be determining in law.

(fol. 20d) **משנה ו**: אֵילּוּ הֵן הַפְּסוּלִין הַמְשַׂחֵק בְּקוּבְיָא וְהַמַּלְוֶה בְרִבִּית וּמַפְרִיחֵי יוֹנִים וְסוֹחֲרֵי שְׁבִיעִית וַעֲבָדִים. אָמַר רַבִּי שִׁמְעוֹן מִתְּחִלָּה לֹא הָיוּ קוֹרִין אוֹתָן אֶלָּא אוֹסְפֵי שְׁבִיעִית. מִשֶּׁרַבּוּ

הָאַנָּסִין חָזְרוּ לִקְרוֹתָן סוֹחֲרֵי שְׁבִיעִית. אָמַר רַבִּי יְהוּדָה אֵימָתַי. בִּזְמַן שֶׁאֵין לָהֶם אוּמָּנוּת אֶלָּא הִיא אֲבָל יֵשׁ לָהֶן אוּמָּנוּת שֶׁלֹּא הִיא הֲרֵי זֶה כָּשֵׁר:

Mishnah 6: The following are disqualified: The dice-player[44], the lender on interest[45], participants in pigeon contests[46], dealers in sabbatical produce[47], and slaves[48]. Rebbi Simeon said, earlier they were listing harvesters of sabbatical produce; but since the increase of oppressors they returned to list only dealers in sabbatical produce[49]. Rebbi Jehudah said, when? If he has no profession but this; but if he has another profession, he is qualified[50].

44 Since the player with honest dice will lose as often as he wins, he cannot possibly live off the income from his wagers. A gambler living off his gambling by necessity must be dishonest.

45 The lender on interest to Jews shows that he is willing to break the law for monetary gain; he will be willing to commit perjury for a fee.

46 Or any sport where money is made by betting.

47 He is willing to break the law for monetary gain.

48 Since a slave has no *persona* in law, he could commit perjury with impunity.

49 Biblical law requires that the produce of fields in a Sabbatical year be abandoned, available to anybody. Therefore, originally the owner of a field who harvested the field for his own use was branded as a scofflaw disqualified as witness or judge. But when Palestine was turned into a Roman province and, after the war of Bar Kokhba, the *annona*, contribution of produce, was imposed yearly, it was necessary to permit harvesting in the Sabbatical year in order to deliver the *annona* and prevent confiscation of the land by the government. Therefore, only actual trade in sabbatical produce was sinful, not harvesting.

50 An occasional gambler and occasional trader in sabbatical produce are qualified.

(21a line 40) **הלכה ו**: אֵילּוּ הֵן הַפְּסוּלִין. הַמְשַׂחֵק בַּקּוּבְיָא כול'. הַמְשַׂחֵק בַּקּוּבְיָא זֶה הַמְשַׂחֵק בִּפְסֵיפָסִין. אֶחָד הַמְשַׂחֵק בִּפְשֵׁיפָשִׁין וְאֶחָד הַמְשַׂחֵק בִּקְלִיפֵּי אֱגוֹזִין וְרִימּוֹנִים לְעוֹלָם אֵין מְקַבְּלִין אוֹתָן עַד שֶׁיְּשַׁבֵּר פְּסֵיפָסָיו אוֹ יִקְרַע שְׁטָרוֹתָיו וְיִבָּדֵק וְיַחְזְרוּ בָהֶן חֲזָרָה גְמוּרָה.

Halakhah 6: "The following are disqualified: The dice-player," etc. [51]The dice player is the one who plays with small stones[52]. [53]"Not only the player with stones, even one who plays with shells of nuts or pomegranates is not accepted unless he break his stones or tear up his IOU's[54], and be checked out and repent in complete repentance."

51 Parallels to the first part of this Halakhah are found in *Roš Haššanah* 1:9 and *Ševuot* 7:4.

52 Greek ψῆφος "pebble, cube; the stones used for mosaics and tokens used in elections." Rashi defines as "marbles".

53 Similar texts are in the Babli 25b, Tosephta 5:2.

54 This should be part of a separate sentence, as in the parallel Yerushalmi texts, Babli, and Tosephta.

The lender on interest cannot repent unless he tear up his IOU's and repent in complete repentance.

(21a line 44) וּמַפְרִיחֵי יוֹנִים. אֶחָד הַמַּמְרֶה יוֹנִים וְאֶחָד הַמַּמְרֶה שְׁאָר בְּהֵמָה חַיָּה וָעוֹף אֵין מְקַבְּלִין אוֹתָן עַד שֶׁיְּשַׁבְּרוּ פְּגִימָיו וְיַחְזְרוּ בָהֶן חֲזָרָה גְמוּרָה.

"Participants in pigeon contests.[55]" [53]Whether one bets on pigeons or bets on any other domesticated animal, wild animal, or bird, he is not accepted unless he break his tools of the catch and repent in complete repentance.

סוֹחֲרֵי שְׁבִיעִית. אֵי זֶהוּ תַּגָּר שְׁבִיעִית. זֶה שֶׁיּוֹשֵׁב וּבָטֵל כָּל־שְׁנֵי שָׁבוּעַ. כֵּיוָן שֶׁבָּא שְׁבִיעִית הִתְחִיל מְפַשֵּׁט יָדָיו וְנוֹשֵׂא וְנוֹתֵן בְּפֵירוֹת שְׁבִיעִית. וּלְעוֹלָם אֵין מְקַבְּלִין אוֹתָן עַד שֶׁתַּגִּיעַ שְׁבִיעִית אַחֶרֶת וְיִבָּדֵק וְיַחְזוֹר בּוֹ חֲזָרָה גְמוּרָה. תַּנֵּי. רִבִּי יוֹסֵי אוֹמֵר. שְׁתֵּי שְׁבִיעִיּוֹת. רִבִּי נְחֶמְיָה אוֹמֵר. חֲזָרַת מָמוֹן לֹא חֲזָרַת דְּבָרִים. שֶׁיֹּאמַר לָהֶם. הֵא לָכֶם ר' זוּז וְחִלְּקוּם לָעֲנִיִּים מַה שֶּׁכָּנַסְתִּי מִפֵּירוֹת עֲבֵירָה. הוֹסִיפוּ עֲלֵיהֶן הָרוֹעִין וְהַחַמְסָנִין וְהַגַּזְלָנִין וְכָל־הַחֲשׁוּדִין עַל הַמָּמוֹן עֵדוּתָן בְּטֵילָה. אָמַר רִבִּי אַבָּהוּ. וּבִלְבַד בְּרוֹעִין בְּהֵמָה דַקָּה.

"Dealers in sabbatical produce." [53]"Who is a dealer in sabbatical produce? One who sits idle all the years of a sabbatical cycle. As soon as the sabbatical year starts, be becomes active and trades in sabbatical produce. One does not accept them before another sabbatical year starts and he can be checked out that he repented in complete repentance." It was stated: Rebbi Yose says, two sabbatical periods. [56]"Rebbi Nehemiah says, repentance in money, not repentance in words; that he say to them, here are 200 denars, distribute them to the poor, for I earned them from forbidden produce." [57]They added shepherds, extortionists, and any who are suspect in money matters, that their testimony be invalid. Rebbi Abbahu said, only shepherds of small animals[58].

55 The parallel sources show that there is a sentence missing here: "This is one who bets on pigeons." Organizing pigeon contests is not dishonest, but making a living by betting on animal contests would be impossible for honest betters.

56 Tosephta 5:2.

57 A similar text in the Babli, 25b.

58 Sheep and goats which are destructive of vegetation in agricultural areas. Herders of sheep and goats are acceptable only in regions devoid of agriculture. The Babli notes that robbers and other felons are excluded by biblical law (*Ex.* 23:2). It concludes that Mishnah and *baraitot* refer to actions classified as extortion or robbery only by rabbinical standards.

(21a line 54) אָמַר רַב הוּנָא. מָאן תַּנָּא מַפְרִיחֵי יוֹנִים. רִבִּי לִיעֶזֶר. דְּתַנִּינָן תַּמָּן. מַפְרִיחֵי יוֹנִים פְּסוּלִין מִן הָעֵדוּת. אָמַר רִבִּי מָנָא קוֹמֵי רִבִּי יוֹסֵי. עוֹד הָדָא דְסַנְהֶדְרִי כְּרִבִּי לִיעֶזֶר. אָמַר לֵיהּ. דִּבְרֵי הַכֹּל הִיא. הָכָא אָמַר רִבִּי יוֹסֵי. יוֹדְעִין הָיִינוּ שֶׁפָּסוּל מֵעֵדוּת מָמוֹן. מַה בָא לְהָעִיד. אֶלָּא כְשֵׁם שֶׁפָּסוּל מֵעֵדוּת מָמוֹן כָּךְ פָּסוּל מֵעֵדוּת נְפָשׁוֹת. וְעֵידֵי הַחוֹדֶשׁ כְּעֵידֵי נְפָשׁוֹת אִינּוּן. דְּתַנִּינָן. זֶה הַכְּלָל. כָּל־עֵדוּת שֶׁאֵין אִשָּׁה כְשֵׁירָה לָהֶן אַף הֵן אֵינָן כְּשֵׁירִין לָהּ. מָאן תַּנִּיתָהּ. רַבָּנִין. רַבָּנִין כְּרִבִּי לְעֶזֶר. מוֹדִין לֵיהּ וּפְלִיגִין עֲלוֹהִי. רִבִּי הוּנָא בְשֵׁם רַב הוּנָא אָמַר. כּוּלָּהּ כְּרִבִּי לְעֶזֶר. וְאַתְיָיא אִילֵּין פְּלוּגְתָא כְאִילֵּין פְּלוּגְתָא. דְּתַנֵּי. עֵד זוֹמֵם פָּסוּל מִכָּל־עֵדִיּוֹת שֶׁבַּתּוֹרָה. דִּבְרֵי רִבִּי מֵאִיר. אָמַר רִבִּי יוֹסֵי. בַּמֶּה דְבָרִים אֲמוּרִים. בִּזְמַן שֶׁנִּמְצָא זוֹמֵם בְּעֵדוּת נְפָשׁוֹת. אֲבָל אִם נִמְצָא זוֹמֵם בְּעֵדוּת מָמוֹן אֵין פָּסוּל אֶלָּא מֵאוֹתָהּ עֵדוּת בִּלְבַד. וַתְיָיא דְּרִבִּי יוֹסֵי כְרַבָּנִין וּדְרִבִּי מֵאִיר כְּרִבִּי לְעֶזֶר.

Rav Huna said: Who is the Tanna of "participants in pigeon contests"? Rebbi Eliezer, as we have stated there[59]: "Participants in pigeon contests are disqualified from testimony." Rebbi Mana said before Rebbi Yose: Is that statement in *Sanhedrin* Rebbi Eliezer's[60]? He told him, it is everybody's opinion. [61]So said Rebbi Yose: We knew that he was disqualified for testimony in money matters. What does he[62] come to testify about? For as he is disqualified in money matters, so he is disqualified to testify in criminal trials. The witnesses for the New Moon are held to the standards of criminal trials, as we have stated[63]: "This is the principle: Any testimony for which a woman is not qualified, they[64] are not qualified for." Who stated this? The rabbis[65]! Do the rabbis follow Rebbi Eliezer? They agree with him and disagree with him. Rebbi Huna[66] in the name of Rav Huna said: It follows Rebbi Eliezer in everything. It turns out that this disagreement[67] parallels another disagreement, as it was stated[68]: A perjured witness is disqualified for any and all testimony required by the Torah, the words of Rebbi Meïr. Rebbi Yose said, when has this been said? When he was found perjured in criminal matters. But if he was found perjured in money matters, he is disqualified only from that particular testimony. It turns out that Rebbi Yose parallels the rabbis and Rebbi Meïr Rebbi Eliezer.

59 Mishnah *Idiut* 2:7, formulated as testimony in R. Aqiba's court in the name of R. Eliezer.

60 If this represents a minority opinion, it should have been labelled as such.

61 There is a sentence missing here. found in *Roš Haššanah*: What is meant by "it is everybody's opinion? That is what R. Yose meant to say:". It makes clear that one refers to the statement of the Amora R. Yose. The entire discussion does not refer to the Mishnah in *Sanhedrin* but the one in *Roš Haššanah*. The text in *Roš Haššanah* has to be considered as the original.

62 The witnesses mentioned in the Mishnah *Roš Haššanah*.

63 Mishnah *Roš Haššanah* 1:10.

64 The people disqualified in Mishnah *Sanhedrin* 3:6.

65 In the anonymous Mishnah.

66 In *Roš Haššanah*: R. Jonah. In *Ševuot*: R. Huna.

67 R. Eliezer and the rabbis, R. Meïr and R. Yose (the Tanna).

68 *Tosephta Makkot* 1:11, in the name of R. Jehudah (student of R. Eliezer's student.)

(21a line 67) רִבִּי שִׁמְעוֹן אוֹמֵר. מִתְּחִילָּה לֹא הָיוּ קוֹרִין אוֹתָן אֶלָּא אוֹסְפֵי שְׁבִיעִית. מִשֶּׁרַבּוּ הָאַנָּסִין חָזְרוּ לִקְרוֹתָן סוֹחֲרֵי שְׁבִיעִית. אָמַר רִבִּי יוּדָן. אֵימָתַי. בִּזְמַן שֶׁאֵין לָהֶן אֶלָּא הִיא. אֲבָל יֵשׁ לוֹ אוּמָנוּת שֶׁלֹּא הִיא הֲרֵי זֶה כָשֵׁר׃ הֵיךְ עֲבִידָא. יוֹשֵׁב וּבָטֵל כָּל־שְׁנֵי שָׁבוּעַ. כֵּיוָן שֶׁבָּאת שְׁבִיעִית הִתְחִיל פּוֹשֵׁט אֶת יָדָיו וְנוֹשֵׂא וְנוֹתֵן בְּפֵירוֹת שְׁבִיעִית. אִם יֵשׁ עִמּוֹ מְלָאכָה אַחֶרֶת כָּשֵׁר. וְאִם לָאו פָּסוּל. אֲבָל אִם הָיָה עָסוּק בִּמְלַאכְתּוֹ כָּל־שְׁנֵי שָׁבוּעַ כֵּיוָן שֶׁבָּאת שְׁבִיעִית הִתְחִיל מְפַשֵּׁט אֶת יָדָיו וְנוֹשֵׂא וְנוֹתֵן בְּפֵירוֹת שְׁבִיעִית אַף עַל פִּי שֶׁאֵין עִמּוֹ מְלָאכָה אַחֶרֶת כָּשֵׁר. רִבִּי בָּא בַּר זַבְדָּא רִבִּי אַבָּהוּ בְשֵׁם רִבִּי לָעְזָר. הֲלָכָה כְּרִבִּי יְהוּדָה דְמַתְנִיתִין. אִיקְלַס רִבִּי בָּא בַּר זַבְדָּא דָּמַר שְׁמוּעָה מִשּׁוּם דִּזְעִיר מִינֵּיהּ.

תַּנֵּי רִבִּי חִיָּיה לְחוּמְרָא. הֵיךְ עֲבִידָא. יוֹשֵׁב וְעוֹסֵק בִּמְלַאכְתּוֹ כָּל־שְׁנֵי שָׁבוּעַ. כֵּיוָן שֶׁבָּאת שְׁבִיעִית הִתְחִיל מְפַשֵּׁיט אֶת יָדָיו וְנוֹשֵׂא וְנוֹתֵן בְּפֵירוֹת שְׁבִיעִית. אַף עַל פִּי שֶׁיֵּשׁ עִמּוֹ מְלָאכָה אַחֶרֶת פָּסוּל. לֹא בְדָא רִבִּי בָּא בַּר זַבְדָּא רִבִּי אַבָּהוּ בְשֵׁם רִבִּי לָעְזָר. הֲלָכָה כְּרִבִּי יְהוּדָה דְמַתְנִיתִין. תַּמָּן רִבִּי בָּא בַּר זַבְדָּא דָּמַר שְׁמוּעָה מִשּׁוּם זְעִיר מִינֵּיהּ. אוּף הָכָא כֵן. אָמַר רִבִּי יוֹסֵי בֵּירִבִּי בוּן. תַּמָּן אֵין מַלְכוּת אוֹנֶסֶת. בְּרַם הָכָא הַמַּלְכוּת אוֹנֶסֶת.

[69]"Rebbi Simeon says, earlier they were listing harvesters of sabbatical produce; but since the increase of oppressors they returned to list only dealers in sabbatical produce. Rebbi Jehudah said, when? If he has no profession but this; but if he has another profession, he is qualified." How is this implemented? If he was sitting idle all the years of the sabbatical cycle but

when the Sabbatical began he became active and traded in sabbatical produce. If at the same time he is engaged in another occupation, he is qualified; otherwise he is disqualified. But if he was working in his profession all the years of the sabbatical cycle and when the Sabbatical began he became active and traded in sabbatical produce, even if he has no other profession on the side he is qualified. Rebbi Abba bar Zavda, Rebbi Abbahu in the name of Rebbi Eleazar: Practice follows Rebbi Jehudah[70] of our Mishnah. Rebbi Abba bar Zavda was praised for formulating the tradition in the name of a person younger than himself.

Rebbi Ḥiyya stated restrictively. How is this implemented? If he was working in his profession all the years of the sabbatical cycle but when the Sabbatical began he became active and traded in sabbatical produce. Even if he has another profession on the side he is disqualified. This is not what Rebbi Abba bar Zavda, Rebbi Abbahu said in the name of Rebbi Eleazar: Practice follows Rebbi Jehudah of our Mishnah. Rebbi Abba bar Zavda was praised for formulating the tradition in the name of a person younger than himself. Here also should it be so? Rebbi Yose ben Rebbi Abun said, there the government is not oppressive, here the government is oppressive.

(21b line 6) בָּרִאשׁוֹנָה כְּשֶׁהָיְתָה הַמַּלְכוּת אוֹנֶסֶת הוֹרֵי רִבִּי יַנַּאי שֶׁיְּהוּ חוֹרְשִׁים חֲרִישָׁה הָרִאשׁוֹנָה. חַד מְשׁוּמָּד הֲוָה אִיעֲבַר .שְׁמִיעֲתָא. חֲמְתוֹן רַמְייָן קוֹבְעֲתֵיהּ. אֲמַר לוֹן. הַסְטוּ. שָׁרָא מררא.[71] שָׁרָא לְכוֹן מִרְמָא קוֹבָעַת.

When the government was oppressing the first time, Rebbi Yannai instructed to plough a single ploughing[72]. An apostate was passing by; he saw the putting up of the harrow. He said to them, hey you! Is it permitted for you to plough? Is it permitted for you to put up the harrow?

(21b line 9) אָמַר רִבִּי יַעֲקֹב בַּר זַבְדִּי. קִשְׁיתָהּ קוֹמֵי רִבִּי אַבָּהוּ. לֹא כֵן אָמַר זְעִירָא וְרִבִּי יוֹחָנָן בְּשֵׁם רִבִּי יַנַּאי רִבִּי יִרְמְיָה רִבִּי יוֹחָנָן בְּשֵׁם רִבִּי שִׁמְעוֹן בֶּן יְהוֹצָדָק. נִמְנוּ בַּעֲלִיַּת בֵּית נִתְזָה בְלוֹד. עַל הַתּוֹרָה מְנַיִין. אִם אָמַר גּוֹי לְיִשְׂרָאֵל לַעֲבוֹר עַל אַחַת מִכָּל־מִצְוֹת הָאֲמוּרוֹת בַּתּוֹרָה חוּץ מֵעֲבוֹדָה זָרָה וְגִילּוּי עֲרָיוֹת וּשְׁפִיכוּת דָּמִים יַעֲבוֹר וְאַל יֵיהָרֵג. הָדָא דְתֵימַר בֵּינוֹ לְבֵין עַצְמוֹ. אֲבָל בְּרַבִּים אֲפִילוּ עַל מִצְוָה קַלָּה אַל יִשְׁמַע לוֹ. כְּגוֹן פַּפּוֹס וְלוּלְייָנוּס אָחִיו שֶׁנָּתְנוּ לָהֶן מַיִם בִּכְלִי זְכוּכִית צְבוּעָה וְלֹא קִיבְּלוּ מֵהֶן. אָמַר. לֹא אִיתְכַּוֵּון מְשַׁמְּדְהוֹן אֶלָּא מַגְבֵּי אַרְנוֹנִין. כַּמָּה הֵן רַבִּים. רַבָּנִן דְּקַיְסָרִין אָמְרִין. עֲשָׂרָה. דִּכְתִיב וְנִקְדַּשְׁתִּי בְּתוֹךְ בְּנֵי יִשְׂרָאֵל.

Rebbi Jacob bar Zavdi said, I asked before Rebbi Abbahu: Did not [Rebbi] Ze`ira and Rebbi Johanan in the name of Rebbi Yannai, Rebbi Jeremiah, Rebbi Johanan in the name of Rebbi Simeon ben Yehosadaq, say that they voted on the upper floor of the Nitzah house in Lydda: About all the Torah, if a Gentile tells a Jew to transgress any commandment of the Torah except those concerning idolatry, incest and adultery, and murder, he should transgress and not be killed[73]. That is in private, but in public he should not follow him even for the slightest commandment, as exemplified by Pappos and his brother Julianus to whom they gave water in a colored glass and they did not accept.

He said, they do not intend to lead you to apostasy, they only want to collect *annona*.

What means "in public"? The rabbis of Caesarea say ten, as it is written[74]: *I shall be sanctified in the midst of the Children of Israel.*

(21b line 17) רִבִּי בִּינָא זְעִירָא חֲמוּנֵיהּ פָּרֵי חוֹרֵי חֲמָרָא בְּשַׁבָּתָא. רִבִּי יוֹנָה וְרִבִּי יוֹסֵי הוֹרוֹן מֵיפֵי לְאֻרְטְקִינָס בְּשׁוּבְתָא. אָמַר רִבִּי מָנִי. קַשִּׁיתָהּ קוֹמֵי רִבִּי יוֹנָה אַבָּא. לֹא כֵן אָמַר רִבִּי זְעִירָא רִבִּי יוֹחָנָן בְּשֵׁם רִבִּי יַנַּאי רִבִּי יִרְמְיָה רִבִּי יוֹחָנָן בְּשֵׁם רִבִּי שִׁמְעוֹן בֶּן יְהוֹצָדָק. נִמְנוּ בַּעֲלִיַּית בֵּית נִתְזָה בְלוֹד וְכול'. לֹא אִיתְכַּוֵּון מְשַׁמְּדָתְהוֹן אֶלָּא אִיתְכַּוֵּון מֵיכוֹל פִּיתָּא חֲמִימָא. כַּמָּה הֵן רַבִּים. רַבָּנָן דְּקַיְסָרִין אָמְרֵי. עֲשָׂרָה. דִּכְתִיב וְנִקְדַּשְׁתִּי בְּתוֹךְ בְּנֵי יִשְׂרָאֵל.

They saw the young Rebbi Bina collecting donkey's dung on the Sabbath. Rebbi Jonah and Rebbi Yose permitted baking for Ursicinus on the Sabbath. Rebbi Mana said, I asked before my father Rebbi Jonah, did not Rebbi Ze`ira and Rebbi Johanan in the name of Rebbi Yannai, Rebbi Jeremiah, Rebbi Johanan in the name of Rebbi Simeon ben Yehosadaq, say that they voted on the upper floor of the Nitzah house in Lydda, etc.? He said, he did not intend to lead you to apostasy, he only wanted to eat warm bread..

What means "in public"? The rabbis of Caesarea say ten, as it is written[74]: *I shall be sanctified in the midst of the Children of Israel.*

(21b line 23) רִבִּי אַבִּינָא בְּעָא רִבִּי אִמִּי. גּוֹיִם מָהוּ שֶׁיְּהוּ מְצוּוִּין עַל קִידּוּשׁ הַשֵּׁם. אָמַר לֵיהּ וְנִקְדַּשְׁתִּי בְּתוֹךְ בְּנֵי יִשְׂרָאֵל. יִשְׂרָאֵל מְצוּוִּין עַל קִידּוּשׁ הַשֵּׁם וְאֵין הַ גּוֹיִם מְצוּוִּין עַל קִידּוּשׁ הַשֵּׁם. רִבִּי נִיסִי בְּשֵׁם רִבִּי לָעְזָר שָׁמַע לָהּ מֵהָדָא. לַדָּבָר הַזֶּה יִסְלַח יי לְעַבְדֶּךָ וגו'. יִשְׂרָאֵל מְצוּוִּין עַל קִידּוּשׁ הַשֵּׁם וְאֵין הַגּוֹיִם מְצוּוִּין עַל קִידּוּשׁ הַשֵּׁם.

Rebbi Abinna asked Rebbi Immi: Are Gentiles required to sanctify the Name? He answered him: *I shall be sanctified in the midst of the Children of Israel.* Israel are required to sanctify the Name; the Gentiles are not required to sanctify the Name. Rebbi Nissai in the name of Rebbi Eleazar understood it from the following: *May the Eternal forgive His servant for this*, etc. Israel are required to sanctify the Name; the Gentiles are not required to sanctify the Name.

(21b line 28) רִבִּי בָּא בַּר זְמִינָא הֲוָה מְחַיֵּט גַּבֵּי חַד בַּר נַשׁ בְּרוֹמֵי. אַיְיתֵי לֵיהּ בְּשַׂר נְבֵילָה. אֲמַר לֵיהּ. אֲכוֹל. אֲמַר לֵיהּ. לֵי נָא אֲכִיל. אֲמַר לֵיהּ. אֲכוֹל דִּילָא כֵן אֲנָא קְטִיל לָךְ. אֲמַר לֵיהּ אִין בְּעִית מִיקְטוֹל קְטוֹל דְּלֵי נָא אֲכִיל בְּשַׂר נְבֵילָה. אֲמַר לֵיהּ. מָאן מוֹדַע לָךְ דְּאִילּוּ אֲכָלְתָּהּ הֲוֵינָא קָטְלִין לָךְ. אוֹ יְהוּדִי יְהוּדִי אוֹ אֲרָמַאי אֲרָמַאי. אָמַר רִבִּי מָנָא. אִילּוּ הֲוָה רִבִּי בָּא בַּר זְמִינָא שָׁמַע מִילֵּיהוֹן דְּרַבָּנִין מֵיזַל הֲוָה בְהָדָא.

Rebbi Abba bar Zemina was working as a tailor for somebody in Rome. He brought him carcass meat and told him to eat. He said to him, I will not eat. He said to him, eat! Otherwise I shall kill you. He said to him, if you have to kill, kill, for I shall not eat carcass meat. He said to him, certainly you should know that I would have killed you, had you eaten. Either one is a Jewish Jew or an Aramean Aramean. Rebbi Mana said, if Rebbi Abba bar Zemina had understood the words of the rabbis, he would have been gone.

69 This and the following paragraphs are from *Ševi`it* 4:2, Notes 20-34. A few passages are reformulated.

70 Babli 26b.

71 Read with the *Ševi`it* text מְרַדֵּי "to plough".

72 Babli 26a. This dates the change in Roman taxation policy to the end of the Severan dynasty. For הסטו cf. *Ševi`it* 4:3, Note 23.

73 Babli 74a.

74 *Lev.* 22:32.

75 *2K.* 5:18.

(21b line 34) טִייֵב בִּזְמַן זֶה מָהוּ. רִבִּי יִרְמְיָה סְבַר מֵימַר. בָּטֵל הַדִּין בְּטֵילָה גְזֵירְתָא. רִבִּי יוֹסֵי סְבַר מֵימַר. לְעוֹלָם הַגְּזֵירָה בִמְקוֹמָהּ עַד שֶׁיַּעֲמוֹד בֵּית דִּין אַחֵר וִיבַטְּלָהּ. וְדִכְווָתָהּ. מֵאֵימָתַי אָדָם זוֹכֶה לְפֵירוֹתָיו בַּשְּׁבִיעִית. רִבִּי יִרְמְיָה סְבַר מֵימַר. מִשֶּׁיִּתְּנֵם לְתוֹךְ כֵּילָיו. רִבִּי יוֹסֵי סְבַר מֵימַר. אֲפִילוּ נְתוּנִין בְּתוֹךְ כֵּילָיו לֹא זָכָה. סְבַר דִּינּוּן דִּידֵיהּ וְלֵית אִינּוּן דִּידֵיהּ.

[76]If somebody improved [his field] today, what is the rule? Rebbi Jeremiah was of the opinion that when the reason disappeared, the ordinance

is void. Rebbi Yose was of the opinion that even if the reason disappeared, the ordinance stands until another court abolishes it.

[77]Similarly, how does an owner acquire his own produce in a Sabbatical year? Rebbi Jeremiah wanted to say, from the moment he put it into his vessel. Rebbi Yose was of the opinion that even if he put it into his vessel he did not acquire, for he thinks that it is his but it is not his.

76 The paragraph is a reformulation of one in *Ševi`it* 4:2, Notes 35-37. The prohibition to work after the Sabbatical a field which was improved in the Sabbatical is purely rabbinical.

77 *Ševi`it* 4:2, Note 43, *Ketubot* 9:3 Notes 109-110. The connection with the preceding is a leniency of R. Jeremiah opposed by R. Yose.

(21b line 38) רִבִּי מָנָא כַּד אָעַל פְּרוֹקְלָא בְּצִיפּוֹרִי הוֹרֵי מַפְקָא נַחְתּוֹמַיָּא בְשׁוּקָא. רַבָּנִין דִּנְוֶה הוֹרוּ מֵיפֵי חֲמִיעַ בְּפִסְחָא.

אָמַר רִבִּי יוֹסֵי בֵּירִבִּי בּוּן. אֲנִי֙ פִּי־מֶ֣לֶךְ שְׁמ֔וֹר. אֲנִי פִּי מֶלֶךְ מַלְכֵי הַמְּלָכִים אֶשְׁמוֹר. שֶׁאָמַר לִי בְּסִינַי אָֽנֹכִ֖י יי אֱלֹהֶ֑יךָ. וְעַ֕ל דִּבְרַ֖ת. לֹֽא־יִהְיֶ֥ה לְךָ֛ אֱלֹהִ֥ים אֲחֵרִ֖ים עַל־פָּנָֽיַ׃ שְׁבוּעַ֥ת אֱלֹהִֽים. לֹ֥א תִשָּׂ֛א אֶת־שֵׁם־יי אֱלֹהֶ֖יךָ לַשָּׁ֑וְא. בַּדָּבָר הַזֶּה נָבוֹא הַהוּא גַבְרָא וְהָהֵן כַּלְבָּא שְׁנֵיהֶן שָׁוִין.

רַב יְהוּדָה בְשֵׁם רַב. הֲלָכָה כְרִבִּי יְהוּדָה.

When Proclus[78] entered Sepphoris, Rebbi Mana instructed the bakers to present their wares in the market. The rabbis of Newe[79] instructed to bake leavened on Passover.

[80]Rebbi Yose ben Abun said: *I shall keep the King's sayings*[81], Who told me at Sinai *I am the Eternal, your God*[82], *on the pronouncement*[81], *you shall not have other gods before Me*[83], *of God's oath*[81], *do not take the Name of the Eternal, your God, in vain*[84]. In this matter we come together, this man[85] and this dog[86] are both equal.

Rav Jehudah in the name of Rav: Practice follows Rebbi Jehudah.

78 Grätz (Geschichte der Juden[3] p. 314) reads *Proculus* and identifies him as an officer of Ursicinus's army (under the emperor Gallus.)

79 Sometimes called *Niniveh*, a place *Nova* in the Golan.

80 The old Midrashim, *Lev. r.* 33:6, shorter *Cant. r. ad* 2:14, *Eccl. r. ad* 8:2 quote this in the name of the older R. Levy. Possibly there is no claim of originality asserted here for R. Yose ben R. Abun, three generations after R. Levy, but the sermon is

quoted as objection to the lenient rulings mentioned before.

81 *Eccl.* 8:2.

82 *Ex.* 20:2.

83 *Ex.* 20:3.

84 *Ex.* 20:7.

85 The speaker.

86 Nebuchadnezzar, who is said to have barked like a dog during his spell of insanity, *Lev. r.* 33(6).

(fol. 20d) **משנה ז** וְאֵילּוּ הֵן הַקְּרוֹבִין אָחִיו וַאֲחִי אָבִיו וַאֲחִי אִמּוֹ וּבַעַל אֲחוֹתוֹ וּבַעַל אֲחוֹת אָבִיו וּבַעַל אֲחוֹת אִמּוֹ וּבַעַל אִמּוֹ וְחָמִיו וַאֲגִיסוֹ הֵן וּבְנֵיהֶן וְחַתְנֵיהֶן וְחוֹרְגוֹ לְבַדּוֹ. אָמַר רַבִּי יוֹסֵי זוֹ מִשְׁנַת רַבִּי עֲקִיבָה. אֲבָל מִשְׁנָה רִאשׁוֹנָה דוֹדוֹ וּבֶן דּוֹדוֹ. וְכָל הָרָאוּי לְיוֹרְשׁוֹ וְכָל הַקָּרוֹב לוֹ בְּאוֹתָהּ שָׁעָה. הָיָה קָרוֹב וְנִתְרַחֵק הֲרֵי זֶה כָּשֵׁר. רַבִּי יְהוּדָה אוֹמֵר אֲפִלּוּ מֵתָה בִתּוֹ וְיֵשׁ לוֹ בָנִים מִמֶּנּוּ הֲרֵי זֶה קָרוֹב׃

Mishnah 7: The following are the relatives:[87] His brother, his father's brother and his mother's brother [88], his sister's husband, his father's sister's husband and his mother's sister's husband, his father-in-law, and his brother-in-law [89]; these, their sons and sons-in-law, but his steps[90] alone. Rebbi Yose said, this is Rebbi Aqiba's teaching; but the original Mishnah was: His uncle and his uncle's son[91], and anybody in line to inherit from him, and any related to him at that moment[92]. If he had been related but became unrelated, he is qualified. Rebbi Jehudah says, even if his daughter had died but he had children from him, he remains a relative[93].

87 Since women are barred from giving formal testimony, only the males are enumerated.

88 The father's brother is a relative; so is the father himself. He is mentioned in some Mishnah mss.

89 אֲגִיס is the Syriac form; the usual Babylonian is גִּיס. In Syriac the word denotes the wife's sister's husband. This is the meaning presumed in the Halakhah, but here it includes the wife's brother.

90 His wife's son from a previous marriage.

91 Quoted as relative *par excellence* in *Lev.* 25:29.

92 Any man married to a woman who is a possible heir (as defined in Mishnah *Bava batra* 8:1) is barred to act as witness. At the dissolution of the marriage, by death or divorce, the relationship is terminated.

93 Since the grandchildren are possible heirs, they are barred from being witnesses, and so is their father. This holds true even if the grandchildren all are female.

(21b line 40) **הלכה ז**: אֵילּוּ הֵן הַקְּרוֹבִין כול'. מִכֵּיוָן דְּתַנֵּינָן אָחִיו מַה צוֹרְכָה לְמִתְנֵי אֲחִי אָבִיו. לוֹמַר בְּנוֹ וַחֲתָנוֹ שֶׁל חָתָן.

אֲחִי אָבִיו. מִכֵּיוָן דְּתַנֵּינָן אֲחִי אָבִיו מַה צוֹרְכָה לְמִתְנֵי אֲחִי אִמּוֹ. לוֹמַר בְּנוֹ וַחֲתָנוֹ שֶׁל חָתָן.

אֲחִי אִמּוֹ. מִכֵּיוָן דְּתַנֵּינָן בַּעַל אֲחוֹתוֹ מַה צוֹרְכָה לְמִתְנֵי בַּעַל אֲחוֹת אָבִיו. . לוֹמַר בְּנוֹ וַחֲתָנוֹ שֶׁלְּחָתָן.

בַּעַל אֲחוֹת אָבִיו. מִכֵּיוָן דְּתַנֵּינָן בַּעַל אֲחוֹת אָבִיו. מַה צוֹרְכָה לְמִתְנֵי בַּעַל אֲחוֹת אִמּוֹ. לוֹמַר בְּנוֹ וַחֲתָנוֹ שֶׁלְּחָתָן.

בַּעַל אֲחוֹת אִמּוֹ. וְהָתַנֵּינָן חוֹרְגוֹ לְבַדּוֹ. רַב אָמַר. אִם חֲתַן חֲמוֹתוֹ אָסוּר בַּעַל חוֹרְגָתוֹ לֹא כָּל־שֶׁכֵּן. תִּיפְתָּר שֶׁיֵּשׁ לָהּ בָּנִים וַחֲתָנִים מִמֶּנּוּ.

אֲגִיסוֹ. אִית תַּנָּיֵי תַנֵּי. יֵשׁ לוֹ בָּנִים וַחֲתָנִים. וְאִית תַּנָּיֵי תַנֵּי. אֵין לוֹ בָּנִים וַחֲתָנִים. מָאן דָּמַר יֵשׁ לוֹ בָּנִים וַחֲתָנִים. מִמֶּנָּה. וּמָאן דָּמַר אֵין לוֹ בָּנִים וַחֲתָנִים. מִמָּקוֹם אַחֵר.

Halakhah 7: "The following are the relatives," etc. Since we have stated "his brother," why does one have to state "his father's brother"[94]? To include the son-in-law's son-in-law[95].

"His father's brother". Since we have stated "his father's brother," why does one have to state "his mother's brother"[96]? To include the son-in-law's son-in-law[97].

"His mother's brother". Since we have stated "his sister's husband," why does one have to state "his father's sister's husband"[98]? To include the son-in-law's son-in-law[97].

"His father's sister's husband". Since we have stated "his father's sister's husband," why does one have to state "his mother's sister's husband"? To include the son-in-law's son-in-law[99].

"His mother's sister's husband". But did we not state: "his stepson alone"[100]? Rav said, if his mother-in-law's son-in-law[101] is forbidden, then certainly his stepdaughter's husband[102]. Explain it that she has sons and sons-in-law from hum[103].

"His brother-in-law". Some Tannaïm state: Including sons and sons-in-law; but some Tannaïm state: Excluding sons and sons-in-law. He who said, including sons and sons-in law, from her[104]. But he who said, excluding sons and sons-in law, from another family[105].

94 Two unexpressed principles are underlying the discussion. The first is symmetry: If A is disqualified for B, then B is disqualified for A. The second one is that

for the definition of "relative", there is no difference between male and female.

[It has to be noted that for the definition of incestuous relations, both principles are accepted by Sadducees and rejected by Pharisees. The father's sister is biblically forbidden (*Lev.* 18:12); the brother's daughter, for whom the husband would be the father's brother, is biblically forbidden by Sadducees and Karaites, permitted (and recommended) by Pharisees and rabbinic Jews. The Midrash which asserts that Sarah was not Abraham's paternal half-sister but his niece (*Yebamot* 10:17 Note 210) is more an anti-Sadducee polemic than a genuine interpretation of the biblical text.]

Since the Mishnah states that sons and in-laws of disqualified relations are also disqualified, the mention of the brother implies that the nephew is also disqualified. But for the nephew, the original person is the father's brother; why does he have to be mentioned?

95 The Mishnah by implication disqualifies the cousin (or cousin's husband); this disqualification is not implied by the disqualification of the brother (Babli 28a).

96 In the Babli, 28a, the mention of the mother's brother is taken as proof of the second rule of Note 92. The same is implied here.

97 The same argument as before, to disqualify cousins from the mother's side.

98 This question presupposes that any person disqualified for A also is disqualified for A's son (Babli 28a). A's sister's husband is the father's sister's husband for A's son.

99 This probably is a scribal error, copied from the preceding paragraph. The only reasonable answer would be: to show that in matters of disqualification as witnesses, relations by females are the equivalent of relations by males.

100 Excluding the stepson's wife and his descendants and in-laws.

101 Husband of his father-in-law's stepdaughter.

102 Since it was established that females be treated like males in this matter, the status of the mother-in-law is that of the father-in-law, and her children and children-in-law also are disqualified. Let A be the person in question, W his wife, F, M, his father and mother, D the mother-in-law's daughter from another man, and H the daughter's husband. The relationship between A and H can be given by a diagram:

```
        F  -  M
        |  /  |
  A  -  W     D  -  H
```

On the other hand, the relationship between a man and his stepdaughter's husband can be described by

```
  A  -  W
        |
        D  -  H
```

This graph clearly is a subgraph of the preceding (up to labelling, replacing F,M by A,W). Therefore, if the first graph describes a disqualifying relationship, *a fortiori* the second also describes one.

103 Since the preceding argument leads to a result contradicting the Mishnah, the premiss of the argument is shown to be false. The only siblings of a person's wife disqualified as witnesses are her full or

paternal siblings. "She" in this sentence is the mother-in-law.

104 His wife's sister.

105 Another wife. In the Babli, 28b, there is a dispute whether "he alone" refers to the stepson or *any* brother-in-law.

(21b line 55) רַב נְפַק לְמיתרי משכין לְרִבִּי חִייָה רַבָּה. עֲבַר בְּחַד אֲתַר וְאַשְׁכַּח רִבִּי יוֹחָנָן יְתִיב וּמַקְשֵׁי. תַּנִּינָן. חוֹרְגוֹ לְבַדּוֹ. אֵשֶׁת חוֹרְגוֹ מָהוּ. בַּעַל חוֹרְגָתוֹ מָהוּ. אִשָּׁה כְבַעֲלָהּ וּבַעַל כְּאִשְׁתּוֹ. וְקָמַת אֵשֶׁת חוֹרְגוֹ כְחוֹרְגוֹ וְהַבַּעַל כְּאִשָּׁה.

רַב חִסְדָּא בָּעֵי. דּוֹר שְׁלִישִׁי מָהוּ שֶׁיְּהֵא מוּתָּר בְּאֵשֶׁת רִאשׁוֹן. מֹשֶׁה מָהוּ שֶׁיְּהֵא מוּתָּר בְּאֵשֶׁת פִּינְחָס. רֵישׁ לָקִישׁ אָמַר. מְקַבְּלִין דּוֹר שֵׁינִי וְדוֹר שְׁלִישִׁי מִדּוֹחַק. רִבִּי יוֹחָנָן אָמַר. אֲפִילוּ מֵרֵיוַח.

Rav went to sell hides[106] for the elder Rebbi Ḥiyya. He passed by a place where he found Rebbi Joḥanan sitting and asking: We have stated, "his stepson alone." What is the situation of his stepson's wife, his stepdaughter's husband? A woman is like her husband and the husband is like his wife[107]. Therefore, the situation of his stepson's wife is that of his stepson, and the husband is like his wife[108].

Rav Ḥisda asked: If the third generation permitted the first generation's wife[109]? Is Phineas's wife permitted to Moses[110]? Rebbi Simeon ben Laqish said, one accepts the second and third generations with difficulty[111]. Rebbi Joḥanan said, even with ease[112].

106 Text and meaning are in doubt. One might read מֵיתְרֵי מְשְׁכִין "to span hides"; this does not make much sense. *Nimmuqe Yosef* (Commentary to Alfasi, 6b in the Wilna ed.) reads נְפַק לְמַזְבַּן מַשְׁכּוֹן "went to sell a pledge". This agrees with the following possessive, לר' חייה. The parallel source in the Babli, 28a/b reads: רב איקלע למזבן גוילי "Rav happened to be selling parchment."

107 The Babli 28b treats the two statements as different; one does not necessarily imply the other.

108 A person is disqualified from being a witness for or against his stepson's wife or stepdaughter's husband, but not for or against the stepchild's children or children-in-law.

109 The brother's children are disqualified by the Mishnah. What about the grandchildren?

110 The question is formulated as one of permitted marriages. This does not fit the context, since that problem was discussed in *Yebamot* 2:4. With all commentators one has to read the question whether Moses be qualified to testify for the wife of Phineas, his brother's grandson.

111 A court will accept testimony from persons one generation removed from the Mishnaic disqualifications only if no other

witnesses are available.

112 Any testimony not disqualified by the Mishnah is qualified.

(21b line 61) כְּהָדָא אֲגִיסֵיהּ דְּרַב הוּנָא הֲוָה לֵיהּ דִּין עִם חַד בַּר נַשׁ. אֲמַר. כָּל־מַה דְּרַב הוּנָא אָמַר אֲנָא מְקַבֵּל עָלַי. שְׁמַע רַב הוּנָא וְאָמַר כְּהָדֵין. יוֹדְעֵנִי כְּשֵׁם שֶׁאָמְרוּ מִלְמַעְלָן כֵּן אָמְרוּ מִלְּמַטָּן. רַב יִרְמְיָה בְשֵׁם רַב. הֲלָכָה כְּרִבִּי יוּדָה.

[113]As the following: A brother-in-law[114] of Rav Huna's had a case with some person. He said, I am accepting anything which Rav Huna will decide[115]. Rav Huna heard it and said, this is it[116]. I know that just as they said for the preceding generations, so it is for the following[117]. Rav Jehudah in the name of Rav: Practice follows Rebbi Jehudah[118].

113 This refers to the last part of the Mishnah, the statement of R. Jehudah.

114 The husband of one of Rav Huna's sisters and one of the sisters had died. He had been a relative but now became unrelated.

115 Since Rav Huna was no longer a relative, he was qualified to be a judge.

116 The statement of the Mishnah.

117 The Mishnah refers to the relation between a person and his son-in-law, two different generations. Since R. Jehudah states that if there be grandchildren, the son-in-law remains related, it follows that the anonymous Tanna holds that in all cases the son-in-law becomes unrelated at the moment his marriage is dissolved by death or divorce.

118 This is also quoted in the Babli, 28b, as Rav's opinion. The school of Samuel, represented by Rav Nahman, holds that practice does not follow R. Jehudah. Rav Nahman's rulings have the status of Supreme Court decisions in Babylonia.

(fol. 20d) **משנה ח**: הָאוֹהֵב וְהַשּׂוֹנֵא. אוֹהֵב, זֶה שׁוּשְׁבִין. שׂוֹנֵא כֹּל שֶׁלֹּא דִבֵּר עִמּוֹ שְׁלֹשָׁה יָמִים בְּאֵיבָה. אָמְרוּ לוֹ לֹא נֶחְשְׁדוּ יִשְׂרָאֵל עַל כָּךְ:

Mishnah 8: [119]The lover and the hater[120]. The lover, that is the best man. The hater, anyone who did not talk to him for three days because of ill-will. They told him, Israel are not suspected of this[121].

(21b line 65) **הלכה ח**: הָאוֹהֵב וְהַשּׂוֹנֵא כול'. רִבִּי טֶבְלַיי רִבִּי אַבִּינָּא בְשֵׁם רַב. בְּשִׁבְעַת יְמֵי מִשְׁתֶּה שָׁנוּ.

Halakhah 8: "The lover and the hater," etc. Rebbi Tevelai, Rebbi Abinna in the name of Rav: They stated this for the seven days of wedding festivities[122].

119 The Mishnah is a continuation of R. Jehudah's statement.

120 Are disqualified as witnesses.

121 To testify falsely because of this. But a judge emotionally involved with one of the parties is disqualified (Babli 29a).

122 The best men are disqualified only during the festivities. Rav's opinion is quoted in the Babli, 29a, where a later authority restricts R. Jehudah's rule to the wedding day only.

(fol. 20d) **משנה ט**: כֵּיצַד בּוֹדְקִין אֶת הָעֵדִים. הָיוּ מַכְנִיסִין אוֹתָן וּמְאַיְּימִין עֲלֵיהֶן וּמוֹצִיאִין אוֹתָן לַחוּץ וּמְשַׁיְּירִין אֶת הַגָּדוֹל שֶׁבָּהֶן וְאוֹמֵר לוֹ אֱמוֹר הֵיאַךְ אַתָּה יוֹדֵעַ שֶׁזֶּה חַיָּב לָזֶה. אִם אָמַר הוּא אָמַר לִי שֶׁאֲנִי חַייָב לוֹ אִישׁ פְּלוֹנִי אָמַר לִי שֶׁהוּא חַייָב לוֹ לֹא אָמַר כְּלוּם עַד שֶׁיֹּאמַר בְּפָנֵינוּ הוֹדָה לוֹ שֶׁהוּא חַייָב לוֹ מָאתַיִם זוּז.

Mishnah 9: How does one check out the witnesses? One brings them to court and instills fear into them[123], then removes them[124] but retains the greatest among them[125]. One says to him, tell why you know that this person owes to the other one. If he said, he himself confessed to me that he owes the money[126], or another person told me that he owes it[127], he did not say anything until he says, before us[128] he confessed to him that he owed him 200 denar.

123 Since witnesses are not interrogated under oath, they have to be informed of the gravity of the crime of perjury.

124 This also is the reading of Alfasi and Rosh. Maimonides and the Venice text of the Babli read: One removes everybody.

125 The witnesses are interrogated separately.

126 He might have said this either to establish credit or to publicize his needy status in order that no public service should be required of him.

127 Hearsay has to be disregarded.

128 At least two witnesses, whose word confirms everything by biblical standards.

(21b line 66) **הלכה ט**: כֵּיצַד בּוֹדְקִין אֶת הָעֵדִים כול'. רִבִּי יוֹסֵי בְּשֵׁם רִבִּי יוֹחָנָן. אִם הָיָה מִתְכַּוֵּין לִמְסוֹר לוֹ עֵדוּת עֵדוּתָן קַיֶּימֶת.

Halakhah 9: "How does one check out the witnesses," etc. Rebbi Yose in the name of Rebbi Johanan: If he had intended to appoint them as witnesses, their testimony is valid[129].

129 Testimony that the debtor admitted to the debt (Note 126) is to be accepted if the debtor explicitly stated that he made the statement to his listeners for the purpose of testimony. There must be two listeners (Halakhah 10, Note 180).

(21b line 68) כֵּיצַד דָּנִין. הַדַּייָנִין יוֹשְׁבִין וְהַנִּידּוֹנִין עוֹמְדִין וְהַתּוֹבֵעַ פּוֹתֵחַ בִּדְבָרָיו רִאשׁוֹן שֶׁנֶּאֱמַר מִי־בַעַל דְּבָרִים יִגַּשׁ אֲלֵיכֶם.

וּמְנַיִין שֶׁהַמּוֹצִיא מֵחֲבֵירוֹ עָלָיו הָרְאָייָה. רִבִּי קְרִיסְפָּא בְשֵׁם רִבִּי חֲנַנְיָה בֶּן גַּמְלִיאֵל. יִגַּשׁ אֲלֵיכֶם. יַגִּישׁ רְאָיוֹתָיו.

רִבִּי יוֹחָנָן בָּעֵי. בִּיבָמָה מִי מְרַדֵּף אַחַר מִי. הָתִיב רִבִּי לָעְזָר. וְהָכְתִיב וְעָלְתָה יְבִמְתּוֹ הַשַּׁעְרָה. אָמַר רִבִּי יוֹחָנָן. יָפֶה לִימְּדָנִי רִבִּי לָעְזָר.

רִבִּי בֶּרֶכְיָה וְרִבִּי חֶלְבּוֹ רִבִּי בָּא בְשֵׁם רִבִּי יַנַּאי. הַתּוֹבֵעַ תּוֹבֵעַ וְהַנִּתְבָּע מֵשִׁיב וְהַדַּייָן מַכְרִיעַ. אָמַר רִבִּי סִימוֹן. צָרִיךְ הַדַּייָן לְשַׁנּוֹת טַעֲנוֹתֵיהֶן. שֶׁנֶּאֱמַר וַיֹּאמֶר הַמֶּלֶךְ זֹאת אֹמֶרֶת זֶה־בְּנִי הַחַי וּבְנֵךְ הַמֵּת וגו'.

How does one judge? The judges are sitting[130], the parties are standing, and the claimant starts first with his words, as it is written[131]: *He who has something to say shall present before you*[132].

From where that the burden of proof is on the claimant? Rebbi Crispus in the name of Rebbi Ḥanina ben Gamliel: *Shall present before you,* shall present his proofs[133].

[134]Rebbi Joḥanan asked, in the case of a sister-in-law, who runs after whom? Rebbi Eleazar answered: *His sister-in-law shall come to the gate*[135]. Rebbi Joḥanan said, Rebbi Eleazar taught me correctly.

Rebbi Berekhiah and Rebbi Ḥelbo, Rebbi Abba in the name of Rebbi Yannai: The claimant claims, the respondent responds, and the judge decides. Rebbi Simon said, the judge has to repeat their arguments[136], as it is said[137]: *The king*[138] *said, this one says, my son is the living and yours is the dead one,* etc.

130 They have to sit during the entire proceedings.

131 A misquote from *Ex.* 24:14.

132 Tosephta 6:3.

133 Babli *Bava qamma* 46b.

134 A slight reformulation of a text in

Yebamot 12:7, Notes 123-124.

135 *Deut.* 25:7.

136 To give each party the opportunity to complain that its arguments were not understood correctly by the judges.

137 *1K.* 3:23.

138 Solomon, acting as judge.

(21c lime 1) רַב הוּנָא כַּד הֲוָה חֲמִי סָהֲדוּ מְכַוּוְנָא הֲוָה חֲקַר וְכַד הֲוָה חֲמִי הָכֵן הֲוָה מְכַוֵּון. רַב הוּנָא מֵיקַל לְדַייָנָא דַאֲמַר. מְקַבְּלִין עֲלֵיכוֹן חַד סָהִיד. אֶלָּא יֵימְרוּן אִינּוּן. רַב הוּנָא כַּד הֲוָה יְדַע זְכוּ לְבַר נָשׁ בְּדִינָא וְלָא הֲוָה יְדַע לֵיהּ הֲוָה פְתַח לֵיהּ. עַל שֵׁם פְּתַח־פִּיךָ לְאִלֵּם.

When Rav Huna saw that witnesses said exactly the same, he was investigating[139]. When he saw them essentially identical, he determined the common element[140]. Rav Huna made light of a judge who said, "accept a single witness," but they should say it themselves[141]. When Rav Huna realized an argument in favor of a person who himself did not know it, he guided him[142], following[143] *open your mouth for the dumb.*

139 Witnesses using exactly the same language either bear false witness or they went over their testimony beforehand. Then they can be counted only as one witness, not as the biblically required two.

140 He summarized the common points.

141 Two independent witnesses are absolutely necessary only in criminal trials. Civil suits may be determined on the basis of documents or, with the agreement of the parties, single witnesses. But accepting a single witness cannot be suggested by the court.

142 Since the parties are not supposed to consult lawyers, the judge may by a Socratic dialogue with the parties steer one of the parties to a certain argument which the latter did not see before.

143 *Prov.* 31:8.

(21c line 4) רִבִּי אַבָּהוּ בְשֵׁם רִבִּי יוֹחָנָן. הַמַּכְמִין עֵידָיו אֲחוֹרֵי גָּדֵר לֹא עָשָׂה כְלוּם. כְּהָדָא. חַד בַּר נַשׁ אַשְׁגַּח לְמֵיגוֹס גַּו אֲרִיסְטוֹן. אֲמַר לֵיהּ. הַב לִי מַה דְאַתְּ חַייָב לִי. אֲמַר לֵיהּ. אִין. בָּתָר דְקָמוּן אֲמַר לֵיהּ. לִי נָא חַייָב לָךְ כְּלוּם. אֲמַר לֵיהּ. אִית לִי סְהָדִין. אֲמַר לֵיהּ. לָא אֲמְרִית אֶלָּא בְגִין דְלָא מֵעִירְבֵּב מְגוֹסְתָךְ. אֲתַא קוֹמֵי רִבִּי אִמִּי וָמַר. הָדָא דָמַר רִבִּי יוֹחָנָן. הַמַּכְמִין עֵידָיו אֲחוֹרֵי גָּדֵר לֹא עָשָׂה כְלוּם.

Rebbi Abbahu in the name of Rebbi Joḥanan: He who hides his witnesses behind a wall did not do anything[144]. As in this case: A man happened to prepare food for a meal[145]. He said to another, give me what you owe me. That one answered, yes. When he rose, he told him, I do not owe you anything. He answered, I have witnesses. The other said, I said that only in order not to spoil your food. The case came before Rebbi Immi, who said, this is what Rebbi Joḥanan said, he who hides his witnesses behind a wall did not do anything[146].

144 Babli 29a.

145 Greek ἄριστον.

146 What a person says not in the presence of witnesses must be interpreted following the speaker's explanation.

(fol. 20d) **משנה י**: הָיוּ מַכְנִיסִין אֶת הַשֵּׁנִי וּבוֹדְקִין אוֹתוֹ. אִם נִמְצְאוּ דִבְרֵיהֶם מְכוּוָּנִים נוֹשְׂאִין וְנוֹתְנִין בַּדָּבָר. שְׁנַיִם אוֹמְרִים זַכַּאי וְאֶחָד אוֹמֵר חַייָב זַכַּאי. שְׁנַיִם אוֹמְרִים חַייָב וְאֶחָד אוֹמֵר זַכַּאי חַייָב. אֶחָד אוֹמֵר זַכַּאי וְאֶחָד אוֹמֵר חַייָב וְאֶחָד אוֹמֵר אֵינִי יוֹדֵעַ יוֹסִיפוּ הַדַּייָנִין: וַאֲפִלּוּ שְׁנַיִם מְזַכִּין אוֹ מְחַייְבִין וְאֶחָד אוֹמֵר אֵינִי יוֹדֵעַ יוֹסִיפוּ הַדַּייָנִין:

Mishnah 10: One calls in the second [witness] and examines him. If their testimonies are found consistent, one argues the case. Two[147] say not guilty[148] and one says guilty, he is not guilty. Two say guilty and one says not guilty, he is guilty. One says not guilty, one says guilty, and one says "I do not know", they shall add judges. Even if two say not guilty or guilty but one says "I do not know", they shall add judges[149]

147 Of the judges.

148 Since one deals with civil cases, this means that the claim is rejected.

149 Since the judge who does not vote is considered absent, judgment cannot be given by two judges. There must be three voting judges for the verdict to stand..

(21c line 10) **הלכה י**: הָיוּ מַכְנִיסִין אֶת הַשֵּׁינִי כול'. שְׂעִירִים. מִיעוּט שְׂעִירִים שְׁנַיִם. מַה תַּלְמוּד לוֹמַר שְׁנֵי. שֶׁיְּהוּ שְׁנֵיהֶן שָׁוִין.

כְּבָשִׂים. מִיעוּט כְּבָשִׂים שְׁנַיִם. מַה תַּלְמוּד לוֹמַר שְׁנֵי. שֶׁיְּהוּ שְׁנֵיהֶן שָׁוִין.

מִיעוּט צִפּוֹרִים שְׁנַיִם. מַה תַּלְמוּד לוֹמַר שְׁתֵּי. שֶׁיְּהוּ שָׁווֹת. מִיעוּט חֲצוֹצְרוֹת שְׁתַּיִם. מַה תַּלְמוּד לוֹמַר שְׁתֵּי. שֶׁיְּהוּ שָׁווֹת.

הָתִיב רִבִּי חַגַּי לְרִבִּי יָסָא. וְהָכְתִיב וְעָמְדוּ שְׁנֵי־הָאֲנָשִׁים. מֵעַתָּה מִיעוּט אֲנָשִׁים שְׁנַיִם. מַה תַּלְמוּד לוֹמַר שְׁנֵי. שֶׁיְּהוּ שָׁוִין. וְהָכְתִיב לֹא תַטֶּה מִשְׁפַּט גֵּר יָתוֹם. הֲרֵי גֵר דָּן עִם מִי שֶׁאֵינוֹ גֵר.

יָתוֹם דָּן עִם מִי שֶׁאֵינוֹ יָתוֹם. אִם כֵּן לָמָּה נֶאֱמַר שְׁנֵי. מוּפְנֶה לְהַקִּישׁ וְלָדוּן מִמֶּנּוּ גְזֵירָה שָׁוָה. נֶאֱמַר כָּאן שְׁנֵי וְנֶאֱמַר לְהַלָּן וַיִּשָּׁאֲרוּ שְׁנֵי־אֲנָשִׁים. מַה לְהַלָּן אֲנָשִׁים וְלֹא נָשִׁים אַף כָּאן אֲנָשִׁים וְלֹא נָשִׁים וְלֹא קְטַנִּים. הֲרֵי לָמַדְנוּ שֶׁאֵין הָאִשָּׁה דָנָה. וְלֹא מְעִידָה.

רִבִּי יוֹסֵי בֵּי רִבִּי בּוּן בְּשֵׁם רַב יוֹסֵף. נֶאֱמַר כָּאן שְׁנֵי וְנֶאֱמַר לְהַלָּן שְׁנֵי. מַה לְהַלָּן עַל־פִּי | שְׁנַיִם עֵדִים אַף כָּאן עַל־פִּי שְׁנַיִם עֵדִים. אִם כֵּן מַה תַלְמוּד לוֹמַר שְׁנֵי. שֶׁלֹּא יְהֵא אֶחָד עוֹמֵד וְאֶחָד יוֹשֵׁב. אֶחָד אוֹמֵר כָּל־צָרְכוֹ וְאֶחָד אוֹמֵר לוֹ. קַצֵּר דְּבָרֶיךָ.

אָמַר רִבִּי יְהוּדָה. שָׁמַעְתִּי שֶׁאִם רָצָה הַדַּיָּין לְהוֹשִׁיב אֶת שְׁנֵיהֶן מוֹשִׁיב. רִבִּי יִשְׁמָעֵאל אוֹמֵר. אוֹמְרִין לוֹ. לְבוֹשׁ כְּשֵׁם שֶׁהוּא לָבוּשׁ אוֹ הַלְבִּישֵׁהוּ כְשֵׁם שֶׁאַתְּ לָבוּשׁ.

אָמַר רִבִּי בָּא בְשֵׁם רַב הוּנָא. צְרִיכִין הָעֵדִים לַעֲמוֹד בְּשָׁעָה שֶׁמְּעִידִין. שֶׁנֶּאֱמַר וְעָמְדוּ שְׁנֵי־הָאֲנָשִׁים. רִבִּי יִרְמְיָה בְשֵׁם רִבִּי אַבָּהוּ. אַף הַנִּידוֹנִין צְרִיכִין לַעֲמוֹד בְּשָׁעָה שֶׁמְּקַבְּלִין דִּינָן. שֶׁנֶּאֱמַר אֲשֶׁר־לָהֶם הָרִיב לִפְנֵי יי.

Halakhah 10: "One calls in the second [witness]," etc. [150]*Rams*[151], the minimum of rams are two. Why does the verse say *two*? That both be equal[152].

Sheep, the minimum of sheep are two. Why does the verse say *two*? That both be equal[153].

The minimum of *birds* are two. Why does the verse say *two*? that both be equal[154]. The minimum of *trumpets* are two. Why does the verse say *two*? that both be equal[155].

Rebbi Ḥaggai objected to Rebbi Yasa. Is there not written: *The two men shall stand*[156]? Now, is not two the minimum of "men"? Why does the verse say *two*? That both be equal? But it is written[157]: *Do not bend the lawsuit of the proselyte, the orphan, . . .* That means that a proselyte can have a lawsuit against one who is not a proselyte, an orphan may have a lawsuit against one who is not an orphan. Then why is there written *two*? It is free to be combined and to infer from it an *equal cut*[158]. It is said here *two* and it is said there *two men were left*[159]. Since there one speaks of men but not women, also here men but not women nor underaged.[160] From this we learn that a woman may not be a judge[161] and may not be a witness.

Rebbi Yose ben Rebbi Abun in the name of Rav Joseph. It is said here *two* and it is said there[162] *two*. Since there it must be by the testimony of two witnesses, also here by the testimony of two witnesses. Then why does the verse say *two*? Lest one of them be standing while the other be sitting; one says everything he has to say, but to the other one says, make your statement short[161].

Rebbi Jehudah said, I heard that if the judge wants to let both of them sit, he may tell them to sit down[163]. Rebbi Ismael says, one says to him,[164] either you dress as he is dressed or pay him to be dressed as you are.

Rebbi Abba said in the name of Rav Huna: The witnesses have to stand while testifying, for it is said: *the two men shall stand.* Rebbi Jeremiah in the name of Rebbi Abbahu: Also the parties have to stand at the moment the verdict is given, as it is said[156]: *who have the quarrel before the Eternal*[165].

150 There are two parallels to this text. The one in *Ševu'ot* 4:1 is almost identical with the present text; the one in *Yoma* 6:1 is slightly rewritten (or changed in transmission.) The *Ševu'ot* text seems to be the original of most of the Halakhah.

As explained in the author's *Logical problems in Jewish tradition* (in: Confrontations with Judaism, ed. Ph. Longworth, London 1966, pp. 171-196, mainly p. 174), talmudic interpretation of pentateuchal verses operates on a *principle of definiteness*: The language always is definite. Since the sequence of integers has a smallest but no largest element, an indefinite plural means "two". Therefore, the explicit mention of "two" always implies some special meaning.

151 *Lev.* 16:5,7,8 speaking of the rams used in the service of the Day of Atonement.

152 Babli *Yoma* 62b, *Sifra Ahare Parašah* 2(1).

153 The daily sacrifice required *two sheep* (*Ex.* 27:38, *Num.* 28:3). In both verses, the numeral is שְׁנַיִם (Babli *Yoma* 62b).

154 The birds required for the purification of the person healed from skin disease, *Lev.* 14:4. Babli *Yoma* 62b, Mishnah *Nega'im* 14:1, *Sifra Meṣora'* Introduction 11.

155 The trumpets to be sounded at the time of sacrifices, *Num.* 10:2. *Sifry Num.* 74.

156 *Deut.* 19:17. The verse can be read either as referring to the parties in a lawsuit or to the witnesses in a civil or criminal suit. Cf. Babli *Ševu'ot* 30a.

157 *Deut.*24:17.

158 Cf. *Berakhot* 1:1 Note 70, *Nedarim* 1 Notes 18,159, *Nazir* 4:1 Note 23, *Logical problems* (Note 150) pp. 185-186. Two identical expressions, written in two different connections, each of which is *free*, i. e., not used for an inference not otherwise possible, can be used to transfer rules from one connection to the other. This hermeneutical principle is accepted by all rabbinic schools.

159 *Num.* 11:27. Since Eldad and Medad are mentioned by name in the verse, it is obvious that two men are meant.

160 Only people potentially acceptable for Moses's council of 70 Elders.

161 Babli *Ševu'ot* 30a, *Sifry Deut.* 190.

162 *Deut.* 19:15. The verse explicitly speaks of witnesses.

163 Babli *Ševu`ot* 30a, Tosephta *Sanhedrin* 6:2, *Sifra Qedošim Pereq* 4(4).

164 A person appearing in court dressed better than usual.

165 Babli *Ševu`ot* 30a.

(21c line 30) כְּתִיב לֹא־יוּמְתוּ אָבוֹת֙ עַל־בָּנִים. וַהֲלֹא כְּבָר נֶאֱמַר אִישׁ בְּחֶטְאוֹ יוּמָת׃ מַה תַלְמוּד לוֹמַר לֹא־יוּמְתוּ אָבוֹת֙ עַל־בָּנִים. לֹא־יוּמְתוּ אָבוֹת בְּעֵדוּת בָּנִים וּבָנִים לֹא־יוּמְתוּ בְעֵדוּת אָבוֹת. מְנַיִין שֶׁלֹּא יְהוּ הָעֵדִים קְרוֹבִין שֶׁלַּנִּידוֹנִין.

וּמְנַיִין שֶׁלֹּא יְהוּ הָעֵדִים קְרוֹבִין זֶה לָזֶה. הַגַּע עַצְמָךְ שֶׁאִם הוּזְמוּ לֹא מִפִּיהֶן נֶהֱרָגִין. וּמְנַיִין שֶׁלֹּא יְהוּ הָעֵדִים קְרוֹבִין שֶׁלַּדַּייָנִים. הַגַּע עַצְמָךְ שֶׁאִם הוּזַּם אֶחָד מֵהֶן כְּלוּם נֶהֱרַג עַד שֶׁיּוּזַּם חֲבֵירוֹ. אִם אַתְּ אוֹמֵר כֵּן לֹא הָיָה נֶהֱרַג עַל פִּיו.

וּמְנַיִין שֶׁלֹּא יְהוּ הַדַּייָנִין קְרוֹבִין זֶה לָזֶה. אָמְרָה תוֹרָה. הֲרוֹג עַל פִּי עֵדִים. הֲרוֹג עַל פִּי דַייָנִין. מָה עֵדִים אֵין קְרוֹבִין זֶה לָזֶה אַף דַּייָנִין אֵין קְרוֹבִין זֶה לָזֶה.

אֵין לִי אֶלָּא אָבוֹת וּבָנִים. שְׁאָר קְרוֹבִין מְנַיִין. אָמַר רִבִּי זְעִירָא וּבָנִים. לְרַבּוֹת שְׁאָר קְרוֹבִין. עַד כְּדוֹן כְּרִבִּי עֲקִיבָה.

[166]It is written[167]: *Fathers shall not be killed because of sons*. Is it not already written, *each one should be killed for his own crime*[167,168]? Why does the verse say, *fathers shall not be killed because of sons*? Fathers shall not be killed on the testimony of sons, and sons shall not be killed on testimony of fathers[169]. From here[169a] that witnesses shall not be relatives of the accused.

From where that witnesses may not be relatives of one another? Think of it, if they be found perjured, would they not be killed by their testimony[170]? From where that witnesses may not be relatives of the judges? Think of it, if one of them be found perjured, he could not be killed unless the other also was found perjured. If you say so, would he not be killed by his sentence[170]?

From where that judges may not be relatives of one another? The Torah said, kill on the testimony of witnesses, kill on the sentence of judges. Since witnesses may not be relatives of one another, neither may judges be relatives of one another[171].

So far[167] only fathers and sons; from where the other relatives? Rebbi Ze`ira sais, *and sons* includes the remaining relatives.

So far according to Rebbi Aqiba[172].

166 This section also has an almost identical copy in *Ševuot* 4:1.

167 *Deut*. 24:16.

168 A slight misquote.

169 Babli 17b, *Sifry Deut.* 280.

169a Read with *Ševuot* 4:1 מכן for מניין.

170 Cf. *Gittin* 9:8, Note 128. Formal perjury, "plotting", is testimony which is impossible, i. e., where it was proven that the witnesses were not at the place about which they testify at the time they assert to have seen the object of their testimony. If only one witness was perjured, there is only one valid witness and his testimony is worthless by biblical standards; for worthless testimony there can be no biblical punishment. Therefore, if the two perjured witnesses were related, each would be convicted by his relatives' testimony; this is forbidden by *Deut.* 24:16. But testimony which would not expose the witnesses to the penalty of perjury is worthless. The Babli, 28a, points out that this argument also eliminates a single relative among the witnesses.

171 *Deut.* 24:16 is indeterminate enough to include both testimony and sentence by relatives.

172 Who will consider any *prefixed* ו which is not 100% necessary for the understanding of the text as an addition which invites extension of the rules. The statement attributed here to the late Amora R. Ze`ira is formulated in *Sifry Deut.* 280 as tannaïtic, representing R. Aqiba's opinion.

(21c line 40) כְּרַבִּי יִשְׁמָעֵאל מְנַיִין. תַּנֵּי רַבִּי יִשְׁמָעֵאל. וְשָֽׁפְטוּ֮ הָֽעֵדָ֒ה וְהִצִּ֣ילוּ הָֽעֵדָ֒ה. שֶׁלֹּא יְהֵא הָעֵדָה לֹא קְרוֹבֵי מַכֶּה וְלֹא קְרוֹבֵי מוּכֶּה. אָמַר רִבִּי יוֹסֵי. אִם אוֹמֵר אַתְּ כֵּן נִמְצֵאת אוֹמֵר. בֵּית דִּין גּוֹאֲלֵי הַדָּם. מִיכָּן שֶׁלֹּא יְהוּ הַדַּייָנִין קְרוֹבֵי הַנִּידּוֹנִין. וּמְנַיִין שֶׁלֹּא יְהוּ הָעֵדִים קְרוֹבֵי הַנִּידּוֹנִין. אָמְרָה תוֹרָה. הֲרוֹג עַל פִּי עֵדִים. הֲרוֹג עַל פִּי דַייָנִין. מַה הַדַּייָנִין אֵינָן קְרוֹבֵי הַנִּידּוֹנִין. אַף הָעֵדִים לֹא יְהוּ קְרוֹבֵי הַנִּידּוֹנִין. וּמְנַיִין שֶׁלֹּא יְהוּ הָעֵדִים קְרוֹבִין זֶה לָזֶה. הַגַּע עַצְמָךְ שֶׁהוּזְמוּ לֹא מִפִּיהֶן הֵן נֶהֱרָגִין.

[173]From where following Rebbi Ismael? Rebbi Ismael stated: *The congregation shall judge*[174]*; the congregation shall save*[175]. The congregation be neither relatives of the murderer nor relatives of the murdered. Rebbi Yose said, otherwise you would say that the court is engaged in vendetta[176]. This implies that the judges may not be related to the accused. And from where that the witnesses may not be related to the accused? The Torah said, kill on the testimony of witnesses, kill on the sentence of judges. Since judges may not be related to the accused, neither may witnesses be related to the accused. From where that witnesses may not be relatives of one another[171]? Think of it, if they be found perjured, would they not be killed by their testimony[170]?

173 A slightly changed parallel is in *Ševu`ot* 4:1.

174 *Num.* 35:24, about the trial of the homicide who fled to a city of asylum. R.

Ismael objects to R. Aqiba's inferences from additional ו, את etc. and insists that any interpretations of verses conform to the plain sense of the verse within the purview of his hermeneutical rules.

175 *Num.* 35:25.

176 This gives the missing argument in R. Ismael's statement.

(21c line 47) בַּכְּשֵׁרִים וְלֹא בִפְסוּלִים. שֶׁנֶּאֱמַר אִם־לֹא יַגִּיד וְנָשָׂא עֲוֹנוֹ׃ אֶת שֶׁמַּגִּיד וַחֲבֵירוֹ מְשַׁלֵּם מָמוֹן. יָצָא פָסוּל שֶׁאֲפִילוּ מַגִּיד אֵין חֲבֵירוֹ מְשַׁלֵּם מָמוֹן.

בִּפְנֵי בֵית דִּין. לְהוֹצִיא עֵד אֶחָד. בְּשֶׁאָמְרוּ לוֹ. הֲרֵי אַתְּ מְקוּבָּל עָלֵינוּ כִשְׁנַיִם. יָכוֹל יְהֵא חַייָב. תַּלְמוּד לוֹמַר אוֹ רָאָה אוֹ יָדָע. אֵת שֶׁהוּא כָשֵׁר לְהָעִיד עֵדוּת תּוֹרָה. יָצָא עֵד אֶחָד שֶׁאֵין כָּשֵׁר לְהָעִיד עֵדוּת תּוֹרָה.

שֶׁלֹּא בִּפְנֵי בֵית דִּין. אִם־לֹא יַגִּיד וְנָשָׂא עֲוֹנוֹ׃ אֶת שֶׁמַּגִּיד וּמְשַׁלֵּם מָמוֹן. יָצָא חוּץ לְבֵית דִּין שֶׁאֲפִילוּ מַגִּיד אֵין חֲבֵירוֹ מְשַׁלֵּם מָמוֹן.

[177]"Qualified one but not disqualified one." For it is said, *if he does not tell, he has to bear his punishment*. If he told, the other would have to pay money. This excludes one where the other would not have to pay money even if he told[178].

"Before the court." To exclude a single witness. If they told him that they would accept his word as if there were two [witnesses], would he be guilty? The verse says, *if he had seen or known*. One who is qualified to testify according to biblical standards; this excludes a single witness who is not qualified to testify according to biblical standards[179].

"Outside of court." *If he does not tell, he has to bear his punishment*. If he told, one would have to pay money. This excludes outside of court where the other would not have to pay money even if he told.

177 These paragraphs all start with quotes from Mishnah *Ševu`ot* 4:1; they are copied from the Halakhah there. The object of discussion is *Lev.* 5:1: *If a person sinned when he heard the sound of an imprecation, being a witness, either having seen or known, if he does not tell he has to bear his punishment.* If one of the parties in a civil suit adresses a potential witness and by an oath tells him to appear as a witness in court, if the person so addressed refuses to appear or to testify he has to confess his sin (5:5) and bring a sacrifice graded according to his means (5:6-13). Mishnah *Ševu`ot* 4:1 details the rules under which a person may be declared guilty of violating the oath put on him.

178 A person disqualified as witness never has to appear in court. Babli *Ševu`ot* 30a.

179 *Deut.* 19:15.

(21c line 54) וּמְנַיִין לִשְׁנֵי עֵדִים. הוּא וְעֵד אַחֵר הֲרֵי כָּאן שְׁנַיִם. וּכְרִבִּי יִשְׁמָעֵאל. דְּרִבִּי יִשְׁמָעֵאל אָמַר. כָּל־מָקוֹם שֶׁכָּתוּב בַּתּוֹרָה עֵד סְתָם הֲרֵי הוּא בִכְלָל שְׁנֵי עֵדִים עַד שֶׁיּוֹדִיעֲךָ הַכָּתוּב שֶׁהוּא עֵד אֶחָד. אַשְׁכַּח תַּנֵּי רִבִּי יִשְׁמָעֵאל. עֵד אֶחָד מָהוּ לְחַיֵּיב עָלָיו מִשּׁוּם שְׁבוּעַת בִּיטּוּי. אֶיפְשַׁר לוֹמַר אַחֵר רָאוּי לְצָרְפוֹ וּלְחַייְבוֹ מִשּׁוּם שְׁבוּעַת עֵדוּת וְאַתְּ מְחַייְבוֹ מִשּׁוּם שְׁבוּעַת בִּיטּוּי.

קָרוֹב מָהוּ לְחַייֵב עָלָיו מִשּׁוּם שְׁבוּעַת בִּיטּוּי. יְיָבֹא כְהָדָא דָּמַר רִבִּי בָּא (בַּר) שְׁמוּאֵל. שְׁבוּעָה שֶׁנָּתַן פְּלוֹנִי לִפְלוֹנִי מָנֶה. נִמְצָא שֶׁלֹּא נָתַן. מֵאַחַר שֶׁאֵין בְּיָדוֹ לָבֹא אֵין בְּיָדוֹ לְשֶׁעָבַר. אוֹ כְהָדָא. אָמַר לוֹ. הֵיכָן שׁוֹרִי. אָמַר לוֹ. אֵינִי יוֹדֵעַ מָה אַתָּה סָח. וְהוּא שֶׁמֵּת אוֹ נִשְׁבַּר אוֹ נִשְׁבָּה אוֹ אָבַד. מַשְׁבִּיעֲךָ אֲנִי. וְאָמַר אָמֵן. פָּטוּר. רַב אָמַר. פָּטוּר מִשְּׁבוּעַת פִּיקָּדוֹן וְחַייָב מִשְּׁבוּעַת בִּיטּוּי. אָמַר רִבִּי יוֹחָנָן. מֵאַחַר שֶׁמִּצְוָה לְהַפִּיסוֹ אֵין חַייָב מִשּׁוּם שְׁבוּעַת בִּיטּוּי. עַל דַּעְתֵּיהּ דְּרַב אֵינוֹ מְצֻוֶּה לְהַפִּיסוֹ. מְפַייְסוֹ עַל הָאֱמֶת וְאֵינוֹ מְפַייְסוֹ עַל הַשֶּׁקֶר.

תַּנֵּי רִבִּי יִשְׁמָעֵאל. וְנָשָׂא עֲוֹנוֹ. קָרְבָּן. מְנָן לֵיהּ בֵּית דִּין. יָֽלְפִין אֲגָדָה אֲגָדָה. מָה אֲגָדָה שֶׁנֶּאֱמַר לְהַלָּן בֵּית דִּין אַף כָּאן בֵּית דִּין.

From where two witnesses[180]? He and another make two[181]. Or following Rebbi Ismael, as Rebbi Ismael said, any place where the Torah mentions a witness without further determination it implies two witnesses[182] unless the verse informs you that a single witness is meant. It was found stated in the name of Rebbi Ismael: Can a single witness be found guilty of a blurted oath[183]? Since it is possible to say that another person could team up with him, then he would be subject to the oath of testimony, how could you find him guilty of a blurted oath[184]?

Should a relative be found guilty of a blurted oath[185]? Does it follow what Rebbi Abba said (ben) [in the name of][186] Samuel: [187]"An oath that X gave a *mina* to Y," and it turns out that X had not given; since there is nothing in the future there is nothing in the past. Or the following: [188]"One said to another, `where is my ox?' He responded, `I do not know what you are referring to.' It so happened that it had died, or was wounded, or captured, or lost. `I require you to swear;' the other said `Amen'. He is not liable.[189]" Rav said, he is not liable for a keeper's oath[190] but is liable because of a blurted oath[191]. Rebbi Joḥanan said, since it is a religious duty to appease him[192], he is not liable because of a blurted oath. In Rav's opinion, is there no religious duty to appease him? One appeases with truthful statements, not with lies.

Rebbi Ismael stated: *He has to bear his punishment*[193], a sacrifice[194]. From where that one needs a court[195]? One learns "telling, telling[196]". Since *telling* mentioned there is before a court, also telling here is before a court.

180 The sacrifice for disregarding an imprecation is due only if two witnesses can testify that the potential witness acknowledged the oath put on him.

181 This is R. Aqiba's argument. Since it is written in *Lev.* 5:1 *and he is a witness*, the copula implies the existence of a counterpart, a second witness.

182 Since a single witness is declared insufficient in *Deut.* 19:15, any mention of valid testimony in the biblical text must refer to two witnesses; cf. *Sotah* 6:2 Note 23; Babli 30a, 31b, *Sotah* 2b.

183 This refers to *Lev.* 5:4: *Or a person who blurts out swearing from his lips, to worsen or to improve, for anything a human might blurt out in an oath, and it slipped his mind but then he remembered and became guilty of one of these.* A blurted oath is one which could have been avoided by some reflection.

184 By its nature, a blurted oath is totally disconnected from any judicial precedure.

185 If only two witnesses are known to the party putting an imprecation on those who would not testify and one of these is a relative who could not testify, is the imprecation a blurted oath?

186 From the text in *Ševu`ot*. Samuel only had daughters.

187 Since *Lev.* 5:4 sanctions only future-directed thoughtless oaths, *to worsen or to improve*, in Samuel's opinion oaths that refer to past acts only are not included in the category of blurted oaths. They are meaningless oaths which might not be reparable by a sacrifice.

188 Mishnah *Ševu`ot* 8:3. The person spoken to was an unpaid keeper responsible only if he appropriated another's property for his own use, not if it was otherwise lost (*Bava mesi`a* 7:9).

189 If the keeper maintains that he never received the ox when he had in fact received it, but it died or was lost under circumstances which do not make the keeper responsible for the loss, he does not have to bring the sacrifice for a false oath since his lie did not result in monetary loss to another person.

190 Since he could have told the truth and still not be liable for damages.

191 Since what he pronounced was an oath which resulted from speaking before thinking.

192 The keeper is under a religious obligation to tell the truth to the ox's owner.

193 *Lev.* 5:1.

194 This supports Rav, that a sacrifice is due for any untruthful oath.

195 That a sacrifice is required only for oaths connected with judicial proceedings.

196 The only *legal* texts in the Pentateuch which use the root נגד are *Lev.* 5:1 and *Deut.* 17:9-11. The latter text contains the rules of the Supreme Court and the punishment for disobeying its rulings.

(21c line 69) כְּהָדָא. אֵין מְקַבְּלִין עֵדִים אֶלָּא אִם כֵּן רָאוּ שְׁנֵיהֶן כְּאַחַת. רִבִּי יְהוֹשֻׁעַ בֶּן קָרְחָה אוֹמֵר. אֲפִילוּ בְזֶה אַחַר זֶה. רִבִּי יִרְמְיָה בְשֵׁם רַב. מוֹדִין חֲכָמִים לְרִבִּי יְהוֹשֻׁעַ בֶּן קָרְחָה בְעֵידֵי בְכוֹרָה וּבְעֵידֵי חֲזָקָה. רִבִּי בָּא בְשֵׁם רִבִּי יִרְמְיָה. אַף בְּעֵידֵי סִימָנִין כֵּן. מַה דִפְשִׁיטָא. בְּשֶׁזֶּה אוֹמֵר. רָאִיתִי שְׁתֵּי שְׂעָרוֹת בְּגַבּוֹ. וְזֶה אוֹמֵר. רָאִיתִי שְׁתֵּי שְׂעָרוֹת בְּגַפּוֹ. אֶחָד אוֹמֵר. רָאִיתִי שְׂעָרָה אַחַת בְּגַבּוֹ. וְאֶחָד אוֹמֵר. רָאִיתִי שְׂעָרָה אַחַת בִּכְרֵיסוֹ. וְלֹא כְלוּם. בָּל־שֶׁכֵּן גַּבּוֹ וְגַפּוֹ. שְׁנַיִם אוֹמְרִים רָאִינוּ שְׂעָרָה אַחַת בְּגַבּוֹ. וּשְׁנַיִם אוֹמְרִים רָאִינוּ שְׂעָרָה אַחַת בִּכְרֵיסוֹ. רַב יוֹסֵי וְרַב הוֹשַׁעְיָה בַּר רַב שַׁמַּי. חַד אָמַר. פָּסוּל. וְחַד אָמַר. כָּשֵׁר. מָאן דָּמַר פָּסוּל. בִּמֵעִיד עַל חֲצִי סִימָן. וּמָאן דָּמַר כָּשֵׁר. אֲנִי אוֹמֵר. שֶׁמָּא נִשְׁרוּ. אֶחָד אוֹמֵר. שְׁתֵּי שְׂעָרוֹת בְּגַבּוֹ. וְאֶחָד אוֹמֵר. שְׁנַיִם בִּכְרֵיסוֹ. רִבִּי בָּא אָמַר. דִּבְרֵי הַכֹּל כָּשֵׁר. אָמַר רִבִּי חַגַּיי. דִּבְרֵי הַכֹּל פָּסוּל. רִבִּי יוֹסֵי אָמַר. בְּמַחֲלוֹקֶת. אָמַר רִבִּי [יוֹסֵי] לְרִבִּי חַגַּיי. הָא רִבִּי יוּדָן אָמַר דִּכְווָתִי. אָמַר לֵיהּ. וְעַל רַבֵּיהּ אֲנָא פְלִיג כָּל־שֶׁכֵּן עֲלוֹי. אָמַר רִבִּי מָנָא. יְאוּת אָמַר רִבִּי חַגָּא. אִילּוּ שְׁטָר שֶׁחָתוּם בְּאַרְבָּעָה חוֹתָמוֹת זֶה מֵעִיד עַל שְׁנַיִם וְזֶה מֵעִיד עַל שְׁנַיִם וְקָרָא עָלָיו עִרְעֵר שֶׁמָּא כְלוּם הוּא. וְאֵין כָּל־חֲתִימָה צְרִיכָה שְׁנֵי עֵדִים. וְהָכָא כָל־סִימָן צָרִיךְ שְׁנֵי עֵדִים. רִבִּי חִינְנָה שָׁמַע לָהּ מִשּׁוּם חֲזָקָה. אִילּוּ אֶחָד מֵעִיד שֶׁאֲכָלָהּ שָׁנָה רִאשׁוֹנָה שְׁנִייָה וּשְׁלִישִׁית וְאֶחָד מֵעִיד שֶׁאֲכָלָהּ רְבִיעִית חֲמִישִׁית וְשִׁישִּׁית שֶׁמָּא כְלוּם הוּא. וְאֵין כָּל־חֲזָקָה וַחֲזָקָה צְרִיכָה שְׁנֵי עֵדִים. וְהָכָא כָּל־סִימָן וְסִימָן צָרִיךְ שְׁנֵי עֵדִים.

[197]Or like the following. “One accepts the witnesses’ testimony only if they saw it together. Rebbi Joshua ben Qorḥa says, even if they saw it one after the other.” Rebbi Jeremiah in the name of Rav: The Sages agree with Rebbi Joshua ben Qorḥa with regard to witnesses of firstlings and witnesses of squatters’ rights. Rebbi Abba in the name of Rebbi Jeremiah: the same holds for testimony regarding signs. In that case, it is obvious if one says, I saw two hairs on his back and the other says, I saw two hairs on his side. If one says, I saw one hair on his back and the other says, I saw one hair on his belly, that is nothing; so much more his back and his side. Two are saying, we saw one hair on his back; and two are saying, we saw one hair on his belly. Rav Yose and Rav Hoshaia ben Rav Shammai, one said, it is invalid, but the other said, it is valid. He who says it is invalid considers him as one who testifies to half a sign. He who says it is valid? I say, maybe they were rubbed off. One says, two hairs on his back; and one says, two on his belly[198]. Rebbi Abba said, everybody agrees that this is valid. Rebbi Ḥaggai said, everybody agrees that this is invalid [testimony]. Rebbi Yose said, this is in disagreement. Rebbi [Yose][199] said to Rebbi Ḥaggai, does not Rebbi Yudan

follow my opinion? He answered, I am disagreeing with his teacher, so much more with him. Rebbi Mama said, Rebbi Ḥaggai was correct. If a document was signed by four seals, if one person verified the signature of two [witnesses], and another those of the other two, and the document was attacked, is that worth anything? Does not every single signature need two witnesses? And here, every single hair needs two witnesses. Rebbi Ḥinena learns it (because of)[200] [from the years of] squatting rights. If one [witness] testified that he ate from the property the first, second, and third years and another testified that he ate it the fourth, fifth, and sixth years, is that worth anything? Does not every single year need two witnesses? And here, every single hair needs two witnesses.

197 This text is an incomplete copy of a text in *Sotah* 1:1, Notes 56-71 (*Ketubot* 2:4, *Ševu`ot* 4:1).

198 It is obvious that one has to read with the *Sotah* text: *Two* say *one* hair.

199 From the text in *Sotah*, missing here.

200 Text here, to be replaced by the *Sotah* text in brackets.

(21d line 13) כְּהָדָא. אֵין שׁוֹמְעִין מִן הָעֵדִים אֶלָּא אִם כֵּן בָּאוּ שְׁנֵיהֶן כְּאַחַת. רִבִּי נָתָן אוֹמֵר. שׁוֹמְעִין דִּבְרֵי רִאשׁוֹן וְלִכְשֶׁיָּבוֹא שֵׁינִי שׁוֹמְעִין אֶת דְּבָרָיו. רִבִּי יוֹנָתָן הֲוָה יְתִיב מַקְשֵׁי. אֶיפְשַׁר אִית הָכָא בַּר נַשׁ דְּשָׁמַע הֲלָכָה כְּרִבִּי נָתָן. אָמַר לֵיהּ רִבִּי יוֹסֵי בַּר חֲנִינָה. הָא רִבִּי שִׁמְעוֹן בַּר יָקִים. אָמַר יָקוּם לָעֵיל. כֵּיוָן דִּסְלַק אֲמַר לֵיהּ. שָׁמַעְתָּ הֲלָכָה כְּרִבִּי נָתָן. אָמַר לֵיהּ. שָׁמַעְתִּי. מוֹדֶה רִבִּי יְהוֹשֻׁעַ בֶּן קָרְחָה לְרִבִּי נָתָן. אָמַר לֵיהּ. לְהָדָא צוֹרְכָה. אָמַר לֵיהּ. וְלֹא אִיתְכַּוֵּון רִבִּי יוֹסֵי בַּר חֲנִינָה אֶלָּא מַסְקָא רִבִּי שִׁמְעוֹן בַּר יָקִים לְעֵיל בְּגִין דַּהֲוָה אִינְשָׁא רַבָּא.

[201]And the following. One does not listen to the witnesses unless they come together; Rebbi Nathan says, one listens to the first and when the second comes, one listens to what he has to say. Rebbi Jonathan was sitting and asking, maybe somebody is here who heard that practice follows Rebbi Nathan? Rebbi Yose bar Ḥanina told him, that is Rebbi Simeon ben Yaqim. He said, may he come up[202]. When he came up, he asked him, did you hear that practice follows Rebbi Nathan? He answered, I heard that Rebbi Joshua ben Qorḥa agrees with Rebbi Nathan. He said, do we need this[203]? He said, Rebbi Yose ben Ḥanina only intended to elevate Rebbi Simeon bar Yaqim because he was an important person.

201 From here on, there is no parallel in *Ševu`ot.* The entire story is told in the Babli, 30 a/b, about R. Johanan instead of R. Jonathan.

202 Sit with the ordained judges.

203 This is obvious since R. Joshua ben Qorha does not require the witnesses to testify from the same point of view. Since he accepts testimonies which are consistent but not identical, he also must accept testimonies that are not synchronous.

(21d line 21) רַב חִסְדָּא בָּעֵי. מָהוּ לְקַבֵּל עֵדִים שֶׁלֹּא בִפְנֵי בַּעַל דִּין. רִבִּי יוֹסֵי בְשֵׁם רִבִּי שַׁבְּתַי. מְקַבְּלִין עֵדִים שֶׁלֹּא בִפְנֵי בַּעַל דִּין וְעָבְדִין לֵיהּ גְּזַר דִּין. אִם בָּא וְעִרְעֵר עִרְעֲרוֹ קַיָּים. אָדָם שֶׁשָּׁלְחוּ אַחֲרָיו בֵּית דִּין ג' פְּעָמִים וְלֹא בָא. רִבִּי יְהוֹשֻׁעַ בֶּן לֵוִי אָמַר. מְקַבְּלִין הָעֵדוּת שֶׁלֹּא בִפְנֵי בַּעַל דִּין וְעָבְדִין לֵיהּ גְּזַר דִּין. כְּהָדָא כַּהֲנָא דְמָךְ וּשְׁבַק יַרְתּוֹ לְרִבִּי יֹאשִׁיָּה וּקְבִיל רִבִּי לָעְזָר סָהֲדוּ דְלָא בְאַפּוֹי וּזְכֵי לְרִבִּי יֹאשִׁיָּה. וְלֹא עוֹד אֶלָּא דִשְׁבַק סְפָרִים. כָּתַב רִבִּי לָעְזָר לְיָרְתוֹי. סְפָרִים שֶׁזָּכַת בָּהֶן אֶרֶץ יִשְׂרָאֵל אֵין מוֹצִיאִין אוֹתָן חוּצָה לָאָרֶץ. רִבִּי נִיסִּי בְשֵׁם רִבִּי לָעְזָר. אִם כָּתַב עַל מְנָת לְהוֹצִיא מוֹצִיא. רִבִּי חִיָּיה בַּר בָּא בְּעָא קוֹמֵי רִבִּי יָסֵי. מָהוּ לְהוֹצִיא. אָמַר לֵיהּ. לְעוֹבְדָא אַתְּ שְׁאַל לִי. אָמַר לֵיהּ. לֹא. וּבְאִישׁ לְרִבִּי זְעִירָא דְלָא אֲמַר לֵיהּ עוֹבְדָא בְּגִין מֵידַע מָהוּ אֲמַר.

Rav Ḥisda asked: May one receive witnesses not in the presence of one of the parties? Rebbi Yose[204] in the name of Rebbi Sabbatai: One may receive witnesses not in the presence of the parties and even issue a decision, but if [the absent party] appeals, their appeal must be heard. If a person was summoned by the court three times and did not appear, Rebbi Joshua ben Levi said that one may receive witnesses not in the presence of the parties and issue a decision[205]. As the following: Cahana[206] died and had willed his estate to Rebbi Joshia. Rebbi Eleazar heard witnesses[207] not in the presence [of the heirs] and handed the estate to Rebbi Joshia. Not only that, but the estate contained Torah scrolls. Rebbi Eleazar wrote to his heirs[208]: Scrolls won by the Land of Israel cannot be taken outside. Rebbi Nissai in the name of Rebbi Eleazar: If they were written for export, they can be exported. Rebbi Ḥiyya bar Abba asked before Rebbi Yasa: May one export? He asked him, do you ask me in a practical case? He answered, no[209]. Rebbi Ze`ira was dissatisfied[210] that he had not asked in a practical case, to know what he would have said.

204 Probably one should read *Yasa* for *Yose*; cf. *Diqduqe Soferim Bava qamma* p. 136b, Note 2.

205 The Babli restricts hearing witnesses not in the presence of both parties to this and similar cases; *Bava qamma* 112b.

206 A Babylonian without relatives in Galilee.

207 That Cahana's will conformed to the law of death-bed wills which supersedes the rights of heirs.

208 In Babylonia.

209 R. Yasa did not answer a purely theoretical question. Therefore, we do not know whether the other students of R. Eleazar accepted R. Eleazar's position.

210 R. Hiyya bar Abba's student and successor.

(21d line 32) רִבִּי יִרְמְיָה הֲוָה לֵיהּ דִּין עִם חַד בַּר נַשׁ וְקִבְּלוּן לְשָׁהֲדַייָא דְלָא בְאַפּוֹי דְרִבִּי יִרְמְיָה וְחִייְבוּן לְרִבִּי יִרְמְיָה. וַהֲוָה יְתִיב וּמִצְטָעֵר. אֵיפְשַׁר מְקַבְּלִין עֵדִים בְּלֹא בַעַל דִּין. רִבִּי הוּנָא רִבִּי פִּינְחָס רִבִּי חִזְקִיָּה חוּקוֹק לָא עָלוּן בְּפִירְקָא בְּהַהוּא יוֹמָא. דָּחַק רִבִּי הוּנָא וְאָעַל וּשְׁכַח לְרִבִּי יִרְמְיָה מִצְטָעֵר וְאָמַר. אֵיפְשַׁר מְקַבְּלִין עֵדִים בְּלֹא בַעַל דִּין אֲפִילוּ עִמָּהֶן בְּאוֹתָהּ הָעִיר. אָמַר לֵיהּ. כֵּן חָמַת דַּעְתּוֹן דְּרַבָּנִן.

Rebbi Jeremiah[211] had a suit against a certain person. They accepted testimony not in the presence of Rebbi Jeremiah, and decided against Rebbi Jeremiah. He was sitting despondent; is it possible that one accepts witnesses not in the presence of the parties? Rebbi Hina, Rebbi Phineas, and Rebbi Hizqiah from Ḥuqoq did not go to the lecture[212] on that day, but Rebbi Huna pushed, went in, and found Rebbi Jeremiah despondent; is it possible that one accepts witnesses not in the presence of the parties even if they are present with them in the same city? He told him, this is seen to be the rabbis' opinion[213].

211 A born Babylonian.

212 During the half-yearly study sessions.

213 Since the decision always could be reversed on appeal and the rabbinic court anyhow acted only as an arbitration panel, in contrast to Babylonia where most of the time the rabbinic court had government backing in civil cases. Cf. the Introduction to Tractate *Neziqin*, pp.3-4.

(fol. 20d) **משנה יא:** גָּמְרוּ אֶת הַדָּבָר הָיוּ מַכְנִיסִין אוֹתָן. הַגָּדוֹל שֶׁבַּדַּייָנִין אוֹמֵר אִישׁ פְּלוֹנִי אַתָּה זַכַּאי אִישׁ פְּלוֹנִי אַתָּה חַייָב. וּמְנַיִין כְּשֶׁיֵּצֵא לֹא יֹאמַר אֲנִי הוּא הַמְזַכֶּה וַחֲבֵרַי מְחַייְבִין וּמָה אֶעֱשֶׂה וְרַבּוּ עָלַי. עַל זֶה נֶאֱמַר הוֹלֵךְ רָכִיל מְגַלֶּה סּוֹד:

Mishnah 11: When they have come to a decision, they bring the parties in. The chief judge says, Mr. X, you are not guilty, Mr. X, you are guilty. From where that afterwards, one may not say, I had found for you but my colleagues found you guilty, but what can I do since they were a majority against me? On such a one it was said: *The gossip uncovers secrets*[214].

(21d line 38) **הלכה יא:** גָּמְרוּ אֶת הַדָּבָר כול'. אָמַר רִבִּי יוֹחָנָן. כּוֹפִין אֶת הַמְחַייֵב שֶׁיִּכְתּוֹב זַכַּאי. רִבִּי שִׁמְעוֹן בֶּן לָקִישׁ אָמַר. הַמְחַייֵב כּוֹתֵב חַייָב וְהַמְזַכֶּה כוֹתֵב זַכַּאי. מַתְנִיתָא פְלִיגָא עַל רֵישׁ לָקִישׁ. מְנַיִין כְּשֶׁיֵּצֵא לֹא יֹאמַר. אֲנִי מְזַכֶּה וַחֲבֵרַיי מְחַייְבִין. מָה עֲבַד לָהּ רִבִּי יוֹחָנָן. דְּלָא יְהֵא מָאן דְּהוּא מֵימַר. כַּמָּה בָעִית לִפְלוֹנִי מְזַכֶּה לִפְלוֹנִי בְדִינָא וְלָא שַׁבְקוֹן לִי. מַאי טַעֲמָא דְרֵישׁ לָקִישׁ. דְּלָא יֵיתֵי חוֹרָן וְיִסְבּוֹר דִּכְווָתֵיהּ וְיֵיצַר. אוּף פְּלָן הֲוָה תַמָּן אוּף הוּא טָעָה.

Halakhah 11: "When they have come to a decision," etc. Rebbi Joḥanan said, one forces the one who finds guilty to write "not guilty.[215]" Rebbi Simeon ben Laqish says, the one who finds guilty, writes "guilty"; the one who finds not guilty, writes "not guilty"[216]. The Mishnah disagrees with Rebbi Simeon ben Laqish: "From where that afterwards, one may not say, I had found for you but my colleagues found you guilty." What does Rebbi Joḥanan do with this? That nobody could say, I really wanted to justify X in his suit but they did not let me do it[217]. What is Rebbi Simeon ben Laqish's reason? That no other person should come, reason as he did, and say, also that one was there and he erred[218].

214 *Prov.* 11:13. Since this is from the Hagiographs, it does not have the force of a Torah verse.

215 The decision has to be signed by all three judges, Babli 30a.

216 The dissenter may write a dissenting opinion, Babli 30a.

217 His rule enforces the Mishnah.

218 The dissenting opinion might in the course of history become the majority opinion; then its author should get due credit.

(fol. 20d) **משנה יב:** כָּל־זְמַן שֶׁמֵּבִיא רְאָיָה סוֹתֵר אֶת הַדִּין. אָמְרוּ לוֹ כָּל־רְאָיוֹת שֶׁיֵּשׁ לְךָ הָבֵא מִכָּאן עַד שְׁלֹשִׁים יוֹם. הֵבִיא בְתוֹךְ שְׁלֹשִׁים יוֹם סוֹתֵר לְאַחַר שְׁלֹשִׁים יוֹם אֵינוֹ סוֹתֵר. אָמַר רַבָּן שִׁמְעוֹן בֶּן גַּמְלִיאֵל מַה יַּעֲשֶׂה לֹא מָצָא בְתוֹךְ שְׁלֹשִׁים וּמָצָא לְאַחַר שְׁלֹשִׁים. אָמְרוּ לוֹ הָבֵא עֵדִים

אָמַר אֵין לִי עֵדִים הָבֵא רְאָיָה אָמַר אֵין לִי רְאָיָה וּלְאַחַר זְמַן מָצָא רְאָיָה וּמָצָא עֵדִים הֲרֵי זֶה אֵינוֹ כְלוּם.

Mishnah 12: Any time one produces a proof he may demand a new trial[219]. If they told him, produce all your proofs within thirty days, if he produced within thirty days, he gets a new trial, after thirty days he does not get a new trial. Rabban Simeon ben Gamliel said, what can one do if he did not find within thirty [days] but found after thirty [days][220]? If they told him, produce witnesses; he said, I have no witness; produce proofs; he said, I have no proofs. If later he found a proof, or he found witnesses, this is irrelevant[221].

219 The person who lost a civil suit may request a new trial based on new documentary evidence ("proof") or new witnesses.

220 He is entitled to a new trial if he can explain the delay. In general, practice follows Rabban Simeon ben Gamliel in the Mishnah.

221 The court has to assume that the documents are forged and the witnesses false.

(21d line 45) **הלכה יב**: כָּל־זְמַן שֶׁהוּא מֵבִיא רְאָיָה כול'. אָמַר רִבִּי אוֹשַׁעְיָא. תַּמָּן שֶׁאֶיפְשַׁר לָהֶן לְהוֹסִיף דָּנִין אֵילּוּ כְנֶגֶד אֵילּוּ. בְּרַם הָכָא אִי אֶיפְשַׁר לָהֶן לְהוֹסִיף. רִבִּי יוֹחָנָן וְרֵישׁ לָקִישׁ תְּרֵיהוֹן מָרִין. אֲפִילוּ הָכָא אֶיפְשַׁר לָהֶן לְהוֹסִיף.

Halakhah 12: "Any time one produces a proof," etc. [222]Rebbi Oshaiah said, there[223], where it is possible to add, they continue to argue. But here it is impossible to add[224]. Rebbi Joḥanan and Rebbi Simeon ben Laqish both teach that even here it is possible to add[225].

222 The discussion of Mishnah 12 is in Halakhah 13. Therefore, the indication of a new Halakhah here is erroneous; the reference still is to Mishnah 11, in reference to a split decision of the court.

223 Mishnah 5:7, referring to criminal proceedings. If the court has the maximum number of members, 71, and 35 each are for conviction and acquittal while one is undecided, they have to continue to argue until the undecided judge makes up his mind.

224 He holds that in civil trials one never adds judges. Therefore, even if there are only three judges, they have to continue to argue among themselves until each one has made up his mind.

225 They hold that the rules of adding judges are identical for civil and criminal trials (Maimonides, *Hilkhot Sanhedrin* 8:2).

(fol. 20d) **משנה יג**: אָמַר רַבָּן שִׁמְעוֹן בֶּן גַּמְלִיאֵל מַה יַּעֲשֶׂה לֹא הָיָה יוֹדֵעַ שֶׁיֵּשׁ לוֹ עֵדִים וּמָצָא עֵדִים וְלֹא הָיָה יוֹדֵעַ שֶׁיֵּשׁ לוֹ רְאָיָה וּמָצָא רְאָיָה. אָמְרוּ לוֹ הָבֵא עֵדִים אָמַר אֵין לִי עֵדִים הָבֵא רְאָיָה אָמַר אֵין לִי רְאָיָה רָאָה שֶׁמִּתְחַיֵּיב בַּדִּין וְאָמַר קִרְבוּ פְּלוֹנִי וּפְלוֹנִי וְהַעִידוּנִי אוֹ שֶׁהוֹצִיא רְאָיָה מִתּוֹךְ אֲפֻנְדָּתוֹ הֲרֵי זֶה אֵינוֹ כְלוּם:

Mishnah 13: Rabban Gamliel said, what should he do who did not know that he had witnesses but found witnesses; he did not know that he had proof, but he found proof[226]? If they told him, produce witnesses; he said, I have no witness; produce proofs; he said, I have no proofs; when he saw that the decision would go against him he said, X and Y shall come and testify for me, or he produced proof from his money belt, this is irrelevant[221].

226 This refers to the last case in Mishnah 12. Late submissions must be accepted if the litigant can prove that he had no knowledge of the witnesses or documents within the period allotted him by the court.

(21d line 48) **הלכה יג**: אָמַר רַבָּן שִׁמְעוֹן בֶּן גַּמְלִיאֵל כול'. רִבִּי יוֹחָנָן בְּשֵׁם רַב הוֹשַׁעְיָה. תְּלָתָא אֲמוֹרִין. חַד אָמַר. כָּל־זְמַן שֶׁמֵּבִיא רְאָיָיה סוֹתֵר אֶת הַדִּין. וְחַד אָמַר. הֵבִיא בְתוֹךְ ל' סוֹתֵר. לְאַחַר ל' אֵינוֹ סוֹתֵר. וְחַד אָמַר. לְעוֹלָם אֵין סוֹתֵר עַד שֶׁיָּבִיא רְאָיָיה שֶׁלֹּא הָיָה יוֹדֵעַ בָּהּ כָּל־עִיקָּר. וְהָתַנִּינָן. אָמַר רַבָּן שִׁמְעוֹן בֶּן גַּמְלִיאֵל. מַה יַּעֲשֶׂה לֹא הָיָה יוֹדֵעַ שֶׁיֵּשׁ לוֹ עֵדִים וּמָצָא עֵדִים. שֶׁיֵּשׁ לוֹ רְאָיָה וּמָצָא רְאָיָה כול'. רִבִּי לָא וְרִבִּי זְעִירָא. חַד אָמַר. עַד שֶׁיְּבַטֵּל רְאָיוֹתָיו. וְ חַד אָמַר. עַד שֶׁיִּכְפּוֹר בִּרְאָיוֹתָיו.

Halakhah 13: "Rabban Simeon ben Gamliel said," etc. Rebbi Joḥanan in the name of Rav Hoshaiah: Three Amoraïm[227]. One said, any time he brings proof he can demand a new trial. The other said, if he brought within 30 days[228], he can demand a new trial, after 30 days he cannot demand a new trial. The other said, he never can demand a new trial unless he prove that he absolutely had no knowledge of it[226]. But did we not state: "Rabban Gamliel said, what should he do who did not know that he had witnesses but found witnesses; that he had no proof, but found proof?" Rebbi La and Rebbi Ze`ira: One said, unless he voided his proofs[229]; the other said, until he disclaimed his proofs[230].

227 They explain Rabban Simeon ben Gamliel's words.

228 Of judgment rendered.

229 Rabban Simeon ben Gamliel will agree that he is restricted in asking for a new trial if he himself had belittled the possibility of finding other proof in a statement before the court.

230 He had affirmed before the court that there was nothing to be added.

(21d line 56) רִבִּי לֵוִי הֲוָה לֵיהּ דִּין עִם חַד בַּר נַשׁ עַל עֶסֶק בָּתִּים. וַהֲווֹן דַּיְינִין קוֹמֵי רִבִּי לָעְזָר. לְאַחַר גְּמַר דִּין הֵבִיא רְאָיָה. שָׁאַל לְרִבִּי יוֹחָנָן. אָמַר לֵיהּ. כָּל־זְמַן שֶׁמֵּבִיא רְאָיָה סוֹתֵר הַדִּין. רִבִּי אֶבְמַכִּיס הֲוָה לֵיהּ דִּין עִם חַד בַּר נַשׁ עַל עֵיסֶק רֵיחַיָּא. וַהֲווֹן אִידַיְינִין קוֹמֵי רִבִּי לָעְזָר. לְאַחַר גְּמַר דִּין הֵבִיא עֵדִים. שָׁאַל לְרִבִּי יוֹחָנָן. אָמַר לֵיהּ. אַדַּיִין אַתְּ לָזוֹ. כָּל־זְמַן שֶׁמֵּבִיא רְאָיָה סוֹתֵר אֶת הַדִּין. וְלָמָּה תְּרֵין עוֹבְדִין. רִבִּי לֵוִי לֹא אִיתְעֲבֵד לֵיהּ גְּזַר דִּין. רִבִּי אֶבְמַכִּיס אִיתְעֲבֵד לֵיהּ גְּזַר דִּין.

Rebbi Levi had a suit against a certain person about houses; they had it judged before Rebbi Eleazar. After a decision was reached he presented proof. He[231] asked Rebbi Joḥanan, who told him, any time one brings proof[232] he can demand a new trial. Rebbi Eumachos had a suit against a certain person about mills; they had it judged before Rebbi Eleazar. After a decision was reached he presented witnesses. He asked Rebbi Joḥanan, who said to him, is that still a problem for you? Any time one brings proof he can demand a new trial. Why did it need two cases? In Rebbi Levy's case, no formal verdict had been rendered, in Rebbi Eumachos's case, a formal verdict had been rendered[233].

231 R. Eleazar.

232 Since in the next case, the same expression of "proof" is used in connection with witnesses, it seems that it refers not to the actual proof submitted to the court but to the justification, submitting proof that the new material was unknown to the litigant during the trial.

233 Since in both cases it seems that the additional material was submitted close to the time of the trial, R. Joḥanan did not indicate which of the three Amoraïm he was following. His instruction is binding precedent.

(21d line 63) אִשֵּׁר הַדַּייָנִין מָהוּ שֶׁיְּהֵא צָרִיךְ בֵּית דִּין. רִבִּי הוֹשַׁעְיָה בְשֵׁם שְׁמוּאֵל רַב בַּנַּיי בְשֵׁם שְׁמוּאֵל. חַד אָמַר. יִתְקַיֵּים אוֹ בִכְתַב יְדֵי עֵדִם אוֹ בִכְתַב יְדֵי הַדַּייָנִים. וְחַד אָמַר. אֲפִילוּ בִכְתַב אֶחָד וּבְדַיָּין אֶחָד.

Does a judicial confirmation need a court[234]? Rebbi Hoshaia in the name of Samuel, Rav Bannai in the name of Samuel. One said, it should be confirmed either by the handwriting of the witnesses or the handwriting of the judges[235]; the other said, even with one handwriting and one judge[236].

234 A mortgage foreclosure was certified by a certain court which confirmed the genuineness of document and claim. The property to be foreclosed was in the domain of another court. Does the second court have to ascertain that the certification be genuine or do we assume that court documents cannot be forged and the second court has to authorize the foreclosure?

235 Either the genuineness of the mortgage or the genuineness of the judicial endorsement has to be determined.

236 Two signatures have to be confirmed, but it may be the signature of one witness and one judge since the judges by their endorsement become witnesses to the genuineness of the document. This is the final determination of the Babli, *Ketubot* 21a.

אחד דיני ממונות פרק רביעי

משנה א: אֶחָד דִּינֵי מָמוֹנוֹת וְאֶחָד דִּינֵי נְפָשׁוֹת בִּדְרִישָׁה וּבַחֲקִירָה שֶׁנֶּאֱמַר מִשְׁפַּט אֶחָד יִהְיֶה לָכֶם. מַה בֵּין דִּינֵי מָמוֹנוֹת לְדִינֵי נְפָשׁוֹת. דִּינֵי מָמוֹנוֹת בִּשְׁלֹשָׁה וְדִינֵי נְפָשׁוֹת בְּעֶשְׂרִים וּשְׁלֹשָׁה. דִּינֵי מָמוֹנוֹת פּוֹתְחִין בֵּין לִזְכוּת בֵּין לְחוֹבָה וְדִינֵי נְפָשׁוֹת פּוֹתְחִין לִזְכוּת וְאֵין פּוֹתְחִין בְּחוֹבָה.

Mishnah 1: Both civil suits and criminal suits require cross-examination and investigation[1], as it is said: *One set of rules shall be for you*[23]. What is the difference between civil suits and criminal suits? Civil suits are tried before three judges, criminal suits before 23. In civil suits one starts with arguments either for acquittal or conviction; in criminal courts one starts with arguments[4] for acquittal but not for conviction.

1 Cross-examination is the interrogation of witnesses which changes from trial to trial. Investigation is the determination of answers to the obligatory questions enumerated in Mishnah 5:1.

2 *Lev*. 24:22.

3 A verdict for the plaintiff means monetary loss for the defendant. A verdict for the defendant means no money for the plaintiff. Therefore, it is irrelevant which side of the argument is discussed first among the judges.

4 In the discussion by the judges after all evidence was presented.

(22a line 47) **הלכה א**: אֶחָד דִּינֵי מָמוֹנוֹת כול'. אָמַר רִבִּי יוֹחָנָן. בִּשְׁבִיל לָחוּס עַל מָמוֹן יִשְׂרָאֵל אָמְרוּ. הֵיאַךְ אַתָּה יוֹדֵעַ שֶׁזֶּה חַיָּב לָזֶה. רִבִּי חִיָּיה בַּר בָּא בְעָא קוֹמֵי רִבִּי יוֹסֵי. הֵיךְ עָבְדִין עוֹבְדָא. אָמַר לֵיהּ. כְּרִבִּי יוֹחָנָן. דְּרִבִּי יוֹחָנָן אָמַר. בִּשְׁבִיל לָחוּס עַל מָמוֹן יִשְׂרָאֵל אָמְרוּ. הֵיאַךְ אַתָּה יוֹדֵעַ שֶׁזֶּה חַיָּב לָזֶה. זְעִיר בַּר חִינְנָא בְשֵׁם רִבִּי חֲנִינָה וְרַב יְהוּדָה. חַד אָמַר. וְדָרַשְׁתָּ וְחָקַרְתָּ וְשָׁאַלְתָּ הֵיטֵב. וְחַד אָמַר. צֶדֶק צֶדֶק תִּרְדֹּף. הָא כֵיצַד. אִם אַתְּ רוֹאֶה הַדִּין שֶׁיּוֹצֵא לַאֲמִיתּוֹ חָקְרֵיהוּ וְאִם לָאו צַדְּקֵיהוּ.

רַב הוּנָא כַּד הֲוָה חֲמִי שֶׁהַדִּין מְכַוְונָא הֲוָה חֲקַר וְכַד הֲוָה חֲמִי הָכֵן וְהָכֵן הֲוָה מְכַוֵּין.

Halakhah 1: "Both civil suits," etc. Rebbi Johanan said, to protect Israel's money they said, "tell why you know that this person owes the other.[5]" Rebbi Ḥiyya bar Abba asked before Rebbi Yasa[6]: What does one do in practice? He answered, following Rebbi Joḥanan, as Rebbi Joḥanan said, to protect Israel's money they said, "tell why you know that this person owes the other."

Ze'ir bar Ḥinena in the name of Rebbi Ḥanina and Rav Jehudah, one said: *You shall cross-examine, investigate, and inquire well*[7]. The other said, *equity, equity you shall pursue.*[8] How is that? If you see that the verdict will be the truth, investigate it[9]; otherwise, act in equity.[10]

[11]When Rav Huna saw that witnesses said exactly the same, he was investigating. When he saw them essentially identical, he determined the common element.

5 While the Mishnah requires the same kind of cross-examinations and determinations in civil as in criminal cases, R. Johanan holds that by rabbinic *fiat*, witnesses in civil cases are not to be subjected to cross-examinations that stray from the main topic. While it is necessary in criminal trials to disqualify any witness whose testimony is not 100% consistent (since God has promised to punish every evildoer who escapes human justice, *Ex.* 23:7), excessively rigid standards in civil cases would prevent most owners of capital from lending it, therefore leading to the ruin of the poor. It is in the public interest that claims be swiftly and easily adjudicated. The question quoted (Mishnah 3:9) is the paradigm for any questions to be asked.

6 One has to read יסא for יוסי. R. Hiyya bar Abba was R. Yasa's student and R. Yose's teacher's teacher.

7 *Deut.* 13:15, referring to a criminal case.

8 *Deut.* 16:20, referring to all judicial proceedings.

9 In criminal cases, there is an obligation on the judges to ascertain the truth as well as possible. In the Babli, 32a, the duty to careful investigation is emphasized in all cases where the judges suspect foul play by one of the parties; cf. Note 10.

10 In civil cases, the judges have to ascertain that the judgment be equitable.

11 Halakhah 3:9, Notes 139-140.

(22a line 55) כֵּיצַד פּוֹתְחִין לִזְכוּת. אוֹמְרִין. אֶיפְשַׁר שֶׁזֶּה הָרַג אֶת הַנֶּפֶשׁ. אָמַר רִבִּי יוֹסֵי. אִין כֵּינִי. אָמַר אֶחָד מִן הָעֵדִים. יֵשׁ לִי לְלַמֵּד עָלָיו זְכוּת. וּבָא חֲבֵירוֹ וְסִייְעוֹ. וְיֵשׁ בָּאן סִיּוּעַ. אִם אוֹמֵר אַתְּ כֵּן לֹא נִמְצֵאתָ חָב לַדַּייָנִים. וְיֵשׁ עֵדִים לְשְׁקָרִן.

How does one start for acquittal? One says, is it possible that this one be a murderer[12]? Rebbi Yose said, if this is so, if one of the witnesses said, I have something to say in his defense, and his colleague comes to support him, is that support? If you say so, would you not put guilt on the judges, to lead witnesses to lie?

12 If the judges in their discussions say this, after the evidence was heard, nothing bad can be said. R. Yose reads the question as one directed towards eye witnesses to a murder. An intimation by the judges that they do not believe the witnesses may lead them to lie to exonerate the murderer; this would make the judges accomplices of the murderer after the fact.

(22a line 58) אָמַר רִבִּי יוֹחָנָן. כָּל־שֶׁאֵינוֹ יוֹדֵעַ לָדוּן אֶת הַשֶּׁרֶץ לְטַהֲרוֹ וּלְטַמְּאוֹ מֵאָה פְעָמִים אֵין יָכוֹל לִפְתּוֹחַ בִּזְכוּת. כֵּיצַד דָּנִין הַשֶּׁרֶץ. אָמַר רִבִּי יַנַּאי. מַה אִם הַנָּחָשׁ שֶׁמֵּמִית טָהוֹר. עַכְבָּר שֶׁאֵין מֵמִית אֵינוֹ דִין לִהְיוֹת טָהוֹר. אוֹ חִילוּף. עַכְבָּר שֶׁאֵין מֵמִית טָמֵא. נָחָשׁ שֶׁמֵּמִית אֵינוֹ דִין לִהְיוֹת טָמֵא. הָתִיב רִבִּי פִּינְחָס. הֲרֵי עַקְרָב מֵמִית וַהֲרֵי הוּא טָהוֹר. אַשְׁכַּח תַּנֵּי אֲמַר. הוּא נָחָשׁ הוּא עַקְרָב.

אָמַר רִבִּי. תַּלְמִיד וָתִיק הָיָה לְרִבִּי וְהָיָה מְטַהֵר אֶת הַשֶּׁרֶץ וּמְטַמְּאוֹ ק' פְּעָמִים. אָמְרִין. הַהוּא תַלְמִידָא לָא הֲוָה יָדַע מוֹרִייָה. אָמַר רִבִּי יַעֲקֹב בַּר דּוֹסַאי. הַהוּא תַלְמִידָא קְטוּעַ מִטּוּרָא דְסִינַי הֲוָה.

Rebbi Johanan said, anybody who cannot argue for the crawling animal to make it pure a hundred times cannot start arguing for acquittal[13]. How does one argue about a crawling animal? Rebbi Johanan said, since a snake which kills[14] is pure, a rat which does not kill logically should be pure. Since a rat which does not kill is impure, a snake which kills logically should be impure. Rebbi Phineas objected: Is there not the scorpion which kills and is pure? It was found that a Tanna said, snake and scorpion both follow the same rules.

[15]Rebbi said, Rebbi [ ] had a self-confident student who was arguing for purity or impurity of the crawling animal a hundred times. They said, this student never could instruct[16]. Rebbi Jacob bar Dositheos said, this student was cut-off from Mount Sinai[17].

13 In the Babli, 17a, Rav states that anybody who cannot argue for the purity of crawling animals is not a candidate for membership in the Synhedrion. *Lev.* 11:29-38 describes the impurity of eight particular crawling animals (mostly reptiles). The list includes the rat. (For some reason, the commentator to the Babli 91a, probably Rashi's son-in-law Jehuda ben Nathan, defines עַכְבָּר as *écureuil*, "squirrel".) All other crawling animals,

including snakes (*Lev.* 11:42), are forbidden as food but their carcasses are not impure.

14 It kills both humans and domestic animals, thereby causing the severe impurities of corpses and animal carcasses. For logical consistency, the agent of impurity should be impure; Babli *Eruvin* 13b.

15 In the Babli *Eruvin* 13b, Rebbi *Johanan* said, Rebbi *Meïr* had a student by the name of Symmachos who could give 49 reasons for everything pure and 49 reasons for everything impure. [In *Midrash Tehillim*, ed. Buber p. 108 Note 37, it is R. Aqiba's student Rebbi Meïr.] Since Symmachos is praised, the stories are not parallel and the names cannot be copied. It is clear that the second "Rebbi" needs to be followed by a name.

The same Babli also quotes a *baraita* that at Jabneh there was a self-confident (ותיק واثق) student who could give 150 reasons for the purity of crawling animals. This is the parallel to the *baraita* here.

16 A Sophist cannot come to a clear decision of what is right.

17 Even though all future Jewish souls, including proselytes, participated in receiving the Torah at Mount Sinai, that student was excluded as not being Jewish. (Cf. H. Guggenheimer, *The Scholar's Haggadah*, Northvale NJ 1995, p. 308-309.)

(fol. 21d) **משנה ב**: דִּינֵי מָמוֹנוֹת מַטִּין עַל פִּי עֵד אֶחָד בֵּין לִזְכוּת בֵּין לְחוֹבָה וְדִינֵי נְפָשׁוֹת מַטִּין עַל פִּי עֵד אֶחָד לִזְכוּת וְעַל פִּי שְׁנַיִם לְחוֹבָה.

Mishnah 2: Civil suits are decided[18] by one witness[19] whether for credit or debit; criminal suits are decided by one witness[19] for acquittal and two for conviction[20].

18 The use of the verb נטה "to bend" referring to judicial decision is from *Ex.* 23:2.

19 This is a rather frequent scribal error (including the *editio princeps* of Maimonides's Code) induced by the common expression "one witness". Decisions are not made by witnesses but by votes of judges. The word "witness" has to be deleted both times (cf.*Diqduqe Soferim Sanhedrin* p. 87, Note 1.)

20 If 12 judges vote for conviction and 11 for acquittal, it is a potential mistrial. A difference of two votes between those voting for conviction or acquittal is possible only if an odd number of judges abstain.

(22a line 67) **הלכה ב**: דִּינֵי מָמוֹנוֹת מַטִּין כול'. אָמַר רִבִּי יַנַּאי. אִילּוּ נִיתְּנָה הַתּוֹרָה חֲתוּכָה לֹא הָיְתָה לָרֶגֶל עֲמִידָה. מַה טַעֲמָא. וַיְדַבֵּר יי אֶל־מֹשֶׁה. אָמַר לְפָנָיו. רִבּוֹנוֹ שֶׁלְּעוֹלָם. הוֹדִיעֵנִי הֵיאָךְ הִיא הַהֲלָכָה. אָמַר לוֹ. אַחֲרֵי רַבִּים לְהַטּוֹת׃ רָבוּ הַמְזַכִּין זָכוּ. רָבוּ הַמְחַייְבִין חִייְבוּ. כְּדֵי

שֶׁתְּהֵא הַתּוֹרָה נִדְרֶשֶׁת מ"ט פָּנִים טָמֵא וּמ"ט פָּנִים טָהוֹר. מִנְייָן ודגלו. וְכֵן הוּא אוֹמֵר אִמְרוֹת יי אֲמָרוֹת טְהֹרוֹת כֶּסֶף צָרוּף בַּעֲלִיל לָאָרֶץ מְזוּקָּק שִׁבְעָתָיִם׃ וְאוֹמֵר מֵישָׁרִים אֲהֵבוּךָ׃

Halakhah 2: "Civil suits are decided," etc. Rebbi Yannai said, if the Torah had been given decided[21], no foot could stand. What is the reason? *The Eternal spoke to Moses*[22]. He said before Him: Master of the Universe, inform me what is the practice. He told him, *to bend*[23] *after the majority.*[18] If there was a majority for acquitting, they acquitted; if there was a majority for convicting, they convicted; so that the Torah[24] could be explained in 49 ways impure and 49 ways pure, the numerical value of[25] ודגלו. And so it says[26]: *the commands of the Eternal are pure sayings; molten silver in an earthenware crucible, refined sevenfold.* And it says[27], *the straightforward love You.*

21 חתך "to cut" in this connection is a translation of Latin *decidere* (literally "to cut off; settle, decide.) There is no reason why R. Yannai could not have acted as a Roman Judge, just like his contemporary R. Jonathan (cf. *Bava batra* 3:4 and *Introduction to Tractate Neziqin.*) R. Yannai counts it as an advantage that the Torah is formulated as a set of potentially ambiguous principles rather than a collection of court decisions which would represent unchangeable precedents.

22 *Qorban He`edah* takes this as a reference to *Ex.* 12:1, where v. 2 continues: *This month is for you the beginning of months; first it shall be for you of the year's months.* The two clauses in the verse have different status. In the first part, God designated the first month of the year of the Exodus. In the second part, Moses and his successors are commanded to determine every year which month should be "first". The Torah does not give an algorithm to determine which lunar month has to serve as "Spring Month" (*Ex.* 13:4). Any calendar system agreed to by Moses's successors has divine sanction. (The current method, concentrating on designating the seventh month, from time to time yields rather questionable results.)

23 This is the opposite of rigidity. The understanding of Torah and with it the entire code of behavior required by it is a function of time. While precedents should be overthrown only for very weighty reasons, no rule is invariable for all times.

24 That means, every precept in the Torah can be explained as having 49 different negative and 49 different positive aspects.

25 *Cant.* 2:4: "His banner over me is love." The numerical value is 6+4+3+30+6 = 49.

26 *Ps.* 12:7. "Sevenfold" is interpreted as $7^2 = 49$.

27 *Cant.* 1:4. Since מישרים is a plural, it indicates that the Torah has a plurality of straightforward interpretations.

(fol. 21d) **משנה ג**: דִּינֵי מָמוֹנוֹת מַחֲזִירִין בֵּין לִזְכוּת בֵּין לְחוֹבָה. דִּינֵי נְפָשׁוֹת מַחֲזִירִין לִזְכוּת וְאֵין מַחֲזִירִין לְחוֹבָה.

Mishnah 3: Civil suits can be retried[28] both for credit and for debit. Criminal suits can be retried for acquittal[29] but not for conviction.

28 As explained in 3:10-13, civil suits can be re-opened if new documents or new witnesses become available.

29 Appeals and retrials are possible only after conviction but never after acquittal.

(22a line 74) **הלכה ג**: דִּינֵי מָמוֹנוֹת מַחֲזִירִין בֵּין לִזְכוּת בֵּין לְחוֹבָה כול'. הֲרֵי שֶׁיָּצָא מִבֵּית דִּין זַכַּאי וּמָצְאוּ לוֹ חוֹבָה. שׁוֹמֵעַ אֲנִי שֶׁיַּחֲזִירוּהוּ. תַּלְמוּד לוֹמַר צַדִּיק אַל תַּהֲרוֹג. הֲרֵי שֶׁיָּצָא מִבֵּית דִּין חַייָב וּמָצְאוּ לוֹ זְכוּת. שׁוֹמֵעַ אֲנִי שֶׁלֹּא יַחֲזִירוּהוּ. תַּלְמוּד לוֹמַר וְנָקִי אַל תַּהֲרוֹג. יָכוֹל אִם צָדַק בְּדִינָךְ יִצְדַּק בְּדִינִי. תַּלְמוּד לוֹמַר כִּי לֹא־אַצְדִּיק רָשָׁע: אָמַר רִבִּי יִצְחָק. אָמַר לִי רִבִּי יוֹסֵי. לֹא שַׁנְייָא אֶלָּא אֲפִילוּ נִזְדַּכֶּה בְטָעוּת מַחֲזִירִין אוֹתוֹ.

Halakhah 3: "Civil suits can be retried both for credit and for debit," etc. [30]If he left the court being acquitted, and they found reasons for conviction, could I understand that one returned him? The verse says[31], *do not slay the acquitted.* If he left the court being convicted, and they found reasons for acquittal, could I understand that one should not return him? The verse[31] says, *but do not slay the innocent*. I could think that if he is acquitted in your court, he is acquitted in My court; the verse[31] says, *I shall not acquit the wicked.*

Rebbi Isaac said, Rebbi Yose told me: There is no difference; if the acquittal was in error[32], one retries him.

30 Babli 33b, *Mekhilta dR. Ismael Mišpatim* 20 (p.327-328), *dR. Simeon ben Iohai* 23:7; shortened *Sifry Deut.* 144.

31 *Ex.* 23:7.

32 For example, if the clerk of court made an error in tallying the votes. The Babli, 33b, holds that a retrial is possible if an acquittal was in clear violation of a biblical verse.

(fol. 22a) **משנה ד**: דִּינֵי מָמוֹנוֹת הַכֹּל מְלַמְּדִין זְכוּת וְחוֹבָה. דִּינֵי נְפָשׁוֹת הַכֹּל מְלַמְּדִין זְכוּת וְאֵין הַכֹּל מְלַמְּדִין חוֹבָה.

Mishnah 4: In civil suits, anybody[33] may argue for credit or debit. In criminal suits, anybody may argue for acquittal but not everybody may argue for conviction[34].

33 Every judge.

34 As explained in Mishnah 5.

(22b line 4) **הלכה ד:** דִּינֵי מָמוֹנוֹת הַכֹּל מְלַמְּדִין זְכוּת וְחוֹבָה כול'. רִבִּי מִי בְעָא קוֹמֵי רִבִּי יוֹחָנָן. אֲפִילוּ נוֹאֵף וְנוֹאֶפֶת. אָמַר לֵיהּ. אִתְקְלַף מַרְקוּעָךְ.

Halakhah 4: "In civil suits, anybody may argue for credit or debit," etc. Rebbi Immi asked before Rebbi Johanan: Even an adulterer and an adulteress[35]? He told him, your patch came off[36].

35 It is obvious that this Halakhah does not refer to Mishnah 4. From the parallel in the Babli, 33b, where R. Ḥiyya bar Abba asked and received an insulting answer, one might refer to the preceding statement in Halakhah 3, whether adulterers who were acquitted after the adultery was proven may be retried. This interpretation requires one to adopt the Babli's explanation of R. Yose's statement.

If the Halakhah belongs to Mishnah 5, the question might be whether a judge who argued for acquittal in the case of an adulterer may argue for conviction in the following trial of the adulteress. Halakhah 9 and Tosephta 7:2 prescribe that adulterer and adulteress have to be tried separately on different days.

36 The question is stupid; it is as if you had a hole in your pants.

(fol. 22a) **משנה ה:** דִּינֵי מָמוֹנוֹת הַמְלַמֵּד זְכוּת מְלַמֵּד חוֹבָה וְהַמְלַמֵּד חוֹבָה מְלַמֵּד זְכוּת וְדִינֵי נְפָשׁוֹת הַמְלַמֵּד חוֹבָה מְלַמֵּד זְכוּת. אֲבָל הַמְלַמֵּד זְכוּת אֵינוֹ יָכוֹל לַחֲזוֹר וּלְלַמֵּד חוֹבָה.

Mishnah 5: In civil suits, one who argued for credit may argue for debit and one who argued for debit may argue for credit; but in criminal suits one who argued for conviction may argue for acquittal but one who argued for acquittal is barred from arguing for conviction.

(22b line 6) **הלכה ה:** דִּינֵי מָמוֹנוֹת הַמְלַמֵּד זְכוּת כול'. רִבִּי אָמַר. וּבִלְבַד שֶׁלֹּא יְהוּ מְחוּסָּרִין לוֹמַר. אִישׁ פְּלוֹנִי אַתָּה זַכַּאי וְאַתָּה חַייָב. אֲבָל אִם הָיוּ מְחוּסָּרִין בְּמַשָּׂה וּבְמַתָּן לֹא בְדָא. רִבִּי יוֹסֵי בֶן חֲנִינָה אָמַר. אֲפִילוּ מְחוּסָּרִין בְּמַשָּׂה וּמַתָּן.

Halakhah 5: "In civil suits, one who argued for credit," etc. Rebbi said, if they only miss saying, Mr. X, you are acquitted, or you are convicted; it does not apply to the discussion[37]. Rebbi Yose ben Ḥanina said, it also applies to the discussion[38].

37 A judge who argued for acquittal during the discussion is barred from voting for conviction during the final vote but a judge originally arguing for acquittal may change his mind during the discussion and later argue for conviction. In the Babli, 34b, Rav reads the Mishnah as implying that during the discussion, a person arguing for acquittal cannot then argue for conviction but the next day he may vote for conviction.

38 A judge originally arguing for acquittal cannot later argue for conviction.

(fol. 22a) **משנה ו**: דִּינֵי מָמוֹנוֹת דָּנִין בַּיּוֹם וְגוֹמְרִין בַּלַּיְלָה וְדִינֵי נְפָשׁוֹת דָּנִין בַּיּוֹם וְגוֹמְרִין בַּיּוֹם.

Mishnah 6: Civil suits are tried during the day and may be decided in the night but criminal suits are tried during the day and decided during daytime.

(22b line 9) **הלכה ו**: דִּינֵי מָמוֹנוֹת דָּנִין בַּיּוֹם כול'. מְנָלָן. וְשָׁפְטוּ אֶת־הָעָם בְּכָל־עֵת. וְאִית קְרִי לְשֶׁעָבַר. אָמַר רַב שְׁמוּאֵל בַּר רַב יִצְחָק. כֵּינִי מַתְנִיתָא. שֶׁאִם טָעוּ וְדָנוּ בַלַּיְלָה שֶׁדִּינָם דִּין. תַּלְמוּד לוֹמַר וְשָׁפְטוּ אֶת־הָעָם בְּכָל־עֵת. אָמַר. הָא אֲמִירָה.

Halakhah 6: "Civil suits are tried during the day," etc. From where this? *They judged the people at all times*[39]. But this is a verse about what happened[40]! Rav Samuel[41] ben Rav Isaac said: so is the *baraita*: If they erred and judged in the night, their judgment stands, as the verse said: *they shall judge the people at all times*[42]. He[43] said, that is a statement[44].

39 *Ex.* 18:26.

40 Information about what Moses had people do in the desert is quite different from prescription of future organization of courts. The context makes it clear that courts organized on Jethro's suggestion only handled civil suits *between a man and his neighbor*.

41 The name must be either *Rebbi* Samuel bar Rav Isaac or Rav *Naḥman* bar Rav Isaac; cf. *Bava qamma* 9:1, Note 12.

42 *Ex.* 18:22, the prescription of future organization. The Babli, 34b, disagrees and permits only finishing a trial which started during daytime.

43 The person who had raised the objection in the first place. In *Bava qamma* 9:1 (Note 16) the expression is used by Rav Nahman bar Jacob.

44 A true statement. Tosaphot *Yebamot* 104a *s. v.* מר feel forced to emend the text. This is unnecessary.

(fol. 22a) **משנה ז**: דִּינֵי מָמוֹנוֹת גּוֹמְרִין בּוֹ בַיּוֹם בֵּין לִזְכוּת בֵּין לְחוֹבָה. וְדִינֵי נְפָשׁוֹת גּוֹמְרִין בּוֹ בַיּוֹם לִזְכוּת וּבְיוֹם שֶׁלְּאַחֲרָיו לְחוֹבָה. לְפִיכָךְ אֵין דָּנִין לֹא בְעֶרֶב שַׁבָּת וְלֹא בְעֶרֶב יוֹם טוֹב׃

Mishnah 7: Civil suits are decided on the same day, whether for credit or debit. But criminal suits are decided the same day for acquittal, the next day[45] for conviction. Therefore one does not judge on Sabbath eve or holiday eve[46].

45 If there be a majority for conviction, one puts off the final vote for reasons for acquittal might be found in the meantime.

46 Neither judgment can be rendered nor the judgment executed on a Sabbath or holiday. The possibility of a trial taking longer than one day is not contemplated.

(22b line 13) **הלכה ז**: דִּינֵי מָמוֹנוֹת גּוֹמְרִין בּוֹ בַיּוֹם כול׳. תַּנֵּי. הָעֵד אֵין מְלַמֵּד לֹא זְכוּת וְלֹא חוֹבָה. מְנָלָן. וְעֵד לֹא־יַעֲנֶה בְנֶפֶשׁ לָמוּת׃ וּמְנַיִן שֶׁאַף הוּא אֵין מְלַמֵּד לֹא זְכוּת וְלֹא חוֹבָה. תַּלְמוּד לוֹמַר וְהוּא לֹא־יַעֲנֶה בְנֶפֶשׁ לָמוּת׃ רֵישׁ לָקִישׁ אָמַר. פְּעָמִים שֶׁאָדָם רוֹאֶה אֶת עַצְמוֹ מִזְדַּמֵּם וּמַפְלִיג דְּבָרָיו שֶׁלֹּא יָמוּת.

Halakhah 7: "Civil suits are decided on the same day," etc. It was stated[47]: A witness may not argue either for acquittal or conviction[48]. From where this? *A witness shall not argue about anybody on trial for his life*[49]. And from where that he himself may not argue either for acquittal or conviction? The verse says, one *shall not argue about anybody on trial for his life*[50]. Rebbi Simeon ben Laqish said, sometimes a person sees himself set up by perjured witnesses and he speaks much lest he be put to death[51].

47 A similar *baraita* is quoted in the Babli, 33b, where, however, a dissent is noted.

48 In the formulation of the Babli: A witness cannot turn judge.

49 *Num*. 35:30. In the Babli, R. Yose ben Jehudah reads the verse only as prohibiting a witness from arguing for conviction.

50 This is not a verse. *Num*. 35:30 reads: *A single witness may not argue* . . . This is split into two sentences: A witness may not, a single person may not.

51 While in the Babli, 34a, R. Simeon ben Laqish is quoted as sustaining the opinion that the accused may not testify for himself since he is party to the proceedings, here it seems clear that he gives the accused the right to point out to the judges the fact that he is accused because of perjured (or otherwise tainted) testimony.

(22b line 17) וּמְנַיִין שֶׁצְּרִיכִין שְׁנֵי יָמִים סְמוּכִין זֶה לָזֶה.

רִבִּי חִזְקִיָּה רִבִּי אַחַי בְשֵׁם רִבִּי אַבָּהוּ. אָסוּר לָדוּן דִּינֵי מָמוֹנוֹת בְּעֶרֶב שַׁבָּת. וְהָדָא מַתְנִיתָא פְלִיגָא. לְפִיכָךְ אֵין דָּנִין לֹא בְעֶרֶב שַׁבָּת וְלֹא בְעֶרֶב יוֹם טוֹב. דִּינֵי נְפָשׁוֹת. הָא דִינֵי מָמוֹנוֹת דָּנִין. וְתַנֵּי רִבִּי חִייָה כֵן. דָּנִין דִּינֵי מָמוֹנוֹת בְּעֶרֶב שַׁבָּת וְאֵין דָּנִין דִּינֵי נְפָשׁוֹת בְּעֶרֶב שַׁבָּת. אָמַר. כָּאן לַהֲלָכָה כָּאן לְמַעֲשֶׂה.

1 אחי | **כב** אחא אבהו | **כ** אבהו אמ' והדה | **כב** והא 3 ואין דנין | **כב** אבל לא בערב שבת. אמר | **כ** - 4 למעשה | **כב** לדבר תורה

וְיִדּוֹנוּ אוֹתוֹ בְעֶרֶב שַׁבָּת וְיִגָּמֵר דִּינוֹ בְשַׁבָּת וְיֵיהָרֵג לְמוֹצָאֵי שַׁבָּת. אִם אוֹמֵר אַתְּ כֵּן נִמְצָא דִינוֹ מִשְׁתַּקֵּעַ. רֵישׁ לָקִישׁ בָּעֵי. וְיִדּוֹנוּ אוֹתוֹ בַשַּׁבָּת וְיִגָּמֵר דִּינוֹ בַשַּׁבָּת וְיֵיהָרֵג בַּשַּׁבָּת. מָה אִם עֲבוֹדָה שֶׁדּוֹחָה שַׁבָּת רְצִיחַת מִצְוָה דוֹחָה אוֹתָהּ. שֶׁנֶּאֱמַר מֵעִם מִזְבְּחִי תִּקָּחֶנּוּ לָמוּת. שַׁבָּת שֶׁהָעֲבוֹדָה דוֹחָה אוֹתָהּ אֵין דִּין שֶׁתְּהֵא רְצִיחַת מִצְוָה דוֹחָה אוֹתָהּ. רִבִּי לָא בְשֵׁם רִבִּי יַנַּאי. מִיכָּן לְבָתֵּי דִינִין שֶׁלֹּא יְהוּ דָנִין בַּשַּׁבָּת. מַאי טַעֲמָא. נֶאֱמַר כָּאן בְּכָל־מוֹשְׁבֹתֵיכֶם וְנֶאֱמַר לְהַלָּן וְהָיוּ אֵלֶּה לָכֶם לְחוּקַּת מִשְׁפָּט לְדֹרֹתֵיכֶם בְּכֹל מוֹשְׁבוֹתֵיכֶם: מַה לְהַלָּן בְּבֵית דִּין הַכָּתוּב מְדַבֵּר. אַף כָּאן בְּבֵית דִּין הַכָּתוּב מְדַבֵּר.

From where that one needs two consecutive days[52]?

[53]Rebbi Ḥizqiah, Rebbi Aḥa, said in the name of Rebbi Abbahu: It is forbidden to judge money matters on Friday. Does not a Mishnah object: "Therefore one does not judge [criminal matters] on Sabbath eve or holiday eve"? Hence, one judges money matters! Also, Rebbi Ḥiyya stated thus: One judges money matters on Friday but not criminal matters. One is for practice, the other for action[53a].

Could one not judge him on Fridays, pass sentence on the Sabbath, and execute him after the Sabbath? If you say so, it turns out that his judgment is delayed[54]. Rebbi Simeon ben Laqish asked, could he not be judged on the Sabbath, have his sentence passed on the Sabbath, and be executed on the Sabbath? Temple service, which supersedes Sabbath prohibitions[55], is pushed aside by obligatory executions, since it is said, *from My altar take him to be executed*[56]. Therefore the Sabbath, which is pushed aside by Temple service, logically should be pushed aside by obligatory executions[57].

Rebbi La in the name of Rebbi Yannai: This[58] implies that courts may not sit on the Sabbath; what is the reason? It is said here, *in all your dwellings*[59], and it is said there, *these shall be for you legal procedures for your generations in all your dwellings*[60]. Since there the verse refers to courts, so also here the verse refers to courts.

52 Since the Mishnah requires sentence to be passed on the day immediately following, there should be some biblical justification. The continuation of the argument shows that a reference is missing which would imply that justice delayed is justice denied.

53 The same text is found in *Ketubot* 1:1 (Notes 43-46,כ) and *Besah* 5:2 (64 l. 59, ב).

53a "Practice" means "code of practice", "action" means actual procedure. The parallel sources read: "one is for practice, the other for words of Torah", meaning that in theory one may judge but in practice one does not.

54 This argument really implies that capital crimes be tried only by the Supreme Court whose decrees are final.

55 The Sabbath Temple service, as prescribed in *Num.* 28:10, requires slaughtering and burning. For any other purpose, these are deadly sins and capital crimes if done on the Sabbath.

56 *Ex.* 21:14. The verse is read, not as a denial of asylum for any murderer, but as a commandment to immediately execute a Cohen even if he was officiating when convicted of murder. (The non-Cohen would commit a deadly sin by touching the altar.)

57 The argument deserves no refutation since the relation "stronger than" underlying an argument *de minore ad majus* is not transitive (*a* stronger than *b*, *b* stronger than *c* does *not* imply *a* stronger than *c*. Babli *Šabbat* 132b; cf. H. Guggenheimer, *Logical Problems in Jewish Tradition*, in: Confrontations with Judaism, London 1967, pp. 182-183.) The Babli, 35b, disproves the argument at length.

58 Mishnah 6.

59 *Ex.* 35:3, the prohibition to start a fire on the Sabbath.

60 *Num.* 35:29, the law of homicide and murder. The argument (Babli 35b) goes as follows. Some capital crimes are punished by burning. *Ex.* 35:3, which has been shown to be applicable to court proceedings, forbids executing a convicted criminal who has to be burned. Therefore no capital punishment can be executed on the Sabbath.

(fol. 22a) **משנה ח**: דִּינֵי מָמוֹנוֹת הַטְּהָרוֹת וְהַטֻּמְאוֹת מַתְחִילִין מִן הַגָּדוֹל דִּינֵי נְפָשׁוֹת מַתְחִילִין מִן הַצַּד. הַכֹּל כְּשֵׁירִין לָדוּן דִּינֵי מָמוֹנוֹת וְאֵין הַכֹּל כְּשֵׁירִין לָדוּן דִּינֵי נְפָשׁוֹת אֶלָּא כֹהֲנִים לְוִיִּם וְיִשְׂרְאֵלִים הַמַּשִּׂיאִין לַכְּהוּנָּה:

Mishnah 8: In cases of money matters, purity, and impurity, one starts with the greatest[61]. In criminal cases, one starts from the side[62]. Everybody is qualified to judge money matters but not everybody is qualified to judge criminal matters, but only Cohanim, Levites and Israel whose daughters may marry into the priesthood[63].

61 The most respected among the judges is requested to give his opinion first.

62 In criminal cases, the most respected judge has to give his opinion last, lest the junior members of the court be influenced by the authoritative voice.

63 None of whose known ancestors are bastards or desecrated priests.

(22b line 31) **הלכה ח:** דִּינֵי מָמוֹנוֹת הַטְּהָרוֹת וְהַטֻּמְאוֹת כול'. רִבִּי אוֹמֵר. לֹא־תַעֲנֶה עַל־רִיב. רִב כָּתוּב. שֶׁלֹּא תַעֲנֶה אַחַר הָרַב אֶלָּא קוֹדֶם לָרַב. רִבִּי יוֹסֵי בֶּן חֲנִינָה אָמַר. לֹא־תַעֲנֶה עַל־רִיב. רִב כָּתוּב. שֶׁלֹּא תַעֲנֶה קוֹדֶם לָרַב אֶלָּא אַחַר הָרַב. רַב אָמַר. לֹא־תַעֲנֶה. אֲפִילוּ אַחַר מֵאָה. דִּבְרֵי רִבִּי פִּינְחָס.

Halakhah 8: "In cases of money matters, purity, and impurity," etc. Rebbi says, *do not argue about a quarrel*[64]. It is written *against the greatest*[65], that one does not argue after the greatest, only prior to the greatest. Rebbi Yose ben Ḥanina said, *do not argue about a quarrel.* It is written *before the greatest*, that one does not argue prior to the greatest, only after the greatest[66]. Rav said, *do not argue*, even after a hundred[67], the words of Rebbi Phineas[68].

64 *Ex.* 23:2.

65 The word is written defective. The masoretic text follows the Talmudim in this (Babli 36a). It is difficult to decide whether the pronunciation of " the greatest" was רִב or רָב.

66 Depending on how one understands the word עַל, one comes to opposite conclusions. R. Yose ben Hanina denies that there be a difference in procedures between civil and criminal cases.

67 He denies that the verse has any relevance for judicial procedures; he reads it as an injunction not to change one's mind even in the face of a hundred opposing opinions unless one is convinced that his earlier opinion was incorrect.

68 No Tanna "R. Phineas" is known, nor any such Amora in the first generation. Either the name has to be deleted or the reference is to R. Phineas ben Yaïr.

(22b line 35) רִבִּי חִלְקִיָּה בְּשֵׁם רִבִּי סִימוֹן. אִיתְפַּלְגוֹן רִבִּי יוֹחָנָן וְרֵישׁ לָקִישׁ. חַד אָמַר. דִּינֵינוּ כְּדִינֵיהֶן. וְחַד אָמַר. אֵין דִּינֵינוּ כְּדִינֵיהֶן. מָאן דָּמַר דִּינֵינוּ כְּדִינֵיהֶן. נִיחָא. וּמָאן דָּמַר אֵין דִּינֵינוּ כְּדִינֵיהֶן. מַה מְקַיֵּים וַיֹּאמֶר יְהוּדָה. וַיֹּאמֶר מְמוּכָן. רָאוּ דִבְרֵי יְהוּדָה. רָאוּ דִבְרֵי מְמוּכָן.

Rebbi Ḥilqiah in the name of Rebbi Simon: Rebbi Joḥanan and Rebbi Simeon ben Laqish disagreed[69]. One said, our procedures are like their procedures, and one said, our procedures are not like their procedures[70]. He who said, our procedures are like their procedures, is understandable. He wo said, our procedures are not like their procedures, how does he understand

Jehudah said[71], *Memukhan said*[72]? They agreed with what Jehudah said, they agreed with what Memukhan said[73].

69 A more complete list of names is in the parallel, *Midrash Esther ad* 1:13.

70 Whether in Gentile courts the presiding judge also votes last in criminal proceedings.

71 When the brothers discussed what to do with Joseph, Jehudah volunteered his plan not to kill Joseph (*Gen.* 37:26) even though he was the fourth of the brothers (but the oldest, Reuben, was absent.) Since this happened before the revelation of Sinai, one has to assume that the brothers followed general Noahide rules.

72 *Esth.* 1:13. In the trial of Washti, the last named of the Persian grandees gave his opinion first.

73 Since in both cases no other opinions are recorded, we do not know in which order they spoke. Only the opinion which was agreed to in the end is mentioned.

(22b line 39) וּמְנַיִין שֶׁמַּתְחִילִין בְּדִינֵי נְפָשׁוֹת מִן הַצַּד. תַּנָּא שְׁמוּאֵל הַזָּקֵן קוֹמֵי רִבִּי אָחָא. וַיֹּאמֶר דָּוִד לַאֲנָשָׁיו חִגְרוּ | אִישׁ חַרְבּוֹ. וְאַחַר כָּךְ יָשְׁבוּ בַדִּין עַל נָבָל. רִבִּי תֵימָא בַּר פַּפַּייָס בְּשֵׁם רַב הוֹשַׁעְיָה. אַף בִּפְסוּל מִשְׁפָּחָה מַתְחִילִין מִן הַצַּד.

[74]From where that in criminal trials the voting starts from the side? Samuel the Elder stated before Rebbi Aḥa: *David told his men, each gird his sword*[75], and after this[76], they were sitting in judgment about Nabal.

Rebbi Thema bar Pappaias in the name of Rav Hoshaia: Also when disqualifying families[77] one starts from the side.

74 This is quoted in Halakhah 2:3 (Note 98).

75 *1S.* 25:13.

76 When everybody had given his opinion that Nabal should be killed, David girded his sword in assent.

77 A determination that daughters of a certain family cannot be married either by born Jews since they are descended from a bastard, or by priests since they are descended from a desecrated priest or a woman desecrated by a priest. All restrictions of criminal cases apply here, in the only cases heard by Amoraic courts in Palestine under the rules of criminal trials.

(22b line 42) הַכֹּל כְּשֵׁירִין לָדוּן דִּינֵי מָמוֹנוֹת. רִבִּי יְהוּדָה אוֹמֵר. אֲפִילוּ מַמְזֵירִין. רִבִּי יְהוּדָה אוֹמֵר. אֵין מְדַקְדְּקִין בְּיֵין נֶסֶךְ.

"Anybody is qualified to judge money matters." Rebbi Jehudah says, even bastards[78]. Rebbi Jehudah says, one does not investigate about libation wine[79].

78 In the Babli, 36b, this is a statement of *Rav* Jehudah.

79 Wine used in a pagan libation ceremony. The statement is out of place here; it is included as one of R. Jehudah's lenient rulings.

The rules of Gentile wine are the main topic of Tractate *`Avodah zarah*. Wine used in a pagan ceremony, even only an invocation at a pagan dinner, is forbidden biblically for all usufruct. All other Gentile wine is only forbidden rabbinically. Since the wine is forbidden anyhow, R. Jehudah states that one does not have to investigate whether the rigid biblical rules apply to a given wine; one follows the rabbinic rules unless it be known that the wine is biblically forbidden.

(fol. 22a) **משנה ט**: סַנְהֶדְרִין הָיְתָה כַּחֲצִי גוֹרֶן עֲגוּלָּה כְּדֵי שֶׁיְּהוּ רוֹאִין זֶה אֶת זֶה. וּשְׁנֵי סוֹפְרֵי דַיָּנִין עוֹמְדִין לִפְנֵיהֶן אֶחָד מִיָּמִין וְאֶחָד מִשְּׂמֹאל וְכוֹתְבִין דִּבְרֵי מְזַכִּין וְדִבְרֵי מְחַיְּבִין. רַבִּי יְהוּדָה אוֹמֵר שְׁלֹשָׁה הָיוּ. אֶחָד כּוֹתֵב דִּבְרֵי מְחַיְּבִין וְאֶחָד כּוֹתֵב דִּבְרֵי מְזַכִּין וְהַשְּׁלִישִׁי כוֹתֵב דִּבְרֵי מְזַכִּין וְדִבְרֵי מְחַיְּבִין:

Mishnah 9: The Synhedrion was like a semicircular threshing floor[80], so that they could see one another. Two court reporters were standing before them, one to the right and one to the left, and they wrote down the arguments of those who argued for acquittal and those who argued for conviction. Rebbi Jehudah says, there were three. One wrote the arguments for conviction, one wrote the arguments for acquittal, and one wrote the arguments for acquittal and for conviction.

80 Not to mention the objectionable word "amphitheater". It is not clear whether this applies only to the original Synhedrion, the High Priest's council, or to any court empowered to try capital cases. It did apply to the Academy of Jabneh, constituted by Rabban Johanan ben Zakkai after the destruction of Jerusalem, but probably not to any of its successor academies.

(22b line 44) **הלכה ט**: סַנְהֶדְרִין הָיְתָה כַּחֲצִי גוֹרֶן עֲגוּלָּה כול'. כְּתִיב לֹא תַטֶּה מִשְׁפַּט אֶבְיוֹנְךָ בְּרִיבוֹ: בְּרִיבוֹ אֵי אַתָּה מַטֶּה. אֲבָל אַתָּה מַטֶּה בְדִינוֹ שֶׁלְּשׁוֹר. רִבִּי אַבָּהוּ בְשֵׁם רִבִּי יוֹחָנָן. וּבִלְבַד בִּדְבָרִים שֶׁבֵּין דִּינֵי מָמוֹנוֹת לְדִינֵי נְפָשׁוֹת. כַּמָּה אִינּוּן. אֲנָן תַּנִּינָן. תֵּשַׁע. תַּנֵּי רִבִּי חִיָּיה. חַד־עָשָׂר. הֵי דִינִין תַּרְתֵּי אוֹחֲרָנְיָיתָא. הַסָּרִיס וְכָל־מִי שֶׁלֹּא רָאָה לוֹ בָנִים כָּשֵׁר לָדוּן דִּינֵי מָמוֹנוֹת וְלֹא דִינֵי נְפָשׁוֹת. רִבִּי אַבָּהוּ בְשֵׁם רִבִּי יוֹחָנָן. אַף פָּחוּת מִבֶּן עֶשְׂרִים וְשֶׁלֹּא הֵבִיא שְׁתֵּי שְׂעָרוֹת כָּשֵׁר בְּדִינֵי מָמוֹנוֹת וְלֹא בְדִינֵי נְפָשׁוֹת. וְיוֹשֵׁב בְּדִינוֹ שֶׁלְּשׁוֹר. רִבִּי יוֹסֵי בֶּן חֲנִינָה אָמַר.

תְּלַת עֶשְׂרֵה. וְהֵי דִינוּן תַּרְתֵּי אוֹחֲרָנְיָיתָא. דָּנִין שְׁנֵי דִינֵי מָמוֹנוֹת בְּיוֹם אֶחָד וְאֵין דָּנִין שְׁנֵי דִינֵי נְפָשׁוֹת בְּיוֹם אֶחָד. אָמַר רִבִּי אָבִין. אֲפִילוּ נוֹאֵף וְנוֹאֶפֶת.

Halakhah 9: "The Synhedrion was like a semicircular threshing floor," etc. It is written: *Do not bend your destitute's proceeding in his trial*[81]. In *his* trial you do not bend; you may bend in the ox's trial[82]. Rebbi Abbahu in the name of Rebbi Johanan: But only in those rules which are different for civil and criminal suits. How many are these? We have stated nine[83]; Rebbi Ḥiyya stated eleven. Which rules are the last two? The castrate and one who never had children[84] is qualified to judge civil suits but not criminal suits. Rebbi Abbahu in the name of Rebbi Johanan: Also one who is less than twenty years of age or who does not have two pubic hairs[85] is qualified to judge civil suits but not criminal suits. Rebbi Yose ben Ḥanina said thirteen. Which rules are the last two? One judges two civil suits on one day but one does not try two criminal suits on one day. Rebbi Abin said, even adulterer and adulteress[86].

81 *Ex*. 23:6. The protection accorded defendants in criminal trials cannot be made dependent on the defendant's status.

82 While the ox who killed a human is on trial for its life, the rules are those of civil suits since the ox represents its owner's money.

83 In Mishnaiot 1-7. The Babli, 36b, points out that there is another difference stated in Mishnah 8, but the exclusion of bastards is implicit already in the choice of 23 judges since these judges must in theory be qualified to serve in Moses's council.

84 The Babli, 36b, also excludes men too old to remember the trouble they had in raising their children, who also would be inclined to cruelty.

85 Although he is past age 20 he still is infantile; cf. *Yebamot* 10:17 Notes 221-227.

86 Where the proof of guilt of one person equally applies to the other. In the Babli, 46a, Rav Ḥisda restricts this to the case where the statutory punishments are different, such as adultery with a Cohen's daughter, where the adulterer is strangled but the adulteress burned. There is no reason to transfer this statement to the Yerushalmi. Cf. Note 35.

(fol. 22a) **משנה י**: וְשָׁלֹשׁ שׁוּרוֹת שֶׁל תַּלְמִידֵי חֲכָמִים יוֹשְׁבִין לִפְנֵיהֶן וְכָל־אֶחָד וְאֶחָד מַכִּיר אֶת מְקוֹמוֹ. צָרְכוּ לִסְמוֹךְ סוֹמְכִין מִן הָרִאשׁוֹנָה. אֶחָד מִן הַשְּׁנִייָה בָּא לוֹ לָרִאשׁוֹנָה וְאֶחָד מִן הַשְּׁלִישִׁית בָּא לוֹ לַשְּׁנִייָה. וּבוֹרְרִין לָהֶן עוֹד אֶחָד מִן הַקָּהָל וּמוֹשִׁיבִין אוֹתוֹ בַּשְּׁלִישִׁית. וְלֹא הָיָה יוֹשֵׁב בִּמְקוֹמוֹ שֶׁל רִאשׁוֹן אֶלָּא יוֹשֵׁב בְּמָקוֹם שֶׁהוּא רָאוּי לוֹ:

Mishnah 10: Three rows of students of the Sages[87] were sitting before them; each one of them knew his place[88]. If they needed to ordain,[89] they ordained one from the first row. One of the second row came to sit in the first, and one of the third came to sit in the second[90]. They chose a person from the general public and placed him in the third row; he did not sit in the place of the one promoted but in the place befitting him[91].

87 Each criminal court was supposed to function as a law school.
88 Determined by their standing in examinations.
89 If there was a vacancy on the bench.
90 Not that he came by himself but was promoted by the court according to his standing.
91 By the result of the entrance examination.

(22b line 54) **הלכה י׃** שָׁלֹשׁ שׁוּרוֹת שֶׁלְּתַלְמִידֵי חֲכָמִים כול'. רִבִּי בָּא בַּר יָסָא בְשֵׁם רִבִּי יוֹחָנָן. נֶאֱמַר כָּאן עֵדָה וְנֶאֱמַר לְהַלָּן עֵדָה. מַייְתֵי לָהּ רַב מִמַּתְנִיתָא. מַתְנִיתָא אָמְרָה. הֱוֵי זָנָב לָאֲרָיוֹת וְלֹא רֹאשׁ לַשּׁוּעָלִים. מַתְלָא אָמְרָה. הֱוֵי רֹאשׁ לַשּׁוּעָלִים וְלֹא זָנָב לָאֲרָיוֹת. דְּתַנִּינָן. צָרְכוּ לִסְמוֹךְ סוֹמְכִין מֵרִאשׁוֹנָה.

Halakhah 10: "Three rows of students of the Sages," etc. Rebbi Abba (bar) [Rebbi][92] Yasa in the name of Rebbi Johanan: It says here *congregation*, and it says there *congregation*.

Rav brought it from a Mishnah; the Mishnah says "be a tail of lions and not a head of jackals. [93]" The parable says, be a head of jackals but not a tail of lions. But we have stated: "If they needed to ordain, they ordained one from the first row.[94]"

92 This is a quote from Halakhah 1:6, Note 338. One has to read with the text there, R. Abba, R. Yasa, rather than introduce an otherwise unknown R. Abba bar Yasa. In the opinion of the Babli, the law school had room for 3 times 23 students. It seems that the Yerushalmi agrees; therefore the derivation of the number 23 of members of the court is hinted at by the quote of its first sentence.
93 *Avot* 4:15.
94 The Mishnah does not require that the occupant of the first seat of the first row be ordained; it could be anyone from the first row. Therefore, the last seat in the first row is better than the top seat in the second row.

(fol. 22a) **משנה יא׃** כֵּיצַד מְאַייְמִין עַל עֵדֵי נְפָשׁוֹת הָיוּ מַכְנִיסִין אוֹתָן וּמְאַייְמִין עֲלֵיהֶן שֶׁמָּא תֹאמְרוּ מֵאֹמֶד וּמִשְּׁמוּעָה עֵד מִפִּי עֵד וּמִפִּי אָדָם נֶאֱמָן שְׁמַעְתֶּם אוֹ שֶׁמָּא אֵי אַתֶּם יוֹדְעִין

שֶׁסּוֹפֵינוּ לִבְדּוֹק אֶתְכֶם בִּדְרִישָׁה וּבַחֲקִירָה. הֱוו יוֹדְעִין שֶׁלֹּא כְדִינֵי מָמוֹנוֹת דִּינֵי נְפָשׁוֹת. דִּינֵי מָמוֹנוֹת אָדָם נוֹתֵן מָמוֹן וּמִתְכַּפֵּר לוֹ. דִּינֵי נְפָשׁוֹת דָּמוֹ וְדַם זַרְעִיּוֹתָיו תְּלוּיִין בּוֹ עַד סוֹף כָּל־הַדּוֹרוֹת. שֶׁכֵּן מָצִינוּ בְקַיִן כְּשֶׁהָרַג אֶת אָחִיו שֶׁנֶּאֱמַר בּוֹ קוֹל דְּמֵי אָחִיךָ צֹעֲקִים אֵלַי מִן־הָאֲדָמָה׃ אֵינוֹ אוֹמֵר דַּם אָחִיךָ אֶלָּא דְּמֵי אָחִיךָ דָּמוֹ וְדַם זַרְעִיּוֹתָיו. דָּבָר אַחֵר דְּמֵי אָחִיךָ שֶׁהָיָה דָמוֹ מוּשְׁלָךְ עַל הָעֵצִים וְעַל הָאֲבָנִים.

Mishnah 11: How does one instill fear in witnesses in criminal cases[95]? One brings them in and instills fear in them. Maybe you would testify by a guess, or by a rumor, or from the mouth of a witness, or you heard it from a trustworthy source[96], or maybe you do not know that we shall examine you by cross-examination and interrogation[1]. You should know that criminal trials are not like civil trials. In civil trials a person[97] pays money and is forgiven. In criminal trials, his blood and the blood of all his descendants hang in the balance, to the end of all generations. So we find when Cain slew his brother, it is said: *The sounds of your brother's bloods cry to me from the earth*[98]. It does not say *your brother's blood* but *your brother's bloods*, his blood and that of his descendants. Another explanation[99]: *Your brother's bloods,* the blood was splashed on trees and stones.

95 A criminal trial is one where the punishment is either death or flogging. Flogging is potentially life-threatening. A crime for which the punishment is a fine is tried as civil infraction under the rules of civil suits.

96 This still is hearsay evidence which is inadmissible.

97 On whose incorrect testimony another person was found owing money.

98 *Gen.* 4:10; cf. *Gen. rabba* 22(21).

99 This is a possible correct interpretation of the verse, not to be used as sermon in court. Cf. *Gen. rabba* 22(22).

(22b line 58) **הלכה יא**: כֵּיצַד מְאַייְמִין כול'. כֵּיצַד מֵאוֹמֶד. לֹא תֹאמְרוּ. רְאִינוּהוּ רוֹדֵף אַחֲרָיו וְסַייִף בְּיָדוֹ. נִכְנַס לַחוּרְבָּה אַחֲרָיו. נִכְנַסְנוּ אַחֲרָיו וּמְצָאנוּהוּ הָרוּג. רְאִינוּהוּ יוֹצֵא וְהַסַּייִף מְטַפְטֶפֶת דָּם. אָמַר רִבִּי שִׁמְעוֹן בֶּן שֶׁטַח. אֶרְאֶה בְנֶחָמָה אִם לֹא רְאִיתִי רוֹדֵף אַחַר אַחֵר נִכְנַס לַחוּרְבָּה. נִכְנַסְתִּי אַחֲרָיו וּמְצָאתִיו הָרוּג וְזֶה יוֹצֵא וְסַייִף מְנַטֵּף דָּם. אָמַרְתִּי לוֹ. אֶרְאֶה בְנֶחָמָה שֶׁזֶּה הֲרָגוֹ. אֲבָל מָה אֶעֱשֶׂה שֶׁאֵין דָּמְךָ מָסוּר בְּיָדִי אֶלָּא הַיּוֹדֵעַ מַחֲשָׁבוֹת יִפָּרַע מֵאוֹתוֹ הָאִישׁ. לֹא הִסְפִּיק לָצֵאת מִשָּׁם עַד שֶׁהִכִּישׁוֹ נָחָשׁ וָמֵת.

Halakhah 11: "How does one instill fear," etc. What is meant by a guess? [100]"Do not say, we saw him with a sword in his hand running after another person. He entered a ruined building after him; we entered after him and found him slain. We saw him coming out and his sword was dripping blood[101]. Simeon ben Shetah[102] said: May I not see consolation[103] if I did not see one running after another person into a ruined building. I entered after him and found him slain while the other left with his sword dripping blood. I said to him, may I not see consolation if you did not kill him. But what can I do since your blood is not delivered into my hands. But He Who knows thoughts may collect from that person. He did not manage to leave before a snake bit him and he died.

100 Babli 37b, Tosephta 8:3.

101 A death sentence can never be pronounced on circumstantial evidence.

102 The head of the Synhedrion under his sister Queen Salome (Shalomsion).

103 I. e., may I not have part in the Future Life if . . .

(fol. 22a) **משנה יב**: לְפִיכָךְ נִבְרָא הָאָדָם יְחִידִי בָעוֹלָם לְלַמֵּד שֶׁכָּל־הַמְאַבֵּד נֶפֶשׁ אַחַת מַעֲלִין עָלָיו כְּאִילּוּ אִיבֵּד עוֹלָם מָלֵא. וְכָל־הַמְקַיֵּים נֶפֶשׁ אַחַת מַעֲלִין עָלָיו כְּאִילּוּ קִייֵּם עוֹלָם מָלֵא. וּמִפְּנֵי שְׁלוֹם הַבְּרִיּוֹת, שֶׁלֹּא יֹאמַר אָדָם לַחֲבֵרוֹ אַבָּא גָדוֹל מֵאָבִיךָ וְשֶׁלֹּא יְהוּ הַמִּינִין אוֹמְרִים הַרְבֵּה רְשׁוּיוֹת יֵשׁ בַּשָּׁמַיִם.

Mishnah 12: Therefore man was created single in the world to teach that for anybody who destroys a single life it is counted as if he destroyed an entire world, and for anybody who preserves a single life it is counted as if he preserved an entire world. And because of peace among men, that nobody could say to another, my father was greater than your father. And that sectarians[104] could not say, there are a plurality of powers in Heaven.

104 In general, מין denotes a Jewish Christian. If Jesus was identical in nature with God, he could not have been created or born. If Jesus was similar in nature to God, his creation would contradict the thesis of unique creation of man. If Jesus was simply referring to himself as God's son in the meaning of *Deut.* 11:1, he is no power in Heaven.

(22b line 65) **הלכה יב**: לְפִיכָךְ נִבְרָא הָאָדָם כול'. אָדָם נִבְרָא יְחִידִי בָעוֹלָם מִפְּנֵי הַמִּשְׁפָּחוֹת שֶׁלֹּא יְהוּ מִתְגָּרוֹת זוֹ בְזוֹ. וַהֲלֹא דְבָרִים קַל וָחוֹמֶר. וּמָה אִם בִּזְמַן שֶׁהֵן בְּנֵי אַב אֶחָד מִתְגָּרוֹת זוֹ

בְזוֹ. אִילוּ הָיוּ בְנֵי שְׁנַיִם עַל אַחַת כַּמָּה וְכַמָּה. דָּבָר אַחֵר. שֶׁלֹּא יְהוּ הַצַּדִּיקִים אוֹמְרִים. אָנוּ בְנֵי צַדִּיק וְאַתֶּם בְּנֵי רְשָׁעִים.

Halakhah 12: "Therefore man was created," etc. [105]"Man was created single in the world because of the families, lest they should attack one another. Is that not argument *de minore ad majus*? Since now that they are all descendants of one father they attack one another, if they had been descendants of two not so much more? Another explanation: The just ones should not say, we are the descendants of a just man, but you are the sons of evildoers[106]."

105 Babli 38a, Tosephta 8:4.

106 There is no predestination, genetic or otherwise.

(fol. 22a) **משנה יג**: וּלְהַגִּיד גְּדוּלָּתוֹ שֶׁל מֶלֶךְ מַלְכֵי הַמְּלָכִים הַקָּדוֹשׁ בָּרוּךְ הוּא שֶׁאָדָם טוֹבֵעַ כַּמָּה מַטְבְּעוֹת בְּחוֹתָם אֶחָד וְכוּלָּן דּוֹמִין זֶה לָזֶה. וּמֶלֶךְ מַלְכֵי הַמְּלָכִים הַקָּדוֹשׁ בָּרוּךְ הוּא טָבַע כָּל־אָדָם בְּחוֹתָמוֹ שֶׁל אָדָם הָרִאשׁוֹן וְאֵין אֶחָד דּוֹמֶה לַחֲבֵרוֹ. לְפִיכָךְ כָּל־אֶחָד וְאֶחָד חַייָב לוֹמַר בִּשְׁבִילִי נִבְרָא הָעוֹלָם.

Mishnah 13: And to proclaim the greatness of the King over kings of kings, the Holy One, praise to Him. For a man coins many coins with one die; they are one like the other. But the King over kings of kings, the Holy One, praise to Him, stamps every man with the stamp of the first man, but no one is like any other. Therefore, everybody is required to say, the world was created for me.

(22b line 70) **הלכה יג**: וּלְהַגִּיד גְּדוּלָּתוֹ שֶׁל מֶלֶךְ מַלְכֵי הַמְּלָכִים הַקָּדוֹשׁ בָּרוּךְ הוּא כול'. לְהַגִּיד גְּדוּלַּת מֶלֶךְ מַלְכֵי הַמְּלָכִים שֶׁמֵּחוֹתָם אֶחָד טוֹבֵעַ כָּל־הַחוֹתָמוֹת וְאֵין אֶחָד מֵהֶן דּוֹמֶה לַחֲבֵרוֹ. שֶׁנֶּאֱמַר תִּתְהַפֵּךְ כְּחוֹמֶר חוֹתָם. וּמִפְּנֵי מַה שִׁינָּה פַּרְצוּפֵיהֶן. שֶׁלֹּא יְהֵא אָדָם קוֹפֵץ וְהוֹלֵךְ לְאֵשֶׁת חֲבֵירוֹ אוֹ לִשְׂדֵה חֲבֵירוֹ. תַּנֵּי בְשֵׁם רִבִּי מֵאִיר. שְׁלֹשָׁה דְבָרִים שִׁינָּה הַקָּדוֹשׁ בָּרוּךְ הוּא בִּבְנֵי אָדָם. מַרְאֶה פָנִים וְדַעַת וְקוֹל. מַרְאֶה וְדַעַת מִפְּנֵי הַגַּזְלָנִין. וְקוֹל מִפְּנֵי הָעֶרְוָה. אָמַר רִבִּי יִצְחָק. אֲפִילוּ תֵּינְתָא אוֹ חִיטְּתָא לָא דַמְיָא לַחֲבֵירְתָהּ. אָדָם נִבְרָא בְעֶרֶב שַׁבָּת כְּדֵי שֶׁיִּיכָּנֵס תְּחִילָּה לְמִצְוָה. דָּבָר אַחֵר. לָמָּה נִבְרָא בָאַחֲרוֹנָה. מָשָׁל לְמֶלֶךְ שֶׁעָשָׂה סְעוּדָה. כְּשֶׁמַּתְקִין הַסְּעוּדָה מַזְמִין הָאוֹרְחִין. כָּךְ חָכְמוֹת בָּנְתָה בֵיתָהּ. זֶה הַקָּדוֹשׁ בָּרוּךְ הוּא שֶׁבָּנָה אֶת הָעוֹלָם בְּחָכְמָה. שֶׁנֶּאֱמַר יְיָ

בְּחָכְמָה יָסַד־אָרֶץ וגו׳. חָצְבָה עַמּוּדֶיהָ שִׁבְעָה. אֵילּוּ שִׁבְעַת יְמֵי בְרֵאשִׁית. טָבְחָה טִבְחָהּ מָסְכָה יֵינָהּ. אֵילּוּ יַמִּים וּנְהָרוֹת וְכָל־צוֹרְכֵי הָעוֹלָם. מִי־פֶתִי יָסֻר הֵנָּה. זֶה אָדָם וְחַוָּה.

Halakhah 13: "And to proclaim the greatness of the King over kings of kings, the Holy One, praise to Him," etc. [106]To proclaim the greatness of the King over kings of kings Who from one die coins all seals and no one is like the other, as it is said: *The seal turns around like clay*[107]. Why did He change their looks[108]? That no man should jump and go to another's wife or another's field. It was stated in the name of Rebbi Meïr: Three things did the Holy One, praise to Him, diversify in humans: looks of the face, understanding, and voice. Looks and understanding because of the robbers, voice because of forbidden women. Rebbi Isaac said, even a fig tree or a wheat plant is not identical to any other. Man was created Sabbath Eve so from the start he should enter with a commandment[109]. Another explanation: Why was he created last? A parable of a king who made a banquet. After he had ordered the meal, he invited the guests. [110]So *wisdom built her house*, that is the Holy One, praise to Him, Who created the world in wisdom, as it is said, *the Eternal in wisdom based the earth*[111], etc. *She quarried its seven pillars*, these are the seven days of creation. *She slaughtered her slaughtering, mixed her wine*, these are seas and rivers and all the needs of the world. *Any silly one shall come here*, that is Adam and Eve.

106 Babli 38a, Tosephta 8:5,6,9.

107 *Job* 38:15; cf. *Kilaim* 9:4 Note 78.

108 Greek πρόσωπος.

109 To celebrate the Sabbath.

110 *Prov.* 9:1,2,4.

111 *Prov.* 3:19.

(fol. 22a) **משנה יד**: וְשֶׁמָּא תֹאמְרוּ מַה לָּנוּ וְלַצָּרָה הַזֹּאת וַהֲלֹא כְבָר נֶאֱמַר וְהוּא עֵד אוֹ רָאָה אוֹ יָדָע וגו׳. שֶׁמָּא תֹאמְרוּ מַה לָּנוּ לָחוּב בְּדָמוֹ שֶׁל זֶה וַהֲלֹא כְבָר נֶאֱמַר וּבַאֲבֹד רְשָׁעִים רִנָּה:

Mishnah 14: Maybe you will say, why should we go to all this trouble? There already is written: *If he is a witness, or saw, or knew*[112], etc. Maybe you will say, why should we be guilty of this man's blood? There already is written: *In destruction of evildoers is clamor*[113].

112 *Lev.* 5:1. As usual, the implication is from the part of the verse which is not quoted: *If he do not tell, he has to bear his sin.*

113 *Prov.* 11:10.

(22c line 8) **הלכה יד**: שֶׁמָּא תֹאמְרוּ מַה לָּנוּ וְלַצָּרָה כול'. כְּתִיב וַיַּעֲבוֹר הָרִנָּה בַּמַּחֲנֶה. מָהוּ הָרִינָּה. הֶירֵינֵי. וְכֵן הוּא אוֹמֵר בְּצֵאת לִפְנֵי הֶחָלוּץ וגו'. לְלַמְּדָךְ שֶׁאַף מַפָּלַת הָרְשָׁעִים אֵינָהּ שִׂמְחָה לִפְנֵי הַמָּקוֹם.

Halakhah 14: "Maybe you will say, why should we go to all this trouble," etc. It is written: *The clamor erupted in the camp*[114]. What is "the clamor"? Quiet[115]. And so it says, *when they went in front of the armed forces*[116], to teach that even the downfall of the evildoers is no joy before the Omnipresent.

114 *1K.* 22:36.

115 According to N. Brüll, *Jahrbuch für jüdische Geschichte und Literatur* 1, p. 134, this is Greek εἰρήνη "peace, quiet". Cf. also *Pesiqta dR. Cahana* 20 (ed. S. Buber p. 141a Note 10, as explanation of the verbal form רָנִּי, *Is.* 54:1). The death of the evil king Ahab (v. 35) brought quiet to everybody.

116 *2Chr.* 20:21. The argument is from the part of the verse which is not quoted. When the Levites went before the army against the Moabites and Edomites, they sang: *give praise to the Eternal, for His Grace is forever*, intentionally changing the traditional text (*Ps.* 118:1,136:1), *give praise to the Eternal* for He is good, *for His Grace is forever.*

היו בודקין פרק חמישי

משנה א: הָיוּ בוֹדְקִין אוֹתָן בְּשֶׁבַע חֲקִירוֹת בְּאֵי זוֹ שָׁבוּעַ בְּאֵי זוֹ שָׁנָה בְּאֵי זֶה חוֹדֶשׁ בְּכַמָּה בַחוֹדֶשׁ בְּאֵי זֶה יוֹם בְּאֵי זוֹ שָׁעָה בְּאֵי זֶה מָקוֹם. רִבִּי יוֹסֵי אוֹמֵר בְּאֵי זֶה יוֹם בְּאֵי זוֹ שָׁעָה בְּאֵי זֶה מָקוֹם מַכִּירִין אַתֶּם אוֹתוֹ וְהִתְרֵיתֶם בּוֹ. הָעוֹבֵד עֲבוֹדָה זָרָה אֶת מֶה עָבַד וּבַמֶּה עָבַד׃

[0]**Mishnah 1**: They were investigating him in seven ways[1]: In which Sabbatical period, in which year[2], in which month, which day of the month, which day, which hour, at which place[3]? Rebbi Yose said, which day, which hour, which place[4], do you recognize him, and did you warn him[5]? If one worshipped idols, what did he worship and how did he worship[6]?

0 For this Chapter and the next, there exists a Genizah text, published by M. Assis in *Tarbiz* 47 (1977) 29-90, 321-329, compared to the Leiden text. Additions from this text will be denoted G.

1 The number seven may be taken from Roman law, formulated in Quintilian's hexameter which enumerates the questions to be answered in a trial: *Quis, quid, ubi, quibus auxiliis, cur, quomodo, quando?* "Who? What? Where? By means of what? For what purpose? How? When?" But questions 4,5,6 are reserved for cross-examination, not investigation (cf. Chapter 4, Note 1) (E. G.).

2 In the Sabbatical period. It is clear from this Mishnah that for capital crimes there is no statute of limitations.

3 The Mishnah is a direct continuation of the preceding Chapter. Testimony is acceptable in court only if given under the possible penalties of perjury. But the only way the biblical penalties can be imposed is that the witnesses are proven not to have been at the indicated place of the crime at the time indicated. Therefore, exact determination of time and place are prerequisites to the trial.

4 He has only three questions before the actual crime is investigated.

5 A conviction in biblical law is possible only if criminal intent is proven. This is provable only by two witnesses who testify that they saw the defendant intent on committing a crime and informed him that his intended action was prohibited and that he exposed himself to such and such penalties.

6 Actions which imitate worship of Heaven or are specific for a certain deity are capital crimes; any other actions are punishable only by whipping or not at all (Mishnah 7:12).

(22c line 55) **הלכה א**: הָיוּ בוֹדְקִין אוֹתָן בְּשֶׁבַע חֲקִירוֹת כול'. וְלֹא תַנִּינָן. בְּאֵי זֶה יוֹבֵל. שֶׁאֵין הַדָּבָר מָצוּי. אַשְׁכַּח תַּנֵּי. רִבִּי שִׁמְעוֹן בֶּן יוֹחַי אוֹמֵר. אַף בְּאֵי זֶה יוֹבֵל. וְקַיְימוּנָהּ בָּהוּא דְעָאַל וּבָהוּא דְנָפַק.

Halakhah 1: "They were investigating him in seven ways," etc. But we did not state, in which Jubilee period? For that is not current[7]. It was found stated: Rebbi Simeon ben Iohai says, also in which Jubilee period[8]? We confirmed that in a year which started or concluded [a Jubilee period][9].

7 Since the Jubilee was not observed during Second Temple times (cf. *Ševi`it* 1:1 Note 7, *Qiddušin* 1:2 Notes 190-191) except possibly for the determination of Sabbatical periods, one cannot assume that the witnesses were able to determine the year by its position in a Jubilee period.

8 Cf. Babli 40b.

9 At least during the existence of the Temple, close to the beginning or the end of a Jubilee period everybody can be assumed to be alerted to the change in computation of Sabbatical periods induced by the (not observed) Jubilee. Everybody agrees that after the destruction of the Temple, the determination of the Jubilee period was meaningless. Therefore, the Mishnaiot dealing with procedures in criminal trials are attempts of reconstruction of Hasmonean or even earlier procedures.

(22c line 57) מְנַיִין לְשֶׁבַע חֲקִירוֹת. תַּנָּא שְׁמוּאֵל הַזָּקֵן קוֹמֵי רִבִּי אָחָא. וְדָרַשְׁתָּ וְחָקַרְתָּ וְשָׁאַלְתָּ הֵיטֵב וְהִנֵּה אֱמֶת נָכוֹן. אָמַר לֵיהּ. לָא תְהֵא קְרָא וַאֲזִיל אֶלָּא וְדָרַשְׁתָּ וְחָקַרְתָּ וְשָׁאַלְתָּ הֵיטֵב וְהוּגַּד לְךָ וְשָׁמַעְתָּ וְשָׁאַלְתָּ הֵיטֵב. הֵיטֵב הֵיטֵב לִגְזֵירָה שָׁוָה. לִיתֵּן [לְ] [G]כָּל־אַחַת וְאַחַת שְׁמוּעָה שְׁאֵלָה דְּרִישָׁה וַחֲקִירָה. רִבִּי יִצְחָק מַקְשֵׁי לָהּ. הֲווֹן תְּפִיסִין בְּחַד לֵיסְטֵיס דְּטִיבֵּרְיָא אָמְרִין. כְּדוֹן קָטוֹל כְּדוֹן קְטַל. וּמְנַיִין לָזֶה שֶׁבַע חֲקִירוֹת. אִיסִּי אָמַר. כָּל־זְמַן שֶׁאִילּוּ הָעֵדִים יְכוֹלִין לְהִזְדַּמֵּם עַל אוֹתוֹ הָעֵדוּת אֵין הַהוֹרֵג נֶהֱרָג.

From where the seven investigations? Samuel the Elder stated before Rebbi Aḥa: *You shall inquire, investigate, ask in depth, and behold, the matter is well founded*[10]. He told him, this verse does not work[11]; but: *you shall inquire, investigate, ask in depth; it will be told to you, you shall listen, ask in depth*[12]. In depth, in depth for an equal cut, to require in each case listening, asking, inquiry, and investigation[13]. Rebbi Isaac asked about this: If they caught an armed robber in Tiberias and said, this is the murderer, this is the murdered; why does this need seven investigations[14]? Issi said, any time that the witnesses could not be proven perjured, the murderer cannot be executed on that testimony[15].

10 *Deut.* 13:15. The judicial inquiry is described by seven words.

11 At least another word has to be added to reach the next dividing accent; stopping at נָכוֹן is unjustified. On the other hand, the two words דָרַשְׁתָּ הֵיטֵב represent a single notion.

12 *Deut.* 17:4.

13 Both verses 13:15 and 17:4 mention five notions each of inquiry; eliminating the words appearing twice one is left with seven different words. Babli 40a, *Sifry Deut.* 93.

14 Is the situation not obvious?

15 Since perjured witnesses in a capital case can be executed if it was shown that they could not have seen the act since at the pretended time they were at another place, a criminal trial can proceed only if the witnesses can be made to testify about the exact time and place where the observed criminal act took place.

(22c line 65) מַכִּירִין אַתֶּם אוֹתוֹ. מֶה הָיָה. גּוֹי הָיָה אוֹ יִשְׂרָאֵל הָיָה. נִישְׁמְעִינָהּ מֵהָדָא דָּמַר רִבִּי יוֹחָנָן. נֶהֱרַג מִטִּיבֵּרִיָּא לְצִיפּוֹרִי חֲזָקָה שֶׁיִּשְׂרָאֵל הָיָה.

"Do you recognize him?" Who was he, a Gentile[16] or an Israel? Let us hear from what Rebbi Johanan said: If he was slain between Tiberias and Sepphoris, it is *prima facie* evidence that he was an Israel[17].

16 Then it would be a case for the king's court, not the Sanhedrin.

17 In order to remove the case to a police court, the defendant would have to prove that the slain person was a Gentile. As a practical matter, an unknown corpse found on the road between Tiberias and Sepphoris is a *corpse of obligation* (*Nazir* 7:1).

(22c line 67) הִתְרֵיתֶם בּוֹ. מְנַיִין לְהַתְרָייָה. רִבִּי שְׁמוּאֵל בַּר נַחְמָן בְּשֵׁם רִבִּי יוֹנָתָן. וְאִ֣ישׁ אֲשֶׁר־יִקַּ֣ח אֶת־אֲחֹת֗וֹ. חֶ֣סֶד ה֔וּא. אָמַר רִבִּי בּוּן. קַיִן נָשָׂה אֲחוֹתוֹ. הֶבֶל נָשָׂה אֲחוֹתוֹ. חֶסֶד עָשִׂיתִי עִם הָרִאשׁוֹנִים שֶׁיִּיבָּנֶה עוֹלָם מֵהֶן. כִּֽי־אָמַ֗רְתִּי עוֹלָ֣ם חֶ֣סֶד יִבָּנֶ֑ה.

תַּנֵּי. רִבִּי שִׁמְעוֹן בֶּן יוֹחַי אוֹמֵר. עַל־פִּ֣י ׀ שְׁנַ֣יִם עֵדִ֗ים יוּמַ֣ת הַמֵּ֑ת. [וְכִי][G] הַמֵּת מֵת. אֶלָּא לְהוֹדִיעוֹ בְּאֵי זֶה מִיתָה מֵת. תַּנֵּי. רִבִּי יוּדָה בֵּירִבִּי אִלְעָאי אוֹמֵר. וְכִֽי־יָזִ֥ד אִ֛ישׁ עַל־רֵעֵ֖הוּ לְהָרְג֣וֹ בְעָרְמָ֑ה. שֶׁיַּעֲרִימוּהוּ בְּאֵי זֶה מִיתָה מֵת.

הָיְתָה מִיתָתוֹ בַחֲמוּרָה וְהִתְרוּ בוֹ בְּקַלָּה. יְכִיל מֵימַר. אִילּוּ הֲוָה יְדַע שֶׁמִּיתָתוֹ בַחֲמוּרָה לָא הֲוָה עֲבַד הָדָא מִילְּתָא. הָיָה מִיתָתוֹ בְקַלָּה וְהִתְרוּהוּ בוֹ בַחֲמוּרָה. עַל דַּעְתֵּיהּ דְּרִבִּי יוּדָן בֵּירִבִּי אִלְעָאי שֶׁיַּעֲרִימוּהוּ בְּאֵי זֶה מִיתָה מֵת.

הָיוּ מַתְרִין בּוֹ וְשׁוֹתֵק. מַתְרִין בּוֹ וּמַרְכִּין בְּרֹאשׁוֹ. אַף עַל פִּי שֶׁאוֹמֵר יוֹדֵעַ אֲנִי. פָּטוּר. עַד שֶׁיֹּאמַר. עַל מְנָת כֵּן אֲנִי עוֹשֶׂה. רָאוּהוּ שׁוֹפֵךְ דָּם. אָמְרוּ לוֹ. הֲוֵי יוֹדֵעַ שֶׁבֶּן בְּרִית הוּא וְהַתּוֹרָה אָמְרָה שֹׁפֵךְ֙ דַּ֣ם הָֽאָדָ֔ם בָּֽאָדָ֖ם דָּמ֣וֹ יִשָּׁפֵ֑ךְ. אַף עַל פִּי שֶׁאָמַר. יוֹדֵעַ אֲנִי. פָּטוּר עַד שֶׁיֹּאמַר. עַל

מְנָת כֵּן אֲנִי עוֹשֶׂה. רָאוּהוּ מְחַלֵּל שַׁבָּת. אָמְרוּ לוֹ. הֲוֵי יוֹדֵעַ שֶׁהוּא שַׁבָּת וְהַתּוֹרָה אָמְרָה מְחַלְלֶיהָ מוֹת יוּמָת. אַף עַל פִּי שֶׁאָמַר. יוֹדֵעַ אֲנִי. פָּטוּר. עַד שֶׁיֹּאמַר. עַל מְנָת כֵּן אֲנִי עוֹשֶׂה.

"Did you warn him?" From where warning? Rebbi Samuel bar Naḥman in the name of Rebbi Jonathan: [18]*A man who would take his sister . . . , it is* ḥesed. Rebbi Bun said, Cain married his sister, Abel married his sister. *It is charitable*, I was charitable with the first generations so the world could be inhabited; *I said, the world was to be built on* ḥesed[19].

It was stated: Rebbi Simeon ben Iohai said, *by the mouth of two witnesses shall the dead die*[20]. Does he die when dead? But to tell him by which kind of death he will be executed.

It was stated: Rebbi Jehudah ben Rebbi Illai said, *and if a man intentionally kill his neighbor knowingly*[21]; they shall inform him by which kind of death he will be executed.

If his death should have been a severe one[22] but they warned him about an easy one. He could say that had he known that his death was to be severe, he would not have committed that crime. If his death should have been an easy one but they warned him about a severe one; in the opinion of Rebbi Jehudah ben Rebbi Illai they have to inform him by which kind of death he will be executed[23].

"If they warned him and he remained silent, they warned him and he nodded his head, even if he said, I know, he cannot be prosecuted unless he say: for that purpose I am doing it.[24]" "If they saw him spilling blood; they told him, know that he is a son of the Covenant[25] and the Torah said, *he who spills a man's blood, by man his blood shall be spilled*[26], even if he said, I know, he cannot be prosecuted unless he say: for that purpose I am doing it[27]." "If they saw him desecrating the Sabbath; they told him, know that today is Sabbath and the Torah said, *its desecrators shall be put to death*[28], even if he said, I know, he cannot be prosecuted unless he say: for that purpose I am doing it[29]."

18 *Lev.* 20:17. In a slightly different setting, this paragraph also is in *Yebamot* 11:1, Notes 25-26. Incest with one's sister is criminal (although by the earthly court only punishable by flogging) while it was permitted to earlier generations. Therefore, it cannot be assumed that everybody knows it to be prohibited. People found engaged in

incestuous acts cannot be prosecuted unless before the act informed of its criminality.

19 *Ps.* 89:3.

20 *Deut.* 17:6. In the Babli, this is an Amoraic argument. The verse is read as: *by the mouth of two witnesses shall the dead kill himself*, i. e., in the presence of two witnesses he accepts to be killed.

21 *Ex.* 21:14, Babli 41a. Babli and *Mekhiltot* read the verse as freeing the mentally disabled from prosecution.

22 Mishnah 7:1, Note 1.

23 R. Jehudah finds the warning deficient, preventing the imposition of a death sentence. By contrast, in the Babli, 80b, it is stated as commonly accepted that a warning about a painful death implies the same of an easy one.

24 Tosephta 11:2. Cf. also Note 20.

25 A Jew.

26 *Gen.* 9:6. The quote seems to be slightly out of place since it is directed at Gentile criminal courts which are not under the severe restrictions imposed at Torah courts.

27 Tosephta 11:4.

28 *Ex.* 31:14.

29 Tosephta 11:3.

(22d line 10) רִבִּי חִיָּה בַּר גַּמְדָּא שָׁאַל. מְקוֹשֵׁשׁ מִשּׁוּם מַה מִיחַייֵב. מִשּׁוּם תּוֹלֵשׁ אוֹ מִשּׁוּם קוֹצֵר. נִישְׁמְעִינָהּ מֵהָדָא. וַיִּהְי֥וּ בְנֵֽי־יִשְׂרָאֵ֖ל בַּמִּדְבָּ֑ר וַֽיִּמְצְא֗וּ. מְלַמֵּד שֶׁמְּצָאוּהוּ תוֹלֵשׁ עֵצִים מִן הַקַּרְקַע.

רִבִּי חִיָּה בַּר גַּמְדָּא שָׁאַל. מְקוֹשֵׁשׁ בַּמֶּה הִיא מִיתָתוֹ. בִּסְקִילָה. נִישְׁמְעִינָהּ מֵהָדָא. יוֹדְעִין הָיוּ שֶׁמְּקוֹשֵׁשׁ חַייָב מִיתָה וְלֹא הָיוּ יוֹדְעִין בַּמֶּה הָיְתָה מִיתָתוֹ. אַשְׁכַּח תַּנָּא רִבִּי חִייָה. הוֹצֵ֣א אֶת־הַֽמְקַלֵּ֗ל מִחוּץ֙ לַֽמַּחֲנֶ֔ה. בַּמֶּה הָיְתָה מִיתָתוֹ. בִּסְקִילָה.

Rebbi Ḥiyya bar Gamda asked[30]: What was the gatherer's guilt? Because of tearing off or because of reaping[31]? Let us hear from the following: *The Children of Israel were in the desert when they found . . .* This teaches that he was tearing wood off the ground[32].

Rebbi Ḥiyya bar Gamda asked: How was the gatherer put to death[33]? By stoning. Let us hear from the following[34]: "They knew that the gatherer should be executed but they did not know how he should be put to death." It was found that Rebbi Ḥiyya stated: *Take the blasphemer outside the camp*[35]. How was he put to death? By stoning.

30 His question is about the degree of specificity required in the warning delivered to a person ready to commit a crime punishable by death. Is it sufficient to deliver a general warning as described in the preceding paragraph (Note 27) or does one have to specify the exact paragraph of the law being violated? In the case of the Sabbath, is it enough to warn a person not to do any work or does he have to be warned about which of the 39 prohibited types of work he is going to perform? The biblical

evidence about the gatherer (*Num.* 15:32-36) shows that the Tosephta was correct in requiring only a general warning.

31 In the list of the forbidden categories of work (Mishnah *Šabbat* 7:2-4) only reaping is mentioned, which means cutting off the produce from its root. All forms of harvesting are forbidden as derivatives of reaping. The question remains whether a warning about tearing off from the ground would also cover reaping; a warning about reaping certainly covers all forms of harvesting.

32 *Sifry Num.* 113.

33 According to R. Jehudah, he could not be put to death if the specific way of execution was not known even though the fact that violating the Sabbath was known to be a capital crime.

34 *Sifra Emor Parashah* 14(5).

35 *Lev.* 24:14. This proves that from the pentateuchal stories nothing can be inferred for the rules of procedure required at later times. While it was known that a Sabbath infraction was punishable by death (Note 28), nothing was known about the penalty for blasphemy. Therefore, the first time these crimes occurred after the epiphany on Sinai, the law was only being formed; it was not yet consolidated (Babli 78b).

(22d line 14) אֶת מֶה עָבַד. לִפְעוֹר אוֹ לְמֶרְקוּלִיס. בַּמֶּה עֲבָדָהּ. בַּעֲבוֹדָתָהּ עֲבָדָהּ אוֹ בַעֲבוֹדַת גָּבוֹהַּ. נִישְׁמְעִינָהּ מֵהָדָא. מַעֲשֶׂה שֶׁבָּאוּ שְׁנַיִם וְאָמְרוּ. רָאִינוּ זֶה עוֹבֵד עֲבוֹדָה זָרָה וְאֵין אָנוּ יוֹדְעִין פְּעוֹר הָיָה אוֹ מֶרְקוּלִיס הָיָה. דָּנִין אוֹתוֹ בִשְׁתֵּיהֶן וּבְאֵי זֶה מִזְדַּכֶּה פּוֹטְרִין אוֹתוֹ.

"What did he worship?" *Peor* or Mercury[36]? "And how did he worship?" In its proper worship or the worship of Heaven[37]? Let us hear from the following: It happened that two [witnesses] came and said, we saw that this one was worshipping idols, but we do not know whether it was *Peor* or Mercury[38]. One judges him for both and for the one in which he was found innocent one lets him go[39].

36 As explained in Mishnah 7:12, the worship of *Ba`al Pe`or* was by defecating in front of his statue; the worship of *Mercurius*, the Greek *Hermes*, was by throwing an additional stone on the heap surrounding the *Hermes*, the pillar representing the divinity. Both forms of worship would be an insult if performed for any other idol and, therefore, not punishable.

37 Any imitation of Temple worship for an idol is a capital crime. Any other sort of worship is punishable only if ordinarily it was performed for that idol.

38 Clearly, this is inadmissible testimony.

39 Since the accused must be found innocent of one of two mutually exclusive allegations, one may accept the witnesses by basing a trial on their testimony even if a not-guilty verdict is a foregone conclusion.

(fol. 22c) **משנה ב**: כָּל הַמַּרְבֶּה בִבְדִיקוֹת הֲרֵי זֶה מְשׁוּבָּח. מַעֲשֶׂה וּבָדַק בֶּן זַכַּאי בְּעוּקְצֵי תְאֵנִים. וּמַה בֵּין חֲקִירוֹת לִבְדִיקוֹת. אֶלָּא שֶׁבַּחֲקִירוֹת אֶחָד אוֹמֵר אֵינִי יוֹדֵעַ עֵדוּתָן בְּטֵילָה. בְּדִיקוֹת אָמַר אֶחָד אֵינִי יוֹדֵעַ וַאֲפִלּוּ שְׁנַיִם אוֹמְרִים אֵין אָנוּ יוֹדְעִין עֵדוּתָן קַייֶמֶת. אֶחָד חֲקִירוֹת וְאֶחָד בְּדִיקוֹת בִּזְמַן שֶׁהֵן מַכְחִישִׁין זֶה אֶת זֶה עֵדוּתָן בְּטֵילָה:

Mishnah 2: Anybody who adds inquiries[40] is praiseworthy. It happened that Ben Zakkai[41] cross-examined about fig stalks. What is the difference between investigations and cross-examinations? In investigations, if one said "I do not know", their testimony is worthless[42]. In cross-examinations, if one said "I do not know", or even two say "we do not know," their testimony remains valid[43]. Both in investigations and cross-examinations, if they contradict one another their testimony is worthless[44].

40 About the details of the crime which are investigated after time and place have been established.

41 According to the Babli, 41a/b, it is possible that he is Rabban Johanan ben Zakkai. During the time that capital jurisdiction was still in the hands of a Jewish court, not yet in that of the Roman governor, he was not yet the head of the Synhedrion and, therefore, had no title.

42 As testimony which cannot be shown to be perjured.

43 The credibility of the witnesses may be impaired. This is a matter to be decided by the judges, not an absolute obstacle.

44 A conviction requires testimony by two witnesses. If there are conflicting testimonies and the judges believe one of them, no conviction could result since it would be based on the word of one witness alone.

(22d line 18) **הלכה ב**: כָּל הַמַּרְבֶּה בִבְדִיקוֹת כול'. בַּמֶּה לְקָטָן. בְּעוּקְצֵיהֶן לְקָטָן. בַּמֶּה אֲכָלָן. בְּגַלְעִינֵיהֶן.

Halakhah 2: "Anybody who adds inquiries," etc. How did he pluck them[45]? He plucked them with their stalks. How did he eat them? With their pits[46].

45 An example of Ben Zakkai's inquiry; cf. Babli 41a.

46 Referring to olives.

(22d line 19) תַּמָּן תַּנִּינָן. מִי שֶׁהָיוּ שְׁתֵּי כִתֵּי עֵדִים מְעִידִין. אֵילּוּ מְעִידִין שֶׁנָּזַר שְׁתַּיִם וְאֵילּוּ מְעִידִין שֶׁנָּזַר חָמֵשׁ. בֵּית שַׁמַּאי אוֹמְרִים. נֶחְלְקָה עֵדוּתָן. אֵין כָּאן נְזִירוּת. וּבֵית הִלֵּל אוֹמְרִים. יֵשׁ בִּכְלַל חָמֵשׁ שְׁתַּיִם. וִיהֵא נָזִיר שְׁתַּיִם: רַב אָמַר. בִּכְלָל נֶחְלְקוּ. אֲבָל בִּפְרָט כָּל־עַמָּא מוֹדוּ

נֶחְלְקָה הָעֵדוּת. וְרִבִּי יוֹחָנָן אָמַר. בְּמוֹנֶה נֶחְלְקוּ. אֲבָל בְּכוֹלֵל כָּל־עַמָּא מוֹדוּ שֶׁיֵּשׁ בִּכְלָל חָמֵשׁ שְׁתַּיִם. הֵידֵינוּ כוֹלֵל וְהֵידֵינוּ מוֹנֶה. כּוֹלֵל. אָהֵן אוֹמֵר תַּרְתֵּי וְאָהֵן אָמַר חָמֵשׁ. מוֹנֶה. אָהֵן אָמַר חָדָא תַרְתֵּי. וְאָהֵן אָמַר תְּלַת אַרְבָּעֵי.

[47]There, we have stated: "If two groups of witnesses were testifying against a person, one group say that he vowed *nazir* twice, the others say that he vowed *nazir* five times. The House of Shammai say, the testimony is split and there is no *nezirut* there. But the House of Hillel say, five contains two; he should be a *nazir* twice." Rav said, they differ in the overall testimony. But in detail, everybody agrees that the testimony is split. Rebbi Johanan said, they differ in counting. But in an overall testimony, everybody agrees that five contains two. What is overall and what is counting? Overall, this one says two, the other one says five. Counting, this one says one, two, the other one says three, four.

47 Parallel texts to this and the following paragraphs are in *Yebamot* 15:5 (Notes 115-134) and Nazir 3:7 (Notes 110-112).

(22d line 26) רַב אָמַר. הִכְחִישׁ עֵדוּת בְּתוֹךְ עֵדוּת לֹא בָֽטְלָה הָעֵדוּת. וְרִבִּי יוֹחָנָן אָמַר. הִכְחִישׁ עֵדוּת בְּתוֹךְ עֵדוּת בָֽטְלָה הָעֵדוּת. דִּבְרֵי הַכֹּל הִכְחִישׁ עֵדוּת לְאַחַר עֵדוּת לֹא בָֽטְלָה הָעֵדוּת. חֵילֵיהּ דְּרִבִּי יוֹחָנָן מֵהָדָא. דָּמַר רִבִּי בָּא בַּר חִייָה בְשֵׁם רִבִּי יוֹחָנָן. הוּחְזַק הַמּוֹנֶה. זֶה אוֹמֵר. מִן הַכִּיס מָנֶה. וְזֶה אוֹמֵר. מִן הַצְּרוֹר מָנֶה. הִכְחִישׁ עֵדוּת בְּתוֹךְ עֵדוּת אוּף רַב מוֹדֶה שֶׁבָּֽטְלָה הָעֵדוּת. מַה פְלִיגִין. בְּשֶׁהָיוּ שְׁתֵּי כִיתֵּי עֵדִים. אַחַת אוֹמֶרֶת. מִן הַכִּיס מָנֶה. וְאַחַת אוֹמֶרֶת. מִצְּרוֹר מָנֶה. הִכְחִישׁ עֵדוּת בְּתוֹךְ עֵדוּת בָּֽטְלָה עֵדוּת. וּכְרַב לֹא בָֽטְלָה עֵדוּת. אַחַת אוֹמֶרֶת. לְתוֹךְ חֵיקוֹ מָנָה. וְאַחַת אוֹמֶרֶת. לְתוֹךְ פּוּנְדָּתוֹ מָנָה. דִּבְרֵי הַכֹּל הִכְחִישׁ עֵדוּת בְּתוֹךְ עֵדוּת לֹא בָֽטְלָה הָעֵדוּת. אֶחָד אוֹמֵר. בְּסַיִיף הֲרָגוֹ. וְאֶחָד אוֹמֵר. בְּמַקֵּל הֲרָגוֹ. הַכְחֵשׁ עֵדוּת בְּתוֹךְ עֵדוּת אוּף רַב מוֹדֶה שֶׁבָּֽטְלָה הָעֵדוּת. מַה פְלִיגִין. בְּשֶׁהָיוּ שְׁתֵּי כִיתֵּי עֵדִים. אַחַת אוֹמֶרֶת. בְּסַיִיף. וְאַחַת אוֹמֶרֶת. בְּמַקֵּל. הַכְחֵשׁ עֵדוּת בְּתוֹךְ עֵדוּת בָּֽטְלָה עֵדוּת. וּכְרַב לֹא בָֽטְלָה עֵדוּת. אַחַת אוֹמֶרֶת. לַצָּפוֹן נָטָה. וְאַחַת אוֹמֶרֶת. לַדָּרוֹם פָּנָה. דִּבְרֵי הַכֹּל הִכְחִישׁ עֵדוּת לְאַחַר עֵדוּת לֹא בָֽטְלָה הָעֵדוּת. חֵיילֵיהּ דְּרַב מֵהָדָא דְתַנִּינָן תַּמָּן. רִבִּי יוּדָן וְרִבִּי שִׁמְעוֹן אוֹמְרִין. הוֹאִיל וְזוֹ וָזוֹ מוֹדוֹת שֶׁאֵינוֹ קַיָּים יִנָּשֵׂאוּ. וְלֹא שְׁמִיעַ דָּמַר רִבִּי לָֽעְזָר. מוֹדֶה רִבִּי יְהוּדָה וְרִבִּי שִׁמְעוֹן בְּעֵדִים. מַה בֵין עֵדִים וּמַה בֵּין צָרָה. לֹא עָשׂוּ דִּבְרֵי צָרָה בַּחֲבֵירָתָהּ כְּלוּם. אָמַר רִבִּי יוֹחָנָן. אִין אֲמָרָהּ רִבִּי לָֽעְזָר מִינִּי שְׁמָעָהּ וַאֲמָרָהּ. מַתְנִיתָא פְלִיגָא עַל רַב. אֶחָד חֲקִירוֹת וְאֶחָד בְּדִיקוֹת בִּזְמַן שֶׁהֵן מַכְחִישִׁין זֶה אֶת זֶה עֵדוּתָן בְּטֵילָה. מָה עֲבַד לָהּ רַב. אָמַר רִבִּי מָנָא. פָּתַר לָהּ רַב עֵד בְּעֵד. אָמַר רִבִּי אָבִין. אֲפִילוּ יִפְתָּר כַּת בְּכַת שַׁנְיָיא הִיא לְדִינֵי נְפָשׁוֹת. דִּכְתִיב צֶדֶק צֶדֶק תִּרְדּוֹף.

Rav said, if testimony was contradictory in its essence, the testimony is not void. Rebbi Johanan said, if testimony is contradictory in itself, the testimony is void. In the opinion of everybody, if testimony was contradictory in aspects that belong after the fact, the testimony is not void. The strength of Rebbi Johanan is consistent with what Rebbi Abba bar[48] Hiyya said in the name of Rebbi Johanan, if it was agreed that he counted but one [witness] said, he counted from a wallet, and the other said, he counted from a bundle, that contradicts the essence of the testimony, and Rav will agree that the testimony be void. Where do they disagree? If there were two groups of witnesses, one says he counted from a wallet and the other says he counted from a bundle. That contradicts the essence of the testimony: the testimony is void, but according to Rav, the testimony is not void. One said, he counted into his bosom, but the other said, he counted into his money-belt: everybody agrees that this contradicts the essence of the testimony but the testimony is not void. If one [witness] said, he killed him with a sword, the other [witness] said, he killed him with a mace, that contradicts the essence of the testimony; Rav will agree that the testimony be void. Where do they disagree? If there were two groups of witnesses, one says he killed him with a sword and the other says, he killed him with a mace. That contradicts the essence of the testimony, the testimony is void, but according to Rav, the testimony is not void. One says, he turned to the North and one says, he ran away to the South, everybody agrees that the testimony was contradictory in aspects that belong after the fact, and the testimony is not void. The strength of Rav comes from what we have stated there: "Rebbi Jehudah and Rebbi Simeon say, since both agree that he is not alive they can be remarried." He did not hear that Rebbi Eleazar said, Rebbi Jehudah and Rebbi Simeon concede in the case of witnesses. What is the difference between witnesses and the co-wife? They do not consider the co-wife's words compared to those of her companion. Rebbi Johanan said, if Rebbi Eleazar said this, he said it because he had heard it from me. The Mishnah disagrees with Rav: "Both in investigations and cross-examinations, if they contradict one another their testimony is worthless." What does Rav do with this? Rebbi Mana said, Rav will explain it as referring to single witness against single witness. Rebbi

Abun said, even if you say groups and groups. There is a difference in criminal cases, as it is written: *Justice, justice you shall pursue.*

48 Read with the parallel sources: R. Abba, R. Hiyya.

(fol. 22c) **משנה ג**: אֶחָד אוֹמֵר בִּשְׁנַיִם בַּחֹדֶשׁ וְאֶחָד אוֹמֵר בִּשְׁלֹשָׁה בַחֹדֶשׁ עֵדוּתָן קַיֶּמֶת שֶׁזֶּה יוֹדֵעַ בְּעִבּוּרוֹ שֶׁל חֹדֶשׁ וְזֶה לֹא יָדַע. אֶחָד אוֹמֵר בִּשְׁלֹשָׁה וְאֶחָד אוֹמֵר בַּחֲמִשָּׁה עֵדוּתָן בְּטֵילָה. אֶחָד אוֹמֵר בִּשְׁתֵּי שָׁעוֹת וְאֶחָד אוֹמֵר בְּשָׁלֹשׁ שָׁעוֹת עֵדוּתָן קַיֶּמֶת. אֶחָד אוֹמֵר בְּשָׁלֹשׁ וְאֶחָד אוֹמֵר בְּחָמֵשׁ עֵדוּתָן בְּטֵילָה. רִבִּי יְהוּדָה אוֹמֵר קַייֶמֶת. אֶחָד אוֹמֵר בְּחָמֵשׁ וְאֶחָד אוֹמֵר בְּשֶׁבַע עֵדוּתָן בְּטֵילָה שֶׁבְּחָמֵשׁ חַמָּה בַמִּזְרָח וּבְשֶׁבַע בַּמַּעֲרָב:

Mishnah 3: One says, on the second of the month, but the other says, on the third of the month[49], their testimony may be valid, since one knew about the addition to the month but the other did not know[50]. One says on the third, the other says on the fifth, their testimony is invalid[51]. One says, at two hours[52] but the other said at three hours, their testimony is valid[53]. One says at three but the other says at five, their testimony is invalid; Rebbi Jehudah says it is valid. One says at five but the other says at seven, their testimony is invalid since at five hours the sun is in the East but at seven in the West[54].

49 In the investigation of the date on which the alleged crime was committed.

50 In the absence of a published calendar, one cannot assume that everybody knew when a thirtieth day was added to a month. In the published calendar used today, only the eighth and ninth months are variable but the Mishnaic calendar (Babli *Arakhin* 8b-10a) admitted up to four variable months. It is up to the court to determine whether the witnesses intended to testify about one and the same day.

51 Two days' difference cannot be explained away.

52 The time between sunrise and sunset is divided into 12 hours. At all calendar dates, 6 hours is about noontime. At the equinoxes, 2 hours is 8 am, 3 hours 9 am, 5 hours 11 am, 7 hours 1 pm.

53 From people who have no watches.

54 The last statement is needed only for R. Jehudah. R. Jehudah does not accept testimony that differs by two hours in all cases; he notes that daylight between 9 am and 11 am is not very different; but the shadows are quite different between am and pm hours.

(22d line 49) **הלכה ג**: אֶחָד אוֹמֵר בִּשְׁנַיִם בַּחֹדֶשׁ כול׳. עַד הֵיכָא. רִבִּי יָסָא בְשֵׁם רִבִּי יוֹחָנָן. עַד רוֹב הַחֹדֶשׁ. אָמַר רִבִּי יוֹחָנָן. כְּגוֹן הָעִירוֹנִין הַלָּלוּ. וַחֲכָמִים אוֹמְרִים. אֵינָן כְּלוּם. וְאָמַר רִבִּי יָסָא. כְּגוֹן אֲנָא דְמִן יוֹמוֹי לָא צְלִית מוּסָפָא דְלָא יְדַע אֵימַת יַרְחָא.

Halakhah 3: "One says, on the second of the month," etc. Until when[55]? Rebbi Yasa in the name of Rebbi Johanan: Up to the greater part of the month[56]. Rebbi Yose said, e. g., those village dwellers[57]. But the Sages say, it is nothing[58], and Rebbi Yasa said, for example I, who never in my life prayed *musaf*[59], since I do not know when the month starts[60].

55 May one assume that people do not know which day of the month a given day is.

56 After the 16th, everybody knows how the month was determined.

57 They have a need to know the day of the week, but not of the month.

58 It is unclear whether the Sages object to the Mishnah or to R. Johanan's statement. From R. Yasa it seems that they object to R. Johanan.

59 The additional prayer which distinguishes the morning service of the New Moon from the weekday services.

60 He and his colleague Immi (Ammi) never were part of the Academy of Tiberias; it seems that they never were invited to the meetings at which the calendar was determined. This was his way of protesting.

(22d line 52) רִבִּי מֵאִיר אוֹמֵר. מִשֵּׁשׁ שָׁעוֹת וּלְמַעְלָן מִדִּבְרֵיהֶן. רִבִּי יוּדָה אוֹמֵר. מִשֵּׁשׁ שָׁעוֹת וּלְמַעְלָה מִדִּבְרֵי תוֹרָה. מַאי טַעְמָא דְרִבִּי מֵאִיר. אַךְ בַּיּוֹם הָרִאשׁוֹן. זֶה חֲמִשָּׁה עָשָׂר. יָכוֹל מִשֶּׁתֶּחְשַׁךְ. תַּלְמוּד לוֹמַר אַךְ חִלֵּק. הָא כֵיצַד. תֵּן לוֹ שָׁעָה אַחַת קוֹדֶם שְׁקִיעַת הַחַמָּה. מַאי טַעְמָא דְרִבִּי יְהוּדָה. אַךְ בַּיּוֹם הָרִאשׁוֹן. זֶהאַרְבָּעָה עָשָׂר. יָכוֹל כָּל־הַיּוֹם. תַּלְמוּד לוֹמַר אַךְ חִלֵּק. חֶצְיוֹ לְחָמֵץ וְחֶצְיוֹ לְמַצָּה. מִחְלֶפֶת שִׁיטַּת רִבִּי מֵאִיר. תַּמָּן אָמַר. אַךְ לְרַבּוֹת. וְכָא אָמַר. אַךְ לְמָעֵט. אָמַר רִבִּי שְׁמוּאֵל בַּר אֶבְדּוּמֵי. מִיעֲטוֹ שֶׁאֵינוֹ מְחָמֵץ. רִבִּי מֵאִיר אוֹמֵר. לֹא־תֹאכַל עָלָיו חָמֵץ. עַל אֲכִילָתוֹ. רִבִּי יְהוּדָה אוֹמֵר. לֹא־תֹאכַל עָלָיו חָמֵץ. עַל עֲשִׂייָתוֹ.

רִבִּי יוּדָן אִית לֵיהּ עֲשֵׂה וְלֹא תַעֲשֶׂה עַל אֲכִילָתוֹ. עֲשֵׂה וְלֹא תַעֲשֶׂה עַל בִּיעוּרוֹ. עֲשֵׂה עַל אֲכִילָתוֹ. שִׁבְעַת יָמִים תֹּאכַל־עָלָיו מַצּוֹת. לֹא חָמֵץ. כָּל־לֹא תַעֲשֶׂה שֶׁבָּא מִכֹּחַ עֲשֵׂה עֲשֵׂה הוּא. וְלֹא תַעֲשֶׂה עַל אֲכִילָתוֹ. לֹא־תֹאכַל חָמֵץ. עֲשֵׂה עַל בִּיעוּרוֹ. שִׁבְעַת יָמִים תַּשְׁבִּיתוּ שְׂאֹר מִבָּתֵּיכֶם. לֹא תַעֲשֶׂה עַל בִּיעוּרוֹ. שִׁבְעַת יָמִים שְׂאֹר לֹא יִמָּצֵא בְּבָתֵּיכֶם.

הָא רִבִּי מֵאִיר אָמַר. מִשֵּׁשׁ שָׁעוֹת וּלְמַעְלָה מִדִּבְרֵיהֶן. שִׁשִּׁית אֲסוּרָה מִשּׁוּם גָּדֵר. חֲמִישִׁית לָמָּה. מִשּׁוּם גָּדֵר. וְיֵשׁ גָּדֵר לְגָדֵר. אֶלָּא חֲמִישִׁית מִתְחַלְּפָה בַשְּׁבִיעִית. מִחְלְפָה שִׁיטַּת רִבִּי יְהוּדָה. תַּמָּן אָמַר. אֵין חֲמִישִׁית מִתְחַלֶּפֶת בַּשְּׁבִיעִית. וְכָא אָמַר. חֲמִישִׁית מִתְחַלֶּפֶת בַּשְּׁבִיעִית. אָמַר רִבִּי יוֹסֵי. תַּמָּן מָסוּר לַנָּשִׁים וְהֵן עֲצֵילוֹת. הָכָא הַדָּבָר מָסוּר לְבֵית דִּין וְהֵן זְרִיזִין. אָמַר

רִבִּי יוֹסֵי בֵּירִבִּי בּוּן. תַּמָּן תְּחִילַּת חֲמִישִׁית סוֹף שְׁבִיעִית. הָכָא סוֹף חֲמִישִׁית תְּחִילַּת שְׁבִיעִית. וְתַנֵּי כֵן. תְּחִילַּת חָמֵשׁ חַמָּה בַּמִּזְרָח וְסוֹף שֶׁבַע חַמָּה בַּמַּעֲרָב. לְעוֹלָם אֵין חַמָּה נוֹטָה לְמַעֲרָב אֶדָּא בְסוֹף שֶׁנַע.

[61]Rebbi Meïr says, from noontime on it is from their words; Rebbi Jehudah says, from noontime on it is biblical[62].

What is Rebbi Meïr's reason? *Only on the first day*[63], that is the fifteenth[64]. I could think at nightfall; the verse says *only*, to separate[65]. How is this? Give it one hour before sundown[66].

What is Rebbi Jehudah's reason? *Only on the first day*[63], that is the fourteenth. I could think the entire day; the verse says *only*, to separate. Half for leavened matter, half for *mazzah*.

Rebbi Meïr's argument seems inverted. There, he said *only* to add; here he said *only* to diminish[67]. Rebbi Samuel bar Eudaimon said, he diminished, lest it be for[68] leavened matter.

Rebbi Meïr said, *do not eat leavened matter with it*[69], while it is eaten. Rebbi Jehudah said, *do not eat leavened matter with it*, while it is prepared[70].

Rebbi Jehudah has both a positive and a negative commandment concerning its eating[71], a positive and a negative commandment concerning its[72] removal. A positive commandment concerning its eating, *seven days you shall eat unleavened bread for it*[69], not leavened. Any prohibition which is implied by a positive commandment has the status of positive commandment[73]. A negative commandment concerning its eating, *do not eat leavened*[74]. A positive commandment concerning its removal, *seven days . . . you shall remove sour dough from your houses*[63]. A negative commandment concerning its removal, *for seven days sour dough shall not be found in your houses*[75].

Now Rebbi Meïr says, after noontime it is forbidden because of their words. The [76](sixth) [seventh] hour it is forbidden because of a fence. Why the (fifth) [sixth]? Because of a fence. Is there a fence around a fence? But the (fifth) [sixth] may be confounded with the seventh[77].

Rebbi Jehudah's argument seems inverted. There[78], he says that the fifth cannot be confounded with the seventh. But here[79], he says that the fifth can be confounded with the seventh. Rebbi Yose said, there[80] the matter is given over to women who are lazy, here[81] the matter is given over to the court who is careful. Rebbi Yose ben Rebbi Abun said, there[81] it is a matter between the beginning of the fifth and the end of the seventh hour. Here[79] it is between the end of the fifth and the start of the seventh[82]. It also was stated thus[83]: At the start of the fifth hour, the sun is in the East, and the end of the seventh the sun is in the West. The sun never starts setting before the end of the seventh hour.

61 Most of this text belongs to *Pesahim* 1:4. The scribe of the Leiden ms., after the text translated here in the first 5 paragraphs, wrote: "one continues in *Sanhedrin* until `the sun never starts setting'." The corrector who prepared the ms. for the Venice printer added the omitted portion; his text differs from the one given here by both an addition and a lacuna. It is impossible to decide whether the corrector's *Pesahim* text is copied from a different ms. or represents the corrector's emendations of the Sanhedrin text. In neither text is the use of references "here" and "there" (either *Pesaḥim* or *Sanhedrin*) completely consistent.

62 The main topic of the following section is the prohibition of leavened matter on Passover. It is agreed by everybody that leavened matter must be disposed of by noontime (the end of the sixth hour) of the 14th of Nisan. In Mishnah *Pesahim* 1:4, R. Meïr states that "one eats [leavened bread] during all of the fifth hour (between 10 and 11 am local time) and burns the remainder at the start of the sixth hour (shortly after 11 am). R. Jehudah says, one eats during the entire fourth hour (9 to 10 am local time), one suspends leavened matter during the fifth hour and burns the remainder at the start of the sixth. ("Suspending" means that eating leavened matter is forbidden but usufruct is permitted.)

The anonymous majority in *Sanhedrin* 5:3 is presumed to represent R. Meïr's opinion. The question now remains whether the disagreement between R. Meïr and R. Jehudah in *Sanhedrin* is the same as in *Pesahim* or not.

63 *Ex.* 12:15: *Seven days you shall eat mazzot; only on the first day you shall eliminate sour dough from your houses . . .* אך might also be translated as "certainly".

64 *Ex.* 12:14 states: *This day shall be a remembrance for you; you shall keep it as a holiday of pilgrimage for the Eternal . . . Num.* 28:15-16 require that the 14th of Nisan be *pesah* for the Eternal; starting from the 15th for seven days it is the holiday of *mazzot*. Since *pesaḥ* (i. e., the day of the slaughter of the *pesah* sacrifice) is connected inextricably with the holiday of *mazzot*, the reference in v. 14 to the "first day" is intrinsically ambiguous, whether it refer to *pesah* or to the holiday.

65 A similar argument is in the Babli, *Pesaḥim* 4b, *Mekhilta dR. Ismael* (ed. Horovitz-Rabin p. 28), *Mekhilta dR. Simeon b. Iohai* (ed. Epstein-Melamed p. 17).

66 I. e., the only biblical requirement is that all leavened matter be completely disposed of before the holiday at sundown.

67 It seems that this refers to *Ex.* 12:16:. . . *no work shall be done [on the holidays],* only *what may be eaten by any soul, it alone*

may be made by you. Everybody agrees that food may be prepared on a holiday. According to R. Meïr (i. e., the anonymous opinion in Mishnah *Megillah* 1:8) *only* food may be prepared, not preparations necessary for the preparation of food. According to R. Jehudah (*Megillah* 1:8), anything that in the end leads to preparation of food is permitted on a holiday. R. Meïr reads *only* as a restriction in v. 16 and as an addition in v. 15!

68 Read with the *Pesahim* text בחמץ instead of מחמץ. The extension of a prohibition parallels the restriction of a permission.

69 *Deut.* 16:3, referring to the *pesah* sacrifice which is slaughtered on the afternoon of the 14th and eaten in the night of the 15th.

70 In the afternoon of the 14th. This supports R. Jehudah's contention that leavened matter is biblically forbidden in the afternoon of the 14th; *Sifry Deut.* 130.

71 "It" here refers to *mazzah.*

72 "It" here refers to leavened matter.

73 It is not an indictable offense; cf. *Bikkurim* 1:5, Note 103. If a positive commandment is in conflict with a negative one (a prohibition), the positive is stronger. But an obligation which is both positive and negative is stronger than anything else.

74 *Deut.* 16:3; the word עָלָיו is missing here, supplied in *Pesahim.*

75 *Ex.* 12:19.

76 The numerals in parentheses are from *Sanhedrin*; those in brackets are the corrected ones from *Pesaḥim*. For R. Meïr, the biblical prohibition of leavened matter starts at the 11th hour (5 pm local time). The earlier afternoon hours, including the 7th, are rabbinically forbidden as a "fence around the law". Then it is difficult to understand why leavened matter has to be burned *at the start* of the 6th, extending the rabbinic prohibition for another hour as a fence around the fence, a practice generally rejected.

77 It is not a fence around a fence but consistent with the opinion of the Sages (R. Meïr) in *Sanhedrin* 5:3. In a society without watches the difference between 11am and 12am is not generally recognized; a prohibition enforced after noontime must practically be enforced starting from 11am.

78 This is here, in the Mishnah *Sanhedrin.* R. Jehudah agrees that while without watches people cannot distinguish between two morning or two afternoon hours, he explicitly agrees that people distinguish between fifth (10-11am) and seventh (12am-1pm).

79 In *Pesahim* he requires one to stop eating leavened matter two hours before the start of the seventh hour when the biblical prohibition begins.

80 In *Pesaḥim* one speaks of household chores.

81 In *Sanhedrin* the Mishnah does not require the court to accept any testimonies where the witnesses differ widely in fixing the time of a crime; R. Jehudah admonishes the court under certain circumstances to investigate whether the witnesses do not in reality testify about the same time; Babli *Pesaḥim* 12b.

82 In *Pesahim* the period of doubt is little more than 60 min., in *Sanhedrin* close to 180 min. The apparent inconsistency is due to the informal use of "hour."

83 A similar *baraita* is in *Pesahim 12b*.

(fol. 22c) **משנה ד**: הָיוּ מַכְנִיסִין אֶת הַשֵּׁנִי וּבוֹדְקִין אוֹתוֹ. נִמְצְאוּ דִבְרֵיהֶן מְכֻוָּנִין פּוֹתְחִין בִּזְכוּת. אָמַר אֶחָד מִן הָעֵדִים יֶשׁ לִי לְלַמֵּד עָלָיו זְכוּת אוֹ אֶחָד מִן הַתַּלְמִידִים יֶשׁ לִי לְלַמֵּד עָלָיו חוֹבָה מְשַׁתְּקִין אוֹתוֹ. אָמַר אֶחָד מִן הַתַּלְמִידִים יֶשׁ לִי לְלַמֵּד עָלָיו זְכוּת מַעֲלִין וּמוֹשִׁיבִין אוֹתוֹ בֵּינֵיהֶן וְלֹא הָיָה יוֹרֵד מִשָּׁם כָּל הַיּוֹם כּוּלּוֹ. אִם יֵשׁ מַמָּשׁ בִּדְבָרָיו שׁוֹמְעִין לוֹ. אֲפִילוּ אָמַר הוּא יֶשׁ לִי לְלַמֵּד עַל עַצְמִי זְכוּת שׁוֹמְעִין לוֹ וּבִלְבַד שֶׁיֵּשׁ מַמָּשׁ בִּדְבָרָיו:

Mishnah 4: They brought in the second [witness] and examined him. If their testimonies were coherent, one starts with arguing for acquittal[84]. If one of the witnesses said, I have an argument for his acquittal[85], or one of the students said, I have an argument for his conviction, one forces them to be silent. If one of the students said, I have an argument for his acquittal, one brings him up and lets him sit among them[86]. He was not demoted from there the entire day; if his argument has substance, one listens to him. Even if he[87] said, I have to argue for my acquittal, one listens to him if there is substance to his words.

משנה ה: אִם מָצְאוּ לוֹ זְכוּת פְּטָרוּהוּ. וְאִם לָאו מַעֲבִירִין דִּינוֹ לְמָחָר. וּמִזְדַּוְּגִין זוּגוֹת זוּגוֹת מְמַעֲטִין בְּמַאֲכָל וְלֹא הָיוּ שׁוֹתִין יַיִן כָּל הַיּוֹם וְנוֹשְׂאִין וְנוֹתְנִין בַּדָּבָר כָּל הַלַּיְלָה וּלַמָּחֳרָת מַשְׁכִּימִין וּבָאִין הַמְזַכֶּה אוֹמֵר אֲנִי הוּא הַמְזַכֶּה וּמְזַכֶּה אֲנִי בִמְקוֹמִי. וְהַמְחַייֵב אוֹמֵר אֲנִי הוּא הַמְחַייֵב וּמְחַייֵב אֲנִי בִמְקוֹמִי. הַמְלַמֵּד חוֹבָה מְלַמֵּד זְכוּת. אֲבָל הַמְלַמֵּד זְכוּת אֵינוֹ יָכוֹל לַחֲזוֹר וּלְלַמֵּד חוֹבָה. וְאִם טָעוּ בַדָּבָר שְׁנֵי סוֹפְרֵי הַדַּיָּנִין מַזְכִּירִין אוֹתָן.

Mishnah 5: If they found him innocent, they free him. Otherwise they hold his case over to the next day, split into groups of two, eat little and refrain from wine the entire day, and discuss during the entire night[88]. The next morning they start early. One who voted for acquittal says, I am for acquittal and I remain for acquittal. One who voted for conviction says, I am for conviction and I remain for conviction. He who voted for conviction may vote for acquittal; but he who voted for acquittal may not change and vote for conviction. If they erred in the matter, the two clerks of court will remind them.

84 Mishnah 4:1.

85 A witness for the prosecution who argues for acquittal undermines his own testimony. Anyhow, no witness can become

judge in the same case (Halakhah 5).

86 The judges.

87 The accused.

88 The topic of discussion is not mentioned; it seems to be the case under consideration. In the Tosephta, the judges are required to review the legal background, if a murder case the laws of murder, if an incest case the laws of incest.

(22d line 75) **הלכה ד**: הָיוּ מַכְנִיסִין אֶת הַשֵּׁינִי כול'. תַּנֵּי. אִם מָצְאוּ לוֹ זְכוּת פְּטָרוּהוּ וְאִם לָאו מַעֲבִירִין דִּינוֹ וּמִזְדַּוְּגִין זוּגוֹת וּמְמַעֲטִין בְּמַאֲכָל וְלֹא הָיוּ שׁוֹתִין יַיִן וְנוֹשְׂאִין וְנוֹתְנִין כָּל הַלַּיְלָה. וּלְמָחָר מַשְׁכִּימִין וּבָאִין. וַחֲזָנֵי כְנֵסִיּוֹת מְחַזְּרִין אַחֲרֵיהֶן וְאוֹמְרִין. אִישׁ פְּלוֹנִי [בֶּן אִישׁ פְּלוֹנִי. וְהוּא אוֹמֵר. בִּמְקוֹמִי אֲנִי.][G] מְחַייֵב הָיִיתִי וּמְחַייֵב אֲנִי. מְזַכֶּה הָיִיתִי וּמְזַכֶּה אֲנִי. מְחַייֵב הָיִיתִי וּמְזַכֶּה אֲנִי. שׁוֹמְעִין לוֹ. מְזַכֶּה הָיִיתִי וּמְחַייֵב אֲנִי. לַמֵּד תְּחִילָּה. תַּנֵּי. טָעָה אֶחָד מִן הַדַּייָנִין. אִם הָיָה מְזַכֶּה סוֹפְרֵי הַדַּייָנִין מַזְכִּירִין אוֹתוֹ. אִם הָיָה מְחַייֵב אוֹמְרִין לוֹ. לַמֵּד תְּחִילָּה.

Halakhah 4: "They brought in the second," etc. It was stated[89]: "If they found him innocent, they freed him; otherwise they hold his case over, split into groups of two, eat little and refrain from wine, and discuss during the entire night. The next morning they start early, the beadles of the synagogues come for them. They ask, Mr. X [ben Mr. Y. He says, present.][90] I was for conviction and I still am for conviction; or I was for acquittal and I still am for acquittal; I was for conviction and now I am for acquittal; one accepts his vote. I was for acquittal and now I am for conviction; argue as before.[99]" It was stated: If one of the judges erred, the clerks of court remind him. If he was for conviction, they tell him, argue as before.

89 Tosephta 9:1.

90 Addition from the Genizah text (Note 0); not absolutely necessary for the understanding of the text and not in the Tosephta.

91 In the Tosephta: "They tell him, consider your earlier argument." This is understood here.

(23a line 6) אָמַר רִבִּי לָא. מִפְּנֵי מַה כּוֹתְבִין דִּבְרֵי הַמְזַכֶּה. מִפְּנֵי הַמְחַייֵב. שֶׁמָּא תִיטָּרֵף דַּעְתּוֹ. וְאִין חֲלִיף מִילָּא יֵימְרוּן לֵיהּ. הָדָא אֲמְרָת הָדָא לָא אֲמְרָת. [הָדָא אֲמְרָה][G]. צְרִיכָה שְׁנֵי [כִיתֵּי][G] עֵדִים. נִמְצָא דִינוֹ מִשְׁתַּקֵּעַ. רִבִּי יוֹדֵי בֵּירִבִּי בּוּן אָמַר. מִפְּנֵי הַמְזַכֶּה.

Rabbi La said, why does one record the argument of him who argues for acquittal? Because of him who argues for conviction, maybe his memory will fail him. If he switches his argument, they could say to him, this you said, this you did not say. [Does this mean] that it needs two [groups of] witnesses[92]? It would mean that the trial would be extended. Rebbi Yose ben Rebbi Abun said, because of him who argues for acquittal[93].

92 The text in brackets is from the Genizah; it is not a better text. The Leiden text seems to follow R. Jehudah (Mishnah 4:9) who requires that the arguments of each judge be recorded by two scribes, i. e., two witnesses who may prevent him from changing his mind. The Genizah text asks whether if an acquitting judge now wants to vote for conviction one has to start the entire proceedings anew. This would preclude pronouncing sentence on that day and would amount to forbidden procrastination in administering justice.

93 Mishnah 5 alone is justification enough.

(fol. 22c) **משנה ו**: וְאִם לָאו עוֹמְדִים לַמִּנְייָן. שְׁנֵי עָשָׂר מְזַכִּין וְאַחַד עָשָׂר מְחַייְבִין זַכַּאי. שְׁנֵים עָשָׂר מְחַייְבִין וְאַחַד עָשָׂר מְזַכִּין וַאֲפִלּוּ עֶשְׂרִים וּשְׁנַיִם מְזַכִּין אוֹ מְחַייְבִין וְאֶחָד אוֹמֵר אֵינִי יוֹדֵעַ יוֹסִיפוּ הַדַּייָנִים.

Mishnah 6: If they found him innocent, they free him; otherwise they tally the vote. If twelve are for acquittal and eleven for conviction, he is found innocent. If twelve are for conviction and eleven for acquittal[94], or even twenty-two are for acquittal or conviction and one says, I do not know[95], they shall add judges.

94 A criminal conviction needs a qualified majority of at last two (Mishnah 4:2). Since there was no majority for acquittal, the accused is neither acquitted nor convicted; this is a case of a hung court.

95 A judge who abstains in the final vote is counted not present. Then the court is no longer composed of 23 members; there is a mistrial.

(23 line 9) **הלכה ה**: אִם מָצְאוּ לוֹ זְכוּת פְּטָרוּהוּ כול'. תַּנֵּי. אֶחָד מִן הָעֵדִים שֶׁאָמַר. יֵשׁ לִי לְלַמֵּד עָלָיו זְכוּת. וּבָא חֲבֵירוֹ וְסִייְעוֹ וּבָא חֲבֵירוֹ וְסִייְעוֹ. אֶת מִי מְמַנִּין. לָרִאשׁוֹן לַשֵּׁינִי לִשְׁנֵיהֶן. נִשְׁמְעִינָהּ מֵהָדָא דְרִבִּי יוֹחָנָן. וְהוּא שֶׁנִּזְדַּכֶּה מִפִּי עַצְמוֹ אֵין מוֹשִׁיבִין אוֹתוֹ דַייָן. הֲרֵי שֶׁנִּזְדַּכֶּה מִפִּי עַצְמוֹ וְנִמְצָא עֵד וְדַייָן לֹא מָצִינוּ עֵד נַעֲשֶׂה דַייָן.

Halakhah 5: "If they found him innocent, they free him," etc. It was stated: If one of the witnesses said, I have an argument for his acquittal, and another came to support him, (and another came to support him,)[96] whom do you co-opt [97]? Let us hear from the following of Rebbi Johanan: If somebody was acquitted following his own pleading, one does not place him with the judges. Therefore, if he was acquitted following (his own)[98] pleading, then one person would be simultaneously witness and judge. We do not find that anybody can be both witness and judge.

96 Corrector's addition, to be deleted.

97 Following Mishnah 4 which, however, speaks of law students, not of witnesses. Only R. Yose ben R. Jehudah admits pleading by a witness (Tosephta 9:4).

98 This must read: "the witness".

(23a line 14) אוֹמְרִים בְּדִינֵי מָמוֹנוֹת. נִזְדַּקֵּן הַדִּין. [וְאֵין אוֹמְרִים בְּדִינֵי נְפָשׁוֹת נִזְדַּקֵּן הַדִּין.][G] וְהַגָּדוֹל שֶׁבַּדַּייָנִין אוֹמֵר. נִזְדַּקֵּן הַדִּין.

In civil suits one declares the judgment as definitive[99] [but in criminal suits one does not declare the judgment as definitive.][100] The greatest among the judges declares the judgment as definitive [101].

99 A strictly literal translation would be: "the judgment became old." The interpretation of this otherwise unknown expression follows Rav Ashi in the Babli, 42a. The case can neither be appealed nor retried.

100 Addition also found in the Babli, implied by the preceding sentence. As long as a criminal sentence was not executed, the trial may be re-opened at any time if a new argument for acquittal can be presented.

101 Babli 42a.

(fol. 22c) **משנה ז**: עַד כַּמָּה מוֹסִיפִין שְׁנַיִם שְׁנַיִם עַד שִׁבְעִים וְאֶחָד. שְׁלֹשִׁים וְשִׁשָּׁה מְזַכִּין וּשְׁלֹשִׁים וַחֲמִשָּׁה מְחַייְבִין זַכַּאי. שְׁלֹשִׁים וְשִׁשָּׁה מְחַייְבִין וּשְׁלֹשִׁים וַחֲמִשָּׁה מְזַכִּין דָּנִין אֵילוּ כְּנֶגֶד אֵילוּ עַד שֶׁיִּרְאֶה אֶחָד הַמְחַייְבִין אֶת דִּבְרֵי הַמְזַכִּין:

Mishnah 7: Up to what number does one add? [One adds] two and two up to 71[102]. If 36 vote for acquittal and 35 for conviction, he is found innocent. If 36 vote for conviction and 35 for acquittal[102], they have to continue to argue with one another until one of the voters for conviction is convinced by the arguments of those in favor of acquittal.

102 The size of the Supreme Court is the upper limit for the size of any court.

103 This is a *de facto* vote for acquittal since for conviction a majority of two votes

is required and the judges voting for acquittal are barred from changing their vote. Since no judges can be added, the only way to conclude the trial is for one of the convicting judges to become one of the acquitting.

(23 line 15) **הלכה ז:** עַד כַּמָּה מוֹסִיפִין כול'. תַּנֵּי. לָמָּה מוֹסִיפִין דַּיָּינִין. שֶׁאִם הָיוּ שְׁנַיִם מִן הָרִשׁוֹנִים מְזַכִּין וְאֶחָד מִן הָאַחֲרוֹנִים לִיגָּמֵר הַדִּין בִּשְׁלֹשָׁה. אָמַר רִבִּי לָא. מִכֵּיוָן שֶׁנִּרְאֶה דִינוֹ לִיגָּמֵר בְּאַרְבָּעָה אֵין גּוֹמְרִין אוֹתוֹ בִשְׁלֹשָׁה.

Halakhah 7: "Up to what number does one add," etc. [104]It was stated: Why does one add judges? For if there were two of the original judges voting affirmatively[105], together with one of the later ones judgment will be rendered by three. Rebbi La said, since the judgment can be rendered by four, one does not render it by three[106].

104 This and the next paragraph refer to Halakhah 3:3; the subject is civil suits.

105 Even if two judges vote for the claimant but the third abstains, no judgment can be rendered by a court of two.

106 Although only one additional judge is needed, one always adds two. If only one judge were added, he would be unable to change the outcome; he is not really a judge of equal standing with the others. But two judges could force the addition of another two by voting for the defendant.

(23 line 18) אָמַר רִבִּי יוֹסֵי. וְתִשְׁמַע מִינֵּיהּ. שְׁלֹשָׁה שֶׁדָּנוּ וּמֵת אֶחָד מֵהֶן. חוֹתְמִין בִּשְׁנַיִם וְכוֹתְבִין. אַף עַל פִּי שֶׁחָתַמְנוּ בִשְׁנַיִם בִּשְׁלֹשָׁה דָּנְנוּ. אָמַר רִבִּי חַגַּיי. מַתְנִיתָא אָמְרָה כֵן. הַדַּייָנִין חוֹתְמִין בּוֹ מִלְּמַטָּה אוֹ הָעֵדִים. וּלְמֵידִין מִידַּת הַדִּין מִפְּרוֹזְבּוֹל. אַשְׁכַּח תַּנֵּי. הוּא לָמַד מִידַּת הַדִּין מִפְּרוֹזְבּוֹל.

Rebbi Yose said, one understands from here: [107]If three sat in judgment and one of them died, two sign and note: Even though we are two who sign, we were three in judging. Rebbi Ḥaggai said, a Mishnah implies this: "The judges sign at the bottom or the witnesses." Does one learn court documents from *prozbol*? It was found stated: This about court documents he inferred from the rules of *prozbol*.

107 This is from *Ševi`it* 10:3, Note 91 where *prozbol* is explained. The text there and in the Babli, *Ketubot* 22a, is in the name of the earlier Amora R. Abba.

(12a line 22) לֹא רָאָה. רִבִּי יוֹחָנָן אָמַר. זַכַּאי. רֵישׁ לָקִישׁ אָמַר. חַייָב. אָמַר לֵיהּ רִבִּי יוֹחָנָן. וַהֲלֹא זַכַּאי הוּא. וְלָמָּה דָנִין יֵלְכוּ כְּנֶגֶד אֵילּוּ. שֶׁלֹּא יֵירָאֶה דִין זֶה יוֹצֵא מְעֻמְעָם.

If nobody changes his opinion[108]? Rebbi Johanan said, he is acquitted[109]. Rebbi Simeon ben Laqish said, he is convicted[110]. Rebbi Johanan said to him, is he not acquitted[111]? Why do they have to continue to argue with one another? So the judgment should not be in question[112].

108 This refers to the Mishnah. If no one voting for conviction changes his mind, at the end of the day judgment must be rendered. What is the practical consequence of 36 votes for conviction, 35 for acquittal?

109 Since the votes for conviction fall short of the majority required, it is an automatic acquittal (Babli 42a).

110 Since there is a majority for conviction, there can be no acquittal. R. Simeon ben Laqish will agree that if it is a capital case, the accused cannot be executed except the missionary for idolatry (Tosephta 10:12).

111 Mishnah 4:2.

112 To discourage any attempt at a retrial.

נגמר הדין פרק שישי

(fol. 23a) **משנה א**: נִגְמַר הַדִּין מוֹצִיאִין אוֹתוֹ לְסוֹקְלוֹ. בֵּית הַסְּקִילָה הָיָה חוּץ לְבֵית דִּין שֶׁנֶּאֱמַר הוֹצֵא אֶת־הַמְקַלֵּל אֶל־מִחוּץ לַמַּחֲנֶה. וְאֶחָד עוֹמֵד עַל פֶּתַח בֵּית דִּין וְהַסּוּדָרִין בְּיָדוֹ וְהַסּוּס רָחוֹק מִמֶּנּוּ כְּדֵי שֶׁיְּהֵא רוֹאֵהוּ. אוֹמֵר אֶחָד יֶשׁ לִי לְלַמֵּד עָלָיו זְכוּת הַלָּה מֵנִיף בַּסּוּדָרִין וְהַסּוּס רָץ וּמַעֲמִידוֹ. אֲפִילוּ הוּא אוֹמֵר יֶשׁ לִי לְלַמֵּד עַל עַצְמִי זְכוּת מַחֲזִירִין אוֹתוֹ וַאֲפִילוּ אַרְבָּעָה וַחֲמִשָּׁה פְּעָמִים וּבִלְבַד שֶׁיְּהֵא מַמָּשׁ בִּדְבָרָיו.

Mishnah 1: If sentence was passed[1], one brings him out to be stoned. The place for stoning was outside the court as it is said: *Bring the blasphemer outside the camp*[2]. One person was standing outside the court building with towels in his hand[3]; a horse[4] was standing ready at a distance but so he could see him[5]. If one said[6], I have an argument in his favor, that one waves his towels, the horse gallops and stops him[7]. Even if he himself says, I have an exculpatory argument for myself, one returns him[8] even four or five times, on condition that his argument be substantial.

1 If in a capital case the accused was condemned to death. In the list of biblical death penalties (Mishnah 7:1) stoning is mentioned first; therefore, the details of the stoning procedure are explained first.

2 *Lev*. 24:14. A walled city is the equivalent of the desert "camp"; the execution took place outside the city walls (*Ketubot* 4:6, Note 132). However, the unfaithful preliminarily married virgin was stoned in front of her parents' house (*Deut*. 22:21, Tosephta 10:10, Babli 45b) and the idolator at his place of worship (*Deut*. 17:5; *Sifry Deut*. 148; Babli *Ketubot* 45b).

3 Latin *sudarium, -i, n.*; in the Talmudim used for any rectangular piece of cloth too small to cover the body. Here it is used for signal flags.

4 Meaning: a man on a horse.

5 The horse was stationed on the road to the place of execution as far away as possible so that the rider still could see the person holding the signal flags.

6 One of the judges or of the law students remaining in the court building.

7 The procession to the place of execution cannot start until the judges reassemble and decide whether the new argument is weighty enough to restart the deliberations towards a new vote.

8 To the court building to present his case to the judges.

(23b line 14) **הלכה א**: נִגְמַר הַדִּין כול'. מַתְנִיתִין אוֹ כְרִבִּי אוֹ כְרַבָּנִן בְּעִיר שֶׁלְּגוֹיִם. דְּתַנֵּי בִּשְׁעָרֶיךָ. רִבִּי אוֹמֵר. בִּשְׁעָרֶיךָ. בְּשַׁעַר שֶׁנִּמְצְאוּ בוֹ. אַתָּה אוֹמֵר כָּךְ אוֹ אֵינוֹ אֶלָּא בְשַׁעַר שֶׁנִּידּוֹנוּ בוֹ. נֶאֱמַר כָּאן בִּשְׁעָרֶיךָ וְנֶאֱמַר לְהַלָּן כִּי־יִמָּצֵא בְקִרְבְּךָ בְּאַחַד שְׁעָרֶיךָ. מַה שְׁעָרֶיךָ הָאָמוּר לְהַלָּן שַׁעַר שֶׁנִּמְצָא בוֹ אַף שְׁעָרֶיךָ הָאָמוּר כָּאן שַׁעַר שֶׁנִּמְצְאוּ בוֹ. וְרַבָּנִן אָמְרֵי. בִּשְׁעָרֶיךָ. בְּשַׁעַר שֶׁנִּידּוֹן בּוֹ. אַתָּה אוֹמֵר כָּךְ אוֹ אֵינוֹ אֶלָּא בְשַׁעַר שֶׁנִּמְצָא בוֹ. נֶאֱמַר כָּאן בִּשְׁעָרֶיךָ וְנֶאֱמַר לְהַלָּן וְהוֹצֵאתָ אֶת־הָאִישׁ הַהוּא אוֹ אֶת־הָאִשָּׁה הַהִוא אֶל־שְׁעָרֶיךָ. מַה שְׁעָרֶיךָ הָאָמוּר לְהַלָּן שַׁעַר שֶׁנִּידּוֹן בּוֹ. אַף שְׁעָרֶיךָ הָאָמוּר כָּאן שַׁעַר שֶׁנִּידּוֹן בּוֹ.

Halakhah 1: "If sentence was passed," etc. The Mishnah[9] either follows Rebbi or the rabbis in a Gentile city[10]. As we have stated: Rebbi said[11], *at your gates*[12], at the gate they were found. You are saying so, or maybe at the gate they were judged? It is said here, *at your gates*, and it says there, *if there be found in your midst, at one of your gates*[13]. Since *gates* mentioned there refers to the gate where he was found, *gates* mentioned here also refers to the gate where he was found. But the rabbis say, *at your gates*, at the gate where he was judged. You are saying so, or maybe at the gate were he was found? It is said here, *at your gates*, and it says there, *take this man or this woman . . . to your gates*[14]. Since *gates* mentioned there refers to the gate where he was judged, *gates* mentioned here also refers to the gate where he was judged.

9 The Mishnah has a blanket statement which treats all kinds of stoning in the same way (cf. Note 2). While it is not specified where the stoning takes place, it is clear that it cannot be in front of the court building, where the rabbis require the idolator to be stoned.

10 The rabbis agree that in a city whose majority population is Gentile and idolatrous, a stoning for idolatry must take place in the Jewish quarter [Tosephta Chapter 10 in the *editio princeps* (10:4 in the Wilna ed.), missing in Zuckermandel's edition, Halakhah 10:10.]

11 A similar text is anonymous in *Sifry Deut.* 148.

12 The paragraph about punishment for idolatry (*Deut.* 17:2-7) mentions that idolatry was practiced *at your gates* (v. 2) and that the idolator should be stoned *at your gates* (v. 5). The context indicates that the first *gate* is the place of worship, the second the place of execution. But the talmudic doctrine of unique meaning of lexemes requires that *at your gates* have the same meaning in both cases. Either the meaning in v. 5 is induced by that of v. 2 (Rebbi) or that in v. 2 by v. 5 (the rabbis). On methodological grounds, Rebbi's position is preferred in the Babylonian sources (*Ketubot* 45b and *Sifry*).

13 *Deut.* 17:2.

14 *Deut.* 17:5.

(23b line 23) אָמַר רִבִּי יוֹחָנָן. כַּתְּחִילָּה בֵּין יֵשׁ מַמָּשׁ בִּדְבָרָיו בֵּין לָאו שׁוֹמְעִין לוֹ. מִיכָּן וְהֵילָךְ יֵשׁ מַמָּשׁ בִּדְבָרָיו שׁוֹמְעִין לוֹ וְאִם לָאו אֵין שׁוֹמְעִין לוֹ. אָמְרֵי. וְהוּא שֶׁיֵּשׁ בִּדְבָרָיו הָאַחֲרוֹנִים מַמָּשׁ. חִזְקִיָּה שָׁאַל. הֲרֵי שֶׁהָיָה יוֹצֵא לֵיהָרֵג וְנִשְׁתַּתֵּק. כֵּן אָנוּ אוֹמְרִים. הָא לֹא נִשְׁתַּתֵּק הָיָה לוֹ לְלַמֵּד עַל עַצְמוֹ זְכוּת. שָׁמַע רִבִּי יוֹחָנָן וָמַר. הֵא שְׁאֵלְתָא דְחַמְרָא. אֶלָּא כֵינִי. הֲרֵי שֶׁהָיָה יוֹצֵא לֵיהָרֵג וְאָמַר. יֵשׁ לִי לְלַמֵּד עַל עַצְמִי זְכוּת וְנִשְׁתַּתֵּק. כֵּן אָנוּ אוֹמְרִים. הָא אִילוּ לֹא נִשְׁתַּתֵּק הָיָה לוֹ לְלַמֵּד עַל עַצְמוֹ זְכוּת. אָמַר. הֵא אֲמִירָה.

Rebbi Johanan said, the first time one listens to him whether or not his arguments are substantial[15]. After that, if his arguments are substantial[16] one listens to him, otherwise one does not listen to him. They said, only if his later arguments are substantial[17].

Hizqiah asked: If he was led out to be executed when he became paralyzed, do we say that had he not become paralyzed, he would have argued for his acquittal? Rebbi Johanan heard this and said, this is a donkey's question[18]. But it must be: If he was led out to be executed and said, I have to argue for my acquittal: when he became paralyzed, do we say that had he not become paralyzed, he would have argued for his acquittal? He said, that is a statement[19].

15 In the Tosephta (9:4): The first three times. In the Babli (45a) Rav Pappa's statement parallels that of R. Johanan here.

16 As the Babli points out, this implies that some persons learned in the law are always near the condemned for preliminary evaluation of his arguments.

17 The statement of the Mishnah that the court is reconvened only if the arguments presented be substantial, refers only to the second and following times, not to the first appeal.

18 It is stated in Mishnah 2 that the entire world is invited to present exculpatory arguments. Do we say that because somewhere in the world a person may be paralyzed now, one can never execute anybody? (Babli 43a in the name of Babylonian scholars.)

19 Hizqiah agrees with the reformulation and its consequence, *viz.*, that the execution cannot proceed. The Babli leaves it as an open question.

(fol. 23a) **משנה ב**: אִם מָצְאוּ לוֹ זְכוּת פְּטָרוּהוּ וְאִם לָאו יוֹצֵא לִיסָּקֵל. וְהַכָּרוֹז יוֹצֵא לְפָנָיו אִישׁ פְּלוֹנִי בֶּן פְּלוֹנִי יוֹצֵא לִסָּקֵל עַל שֶׁעָבַר עֲבֵרָה פְּלוֹנִית וּפְלוֹנִי וּפְלוֹנִי עֵדָיו וְכָל־מִי שֶׁהוּא יוֹדֵעַ לוֹ זְכוּת יָבוֹא וִילַמֵּד:

Mishnah 2: If they found him innocent[20], they free him, otherwise he is led to be stoned. The herald[21] goes before him: "X ben Y is led to be stoned because he committed crime Z; U and V testified against him[22]. Anybody who knows of his innocence shall come and argue."

20 Upon reconsideration.

21 Greek κῆρυξ.

22 The call is for witnesses who can prove the original witnesses to be perjured.

(23b line 31) **הלכה ב**: אִם מָצְאוּ לוֹ זְכוּת כול'. תַּנֵּי. שׁוֹר הַיּוֹצֵא לִיסָּקֵל וְנִמְצְאוּ עֵידָיו זוֹמְמִין. רִבִּי יוֹחָנָן אָמַר. כָּל־הַקּוֹדֵם בּוֹ זָכָה. רֵישׁ לָקִישׁ אָמַר. הֶפְקֵר טָעוּת הוּא. וְכֵן עֶבֶד הַיּוֹצֵא לִיסָּקֵל וְהִקְדִּישׁוֹ בְעָלָיו. רִבִּי יוֹחָנָן אָמַר. זָכָה לְעַצְמוֹ. רֵישׁ לָקִישׁ אָמַר. יֵיאוּשׁ שֶׁלְּטָעוּת הוּא.

Halakhah 2: "If they found him innocent," etc. [23]It was stated: If a bull was led out to be stoned when its witnesses were found to be perjured, Rebbi Johanan said, the first to come acquires it; Rebbi Simeon ben Laqish said, it was a false declaration of ownerlessness[24]. Similarly, if a slave was led out to be stoned when his owner dedicated him to the Temple[25], Rebbi Johanan said, he acquired himself; Rebbi Simeon ben Laqish said, it was false despair.

23 Better versions of this paragraph are in 10:8 Note 337, *Bava qamma* 4:9 Notes 122-125.

24 This is Babylonian spelling. The Yerushalmi form is הבקר.

25 One has to read with the parallel sources: When his witnesses were found perjured. At the moment the slave is condemned to death, he loses all value for his owner; valueless objects cannot be dedicated. Therefore the dedication is the equivalent of declaring the slave ownerless.

(fol. 23a) **משנה ג**: רָחוֹק מִבֵּית הַסְּקִילָה עֶשֶׂר אַמּוֹת אוֹמֵר לוֹ הִתְוַדֵּה שֶׁכֵּן דֶּרֶךְ כָּל־הַמּוּמָתִין מִתְוַדִּין שֶׁכָּל־הַמִּתְוַדֶּה יֶשׁ לוֹ חֵלֶק לָעוֹלָם הַבָּא. שֶׁכֵּן מָצִינוּ בְעָכָן שֶׁאָמַר לוֹ יְהוֹשֻׁעַ בְּנִי שִׂים־נָא כָבוֹד לַיי אֱלֹהֵי יִשְׂרָאֵל וְתֶן־לוֹ תוֹדָה וְהַגֶּד־נָא לִי מֶה עָשִׂיתָ אַל־תְּכַחֵד מִמֶּנִּי׃ וַיַּעַן עָכָן אֶת־יְהוֹשֻׁעַ וַיֹּאמַר אָמְנָה אָנֹכִי חָטָאתִי לַיי אֱלֹהֵי יִשְׂרָאֵל וְכָזֹאת וְכָזֹאת עָשִׂיתִי׃ וּמְנַיִין שֶׁנִּתְכַּפֵּר לוֹ וִדּוּיוֹ שֶׁנֶּאֱמַר וַיֹּאמֶר יְהוֹשֻׁעַ מֶה עֲכַרְתָּנוּ יַעְכָּרְךָ יי בַּיּוֹם הַזֶּה. הַיּוֹם הַזֶּה אַתָּה עָכוּר וְאֵי אַתָּה עָכוּר לֶעָתִיד לָבוֹא.

Mishnah 3: Ten cubits' distance from the place of stoning one tells him: confess! So is the way of any dying person to confess, since anyone who confesses has part in the World to Come. For so we find about Achan to whom Joshua said, *my son, honor the Eternal, the God of Israel, confess to Him, and tell me what you did, do not hide it from me. Achan answered Joshua and said, in fact I sinned against the Eternal, the God of Israel, and such and such I did*[26]. From where that his confession atoned for him? For it is said, *Joshua said to him, how did you devastate us; may the Eternal devastate you on this day*[27]. This day you are devastated; you are not devastated in the Future World.

26 *Jos.* 7:19-20.

27 *Jos.* 7:25.

(23b line 35) **הלכה ג**: רָחוֹק מִבֵּית הַסְּקִילָה עֶשֶׂר אַמּוֹת כול'. אַתְּ מוֹצֵא שֶׁכְּשֶׁמָּעַל עָכָן בַּחֶרֶם הִתְחִיל יְהוֹשֻׁעַ מְפַייֵס לִפְנֵי הַקָּדוֹשׁ בָּרוּךְ הוּא וְאוֹמֵר. רִבּוֹנוֹ שֶׁלְּעוֹלָם. הוֹדִיעֵינִי מִי זֶה הָאִישׁ. אָמַר לוֹ הַקָּדוֹשׁ בָּרוּךְ הוּא. אֵינִי מְפַרְסֵם כָּל־בִּרְייָה וְלֹא עוֹד אֶלָּא נִמְצֵאתִי אוֹמֵר לָשׁוֹן הָרַע. אֶלָּא לֵךְ וְהַעֲמֵיד אֶת יִשְׂרָאֵל לִשְׁבָטָיו וְהַפֵּל עֲלֵיהֶן גּוֹרָלוֹת. מִיַּד אֲנִי מוֹצִיאוֹ. הָדָא הִיא דִכְתִיב וַיַּשְׁכֵּ֤ם יְהוֹשֻׁ֙עַ֙ בַּבֹּ֔קֶר וַיַּקְרֵ֥ב אֶת־יִשְׂרָאֵ֖ל לִשְׁבָטָ֑יו וַיִּלָּכֵ֗ד עָכָ֞ן בֶּן־כַּרְמִ֤י בֶּן־זֶ֙רַח֙ לְמַטֵּ֣ה יְהוּדָ֔ה׃ אָמַר לוֹ עָכָן. מַה. בַּגּוֹרָל אַתָּה תוֹפְשֵׂינִי. לֵית בְּכָל־הָהֵן דָּרָא כָּשֵׁר אֶלָּא אַתְּ וּפִינְחָס. אַסְקוּן נִיבְזִין בֵּינֵיכוֹן. פִּנְטוֹס דְּמִתְפַּייֵס חַד מִינְּכוֹן. וְלֹא עוֹד אֶלָּא לְמֹשֶׁה רַבָּךְ לֵית מִידְמוֹךְ אֶלָּא תַּלְתִּין אוֹ אַרְבָּעִין יוֹמִין. לֹא כֵן אַלְפָּן מֹשֶׁה רַבָּן עַל־פִּ֣י ׀ שְׁנַ֣יִם עֵדִ֗ים. שְׁרִיתָה טָעֵי. בְּאוֹתָהּ שָׁעָה צָפָה יְהוֹשֻׁעַ בְּרוּחַ הַקּוֹדֶשׁ שֶׁהוּא מְחַלֵּק לְיִשְׂרָאֵל אֶת הָאָרֶץ בַּגּוֹרָל. הָדָא הִיא דִכְתִיב וַיַּשְׁלֵ֨ךְ לָהֶ֤ם יְהוֹשֻׁ֙עַ֙ גּוֹרָ֔ל. אֱמוֹר מֵעַתָּה. אָנוּ מוֹצִיאִין שֵׁם רַע עַל הַגּוֹרָלוֹת. וְלֹא עוֹד אֶלָּא שֶׁאִם נִתְקַייְמוּ עַכְשָׁיו יְהוּ כָּל־יִשְׂרָאֵל אוֹמְרִים. בְּדִינֵי נְפָשׁוֹת נִתְקַייְמוּ כָּל־שֶׁכֵּן בְּדִינֵי מָמוֹנוֹת. וְאִם בָּטְלוּ עַכְשָׁיו יְהוּ כָּל־יִשְׂרָאֵל אוֹמְרִים. בְּדִינֵי נְפָשׁוֹת בָּטְלוּ כָּל־שֶׁכֵּן בְּדִינֵי מָמוֹנוֹת. בְּאוֹתָהּ שָׁעָה הִתְחִיל יְהוֹשֻׁעַ מְפַייֵס לְעָכָן וּמַשְׁבַּע לֵיהּ בֵּאלֹהֵי יִשְׂרָאֵל וְאוֹמֵר לוֹ. בְּנִ֗י שִֽׂים־נָ֨א כָב֜וֹד לַיי אֱלֹהֵ֤י יִשְׂרָאֵל֙. וַיַּ֧עַן עָכָ֛ן אֶת־יְהוֹשֻׁ֖עַ וַיֹּאמַ֑ר. אָמְנָ֗ה. מָהוּ אָמְנָה. קוּשְׁטָא. אָנֹכִ֤י חָטָ֙אתִי֙ לַיי אֱלֹהֵ֣י יִשְׂרָאֵ֔ל. אֲמַר לֵיהּ. מָה אֲנָא בְעֵי מִינָּךְ חָדָא וְאַתְּ אָמְרַת לִי תַּרְתֵּי. אֲמַר לֵיהּ. אֲנִי הוּא שֶׁמָּעַלְתִּי בְחֶרֶם מִדְיָן וּבְחֶרֶם יְרִיחוֹ. אָמַר רִבִּי תַנְחוּמָא. בְּאַרְבָּעָה חֲרָמִים מָעַל. בְּחֶרֶם כְּנַעֲנִי מֶלֶךְ עֲרָד. בְּחֶרֶם סִיחוֹן וְעוֹג. בְּחֶרֶם מִדְיָן. בְּחֶרֶם יְרִיחוֹ. וּמְנַיִין שֶׁכִּיפֵּר לוֹ ווִידּוּיוֹ. שֶׁנֶּאֱמַר וּבְנֵ֣י זֶ֔רַח זִמְרִ֣י וְאֵיתָ֗ן וגו'. רִבִּי יְהוֹשֻׁעַ בֶּן לֵוִי אָמַר. זִמְרִי זֶה עָכָן שֶׁעָשָׂה מַעֲשֵׂה זִמְרִי. רִבִּי שְׁמוּאֵל בַּר נַחְמָן אָמַר. הֵימָן זֶה עָכָן. אָמְנָה אָנֹכִי חָטָ֙אתִי֙. כּוּלָּם חֲמִשָּׁה. וְכִי אֵינִי יוֹדֵעַ שֶׁהֵן חֲמִשָּׁה. אֶלָּא מְלַמֵּד שֶׁאַף עָכָן יֵשׁ לוֹ חֵלֶק לֶעָתִיד לָבוֹא.

Halakhah 3: "Ten cubits' distance from the place of stoning," etc. You find that when Achan stole from the ban, Joshua started supplicating before the Holy One, praise to Him, and said: Master of the Universe, inform me who is the man. The Holy One, praise to Him, answered: I never publicize any creature. In addition, would I not be guilty of slander[28]? But go and let Israel stand up by its tribes and throw lots, then immediately I shall draw him out. That is what is written: *Joshua got up early in the morning and summoned Israel by its tribes. Achan ben Karmi ben Zeraḥ from the tribe of Jehudah was caught*[29]. Achan told him, how? Do you catch me by lots[30]? There is nobody more pious in the present generation than you or Phineas. Let lots be thrown between you, certainly[31] one of you will be caught. Not only this, but your teacher Moses died only 30 or 40 days ago. Did not our teacher Moses instruct us: *By the testimony of two witnesses*[32]? You started erring. At that moment did Joshua have a vision by the holy spirit how he distributes the Land to Israel by lots. That is what is written: *Joshua threw lots for them*[33]. This means, we are giving lots a bad name. Not only this, but if lots are confirmed now, all of Israel will say, since the lots were true in criminal matters, so much more in money matters. But if they are repudiated now, all of Israel will say, since the lots were repudiated in criminal matters, so much more in money matters. At that moment, Joshua started supplicating Achan, entreated him in the name of Israel's God, and said to him: *my son, honor the Eternal, the God of Israel, . . . Achan answered Joshua and said, in fact*[26]. What means אָמְנָה? Truth[34]. *I sinned against the Eternal, God of Israel.* He told him, I asked you for one and you are answering me two[35]? he answered, I stole from the ban of Midian and the ban of Jericho. Rebbi Tanḥuma said, he stole from four bans: The ban of the Phoenician, king of Arad, the ban of Siḥon and Og, the ban of Midian, the ban of Jericho.

From where that his confession atoned for him? It is said[36], *the sons of Zeraḥ: Zimri and Ethan,* etc. Rebbi Joshua ben Levi said, Zimri is Achan who behaved like Zimri[37]. Rebbi Samuel bar Naḥman said, *Heman*[38] that is Achan, *omna* I sinned. *Altogether five*. Did I not know that they were five[39]? But it teaches that Achan also has part in the World to Come[40].

28 Babli 11a, 43b. An expanded version in *Tanhuma Mas`e* 5.

29 *Jos.* 7:16.

30 The entire procedure described in *Jos.* 7:16-26 cannot be justified either in pentateuchal or in rabbinic law.

31 Greek πάντως. The outcome of drawing of lots is essentially predetermined by the set from which the lot is drawn.

32 *Deut.* 19:15.

33 *Jos.* 18:10.

34 Deriving אמנה from the root אמן.

35 Referring to the doubling *such and such* in v. 7:20.

36 The assassin of king Ela, *1K.* 16:10. In *Jos.* 7:19, the son of Zerah and father of Carmi is called *Zavdi*, not *Zimri*. This underlies the talmudic doctrine that all of Chronicles is to be explained alegorically.

38 Aramaic הֵימָן is Hebrew נֶאֱמָן, cf. Note 34.

39 Since the verse enumerates five sons of Zerah.

40 Since he is counted together with Ethan and Heman, the composers of psalms. Tosephta 9:5.

(fol. 23a) **משנה ד**: וְאִם אֵינוֹ יוֹדֵעַ לְהִתְוַדּוֹת אוֹמְרִים לוֹ אֱמוֹר תְּהֵא מִיתָתִי כַּפָּרָה עַל כָּל עֲווֹנוֹתַי. רַבִּי יְהוּדָה אוֹמֵר אִם הָיָה יוֹדֵעַ שֶׁהוּא מְזוּמָּם אוֹמֵר תְּהֵא מִיתָתִי כַּפָּרָה עַל כָּל עֲווֹנוֹתַי חוּץ מֵעָוֹן זֶה. אָמְרוּ לוֹ אִם כֵּן יְהוּ כָל־אָדָם אוֹמֵר כָּךְ כְּדֵי לְנַקּוֹת אֶת עַצְמָן:

Mishnah 4: If he does not know how to confess, one tells him, say: "My death shall be atonement for all my sins." Rebbi Jehudah said, if he knows that he was the victim of perjurers, he says: "My death shall be atonement for all my sins except this one.[41]" They told him, if so, everybody would say so to declare themselves innocent[42].

41 For which he is being stoned.

42 And to declare the witnesses perjured and the judges bribed or incompetent.

(23 c line 61) **הלכה ד**: וְאִם אֵינוֹ יוֹדֵעַ לְהִתְוַדּוֹת כול'. מַעֲשֶׂה בְאֶחָד שֶׁהָיָה יוֹצֵא לֵיהָרֵג. אָמְרוּ לוֹ. אֱמוֹר. תְּהֵא מִיתָתִי כַּפָּרָה עַל־כָּל עֲווֹנוֹתַי. אָמַר. תְּהֵא מִיתָתִי כַּפָּרָה עַל־כָּל עֲווֹנוֹתַי חוּץ מִן עָוֹן זֶה. אִם עֲשִׂיתִיו אַל יִמְחוֹל לִי. וּבֵית דִּין יִשְׂרָאֵל יְהֵא נָקִי. וּכְשֶׁבָּא דָבָר אֵצֶל חֲכָמִים זָלְגוּ עֵינֵיהֶם. אָמְרוּ. לְהַחֲזִירוֹ אִי אֶפְשַׁר שֶׁאֵין לְדָבָר סוֹף. אֶלָּא הֲרֵי דָמוֹ תָלוּי בְּצַוַּאר עֵדִים.

Halakhah 4: "If he does not know how to confess," etc. [43]"It happened that one was led out to be executed. They told him, say: `My death shall be atonement for all my sins.' He said, `my death shall be atonement for all my sins except for this sin; if I committed it, He[44] should never forgive me, but the court of Israel is innocent.' When the case came before the Sages, their tears flowed. They said, it is impossible to reopen the case[45], since it would never end. But this person's blood hangs on the witnesses' necks."

43 Babli 44b, Tosephta 9:5.

44 God.

45 Since the statement was not accompanied by any argument or proof of perjury. The Babli version is very difficult at this point.

(fol. 23a) **משנה ה**: רָחוֹק מִבֵּית הַסְּקִילָה אַרְבַּע אַמּוֹת מַפְשִׁיטִין אֶת בְּגָדָיו. הָאִישׁ מְכַסִּין אוֹתוֹ מִלְּפָנָיו וְהָאִשָּׁה מִלְּפָנֶיהָ וּמֵאַחֲרֶיהָ דִּבְרֵי רִבִּי יְהוּדָה. וַחֲכָמִים אוֹמְרִים הָאִישׁ נִסְקָל עָרוֹם וְאֵין הָאִשָּׁה נִסְקֶלֶת עֲרוּמָּה:

Mishnah 5: At a distance of four cubits from the place of stoning one removes his clothes. One covers a man in front, a woman one covers front and back, the words of Rebbi Jehudah; but the Sages say, a man is stoned naked[46], but no woman is stoned naked[47].

46 Except for a loin cloth.

47 She may not be touched by men.

(23c line 16) **הלכה ח**: אָמַר רִבִּי אֱלִיעֶזֶר כול'. מִחְלְפָה שִׁיטַּת רִבִּי יְהוּדָה. תַּמָּן אָמַר. אִם הָיָה שְׂעָרָהּ נָאֶה לֹא הָיָה סוֹתְרוֹ. וְכָא הוּא אוֹמֵר אָכֵין. הָכָא מִכָּל־מָקוֹם לְמִיתָה אָזְלָה. בְּרַם תַּמָּן שֶׁאִם תִּימָּצֵא טְהוֹרָה וְיִתְגָּרוּ בָהּ פִּירְחֵי כְהוּנָּה. מִחְלְפָה שִׁיטַּת רַבָּנִן. תַּמָּן אָמְרִין. הָאִישׁ נִסְקָל עָרוֹם וְאֵין הָאִשָּׁה נִסְקֶלֶת עֲרוּמָּה. וְכָא אִינּוּן אָמְרִין הָכֵין. הָכָא וְאָהַבְתָּ לְרֵעֲךָ כָּמוֹךָ. בְּרוֹר לוֹ מִיתָה יָפָה. בְּרַם תַּמָּן וְנִיוַּסְּרוּ כָּל־הַנָּשִׁים.

[48]**Halakhah 8**: "Rebbi Eliezer said," etc. The argument of Rebbi Jehudah seems inverted. There, he says: "If her hair was beautiful, he did not uncover it." And here, he says so? Here, anyhow she goes to her death, but there, maybe she will be found to be pure and the young priests would attack her. The argument of the rabbis seems inverted. There[49], they say: "A man is stoned naked , but no woman is stoned naked ." And here[50], they say so? Here, *you shall love your neighbor as yourself*, choose for him a decorous death. But here, *all women should be taught*.

48 For the rest of this Chapter, Mishnaiot and Halakhot do not fit together in the ms. and *editio princeps*. The quotes at the start refer to the Mishnaiot indicated by the Halakhah; the text has been placed after the Mishnah to which it belongs. The text in this Halakhah is essentially a copy from *Sotah* 1:5, Notes 226-232.

49 This should be "here", showing that the original is in *Sotah*.

50 This should be "there".

(fol. 23a) **משנה ו**: בֵּית הַסְּקִילָה הָיָה גָבוֹהַּ שְׁתֵּי קוֹמוֹת וְאֶחָד מִן הָעֵדִים דּוֹחֲפוֹ עַל מָתְנָיו. נֶהְפַּךְ עַל לִבּוֹ הוֹפְכוֹ עַל מָתְנָיו אִם מֵת בָּהּ יָצָא. וְאִם לָאו נוֹטֵל אֶת הָאֶבֶן וְנוֹתְנָהּ עַל לִבּוֹ. אִם מֵת בָּהּ יָצָא וְאִם לָאו הָעֵד הַשֵּׁנִי נוֹטֵל אֶת הָאֶבֶן וְנוֹתְנָהּ עַל לִבּוֹ. אִם מֵת בָּהּ יָצָא וְאִם לָאו רְגִימָתוֹ בְכָל יִשְׂרָאֵל שֶׁנֶּאֱמַר יַד הָעֵדִים תִּהְיֶה־בּוֹ בָרִאשֹׁנָה לַהֲמִיתוֹ וְיַד כָּל־הָעָם בָּאַחֲרֹנָה.

Mishnah 6: The place of stoning was two man-sizes high; one of the witnesses pushed him at his hips[51]. If he fell on his breast, he turns him around on his back. If he died from this, it is sufficient; otherwise he takes the stone[52] and puts it on his breast. If he died from this, it is sufficient; otherwise the second witness takes the stone and puts it on his breast[53]. If he died from this, it is sufficient; otherwise the stoning is on all of Israel as it is said: *The witnesses' hand shall be first on him to kill him, the hand of the entire people afterwards*[54].

51 As both Talmudim state, *Ex*. 19:13 implies that throwing down is part of stoning.

52 According to Tosephta 9:6, a stone which needed two people to be lifted.

53 This sentence is missing in all parallels; it may be a case of dittography.

54 *Deut*. 17:7.

(23c line 6) **הלכה ז**: כָּל הַנִּסְקָלִין נִתְלִין דִּבְרֵי רִבִּי לִיעֶזֶר כול׳. תַּנֵּי. וְכִמְלוֹא קוֹמָתוֹ שֶׁלְּנוֹפֵל הֲרֵי חֲמִשָּׁה. הָכָא אַתְּ מַר. וְכִמְלוֹא קוֹמַת הַנּוֹפֵל הֲרֵי חֲמִשָּׁה. וּבְבוֹר שֶׁלְּנִיזָּקִין אַתְּ מַר. עַד עֲשָׂרָה טְפָחִים. לֹא דוֹמֶה נוֹפֵל מִדַּעַת לַנּוֹפֵל שֶׁלֹּא מִדַּעַת. רִבִּי יוֹנָתָן בֶּן חָלִי רִבִּי אֶבְדּוּמֵי בֶּן בְּרַתֵּיהּ דְּרִבִּי טָבִי בְּשֵׁם רִבִּי יֹאשִׁיָּה. אִילֵּין דְּחַבְטִין תּוֹרָא בְּחֵיילֵיהּ אֵין בּוֹ מִשּׁוּם רִיסּוּק אֵיבָרִים. בְּיוֹמוֹי דְּרִבִּי פִּינְחָס חַבְטוּ תּוֹרָא בְּחֵיילֵיהּ. אֲמַר לוֹן. בְּחַיֵּיכוֹן שָׁרוּנֵיהּ. שָׁרוּנֵיהּ וְקוֹם וַעֲרַק. אָמַר. בָּרוּךְ שֶׁבָּחַר בַּחֲכָמִים וּבְדִבְרֵיהֶם. דְּאָמְרֵי. אִילֵּין דְּחַבְטִין תּוֹרָא בְּחֵילֵיהּ אֵין בּוֹ מִשּׁוּם רִיסּוּק אֵיבָרִים.

Halakhah 7: "All those stoned are hanged, the words of Rebbi Eliezer," etc. It was stated[55]: "Adding his own height, these are five." Here you say, adding his own height, these are five. But for a pit in matters of damages, you say even ten handbreadths[56]. One cannot compare one who falls consciously, and one who falls accidentally.

Rebbi Jonathan ben Hali, Rebbi Eudaimon the son of Rebbi Tabi's daughter, in the name of Rebbi Josia: Those who throw down an ox with all their might[57] do not cause any of its limbs to break[58]. In the days of Rebbi Phineas they threw down an ox with all their might. He told them, By your lives, free it. They freed it, it got up and fled. He said, praised be He Who selected the Sages and their pronouncements, for they say, those who throw down an ox with all their might not cause any of its limbs to break.

55 In the Babli, 45a, and Tosephta 9:6, the height of the fall is 3 = 2+1 man-sizes.

56 A pit 10 handbreadths deep ($1\frac{2}{3}$ cubits) already is life-threatening (Mishnah *Bava qamma* 5:7).

57 Cattle is slaughtered lying down. To push down an ox for slaughter may need great force; does one have to limit the force for fear of causing injuries to the ox, which would make it unfit as food?

58 Babli *Hulin* 51b.

(23c line 14) וּמְנַיִין שֶׁטָּעוּן סְקִילָה. שֶׁנֶּאֱמַר סָקוֹל יִסָּקֵל. וּמְנַיִין שֶׁטָּעוּן דְּחִיָּה. שֶׁנֶּאֱמַר יָרֹה יִיָּרֶה. וּמְנַיִין שֶׁטָּעוּן דְּחִיּוֹת. תַּלְמוּד לוֹמַר יִיָּרֶה.

[59]From where that he needs to be stoned? For it is said[60], *by stoning he be stoned.* From where that he needs to be pushed? For it is said, *by pushing he be pushed.* [61]From where that he needs two pushings? The verse says, *to be pushed.*

59 Babli 45a; *Mekhilta dR. Ismael Yitro* 3 (p. 212); *Mekhilta dR. Simeon ben Johai Yitro* p. 141.

60 *Ex.* 19:13.

61 In the parallel sources: From where that is is sufficient if he dies from being pushed? In the opinion of *Pene Moshe*, the second pushing is the turning on his back if he lands on his face.

(fol. 23a) **משנה ז**: כָּל הַנִּסְקָלִין נִתְלִין דִּבְרֵי רִבִּי אֱלִיעֶזֶר וַחֲכָמִים אוֹמְרִים אֵינוֹ נִתְלֶה אֶלָּא הַמְגַדֵּף וְהָעוֹבֵד עֲבוֹדָה זָרָה. הָאִישׁ תּוֹלִין אוֹתוֹ פָּנָיו כְּלַפֵּי הָעָם וְהָאִשָּׁה פָּנֶיהָ כְּלַפֵּי הָעֵץ דִּבְרֵי רִבִּי לִיעֶזֶר וַחֲכָמִים אוֹמְרִים הָאִישׁ נִתְלֶה וְאֵין הָאִשָּׁה נִתְלֵית.

Mishnah 7: Anyone who was stoned is hanged[62], the words of Rebbi Eliezer. But the Sages say, only the blasphemer and the idolator are hanged. A man is hanged face to the people and a woman face to the pole, the words of Rebbi Eliezer. But the Sages say, a man is hanged[63], a woman is not hanged.

משנה ח: אָמַר לָהֶן רִבִּי אֱלִיעֶזֶר מַעֲשֶׂה בְשִׁמְעוֹן בֶּן שֶׁטָח שֶׁתָּלָה נָשִׁים בְּאַשְׁקְלוֹן. אָמְרוּ לוֹ שְׁמוֹנִים נָשִׁים תָּלָה וְאֵין דָּנִין שְׁנַיִם בְּיוֹם אֶחָד.

Mishnah 8: Rebbi Eliezer said, it happened that Simeon ben Shetaḥ hanged women in Ascalon. They told him, he hanged eighty women, but one does not try two on the same day[64].

משנה ט: כֵּיצַד תּוֹלִין אוֹתוֹ. מְשַׁקְּעִין אֶת הַקּוֹרָה בָאָרֶץ וְהָעֵץ יוֹצֵא מִמֶּנּוּ. וּמַקִּיף שְׁתֵּי יָדָיו זוֹ עַל גַּבֵּי זוֹ וְתוֹלֶה אוֹתוֹ. רִבִּי יוֹסֵי אוֹמֵר הַקּוֹרָה מֻטָּה עַל הַכּוֹתֶל וְתוֹלֶה אוֹתוֹ כְּדֶרֶךְ שֶׁהַטַּבָּחִין עוֹשִׂין. תּוֹלִין וּמַתִּירִין אוֹתוֹ מִיָּד וְאִם לָן עוֹבֵר עָלָיו בְּלֹא תַעֲשֶׂה שֶׁנֶּאֱמַר לֹא־תָלִין נִבְלָתוֹ עַל־הָעֵץ כִּי־קָבוֹר תִּקְבְּרֶנּוּ בַּיּוֹם הַהוּא כִּי־קִלְלַת אֱלֹהִים תָּלוּי כְּלוֹמַר מִפְּנֵי מַה זֶה תָּלוּי. מִפְּנֵי שֶׁבֵּרַךְ אֶת הַשֵּׁם וְנִמְצָא שֵׁם שָׁמַיִם מִתְחַלֵּל:

Mishnah 9: How does one hang him? One sinks a stake into the ground, wood is sticking out from there. One binds both hands, one on top of the other, and hangs him. Rebbi Yose says, the beam is leaning on the wall[66]; one hangs him in the way butchers do. One hangs him and takes him down immediately; if he were left overnight, one would transgress a prohibition, as it is said[67]: *Do not leave his corpse on the wood overnight, but certainly bury him on the same day, for a hanged person is blasphemy.* This means, why was he hanged? Because he blasphemed; it turns out that the name of Heaven would be desecrated[68].

62 *Deut.* 21:22 is read as a requirement that the corpse of the criminal be hanged after execution, not as recognizing hanging as a legitimate form of execution.

63 Since *Deut.* 21:21 refers to *a man* being executed.

64 In addition, he used hanging as a form of execution, which is forbidden.

65 By his hands.

66 He rejects a form which might resemble a Roman cross. He requires the corpse to he hung from a horizontal beam like an animal carcass.

67 *Deut.* 21:23.

68 This is the rabbis' reason to restrict hanging to the blasphemer and those guilty of related crimes (Mishnah 7, Halakhah 9, *Sifry Deut.* 221). The verse is read following the Roman custom of noting the condemned person's crime on his cross, restricting hanging to crimes having an element of blasphemy.

(23b line 66) **הלכה ה**: רָחוֹק מִבֵּית הַסְּקִילָה אַרְבַּע אַמּוֹת כול'. אָמַר רִבִּי יְהוּדָה בַּר טַבַּאי. אֶרְאֶה בְנֶחָמָה אִם לֹא הָרַגְתִּי עֵד זוֹמֵם. שֶׁהָיוּ אוֹמְרִים. עַד שֶׁיֵּיהָרֵג. שֶׁנֶּאֱמַר נֶפֶשׁ תַּחַת נָפֶשׁ. אָמַר לוֹ שִׁמְעוֹן בֶּן שֶׁטַח. אֶרְאֶה בְנֶחָמָה אִם לֹא מַעֲלִים עָלֶיךָ כְּאִילּוּ שָׁפַכְתָּ דָּם נָקִי. בְּאוֹתָהּ שָׁעָה קִיבֵּל עָלָיו שֶׁלֹּא יוֹרֶה אֶלָּא מִפִּי שִׁמְעוֹן בֶּן שֶׁטַח.

Halakhah 5: "At a distance of four cubits from the place of stoning," etc. [69]"Rebbi Jehudah ben Ṭabbai said, may I never see consolation if I did not execute a perjured witness, for they were saying, until he was executed, as it is said, *a life for a life*. Simeon ben Sheṭaḥ told him, may I never see consolation if it is not held against you that you spilled innocent blood. At that time, he took it upon himself not to teach except what he heard from Simeon ben Sheṭaḥ."

69 Babli *Makkot* 5b, Hagigah 16b; Tosephta 6:6. The text is badly truncated; following the parallel sources it should read approximately:

Jehudah ben Ṭabbai said, may I never see consolation if I did not execute a perjured witness, for the Sadducees were saying, a perjured witness is not executed unless the accused was executed, as it is said, *a life for a life*. Simeon ben Shetah told him, may I never see consolation if it is not held against you that you spilled innocent blood since no perjured witness is executed unless both of them are shown to be perjured. At that time, he took it upon himself not to teach except what he heard from Simeon ben Sheṭaḥ.

This is the first of a series of treatments of the Simeon ben Shetaḥ legend (Mishnah 8) before one returns to a discussion of the Mishnah.

If only one of the witnesses is found perjured, neither his testimony nor that of the other witness can be used against the accused since both are testimonies of single witnesses unsupported by a second witness. The case against the accused has to be dismissed; there is no case.

(23b line 71) שִׁמְעוֹן בֶּן שֶׁטַח הָיוּ יָדָיו חֲמוּמוֹת. אֲתַר סִיעַת לֵיצָנִין אָמְרֵי. הָבוּ עֵצָה נִיסְהוֹד עַל בְּרֵיהּ וְנִיקְטְלִינֵיהּ. אַסְהִידוּ עֲלוֹי. וְנִגְמַר דִּינוֹ לֵיהָרֵג. מִי נְפַק לְמִיתְקַטְלָא אָמְרֵי לֵיהּ. מָרִי שִׁיקְרִין אֲנָן. בְּעָא אֲבוֹי מַחְזַרְתֵּיהּ. אֲמַר לֵיהּ. אַבָּא. אִם בִּיקַּשְׁתָּה לָבוֹא תְשׁוּעָה עַל יָדֶךָ עֲשֵׂה אוֹתִי כְאֶסְקוּפָּה.

Simeon ben Sheṭaḥ's hands were hot[70]. There came a group of scoffers who said, let us take counsel, testify against his son, and kill him. They testified against him. He was sentenced to be executed. When he was taken to be killed, they told him, our Master, we are liars[71]. His father wanted to return him[72]; he told him, my father, if you want that salvation come through you[73], treat me as a target[74].

70 He was quick in persecuting persons not conforming to pharisaic standards (cf. H. Graetz, *Geschichte der Juden* 3-1[5], p. 146).

71 They could confess their perjury with impunity. By Sadducee standards, a false witness in a capital case cannot be punished

as long as the victim was not executed. By pharisaic standards, no self-incrimination is admissible in court.

72 To have the conviction overturned, Halakhah 1.

73 By strict pharisaic (rabbinical) rules, witnesses cannot change their story once the phase of testimony was concluded and deliberations started (*Bava mesia`* 1:2 Note 30; *Ševi`it* 10:5 Note 96). By the strict letter of the law, there was no ground for reconsideration.

74 Greek σκοπός, Latin *scopus*, "goal, target" (E. G.).

(23b line 75) **הלכה ו**: בֵּית הַסְּקִילָה הָיָה גָבוֹהַּ כול'. מַעֲשֶׂה בְחָסִיד אֶחָד שֶׁהָיָה מְהַלֵּךְ בַּדֶּרֶךְ וְרָאָה שְׁנֵי בְנֵי אָדָם נִזְקָקִין לְכַלְבָּה. אָמְרִין. נָן יָדְעִין דּוּ גַּבְרָא חֲסִידָא אֲזִיל וּמַסְהִיד עֲלָן וּמָרָן דָּוִד קְטִיל לָן. אֶלָּא נַיקְדִּימֵיהּ וְנִיסְהוֹד עֲלוֹי. אַסְהִידוּ עֲלֵיהּ. וְנִגְמַר דִּינוֹ לֵיהָרֵג. הוּא שֶׁדָּוִד אָמַר. הַצִּילָה מֵחֶרֶב נַפְשִׁי מִיַּד־כֶּ֫לֶב יְחִידָתִי׃ מֵחֶרֶב. מֵחֶרֶב אוּרִיָּה. מִכֶּלֶב. מִכַּלְבּוֹ שֶׁלְּחָסִיד.

רִבִּי יוּדָה בֶּן פָּזִי סָלַק לְעִילִיתָא דְבֵי מִדְרָשָׁא וְרָאָה שְׁנֵי בְנֵי אָדָם נִזְקָקִין זֶה לָזֶה. אָמְרוּ לֵיהּ. רִבִּי. הַב דַּעְתָּךְ דְּאַתְּ חַד וַאֲנָן תְּרֵי.

Halakhah 6: "The place of stoning was two man-sizes high," etc. It happened that a pious man was walking on the road when he saw two people having sex with a bitch. They said, we know that this is a pious man, he will go, testify against us, and our lord David will kill us[75]. Therefore, we shall be quicker than him and testify against him. They testified against him and he was sentenced to be executed. That is what David said[76], *Rescue my soul from the sword, From the dog my only one! From the sword*, Uriah's sword. *From the dog*, the pious man's dog.

Rebbi Jehudah ben Pazi went to the upper floor of the House of Study and saw two men in homosexual activity. They said to him, Rebbi! Realize that you are one and we are two!

75 Which the king by his police powers could do on the information of one witness.

76 *Ps*. 22:21.

(23c line 26) אִית תַּנָּיֵי תַנֵּי. יְהוּדָה בֶּן טַבַּאי נָשִׂיא. אִית תַּנָּיֵי תַנֵּי. שִׁמְעוֹן בֶּן שֶׁטַח נָשִׂיא.

מָאן דָּמַר. יְהוּדָה בֶּן טַבַּאי נָשִׂיא. עוֹבְדָא דַאֲלֶכְּסַנְדְּרִיָּאה מְסַיֵּיעַ לֵיהּ. וַהֲווֹן בְּנֵי יְרוּשָׁלַםִ כּוֹתְבִין. מִיְּרוּשָׁלַםִ הַגְּדוֹלָה לַאֲלֶכְּסַנְדְּרִיָּאה הַקְּטַנָּה. עַד מָתַי בַּעֲלִי שָׁרוּי בְתוֹכֵךְ וַאֲנִי יוֹשֶׁבֶת עֲגוּמָה בְּבֵיתִי.

Text of G

מָאן דָּמַר. יְהוּדָה בֶּן טַבַּאי נָשִׂיא. עוֹבְדָא דַאֲלֶכְסַנְדְּרִיָּה מְסַייֵעַ לֵיהּ. וּמָאן דָּמַר. שִׁמְעוֹן בֶּן שֶׁטַח נָשִׂיא. עוֹבְדָה דְאַשְׁקְלוֹן מְסָייְעָא לֵיהּ. יְהוּדָה בֶּן טַבַּאי הֲווֹן בְּנֵי יְרוּשָׁלַםִ בְּעַייָן מַמְנִיתֵיהּ נָשִׂיא וְלָא קִבֵּל עֲלוֹי. עֲרַק וַאֲזַל לַאֲלֶכְסַנְדְּרִיָּה. וַהֲווֹן בְּנֵי יְרוּשָׁלַםִ כּוֹתְבִין. מִיְּרוּשָׁלַםִ הַגְּדוֹלָה לַאֲלֶכְסַנְדְּרִיָּה הַקְּטַנָּה. עַד מָתַי בַּעֲלִי שָׁרוּי בְּתוֹכֵךְ וַאֲנִי יוֹשֶׁבֶת עֲגוּמָה בְּבֵיתִי. פָּרַשׁ מֵייתֵי לֵיהּ גַּו אִסְרָטָא. אֲמַר. דְּכִירָה מָרְתָא דְבַייְתָא דִיאוּת קִבַּלְתּוֹן וַחֲסִידָה הֲוָות. אֲמַר לֵיהּ חַד מִן תַּלְמִידוֹי. חָדָא עֵינָא הֲוָות שְׁוּרָה. אֲמַר לֵיהּ. אִית גַּבָּךְ תַּרְתֵּיי. חָדָא דְאִיסְתַּכַּלְתְּ בָּהּ וְחָדָא דַחֲשַׁדְתָּנִי דְאִיסְתַּכְּלִית בָּהּ. מָה אֲמְרִית יָאָה בְרֵיוָאה לָא אֲמְרִית וְאֶלָּא יָאָה בְעוֹבְדָהּ. וְאִקְפַּד עֲלוֹי וָמִית.

Some Tannaïm state: Jehudah ben Ṭabbai was president; some Tannaïm state, Simeon ben Sheṭah was president[77].

[78]What happened in Alexandria supports him who said, Jehudah ben Ṭabbai was president, since the people from Jerusalem did write: From the great Jerusalem to the small Alexandria: How long still will my husband live in your midst and I am sitting sorrowful in my house?

Text of G

[79]What happened in Alexandria supports him who said, Jehudah ben Ṭabbai was president; what happened in Ascalon supports him who said, Simeon ben Sheṭah was president. The people of Jerusalem wanted to appoint Jehudah ben Ṭabbai as president[80], but he fled and went to Alexandria. The people from Jerusalem did write: From the great Jerusalem to the small Alexandria: How long still will my husband live in your midst and I am sitting sorrowful in my house? He took leave and started on the road trip[81]. He said, I remember the lady of the house who received us well and was so gracious. One of his students told him, one of her eyes was damaged. He told him, you have sinned twice; first that you looked at her, and second that you suspected me of having looked at her. I did not say that she was beautiful in looks; I only said that she was beautiful in her deeds. He was taking offense and he died[82].

77 This refers to Mishnah *Hagigah* 2:2 (Babli *Hagigah* 16b) where early disagreements between the presidents of the Supreme Court and their deputies over an aspect of Temple service are reported. The paragraph shows that this and the following paragraphs are originally from *Hagigah* (77d l. 33). In the Babli, Joshua ben

Perahia everywhere replaces Jehudah ben Tabbai.

The Aramaic of the following texts shows that one deals with popular tales.

78 This is a short excerpt of the text in *Hagigah*; the full text is given in G. But since the introductory sentence makes sense only in *Hagigah*, it may well be that the short reference here is original since the interest of the Halakhah is in the Simeon ben Shetah story, and the Genizah text is an enlargement. Therefore, each text is presented separately.

79 *Hagigah* 2:2 (77d l. 33), Babli *Sotah* 47a (in the edition of the Complete Israeli Talmud, p. 301 ff.). The paragraph was eliminated by the censor from the printed editions of the Babli starting with the Basel edition since the Babli named the wayward student יֵשׁוּ "Jesus".

80 The information of the Babli, that he fled when king Yannai turned against the Pharisees, is generally accepted as historical.

81 In the Babli, he went by ship.

82 Jehudah ben Tabbai took offense; the student died.

(23c line 30)[83] וּמָאן דָּמַר. שִׁמְעוֹן בֶּן שֶׁטַח נָשִׂיא. עוֹבְדָה דְאַשְׁקְלוֹן מְסַייֵעַ לֵיהּ. תְּרֵין תַּלְמִידִין הֲווּ בְּאַשְׁקְלוֹן אָכְלִין כְּחָדָא וְשָׁתִין כְּחָדָא וְלָעְיין בְּאוּרַייְתָא כְּחָדָא. מִית חַד מִינּוֹן וְלָא אִתְגְּמַל חֶסֶד. מִית בַּר מַעְיָין מוֹכֵס וּבְטֵילַת כָּל־מְדִינְתָּא מִגְמְלִינֵיהּ חֶסֶד. שְׁרֵי הַהוּא תַלְמִידָא בְכֵי וַאֲמַר. וַוי. דִּילְמָא לֵית לְשׂוֹנְאֵי יִשְׂרָאֵל כְּלוּם. אִיתְחֲמִיהּ לֵיהּ בְּחֶלְמֵיהּ וַאֲמַר. לָא תִיבְזֵי בְּנֵי מָרֵיךְ. דֵּין עֲבַד חַד זְכוּ וַאֲזַל בֵּיהּ וְדֵין עֲבַד חַד חוֹבָה וַאֲזַל בֵּיהּ. וּמַה חוֹבָה עֲבַד. חַס דְּלָא עֲבַד חוֹבָה מִן יוֹמוֹי. אֶלָּא זִימְנָא חָדָא הִקְדִּים תְּפִילִּין שֶׁלְּרֹאשׁ לִתְפִילִּין שֶׁלְּיָד. וּמַה זְכוּ עֲבַד בַּר מַעְיָין מוֹכֵס. חַס לֵיהּ דְּלָא עֲבַד זְכוּ מִן יוֹמוֹי. אֶלָּא זִימְנָא חָדָא עֲבַד אֲרִסְטוֹן לְבוּלֶבוּטַיָּא וְלָא אָתוֹן. אֲמַר. יֵיתוּן מִיסְכֵּינֵי וְיֵיכְלוּנֵיהּ דְּלָא לִיקַּלְקֵל. וְאִית דָּמְרִין. הֲוָה סַגֵּי בְאוֹרְחָא וַהֲוָה תְחוֹת שִׁיחֵיהּ חַד עִיגּוּל. וּנְפַל וְנַסְתֵּיהּ חַד מִסְכֵּן וְלָא מַר לֵיהּ מִידֵּי בְּגִין דְּלָא מְסַמְּקָא אַפּוֹי. וַחֲמָא הַהוּא תַלְמִידָא גַּו גַּנִּין גַּו פַּרְדֵּיסִין גַּו מַבּוּעִין דְּמַיָּא. וַחֲמָא לְבַר מַעְיָין מוֹכֵס קַיָּים עַל גֵּיף נַהֲרָא. בָּעֵי מַמְטֵי מַיָּא וְלָא מַטֵּי. וַחֲמָא לְמִרְיָם בַּת עֲלֵי בְצָלִים תַּלְיָיא בְחִיטֵּי בִיזַיָּא. וְאִית דָּמְרִין. תִּרְעַת גֵּהִינָּם קְבִיעָא גַּו אוּדְנָהּ. אֲמַר לוֹן. [לָמָּה. אָמְרִין לֵיהּ. בְּגִין דַּהֲוָת צַיְימָא וּמְפַרְסְיָיהּ לִמְגִי[ר]תָהּ. וְאִית דָּמְרִין. דַּהֲוָת צַיְימָא חַד יוֹם וּמְקַזָּה לָהּ תְּרֵי. אֲמַר לוֹן.][G] עַד אֵימַת כָּדֵין. אָמְרֵי לֵיהּ. עַד דְּיֵיתֵי שִׁמְעוֹן בֶּן שֶׁטַח נַסְבִּין לָהּ מִן גַּוֹא אוּדְנָהּ וִיהָבִין לָהּ גַּו אוּדְנֵיהּ. אֲמַר לוֹן. וּמַה הוּא סוּרְחָנֵיהּ. אָמְרֵי לֵיהּ. דִּנְדַר עַל נַפְשֵׁיהּ וַאֲמַר. אִי אִתְעֲבִיד נְשִׂיָא קָטְלֵי לְכָל־חָרַשַׁיָּא. וְהֵיידַן עֲבִיד לֵיהּ נָשִׂיא וְלָא קָטְלוֹן. אֶלָּא תוּמָנִין נָשִׁים בִּמְעָרַת אַשְׁקְלוֹן מְחַבְּלִין עָלְמָא. זִיל וָמַר לֵיהּ. אֲמַר לוֹן. גַּבְרָא רַבָּא הוּא וְלֵית הוּא מְהֵימְנָתִי. אָמְרֵי לֵיהּ. עִינְוָון הוּא סַגֵּי וּמְהֵימְנָתִיךְ. וְאִין לֵית מְהֵימְנָתִיךְ אַפִּיק עֵינֵיךְ וְיָבֵא גַּוֹא יָדָךְ. אַפִּיק עֵינֵיהּ וִיהַב גַּו יָדֵיהּ. אָמְרוּ. חָזְרַת וְאִשְׁתָּוֵות לַחֲבֵירְתָהּ. אֲזַל וָמַר לֵיהּ. בָּעָא מֵיעְבַד סֵימָנֵיהּ קוֹמוֹי אֲמַר לֵיהּ. לֵית אַתְּ צָרִיךְ. אֲנָא יְדַע דְּאַתְּ גַּבְרָא חֲסִידָא. אַף עַל פִּי כֵן בְּלִיבִּי חַשְׁבֵית בְּפוּמִי לָא אַמְרֵית. וַהֲוָה יוֹם סַגְרִיר. נְטַל תְּמַנִּין גּוּבְרִין בְּחִירִין לְבוּשִׁין מָאנִין נְקִיין וּנְסַב עִמּוֹן תְּמַנִּין קִידְרִין חֲדוּתִין.

אֲמַר לוֹן. כַּד נָא צְפַר לַבְּשִׁין מָנֵיכוֹן. וְכַד נָא צְפַר תִּנְייָנוּת עוּלּוּ. כֵּיוָן דְּאָעַל לִמְעָרַת אַשְׁקְלוֹן אֲמַר. אוּים אוּים. פִּתְחוּן לִי. מִן דִּידְכוֹן אֲנָא. כֵּיוָן דְּכָנַס. חָדָא אֲמְרָה מַה דָאֲמְרָה וּמַייתֵי פִיתָּה. חָדָא אֲמְרָה מַה דָאֲמְרָה וּמַייתֵי תַבְשִׁילָה. חָדָא אֲמְרָה מַה דָאֲמְרָה וּמַייתֵי חַמְרָא. אֲמְרוּן לֵיהּ. מָה אִי[ת] בָּךְ עֲבַד. אֲמַר לוֹן. אִי בִּי עֲבִידְנָא צְפַר תְּרֵין זִימְנִין וּמְעַיֵּל לְהָכָא תּוּמְנִין גּוּבְרִין בְּחִירִין לְבוּשִׁין מָאנִין נְקִיים חֲדֵי וּמַחְדֵּי לְכוֹן. אֲמְרִין לֵיהּ. לוֹן נָן בְּעַיִין. כֵּיוָן דִּצְפַר לְבֵשׁוּ מָנִין נְקִיִים. כֵּיוָן דִּצְפַר תִּנְייָנוּ עָלוּ כּוּלְהוּ כְּחָדָא. רְמַז לוֹן. כָּל־חַד מִינְּכוֹן יִטּוֹל חָדָא וִיטַלְטְלֵינָּה מֵאַרְעָא. וְלָא מַצְלַח מַי דוּ עַבְדָּה. וַהֲוָה אֲמַר לְהַהִיא דְאַייְתַת פִּיתָּה. אַייְתִי פִּיתָּא. וְלָא מַתְיָיא. וְהוּא אֲמַר. אַייְתִי לִצְלִיבָא. אַייְתִי תַבְשִׁילָא. וְלָא מַתְיָיא. וְהוּא אֲמַר. אַייְתִי לִצְלִיבָא. אַייְתִי חֲמַר. וְלָא מַתְיָיא. וְהוּא אֲמַר. אַייְתִי לִצְלִיבָא. כֵּן עֲבַד לְכוּלְּהִי. הַיְינוּ דְּתַנִּינָן. שְׁמוֹנִים נָשִׁים תָּלָה שִׁמְעוֹן בֶּן שֶׁטַח בְּאַשְׁקְלוֹן. וְאֵין דָּנִין שְׁנַיִם בְּיוֹם אֶחָד. אֶלָּא שֶׁהַשָּׁעָה צְרִיכָה לְכֵן.

What happened in Ascalon supports him who said, Simeon ben Shetaḥ was president. Two students were in Ascalon. They ate together, drank together, and studied Torah together. One of them died, and nobody attended his funeral. The son of Ma`yan[84] the publican died; the entire city stopped working to attend his funeral. The other student started crying and said woe, do the haters of Israel[85] have no hope? It was shown to him in his dream and said, do not denigrate your Master's children. This one did one good deed and died with it, the other one committed one sin and died with it[86]. What sin did he commit? Far be it that he committed a sin, but once he put on his head phylacteries before his arm phylacteries[87]. What good deed did the son of publican Ma`yan do? Far be it that he committed a good deed, but once he prepared a breakfast for the city council but they did not show up. He said, let the poor come and eat it, so it should not go to waste. Some say, he was walking in the street, having a loaf under his shoulder. It fell down[88] and a poor person picked it up. He did not say anything in order not to embarrass him. This student saw gardens and water sources. He saw the son of Ma`yan the publican standing on the river bank trying in vain to reach the water. He also saw Miriam, Onion-leaf's daughter, hanging on her breast nipples; but some say, the door of Hell was fixed in her ear. He asked, [why? They told him, because she fasted and made herself famous among her neighbors. Some say, she fasted one day and was dissolute two days. He asked them][G] for how long? They told him, when Simeon ben Shetaḥ comes, we shall remove it from her ear and put is in his ear. He asked them, what is his misdeed? They told him, because he made a personal vow that if he were elected president, he would kill all sorcerers. But now he was made president and he did not kill them. In fact, there are eighty women in the cave of Ascalon who hurt the world; go and tell him! He told them, he is an important personality, he will not believe me. They told him, he is very meek and will believe you. In case that he will not believe you, take out one of your eyes and put it in your hand. He took out one of his eyes and put it in his hand. They said, return it; it was even with the other. He went and told him. He wanted to perform his miracle before him, but he told him, you do not need to. I know that you are a pious person. Even though I intended so in my thoughts, I never spoke it with my mouth[91]. It was a day of rainstorms. He took eighty select men in clean garments and took with them eighty amphoras[92]. He told them, when I whistle once, put on your garments. When I whistle for the second time, come. When he came to the cave of Ascalon, he said אוים, אוים[93], open for me, I am one of yours. When he entered, one said what she said and produced bread. One said what she said and produced a dish. One said what she said and produced wine. They asked him, what can you do? He told them, when I whistle twice, I shall bring here eighty select men in dry garments for your pleasure and entertainment. They told him, we desire them. When he whistled, they put on their garments; when he whistled for the second time, they all entered together. He made them a sign for each one to grab one of them and lift her from the earth[94]. Then they did not succeed in what they were trying to do. He told the one who brought bread, bring bread! She did not succeed. He said, take her to be crucified[95]. Bring a dish! She did not succeed. He said, take her to be crucified. Bring wine! She did not succeed. He said, take her to be crucified. This he did to all of them. That is what we have stated: "Simeon ben Shetaḥ hanged eighty women in Ascalon, but one does not try two on the same day." But the hour needed it[96].

83 Single letters added in brackets are added from *Ḥagigah* (Note 77) for correct spelling. The text, including the addition from G, is a slight reformulation of the text in *Ḥagigah.*

84 "The source", a symbolic name to contrast with the punishment of his son by eternal thirst.

85 I. e., the Jews. It is common that bad things should be said of your enemies, not of

yourself.

86 It is a general answer to the question צדיק ורע לו רשע וטוב לו "why do the just suffer and the wicked enjoy their lives?" that the wicked enjoy the rewards for their few good deeds and the just are punished for their few sins in this world, to create a clean slate for reward and punishment in the World to Come.

87 *Ex*. 13:9,16 require that the sign (*tefillin*, phylacteries) carried by the faithful be on the arm before being put on the head. The repetition emphasizes the importance of this feature.

88 And he would not have eaten it afterwards.

89 In the Future World.

90 Fasting without repentance is sinful (*Nedarim* 9:1 Note 25.)

91 He never made a vow valid in the eyes of the earthly court; he understood that the Heavenly Court uses other yardsticks for pious people. Since *Deut*. 23:22 declares an unfulfilled vow to fill the vower with sin; the fear of accidental, undeclared vows underlies a number of Jewish rituals.

92 I. e., he took 80 fresh garments in 80 amphoras to protect them from the rain.

93 The meaning of these words is unknown. Neither Rapoport's ἅγιον, ἅγιον (holy, holy) nor Levy's ὁμοία,ὁμοία (equals, equals), nor Dalmann's ὠή or Jastrow's εὔαν (hallo!) make any sense in the context. But compare Greek εὐοῖ, Latin *euhoe, euoe, ēvoe*, shout of joy at the festivities of Dionysos-Bacchus, possibly intended for emphasis on the idolatrous aspects of sorcery (E. G.). If the witches spoke Phoenician or Hebrew, the expression could be part of a Semitic oath formula from the root ימין like أيمن لله "by God".

94 Their witchcraft was an expression of chthonic powers which were only active while they were in connection with the earth. This in itself is proof of forbidden sorcery.

95 Which is not a form of execution sanctioned by the Torah.

96 He acted under the king's police powers, disregarding all judicial rules.

(23c line 69) תַּנֵּי. רִבִּי אֱלִיעֶזֶר בֶּן יַעֲקֹב אוֹמֵר. זֶה חוֹמֶר בִּמְחַלֵּל מִבִּמְגַדֵּף וְזֶה זֶה חוֹמֶר בִּמְגַדֵּף מִבִּמְחַלֵּל. בִּמְגַדֵּף כְּתִיב לֹא־תָלִין נִבְלָתוֹ עַל־הָעֵץ. וּבִמְחַלֵּל כְּתִיב וַתִּקַּח רִצְפָּה בַת־אַיָּה אֶת־הַשַּׂק וַתַּטֵּהוּ עַל הַצּוּר מִתְּחִילַּת קָצִיר עַד נִתַּךְ־מַיִם עֲלֵיהֶם. מְלַמֵּד שֶׁהָיוּ תְלוּיִין מִי״ו בְּנִיסָן עַד י״ז בְּמַרְחֶשְׁוָן.

[97]It was stated: Rebbi Eliezer ben Jacob said, this is worse for the desecrator[98] than for the blasphemer and worse for the blasphemer than the desecrator. About the blasphemer it is written[67]: *Do not leave his corpse on the gallows overnight.* But about the desecrator it is written[99]: *Rispa bat Aya took sackcloth and spread it on the rock from the start of harvest until water*

was poured on them. This teaches that they were hanging from the sixteenth of Nisan to the seventeenth of Marḥeshwan.

97 Here starts the discussion of the duty to see to the immediate burial of a corpse, and the difficulty of reconciling this biblical duty with king David's conduct in the matter of the Gibeonites and king Saul's sons (*2S.* 21). The argument in the following text is a shortened and partially elliptic rewriting of *Qiddušin* 4:1. The commentary for the full text of *Qiddušin* 4:1 (Notes 46-85) may serve here also. Other parallels are Babli *Yebamot* 78b-79a, *Num. rabba* 8(4), *Midrash Samuel* 28(5).

98 The person who desecrates the Name of God; he committed the one sin which in Judaism can only be atoned for by death (Babli *Yoma* 87a).

99 *2S.* 20:10.

(23c line 74) כְּתִיב וַיִּתְּנֵם יְהוֹשֻׁעַ בַּיּוֹם הַהוּא חוֹטְבֵי עֵצִים וְשׁוֹאֲבֵי מַיִם לָעֵדָה. נִיחָא לָעֵדָה. וּלְמִזְבַּח יי. אֶלָּא שֶׁתְּלָייָן יְהוֹשֻׁעַ בריפן[100]. אָמַר. אֲנִי [לֹא] מַרְחִיקָן וְלֹא מְקָרְבָן. אֶלָּא מִי שֶׁעָתִיד לִבְנוֹת בֵּית הַבְּחִירָה דְּאֵת[101] דַּעְתּוֹ לְקָרֵב יְקָרֵב וְאֵת דַּעְתּוֹ לְרַחֵק יְרַחֵק. וּבָא דָוִד וְרִיחֲקָן. וְהַגִּבְעוֹנִים לֹא מִבְּנֵי יִשְׂרָאֵל הֵמָּה. וְלָמָּה רִיחֲקָן. עַל שֵׁם וַיְהִי רָעָב בִּימֵי דָוִד שָׁלֹשׁ שָׁנִים וגו'. אָמַר דָּוִד. בַּעֲוֹן ג' דְּבָרִים גְּשָׁמִים נֶעֱצָרִין. עֲבוֹדָה זָרָה וְגִילּוּי עֲרָיוֹת וּשְׁפִיכוּת דָּמִים. עֲבוֹדָה זָרָה דִּכְתִיב פֶּן־יִפְתֶּה לְבַבְכֶם וְסָמִיךְ לֵיהּ וְעָצַר אֶת־הַשָּׁמַיִם. גִּילּוּי עֲרָיוֹת דִּכְתִיב וַיִּמָּנְעוּ רְבִיבִים וּמַלְקוֹשׁ לֹא הָיָה וּמֵצַח אִשָּׁה זוֹנָה הָיָה לָךְ. שְׁפִיכוּת דָּמִים שֶׁנֶּאֱמַר כִּי הַדָּם הוּא יַחֲנִיף אֶת־הָאָרֶץ. וְיֵשׁ אוֹמְרִים. אַף פּוֹסְקֵי צְדָקָה בָּרַבִּים וְאֵינָן נוֹתְנִין. דִּכְתִיב נְשִׂיאִים וְרוּחַ וְגֶשֶׁם אָיִן אִישׁ מִתְהַלֵּל בְּמַתַּת־שָׁקֶר׃ בָּדַק דָּוִד בְּכָל־דְּרָכָיו וְלֹא מָצָא אֶחָד מֵהֶן. הִתְחִיל שׁוֹאֵל בְּאוּרִים וְתוּמִּים. הָדָא הוּא דִכְתִיב וַיְבַקֵּשׁ דָּוִד אֶת־פְּנֵי יי. אָמַר רִבִּי לָעְזָר. כְּתִיב בַּקְּשׁוּ יי כָּל־עַנְוֵי אָרֶץ אֲשֶׁר מִשְׁפָּטוֹ פָּעָלוּ וגו'. וַיֹּאמֶר יי עַל שָׁאוּל וְעַל בֵּית הַדָּמִים עַל־אֲשֶׁר־הֵמִית אֶת־הַגִּבְעוֹנִים׃ עַל שָׁאוּל. שֶׁלֹּא עֲשִׂיתֶם עִמּוֹ חֶסֶד. וְעַל בֵּית הַדָּמִים עַל־אֲשֶׁר־הֵמִית אֶת־הַגִּבְעוֹנִים׃ שָׁלַח דָּוִד וּקְרָאָן. אָמַר לָהֶם. מַה לָּכֶם וּלְבֵית שָׁאוּל. אָמְרוּ לוֹ. עַל יְדֵי שֶׁהֵמִית מִמֶּנּוּ שִׁבְעָה אֲנָשִׁים שְׁנֵי חוֹטְבֵי עֵצִים וּשְׁנֵי שׁוֹאֲבֵי מַיִם וְסוֹפֵר וְחַזָּן וְשַׁמָּשׁ. אֲמַר לוֹן. מַה תּוּן בְּעוּן. אָמְרוּ לֵיהּ. יֻתַּן־לָנוּ שִׁבְעָה אֲנָשִׁים... וְהוֹקַעֲנוּם לַיי בְּגִבְעוֹן. אֲמַר לוֹן. וּמָה הֲנָייָה יֵשׁ לְכוֹן אִין אִינּוּן מִתְקַטְּלִין. סְבוּ לְכוֹן כְּסַף וּדְהַב. אָמְרוּ לֵיהּ. אֵין־לָנוּ כֶּסֶף וְזָהָב עִם־שָׁאוּל וְעִם־בֵּיתוֹ. אֲמַר. דִּילְמָא בְּהַתִּין אִילֵּין מִן אִילֵּין. הֲוָה נְסִיב כָּל־חַד וְחַד מִינּוֹן וּמְפַייֵס לֵיהּ קוֹמֵי נַפְשֵׁיהּ וְהוּא לָא מְקַבֵּל עֲלוֹי. הָדָא הוּא דִכְתִיב אֵין־[לָנוּ] כֶּסֶף וְזָהָב. אֵין לִי כְּתִיב. בְּאוֹתָהּ שָׁעָה אָמַר דָּוִד. שָׁלֹשׁ מַתָּנוֹת טוֹבוֹת נָתַן הַקָּדוֹשׁ לְיִשְׂרָאֵל. בּוֹייְשָׁנִין וְרַחֲמָנִין וְגוֹמְלֵי חֲסָדִים. בּוֹייְשָׁנִין דִּכְתִיב לְבַעֲבוּר תִּהְיֶה יִרְאָתוֹ עַל־פְּנֵיכֶם וגו'. רַחֲמָנִין דִּכְתִיב וְנָתַן־לְךָ רַחֲמִים וְרִחַמְךָ וְהִרְבֶּךָ. גּוֹמְלֵי חֲסָדִים דִּכְתִיב וְשָׁמַר יי אֱלֹהֶיךָ לְךָ אֶת־הַבְּרִית וְאֶת־הַחֶסֶד. וְאִילּוּ אֵין בָּהֶן אַחַת מֵהֶן וְרִיחֲקָן. וְהַגִּבְעוֹנִים לֹא מִבְּנֵי יִשְׂרָאֵל הֵמָּה. וְאַף עֶזְרָא בָא וְרִיחֲקָן. וְהַנְּתִינִים הָיוּ יוֹשְׁבִים

בָּעוֹפֶל וְצִיתָא וְגִישְׁפָּא מִן הַגִּבְעוֹנִים. וְאַף לְעָתִיד הַקָּדוֹשׁ בָּרוּךְ הוּא מְרַחֲקָן. דִּכְתִיב וְהָעוֹבֵד הָעִיר יַעַבְדוּהוּ מִכֹּל שִׁבְטֵי יִשְׂרָאֵל: יַאֲבִידוּהוּ מִכָּל־שִׁבְטֵי יִשְׂרָאֵל.

וַיֹּאמֶר הַמֶּלֶךְ אֲנִי אֶתֵּן׃ וַיִּקַּח הַמֶּלֶךְ אֶת־שְׁנֵי בְּנֵי רִצְפָּה. וּלְמִיכַל בַּת־שָׁאוּל לֹא־הָיָה לָהּ וָלֶד. וְתֵימַר אָכֵן. אֱמוֹר מֵעַתָּה. בְּנֵי מֵרַב הָיוּ וְגִידְּלָתָם מִיכַל וְנִקְרְאוּ עַל שְׁמָהּ. וַיִּתְּנֵם הַמֶּלֶךְ בְּיַד הַגִּבְעוֹנִים וַיּוֹקִיעוּם בָּהָר לִפְנֵי יי וַיִּפְּלוּ שְׁבַעְתָּם יָחַד. שְׁבַעְתָּיִם כְּתִיב חָסֵר חָד. זֶה מְפִיבוֹשֶׁת שֶׁנִּתְפַּלֵּל עָלָיו דָּוִד וּקְלָטוֹ הַמִּזְבֵּחַ. אָמַר לָהֶן. הֲרֵינִי מַעֲבִירָן לִפְנֵי הַמִּזְבֵּחַ. כָּל־שֶׁהַמִּזְבֵּחַ קוֹלְטוֹ הֲרֵי הוּא שֶׁלּוֹ. מִפְּנֵי מְפִיבוֹשֶׁת שֶׁהָיָה גָדוֹל בַּתּוֹרָה. וְהֶעֱבִירוֹ לִפְנֵי הַמִּזְבֵּחַ וְקָלְטוֹ. אָמַר רִבִּי אָבִין. אֶקְרָא לֵאלֹהִים עֶלְיוֹן לָאֵל גּוֹמֵר עָלָי׃ שֶׁהִסְכִּים הַקָּדוֹשׁ בָּרוּךְ הוּא עִם דָּוִד. וְהֵמָּה הוּמְתוּ בִּימֵי קָצִיר בִּתְחִילַּת קְצִיר שְׂעֹרִים. וַתִּקַּח רִצְפָּה בַת־אַיָּה אֶת הַבֶּגֶד וַתַּטֵּהוּ לָהּ עַל הַצּוּר. מָהוּ עַל הַצּוּר. אָמַר רִבִּי הוֹשַׁעְיָה. שֶׁהָיְתָה אוֹמֶרֶת הַצּוּר תָּמִים פָּעֳלוֹ. רִבִּי נָא בַּר זְמִינָא בְשֵׁם רִבִּי הוֹשַׁעְיָה. גָּדוֹל הוּא קִידּוּשׁ הַשֵּׁם מֵחִילּוּל הַשֵּׁם. בְּקִידּוּשׁ הַשֵּׁם כָּתוּב לֹא־תָלִין נִבְלָתוֹ. וּבְחִילּוּל הַשֵּׁם כָּתוּב וַיִּהְיוּ תְלוּיִים עַד נִתַּךְ־מַיִם עֲלֵיהֶם. מְלַמֵּד שֶׁהָיוּ תְלוּיִין מִי״ו בְּנִיסָן עַד י״ז בְּמַרְחֶשְׁוָן. וְהָיוּ הָעוֹבְרִין וְשָׁבִין אוֹמְרִים. מַה חָטְאוּ שֶׁנִּשְׁתַּנָּה עֲלֵיהֶן מִידַּת הַדִּין. וְהָיוּ אוֹמְרִים לָהֶן. עַל שֶׁפָּשְׁטוּ יְדֵיהֶן בַּגֵּרִים אֲרוּרִים. וַהֲרֵי דְבָרִים קַל וָחוֹמֶר. וּמָה אֵילּוּ שֶׁלֹּא נִתְגַּיְּירוּ לְשׁוּם שָׁמַיִם תָּבַע הַקָּדוֹשׁ בָּרוּךְ הוּא דָּמָן. הַמִּתְגַּיְּירִין לְשׁוּם שָׁמַיִם לֹא כָּל־שֶׁכֵּן. הַרְבֵּה גֵרִים נִתְגַּיְּירוּ בְּאוֹתוֹ הַיּוֹם. שֶׁנֶּאֱמַר וַיְסַפֵּר שְׁלֹמֹה כָּל־הָאֲנָשִׁים הַגֵּירִים וַיַּעַשׂ מֵהֶם שִׁבְעִים אֶלֶף נוֹשֵׂא סַבָּל וגו'.

It is written[102]: *At that moment Joshua dedicated them as hewers of wood and drawers of water for the congregation.* One understands "for the congregation." But "for the Eternal's altar"? But Joshua kept them in limbo. He said, I shall [neither][103] exclude nor include them. But he who sometime in the future will build the Temple, if he wants to include he may include, if he wants to exclude he may exclude. David came and excluded them as it is said[104]: *But the Gibeonites are not part of the Children of Israel.* Why did he exclude them? Because *there was a famine in David's time, three years year after year.* David said, for three sins the rains are locked away: Foreign worship, incest and adultery, and murder. Foreign worship, as it is written[105]: *Beware, lest you be seduced* and next to it, *He locks the sky up*. Incest and adultery, as it is written[106] *Rain-showers were withheld, there was no late rain, for you had the forehead of a whoring woman.* Murder, as it is written[107]: *Because blood will distort the Land.* Some say, also those who publicly promise money for welfare but do not pay, as it is written[108]: *Clouds and wind but no rain means the man who boasts with lying gifts.* David checked on all his ways and did not find any of them. He turned to ask the Urim and Tummim. That is what is written[104]: *David asked before the Eternal.* Rebbi Eleazar said, it is written[109]: *Ask the Eternal, all the meek of the Land, who execute His Law*, etc. [104]*The Eternal said, because of Saul and the House of blood-guilt, for he had killed the Gibeonites. Because of Saul*, whom you did not grant the last favor, *and because of the House of blood-guilt, for he had killed the Gibeonites.* David sent and called them. He asked them, what is between you and the House of Saul? They told him, because he killed seven of our men, two hewers of wood, two drawers of water, a scribe, a religious leader, and a beadle. He asked them, what do you want now? They said to him, *May there be given to us seven men . . . and we shall hang them before the Eternal in Gibeon*[110]. He said to them, what use is it to you that they be killed? Take silver and gold for yourselves! But they answered, *there is no silver or gold for us from Saul and his house*[111]. He said, maybe they are afraid one of the other; he dealt which each of them separately, trying to mollify him by himself, but nobody accepted it. That is what is written, *there is no silver or gold for us*, it is written *for me.* At this moment, David said that the Holy One gave three good gifts to Israel: They are decent, merciful, and charitable. Decent, for it is written[112]: *that His fear be on your faces.* Merciful, for it is written[113]: *He gave you mercy, had mercy on you and increased you.* Charitable, for it is written[114]: *The Eternal, your God, kept for you covenant and charity.* But these, nothing of this is found in them; he excluded them: *But the Gibeonites are not of the Children of Israel*[104]. And Ezra also excluded them, as it is said:[115] *And the dedicated ones dwelt in the Ophel; Ziha and Gishpa were of the dedicated ones.* Also in the future, the Holy One, praise to Him, will exclude them as it is written[116]: *The city worker will cultivate it, from all tribes of Israel.* He will eliminate them from all tribes of Israel.

[117]*The king said, I shall give*[110]. *The king took the two sons of Rispah bat Ayah*[118]. *Michal, Saul's daughter, did not have a child*[119], and you say so? Say now that they were sons of Merab but Michal raised them, so they were named after her. *The king gave them into the hand of the Gibeonites who hanged them on the mountain before the Eternal*[120]. *All seven* is written

defective of one letter. That refers to Mephiboshet, for whom David prayed and whom the altar received. He told them, I let them pass by the altar and anyone whom the altar receives will be his, because of Mephiboshet who was great in Torah. He let him pass by the altar, which received him. Rebbi Avin said, *I shall call to the Most High God, to the Power Who has the ultimate decision over me*[121]. For the Holy One, praise to Him, agreed with David. *They were killed on the day of harvest . . .at the start of the barley harvest*[120]. *Rispah bat Ayah took a garment and laid it out on the rock*[122]. What means *on the rock*? Rebbi Hoshaia said, she was reciting: *The rock, perfect is His action*[123]. Rebbi Abba bar Zamina in the name of Rebbi Hoshaia: Sanctification of the Name is greater than desecration of the Name. Referring to sanctification of the Name it is written: *Do not leave his corpse overnight*[67]. But referring to desecration of the Name it is written that they were left hanging *until water was poured on them*[120]. This teaches that they were hanging from the sixteenth of Nisan to the seventeenth of Marheshwan. The passers-by were saying: How did these people sin that the rules of justice were changed for them? They were answered: Because these had attacked cursed proselytes. Is that not an argument *de minore ad majus*? Since even for those who did not convert for the sake of Heaven, the Eternal avenged their blood; if one would convert for the sake of Heaven not so much more? Many converts were converted at that time; that is what is written[124]: *Solomon counted all proselytes . . . and appointed from them 70'000 carriers*, etc.

100 Reading with the *Qiddušin* text: בדופן.

101 Reading with the *Qiddušin* text: ואת.

102 *Jos.* 9:27.

103 Added from the *Qiddušin* text.

104 *2S.* 21:1-2.

105 *Deut.* 11:16-17.

106 *Jer.* 3:2-3.

107 *Num.* 35:33.

108 *Prov.* 25:14.

109 *Zeph.* 2:3.

110 *2S.* 21:6.

111 *2S.* 21:4.

112 *Ex.* 20:20.

113 *Deut.* 13:18,

114 *Deut.* 7:12.

115 *Neh.* 3:26, 11:21.

116 *Ez.* 48:19.

117 Several passages in this paragraph are truncated; refer to the *Qiddušin* text.

118 *2S.* 21:8.

119 *2S.* 6:23.

120 *2S.* 21:9.

121 *Ps.* 57:3.

122 *2S.* 21:10.

123 *Deut.* 32:4.

124 *2Chr.* 2:16-17.

(fol. 23a) **משנה י**: אָמַר רַבִּי מֵאִיר בִּזְמַן שֶׁאָדָם מִצְטַעֵר שְׁכִינָה מָה הַלָּשׁוֹן אוֹמֶרֶת. כִּבְיָכוֹל קַלַּנִי מֵרֹאשִׁי קַלַּנִי מִזְּרוֹעִי. אִם כָּךְ אָמַר הַכָּתוּב מִצְטַעֵר אֲנִי עַל דָּמָן שֶׁל רְשָׁעִים קַל וָחֹמֶר עַל דָּמָן שֶׁל צַדִּיקִים שֶׁנִּשְׁפַּךְ.

Mishnah 10: Rebbi Meïr said: When a human suffers, how does the Divine presence[125] express Itself? If it could be said[126], my head is light, my arm is light[127]. If Scripture says so, I am suffering about the blood of evildoers, so much more if blood of the just is spilled.

125 The *Šekhinah* is God's Presence among men, *Ex*. 29:46.

126 The usual expression to justify an anthropomorphism. We know that human behavior cannot be attributed to the *Šekhinah*, but if it could, one could say . . .

127 This translation is tentative; see the Halakhah.

(23d line 50) **הלכה י**: אָמַר רַבִּי מֵאִיר כול'. אֲנָן תַּנִּינָן. קַלֵּינִי. אִית תַּנָּיֵי תַנֵּי. קַל אֲנִי. מָאן דָּמַר קַלֵּינִי. לֵית הוּא אֶלָּא קָלִיל. מַה דָּמַר. קַל אֲנִי. לֵית הוּא אֶלָּא נְטִיל.

מַתְנִיתָא דְלָא כְרַבִּי מֵאִיר דְּאָמַר. אַף הַמְגַדֵּף עוֹבֵר בְּלֹא תַעֲשֶׂה.

Halakhah 10: "Rebbi Meïr said," etc. We have stated קַלֵּינִי. Some Tannaïm state קַל אֲנִי. [128]He who says קַלֵּינִי uses only an expression of lightness. He who says קַל אֲנִי uses a language of load.

The Mishnah does not follow Rebbi Meïr because he said, also for the blasphemer one violates a prohibition[129].

128 It seems that one should follow R. David Fraenckel and switch the references. This also would follow Talmudic style: readings AB are discussed as BA: "He who says קַל אֲנִי (I am light) uses an expression of lightness. He who says קַלֵּינִי (קַל אֵינִי I am not light) uses a language of load."

The Babli, 46b, only discusses the second alternative, or a possibility of deriving the expression from the root קלל "to curse."

129 It is a question of interpretation of *Deut*. 21:23: *Do not leave his corpse on the gallows overnight* (a prohibition), *but burying you shall bury him on the same day* (a positive commandment). It is agreed that the positive commandment applies to all burials (Mishnah 11). The question is the domain of applicability of the prohibition.

In Mishnah 9, the rabbis hold that only people attacking the essence of the faith are hanged. The question remains what their position is about witnesses who falsely accuse somebody of blasphemy. It may be that *Sifry Deut.* 221, which excludes the perjured witnesses from being hanged, represents R. Meïr's position, which is not documented elsewhere. Then the sentence should be read: *Only for the blasphemer does one violate the prohibition . . .*, since only concerning the blasphemer there is a duty to hang his corpse.

(fol. 23a) **משנה יא**: וְלֹא זוֹ בִלְבַד אֶלָּא כָּל הַמֵּלִין אֶת מֵתוֹ עוֹבֵר בְּלֹא תַעֲשֶׂה. הֱלִינוּ לִכְבוֹדוֹ לְהָבִיא לוֹ אָרוֹן וְתַכְרִיכִין אֵינוֹ עוֹבֵר עָלָיו בְּלֹא תַעֲשֶׂה. וְלֹא הָיוּ קוֹבְרִין אוֹתוֹ בְּקִבְרוֹת אֲבוֹתֵיהֶן. אֶלָּא שְׁנֵי קְבָרוֹת הָיוּ מְתוּקָּנִין לְבֵית דִּין אֶחָד לַנִּסְקָלִין וְלַנִּשְׂרָפִין וְאֶחָד לַנֶּהֱרָגִין וְלַנֶּחֱנָקִין:

Mishnah 11: Not only this, but anybody who leaves his dead[130] overnight violates a prohibition. If he left him overnight for his honor, to provide him with a coffin and shrouds[131], he does not violate a prohibition in his regard. They did not bury them[132] in their family graves, but two graves[133] were prepared, one for those stoned or burned, the other for those beheaded or strangled[134].

130 Any deceased whose burial is his personal responsibility.

131 These are examples rather than an exhaustive list of reasons for a delayed funeral.

132 People executed by a court verdict.

133 In all printed Babli editions בתי קברות "cemetaries". This reading has no parallel in Babli mss. (*Diqduqe Soferim* 36a Note ל). Maimonides's autograph Mishnah text has קבורות, read קְבוּרוֹת "burial sites". This seems to be the best reading.

134 The sins of those executed by the two cruel methods are incomparably worse than those of persons executed by the two swift methods.

(23d line 53) **הלכה יא**: וְלֹא זוֹ בִלְבַד כול'. תַּנֵּי. הַמַּעֲבִיר אָרוֹן מִמָּקוֹם לְמָקוֹם אֵין בּוֹ מִשּׁוּם לִיקּוּט עֲצָמוֹת. אָמַר רִבִּי אָחָא. הָדָא דְתֵימַר בַּאֲרוֹן שַׁיִישׁ. אֲבָל בַּאֲרוֹן עֵץ יֵשׁ בּוֹ מִשּׁוּם לִיקּוּט עֲצָמוֹת. אָמַר רִבִּי יוֹסֵי. אֲפִילוּ בַּאֲרוֹן עֵץ אֵין בּוֹ מִשּׁוּם לִיקּוּט עֲצָמוֹת. אֵי זֶהוּ לִיקּוּט עֲצָמוֹת.

אָמַר רִבִּי חַגַּיי. וְהוּא שֶׁשָּׁמַע לְמָחָר. אֲבָל בּוֹ בַּיּוֹם יֵשׁ שְׁמוּעָה לְלִיקּוּט עֲצָמוֹת. תַּנֵּי נִיקוֹמַכֵי קוֹמֵי רִבִּי זְעִירָא. אֵין שִׁיעוּר לְלִיקּוּט עֲצָמוֹת. רִבִּי מָנִי הוֹרֵי לְרִבִּי לָא דְכֵפְרָא לִקְרוֹעַ וּלְהִתְאַבֵּל כְּרִבִּי אָחָא וְלֹא לִיטַּמּוֹת כְּרִבִּי יוֹסֵי.

תַּנֵּי. לִיקּוּטֵי עֲצָמוֹת כִּשְׁמוּעָן. אֵי זֶהוּ לִיקּוּט עֲצָמוֹת. הַמְלַקֵּט עֶצֶם עֶצֶם מִשֶּׁיִּתְאַכֵּל הַבָּשָׂר. תַּנֵּי. לִיקּוּט עֲצָמוֹת אֵין אוֹמְרִים עֲלֵיהֶן קִינִּים וָנֶהִי וְלֹא בִרְכַּת אֲבֵלִים וְלֹא תַנְחוּמֵי אֲבֵלִים. אֵילּוּ הֵן בִּרְכַּת אֲבֵילִים. שֶׁאוֹמְרִים בְּבֵית הַכְּנֶסֶת. אֵילּוּ הֵן תַּנְחוּמֵי אֲבֵילִים. שֶׁהֵן אוֹמְרִים בַּשּׁוּרָה. תַּנֵּי. אֲבָל אוֹמְרִים עֲלֵיהֶן דְּבָרִים. מָה הֵן דְּבָרִים. רַבָּנִן דְּקֵיסָרִין אָמְרִין. קִילּוּסִין.

Halakhah 11: "Not only this," etc. It was stated: [135]If somebody transports a coffin from one place to the other, the rules of collecting bones do not apply[136]. Rebbi Aḥa said, this means in a marble[137] coffin. But in a wooden coffin, the rules of collecting bones do apply. Rebbi Yose said, even for a wooden coffin the rules of collecting bones do not apply. What is "collecting bones"[138]?

Rebbi Ḥaggai said, only if he heard it the next day. But on the same day notice must be taken of collecting bones[139]. Nikomachos stated before Rebbi Ze`ira: Collecting bones has no [minimal] amount[140]. Rebbi Mani instructed Rebbi La from Kufra[141] to tear his garment and mourn following Rebbi Aḥa[142], not to pollute himself following Rebbi Yose[143].

It was stated: Collecting bones, following the information[144]. What is collecting bones? One collects every single bone after the flesh has rotted away[138].

It was stated: When collecting bones one does not recite lamentations and wailing, nor the benediction of mourners, nor consolation of mourners. The benediction of mourners, what is said in the synagogue. Consolation of mourners, what is said in the row[145]. It was stated: But one spoke words on the occasion. What are words? The rabbis of Caesarea said, eulogies[146].

135 The Halakhah really belongs to the next Mishnah, which refers to collecting bones. The text as it stands here is missing a few lines which in part make it incomprehensible. The origin is in *Mašqin* (*Mo`ed qatan*) 1:5 (80d ll. 1-14); it also is found in *Pesahim* 8:7 (36b ll. 22-37).

136 This refers to Mishnah *Mo`ed qaṭan* 1:3: "R. Meïr says, a person may collect his parents' bones on a semi-holiday because it makes him happy; R. Yose says, it is an occasion of mourning. Halakhah 12 (*Mo`ed qatan* 1:5) determines that the day of collecting the bones (transferring them from burial in the ground to an ossuary to be stored in a cave) is a day of mourning (prohibited one a semi-holiday) but the day following is a holiday since the person is assured that his parents were freed from punishment in the world of souls. [Only extremely vicious souls are punished in eternity, cf. Chapter 10. For all other

evildoers, the punishment in hell is for 12 months or until the flesh has disappeared from the bones, whichever comes sooner. For this reason, a mourner may not recite the prayer for the dead (customary since the last millennium) for more than 11 months; if he did recite it in the 12th month he would declare his parent an evildoer, in itself a sin.]

137 In the parallels: stone.

138 The missing answer, found in the parallels, is: One transports them in an ἐπικάρσιον ("cloth hanging down", used for striped cloth) from place to place.

139 The text to which this remark belongs again is missing. It starts with the sentence of Note 144.

In case of a death, the relatives near the deceased have to see to his burial and start the mourning rites immediately. Those farther away have to start when they are informed. There is a difference in the rules between "recent information" (within 30 days of the death) or "distant information" (after 30 days). The same is true for collecting the bones. Not only the person actually collecting the bones has to observe the rites of mourning, but all his close relatives who in theory also could have collected the bones. But since the day following already is a day of joy (Note 136), only information which reaches the relative on the day itself forces the recipient to observe mourning.

140 Mourning while collecting the bones is required even for a single bone. In the parallels, this is the answer to the question: Is there a minimal amount required when collecting bones?

141 In the parallels: R. Mana instructed R. Hillel from Kifra.

142 Transporting a wooden coffin is subject to all rules of mourning.

143 A Cohen is not permitted to transport a wooden coffin, even if it is for one of the close relatives for whom he is obligated to pollute himself.

144 Cf. Note 139.

145 After burial, the participants in the funeral form two rows; the mourners walk in between while the participants recite formulas of consolation; cf. *Berakhot* 3:2, Note 121.

146 Praises of the deceased. According to H. L. Fleischer, this word קילוס, which also exists in Syriac, and a related verb in Arabic are derived from Greek καλῶς! "beautiful, excellent."

(fol. 23b) **משנה יב**: נִתְעַכֵּל הַבָּשָׂר הָיוּ מְלַקְּטִין אֶת הָעֲצָמוֹת וְקוֹבְרִין אוֹתָן בִּמְקוֹמָן. וְהַקְּרוֹבִין בָּאִין וְשׁוֹאֲלִין אֶת שְׁלוֹם הָעֵדִים וְאֶת שְׁלוֹם הַדַּיָּנִין כְּלוֹמַר דְּעוּ שֶׁאֵין בְּלִבֵּינוּ עֲלֵיכֶם שֶׁדִּין אֱמֶת דַּנְתֶּם. וְלֹא הָיוּ מִתְאַבְּלִין אֲבָל אוֹנְנִין שֶׁאֵין אֲנִינָה אֶלָּא בַלֵּב:

Mishnah 12: If the flesh has rotted away, one collects the bones and buries them at their place[146]. The relatives come[147] and greet the witnesses and judges, implying that "we hold no grudge against you because you delivered a true judgment." They did not mourn but were in deep sorrow[148], since deep sorrow is only in the mind.

146 The bones of the person executed are exhumed from the court's burial site and reburied in the family grave or cave.

147 Immediately after the execution.

148 The day of execution itself, when the deep mourner is barred from all religious acts (*Deut.* 26:14). Mourning rites only start after burial.

(23 line 65) **הלכה יב**: נִתְעַכֵּל הַבָּשָׂר כול'. תַּנֵּי. בָּרִאשׁוֹנָה הָיוּ מְלַקְּטִין אֶת הָעֲצָמוֹת וְקוֹבְרִין אוֹתָן בְּמַהֲמוֹרוֹת. נִתְעַכֵּל הַבָּשָׂר הָיוּ מְלַקְּטִין אוֹתָן וְקוֹבְרִין אוֹתָן בַּאֲרָזִים. אוֹתוֹ הַיּוֹם מִתְאַבֵּל וּלְמָחָר הָיָה שָׂמֵחַ. לוֹמַר שֶׁנַּיְיחוּהוּ אֲבוֹתָיו מִן הַדִּין.

Halakhah 12: "If the flesh has rotted away," etc. [149]It was stated: In earlier times, they were collecting the bones after burying them in ditches[150]. When the flesh had rotted away, they collected them and buried them in cedar wood. On the day itself he was mourning, the day after he was happy[151], implying that his parents were at rest[152] from judgment.

149 The parallel is in *Mašqin* (*Mo`ed qatan*) 1:5 (80c l. 74). The subject is a common person, not a criminal.

150 The translation is tentative; the word appears only in this *baraita* and *Ps.* 140:11.

151 Cf. Note 136. In the Babli, *Mo`ed qatan* 8a, the quote appears in a different context.

152 Reading ניניחו with the parallel text.

(23d line 68) וְלֹא עוֹד אֶלָּא הָיוּ קוֹבְרִין אוֹתָן בִּפְנֵי עַצְמָן. הַנִּסְקָלִין בַּנִּשְׂרָפִין וְהַנֶּהֱרָגִין בַּנֶּחֱנָקִין. הוּא שֶׁדָּוִד אוֹמֵר אַל־תֶּאֱסוֹף עִם־חַטָּאִים נַפְשִׁי. הַנִּסְקָלִין וְהַנִּשְׂרָפִין. וְעִם־אַנְשֵׁי דָמִים חַיָּי. הַנֶּהֱרָגִין וְהַנֶּחֱנָקִין.

[153]Not only this, but they were buried separately, those stoned with the burned, those beheaded with the strangled. This as what David said[154], *Do not*

collect my soul with sinners, those stoned or burned; *nor my life with men of blood guilt,* those beheaded or strangled.

153 This refers to the end of Mishnah 11.

154 *Ps.* 26:9.

(23d line 71) רִבִּי אַבָּהוּ מֲטְתֵיהּ אוֹנֵס. אֲזַל לֵיהּ חַד מִינוּק. עָלוֹן רִבִּי יוֹנָה וְרִבִּי יוֹסֵי מִי חֲמִי לֵיהּ אַפִּין. מֵאֵימָתֵיהּ עָלֵיה לָא אֲמְרוּ לֵיהּ מִילָּא דְאוֹרַייָא. אֲמַר לוֹן. מַשְׁגְּחִין רַבָּנִן מֵימַר מִילָּא דְאוֹרַייָא. אֲמְרוּ לֵיהּ. אַשְׁגַּח מָרָן. אֲמַר לוֹן. מָה אִם רְשׁוּת שֶׁלְּמַטָּן שֶׁיֵּשׁ בּוֹ כָּזָב וְשֶׁקֶר וּגְנֵיבוּת דַּעַת וּמַשּׂוֹא פָנִים וּמִקַּח שׁוֹחַד וְהַיּוֹם עוֹדֶנּוּ וּמָחָר אֵינֶנּוּ נֶאֱמַר בָּהּ הַקְּרוֹבִין בָּאִין וְשׁוֹאֲלִין שְׁלוֹם הַדַּיָּנִין וְהָעֵדִים לוֹמַר שֶׁאֵין בְּלִיבֵּינוּ עֲלֵיכֶם כְּלוּם. שֶׁדִּין אֱמֶת דַּנְתֶּם. רְשׁוּת שֶׁלְּמַעֲלָן שֶׁאֵין בָּהּ לֹא כָזָב וְלֹא שֶׁקֶר וְלֹא גְנֵיבוּת דַּעַת וְלֹא מַשּׂוֹא פָנִים וְלֹא מִקַּח שׁוֹחַד וְהוּא חַי וְקַיָּים לְעוֹלָם ולְעוֹלְמֵי עוֹלָמִים. עַל אַחַת כַּמָּה וְכַמָּה שֶׁחַייָבִים אָנוּ לְקַבֵּל עָלֵינוּ מִידַּת הַדִּין. וְאוֹמֵר וְנָתַן־לְךָ֨ רַחֲמִים֙ וְרִחַמְךָ֣ וְהִרְבֶּ֔ךָ כַּאֲשֶׁ֥ר נִשְׁבַּ֖ע לַאֲבֹתֶֽיךָ׃

An accident happened to Rebbi Abbahu; he lost a baby. Rebbi Jonah and Rebbi Yose ascended[155] to visit him. Out of respect for him,[156] they did not speak to him words of Torah. He told them, would the rabbis think saying a word of Torah? They answered, think of it, our teacher. He said to them: If about a terrestrial authority, where one finds lies, and untruth, and misleading statements, and favoritism, and bribery, and they are here one day and gone the next, it was said: "the relatives come and greet the judges and witnesses, implying that we hold no grudge against you because you delivered a true judgment," the Heavenly authority, before which there are no lies, no untruth, no misleading statements, no favoritism, and no bribery, and He exists forever in all worlds, so much more are we obligated to accept His judgment. And it is said[113], *May He give you mercy, have mercy on you, and make you increase as He has sworn to your ancestors.*

155 They came from Tiberias below sea level to Caesarea Philippi in the foothills of the Golan Heights to offer their condolences.

156 The great man of the generation of their teachers.

ארבע מיתות פרק שביעי

(fol. 24a) **משנה א**: אַרְבַּע מִיתוֹת נִמְסְרוּ לְבֵית דִּין סְקִילָה שְׂרֵפָה הֶרֶג וָחֶנֶק. רִבִּי שִׁמְעוֹן אוֹמֵר שְׂרֵפָה סְקִילָה חֶנֶק וָהֶרֶג. זוֹ מִצְוַת הַנִּסְקָלִין:

Mishnah 1: Four kinds of execution was the court empowered to impose: Stoning, burning, decapitation, and strangling. Rebbi Simeon says: Burning, stoning, strangling, and decapitation[1]. The preceding was prescribed for stoning.

1 They differ in the evaluation of which type of execution inflicts more pain on the condemned, starting with the worst and ending with the easiest.

(24b line 9) **הלכה א**: אַרְבַּע מִיתוֹת נִמְסְרוּ לְבֵית דִּין כול׳. וְלָרָשׁוּת לֹא נִיתַּן אֶלָּא דִין הֶרֶג בִּלְבַד. סְקִילָה מְנַיִין. וּסְקַלְתֶּם בָּאֲבָנִים וָמֵתוּ׃ שְׂרֵיפָה. שֶׁנֶּאֱמַר בָּאֵשׁ יִשְׂרְפוּ אֹתוֹ וְאֶתְהֶן. הֶרֶג. נֶאֱמַר כָּאן נְקִימָה וְנֶאֱמַר לְהַלָּן וְהֵבֵאתִי עֲלֵיכֶם חֶרֶב נֹקֶמֶת נְקַם־בְּרִית. מַה נְקִימָה הָאֲמוּרָה לְהַלָּן חֶרֶב. אַף נְקִימָה הָאֲמוּרָה כָאן חֶרֶב. חֶנֶק. לֵית מַשְׁכַּח לֵיהּ. אָמְרַת. כָּל־מִיתָה הָאֲמוּרָה בַּתּוֹרָה סְתָם אֵין אַתָּה רַשַּׁאי לְהַחֲמִיר עָלֶיהָ אֶלָּא לְהָקֵל עָלֶיהָ וְתָלוּ אוֹתָהּ בַּחֶנֶק.

Halakhah 1: "Four kinds of execution was the court empowered to impose," etc. But to the government[2] only decapitation was given.

From where stoning? *You shall stone them with stones that they die*[3]. Burning, for it is written, *in fire you shall burn him and them*[4]. Avenging is written here[5], and there it is written: *I shall bring over you a sword which avenges the vengeance of the Covenant*[6]. Since avenging mentioned there is by the sword, also avenging mentioned here is by the sword. Strangling? You do not find it[7]. You say that for any death penalty mentioned in the Torah with no particular indication, you are not empowered to make it more stringent, but only to make it less so; they assigned this to strangling.

2 The Roman Imperial government. When Caracalla extended Roman citizenship to all free inhabitants of the empire, he thereby abolished crucifixion (except for slaves).

3 *Deut*. 17:5.

4 *Lev*. 20:14.

5 *Ex*. 21:20. The slave slain by his master shall be avenged. Babli 52b; the

Babli text in *Mekhilta dR. Ismael* p. 273, *dR. Simeon bar Iohai* p. 175.

6 *Lev*. 26:25.

7 It is not mentioned anywhere in biblical literature as a recognized form of execution. The Babli's discussion, 52b, is inconclusive.

(24b line 15) רִבִּי שִׁמְעוֹן אוֹמֵר. שְׂרֵיפָה חֲמוּרָה מִסְּקִילָה. וְרַבָּנִין מָרִין. סְקִילָה חֲמוּרָה מִשְּׂרֵיפָה. רִבִּי שִׁמְעוֹן אוֹמֵר. חֶנֶק חֲמוּרָה מֵהֶרֶג. וְרַבָּנִין מָרִין. הֶרֶג חָמוּר מֵחֶנֶק. רִבִּי שִׁמְעוֹן דָּרַשׁ. כָּל־שֵׁם בַּת כֹּהֵן בִּשְׂרֵיפָה. וְרַבָּנִין מָרִין. כָּל־שֵׁם אֲרוּסָה בִסְקִילָה. רִבִּי שִׁמְעוֹן דָּרַשׁ. מַה בַּת כֹּהֵן שֶׁהֶחֱמִירָה תוֹרָה בָּאֲרוּסָה שֶׁתְּהֵא בִּשְׂרֵיפָה הֵיקִילָה בִנְשׂוּאָה שֶׁתְּהֵא בִסְקִילָה. בַּת יִשְׂרָאֵל שֶׁהֵיקִילָה תוֹרָה בָּאֲרוּסָה שֶׁתְּהֵא בִסְקִילָה אֵינוֹ דִין שֶׁנָּקֵל עָלֶיהָ בִנְשׂוּאָה שֶׁתְּהֵא בַהֲרִיגָה. וְרַבָּנִין דָּרְשִׁין. מַה אִם בַּת יִשְׂרָאֵל שֶׁהֶחֱמִירָה הַתּוֹרָה בָּאֲרוּסָה שֶׁתְּהֵא בִסְקִילָה הֵיקִילָה בִנְשׂוּאָהּ שֶׁתְּהֵא בִשְׂרֵיפָה. בַּת כֹּהֵן שֶׁהֵיקִילָה הַתּוֹרָה בָּאֵירוּסֶיהָ שֶׁתְּהֵא בִשְׂרֵיפָה אֵינוֹ דִין שֶׁנָּקֵל בְּנִישּׂוּאֶיהָ שֶׁתְּהֵא בַחֲנִיקָה.

Rebbi Simeon says, burning is worse than stoning, but the rabbis teach that stoning is worse than burning. Rebbi Simeon says, strangulation is worse than decapitation; but the rabbis teach that decapitation is worse than strangulation[1].

Rebbi Simeon explained that any reference to "Cohen's daughter" implies burning, but the rabbis teach that any reference to "preliminarily married" implies stoning[8].

Rebbi Simeon explained: The Torah was stringent with a Cohen's daughter and ordered that as preliminarily married she be burned, but was lenient with the definitively married one that she be stoned[9]. The Torah was lenient with the preliminarily married daughter of an Israel and ordered that she be stoned; it is logical that we be lenient with the definitively married one that she be decapitated[10]. But the rabbis explain, since the Torah was stringent with the preliminarily married daughter of an Israel and ordered that she be stoned, it was lenient with her in her definitively married status to be burned[11]. The Torah was lenient with the daughter of a Cohen in her pleliminarily married status and ordered that she be burned; it is logical that we be lenient with her in her definitively married status that she be strangled[12].

8 Adultery by a preliminarily married virgin is punishable by stoning (*Deut*. 22:24), by a definitively married woman by "death" (*Lev*. 20:10), which by the preceding argument means the least painful of the four kinds of execution. *Lev*. 21:9

prescribes death by burning for the whoring daughter of a Cohen. The status (unmarried, preliminarily or definitively married) of the Cohen's daughter is not spelled out. Since sexual activity of an unmarried woman is nowhere in the Bible classified as a capital crime [*Sifra Emor Pereq* 1(15)], it is assumed that the Cohen's daughter mentioned in the verse cannot be unmarried (virgin or widowed). The problem remains whether *Lev*. 21:9 refers to a preliminarily or definitively married woman.

For R. Simeon, who holds that burning is more painful than stoning, *Lev*. 21:9 refers to any adulterous daughter of a Cohen, irrespective of the status of her marriage (Babli 50a). For the rabbis who hold that stoning is more painful than burning, *Lev*. 21:9 cannot refer to a preliminarily married maiden since then it would treat a Cohen's daughter more leniently than an Israel's, which contradicts the entire tenor of *Lev*. 21:1-9.

The formulation of the rabbis' position is not quite correct since *Deut*. 22:24 applies only to a preliminarily married maiden (between the ages of 12 and 12 years 6 months; cf. *Yebamot* 1:3, Notes 159-160). In the text following, "preliminarily married" means "preliminarily married maiden"; "definitively married" means "definitively married or adult preliminarily married".

9 This statement contradicts the assertion in the previous paragraph that R. Simeon applies *Lev*. 21:9 to any married daughter of a Cohen; it also contradicts both the principles that (1) penalties must be spelled out in Scripture, cannot be inferred by hermeneutical rules, and (2) in any argument *de minore ad majus* only the data of the rules which are compared can be used; only identical terms can be transferred. Both objections again lead to the conclusion that R. Simeon cannot differentiate between a preliminarily and a definitively married daughter of a Cohen.

10 This is no logical argument at all but a clear reference to biblical verses; cf. Note 8. The only inference is that for R. Simeon the standard method of execution must be beheading.

11 A clear scribal error; it must be "strangled" (Note 8).

12 This proves that at the end of the preceding sentence one has to read "strangled".

(24b line 25) רִבִּי אַבָּהוּ בְשֵׁם רִבִּי יוֹסֵי בֶּן חֲנִינָה. כָּל־מִיתָה שֶׁהִיא לְמַטָּה מִמִּיתַת אָבִיהָ בִשְׂרֵיפָה. כְּשֶׁהִיא אֶצֶל אָבִיהָ עִם אָבִיהָ בִשְׂרֵיפָה וְעִם חָמִיהָ בִסְקִילָה. אֶת־אָבִיהָ הִיא מְחַלֶּלֶת בָּאֵשׁ תִּשָּׂרֵף׃ רִבִּי לִיעֶזֶר אוֹמֵר. עִם אָבִיהָ בִשְׂרֵיפָה עִם חָמִיהָ בִסְקִילָה. הִיא בִשְׂרֵיפָה וְאֵין בּוֹעֲלָהּ בִּשְׂרֵיפָה. הִיא בִשְׂרֵיפָה וְאֵין זוֹמְמֶיהָ בִּשְׂרֵיפָה. כְּיוֹצֵא בָהֶם בִּשְׂרֵיפָה הִיא וָהֵן בִּשְׂרֵיפָה. כְּיוֹצֵא בָהֶן בִּסְקִילָה הִיא וָהֵן בִּסְקִילָה. כְּיוֹצֵא בָהֶן בְּחֶנֶק הֵן בִּשְׂרֵיפָה וְהוּא בְּחֶנֶק.

Rebbi Abbahu in the name of Rebbi Yose ben Ḥanina: Anyone who is executed less cruelly than her father's death is by burning[13]. As long as she is with her father, with her father she is burned, with her father-in-law stoned.

With her father she is desecrating, in fire she should be burned[14]. Rebbi Eliezer says, with her father she is burned, with her father-in-law stoned[15]. She by burning, her paramour not by burning[16]. She by burning, her perjured witnesses not by burning. Similarly by burning, she and they by burning. Simnilarly by stoning, she and they by stoning. Similarly by strangulation, they by burning but he by strangulation[17].

13 The discussion follows the rabbis, for whom stoning is more severe than burning. The statement is a little more explicit in the Babli, 51a.

A definitively married Israel woman who commits adultery is strangled, except that if she commit incest with her father both are burned (*Lev.* 20:14). As a preliminarily married maiden she would be stoned. Therefore, it is clear that for the rabbis the daughter of a Cohen is burned only if either she commits incest with her father or adultery when definitively married.

14 *Lev.* 21:9, reading אֶת as "with". The quote with the following two sentences is a *baraita*, *Sifra Emor Pereq* 1(19); Tosephta 14:17.

15 *Lev.* 20:12. From *Lev.* 20:27: *they shall be put to death, by a stone they shall be stoned, their blood be on them,* it is inferred that any expression "their blood be on them" means execution by stoning. Babli 54a.

16 The singular used in *Lev.* 21:9 implies that only she is executed by burning; her paramour is punished, like any adulterer with a married woman, by strangulation (Babli 51a).

17 The last three sentences are repeated as last sentences of this Tractate, Halakhah 11:8; Tosephta 14:17. "They" are perjured witnesses who falsely accuse her. If they accuse her of adultery as a definitively married woman, then the perjured witnesses are strangled, the prescribed punishment of the paramour. If they accuse her of incest with her father, they are burned, the prescribed punishment of her father. If they accuse her of adultery as preliminarily married maiden, they are stoned, the prescribed punishment both of her and her paramour.

The last sentence cannot stand as it appears here. In Chapter 11, one reads כְּיוֹצֵא בָהֶן בְּחֶנֶק הִיא וָהֵן בְּחֶנֶק "similarly by strangulation, she and they by strangulation." In the Tosephta כְּיוֹצֵא בָהֶן בְּחֶנֶק הוּא בִּשְׂרֵיפָה וְהֵן בְּחֶנֶק "similarly by strangulation, he is burned and they by strangulation." One sees that none of the scribes understood what he was writing. One may read in Chapter 11 "*he* and they by strangulation," or in the Tosephta "*she* is burned and they strangled". In the text here, one has to read: "*she* by burning but he (or *they*) by strangulation."

(24b line 32) רִבִּי אַבָּהוּ בְשֵׁם רִבִּי יוֹסֵי בֶן חֲנִינָה. רַבָּנִין דָּֽרְשִׁין. אַנְשֵׁי עִיר הַנִּדַּחַת בִּכְלָל עוֹבְדֵי עֲבוֹדָה זָרָה הָיוּ בִסְקִילָה. יָֽצְאוּ לִידּוֹן בְּקַלָּה שֶׁבְּמִיתוֹת בִּשְׂרֵיפָה. לֹא דַייֵךְ שֶׁאַתְּ מוֹצִיאָהּ לִידּוֹן

בְּקַלָּה שֶׁבְּמִיתוֹת בִּשְׂרֵיפָה אֶלָּא שֶׁאַתְּ מוֹצִיאָן לָדוּן בְּקַלָּה שֶׁבְּמִיתוֹת בַּחֲנִיקָה. רִבִּי שִׁמְעוֹן דָּרַשׁ. נָבִיא הַשֶּׁקֶר בִּכְלָל עוֹבְדֵי עֲבוֹדָה זָרָה הָיוּ בִשְׂרֵיפָה. יָצְאוּ לִידּוֹן בְּקַלָּה שֶׁבְּמִיתוֹת בִּסְקִילָה. לֹא דַייֶךְ שֶׁאַתְּ מוֹצִיאָן לִידוֹן בְּקַלָּה שֶׁבְּמִיתוֹת בִּסְקִילָה אֶלָּא שֶׁאַתְּ רוֹצֶה לְהוֹצִיאָן לָדוּן בַּקַּלָּה שֶׁבְּמִיתוֹת בַּהֲרִיגָה.

רִבִּי שְׁמוּאֵל בַּר סוֹסְרְטַאי בְּשֵׁם רִבִּי אַבָּהוּ מַחֲלִף. רַבָּנִין דָּרְשִׁין. נָבִיא הַשֶּׁקֶר בִּכְלָל עוֹבְדֵי עֲבוֹדָה זָרָה הָיָה בִסְקִילָה. יָצָא לִידוֹן בְּקַלָּה שֶׁבְּמִיתוֹת בִּשְׂרֵיפָה. לֹא דַייֶךְ שֶׁאַתְּ מוֹצִיאוֹ בִשְׂרֵיפָה אֶלָּא שֶׁאַתְּ מוֹצִיאוֹ לִידוֹן בַּקַּלָּה שֶׁבְּמִיתוֹת בַּחֲנִיקָה.

רִבִּי שִׁמְעוֹן דָּרַשׁ. אַנְשֵׁי עִיר הַנִּדַּחַת בִּכְלָל עוֹבְדֵי עֲבוֹדָה זָרָה הָיוּ בִשְׂרֵיפָה. יָצְאוּ לִידּוֹן בְּקַלָּה שֶׁבְּמִיתוֹת בִּסְקִילָה. לֹא דַייֶךְ אֶלָּא שֶׁאַתְּ מוֹצִיאָן לִידוֹן בַּקַּלָּה שֶׁבְּמִיתוֹת בַּהֲרִיגָה.

Rebbi Abbahu in the name of Rebbi Yose ben Ḥanina: The rabbis explain that the inhabitants of a seduced city[18] should have been included in the category of idolaters, by stoning. They were treated to a less painful way of execution; that should be by burning[19]. It is not enough that you decree for them an easier death by burning, but should you have them judged by the easiest way, by strangulation[20]? Rebbi Simeon explained: The false prophet[21] should have been included in the category of idolaters, by burning[22]. He was treated to a less painful way of execution, which should be by stoning. It is not enough that you decree for them an easier death by stoning, but you have him judged by the easiest way, by beheading[23].

Rebbi Samuel ben Sosartai in the name of Rebbi Abbahu switches the arguments. The rabbis explained: The rabbis explain that the false prophet should have been included in the category of idolaters, by stoning. He was treated to a less painful way of execution, [this should have been] by burning. It is not enough that you decree burning for them, but you have him judged by the easiest way, by strangulation[24]. Rebbi Simeon explained: The inhabitants of a seduced city should have been included in the category of idolaters, by burning. They were treated to a less painful way of execution; that should be by stoning[22]. This is not enough for you but you have them judged by the easiest way, by beheading[25].

18 A city which by vote of city council and population decides to become pagan. Its inhabitants have to be killed by the sword (*Deut.* 13:13-19). Individual apostates to paganism have to be stoned (*Deut.* 17:5).

19 Just one degree less than stoning.

20 This is the rabbis' argument to prove that beheading is worse than strangulation. If the punishment of the inhabitants of the seduced city were the easiest way of execution, the verse simply should have decreed the unspecified death penalty. Since beheading was specified, it must be worse than the unspecified death penalty.

The reason behind the argument is R. Ismael's tenth hermeneutical principle [*Sifra Wayyiqra Pereq* 1(2)], that special treatment for a crime already treated in general always expresses a leniency, not greater strictness.

21 *Deut.* 13:2-6. He is described as a missionary for paganism; his sentence is "death" which means strangulation for the rabbis and beheading for R. Simeon.

22 This makes no sense since it contradicts *Deut.* 17:5. The first two sentences of the argument attributed to R. Simeon are simply taken from the rabbis' argument with stoning and burning switched, even though the argument is irrelevant.

23 Since the rabbis must agree that the false prophet be executed in the least painful way, they agree that once a punishment is reduced, it may be reduced to the lowest level; the rabbis' argument in Note 20 is contradicted. The mention of death by the sword in *Deut.* 13:16 may be an example of the third hermeneutical rule, "a general principle exemplified once".

24 This adapts for the rabbis the argument ascribed to R. Simeon in the preceding paragraph.

25 In this version, the arguments of both parties are completely parallel; each one is consistent within its own system. Both systems are compatible with the biblical verses.

(fol. 24a) **משנה ב**: מִצְוַת הַנִּשְׂרָפִין הָיוּ מְשַׁקְּעִין אוֹתוֹ בַּזֶּבֶל עַד אַרְכּוּבוֹתָיו וְנוֹתְנִין סוּדָרִין קָשָׁה לְתוֹךְ הָרַכָּה וְכוֹרֵךְ עַל צַוָּארוֹ. זֶה מוֹשֵׁךְ אֶצְלוֹ וְזֶה מוֹשֵׁךְ אֶצְלוֹ עַד שֶׁהוּא פוֹתֵחַ אֶת פִּיו וּמַדְלִיק אֶת הַפְּתִילָה וְזוֹרְקָהּ לְתוֹךְ פִּיו וְיוֹרֶדֶת לְתוֹךְ מֵעָיו וְחוֹמֶרֶת אֶת בְּנֵי מֵעָיו. רִבִּי יְהוּדָה אוֹמֵר אַף הוּא אִם מֵת בְּיָדָם לֹא הָיוּ מְקַייְמִין בּוֹ מִצְוַת שְׂרֵפָה אֶלָּא פּוֹתְחִין אֶת פִּיו בִּצְבַת שֶׁלֹּא בְטוֹבָתוֹ וּמַדְלִיק אֶת הַפְּתִילָה וְזוֹרְקָהּ לְתוֹךְ פִּיו וְיוֹרֶדֶת לְתוֹךְ מֵעָיו וְחוֹמֶרֶת אֶת בְּנֵי מֵעָיו. אָמַר רִבִּי אֶלְעָזָר בֶּן צָדוֹק מַעֲשֶׂה בְּבַת כֹּהֵן שֶׁזִּנְּתָה וְהִקִּיפוּהָ חֲבִילֵי זְמוֹרוֹת וּשְׂרָפוּהָ. אָמְרוּ לוֹ מִפְּנֵי שֶׁלֹּא הָיָה בֵית דִּין שֶׁבְּאוֹתָהּ שָׁעָה בָּקִי׃

Mishnah 2: The order of burning: One makes him sink into manure up to his knees[26], puts a stiff cloth into soft ones and winds them around his throat. One person draws in his direction, the other draws in his direction until he opens his mouth[27]. Then one lights a wick[28] and throws it into his mouth that it enters his innards and chars his intestines. Rebbi Jehudah says, in that case, if he would die in their hands they would not have fulfilled the duty of burning[29]; one opens his mouth forcefully with tongs, lights a wire and throws it into his mouth that it enters his innards and chars his intestines. Rebbi Eleazar ben Ṣadoq said, it happened that a Cohen's daughter whored; they surrounded her with firewood and burned her. They told him, because the court at that time was incompetent[30].

26 To make the condemned lose partial consciousness from the methane gas coming from the manure.

27 The two witnesses stand to either side of the condemned and choke him to force him to open his mouth. The coarse cloth is the one which chokes; the soft cloth is to shield the skin from injury. The entire procedure is modelled on the death of Nadab and Abihu (*Lev.* 10:1-6) which is called "burning" (v. 6) but whose bodies were not injured externally (v. 5), and similarly the deaths of the 250 followers of Korah (*Num.* 16:35); Babli 52a.

28 Not really a wick but either liquid metal (Babli 52a) or burning oil.

29 By refusing to open his mouth, the condemned could force his executioners to choke him to death, which is considered the least painful kind of execution.

30 Not incompetent but Sadducee (or in any case anti-Pharisee).

(24b line 45) **הלכה ב**: מִצְוַת הַנִּשְׂרָפִין כול'. וְיִתֵּן קָשָׁה בִּפְנֵי עַצְמוֹ. אָמַר. שֶׁלֹּא יָמוּת. שֶׁכֵּן מָצִינוּ שֶׁבְּשָׁעָה שֶׁסָּתַם חִזְקִיָּהוּ אֶת מוֹצָא מֵימֵי גִיחוֹן הָעֶלְיוֹן בְּמָנִים דַּקִּים סְתָמָן.

Halakhah 2: "The order of burning," etc. Why does one not use the hard cloth alone? One said, that he should not die[31]; as we find that when Hezekias closed the waters of the upper Giḥon spring[32], he stopped it with soft clothing.

31 To avoid strangling him.

32 *2Chr.* 32:2,4.

(24b line 47) רִבִּי קְרִיסְפָּא בְשֵׁם רִבִּי יוֹחָנָן. בִּפְתִילָה שֶׁלְּבַעַץ הִיא מַתְנִיתָא. מָהוּ בִּפְתִילָה שֶׁלְּבַעַץ. רַבָּנִין דְּקֵיסָרִין אָמְרִין. אֵבֶר וְקַסִּיטֵירִיּוֹן מְעוּרָבִין. אָמַר רִבִּי יוֹסֵי בֵּירִבִּי בּוּן. אַתְיָא כְּמָאן דָּמַר. מַדְלִיק אֶת הַפְּתִילָה וְזוֹרְקָהּ לְתוֹךְ פִּיו. בְּרַם כְּמָאן דָּמַר. יוֹרֶדֶת לְתוֹךְ מֵעָיו וְחוֹמֶרֶת אֶת בְּנֵי מֵעָיו. בִּפְתִילָה שֶׁלְּנֶפֶט הִיא מַתְנִיתָא.

[33]Rebbi Crispus in the name of Rebbi Joḥanan: The Mishnah speaks of a *ba`aṣ*[34] wire. What is a *ba`aṣ* wire? The rabbis of Caesarea say, a mixture of lead and tin[35]. Rebbi Yose ben Rebbi Abun said, this follows him who said, "one lights a wire and throws it into his mouth." But for him, who says, "it enters his innards and chars his intestines," the Mishnah speaks of a wick of Naphtha[36].

33 From here to the middle of Halakhah 5 there exists a (frequently lacunary) Genizah text (G) in pure Galilean spelling (L. Ginzberg, *Yerushalmi Fragments*, pp. 258-259).

34 Usually, בעץ is translated as "tin." But since the pure metal appears in the text under its Greek name, the Hebrew word (and its Aramaic counterpart אֲבָצָא) denote the commercial product, a lead-tin alloy.

35 Greek κασσίτερος, ὁ, "tin". In G: וקסיטיר.

36 The Babli, 52a, only recognizes a wire of lead.

(24b line 52) תַּנֵּי. קוֹדֶם לְאַרְבָּעִים שָׁנָה עַד שֶׁלֹּא חָרֵב הַבַּיִת נִיטְלוֹ דִינֵי נְפָשׁוֹת מִיִּשְׂרָאֵל. בִּימֵי רִבִּי שִׁמְעוֹן בֶּן יוֹחַי נִיטְלוּ דִינֵי מָמוֹנוֹת מִיִּשְׂרָאֵל. אָמַר רִבִּי שִׁמְעוֹן בֶּן יוֹחַי. בְּרִיךְ רַחֲמָנָא דְלֵי נָא חֲכִים מֵידוֹן.

[37]It was stated: Forty years before the Temple was destroyed, criminal jurisdiction was removed from Israel, and in the days of Simeon ben Iohai civil jurisdiction was removed from Israel. Rebbi Simeon ben Iohai said, praised be the Merciful, for I am not wise enough to judge.

37 Halakhah 1:1, Notes 31-35.

(24b line 54) אָמַר רִבִּי לְעֶזָר בֵּירִבִּי צָדוֹק. תִּינוֹק הָיִיתִי וְרוֹכֵב עַל כְּתֵיפוֹ דְאַבָּא. וְרָאִיתִי בַת כֹּהֵן שֶׁזִּינָּת וְהִקִּיפוּהָ חֲבִילֵי זְמוֹרוֹת וּשְׂרָפוּהָ. אָמְרוּ לוֹ. תִּינוֹק הָיִיתָ וְאֵין עֵדוּת לְתִינוֹק. כַּד חָמָא הָא מִילְּתָא לָא הֲוָה פָּחוּת מִבֶּן עֶשֶׂר שְׁנִין. כַּד הֲוָה מְהַלֵּךְ עִם רִבִּי לָא הֲוָה פָּחוּת מִן תַּלְתִּין שְׁנִין. דְּלֵית אוֹרְחָא דְגַבְרָא רַבָּא מְהַלֵּךְ עִם בַּר נַשׁ פָּחוּת מִן תַּלְתִּין שְׁנִין. וְתַנֵּי כֵן. אָמַר רִבִּי. מַעֲשֶׂה שֶׁהָיִיתִי אֲנִי בָא וְרִבִּי אֶלְעָזָר בֵּירִבִּי צָדוֹק מִבֵּית שִׁירְיין וְאָכַלְנוּ תְאֵנִים וַעֲנָבִים עֲרַאי חוּץ לַסּוּכָּה.

"Rebbi Eleazar ben Rebbi Ṣadoq said, I was a child riding on my father's shoulder when I saw the daughter of a Cohen who had whored; they surrounded her with firewood and burned her. They told him, you were a child; a child cannot testify."[38] When he saw this, he[39] was no less than ten years old. When he walked with Rebbi, he must have been no less than thirty years old since it is not fitting for a great personality to be accompanied by anybody less than thirty years of age. As we have stated: "Rebbi said, I was coming from bet Sirin with Rebbi Eleazar ben Rebbi Ṣadoq when we ate figs and grapes outside the tabernacle[40].

38 Babli 52b, Tosephta 9:11.

39 This is rather old for a child riding on his father's shoulder. Probably it means "older than 5 years." [More than 150 years separate the burning reported by R. Eleazar ben R. Sadoq I from R. Eleazar ben R. Sadoq II accompanying Rebbi.]

40 On Tabernacles, only full meals have to be eaten in the *sukkah*; snacks may be eaten outside.

(fol. 24a) **משנה ג**: מִצְוַת הַנֶּהֱרָגִין. הָיוּ מַתִּיזִין אֶת רֹאשׁוֹ בַּסַּיִיף כְּדֶרֶךְ שֶׁהַמַּלְכוּת עוֹשָׂה. רִבִּי יְהוּדָה אוֹמֵר, נִיוּוּל הוּא זֶה אֶלָּא מַנִּיחַ אֶת רֹאשׁוֹ עַל הַסַּדָּן וְקוֹצֵץ בַּקּוֹפִיץ. אָמְרוּ לוֹ אֵין מִיתָה מְנוּוֶּלֶת מִזּוֹ.

Mishnah 3: The order of beheading. They were chopping off his head with a sword just as the [Roman] government does. Rebbi Jehudah says, this is ugliness but one puts his head on the block and cuts it with a butcher knife. They told him, there is no death uglier than this.

(24b line 62) **הלכה ג**: מִצְוַת הַנֶּהֱרָגִין כול'. מוֹדֶה רִבִּי יְהוּדָה שֶׁאֵין מִיתָה מְנוּוֶּלֶת מִזּוֹ. אֶלָּא שֶׁאָמְרָה תוֹרָה וּבְחֻקּוֹתֵיהֶם לֹא תֵלֵכוּ׃ אָמַר רִבִּי יוֹחָנָן. וְתַנֵּי כֵן. יִרְצַח הָרוֹצֵחַ. בְּמַה שֶׁרָצַח. יָכוֹל אִם הֲרָגוֹ בְסַיִיף יַהַרְגֶנּוּ בְסַיִיף. בַּמַּקֵּל יַהַרְגֶנּוּ בַמַּקֵּל. נֶאֱמַר כָּאן נְקִימָה וְנֶאֱמַר לְהַלָּן וְהֵבֵאתִי עֲלֵיכֶם חֶרֶב נֹקֶמֶת נְקַם־בְּרִית. מַה נְקִימָה שֶׁנֶּאֶמְרָה לְהַלָּן בְּחֶרֶב. אַף נְקִימָה שֶׁנֶּאֶמְרָה כָּאן מִיתָה בַּחֶרֶב. יָכוֹל יִטְלֶינּוּ מִבֵּין הָאַגַּפַּיִים. נֶאֱמַר כָּאן וּבִעַרְתָּ הָרָע מִקִּרְבֶּךָ׃ וְנֶאֱמַר לְהַלָּן וְאַתָּה תְּבַעֵר הַדָּם הַנָּקִי מִקִּרְבֶּךָ. הַבְעָרָה הַבְעָרָה. עֲרִיפָה עֲרִיפָה. מָה הַבְעָרָה שֶׁנֶּאֶמְרָה לְהַלָּן מוּל הָעוֹרֶף אַף כָּאן מוּל הָעוֹרֶף. מָה עֲרִיפָה שֶׁנֶּאֶמְרָה לְהַלָּן הַתָּזַת הָרֹאשׁ אַף כָּאן הַתָּזַת הָרֹאשׁ.

Halakhah 3: "The order of beheading," etc. [41]"Rebbi Jehudah agrees that there is no death uglier than this but the Torah said[42], *in their statutes you shall not walk.*" Rebbi Joḥanan said, also it was stated thus: *One shall murder the murderer*[43], the way he murdered. I could think that if he killed with a sword, one should kill him with a sword, with a rod one should kill him with a rod? Avenging is written here[5], and there it is written: *I shall bring over you a sword which avenges the vengeance of the Covenant*[6]. Since avenging mentioned there is by the sword, also avenging mentioned here is by the sword. I could think that he[44] should kill him between the arms? It is said here[45], *you shall eliminate the evil from your midst*, and it is said there[46], *you shall eliminate the innocent blood from your midst.* Elimination, elimination;

breaking the neck, breaking the neck[47]. Since elimination here is at the neck, also there it is at the neck. Since breaking the neck there implies chopping off the head, also here chopping off the head.

41 Babli 52b; Tosephta 9:11.

42 *Lev.* 18:3.

43 *Num.* 35:30: *Any homicide; following witnesses one shall murder the murderer.*

44 The avenger.

45 *Deut.* 19:19. Since this refers to perjured witnesses, it includes all kinds of death penalties.

46 *Deut.* 21:9.

47 By the doctrine of invariability of lexemes the meaning of "elimination" must be the same in *Deut.* 19:19 and *Deut.* 21:9. That of "breaking the neck" in *Deut.* 21:4 is defined by "neck" in *Lev.* 5:8. Since elimination in *Deut.* 21 is by breaking the neck, *Deut.* 19:19 also must refer to the neck. Since strangulation is not mentioned in the Pentateuch, the only method of execution to which this may refer is beheading.

(fol. 24a) **משנה ד**: מִצְוַת הַנֶּחֱנָקִין הָיוּ מְשַׁקְּעִין אוֹתוֹ בַּזֶּבֶל עַד אַרְכּוּבּוֹתָיו. וְנוֹתְנִין סוּדָרִין קָשָׁה לְתוֹךְ הָרַכָּה וְכוֹרֵךְ עַל צַוָּארוֹ. זֶה מוֹשֵׁךְ אֶצְלוֹ וְזֶה מוֹשֵׁךְ אֶצְלוֹ עַד שֶׁנַּפְשׁוֹ יוֹצְאָה:

Mishnah 4: The order of the strangled: One makes him sink into manure up to his knees[26], puts a stiff cloth into soft ones and winds them around his throat. One person draws in his direction, the other one draws in his direction until he expires.

הלכה ד: מִצְוַת הַנֶּחֱנָקִין כול'. חֶנֶק לֵית מַשְׁכַּח. אֱמְרַת. הֲרֵי זוֹ מִיתָה בַּתּוֹרָה. כָּל־מִיתָה שֶׁנֶּאֶמְרָה בַּתּוֹרָה סְתָם אֵין אַתְּ רַשַּׁאי לְמוֹשְׁכָהּ לְהַחֲמִיר עָלֶיהָ אֶלָּא לְהָקֵל עָלֶיהָ. דִּבְרֵי רִבִּי יֹאשִׁיָּה. אָמַר לוֹ רִבִּי יוֹנָתָן. לֹא מִפְּנֵי שֶׁהִיא קַלָּה אֶלָּא שֶׁנֶּאֶמְרָה סְתָם. כָּל־מִיתָה שֶׁנֶּאֶמְרָה סְתָם אֵי אַתָּה רַשַּׁאי לְהַחֲמִיר עָלֶיהָ אֶלָּא לְהָקֵל עָלֶיהָ. תָּלוּ אוֹתָהּ בַּחֶנֶק.

Halakhah 4: "The order of the strangled," etc. Strangling? You do not find it[7]. This refers to death penalty in the Torah. For any death penalty mentioned in the Torah with no particular indication, you are not empowered to try to make it more stringent, only to make it less so, the words of Rebbi Josia. Rebbi Jonathan said to him, not because it is the least painful, but because it is mentioned in the Torah with no specific indication. For any death penalty mentioned in the Torah with no particular indication, you are not empowered to try to make it more stringent but only to make it less so; they ascribed this to strangling.

48 Babli 52b.

49 He agrees with R. Simeon that beheading is the least painful.

50 This seems to be a *non sequitur*. The text is confirmed by the Genizah fragment; this forbids emendations. In the Babli (*loc. cit.*), Rebbi Jonathan is quoted as stating that "because it is mentioned in the Torah with no particular indication, it is strangling." This statement is omitted by R. Hananel in his commentary to the Babli.

Probably the text should be interpreted as follows. An unspecified death penalty cannot be one of the three specified ones, otherwise the exact method of execution would have been mentioned. Therefore, one must rely on tradition to specify the method which, however, has to approximate the least painful of the specified ones in severity.

(24c line 3) אָמַרְתָּ. סֶדֶר חֶנֶק כָּךְ הוּא. זֶה מוֹשֵׁךְ אֶצְלוֹ וְזֶה מוֹשֵׁךְ אֶצְלוֹ. כַּהֲנָא בְעָא קוֹמֵי רַב. תַּמָּן אַתְּ מַר. זֶה מוֹשֵׁךְ הֵילָךְ וְזֶה מוֹשֵׁךְ הֵילָךְ. וְכָא אַתְּ מַר. זֶה מוֹשֵׁךְ אֶצְלוֹ וְזֶה מוֹשֵׁךְ אֶצְלוֹ. אָמַר לֵיהּ. תַּמָּן זֶה מִלְּפָנָיו וְזֶה מִלְּאַחֲרָיו. בְּרַם הָכָא דֵּין מִן דֵּין סִיטְרָא וְדֵין מִן דֵּין סִיטְרָא.

You said, the order of strangling is the following: "One person draws in his direction, the other one draws in his direction." Cahana asked before Rav: There[51], you say, "one draws in *one* direction, the other draws in *one* direction." But here, you say, "one draws in *his* direction, the other draws in *his* direction.[52]" He told him, there one is in front, the other in the back. But here, one is on one side, the other one is on the other side.

51 Mishnah *Zavim* 3:2. The sufferer from gonorrhea causes impurity to everything he sits on and everything which is moved either by his force or on which he sits (*Lev.* 15:10). For example, a sufferer from gonorrhea and a pure person sit in the same boat but do not touch at all. The moment the boat moves, the pure person and his garments become impure. This impurity is known as מִדְרָס "[caused by] stepping upon." The Mishnah refers to two persons, one suffering from gonorrhea and one pure, who together are splicing the same rope, working at different ends. Since each of them moves the rope in his direction, the pure person and his garments become impure the moment the impure person moves the rope while the pure one is holding it.

52 Why the change in language?

(fol. 24a) **משנה ה:** אֵילּוּ הֵן הַנִּסְקָלִין. הַבָּא עַל הָאֵם וְעַל אֵשֶׁת אָב וְעַל הַכַּלָּה וְעַל הַזָּכָר וְעַל הַבְּהֵמָה וְהָאִשָּׁה הַמְבִיאָה עָלֶיהָ אֶת הַבְּהֵמָה וְהַמְגַדֵּף וְהָעוֹבֵד עֲבוֹדָה זָרָה וְהַנּוֹתֵן מִזַּרְעוֹ לַמֹּלֶךְ וּבַעַל אוֹב וְיִדְּעוֹנִי וְהַמְחַלֵּל אֶת הַשַּׁבָּת וְהַמְקַלֵּל אָבִיו וְאִמּוֹ וְהַבָּא עַל נַעֲרָה הַמְאוֹרָסָה וְהַמֵּסִית וְהַמַּדִּיחַ וְהַמְכַשֵּׁף וּבֵן סוֹרֵר וּמוֹרֶה.

Mishnah 5: The following are stoned: A male having sexual relations with the mother, or the father's wife[53], or the daughter-in-law, or a male, or an animal; or a female bringing an animal onto herself[54]. Also the blasphemer[55], the worshipper of idols[56], he who gives one of his descendants to the Moloch[57], and the necromancer, and the medium[58]. Also one who desecrates the Sabbath[59], or who curses father or mother[60], or who has sexual relations with a preliminarily married maiden[8], or who leads astray[61], or who seduces[62], or the sorcerer[63], or the deviant and rebellious son[64].

53 Even if she is not his mother, *Lev.* 20:11. One infers from *Lev.* 20:27 that *their blood be on them* means that the punishment is stoning (Halakhah 9).

54 *Lev.* 20:12,13,15,16.

55 *Lev.* 24:23. It is a capital crime only if the Divine Name (which today is unknown) was used in the blasphemy.

56 *Deut.* 17:5.

57 *Lev.* 20:2.

58 *Lev.* 20:27. The necromancer is the person who raises the spirits of the dead; cf. *1S.* 28. The medium is one who incorporates a spirit which predicts the future, speaking from the medium's body, not his mouth.

59 *Num.* 15:36.

60 *Lev.* 20:9.

61 The missionary for another faith who addresses individuals in private; *Deut.* 13:11, cf. Mishnah 16.

62 He acts in public; Halakhah 16.

63 Halakhah 19.

64 *Deut.* 21:21.

(24c line 7) **הלכה ה:** אֵילּוּ הֵן הַנִּסְקָלִין כול'. לָכֵן צְרִיכָה בְּהֶעְלֵם אֶחָד. אֲבָל בִּשְׁנֵי הֶעֱלֵימוֹת. שֶׁכֵּן אֲפִילוּ בְאִשָּׁה אַחַת בָּא עָלֶיהָ וְחָזַר וּבָא עָלֶיהָ בְּהֶעְלֵם אֶחָד. חַייָב עַל כָּל־אַחַת וְאַחַת. רִבִּי שִׁמְעוֹן בְּרֵיהּ דְּרִבִּי הִלֵּל בֶּן פָּזִי בְּעָא קוֹמֵי רִבִּי הִלֵּל בֶּן פָּזִי. מַתְנִיתָא בְאִשָּׁה אַחַת שֶׁיֵּשׁ לָהּ שֵׁמוֹת הַרְבֵּה. אֲבָל אִם הָיוּ נָשִׁים הַרְבֵּה וְהֶעֱלֵימוֹת הַרְבֵּה בְּהֶעְלֵם אֶחָד הוּא. אָמַר לֵיהּ. לָכֵן צְרִיכָה בְּהֶעְלֵם אֶחָד. דְּאִיתְפַּלְּגוֹן. הוּא בְּהֶעְלֵם אֶחָד וְהִיא בַּחֲמִשָּׁה הֶעֱלֵימוֹת. רִבִּי יוֹחָנָן אָמַר. הוּא מֵבִיא קָרְבָּן אֶחָד וְהִיא מְבִיאָה ה' קָרְבָּנוֹת. רִבִּי שִׁמְעוֹן בֶּן לָקִישׁ אָמַר. כְּשֵׁם שֶׁאֵינוֹ מֵבִיא [אֶלָּא][G] קָרְבָּן אֶחָד כָּךְ אֵינָהּ מְבִיאָה אֶלָּא קָרְבָּן אֶחָד. שֶׁלֹּא תֹאמַר. יֵעָשׂוּ נָשִׁים הַרְבֵּה וְהֶעֱלֵימוֹת הַרְבֵּה בְּהֶעְלֵם אֶחָד אֵינוֹ חַייָב אֶלָּא אַחַת. לְפוּם כָּךְ צָרַךְ מֵימַר. חַייָב עַל כָּל־אַחַת וְאַחַת.

Halakhah 5: "The following are stoned," etc. [65]It is necessary in one forgetting[66], but in two forgettings? Since even for one woman, if he had relations with her several times in one forgetting, he is liable for each one[67].

Rebbi Simeon ben Rebbi Hillel ben Pazi asked before Rebbi Hillel ben Pazi: The Mishnah refers to one woman who is forbidden under many names[65]. But if there were many women, or many forgettings, is that in one forgetting[68]? He told him, it is necessary to state for one forgetting, since they disagreed: He acts in one forgetting but she in five forgettings. Rebbi Johanan said, he brings one sacrifice but she brings five sacrifices[69]. Rebbi Simeon ben Laqish said, since he brings [only][70] one sacrifice, she brings only one sacrifice; lest you say that many women, or many forgettings, be treated as one forgetting. Therefore, it is necessary to say[71], he is liable for each one.

65 This Halakhah refers more to Mishnah *Keritut* 1:1 (for which no Yerushalmi exists) than to the present Mishnah which rather serves as a header for the following Mishnaiot (6-19) which take up all cases mentioned in the Mishnah. Since the rules of evidence essentially guarantee that nobody can be executed, it is asserted, and shown in detail in the following Halakhot, that a criminal who escapes the earthly court is condemned by the Heavenly court to extirpation. If a sin punishable by extirpation was committed inadvertently, it can be atoned for by a purification sacrifice. (No sin committed intentionally can be atoned for by a sacrifice.) *Keritut* 1:1 contains a list of 36 sins punishable by extirpation, including those mentioned in the Mishnah here. That the number 36 is mentioned in the Mishnah is interpreted to mean that for each category a separate sacrifice is needed. For example, a person who inadvertently sleeps with a woman who is his mother married to his father has to bring two sacrifices, one for sleeping with his mother and one for his father's wife.

66 It is emphasized repeatedly (*Lev*. 4:13, 5:2,3) that an inadvertent sin, for which atonement by a sacrifice is possible, must involve an element of forgetting, either of the law which forbids the action, or of the identity of the person with whom the forbidden act was committed; this includes ignorance of the law or identity of the person. It is clear that a sacrifice is possible only if the person realizes the criminality of his act, i. e., he came to know the law or the identity. If then he forgets the information again, a new situation is created which is not a continuation of the previous one. This is a major topic of Tractate *Ševu`ot*.

It seems that הֶעֱלֵם, הֶעֱלֵימוֹת are Babylonisms in the text; G writes עֲלֵם, עֲלָמוֹת, יעלמות.

67 It seems impossible to make sense of this sentence. The most probable emendation is to read "two forgettings", see the preceding Note.

68 If in ignorance of the law, he slept with many menstruating women, or with several of his sisters, does this trigger the obligation of one or of several sacrifices? Similarly, if he repeatedly inadvertently slept with the same forbidden woman but in the intervals had realized the criminal character of his deed, does this trigger the obligation of one or of several sacrifices?

69 In the Babli, *Keritutl* 15a, this is a tannaïtic statement. The dissenting opinion is not mentioned there.

70 The word is missing in the Leiden ms., in G only the last א is clearly readable but the reconstruction of the word is quite certain.

71 In the missing Halakhah to *Keritut* 1:1, it is stated that the number of possible cases is stated to stress that each sin represents a different obligation, following R. Johanan. In both questions of Note 68 the answer is that several sacrifices are required.

(24c line 7) אָמַר רִבִּי בּוּן בַּר חִייָה. תַּנֵּי רִבִּי יִשְׁמָעֵאל כֵּן. לֹא תְנַחֲשׁוּ וְלֹא תְעוֹנֵנוּ׃ וַהֲלֹא הַנִּיחוּשׁ וְהָעִינּוּן בִּכְלָל הָיוּ וְיָצְאוּ מִן הַכְּלָל לַחֲלוֹק עַל הַכְּלָל. כְּלָל בְּהִיכָּרֵת וּפְרָט בְּהִיכָּרֵת. מִילְּתֵיהּ דְּרִבִּי יוֹחָנָן אָמְרָה. כְּלָל וּפְרָט הוּא. דָּמַר רִבִּי אַבָּהוּ בְשֵׁם רִבִּי יוֹחָנָן. כִּי כָּל־אֲשֶׁר יַעֲשֶׂה מִכֹּל הַתּוֹעֵבוֹת הָאֵלֶּה וְנִכְרְתוּ וגו'. וַהֲלֹא אֲחוֹתוֹ בִּכְלָל הָיְתָ וְיָצְאת מִן הַכְּלָל לַחֲלוֹק עַל הַכְּלָל. הָתִיב רִבִּי לָעְזָר. וְהָכְתִיב עֶרְוַת אֲחוֹת אִמְּךָ וְעֶרְוַת אֲחוֹת אָבִיךָ לֹא תְגַלֵּה. אָמַר לֵיהּ. לְצוֹרֶךְ יָצָאת לִידוֹן בַּעֲרָיָה. וְהָכְתִיב וְאִ֠ישׁ אֲשֶׁר־יִשְׁכַּ֨ב אֶת־אִשָּׁה דָּוָה וְגִלָּתָה אֶת־עֶרְוָתָהּ֙ אֶת־מְקֹרָ֣הּ הֶעֱרָ֔ה וְה֕וּא גִּילְּתָה אֶת־מְקוֹר דָּמֶיהָ. אָמַר לֵיהּ. לְצוֹרֶךְ יָצָאת לִידוֹן בַּעֲרָייָה. שֶׁלֹּא תֹאמַר. הוֹאִיל וְאֵין חַייָבִין עָלֶיהָ אֶלָּא מִשּׁוּם טוּמְאַת עֲרָייָה לֹא נַעֲשֶׂה בָהּ אֶת הַמְעָרֶה כְגוֹמֵר. לְפוּם כֵּן צָרִיךְ מֵימַר. [חַייָב עַל כָּל־אַחַת וְאַחַת.] וְהָכְתִיב וְאִישׁ אֲשֶׁר יִשְׁכַּב֙ אֶת־דּוֹדָתוֹ עֶרְוַת דּוֹדוֹ גִּלָּה. אָמַר לֵיהּ. לְצוֹרֶךְ יָצָאת לִידוֹן בַּעֲרִירִי. דְּאָמַר רִבִּי יוּדָן. כָּל־אֲתַר דְּתֵימַר עֲרִירִים יִהְיוּ הַוּוֹיָן בְּלֹא וְוֹלָד. וְכָל־אֲתַר דְּתֵימַר עֲרִירִים יָמוּתוּ קוֹבְרִין אֶת בְּנֵיהֶן.

[72]Rebbi Abun bar Hiyya said[73,74]: Rebbi Ismael stated so: *You shall not divine nor cast spells*[75]. Were not divination and spellbinding included in the general class but were mentioned separately to be treated differently from the general case? In general by extirpation, the separate cases for extirpation[76]. A statement of Rebbi Johanan says, it is a case of general case and detail[77], as Rebbi Abbahu said in the name of Rebbi Johanan, *for anybody who would perform any of these abominations will be extirpated*[78], etc. Was not his sister included in the general class[79]? Rebbi Eleazar objected: Was it not written, *the nakedness of your mother's sister and your father's sister you shall not uncover*[80]? He told him, it was stated separately for a reason, to judge it by touching[81]. But is it not written[82]: *A man who would lie with an unwell*

woman, who uncovered her nakedness, he touched her source, and she uncovered the source of her blood? He told him, it was stated separately for a reason, to judge it by touching. That you should not say, since one is guilty about her already by the impurity of touching, we should not treat the one who touched equal to the one who had full intercourse. Therefore, it was necessary to say it[83]. But is it not written[84]: *A man who would sleep with his aunt uncovered his uncle's nakedness*? He told him, it was stated separately for a reason, to judge it by destruction[85], as Rebbi Yudan said, at all places where *they will be destroyed* is mentioned, they will be childless; where *they shall die destroyed* is mentioned, they shall bury their children.

72 This paragraph and the following almost to the end of the Halakhah have a slightly more complete parallel in *Šabbat* 7:2 (9c l.62-9d l.59).

73 In *Šabbat*, there is here a sentence connecting the text to the preceding discussion, not applicable here. This shows that the text here is not a mechanical copy of the text in *Šabbat*.

74 One of R. Ismael's hermeneutical principles is that "a detail which was singled out from a general class was singled out not for itself but as an example for the entire class." In *Šabbat*, R. Abun bar Hiyya is reported here to have stated that according to R. Ismael this holds only for a single detail, not for two or more. (As a statement of R. Johanan see below, Notes 95 ff.).

75 *Lev*. 19:26. Divination is an attempt to predict the future by magical means; spellbinding is practical witchcraft. Both are particular examples of the prohibition of witchcraft (*Ex*. 22:17), but no penalty is indicated.

76 To use witchcraft is a capital crime as indicated in the Mishnah; in the absence of witnesses there is an automatic Divine verdict of extirpation. But the special cases of divination and spellbinding only trigger a verdict of extirpation; they are not cases for the human court. This illustrates R. Ismael's principle. In *Sifra Qedošim Pereq* 6(2), R. Ismael and R. Aqiba identify divination and spellbinding as examples of make-believe witchcraft which according to Mishnah 19 is not punishable by the human court. Automatically, these are separate examples of sins which require a purification sacrifice if done without criminal intent. A person who unintentionally acts as sorcerer, divinator, and spellbinder has to bring three sacrifices.

77 The wording might be slightly misleading. There is a hermeneutical principle (#5 on R. Ismael's list) which states that a general expression followed by particulars only refers to the particulars. This presupposes that both general expression and details are in the same paragraph. For example, *Lev*. 1:2 describes sacrificial animals as *animals, cattle, sheep, or goats*. In the context, "animals" means "cattle, sheep, and goats". In the discussion here, the details are mentioned in paragraphs

other than the one describing the general category. Then one has to find a reason why the details have to be mentioned separately.

78 *Lev.* 18:29. This verse decrees a general verdict of extirpation on any violation of sexual taboos spelled out in *Lev.* 18, whether or not they are criminally punishable.

79 The sister is forbidden in *Lev.* 18:9 but in the chapter about penalties, *Lev.* 20:17, the punishment is reserved for Heaven.

80 A misquote from *Lev.* 18:7,8. It seems that in G the verses were quoted correctly. It is incorrect also in *Šabbat*. It seems from the context that the text in G is a learned scribe's correction of the original which, however, did not refer to *Lev.* 18:7,8 but to *Lev.* 20:19: T*he nakedness of your mother's sister and your father's sister you shall not uncover, for his close relative he touched, their sin they have to carry.* Cf. Babli *Yebamot* 54a.

81 *Lev.* 20:19 makes two statements: The punishment is reserved for Heaven and the sin is committed the moment the genitals of the parties touch, without any penetration. Mishnah *Yebamot* 6:2 extends the equivalence of touching and penetration to all sexual offenses.

82 *Lev.* 20:18. The implications are the same as for v. 19.

83 In G and *Šabbat*: "Therefore, it was necessary to say that he is liable for each one," cf. Note 71. It is possible to justify the addition by noting that *Lev.* 18:29 decrees separate extirpation and, therefore, separate sacrifices for unintentional sin, for each separate category of incest.

84 *Lev.* 20:20.

85 In *Šabbat* there is a reference here to *Lev.* 20:21. This also is missing in G, showing that the text here is secondary to that in *Šabbat*, since *Lev.* 20:20 says *they shall die destroyed* whereas v. 21 notes *they shall be destroyed.* The difference is explained in the following statement by R. Yudan. The Babli (*Yebamot* 55a) applies both statements to both verses.

86 The Amora. His counterpart in the Babli is the third generation Amora Rabba (Rav Abba bar Nahmani).

(24c line 33) אָמַר רִבִּי יוֹסֵי. דּוֹדָתוֹ לְצוֹרֶךְ יָצָאת. לְמָעֵט אֶת אֵשֶׁת אָחִיו מֵאִמּוֹ. מַה טַעְמָא. נֶאֱמַר כָּאן דּוֹדָתוֹ וְנֶאֱמַר לְהַלָּן אוֹ־דוֹדוֹ אוֹ בֶן־דּוֹדוֹ יִגְאָלֶנּוּ. מַה דּוֹדוֹ שֶׁנֶּאֱמַר לְהַלָּן בַּאֲחִי אָבִיו מֵאָבִיו הַכָּתוּב מְדַבֵּר. אַף דּוֹדָתוֹ שֶׁנֶּאֶמְרָה כָאן בְּאֵשֶׁת אֲחִי אָבִיו מֵאָבִיו הַכָּתוּב מְדַבֵּר. אַף אֵשֶׁת אָחִיו לִימְדָה מִדּוֹדָתוֹ. מַה דּוֹדָתוֹ שֶׁנֶּאֶמְרָה לְהַלָּן בְּאֵשֶׁת אֲחִי אָבִיו מֵאָבִיו הַכָּתוּב מְדַבֵּר. אַף אֵשֶׁת אָחִיו שֶׁנֶּאֶמְרָה כָאן בְּאֵשֶׁת אָחִיו מֵאָבִיו הַכָּתוּב מְדַבֵּר. עַד כְּדוֹן כְּרִבִּי עֲקִיבָה. כְּרִבִּי יִשְׁמָעֵאל. תַּנֵּי רִבִּי יִשְׁמָעֵאל. נֶאֱמַר כָּאן אֵשֶׁת אָחִיו וְנֶאֱמַר לְהַלָּן וְאִישׁ אֲשֶׁר יִקַּח אֶת־אֵשֶׁת אָחִיו נִדָּה הִוא. מַה נִידָּה יֵשׁ לָהּ הֵיתֵר אַחַר אִיסּוּרָהּ. אַף אֵשֶׁת אָחִיו [מֵאָבִיו][G] יֵשׁ לָהּ הֵיתֵר [לְאַחַר אִיסּוּרָהּ][G]. יָצָאת אֵשֶׁת אָחִיו מֵאִמּוֹ שֶׁאֵין לָהּ הֵיתֵר אַחַר אִיסּוּרָהּ.

Rebbi Yose said, it was necessary that *his aunt* be mentioned separately, to exclude his mother's brother's wife[87]. What is the reason? It is said here *his aunt*, and it is said there[88], *either his uncle or his uncle's son shall free him*. Since by *his uncle* mentioned there, the verse understands his father's paternal brother, also by *his aunt* mentioned here, the verse speaks of his father's paternal brother's wife. Also *his brother's wife*[89] can be inferred[90] from *his aunt*. Since by *his aunt* mentioned there, the verse speaks of his father's paternal brother's wife, also by *his brother's wife* mentioned here, the verse speaks of his paternal brother's wife. So far following Rebbi Aqiba. Following Rebbi Ismael? Rebbi Ismael stated: It is said here *his brother's wife* and it is said there[91], *a man who would take his brother's wife, she is niddah*[92]. Since a menstruating woman will be permitted after being forbidden, also his [paternal] brother's wife may be permitted [after being forbidden.[93]] This excludes his maternal brother's wife, who cannot be permitted after being forbidden[94].

87 From punishment by loss of children (rejected in the Babli, *Yebamot* 55a).

88 *Lev*. 25:49. Since the subject of the entire Chapter is inheritance, it is understood that only the male line is addressed.

89 Who is forbidden in *Lev*. 18:16.

90 The reading of G and *Šabbat*, לְמֵידָה, seems preferable.

91 *Lev*. 20:21, the penalty clause referring to the prohibition formulated in *Lev*. 18:16.

92 In biblical Hebrew, the meaning of the root נדד is the same as Arabic ندّ "to separate, to disperse". This applies both to the menstruating woman (*Lev*. 18:19), who is forbidden relations with her husband, and to the person excommunicated (מְנֻדֶּה) who is separated from the community. In rabbinic Hebrew, the word נִדָּה is used exclusively for the menstruating woman; this is the reference made here, even though the argument is equally valid for the excommunicated person. (Babli *Yebamot* 54b.)

93 The words in brackets are added from G and *Šabbat*. The menstruating woman *is* permitted after her purification; the brother's wife *may be* permitted, *viz*., if the brother dies childless. In the latter case, "brother" means paternal brother (*Yebamot* 1:1, Note 45).

94 But for whom no punishment is spelled out.

(24c line 44) וְהָא רִבִּי יוֹחָנָן מַקְשֵׁי לָהּ מְנָן תֵּיתֵי לֵיהּ. רִבִּי אַבָּהוּ בְּשֵׁם רִבִּי לָעְזָר בְּשֵׁם רִבִּי הוֹשַׁעְיָה. שְׁנֵי לָאוִין וְכָרֵת אֶחָד לָאוִין חוֹלְקִין אֶת הַהִכָּרֵת. מַה טַעַם. עַל־בְּשַׂר אָדָם לֹא יִיסָךְ וּבְמַתְכֻּנְתּוֹ לֹא תַעֲשׂוּ כָּמוֹהוּ. וְכָתוּב אִישׁ אֲשֶׁר יִרְקַח כָּמוֹהוּ וַאֲשֶׁר יִתֵּן מִמֶּנּוּ עַל־זָר וְנִכְרַת מֵעַמָּיו׃ הֲרֵי כָאן שְׁנֵי לָאוִין וְכָרֵת אֶחָד. לָאוִין חוֹלְקִין אֶת הַהִכָּרֵת. וְעוֹד מִן הָדָא. שְׁמוּאֵל בַּר אַבָּא בְעָא קוֹמֵי רִבִּי זְעוּרָה. וְיֵצְאוּ שְׁלָמִים וִיחַלְּקוּ עַל כָּל־ הַקֳּדָשִׁים בְּטוּמְאָה. אָמַר לֵיהּ.

לְצוֹרֶךְ יָצְאוּ. לְמָעֵט קָדְשֵׁי בֶדֶק הַבַּיִת [לִמְעִילָה][G] שֶׁאֵין חַייָבִין עֲלֵיהֶן מִשּׁוּם פִּיגּוּל וְנוֹתָר וְטָמֵא. וְלָא מַתְנִיתָא הִיא. קָדְשֵׁי הַמִּזְבֵּחַ מִצְטָרְפִין זֶה עִם זֶה לִמְעִילָה וְחַייָבִין עֲלֵיהֶן מִשּׁוּם פִּגּוּל נוֹתָר וְטָמֵא. מַה שֶׁאֵין כֵּן בְּקָדְשֵׁי בֶדֶק הַבַּיִת מִכֵּיוָן שֶׁאֵינָן מִצְטָרְפִין (אֵינָן) חוֹלְקִין. אָמַר רִבִּי חֲנִינָה. וְכֵן הִיא צְרִיכָה לֵיהּ. וְיֵחַלְקוּ וְלֹא יִצְטָרְפוּ.

But Rebbi Johanan himself had a problem: from where does one prove it[95]? Rebbi Abbahu in the name of Rebbi Eleazar in the name of Rebbi Hoshaia: Two prohibitions and one extirpation, the prohibitions split the extirpation[96]. For example[97], *it should not be used to be rubbed on anybody's skin and in its proportions you shall not imitate it*, and it is written, *a person who would compound similarly, or who would put it on a stranger, will be extirpated from his people*, that is two prohibitions and one extirpation. The prohibitions split the extirpation[98]. Also from the following: Samuel bar Abba asked before Rebbi Ze`ura, should not well-being sacrifices, being treated separately, split all *sancta* regarding impurity[99]? He told him, it was necessary that they be treated separately, to eliminate *sancta* destined for the upkeep of the Temple [regarding larceny][100], lest one be liable for them because of mushiness[101], leftovers[102], and impurity. But is that not a Mishnah? "All *sancta* destined for the altar combine with one another with respect to liability for mushiness, leftovers, and impurity[103]," in contrast to *sancta* destined for the upkeep of the Temple[104]. Since they do not combine, they do (not)[105] split[106]. Rebbi Hanina[107] said, what he really questioned, should they not split but combine [108]?

95 This refers to the paragraph before the last, where R. Johanan explained that the sister had a special role in the list of incest prohibitions, to deduce that from the different levels of punishment the blanket decree of extirpation really represents separate decrees for each kind of infraction. In *Šabbat*, the name is Ismael; this may be the correct attribution, cf. Note 124.

96 This answers R. Johanan's question. It is rather frequent to find verses containing multiple prohibitions covered by one mention of extirpation where the context makes it clear that each single infraction triggers extirpation.

97 *Ex.* 30:32,33 regarding the holy oil. Only v. 33 is discussed.

98 A person who inadvertently compounds aromatic oil in the same composition as holy oil and uses it on people has to bring two sacrifices. The argument is repeated in Halakhah 9:1 (end of fol. 26d) and accepted in the Babli, *Makkot* 14b.

99 Impurity of well-being sacrifices, the only ones available to lay people, is treated

at length in *Lev.* 7:11-27. Impurity of sacrifices available to priests is treated in *Lev.* 22:1-16. One should assume that a priest who inadvertently eats a combination of impure well-being and other sacrifices has to bring separate purification sacrifices; but this is not the case.

100 The text in brackets is found in G and in *Šabbat*. While misuse of all kinds of sacrifices is also larceny, it is punishable only if the monetary value of the misuse is at least one *perutah*. Misuse of one half *perutah*'s worth of Temple donations and one half *perutah*'s worth of sacrifices is not punishable.

101 Sacrificing with the intent of eating of the sacrificial meat out of its time and place.

102 Eating of sacrificial meat after its allotted time.

103 This shows that well-being and other sacrifices are equal in the hand of the Cohen.

104 Mishnah *Me`ilah* 4:1. The categories of mushiness, leftovers, and impurity do not apply to monetary gifts to the Temple. Anything donated to the Temple which is not a sacrifice or a temple vessel is sold by the Temple treasurer and thereby reverts to fully profane status.

105 The word is not in G and *Šabbat*; it should be deleted.

106 Somebody committing simultaneous larceny involving gifts to the Temple and sacrifices has to atone separately for the two offenses.

107 G reads: Hinena, preferable for chronological reasons.

108 The question remains unanswered why the rules for well-being are no different from those for other sacrifices even for Cohanim. In *Šabbat*, R. Ḥanina's statement is an assertion that the rules *are* different for well-being and other sacrifices. This would agree with the Babli, *Me`ilah* 15a, that in fact well-being and purification offerings do not combine; the contrary statement of the Mishnah is classified as a rabbinic stringency.

(24c line 55) כָּלַל בַּעֲשֵׂה וּפָרַט בְּלֹא תַעֲשֶׂה. מִילְּתֵיהּ דְּרִבִּי לָעְזָר אָמְרָה. כְּלָל וּפְרָט הוּא. רִבִּי לָעְזָר אָמַר. לוֹקִין עַל יְדֵי חֲרִישָׁה בַּשְּׁבִיעִית. רִבִּי יוֹחָנָן אָמַר. אֵין לוֹקִין עַל יְדֵי חֲרִישָׁה בַּשְּׁבִיעִית. מַה טַעֲמָא דְרִבִּי לָעְזָר. וְשָֽׁבְתָ֣ה הָאָ֔רֶץ שַׁבָּ֖ת לַיי כְּלָל. שָֽׂדְךָ֙ לֹ֣א תִזְרָ֔ע וְכַרְמְךָ֖ לֹ֥א תִזְמֹֽר פְּרָט. הַזּוֹרֵעַ וְהַזּוֹמֵר בִּכְלָל הָיוּ. וְלָמָּה יָצְאוּ. לְהַקִּישׁ אֲלֵיהֶם. אֶלָּא מַה הַזּוֹרֵעַ וְהַזּוֹמֵר מְיוּחָדִין שֶׁהֵן עֲבוֹדָה בָאָרֶץ וּבְאִילָן אַף אֵין לִי אֶלָּא דָבָר שֶׁהוּא עֲבוֹדָה בָאָרֶץ וּבְאִילָן. מָה עֲבַד לָהּ רִבִּי יוֹחָנָן. שְׁנֵי דְבָרִים הֵן. וּשְׁנֵי דְבָרִים שֶׁיָּֽצְאוּ מִן הַכְּלָל חוֹלְקִין. עַל דַּעְתֵּיהּ דְּרִבִּי אֶלְעָזָר אֵינָן חוֹלְקִין. וְאִית לֵיהּ. לַחֲלוֹק אֵינָן חוֹלְקִין הָא לְלַמֵּד מְלַמְּדִין. עַל דַּעְתֵּיהּ דְּרִבִּי יוֹחָנָן אֵינָן מְלַמְּדִין. שַׁנְיָא הִיא שֶׁכָּלַל בַּעֲשֵׂה וּפָרַט בְּלֹא תַעֲשֶׂה. וְאֵין עֲשֵׂה מְלַמֵּד עַל לֹא תַעֲשֶׂה וְאֵין לֹא תַעֲשֶׂה מְלַמֵּד עַל עֲשֵׂה. עַל דַּעְתֵּיהּ דְּרִבִּי לָעְזָר עֲשֵׂה מְלַמֵּד עַל לֹא תַעֲשֶׂה אֲבָל לֹא תַעֲשֶׂה אֵינוֹ מְלַמֵּד עַל עֲשֵׂה. עַל דַּעְתֵּיהּ דְּרִבִּי יוֹחָנָן נִיחָא מוּתָּר לַחְפּוֹר בָּהּ בּוֹרוֹת שִׁיחִין וּמְעָרוֹת. עַל דַּעְתֵּיהּ דְּרִבִּי לָעְזָר מָהוּ לַחְפּוֹר בָּהּ בּוֹרוֹת שִׁיחִין וּמְעָרוֹת. כְּשֵׁם שֶׁאֵין מְלַמְּדִין לְעִנְיָן אִיסּוּר כָּךְ

לְעִנְיָין הֵיתֵר לֹא יְלַמְּדוּ. אָמַר רִבִּי בָּא קַרְתִּיגִינָאָה. טַעֲמָא דְּרִבִּי יוֹחָנָן שֵׁשׁ שָׁנִים֙ תִּזְרַ֣ע שָׂדֶ֔ךָ לֹא בַּשְּׁבִיעִית וְשֵׁשׁ שָׁנִים תִּזְמֹר כַּרְמֶךָ לֹא בַשְּׁבִיעִית. כָּל־ לֹא תַעֲשֶׂה שֶׁהוּא בָא מִכֹּחַ עֲשֵׂה עֲשֵׂה הוּא וְעוֹבֵר בַּעֲשֵׂה. רִבִּי יִרְמְיָה אָמַר. עוֹבֵר בַּעֲשֵׂה. רִבִּי יוֹסֵי אוֹמֵר. אֲפִילוּ בַעֲשֵׂה אֵין בּוֹ. וְהָכְתִיב מָלֵא וְשָׁבְתָה הָאָרֶץ שַׁבָּת לַיי. לְעִנְיָין לֹא תַעֲשֶׂה שֶׁבּוֹ.

יְהוּ לוֹקִין עַל הַתּוֹסֶפֶת. רִבִּי יוֹחָנָן פָּתַר מַתְנִיתָא יָכוֹל יְהוּ לוֹקִין עַל יְדֵי חֲרִשָׁה בַשְּׁבִיעִית. הֲרֵי רִבִּי לָעְזָר פָּתַר מַתְנִיתָא יָכוֹל יְהוּ לוֹקִין עַל אִיסּוּר שְׁנֵי פְרָקִים הָרִאשׁוֹנִים. אִית תַּנָּיֵי תַנֵּי שֵׁשׁ שָׁנִים֙ תִּזְרַ֣ע שָׂדֶ֔ךָ וְשֵׁשׁ שָׁנִים תִּזְמֹר כַּרְמֶךָ. וְאִית תַּנָּיֵי תַנֵּי שָׂדְךָ֙ לֹא תִזְרָ֔ע וגו'. מָאן דָּמַר שֵׁשׁ שָׁנִים֙ מְסַייֵעַ לְרִבִּי יוֹחָנָן. וּמָאן דָּמַר שָׂדְךָ֙ לֹא תִזְרָע מְסַייֵעַ לְרִבִּי לָעְזָר.

מַתְנִיתָא מְסַייְעָא לְרִבִּי לָעְזָר. הִשָּׁמֵר בְּלֹא תַעֲשֶׂה. פֶּן לֹא תַעֲשֶׂה. וְכָתוּב שָׁם תַּעֲלֶה עוֹלוֹתֶיךָ וְשָׁם תַּעֲשֶׂה. שָׁם תַּעֲלֶה זוֹ הַעֲלִייָה. וְשָׁם תַּעֲשֶׂה זוֹ הַשְּׁחִיטָה וּזְרִיקָה. מָה הָעֲלִייָה שֶׁהִיא בַעֲשֵׂה הֲרֵי הִיא בְלֹא תַעֲשֶׂה. אַף שְׁחִיטָה וּזְרִיקָה שֶׁהֵן בַּעֲשֵׂה יְהוּ בְלֹא תַעֲשֶׂה. בְּגִין דִּכְתִיב שָׁם תַּעֲלֶה וְשָׁם תַּעֲשֶׂה. הָא אִילּוּ לֹא כָתַב שָׁם תַּעֲלֶה וְשָׁם תַּעֲשֶׂה אֵין עֲשֵׂה מְלַמֵּד עַל לֹא תַעֲשֶׂה וְאֵין לֹא תַעֲשֶׂה מְלַמֵּד עַל עֲשֵׂה. מָה עֲבַד לָהּ רִבִּי יוֹחָנָן. שֶׁלֹּא תֹאמַר כְּמָה דְּתֵימַר גַּבֵּי שַׁבָּת חָפַר חָרַץ נָעַץ אֵינוֹ חַייָב אֶלָּא אַחַת. וְדִכְווָתָהּ שָׁחַט וְהֶעֱלָה לֹא יְהֵא חַייָב אֶלָּא אַחַת. לְפוּם כָּךְ צָרַךְ מֵימַר. חַייָב עַל־כָּל אַחַת וְאַחַת.

If He stated a general principle as a positive commandment but the detail as a prohibition[109], the word of Rebbi Eleazar is that this is a general principle followed by a detail[110]. [111]Rebbi Eleazar said, one whips for ploughing in the Sabbatical year. Rebbi Joḥanan said, one does not whip for ploughing in the Sabbatical year. What is Rebbi Eleazar's reason? *The Land shall keep a Sabbath for the Eternal*[112], a general principle. *Your field you shall not sow, your vineyard you shall not prune*[113], detail. The sower and the pruner were included in the general case; why were they mentioned separately? To include with them; since the sower and the pruner are particular in that they perform work on the ground or on a tree, I have only what is work on the ground or on a tree. How does Rebbi Joḥanan treat this? They are two different things, and two different details for one general principle do divide. In Rebbi Eleazar's opinion they do not divide[114]. But he holds that because they do not divide, they are for making inferences. In Rebbi Joḥanan's opinion, they are not for making inferences. There is a difference here because He stated a general principle as a positive commandment but the detail as prohibitions. No positive commandment allows inferences for a prohibition and no prohibition allows inferences for a positive commandment.

In Rebbi Eleazar's opinion a positive commandment allows inferences for a prohibition but no prohibition allows inferences for a positive commandment. In Rebbi Johanan's opinion it is obvious that one may dig cisterns, ditches, and caves during it. In Rebbi Eleazar's opinion, may one dig cisterns, ditches, and caves during it? Just as one cannot make inferences for prohibitions, so one should not be able to make inferences for permissions[115]. Rebbi Abba from Carthage said, Rebbi Johanan's reason is *six years you shall sow your field*, not in the Sabbatical; *and six years you shall prune your vineyard*[116], not in the Sabbatical. Any prohibition inferred from a positive commandment is a positive commandment; one violates a positive commandment[117]. Rebbi Jeremiah said, one violates a positive commandment. Rebbi Yose said, there is not even a positive commandment. But is it not written that *the Land shall rest as a repose for the Eternal*? That is for the prohibition implied by it[118].

[119][I could think that] they should be giving lashes for the addition. Rebbi Johanan explains the *baraita*: I could think that one gives lashes for ploughing during the Sabbatical year, but Rebbi Eleazar explains the *baraita*: I could think that one gives lashes for the first two terms[120]. Some Tannaïm state: *Six years you shall sow your field, and six years you shall prune your vineyard*; but some Tannaïm state: *Your field you shall not sow*, etc. He who says *six years* supports Rebbi Johanan; he who says *your field you shall not sow* supports Rebbi Eleazar.

A *baraita* supports[121] Rebbi Eleazar: *Be on guard*, a prohibition. *Lest*, a prohibition. And it is written[122]: *There, you shall offer your elevation offerings and there you shall make. There, you shall offer*, that is the offering; *and there you shall make*, that is slaughtering and sprinkling. Just as offering is a positive commandment and a prohibition, so slaughtering and sprinkling which are positive commandments should be covered by a prohibition. Because it is written *there you shall offer, and there you shall make.* Therefore, if *there you shall offer, and there you shall make* were not written, no positive commandment would allow inferences for a prohibition and no prohibition would allow inferences for a positive commandment. How does Rebbi Johanan handle this? That you should not say as you say referring to the Sabbath: If one dug a hole, made a ditch, or dug to put in a pole, he is guilty only of one offense[123]. Similarly, if he slaughtered and offered, he should be guilty only of one offense; therefore, it was necessary to say, he is liable for every single action[124].

109 The vocalization and, consequently, the interpretation of כלל and פרט as verbs rather than nouns, is from G. Here ends the Genizah fragment.

110 If a pentateuchal verse partially is an exhortation to action and partially a prohibition, it nevertheless forms a logical unit.

111 From here to the end of the Halakhah there also is a parallel in *Kilaim* 8:1, Notes 20-36 (Babli *Mo`ed qaṭan* 3a). The text in *Kilaim* practically is identical with that in *Šabbat*; the text here is slightly abbreviated. The punishment for violating a biblical prohibition for which no penalty is specified is by flogging. The problem is that ploughing is not specifically mentioned in *Lev.* 25.

112 *Lev.* 25:3.

113 *Lev.* 25:4.

114 To require separate atonement if performed inadvertently.

115 For R. Johanan, if ploughing is not sanctionable, digging for other than agricultural purposes certainly is permitted. But for R. Eleazar digging is work on the ground (in the language of his argument) but not in the field (as forbidden in the verse.)

116 *Lev.* 25:3.

117 As such it is not sanctionable; cf. Halakhah 5:3, Note 73.

118 He takes R. Eleazar literally at his word. If *Lev.* 25:3-4 represents a general principle followed by a detail (even if the principle is a positive commandment and the detail a prohibition) then by R. Ismael's hermeneutical rule כְּלָל וּפְרָט אֵין בִּכְלָל אֶלָּא מַה שֶׁבִּפְרָט "general principle followed by detail: the general principle only applies to the detail", nothing not mentioned in the verse is prohibited.

119 This paragraph is slightly shortened from *Kilaim* and *Šabbat*, explained in *Kilaim* 8:1, Notes 26-28. As the other sources show, the first sentence is a rhetorical question from a *baraita* referring to rabbinic additions to Sabbatical prohibitions. The words in brackets represent the introductory formula יָכוֹל added from the parallel sources, "I could think that . . ." which has to be disproved. Since this formula is central to the understanding of the paragraph, one has an additional indication of the secondary character of the text here.

120 The prohibition of agricultural work after the harvest of the preceding year, different for work on the ground or on trees.

121 In both parallels: *disagrees with*. The latter is the correct version as explained at length in *Kilaim* 8:1 Note 29 and refers to *Sifry Deut.* 70-71. The example refers to sacrificing outside the Temple district (or another holy place designated by God) and is missing in *Kilaim*. The statement itself is found in the Babli, *Zebaḥim* 106a.

122 *Deut.* 12:13-14: Be on guard, *and do not offer your elevation sacrifices at any place which you see. Only at the place which the Eternal will choose* . . . there you

shall offer *your elevation sacrifices* and there you shall do *everything which I am commanding you.* This is a general prohibition followed by two specific positive commandments.

123 Sabbath prohibitions are classified into 39 different categories (Mishnah *Šabbat* 7:2). Different actions all of which are classified under the same category are considered one and the same violation of the Sabbath. The activities quoted here are all derivatives of ploughing (Babli *Šabbat* 73b).

124 In the Babli, *Zebaḥim* 107b, according to one opinion this is R. Ismael's position.

(24d line 14) רִבִּי זְעִירָה רַב חִייָה בַּר אַשִׁי בְשֵׁם כָּהֲנָא. הַנּוֹטֵעַ בַּשַּׁבָּת חַייָב מִשּׁוּם זוֹרֵעַ. רִבִּי זְעוּרָה אָמַר. זוֹמֵר כְּנוֹטֵעַ. נָטַע וְזָמַר בַּשַּׁבָּת. עַל דַּעְתֵּיהּ דְּכָהֲנָא חַייָב שְׁתַּיִם. עַל דַּעְתֵּיהּ דְּרִבִּי זְעוּרָה אֵינוֹ חַייָב אֶלָּא אַחַת. כְּלוּם אָמַר רִבִּי זְעוּרָה אֶלָּא זוֹמֵר כְּנוֹטֵעַ. דִּילְמָא נוֹטֵעַ כְּזוֹמֵר. הַכֹּל הָיָה בִכְלָל זְרִיעָה וְיָצָאת זְמִירָה לְהַחֲמִיר עַל עַצְמָהּ. מִפְּנֵי שֶׁיָּצָאת זְמִירָה לְהַחֲמִיר עַל עַצְמָהּ אַתְּ פּוֹטְרוֹ מִשּׁוּם זוֹרֵעַ. הוֹי לֹא שַׁנְייָא. נָטַע וְזָמַר בַּשַּׁבָּת. בֵּין עַל דַּעְתֵּיהּ דְּכָהֲנָא בֵּין עַל דַּעְתֵּיהּ דְּרִבִּי זְעוּרָה חַייָב שְׁתַּיִם.

1 זעירה | ד זעירא חייה | ד חייא זעורה | ד זעירא 2 זומר | ד הזומר 3 זעורה | ד זעירא (twice) זומר | ד הזומר דילמא | ד שמא נוטע | ד הנוטע 4 ויצאת | ד יצאת 6 זעורה | ד זעירא

[125]Rebbi Ze`ira, Rav Ḥiyya bar Ashi in the name of Cahana: He who is planting on the Sabbath is guilty because of sowing. Rebbi Ze`ura said, he who prunes is like one who plants. If he planted and pruned on the Sabbath, according to Cahana he is guilty on two counts, according to Rebbi Ze`ura only on one count. Did not Rebbi Ze`ura say the pruner is like the planter, did perhaps he say the planter is like the pruner? All was included in the category of sowing; pruning was singled out for particular stringency. Because pruning was singled out for particular stringency you want to exempt it because of sowing? This means, there is no difference. If he planted and pruned on the Sabbath, according to both Cahana and Rebbi Ze`ura he is guilty on two counts

125 This paragraph is from *Kilaim* (ד) 8:1, Notes 33-36.

(fol. 24a) **משנה ו**: הַבָּא עַל הָאֵם חַייָב עָלֶיהָ מִשּׁוּם אֵם וּמִשּׁוּם אֵשֶׁת אָב. רִבִּי יְהוּדָה אוֹמֵר אֵינוֹ חַייָב אֶלָּא מִשּׁוּם הָאֵם בִּלְבַד.

Mishnah 6: A person having sexual relations with the mother is guilty because of mother and because of father's wife[126]. Rebbi Jehudah say, he is guilty only because of mother[127].

משנה ז: הַבָּא עַל אֵשֶׁת אָב חַייָב עָלֶיהָ מִשּׁוּם אֵשֶׁת אָב וּמִשּׁוּם אֵשֶׁת אִישׁ בֵּין בְּחַיֵּי אָבִיו בֵּין לְאַחַר מִיתַת אָבִיו בֵּין מִן הָאֵירוּסִין בֵּין מִן הַנִּישּׂוּאִין.

Mishnah 7: A person having sexual relations with the father's wife is guilty because of father's wife and because of married woman, whether during his father's lifetime or after his father's death[128], whether preliminarily married or definitively married.

126 If he committed the incest in ignorance either of the person or the law, he owes two purification sacrifices.

127 He holds that *Lev*. 18:7 only forbids the mother; 18:8 only forbids the step-mother.

128 But if the widowed stepmother is not remarried, he is not guilty for sleeping with an otherwise married woman. Similarly, a man sleeping with his daughter-in-law (Halakhah 8) is not guilty of adultery with a married woman if at the moment of the crime she was not married to anybody. Neither the prohibition of the stepmother nor that of the daughter-in-law are removed by divorce and remarriage to a third party.

(24d line 21) **הלכה ו**: הַבָּא עַל הָאֵם כול'. **הלכה ז**: הַבָּא עַל אֵשֶׁת אָב כול'. אַזְהָרָה לָבֹא עַל הָאֵם מְנַיִין. עֶרְוַת אִמְּךָ לֹא תְגַלֵּה. כָּרֵת מְנַיִין. כִּי כָּל־אֲשֶׁר יַעֲשֶׂה מִכֹּל הַתּוֹעֵבוֹת הָאֵלֶּה וְנִכְרְתוּ הַנְּפָשׁוֹת הָעוֹשׂוֹת מִקֶּרֶב עַמָּם: אַזְהָרָה לָבֹא עַל אֵשֶׁת אָב מְנַיִין. עֶרְוַת אֵשֶׁת־אָבִיךָ לֹא תְגַלֵּה. כָּרֵת מְנַיִין. כִּי כָּל־אֲשֶׁר יַעֲשֶׂה וגו'. עוֹנֶשׁ מְנַיִין. וְאִישׁ אֲשֶׁר יִשְׁכַּב֙ אֶת־אֵשֶׁת אָבִיו עֶרְוַת אָבִיו גִּלָּה מוֹת־יוּמְתוּ וגו'.

Halakhah 6: "A person having sexual relations with the mother," etc. **Halakhah 7**: "A person having sexual relations with the father's wife," etc. From where the warning[129] for a person having sexual relations with the mother? *Your mother's nakedness you shall not uncover.*[130] From where extirpation? *For anybody who would commit any of these abominations, the guilty persons will be extirpated from their people*[131].

From where the warning for a person having sexual relations with the father's wife? *Your father's wife's nakedness you shall not uncover.*[132] From where extirpation? *For anybody who would commit,*[131] etc. Punishment from where? *A man who would sleep with his father's wife, his father's nakedness he uncovered; they shall be put to death,*[133] etc.

129 A prohibition the penalty for which is not spelled out carries a penalty of flogging (*Deut*. 25:2l). For any more serious infraction the pentateuchal style requires that separate verses must spell out (1) the prohibition, (2) the penalty to be imposed by the court, (3) the penalty imposed by Heaven in case the crime was not observed by two blameless adult male witnesses and, therefore, no court case was possible. In case of sexual crimes this would mean that the witnesses have to see the sex act. For a civil case, such as a husband wishing to divorce his wife because of her adultery, without paying her *ketubah*, it is enough for witnesses to testify to her going to a room with another man, locking the door, and extinguishing the lights. But this is not enough for a criminal conviction.

130 *Lev*. 18:7.

131 *Lev*. 18:29.

132 *Lev*. 18:8

133 *Lev*. 20:11. Even R. Jehudah will agree that this verse also refers to the mother. The verse ends: *their blood be on them*. In the next Halakhah it will be determined that this expression implies stoning; cf. Babli 54a.

(fol. 24a) **משנה ח**: הַבָּא עַל כַּלָּתוֹ חַייָב עָלֶיהָ מִשּׁוּם כַּלָּתוֹ וּמִשּׁוּם אֵשֶׁת אִישׁ בֵּין בְּחַיֵּי בְנוֹ בֵּין לְאַחַר מִיתַת בְּנוֹ בֵּין מִן הָאֵירוּסִין בֵּין מִן הַנִּישּׂוּאִין.

Mishnah 8: A person having sexual relations with his daughter-in-law is guilty because of his daughter-in-law and because of a married woman, whether during his son's lifetime or after his son's death[128], whether preliminarily married or definitively married.

(24d line 27) **הלכה ח**: הַבָּא עַל כַּלָּתוֹ כול'. אַזְהָרָה לְבָא עַל כַּלָּתוֹ מְנַיִין. עֶרְוַת כַּלָּתְךָ לֹא תְגַלֶּה. כָּרֵת מְנַיִין. כִּי כָּל־אִישׁ אֲשֶׁר יַעֲשֶׂה מִכֹּל הַתּוֹעֵבוֹת הָאֵלֶּה וְנִכְרְתוּ. עוֹנֶשׁ מְנַיִין. וְאִישׁ אֲשֶׁר יִשְׁכַּב אֶת־כַּלָּתוֹ וגו'.

Halakhah 8: From where the warning[129] for a person having sexual relations with his daughter-in-law? *Your daughter-in-law's nakedness you shall not uncover*.[134] From where extirpation? *For any man who would commit any of these abominations will be extirpated*,[131,135] etc. Punishment from where? A *man who would sleep with his daughter-in-law*[136] etc.

134 *Lev*. 18:15.

135 The verse is slightly misquoted.

136 *Lev*. 20:12.

(24d line 30) תַּנִּיתָהּ הָכָא תַּנִּיתָהּ בִּכְרִיתוּת. נִיחָא בִּכְרִיתוּת. שֶׁהוּא מֵבִיא קָרְבָּן וְחוֹזֵר וּמֵבִיא קָרְבָּן. אִית לָךְ מֵימַר בְּסַנְהֶדְרִין. שֶׁהוּא נִסְקַל וְחוֹזֵר וְנִסְקַל. אָמַר רִבִּי יוּדָן אָבוֹי דְרִבִּי מַתַּנְיָיָה. לְהַתְרָיָיה אִיתְאֲמָרַת. שֶׁאִם הִתְרוּ בוֹ מִשּׁוּם אֵשֶׁת אָב לוֹקֶה. מִשּׁוּם אֵם לוֹקֶה. וְיִתְרוּ בוֹ מִשּׁוּם אֵשֶׁת אִישׁ. אָמַר רִבִּי אָבוּן. תִּיפְתָּר בִּפְנוּיָה.

We have it stated here, we have it stated in *Keritut*[137]. One understands in *Keritut*[138] that he brings one sacrifice and then has to bring a second. What can you say in *Sanhedrin*[139]? That he is stoned and then stoned again? Rebbi Yudan, Rebbi Mattaniah's father, said: explain it for warnings[140]. For if they warned him because of the father's wife, he is hit,[141] because of the mother, he is hit. Could they not also warn him because of a married woman? Rebbi Abun said, explain it if she was unmarried[128].

137 The multiple transgressions committed by one act mentioned in the last three Mishnaiot are also implied by Mishnah *Keritut* 1:1.

138 If the sin was committed inadvertently, one act may require multiple sacrifices for atonement.

139 A person can be executed only once.

140 Since a person can only be convicted if he was warned in appropriate fashion (Halakhah 5:1), he will be convicted for the single transgression about which he had been warned.

141 As the commentaries point out, one cannot translate לוֹקֶה by "being flogged", since one refers to capital crimes.

(24d line 34) תַּמָּן תַּנִּינָן. רִבִּי יְהוּדָה אוֹמֵר. אִם לֹא הָיְתָה אִמּוֹ רְאוּיָה לְאָבִיו אֵינוֹ חַיָּב אֶלָּא אַחַת. הָא אִם הָיְתָה אִמּוֹ רְאוּיָה לְאָבִיו חַיָּב שְׁתַּיִם. רִבִּי אַבָּהוּ בְשֵׁם רִבִּי יוֹחָנָן. לֹא שַׁנְייָא. בֵּין שֶׁהָיְתָה אִמּוֹ רְאוּיָה לְאָבִיו בֵּין שֶׁאֵין אִמּוֹ רְאוּיָה לְאָבִיו אֵינוֹ חַיָּב אֶלָּא אַחַת. טַעֲמֵיהּ דְּרִבִּי יוֹחָנָן. אִמְּךָ הִיא. מִשּׁוּם אִמּוֹ אַתָּה מְחַייְבוֹ. עֲרָה אֶת כָּל־הַפָּרָשָׁה לָאֵם. רִבִּי בּוּן בַּר חִייָה בְּעָא קוֹמֵי רִבִּי זְעִירָא. מָה רָאָה רִבִּי יוֹחָנָן לִתְפּוֹשׂ אֶת הָאֵם וּלְהָנִיחַ אֶת אֵשֶׁת הָאָב. אָמַר לֵיהּ. דְּהוּא סָבַר כְּרִבִּי יִשְׁמָעֵאל. דְּרִבִּי יִשְׁמָעֵאל דָּרַשׁ. עֶרְוַת אֵשֶׁת־אָבִיךָ. בְּזָכוּר הַכָּתוּב מְדַבֵּר. וְאֵין אָבִיו בִּכְלַל הַזָּכוּר. אֶלָּא לְחַייְבוֹ שְׁתַּיִם. דְּתַנֵּי. הַבָּא עַל אָבִיו חַיָּב עָלָיו שְׁתַּיִם. וְנִיתְנֵי. שְׁלֹשִׁים וָשֶׁבַע כְּרִיתוּת בַּתּוֹרָה. רִבִּי מָנָא אָמַר. כָּל־שֵׁם זָכוּר אֶחָד. עֶרְוַת אֵשֶׁת־אָבִיךָ בְּאֵשֶׁת אָב הַכָּתוּב מְדַבֵּר. עֶרְוַת אִמְּךָ זוֹ אִמּוֹ שֶׁהִיא אֵשֶׁת אָבִיו. אִמּוֹ שֶׁאֵינָהּ אֵשֶׁת אָבִיו מְנַיִין. אִמְּךָ הִוא לֹא תְגַלֶּה עֶרְוָתָהּ׃ מָה עֲבַד לָהּ רִבִּי יִשְׁמָעֵאל. פָּתַר לָהּ לְאַחַר מִיתָה. וְלֵית לֵיהּ לְרִבִּי עֲקִיבָה כֵּן עֶרְוַת אָבִיךָ הִיא׃ לֹא שַׁנְייָא בֵּין בְּחַיֶּיהָ בֵּין לְאַחַר מִיתָה. רִבִּי עֲקִיבָה דָּרַשׁ. עֶרְוַת אֵשֶׁת־אָבִיךָ. בְּאֵשֶׁת אָב הַכָּתוּב מְדַבֵּר. עֶרְוַת אִמְּךָ זוֹ אִמּוֹ שֶׁהִיא אֵשֶׁת אָבִיו. אִמּוֹ שֶׁאֵינָהּ אֵשֶׁת אָבִיו מְנַיִין. אִמְּךָ הִוא לֹא תְגַלֶּה עֶרְוָתָהּ׃ מָה עֲבַד לָהּ רִבִּי יִשְׁמָעֵאל. פָּתַר לָהּ לְאַחַר מִיתָה. וְלֵית לֵיהּ לְרִבִּי עֲקִיבָה כֵּן עֶרְוַת אָבִיךָ עֶרְוַת אִמְּךָ. מָה אָבִיךָ כָּל־שֶׁהוּא אָבִיךָ בֵּין לָעוֹנֶשׁ בֵּין לָאַזְהָרָה. אַף אִמְּךָ

כָּל־שֶׁהִיא אִמְּךָ בֵּין לָעוֹנֶשׁ בֵּין לָאַזְהָרָה. לָא מִסְתַּבְּרָה דְּדָרִישׁ אָהֵן קִרְיָיה. אֶלָּא רִבִּי יוּדָה דְּלֵית לֵיהּ אִמּוֹ שֶׁהִיא אֵשֶׁת אָבִיו צָרִיךְ מִידְרוֹשׁ עֶרְוַת אָבִיךָ וְעֶרְוַת אִמְּךָ. מָה אָבִיךָ כָּל־שֶׁהוּא אָבִיךָ בֵּין לָעוֹנֶשׁ בֵּין לָאַזְהָרָה. אַף אִמְּךָ כָּל־שֶׁהִיא אִמְּךָ בֵּין לָעוֹנֶשׁ בֵּין לָאַזְהָרָה. אָמַר רִבִּי זְעִירָה. הָדָא אָמְרָה. לְמֵידִין מִגְּזֵירָה שָׁוָה אֲפִילוּ מוּפְנָה מִצַּד אֶחָד. אָמַר לֵיהּ רִבִּי יוּדָן. לֵית דָּא פְשִׁיטָא עַל דְּרִבִּי עֲקִיבָה. דְּרִבִּי עֲקִיבָה אָמַר. גְּזֵירָה שָׁוָה אַף עַל פִּי שֶׁאֵינָהּ מוּפְנָה.

[142]There, we have stated[143]: Rebbi Jehudah says, if his mother was not fit for his father, he is liable only for one [sacrifice]. Therefore, if his mother was fit for his father, he is liable for two. Rebbi Abbahu in the name of Rebbi Joḥanan: There is no difference. Whether his mother was fit for his father or unfit for his father, he is liable only once. The reason of Rebbi Joḥanan[144]: *Your mother is she*, you find him guilty because of his mother; this directs the entire chapter towards his mother[145]. Rebbi Abun bar Ḥiyya asked before Rebbi Ze`ira: What caused Rebbi Joḥanan[144] to concentrate on the mother and to leave the father's wife aside? He told him, for he argues with Rebbi Ismael, as Rebbi Ismael explained: *Your father's wife's nakedness*[146]; the verse refers to the male. Is not his father included in the category of the male[147]? Only to make him liable twice, as we have stated: A person having sexual relations with his father is doubly liable about him[148]. Then should we not state "thirty-seven extirpations in the Torah"[149]? Rebbi Mana said, all denotations of males are one.

[150]*Your father's wife's nakedness*; the verse refers to the father's wife. *Your mother's nakedness*, that is his mother who is his father's wife. From where his mother who is not his father's wife? *Your mother is she; do not uncover her nakedness*. How does Rebbi Ismael treat this? He explains it to apply after [the father's] death[151]. Does Rebbi Aqiba not explain *she is your father's nakedness*[152]? There is no difference whether during lifetime or after death. Rebbi Aqiba explains: *Your father's wife's nakedness*[146], the verse refers to the father's wife. *Your mother's nakedness*, that is his mother who is his father's wife. From where his mother who is not his father's wife? *Your mother is she; do not uncover her nakedness*. How does Rebbi Ismael treat this? He explains it to apply after [the father's] death[153]. Does not Rebbi Aqiba treat *your father's nakedness, your mother's nakedness*[154]? Since *your father* refers to your father in any capacity[155] both for punishment[156] and

warning, so also *your mother* refers to one's mother in any capacity both for punishment and warning. Is it not reasonable to explain that verse except following Rebbi Jehudah who because he does not accept "his mother who is his father's wife"[157] must explain that *your father's nakedness, your mother's nakedness* refers to your father in any capacity both for punishment and warning, so also *your mother* refers to your mother in any capacity both for punishment and warning. Rebbi Ze`ira said, this implies that one infers from parallel language[158] even if it is free only from one side[159]. Rebbi Yudan said to him[160], this is obvious for Rebbi Aqiba since Rebbi Aqiba infers from parallel language even if it is not free[161].

142 These two paragraphs are partially corrupt. In a few places, the required corrections are obvious; other passages are not so simple. The text was treated at length by M. Assis לפירושה של סוגיא אחת בירושלמי סנהדרין Sinai 99(1986) pp. 110-127. The parallel in the Babli is 53a-54a.

143 In the Yerushalmi תַּמָּן תַּנִּינָן always introduces a Mishnah quote. Already J. N. Epstein in מבוא לנוסח המשנה p. 150 has noted that one should read תַּמָּן תְּנַיִין "there (in Babylonia) one states." The Babylonian *baraita* is quoted in the Babli, 53a.

144 It seems that one has to read "R. Jehudah" since R. Johanan opposes the conclusion of the argument.

145 This is only the end of an argument which can be reconstructed from *Sifra Qedošim Pereq* 9(12). *Lev.* 18:7 reads: *Your father's nakedness and your mother's nakedness you shall not uncover; she is your mother, do not uncover her nakedness.* The unusual wordiness of the verse has to be explained. Later in the paragraph there is disagreement whether *your father's nakedness* refers to homosexual relations or describes a woman other than the mother who had sexual relations with the father. R. Jehudah opts for the first alternative. The mother then is singled out; she is equally forbidden whether she is or ever was his father's wife or not, just as the father is forbidden whether he ever was married to his mother or not. This excludes any possibility to charge relations with her as father's wife as a separate crime.

146 Obviously one has to read *your father's nakedness* (v. 7) instead of a quote from v.8.

147 Since homosexual intercourse also is a capital crime.

148 Babli 54a; Tosaphot *s. v.* הבא.

149 Mishnah *Keritut* 1:1 lists 36 separate cases of extirpation; homosexual acts with the father are not listed.

150 This text is repeated later as R. Aqiba's opinion. Since R. Ismael was quoted as opposing this interpretation, it is not his opinion. The text is dittography from the following.

151 Why is the mother mentioned twice, once in parallel with the father and once separately?

152 *Lev*. 18:8, referring to the stepmother.

153 Dittography from above.

154 M. Assis here sees a lacuna referring to the earlier statement that the mother remains equally forbidden whether or not the father is alive. This is not a necessary inference.

155 Whether married, seducer, rapist or paying for sexual services.

156 Punishment is spelled out in *Lev*. 20:11, warning in 18:7.

157 He rejects the interpretation that the first mention of *your mother* in v. 7 refers to the father's wife, the second mention to a mother not married to his father.

158 גְּזֵירָה שָׁוָה "equal cut" is the transfer of rules from one law to another if identical language was used. The majority opinion accepts inferences from "equal cut" only if (a) there exists a tradition that the words in question were written for this purpose and (b) no other inferences are drawn from the expressions in question (Babli *Niddah* 22b). Property (b) is meant if an expression is called "free". The equal cut here is the use of *your father's nakedness* both in v.7 and v.8. As we have seen, in v.7 the expression clearly is not "free".

159 M. Assis rightly points out that it is not free even in v.8 since the expression is used to forbid the stepmother after the father's death.

160 As M. Assis points out, the statement also is quoted in *Yoma* 8:3 (45a l. 48) where R. Yudan's statement is an independent remark. Since R. Yudan lived a generation after R. Ze`ira, the *Yoma* version has to be accepted.

161 This statement is unknown to Babylonian sources; the statement of the Babylonian R. Ze`ira is found in the Babli, *Šabbat* 64a, *Niddah* 22b.

(24d line 60) רִבִּי יִרְמְיָה בָעֵי. הַבָּא עַל אִמּוֹ מָהוּ שֶׁיְּהֵא חַייָב מִשֵּׁם אֵשֶׁת אִישׁ. תָּא חֲמִי. אִילּוּ בָא אַחֵר עָלֶיהָ חַייָב מִשּׁוּם אֵשֶׁת אִישׁ בְּנָהּ לֹא כָל־שֶׁכֵּן. הָתִיב רִבִּי יוֹסֵי. הֲרֵי חוֹרְגָהּ הֲרֵי הוּא חַייָב עָלֶיהָ מִשּׁוּם אֵשֶׁת אִישׁ. וּבְנָהּ אֵינוֹ חַייָב עָלֶיהָ מִשּׁוּם אֵשֶׁת אִישׁ. דְּתַנֵּי. אַף בִּשְׁאָר כָּל־הָעֲרָיוֹת כֵּן. חֲמוֹתוֹ וְאֵשֶׁת אִישׁ אַתְּ תּוֹפְשׂוֹ מִשּׁוּם חֲמוֹתוֹ. כַּלָּאוֹ וְאֵשֶׁת אִישׁ אַתְּ תּוֹפְשׂוֹ מִשּׁוּם כַּלָּתוֹ. אֲחוֹתוֹ וְאֵשֶׁת אִישׁ אַתְּ תּוֹפְשׂוֹ מִשּׁוּם אֲחוֹתוֹ. מַבְרִיחוֹ מִן הַחֲמוּרָה וּמְקַנְתְּרוֹ בַקַּלָּה לֵית יְכִיל. דְּתַנֵּי. הַבָּא עַל אֲחוֹתוֹ חַייָב עָלֶיהָ מִשּׁוּם אֲחוֹתוֹ וּמִשּׁוּם בַּת אֵשֶׁת אָבִיו. רִבִּי יוֹסֵי בֵּירִבִּי יוּדָה אוֹמֵר. הַבָּא עַל אֲחוֹתוֹ אֵינוֹ חַייָב עָלֶיהָ אֶלָּא מִשּׁוּם שֵׁם אֶחָד בִּלְבַד. וְכֵן הַבָּא עַל כַּלָּתוֹ. רִבִּי יִרְמְיָה רִבִּי אַבָּהוּ בְשֵׁם רִבִּי יוֹחָנָן. אַתְיָיא דְרִבִּי יוֹסֵי בֵּירִבִּי יוּדָה בְשִׁיטַּת רִבִּי יוּדָה אָבִיו. כְּמַה דְרִבִּי יוּדָה תוֹפֵשׂ שֵׁם רִאשׁוֹן. כֵּן רִבִּי יוֹסֵי בֵּירִבִּי יוּדָה תוֹפֵשׂ שֵׁם רִאשׁוֹן. חָזַר רִבִּי יִרְמְיָה רִבִּי אַבָּהוּ בְשֵׁם רִבִּי יוֹחָנָן. לֵית לְרִבִּי יוֹסֵי בֵּירִבִּי יוּדָה בְשִׁיטַּת רִבִּי יוּדָה אָבִיו. תַּמָּן אִמּוֹ בְלֹא אֵשֶׁת אָבִיו חַייָב. אֵשֶׁת אָבִיו בְּלֹא אִמּוֹ חַייָב. בְּרַם הָכָא מָצִינוּ בַּת אֵשֶׁת אָבִיו בְּלֹא אֲחוֹתוֹ הוּא מוּתָּר בָּהּ.

Rebbi Jeremiah asked: Is a person having sexual relations with his mother guilty [of adultery] with her as a married woman[162]? Come and see: if a third person had sexual relations with her, would he not be guilty [of adultery] with her as a married woman? Her son not so much more? Rebbi Yose objected: is not her stepson guilty [of adultery] with her as a married woman, but her son is not guilty [of adultery] with her as a married woman[163]? As we have stated:[164] Also with all other cases of incest and adultery the situation is the same. His mother-in-law as a married woman, you catch him because of his mother-in-law[165]. His daughter-in-law as a married woman, you catch him because of his daughter-in-law[166]. His sister as a married woman, do you catch him because of his sister? You smuggle him away from the serious crime and strike him for the easier one[167]; this you cannot do as we have stated: A person having sexual relations with his sister is liable because of her as his sister and as a daughter of his father's wife[168]. Rebbi Yose ben Rebbi Jehudah says, a person having sexual relations with his sister[169] is only liable because of her as his sister; the same is true for his daughter-in-law. Rebbi Jeremiah, Rebbi Abbahu in the name of Rebbi Johanan: Rebbi Yose ben Rebbi Jehudah follows the argument of his father Rebbi Jehudah. Just as Rebbi Jehudah accepts the description mentioned first, so Rebbi Yose ben Rebbi Jehudah accepts the description mentioned first. Rebbi Jeremiah, Rebbi Abbahu in the name of Rebbi Joḥanan turned around: Rebbi Yose ben Rebbi Jehudah does not follow the argument of his father Rebbi Jehudah. There he is liable because of his mother, who is not his father's wife; he is liable because of his father's wife who is not his mother. But here we find that he is permitted his father's wife's daughter, who is not his sister[170].

162 This is a question only for R. Jehudah; for the majority it already was answered positively, Note 128.

163 To make sense of this objection, one has to read אֵשֶׁת אָב "the father's wife" instead of אֵשֶׁת אִישׁ "a married woman". R. Jehudah in the Mishnah explicitly declares the prohibition of the father's wife inapplicable to the mother.

164 A similar text is in Tosephta 10:2.

165 The mother-in-law is forbidden as the wife's mother (*Lev.* 18:17); the penalty for the willful crime is burning (20:14), more serious than strangling, the penalty for adultery (20:10).

166 The penalty is stoning (20:10). Even though the question here is about the number of sacrifices due for an unintended crime, the more serious crime is the only one counted. But, naturally, if in case of intentional crime the warning was given

only about adultery, not about any incestuous aspect, the perpetrator is tried for adultery. This *baraita* contradicts the Mishnah.

167 Adultery is a capital crime; sleeping with one's sister is punishable only by Heaven, not the human court.

The verb קנתר used here is Greek κεντρόω "to strike with a stick" (to goad an animal.)

168 The sister is always characterized as *your father's daughter or your mother's daughter* (18:9,20:17), describing the full sister or the maternal half-sister, or *your father's wife's daughter from your father* (18:11), describing the paternal half-sister. It seems that there is no biblical penalty attached to relations with the paternal extramarital half-sister. Babli *Yebamot* 22b.

169 The unmarried sister.

170 Children from previous marriages who are not related to one another are encouraged to marry. Rav was the son of R. Hiyya's unrelated half-brother and half-sister from previous marriages of his parents.

(fol. 24a) **משנה ט**: הַבָּא עַל הַזָּכָר וְעַל הַבְּהֵמָה וְהָאִשָּׁה הַמְּבִיאָה אֶת הַבְּהֵמָה. אִם אָדָם חָטָא בְּהֵמָה מֶה חָטָאת. אֶלָּא לְפִי שֶׁבָּאת לְאָדָם תַּקָּלָה עַל יָדָהּ לְפִיכָךְ אָמַר הַכָּתוּב תִּיסָּקֵל. דָּבָר אַחֵר שֶׁלֹּא תְהֵא הַבְּהֵמָה עוֹבֶרֶת בַּשּׁוּק וְיֹאמְרוּ זוֹ הִיא שֶׁנִּסְקַל אִישׁ פְּלוֹנִי עַל יָדֶיהָ:

Mishnah 9: A man who had sexual relations with a male or an animal, or a woman who brings an animal [upon herself][171]. If a human sinned, what did the animal sin[172]? But because it caused a mishap to a human, therefore the verse decreed that it should be stoned. Another explanation: Lest the animal be seen in public and people say, this is the one because of which X was stoned.

171 These are to be stoned, Mishnah 5.

172 *Lev*. 20:15 decrees that a male who had relations with an animal shall be killed together with the animal, while v. 16 decrees that a woman who had relations with an animal shall be stoned together with the animal. The two verses are considered a unit, so that *killing* in v. 15 is read as *stoning*.

(24d line 76) **הלכה ט**: הַבָּא עַל הַזָּכוּר. אַזְהָרָה לָבֹא עַל הַזְּכוּר מְנַיִין. וְאֶת־זָכָר לֹא תִשְׁכַּב מִשְׁכְּבֵי אִשָּׁה. כָּרֵת מְנַיִין. כִּי כָּל־אֲשֶׁר יַעֲשֶׂה מִכֹּל הַתּוֹעֵבוֹת הָאֵלֶּה וְנִכְרְתוּ וגו׳: עוֹנֶשׁ מְנַיִין. וְאִישׁ אֲשֶׁר יִשְׁכַּב אֶת־זָכָר מִשְׁכְּבֵי אִשָּׁה תּוֹעֵיבָה עָשׂוּ שְׁנֵיהֶם מוֹת יוּמָתוּ דְּמֵיהֶם בָּם: אַתְּ יְלִיף דְּמֵיהֶם הָךְ מִדְּמֵיהֶם בָּם. עַד כְּדוֹן לַשּׁוֹכֵב. לַנִּשְׁכָּב מְנַיִין. וְאֶת־זָכָר לֹא תִשְׁכַּב מִשְׁכְּבֵי אִשָּׁה.

קְרֵי בֵיהּ. לֹא תִישַּׁכֵּב. עַד כְּדוֹן כְּרִבִּי עֲקִיבָה. כְּרִבִּי יִשְׁמָעֵאל. לֹא־יִהְיֶה קָדֵשׁ מִבְּנֵי יִשְׂרָאֵל׃. כָּרֵת לַנִּשְׁכַּב כְּרִבִּי יִשְׁמָעֵאל מְנַיִין. רִבִּי יִרְמְיָה בְשֵׁם רִבִּי אַבָּהוּ. נֶאֱמַר כָּאן קָדֵשׁ וְנֶאֱמַר לְהַלָּן וְגַם־קָדֵשׁ הָיָה בָאָרֶץ. אַתְּ לָמֵד קָדֵשׁ מִקָּדֵשׁ וְקָדֵשׁ מִתּוֹעֵבָה. רִבִּי חִייָה בַּר אָדָא בְשֵׁם רִבִּי חֲנִינָה. תּוֹעֵיבָה מִתּוֹעֵיבָה. אָמַר רִבִּי יוֹסֵי בֵּרִבִּי בּוּן. מַתְנִיתָה אָמְרָה כֵן. תּוֹעֵבָה עָשׂוּ שְׁנֵיהֶם. שְׁנֵיהֶם בִּסְקִילָה. שְׁנֵיהֶם בְּאַזְהָרָה. שְׁנֵיהֶן בְּהִכָּרֵת.

Halakhah 9: "A man who had sexual relations with a male." From where the warning[129] for a person having sexual relations with a male[173]? *With a male you shall not sleep in women's ways*[174]. From where extirpation? *For anybody who would commit any of these abominations will be extirpated*[131,135], etc. Punishment from where? *A man who would sleep with a male in women's ways, an abomination did both of them commit; they shall be put to death; their blood be on them*[175]. You learn *their blood be on them* from *their blood be on them*[15]. That is for the active one. For the passive one from where? *With a male you shall not sleep in women's ways*, read: *to be slept with*[176]. So far following Rebbi Aqiba. Following Rebbi Ismael? *There shall be no qadeš among the sons of Israel*[177]. From where extirpation for the passive homosexual following Rebbi Ismael? Rebbi Jeremiah in the name of Rebbi Abbahu. It says here *qadeš* and it says there, *also a qadeš was in the land*[178]. You learn *qadeš* from *qadeš* and *qadeš* from *abomination*[179]. Rebbi Ḥiyya bar Ada in the name of Rebbi Ḥanina: *Abomination* from *abomination*[180]. Rebbi Yose ben Rebbi Abun said, a *baraita*[181] states this: *Both committed an abomination*[174]. Both are stoned, both are subject to warning, both by extirpation.

173 The form זָכוּר denotes, if not the penis, then the male as appendix to his sex organ.

174 *Lev.* 18:22. A general parallel to this paragraph is in the Babli, 54b.

175 *Lev.* 20:13.

176 The unvocalized text תשכב can be read either with the masoretes as active תִּשְׁכַּב "you shall sleep" or as passive תִּשָּׁכֵב "you shall be slept with". The nonstandard vocalization in the text is from the ms. (Babli 54b).

177 *Deut.* 23:18. The identification of the *qadeš* as the male prostitute follows later from the verse in *Kings*.

178 *1K.* 14:24.

179 It is assumed that *qadeš* means the same in both verses. Also, *qadeš* must refer to the male since the feminine form *qedešah* is explicitly mentioned in *Deut.* 23:18. *1K.* 14 continues: *They did all the* abominations *of the peoples whom the Eternal had uprooted from before the Children of Israel.*

These *abominations* are referred to in *Lev.* 18:29 and the only abominations unique to a male are homosexuality and active bestiality. In the Babli, 54b, both R. Ismael's and R. Aqiba's statements are quoted as *baraitot*; partially also in *Sifra Qedošim Pereq* 9(12).

180 In *Lev.*20, the expression *abomination* is only used for the homosexual. This implies that the *qadeš* in *1K.* 14:24, and therefore in *Deut.* 23:18 is engaged in homosexual acts.

181 Not recorded elsewhere.

(25c line 11) אַזְהָרָה לָבֹא עַל הַבְּהֵמָה מְנַיִין. וּבְכָל־בְּהֵמָה לֹא־תִתֵּן שְׁכָבְתְּךָ לְטָמְאָה־בָהּ. כָּרֵת מְנַיִין. כִּי כָּל־אֲשֶׁר יַעֲשֶׂה מִכֹּל הַתּוֹעֵבוֹת הָאֵלֶּה וְנִכְרְתוּ וגו׳: עוֹנֶשׁ מְנַיִין. וְאִישׁ אֲשֶׁר יִתֵּן שְׁכָבְתּוֹ בִּבְהֵמָה מוֹת יוּמָת: אַתְּ יְלִיף דְּמֵיהֶם בָּם מִדְּמֵיהֶם בָּם. עַד כְּדוֹן כְּרִבִּי עֲקִיבָה. כְּרִבִּי יִשְׁמָעֵאל. רִבִּי יִשְׁמָעֵאל מִן אַתְרֵיהּ וְרִבִּי עֲקִיבָה מִן אַתְרֵיהּ. כָּרֵת לַנִּשְׁכָּב עַל דְּרִבִּי יִשְׁמָעֵאל לֵית מַשְׁכַּח. עוֹנֶשׁ לַנִּשְׁכָּב בֵּין עַל דְּרִבִּי יִשְׁמָעֵאל בֵּין עַל דְּרִבִּי עֲקִיבָה לֵית מַשְׁכַּח. וּכְתִיב זֹבֵחַ לָאֱלֹהִים יָחֳרָם. מַה זֶּה בִסְקִילָה וְכָרֵת אַף זֶה בִסְקִילָה וְכָרֵת. מַה נַפְקָא מִבֵּינֵיהוֹן. שָׁכַב אֶת הַזָּכוּר וְנִשְׁכַּב מִמֶּנּוּ. עַל דַּעְתֵּיהּ דְּרִבִּי יִשְׁמָעֵאל אֵינוֹ חַייָב אֶלָּא אַחַת. עַל דַּעְתֵּיהּ דְּרִבִּי עֲקִיבָה חַייָב שְׁתַּיִם. שָׁכַב אֶת הַבְּהֵמָה וְנִשְׁכַּב מִמֶּנָּהּ. בֵּין עַל דַּעְתֵּיהּ דְּרִבִּי עֲקִיבָה בֵּין עַל דַּעְתֵּיהּ דְּרִבִּי יִשְׁמָעֵאל חַייָב שְׁתַּיִם. שָׁכַב אֶת הַזָּכוּר וְאֶת הַבְּהֵמָה חַייָב שְׁתַּיִם. נִשְׁכַּב מִן הַזָּכוּר וּמִן הַבְּהֵמָה חַייָב שְׁתַּיִם. שָׁכַב שְׁנֵי זְכָרִים כְּאַחַת. מֵאַחַר שֶׁמִּתְחַייְבִין עַל יָדוֹ שְׁנַיִם חַייָב שְׁתַּיִם. נִשְׁכַּב מִשְּׁנֵי זְכָרִים כְּאַחַת. מֵאַחַר שֶׁמִּתְחַייְבִים עַל יָדוֹ שְׁנַיִם חַייָב שְׁתַּיִם. תַּנֵּי. הַזָּכוּר לֹא עָשָׂה בוֹ הַקָּטָן כְּגָדוֹל וְהַבְּהֵמָה עָשָׂה בָהּ הַקְּטַנָּה כִּגְדוֹלָה. אָמַר רִבִּי לָעְזָר. לְעוֹלָם אֵינוֹ מִתְחַייֵב עָלֶיהָ עַד שֶׁתְּהֵא בַּת שָׁלֹשׁ שָׁנִים וְיוֹם אֶחָד.

From where the warning[129] for a person having sexual relations with an animal? *Do not give your emission into an animal to defile yourself by it*[182]. From where extirpation? *For anybody who would commit any of these abominations will be extirpated*[131,135], etc. Punishment from where? *A man who would sleep with a animal shall be put to death*[183]. You infer *their blood be on them* from *their blood be on them*[15,184]. So far following Rebbi Aqiba. Following Rebbi Ismael? Rebbi Ismael from his source[179] and Rebbi Aqiba from his source[185]. Extirpation for a male passive partner is not found for Rebbi Ismael[186]. Punishment for a male passive partner is not found for Rebbi Ismael or Rebbi Aqiba[187], but it is written: *One who sacrifices to the forces of nature shall be banned.* Since this one is in for stoning and extirpation, also that one is in for stoning and extirpation[188]. What is the difference between them? If one had active homosexual relations followed by passive ones, in

Rebbi Ismael's opinion he is liable only once; in Rebbi Aqiba's opinion he is liable twice[189]. If one had active relations with an animal followed by passive ones. Both in Rebbi Aqiba's as in Rebbi Ismael's opinions he is liable twice[190]. If he had active homosexual relations with both a male and an animal he is liable twice. If he had passive homosexual relations with both a male and an animal he is liable twice. If he had simultaneous active sexual relations with two males, since both of them became guilty because of him, he is liable twice. If he had simultaneous passive sexual relations with two males, since both of them became guilty because of him, he is liable twice

It was stated: For males, an underage boy does not have the status of an adult[191]; a young animal has thc status of a fully grown one. Rebbi Eleazar said, he cannot become liable because of it unless it be three years and one day of age[192].

182 *Lev*. 18:23. The entire paragraph has a parallel in the Babli, 54b.

183 *Lev*.20:15. The corresponding verse for a woman is 20:16.

184 The expression is used only in v. 16. It is implied that the punishment for male bestiality cannot be less than that of female bestiality.

185 R. Ismael includes bestiality in the actions of a *qadeš*. R. Aqiba always refers to *Lev*. 18:29.

186 The Babli disagrees and finds the passive participant in bestiality in *Ex*. 22:18.

187 In *Lev*. 20.

188 The worshipper of the forces of nature is banned *Ex*. 22:19, but as adherent of foreign worship he is stoned. It is implied that the death penalty decreed in the preceding verse, *anybody lying with an animal shall be put to death*, for the passive participant in bestiality also must be executed by stoning.

189 In the Babli, 54b, the attributions are switched. One has to follow the classical commentaries in correcting the Yerushalmi following the Babli since, as explained in Notes 175-178, R. Aqiba finds the prohibition of active and passive homosexuality in the same verse whereas R. Ismael defines the passive homosexual as *qadeš*. Therefore, combined active and passive homosexual activity violates one verse for R. Aqiba, two for R. Ismael.

190 For both R. Aqiba and R. Ismael both *Lev*. 18:22 (or 23) and *Ex*. 22:18 are violated. The Babli disagrees, 54b.

191 Sexual relations with males under the age of nine years and one day, and females under three years and one day, are not considered as sexual activities; cf. *Ketubot* 1:3 Notes 147,152.

192 This does not refer to bestiality but to homosexuality. Homosexual relations of a male with an underage boy are not punishable unless the boy is at least three

years and one day of age, i. e., that a valid sex act would have been performed if the child had been a girl. In the Babli, 54b/55a, Samuel derives this from *Lev.* 18:22 where homosexual acts are called *lyings in woman's way*.

(25a line 28) רִבִּי בּוּן בַּר חִייָה בְּעָא מֵרִבִּי זְעִירָא. מָה רָאָה רִבִּי יִשְׁמָעֵאל וְרִבִּי עֲקִיבָה לֵיחָלֵק בִּזְכוּר וּבִבְהֵמָה וּבִשְׁאָר כָּל־הָעֲרָיוֹת לֹא נֶחְלְקוּ. אָמַר לֵיהּ. שֶׁבְּכָל־הָעֲרָיוֹת כָּתוּב בָּהֶן שְׁאֵר בָּשָׂר וְאֵילּוּ אֵין כָּתוּב בָּהֶן שְׁאֵר בָּשָׂר. הָתִיבוּן. הֲרֵי נִידָּה אֵין כָּתוּב בָּהּ שְׁאֵר בָּשָׂר וְנֶחְלְקוּ עָלֶיהָ. רִבִּי יִרְמְיָה בְּשֵׁם רִבִּי אַבָּהוּ. מִכֵּיוָן דִּכְתִיב קְרֵיבָה קְרֵיבָה. כְּמִי שֶׁכּוּלְּהֶם כָּאן וְכוּלְּהֶם כָּאן. רִבִּי חִייָא בַּר אָדָא בְּשֵׁם רִבִּי חֲנִינָה. וְאֶל־אִשָּׁה בְּנִדַּת טוּמְאָתָהּ לֹא תִקְרַב לְגַלּוֹת עֶרְוָתָהּ׃ אָמַר רִבִּי יוֹסֵי בֵּירִבִּי בוּן. הִיא בַּל תִּקְרַב הִיא בַּל תְּגַלֶּה.

Rebbi Abun bar Ḥiyya asked of Rebbi Ze`ira: For what reason did Rebbi Ismael and Rebbi Aqiba disagree about a male and an animal but did not disagree about any incest prohibition[193]? He told him, because for all incest prohibitions it is written *blood relative,*[194] and about these it is not written *blood relative.* They objected: About the menstruating woman it is not written *blood relative*; did they disagree about her[195]? Rebbi Jeremiah in the name of Rebbi Abbahu: For it is written *approach, approach*; it is as if all were here and there[196]. Rebbi Ḥiyya bar Aba in the name of Rebbi Ḥanina: *To the wife in the separation of her impurity you shall not come near to uncover her nakedness*[197]. Rebbi Yose ben Rebbi Abun said, "not to come near" is "not to uncover.[198]"

193 For all other sexual prohibitions they agree that the warnings and punishments equally apply to both partners.

194 The introductory clause *Lev.* 18:6: *No human shall come near to his blood relative to uncover nakedness* refers to both sexes. The detailed prohibitions always are formulated for the male and mention the female's nakedness, but here nakedness is mentioned without any pronoun, masculine or feminine.

195 Both agree that for both partners the warning is *Lev.* 18:19 and the punishment, explicitly for both sexes, is 20:18.

196 The singular in 18:19 is equivalent to the plural used in 18:6; it is as if "blood relative" were written there.

197 *Lev.* 18:19. The verse seems to refer exclusively to the male; it is quoted as an objection.

198 Since "not to uncover" is used in 20:18 explicitly for both sexes, "not to come near" in 18:19 also must apply to both sexes.

(25a line 35) אַזְהָרָה לָאִשָּׁה הַמֵּבִיאָה אֶת הַבְּהֵמָה עָלֶיהָ מְנַיִין. וְאִשָּׁה לֹא־תַעֲמֹד לִפְנֵי בְהֵמָה לְרִבְעָהּ תֶּבֶל הוּא׃ כָּרֵת מְנַיִין. כִּי כָּל־אֲשֶׁר יַעֲשֶׂה מִכֹּל הַתּוֹעֵבוֹת הָאֵלֶּה וְנִכְרְתוּ׃ עוֹנֶשׁ מְנַיִין. וְאִשָּׁה אֲשֶׁר תִּקְרַב אֶל־כָּל־בְּהֵמָה לְרִבְעָה אֹתָהּ וְהָרַגְתָּ אֶת־הָאִשָּׁה וְאֶת־הַבְּהֵמָה מוֹת יוּמָתוּ דְּמֵיהֶם בָּם׃ אַתְּ יְלִיף הֲרִיגָה מֵהֲרִיגָה. סְקִילָה מִסְּקִילָה. דְּמֵיהֶם בָּם מִדְּמֵיהֶם בָּם.

From where the warning[129] for a woman bringing an animal upon herself? *A woman should not stand before an animal to be impregnated; it is mixture*[199]. Extirpation from where? *For anybody who would commit any of these abominations will be extirpated*[131,135]. Punishment from where? *If a woman* stood before an animal *to be impregnated, you should slay the woman and the animal; dying they shall be put to death, their blood be on them*[200]. One infers slaying from slaying, stoning from stoning, *their blood be on them* from *their blood be on them*[201].

199 *Lev*. 18:19.

200 Misquoted from *Lev*. 20:16.

201 Both for male and female bestiality it is said that the animal has to be *slain*; this shows that in both cases the animal has to be killed in the same way. Stoning is to be inferred from *their blood be on them* (Notes 15,184) referring to the female; this then is transferred also to apply to the male.

(25a line 41) רִבִּי בָּא בַּר מָמָל בָּעֵי. הַגַּע עַצְמָךְ שֶׁבָּא עָלֶיהָ שׁוֹגֵג. הֲרֵי הִיא נִסְקֶלֶת עַל יָדוֹ וְהוּא פָטוּר. רִבִּי שִׁמְעוֹן בָּעֵי. הַגַּע עַצְמָךְ שֶׁחָרַשׁ בָּהּ בַּשַּׁבָּת. הֲרֵי הוּא נִסְקַל עַל יָדָהּ וְהִיא פְטוּרָה. לֵית לָךְ אֶלָּא כְהָדָא דָּמַר רִבִּי שְׁמוּאֵל בַּר רַב יִצְחָק. כַּסְפָּם וּזְהָבָם עָשׂוּ לָהֶם עֲצַבִּים לְמַעַן יִכָּרֵתוּן אֵין כָּתוּב כָּאן אֶלָּא לְמַעַן יִכָּרֵת. כְּאִינָשׁ דָּמַר. שְׁחִיק טִימַיָּיא דְפַלָן. דְּאַפִּיק בְּרֵיהּ לְעַבְדָּא בִישָׁא.

Rebbi Abba bar Mamal asked: Think of it, if he erroneously has sexual relations with it[202]. Should it be stoned because of him while he is not liable[203]? Rebbi Simeon asked: Think of it, if he used it to plough on the Sabbath. Is he not being stoned while it is not liable[204]? You have only, as Rebbi Samuel ben Rav Isaac explained: [205]*With their silver and gold they made idols for themselves*; it is not written "that they be extirpated" but *that he be extirpated*[206]. As if a person say: the bones of X be ground up for he led his son to evil ways.

202 If a male thought that bestiality was not forbidden.

203 Instead of simply stating that the verse requires that the animal be killed, the

Mishnah states two different reasons for it. The first reason, that it led a human into sin, applies even if the human is not prosecutable because he was not duly warned of the criminality of the intended act. The second reason, that the animal was known as the one for which a human was stoned, does not apply. Babli 55b in the name of Babylonian Amoraïm.

204 The second reason stated in the Mishnah would apply here, but no animal can be stoned for a Sabbath violation.

Since R. Simeon is quoted after R. Abba bar Mamal, it seems that he is to be identified with R. Simeon ben Laqish.

205 *Hos*. 8:4.

206 It is possible that of a group of criminals only one actually is prosecutable. There is nothing remarkable if human and animal are treated differently.

(fol. 24a) **משנה י׳** הַמְגַדֵּף אֵינוֹ חַיָּיב עַד שֶׁיְּפָרֵשׁ אֶת הַשֵּׁם. אָמַר רִבִּי יְהוֹשֻׁעַ בֶּן קָרְחָה בְּכָל־יוֹם דָּנִין אֶת הָעֵדִים בְּכִינּוּי יַכֶּה יוֹסֵה אֶת יוֹסֵה. נִגְמַר הַדִּין לֹא הָיוּ הוֹרְגִין בְּכִינּוּי אֶלָּא מוֹצִיאִין אֶת כָּל־הָאָדָם לַחוּץ וּמְשַׁיְּירִין אֶת הַגָּדוֹל שֶׁבָּהֶן וְאוֹמֵר לוֹ אֱמוֹר מַה שֶּׁשָּׁמַעְתָּ בְּפֵרוּשׁ. וְהוּא אוֹמֵר וְהַדַּיָּינִים עוֹמְדִין עַל רַגְלֵיהֶן וְקוֹרְעִין וְלֹא מְאַחִין. וְהַשֵּׁנִי אוֹמֵר אַף אֲנִי כָּמוֹהוּ וְהַשְּׁלִישִׁי אוֹמֵר אַף אֲנִי כָּמוֹהוּ׃

Mishnah 10: The blasphemer is not liable unless he explicitly use the Name[207]. Rebbi Joshua ben Qorḥa said, during the trial one deals with the witnesses by substitute name, may Yose hit[208] Yose. At the end of the proceedings one does not sentence him to death by substitute name but one dismisses the public, retains the most prestigious among them[209] and says to him, tell us explicitly what you heard. He says it while the judges are standing; they tear their garments[210] and never mend them[211]. The second one[209] says, also I [heard] like him; the third[209] one says, also I [heard] like him.

207 The Tetragrammaton in its original pronunciation, now lost.

208 An expression of curse, *Deut*. 28:22.

209 The witnesses.

210 Since everybody who hears a blasphemy using the Name has to rend his garment, as if a close relative had died.

211 As for garments rent because of the death of a parent, the tear cannot be mended invisibly.

(25a line 46) **הלכה י׳** הַמְגַדֵּף אֵינוֹ חַיָּיב כול׳. אַזְהָרָה לַמְגַדֵּף מְנַיִין. אֱלֹהִים לֹא תְקַלֵּל. כָּרֵת מְנַיִין. אִישׁ אִישׁ כִּי־יְקַלֵּל אֱלֹהָיו וְנָשָׂא חֶטְאוֹ. עוֹנֶשׁ מְנַיִין. וְנוֹקֵב שֵׁם־יי מוֹת יוּמָת. וּכְרִבִּי

יִשְׁמָעֵאל. דְּרִבִּי יִשְׁמָעֵאל אָמַר. בַּדַּיְינִים הַכָּתוּב מְדַבֵּר. אִם עַל הַדַּיְינִים הוּא מַזְהִיר לֹא כָל־שֶׁכֵּן עַל הַכִּינּוּיִים. אִם עַל הַכִּינּוּיִים הוּא עוֹנֵשׁ כָּרֵת לֹא כָל־שֶׁכֵּן עַל שֵׁם הַמְיוּחָד. אִית תַּנָּיֵי תַנֵּי. עַל הַכִּינּוּיִים בְּאַזְהָרָה וְכָרֵת. עַל שֵׁם הַמְיוּחָד בְּמִיתָה. אִית תַּנָּיֵי תַנֵּי. עַל הַכִּינּוּיִים בְּאַזְהָרָה וְעַל שֵׁם הַמְיוּחָד בְּמִיתָה וְכָרֵת. מָאן דָּמַר. עַל הַכִּינּוּיִים בְּאַזְהָרָה וְכָרֵת. אֱלֹהִים לֹא תְקַלֵּל. וְעוֹד אִישׁ אִישׁ כִּי־יְקַלֵּל אֱלֹהָיו וְנָשָׂא חֶטְאוֹ. בְּכָרֵת. וְעַל שֵׁם הַמְיוּחָד בְּמִיתָה. וְנוֹקֵב שֵׁם־יי מוֹת יוּמָת. וּמָאן דָּמַר. עַל הַכִּינּוּיִין בְּאַזְהָרָה. אֱלֹהִים לֹא תְקַלֵּל. וְעַל שֵׁם הַמְיוּחָד בְּמִיתָה וְכָרֵת. וְנוֹקֵב שֵׁם־יי מוֹת יוּמָת. אִישׁ אִישׁ כִּי־יְקַלֵּל אֱלֹהָיו וגו'.

Halakhah 10: "The blasphemer is not liable," etc. [212]From where a warning for the blasphemer? *You shall not curse God*[213]. Extirpation from where? *Anybody who curses his God shall bear his sin*[214]. Punishment from where? *He who curses the Name of the Eternal shall be put to death*[215]. But according to Rebbi Ismael, since Rebbi Ismael said that the verse refers to judges[216]? If he is warned about judges, then so much more about [divine] substitute names[217]. If he is subject to extirpation for substitute names, so much more for the Unique Name.

Some Tannaïm state: for substitute names warning and extirpation, for the Unique Name the death penalty. Some Tannaïm state: for substitute names warning, for the Unique Name the death penalty or extirpation[218]. He who says, for substitute names warning and extirpation, *you shall not curse God* and *anybody who curses his God shall bear his sin* by extirpation; for the Unique Name the death penalty, *he who curses the Name of the Eternal shall be put to death.* He who says, for substitute names warning, *you shall not curse God,* for the Unique Name the death penalty or extirpation, *he who curses the Name of the Eternal shall be put to death; anybody who curses his God shall bear his sin*[219], etc.

212 The parallel in the Babli is 56a.

213 *Ex.* 22:27. Since *El* means "power", *Elohim* as a plural of majesty means "superior power"; in this case "supreme power" in contrast to *elohim aḥerim* which are not other gods" but "other powers", such as the rain worshipped by Semites as Baal and by the Greeks as Zeus.

214 *Lev.* 24:15. In *Num.* 9:13, referring to the Second Passover, it is spelled out that "carrying one's sin" is equivalent to "being subject to extirpation" [*Sifra Emor Pereq* 19(6), in the name of R. Jehudah.]

215 *Lev.* 24:16.

216 He reads *Ex.* 22:27 as referring to judges, who are called *elohim* in *Ex.* 22:7, *Ps.* 82:1. Babli 66a, *Mekhilta dR. Ismael*

Mišpatim 19 (p. 317). The previous argument is R. Aqiba's.

217 Any reference to the Deity other than the Tetragrammaton, the Unique name. Babli 56a, *Mekhilta dR. Simeon ben Iohai* p. 213. The argument seems to contradict the principle that "one may not punish on the basis of a logical argument" (cf. Halakhah 7:1 Note 9). But since the argument refers only to warning and Heavenly retribution, not to penalties imposed by the court, there is no contradiction.

218 *Sifra Emor Pereq* 19(5), opinion of the rabbis opposing Rebbi Meïr who equates the Unique Name and its substitute names.

219 The same group of verses can lead to two different conclusions without possibility of deciding between them.

(25a line 57) רִבִּי יִרְמְיָה בְשֵׁם רִבִּי שְׁמוּאֵל בַּר רַב יִצְחָק. זֹאת אוֹמֶרֶת שֶׁדָּנִין מִסָּפֵק. הֵיךְ עֲבִידָא. פְּלוֹנִי הָרַג אֶת הַנֶּפֶשׁ. יְהֵא נִידּוֹן עַד שֶׁיָּבוֹאוּ עֵדָיו. אָמַר לֵיהּ רִבִּי יוֹסֵי. וְתָפְשִׂין בַּר נַשָּׁא בְשׁוּקָא וּמְבַזִּין לֵיהּ. אֶלָּא כֵינִי. פְּלוֹנִי הָרַג אֶת הַנֶּפֶשׁ וַהֲרֵי עֵידָיו שֶׁהָרַג אֶת הַנֶּפֶשׁ. יְהֵא תָפוּשׂ עַד שֶׁיָּבוֹאוּ עֵדָיו.

Rebbi Jeremiah in the name of Rebbi Samuel bar Rav Isaac: This[220] implies that one proceeds on the basis of a doubt. How is this? "X killed a person." One proceeds to try him until his witnesses come. Rebbi Yose said to him, does one arrest a person in the market and insult him[221]? But is it as follows: "X killed a person, and there are witnesses." Let him be put under arrest until his witnesses come.

220 The Mishnah which states that the trial of the blasphemer proceeds before the court did hear the exact wording of the offensive statement.

221 The court, acting as inquisitor, cannot arrest a person without a reasonable probability of conviction.

(25a line 61) וְאָמְרִין לֵיהּ. גַּדֵּף. אֶלָּא אוֹתוֹ הַשֵּׁם שֶׁאֲמַרְתִּי לִפְנֵיכֶם אוֹתוֹ קִלֵּל. וּבוֹ קִלֵּל. וְאֵין הָעֵדִים צְרִיכִין לִקְרוֹעַ שֶׁכְּבָר קָרְאוּ בְשָׁעָה שֶׁשָּׁמְעוּ.

רִבִּי שִׁמְעוֹן בֶּן לָקִישׁ אָמַר. מִכָּן לַדַּייָנִים שֶׁקִּיבְּלוּ עֵדוּת עוֹמְדִין שֶׁדִּינָן דִּין. אַתְּ שְׁמַע מִינָּהּ שִׁית. אַתְּ שְׁמַע מִינָּהּ כָּהִיא דְאָמַר רִבִּי שְׁמוּאֵל בַּר רַב יִצְחָק. וְאַתְּ שְׁמַע מִינָּהּ כָּהִיא דְאָמַר רִבִּי שִׁמְעוֹן בֶּן לָקִישׁ. וְאַתְּ שְׁמַע מִינָּהּ . שׁוֹמֵעַ מִפִּי שׁוֹמֵעַ חַייָב לִקְרוֹעַ. וְאַתְּ שְׁמַע מִינָּהּ. מִכָּן לָעֵד שֶׁהֵעִיד עֵדוּתוֹ הַשֵּׁינִי אוֹמֵר. אַף אֲנִי כָמוֹהוּ. וְהַשְּׁלִישִׁי אוֹמֵר. אַף אֲנִי כָמוֹהוּ. וְאַתְּ שְׁמַע מִינָּהּ שֶׁהוּא אֶחָד מִן הַקְּרָעִים שֶׁאֵינָן מִתְאַחִין. וְאַתְּ שְׁמַע מִינָּהּ. מִכֵּיוָן שֶׁהָיוּ יוֹדְעִין מִשָּׁעָה הָרִאשׁוֹנָה שֶׁהוּא שֵׁם הַמְיוּחָד שֶׁהוּא צָרִיךְ לִקְרוֹעַ.

רִבִּי חִייָה אָמַר רִבִּי יָסָא מַקְשֵׁי. תַּנִּינָן. הַכָּרוֹז יוֹצֵא לְפָנָיו. אִישׁ פְּלוֹנִי בֶּן פְּלוֹנִי יוֹצֵא לִיסָּקֵל עַל שֶׁעָבַר עֲבֵירָה פְלוֹנִית. וּפְלוֹנִי וּפְלוֹנִי עֵדָיו. כָּל מִי שֶׁיּוֹדֵעַ לוֹ זְכוּת יָבוֹא וִילַמֵּד. שָׁמַעְנוּ. שׁוֹמֵעַ מִפִּי שׁוֹמֵעַ צָרִיךְ לִקְרוֹעַ. שְׁמָעִינָן. שׁוֹמֵעַ מִפִּי שׁוֹמֵעַ וְשׁוֹמֵעַ מִפִּי שׁוֹמֵעַ צָרִיךְ לִקְרוֹעַ.

מָהוּ לִקְרוֹעַ עַל קִילְלַת הַשֵּׁם. נִישְׁמְעִינָהּ מִן הָדָא. וַיְהִ֗י כִּשְׁמֹ֙עַ֙ הַמֶּ֣לֶךְ חִזְקִיָּ֔הוּ אֶת דִּבְרֵי רַב שָׁקֵה וַיִּקְרַ֖ע אֶת־בְּגָדָ֑יו. מָהוּ לִקְרוֹעַ עַל קִילְלַת הַגּוֹי. מָאן דְּאָמַר. רַב שָׁקֵה גּוֹי הָיָה. קוֹרְעִין. מָאן דָּמַר. יִשְׂרָאֵל הָיָה. אֵין קוֹרְעִין. תַּנֵּי רִבִּי הוֹשַׁעְיָה. אֶחָד הַשּׁוֹמֵעַ קִלְלַת הַשֵּׁם מִיִּשְׂרָאֵל וְאֶחָד הַשּׁוֹמֵעַ מִפִּי הַגּוֹי חַייָב לִקְרוֹעַ. מַה טַעֲמָא. הִנֵּה֙ יי אֱלֹהֵ֖י כָּל־בָּשָׂ֑ר הֲמִמֶּ֕נִּי יִפָּלֵ֖א כָּל־דָּבָֽר׃

Does one tell him, blaspheme[222]? But that Name which I am saying before you, that one he cursed or by that one he cursed[223]. But the witnesses need not rend their garments since they already rent them when they heard it the first time. Rebbi Simeon ben Laqish said, from here[224] that in case the judges heard testimony while standing, their judgment is valid.

You infer six statements from this[224]. One infers the statement of Rebbi Samuel bar Rav Isaac[220], and one infers the statement of Rebbi Simeon ben Laqish. Also one infers that he who hears from one who heard has to rend[225], and one infers that if one witness testified, the second one says, I testify to the same, and the third says, I testify to the same[226]. Also one infers that this is one of the tears which are not mended[211], and one infers that even when they know from the start that it is the Unique Name, they have to rend.

Rebbi Ḥiyya said that Rebbi Yasa asked: We have stated[227]: "The herald goes before him: 'X ben Y is led to be stoned because he committed crime Z; U and V testified against him. Anybody who knows of his innocence shall come and argue.'" We inferred that he who hears from one who heard has to rend. Does he who hears from one who heard from one who heard have to rend[228]?

Does one have to rend one's garments for blasphemy?[229] Let us hear from the following: *When king Hezekias heard* the words of Rab Šake, *he rent his garment*[230]. Does one have to rend for a Gentile's blasphemy? According to him who said that Rab Šake was a Gentile, one rends. According to him who said that Rab Šake was an Israel, one does not rend[231]. Rebbi Hoshaia stated: Both one who heard blasphemy from an Israel or one who heard from the mouth of a Gentile has to rend his garment. What is the reason? *Since I am the Eternal, God over all flesh, should anything be extraordinary for me*[232]?

222 This is a question about the Mishnah. How can the court require the witness to sin by repeating the entire blasphemy?

223 The witness is not asked to blaspheme. The text of the blasphemy except for the Name had been testified to earlier; now it is only necessary to confirm that the Name was used, which alone makes the blasphemy a capital crime.

The text makes it clear that blasphemy is not only cursing God by His Name but also cursing another person using the Name, including any magical practices using the Name.

224 From the Mishnah.

225 Since the judges have to tear their garments, even though they are hearing the blasphemy only indirectly.

226 This statement seems to apply only to the case of the blasphemer. Witnesses have to be heard one at a time (5:3-4) to determine that they are not perjured. The speaking of the Name is the only case in which witnesses appear together, after having been interrogated separately about all other aspects of the case. However, the Babli (60a) reads the statement as implying that by biblical standards a witness may state that his testimony is identical with that of the first witness and that the rules of 5:3-4 are rabbinic only.

227 Mishnah 6:2.

228 Does everybody who hears the herald have to rend his garment? Since this is not mentioned in the Mishnah, the implied answer to the question is negative.

229 Finally one asks why one has to rend his garment when he hears blasphemy since this obligation is not mentioned in the Torah.

230 *2K.* 19:1. Since the king heard the blasphemy from his ministers, it proves that one has to rend his garment even if he hears it indirectly. Babli 69a.

231 On the one hand, it is not likely that a high official of the king of Assyria was not an Assyrian. On the other hand, why should a high Assyrian official be able to speak Hebrew unless he was a Jewish apostate? *Mo`ed qaṭan* 3:6 (83b l. 32); Babli 60a. M. Cogan and H. Tadmor, *II Kings*, The Anchor Bible vol. 11 (1988) p. 230.

232 *Jer.* 32:26.

(25b line 3) מָהוּ לִקְרוֹעַ בִּזְמַן הַזֶּה. רִבִּי יוֹסֵה רִבִּי יִרְמְיָה בְשֵׁם רִבִּי חִייָה בַּר בָּא רִבִּי חִזְקִיָּה רִבִּי יִרְמְיָה בְשֵׁם רִבִּי יוֹחָנָן. מִשֶּׁרָבוּ הַגּוֹדְפָנִים פָּסְקוּ מִלִּקְרוֹעַ. מָהוּ לִקְרוֹעַ עַל הַכִּינּוּיִין בִּזְמַן הַזֶּה. נִישְׁמְעִינָהּ מֵהָדָא. רִבִּי שִׁמְעוֹן בֶּן לָקִישׁ הֲוָה מְהַלֵּךְ בְּאִיסְרָטָא. פָּגַע בֵּיהּ חַד כּוּתַיי וַהֲוָה מְגַדֵּף וְהוּא קָרַע מְגַדֵּף וְהוּא קָרַע. נְחַת לֵיהּ מִן חַמְרָא וִיהַב לֵיהּ מַרְתּוּקָא גַו לִיבֵּיהּ. אֲמַר לֵיהּ. בַּר כּוּתַיי. אִית לְאִימָּךְ מָאנִין מְסַפְּקָא לִי. מִילְּתֵיהּ הָדָא אֲמְרָה שֶׁקּוֹרְעִין עַל הַכִּינּוּיִין וְשֶׁקּוֹרְעִין בִּזְמַן הַזֶּה.

Does one rend his garment nowadays[233]? Rebbi Yose, Rebbi Jeremiah in the name of Rebbi Ḥiyya bar Abba, Rebbi Ḥisqiah, Rebbi Jeremiah in the name of Rebbi Joḥanan: When blasphemers proliferated, they stopped rending[234]. Does one rend for substitute names today? Let us hear from the following: Rebbi Simeon ben Laqish was travelling on the highway. He met a Samaritan who was repeatedly blaspheming, and he was rending. He dismounted from the donkey and gave him a blow on his heart saying to him: Samaritan! Does your mother have garments to supply me with? [His word] This implies[235] that one rends for substitute names[236] and rends his garments at the present time.

233 Since the pronunciation of the Name is unknown, an obligation to rend one's garments would imply that it applies to substitutes of the Name. The paragraph has a parallel in *Mo`ed qatan* 3:6, 83b l. 38.

234 The same statement in the Babli 60a in the name of R. Hiyya (bar Abba). The implication is that the status of substitute names is the same as that of the Name.

235 The scribe wrote הדא אמרה "this implies". The corrector added מילתיה but then forgot to cross out הדא. One should read either "his word" or "this".

236 Disagreeing with R. Johanan and the latter's student R. Hiyya bar Abba.

(fol. 24a) **משנה יא**: הָעוֹבֵד עֲבוֹדָה זָרָה אֶחָד הָעוֹבֵד וְאֶחָד הַזּוֹבֵחַ וְאֶחָד הַמְקַטֵּר וְאֶחָד הַמְנַסֵּךְ וְאֶחָד הַמִּשְׁתַּחֲוֶה וְהַמְקַבְּלוֹ עָלָיו לֶאֱלוֹהַּ וְהָאוֹמֵר לוֹ אֵלִי אַתָּה.

Mishnah 11: The worshipper of strange worship[237] whether he worships[238], or sacrifices[239], or burns incense, or makes a libation, or prostrates himself; also one who accepts it as a god and says to it: you are my god[240].

משנה יב: אֲבָל הַמְגַפֵּף וְהַמְנַשֵּׁק וְהַמְכַבֵּד וְהַמַּרְבִּיץ הַמַּרְחִיץ הַסָּךְ הַמַּלְבִּישׁ וְהַמַּנְעִיל עוֹבֵר בְּלֹא תַעֲשֶׂה. הַנּוֹדֵר בִּשְׁמוֹ וְהַמְקַיֵּם בִּשְׁמוֹ עוֹבֵר בְּלֹא תַעֲשֶׂה. הַפּוֹעֵר עַצְמוֹ לְבַעַל פְּעוֹר זוֹ הִיא עֲבוֹדָתוֹ. הַזּוֹרֵק אֶבֶן לְמַרְקוּלִיס זוֹ הִיא עֲבוֹדָתוֹ:

Mishnah 12: But one who embraces[241], or kisses, or sweeps clean[242], or sprinkles water[243]; one who washes, rubs with oil, clothes, or puts shoes on it, violates a prohibition[244]. He who makes a vow in its name or keeps one in its name violates a prohibition. One who defecates in front of *Baal Pe`or* follows its worship[245]. One who throws a stone at a statue of Mercury follows its worship[246].

237 Who is mentioned in Mishnah 5 as subject to stoning.

238 In a way customary for the worship of the idol even if it does not resemble any

approved worship of Heaven.

239 Any of the acts required in the Temple proffered to an idol is a capital crime even if ordinarily this is not the worship of this idol.

240 Without any other action.

241 A statue.

242 The floor on which the statue stands.

243 To settle the dust on the dirt floor on which the statue is standing.

244 The penalty would be flogging, not stoning.

245 While in later biblical texts (*Is.* 5:14, *Job* 6:10) פער فعر means "to open one's mouth wide", in rabbinic Hebrew it always means "to defecate". Therefore *Ba`al Pe`or* is interpreted as a deity worshipped by defecating in front of it. The defecation then becomes a capital crime.

246 While in general throwing a stone at an idol would be a commendable sign of disrespect, throwing a stone at a Hermes stele is a capital crime.

(25b line 10) **הלכה יא:** הָעוֹבֵד עֲבוֹדָה זָרָה כול'. אַזְהָרָה לָעוֹבֵד עֲבוֹדָה זָרָה מְנַיִין. לֹא תָעָבְדֵם. כָּרֵת מְנַיִין. אֶת־יי הוּא מְגַדֵּף וְנִכְרְתָה. וְלֹא מְגַדֵּף כָּתוּב. כְּאָדָם שֶׁהוּא אוֹמֵר לַחֲבֵירוֹ. גִּידַּפְתָּה אֶת כָּל־הַקְּעָרָה וְלֹא שִׁייַרְתָּה בָהּ כְּלוּם. מָשָׁל רִבִּי שִׁמְעוֹן בֶּן לְעָזָר אוֹמֵר. לִשְׁנַיִם שֶׁהָיוּ יוֹשְׁבִין וּקְעָרָה שֶׁלְּגְרִיסִין בֵּינֵיהוֹן. פָּשַׁט אֶחָד אֵת יָדָיו וְגִידֵּף אֶת כָּל־הַקְּעָרָה וְלֹא שִׁייֵר בָּהּ כְּלוּם. כָּךְ הַמְגַדֵּף וְהָעוֹבֵד עֲבוֹדָה זָרָה אֵינוֹ מְשַׁייֵר לְאַחֲרָיו מִצְוָה. עוֹנֶשׁ מְנַיִין. וְהוֹצֵאתָ אֶת־הָאִישׁ הַהוּא אוֹ אֶת־הָאִשָּׁה הַהִיא אֲשֶׁר עָשׂוּ אֶת־הַדָּבָר הַזֶּה אֶל־שְׁעָרֶיךָ וגו' עַד וּסְקַלְתָּם אוֹתָם בָּאֲבָנִים וָמֵתוּ׃

Halakhah 11: "The worshipper of strange worship," etc. From where warning about strange worship? *Do not worship them*[247]. Extirpation from where? *He blasphemed the Eternal and will be extirpated*[248]. But is there not written "blasphemed"? As one would say to another, you scraped out the entire pot[249] and did not leave anything; a parable which Rebbi Simeon ben Eleazar formulated: Two people were sitting with a pot of porridge between them. One of them stretched out his hand, scraped out the entire pot, and did not leave anything in it. So both the blasphemer and the worshipper of strange worship do not leave any commandment as residue[250].

From where the punishment? *You shall lead out that man, or that woman, who did this deed to your gates*, etc., up to *and stone them with stones until they die*[251].

247 *Ex.* 20:5, *Deut.* 5:9 the Second Commandment.

248 *Num.* 15:30. The verse describes any person who sins intentionally as a blasphemer. The verse decrees extirpation as punishment for any willful deed for which a sacrifice would be required if done inadvertently, in case it cannot be

prosecuted in court for lack of witnesses.

The traditional interpretation of the purification sacrifices prescribed in *Num.* 15:22-29, which differ from those prescribed under similar headings in *Lev.* 4:1-5:14, assigns the sacrifices prescribed in *Num.* exclusively to sins of idolatry; those of *Lev.* to the atonement of all other transgressions (*Sifry Num.* 111-112). Therefore, the following verse 15:30 can also be interpreted as specifically referring to idolatry.

249 It seems that in Galilean dialect גדף جحّف "to blaspheme" was pronounced like גדף جذف "to fly quickly" and this in turn sounded like גרף جرف "to scoop out with a shovel, to scratch out completely." The parallel in the Babli, *Keritut* 7b, formulates גִּירַפְתָּ הַקְּעָרָה "you scratched out the pot" and Rashi comments: ד can be replaced by ר.

250 Obeying a Divine command after blaspheming or worshipping a strange deity is an empty gesture, devoid of all value.

251 *Deut.* 17:5.

(25b line 18) לֹא תָעָבְדֵם. הָיִיתִי אוֹמֵר. עַד שֶׁיַּעֲבוֹד כָּל־עֲבוֹדָה זָרָה שֶׁבָּעוֹלָם. תַּלְמוּד לוֹמַר לֹא־תִשְׁתַּחֲוֶה לָהֶם. הִשְׁתַּחֲוָיָה בִּכְלָל הָיְתָה וְלָמָּה יָצָאת. לְהַקִּישׁ אֵלֶיהָ. אֶלָּא מַה הִשְׁתַּחֲוָיָה מְיוּחֶדֶת מַעֲשֶׂה יָחִיד וְחַייָבִין עָלֶיהָ בִּפְנֵי עַצְמָהּ. אַף אֲנִי אַרְבֶּה כָּל־מַעֲשֶׂה וּמַעֲשֶׂה שֶׁיֵּשׁ בָּהּ חַייָבִין עָלָיו בִּפְנֵי עַצְמוֹ. אַף עַל גַּב דְּרִבִּי שִׁמְעוֹן בֶּן לְעָזָר אָמַר. זִיבֵּחַ וְקִיטֵּר וְנִיסֵּךְ בְּהֶעֱלֵם אֶחָד אֵינוֹ חַייָב אֶלָּא אַחַת. מוֹדֶה שֶׁאִם עֲבָדָהּ בַּעֲבוֹדָתָהּ בַּעֲבוֹדַת הַגָּבוֹהַּ בַּעֲבוֹדַת הִשְׁתַּחֲוָיָה שֶׁהוּא חַייָב עַל כָּל־אַחַת וְאַחַת. כְּדָמַר רִבִּי שְׁמוּאֵל בְּשֵׁם רִבִּי זְעִירָא. וְלֹא־יִזְבְּחוּ עוֹד אֶת־זִבְחֵיהֶם לַשְּׂעִירִ͏ם. אָמְרוּ לֵיהּ. מְטִי תָּנָה לְקֳדָשִׁים.

Do not worship them[247]. Should I say, not unless he worshipped every single strange worship in the world? The verse says, *do not prostrate yourself before them*[247]. [252]Prostration was included[253]; why is it mentioned separately? To tie to it: Prostration is special in that it is the act of a single person and is punishable separately, so I am adding any single act that one is liable for separately. Even though Rebbi Simeon ben Eleazar said[254], if one sacrificed, and burned incense, and poured a libation in one forgetting[255] he is liable only for one; he agrees that if one worshipped it in its proper worship which is identical with the worship of Heaven like prostrating, he is liable for each single action[256]. As Rebbi Samuel said in the name of Rebbi Ze`ira: *They should not continue to offer their sacrifices to spirits.*[257] They said to him, turn and refer it to sacrifices[258].

252 The argument is hinted at in the Babli, 60b.

253 Even though in the verse prostrating is mentioned before worshipping, it clearly is

an act of worship and on purely logical grounds would not have to be mentioned separately.

254 Halakhah 13, 25c l. 18, the entire argument is attributed to R. Jehudah ben Tanhum.

255 If he was oblivious to the fact that worshipping other gods was forbidden, he only has to bring one purification sacrifice.

256 Applying any forms of worship of Heaven to any other purpose is sinful. Therefore, using it for pagan worship is not the same as accepting pagan rites of other forms.

257 *Lev.* 17:7.

258 The paragraph forbids any sacrificial act outside the holy precinct. It is not applicable to the question at hand.

(25b line 27) רִבִּי יָסָא בְשֵׁם רִבִּי יוֹחָנָן. זִיבֵּחַ לָהּ טָלֶה בַעַל מוּם חַייָב. מַאי כְדוֹן. כַּיי דָמַר רִבִּי הִילָא. לֹא־תַעֲשׂוּן כֵּן לַיי אֱלֹהֵיכֶם׃ כָּל־לַיי אֱלֹהֵיכֶם לֹא־תַעֲשׂוּן כֵּן.

Rebbi Yasa in the name of Rebbi Johanan: If he sacrificed a defective lamb to it, he is guilty[259]. From where this? As Rebbi Hila said, *do not do such to the Eternal, your God*[260]. Anything that you might do for the Eternal, your God, you may not do in this case.

259 It is forbidden to sacrifice defective animals to God (*Lev.* 22:20). Nevertheless, if regular pagan worship does not include animal sacrifices but a Jew chooses to sacrifice a defective animal to that idol, he is guilty of idolatry. The Babli, *Avodah zarah* 51a, quotes R. Abbahu in the name of R. Johanan in the opposite sense.

260 *Deut.* 12:4. The paragraph deals with the destruction of places of pagan worship. It is interpreted to mean that anything similar to Temple worship, even if executed in an unacceptable way, is forbidden as pagan worship. *Sifry Deut.* 81 follows the Yerushalmi: "Anything which cannot be sacrificed in the Temple but somebody sacrificed it as foreign worship, if its kind might be sacrificed to God he is guilty; otherwise he cannot be prosecuted."

(25b line 31) רִבִּי בּוּן בַּר חִייָה בְּעָא קוֹמֵי רִבִּי זְעִירָה. לֹא תָעָבְדֵם כְּלָל. לֹא־תִשְׁתַּחֲוֶה לָהֶם פְּרָט. כִּי לֹא תִשְׁתַּחֲוֶה לְאֵל אַחֵר חָזַר וְכָלַל. כְּלָל וּפְרָט וּכְלָל אֵין בִּכְלָל אֶלָּא מַה שֶׁבִּפְרָט. רִבִּי בּוּן בַּר כָּהֲנָה בְּעָא קוֹמֵי רִבִּי הִילָא. לֹא־תַעֲשׂוּן כֵּן כְּלָל. זֹבֵחַ לָאֱלֹהִים יָחֳרָם פְּרָט. בִּלְתִּי לַיי לְבַדּוֹ. חָזַר וְכָלַל. כְּלָל וּפְרָט וּכְלָל וְהַכֹּל בִּכְלָל. וְרִיבָה אֶת הַמְגַפֵּף וְהַמְנַשֵּׁק. אָמַר לֵיהּ. לְאֵי זֶה דָּבָר נֶאֶמְרָה הִשְׁתַּחֲוָיָה. לֹא לְלַמֵּד עַל עַצְמוֹ שֶׁהוּא מַעֲשֶׂה. הַמְגַפֵּף וְהַמִּשְׁתַּחֲוֶה שֶׁאֵינָן מַעֲשֶׂה.

Rebbi Abun bar Hiyya asked before Rebbi Ze`ira: *Do not worship them*[247], a principle. *Do not prostrate yourself before them*[247], a detail. *For you shall not prostrate yourself before another god*[261]; He again stated the principle. Principle, detail, and principle: is nothing covered but the detail[262]?

Rebbi Abun bar Cahana asked before Rebbi Hila: *Do not do such*[260], a principle. *One who sacrifices to gods shall be banned*[263], a detail. *Only for the Eternal alone*[263], He again stated the principle. Principle, detail, and principle; is not everything included[264]? Does it not add one who embraces and one who kisses[268]? He told him, why is prostrating mentioned? Not to infer from it that it is an action? He who embraces and he who (prostrates himself)[266] do not exemplify actions.

261 *Ex.* 34:14.

262 Since in the Ten Commandments prostrating is mentioned before worshipping, the order really should be detail, principle, principle. Also, in our text of the *Introduction to Sifra*, "principle, detail, principle has to be judged in light of the detail," adding anything similar to detail. The passage supports the thesis of Menahem Cahana [קוים לתולדות התפתחותה של מידת כלל ופרט בתקופת התנאים, ספר זיכרון לתרצה ליפשיץ, ed. א. אדרעי, מ. בראשי, י. לוינסון Jerusalem 2005, pp. 173-216] that only the list of hermeneutical rules is original but the detailed interpretation of the rules is Babylonian (following R. Aqiba), never accepted in the Yerushalmi. The latter does not differentiate between כְּלָל וּפְרָט, פְּרָט וּכְלָל, כְּלָל וּפְרָט וּכְלָל and in all cases reduces the validity of the principle to the case of the detail. The question naturally deserves no answer since it is not כְּלָל וּפְרָט וּכְלָל but פְּרָט וּכְלָל וּכְלָל, which is not the subject of any hermeneutical rule.

263 *Ex.* 22:19.

264 This statement is not found elsewhere in talmudic texts. But in R. Aqiba's system of additions (רִבּוּי) and subtractions (מִעוּט), addition + subtraction + addition implies that almost everything corresponding to the broad description of the additions is included (Tosephta *Ševu`ot* 1:7, Babli *Nazir* 35b).

265 But according to Mishnah 12, embracing or kissing an idol is not a capital crime.

266 It is clear that one has to read ומנשק "and kisses" instead of ומשתחוה "and prostrates himself". Embracing and kissing are not acts of worship.

(25b line 36) מְנַיִין לָאוֹמֵר לוֹ. אֵלִי אַתָּה. רַב אָבוּן בְּשֵׁם רַבָּנִין דְּתַמָּן. וַיִּשְׁתַּחֲווּ־לוֹ֙ וַיִּזְבְּחוּ־ל֔וֹ וַיֹּ֣אמְר֔וּ אֵ֥לֶּה אֱלֹהֶ֖יךָ֙ יִשְׂרָאֵל וגו'. מֵעַתָּה אֵינוֹ מִתְחַייֵב עַד שֶׁיִּזְבַּח וִיקַטֵּר וְיֹאמַר. אָמַר רִבִּי יוֹסֵי. לֹא בָא הַכָּתוּב לְהַזְכִּיר אֶלָּא גְּנָייָן שֶׁלְּיִשְׂרָאֵל. וַיִּשְׁתַּחֲווּ־לוֹ֙ וְלֹא לַגָּבוֹהַּ. וַיִּזְבְּחוּ־ל֔וֹ לֹא לַגָּבוֹהַּ. וַיֹּ֣אמְר֔וּ לוֹ. לֹא לַגָּבוֹהַּ. מַאי כְדוֹן. נֶאֱמַר כָּאן אֲמִירָה וְנֶאֶמְרָה אֲמִירָה בַּמֵּסִית. מָה אֲמִירָה הָאֲמוּרָה בַמֵּסִית עָשָׂה בָהּ אֲמִירָה כְּמַעֲשֶׂה. אַף אֲמִירָה הָאֲמוּרָה כָאן נַעֲשֶׂה בָהּ אֲמִירָה כְּמַעֲשֶׂה.

כָּתוּב וַיֵּ֗לֶךְ וַֽיַּעֲבֹד֙ אֱלֹהִ֣ים אֲחֵרִ֔ים וַיִּשְׁתַּחֲוּ לָהֶ֑ם וְלַשֶּׁ֣מֶשׁ | א֣וֹ לַיָּרֵ֔חַ. אָמַר רִבִּי זְעוּרָה. לַשֶּׁמֶשׁ אֵין כָּתוּב כָּאן אֶלָּא וְלַשֶּׁמֶשׁ. אֵין כָּאן כְּלָל וּפְרָט אֶלָּא רִיבּוּיִים. הָתִיב רִבִּי אַבָּא בַּר

זְמִינָא קוֹמֵי רִבִּי זְעוּרָה .וְהָא כָתוּב כֹּל אֲשֶׁר־לוֹ סְנַפִּיר וְקַשְׂקֶשֶׂת וְכֹל אֲשֶׁר אֵין־לוֹ סְנַפִּיר וְקַשְׂקֶשֶׂת. מֵעַתָּה אֵין כָּאן כְּלָל וּפְרָט אֶלָּא רִיבּוּיִים. אֶלָּא בְגִין דִּכְתַב וָי"ו. אָמַר רִבִּי יוֹחָנָן בַּר מַרְיָיא. כָּל־הֵן דַּאֲנָא מַשְׁכַּח וָי"ו אֲנָא מְחִיק לֵיהּ. אָמַר רִבִּי שְׁמוּאֵל בַּר אֶבוּדֶּמָא. הָיִיתִי אוֹמֵר. מַה שֶׁבַּיַּמִּים יְהוּא אֲסוּרִין וּמַה שֶׁבַּגִּיגִּיּוֹת וְשֶׁבַּבֵּיבָרִים יְהוּא מוּתָּרִין. תַּלְמוּד לוֹמַר וְכָל־אֲשֶׁר בַּמָּיִם. רִיבָּה.

רִבִּי שְׁמוּאֵל בַּר נַחְמָנִי בְּשֵׁם רִבִּי הוֹשַׁעְיָה. הָאוֹמֵר לוֹ. אֵלִי אַתָּה. מַחֲלוֹקֶת רִבִּי וַחֲכָמִים. הִשְׁתַּחֲוֶה לָהּ מָהוּ. רִבִּי יוֹחָנָן אָמַר. דִּבְרֵי הַכֹּל מוֹדִין בִּכְפִיפַת קוֹמָה שֶׁהוּא חַייָב. מַה בֵין הַמַּעֲלֶה וְהַמּוֹרִיד קוֹמָתוֹ וְהַמַּעֲלֶה וְהַמּוֹרִיד שִׂפְתוֹתָיו. רִבִּי יוֹחָנָן אָמַר. כַּמַּחֲלוֹקֶת. וְרֵישׁ לָקִישׁ אָמַר. כַּמַּחֲלוֹקֶת. אָמַר רִבִּי זְעִירָא. קִרְייָא מְסַייֵעַ לְרֵישׁ לָקִישׁ. תּוֹרָה אַחַת יִהְיֶה לָכֶם לָעוֹשֶׂה בִּשְׁגָגָה׃ אֵין לִי אֶלָּא דָבָר שֶׁהוּא מַעֲשֶׂה. הַמְגַפֵּף וְהַמִּשְׁתַּחֲוֶה שֶׁאֵינָן מַעֲשֶׂה מְנַיִין.

From where about him who says, "you are my god"[267]? Rav Abun in the name of the rabbis there[268]: *They prostrated themselves before it, and sacrificed to it, and said, these are your gods, Israel.* Then he should not be guilty unless he sacrifice, burn incense, and declare. Rebbi Yose said, the verse is written only for the disgrace of Israel. *They prostrated themselves before it,* not before Heaven. *And sacrificed to it,* not to Heaven. *And said,* not to Heaven. What about this[269]? *Saying* is mentioned here and *saying* is said about one who leads astray[61,270]. Since for *saying* mentioned about one who leads astray, saying is equated with acting, also for the *saying* mentioned here, we have to equate saying with acting.

It is written[271]: *He went and worshipped other powers and prostrated himself before them, and to the sun, and to the moon.* Rebbi Ze`ira said, it is not said *to the sun* but *and to the sun.* That is not principle and detail but addition[272]. Rebbi Abba bar Zemina objected before Rebbi Ze`ura; is it not written *any which have fins and scales, and any which do not have fins and scales*[273]? Then this is not principle and detail but additions since there is written *and*[274]? Rebbi Johanan bar Marius said, anywhere I am encountering *and*, I am deleting it[275]. Rebbi Samuel ben Eudaimon said, I would have said that anything in the oceans is forbidden, what is in barrels and vivaria[276] should be permitted. The verse says, *and anything which lives in water*, an addition[277].

Rebbi Samuel bar Nahmani in the name of Rebbi Hoshaia: If one says to it, you are my god, there is disagreement between Rebbi[278] and the Sages. If he (prostrated himself)[266], what is the rule? Rebbi Joḥanan said, everybody agrees that if he lowered his body[279], he is guilty. What is the difference between raising and lowering his body, and raising and lowering his lips[280]? Rebbi Joḥanan said, following disagreement[281]. Rebbi Simeon ben Laqish said, following the distinction[282]. Rebbi Ze`ira said, a verse supports Rebbi Simeon ben Laqish: *One rule should be for you, for the one* acting *in error*[283]. This only refers to what represents an action. The one who embraces (and who prostrates himself)[266], which are not action, from where[284]?

267 That it is a capital crime.

268 *Ex*. 32:8, speaking of the Golden Calf.

269 How does the verse imply that declaring one's allegiance to another power constitutes a capital crime?

270 An example of הֶקֵּשׁ "trapping", or בִּנְיַן אָב מִכָּתוּב אֶחָד, the third hermeneutical rule. Since in one case it is established that by talking alone one may commit a capital crime, in all other cases where talking is equated to actions constituting capital crimes, it is a capital crime in itself.

271 *Deut*. 17:3. If not for R. Ze`ira's interpretation, one would translate *or to the sun, or to the moon.*

272 By the rule כְּלָל וּפְרָט וּכְלָל אֵין בִּכְלָל אֶלָּא מַה שֶׁבִּפְרָט "principle, detail, and principle: nothing is covered but the detail," the verse seems to imply that only worship of sun or moon are capital crimes, not the worship of other gods (cf. Note 213). Since the detail is not standing alone but is connected to the general category by *and*, even R. Ismael will agree that the verse adds the worship of celestial bodies as bodies, rather than deities, to the definition of pagan worship.

273 *Lev*. 11:9: *This you may eat from anything which is in the water: Any with fin and scale in the water,* in seas and rivers, *those you may eat.* On the face of it, the verse declares a principle of what may be eaten from the water, followed by a detail, from lakes (standing water) and rivers (flowing water).

274 As explained later, the preceding argument would allow to eat seafood grown in barrels and aquariums, against the received rules, unless one accepts every *and*, even those needed by the rules of grammar, as additions. This may be R. Aqiba's approach; it certainly is unacceptable for R. Ismael's hermeneutical rules. Babli *Ḥulin* 66b.

275 This is essentially R. Ismael's approach that "the Torah speaks human speech;" no word needed by the basic rules of grammar and syntax carries a hidden meaning.

276 Latin *vivarium* "game, fish preserve".

277 Because of the introductory clause, the verse must be read as principle, principle, and detail; this does not fit the scheme of "principle and detail" but the wordiness must be interpreted as intended to cover all possible cases.

The verse as quoted does not exist; in *Lev*. 11:9-10, *Deut*. 14:9 one reads מִכֹּל אֲשֶׁר בַּמָּיִם, the partitive *mem* indicating that not everything living in the water can be eaten, but not referring to the varieties of water.

278 This disagreement is not mentioned in any other source. It is possible that a name should be inserted here.

279 This is prostrating which by the verse was defined as an idolatrous act.

280 This is declaring the idol as one's god, which also can be done by only moving body parts, the lips. In the Babli, 65b, R. Johanan extends his argument by criminalizing a person who prevents his ox from eating while threshing by shouting at it.

281 The nature of this disagreement cannot be determined. It is possible that R. Johanan by his argument implies that embracing and kissing idols are capital crimes.

282 The distinction made in the Mishnah between idolatrous acts which are capital crimes and those which are simple transgressions.

283 *Num.* 15:29; the reference to idolatrous acts is explained in Note 248.

284 Therefore, embracing and kissing cannot be capital crimes since they do not fit the criterion for a purification sacrifice in case the act was unintentional.

(fol. 24a) **משנה יג**: הַנּוֹתֵן מִזַּרְעוֹ לַמּוֹלֶךְ אֵינוֹ חַייָב עַד שֶׁיִּמְסוֹר לַמּוֹלֶךְ וְיַעֲבִיר בָּאֵשׁ. מָסַר לַמּוֹלֶךְ וְלֹא הֶעֱבִיר בָּאֵשׁ. הֶעֱבִיר בָּאֵשׁ וְלֹא מָסַר לַמּוֹלֶךְ אֵינוֹ חַייָב עַד שֶׁיִּמְסוֹר לַמּוֹלֶךְ וְיַעֲבִיר בָּאֵשׁ. בַּעַל אוֹב זֶה פִּיתוֹם וְהַמְדַבֵּר מִשֶּׁחְיוֹ וְיִדְּעוֹנִי זֶה הַמְדַבֵּר בְּפִיו. הֲרֵי אֵלּוּ בִסְקִילָה וְהַנִּשְׁאָל בָּהֶן בְּאַזְהָרָה׃

Mishnah 13: One who gives any of his descendants to the Moloch is only guilty if he delivers him to the Moloch and makes him pass through fire. If he delivered him to the Moloch but did not make him pass through fire, or made him pass though fire but did not deliver him to the Moloch, is only guilty if he delivers him to the Moloch and makes him pass through fire.

The necromancer is the Πύθων[285] and one who[286] speaks from his armpit. The medium[58] speaks through his mouth. These are stoned but one who consults them is forewarned[287].

285 Πύθων, -ωνος, ὁ, "the serpent Python", a spirit of divination. The plural πύθωνες "ventriloquists".

286 In the Babli and the independent Mishnah mss: the Πύθων who speaks from his armpit.

287 While turning to necromancers and fortune-tellers is repeatedly forbidden (*Lev.* 19:31, *Deut.* 18:10-11), no punishment is spelled out in the biblical text.

(25b line 56) **הלכה יג:** הַנּוֹתֵן מִזַּרְעוֹ לַמּוֹלֶךְ. אַזְהָרָה לַנּוֹתֵן מִזַּרְעוֹ לַמּוֹלֶךְ מְנַיִין. וּמִזַּרְעֲךָ לֹא־תִתֵּן לְהַעֲבִיר לַמּוֹלֶךְ. כָּרֵת מְנַיִין. כִּי מִזַּרְעוֹ נָתַן לַמּוֹלֶךְ וְנִכְרְתָה. עוֹנֶשׁ מְנַיִין. אִישׁ אִישׁ מִבְּנֵי יִשְׂרָאֵל וּמִן־הַגֵּר | הַגָּר בְּיִשְׂרָאֵל אֲשֶׁר יִתֵּן מִזַּרְעוֹ לַמּוֹלֶךְ מוֹת יוּמָת עַם הָאָרֶץ יִרְגְּמוּהוּ בָאָבֶן: וּמִזַּרְעֲךָ לֹא־תִתֵּן. יָכוֹל אֲפִילוּ מָסַר וְלֹא הֶעֱבִיר יְהֵא חַייָב. תַּלְמוּד לוֹמַר וּמִזַּרְעֲךָ לֹא־תִתֵּן לְהַעֲבִיר. יָכוֹל אֲפִילוּ מָסַר וְהֶעֱבִיר שֶׁלֹּא לַמּוֹלֶךְ יְהֵא חַייָב. תַּלְמוּד לוֹמַר וּמִזַּרְעֲךָ לֹא־תִתֵּן לְהַעֲבִיר לַמּוֹלֶךְ. יָכוֹל אֲפִילוּ מָסַר וְהֶעֱבִיר לַמּוֹלֶךְ שֶׁלֹּא בָאֵשׁ יְהֵא חַייָב. תַּלְמוּד לוֹמַר לֹא־יִמָּצֵא בְךָ מַעֲבִיר בְּנוֹ־וּבִתּוֹ בָּאֵשׁ. עֲבָרָה עֲבָרָה לִגְזֵירָה שָׁוָה. מָה הָעֲבָרָה שֶׁנֶּאֶמְרָה לְהַלָּן בָּאֵשׁ אַף כָּאן בָּאֵשׁ. נִמְצֵאתָה אוֹמֵר. לְעוֹלָם אֵינוֹ חַייָב עַד שֶׁיִּמְסוֹר וְיַעֲבִיר בָּאֵשׁ לַמּוֹלֶךְ. רִבִּי נָסָה בְשֵׁם רִבִּי לָעְזָר. לְעוֹלָם אֵינוֹ מִתְחַייֵב עַד שֶׁיִּמְסְרֶנּוּ לַכּוֹמָרִים וִיטִּילֶנּוּ וְיַעֲבִירֶנּוּ. הֶעֱבִירוֹ כְדַרְכּוֹ מָהוּ. הָיָה מוֹשְׁכוֹ וּמַעֲבִירוֹ. תַּנֵּי. הֶעֱבִירוֹ בְרַגְלוֹ פָּטוּר. רִבִּי לָעְזָר בֵּירִבִּי שִׁמְעוֹן מְחַייֵב. אֶחָד הַמּוֹלֶךְ וְאֶחָד שְׁאָר עֲבוֹדָה זָרָה. רִבִּי לָעְזָר בֵּירִבִּי שִׁמְעוֹן אוֹמֵר. אֵינוֹ חַייָב אֶלָּא לַמּוֹלֶךְ בִּלְבַד. אֵינוֹ חַייָב אֶלָּא עַל יוֹצְאֵי יְרֵיכוֹ. אָמַר רִבִּי יוֹחָנָן. טַעֲמָא דְרִבִּי לָעְזָר בֵּירִבִּי שִׁמְעוֹן מֵהָכָא. לֹא־יִמָּצֵא בְךָ בְּגוּפְךָ לֹא יִמָּצֵא מַעֲבִיר. וְהִכְרַתִּי אֹתוֹ מִקֶּרֶב עַמּוֹ: לְרַבּוֹת שְׁאָר עֲבוֹדָה זָרָה בְּהִיכָּרֵת. עוֹנֶשׁ מְנַיִין. מִזַּרְעוֹ נָתַן לַמֹּלֶךְ מוֹת יוּמָת. והוּא שֶׁהֶעֱבִיר עַצְמוֹ. לֹא בְרַגְלוֹ הוּא עוֹבֵר. מִפְּנֵי שֶׁהֶעֱבִיר אֶת עַצְמוֹ. אֲבָל אִם הָיָה מוֹשֵׁךְ בּוֹ וּמַעֲבִירוֹ חַייָב. מָה הִיא דְאָמַר רִבִּי לָעְזָר בֵּירִבִּי שִׁמְעוֹן. הֶעֱבִירוֹ בְרַגְלוֹ פָּטוּר. בְּהוּא דְעַבְרֵיהּ מִזְקָר.

Halakhah 13: "One who gives any of his descendants to the Moloch." From where a warning not to give any of his descendants to the Moloch? *Do not give any of your descendants to the Moloch*[288]. Extirpation from where? *For he gave one of his descendants to the Moloch*[289] *and shall be extirpated*[290]. Punishment from where? *Each one of the Children of Israel, or of the sojourner in Israel, who would give any of his descendants to the Moloch shall be made to die; the people of the Land shall smash him with stones*[291]. *Do not give any of your descendants,* I could think that he was guilty if he handed over but did not make him pass[292]; the verse says: *Do not give any of your descendants to pass through.* I could think that he was guilty if he handed over and made him pass through but not for the Moloch; the verse says: *Do not give any of your descendants to pass through* for the Moloch[293]. I could think that he was guilty if he handed over and made him pass through for the Moloch but without fire; the verse says: *among you, nobody should be found to make his son or his daughter pass through fire*[294]. Passing through, passing through as an equal cut[295]. Since "passing through" mentioned there is through fire, so "passing through" mentioned here also is through fire. You have to say that he is not guilty unless he handed over and made him pass through fire for the Moloch.

Rebbi Nasa in the name of Rebbi Eleazar: He is guilty only if he hand him over to the priests, takes him, and makes him pass. What if he lets him walk normally? It was stated: one was drawing him and made him pass through. It was stated: if he made him walk through on his feet he is not prosecutable[296]. Rebbi Eleazar ben Rebbi Simeon declares him guilty. Whether for the Moloch or for any other foreign worship; Rebbi Eleazar ben Rebbi Simeon says, he is guilty only for the Moloch[297], he is guilty only for his descendants. Rebbi Joḥanan said, Rebbi Eleazar ben Rebbi Simeon's reason is from here: *It shall not be found in you*[298], from your body you should not be found making pass through.

I shall extirpate him . . . from among his people[299]. To include all other foreign worship for extirpation[300]. From where punishment? *Of his descendants he gave to the Moloch*[289], *death he shall be made to die*[291], if he made him pass through himself. Does he not pass through on his feet? Because he made him pass through himself, but if he was drawing him and made him pass through, he is guilty. What does Rebbi Eleazar ben Rebbi Simeon mean, if he made him walk through on his feet he is not prosecutable? He has to make him pass through jumping.

288 *Lev*. 18:21.

289 *Lev*. 20:3

290 A wrong quote from *Lev*. 20:5. It should read: *I shall extirpate him*.

291 *Lev*. 20:2.

292 In the interpretation of the Talmudim, the child was handed over to the Moloch priests and then made to pass or be carried between two fires. It is not assumed that the child was burned since that would be murder which in itself is a capital crime and would obviate the discussion of the exact conditions which make Moloch worship a capital crime. In the Babli, 64b, it is assumed that there is one fire in a ditch and the Moloch worship requires to jump, not to walk, over the fire. This interpretation also is possible for the Yerushalmi.

The paragraphs have a parallel in the Babli, 64b, partially with different attributions.

293 Since passing through (or jumping over) fire is characteristic for Moloch worship and not part of worship of Heaven, doing this for any other deity is forbidden foreign worship, subject to divine extirpation, but not a prosecutable capital crime.

294 *Deut*. 18:10. In the Moloch paragraphs in *Lev*., the nature of "passing

through" is never spelled out; by the doctrine of invariability of lexemes it is only made definite in this quote. *Sifra Qedošim Parašah* 10(3).

295 Cf. 3:10, Note 158.

296 Babli 64b. In neither Talmud is it totally clear whether father or priests make the child pass through or over the fire.

297 Bablt 64a.

298 The word בְּךָ in *Deut.* 18:10 is read as *in you*; this is interpreted to describe one's bodily issue, the children.

299 A not quite correct quote from *Lev.* 20:5.

300 In the Moloch paragraph *Lev.* 20:1-5 extirpation is mentioned twice, in vv. 3 and 5. One refers to Moloch worship; the other then must refer to any other worship using fire. *Sifra Qedošim Parašah* 10(15).

(25c line 1) רִבִּי בּוּן בַּר חִייָה בְּעָא קוֹמֵי רִבִּי זְעִירָא. מְסַר וְלֹא הֶעֱבִיר תַּפְלוּגְתָא דְּחִזְקִיָּה וְרִבִּי יוֹחָנָן. גְּאִיתְפָּלְגוּן. טָבַח וְלֹא מָכַר. חִזְקִיָּה אָמַר חַייָב. וְרִבִּי יוֹחָנָן אָמַר פָּטוּר.

Rebbi Abun bar Ḥiyya asked before Rebbi Ze`ira: If he handed over but did not make to pass through,[391] is that the disagreement between Ḥizqiah and Rebbi Joḥanan? Fore they disagreed: If he slaughtered but did not sell, Ḥizqiah said he is liable, but Rebbi Joḥanan said, he is not liable [392].

301 At the start of the Halakhah it was noted that if somebody handed over his child to the Moloch priests but did not make him pass over the fire, he is not guilty under the Moloch paragraph. One has to read that to mean that the intent had been for a full Moloch ceremony but that for some reason it was not executed. Then the question here is, whether there is any guilt in handing over the child knowing that the ceremony cannot be performed.

302 The thief of livestock who *slaughters and sells* stolen animals is liable to fourfold or fivefold restitution (*Ex.* 21:37). The question arises whether stealing and slaughtering an animal which cannot be sold, e. g., one dedicated as sacrifice but still in its owner's hand, triggers liability for quadruple or only double restitution. The problem is not mentioned elsewhere; a related one is in *Ševu`ot* 8:8. The comparison of civil and criminal law is unfounded; the question merits no answer.

(25c line 4) רִבִּי בָּא רִבִּי חִייָה בְּשֵׁם רִבִּי יוֹחָנָן. רְאֵה לָשׁוֹן שֶׁלִּימְּדַתְךָ הַתּוֹרָה. מוֹלֶךְ. כָּל־שֶׁתַּמְלִיכֵהוּ עָלֶיךָ. אֲפִילוּ קֵיסֵם אֲפִילוּ צְרוֹר. וְהִכְרַתִּי אֹתוֹ מִקֶּרֶב עַמּוֹ. לְרַבּוֹת שְׁאָר עֲבוֹדָה זָרָה בְּהִיכָּרֵת. רִבִּי נָסָה בְּשֵׁם רִבִּי לָעְזָר. לְרַבּוֹת שְׁאָר עֲבוֹדָה זָרָה לְבָנִים וּלְבָנוֹת. דְּתַנֵּי. אֶחָד הַמּוֹלֶךְ וְאֶחָד שְׁאָר עֲבוֹדָה זָרָה. בֵּין שֶׁעֲבָדָהּ בְּבָנִים וּבְבָנוֹת בֵּין שֶׁעֲבָדָהּ בְּאָבוֹת וּבְאִמָּהוֹת. חַייָב. אָמַר רִבִּי זְעִירָה. בְּשֶׁאֵין עֲבוֹדָתָהּ לָכֵן. אֲבָל אִם הָיְתָה עֲבוֹדָתָהּ לָכֵן פָּטוּר. אָמַר רִבִּי הִילָא. אֲפִילוּ עֲבוֹדָתָהּ לָכֵן חַייָב שְׁתַּיִם. מַתְנִיתָא מְסַייְעָא לְרִבִּי הִילָא. מוֹלֶךְ בִּכְלַל עֲבוֹדָה זָרָה הָיָה וְיָצָא

לִידוֹן לְהָקֵל עָלָיו שֶׁלֹּא יְהֵא חַייָב אֶלָּא עַל יוֹצְאֵי יְרֵיכוֹ. אָמַר רִבִּי תַנְחוּם בַּר יִרְמְיָה. אַתְייָא דְּרִבִּי לָעְזָר בֵּירִבִּי שִׁמְעוֹן כְּשִׁיטַּת רִבִּי שִׁמְעוֹן אָבִיו. כְּמָה דְרִבִּי שִׁמְעוֹן אָמַר. מוֹלֶךְ בִּכְלַל עוֹבְדֵי עֲבוֹדָה זָרָה הָיָה. יָצָא לִידוֹן לְהָקֵל עָלָיו שֶׁלֹּא יְהֵא חַייָב אֶלָּא עַל יוֹצְאֵי יְרֵיכוֹ. כֵּן רִבִּי לָעְזָר בֵּירִבִּי שִׁמְעוֹן אָמַר. בִּכְלַל עוֹבְדֵי עֲבוֹדָה זָרָה הָיָה. יָצָא לִידוֹן לְהָקֵל עָלָיו שֶׁלֹּא יְהֵא חַייָב אֶלָּא עַל יוֹצְאֵי יְרֵיכוֹ.

אָמַר רִבִּי תַנְחוּם בַּר יוּדָן. אַף עַל גַּב דְּרִבִּי לָעְזָר בֵּירִבִּי שִׁמְעוֹן אָמַר. זִיבֵּחַ וְקִיטֵּר נִיסֵּךְ בְּהֶעֱלֶם אֶחָד אֵינוֹ חַייָב אֶלָּא אַחַת. מוֹדֶה שֶׁאִם עֲבָדָהּ בַּעֲבוֹדָתָהּ בַּעֲבוֹדַת הַגָּבוֹהַּ כַּעֲבוֹדַת הִשְׁתַּחֲוָיָה שֶׁהוּא חַייָב עַל כָּל־אַחַת וְאַחַת. מְנַיִין שֶׁאִם עֲבָדָהּ בַּעֲבוֹדָתָהּ בַּעֲבוֹדַת הַגָּבוֹהַּ בַּעֲבוֹדַת הִשְׁתַּחֲוָיָה שֶׁהוּא חַייָב עַל כָּל־אַחַת וְאַחַת. רִבִּי שְׁמוּאֵל בְּשֵׁם רִבִּי זְעוּרָה. וְלֹא־יִזְבְּח֥וּ עוֹד֙ אֶת־זִבְחֵיהֶ֔ם לַשְּׂעִירִ֕ם. אָֽמְרוּ לֵיהּ. מַטִּי תָנָהּ לַקֳּדָשִׁים.

רִבִּי יָסָא בְשֵׁם רִבִּי יוֹחָנָן. זִיבֵּחַ לָהּ טָלֶה בַּעַל מוּם חַייָב. מַאי כְדוֹן. כִּדְאָמַר רִבִּי הִילָא. לֹא־תַעֲשׂ֣וּן כֵּ֔ן לַיי אֱלֹהֵיכֶ֑ם׃ כָּלַיי אֱלֹהֵיכֶם לֹא־תַעֲשׂ֣וּן כֵּֽן.

אָמַר רִבִּי פִינְחָס קוֹמֵי רִבִּי יוֹסֵה בְשֵׁם רַב חִסְדָּא. הָיְתָה עֲבוֹדָתָהּ בְּבָנִים וּבְבָנוֹת וַעֲבָדָהּ בָּאָבוֹת וּבָאִמָּהוֹת חַייָב שְׁתַּיִם. וַהֲוָה רִבִּי זְעוּרָה חֲדִי בָהּ. סָבַר מֵימַר. בְּשִׁיטַּת רִבִּי הִילָא רַבֵּיהּ אִיתְאֲמָרַת. וְעַל דְּרִבִּי לָעְזָר בֵּירִבִּי שִׁמְעוֹן אִיתְאֲמָרַת. אֲמַר לֵיהּ. וּמַה בְיָדָךְ. וְעַל דְּרַבָּנִין אִיתְאֲמָרַת. אֲמַר לֵיהּ. וּלְהָדָא צוֹרְכָת.

Rebbi Abba bar Ḥiyya in the name of Rebbi Joḥanan[303]: Look at the expression which the Torah taught you, *Moloch*; anything that you make king over yourself, even a chip of wood, even a pebble[304]. *I shall extirpate him from amidst his people,* to include all other foreign worship in extirpation[300]. Rebbi Nasa in the name of Rebbi Eleazar: to include all other foreign worship relating to sons and daughters, as it was stated: He is guilty whether for the Moloch or any other foreign worship, whether he worshipped them with sons and daughters, or worshipped them with fathers and mothers. Rebbi Ze`ira said: if its worship did not prescribe this; but if its worship did prescribe it, he is free from prosecution[305]. Rebbi Hila said, even if its worship did prescribe it, he is twice guilty[306]. A *baraita* supports Rebbi Hila: The Moloch was included in all other foreign worships; it is mentioned separately to be lenient in this regard that he be guilty only for his descendants[307].

Rebbi Tanḥum bar Jeremiah said, it follows that Rebbi Eleazar ben Rebbi Simeon follows the argument of his father Rebbi Simeon. Just as Rebbi Simeon said, the Moloch was included in all other foreign worships; it is mentioned separately to be lenient in this regard that he be guilty only for his descendants, so Rebbi Eleazar ben Rebbi Simeon said, the Moloch was included in all other foreign worships; it is mentioned separately to be lenient in this regard that he be guilty only for his descendants[298].

Rebbi Tanḥum ben Yudan said, even though Rebbi Eleazar ben Rebbi Simeon said[254], if one sacrificed, and burned incense, and poured a libation in one forgetting[255] he is liable only for one; he agrees that if one worshipped it in its proper worship which is identical to the worship of Heaven like prostrating, he is liable for each single action[256]. From where that if one sacrificed, and burned incense, and poured a libation in one forgetting he is liable only for one; he agrees that if one worshipped it in its proper worship which is identical with the worship of Heaven like prostrating, he is liable for each single action? As Rebbi Samuel said in the name of Rebbi Ze`ira: *They should not continue to offer their sacrifices to spirits*[257]. They said to him, turn and refer it to sacrifices.

Rebbi Yasa in the name of Rebbi Joḥanan: If he sacrificed a defective lamb to it, he is guilty[259]. From where this? As Rebbi Hila said, *do not do such to the the Eternal, your God*[260]. Anything that be for the Eternal, your God, you may not do.

Rebbi Phineas said before Rebbi Yose in the name of Rav Ḥisda[308]: If its worship prescribed sons or daughters but he worshipped it with fathers or mothers, he is twice guilty. Rebbi Ze`ira enjoyed this; he thought that this was said following his teacher's Rebbi Hila's system and referred to Rebbi Eleazar ben Rebbi Simeon. He told him, what do you have in your hand? It referred to the rabbis! He answered, did you need it for this[309]?

303 In the Babli, 64a, this is a tannaïtic statement attributed to R. Hanina ben Antigonos.

304 Since the root *mlk* of "Moloch" means "to rule".

305 He holds that Moloch worship is defined by its rules, not by the name given to the deity being worshipped. Since R. Eleazar ben R. Simeon was quoted earlier that in Moloch worship one is guilty only for his descendants; if the rules of worship require descendants, the rules of Moloch worship apply. But if the Moloch rules are applied to the worship of a deity whose published rules do not include the Moloch rules, then it is an act of idolatry irrespective of the nature of the participants.

306 Once for idolatry and once for following the Moloch rules.

307 The following paragraph shows that

this *baraita* must be attributed to R. Simeon.

308 The name tradition here is impossible. R. Phineas, student of the last generation Amora R. Yose who was R. Ze`ira's student's student, could not have been R. Ze`ira's discussion partner and was an unlikely source for the statement of the second generation Rav Hisda.

309 Since the rabbis do not accept that the rules of the Moloch include any leniency, it is obvious that a person who worships any other deity by the Moloch ritual is guilty both of idolatry and of following the Moloch.

(25c line 31) אַזְהָרָה לְבַעַל אוֹב מְנַיִין. אַל־תִּפְנ֣וּ אֶל־הָאוֹבוֹת. כָּרֵת מְנַיִין. הַנֶּ֗פֶשׁ אֲשֶׁר תִּפְנֶ֣ה אֶל־הָאוֹבוֹת וְאֶל־הַיִּדְּעוֹנִים וגו'. עוֹנֶשׁ מְנַיִין. וְאִ֣ישׁ אֽוֹ־אִשָּׁה כִּֽי־יִֽהְיֶ֨ה בָהֶ֥ם א֛וֹב א֥וֹ יִדְּעוֹנִ֖י מ֣וֹת יוּמָ֑תוּ. וְלָמָּה לֹא תַנִּינָן יִדְּעוֹנִי בִּכְרֵיתוּת. רִבִּי חִזְקִיָּה בְשֵׁם רֵישׁ לָקִישׁ. מִפְּנֵי שֶׁנִּכְלְלוּ כוּלָּם בְּלָאו אֶחָד אַל־תִּפְנ֣וּ אֶל־הָאוֹבוֹת וגו'. רִבִּי יָסָא בְשֵׁם רֵישׁ לָקִישׁ. שֶׁהוּא בְלֹא תַעֲשֶׂה שֶׁהוּא בָא מִכֹּחַ עֲשֵׂה. אָמַר רִבִּי זְעוּרָה קוֹמֵי רִבִּי יָסָא. הָכֵן לָא אֲתָא מַתְנֵי בַר נַשׁ מַתְנֵי יִדְּעוֹנִי בִּכְרֵיתוּת אֶלָּא אַתְּ. אֲמַר לֵיהּ. כְּמָה דְאִישְׁתָּעֵי קְרָא אִישְׁתָּעַיַּית מַתְנִיתָה. אוֹב אוֹ יִדְּעוֹנִי.

אוֹ[325] זֶה פִיתוֹם הַמְדַבֵּר מִשֶּׁיחְיו. וְיִדְּעוֹנִי זֶה הַמְדַבֵּר בְּפִיו. הֲרֵי אֵלּוּ בִסְקִילָה וְהַנִּשְׁאָל בָּהֶן בְּאַזְהָרָה׃ וְדֹרֵ֖שׁ אֶל־הַמֵּתִֽים. אִית תַּנָּיֵי תַנֵּי. זֶה הַנִּשְׁאַל בַּגּוּלְגּוֹלֶת. אִית תַּנָּיֵי תַנֵּי. זֶה הַנִּשְׁאַל בִּזְכוּרוֹ. מַה בֵין הַנִּשְׁאַל בַּגּוּלְגּוֹלֶת לַמַּעֲלֶה בִזְכוּרוֹ. שֶׁהַנִּשְׁאַל בַּגּוּלְגּוֹלֶת עוֹלֶה כְדַרְכּוֹ וְעוֹלֶה בַשַּׁבָּת וְהַהֶדְיוֹט מַעֲלֶה אֶת הַמֶּלֶךְ. וְהַמַּעֲלֶה בִזְכוּרוֹ אֵינוֹ עוֹלֶה כְדַרְכּוֹ וְאֵינוֹ עוֹלֶה בַשַּׁבָּת וְאֵין הַהֶדְיוֹט מַעֲלֶה אֶת הַמֶּלֶךְ.

אָמַר רִבִּי הוּנָא. קִרְייָא מְסַייֵעַ לְמָאן דְּאָמַר. אוֹב זֶה הַמַּעֲלֶה בִזְכוּרוֹן. מַה טַעֲמָא. קָֽסֳמִי־נָ֥א לִי֙ בָּא֔וֹב וְהַ֣עֲלִי לִ֔י אֵ֥ת אֲשֶׁר־אֹמַ֖ר אֵלָֽיִךְ׃ מַה אַתְּ שְׁמַע מִינָּהּ. אָמַר רִבִּי מָנָא. מִיכָּן דַּהֲוָת יָדְעָה מִילִּין מִלִּין סַגִּין. מַאי כְדוֹן. וְֽהָיָ֨ה כְּא֤וֹב מֵאֶ֙רֶץ֙ קוֹלֵ֔ךְ.

מִילֵּיהוֹן דְּרַבָּנִין מְסַייְעָן לְרִבִּי יָסָא. דְּאָמַר רִבִּי יָסָא בְשֵׁם רַבָּנִין. מִפְּנֵי שֶׁהֵן מַקְטִירִין לַשֵּׁדִים. רִבִּי הִילָא בְשֵׁם רִבִּי יָסָא. מִפְּנֵי שֶׁנִּכְלְלוּ כוּלָּן עַל יְדֵי מַעֲשֶׂה.

From where the warning about the necromancer? *Do not turn to the necromancers*[326]. From where extirpation? *A person who would turn to necromancers and mediums*[327], etc. Punishment from where? *A man or woman, impersonating a necromancer or a medium, shall be put to death*[328]. Why is the medium not mentioned in *Keritut*[329]? Rebbi Ḥizqiah in the name of Rebbi Simeon ben Laqish: Because they are taken together in one prohibition, *do not turn to the necromancers*[330], etc. Rebbi Yasa in the name of Rebbi Simeon ben Laqish: Because it is a prohibition implied by a positive commandment[331]. Rebbi Ze`ira said before Rebbi Yasa: No person except you thought of stating the medium in this way in *Keritut*. He told him, because as the verse formulated it so the Mishnah formulates it, *a necromancer or a medium*[330].

"The necromancer is the πύθων[285] and one who[286] speaks from his armpit. The medium[58] speaks through his mouth. These are stoned but one who consults them is forewarned[287]. *And one who asks the dead*[332]. [333]Some Tannaïm state: this is one who interrogates a skull. Some Tannaïm state: this is one who interrogates his[334,173] masculinity. What is the difference between one interrogated by his skull or one raised by his masculinity? The one interrogated by his skull rises normally, rises on the Sabbath, and a commoner can raise a king. But one raised by his masculinity does not rise normally[335], does not rise on the Sabbath, and a commoner cannot raise a king.

Rebbi Huna said, a verse supports him who said, the necromancer is the one who raises by his masculinity. What is the reason? *Please apply necromancer's magic and raise for me whom I shall tell you*[336]. What do you understand from here? Rebbi Mana said, it implies that she was competent in many ways[337]. What about it? *Your voice will be from the earth like that of a necromancer*[338].

The words of the rabbis support Rebbi Yasa, as Rebbi Yasa said in the rabbis' name: Because they burn incense to spirits[339]. Rebbi Hila in the name of Rebbi Yasa: Because they all were included by actions[340].

325 Read אוֹב.

326 *Lev.* 19:31. Here starts the discussion of the second part of the Mishnah.

327 *Lev.* 20:6.

328 *Lev.* 20:27.

329 Mishnah *Keritut* 1:1 mentions only the necromancer, not the medium.

330 In *all* pentateuchal verses mentioning אוֹב it is paired with יִדְּעוֹנִי (the verses quoted plus *Deut.* 18:11). Babli 65b.

331 Cf. 5:3, Note 73. This formulation does not make any sense, as indicated by R. Ze`ira's question. It should have been formulated: Because the medium is treated as an appendix to the necromancer. The medium never creates an obligation for a purification offering if one for necromancy already was established; he cannot be mentioned in *Keritut* 1:1 separately from the necromancer.

332 *Deut.* 18:11. No criminal sanction is spelled out for this.

333 Tosephta 10:7, explaining the term "interrogating the dead". In the Babli, 65b, the same *baraita* explains the term "necromancer".

334 The dead.

335 The dead appears feet up, head down.

336 *1S.* 28:8.

337 Since Saul had to request a particular

method, the woman must have been competent in all sorts of sorcery. She realized that her customer was Saul because she recognized Samuel whose status was that of a king.

338 *Is.* 29:4.

339 This returns to the statement of R. Yasa in the first paragraph here. The user of necromancy is a potential candidate for a purification offering since it depends on an action, *viz.*, burning incense to spirits. But a medium who is totally passive does not qualify.

340 A different formulation of the argument of Note 339; all transgressions mentioned in *Keritut* 1:1 involve some action.

(fol. 24a) **משנה יד**: הַמְחַלֵּל אֶת הַשַּׁבָּת בְּדָבָר שֶׁחַייָבִין עַל זְדוֹנוֹ כָּרֵת וְעַל שִׁגְגָתוֹ חַטָּאת. וְהַמְקַלֵּל אָבִיו וְאִמּוֹ אֵינוֹ חַייָב עַד שֶׁיְּקַלְּלֵם בַּשֵּׁם. קִלְּלָם בְּכִנּוּי רַבִּי מֵאִיר מְחַייֵב וַחֲכָמִים פּוֹטְרִין:

Mishnah 14: One who desecrates the Sabbath[59,341] by something which if performed intentionally makes him liable to extirpation, or to a purification sacrifice if in error. But he who curses father or mother[60] is guilty only of he cursed them by the Name[207]. If he cursed them by a substitute name, Rebbi Meïr declares him guilty but the Sages free him from prosecution.

משנה טו: הַבָּא עַל נַעֲרָה הַמְאוֹרָסָה אֵינוֹ חַייָב עַד שֶׁתְּהֵא נַעֲרָה בְתוּלָה מְאוֹרָסָה בְּבֵית אָבִיהָ. בָּאוּ עָלֶיהָ שְׁנַיִם הָרִאשׁוֹן בִּסְקִילָה וְהַשֵּׁנִי בְּחֶנֶק:

Mishnah 15: One who has sexual relations with a preliminarily married adolescent[7] is only liable if she was an adolescent, a virgin, and preliminarily married, in her father's house. If two [men] had relations with her, the first one is stoned, the second is subject to strangling[342].

341 If duly warned by two witnesses about the criminality of his intent, he can be prosecuted if in the absence of witnesses he would be subject to Divine extirpation. But if he violates any of the positive commandments for the Sabbath he cannot be prosecuted by biblical standards; for violating a simple prohibition he at most could be sentenced to 39 lashes.

342 As a common adulterer.

(25c line 51) **הלכה יד**: הַמְחַלֵּל אֶת הַשַּׁבָּת כול'. אַזְהָרָה לַמְחַלֵּל מְנַיִין. לֹא־תַעֲשֶׂה כָל־מְלָאכָה. כָּרֵת מְנַיִין. כִּי כָּל־הָעוֹשֶׂה בָהּ מְלָאכָה וְנִכְרְתָה. עוֹנֶשׁ מְנַיִין. מְחַלְלֶיהָ מוֹת יוּמָת.

וְתַנֵּי שְׁלֹשִׁים וְשֶׁבַע כָּרֵיתוֹת בַּתּוֹרָה. אָמַר רִבִּי יוֹסֵי בֵּירִבִּי בּוּן. שֶׁאִם עָשָׂה כוּלָּן בְּזָדוֹן שַׁבָּת וּבְזָדוֹן מְלָאכָה שֶׁהוּא חַייָב עַל כָּל־אַחַת וְאַחַת.

Halakhah 14: "One who desecrates the Sabbath," etc. From where warning for the desecrator? *Do not perform any work*[343]. From where extirpation? *For any who would perform work on it would be extirpated*[344]. From where punishment? *Its desecrator shall be made to die the death.* Should we not state 37 kinds of extirpation in the Torah[345]? Rebbi Yose ben Rebbi Abun said, because if he performs all of them, intentionally on the Sabbath and intentionally for the work, he is liable for each one singly.

343 *Ex.* 20:10.

344 *Ex.* 31:14.

345 This is a copy from Halakhah 9, Note 149. The question should be that in *Keritut* 1:1 74 kinds of extirpation should be mentioned since, as R. Yose ben Abun explains, each one of the 39 categories of work forbidden on the Sabbath defines its own obligation for a purification sacrifice if the person was aware that it was Sabbath and that he was performing this kind of work, and only had forgotten that it was forbidden. Then a single person could be obligated for up to 39 sacrifices for desecrating a single Sabbath. But if he simply had forgotten that it was Sabbath, a single sacrifice is due and this is what is counted in *Keritut*.

(25c line 55) אַזְהָרָה לַמְקַלֵּל אָבִיו וְאִמּוֹ מְנַיִין. אִישׁ אִמּוֹ וְאָבִיו תִּירָאוּ. עוֹנֶשׁ וְכָרֵת מְנַיִין. וּמְקַלֵּל אָבִיו וְאִמּוֹ מוֹת יוּמָת: וְאוֹמֵר כִּי כָּל־אֲשֶׁר יַעֲשֶׂה מִכֹּל הַתּוֹעֵבֹת הָאֵלֶּה וְנִכְרְתוּ.

From where a warning for the one who curses father or mother? *Everybody has to fear his mother and father*[346]. From where punishment and extirpation? *And he who curses his father or mother shall be made to die the death*[347]. And it says, *for anybody who would commit any of these abominations will be extirpated*[349,131].

346 *Lev.* 19:3.

347 *Ex.* 21:17.

348 A verse introduced by "and it says" is quoted as indirect support of a thesis, not a proof. The verse decrees extirpation only for sexual crimes; it precedes *Lev.* 19:3 by 4 verses. But cursing or injuring father or mother are the only capital crimes for which no verse decrees extirpation. One might consider cursing a parent as an abomination.

(25c line 58) הַבָּא עַל נַעֲרָה הַמְאוֹרָסָה. רִבִּי יָסָא בְשֵׁם רִבִּי יוֹחָנָן רִבִּי חִייָה בְשֵׁם רִבִּי לָעְזָר. דְּרִבִּי מֵאִיר הִיא. בְּרַם לְרַבָּנִין אֲפִילוּ קְטַנָּה. מַה טַעֲמָא דְּרִבִּי מֵאִיר. נַעַר חָסֵר אָמוּר בַּפָּרָשָׁה.

מַה מְקַייְמִין רַבָּנִן נַעַר. רִבִּי אַבָּהוּ בְשֵׁם רֵישׁ לָקִישׁ. נַעֲרָה אַחַת שְׁלֵימָה אֲמוּרָה בַפָּרָשָׁה וְלִימְּדָה עַל כָּל־הַפָּרָשָׁה כוּלָּהּ שֶׁהִיא גְדוֹלָה. מְתִיב רִבִּי מֵאִיר לְרַבָּנִין. הֲרֵי הַמּוֹצִיא שֵׁם רַע הֲרֵי אֵין כָּתוּב בּוֹ אֶלָּא נַעַר וְהִיא גְדוֹלָה. שֶׁאֵין קְטַנָּה נִסְקֶלֶת. מָה עַבְדִּין לָהּ רַבָּנִין. אָמַר רִבִּי אָבִין. תִּיפְתָּר שֶׁבָּא עָלֶיהָ דֶּרֶךְ זְכָרוּת. רִבִּי יַעֲקֹב בַּר אַבָּא בְּעָא קוֹמֵי רַב. הַבָּא עַל הַקְּטַנָּה מָהוּ. אָמַר לֵיהּ. בִּסְקִילָה. הַבָּא עַל הַבּוֹגֶרֶת מָהוּ. אָמַר לֵיהּ. אֲנִי אֶקְרָא נַעֲרָה וְלֹא בוֹגֶרֶת. וּקְרָא נַעֲרָה וְלֹא קְטַנָּה. וְלֵית מוֹדֶה לִי שֶׁהִיא בִקְנָס. אָמַר לֵיהּ. תַּחַת אֲשֶׁר עִינָּהּ. לְרַבּוֹת אֶת הַקְּטַנָּה לִקְנָס. וּקְרָא תַּחַת אֲשֶׁר עִינָּהּ. לְרַבּוֹת אֶת הַבּוֹגֶרֶת בִּקְנָס. אָמַר רַב. אַף עַל גַּב דְּנִצְחִי רִבִּי יַעֲקֹב בַּר אַבָּא בְדִינָא הֲלָכָה הַבָּא עַל הַקְּטַנָּה בִסְקִילָה וְהִיא פְטוּרָה. רִבִּי אָבוּן בְּשֵׁם רִבִּי שְׁמוּאֵל. וְלָמָּה לֹא פָתַר לֵיהּ מִן הָדָא. וּמֵ֗ת הָאִ֛ישׁ אֲשֶׁר־שָׁכַ֥ב עִמָּ֖הּ לְבַדּֽוֹ׃ וְכִי אֵין אָנוּ יוֹדְעִין שֶׁאֵין לַנַּעֲרָה חֵט מָוֶת. וּמַה תַלְמוּד לוֹמַר וְלַֽנַּעֲרָ֙ לֹא־תַעֲשֶׂ֣ה דָבָ֔ר אֵ֥ין לַֽנַּעֲרָ֖ה חֵ֣טְא מָ֑וֶת. אֶלָּא מִכָּן הַבָּא עַל הַקְּטַנָּה בִסְקִילָה וְהִיא פְטוּרָה.

349"One who has sexual relations with a preliminarily married maiden." Rebbi Yasa in the name of Rebbi Johanan, Rebbi Hiyya in the name of Rebbi Eleazar: This is Rebbi Meïr's. But for the rabbis even if she is a minor. What is Rebbi Meïr's reason? "*Lad*" is written defectively in the paragraph. How do the rabbis explain "*a lad*"? Rebbi Abbahu in the name of Rebbi Simeon ben Laqish: Once in the paragraph it is written *a young woman*; this teaches that in the entire paragraph she is an adult. Rebbi Meïr objected to the rabbis: In the matter of the calumniator, *a lad* is written and she is an adult since a minor is not stoned? What do the rabbis do with this? Rebbi Abin said, explain it that he came to her as a male.

Rebbi Jacob bar Abba asked before Rav: What is the law of him who comes to a minor? He said to him, by stoning. What is the law of him who comes to an adult? He said to him, I am reading *an adolescent*, not an adult. Read *an adolescent*, not a minor! Do you not agree with me that she has the right to a fine? He answered, *because he mistreated her*, that includes a minor for a fine. Read *because he mistreated her*, that includes an adult for a fine! Rav said, even though Rebbi Jacob bar Abba won the logical argument, practice is that he who comes to a minor is [punished] by stoning but she is free. Rebbi Abun in the name of (Rebbi)[350] Samuel. Why? He understood it from the following: *The man who had lain with her alone shall die*. Do we not know that the girl has not committed a capital crime? Why does the verse say, *do not do anything to the girl; the girl has not committed a capital crime*?

That includes him who has sexual relations with a [preliminarily married] underage girl; he is stoned and she is free.

349 This text is also in *Ketubot* 3:9, explained there with a list of readings in Notes 126-135. The parallel in the Babli is 66b.

350 It is clear from *Ketubot* and the Babli that the speaker is Samuel, Rav's contemporary, and not the later Galilean R. Samuel. *Sifry Deut* 243 disagrees with Samuels' argument.

(fol. 24a) **משנה יו:** הַמֵּסִית זֶה הֶדְיוֹט הַמֵּסִית אֶת הַהֶדְיוֹט. אָמַר לוֹ יֵשׁ יִרְאָה בְּמָקוֹם פְּלוֹנִי כָּךְ אוֹכֶלֶת כָּךְ שׁוֹתָה כָּךְ מְטִיבָה כָּךְ מְרִיעָה. כָּל חַיָּבֵי מִיתוֹת שֶׁבַּתּוֹרָה אֵין מַכְמִינִין עֲלֵיהֶם חוּץ מִזּוֹ. אָמַר לִשְׁנַיִם וְהֵן עֵדָיו, מְבִיאִין אוֹתוֹ לְבֵית דִּין וְסוֹקְלִין אוֹתוֹ.

Mishnah 16: The one who leads astray[351] is a commoner who leads a commoner astray, by saying to him: There is something to worship at place X; it eats such and such, drinks such and such; it gives such and such benefits, can do such and such evil. For no capital crime in the Torah may one use entrapment[352], except for this one. If he said it to two persons, they become his witnesses, bring him to court, and stone him.

משנה יז: אָמַר לְאֶחָד הוּא אוֹמֵר יֶשׁ לִי חֲבֵרִים רוֹצִים בְּכָךְ. אִם הָיָה עָרוּם וְאֵינוֹ מְדַבֵּר בִּפְנֵיהֶם מַכְמִינִין מֵאֲחוֹרֵי הַגָּדֵר וְהוּא אוֹמֵר לוֹ אֱמוֹר מַה שֶּׁאָמַרְתָּ לִי בְּיִיחוּד וְהַלָּה אוֹמֵר לוֹ וְהוּא אוֹמֵר לוֹ הֵיאַךְ נַנִּיחַ אֱלֹהֵינוּ שֶׁבַּשָּׁמַיִם וְנַעֲבוֹד עֵצִים וַאֲבָנִים. אִם חָזַר בּוֹ מוּטָב. אִם אָמַר כָּךְ הִיא חוֹבָתֵנוּ וְכָךְ יָפֶה לָנוּ הָעוֹמְדִין מֵאֲחוֹרֵי הַגָּדֵר מְבִיאִין אוֹתוֹ לְבֵית דִּין וְסוֹקְלִין אוֹתוֹ.

Mishnah 17: If he said this to a single person, he should tell him, I have friends who also want this[353]. If he was sly[354] and did not talk in their presence, one sets a trap behind a wall[355]; he tells him, repeat what you told me alone; then he tells him, how can we abandon our God in Heaven and worship wood and stones[356]? If he repents, it is good[357]; if he says, it is our duty, or so it is good for us, those who stand behind the wall bring him to court and stone him.

משנה יח: הָאוֹמֵר אֶעֱבוֹד אֵלֵךְ וְאֶעֱבוֹד נֵלֵךְ וְנַעֲבוֹד. אֲזַבֵּחַ אֵלֵךְ וַאֲזַבֵּחַ נֵלֵךְ וּנְזַבֵּחַ. אַקְטִיר אֵלֵךְ וְאַקְטִיר נֵלֵךְ וְנַקְטִיר. אֲנַסֵּךְ אֵלֵךְ וַאֲנַסֵּךְ נֵלֵךְ וּנְנַסֵּךְ. אֶשְׁתַּחֲוֶה אֵלֵךְ וְאֶשְׁתַּחֲוֶה נֵלֵךְ וְנִשְׁתַּחֲוֶה. הַמַּדִּיחַ זֶה הָאוֹמֵר נֵלֵךְ וְנַעֲבוֹד עֲבוֹדָה זָרָה:

Mishnah 18: He says, I shall worship, I shall go and worship, let us go and worship; I shall sacrifice, I shall go and sacrifice, let us go and sacrifice; I shall burn incense, I shall go and burn incense, let us go and burn incense; I shall pour libations, I shall go and pour libations, let us go and pour libations; I shall prostrate myself, I shall go and prostrate myself, let us go and prostrate ourselves. The seducer[351] is one who says, let us go and profess a strange worship.

351 The one who leads astray (Note 61) presents a problem for law enforcement since a single listener cannot appear in court as a witness. In the Babli, the seducer (Note 62) is one who openly propagates another faith, who is easily prosecuted. But in the Yerushalmi the difference between *him who leads astray* and the *seducer* is that the former speaks Hebrew while the latter speaks in the vernacular.

352 By the prosecution, as spelled out in Mishnah 17.

353 In order to have him speak before two witnesses.

354 He knows that if he only speaks to a single listener, he may with impunity try to convert a thousand people since no two of them can testify to the same occurrence and, therefore, cannot appear as witnesses in court.

355 A rural wall of stones without mortar.

356 This is the required warning, *viz.*, that apostasy is a crime.

357 Then he cannot be prosecuted since what he said was before he was duly warned, which is not prosecutable in court.

(25c line 74) **הלכה יו**: הַמֵּסִית זֶה הֶדְיוֹט כול'. הָא חָכָם לֹא. מִכֵּיוָן שֶׁהוּא מֵסִית אֵין זֶה חָכָם. מִכֵּיוָן שֶׁהוּא נִיסֵּת אֵין זֶה חָכָם. כֵּיצַד עוֹשִׂין לְהַעֲרִים עָלָיו. מַכְמִינִין עָלָיו שְׁנֵי עֵדִים בַּבַּיִת הַפְּנִימִית וּמוֹשִׁיבִין אוֹתוֹ בַּבַּיִת הַחִיצוֹן וּמַדְלִיקִין אֶת הַנֵּר עַל גַּבָּיו כְּדֵי שֶׁיְּהוּ רוֹאִין אוֹתוֹ וְשׁוֹמְעִין אֶת קוֹלוֹ. שֶׁכֵּן עָשׂוּ לְבֶן סוֹטֶדָא בְּלוֹד וְהִכְמִינוּ עָלָיו שְׁנֵי תַלְמִידֵי חֲכָמִים וְהֶבִיאוּהוּ לְבֵית דִּין וּסְקָלוּהוּ. וָכָה אַתְּ אָמַר הָכֵן. שַׁנְייָא הִיא דְּאָמַר. אֲנִי. וְאָמַר אוֹף הָכָא. אֲנִי. שֶׁלֹּא יַעֲרִים. וְיַעֲרִים. שֶׁלֹּא יֵלֵךְ וְיַסִּית עַצְמוֹ וְיַסִּית אֲחֵרִים עִמּוֹ.

2 ניסת | י ניסית מכמינין | י מכמינים עדים | י עדים בני אדם 3 את הנר | י נר 4 סוטדא | י סטרא והכמינו | י שהכמינו 5 את אמר | י תמר ואמר אוף | י אף שלא יערים. ויערים | י - 6 ילך ויסית עצמו ויסית | י יברח וילך לו וילך ויסית את

Halakhah 16: "The one who leads astray is a commoner," etc. [358]Therefore, not a Sage? Since he seduces, he is not a Sage. Since he is seduced, he is not a Sage. What does one do to outwit him? One hides two witnesses in an inner room and puts him into the outer room, lights a candle near him so they can see him and hear his voice. That is what they did to Ben Sateda in Lydda, where they hid two Sages, brought him to court, and stoned him. And here, you say so? It is different because he said, "I am". Here also, "I am"? That he should not get wise to it. And what if he got wise to it? That he should not go away, and continue to seduce himself and others with him.

358 The parallel text is in *Yebamot* 16:6 (י) Notes 125-132. The text there is the original, since only there the question "and here, you say so?" and the answer to it make sense.

(25d line 5) מֵסִית אוֹמֵר בְּלָשׁוֹן גָּבוֹהַּ וְהַמֵּדִיחַ אוֹמֵר בְּלָשׁוֹן נָמוּךְ. מֵסִית שֶׁאָמַר בְּלָשׁוֹן נָמוּךְ נַעֲשֶׂה מֵדִיחַ. וּמֵדִיחַ שֶׁאָמַר בְּלָשׁוֹן גָּבוֹהַּ נַעֲשֶׂה מֵסִית. מֵסִית אוֹמֵר בְּלָשׁוֹן הַקּוֹדֶשׁ וּמֵדִיחַ אוֹמֵר בְּלָשׁוֹן הֶדְיוֹט. מֵסִית שֶׁאָמַר בְּלָשׁוֹן הֶדְיוֹט נַעֲשֶׂה מֵדִיחַ. וּמֵדִיחַ שֶׁאָמַר בְּלָשׁוֹן הַקּוֹדֶשׁ נַעֲשֶׂה מֵסִית.

The one who leads astray says it aloud, the seducer speaks in a low voice. One who leads astray who spoke in a low voice becomes a seducer; a seducer who spoke in a low voice becomes one who leads astray. The one who leads astray speaks in Hebrew, the seducer speaks in a vernacular. One who leads astray who spoke in a vernacular becomes a seducer; a seducer who spoke in Hebrew becomes one who leads astray[351,359].

345 Since one who leads astray and the seducer are two different biblical categories, a missionary for paganism cannot be condemned if the paragraph under which he is condemned is not determined.

(fol. 24b) **משנה יט**: הַמְכַשֵּׁף הָעוֹשֶׂה מַעֲשֶׂה וְלֹא הָאוֹחֵז אֶת הָעֵינַיִם. רִבִּי עֲקִיבָה אוֹמֵר מִשּׁוּם רִבִּי יְהוֹשֻׁעַ שְׁנַיִם לוֹקְטִים קִשּׁוּאִין אֶחָד לוֹקֵט פָּטוּר וְאֶחָד לוֹקֵט חַייָב. הָעוֹשֶׂה מַעֲשֶׂה חַייָב וְהָאוֹחֵז אֶת הָעֵינַיִם פָּטוּר:

Mishnah 19: The sorcerer is one who does a deed[360] but not one who creates an illusion[361]. Rebbi Aqiba says in the name of Rebbi Joshua: Two are collecting green melons[362]; one who collected cannot be prosecuted, the other one is guilty. The who does a deed is guilty; he who creates an illusion cannot be prosecuted.

360 To convict somebody of sorcery, to be punished by stoning (Mishnah 5), the

witnesses have to prove that he created something contradicting the laws of nature; at the end of the Halakhah this seems to be restricted to the creation of a parentless living creature.

361 In this matter, visual impressions do not count.

362 In modern Hebrew "zucchini"; cf. *Kilaim* Chapter 1, Note 38.

(25d line 10) **הלכה יט**: הַמְכַשֵּׁף הָעוֹשֶׂה מַעֲשֶׂה כול'. מְכַשֵּׁפָה לֹא תְחַיֶּה: אֶחָד הָאִישׁ וְאֶחָד הָאִשָּׁה. אֶלָּא שֶׁלִּימְּדָתְךָ הַתּוֹרָה דֶּרֶךְ אֶרֶץ מִפְּנֵי שֶׁרוֹב הַנָּשִׁים כַּשְׁפָנִיּוֹת. אָמַר רִבִּי לְעֶזֶר. מְכַשֵּׁף בִּסְקִילָה. מַה טַעֲמָא דְּרִבִּי לְעֶזֶר. נֶאֱמַר כָּאן מְכַשֵּׁפָה לֹא תְחַיֶּה. וְנֶאֱמַר לְהַלָּן אִם־בְּהֵמָה אִם־אִישׁ לֹא יִחְיֶה. מַה לֹא יִחְיֶה שֶׁנֶּאֱמַר לְהַלָּן בִּסְקִילָה אַף כָּאן בִּסְקִילָה. מַה טַעֲמוֹן דְּרַבָּנִין. נֶאֱמַר כָּאן מְכַשֵּׁפָה לֹא תְחַיֶּה. וְנֶאֱמַר לְהַלָּן לֹא תְחַיֶּה כָּל־נְשָׁמָה. מַה לֹא תְחַיֶּה שֶׁנֶּאֱמַר לְהַלָּן מִיתָה בַּחֶרֶב. אַף לֹא תְחַיֶּה שֶׁנֶּאֱמַר כָּאן מִיתָה בַּחֶרֶב. אָמַר רִבִּי עֲקִיבָה. מִן הַדָּבָר הַזֶּה אֲנִי מַכְרִיעוֹ. מוּטָּב שֶׁיִּלָּמֵד לֹא תְחַיֶּה מִלֹּא תְחַיֶּה וְאַל יוֹכִיחַ לֹא יִחְיֶה. מַה טַעֲמָא דְּרִבִּי יְהוּדָה. נֶאֱמַר כָּאן מְכַשֵּׁפָה לֹא תְחַיֶּה וְנֶאֱמַר לְהַלָּן כָּל־שֹׁכֵב עִם־בְּהֵמָה מוֹת יוּמָת: מַה מִיתַת הַבְּהֵמָה בִּסְקִילָה אַף כָּאן בִּסְקִילָה.

Halakhah 19: "The sorcerer is one who does a deed," etc. *A sorceress you shall not let live*[363], whether man or woman, but the Torah taught you the way of the world that most women have a tendency to sorcery[364]. Rebbi Eliezer said, a sorcerer is [executed] by stoning. What is Rebbi Eliezer's reason? It says here, *a sorceress you shall not let live*, and it says there, *whether human or animal they shall not live*[365]. Since *shall not live* there means by stoning, also here by stoning. What is the rabbis'[366] reason? It says here, *a sorceress you shall not let live*, and it says there, *you shall not let live anybody*[367]. Since *you shall not let live* there means death by the sword, also *you shall not let live* here means death by the sword. Rebbi Aqiba said, from this argument I am deciding. It is preferable to learn *you shall not let live* from *you shall not let live* rather than from *shall not live*. What is Rebbi Jehudah's reason[368]? It says here, *a sorceress you shall not let live,* and it says there, *anybody lying with an animal shall die the death*[369]. Since the execution of the animal is by stoning, so here also by stoning[370].

363 *Ex.* 22:17.

364 Babli 67a and *Mekhilta dR. Simeon ben Iohai, ad loc.*, the first part only in *Mekhilta dR. Ismael, ad loc.*

365 *Ex.* 19:13. The verse requires *stoning or shooting* the transgressor.

In the Babylonian sources (Babli and the two *Mekhiltot*), this argument is attributed to R. Aqiba, who in the Yerushalmi rejects it.

366 There "rabbis" oppose the Mishnah and decree beheading for the sorcerer; in Babli and *Mekhilta dR. Simeon ben Iohai* the author is R. Yose the Galilean, in *Mekhilta dR. Ismael* it is R. Ismael.

367 *Deut.* 20:16.

368 The student of R. Eliezer's student gives the final argument for the Mishnah. In the Babli (here and *Berakhot* 21b) and *Mekhilta dR. Simeon ben Iohai* his argument is attributed to Ben Azzai, in *Mekhilta dR. Ismael* to R. Yose the Galilean.

369 *Ex.* 22:18, the verse following the one about the sorceress. Since in v. 17 the method of execution is not indicated, the instruction of v. 18 is interpreted in the light of *Lev.* 20:15-16 and applied to both verses.

370 Since for animals the only explicitly mentioned example of execution is the stoning of the notorious bull.

(25d line 21) דִּלְמָא. רִבִּי לִעֶזֶר וְרִבִּי יְהוֹשֻׁעַ וְרִבִּי עֲקִיבָה עָלוֹן לְמִסְחֵי בְהָדֵין דֵּימוֹסִין דְּטִיבֵּרִיָּא. חַמְתּוֹן חַד מִינַיי. אָמַר מַה דָּמַר וּתְפַשִׂיתוֹן כִּיפָּה. אָמַר רִבִּי לִיעֶזֶר לְרִבִּי יְהוֹשֻׁעַ. מַה יְהוֹשֻׁעַ בֶּן חֲנַנְיָה. חֲמִי מַה דְאַתְּ עֲבַד. מִי נְפַק אָהֵן מִינַייָא אָמַר רִבִּי יְהוֹשֻׁעַ מַה דָּמַר וְתָפַשׂ יָתֵיהּ תַּרְעָה. וַהֲוָה כָּל־מָאן דַּעֲלֵיל הֲוָה יְהִיב לֵיהּ חַד מַרְתּוּקָה וְכָל־מָאן דִּנְפַק הֲוָה יְהִיב לֵיהּ בְּנִתִּיקָא. אֲמַר לוֹן. שְׁרוֹן מַה דַּעֲבַדְתּוֹן. אָמְרִין לֵיהּ. שְׁרִי וַאֲנָן שָׁרֵיי. שָׁרוֹן אִילֵּין וְאִילֵּין. מִן דִּנְפַקוֹן אֲמַר רִבִּי יְהוֹשֻׁעַ לְהַהוּא מִינַייָה. הָא מַה דְאַתְּ חֲכַם. אֲמַר נֵיחוֹת לְיַמָּא. מִן דְּנַחְתִּין לְיַמָּא אֲמַר הַהוּא מִינַייָא מַה דַּאֲמַר וְאִיתְבְּזַע יַמָּא. אֲמַר לוֹן. וְלָא כֵן עֲבַד מֹשֶׁה רַבְּכוֹן בְּיַמָּא. אָמְרִין לֵיהּ. לֵית אַתְּ מוֹדֶה לוֹן דַּהֲלִיךְ מֹשֶׁה רַבָּן בְּגַוֵּיהּ. אֲמַר לוֹן. אִין. אָמְרוּן לֵיהּ. וַהֲלִיךְ בְּגַוֵּיהּ. הָלַךְ בְּגַוֵּיהּ. גְּזַר רִבִּי יְהוֹשֻׁעַ עַל שָׂרָהּ דְּיַמָּא וּבְלָעֵיהּ.

Example. Rebbi Eliezer, Rebbi Joshua, and Rebbi Aqiba went to bathe at the public baths[371] of Tiberias. A Minean[372] saw them, said what he said, and the cupola caught them[373]. Rebbi Eliezer said to Rebbi Joshua:[374] Joshua ben Ḥanania, look what you can do. When this Minean was leaving, Rebbi Joshua said what he said and the door trapped him. Anybody who entered hit him with his fist, anybody leaving hit him when forcing the door open. He told them, undo what you did; they told him, you undo, then we shall undo. They mutually undid. When they left, Rebbi Joshua said to this Minean, is that all you are wise to? He answered, let us go down to the sea. When they had descended to the sea, this Minean said what he said and the sea was split. He told them, is that not what your teacher Moses did to the sea? They answered, do you not agree that our teacher Moses walked through it? He said to them, yes. They told him, enter it. He entered it. Rebbi Joshua commanded the prince of the sea[375] who swallowed him.

371 δημόσια (*scil.*, βαλανεῖα).

372 A Jewish heretic; a name frequently but not exclusively applied to Jewish Christians.

373 They were put under a spell so they could not leave the space under the cupola of the main room of the thermal baths.

374 In the rules of witchcraft all Sages of his generation were students of R. Eliezer, as told at the end of the Halakhah.

375 The angel running the Sea of Genezareth. The idea of angels running natural phenomena is a Jewish adaptation of the Greek myth of gods of the sea and nymphs of sources.

(25d line 33) דִּלְמָא. רִבִּי לְעֶזֶר וְרִבִּי יְהוֹשֻׁעַ וְרַבָּן גַּמְלִיאֵל סְלָקוּן לְרוֹמֵי. עָלוֹן לְחַד אֲתַר וְאַשְׁכְּחוֹן מֵיינוּקַיָּא עָבְדִין גַּבְשׁוּשִׁין וְאָמְרִין הָכֵין. בְּנֵי אַרְעָא דְיִשְׂרָאֵל עָבְדִין וְאָמְרִין. הָהֵן תְּרוּמָה וְהָהֵן מַעֲשֵׂר. אָמְרִין מִסְתַּבְּרָא דְאִית הָכָא יְהוּדָאִין. עָלוֹן לְחַד אֲתַר וְאִתְקַבְּלוּן בְּחַד כיי[376]. יְתָבוּן לְמֵיכַל וַהֲוָה כָּל־תַּבְשִׁיל דַּהֲוָה עֲלִיל קוֹמֵיהוֹן אִי לָא הֲווֹן מַעֲלִין לֵיהּ בְּחַד קִיטוֹן לָא הֲוָה מַייתֵי לֵיהּ קוֹמֵיהוֹן. וְחָשׁוּן דִּילְמָא דְאִינּוּן אָכְלִין זִבְחֵי מֵתִים. אָמְרִין לֵיהּ. מָה עִסְקָךְ דְּכָל־תַּבְשִׁיל דְּאַתְּ מַייתֵי קוֹמֵינָן אִין לֵית אַתְּ מְעַייֵל לָהֵן קִיטוֹנָא לֵית אַתְּ מַייתֵי לָן קוֹמֵינָן. אֲמַר לוֹן. חַד אַבָּא גְבַר סָב אִית לִי וּגְזַר עַל נַפְשֵׁיהּ דְּלָא נְפַק מִן הָדָא קִיטוֹנָא כְּלוּם עַד דְּיֵיחְמֵי לְחַכְמֵי יִשְׂרָאֵל. אָמְרִין לֵיהּ. עוֹל וֶאֱמוֹר לֵיהּ. פּוּק הָכָא לְגַבֵּיהוֹן דְּאִינּוּן הָכָא. נְפַק לְגַבּוֹן. אָמְרִין לֵיהּ. מָה עִיסְקָךְ. אֲמַר לוֹן. צְלוֹן עַל בְּרִי דְלָא מוֹלִיד. אָמַר רִבִּי לְעֶזֶר לְרִבִּי יְהוֹשֻׁעַ. מַה יְהוֹשֻׁעַ בֶּן חֲנַנְיָה. חֲמִי מַה דְּאַתְּ עֲבִיד. אֲמַר לוֹן. אַייתוֹן לִי זֶרַע דְּכִיתָּן. וְאַייְתוֹן לֵיהּ זֶרַע דְּכִיתָּן. אִיתְחֲמֵי לֵיהּ זָרַע לֵיהּ עַל גַּבֵּי טַבְלָה. אִיתְחֲמֵי מַרְבֵּץ לֵיהּ. אִיתְחֲמֵי דְסָלְקַת. אִיתְחֲמֵי מִתְלַשׁ בָּהּ. עַד דַּאֲסַק חָדָא אִיתָא בְּקַלְעִיתָא דְשַׂעֲרָה. אֲמַר לָהּ. שְׁרֵי מַה דַּעֲבַדְתִּין. אָמְרָה לֵיהּ. לֵי נָא שָׁרְיָיה. אֲמַר לָהּ. דְּלָא כֵן אֲנָא מְפַרְסֵם לִיךְ. אָמְרָה לֵיהּ. לֵי נָא יָכְלָה דְאִינּוּן מְטַלְקִין בְּיַמָּא. וּגְזַר יְהוֹשֻׁעַ עַל שַׂרְיָא דְיַמָּא וּפְלָטוֹן. וְצָלוֹן עֲלוֹי וְזָכָה לְמוֹקְמֵי לְרִבִּי יוּדָה בֶּן בַּתִירָה. אָמְרוּ. אִילּוּ לֹא עָלִינוּ לְכָאן אֶלָּא לְהַעֲמִיד הַצַּדִּיק הַזֶּה דַּיֵּינוּ.

Example. Rebbi Eliezer, and Rebbi Joshua, and Rabban Gamliel travelled to Rome. They came to a place where they found children making stone heaps and saying as follows: What they do in the Land of Israel is to say, this is heave, this is tithe. They said, it is clear that Jews live here. They entered a place and were received at a house. They sat down to eat. It happened that no dish was brought to them unless it was brought [first] to a certain bedroom[377]. They became afraid that perhaps they were eating offerings to the dead[378]. They asked him, why is it that you bring no dish before us unless you brought it first to that bedroom? He told them, I have an old father who vowed not to leave that bedroom until he might see the Sages of Israel. They told him, go and tell him to come out because they are here. He came out; they asked him, what is your problem? He told them, pray for my son because he is sterile. Rebbi Eliezer said to Rebbi Joshua:[374] Joshua ben Ḥanania, look what you can do. He told them, bring me linseed; they brought him linseed. It appeared to them as if he was sowing it on a table[379]. It appeared as if he was watering it; it appeared to grow; it appeared that he was plucking out of it, until there appeared a woman with braided hair. He told her, undo what you did. She answered, I shall not undo. He told her, then I shall make you known. She said, I cannot, because they[380] were thrown into the sea. Rebbi Joshua commanded the prince of the sea[375] who disgorged them. Then they prayed for him and he had the merit of raising Rebbi Jehudah ben Bathyra[381]. They said, if we came here only to bring the just person to the world, it would have been enough.

376 Read ביי for בַּיִת.

377 Greek κοιτών.

378 Since it is not usual to eat in a bedroom, they were afraid that the food was first offered to a corpse in a pagan ceremony which would make the food forbidden to them.

379 Latin *tabula*.

380 The charms used for the spell put on the son to make him sterile.

381 The family Ben Bathyra is placed in both Talmudim (cf. *Berakhot* 3:4 Note 391) at Nisibis in Kurdistan, not on the road from Palestine to Rome. The source of the stories, characterized as non-legal texts by their Aramaic language, is a problem because it mixes Palestinian חמי "to see" with the Babylonian meaning "to decree" of the root גזר instead of Galilean "to decide".

(25d line 53) אָמַר רִבִּי יְהוֹשֻׁעַ בֶּן חֲנַנְיָה. יְכִיל אֲנָא נְסִיב קָרְיָין וַאֲבַטִּיחִין וַעֲבִיד לוֹן אַיְילִין טַבִּין וְהִידְנוֹן עֲבִידִין אַיְילִין וְטַבִּין. אֲמַר רִבִּי יַנַּאי. מְהַלֵּךְ הֲוֵינָא בְּהָדָא אִסְרָטָא דְצִיפּוֹרִי וַחֲזִית חַד מִינַיי נְסִיב חַד צְרִיר וּזְרַק לֵיהּ לְרוּמָא וַהֲוָה נְחַת וּמִתְעֲבֵד עֵגֶל. וְלֹא כֵן אָמַר רִבִּי לָעְזָר בְּשֵׁם רִבִּי יוֹסֵי בַּר זִמְרָא. אִם מִתְכַּנְּסִין הֵן כָּל־בָּאֵי עוֹלָם אֵינָן יְכוּלִין לִבְרָאוֹת יִתּוּשׁ אֶחָד וְלִזְרוֹק בּוֹ נְשָׁמָה. נֵימַר. לָא נֶסְבָה הוּא מִינַיָּא חַד צְרוֹר וּזְרָקֵיהּ לְרוּמָא וּנְחַת וּמִתְעֲבֵד חַד עֵגֶל. אֶלָּא לְסָרֵיהּ קָרָא וְגָנַב לֵיהּ עֵגֶל מִן בָּקוֹרְתָא וְאַייתֵי לֵיהּ.

אָמַר רִבִּי חִינְנָא בֵּירִבִּי חֲנַנְיָה. מְטַייֵל הֲוֵינָא בְּאִילֵּין גּוּפְתָּא דְצִיפּוֹרִין וַחֲמִית חַד מִינַיי נְסִיב חָדָא גּוּלְגְּלָא וּזְרָקָהּ לְרוּמָא וְהִיא נַחְתָּא וּמִתְעַבְדָא עֵגֶל. אֲתִית וַאֲמָרִית לְאַבָּא. אֲמַר לִי. אִין אֲכָלִית מִינָּהּ מַעֲשֶׂה הוּא. וְאִילָא אֲחִיזַת עֵינַיִם הוּא.

Rebbi Joshua ben Hanania said: I am able to take gourds and watermelons and turn them into rams and deer who would produce rams and deer. Rebbi

Yannai said, I was walking on a road in Sepphoris when I saw a Minean[372] taking a pebble, throwing it into the air, after which it came down transforming itself into a calf. But did not Rebbi Eleazar say in the name of Rebbi Yose ben Zimra: If all people of the world came together, they could not create one mosquito and bring it to life[382]. Let us say that this Minean did not take a pebble, threw it into the air, after which it came down transforming itself into a calf, but he called on his genie[383] who stole a calf for him from a cattle barn and brought it to him.

Rebbi Ḥinena ben Ḥanania said: I was promenading at Gufta[384] of Sepphoris when I saw a Minean taking a skull, throwing it into the air, after which it came down transforming itself into a calf. I went and told it to my father. He said, if you ate from it, it was an action; otherwise it was an illusion.

382 Since the objection is not raised against R. Joshua, plants are recognized as living things parallel to animals. Babli 67b.

383 Both vocalization and translation are tentative.

384 An unidentified suburb of Sepphoris; cf. *Kilaim* 9:4 Note 85.

(25d line 65) אָמַר רִבִּי יְהוֹשֻׁעַ בֶּן חֲנַנְיָה. שְׁלֹשׁ מֵאוֹת פַּרְשִׁיּוֹת הָיָה רִבִּי לִיעֶזֶר דּוֹרֵשׁ בְּפָרָשַׁת מְכַשֵּׁפָה וּמִכּוּלָּם לֹא שָׁמַעְתִּי אֶלָּא שְׁנֵי דְבָרִים. שְׁנַיִם לוֹקְטִין קִישּׁוּאִין אֶחָד לוֹקֵט פָּטוּר וְאֶחָד לוֹקֵט חַיָּב. הָעוֹשֶׂה מַעֲשֶׂה חַיָּב וְהָאוֹחֵז אֶת הָעֵינַיִם פָּטוּר. אָמַר רִבִּי דָּרוֹסָא. תְּשַׁע מֵאוֹת פַּרְשִׁיּוֹת הָיוּ. שְׁלֹשׁ מֵאוֹת לְחִיּוּב וּשְׁלֹשׁ מֵאוֹת לִפְטוֹר וּשְׁלֹשׁ מֵאוֹת לְחִיּוּב שֶׁהוּא פְטוֹר.

Rebbi Joshua ben Ḥanania said: Rebbi Eliezer used to explain 300 chapters in the matter of the sorceress, but from all of them I understood only two things: "Two are collecting green melons[362]; one who collected cannot be prosecuted, the other one is guilty. He who does a deed is guilty; he who creates an illusion cannot be prosecuted." Rebbi Darosa said, there were 900 chapters. 300 where one is guilty, 300 where one is free[385], and 300 where one is guilty but cannot be prosecuted.[386]

385 Creating the illusion of witchcraft is not forbidden.

386 Forbidden action which nevertheless cannot lead to prosecution. A similar situation exists for Sabbath prohibitions where only a small part of Sabbath violations are of the kind that could be prosecuted in court. Babli 68a.

בן סורר ומורה פרק שמיני

(fol. 26a) **משנה א**: בֵּן סוֹרֵר וּמוֹרֶה מֵאֵימָתַי נַעֲשֶׂה בֵן סוֹרֵר וּמוֹרֶה מִשֶּׁיָּבִיא שְׁתֵּי שְׂעָרוֹת וְעַד שֶׁיַּקִּיף זָקָן הַתַּחְתּוֹן וְלֹא הָעֶלְיוֹן אֶלָּא שֶׁדִּבְּרוּ חֲכָמִים בְּלָשׁוֹן נְקִייָה. שֶׁנֶּאֱמַר כִּי־יִהְיֶה לְאִישׁ בֵּן. בֵּן וְלֹא בַת. בֵּן וְלֹא אִישׁ. הַקָּטָן פָּטוּר שֶׁלֹּא בָא לִכְלַל הַמִּצְוֹת:

Mishnah 1: The deviant and rebellious son[1]. When can one become a deviant and rebellious son? From the moment he grows two [pubic] hairs to when he sports a beard, the lower, not the upper[2], because the Sages used clean language[3]. For it is written: *If a man have a [deviant and rebellious] son*[4]. A son but not a daughter, a son but not a father[5]. The underage [son] is not liable since he does not have any obligation[6].

1 Who has to be stoned according to Mishnah 7:5.

2 If the pubic area is fully covered by hair.

3 To avoid mentioning genitals.

4 *Deut*. 21:18.

5 From the moment that a son is sexually mature, he can no longer be tried as deviant and rebellious son.

6 An underage child never has any obligation; his parents have the duty to educate him.

(26a line 45) **הלכה א**: בֵּן סוֹרֵר וּמוֹרֶה כול'. רִבִּי זְעִירָא רִבִּי אַבָּהוּ רִבִּי יוֹסֵי בֶּן חֲנִינָה בְשֵׁם רִבִּי שִׁמְעוֹן בֶּן לָקִישׁ. כָּתוּב וְכִי־יָזִד אִישׁ עַל־רֵעֵהוּ לְהוֹרְגוֹ בְעָרְמָה. מֵאֵימָתַי הוּא נַעֲשֶׂה אִישׁ. מִשֶּׁיָּזִיד. מֵאֵימָתַי הוּא מֵזִיד. מִשֶּׁתִּתְפַּשֵּׁט הַכַּף. מָשָׁל בָּשֵׁל הַזֶּרַע מִבִּפְנִים חִשְׁחִירָה הַקְּדֵירָה מִבַּחוּץ. אָמַר רִבִּי זְעִירָא. תַּנָּא רִבִּי שִׁילָא בַּר בִּינָא. כִּי־יִהְיֶה לְאִישׁ בֵּן. לֹא שֶׁיְּהֵא הַבֵּן אָב. מִכֵּיוָן שֶׁהוּא רָאוּי לָבוֹא עַל אִשָּׁה וּלְעַבְּרָהּ הֲיי דִי לֵיהּ אָב וְלֹא בֵן. וְאָֽמְרָה תוֹרָה. בֵּן וְלֹא אָב. וְאַתְיָא כַּיי דָמַר רִבִּי יָסָא בְשֵׁם רִבִּי שַׁבְּתַי. כָּל־יָמָיו שֶׁלְּבֵן סוֹרֵר וּמוֹרֶה אֵינָן אֶלָּא שִׁשָּׁה חֳדָשִׁים בִּלְבַד.

Halakhah 1: "The deviant and rebellious son," etc. Rebbi Ze`ira, Rebbi Abbahu, Rebbi Yose ben Ḥanina in the name of Rebbi Simeon ben Laqish. It is written: *If a man would concoct against his neighbor to kill him slyly*[7]. When does he become a man? When he concocts. When is he done cooking? When his *palm*[8] expands. A simile: If the seed is fully cooked inside, the pot becomes black on the outside. Rebbi Ze`ira said that Rebbi Shila bar Bina stated: *If a man have a son*, not that the son be a father. From the moment that he may come to a woman and make her pregnant, he is a potential father, not a son[9]. But the Torah said, a son, not a father. It parallels what Rebbi Yasa said in the name of Rebbi Sabbatai: The entire period of a "deviant and rebellious son" is only six months[10].

7 *Ex*. 21:14. The argument is an almost untranslatable pun, identifying the two meanings of the root זיד "to plot, to be mischievous" and "to cook" (Babli 69a). (Gesenius-Buhl also notes the two meanings for the root; modern Jewish lexicographers following Ben Jehudah prefer to derive the *hapax* "to cook" from a root נזד.)

8 *Palm* as anatomic detail denotes the *mons veneris* of a woman (*Yebamot* 1:2, Note 143); it is used here for the corresponding pubic area of the man.

9 While it is accepted that from the age of 9 years a male may be able to have full intercourse with a woman (*Yebamot* 3:10 Note 143), he cannot be held responsible for his actions before he reaches age 13. Therefore, he can be a responsible father only at age 13. The Babli (68b,69b) and the Yerushalmi (*Yebamot* 10:14, Notes 209-211; copied *Qiddušin* 1:2 59c l. 26, p. 73) recognize the fact that an underage male may become a father. The son born to an underage father can never become *deviant and rebellious* since he is not the son of a *man* as required by the verse.

10 Since everywhere in talmudic literature the period between onset of female puberty and full feminine development is taken to be six months, the same is asserted here for the male. In the Babli, 69a, R. Sabbatai determines this period as three months.

(26a line 53) אָמַר רִבִּי יָסָא. כָּל־אִילֵּין מִילַּייָא לָא מִסְתַּבְּרִין דְּלָא חִילוּפִין. תַּנֵּי. תֵּדַע לָךְ שֶׁהוּא כֵן. מִי הָיָה בְדִין שֶׁיְּהֵא חַייָב הַבֵּן אוֹ הַבַּת. הֲוֵי אוֹמֵר. הַבַּת. וּפָטְרָה הַתּוֹרָה אֶת הַבַּת וְחִייְבָה אֶת הַבֵּן. מִי הָיָה בְדִין שֶׁיְּהֵא חַייָב קָטוֹן אוֹ גָדוֹל. הֲוֵי אוֹמֵר. גָּדוֹל. פָּטְרָה הַתּוֹרָה אֶת הַגָּדוֹל וְחִייְבָה אֶת הַקָּטָן. מִי הָיָה בְדִין שֶׁיְּהֵא חַייָב הַגּוֹנֵב מִשֶּׁלַּאֲחֵרִים אוֹ הַגּוֹנֵב מִשֶּׁלְּאָבִיו וְאִמּוֹ. הֲוֵי אוֹמֵר. הַגּוֹנֵב מִשֶּׁלַּאֲחֵרִים. פָּטְרָה הַתּוֹרָה הַגּוֹנֵב מִשֶּׁלַּאֲחֵרִים וְחִייְבָה הַגּוֹנֵב מִשֶּׁלְּאָבִיו וְאִמּוֹ. לְלַמְּדָךְ שֶׁכּוּלָּן אֵינָן אֶלָּא בִגְזֵירַת מֶלֶךְ.

Rebbi Yasa said, all these rules would be reasonable if they were the opposite. It was stated: You should know that this is the case. Who according to reason should be guilty, son or daughter? One would say, a daughter[11]. But the Torah freed the daughter and declared the son guilty[12]. Who according to reason should be guilty, the younger or the older? One would say, the older. But the Torah freed the older and declared the younger guilty[12]. Who according to reason should be guilty, one who steals from others or one who steals from father or mother? One would say, one who steals from others. But the Torah freed the one who steals from others and declared the one who steals from father or mother guilty[13]. To teach that all of these [rules] are only the King's decisions[14].

11 Who in her youth has to be obedient to her parents and later in life to her husband.

12 As stated in the Mishnah.

13 Mishnah 5.

14 Even though this seems to contradict Halakhah 7.

(fol. 26a) **משנה ב:** מֵאֵימָתַי הוּא חַיָּיב מִשֶּׁיֹּאכַל טרטימר בָּשָׂר וְיִשְׁתֶּה חֲצִי לוֹג יַיִן בָּאִיטַלְקִי. רַבִּי יוֹסֵי אוֹמֵר, מְנֶה בָּשָׂר וְלוֹג יַיִן. אָכַל בַּחֲבוּרַת מִצְוָה אָכַל בְּעִבּוּר הַחֹדֶשׁ אָכַל מַעֲשֵׂר שֵׁנִי בִּירוּשָׁלַם. אָכַל נְבֵלוֹת וּטְרֵפוֹת וּשְׁקָצִים וּרְמָשִׂים. אָכַל דָּבָר שֶׁהוּא מִצְוָה וְדָבָר שֶׁהוּא עֲבֵרָה אָכַל כָּל־מַאֲכָל וְלֹא אָכַל בָּשָׂר שָׁתָה כָל־מַשְׁקֶה וְלֹא שָׁתָה יַיִן אֵינוֹ נַעֲשֶׂה בֵן סוֹרֵר וּמוֹרֶה עַד שֶׁיֹּאכַל בָּשָׂר וְיִשְׁתֶּה יַיִן שֶׁנֶּאֱמַר זוֹלֵל וְסֹבֵא. וְאַף עַל פִּי שֶׁאֵין רְאָיָה לַדָּבָר זֵכֶר לַדָּבָר שֶׁנֶּאֱמַר אַל־תְּהִי בְסֹבְאֵי יָיִן בְּזֹלְלֵי בָשָׂר לָמוֹ׃

Mishnah 2: When is he guilty? From the moment he eats a fourfold[15] portion of meat and drinks half a *log* of wine. Rebbi Yose says, a *mina* of meat[16] and a *log* of wine. If he ate in a company of obligation[17], or at the lengthening of a month[18], or ate Second Tithe in Jerusalem, or ate torn or carcass meat, abominations and crawling things, i. e., if he ate anything which either is an obligation or anything forbidden, or ate any food but not meat, or drank any drink but not wine, he does not turn into a deviant and rebellious son unless he ate meat and drank wine, since it is said: *gorging and drinking to excess*[4]. Even if it is not proof, there is a hint in what is said: *Do not be among those who drink wine excessively, nor with those who are gorging themselves on meat*[19].

15 Greek τετραμοιρία "fourfold portion", cf. H. and E. Guggenheimer, תרטימר בשר Sinai 83(1978) p. 191. A *baraita* in the Babli (*Pesahim* 86b, *Besah* 25b) states that a civilized person drinks a cup of wine (a quarter *log*, about 130 cm^3) in two sips. One becomes deviant in drinking half a *log* in one gulp; this is the fourfold amount of a civilized person. The "fourfold amount" of meat is defined in the Halakhah

(and the Babli) as half a Roman pound. Therefore, a civilized person will eat meat in portions no larger than $1\frac{1}{2}$ Roman oz. per bite. The amount mentioned in the Mishnah refers to a single bite or sip, not the total amounts consumed during a meal (Maimonides *Mamrim* 7:2).

The form טרטימר instead of טטרמור is not unusual since Greek words copied into Aramaic or Hebrew often exhibit metathesis if one of the consonants λμνρ is involved [H. and E. Guggenheimer, למילון התלמודי יב *Lešonenu* 39(1975) 59-60.]

16 A Greek *mina* of 100 drachmas, not a Semitic *maneh* of 60 šeqels (between 120 and 240 drachmas), cf. Note 20.

17 In modern Hebrew this is called סְעוּדַת מִצְוָה "a meal of obligation", the festive meal at religious occasions such as weddings, circumcisions, redemption of firstborns, etc.

18 Before the publication of the calendar computations the Synhedrion, and its successor, the Academy of Tiberias, had to determine for every month whether it should have 29 or 30 days. This meeting always was the occasion of a festive meal.

19 *Prov.* 23:20.

(26a line 61) **הלכה ב**: מֵאֵימָתַי הוּא חַייָב כול'. אָמַר רִבִּי יוֹסֵי. טרטימר חֲצִי לִטְרָא הוּא.

Halakhah 2: "When is he guilty," etc. Rebbi Yose said[20], the fourfold portion is half a Roman pound.

20 The Amora R. Yose determines the amount required by the Sages as half that indicated by the Tanna R. Yose, a statement ascribed in the Babli to his teacher's teacher R. Ze`ira. His statement implies that. as a weight, a mina (100 drachmas) was identified with the pound of 12 ounces, i. e. 96 denars. Since other talmudic data indicate that as a coin, *drachma* in the Eastern Roman Empire was the name of the silver denar, one has to assume that *mina* as a weight simply was a name for the Roman pound. [D. Sperber (*Roman Palestine 200-400, Money and Prices*, Ramat Gan 1974) consistently writes *mina* for the weight and *maneh* for the coin. But since a talmudic מנה always denotes 100 denars, there is no reason not to read the word as Μνᾶ, מְנָה.]

(26a line 62) אֵינוֹ חַייָב עַד שֶׁיֹּאכְלֶנּוּ מְהוּבְהָב. אֲכָלוֹ חַי כֶּלֶב הוּא. אֲכָלוֹ מְבוּשָּׁל בַּר נַשׁ הוּא. אֲכָלוֹ הסוקים מָהוּ. גִּידִים הָרַכִּים מָה הֵן. רִבִּי יוֹחָנָן אָמַר. נִימְנִין עֲלֵיהֶן. רִבִּי שִׁמְעוֹן בֶּן לָקִישׁ אָמַר. אֵין נִימְנִין עֲלֵיהֶן. רִבִּי יַעֲקֹב בַּר אָחָא בְשֵׁם רִבִּי זְעִירָא. אִיתְפַּלְּגוֹן רִבִּי יוֹחָנָן וְרִבִּי שִׁמְעוֹן בֶּן לָקִישׁ. דְּתַנִּינָן תַּמָּן. אֵילּוּ שֶׁעוֹרוֹתֵיהֶן כִּבְשָׂרָן. אָמַר רִבִּי יוֹחָנָן. עוֹד זֶה לֹא שָׁנוּ אֶלָּא לְאִיסּוּר וּלְטוּמְאָה. הָא לִלְקוֹת לֹא. רִבִּי שִׁמְעוֹן בֶּן לָקִישׁ אָמַר. מִשְׁנָה תְמִימָה שָׁנָה רִבִּי. בֵּין לְאִיסּוּר בֵּין לְטוּמְאָה. מִחְלְפָה שִׁיטָּתֵיהּ דְּרִבִּי שִׁמְעוֹן בֶּן לָקִישׁ. תַּמָּן הוּא עֲבַד לָהּ בָּשָׂר. וְכָא לָא עֲבַד לָהּ בָּשָׂר. אָמַר רִבִּי יוּדָה בַּר פָּזִי. שַׁנְייָא הִיא תַמָּן שֶׁהוּא עוֹר וְסוֹפוֹ לְהַקְשׁוֹת. כָּל־שֶׁכֵּן מִחְלְפָה

שִׁיטָּתֵיהּ דְּרִבִּי שִׁמְעוֹן בֶּן לָקִישׁ. וּמַה תַּמָּן שֶׁסּוֹפוֹ לְהַקְשׁוֹת הוּא עֲבַד לָהּ בָּשָׂר. כָּאן שֶׁאֵין סוֹפוֹ לְהַקְשׁוֹת לֹא כָל־שֶׁכֵּן. אָמַר רִבִּי אַבָּהוּ. טַעֲמָא דְרִבִּי יוּדָה בַּר פָּזִי וְאָכְלוּ אֶת־הַבָּשָׂר. לֹא גִידִים.

He is guilty only it he ate it rare[21]. If he ate it raw, he is a dog. If he ate it cooked, he is a human. If he ate cartilage[22], what is the rule? What is the rule about soft sinews? [23]Rebbi Johanan said, one subscribes to them; Rebbi Simeon ben Laqish said, one does not subscribe to them. Rebbi Jacob bar Aḥa in the name of Rebbi Ze`ira: Rebbi Johanan and Rebbi Simeon ben Laqish disagreed about what is stated there[24]: "The following have their hides treated like their flesh." Rebbi Johanan said, this was only said as prohibition and regarding impurity, but not for flogging. Rebbi Simeon ben Laqish said, Rebbi stated a complete Mishnah, not only for prohibition and regarding impurity[25].

The reasoning of Rebbi Simeon ben Laqish seems inverted. There, he treats it as flesh, but here, he does not treat it as meat[26]. Rebbi Judah bar Pazi said, there is a difference, since there one refers to skin which in the end will become hard. This emphasizes that the reasoning of Rebbi Simeon ben Laqish seems inverted! Since there, where in the end it will harden, he treats it as flesh, here where in the end it will not harden[27], not so much more? Rebbi Abbahu[28] said, the reason of Rebbi Judah bar Pazi is: *they shall eat the meat in that night*[29], not sinews.

21 Superficially grilled. Eating grilled meat rare is not human. In the Babli (70a) this is called "cooked and uncooked".

22 The word הסוקים is a *hapax* and probably corrupt. It is translated as if it were written חסוכים.

23 This text to the end of the paragraph is a shortened form of a discussion in *Pesahim* 7:11 (35a l. 62); the final result there and here is that the discussion is irrelevant for the rules regarding the deviant and rebellious son, which implies that for the *fourfold portion* nothing can be included that is not regularly counted as food.

The paschal lamb may be eaten only by persons who had subscribed to it, i. e., who were part of the group for whom the lamb was slaughtered during the afternoon of the 14th of Nisan. The lamb should be eaten in small quantities at the end of the meal; the minimum quantity per person is the volume of an average olive (כְּזַיִת). The question now arises whether barely edible parts, such as cartilage and soft sinews, can be used to fulfill the duty of eating from the paschal lamb and the number of subscribers increased accordingly.

24 Mishnah *Hulin* 9:2. Mishnah 9:1 states that in general the hide of an animal is

subject to the rules of impurity of food, but not to those of impurity of carcasses. Then Mishnah 2 lists some animals whose hides follow the rules of flesh in all respects (general consensus exists only for humans and domesticated pigs.) R. Johanan holds that for eating pigskin one never can be prosecuted, while R. Simeon ben Laqish holds that eating pigskin, not yet transformed into leather, is as punishable as eating pork.

25 In *Pesaḥim* it is stated explicitly that the differences among the rabbis are about whipping offenders.

26 "There" is *Ḥulin, "here" is Pesaḥim.*

27 Animal hide will become inedible; soft sinews and cartilage will remain edible after cooking.

28 In *Pesaḥim*" R. Abun".

29 *Ex.* 12:8, a verse about the paschal lamb, irrelevant for the rules about the deviant and rebellious son.

(26a line 74) אָכַל בַּחֲבוּרַת מִצְוָה. אָכַל בְּעִבּוּר הַחֹדֶשׁ. אָכַל מַעֲשֵׂר שֵׁנִי בִּירוּשָׁלֵם. וְיִסְּרוּ אֹתוֹ וְאֵינֶנּוּ שׁוֹמֵעַ בְּקוֹלָם. יָצָא זֶה שֶׁהוּא שׁוֹמֵעַ בְּקוֹל אָבִיו שֶׁבַּשָּׁמַיִם.

"If he ate in a company of obligation[17], or at the lengthening of a month[18], or ate Second Tithe in Jerusalem." *They would discipline him,* but he does not listen to their voice[30]. This excludes one who listens to the voice of his Father in Heaven[31].

30 A slight misquote from *Deut.* 21:18, for: *but he does not listen to the voice of his father or his mother.*

31 Cf. *Qiddušin* 1:2, Note 630.

(26a line 76) אָמַר רִבִּי יוֹחָנָן. אִם הִזְכִּירוּךְ לְבוּלֵי יְהְיֶה יַרְדֵּן בַּעַל גְּבוּלְךְ. אָמַר רִבִּי יוֹחָנָן. קוֹבְלִין לָרָשׁוּת לְהִיפָּטֵר מִבּוּלֵי. אָמַר רִבִּי יוֹחָנָן. לוֹוִין בְּרִיבִּית לַחֲבוּרַת מִצְוָה וּלְקִידּוּשׁ הַחוֹדֶשׁ. רִבִּי יוֹחָנָן הֲוָה עֲלִיל לִכְנִשְׁתָּא בְּצַפְרָא וּמְלַקֵּט פֵּירוּרִין וַאֲכִיל וַאֲמַר. יְהֵא חֶלְקִי עִם מָאן דְּקַדֵּשׁ יַרְחָא הָכָא רוּמְשִׁית.

[32]Rebbi Joḥanan said, if you were nominated for the city council, may the Jordan be the master of your border[33]. Rebbi Joḥanan said, one complains to the government to be freed from the city council[34]. Rebbi Joḥanan said, one borrows against interest for a company of obligation and the sanctification of the month. Rebbi Joḥanan used to go to the assembly hall in the morning[35], collect the crumbs, and eat them, saying: May my part be with those who in the evening were sanctifying the month.

32 This paragraph does not belong here. It is a slight reformulation of a paragraph in *Mo`ed qatan* 2:3 (81b l. 33). There it was stated that one is permitted to earn money on the intermediate days of a holiday in order to have more money to spend on festive meals. The connection to this Chapter is that the deviant and rebellious son is absolved if he partakes of festive meals.

33 Since the Roman government never allowed local taxes, it appointed rich people to the council (βουλή); these had to provide public services at their own expense. To avoid such an onerous *leiturgia*, one is permitted to leave the Land of Israel.

34 While in general one should avoid contact with Roman imperial officials, it is permitted to file complaints to make oneself undesirable, so as not to be considered for a council appointment.

35 Before he became a member of the body fixing the calendar.

(26b line 4) אָכַל נְבֵלוֹת וּטְרֵפוֹת שְׁקָצִים וּרְמָשִׂים. וְיִסְּרוּ אוֹתוֹ וְלֹא יִשְׁמַע בְּקוֹלָם. יָצָא זֶה אֲפִילוּ בְקוֹל אָבִיו שֶׁבַּשָּׁמַיִם אֵינוֹ שׁוֹמֵעַ.

"Or ate torn or carcass meat, abominations and crawling things." *They would discipline him,* but he would not listen to their voice[30]. This excludes one who even to the voice of his Father in Heaven[31] does not listen[36].

36 Babli 70b.

(fol. 26a) **משנה ג**: גָּנַב מִשֶּׁל אָבִיו וְאָכַל בִּרְשׁוּת אָבִיו מִשֶּׁל אֲחֵרִים וְאָכַל בִּרְשׁוּת אֲחֵרִים מִשֶּׁל אֲחֵרִים וְאָכַל בִּרְשׁוּת אָבִיו אֵינוֹ נַעֲשָׂה בֵן סוֹרֵר וּמוֹרֶה עַד שֶׁיִּגְנוֹב מִשֶּׁל אָבִיו וְיֹאכַל בִּרְשׁוּת אֲחֵרִים. רַבִּי יוֹסֵי בֵּי רַבִּי יְהוּדָה אוֹמֵר עַד שֶׁיִּגְנוֹב מִשֶּׁל אָבִיו וּמִשֶּׁל אִמּוֹ:

Mishnah 3: If he stole from his father and ate at his father's property, or from others and ate at others' property, or from others and ate at his father's property, he is not treated as deviant and rebellious son unless he stole from his father and ate at others' property[37]. Rebbi Yose ben Rebbi Jehudah says, unless he stole both from his father and his mother[38].

37 That he stole money from his father to which he has easy access and ate at other's premises where does not have to fear to be easily discovered. The facility of the crime will turn him into a habitual criminal (Babli 71a).

38 Since in the relevant paragraph the Torah insists to mention the mother on equal footing with the father. If the mother has no separate property of her own, there is a

question whether according to this opinion the son can never become deviant and rebellious (Note 50).

הלכה ג: (26b line 7) גָּנַב מִשֶּׁלְּאָבִיו כול'. אַזְהָרָה לַגְּנֵיבָה הָרִאשׁוֹנָה מְנַיִין. לֹא תִּגְנוֹבוּ. אַזְהָרָה לַגְּנֵיבָה שְׁנִייָה מְנַיִין. לֹא תִגְנוֹבוּ. לֹא תִגְנוֹבוּ עַל מְנָת לְמַקֵּט. לֹא תִגְנוֹבוּ עַל מְנָת לְשַׁלֵּם תַּשְׁלוּמֵי כֶפֶל. עַל מְנָת לְשַׁלֵּם תַּשְׁלוּמֵי אַרְבָּעָה וַחֲמִשָּׁה. בֶּן בַּגְבַּג אוֹמֵר. לֹא תִגְנוֹב אֶת שֶׁלָּךְ מֵאַחַר הַגַּנָּב. שֶׁלֹּא תֵרָאֶה גוֹנֵב.

רִבִּי בָּא רִבִּי יוֹחָנָן בְּשֵׁם רַב הוֹשַׁעְיָה. אֵינוֹ חַייָב עַד שֶׁיִּגְנוֹב מָעוֹת. רִבִּי זְעִירָה בְשֵׁם רִבִּי הוֹשַׁעְיָה. אֵינוֹ חַייָב עַד שֶׁיְּזַלְזֵל מָעוֹת. מָהוּ שֶׁיְּזַלְזֵל מָעוֹת. מָה אֲנָן קַייָמִין. אִם בָּהוּ דְאָמַר. הֵא לָךְ חֲמִשָּׁה וְהַב לִי תְלָתָא. שַׁטְיָא הוּא. הֵא לָךְ תְּלָתָא וְהַב לִי חֲמִשָּׁה. בַּר נַשׁ הוּא. אֶלָּא כִּי נָן קַייָמִין בְּהוּא דָמַר. הֵא לָךְ חֲמִשָּׁה וְהַב לִי חֲמִשָּׁה.

הֵי דֵינוֹ גַנָּב וְהֵי דֵינוֹ גַזְלָן. אָמַר רִבִּי הִילָא. גָּנַב בִּפְנֵי עֵדִים גַּנָּב. בִּפְנֵי הַבְּעָלִים גַּזְלָן. רִבִּי זְעוּרָה בָעֵי. מֵעַתָּה אֲפִילוּ נִתְכַּוֵון לִגְזֵילָה וּלְבַעֲלֶיהָ אֵין זֶה גוֹזְלָן. וְהֵידֵינוּ גוֹזְלָן עַל דַּעְתֵּיהּ דְּרִבִּי זְעוּרָה. רִבִּי שְׁמוּאֵל בַּר סוֹסַרְטָא בְשֵׁם רִבִּי אַבָּהוּ. עַד שֶׁיִּגְזְלֶנּוּ בִפְנֵי עֲשָׂרָה בְנֵי אָדָם. בִּנְייָן אָב שֶׁבְּכוּלָּן וַיִּגְזוֹל אֶת־הַחֲנִית מִיַּד הַמִּצְרִי וַיַּהַרְגֵהוּ בַּחֲנִיתוֹ:

1 תגנובו | א תגנוב 2 שנייה | א השנייה תגנובו | א תגנוב 3 תגנוב | א תגנב 5 רב | א ר' זעירה | א זעירא 6 שיזלזל | א עד שיזלזל בהו | א באו 7 שטי | א שוטה 8 בהוא | א באו 9 הי דינו | א היידינו (2 times) גזלן | א גוזלן 9-10 ר' זעורה בעי | א אמ' ר' זעירה 10 לגזילה | א לגוזלה ולבעליה | א ולבעילה אזלה זה | א - והידינו | א והיי דינו דעתיה | א - 11 שיגזלנו | א שיגזול 12 ויהרגהו בתניתו | א וגו'

Halakhah 3: "If he stole from his father," etc. [39]From where a first warning about stealing: *you shall not steal*[40]. From where a second warning about stealing: *you shall not steal*[41]. *You shall not steal*, in order to aggravate; *you shall not steal,* in order to pay double restitution, in order to pay quadruple or quintuple restitution. Ben Bagbag says, do not steal your own property from the thief, lest you be seen stealing.

Rebbi Abba, Rebbi Joḥanan in the name of Rav[42] Hoshaia: he is guilty only if he steals money. Rebbi Ze`ira in the name of Rebbi Hoshaia: he is guilty only if he shows contempt for money. What means showing contempt for money? Where do we hold? If about him who says, here you have five and give me for three, he is an idiot. Here you have three and give me for five, he is a regular person. But we deal with one who says, here you have five and give me for five[43].

What is a thief and what is a robber[44]? Rebbi Hila said, if he stole in the presence of witnesses, he is a thief, in the presence of the owners he is a robber. Rebbi Ze`ura asked[45]: but if he intended to rob in front of its owners, he is not a robber. What is a robber according to Rebbi Ze`ura? Rebbi Samuel ben Sosarta in the name of Rebbi Abbahu: only if he rob in the presence of ten people. The prototype for all these: *He robbed the spear from the hand of the Egyptian and killed him with his own spear*[46].

39 This Halakhah also is Halakhah 11:2 (**א**); only the second paragraph is relevant here.

40 As in 11:2 one should read *do not steal* לֹא תִּגְנוֹב, *Ex.* 20:16. The Ten Commandments only refer to the worst of crimes; *stealing* referred to there is kidnapping of humans, a capital crime (Babli 86a, *Bava meṣia`* 61b).

41 Stealing as a civil offense is prohibited in *Lev.* 19:11. The remainder of the paragraph is a *baraita* also in *Sifra Qedošim Parašah* 2(2), Tosephta *Bava qamma* 10;37-38, Babli *Bava qamma* 27b (*Tanhuma Noah* 4). Stealing is forbidden even if one intends to return the stolen goods after teaching the owner a lesson, or to have a pretext to give a poor person money in the shape of a fine.

42 With 11:2 read "Rebbi".

43 Since he has money, he has the urge to spend all of it even if it means that he buys more than he actually needs.

44 With 11:2 read: "R. Ze`ira said."

45 While the thief pays double to quintuple restitution, the robber only has to return the robbed goods. The distinction between thief and robber has far-reaching consequences. The thief takes by stealth, the robber in public. The question is, what is the definition of "in public"?

46 *2S.* 23:21. R. Ze`ira insists that the characteristic of the robber is not that he takes by force, even in the presence of the owners, but that he does it in public. As always, "in public" is defined as in the presence of ten adult males. Babli *Bava qamma* 79b.

(fol. 26a) **משנה ד**: הָיָה אָבִיו רוֹצֶה וְאִמּוֹ אֵינָהּ רוֹצָה אָבִיו אֵינוֹ רוֹצֶה וְאִמּוֹ רוֹצָה אֵינוֹ נַעֲשֶׂה בֵּן סוֹרֵר וּמוֹרֶה עַד שֶׁיְּהוּ שְׁנֵיהֶם רוֹצִים. רִבִּי יְהוּדָה אוֹמֵר אִם לֹא הָיְתָה אִמּוֹ רְאוּיָה לְאָבִיו אֵינוֹ נַעֲשֶׂה בֵּן סוֹרֵר וּמוֹרֶה.

Mishnah 4: If his father was willing but not his mother, or his father unwilling but his mother willing, he cannot be treated as deviant and rebellious son unless both be willing[47]. Rebbi Jehudah says if his mother was inappropriate for his father[48], he cannot be treated as deviant and rebellious son.

47 The son can be brought before the court only by unanimous consent of his parents. This usually is derived from *Deut.* 21:20 where the parents have to complain that the son does not listen to their voice. The singular used, voice, implies common voice. (The Babli 71a infers that the parents actually have to speak with one voice; their voices have to sound the same. This is not mentioned in Yerushalmi or *Sifry*.)

48 Usually this means that his mother is (biblically or rabbinically) forbidden to his father. Here one could not exclude the disqualification of a mismatch.

(26b line 22) **הלכה ד**: הָיָה אָבִיו רוֹצֶה כול'. אָמַר רִבִּי יוֹחָנָן. וַאֲפִילוּ אֵין אִמּוֹ רְאוּיָה לְאָבִיו. וְכָל־מַה שֶׁיֵּשׁ לְאִמּוֹ לֹא מִשֶּׁלְּאָבִיו הֵם. אָמַר רִבִּי יוֹסֵי בֵּירִבִּי בוּן. תִּיפְתָּר בָּהוּ דַהֲבַת נָסְבָה דִיּוּרִין וְעָבְדָת שֵׁרוּ וְגָנַב מִנְּהוֹן.

Halakhah 4: "If his father was willing," etc. Rebbi Johanan said, even if his mother was not suitable for his father[49]. But is not all of his mother's property also his father's[50]? Rebbi Yose ben Abun said, explain it about one who took in lodgers, made repasts, and he stole from there.[51]

49 Practice should not follow R. Jehudah.

50 Only if his mother be married to his father; an illegitimate son is not excluded either from inheritance or filial obligations. The question is relevant only for R. Jehudah in Mishnah 3, who requires that the son had stolen from his mother's property which was not his father's.

51 This explanation really is unnecessary; in Tractate *Ketubot* many exceptions are noted to the rule that the husband has the usufruct of the wife's property or the right to her earnings.

(fol. 26a) **משנה ה**: הָיָה אֶחָד מֵהֶם גִּידֵּם אוֹ חִיגֵּר אוֹ אִילֵּם אוֹ סוּמֶא אוֹ חֵרֵשׁ אֵינוֹ נַעֲשֶׂה בֵן סוֹרֵר וּמוֹרֶה שֶׁנֶּאֱמַר וְתָפְשׂוּ בוֹ אָבִיו וְאִמּוֹ וְלֹא גִידְּמִין. וְהוֹצִיאוּ אֹתוֹ וְלֹא חִיגְּרִים וְאָמְרוּ וְלֹא אִלְּמִין בְּנֵנוּ זֶה וְלֹא סוּמִים אֵינֶנּוּ שֹׁמֵעַ בְּקֹלֵנוּ וְלֹא חֵרְשִׁים. מַתְרִין בּוֹ בִּפְנֵי שְׁלֹשָׁה וּמַלְקִין אוֹתוֹ. חָזַר וְקִילְקֵל נִדּוֹן בְּעֶשְׂרִים וּשְׁלֹשָׁה. וְאֵינוֹ נִסְקַל עַד שֶׁיְּהוּ שָׁם שְׁלֹשָׁה הָרִאשׁוֹנִים שֶׁנֶּאֱמַר בְּנֵנוּ זֶה זֶה הוּא שֶׁלָּקָה בִּפְנֵיכֶם.

Mishnah 5: If one of them[52] was one-armed, or lame, or mute, or deaf, he cannot be tried as deviant and rebellious son, as it is said:[53] *His father and mother shall grab him,* not one-armed ones, *bring him out*, not lame ones, *and say*, not mute ones, *this son of ours*, and not blind ones[54], *he does not listen to our voice*, not deaf ones. One warns him before three [judges] and whips him.

If he becomes a repeat offender, he is tried by 23 but cannot be stoned unless the original three were present, since it is said *this son of ours*, this is the one who was whipped before you[55].

52 Of the parents.

53 *Deut*. 21:19.

53 Blind persons cannot point their fingers at the accused, they cannot know where in the room he is.

54 The original judges become the witnesses who can testify to a proper warning given to the deviant son.

(26b line 25) **הלכה ה**: הָיָה אֶחָד מֵהֶם גִּידֵּם כול'. כְּשֵׁם שֶׁאַתְּ דּוֹרֵשׁ בְּאָבִיו וּבְאִמּוֹ כָּךְ אַתְּ דּוֹרֵשׁ בְּזִקְנֵי בֵית דִּין. שֶׁנֶּאֱמַר וְיָצְאוּ פְּרָט לְחִיגְּרִים. וְאָמְרוּ פְּרָט לְאִילְּמִים. יָדֵינוּ לֹא שָׁפְכוּ פְּרָט לְגִידְּמִים. וְעֵינֵינוּ לֹא רָאוּ פְּרָט לְסוּמִין. מַגִּיד הַכָּתוּב כְּשֵׁם שֶׁזִּקְנֵי בֵית דִּין שְׁלֵימִין בְּצֶדֶק כָּךְ הֵם צְרִיכִין לִהְיוֹת שְׁלֵימִין בְּאֵיבְרֵיהֶן.

Halakhah 5: "If one of them was one-armed." etc. Just as one explains for his father and mother, so one explains for the Elders of the Court,[56] as it is said [57]: *They shall go out*, to exclude lame ones; *and say* [58], to exclude mute ones; *our hands did not spill*, to exclude one-armed ones; *and our eyes did not see*, to exclude blind ones. The verse tells you that just as the Elders of the Court must be unblemished morally, so they must be unblemished physically[59].

56 The Supreme Court.

57 *Deut*. 21:2.

58 *Deut*. 21:7.

59 Rejected by the Babli, 36b. Moses, the president of the first Supreme Court, had a speech defect.

(26b line 29) אָמַר רִבִּי יוֹחָנָן. מֵת אֶחָד מִן הָרִאשׁוֹנִים אֵינוֹ נִסְקָל. וְלֹא מַתְנִיתָא הִיא. אֵינוֹ נִסְקַל עַד שֶׁיְּהוּ שָׁם שְׁלֹשָׁה הָרִאשׁוֹנִים. אָמַר רִבִּי הוֹשַׁעְיָה. שֶׁלֹּא תֹאמַר. יֵעָשֶׂה דִין שֵׁינִי רִאשׁוֹן. לְפוּם כָּךְ צָרַךְ מַתְנִיתָהּ.

Rebbi Johanan said, if one of the first [judges] died, he cannot be stoned. Is that not the Mishnah: "he cannot be stoned unless the original three were present"? Rebbi Hoshaia said, you should not say that the second trial should become the first[60]; therefore, one had to state this.

60 If a member of the original court had died, the second court cannot warn and whip the deviant son and set him up to be executed by a third court.

(fol. 26a) **משנה ו**: בָּרַח עַד שֶׁלֹּא נִגְמַר דִּינוֹ וְאַחַר כָּךְ הִקִּיף זָקָן הַתַּחְתּוֹן פָּטוּר. וְאִם מִשֶּׁנִּגְמַר דִּינוֹ בָּרַח וְאַחַר כָּךְ הִקִּיף זָקָן הַתַּחְתּוֹן חַייָב:

Mishnah 6: If he escaped before sentence was passed and then grew the lower beard, he is not liable[61]; but if he escaped after sentence was passed and then grew the lower beard, he is liable.

61 If he is recaptured, he needs a new trial. But since by then he already is an adult able to have children, he cannot be tried as a deviant and rebellious son. If sentence already was passed, no new trial is needed; the prior sentence can be carried out.

(26b line 32) **הלכה ו**: בָּרַח עַד שֶׁלֹּא נִגְמַר דִּינוֹ כול'. אָמַר רִבִּי יֹאשִׁיָּה. סָח לִי זְעִירָה מִשֵּׁם אַנְשֵׁי יְרוּשָׁלֵם. שְׁלֹשָׁה הֵן שֶׁאִם בִּקְשׁוּ לִמְחוֹל מוֹחֲלִין. וְאֵילוּ הֵן. סוֹטָה וּבֵן סוֹרֵר וּמוֹרֶה וְזָקֵן מַמְרֵא עַל פִּי בֵית דִּין.

סוֹטָה. וְלֹא מַתְנִיתָא הִיא. שֶׁבַּעֲלָהּ אֵינוֹ רוֹצֶה לְהַשְׁקוֹתָהּ. סָבְרִין מֵימַר. עַד שֶׁלֹּא נִכְתְּבָה הַמְּגִילָּה. אֲתָא מֵימַר. וַאֲפִילוּ מִשֶּׁנִּכְתְּבָה הַמְּגִילָּה. וּבְשֶׁלֹּא נִמְחֲקָה הַמְּגִילָּה. אֲבָל אִם נִמְחֲקָה הַמְּגִילָּה לֹא בְדָא.

בֵּן סוֹרֵר וּמוֹרֶה. וְלֹא מַתְנִיתָא הִיא. הָיָה אָבִיו רוֹצֶה וְאִמּוֹ אֵינָהּ רוֹצָה. אִמּוֹ רוֹצָה וְאָבִיו אֵינוֹ רוֹצֶה. סָבְרִין מֵימַר. עַד שֶׁלֹּא עָמַד בְּדִין. אֲתָא מֵימַר לָךְ. וַאֲפִילוּ עָמַד בְּדִין. וּבְשֶׁלֹּא נִגְמַר דִּינוֹ. אֲבָל אִם נִגְמַר דִּינוֹ לֹא בְדָא.

זָקֵן מַמְרֵא. הָדָא דְתֵימַר שֶׁלֹּא לְהוֹרְגוֹ. אֲבָל לְהַחֲזִירוֹ לֹא הָיוּ מַחֲזִירִין אוֹתוֹ לִמְקוֹמוֹ.

וּכְשֶׁבָּאתִי אֶצֶל רִבִּי יְהוּדָה בֶּן בָּתֵירָה לִנְצִיבִין עַל שְׁנַיִם הוֹדָה לִי וְעַל אֶחָד לֹא הוֹדָה לִי. עַל זָקֵן מַמְרֵא לֹא הוֹדָה לִי כְּדֵי שֶׁלֹּא יִרְבּוּ מַחֲלוֹקוֹת בְּיִשְׂרָאֵל.

Halakhah 6: "If he escaped before sentence was passed," etc. [62]Rebbi Joshia said, Ze`ira told me in the name of the people of Jerusalem: In three cases, if they want to forgive, they may forgive. These are: The suspect wife, the deviant son, and the Elder rebelling against the [Supreme] Court.

The suspect wife, is that not a Mishnah, "one whose husband refuses to let her drink"? They wanted to say, before the scroll was written. He comes to tell, even after the scroll was written. But it does not apply to the case where the scroll had been erased[63].

The deviant son, is that not a Mishnah, "if his father was willing but not his mother, or his mother willing but his father unwilling"? They wanted to say, before he was tried. He comes to tell, even after he was tried. But it does not apply to the case where judgment had been passed.

The rebellious Elder[64]; that means not to kill him. But they cannot let him return to his place.

[65]But when I came to Rebbi Jehudah ben Bathyra at Nisibis, he agreed with me in two cases and disagreed in one. He disagreed about the rebellious Elder, lest quarrels increase in Israel[66].

62 This paragraph is quoted in *Sotah* 4:3, Notes 39-41. This is one of the few cases where the Leiden ms. does not copy the text but simply refers to it by "etc." The parallel quotes in the Babli are *Sotah* 25a, *Sanhedrin* 88a.

63 In the ordeal of the suspected adulteress, if the text of the curses involving the Divine Name has been erased, the procedure is irreversible, just as a judicial procedure is after judgment was passed.

64 Who refuses to follow the ruling of the Supreme Court sitting on the Temple Mount, *Deut.* 17:8-13. Even if he is not executed, he has to be stripped of his judicial functions.

65 This continues the statement of Rebbi Joshia which was interrupted by the discussion of the three cases. In the Babli, the dissenters are "my colleagues in the South."

66 The suspected adulteress and the deviant and rebellious son can be prosecuted only on request of the injured party; refusal to obey the instructions of the Supreme Court must be prosecuted automatically.

(26b line 46) מַה טַעֲמוֹן דְּבֵית שַׁמַּי. הָבֵא לִי בַּעֲלִי וַאֲנִי שׁוֹתָה. מַה טַעֲמוֹן דְּבֵית הִלֵּל. הוֹאִיל וְאֵין כָּאן בַּעַל לְהַשְׁקוֹתָהּ הֶחֱזִירָתָהּ הַתּוֹרָה לִסְפֵיקָהּ וּסְפֵיקָהּ לִסְפֵיקָהּ. וּסְפֵיקָהּ לְחוּדֵיהּ.

What is the reason of the House of Shammai? "Bring me my husband and I shall drink." What is the reason of the House of Hillel? Since there is no husband to let her drink, the Torah returns her to a state of doubt, which induces another doubt, which remains a doubt[67].

67 This paragraph has nothing to do with the current subject but belongs to *Sotah* 4:3. It was omitted there together with the preceding four paragraphs.

If a husband suspects his wife of adultery and warns her in the presence of two adult witnesses not to be with her suspected paramour, then if there is circumstantial evidence of adultery but no proof which would hold up in court, the wife is forbidden to her husband until she undergoes the ordeal by drinking the magic water in the Temple court (*Num.* 11:5-31). If the ordeal confirms her adultery, she is divorced as adulteress without any money.

The ordeal must take place in the presence of the husband. If the husband dies before the ordeal can take place, the woman cannot drink. The House of Shammai rules that she is a widow, entitled to all benefits due to a widow, since the death of her husband barred her from clearing her name without her fault. The House of Hillel hold that as suspected adulteress she cannot go to court to collect money from the heirs to the estate since only valid claims can be enforced in court; it is not the heirs' doing that she cannot prove her case (*Sotah* 4:1 Notes 13-16).

(26b line 49) תַּמָּן תַּנִּינָן. הַפּוֹגֶמֶת כְּתוּבָּתָהּ לֹא תִיפָּרַע אֶלָּא בִשְׁבוּעָה. תַּנֵּי הַפּוֹגֶמֶת לֹא הַפּוֹחֶתֶת. כֵּיצַד. הָיְתָה כְתוּבָּתָהּ מָאתַיִם וְהִיא אוֹמֶרֶת מְנָה נִפְרַעַת שֶׁלֹּא בִשְׁבוּעָה. מַה בֵּין הַפּוֹגֶמֶת וּמַה בֵּין הַפּוֹחֶתֶת. אָמַר רִבִּי חֲנִינָה. [פּוֹגֶמֶת][68] בָּא מַשָּׂא וּמַתָּן בֵּינְתַיִים. פּוֹחֶתֶת לֹא בָא מַשָּׂא וּמַתָּן בֵּינְתַיִים.

[69]There, we stated: "If she had compromised her *ketubah*, she shall not be able to collect without an oath." It was stated "compromised", not that she reduced [her *ketubah*]. How? If her *ketubah* was 200 but she claims a mina, she is paid without an oath. What is the difference between one who did compromise and one who claims less? Rebbi Ḥanina said, if she compromises there was a transaction between them; if she claims less there was no transaction between them.

רִבִּי יִרְמְיָה בָּעֵי. כְּמָה דְּתֵימַר תַּמָּן. וְעֵד אֶחָד מְעִידָהּ שֶׁהִיא פְרוּעָה לֹא תִיפָּרַע אֶלָּא בִשְׁבוּעָה. וְדִכְוָותָהּ וְעֵד אֶחָד מְעִידָהּ שֶׁהִיא פְחוּתָה לֹא תִיפְחַת אֶלָּא בִשְׁבוּעָה. אָמַר רִבִּי יוֹסֵי. בְּשָׁעָה שֶׁעֵד אֶחָד מְעִידָהּ שֶׁהִיא פְרוּעָה אֵינוֹ מַכְחִישׁ שְׁנַיִם. וּבְשָׁעָה שֶׁמֵּעִיד שֶׁהִיא פְחוּתָה מַכְחִישׁ אֶת שְׁנַיִם.

Rebbi Jeremiah asked: Since we stated there: "If one witness testified that [the *ketubah*] was paid, she shall not be able to collect without an oath"; should it be similar that if one witness testifies that [the *ketubah*] was reduced, she shall not be able to collect the reduced amount without an oath? Rebbi Yose said, at the moment when one witness testified that it was paid, he does not contradict two [witnesses]; but when he testifies that it was reduced he would contradict two [witnesses.]

תַּנֵּי. וְהַנִּפְרַעַת שֶׁלֹּא בְפָנָיו לֹא תִיפָּרַע אֶלָּא בִשְׁבוּעָה. וְנִפְרָעִים מֵאָדָם שֶׁלֹּא בְפָנָיו. אָמַר רִבִּי יִרְמְיָה. תִּיפְתָּר בִּשְׁטָר שֶׁהָרִיבִּית אוֹכֶלֶת בּוֹ. וּבֵית דִּין גּוֹבִין רִיבִּית. תִּיפְתָּר שֶׁעָרַב לוֹ מִגּוֹי.

[70]It was stated: "If she collects in his absence, she shall not be able to collect without an oath." Can one collect from a person in his absence?

Rebbi Jeremiah said, explain it about a contract for which interest is due. Would the court collect interest? Explain that it was guaranteed for a Gentile.

וְהָתַנֵּי. יוֹרֵשׁ שֶׁפָּגַם אָבִיו שְׁטָר חוֹב הַבֵּן גּוֹבֶה בְלֹא שְׁבוּעָה. בָּזֶה יָפֶה כֹּחַ הַבֵּן מִכֹּחַ הָאָב. שֶׁהָאָב אֵינוֹ גוֹבֶה אֶלָּא בִשְׁבוּעָה. אָמַר רִבִּי לָעְזָר. וְנִשְׁבַּע שְׁבוּעַת יוֹרֵשׁ. שֶׁלֹּא פִיקְּדָנוּ אַבָּא וְשֶׁלֹּא אָמַר לָנוּ אַבָּא וְשֶׁלֹּא מָצִינוּ שְׁטָר בֵּין שְׁטָרוֹתָיו שֶׁלְּאַבָּא שֶׁשְּׁטָר זֶה פָּרוּעַ. הָא אִם נִמְצָא פָּרוּעַ. רַב הוֹשַׁעְיָה בָּעֵי. מַתְנִיתָא דְבֵית שַׁמַּי. דְּבֵית שַׁמַּי אוֹמְרִים. נוֹטֶלֶת כְּתוּבָּתָהּ וְלֹא שׁוֹתָה. אָמַר רִבִּי יוֹסֵי. טַעֲמוֹן דְּבֵית שַׁמַּי הָבֵא לִי בַעֲלִי וַאֲנִי שׁוֹתָה. בְּרַם הָכָא בְּדִין הָיָה אֲפִילוּ אָבִיו לֹא יִשָּׁבַע. תַּקָּנָה תִקְּנוּ בוֹ שֶׁיִּשָּׁבַע. בּוֹ תִיקְּנוּ וּבִבְנוֹ לֹא תִיקְּנוּ. כֵּיוָן שֶׁמֵּת הֶעֱמַדְתָּ אֶת בְּנוֹ עַל דִּין תּוֹרָה.

It was stated: If an heir's father held a partially paid promissory note, the son collects without swearing. In this the son's power is greater than the father's since the father can collect only by swearing. Rebbi Eleazar said, nevertheless he has to execute an heir's oath, "that our father did not charge us, that our father did not tell us, that we did not find a document among our father's documents stating that this note was paid." Therefore, if there was a document, the note was paid. Rebbi Hoshaia asked, does the *baraita* follow the House of Shammai? For the House of Shammai say, "she collects her *ketubah* and does not drink." Rebbi Yose said, there the reason of the House of Shammai is: bring my husband and I shall drink! But here, it would be in order that even his father would not have to swear. They instituted a rule that he has to swear. They instituted this for him, but not for his son. When he died, you put his son on the biblical rule.

נִתְחַייֵב אָבִיו שְׁבוּעָה בְּבֵית דִּין וּמֵת אֵין בְּנוֹ גוֹבֶה. דְּלֹא כֵן מָה נָן אָמְרִין. יֵשׁ אָדָם מוֹרִישׁ שְׁבוּעָתוֹ לִבְנוֹ. אָמַר רִבִּי בָּא. הָכֵין אִתְאֲמָרַת. פָּגַם אָבִיו שְׁטָרוֹ בְּבֵית דִּין וּמֵת אֵינוֹ גוֹבֶה. רַב חִסְדָּא בָּעֵי. בְּגִין דַּהֲלִיךְ תַּרְתֵּין פְּסִיעָן הוּא מַפְסִיד. אִילּוּ פְגָמוֹ חוּץ לְבֵית דִּין אַתְּ אֲמַר. גּוֹבֶה. מִפְּנֵי שֶׁפְּגָמוֹ בְבֵית דִּין אַתְּ מַר. אֵינוֹ גוֹבֶה.

If a father became obligated to swear in court and died, his son cannot collect. If it were otherwise, what could we say? Can a man let his son inherit an obligation to swear? Rebbi [71]Ba said, it was said as follows: if a man compromised his document in court, his son cannot collect. [72]Rav Ḥisda asked: Because he walked two steps, does he lose? If he compromised it outside the court, he collects. Because he compromised it in court, he cannot collect?

68 Needed word added from the text in *Ketubot*.

69 The text from here to the end of the Halakhah is mainly from *Ketubot* 9:7, Notes 167-185. It has no connection with the theme in *Sanhedrin*, only a tenuous one with the previously quoted text from *Sotah*. The text here is secondary as shown by a few omissions.

70 This paragraph is from *Ketubot* 9:9, Notes 200-204.

71 In *Ketubot*: Abun.

72 This is also quoted in *Ševuot* 7:6 (38a l. 25).

(fol. 26a) **משנה ז**: בֵּן סוֹרֵר וּמוֹרֶה נִדּוֹן עַל שֵׁם סוֹפוֹ. אָמְרָה תוֹרָה יָמוּת זַכַּאי וְאַל יָמוּת חַייָב. שֶׁמִּיתָתָן שֶׁל רְשָׁעִים הֲנָיָה לָהֶן וַהֲנָייָה לָעוֹלָם וְהַצַּדִּיקִים רַע לָהֶן וְרַע לָעוֹלָם. יַיִן וְשֵׁינָה לָרְשָׁעִים הֲנָייָה לָהֶן וַהֲנָיָה לָעוֹלָם וְלַצַּדִּיקִים רַע לָהֶן וְרַע לָעוֹלָם. פִּזּוּר לָרְשָׁעִים הֲנָייָה לָהֶן וַהֲנָייָה לָעוֹלָם וְלַצַּדִּיקִים רַע לָהֶן וְרַע לָעוֹלָם. כִּינּוּס לָרְשָׁעִים רַע לָהֶן וְרַע לָעוֹלָם וְלַצַּדִּיקִים הֲנָייָה לָהֶן וַהֲנָייָה לָעוֹלָם. שֶׁקֶט לָרְשָׁעִים רַע לָהֶן וְרַע לָעוֹלָם וְלַצַּדִּיקִים הֲנָייָה לָהֶן וַהֲנָייָה לָעוֹלָם:

Mishnah 7: The deviant and rebellious son is judged because of his end; the Torah said, it is better that he should die innocent rather than guilty, for death of the evildoers is an enjoyment for them and enjoyment for the world, but concerning the just it is bad for them and bad for the world. Wine and sleep of the evildoers is an enjoyment for them and enjoyment for the world, but concerning the just it is bad for them and bad for the world. Scattering of the evildoers is an enjoyment for them and enjoyment for the world, but concerning the just it is bad for them and bad for the world. Coming together of the evildoers is bad for them and bad for the world, but concerning the just it is an enjoyment for them and enjoyment for the world. Quiet of the evildoers is bad for them and bad for the world, but concerning the just it is an enjoyment for them and enjoyment for the world.

(26b line 74) **הלכה ז**: בֵּן סוֹרֵר וּמוֹרֶה כול'. צָפָה הַקָּדוֹשׁ בָּרוּךְ הוּא שֶׁסּוֹף זֶה עָתִיד לְגַמֵּר נִיכְסֵי אָבִיו וְאֶת נִיכְסֵי אִמּוֹ וְיוֹשֵׁב לוֹ בְּפָרָשַׁת דְּרָכִים וּמְקַפֵּחַ אֶת הַבְּרִיּוֹת וְהוֹרֵג אֶת הַנְּפָשׁוֹת וְסוֹפוֹ לְשַׁכֵּחַ אֶת תַּלְמוּדוֹ. וְאָמְרָה תוֹרָה מוּטָּב שֶׁיָּמוּת זַכַּאי וְאַל יָמוּת חַייָב. שֶׁמִּיתָתָן שֶׁלָּרְשָׁעִים הֲנָייָה לָהֶן וַהֲנָייָה לָעוֹלָם וְלַצַּדִּיקִים רַע לָהֶן וְרַע לָעוֹלָם.

Halakhah 7: "The deviant and rebellious son," etc. The Holy One, praise to Him, saw that this one in the end will waste his father's and his mother's properties, will sit at road crossings, rob people, and kill them, and in the end will forget all he has learned[73]. Therefore, the Torah said, he should die innocent rather than die guilty, for death of the evildoers is an enjoyment for them and enjoyment for the world, but concerning the just it is bad for them and bad for the world.

73 And therefore descend to the level of animals. While the opinion voiced in the Babli (71a) that "the case of the deviant and rebellious son never happened and never will happen" is not found in the Yerushalmi, the detailed rabbinic rules certainly are intended to make sure it never can happen in rabbinic Judaism. But apart from offering ample material for sermons, the rules clearly are intended to show that in biblical law the father has no power over the life of his children; any action against a child needs not only the consent of the mother but a court proceeding, in stark contrast to ancient Roman law (Babli 72a).

(26c line 3) יַיִן וְשֵׁינָה לָרְשָׁעִים הֲנָייָה לָהֶן וַהֲנָייָה לָעוֹלָם וְלַצַּדִּיקִים רַע לָהֶן וְרַע לָעוֹלָם. אָמַר רִבִּי אַבָּהוּ. וּבִלְבַד יַיִן עִם רוֹב שֵׁינָה. אָמַר רִבִּי יוֹנָתָן. יְשֵׁינִים הֵן קִימְעָא שֶׁתְּהֵא דַעְתָּן מְיוּשֶּׁבֶת.

"Wine and sleep of the evildoers is an enjoyment for them and enjoyment for the world, but concerning the just it is bad for them and bad for the world." Rebbi Abbahu said, only wine with an excess of sleep[74]. Rebbi Jonathan said, they sleep a little so they can concentrate better.

74 Even the just have to sleep and to drink some wine, as long as one does not drink so much that he has to sleep off his alcohol.

(fol. 26a) **משנה ח**: הַבָּא בַמַּחְתֶּרֶת נִידּוֹן עַל שֵׁם סוֹפוֹ. הָיָה בָא בַמַּחְתֶּרֶת וְשָׁבַר אֶת הֶחָבִית אִם יֶשׁ לוֹ דָמִים חַייָב אִם אֵין לוֹ דָמִים פָּטוּר:

Mishnah 8: The intruder by stealth is judged because of his end[75]. If in the course of a burglary he broke an amphora, if he has blood-guilt attached to him[76], he is liable[77]; if he has no blood-guilt attached to him, he is not liable[78].

75 *Ex.* 22:1 permits the residents of a house to kill the stealth intruder since it is assumed that he would kill anybody offering resistance to his burglary.

76 *If the sun shone on him*, *Ex.* 22:2.

77 *Ex.* 22:2.

78 Since he can be killed, his burglary is the equivalent of a capital crime cf. Note 102.

(26d line 5) **הלכה ח**: הַבָּא בַמַּחְתֶּרֶת כול׳. תַּנֵּי רִבִּי יִשְׁמָעֵאל. זֶה אֶחָד מִשְּׁלֹשָׁה מִקְרִיּוֹת שֶׁנֶּאֶמְרוּ בַתּוֹרָה כְמָשָׁל. אִם־יָקוּם וְהִתְהַלֵּךְ בַּחוּץ עַל־מִשְׁעַנְתּוֹ. אִם־בַּמַּחְתֶּרֶת יִמָּצֵא הַגַּנָּב. אִם־זָרְחָה הַשֶּׁמֶשׁ עָלָיו דָּמִים לוֹ. וְכִי עָלָיו לְבַדּוֹ הַחַמָּה זוֹרַחַת. וַהֲלֹא עַל כָּל־בָּאֵי הָעוֹלָם זוֹרַחַת הַחַמָּה. אֶלָּא מַה זְרִיחַת הַחַמָּה מְיוּחֶדֶת שֶׁהוּא שָׁלוֹם לְכָל־בָּאֵי הָעוֹלָם. כָּךְ כָּל־זְמַן שֶׁאַתְּ יוֹדֵעַ שֶׁאַתְּ שָׁלוֹם מִמֶּנּוּ בֵּין בַּיּוֹם וּבֵין בַּלַּיְלָה הַהוֹרְגוֹ נֶהֱרַג. פְּעָמִים שֶׁהוּא בָא לִגְנוֹב פְּעָמִים שֶׁהוּא בָא לַהֲרוֹג. אָמְרַתְּ שֶׁאִם בָּא לִגְנוֹב וַדַּאי וַהֲרָגוֹ הַהוֹרְגוֹ נֶהֱרַג. פְּעָמִים שֶׁהוּא בָא לַהֲרוֹג נֶהֱרַג. מִיכָּן אַתְּ דָן לְפִיקּוּחַ נֶפֶשׁ. לוֹמַר. מַה עֲבוֹדָה זָרָה מְיוּחֶדֶת שֶׁהִיא מְטַמְּאָה אֶת הָאָרֶץ וּמְחַלֶּלֶת אֶת הַשֵּׁם וּמְסַלֶּקֶת אֶת הַשְּׁכִינָה וּדוֹחִין בָּהּ אֶת הַסָּפֵק. כָּל־שֶׁכֵּן לְפִיקּוּחַ נֶפֶשׁ שֶׁיִּדְחֶה אֶת הַסָּפֵק.

Halakhah 8: "The intruder by stealth," etc. [79]Rebbi Ismael stated: This is one of three verses[80] which in the Torah have been formulated as a simile: *If he gets up and walks outside on his support*[81]. *If the thief is found in the digging, if the sun shone on him, he has blood*[77]. Does the sun shine only on him? Does the sun not shine on all beings in the world? But just as sunshine is special in that it brings peace to the entire world, so in any case in which you know that you are at peace with him, whether it be day or night his killer will be killed[82]. If sometimes he comes to steal, sometimes he comes to kill, you say that if certainly he comes to steal, his killer will be killed[83]? Since sometimes he comes to kill, he may be killed. From here you argue about danger to life, to say that just as (foreign worship)[84] is special in that it defiles the Land, desecrates the Name, removes the Divine Presence, and doubts are disregarded, so much more that doubts have to be disregarded in cases of danger to life[85].

79 Parallel texts are in the Babli 72a, *Mekhilta dR.. Ismael Mišpaṭim* 13, *dR. Simeon ben Iohai* p. 192, *Sifry Deut.* 217; partially *Yerushalmi Ketubot* 4:4 (Notes 88-93).

80 To the verses *Ex.* 21:19 and 22:2 mentioned here one has to add *Deut.* 22:17.

81 *Ex.* 21:19

82 The Babli, 79b, states that if a father intrudes in the son's home, the son does not have the right to kill him. The Yerushalmi does not have this good opinion of family relationships, cf. the next paragraph.

83 In Tosephta 11:9, this is a declarative sentence; the next sentence is missing there.

84 Obviously, *foreign worship* has to be

deleted since Mishnah 9 states clearly that a person intent on idolatry cannot be killed before he acts. One must read שְׁפִיכוּת דָּמִים "bloodshed" which defiles the Land (*Num.* 35:33; Babli *Šabbat* 33a, *Yoma* 85a); by Mishnah 9 a person intent on committing murder may be killed by any bystander before he commits the murder. If a person with a drawn sword runs after another, it is only a surmise but one which allows the bystander to kill the attacker; maybe the pursuer would not kill his victim. This is the "action in doubt" referred to in this sentence.

85 The Sabbath must be desecrated for the possibility of saving a life. For example, if there was a landslide on the Sabbath and it is only surmised that somebody was buried in it, one starts digging without delay.

(26d line 17) כְּתִיב אִם־בַּמַּחְתֶּרֶת יִמָּצֵא הַגַּנָּב וְהֻכָּה וָמֵת אֵין לוֹ דָּמִים. תַּנֵּי רִבִּי חִייָה. בַּמַּחְתֶּרֶת אֵין לוֹ דָּמִים חוּץ לַמַּחְתֶּרֶת יֵשׁ לוֹ דָּמִים. תַּנֵּי רִבִּי שִׁמְעוֹן בֶּן יוֹחַי. אֲפִילוּ חוּץ לַמַּחְתֶּרֶת אֵין לוֹ דָּמִים. לְפִי שֶׁמָּמוֹנוֹ שֶׁל אָדָם חָבִיב עָלָיו כְּנַפְשׁוֹ. חֲמִי לֵיהּ אֲזִיל בָּעֵי מֵיסַב מָמוֹנֵיהּ מִינֵּיהּ וְקָאִים עֲלוֹי וְקָטְלֵיהּ. רַב הוּנָא אָמַר. נָטַל אֶת הַכִּיס וְהָפַךְ אֶת פָּנָיו לָצֵאת וְהָלַךְ לוֹ וְעָמַד עָלָיו וַהֲרָגוֹ אֵין הַהוֹרֵג נֶהֱרַג. מַה טַעֲמָא דְרַב הוּנָא. כִּי יֵחַם לְבָבוֹ. רַב אָמַר. כָּל־דְּיֵיתֵי עֲלַי אֲנָא קְטַל לֵיהּ חוּץ מֵחֲנַנְיָה בֶן שִׁילָא דַּאֲנָא יְדַע דְּלָא אֲתֵי אֶלָּא מֵיסַב מְגוּסְתֵיהּ מִינַּיי. אֲמַר רִבִּי יִצְחָק. מִכֵּיוָן דְּאַבְרֵי לִיבֵּיהּ עֲלוֹי לְמֵיעֲבֵד לֵיהּ דָּא מִילְּתָא אֵין זֶה חֲנַנְיָה בֶן שִׁילָא.

It is written: *If the thief was found in a tunnel, was smitten, and died, there is no blood-guilt*[75]. Rebbi Ḥiyya stated: In the tunnel[86] there is no blood-guilt, outside the tunnel there is blood guilt. Rebbi Simeon ben Ioḥai stated: Even outside the tunnel there is no blood-guilt, for a person's property is beloved by him like his own soul. He[87] sees him[88], that he[88] comes to take his[87] money away from him, stands up against him[88] and kills him[88,89]. Rav Huna said, if he took a wallet, turned to leave and went, if then one stood up against him and killed him[88] the killer will not be killed. What is Rav Huna's reason? *For his temper is hot*[90]. Rav said, I would kill anybody who would come against me, except Ḥanania ben Shila[91], of whom I know that he would come only to take his meal from me. Rebbi Isaac said, if he has the temerity to do something like that, he cannot be Ḥanania ben Shila[92].

86 From חתר "to undermine". The thief digs under the wall to enter the house.

87 The property owner.

88 The thief.

89 A similar statement is anonymous in the Babli, *Yoma* 85b.

90 *Deut.* 19:6, another case of non-prosecutable homicide.

91 A cousin of Rav, lover of roast pigeon (Babli *Pesaḥim* 10:8).

92 Therefore, any thief caught in a house may be killed by the owner.

(fol. 26a) **משנה ט**: וְאֵילּוּ שֶׁמַּצִּילִין אוֹתָן בְּנַפְשָׁן. הָרוֹדֵף אַחַר חֲבֵירוֹ לְהוֹרְגוֹ אַחַר הַזָּכָר וְאַחַר נַעֲרָה הַמְאוֹרָסָה. אֲבָל הָרוֹדֵף אַחַר הַבְּהֵמָה וְהַמְחַלֵּל אֶת הַשַּׁבָּת וְהָעוֹבֵד עֲבוֹדָה זָרָה אֵין מַצִּילִין אוֹתָן בְּנַפְשָׁן:

Mishnah 9: The following ones one saves at the cost of their own persons[93]: He who purses another to kill him, the male[94], or the preliminarily married virgin girl[95]. But he who pursues an animal[96], or who desecrates the Sabbath, or who worships strange worship, one may not save at the cost of their own persons.

93 Preferably by injuring him; if this is not possible by killing him (Babli).

94 In order to commit homosexual rape.

95 Whose rape is equated with murder, *Deut*. 22:26.

96 To commit bestiality. It is not permitted to kill a person intending to commit a capital crime; only a person bent on committing murder or a crime against a human comparable to murder has to be killed if caught *in flagranti*.

(26c line 26) **הלכה ט**: אֵילּוּ שֶׁמַּצִּילִין אוֹתָן בְּנַפְשָׁן כול'. הָרוֹדֵף אַחַר חֲבֵירוֹ לְהוֹרְגוֹ בֵּין בַּבַּיִת בֵּין בַּשָּׂדֶה מַצִּילִין אוֹתוֹ בְנַפְשׁוֹ. אֶחָד הָרוֹדֵף אַחַר חֲבֵירוֹ לְהוֹרְגוֹ וְאֶחָד הָרוֹדֵף אַחַר כָּל־שְׁאָר עֲבֵירוֹת שֶׁבַּתּוֹרָה מַצִּילִין אוֹתוֹ בְּנַפְשׁוֹ. אֲבָל אִם הָיְתָה אַלְמָנָה לְכֹהֵן גָּדוֹל. גְּרוּשָׁה וַחֲלוּצָה לְכֹהֵן הֶדְיוֹט. מַמְזֶרֶת וּנְתִינָה לְיִשְׂרָאֵל. בַּת יִשְׂרָאֵל לְנָתִין וּלְמַמְזֵר. אֵין מַצִּילִין אוֹתוֹ בְּנַפְשׁוֹ. נַעֲשָׂה הַמַּעֲשֶׂה אֵין מַצִּילִין אוֹתוֹ בְּנַפְשׁוֹ. אִם יֵשׁ שָׁם מוֹשִׁיעִים אֵין מַצִּילִין אוֹתוֹ בְּנַפְשׁוֹ. רִבִּי יוּדָה אוֹמֵר. אִם אָמְרָה. הַנַּח לוֹ. אֵין מַצִּילִין אוֹתוֹ בְּנַפְשׁוֹ. שֶׁאִם מְמָחִין הֵן עַל יָדָיו נִמְצְאוּ בָאִין לִידֵי שְׁפִיכוּת דָּמִים.

Halakhah 9: "The following ones one saves at the cost of their own persons" etc. [97]"He who pursues another to kill him, whether in a house or on the field one saves at the cost of his own person, both him who pursues another to kill him or him who pursues any of the transgressions[98] in the Torah one saves at the cost of his own person. But if it was a widow for a High Priest, a divorcee or one who had received *ḥalîṣah* for a common priest, a bastard or a Gibeonite for an Israel, an Israel woman for a bastard or a Gibeonite, one does not save him at the cost of his own person[99]. If the deed had been done, one does not save him at the cost of his own person[100]. If there are people to save her, one does not save him at the cost of his own person[100]. Rebbi Jehudah says, if she[101] said, let him do it, one does not save at the cost of his own person. For if they would injure him, they through him would come to spill blood."

97 Similar texts are in the Babli 73a, Tosephta 11:10-11.

98 The parallel texts and the continuation of the *baraita* make it likely that one should not read עֲבֵירוֹת "transgressions" but עֲרָיוֹת "nakednesses; acts of incest and adultery which constitute either capital crimes or deadly sins."

99 Sexual offenses which are simple misdemeanors cannot be prevented by killing the offender.

100 This is a case for the police and regular administration of justice.

101 The victim of sexual agression who is afraid she might be killed.

(26c line 35) פְּשִׁיטָא דָא מִילְּתָא. רוֹצֵחַ שֶׁשִּׁיבֵּר אֶת הַכֵּלִים אוֹ שֶׁהִזִּיק חַייָב לְשַׁלֵּם. הָיָה מְשַׁבֵּר עַד שֶׁהוּא מַגִּיעַ לָעִיר. רִבִּי זְעִירָא וְרִבִּי הוֹשַׁעְיָה. חַד אָמַר. נוֹתֵן דָּמִים. וְחָרָנָא אָמַר. אֵינוֹ נוֹתֵן דָּמִים. רוֹדֵף שֶׁנַּעֲשָׂה נִרְדָּף מָהוּ לְהַצִּיל אֶת הָרוֹדֵף בְּנַפְשׁוֹ שֶׁלְּנִירְדָּף. גָּדוֹל שֶׁנַּעֲשָׂה קָטוֹן מָהוּ לְהַצִּיל אֶת הַגָּדוֹל בְּנַפְשׁוֹ שֶׁלְּקָטָן. הָתִיב רִבִּי יִרְמְיָה. וְהָתַנִּינָן. יָצָא רֹאשׁוֹ וְרוּבּוֹ אֵין נוֹגְעִין בּוֹ. שֶׁאֵין דּוֹחִין נֶפֶשׁ מִפְּנֵי נֶפֶשׁ: רִבִּי יוֹסֵי בֵּירִבִּי בּוּן בְּשֵׁם רַב חִסְדָּא. שַׁנְייָא הִיא תַמָּן שֶׁאֵין אַתְּ יוֹדֵעַ מִי הָרַג אֶת מִי.

The following is obvious: A murderer who broke vessels or otherwise caused damage is liable to pay[102]. If he continued to break until he came to the town, Rebbi Ze`ira and Rebbi Hoshaia: One said, he pays, the other said, he does not pay. If the pursuer becomes the pursued, may one save the pursuer through the person of the pursued[103]? An adult (who became)[104] a minor, may one save the adult through the person of the minor? Rebbi Jeremiah objected, did we not state[105]: "If his head and most of his body were born, one does not touch him, for one does not push aside one life for another." Rebbi Yose ben Rebbi Abun said in the name of Rav Hisda: It is different there since you do not know who is killing whom[106].

102 Since no crime can be punished more than once (*Terumot* 7:1 Notes 3-73, *Ketubot* 3:1 Note 29; Babli *Ketubot* 32b, *Bava qamma* 36a, *Makkot* 7b, 13b), any damage done during the commission of a crime cannot be recovered from the criminal. Any damage caused before and after the crime has been committed can be recovered. The

only question, the subject of the next two sentences, is whether the pursuit of the victim is part of the crime and protects the murderer from damage claims or not.

103 If the intended victim gets hold of a weapon and turns against the agressor, is there any cause for the uninvolved to act? The question is not answered.

104 From the following text it seems clear that one has to read: If an adult was pursued by a minor, may one save the adult through the minor's life? In a parallel text, *Šabbat* 14 (14d l. 67), the question is attributed to Rav Hisda, mentioned later here also.

105 Mishnah *Ahilut* 7:6. If the life of the mother is endangered during childbirth, the attendants must kill the fetus by cutting it into pieces and removing it. But if head and torso are already outside, so that the baby is breathing on his own, he cannot be killed even if he is endangering his mother's life. This is a case of a minor pursuing an adult.

106 Since the life of the baby is equally endangered, one cannot conclude that a minor intent on murder may not be killed by bystanders.

(26c line 42) תַּנֵּי רִבִּי לָעְזָר בֵּירִבִּי שִׁמְעוֹן אוֹמֵר. הַהוֹלֵךְ לַעֲבוֹד עֲבוֹדָה זָרָה מַצִּילִין אוֹתוֹ בְנַפְשׁוֹ. אִם מִפְּנֵי כְבוֹד בָּשָׂר וָדָם מַצִּילִין אוֹתוֹ בְנַפְשׁוֹ לֹא כָּל־שֶׁכֵּן מִפְּנֵי חַי הָעוֹלָמִים.

It was stated[107]: "Rebbi Eleazar ben Rebbi Simeon says, one who goes to worship a strange worship is saved at the cost of his own person." If one saves at the cost of his own person to protect the honor of flesh and blood[108], so much more because of the Life of the World[109].

107 Tosephta 11:12 in the name of R. Eleazar ben R. Ṣadoq.

108 To save a woman from being raped.

109 Cf. *Daniel* 12:7. The vocalization חַי is standard Sephardic; traditional Ashkenazic is חֵי (cf. M. Hershler, *Siddur of R. Solomon ben Samson of Garmaise including the Siddur of the Haside Ashkenas*, Jerusalem 1971, pp. 21-22.)

אילו הן הנשרפין פרק תשיעי

(fol. 26c) **משנה א**: אֵילוּ הֵן הַנִּשְׂרָפִין הַבָּא עַל אִשָּׁה וּבִתָּהּ וּבַת כֹּהֵן שֶׁזִּינְּתָה. יֵשׁ בִּכְלָל אִשָּׁה וּבִתָּהּ בִּתּוֹ וּבַת בִּתּוֹ וּבַת בְּנוֹ וּבַת אִשְׁתּוֹ וּבַת בִּתָּהּ וּבַת בְּנָהּ. וְאֵילוּ הֵן הַנֶּהֱרָגִין הָרוֹצֵחַ וְאַנְשֵׁי עִיר הַנִּדַּחַת.

Mishnah 1: The following are to be burned: one who copulates with a woman and her daughter,[1] and the daughter of a Cohen who committed adultery[2]. In the category of *a woman and her daughter* are included his daughter, his daughter's daughter, his son's daughter, his wife's daughter, her daughter's daughter, and her son's daughter[3]. The following are to be beheaded: the murderer,[4] and the inhabitants of a seduced town[5].

1 *Lev.* 20:14.

2 *Lev.* 21:9.

3 *Lev.* 18:17 includes relations with a woman and her granddaughter with the prohibition of a woman and her daughter. The Mishnaiot in the Babli and most independent Mishnah mss. include mention of the mother and the grandmother-in-law. This is logically redundant.

4 Chapter 7, Note 4.

5 *Deut.* 13:16; Halakhot 7:1,10:7,8.

(26d line 21) **הלכה א**: אֵילוּ הֵן הַנִּשְׂרָפִין כול'. תַּמָּן תַּנִּינָן.

Halakhah 1: "The following are to be burned," etc. There, we have stated[6]:

6 The entire following Halakhah is a copy of *Yebamot* 11:1, explained there in Notes 4-65. The text here does not always follow the same order as given there. The Notes here are restricted to indicate where the text of *Yebamot* (Y) was preferred for translation. The corruptions in the *Sanhedrin* text make it clear that the Y text is original.

(26d line 21; Y 11c l.58) נוֹשְׂאִין עַל הָאֲנוּסָה וְעַל הַמְפוּתָּה. כֵּינִי מַתְנִיתִין. נוֹשְׂאִין אחד הָאֲנוּסָה וְאחד הַמְפוּתָּה. אָנַס אִשָּׁה מוּתָּר בְּאִמָּהּ. פִּיתָּה אִשָּׁה מוּתָּר בְּבִתָּהּ.

"One may marry [relatives of] a rape victim or a seduced woman." So is the Mishnah: One may marry after[7] a rape or after a seduction. If he raped a woman, her mother is permitted. If he seduced a woman, he daughter is permitted.

7 The reading of Y אחר clearly is the correct one, not אחד "one," as written here.

(26d line 24; Y 11c l.60) הָאוֹנֵס וְהַמְפַתֶּה עַל הַנְּשׂוּאָה חַייָב. אָמַר רִבִּי יוֹחָנָן. דֶּרֶךְ נִישּׂוּאִין שָׁנוּ. נָשָׂא אִשָּׁה וְאַחַר כָּךְ אָנַס אֶת אִמָּהּ חַייָב. נָשָׂא אִשָּׁה וְאַחַר כָּךְ פִּיתָּה אֶת בִּתָּהּ חַייָב.

"He who rapes or seduces [a relative of] a married woman is [criminally] liable." Rebbi Joḥanan said, one stated this for marriage. If he married a woman and then raped her mother, he is [criminally] liable. If he married a woman and then seduced her daughter, he is [criminally] liable.

(26d line 26; Y 11c l.62) אָמַר רִבִּי לָעְזָר. סוּמָכוֹס וְרִבִּי יוֹחָנָן בֶּן נוּרִי אָמְרוּ דָּבָר אֶחָד. דְּתַנִּינָן תַּמָּן. שְׁחָטָהּ וְאֶת בַּת בִּתָּהּ וְאַחַר כָּךְ שָׁחַט אֶת בִּתָּהּ סוֹפֵג אֶת הָאַרְבָּעִים. סוּמָכוֹס אוֹמֵר מִשּׁוּם רַבִּי מֵאִיר. סוֹפֵג אֶת שְׁמוֹנִים. תַּמָּן תַּנִּינָן. רַבִּי יוֹחָנָן בֶּן נוּרִי אוֹמֵר. הַבָּא עַל חֲמוֹתוֹ חַייָב עָלֶיהָ מִשּׁוּם חֲמוֹתוֹ וְאֵם חֲמוֹתוֹ וְאֵם חָמִיו. אָמְרוּ לוֹ. שְׁלָשְׁתָּן שֵׁם אֶחָד הֵן׃ רִבִּי יוּדָה בַּר פָּזִי בְּשֵׁם רִבִּי יוֹחָנָן. מוֹדֶה סוּמָכוֹס לְרִבִּי יוֹחָנָן. אַשְׁכַּח תַּנֵּי. עוֹד הִיא בְמַחֲלוֹקֶת. מַאי טַעֲמָא דְרִבִּי יוֹחָנָן בֶּן נוּרִי. מַה אִשָּׁה וּבִתָּהּ וּבַת בִּתָּהּ בִּשְׁנֵי לָאוִין. אַף אִשָּׁה (וּבִתָּהּ) וּבַת בִּתָּהּ בִּשְׁנֵי לָאוִין. מַה טַעֲמוֹן דְּרַבָּנִין. מַה בַּת בִּתָּהּ וּבַת בְּנָהּ בְּלָאו אֶחָד אַף אִשָּׁה וּבַת בִּתָּהּ וּבַת בְּנָהּ בְּלָאו אֶחָד.

Rebbi Eleazar said, Symmachos and Rebbi Joḥanan ben Nuri said the same thing, since we stated there: "If he slaughtered her, her daughter's daughter, and afterwards her daughter, he absorbs forty [lashes]. Symmachos said in Rebbi Meïr's name, he absorbs eighty." There, we have stated: "Rebbi Joḥanan ben Nuri said, he who copulates with his mother-in-law may be liable because of his mother-in-law, his mother-in-law's mother, and his father-in-law's mother. They said to him, all three fall under the same law." Rebbi Jehudah bar Pazi in the name of Rebbi Joḥanan: Symmachos agrees with Rebbi Joḥanan. It was found stated: it still is in dispute. What is Rebbi Joḥanan ben Nuri's reason? Since a woman and her daughter and a woman and her daughter's daughter fall under two separate prohibitions, also a woman and (her daughter) [her son's daughter][8] and her daughter's daughter fall under two separate prohibitions. What is the reason of the rabbis? Since a woman and her daughter and a woman and her daughter's daughter fall under one and the same prohibition, also a woman and her son's daughter and her daughter's daughter fall the under same prohibition.

8 Text of Y. The text of *Sanhedrin* (in parentheses) simply is a copy of the preceding sentence.

(26d line 35, Y 11c l.76) כְּתִיב עֶרְוַת אִשָּׁה וּבִתָּהּ לֹא תְגַלֶּה. וּכְתִיב וְאִישׁ אֲשֶׁר יִקַּח אֶת־אִשָּׁה וְאֶת־אִמָּהּ זִימָּה הִיא. בְּכוּלְּהֹם כְּתִיב שְׁכִיבָה וּבָהּ כְּתִיב לְקִיחָה. לְלַמְּדָךְ שֶׁאֵינוֹ חַייָב עַל הַשְּׁנִייָה עַד שֶׁתְּהֵא לְקוּחָה לוֹ. אוֹ אֵינוֹ מִתְחַייֵב עָלֶיהָ אֶלָּא עַל דֶּרֶךְ נִישּׂוּאִין. לָמַדְנוּ שֶׁאֵין קִידּוּשִׁין מִתּוֹפְסִין בָּעֲרָיוֹת. וְהֶכְתִיב לֹא־יִקַּח אִישׁ אֶת־אֵשֶׁת אָבִיו וְלֹא יְגַלֶּה כְּנַף אָבִיו׃ בָּא לְהוֹדִיעֲךָ שֶׁהָיָה מוּתָּר בָּהּ עַד שֶׁלֹּא נִישֵּׂאת לְאָבִיו. וְהֶכְתִיב וְאִישׁ אֲשֶׁר יִקַּח אֶת־אֵשֶׁת אָחִיו. מָה הוּא בָא לְהוֹדִיעָךְ. שֶׁהָיָה מוּתָּר בָּהּ עַד שֶׁלֹּא נִישֵּׂאת לְאָחִיו. וְתוּבָן עַל יְדֵי יִיבּוּם. וְהֶכְתִיב וְאִשָּׁה אֶל אֲחוֹתָהּ לֹא תִקָּח. בָּא לְהוֹדִיעָךְ שֶׁהָיָה מוּתָּר בָּהּ עַד שֶׁלֹּא נָשָׂא אֲחוֹתָהּ. וְתוּבָן לְאַחַר מִיתַת אֲחוֹתָהּ. וְהֶכְתִיב וְאִישׁ אֲשֶׁר־יִקַּח אֶת־אֲחוֹתוֹ בַּת־אָבִיו אוֹ בַת־אִמּוֹ וְרָאָה אֶת־עֶרְוָתָהּ וְהִיא תִרְאֶה אֶת־עֶרְוָתוֹ חֶסֶד הוּא. שֶׁלֹּא תֹאמַר. קַיִן נָשָׂא אֶת אֲחוֹתוֹ. הֶבֶל נָשָׂא אֶת אֲחוֹתוֹ. חֶסֶד עָשִׂיתִי עִם הָרִאשׁוֹנִים שֶׁיִּיבָּנֶה הָעוֹלָם מֵהֶם. אָמַרְתִּי עוֹלָם חֶסֶד יִבָּנֶה. וְהֶכְתִיב אַלְמָנָה וּגְרוּשָׁה וַחֲלָלָה זוֹנָה אֶת־אֵלֶּה לֹא יִקָּח. בָּא לְהוֹדִיעָךְ שֶׁאִם קִידְּשָׁהּ תָּפְסוּ בָהּ קִידּוּשִׁין.

It is written, *the genitals of a woman and her daughter you shall not uncover,* and it is written, *if a man take a woman and her mother, it is taboo.* Everywhere is written *lying with*, but here is written *taking*, to teach you that he cannot be [criminally] liable for the second woman unless she be taken by him. Or maybe he is [criminally] liable only by marriage? We already said that there is no valid incestuous marriage. But is it not written: *Nobody may marry his father's wife, and he should not uncover his father's garment's corner*? This comes to tell that she was permitted to him before his father married her. But is it not written: *If a man take his brother's wife*? This comes to tell you that she was permitted to him before his brother married her. This is understood by levirate. But is it not written: *You should not take a woman in addition to her sister*? This comes to tell you that she was permitted to him before he married her sister. This is understood after her sister's death. But is it not written: *A man who would take his sister, his father's daughter or his mother's daughter, it is ḥesed*? That you should not say that Cain married his sister, Abel married his sister, *it is charitable*, I was charitable with the first generations so the world could be inhabited; *I said, the world was built on ḥesed.* But is it not written: *Widow, divorcee, and desecrated, these he shall not take*? This comes to tell you that if he became betrothed to her, the betrothal is valid.

(26d line 51, Y 11d l.26) רַב הוּנָא אָמַר. עַד כְּדוֹן בַּת בִּתּוֹ לְנִישּׂוּאִין. בַּת בִּתּוֹ מִן הָאוֹנְסִין. כְּתִיב עֶרְוַת בַּת־בִּנְךָ אוֹ בַת־בִּתְּךָ לֹא תְגַלֶּה עֶרְוָתָן. מָה אֲנָן קַייָמִין. אִם לְנִישּׂוּאִין הֲרֵי כְּבָר אָמוּר. אֶלָּא אִם אֵינוֹ עִנְייָן לְנִישּׂוּאִין תְּנֵיהוּ עִנְייָן לְאוֹנְסִין. עַד כְּדוֹן בַּת בִּתּוֹ. בִּתּוֹ מְנַיִין. רַב אָמַר. אִם עַל בַּת בִּתּוֹ הוּא מוּזְהָר עַל בִּתּוֹ לֹא כָל־שֶׁכֵּן. אִם עַל בַּת בִּתּוֹ הוּא עָנוּשׁ כָּרֵת לֹא כָל־שֶׁכֵּן עַל בִּתּוֹ.

מְנָא לֵיהּ. אַשְׁכַּח תַּנֵּי חִזְקִיָּה. וּבַת אִישׁ כֹּהֵן כִּי תֵחֵל לִזְנוֹת. מַה תַּלְמוּד לוֹמַר אִישׁ. אֶלָּא לְהָבִיא הַבָּא עַל בִּתּוֹ מִן הָאוֹנְסִין שֶׁהוּא בִשְׂרֵיפָה.

(Rav Huna said:)[9] so far his daughter's daughter from marriage. His daughter's daughter from a rape? It is written, *the genitals of your son's daughter or your daughter's daughter you shall not uncover*. Where do we hold? If from marriage, it already had been said. So it cannot refer to marriage but must refer to rape. So far about his daughter's daughter; from where his daughter? Rav said, if he is forewarned about his daughter's daughter, so much more for his daughter! If for his daughter's daughter he is subject to punishment (by extirpation)[9], so much more for his daughter!

[10]From where does he have this? If was found stated by Ḥizqiah: *And if the daughter of a Cohen man start to whore* [11]. Why does the verse say *man*? To include one who copulates with his daughter from a rape among the burned [12].

9 Missing in Y, probably spurious.

10 Missing in Y. Rav's argument is rejected in the Babli 76a since it violates a fundamental principle of criminal law that no act is punishable which is not listed as punishable in the written law. Therefore one needs a verse which punishes sexual relations with an illegitimate daughter.

11 *Lev*. 21:9.

12 The verse states clearly that the priesthood is inherited from the male line. A daughter of a Cohen who is not the daughter of the Cohen's wife still is a Cohen's daughter and subject to the rules of the priesthood. But the Babli 76a rejects the argument given here since the verse states that the Cohen's daughter has to be burned because *she desecrates her father*; this excludes an incestuous relationship, in which the father desecrates his daughter.

(26d line 59, Y 11d l.15) רַב חוּנָה שָׁמַע כּוּלְּהוֹן מִן הָכָא. עֶרְוַת אִשָּׁה וּבִתָּהּ לֹא תְגַלֵּה. וּכְתִיב וְאִישׁ אֲשֶׁר יִקַּח אֶת־אִשָּׁה וְאֶת־אִמָּהּ זִמָּה הִיא. זִמָּה זִמָּה לִגְזֵירָה שָׁוָה. מַה לְמַתָּן שְׁלֹשָׁה דוֹרוֹת אַף לְמַעְלָן שְׁלֹשָׁה דוֹרוֹת. מַה לְמַתָּן בְּלֹא תַעֲשֶׂה אַף לְמַעְלָן בְּלֹא תַעֲשֶׂה. מַה לְמַטָּן דֶּרֶךְ

נִישּׂוּאִין אַף לְמַעְלָן דֶּרֶךְ נִישּׂוּאִין. מַה לְמַטָּן בִּשְׂרֵיפָה אַף לְמַעְלָן בִּשְׂרֵיפָה. מַה לְמַטָּן עָשָׂה בַת זָכָר כְּבַת נְקֵיבָה אַף לְמַעְלָן נַעֲשֶׂה בַת זָכָר כְּבַת נְקֵיבָה.

[13]<u>Rav</u> Huna understood all of these [rules] from this verse: *The genitals of a woman and her daughter you should nor uncover*. <u>And it is written, *if a man take a woman and her daughter, it is taboo*</u>. Taboo-taboo for an equal cut. Since there are three generations downwards, so there are three generations upwards. Since there is a prohibition downwards, there is a prohibition upwards. Since <u>downwards</u> one requires marriage, so <u>upwards</u> one requires marriage. Since <u>downwards</u> they are burned, so <u>upwards</u> they are burned. Since downwards He gave the male's daughter the same status as the female's daughter, so upwards we give the male's <u>daughter</u> the same status as the female's <u>daughter</u>.

13 The changes from or additions to the text in Y are <u>underlined</u>. It is clear that the *Yebamot* text is the correct one, where in the references to *Lev*. 20:14 "upwards" and "downwards" have to be interchanged and in the last sentence "mother" replaces "daughter".

((26d line 65, Y 11d l.21) וּכְרִבִּי מֵאִיר. דְּרִבִּי מֵאִיר אָמַר. גְּזֵירָה שָׁוָה בְּמָקוֹם שֶׁבָּא. דּוֹר שְׁלִישִׁי לְמַטָּה מְנַיִין שֶׁהוּא בְלֹא תַעֲשֶׂה. (וּכְרַבָּנִין דִּינּוּן אָמְרִין. גְּזֵירָה שָׁוָה בְּמָקוֹם שֶׁבָּאת. דּוֹר שְׁלִישִׁי לְמַטָּה מְנַיִין שֶׁהוּא בָא בְלֹא תַעֲשֶׂה.) וּכְרַבָּנִין דִּינּוּן אָמְרִין. גְּזֵירָה שָׁוָה כָּאָמוּר בָּהּ. דּוֹר שְׁלִישִׁי לְמַעְלָה מְנַיִין שֶׁהוּא בִשְׂרֵיפָה. בֵּין כְּרַבָּנִין בֵּין כְּרִבִּי מֵאִיר דּוֹר שְׁלִישִׁי לְמַטָּה מְנַיִין שֶׁהוּא בְלֹא תַעֲשֶׂה. אָמַר רִבִּי יוֹסֵי. מִכֵּיוָן דִּכְתִיב זִמָּה זִמָּה כְּמִי שֶׁכּוּלְּהֹם כָּאן.

And following Rebbi Meïr? Since Rebbi Meïr said, a *gezerah šawah* is at the place it comes from, from where is the third generation downwards forbidden? (And following the rabbis, who say, a *gezerah šawah* is at the place it comes from, from where is the third generation downwards forbidden?)[9] And following the rabbis, who say, a *gezerah šawah* is said about them, from where is the third generation upwards punished by burning? Both for Rebbi Meïr and the rabbis, from where that the third generation downwards is forbidden? (Rebbi Yose said,)[9] since it is written *taboo-taboo*, it is as if all were there.

(26d line 71, Y 77d l.46) אָמַר רִבִּי יוֹסֵי בֵּירִבִּי בוּן. עוֹד הוּא אִית לֵיהּ אַזְהָרָה מִן תַּמָּן. אַל־תְּחַלֵּל אֶת־בִּתְּךָ לְהַזְנוֹתָהּ.

[14]Rebbi Yose ben Rebbi Abun said, one may even understand this from the warning: *Do not desecrate your daughter to force her into prostitution.*

14 This sentence is quite out of place here; in *Yebamot* it follows the paragraph after the next. All sexual offenses against a daughter are covered by *Lev.* 19:29; punishment only has to be specified in different cases. Babli 76a.

(26d line 73, Y 11d l.37) רִבִּי חַגַּיי בְּעָא קוֹמֵי רִבִּי יוֹסֵי. לָמָּה לֵי נָן אָֽמְרִין. בִּתְּךָ לֹא תְגַלֶּה בַּת בִּתְּךָ לֹא תְגַלֶּה. אָמַר לֵיהּ. וְיֵימַר קִרְייָא עֶרְוַת אִשָּׁה וּבַת בִּתָּהּ לֹא תְגַלֶּה וַאֲנָן אָֽמְרִין. בִּתְּךָ לֹא תְגַלֶּה בַּת בִּתְּךָ לֹא תְגַלֶּה.

Rebbi Ḥaggai asked before Rebbi Yose: Why do we not say, "your daughter you should not uncover, your daughter's daughter you should not uncover"? He said, if it were written "the genitals of a woman and her daughter's daughter you shall not uncover," we would have said "your daughter you should not uncover, your daughter's daughter you should not uncover".

(26d line 76, Y 11d l.40) שְׁנַיִם לָאוִין וְכָרֵת אֶחָד לָאוִין חוֹלְקִין אֶת הַהִכָּרֵת. וּמַה טַעֲמָא. עַל־בְּשַׂ֤ר אָדָם֙ לֹ֣א יִיסָ֔ךְ וּבְמַתְכֻּנְתּ֕וֹ לֹ֥א תַעֲשׂ֖וּ כָּמֹ֑הוּ וגו'. וּכְתִיב אִ֚ישׁ אֲשֶׁ֣ר יִרְקַ֣ח כָּמֹ֔הוּ וגו'. הָדָא אָמְרָה. שְׁנֵי לָאוִין וְכָרֵת אֶחָד חוֹלְקִין אֶת הַהִכָּרֵת.

If there are two prohibitions and one liability to extirpation, the prohibitions split the extirpation. What is the reason? *On human flesh it may not be rubbed and in its proportions you should not make [a compound] like it,* etc.. And it is written: *A man who would compound like it, etc.* This implies that for two prohibitions and one liability to extirpation, the prohibitions split the extirpation.

(27a line 3, Y 11d l.34) בְּעוֹן קוֹמֵי רִבִּי אַבָּהוּ. הַבָּא עַל אִשָּׁה וְיָֽלְדָה בַת וְחָזַר וּבָא עָלֶיהָ חַייָב עָלֶיהָ מִשּׁוּם אִשָּׁה וּבִתָּהּ וּבַת בִּתָּהּ וּבַת בְּנָהּ. אָמַר לוֹן שַׁאֲרָ֥ה הֵ֖נָּה זִמָּ֥ה הִֽוא׃ כּוּלְּהֹם מִשּׁוּם זִימָּה.

They asked before Rebbi Abbahu: If [a man] copulated with a woman, she had a daughter, and after that he came and copulated with the latter. Is he [criminally] liable about her because of a woman and her daughter, her daughter's daughter, and her son's daughter? He said to them, *they are relatives, it is taboo*, all because of taboo.

(27a line 5, Y 11d l.47) מַה טַעֲמָא דְרִבִּי יְהוּדָה. לֹא־יִקַּח אִישׁ אֶת־אֵשֶׁת אָבִיו לֹא יְגַלֶּה כְּנַף אָבִיו׃ זוֹ אֲנוּסָתוֹ. מַה מְקַיְּימִין רַבָּנִין כְּנַף. תַּמָּן אָמְרִין וְלָא יָדְעִין אִין שְׁמוּעָה זוֹ. כָּנָף זוֹ שֶׁהוּא זְקוּקָה לְאָבִיו. וְלֹא כָךְ אֵינוֹ חַייָב עָלֶיהָ מִשּׁוּם אֵשֶׁת אָבִיו. אָמַר רִבִּי הִילָא. לְהַתְרָייָה. שֶׁאִם הִתְרוּ בוֹ מִשּׁוּם אֵשֶׁת אָב לוֹקֶה. מִשּׁוּם כָּנָף לוֹקֶה. מוֹדֶה רִבִּי יוּדָה בְמַכּוֹת. מוֹדֶה רִבִּי יוּדָה בְקָרְבָּן. מוֹדֶה רִבִּי יוּדָה בִשְׁאָר כָּל־הָאֲנָשִׁים שֶׁהוּא פָטוּר. מוֹדֶה רִבִּי יוּדָה שֶׁאִם קִידְּשָׁהּ תָּפְסוּ בָהּ קִידּוּשִׁין.

What is the reason of Rebbi Jehudah? *A man may not take his father's wife, and he should not uncover his father's wing;* that is his rape victim. How do the rabbis explain "his father's wing"? There, they say and they do not know the origin of the tradition, that refers to a wing which is in need of his father. Would he not anyhow be [criminally] liable for her because of "his father's wife"? Rebbi Hila said, because of forewarning; if he was warned because of his father's wife he will be whipped, and because of his father's wing he will be whipped. Rebbi Jehudah agrees about whipping. Rebbi Jehudah agrees about sacrifice. Rebbi Jehudah agrees about all other men[15] that he is free. Rebbi Jehudah agrees that if he marries her preliminarily that the preliminary marriage is legally valid.

15 Probably for האנשים one should read האנסים "the rapists." A man can have relations with a woman raped or seduced by any close relative except his father, and even marry her. In Y the reading is הספיקות "the doubts" (see there, Note 61.)

(27a line 12 Y 11d l.54) רִבִּי חַגַּיי בְּעָא קוֹמֵי רִבִּי יוֹסֵי. מַהוּ שֶׁיְּהֵא הַוְולָד מַמְזֵר כְּרִבִּי יוּדָה. אָמַר לֵיהּ. לֹא־יָבוֹא פְצוּעַ־דַּכָּה וּכְרוּת שָׁפְכָה בִּקְהַל יי הִפְסִיק הָעִנְייָן. וַיַּפְסִיק הָעִנְייָן לְעִנְייַן אֵשֶׁת אָב. אֵשֶׁת אָב בִּכְלָל כָּל־הָעֲרָיוֹת הָייְתָה וְיָצָאת מִכְּלָלָהּ לְלַמֵּד עַל כָּל־הָעֲרָיוֹת לְמַמְזֵר. וְתֵצֵא אֲנוּסָה וּתְלַמֵּד עַל כָּל־הָאֲונֵסִים לְאִסּוּר. אֵשֶׁת אָב בִּכְלָל כָּל־הָעֲרָיוֹת הָיָית וְיָצָאת מִכְּלָלָהּ לְלַמֵּד עַל כָּל־הָעֲרָיוֹת לְמַמְזֵר. אִית לָךְ מֵימַר הָכָא. אֲנוּסָה בִּכְלָל הָיָית וְיָצָאת מִכְּלָלָהּ לְלַמֵּד עַל כָּל־הָאֲונֵסִים. וְתֵצֵא אֵשֶׁת אָב וּתְלַמֵּד עַל כָּל־אֲנוּסָתָהּ. אָמַר לֵיהּ. אִם אֵשֶׁת אָב הִיא אֵינָהּ אֲנוּסָה. וְאִם אֲנוּסָה הִיא אֵינָהּ אֵשֶׁת אָב.

[16]Rebbi Haggai asked before Rebbi Yose: Is the child a bastard following Rebbi Jehudah? He said to him, *No one with a damaged testicle or with cut-off penis may marry into the Eternal's congregation* interrupts the argument. It interrupted the argument in the matter of the father's wife. The father's wife was part of the set of all incest prohibitions; it was selected from

this set to teach about bastardy for all incest prohibitions. Similarly, let the rape victim be selected to teach a prohibition concerning all rape victims. The father's wife was part of the set of all incest prohibitions; it was selected from this set to teach about bastardy for all incest prohibitions. Can you say here that the rape victim was in the set, that it could teach a prohibition concerning all rape victims? Why cannot the father's wife be selected to teach about the rape victim in her case? He said to him, if she is his father's wife, she is not his rape victim; if she is the father's rape victim, she is not his wife.

16 In this paragraph, the indications of who is the speaker of each sentence are given in *Yebamot* 11:1, Notes 62-65.

(fol. 26c) **משנה ב**: רוֹצֵחַ שֶׁהִכָּה אֶת רֵעֵהוּ בָּאֶבֶן אוֹ בַבַּרְזֶל וְכָבַשׁ עָלָיו לְתוֹךְ הַמַּיִם אוֹ לְתוֹךְ הָאוּר וְאֵינוֹ יָכוֹל לַעֲלוֹת מִשָּׁם וָמֵת חַייָב. דְּחָפוֹ לְתוֹךְ הַמַּיִם אוֹ לְתוֹךְ הָאוּר וְיָכוֹל הוּא לַעֲלוֹת מִשָּׁם וָמֵת פָּטוּר. שִׁיסָּה בוֹ אֶת הַכֶּלֶב שִׁיסָּה בוֹ אֶת הַנָּחָשׁ פָּטוּר. הִשִּׁיךְ בּוֹ אֶת הַנָּחָשׁ רִבִּי יְהוּדָה מְחַייֵב וַחֲכָמִים פּוֹטְרִין.

Mishnah 2: A murderer who attacked someone with a stone or an iron[17], or forced him under water or into fire so he could not escape from there and died, is [criminally] liable. If he pushed him into water or fire and he could have escaped from there by himself but died, he is not [criminally] liable[18]. If he provoked a dog or a snake against him, he is not [criminally] liable[18]. If he let a snake bite him[19], Rebbi Jehudah declares him [criminally] liable but for the Sages he is not [criminally] liable.

17 These are the cases described in the Torah, *Num*. 35:16,17.

18 This is a case of indirect causation, not covered by biblical law.

19 The murderer held the poisonous snake until it started to bite the victim. For R. Jehudah it is a case of murder, for the Sages one of indirect causation.

(27a line 21) **הלכה ב**: רוֹצֵחַ שֶׁהִכָּה אֶת רֵעֵהוּ כול'. כְּתִיב וְאִ֠ם בְּאֶ֨בֶן יָ֜ד אֲשֶׁר־יָמ֥וּת בּוֹ הִכָּ֛הוּ וַיָּמֹ֖ת מוֹת־יוּמַ֣ת הַמַּכֶּ֑ה רוֹצֵ֣חַ ה֔וּא מ֖וֹת יוּמַ֥ת הָרוֹצֵֽחַ׃ א֡וֹ בִּכְלִ֣י עֵֽץ־יָד֩ אֲשֶׁר־יָמ֨וּת בּ֥וֹ הִכָּ֖הוּ וַיָּמֹ֑ת רוֹצֵ֣חַ ה֔וּא מ֥וֹת יוּמַ֖ת הָרוֹצֵֽחַ׃ כְּשֶׁהוּא בָא אֵצֶל הַבַּרְזֶל אֵינוֹ אוֹמֵר לֹא שֶׁיָּמוּת בּוֹ וְלֹא שֶׁלֹּא יָמוּת בּוֹ. אֶלָּא אֲפִילוּ צִינּוֹרָה קְטַנָּה דְהִיא יָכְלָה מֵקִים גּוּ וֶשְׁטָא וּמִקְטְלִינֵיהּ. וְהוּא שֶׁיְּהֵא בָאֶבֶן כְּדֵי

לַהֲמִיתוֹ. בָּעֵץ כְּדֵי לַהֲמִיתוֹ. כִּוְּנוֹ כְּנֶגֶד הַסּוּס. כִּוְּנוֹ כְּנֶגֶד הַחֵץ. כִּוְּנוֹ כְּנֶגֶד הָרוֹמַח. הֶעֱמִידוֹ בַצִּינָּה. הִשְׁקָה אוֹתוֹ מַיִם רָעִים. הֶעֱבִיר אֶת הַתִּקְרָא מֵעָלָיו וְיָרְדוּ גְּשָׁמִים וַהֲרָגוּהוּ. פָּתַק אַמַּת הַמַּיִם עָלָיו וּבָאוּ עָלָיו הַמַּיִם וּשְׁטָפוּהוּ.

Halakhah 2: "A murderer who attacked someone," etc. It is written[20]: *If he hit him with a lethal stone in his hand so that he died, (the hitter shall die, he is a murderer,)*[21] *the murderer shall be put to death. Or he hit him with a lethal wooden implement in his hand so that he died, the murderer shall be put to death*[22]. When He comes to iron[23], He does not speak of lethal or not lethal, but even a small hook when applied to the esophagus could kill him; but a stone must be lethal, wood must be lethal[24]. If he put him in front of a horse[25], in front of an arrow, in front of a spear, put him out in the cold, gave him bad water to drink, removed the ceiling over him and the rains came down and killed him, or he opened a water canal whose waters swept over him[26].

20 *Num.* 35:17.

21 *Num.* 35:21; the quote is not appropriate

22 *Num.* 35:18.

23 *Num.* 35:16. Babli 76b.

24 Prosecution of murder with a stone or wood is possible only if the stone or wood can be classified as lethal; otherwise the murderer can claim that the slain person was the victim of an accident.

25 In the following cases, it is presumed that the murderer somehow immobilized his victim. In these cases, the murderer is guilty if the horse already was galloping, or the arrow or spear already flying, etc. Then the action of the murderer is murder. But according to the Mishnah, tying a person as a target for other people's future shots is indirect causation. Babli 77a.

26 It is murder if the first wave of water is lethal.

(27a line 30) מַה טַעֲמָא דְרִבִּי יוּדָה. מִפְּנֵי הָאֶרֶס הַנָּתוּן בֵּין הַנְּקָבִים. מַה טַעֲמוֹן דְּרַבָּנִין. לְעוֹלָם אֵין הָאֵירֶס נָתוּן בֵּין הַנְּקָנִים עַד שֶׁיַּחֲזוֹר וְיָקִיא.

What is Rebbi Jehudah's reason? Because of the poison in the hollow teeth[27]. What is the reason of the rabbis? There is no poison in the hollow teeth until it excretes it.

27 For R. Jehudah, the moment when the snake starts biting, the poison starts to flow. Therefore holding a snake is no different from holding a dagger. The rabbis hold that the snake has to push out the poison by the action of some of its muscles; this makes the

action of the murderer indirect causation; Babli 78a.

(fol. 26c) **משנה ג**: הַמַּכֶּה אֶת חֲבֵרוֹ בֵּין בָּאֶבֶן בֵּין בָּאֶגְרוֹף וַאֲמָדוּהוּ לְמִיתָה וְהֵיקֵל מִמַּה שֶּׁהָיָה וּלְאַחַר מִכָּאן הִכְבִּיד וָמֵת חַיָּיב. רִבִּי נְחֶמְיָה אוֹמֵר פָּטוּר שֶׁרַגְלַיִם לַדָּבָר׃

Mishnah 3: If somebody injures another person by a stone or with his fist[28] and they expected him to die, but he got better and only afterwards deteriorated and died; he is [criminally] liable. Rebbi Neḥemiah declares him not liable since it is not unsubstantiated[29].

28 The language is from *Ex*. 21:18.

29 For R. Nehemiah it is probable that the death was not caused by the injury; for the rabbis the opposite is true.

(27a line 32) **הלכה ג**: הַמַּכֶּה אֶת חֲבֵרוֹ כול'. כֵּינִי מַתְנִיתָא. רִבִּי נְחֶמְיָה פוֹטֵר וַחֲכָמִים מְחַייְבִין. שֶׁרַגְלַיִם לַדָּבָר. רַבָּנִין אָמְרִין. שְׁנֵי אֲמוּדִין רָבִים עַל עוֹמֶד אֶחָד. רִבִּי נְחֶמְיָה אוֹמֵר. עוֹמֶד הָאֶמְצָאִי רָבָה עַל שְׁנֵיהֶן. מַה טַעֲמָה דְּרִבִּי נְחֶמְיָה. אִם־יָקוּם וְהִתְהַלֵּךְ בַּחוּץ עַל־מִשְׁעַנְתּוֹ וְנִקָּה הַמַּכֶּה. וְכִי עָלְתָה עַל דַּעְתָּךְ שֶׁיְּהֵא זֶה מְהַלֵּךְ בַּשּׁוּק וַהֲלָה נֶהֱרַג עַל יָדוֹ. אֶלָּא אֲפִילוּ מֵת בָּעֲמִידָה רִאשׁוֹנָה פָּטוּר. מַה טַעֲמוֹן דְּרַבָּנִין. וְלֹא יָמוּת וְנָפַל לְמִשְׁכָּב. וְכִי אֵין אָנוּ יוֹדְעִין שֶׁאִם לֹא יָמוּת וְנָפַל לְמִשְׁכָּב. אֶלָּא בְּשֶׁלֹּא עֲמָדוּהוּ לְמִיתָה. אִם בְּשֶׁלֹּא עֲמָדוּהוּ לְמִיתָה בְּדָא כְתִיב אִם־יָקוּם וְהִתְהַלֵּךְ בַּחוּץ עַל־מִשְׁעַנְתּוֹ וְנִקָּה הַמַּכֶּה. הָא אִם לֹא קָם חַייָב. אֶלָּא בְּשֶׁעֲמָדוּהוּ לְמִיתָה. אִם בְּשֶׁעֲמָדוּהוּ לְמִיתָה בְּדָא כְתִיב רַק שִׁבְתּוֹ יִתֵּן וְרַפֹּא יְרַפֵּא׃ רִבִּי הִילָא בְשֵׁם רִבִּי שִׁמְעוֹן בֶּן לָקִישׁ. חִידּוּשׁ מִקְרָא הוּא שֶׁיִּתֵּן. רִבִּי אַבָּהוּ בְשֵׁם רִבִּי יוֹסֵי בֶּן חֲנִינָה. עוֹמֶד שֶׁלְּקָטָעוּת הָיִיתָה. מַה מַפְקָה מִבֵּינֵיהוֹן. הֵיקֵל מִמַּה שֶׁהָיָה וְאַחַר כָּךְ הִכְבִּיד וָמֵת חַייָב. רִבִּי נְחֶמְיָה פוֹטֵר. שֶׁרַגְלַיִם לַדָּבָר. מָאן דְּאָמַר. חִידּוּשׁ מִקְרָא הוּא שֶׁיִּתֵּן. נָתַן נָתַן. לֹא נָתַן מָהוּ שֶׁיִּתֵּן. מָאן דְּאָמַר. עוֹמֶד שֶׁלְּקָטָעוּת הָיָה. לֹא נָתַן אֵין אוֹמְרִים לוֹ שֶׁיִּתֵּן. נָתַן מָהוּ שֶׁיִּטּוֹל. מַתְנִיתָא מְסַייְעָה לְדֵין וּמַתְנִיתָא מְסַייְעָה לְדֵין. מַתְנִיתָא מְסַייְעָה לְרִבִּי יוֹסֵי בַּר חֲנִינָה. אֲמָדוּהוּ לְחַיִּים וָמֵת. מֵאֵימָתַי מוֹנִין לוֹ. מִשֶּׁיַּכְבִּיד. הָדָא אָמְרָה. עוֹמֶד שֶׁלְּקָטָעוּת הָיְתָה. וְאִין תֵּימַר. חִידּוּשׁ מִקְרָא הוּא שֶׁיִּתֵּן. יִתֵּן מִשָּׁעָה הָרִאשׁוֹנָה. מַתְנִיתָא מְסַייְעָא לְרִבִּי שִׁמְעוֹן בֶּן לָקִישׁ. עֲמָדוּהוּ לְמִיתָה וְחָיָה. מֵאֵימָתַי מוֹנִין לוֹ. מִשֶּׁיַּכְבִּיד. אָמַר רִבִּי יָסֵי. לֵית כָּאן מִשֶּׁיַּכְבִּיד אֶלָּא מִשָּׁעָה הָרִאשׁוֹנָה. הָדָא אָמְרָה. חִידּוּשׁ מִקְרָא הוּא שֶׁיִּתֵּן. וְאִין תֵּימַר. עוֹמֶד שֶׁלְּקָטָעוּת הָיְתָ. נוֹתֵן עַד שָׁעָה שֶׁיָּמוּת.

Halakhah 3: "If somebody injures another person," etc. So is the Mishnah: [30]"Rebbi Neḥemiah declares him not [criminally] liable but the Sages declare him [criminally] liable since it is not unsubstantiated." The

Sages say, two estimations have precedence over one estimation; Rebbi Nehemiah says, the intermediate estimation has precedence over the two. What is Rebbi Nehemiah's reason? *If he gets up and walks outside on his cane, the attacker is exonerated.* Could you think that this one walks in the market and the other one is executed because of him? But even if he dies according to the first estimation, he cannot be prosecuted. What is the rabbi's reason? *If he does not die but is bedridden.* Would we not know that even if he does not die that he will be bedridden? But if they did not estimate that he would die. If they did not estimate that he would die, that is what is written: *If he gets up and walks outside on his cane, the attacker is exonerated.* Therefore, if he does not get up, [the attacker] is [criminally] liable. But if they estimated that he would die? If they estimated that he would die, that is what is written: *But he has to pay for his disability and the medical costs.* Rebbi Hila in the name of Rebbi Simeon ben Laqish: It is an extraordinary decree of Scripture that he has to pay. Rebbi Abbahu in the name of Rebbi Yose ben Ḥanina: It was an erroneous estimation. What is the difference between them? "But he got better and only afterwards deteriorated and died; he is [criminally] liable. Rebbi Nehemiah declares him not liable since it is not unsubstantiated." For him who said, it is an extraordinary decree of Scripture that he has to pay; if he paid, he paid. If he did not pay, does he have to pay? For him who said, it was an erroneous estimation; if he did not pay, one does not order him to pay. If he paid, can he take it back? A *baraita* supports one and a *baraita* supports the other. A *baraita* supports Rebbi Yose bar Ḥanina: If they estimated that he would live but he died, from when does one count for him? From the moment he turns worse[31]. This implies that the estimate was wrong. If you would say, it is an extraordinary decree of Scripture that he has to pay, he should pay from the first moment. A *baraita* supports Rebbi Simeon ben Laqish: If they estimated that he would die but he lived, from when does one count for him? From the moment he turns worse. Rebbi Yose said, it does not say here "from the moment he turns worse" but "from the moment he turns better." That means, it is an extraordinary decree of Scripture that he has to pay. But if you say, it was an erroneous estimation, he has to pay until [the victim] dies.

30 The entire Halakhah is also *Nazir* 9:5, explained there in Notes 163-186 with due attention given to the differences in reading in *Sanhedrin*.

31 A Genizah reading: "improves" (*Nazir* Note 179).

(27a line 56, *Nazir* 58a l.28) הִכָּהוּ עַל יָדוֹ וְצָבַת. אָמְרִין אַסָּיָא. אִין מִקְטְעָא יָדֵיהּ חַיי הוּא. מָהוּ שֶׁיִּתֵּן דְּמֵי הַיָּד. נִישְׁמְעִינָהּ מִן הָדָא. וְכִי יִנָּצוּ אֲנָשִׁים . וְכִי־יְרִיבוּן אֲנָשִׁים. הִיא מְרִיבָה הִיא מַצּוּת. מַה תַלְמוּד לוֹמַר כִּי יִנָּצוּ כִּי יְרִיבוּן. כִּי יְרִיבוּן כִּי יִנָּצוּ. אֶלָּא לִיתֵּן הַמִּתְכַּוֵּין עַל שֶׁאֵינוֹ מִתְכַּוֵּין וְאֶת שֶׁאֵינוֹ מִתְכַּוֵּין עַל הַמִּתְכַּוֵּין. נִיחָא אֶת הַמִּתְכַּוֵּין עַל שֶׁאֵינוֹ מִתְכַּוֵּין. וְאֶת שֶׁאֵינוֹ מִתְכַּוֵּין עַל הַמִּתְכַּוֵּין. אִם שֶׁאֵינוֹ מִתְכַּוֵּין הוּא מִתְחַייֵב לֹא כָל־שֶׁכֵּן עַל הַמִּתְכַּוֵּין. אֶלָּא כֵינִי. הִכָּהוּ עַל יָדוֹ וְצָבַת. אָמְרִין אַסָּיָא. אִין מִקְטְעָא יָדֵיהּ חַיי הוּא. מָהוּ שֶׁיִּתֵּן דְּמֵי הַיָּד. כְּמַה דַּתְּ אָמַר תַּמָּן. חִידּוּשׁ מִקְרָא הוּא שֶׁיִּתֵּן דְּמֵי הַיָּד. וּמַה חִידּוּשׁ מִקְרָא הוּא שֶׁיִּתֵּן דְּמֵי הַיָּד.

[30]If he hit him on his hand and it withered. The physicians said, if his hand is amputated he will live. Does he have to pay for the hand? Let us hear from the following: *If people quarrel, if people brawl.* Is not brawl quarrel? Why does the verse say, *if people quarrel, if people brawl*? To apply the rules of the intended to the unintended and of the unintended to the intended. One understands from the intended to the unintended. Of the unintended to the intended? It must be the following: If he hit him on his hand and it withered. The physicians said, if his hand is amputated he will live. Does he have to pay for the hand? Since you say there, it is an extraordinary decree of Scripture that he pay for the hand, so here it is an extraordinary decree of Scripture that he pay for the hand.

(fol. 26c) **משנה ד**: נִתְכַּוֵּין לַהֲרוֹג אֶת הַבְּהֵמָה וְהָרַג אֶת הָאָדָם לַנָּכְרִי וְהָרַג אֶת יִשְׂרָאֵל לַנְּפָלִים וְהָרַג בֶּן קַייָמָא פָּטוּר.

Mishnah 4: If one intended to kill an animal but he killed a human, a Non-Jew but he killed a Jew, a stillborn[32] but he killed a viable baby, he is not criminally liable[33].

משנה ה: נִתְכַּוֵּין לְהַכּוֹתוֹ עַל מָתְנָיו וְלֹא הָיָה בָהּ כְּדֵי לְהָמִית עַל מָתְנָיו וְהָלְכָה לָהּ עַל לִבּוֹ וְהָיָה בָהּ כְּדֵי לְהָמִית עַל לִבּוֹ וָמֵת פָּטוּר. נִתְכַּוֵּין לְהַכּוֹתוֹ עַל לִבּוֹ וְהָיָה בָהּ כְּדֵי לְהָמִית עַל לִבּוֹ וְהָלְכָה לָהּ עַל מָתְנָיו וְלֹא הָיָה בָהּ כְּדֵי לְהָמִית עַל מָתְנָיו וָמֵת פָּטוּר. נִתְכַּוֵּין לְהַכּוֹת אֶת הַגָּדוֹל וְלֹא הָיָה בָהּ כְּדֵי לְהָמִית אֶת הַגָּדוֹל וְהָלְכָה לָהּ עַל הַקָּטָן וְהָיָה בָהּ כְּדֵי לְהָמִית אֶת הַקָּטָן וָמֵת פָּטוּר.

נִתְכַּוֵון לְהַכּוֹת אֶת הַקָּטָן וְהָיָה בָהּ כְּדֵי לְהָמִית אֶת הַקָּטָן וְהָלְכָה לָהּ עַל הַגָּדוֹל וְלֹא הָיָה בָהּ כְּדֵי לְהָמִית אֶת הַגָּדוֹל וָמֵת פָּטוּר.

Mishnah 5: If one intended to hit someone on his hips where it would not have been enough to kill but it went on his heart where it was enough to kill and he died, he cannot be prosecuted. If one intended to hit someone on his heart where it would have been enough to kill but it went on his hips where it was not enough to kill but he died, he cannot be prosecuted. If one intended to hit someone big whom it would not have been enough to kill but it went on somebody small whom it was enough to kill and he died, he cannot be prosecuted. If one intended to hit someone small whom it would have been enough to kill but it went on somebody big whom it was not enough to kill but he died, he cannot be prosecuted.

32 A newborn who is not expected to live for 30 days is considered stillborn.

33 Biblical law provides sanctions for murder and unintentional homicide, but not for intentional homicide that fails to qualify as murder. Similarly, biblical law is not applicable to Gentiles (*Tanhuma Mišpatim* 3, based on *Ex*. 21:1). These cases cannot be tried in rabbinic court; they are cases for the king's police powers or extrajudicial powers of the communal court (Mishnah 10).

(27a line 66) **הלכה ד**: נִתְכַּוֵון לַהֲרוֹג אֶת הַבְּהֵמָה כול'. רִבִּי יִצְחָק שָׁאַל. עֲמָדוּהוּ לְחַיִּים וָמֵת. וְדֶרֶךְ הַחַיִּים לָמוּת. מִכֵּיוָן דִּכְתִיב רַק שִׁבְתּוֹ יִתֵּן וְרַפֹּא יְרַפֵּא חַייָב לִיתֵּן לוֹ שֶׁבֶת וְרִיפּוּי. רִבִּי יִצְחָק שָׁאַל. עֲמָדוּהוּ לְמִיתָה וְחָיָה.. וְאֵין דֶּרֶךְ הַמֵּתִים לִחְיוֹת. מִכֵּיוָן דִּכְתִיב רַק שִׁבְתּוֹ יִתֵּן וְרַפֹּא יְרַפֵּא חַייָב לִיתֵּן לוֹ שֶׁבֶת וְרִיפּוּי.

Halakhah 4: "If one intended to kill an animal," etc. Rebbi Isaac asked: If they estimated that he would survive but he died; is it not common for the living to die? Since it is written[34] *but he has to pay for his disability and the medical costs*, he is liable to pay for disability and medical costs[35]. Rebbi Isaac asked: If they estimated that he would die but he survived; is it not common for the dying to live. Since it is written *but he has to pay for his disability and the medical costs*, he is liable to pay for disability and medical costs[36].

34 *Ex.* 21:19.

35 This still belongs to Halakhah 3. Since we have a principle that nobody subject to criminal punishment pays damages, why

was it stated earlier that if medical opinion was that the victim would survive, the attacker has to pay the victim's expenses and loss of earnings even though in the end he faces prosecution for murder? His monetary obligation starts immediately with the act of agression; he faces trial only after the victim's death.

36 The moment it becomes clear that the agressor does not face criminal charges, the monetary obligations are activated.

(fol. 26c) **משנה ו**: נִתְכַּוֵּן לְהַכּוֹתוֹ עַל מָתְנָיו וְהָיָה בָהּ כְּדֵי לְהָמִית עַל מָתְנָיו וְהָלְכָה לָהּ עַל לִבּוֹ וָמֵת חַייָב. נִתְכַּוֵּן לְהַכּוֹת אֶת הַגָּדוֹל וְהָיָה בָהּ כְּדֵי לְהָמִית אֶת הַגָּדוֹל וְהָלְכָה לָהּ עַל הַקָּטָן וָמֵת חַייָב. רִבִּי שִׁמְעוֹן אוֹמֵר אֲפִלּוּ נִתְכַּוֵּן לַהֲרוֹג אֶת זֶה וְהָרַג אֶת זֶה פָּטוּר:

Mishnah 6: If one intended to hit someone on his hips where it was enough to kill but it went on his heart and he died; [or] if one intended to hit someone big and it was enough to kill but it went on somebody small and he died; he is [criminally] liable[37]. Rebbi Simeon says, even if he intended to kill one person but killed another, he is not criminally liable[38].

37 These cases all fit the definition of premeditated murder.

38 Cf. Mishnah 4 and Note 33. In his opinion, not only is it homicide if a human is killed instead of an animal, but even if a different human is killed than the intended victim. In Tosephta 12:4 he is opposed by R. Jehudah.

(27a line 71) **הלכה ו**: נִתְכַּוֵּן לְהַכּוֹתוֹ עַל מָתְנָיו כול'. חִזְקִיָּה שָׁאַל. זָרַק אֶת הָאֶבֶן וְהָיָה בָהּ כְּדֵי לְהָמִית. הֵמִית אֶת זֶה וְשִׁיבֵּר אֶת כֵּילָיו שֶׁלָּזֶה. בָּזֶה חִידֵּשׁ הַכָּתוּב וּבָזֶה לֹא חִידֵּשׁ. חִזְקִיָּה שְׁאִיל. זָרַק אֶת הָאֶבֶן וְלֹא הָיָה בָהּ כְּדֵי לְהָמִית. הֵמִית אֶת זֶה וְשִׁיבֵּר אֶת כֵּילָיו שֶׁלָּזֶה. בָּזֶה חִידֵּשׁ הַכָּתוּב וּבָזֶה לֹא חִידֵּשׁ.

Halakhah 6: "If one intended to hit someone on his hips," etc. Ḥizqiah asked: If one threw a deadly stone which killed one person and broke another's vessels, did the verse give the law for one but not for the other[39]? Ḥizqiah asked: If one threw a stone which was not deadly but which killed one person[40] and broke another's vessels, did the verse give the law for one but not for the other?

39 In *Ex*. 21:22-23 it is spelled out that in case of injuries, payment is due only if there is no criminal case. But this refers only to one person. If the stone had killed one

person and broke the same person's vessels, no payment for the vessels would be due. But this says nothing about the obligations of the thrower towards a third person, not involved in the personal injury case.

40 Assuming that in the previous case the law was that the thrower could not be sued by the owner of the vessels, the question remains open whether he can be sued if the thrower cannot be sued for murder (*Num.* 35:17) but only sued for money by the heirs of the slain person. In the Babli 79b both questions are answered in the negative.

(27a line 75) אָמַר רִבִּי שִׁמְעוֹן. אִילֵּין דְּבֵית רִבִּי תְּנַיִין. אֲפִילוּ נִתְכַּוֵּין לַהֲרוֹג אֶת זֶה וְהָרַג אֶת זֶה פָּטוּר. וְאַתְיָיא דְּבֵי רִבִּי כְּרִבִּי נָתָן. דְּתַנֵּי בְשֵׁם רִבִּי נָתָן. הָיָה עוֹמֵד בְּצַד סִיעָה שֶׁלִּבְנֵי אָדָם. אָמַר. לְאֶחָד מִכֶּם אֲנִי מִתְכַּוֵּן לַהֲרוֹג. אֲפִילוּ נִתְכַּוֵּין לַהֲרוֹג אֶת זֶה וְהָרַג אֶת זֶה פָּטוּר.

Rebbi Simeon[41] says, those of the House of Rebbi state: even if he intended to kill one person but killed another, he is not criminally liable[42]. The House of Rebbi follows Rebbi Nathan, as it was stated in the name of Rebbi Nathan: If one was standing next to a group of people and said, I am intending to kill one of you[43]. Even if he intended to kill one person but killed another, he is not criminally liable.

41 This R. Simeon must be the Amora R. Simeon ben Laqish; he cannot be the Tanna R. Simeon ben Iohai mentioned in the Mishnah, who lived a full generation before Rebbi.

42 He cannot be prosecuted for premeditated murder unless he stated before witnesses the name of the person whom he intended to kill. All other cases are cases of willful homicide, not covered by biblical law (Note 33).

43 But he did not specify whom he intended to kill.

(fol. 26c) **משנה ז**: רוֹצֵחַ שֶׁנִּתְעָרֵב בַּאֲחֵרִים כּוּלָּן פְּטוּרִין. רִבִּי יְהוּדָה אוֹמֵר כּוֹנְסִין אוֹתָן לַכִּיפָּה. כָּל חַייָבֵי מִיתוֹת שֶׁנִּתְעָרְבוּ זֶה בָזֶה יִדּוֹנוּ בַקַּלָּה. הַנִּסְקָלִין בַּנִּשְׂרָפִין רִבִּי שִׁמְעוֹן אוֹמֵר יִידּוֹנוּ בִסְקִילָה שֶׁהַשְּׂרֵיפָה חֲמוּרָה וַחֲכָמִים אוֹמְרִים יִידּוֹנוּ בִשְׂרֵיפָה שֶׁהַסְּקִילָה חֲמוּרָה.

Mishnah 7: If a murderer was mixed up with others, none of them are criminally liable[44]. Rebbi Jehudah says, one keeps them in jail[45]. Any condemned to death who were mixed up with others[46] shall be executed by the easier way. Those to be stoned with those to be burned, Rebbi Simeon says they shall be stoned because burning is more painful, but the Sages say they shall be burned since stoning is more painful.

משנה ח: אָמַר לָהֶן רַבִּי שִׁמְעוֹן אִילּוּ לֹא הָיְתָה שְׂרֵיפָה חֲמוּרָה לֹא נִיתְּנָה לְבַת כֹּהֵן שֶׁזִּינָּת. אָמְרוּ לוֹ אִילּוּ לֹא הָיְתָה סְקִילָה חֲמוּרָה לֹא נִתְּנָה לַמְגַדֵּף וְלָעוֹבְדֵי עֲבוֹדָה זָרָה. הַנֶּהֱרָגִין בַּנֶּחֱנָקִין רַבִּי שִׁמְעוֹן אוֹמֵר בְּסַיִיף וַחֲכָמִים אוֹמְרִים בְּחֶנֶק:

Mishnah 8: Rebbi Simeon told them, if burning were not more painful it would not have been prescribed for a Cohen's daughter who committed adultery. They answered him, if stoning were not more painful, it would not have been prescribed for the blasphemer and those who worship strange cults. Those to be slain with those to be strangled, Rebbi Simeon says by the sword, but the Sages say by strangulation[47].

44 Since nobody can be convicted if he was not identified by witnesses.

45 Until each person be identified by witnesses.

46 Also condemned to death.

47 Mishnah 7:1.

(27b line 3) **הלכה ז**: רוֹצֵחַ שֶׁנִּתְעָרֵב בַּאֲחֵרִים כול'. אָמַר רַבִּי יוֹחָנָן. בְּרוֹצֵחַ שֶׁנִּתְעָרֵב בִּכְשֵׁירִין הִיא מַתְנִיתָא. רִבִּי שִׁמְעוֹן בֶּן לָקִישׁ אָמַר. בְּרוֹצֵחַ שֶׁלֹּא נִגְמַר דִּינוֹ שֶׁנִּתְעָרֵב בְּרוֹצֵחַ שֶׁנִּגְמַר דִּינוֹ הִיא מַתְנִיתָא. שְׁמוּאֵל אָמַר. בְּשׁוֹר בַּשְּׁוָורִים הִיא מַתְנִיתָא. אִם בְּשׁוֹר בַּשְּׁוָורִים הִיא מַתְנִיתָא בְּדָא תַנִּינָן כּוֹנְסִין אוֹתָן לַכִּיפָּה.

Halakhah 7: "If a murderer was mixed up with others," etc. Rebbi Joḥanan said, the Mishnah deals with a murderer mixed up with innocent people[48]. Rebbi Simeon ben Laqish said, the Mishnah deals with a murderer being tried mixed up with a murderer who already was convicted. Samuel said, the Mishnah deals with a bull mixed up with other bulls. If the Mishnah referred to a bull[50] mixed up with other bulls, would we state about them that "one keeps them in jail"?

48 In this interpretation, R. Jehudah allows the police to arrest innocent people and keep them in prison until they have proven their innocence.

49 In the Babli, 79b, this is Samuel's interpretation. What is given here as Samuel's is in the Babli attributed to R. Simeon ben Laqish.

50 A bull which has killed a human and must be stoned by the verdict of a court of 23. Humans can be identified by witnesses; cattle all look alike.

(27b line 7) רִבִּי שִׁמְעוֹן אוֹמֵר. חֲמוּרָה שְׂרֵיפָה מִסְּקִילָה. וְרַבָּנִין אָמְרִין. חֲמוּרָה סְקִילָה מִשְּׂרֵיפָה. רִבִּי שִׁמְעוֹן אוֹמֵר. חָמוּר חֶנֶק מֵהֶרֶג. וְרַבָּנִין אָמְרִין. חָמוּר הֶרֶג מֵחֶנֶק.

Rebbi Simeon says, burning is worse than stoning, but the rabbis teach that stoning is worse than burning. Rebbi Simeon says, strangulation is worse than decapitation; but the rabbis teach that decapitation is worse than strangulation[51].

51 Halakhah 7:1, first sentences.

(fol. 26d) **משנה ט**: מִי שֶׁנִּתְחַייֵב שְׁתֵּי מִיתוֹת בֵּית דִּין יִידּוֹן בַּחֲמוּרָה. עָבַר עֲבֵרָה שֶׁיֵּשׁ בָּהּ שְׁתֵּי מִיתוֹת יִידּוֹן בַּחֲמוּרָה. רִבִּי יוֹסֵי אוֹמֵר יִידּוֹן בְּזִיקָה הָרִאשׁוֹנָה שֶׁבָּאָת עָלָיו:

Mishnah 9: Somebody who was found guilty of two death penalties shall be convicted to the more painful one. One who committed one crime punishable by two death penalties shall be convicted to the more painful one. Rebbi Yose says, he shall be convicted for the first connection.

משנה י: מִי שֶׁלָּקָה וְשָׁנָה בֵּית דִּין מַכְנִיסִים אוֹתוֹ לַכִּיפָּה וּמַאֲכִילִין אוֹתוֹ שְׂעוֹרִין עַד שֶׁכְּרֵיסוֹ מִתְבַּקַּעַת. הַהוֹרֵג נֶפֶשׁ שֶׁלֹּא בְעֵדִים מַכְנִיסִין אוֹתוֹ לַכִּיפָּה וּמַאֲכִילִין אוֹתוֹ לֶחֶם צַר וּמַיִם לַחַץ:

Mishnah 10: If somebody was repeatedly whipped, the court sends him to jail[52] where he is fed barley until his belly bursts. One sends the murderer without witnesses to jail and feeds him scanty bread and sparing water[53].

52 For the third conviction of the same kind. These rules have no biblical justification.

53 *Is*. 30:20.

(27b line 10) **הלכה ט**: מִי שֶׁנִּתְחַייֵב שְׁתֵּי מִיתוֹת בֵּית דִּין כול'. תַּמָּן תַּנִּינָן. תַּנֵּי. רִבִּי יוֹסֵי אוֹמֵר יִדּוֹן בְּזִיקָה הָרִאשׁוֹנָה שֶׁבָּאָת עָלָיו. כֵּיצַד. חֲמוֹתוֹ וְנַעֲשִׂית אֵשֶׁת אִישׁ הֲרֵי זוֹ בִשְׂרֵיפָה. אֵשֶׁת אִישׁ וְאַחַר בָּךְ נַעֲשִׂית חֲמוֹתוֹ בַחֲנִיקָה. בָּא עַל חֲמוֹתוֹ. וְהֵיי דָא לָהּ חֲמוֹתוֹ וְכַלּוֹתוֹ. הֵיךְ עֲבִידָא. גְּבַר נְסַב אִיתָא וְלִבְרַתֵּיהּ דַּאֲחָוָהּ וְלִבְרַתֵּיהּ דְּאִיתְתֵיהּ. אֲתָא עַל סַבְתָּא חַייָב עָלֶיהָ מִשּׁוּם חֲמוֹתוֹ וְאֵם חֲמוֹתוֹ וְאֵם חָמִיו. חֲמוֹתוֹ וְכַלּוֹתוֹ כְּאַחַת מָה אָמַר בָּהּ רִבִּי יוֹסֵה. חוֹמֶר בַּקַּל מָה אָמַר בָּהּ רִבִּי יוֹסֵי. שְׁנֵי אִיסּוּרִין כְּאַחַת מָה אָמַר בָּהּ רִבִּי יוֹסֵי.

Halakhah 9: "Somebody who was found guilty of two death penalties," etc. There[54] it was stated that one states: "Rebbi Yose says, he shall be convicted for the first connection." How is this? His mother-in-law[55] who then became a married woman[56] is [executed] by burning. As a married woman[57] who later became his mother-in-law it is by strangulation, if he copulated with his mother-in-law. How with his mother-in-law and daughter-in-law? How can this be? A man married a woman, and her brother's daughter, and the woman's daughter. If he copulated with the old woman[58] he is liable for her because of his mother-in-law, the mother of his mother-in-law, and the mother of his father-in-law. If his mother-in-law is simultaneously his daughter-in-law[59], how does Rebbi Yose treat this? The more severe and the lesser, how does Rebbi Yose treat this[60]? Two simultaneous prohibitions, how does Rebbi Yose treat this[61]?

54 In Babylonia, Babli 81a.

55 Who was a widow or a single parent at the moment of his marriage.

56 If he sleeps with her after her remarriage.

57 If she was forbidden to him as a married woman before his marriage.

58 The first wife's mother who is his other two wives' grandmother.

59 He married a woman whose mother was married to his son.

60 The Babli indicates that R. Yose might accept that a more general and more stringent prohibition supersedes the more narrow one. The Yerushalmi strongly disagrees, as explained in the next paragraph.

61 In the example of the man with three wives his mother-in-law who is the mother of his father-in-law is doubly forbidden in the same degree. For which crime does he have to be prosecuted first and, since a person can be executed only once, the only time?

(27b line 17) אָמְרִין. כְּמַה דְאִשְׁתָּאִלַת עַל דְּרִבִּי יוֹסֵי כָּךְ אִשְׁתָּאִלַת עַל דְּרִבִּי יִשְׁמָעֵאל. דְּתַנֵּי בְשֵׁם רִבִּי יִשְׁמָעֵאל. נִתְאַלְמְנָה וְנִתְגָּרְשָׁה נִתְחַלְּלָה זִינָת וְאַחַר כָּךְ בָּא עָלֶיהָ אֵינוֹ חַיָּב אֶלָּא אַחַת. זִינָת וְנִתְחַלְּלָה וְאַחַר כָּךְ בָּא עָלֶיהָ חַיָּב עַל כָּל־אַחַת וְאַחַת. נִתְאַלְמְנָה וְנִתְגָּרְשָׁה כְּאַחַת מָה אָמַר בָּהּ רִבִּי יִשְׁמָעֵאל. חוֹמֶר בַּקַּל מָה אָמַר בָּהּ רִבִּי יִשְׁמָעֵאל. שְׁנֵי אִיסּוּרִין כְּאַחַת מָה אָמַר בָּהּ רִבִּי יִשְׁמָעֵאל.

They said, what was asked of Rebbi Yose also can be asked of Rebbi Ismael since it was stated in the name of Rebbi Ismael: If she became widowed, divorced, desecrated, and a whore in this order[62]: when afterwards he copulated with her, he is liable only once. If she whored, was desecrated[63], and after that he copulated with her, he is liable for every single [transgression]. If she became widowed and divorced simultaneously[64], how does Rebbi Ismael treat this? The more severe and the lesser, how does Rebbi Ismael treat this[60]? Two simultaneous prohibitions, how does Rebbi Ismael treat this[61]?

62 This refers to *Lev.* 21:14, speaking of the High Priest: *A widow, divorcee, desecrated woman, whore, these he may not take.*

A desecrated woman is one who had forbidden sexual contact with a Cohen, e. g., a divorcee who is forbidden to a common priest. A whore is a woman who slept with a man whom she could not marry, e. g., a close relative or a Gentile.

Since the verse treats the four prohibitions as one, a High Priest who inadvertently sleeps with a woman who became forbidden to him on all four counts in the order enumerated in the verse has to bring a single purification offering.

In the Babli, *Qiddušin* 77a, the argument is the opposite one. A widow is forbidden only to the high priest. A divorcee is also forbidden to a common priest. A desecrated woman of priestly descent in addition of being barred from marrying a priest is barred from eating heave. A whore may also be forbidden to an Israel; in case she was a married woman who committed adultery she becomes forbidden to her husband. Since the prohibitions cover an ever wider circle, they are cumulative. Therefore, for the Babli, a High Priest who sleeps with a divorcee who afterwards became a widow is liable only for one purification offering, whereas the next sentence shows that for the Yerushalmi he is liable for two.

63 A whore is forbidden to a priest. If he sleeps with her the first time, he desecrates her. If then she again sleeps with a priest, this one sleeps with a woman who first whored and then became desecrated.

64 If a first man had contracted with her a legally defective preliminary marriage and then a second man contracted a clearly legal preliminary marriage, the first man has to divorce her and the second may marry her (Babli *Gittin* 89b). If then the second man dies exactly at the moment when she receives the first man's bill of divorce, she becomes simultaneously a widow and a divorcee.

(27b line 23) רַב אָמַר. בְּמִפְּנִים עֵדָיו הִיא מַתְנִיתָא. רִבִּי יוֹסֵי בֶּן חֲנִינָה אָמַר. בְּשֶׁאֵינוֹ יָכוֹל לְקַבֵּל הַתְרָייָה.

Rav said, the Mishnah [deals with the case that the crime was committed] inside from the witnesses. Rebbi Yose ben Ḥanina said, when he could not receive warning[65].

65 This refers to Mishnah 10. While for all other death penalty cases one can be satisfied with letting Heaven mete out the penalty (*Ex.* 23:7), no commonwealth can exist which lets 99.99% of all murders go unpunished. It is agreed that the death penalty cannot be imposed if not all conditions for such a judgment are satisfied. A rabbinic court cannot be oblivious of *Deut.* 19:15 which clearly requires two eye witnesses for criminal conviction and excludes circumstantial evidence and testimony of a single witness. It is explained that a sentence of life in jail can be imposed on the testimony of two witnesses whose testimony would be inadmissible in a death penalty case. According to Rav, one possible scenario is that of Halakhah 4:11, where two witnesses testify that the accused entered a room where the victim was alive, left with a bloody sword, and the victim was found inside stabbed to death. R. Yose ben Hanina points to another scenario, where there were eye witnesses to the murder but it had not been possible to deliver the statutory warning before the murder was committed.

(fol. 26d) **משנה יא:** הַגּוֹנֵב אֶת הַקַּסְוָה וְהַמְקַלֵּל בַּקֶּסֶם וְהַבּוֹעֵל אֲרַמִּית פּוֹגְעִין בָּהֶן. כֹּהֵן שֶׁשִּׁימֵּשׁ בְּטוּמְאָה אֵין אֶחָיו הַכֹּהֲנִים מְבִיאִין אוֹתוֹ לְבֵית דִּין אֶלָּא פִּירְחֵי כְהוּנָּה מוֹצִיאִין אוֹתוֹ חוּץ לָעֲזָרָה וּמְפַצְּעִין אֶת מוֹחוֹ בְּגִיזִירִין. זָר שֶׁשִּׁמֵּשׁ בַּקּוֹדֶשׁ רִבִּי עֲקִיבָה אוֹמֵר בְּחֶנֶק וַחֲכָמִים אוֹמְרִים בִּידֵי שָׁמַיִם:

Mishnah 11: He who steals the chalice[66], or who curses by charms, or who copulates with a Gentile woman, one[67] strikes him. If a priest officiated while impure, his brother priests do not bring him to court but the young priests take him outside the courtyard and smash his brain with bats[68]. A non-priest who officiated in the Temple: Rebbi Aqiba said, by strangulation, but the Sages say, by the hands of Heaven.

66 A Temple vessel.

67 In all other sources of the Mishnah, and an indirect quote in the Hahakhah: Zealots hit him, referring to *Num.* 25:11 where Phineas is praised for being a zealot by killing the chieftain who copulated with the Midianite princess. The Babli 82a makes clear that the offender may be killed with impunity only during the act. If the parties are still together naked but not engaged in actual intercourse, killing them is prosecutable murder.

68 These are straight pieces of lumber which are impervious to impurity. The offending priest is killed without his executioners becoming impure.

(27b line 25) **הלכה יא:** הַגּוֹנֵב אֶת הַקַּסְוָה כול'. קַסְוָה. קִיסְטָא. רַב יְהוּדָה אָמַר. כְּלִי מִשֶּׁל בֵּית הַמִּקְדָּשׁ הָיָה. כְּמַה דְתֵימַר וְאֵת קְשׂוֹת הַנָּסֶךְ.

Halakhah 11: "He who steals the chalice," etc. קסווה *cista*[69]. Rav Jehudah said, it was a Temple vessel, as one says *and the libation chalices*[70].

69 Also cf. Greek κίστη "basket, hamper; writing case; voting urn" .

70 *Num.* 4:7. The same explanation in the Babli, 81b.

(27b line 25) הַמְקַלֵּל בַּקֶּסֶם. כְּגוֹן אִילֵּין נַפָּתַיֵּי דִּמְקַלְּלִין לְקָנְייָךְ קַייְנָךְ קָנְווּךְ.

"He who curses by a charm." Like those Nabateans who curse "your creator, your smith, your acquisition[71].

71 Explanation of J. Levy in his Dictionary, based on Arabic קני "to acquire, to create", קין "smith; any craftsman"; a similar but Hebrew formulation in the Babli 81a. He also notes that the words might be substitutes for others, similar to קונם, קונח, קונס used for קָרְבָּן in vows (cf. Mishnah *Nedarim* 1:2).

(27b line 25) הַבּוֹעֵל אֲרַמִּית. תַּנֵּי רִבִּי יִשְׁמָעֵאל. זֶה שֶׁהוּא נוֹשֵׂא גוֹיָה וּמוֹלִד בָּנִים וּמַעֲמִיד אוֹיְבִים מִמֶּנָּה לַמָּקוֹם. כְּתִיב וַיַּרְא פִּינְחָס בֶּן־אֶלְעָזָר בֶּן־אַהֲרוֹן הַכֹּהֵן. מָה רָאָה. רָאָה אֶת הַמַּעֲשֶׂה וְנִזְכַּר לַהֲלָכָה הַבּוֹעֵל אֲרַמִּית הַקַּנָּאִים פּוֹגְעִין בָּהֶן. תַּנֵּי. שֶׁלֹּא כִרְצוֹן חֲכָמִים. וּפִינְחָס שֶׁלֹּא כִרְצוֹן חֲכָמִים. אָמַר רִבִּי יוּדָה בַּר פָּזִי. בִּיקְשׁוּ לְנַדּוֹתוֹ אִילוּלֵי שֶׁקָּפְצָה עָלָיו רוּחַ הַקּוֹדֶשׁ וְאָמְרָה וְהָיְתָה לּוֹ וּלְזַרְעוֹ אַחֲרָיו בְּרִית כְּהוּנַּת עוֹלָם וגו'.

"One who copulates with a Gentile woman," etc. Rebbi Ismael stated: This is one who marries a Gentile woman, sires children, and from her raises enemies of the Omnipresent[72].

[73]It is written: *Phineas ben Eleazar ben Aharon the priest saw.* What did he see[74]? He understood what happened and remembered practice: "One who copulates with a Gentile woman, zealots strike him." It was stated: not with the agreement of the Sages[75]. Would Phineas act against the Sages? Rebbi Jehudah bar Pazi said, they wanted to excommunicate him had not the Holy Spirit jumped on him and declared that *an eternal covenant of priesthood shall be for him and his descendants after him*[76], etc.

72 In *Megillah* 4:10 (Babli 25a) this is R. Ismael's explanation of *Lev.* 18:21, giving one's descendants to the Moloch.

73 Babli 82a, *Num. rabba* 20(26), *Tanhuma Balaq* 21, *Tanhuma Buber Balaq* 30. *Num.* 25:7.

74 Since Zimri did his deed in public, everybody saw.

75 Since in most cases the zealot's intervention would be first degree murder.

76 *Num.* 25:12.

(27b line 34) מַה טַעֲמֵיהּ דְּרִבִּי עֲקִיבָה. נֶאֱמַר כָּאן מוֹת־יוּמַת וְנֶאֱמַר לְהַלָּן כֹּל הַקָּרֵב | הַקָּרֵב אֶל־מִשְׁכַּן יְי יָמוּת וגו'. מַה טַעֲמוֹן דְּרַבָּנִין. נֶאֱמַר כָּאן מוֹת־יוּמַת וְנֶאֱמַר לְהַלָּן וְהַזָּר הַקָּרֵב יוּמָת. מוּטָּב שֶׁיִּלָּמֵד יוּמַת מִיּוּמָת וְאַל יִלָּמֵד יוּמָת מִיָּמוּת.

What is Rebbi Aqiba's reason? It says here, *dying he shall be put to death*[77], and it says there, *anybody acceding to the Eternal's abode will die, etc.*[78] What is the rabbis' reason? It says here, *dying he shall be put to death*, but it says there, *any outsider coming close shall be put to death*[79]. It is better to compare *shall be put to death* with *shall be put to death* and not *shall be put to death* with *shall die*[80].

77 E. g. *Lev.* 20:10. An unspecified death penalty is by strangling;

78 *Num.* 17:28. While the verse speaks of the access of non-priests to the Sanctuary, it supports only the rabbis' argument since it clearly refers to Heaven's actions. The parallel in the Babli 84a (*Sifry Deut.* 116, end) makes more sense.

79 *Num.* 18:7. This verse supports R. Aqiba.

80 To transfer the interpretation of one word to another verse, the word has to be in the same grammatical form. It is clear that the positions of יומת and ימות have to be switched.

כל ישראל פרק עשירי

(fol. 27b) **משנה א**: כָּל־יִשְׂרָאֵל יֵשׁ לָהֶם חֵלֶק לָעוֹלָם הַבָּא. וְאֵילּוּ שֶׁאֵין לָהֶן חֵלֶק לָעוֹלָם הַבָּא הָאוֹמֵר אֵין תְּחִייַת הַמֵּתִים מִן הַתּוֹרָה וְאֵין תּוֹרָה מִן הַשָּׁמַיִם וְאֶפִּיקוּרוֹס. רַבִּי עֲקִיבָה אוֹמֵר אַף הַקּוֹרֵא בִסְפָרִים הַחִיצוֹנִים וְהַלּוֹחֵשׁ עַל הַמַּכָּה וְאוֹמֵר כָּל־הַמַּחֲלָה אֲשֶׁר שַׂמְתִּי בְמִצְרַיִם לֹא אָשִׂים עָלֶיךָ כִּי אֲנִי יי רֹפְאֶךָ. אַבָּא שָׁאוּל אוֹמֵר אַף הַהוֹגֶה אֶת הַשֵּׁם בְּאוֹתִיּוֹתָיו.

Mishnah 1: All of Israel[1] have a part in the World to Come. But the following have no part in the World to Come: One who says that the resurrection of the dead is not biblical[3], or that the Torah is not from Heaven, or the Epicurean[4]. Rebbi Aqiba says, also one who reads outside books[5], or who whispers over a wound[6] and says, *any sickness that I put on Egypt I shall not put on you, for I am the Eternal, your Healer*. Abba Shaul said, also one who pronounces the Name[7] by its letters.

1 Even those executed for a capital crime. In contrast to Christian (Pauline) teaching that everybody is damned unless he be saved by his particular faith, it is asserted that everybody is saved except when he denies himself salvation .

2 In the Babli and the independent Mishnah mss. the statement is proved by quoting *Is.* 60:21.

3 Since he denies the existence of the World to Come, it cannot exist for him.

4 Who holds that the world is an assembly of atoms subject to random effects.

5 Sectarian religious literature.

6 Or any sick person. It is blasphemous to use biblical verses to heal through miracles.

7 YHWH, whose vocalization does not follow grammatical rules. In cabbalistic invocations of the Name, therefore, one never mentions the letters of the Name in straight sequence but says: YH *in* WH.

(27c line 28) **הלכה א**: אֵילּוּ שֶׁאֵין לָהֶן חֵלֶק לָעוֹלָם הַבָּא כול'. הוֹסִיפוּ עֲלֵיהֶן הַפּוֹרֵק עוֹל וְהַמֵּיפֵר בְּרִית וְהַמְגַלֶּה פָּנִים בַּתּוֹרָה אֵין לָהֶן חֵלֶק לָעוֹלָם הַבָּא. הַפּוֹרֵק עוֹל. זֶה שֶׁהוּא אוֹמֵר. יֵשׁ תּוֹרָה וְאֵינִי סוֹפְנָהּ. הַמֵּיפֵר בְּרִית. זֶה שֶׁהוּא מוֹשֵׁךְ לוֹ עָרְלָה. הַמְגַלֶּה פָּנִים בַּתּוֹרָה. זֶה שֶׁהוּא אוֹמֵר. לֹא נִיתְּנָה תוֹרָה מִן הַשָּׁמַיִם. וְלֹא כְבָר תַּנִּיתָהּ. הָאוֹמֵר אֵין תּוֹרָה מִן הַשָּׁמַיִם. תַּנֵּי רַבִּי חֲנִינָה עֶנְתּוֹנָיָה קוֹמֵי רַבִּי מָנָא. זֶה שֶׁהוּא עוֹבֵר עַל דִּבְרֵי תוֹרָה בְּפַרְהֶסְיָא כְּגוֹן יְהוֹיָקִים בֶּן יֹאשִׁיָּהוּ מֶלֶךְ יְהוּדָה וַחֲבֵירָיו.

Halakhah 1: "The following have no part in the World to Come," etc. [8]They added one who tears away the yoke, one who breaks the Covenant, and one who finds aspects in the Torah, to those who have no part in the World to Come. He who tears away the yoke is one who says the Torah is obligatory but I cannot stand it. He who breaks the Covenant is one who pulls himself a prepuce. He who finds aspects in the Torah is one who says that the Torah was not given from Heaven. But did we not state separately: "He who says that the Torah is not from Heaven?" Rebbi Ḥanina Entanaya stated before Rebbi Mana: This is one who publicly transgresses the words of the Torah in the manner of Joiakim ben Josia, king of Judah, and his circle.

8 This and the following paragraphs are from *Peah* 1:1 (Notes 199-213,P) and partially also from *Qiddušin* 1:10 (Notes 657-680,Q), where the differences in readings are noted.

For this paragraph, cf. Babli 99a, *Sifry Num*. 112, Mishnah *Avot* 3:15.

(27c line 35, P 16b l.29) עֲבוֹדָה זָרָה וְגִילּוּי עֲרָיוֹת. רִבִּי יוֹנָה וְרִבִּי יוֹסֵה. חַד אָמַר. כְּקַלּוֹת. וְחַד אָמַר. כַּחֲמוּרוֹת. מַה נָן קַייָמִין. אִם בְּאוֹתוֹ שֶׁעָשָׂה תְשׁוּבָה. אֵין כָּל־דָּבָר עוֹמֵד בִּפְנֵי כָל־בַּעֲלֵי תְשׁוּבָה. אֶלָּא כֵן אֲנָן קַייָמִין בְּאוֹתוֹ שֶׁלֹּא עָשָׂה תְשׁוּבָה וּמֵת בְּהִיכָּרֵת.

Idolatry and incest and adultery. Rebbi Jonah and Rebbi Yose, one said, like the easy ones[9], and one says, like the hard ones. What are we talking about? If he repented, there is nothing that stands in the way of those who repent. But what we are talking about is one who did not repent and died through extirpation.

9 As explained in *Peah* and qualified in the next paragraph, easy sins are those for which a person is punished in this world so that they will not diminish his bliss in the World to Come. Hard ones are those for which a person will suffer in Hell.

(27c line 38) רוּבּוֹ זְכִיּוֹת וּמִיעוּטוֹ עֲבֵירוֹת נִפְרָעִין מִמֶּנּוּ מִיעוּט עֲבֵירוֹת קַלּוֹת שֶׁיֵּשׁ בְּיָדוֹ בָּעוֹלָם הַזֶּה כְּדֵי לִיתֵּן לוֹ שְׂכָרוֹ מֱשְׁלָם לֶעָתִיד לָבוֹא. רוּבּוֹ עֲבֵירוֹת וּמִיעוּטוֹ זְכִיּוֹת נוֹתְנִין לוֹ שְׂכַר מִצְוֹת קַלּוֹת שֶׁיֵּשׁ בְּיָדוֹ בָּעוֹלָם הַזֶּה כְּדֵי לִיפָּרַע מִמֶּנּוּ מֱשְׁלָם לֶעָתִיד לָבוֹא.

A majority of merits and a minority of transgressions: they[10] let him pay for the minority of transgressions in this world in order to give him his complete recompense in the Future World. A majority of transgressions and a minority of merits: they give him the reward for his merits in this world in order to make him pay completely in the Future World.

10 The Heavenly Court.

(27c line 41, P 16b l.43, Q 61d l.55) רוּבּוֹ זְכִיּוֹת יוֹרֵשׁ גַּן עֵדֶן. רוּבּוֹ עֲבֵירוֹת יוֹרֵשׁ גֵּיהִנָּם. הָיָה מְעוּיָּין. אָמַר רִבִּי יוֹסֵי בֶּן חֲנִינָה. נוֹשֵׂא עֲווֹנוֹת אֵין כָּתוּב כָּאן אֶלָּא נֹשֵׂא עָוֹן. הַקָּדוֹשׁ בָּרוּךְ הוּא חוֹטֵף שְׁטָר אֶחָד מִן הָעֲבֵירוֹת וְהַזְּכִיּוֹת מַכְרִיעוֹת. אָמַר רִבִּי לָעְזָר. וּלְךָ יי חָסֶד כִּי־אַתָּה תְשַׁלֵּם לְאִישׁ כְּמַעֲשֵׂהוּ׃ מַעֲשֵׂהוּ אֵין כָּתוּב כָּאן אֶלָּא כְּמַעֲשֵׂהוּ. וְאִין לֵית לֵיהּ אַתְּ יְהִיב לֵיהּ מִן דִּידָךְ. הִיא דַעְתֵּיהּ דְּרִבִּי לָעְזָר. דְּרִבִּי לָעְזָר אָמַר וְרַב־חֶסֶד מַטֶּה כְלַפֵּי חֶסֶד.

He who has a preponderance of merit inherits paradise. He who has a preponderance of sins inherits hell. What if he is in equilibrium? Rebbi Yose ben Ḥanina said, it does not say "He lifts sins" but rather *He lifts sin*[11]. The Holy One, praise to Him, removes one document from the sins and the merits tilt. Rebbi Eleazar said, *kindness is Yours, o Master, because You repay everyone according to his deeds*[12], and if he has none, You give him from Yours. This is the opinion of Rebbi Eleazar, because Rebbi Eleazar said, *and much kindness*[13], He turns towards kindness.

11 *Ex.* 34:7, *Micha* 7:18. 12 *Ps.* 62:13. 13 *Ex.* 34:7.

(27c line 52, P 16b l. 53, Q 61d l. 60) רִבִּי יִרְמְיָה אָמַר. רִבִּי שְׁמוּאֵל בַּר רַב יִצְחָק בְּעָה. צְדָקָה תִּצֹּר תָּם־דָּרֶךְ וְרִשְׁעָה תְּסַלֵּף חַטָּאת. חַטָּאִים תְּרַדֵּף רָעָה וְאֶת־צַדִּיקִים יְשַׁלֶּם־טוֹב. אִם־לַלֵּצִים הוּא יָלִיץ וְלַעֲנָוִים יִתֶּן־חֵן׃ רַגְלֵי חֲסִידָיו יִשְׁמֹר וּרְשָׁעִים בַּחוֹשֶׁךְ יִדָּמּוּ. כָּבוֹד חֲכָמִים יִנְחָלוּ וּכְסִילִים מֵרִים קָלוֹן׃ וּסְיָיגִין סְיָיגָה וְתַרְעִין תְּרִיעָה. וְכֵינִי. סְיָגִין סְיָיגָה וְתַרְעִין תְּרִיעָה. אֶלָּא כֵינִי. רִבִּי יִרְמְיָה בְּשֵׁם רִבִּי שְׁמוּאֵל בַּר רַב יִצְחָק. שׁוֹמֵר אָדָם אֶת עַצְמוֹ מִן הָעֲבֵירָה פַּעַם רִאשׁוֹנָה שְׁנִיָּיה וּשְׁלִישִׁית. מִכָּן וָהֵילַךְ הַקָּדוֹשׁ בָּרוּךְ הוּא מְשַׁמְּרוֹ. מַה טַעַם. הֶן־כָּל־אֵלֶּה יִפְעַל־אֵל פַּעֲמַיִים שָׁלוֹשׁ עִם־גָּבֶר. אָמַר רִבִּי זְעִירָא. וּבִלְחוּד דְּלָא יְתִיב לֵיהּ. וּמַה טַעַם. וְהַחוּט הַמְשׁוּלָּשׁ לֹא לְעוֹלָם יִנָּתֵק אֵין כָּתוּב כָּאן אֶלָּא לֹא בִמְהֵרָה יִנָּתֵק. אִין אַטְרַחַת עֲלוֹי הוּא מַפְסִק.

Rebbi Jeremiah said that Rebbi Samuel bar Rav Isaac asked: *Justice protects the one on the straight path but sin destroys the sinner*[14]. *Evil deeds will pursue the sinner but He will reward the just*[15]. *While He makes scoffers targets of scoffing, He will bestow grace on the meek*[16]. *He will watch over the feet of his pious ones, but evildoers will be silent in the darkness*[17]. *The wise will inherit honor, but shame will mark the stupid ones*[18]. Fences are made fences and doors doors. Is it so that fences make fences and doors doors? But so it is: Rebbi Jeremiah in the name of Rebbi Samuel ben Rav Isaac: If a person is careful the first, second, and third times not to commit a sin, then in the future the Holy One, praise to Him, will watch over him. What is the reason? *All this God will do twice, three times with a man*[19]. Rebbi Ze`ira said, but only if the person does not revert [to sin]. What is the reason? It does not say *the triple thread* "will never snap" but rather *will not quickly snap*[20]. If you work on it, it will split.

14 *Prov.* 13:6.

15 *Prov.* 13:21.

16 *Prov.* 3:34.

17 *I Sam..* 2:9.

18 *Prov.* 3:35.

19 *Job* 33:29.

20 *Eccl.* 4:12.

(27c line 58, P 16b l.58, Q 61d l. 70) רִבִּי הוּנָא בְשֵׁם רִבִּי אַבָּהוּ. הַקָּדוֹשׁ בָּרוּךְ הוּא אֵין לְפָנָיו שִׁכְחָה. כִּבְיָכוֹל הָא בִשְׁבִיל יִשְׂרָאֵל נַעֲשָׂה שָׁכְחָן. מַה טַעַם. נוֹשֵׂא עָוֹן. נוֹשֵׁא כְתִיב. וְכֵן דָּוִד אָמַר נָשָׂאתָ עֲוֺן עַמֶּךָ כִּסִּיתָ כָל־חַטָּאתָם סֶלָה׃

Rebbi Huna said in the name of Rebbi Abbahu: There is no forgetting before the Holy One, but for Israel He becomes forgetful. What is the reason? *He forgives sin*[11]; "He forgets[21]" is written. And so David said, *You forgot Your people, You covered up all their misdeeds, Selah*[22]".

21 Identifying the Hebrew root נשא "to carry" with the Aramaic נשי "to forget."

22 *Ps.* 85:3.

(27c line 60) שָׁאַל רִבִּי מַתְיָה בֶּן חָרָשׁ אֶת רִבִּי אֶלְעָזָר בֶּן עֲזַרְיָה בִּישִׁיבָה אָמַר לוֹ. שְׁמַעְתָּה אַרְבָּעָה חִלּוּקֵי כַפָּרָה שֶׁהָיָה רִבִּי יִשְׁמָעֵאל דּוֹרֵשׁ. אָמַר לוֹ. שְׁלֹשָׁה הֵן חוּץ מִן הַתְּשׁוּבָה. כָּתוּב אֶחָד אוֹמֵר שׁוּבוּ בָּנִים שׁוֹבָבִים אֶרְפָּה מְשׁוּבוֹתֵיכֶם. וְכָתוּב אֶחָד אוֹמֵר כִּי־בַיּוֹם הַזֶּה יְכַפֵּר עֲלֵיכֶם לְטַהֵר אֶתְכֶם וגו'. וְכָתוּב אֶחָד אוֹמֵר וּפָקַדְתִּי בְשֵׁבֶט פִּשְׁעָם וּבִנְגָעִים עֲוֺנָם. וְכָתוּב אֶחָד אוֹמֵר אִם־יְכֻפַּר הֶעָוֹן הַזֶּה לָכֶם עַד־תְּמוּתוּן וגו'. כֵּיצַד. הָעוֹבֵר עַל מִצְוַת עֲשֵׂה וְשָׁב מִיָּד אֵינוֹ זָז מִמְּקוֹמוֹ עַד שֶׁיִּמְחוֹל לוֹ הַקָּדוֹשׁ בָּרוּךְ הוּא. וְעָלָיו הוּא אוֹמֵר שׁוּבוּ בָּנִים שׁוֹבָבִים אֶרְפָּה מְשׁוּבוֹתֵיכֶם. הָעוֹבֵר עַל מִצְוַת בְּלֹא תַעֲשֶׂה הַתְּשׁוּבָה תוֹלָה וְיוֹם הַכִּיפּוּרִים מְכַפֵּר. וְעָלָיו הוּא אוֹמֵר כִּי־בַיּוֹם הַזֶּה יְכַפֵּר עֲלֵיכֶם וגו'. הָעוֹבֵר עַל הַכְּרִיתוֹת וּמִיתוֹת בֵּית דִּין בְּמֵזִיד הַתְּשׁוּבָה וְיוֹם הַכִּיפּוּרִים מְכַפְּרִין מֶחֱצָה וְהַיִּיסּוּרִין מְכַפְּרִין מֶחֱצָה. וְעָלָיו הוּא אוֹמֵר וּפָקַדְתִּי בְשֵׁבֶט פִּשְׁעָם וגו'. אֲבָל מִי שֶׁנִּתְחַלֵּל בּוֹ שֵׁם שָׁמַיִם אֵין כֹּחַ בַּתְּשׁוּבָה לִתְלוֹת וְלֹא יוֹם הַכִּיפּוּרִם לְכַפֵּר וְלֹא

הַיִּיסוּרִין לְמָרֵק. אֶלָּא הַתְּשׁוּבָה וְיוֹם הַכִּיפּוּרִים מְכַפְּרִין שְׁלִישׁ וְיִיסוּרִין שְׁלִישׁ וּמִיתָה מְמָרֶקֶת שְׁלִישׁ. וְעָלָיו הוּא אוֹמֵר אִם־יְכֻפַּר הֶעָוֹן הַזֶּה לָכֶם עַד־תְּמוּתוּן. הָא לָמַדְנוּ שֶׁהַמִּיתָה מְמָרֶקֶת.

1 אלעזר | **ש** לעזר שמעתה | **ו** שמעת 2 הם | **ו** הן 3 ארפה משובותיכם | **וש** - 4 לטהר אתכם וגו' | **וש** - ובנגעים חטאתכם | **וש** וגו' 5 וגו' | **וש** - כיצד | **ו** הא כיצד העובר | **וש** עבר מיד | **ש** - 6 הקב"ה | **וש** - ועליו | **וש** עליו הוא | **ש** הכת' ארפה משובותיכם | **וש** - 7 מצות | **ו** מצוה - | **ש** ושב מיד ועליו | **וש** עליו הוא | **וש** הכת' 8 וגו' | **ש** - העובר | **ש** עבר 9 והייסורין | **ו** והייסורין בשאר ימות השנה ועליו | **וש** עליו הוא | **ש** הכת' 10 וגו' | **וש** ובנגעים חטאתכם בתשובה | **ו** לא בתשובה **ש** לתשובה יום | **ש** ליום | **ו** ביום 11 הייסורין | **ש** לייסורין התשובה | **וש** תשובה מכפרין שליש | **ש** תולין וייסורין שליש | **ו** והייסורין מכפרין שליש **ש** - 12 שליש | **ו** בייסורין **ש** עם הייסורין ועליו | **ו** עליו

[23]Rebbi Matthew ben Ḥarash asked Rebbi Eleazar ben Azariah in the Academy[24]. He told him, did you hear the four types of Atonement which Rebbi Ismael explained? He answered him, there are three in addition to repentance. One verse says[25], *return, naughty children, I shall heal your waywardness*. But another verse says[26], *for on that day, He shall pardon you, to cleanse you.* And another verse says[27], *I shall visit their crime with the rod, and their iniquity with plagues.* And another verse says[28], *the iniquity of this people shall not be atoned for until you die.* How is this? If somebody violates a positive commandment and repents, immediately before he moves from there the Holy One, praise to Him, would forgive him. About this one it says, *return, naughty children, I shall heal your waywardness*. If one transgresses a prohibition, repentance suspends judgment, and the Day of Atonement pardons. About this one it says, *for on that day, He shall pardon you,* etc. If one intentionally transgressed [sins punishable by] extirpations or death penalties, repentance and the Day of Atonement pardon half, and sufferings pardon half. About this one it says, *I shall visit their crime with the rod,* etc. But by whom the Name of Heaven was desecrated, there is no power in repentance to suspend judgment, nor in the Day of Atonement to pardon, nor in sufferings to scour; but repentance and the Day of Atonement pardon a third, and suffering a third, and death scours[29] a third. About this one it says, *the iniquity of this people shall not be atoned for until you die.* From this we learn that death scours.

23 The same text in *Yoma* 8:8 (45b l.70, ו), *Ševuot* 1:9 (33b l.60, ש); similar texts in the Babli *Yoma* 86a, Tosephta *Yom Hakippurim* 5:6, *Mekhilta dR. Ismael Yitro* 7, *Avot dR. Nathan A* 29, *Midrash Mishle* 10(6) [*Yalqut Šim`ony Jeremiah* 269, *Wehizhir* part 1 p. 54].

24 In Babylonian sources he either asked

R. Eleazar ben Azariah in Rome or R. Eleazar the Caper grower in Laodicea.

25 *Jer*. 3:22.

26 *Lev*. 16:30.

27 *Ps*. 89:33.

28 *Is*. 22:14.

29 The root מרק is used in *Lev*. 6:21 to describe the thorough cleansing of a metal vessel by scouring.

In the *Ševuot* text, punishment for behavior that amounts to Desecration of the Name, i. e., unethical behavior by reputedly religious persons, can be suspended by repentance and the Day of Atonement, but only death in suffering scours.

(27d line 1) אָמַר רִבִּי יוֹחָנָן. זוֹ דִבְרֵי רִבִּי אֶלְעָזָר בֶּן עֲזַרְיָה וְרִבִּי יִשְׁמָעֵאל וְרִבִּי עֲקִיבָה. אֲבָל דִּבְרֵי חֲכָמִים. שָׂעִיר הַמִּשְׁתַּלֵּחַ מְכַפֵּר. כֵּיצַד הוּא מְכַפֵּר. רִבִּי זְעִירָא אָמַר. כָּל־שֶׁהוּא כָּל־שֶׁהוּא. רִבִּי חֲנִינָה אָמַר. בַּסּוֹף. מַה מַפְקָא מִבֵּינֵיהוֹן. מֵת מִיָּד. עַל דַּעְתֵּיהּ דְּרִבִּי זְעִירָא כְּבָר כִּפֵּר. עַל דַּעְתֵּיהּ דְּרִבִּי חֲנִינָה לֹא כִּיפֵּר. אָמַר רִבִּי חֲנִינָה. מַתְנִיתָא מְסַייְעָה לְרִבִּי זְעִירָה. חוֹמֶר בַּשָּׂעִיר מַה שֶׁאֵין כֵּן בְּיוֹם הַכִּיפּוּרִים וּבַיּוֹם הַכִּיפּוּרִים מַה שֶׁאֵין כֵּן בַּשָּׂעִיר. שֶׁיּוֹם הַכִּיפּוּרִים מְכַפֵּר בְּלֹא שָׂעִיר וְשָׂעִיר אֵינוֹ מְכַפֵּר בְּלֹא יוֹם הַכִּיפּוּרִים. חוֹמֶר בַּשָּׂעִיר שֶׁהַשָּׂעִיר מְכַפֵּר מִיָּד וְיוֹם הַכִּיפּוּרִים מִשֶּׁתֶּחְשַׁךְ. אָמַר רִבִּי הוּנָא. אִיתְתָּבַת קוֹמֵי רִבִּי יִרְמְיָה וְאָמַר. תִּיפְתָּר שֶׁהָיָה בְדַעְתָּן לְהָבִיא שָׂעִיר אַחֵר וְלֹא הֱבִיאוּ. אָמַר רִבִּי יוֹסֵה בֶּן יוֹסֵה. וְאֵין הַקָּדוֹשׁ בָּרוּךְ הוּא רוֹאֶה אֶת הַנּוֹלָד. וִיכַפֵּר מִיָּד.

1 אלעזר | וש לעזר 2 - | ו אם אין שעיר היום מכפר ש ואם אין שעיר יום הכיפורים מכפר זעירא | ו זעורה ש זירא כל 'הוא | ו - 3 חנינה | וש חנניה אמ' | ו או' מפקא מביניהון | ש ביניהון מיד | ו מרד זעירא | ו זעורה ש זירא כפר | ו כיפר ש כיפר מיד 4 חנינה | וש חנניה חנינה | ו זעורה ש זירא מתנית' | ש ומתנית' זעירה | ו חנניה ש חנינה 5 כן | ו - (twice) שיום | ו יום 6 אינו | ש אין ושעיר | ו והשעיר שהשעיר | ש והשעיר 7 הונא | ו חונה איתתבת | ש איתותב ואמ' | ש ומר 8 אמ' | ו - בן יוסי | ו ביר' בון בעי ש -

[30]Rebbi Johanan said, these are the words of Rebbi Eleazar ben Azariah, Rebbi Ismael, and Rebbi Aqiba. But the words of the Sages are that the sent-away ram[31] pardons. How does it pardon? Rebbi Ze`ira said, by and by. Rebbi Hanina said, at the end[32]. What is the difference between them? If somebody died in-between[33]. In the opinion of Rebbi Ze`ira, he already was pardoned. In the opinion of Rebbi Hanina, he was not pardoned. Rebbi Hanina said, a *baraita* supports Rebbi Ze`ira[34]: There is strength in the ram which is not in the Day of Atonement, and in the Day of Atonement which is not in the ram, for the Day of Atonement pardons without a ram, but the ram does not atone except on the Day of Atonement. There is strength in the ram, for it pardons immediately but the Day of Atonement only at nightfall. Rebbi Huna said, the question was raised before Rebbi Jeremiah[35] and he said, explain it if they intended to bring another ram but they did not bring it[36].

Rebbi Yose ben Yose said, but does the Holy One, praise to Him, not see into the future? Then He should pardon immediately[37].

30 *Yoma* 8:8 (45c l.12, ו), *Ševuot* 1:9 (33b l.75, ש).

31 The scapegoat which carries the sins to the desert. The other two sources have a statement that in the absence of a scapegoat the day of Atonement alone pardons. This is necessary for an understanding of the text.

32 The moment when the scapegoat falls down the cliff (אֶרֶץ גְּזֵרָה the cut-off land"), *Lev*. 16:22.

33 In the time interval between the High Priest's confession which puts the sins on the ram and its arrival at the cliff.

34 Tosephta *Kippurim* 4:16. Rashi deleted the parallel quote from the Babli *Ševuot* 13b, *s. v.* דתניא חומר בשעיר.

35 Is not the ram atoning when there is a Temple, the Day of Atonement when there is none?

36 In case the original ram developed a bodily defect before it was sent away, a substitute has to be chosen. If none was found, the Day must pardon even if there is a Temple.

37 The questioner (Note 35) is correct.

(27d line 12) כְּתִיב כִּי דְבַר־יְי בָּזָה. אֵין לִי אֶלָּא בִזְמַן שֶׁבִּיזָּה דִבְרֵי תוֹרָה. מְנַיִין אֲפִילוּ כָּפַר בְּמִקְרָא אֶחָד בְּתַרְגּוּם אֶחָד בְּקַל וָחוֹמֶר אֶחָד. תַּלְמוּד לוֹמַר וְאֶת־מִצְוָתוֹ הֵפַר. בְּמִקְרָא אֶחָד וַאֲחוֹת לוֹטָן תִּמְנָע. בְּתַרְגּוּם אֶחָד וַיִּקְרָא־לוֹ לָבָן יְגַר שָׂהֲדוּתָא. בְּקַל וָחוֹמֶר אֶחָד כִּי שִׁבְעָתַיִם יֻקַּם־קָיִן וגו'.

דָּבָר אַחֵר. כִּי דְבַר־יְי בָּזָה. זֶה שֶׁהוּא מַזְכִּיר דִּבְרֵי תוֹרָה בְּמָקוֹם מְטוּנָּף. כְּהָדָא רִבִּי אִילָא וַחֲבֵרַייָא יְתִיבִין קוֹמֵי פוּנְדָּקִיָּה בְרַמְשָׁא. אָמְרִין. מָהוּ מֵימַר מִילָּא דְאוֹרַייָא. אָמְרִין. מִכֵּיוָן דְּאִילּוּ הֲוָה אִימָּמָא הֲוֵינָן חֲמֵיי מַה קוֹמֵינָן. בְּרַם כְּדוֹן אֲסִיר.

[38]It is written[39]: *For he showed contempt for the Eternal's Word.* Not only if he was contemptuous of the teachings of the Torah, from where if he denied one verse, one Aramaic expression, one argument *de minore ad majus*? The verse says, *His command he violated.* One verse, *Lotan's sister was Timna*[40]. One Aramaic expression, *Laban called it Ygar Sahdūta*[41]. One argument *de minore ad majus*: *For Cain would be avenged sevenfold,* etc. [42].

Another interpretation: That is one who mentions teachings of the Torah at a filthy place. [43]As the following: Rebbi Hila and the colleagues were sitting in front of a hostelry in the evening. They asked, may one say words of the Torah? They said, since if it were daytime we would see what is before us, therefore now it is forbidden.

38 Babli 99a, *Sifry Num*. 112.

39 *Num*.15:31.

40 *Gen*. 36:22; cf. *Gen. rabba* 82(15).

41 *Gen*. 31:47. In *Gen. rabba* 72(12) the expression is characterized as Syriac.

42 *Gen*. 4:24. While Lemekh's song violates the formal rules of an argument *de minore ad majus*, the verse is Divine approval of poetry.

43 *Berakhot* 3:5 (Notes 222-223), Babli *Berakhot* 24b.

(27d line 12) בַּר קַפָּרָא אָמַר. אָחָז וְכָל־מַלְכֵי יִשְׂרָאֵל הָֽרְשָׁעִים אֵין לָהֶן חֵלֶק לְעוֹלָם הַבָּא. מַה טַעַם. כָּל־מַלְכֵיהֶ֣ם נָפָ֔לוּ אֵין־קֹרֵ֥א בָהֶ֖ם אֵלָֽי׃ מְתִיבִין לֵיהּ. הֲרֵי הוּא נִמְנֶה בְּפַטֵּיָיה שֶׁל מְלָכִים. בִּימֵ֨י עֻזִּיָּ֧הוּ יוֹתָ֛ם אָחָ֥ז יְחִזְקִיָּ֖הוּ מַלְכֵ֣י יְהוּדָ֑ה׃ אֲמַר לוֹן. מִפְּנֵי שֶׁהָיָה בוֹ בוֹשֶׁת פָּנִים. מַה בוֹשֶׁת הָיָה בוֹ. רִבִּי אָחָא בְשֵׁם רִבִּי לָעְזָר רִבִּי יוֹסֵי בְשֵׁם רִבִּי יְהוֹשֻׁעַ בֶּן לֵוִי. אַתְּ מוֹצֵא בְשָׁעָה שֶׁהָיָה הַנָּבִיא בָּא לְקַטְרְגוֹ הָיָה בוֹרֵחַ לְמָקוֹם טוּמְאָה וְכוֹבֵשׁ אֶת פָּנָיו בְּמָקוֹם טוּמְאָה. לוֹמַר שֶׁאֵין שְׁכִינָה שׁוֹרָה בְמָקוֹם טוּמְאָה. הָדָא הִיא דִכְתִיב וַיֹּ֣אמֶר יי אֶל־יְשַֽׁעְיָ֗הוּ צֵא־נָ֞א לִקְרַ֣את אָחָ֔ז אַתָּ֕ה וּשְׁאָ֥ר יָשׁ֖וּב בְּנֶ֑ךָ אֶל־קְצֵ֗ה תְּעָלַת֙ הַבְּרֵכָ֣ה הָֽעֶלְיוֹנָ֔ה אֶל־מְסִלַּ֖ת שְׂדֵ֥ה כוֹבֵֽס׃ אַל תְּהֵי קוֹרֵא כוֹבֵס אֶלָּא כוֹבֵשׁ. שֶׁהָיָה כוֹבֵשׁ פָּנָיו וּבוֹרֵחַ מִמֶּנּוּ. הָא כֵיצַד. בְּשָׁעָה שֶׁהָיָה הַנָּבִיא בָּא לְקַטְרְגוֹ הָיָה בוֹרֵחַ לְמָקוֹם טוּמְאָה וְכוֹבֵשׁ אֶת פָּנָיו בְּמָקוֹם טוּמְאָה. רִבִּי יְהוּדָה אוֹמֵר. מִפְּנֵי שֶׁנִּתְיַיסֵּר בִּבְנוֹ הַבְּכוֹר. מַה טַעַם. וַיַּהֲרֹ֞ג זִכְרִ֣י ׀ גִּבּ֣וֹר אֶפְרַ֗יִם וגו'. רִבִּי הוֹשַׁעְיָה רַבָּה אָמַר. מִפְּנֵי שֶׁהָיָה אָבִיו צַדִּיק. וּמְנַשֶּׁה לֹא הָיָה אָבִיו צַדִּיק. מְנַשֶּׁה אָבִיו צַדִּיק וּבְנוֹ רָשָׁע. יְחִזְקִיָּהוּ אָבִיו רָשָׁע וּבְנוֹ רָשָׁע. הוּא שֶׁיְּחִזְקִיָּהוּ אוֹמֵר הִנֵּ֥ה לְשָׁל֖וֹם מַר־לִ֣י מָ֑ר. מַר לִי מִלְּפָנַיי מֵאָחָז. מַר לִי מֵאֲחוֹרַיי מִמְּנַשֶּׁה. אָחָז אָבִיו צַדִּיק וּבְנוֹ צַדִּיק. הָדָא הִיא דִכְתִיב. יָ֣ד לְ֭יָד לֹא־יִנָּ֣קֶה רָּ֑ע וְזֶ֖רַע צַדִּיקִ֣ים נִמְלָֽט׃ וְזֶרַע צַדִּיק נִמְלָט אֵין כָּתוּב כָּאן אֶלָּא וְזֶ֖רַע צַדִּיקִ֣ים נִמְלָט. זֶרַע שֶׁהוּא מוּטָּל בֵּין שְׁנֵי צַדִּיקִים נִמְלָט.

[44]Bar Qappara said, Aḥaz and all evil kings of Israel have no part in the World to Come. What is the reason? *All their kings fell, not one of them calls to Me*[45]. They objected to him: Is he not mentioned in the era[46] of kings, *in the days of Uzziahu, Yotham, Aḥaz, Yeḥizqiahu the kings of Jehudah*[47]? He answered them, because he showed shame. How did he show shame? Rebbi Aḥa in the name of Rebbi Eleazar, Rebbi Yose in the name of Rebbi Joshua ben Levi: You find that when the prophet came to accuse him[48], he fled to an impure place and buried his face in an impure place, implying that the Divine Presence does not dwell at an impure place. That is what is written[49]: *The Eternal said to Isaiah, please go out towards Aḥaz, you and your son Še'ar Yašuv, to the end of the canal of the upper pond, to the path of the fuller's field.* Do not read *fuller's* but *suppressing*[50]. He hid his face and fled before him. (How is that? When the prophet came to accuse him, he fled to an

impure place and buried his face in an impure place.)[51] Rebbi Jehudah[52] says, because he was made to suffer about his firstborn son. What is the reason? *Zimri, the strongman of Ephraim, killed*[53] etc. Rebbi Hoshaia the Elder said, because his father was just. [54]But was Manasse's father not just[55]? Manasse's father was just but his son was evil. Hezekias's father was evil and his son was evil. That is what Hezekias says[56]: *Behold, about peace, bitter is bitter for me.* Bitter before me, from Aḥaz. Bitter after me, from Manasse. Aḥaz's father was just and his son just, that is what is written[57]: *hand to hand will not cleanse evil, but the seed of the just will escape.* [Rebbi Phineas said.][58] it is not written "the seed of a just will escape" but *the seed of the just will escape.* The seed lying[59] between two just men will escape[60].

44 A complete parallel to this paragraph is in *Lev. rabba* 36(3); a short reference is in the Babli, 104a.

45 *Hos.* 7:7. This seems to contradict Misnhah 2, where only two kings of Israel are denied part in the World to Come.

46 Greek ὑπατεία, ἡ, "consulate", for which years are counted.

47 *Is.* 1:1.

48 In the Midrash, "to needle him". The change from קנטר to קטרג may be a scribal error.

49 *Is.* 7:3.

50 The argument suggests that under the influence of the Greek, ס,ש,שׁ all sounded the same.

51 The repetition of the sentence looks like dittography, but it also appears in the Midrash text.

52 He is Rebbi. R. Jehudah ben Rabban Simeon, as spelled out in the Midrash and required for chronological reasons.

53 *2Chr.* 28:7. The name should be זִכְרִי not זִמְרִי.

54 From here on exists a Genizah fragment (G): L. Ginzberg, *Yerushalmi Fragments*, New York 1909, pp. 260-264.

55 Mishnah 2 declares that Manasse has no part in the World to Come. It implies that Ahaz has part in the World to Come.

56 *Is.* 38:17.

57 *Prov.* 11:21. The first part of the verse has differing interpretations below and in *Midrash Prov.* 11:21, Babli *Berakhot* 61a, *Eruvin* 18b, *Sotah* 4b.

58 Addition from G. In the Midrash: R. Simon.

59 In G: "planted between" מושתת.

60 The Babli 104a states categorically that the good deeds of the son save the father from judgment but the merits of the father cannot save the son. This is the basis of the *Qaddish* ritual of modern Judaism.

(27d line 40) דָּבָר אַחֵר. יָד לְיָד לֹא־יִנָּקֶה רָע. אָמַר רִבִּי פִּינְחָס. זֶה שֶׁהוּא עוֹשֶׂה צְדָקָה וּמְבַקֵּשׁ לִיטּוֹל שְׂכָרָהּ מִיָּד. אָמַר רִבִּי סִימוֹן. כְּאִינַשׁ דְּאָמַר. הָא שַׂקָּא וְהָא סִלְעָא וְהָא סְאָתָא. קוּם

כּוּל. תֵּדַע לָךְ שֶׁהוּא כֵן. שֶׁהֲרֵי אָבוֹת הָעוֹלָם אִילּוּ בִיקְּשׁוּ לִיטּוֹל שְׂכַר מִצְוֹת שֶׁעָשׂוּ בָּעוֹלָם הַזֶּה מֵאֵיכָן הָיְתָה הַזְּכוּת קַייֶמֶת לִבְנֵיהֶם אַחֲרֵיהֶם. הוּא שֶׁמֹּשֶׁה אָמַר לְיִשְׂרָאֵל וְזָכַרְתִּי אֶת־בְּרִיתִי יַעֲקוֹב וגו'.

עַד אֵיכָן הָיְתָה זְכוּת אָבוֹת קַייֶמֶת. רִבִּי תַנְחוּמָא אָמַר לָהּ בְּשֵׁם רִבִּי חִיָּה רַבָּה. בַּר נַחְמָן אָמַר לָהּ בְּשֵׁם רִבִּי בֶּרֶכְיָה. רִבִּי חֶלְבּוֹ בְשֵׁם רִבִּי בָּא בַּר זַבְדָּא. עַד יוֹאָחָז. וַיָּחָן יי אֹתָם וַיְרַחֲמֵם וגו' עַד־עָתָּה׃ עַד אוֹתָהּ שָׁעָה זְכוּת אָבוֹת קַייֶמֶת. שְׁמוּאֵל אָמַר. עַד הוֹשֵׁעַ. וְעַתָּה אֲגַלֶּה אֶת־נַבְלוּתָהּ לְעֵינֵי מְאַהֲבֶיהָ וְאִישׁ לֹא־יַצִּילֶנָּה מִיָּדִי׃ וְאֵין אִישׁ אֶלָּא אַבְרָהָם. כְּמָה דְתֵּמַר וְעַתָּה הָשֵׁב אֵשֶׁת־הָאִישׁ כִּי־נָבִיא הוּא. וְאֵין אִישׁ אֶלָּא יִצְחָק. כְּמָה דְתֵּמַר מִי־הָאִישׁ הַלָּזֶה הַהֹלֵךְ בַּשָּׂדֶה לִקְרָאתֵנוּ. וְאֵין אִישׁ אֶלָּא יַעֲקֹב. כְּמָה דְתֵימַר וְיַעֲקֹב אִישׁ תָּם. רִבִּי יְהוֹשֻׁעַ בֶּן לֵוִי אָמַר. עַד אֵלִיָּהוּ. וַיְהִי | בַּעֲלוֹת הַמִּנְחָה וַיִּגַּשׁ אֵלִיָּהוּ הַנָּבִיא וַיֹּאמַר יי אֱלֹהֵי אַבְרָהָם יִצְחָק וְיִשְׂרָאֵל הַיּוֹם יִוָּדַע כִּי־אַתָּה אֱלֹהִים בְּיִשְׂרָאֵל וַאֲנִי עַבְדֶּךָ וגו'. רִבִּי יוּדָן אָמַר. עַד חִזְקִיָּהוּ. לְמַרְבֵּה הַמִּשְׂרָה וּלְשָׁלוֹם אֵין־קֵץ. אָמַר רִבִּי אָחָא. זְכוּת אָבוֹת לְעוֹלָם קַייֶמֶת. כִּי אֵל רַחוּם יי אֱלֹהֶיךָ וגו' עַד וְלֹא יִשְׁכַּח אֶת־בְּרִית אֲבֹתֶיךָ. מְלַמֵּד שֶׁהַבְּרִית כְּרוּתָה לַשְּׁבָטִים. רִבִּי יוּדָן בַּר חָנָן בְּשֵׁם רִבִּי בֶּרֶכְיָה. אָמַר הַקָּדוֹשׁ בָּרוּךְ הוּא לְיִשְׂרָאֵל. בָּנַיי. אִם רְאִיתֶם זְכוּת אָבוֹת שֶׁמָּטָה וּזְכוּת אִמָּהוֹת שֶׁנִּתְמוֹטְטָה לְכוּ וְהִידַּבְּקוּ[61] בַחֶסֶד. מַה טַעַם. כִּי הֶהָרִים יָמוּשׁוּ וְהַגְּבָעוֹת תְּמוּטֶינָה. כִּי הֶהָרִים יָמוּשׁוּ זֶה זְכוּת אָבוֹת. וְהַגְּבָעוֹת תְּמוּטֶינָה זֶה זְכוּת אִמָּהוֹת. מִיכָּן וְאֵילָךְ וְחַסְדִּי מֵאִתֵּךְ לֹא־יָמוּשׁ וּבְרִית שְׁלוֹמִי לֹא תָמוּט אָמַר מְרַחֲמֵךְ יי׃

[62]Another explanation: *Hand to hand will not cleanse evil.* Rebbi Phineas said, that is one who gives alms and expects an immediate reward. Rebbi Simon said, like a man who says, here is a sack, here is a tetradrachma, and here is a *se`ah*, go and fill it. You should know that this is so, for if the patriarchs had demanded to receive the reward in this world for the good deeds which they did, from where would their merit remain for their descendants after them? That is what Moses told Israel[63]: *I shall remember My covenant with Jacob*, etc.

[64]How far did the merit of the forefathers extend? Rebbi Tanḥuma said in the name of the Elder Rebbi Ḥiyya, (Bar) [Rebbi][G] Naḥman said it in the name of Rebbi Berekhiah, Rebbi Ḥelbo in the name of Rebbi Abba bar Zavda, up to Joaḥaz. *The Eternal was compassionate about them and had mercy for them* etc., *up to now*[65]. Up to that moment, the merit of the forefathers existed.

Samuel said, up to Hosea's [time]. *But now, I shall uncover her scandalous behavior before the eyes of her lovers, and no man may save her from My hand*[66]. *Man* can only mean Abraham, as you say, *but now return the man's wife, for he is a prophet*[67]. *Man* can only mean Isaac, as you say, *who is this man coming in the field towards us*[68]? *Man* can only mean Jacob, as you say, *but Jacob was a simple man*[69].

Rebbi Joshua ben Levi said, up to Elijah: *It was when the time of the afternoon service came that Elijah the prophet approached and said, O Eternal, God of Abraham, Isaac, and Jacob, today it shall be proclaimed that You are God in Israel and I am Your servant*[70] etc.

Rebbi Yudan said, up to Hezekias, *to increase dominion and peace without end*[71].

[72]Rebbi Aḥa said, the merit of the forefathers extends forever: *For the Eternal is a Merciful Power,* etc., up to *and He shall not forget your forefather's covenant*[73]. This teaches that the covenant was sealed with the tribes. Rebbi Yudan bar Ḥanan in the name of Rebbi Berekhiah: The Holy One, praise to Him, said to Israel: If you see that the merit of the fathers reels, and the merit of the mothers trembles, go and cling to grace. [74]*For mountains may reel, and hills tremble; for mountains may reel,* this is the fathers' merit, *and hills tremble*, this is the mothers' merit. After that, *but My Grace will not leave you and My Covenant of Peace will not reel, says the One Who has mercy on you, the Eternal.*

61 Vocalization of G.

62 *Lev. rabba* 36(3).

63 *Lev.* 26:42.

64 *Lev. rabba* 36(5).

65 *2K.* 13:23.

66 *Hos.* 2:12.

67 *Gen.* 20:7.

68 *Gen.* 24:65.

69 *Gen.* 25:27.

70 *1K.* 18:36. Since Elijah's prayer was granted, this gives a *terminus post quem.*

71 *Is.* 9:6.

72 *Sifra Behuqqotai Pereq* 7(11), *Ex. rabba* 44(3). The argument really is not about the patriarchs' merits but about the validity of the Covenant.

73 *Deut.* 4:31.

74 *Is.* 54:10.

(27d line 65) הָאֶפִּיקוּרוֹס. רִבִּי יוֹחָנָן וְרִבִּי לָעְזָר. חַד אָמַר. כָּהֵן דְּאָמַר. אָהֵן סִפְרָא. וְחָרָנָה אָמַר. כָּהֵן דְּאָמַר. אִילֵּין רַבָּנִין. רִבִּי אֶלְעָזָר וְרִבִּי שְׁמוּאֵל בְּרִבִּי נַחְמָן. חַד אָמַר. לְכִיפָּה שֶׁלָּאֲבָנִים. כֵּיוָן שֶׁנִּתְרוֹעָעָה אַחַת מֵהֶן נִתְרוֹעֲעוּ כוּלָּן. וְחָרָנָה אָמַר. לְבַיִת שֶׁהוּא מָלֵא תֶבֶן. אַף עַל גַּו דְּאַתְּ מַעֲבַר לֵיהּ מִינָּהּ אָהֵן מוֹצָא דִבְגַוֵּיהּ הוּא מְרַעְרַע כָּתְלַיָּא.

"The Epicurean." Rebbi Joḥanan and Rebbi Eleazar, one said, like him who said "this book[75]", and one said, like him who said "these rabbis[76]". Rebbi Eleazar and Rebbi Samuel ben Rebbi Naḥman, one said, [it[77] is comparable] to a stone cupola. If one stone is weakened, all are weakened. The other said, [it is comparable] to a house full of chaff. Even if one removes it from there one finds that it weakened the walls.

75 Speaking of the Torah.

76 In a contemptuous way. In the Babli 100a, a person is defined as Epicurean who is not sufficiently respectful towards his teacher.

77 The influence of an Epicurean.

(27d line 70) רַב אָמַר. קֹרַח עָשִׁיר גָּדוֹל הָיָה. תֵּיסַבְרִין שֶׁלְּפַרְעוֹ נִגְלָה לוֹ בֵּין מִגְדּוֹל וּבֵין הַיָּם. רַב אָמַר. קֹרַח אֶפִּיקְרֹסִי הָיָה. מֶה עָשָׂה. עָמַד וְעָשָׂה טַלִּיּוֹת שֶׁכּוּלָּן תְּכֵלֶת. אֲתַא גַבֵּי מֹשֶׁה. אֲמַר לֵיהּ. מֹשֶׁה רַבֵּינוּ. טַלִּית שֶׁכּוּלָּהּ תְּכֵלֶת מָהוּ שֶׁתְּהֵא חַייֶבֶת בַּצִּיצִית. אָמַר לוֹ. חַייֶבֶת. דִּכְתִיב גְּדִלִים תַּעֲשֶׂה־לָּךְ וגו'. בַּיִת שֶׁהוּא מָלֵא סְפָרִים מָהוּ שֶׁיְּהֵא חַייָב בִּמְזוּזָה. אָמַר לוֹ. חַייָב בִּמְזוּזָה. דִּכְתִיב וּכְתַבְתָּם עַל־מְזוּזוֹת בֵּיתֶךָ וגו'. אָמַר לוֹ. בַּהֶרֶת כִּגְרִיס מָהוּ. אָמַר לוֹ. טָמֵא. פָּֽרְחָה בְכוּלּוֹ. אָמַר לוֹ. טָהוֹר. בְּאוֹתָהּ שָׁעָה אָמַר קֹרַח. אֵין תּוֹרָה מִן הַשָּׁמַיִם וְלֹא מֹשֶׁה נָבִיא וְלֹא אַהֲרוֹן כֹּהֵן גָּדוֹל. בְּאוֹתָהּ שָׁעָה אָמַר מֹשֶׁה. רִבּוֹן כָּל־הָעוֹלָמִים. אִם נִבְרָא לָאָרֶץ פֶּה מִשֵּׁשֶׁת יְמֵי בְרֵאשִׁית הֲרֵי מוּטָב. וְאִם לָאו יִבָּרֵא לָהּ מֵעַכְשָׁיו. וְאִם־בְּרִיאָה יִבְרָא יי.

אָמַר רִבִּי שִׁמְעוֹן בֶּן לָקִישׁ. שְׁלֹשָׁה כָּפְרוּ בִנְבוּאָתָן מִפְּנֵי פוּנָרִייָה וְאֵילוּ הֵן. מֹשֶׁה וְאֵלִיָּהוּ וּמִיכָה. מֹשֶׁה אָמַר. אִם־כְּמוֹת כָּל־הָאָדָם יְמוּתוּן אֵלֶּה וגו'. אֵלִיָּהוּ אָמַר. עֲנֵנִי יי עֲנֵנִי וְיֵֽדְעוּ הָעָם הַזֶּה. וְאִם לָאו וְאַתָּה הֲסִבֹּתָ אֶת־לִבָּם אֲחוֹרַנִּית: מִיכָה אָמַר. אִם־שׁוֹב תָּשׁוּב בְּשָׁלוֹם לֹא־דִבֶּר יי בִּי.

וַיֵּרְדוּ הֵם וְכָל־אֲשֶׁר לָהֶם חַיִּים שְׁאֹלָה. רִבִּי בֶּרֶכְיָה בְשֵׁם רִבִּי חֶלְבּוֹ. אַף שְׁמוּתֵיהֶם פָּֽרְחוּ מִתּוֹךְ טוֹמְסוֹתֵיהֶם. אָמַר רִבִּי יוֹסֵי בַּר חֲנִינָה. אֲפִילוּ מַחַט שֶׁהָיְתָה שְׁאוּלָה בְּיַד יִשְׂרָאֵל מִיָּדָם אַף הִיא נִבְלְעָה עִמָּהֶן. דִּכְתִיב וַיֵּרְדוּ הֵם וְכָל־אֲשֶׁר לָהֶם חַיִּים שְׁאוֹלָה. וּמִי נִתְפַּלֵּל עֲלֵיהֶם. רִבִּי שְׁמוּאֵל בַּר נַחְמָן אָמַר. מֹשֶׁה נִתְפַּלֵּל עֲלֵיהֶם. יְחִי רְאוּבֵן וְאַל־יָמוֹת. רִבִּי יְהוֹשֻׁעַ בֶּן לֵוִי אָמַר. חַנָּה נִתְפַּלְּלָה עֲלֵיהֶן. הִיא דַעְתֵּיהּ דְּרִבִּי יְהוֹשֻׁעַ בֶּן לֵוִי. דְּאָמַר רִבִּי רִבִּי יְהוֹשֻׁעַ בֶּן לֵוִי בְשֵׁם רִבִּי יוֹסֵי. כָּךְ הָיְתָה (דַּעְתּוֹ) [עֲדָתוֹ] שֶׁלְּקֹרַח שׁוֹקַעַת וְיוֹרֶדֶת עַד שֶׁעָמְדָה חַנָּה וְנִתְפַּלְּלָה עֲלֵיהֶם וְאָמְרָה: יי מֵמִית וּמְחַיֶּה מוֹרִיד שְׁאוֹל וַיָּעַל:

Rav said, Korah was very rich; the treasury[78] of Pharao was discovered by him between Migdol and the Sea.

[79]Rav said, Korah was an Epicurean. What did he do? He went and made togas completely of blue wool. He came before Moses and asked him, does a

toga made completely out of blue wool need *sisit*? He answered, it is an obligation since it is written[80]: *braids you shall make for yourselves*. Does a house full of Torah scrolls need a *mezuzah*? He answered, it needs a *mezuzah* since it is written[81], *you shall write them on the door-posts of your house*, etc. He asked him, what is the rule for a white spot the size of a bean[82]? He answered him, it is impure. If it spread over his entire body? He answered him, it is pure[83]. At that moment, Koraḥ said that the Torah is not from Heaven, nor is Moses a [true]G prophet, nor Aaron a High Priest. [84]Then Moses said, Master of all worlds! If a mouth of the earth had been created during the Six Days of Creation, it is fine. Otherwise it should be created now: *If the Eternal would create a Creation*[85].

Rebbi Simeon ben Laqish said, three [persons] were untrue to their prophetic insights because of *ponaria*[86], *viz*., the following: Moses, Elijah, and Micha. Moses said, *if an everyman's death these should die*[87], etc. Elijah said, *hear me, o Eternal, hear me, so this people will know*, otherwise *You would have turned their hearts backwards*[88]. Micha said, *if you would return in peace, the Eternal did not speak through me*[89].

[90]*They and everything that belonged to them descended alive into the pit.* Rebbi Berekhiah in the name of Rebbi Ḥelbo, even their names flew away from their papyrus rolls[90a]. Rebbi Yose ben Ḥanina said, even one of their needles that was in the hand of an Israel as a loan was swallowed up with them, for it is written: *They and everything that belonged to them descended alive into the pit.* Who prayed for them? Rebbi Samuel bar Naḥman said, Moses prayed for them, *Reuben shall live and not die*[91]. [92]Rebbi Joshua ben Levi said, Hannah prayed for them. This is Rebbi Joshua ben Levi's opinion, as Rebbi Joshua ben Levi said in the name of Rebbi Yose: Koraḥ's (opinion) [band]G was continuously sinking until Hannah stood up and said, *the Eternal kills and brings to life, He sends down into the pit and lifts*[93].

78 Greek θησαυρός. In the Babli 110a Korah found Joseph's treasures. In the Babli 110a he found the treasures of Joseph.

79 Similar texts are in *Tanhuma Qorah* 2 (Buber 4), *Num. rabba* 18(2), *Midrash Prov.* 11(27).

80 *Deut.* 22:12. While from *Num.* 15:37-41 one might free a blue toga from exhibiting a blue thread, this verse makes it clear that a knotted appendage is needed.

81 *Deut*. 6:9, 11:20.

82 *Lev*. 13:18-23. By rabbinic interpretation, a white spot indicates skin disease only if it is at least the size of a Cilician bean.

83 *Lev*. 13:13.

84 Cf. *Num. rabba* 18(15), *Midrash Prov*. 11(27).

85 *Num*. 16:30.

86 Latin *poenariae (scil., actiones)* "criminal" (actions), a post-Augustean word (E.G.). The criticism levelled at Moses, Elijah, and Micha (i. e., Michaihu ben Nimla) is that they formulated as a possibility what they prophetically knew was a certainty.

87 *Num*. 16:29.

88 *1K*. 18:37.

89 *1K*. 22:28.

90 *Num*. 16:33.

90a Greek τόμος, "piece, roll of papyrus, volume".

91 *Deut*. 33:6, this refers to Datan and Abiram from the tribe of Reuben.

92 *Midrash Shemuel* ed. Buber 5(12).

93 *1S*. 2:6. She was married to a descendant of Korah's (*2 Chr*. 6:18-23).

(28a line 17) רִבִּי עֲקִיבָה אוֹמֵר. אַף הַקּוֹרֵא בִסְפָרִים הַחִיצוֹנִים. כְּגוֹן סִפְרֵי בֶּן סִירָא וְסִפְרֵי בֶּן לענה. אֲבָל סִפְרֵי הוֹמֵירָס וְכָל־הַסְּפָרִים שֶׁנִּכְתְּבוּ מִיכָּן וָהֵילָךְ הַקּוֹרֵא בָהֶן כְּקוֹרֵא בְאִיגֶּרֶת. מַאי טַעַם. וְיוֹתֵר מֵאֵלֶּה בְּנִי הִזָּהֵר וגו'. לְהִגָּיוֹן נִתְּנוּ. לִיגִיעָה לֹא נִיתְּנוּ.

"Rebbi Aqiba says, also he who reads outside books." [94]For example, the books of Ben Sirach and Ben Laana[95]. But the books of Homer and all books written from now on, one who reads them is like one who reads a letter. What is the reason? *More than these, my son, be careful* [96]etc. They are given to be read, not given for exertion.

94 Babli 100b, *Eccl. rabba* 12(13).

95 The name of the second, otherwise unknown, author is בן לענא in G and בן תגלא in the Midrash. Rav Saadya Gaon in his *Egron* (Note 152) seems to read בן עיראי. In the Babli: books of heretics (מינין). The only books forbidden to study are non-canonical books claiming biblical status.

96 *Eccl*. 12:12. The reference is to the end of the verse, not quoted here: לַהַג הַרְבֵּה. The quote leads to a digression about *Eccl*. 12:11.

(28a line 20) דִּבְרֵי חֲכָמִים כַּדָּֽרְבוֹנוֹת. אָמַר רִבִּי חוּנָה. כִּדְרוֹר נָאוֹת. תַּמָּן קָרֵיי̇ן לְמַרְגָּלִיתָא דִירָה. דָּבָר אַחֵר. כַּדָּֽרְבוֹנוֹת. כְּכַדּוּר הַזֶּה בֵּין הַבָּנוֹת. מַה הַכַּדּוּר הַזֶּה מְקַלֶּטֶת מִיָּד לְיָד וְסוֹפָהּ לָנוּחַ בְּיָד אֶחָד. כָּךְ מֹשֶׁה קִבֵּל תּוֹרָה מִסִּינַי וּמְסָרָהּ לִיהוֹשֻׁעַ וִיהוֹשֻׁעַ לִזְקֵינִים וּזְקֵינִים לִנְבִיאִים וּנְבִיאִים מְסָרוּהָ לְאַנְשֵׁי כְנֶסֶת הַגְּדוֹלָה. דָּבָר אַחֵר. כַּדָּֽרְבוֹנוֹת. שְׁלֹשָׁה שֵׁמוֹת יֵשׁ לוֹ. מַרְדֵּעַ דָּֽרְבָן וּמַלְמֵד. מַרְדֵּעַ שֶׁהוּא מוֹרֶה דֵיעָה בַּפָּרָה. דָּֽרְבָן שֶׁהוּא מַשְׁרֶה בִינָה בַּפָּרָה. מַלְמַד שֶׁהוּא מְלַמֵּד אֶת הַפָּרָה לַחֲרוֹשׁ בִּשְׁבִיל לִיתֵּן חַיִּים לְבַעֲלֶיהָ. אָמַר רִבִּי חָמָא בַּר חֲנִינָה. אִם לְפָרָתוֹ עוֹשֶׂה

אָדָם דָּרְבָן. לְיִצְרוֹ הָרַע שֶׁהוּא מַעֲבִירוֹ מֵחַיֵּי הָעוֹלָם הַזֶּה וּמֵחַיֵּי הָעוֹלָם הַבָּא עַל אַחַת כַּמָּה וְכַמָּה.

וּכְמַסְמְרוֹת נְטוּעִים. וְלָמָּה לֹא אָמַר וּכְמַסְמְרוֹת קְבוּעִים וּכְאִילָנוֹת נְטוּעִים. בָּחֲרוּ לָהֶם בֵּירְרוּ הַבַּרְזֶל וְשִׁיבְּחוּ הַמַּטָּע שֶׁלְּמַטִּיל. דָּבָר אַחֵר. וּכְמַסְמְרוֹת נְטוּעִים. מַה הַמַּסְמֵר הַזֶּה אַתְּ קוֹבְעוֹ. אַף עַל פִּי שֶׁאַתְּ חוֹזֵר וְנוֹטְלוֹ מִמְּקוֹמוֹ מְקוֹמוֹ נִיכָּר. כָּךְ כָּל־מִי שֶׁפָּשְׁטוּ יְדֵיהֶם הָרַבִּים בּוֹ יָד. אַף עַל פִּי שֶׁחָזְרוּ וְקֵרְבוּ אוֹתוֹ סוֹפוֹ לִיטּוֹל אֶת שֶׁלּוֹ מִתַּחַת יְדֵיהֶם. דָּבָר אַחֵר. וּכְמַסְמְרוֹת נְטוּעִים. מַשְׂמֵרוֹת כָּתוּב. מַה מִשְׁמָרוֹת עֶשְׂרִים וְאַרְבָּעָה אַף הַמַּסְמֵרִים עֶשְׂרִים וְאַרְבָּעָה. כַּמָּה מַסְמֵרִים יְהוּ בָהּ. רִבִּי יוֹחָנָן אָמַר. חֲמִשָּׁה. כְּנֶגֶד חֲמִשָּׁה חוּמְשֵׁי תוֹרָה. רִבִּי חִינְנָא אָמַר. שִׁבְעָה. וּכְיָמֶיךָ דָּבְאֶךָ: דָּרַשׁ רִבִּי אָחָא בְשֵׁם רִבִּי חֲנִינָה. תִּשְׁעָה. רִבִּי הָיָה נוֹתֵן אַחַד עָשָׂר עַל זֶה וּשְׁלֹשָׁה עָשָׂר עַל זֶה. מִנְיַן מִשְׁמָרוֹת. רִבִּי יוֹסֵי בֶּן חֲנִינָה אָמַר. כַּלְבַּת אֵינָהּ עוֹלָה לְחֶשְׁבּוֹן מַסְמֵרִים. רִבִּי בָּא בַּר זַבְדָּא בְעָא קוֹמֵי רִבִּי זְעִירָא. מָהוּ לִיתֵּן כּוּלָּן עַל גַּבֵּי מִנְעָל אֶחָד. אֲמַר לֵיהּ. שָׁרֵי. מָהוּ לִיתֵּן כּוּלָּן עַל גַּבֵּי סַנְדָּל אֶחָד. אֲמַר לֵיהּ. שָׁרֵי. תַּנֵּי. אֵין מְגָרְדִין סַנְדָּלִים וּמִנְעָלִים יְשָׁנִים אֲבָל סָכִין וּמַדִּיחִין אוֹתָן. רִבִּי קְרִיסְפָּא בְשֵׁם רִבִּי יוֹחָנָן. תַּלְמִידוֹי דְרִבִּי חִיָּיה רַבָּה אָמְרִין. הָרִאשׁוֹנִים הָיוּ אוֹמְרִין. מְגָרְדִין. שְׁנִיִּים הָיוּ אוֹמְרִין. אֵין מְגָרְדִין. שְׁאָלוֹן לְרִבִּי. אֲמַר לוֹן. אֵין מְגָרְדִין. אֲמַר רִבִּי זְעוּרָה. הָא אֲזִילָה חָדָא מִן תַּלְמִידוֹי דְרִבִּי חִיָּיה רַבָּה. אָמַר רִבִּי חִיָּיה בַּר אַשִּׁי. נְהִיגִין הֲוֵינָא יָתְבִין קוֹמֵי רַב וּמַשְׁחִין וּמַשִּׂיגִין אֲבָל לֹא מְגָרְדִין. תַּנֵּי. לֹא יִלְבַּשׁ אָדָם מִנְעָלִים וְסַנְדָּלִים חֲדָשִׁים אֶלָּא אִם כֵּן הִילֵּךְ בָּהֶן מִבְּעוֹד יוֹם. כַּמָּה יְהֵא בְהִילּוּכָן. בְּנֵי בֵייתֵיהּ דְּבַר קַפָּרָא אָמְרִין. מִן דְּבֵית רַבָּה דְּבַר קַפָּרָא עַד בֵּית רַבָּה דְרִבִּי הוֹשַׁעְיָה. צִיפּוֹרָאֵי אָמְרִין. מִכְּנִישְׁתָּה דְבַבְלָאֵי עַד דִּרְתָּה דְרִבִּי יוֹסֵי בַּר חֲנִינָה. טִיבֵּרָאֵי אָמְרִין. מִן סִידְרָא רַבָּה עַד חָנוּתֵי דְרִבִּי הוֹשַׁעְיָה. תַּנֵּי. לֹא יָסוּךְ אָדָם מִנְעָלִים וְסַנְדָּלִים חֲדָשִׁים. לֹא יָסוּךְ אָדָם אֶת רַגְלוֹ וְהִיא בְתוֹךְ הַמִּנְעָל וְאֶת רַגְלוֹ וְהִיא בְתוֹךְ הַסַּנְדָּל. אֲבָל סָךְ הוּא אֶת רַגְלוֹ וְנוֹתְנָהּ בְּתוֹךְ הַמִּנְעָל אֶת רַגְלוֹ וְנוֹתְנָהּ לְתוֹךְ הַסַּנְדָּל. סָךְ אָדָם שֶׁמֶן וּמִתְעַגֵּל עַל גַּבֵּי קַטַבֹּלְיָא חֲדָשָׁה וְאֵינוֹ חוֹשֵׁשׁ. לֹא יִתְנֶנָּה עַל גַּבֵּי טַבְלָה שֶׁלְּשַׁיִישׁ לְהִתְעַגֵּל עָלֶיהָ. רַבָּן שִׁמְעוֹן בֶּן גַּמְלִיאֵל מַתִּיר. דָּבָר אַחֵר. וּכְמַסְמְרוֹת נְטוּעִים. בְּשָׁעָה שֶׁדִּבְרֵי תוֹרָה יוֹצְאִין מִפִּי בַעֲלֵיהֶן כְּתִיקְנָן הֵן עֲרֵיבִין לְשׁוֹמְעֵיהֶן כְּמַסְמְרוֹת נְטוּעִים. וּבְשָׁעָה שֶׁהֵם יוֹצְאִין מְמוּסְמָסִין הֵם מָרִין לְשׁוֹמְעֵיהֶן כְּמַסְמְרוֹת.

בַּעֲלֵי אֲסוּפּוֹת. אֵין אֲסוּפּוֹת אֶלָּא סַנְהֶדְרִין. כְּמָה דְתֵימַר אֶסְפָה־לִּי שִׁבְעִים אִישׁ מִזִּקְנֵי יִשְׂרָאֵל. דָּבָר אַחֵר. בַּעֲלֵי אֲסוּפּוֹת. שֶׁנֶּאֶמְרִים בָּאֲסֵיפָה. אָמַר רִבִּי שִׁמְעוֹן בֶּן לָקִישׁ. אִם יֹאמַר לִי אָדָם שֶׁיֵּשׁ דִּבְרֵי הַיָּמִים בְּבָבֶל הֲרֵי אֲנִי הוֹלֵךְ וּמְבִיאוֹ מִשָּׁם. וְעַכְשָׁיו אִם מִתְכַּנְּסִין כָּל־רַבּוֹתֵינוּ אֵין יְכוֹלִין לַהֲבִיאוֹ מִשָּׁם.

נִתְּנוּ מֵרוֹעֶה אֶחָד. אָמַר הַקָּדוֹשׁ. אִם שָׁמַעְתָּה דָבָר מִפִּי קָטָן יִשְׂרָאֵל וַהֲנָיֶיךָ. לֹא יְהֵא בְעֵינֶיךָ כְּשׁוֹמְעוֹ מִפִּי קָטָן אֶלָּא כְשׁוֹמְעוֹ מִפִּי גָדוֹל. וְלֹא כְשׁוֹמְעוֹ מִפִּי גָדוֹל אֶלָּא כְשׁוֹמְעוֹ מִפִּי חָכָם. וְלֹא כְשׁוֹמְעוֹ מִפִּי חָכָם אֶלָּא כְשׁוֹמְעוֹ מִפִּי נָבִיא. וְלֹא כְשׁוֹמְעוֹ מִפִּי נָבִיא אֶלָּא כְשׁוֹמְעוֹ מִפִּי רוֹעֶה. וְאֵין רוֹעֶה אֶלָּא מֹשֶׁה. כְּמָה דְתֵימַר וַיִּזְכֹּר יְמֵי־עוֹלָם מֹשֶׁה עַמּוֹ אַיֵּה | הַמַּעֲלֵם מִיָּם אֵת רוֹעֵה צֹאנוֹ אַיֵּה הַשָּׂם בְּקִרְבּוֹ אֶת־רוּחַ קָדְשׁוֹ. לֹא כְשׁוֹמְעוֹ מִפִּי רוֹעֶה אֶלָּא כְשׁוֹמְעוֹ מִפִּי

הַגְּבוּרָה. נִתְּנוּ מֵרוֹעֶה אֶחָד. וְאֵין אֶחָד אֶלָּא הַקָּדוֹשׁ בָּרוּךְ הוּא. כְּמָה דְתָּ מַר שְׁמַע יִשְׂרָאֵל יְי אֱלֹהֵינוּ יְי אֶחָד׃

[97]*The words of the Sages are like goads;* Rebbi Huna said, like a pearl. There, they call a pearl *dirah*[98].

Another explanation, *like goads*, like a girl's ball. Just as this ball is caught from hand to hand but in the end will come to rest in one hand, so "Moses received the Torah from Sinai and transmitted it to Joshua, Joshua to the Elders, the Elders to the Prophets, and the Prophets transmitted it to the Men of the Great Assembly[99]."

Another explanation, *like goads*. It has three names, *mardea`, dārᵉvān, malmad. Mardea`,* because it teaches knowledge to the cow[100]. *Dārᵉvān,* because it plants understanding in the cow. *Malmad*, because it teaches the cow to plough, to keep its owners alive. Rebbi Ḥama bar Ḥanina said, if a person makes a goad for his cow, certainly [he has to make one] for his bad inclinations which will remove him from this world and the World to Come.

[97]*And like planted nails.* Why does he not say, "like fixed nails and planted trees"? They chose and selected the iron and improved the planting of iron rods.

Another explanation, *and like planted nails*. Just as this nail, once it has been fixed, if you then remove it from its place, its place remains visible; so everybody against whom the rabbis[101] stretched out their hand[102], even if afterwards they took him back, in the end he will take what is coming to him from their hands.

Another explanation, *and like planted nails*; it is written *watches*[103]. Since there are 24 watches, there should be 24 nails[104]. How many nails should it have? Rebbi Joḥanan said five, corresponding to the five books of the Torah. Rebbi Ḥinena said seven, *corresponding to your days are your steps*[105]. Rebbi Aḥa explained following Rebbi Ḥanina: nine. Rebbi put eleven on one [shoe] and thirteen on the other, for the number of watches. Rebbi Yose ben Ḥanina said, a crooked nail is not counted with the nails[106]. Rebbi Abba bar Zavda asked before Rebbi Ze`ira[107]: may one put all of them on one boot? He told him, it is permitted. May one put all of them on one sandal? He told him, it is permitted. It was stated: One does not scrape[108] old boots or sandals but one may anoint them or dip them in water. Rebbi Crispus in the name of Rebbi Joḥanan: The students of the Elder Rebbi Ḥiyya say that those of first rank said, one may scrape, those of second rank said, one may not scrape. They asked Rebbi, who told them, one does not scrape. Rebbi Ze`ira said, here goes one of the students of the Elder Rebbi Ḥiyya[109]. Rebbi Ḥiyya bar Ashi said, we used to sit before Rav and were anointing and rinsing, but not scraping. It was stated: A person should wear new boots and sandals only if he walked in them during daytime[110]. How far should he walk? The people from the house of Bar Qappara said, from the House of Study of Bar Qappara to the House of Study of Rebbi Hoshaia[111]. The Sepphoreans say, from the Babylonian synagogue to Rebbi Ḥama bar Ḥanina's house. The Tiberians say, from the Academy to Rebbi Hoshaia's store. It was stated[112]: Nobody should anoint his foot in a shoe or sandal but he may anoint his foot and step into his shoe or his sandal. One may anoint himself and roll on a tarpaulin without worry. One should not put it on a marble slab to roll himself in it, but Rabban Gamliel permits it.

Another explanation, *and like planted nails*. If words about Torah are spelled out clearly by their authors, they are sweet to their listeners like well-ordered saplings. But if they come out confused, they are as bitter for their listeners as nails.

[97]*Masters of assembly*[113]. "Assembly" only means the Synhedrion, as you say: *Assemble for Me seventy men from the Elders of Israel*[114].

Another explanation, *masters of assembly*, it was said in an assembly. Rebbi Simeon ben Laqish said, if somebody told me that Chronicles[115] was to be found in Babylonia, I would go and fetch it from there. But now, if all our rabbis came together, they could not bring it from there.

[97]*They were given from one shepherd.* The Holy One[116] said, if you heard something[117] from the most insignificant one of Israel and it gave you satisfaction, it should not be in your eyes as if you heard it from an insignificant one but from an important one; and not as if you heard it from an

important one but from a Sage; and not as if you heard it from a Sage but from a prophet; and not as if you heard it from a prophet but from a shepherd (and shepherd only means Moses, as it is said[118]: *He remembered the days of old, Moses with his people; where is He Who brought them up from the Sea with his people's shepherd; where is He Who gave His Holy Spirit in its midst*); not as if you heard it from a shepherd but from Divinity. *They were given from one shepherd*, but "One" is only the Holy One, praise to Him, as it is said[119]: *Hear, o Israel, the Eternal is our God, the Eternal is One.*

97 The following is a series of homilies on *Eccl.* 12:11, without direct connection with the theme of the Chapter; cf. Note 96. Parallels are found in *Pesiqta rabbati* 3 (ed. Ish-Shalom 7b-8a); *Midrash Qohelet* 12:11-12; *Lev. rabba* 129(6), *Num. rabba* 13:11-13).

98 In Babylonia one uses the Arabic דּוּרָה. Read דורה with G.

99 Mishnah *Avot* 1:1.

100 It already is noted in the *Pesiqta* that מרדע is a Mishnaic, not a biblical word.

101 Plural of רַבִּי as recognized by E. S. Rosenthal (M. Cahana in *Mehqere Talmud* I, ed. Y. Sussman, D. Rosenthal, Jerusalem 1990, p. 6 Note 17).

102 They put him in ban.

103 Cf. also E. Porath, *Mishnaic Hebrew*, Jerusalem 1938, p. 130 Note 4.

The *watches* are the 24 clans of priests (*1Chr.* 24), each of which was serving in the Temple for one week.

104 The following has a parallel in *Šabbat* 6:1 (8a l. 21 ff.), Babli *Šabbat* 60b. It is forbidden to wear nail-studded work-boots on the Sabbath. But it is permitted to wear shoes decorated with nails. There are different traditions about the number of nails which will constitute a decoration.

105 *Deut.* 33:24.

106 In the Babli, the equivalent of כלבת is כלבוס.

107 For reasons of chronology, one has to switch the position of the names, as in *Šabbat*: The third generation R. Ze`ira asked the second generation R. Abba bar Zavda. Here ends the Genizah fragment.

108 Again this belongs to the rules of the Sabbath (Babli *Šabbat* 141b); it is forbidden to scrape off dirt from one's shoes on the Sabbath.

109 Rebbi certainly is of the authorities of first rank.

110 On Friday.

111 In the village of Dabbara (Golan) where the lintel of Bar Qappara's House of Study was excavated.

112 The following is from *Ševi`it* 8:8, Notes 119-124. Olive oil produced in the Sabbatical year has to be used for the personal needs of man or animal; it is permitted to use it to daub one's body but not to prepare leather or leather products.

113 The translation chosen follows the explanation given here as second possibility. Rashi (following Dunash), Ibn Janah, and Qimhi: "collectors." Levy/Torczyner: "set in frames."

114 *Num.* 11:16.

115 Not the book of Chronicles but a coherent interpretation of its genealogical part, known as 'book of genealogies" (Babli *Pesahim* 62b).

116 One has to add, "praise to him."

117 An explanation of a topic in the Torah.

118 *Is.* 63:11

119 *Deut.* 6:4.

(28a line 76) וְהַלּוֹחֵשׁ עַל הַמַּכָּה וְאוֹמֵר כָּל־הַמַּחֲלָה אֲשֶׁר־שַׂמְתִּי בְמִצְרַיִם לֹא־אָשִׂים עָלֶיךָ כִּי אֲנִי יי רֹפְאֶךָ׃ רַב אָמַר. וּבִלְבַד בְּרוֹקֵק. רִבִּי יְהוֹשֻׁעַ בֶּן לֵוִי אָמַר. אֲפִילוּ אָמַר נֶגַע צָרַעַת כִּי תִהְיֶה בְּאָדָם וְרוֹקֵק אֵין לוֹ חֵלֶק לְעָתִיד לָבוֹא.

אַבָּא שָׁאוּל אוֹמֵר אַף הַהוֹגֶה אֶת הַשֵּׁם בְּאוֹתִיּוֹתָיו. רִבִּי מָנָא אָמַר. כְּגוֹן אִילֵּין כּוּתָאֵי דְּמִשְׁתַּבְּעִין. רִבִּי יַעֲקֹב בַּר אָחָא אָמַר. נִכְתָּב בְּיוּ"ד הֵ"א וְנִקְרָא בְּאָלֶ"ף דָּלֶ"ת.

"One who whispers over a wound and says, *any sickness that I put on Egypt I shall not put on you, for I am the Eternal, your Healer*." Rav said, only one who spits. Rebbi Joshua ben Levi said, even if he only said, *damage by skin disease if it be on a human*[120] and spits, he has no part in the Future World[121].

Abba Shaul said, also one who pronounces the Name[7] by its letters. Rebbi Mana said, for example, those swearing Samaritans[122]. Rebbi Jacob bar Aha said, it is written as *yod he* but read as *alef dalet*[123].

120 *Lev.* 15:26.

121 Using verses as part of magical rites is an unpardonable sin (in the absence of genuine repentance.)

122 It is not known what Samaritans did in those days. Modern Samaritans use the equivalent of *the Name* for all mentions of the Name.

123 The Name has to be pronounced as if written אדני. It seems that he prohibits *any* pronunciation of YHWH even if demonstrably unhistorical (cf. *Berakhot* 1:1, Note 14.)

(fol. 27b) **משנה ב**׃ שְׁלֹשָׁה מְלָכִים וְאַרְבָּעָה הֶדְיוֹטוֹת אֵין לָהֶם חֵלֶק לָעוֹלָם הַבָּא. שְׁלֹשָׁה מְלָכִים אַחְאָב יָרָבְעָם מְנַשֶּׁה. רִבִּי יְהוּדָה אוֹמֵר מְנַשֶּׁה יֵשׁ לוֹ חֵלֶק לָעוֹלָם הַבָּא שֶׁנֶּאֱמַר וַיִּתְפַּלֵּל אֵלָיו וַיֵּעָתֶר לוֹ וַיִּשְׁמַע תְּחִנָּתוֹ וַיְשִׁיבֵהוּ יְרוּשָׁלַיִם לְמַלְכוּתוֹ. אָמְרוּ לוֹ לְמַלְכוּתוֹ הֱשִׁיבוֹ. לֹא הֱשִׁיבוֹ לְחַיֵּי הָעוֹלָם הַבָּא. אַרְבָּעָה הֶדְיוֹטוֹת בִּלְעָם וְדוֹאֵג אֲחִיתֹפֶל וְגֵחֲזִי׃

Mishnah 2: Three kings and four private persons have no part in the Future World[123]. Three kings: Ahab, Jeroboam, Manasse. Rebbi Jehudah says, Manasse has part in the Future World, as it is said:[124] *he prayed to Him. He let Himself be petitioned, and heard his supplications, and returned him to Jerusalem, to his kingdom.* They told him, He returned him to his kingdom; He did not return him to life in the Future World[125]. Four private persons: Bileam and Doëg[126], Aḥitophel[130] and Gehazi[131].

123 Out of all persons mentioned in the Hebrew Bible.

124 *2Chr.* 33:13.

125 R. Jehudah's position is that of the author of Chronicles, the rabbis' that of the author of Kings (*2K.* 21).

126 While in the Talmudim *Doëg the Edomite* is treated as a Jew, his being grouped in the Yerushalmi Mishnah with the Midianite Bileam, separate from the two Israelites, may indicate that for the Yerushalmi Mishnah Gentiles (at least those who are descendants of Abraham) have part in the Future World unless they act to lose it.

127 The paradigmatic suicide.

128 Who was cursed by Elisha.

(28b line 6) **הלכה ב**: שְׁלֹשָׁה מְלָכִים וְאַרְבָּעָה הֶדְיוֹטוֹת כול'. וְכוּלְּהֶם חִידְּשׁוּ עֲבֵירוֹת.

Halakhah 2: "Three kings and four private persons," etc. All of these invented new kinds of sins.

(28b line 7) וְכִי מֶה עָשָׂה יָרָבְעָם. עַל שֶׁעָשָׂה שְׁנֵי עֶגְלֵי זָהָב. וַהֲלֹא כַּמָּה עֲגָלִים עָשׂוּ יִשְׂרָאֵל. תַּנֵּי רִבִּי שִׁמְעוֹן בֶּן יוֹחַי. שְׁלֹשָׁה עָשָׂר עֲגָלִים עָשׂוּ יִשְׂרָאֵל וְאֶחָד דֵּימוֹסִיָּא לְכוּלָּן. וּמַה טַעַם וַיֹּאמְרוּ אֵלֶּה אֱלֹהֶיךָ יִשְׂרָאֵל. הֲרֵי לִשְׁנֵים עָשָׂר שְׁבָטִים. זֶה אֱלֹהֶיךָ הֲרֵי דֵּימוֹסִיָּא אַחַת לְכוּלָּן.

So what did Jeroboam do[129]? Because he made two golden calves. But did Israel not make many calves[130]? Rebbi Simeon ben Iohai stated: Thirteen calves did Israel make[131]; of these one was common property[132] to all of them. What is the reason? *They said, these are your gods, Israel*[133]; this refers to the twelve tribes. *This is your god*[134], i. e., one common property for all of them.

129 To commit a new kind of sin.

130 The sin is not new; for the Yerushalmi Jeroboam has part in the World to Come.

131 Not a single golden calf but 13.

132 Greek δημόσιος, -α, -ον, adj. "belonging to the people". Also used as noun.

133 *Ex.* 32:4,8.

134 *Neh.* 9:18.

(28b line 11) וְכִי מֶה עָשָׂה אַחְאָב. כָּתוּב וַיְהִ֗י הֲנָקֵ֣ל לֶכְתּ֔וֹ בְּחַטֹּ֖אות יָרָבְעָ֣ם בֶּן־נְבָ֑ט. וַהֲלֹא קוּלּוֹתָיו שֶׁל אַחְאָב הֵם כְּחוּמְרוֹתָיו שֶׁלְּיָרָבְעָם. וְלָמָּה נִמְנָה יָרָבְעָם תְּחִילָּה. שֶׁהוּא הִתְחִיל בַּקַּלְקָלָה תְחִילָּה. מָה הֲוָה אַחְאָב עֲבִיד. הֲוָה מְקַשֵּׁט גַּרְמֵיהּ בְּכָל־יוֹם וְקָאִים לֵיהּ קוֹמֵי חִיאֵל אִסְרָטִילָטֵיהּ. וְהוּא אֲמַר לֵיהּ. בְּכַמָּה אֲנָא טָב יוֹמָא דֵין. וְהוּא אֲמַר לֵיהּ. כֵּן וָכֵן. וְהוּא מַפְרִישׁ טִימִיתֵיהּ לַעֲבוֹדָה זָרָה. הָדָא הוּא דִכְתִיב יַ֚עַן הִֽתְמַכֶּרְךָ֔ לַעֲשׂ֥וֹת הָרַ֖ע בְּעֵינֵ֥י יְיָ. רִבִּי לֵוִי עֲבַד דָּרַשׁ הָדֵין קְרָייָא אֲשִׁתָּא יַרְחִין לִגְנַאי. רַ֣ק לֹֽא־הָיָ֔ה כְאַחְאָ֔ב אֲשֶׁ֣ר הִתְמַכֵּ֔ר לַעֲשׂ֥וֹת הָרַ֖ע בְּעֵינֵ֣י יְיָ. אֲתָא לְגַבֵּיהּ בַּלֵּילְיָא. אֲמַר לֵיהּ. מֶה חָטִית לָךְ וּמַה סָרְחִית קֳדָמָךְ. אִית לָךְ רֵישֵׁיהּ דִּפְסוּקָה וְלֵית לָךְ סוֹפֵיהּ אֲשֶׁר־הֵסַתָּה אוֹתוֹ אִיזֶבֶל אִשְׁתּוֹ׃ עֲבַד דְּרַשׁ לֵיהּ שִׁתָּא יַרְחִין לִשְׁבָח. רַ֣ק לֹֽא־הָיָ֔ה כְאַחְאָ֔ב אֲשֶׁר־הֵסַ֥תָּה אֹת֖וֹ אִיזֶ֥בֶל אִשְׁתּֽוֹ׃

So what did Aḥab do[129]? It is written[135]: *If it would have been too easy to follow the sins of Jeroboam ben Nevaṭ.* Are not the light sins of Aḥab the serious sins of Jeroboam? Why was Jeroboam counted first[136]? Because he started the misconduct. What did Aḥab do? He adorned himself every day and stood before his army commander[137] Ḥiel, asking him, for how much am I good today? He answered him, so and so much; then he donated its value[138] to foreign worship. That is what is written[139] *Because you sold yourself to do evil in the Eternal's eyes.*

Rebbi Levi continued for six months to explain the following verse to shame[140] *There never was anyone like Aḥab who sold himself to do evil in the Eternal's eyes.* He came to him at night[141] and asked him, how did I sin against you, what did I do before you? You have the first part of the verse, but you do not have the end of the verse: *whom his wife Jezebel had misguided.* He[142] continued for six months to explain it as praise, *only one should not be like Aḥab . . . whom his wife Jezebel had misguided.*

135 *1K.* 16:31.

136 This shows that the Mishnah underlying the Halakhah was not the Mishnah as quoted in the ms. but followed the order of the Yerushalmi: Jeroboam, Ahab, Manasse.

137 The word probably represents Greek στρατηλάτης "army commander".

138 Greek τίμησις "estimation, valuation".

139 *1K.* 21:20.

140 *1K.* 21:25.

141 This shows that Ahab has part in the World to come, against the Mishnah.

142 R. Levi.

(28b line 22) כָּתוּב בְּיָמָיו בָּנָה חִיאֵל בֵּית הָאֱלִי אֶת־יְרִיחוֹ בַּאֲבִירָם בְּכֹרוֹ יִסְּדָהּ וּבִשְׂגוּב צְעִירוֹ הִצִּיב דְּלָתֶיהָ. חִיאֵל מִן יְהוֹשָׁפָט. יְרִיחוֹ מִבִּנְיָמִין. אֶלָּא שֶׁמְּגַלְגְּלִין זְכוּת עַל יְדֵי זַכַּאי וְחוֹבָה עַל יְדֵי חַיָּיב. וְכֵן הוּא אוֹמֵר בַּאֲבִירָם בְּכֹרוֹ יִסְּדָהּ וּבִשְׂגוּב צְעִירוֹ הִצִּיב דְּלָתֶיהָ. בַּאֲבִירָם בְּכֹרוֹ לֹא הָיָה מְאַיֵּין לְלַמֵּד. וּבִשְׂגוּב הָרָשָׁע הָיָה לוֹ מְאַיֵּין לְלַמֵּד. לְפִי שֶׁרָצוּ לְרַבּוֹת אֶת מָמוֹנָן וְשַׁלְטָה בָהֶן מְאֵירָה וְהָיוּ מִתְמוֹטְטִין וְהוֹלְכִין. לְקַיֵּים מַה שֶּׁנֶּאֱמַר כִּדְבַר יי אֲשֶׁר דִּבֶּר בְּיַד יְהוֹשֻׁעַ בִּן־נוּן. כָּתוּב וַיֹּאמֶר אֵלִיָּהוּ הַתִּשְׁבִּי מִתֹּשָׁבֵי גִלְעָד אֶל־אַחְאָב חַי־יי אֱלֹהֵי יִשְׂרָאֵל אֲשֶׁר עָמַדְתִּי לְפָנָיו אִם־יִהְיֶה הַשָּׁנִים הָאֵלֶּה טַל וּמָטָר כִּי אִם־לְפִי דְבָרִי׃ וְכִי מָה עִנְיָין זֶה אֵצֶל זֶה. אֶלָּא אָמַר הַקָּדוֹשׁ בָּרוּךְ הוּא לְאֵלִיָּהוּ. הָדֵין חִיאֵל גַּבְרָא רַבָּא הוּא. אֵיזִיל חֲמִי לֵיהּ אַפִּין. אֲמַר לֵיהּ. לִי נָה מֵיזַל. אֲמַר לֵיהּ. לָמָּה. אֲמַר לֵיהּ. דְּנָא מֵיזַל וִינוּן אָמְרִין מִילִּין דְּמַכְעִיסִין לָךְ וְלֵינָה יְכִיל מִיסְבּוֹל. אֲמַר לֵיהּ. וְאִין אָמְרִין מִילָּה דְּמַכְעֲסָה לִי כָּל־מַה דְאַתְּ גְּזַר אֲנָא מְקַיֵּים. אֲזַל וְאַשְׁכְּחוֹן עֲסִיקִין בְּהֵן קִרְיָיא וַיַּשְׁבַּע יְהוֹשֻׁעַ בָּעֵת הַהִיא לֵאמֹר אָרוּר הָאִישׁ לִפְנֵי יי אֲשֶׁר יָקוּם וּבָנָה אֶת־הָעִיר הַזֹּאת אֶת־יְרִיחוֹ בִּבְכֹרוֹ יְיַסְּדֶנָּה וּבִצְעִירוֹ יַצִּיב דְּלָתֶיהָ׃ אֲמַר. בְּרִיךְ הוּא אֱלָהֵהוֹן דְּצַדִּיקַיָּיא דִּמְקַיֵּים מִילֵּי דְצַדִּיקָא. וַהֲוָה תַמָּן אַחְאָב. אֲמַר לוֹן אַחְאָב. וְכִי מִי גָדוֹל מִמִּי מֹשֶׁה אוֹ יְהוֹשֻׁעַ. אָמְרִין לֵיהּ. מֹשֶׁה. אֲמַר לוֹן. בְּתוֹרָתוֹ שֶׁלְּמֹשֶׁה כָּתוּב הִשָּׁמְרוּ לָכֶם פֶּן־יִפְתֶּה לְבַבְכֶם וְסַרְתֶּם וַעֲבַדְתֶּם אֱלֹהִים אֲחֵרִים וְהִשְׁתַּחֲוִיתֶם לָהֶם׃ וּמַה כְתִיב בַּתְרֵיהּ. וְחָרָה אַף־יי בָּכֶם וְעָצַר אֶת־הַשָּׁמַיִם וְלֹא־יִהְיֶה מָטָר. וְלֹא הִינַּחְתִּי עֲבוֹדָה זָרָה בָעוֹלָם שֶׁלֹּא עֲבַדְתִּי אוֹתָהּ. וְכָל־טָבָן וְחָמָן דְּאִית בְּעָלְמָא אָתוּן בְּדָרִי. מִילּוֹי דְמֹשֶׁה לֹא קָמָן וּמִילֵּי דִיהוֹשֻׁעַ מְקַיֵּם. אֲמַר לֵיהּ אֵלִיָּהוּ. אִם כִּדְבָרֶיךָ חַי־יי אֱלֹהֵי יִשְׂרָאֵל אֲשֶׁר עָמַדְתִּי לְפָנָיו אִם־יִהְיֶה הַשָּׁנִים הָאֵלֶּה טַל וּמָטָר כִּי אִם־לְפִי דְבָרִי׃ כֵּיוָן שֶׁשָּׁמַע כֵּן הִתְחִיל בּוֹכֶה. הָדָא הִיא דִכְתִיב וַיְהִי כִשְׁמוֹעַ אַחְאָב אֶת־הַדְּבָרִים הָאֵלֶּה וַיִּקְרַע אֶת בְּגָדָיו וַיָּשֶׂם־שַׂק עַל־בְּשָׂרוֹ וַיָּצוֹם וַיִּשְׁכַּב בַּשָּׂק וַיְהַלֵּךְ אַט׃ כַּמָּה נִתְעַנֶּה. שָׁלֹשׁ שָׁעוֹת נִתְעַנֶּה. אִם הָיָה לָמוּד לוֹכַל בְּשָׁלֹשׁ הָיָה אוֹכֵל בְּשֵׁשׁ. אִם לָמוּד לוֹכַל בְּשֵׁשׁ הָיָה אוֹכֵל בְּתֵשַׁע. וַיְהַלֵּךְ אַט. מָהוּ אַט. רִבִּי יְהוֹשֻׁעַ בֶּן לֵוִי אָמַר. שֶׁהָיָה מְהַלֵּךְ יָחֵף. כְּתִיב וַיְהִי דְּבַר־יי אֶל־אֵלִיָּהוּ הַתִּשְׁבִּי לֵאמֹר׃ הֲרָאִיתָ כִּי־נִכְנַע אַחְאָב מִלְּפָנָיי. אָמַר הַקָּדוֹשׁ בָּרוּךְ הוּא לְאֵלִיָּהוּ. רְאֵה מָנָה טוֹבָה שֶׁנָּתַתִּי בְעוֹלָמִי. אָדָם חוֹטֵא לְפָנַי כַּמָּה וְעוֹשֶׂה תְשׁוּבָה וַאֲנִי מְקַבְּלוֹ. הָדָא הִיא דִכְתִיב הֲרָאִיתָ כִּי־נִכְנַע אַחְאָב מִלְּפָנָיי. חֲמִית אַחְאָב עֲבַד תְּשׁוּבָה. יַעַן כִּי־נִכְנַע אַחְאָב מִפָּנַיי לֹא־אָבִיא הָרָעָה בְּיָמָיו בִּימֵי בְנוֹ אָבִיא הָרָעָה עַל־בֵּיתוֹ׃

It is written[143]: *In his days did Ḥiel from Bet-El build Jericho; with his first-born Aviram he set the foundation and with his youngest son Seguv he put in the doors.* Hiel is from the descendants of Josaphat[144], Jericho is in the territory of Benjamin. Only that good deeds are put in the hands of the worthy and bad deeds in the hands of the unworthy; therefore, it is said, *with his first-born Aviram he set the foundation and with his youngest son Seguv he put in the doors.* If it was not appropriate for him to learn from his firstborn Aviram, should he not have learned from the wicked Seguv[145]? Because they wanted to make more money[146], the curse ruled over them and they were continuously weakened to confirm what was said[143], *following the word of the Eternal, the God of Israel, which He had spoken through Joshua ben Nun.*

It is written[147]: *Elijah the Tisbite, from the inhabitants of Gilead, said to Aḥab: By the Living Eternal, the God of Israel, before Whom I stood, there will not be dew or rain in the coming years except by my word.* What is the connection between these[148]? The Holy One, praise to Him, had said to Elijah: this Ḥiel is an important personality, go and pay a visit of condolence. He answered, I do not want to go. He asked, why? He said, for if I go and they say things that enrage You, I shall not be able to bear it. He told him, If they say anything that would enrage Me, anything that you decide I shall fulfill. He went and found them discussing the verse[149]: *At that time, Joshua imprecated as follows: Cursed be the man before the Eternal who would build this town, Jericho; with his first-born he shall put in the foundation and with his youngest set the doors.* He said, praised be the God of the just, Who fulfills the words of the just. Aḥab also was there. Aḥab said to them, who is greater, Moses or Joshua? They told him, Moses. He said to them, in Moses's Torah it is written[150]: *Watch yourselves, lest your hearts be seduced, you deviate, and worship other powers and bow down before them.* What is written next? *The rage of the Eternal will burn against you, He will lock up the sky and there will be no rain.* But I did not leave any strange worship that I would not have worshipped, and all good and comforting things came in my generation. He did not uphold the words of Moses; would He uphold Joshua's words? Elijah told him, it is as you say, *by the Living Eternal, the God of Israel, before Whom I stood, there will not be dew or rain in the coming years except by my word.* When he heard this, he started crying. That is what is written[151]: *When Aḥab heard these words, he tore his garments, put sackcloth on his flesh, fasted, slept in sackcloth and went aṭ.* How long did he fast? He fasted for three hours. If he was used to eat at 6 o'clock, he ate at noontime. If he was used to eat at noontime, he ate at three p.m. *He went aṭ.* What is *aṭ?* Rebbi Joshua ben Levi said, he went barefoot[152].

It is written:[153] *The word of the Eternal went to Elijah the Tisbite as follows: Did you see that Aḥab surrendered before me?* The Holy One, praise to Him, said to Elijah: See the good part which I put in My world. A person may sin greatly before Me, but if he repents I am accepting him[141]. That is what is written, *did you see that Ahab surrendered before Me?* You saw that Ahab repented. *Because Ahab surrendered before me, I shall not bring the evil in his days; in his son's days I shall bring the evil over his dynasty.*

143 *1K.* 16:34; cf. Babli 113a, Tosephta 14:6-9.

144 Identifying this Hiel with Yehiel, *2K.* 21:2.

145 The death of the firstborn could have been an accident; the death of the youngest certainly must be ascribed to Joshua's curse. (It is presumed here that the children died a natural death, not that they were killed by their father as building sacrifice.)

146 The rebuilding of Jericho was a real estate investment.

147 *1K.* 17:1, the verse immediately following 16:34; the medieval division into chapters is misleading.

148 *1K.* 17:1, and *1K.* 16:34.

149 *Jos.* 6:26.

150 *Deut.* 11:16-17.

151 *1K.* 21:27. This belongs to the Nabot affair, not the drought.

152 The early Medieval translator Daud ben Abraham Alfasi in his *Jamu`* (S. L. Skoss, *Kitab Jamu` Al Alfāz,* New Haven 1935) accepts the Jerushalmi's explanation. Rav Saadya Gaon (נחמיה אלוני, האגרון לרב סעדיה גאון, י״ם תשכט) translates אט as رفق "to be sweet. Compare Arabic اطّ "to creak, to groan".

153 *1K.* 21:28-29.

(28b line 57) וְכִי מֶה עָשָׂה אָחָז. עַל יְדֵי שֶׁבָּנָה כִסֵּא בָעֲזָרָה. הָדָא הִיא דִכְתִיב וְאֶת אוּלָם הַכִּסֵּא אֲשֶׁר בָּנוּ בַבַּיִת וגו'. רִבִּי חוֹנְיָה בְשֵׁם רִבִּי לְעָזָר. לָמָּה נִקְרָא שְׁמוֹ אָחָז. שֶׁאָחַז בַּבָּתֵּי כְנֵסִיּוֹת וּבְבָתֵּי מִדְרָשׁוֹת. לְמָה הָיָה אָחָז דוֹמֶה. לְמֶלֶךְ שֶׁהָיָה לוֹ בֵן וּמְסָרוֹ לְפֵידָגוֹגוֹ וְהָיָה מְבַקֵּשׁ לְהוֹרְגוֹ. אָמַר. אִם אֲנִי הוֹרְגוֹ הֲרֵי אֲנִי מִתְחַייֵב מִיתָה. אֶלָּא אֲנִי מוֹשֵׁךְ אֶת מֵינִיקְתּוֹ מִמֶּנּוּ וּמֵעַצְמוֹ הוּא מֵת. כָּךְ אָמַר אָחָז. אִם אֵין גְּדָיִים אֵין תַּיָישִׁים. אִין אֵין תַּייָשִׁים אֵין צֹאן. אִם אֵין צֹאן אֵין רוֹעֶה. אִם אֵין רוֹעֶה אֵין עוֹלָם. אִם אֵין עוֹלָם כִּבְיָכוֹל. כָּךְ הָיָה אָחָז סָבוּר בְּדַעְתּוֹ לוֹמַר. אִם אֵין קְטַנִּים אֵין גְּדוֹלִים. אִם אֵין גְּדוֹלִים אֵין חֲכָמִים. אִם אֵין חֲכָמִים אֵין נְבִיאִים. אִם אֵין נְבִיאִים אֵין רוּחַ הַקּוֹדֶשׁ. אִם אֵין רוּחַ הַקּוֹדֶשׁ אֵין בָּתֵּי כְנֵסִיּוֹת וּבָתֵּי מִדְרָשׁוֹת. כִּבְיָכוֹל אֵין הַקָּדוֹשׁ בָּרוּךְ הוּא מַשְׁרֶה שְׁכִינָתוֹ עַל יִשְׂרָאֵל. רִבִּי יַעֲקֹב בַּר אַבַּיי בְשֵׁם רִבִּי אָחָא מַייְתֵי לָהּ מִן הָדָא וְחִכִּיתִי לַיי הַמַּסְתִּיר פָּנָיו מִבֵּית יַעֲקֹב וְקִוֵּיתִי לוֹ: אֵין לָךְ שָׁעָה קָשָׁה בָעוֹלָם מֵאוֹתָהּ שָׁעָה שֶׁאָמַר לוֹ הַקָּדוֹשׁ בָּרוּךְ הוּא לְמֹשֶׁה וְאָנֹכִי הַסְתֵּר אַסְתִּיר פָּנַי בַּיּוֹם הַהוּא. מֵאוֹתָהּ שָׁעָה וְקִוֵּיתִי לוֹ שֶׁאָמַר לוֹ בְסִינַי כִּי לֹא תִשָּׁכַח מִפִּי זַרְעוֹ. וּמָה אַתְּ מוֹעִיל. הִנֵּה אָנֹכִי וְהַיְלָדִים אֲשֶׁר

נָתַן־לִ֥י יְי. וְכִי יְלָדָיו הָיוּ וַהֲלֹא תַלְמִידָיו הָיוּ. אֶלָּא מְלַמֵּד שֶׁהָיוּ חֲבִיבִין עָלָיו וְהָיָה קוֹרֵא אוֹתָם בָּנַיי.

[154]But what did Aḥaz do? He built a throne in the Temple Court. That is what is written: "The throne-hall which they built in the Temple,[155]" etc. Rebbi Onias in the name of Rebbi Eleazar. Why is he called "the grabber[156]"? For he grabbed synagogues and houses of study[157]. To what may Aḥaz be compared? To a king who had a son whom he entrusted to his pedagogue[158]. The latter wanted to kill him. He said, if I kill him, I will be put to death. But I shall draw his wet-nurse away from him and he will die of himself. So Aḥaz said, if there are no kid goats there are no he-goats. If there are no he-goats there are no goats. If there are no goats there is no shepherd[159]. If there is no shepherd there is no world; if it were thinkable that there be no world. So Aḥaz was thinking, if there are no children[160] there are no adults. If there are no adults, there are no Sages. If there are no Sages, there are no prophets. If there are no prophets, there is no Holy Spirit. If there is no Holy Spirit, there are no synagogues and no houses of study. If it were thinkable, the Holy One, praise to Him,. will not let His Presence rest over Israel.

Rebbi Jacob bar Abbai in the name of Rebbi Aḥa brings it from the following[161] *I shall wait for the Eternal, Who hid His Face from the House of Jacob, and put my hope in Him.* There was no worse moment in the world than when the Holy One, praise to Him, said to Moses[162]: *I shall certainly hide My Face at that time.* From that moment on, *I put my hope in Him,* Who said at Sinai,[163] *for it shall not be forgotten by his descendants.* What would its use be[164]? *Behold, I and the children which the Eternal has given me.* Were they his children? Were they not his students? But this teaches he loved them as if they were his sons and called them "my sons".

154 *Gen. rabba* 42(4), *Esther rabba Introduction*, *Lev. rabba* 11, *Ruth rabba* 1(7).

155 This exists no such verse. Probably, as indicated by *Qorban ha`Edah*, the reference is to *2K*. 16:18: The Sabbath shelter which they had built in the temple . . ."

156 אחז "to grab".

157 To close them down.

158 Greek παιδαγωγός, the slave accompanying the child.

159 God.

160 Going to school.

161 That Ahaz had eliminated all religious instruction, *Is*. 8:17.

162 *Deut*. 31:18.

163 *Deut.* 31:21. This was not said at Sinai but in the steppes of Moab; it is a promise that the study of Torah will never cease.

157 *Is.* 8:18. A different interpretation in the Babli 19b.

(28b line 75) וְכִי מֶה עָשָׂה מְנַשֶּׁה. כָּתוּב בַּיָּמִים הָהֵם חָלָה חִזְקִיָּהוּ לָמוּת וגו' עַד כִּי מֵת אַתָּה וְלֹא תִחְיֶה׃ כִּי מֵת אַתָּה. בְּעוֹלָם הַזֶּה. וְלֹא תִחְיֶה. לֶעָתִיד לָבוֹא. וְלָמָּה. אֲמַר לֵיהּ. דְּלָא בְעִית מִיקְמָה לָךְ בְּנִין. אֲמַר לֵיהּ. לָמָּא לָא בְעִית מִיקְמָה לָךְ בְּנִין. אֲמַר לֵיהּ. חֲמִית דַּאֲנָא מְקִים בַּר רְשִׁיעַ. בְּגִין כֵּן לָא בְעִית מִיקְמָה בְנִין. אֲמַר לֵיהּ. סַב בְּרַתִּי. דִּילְמָא מִינִּי וּמִינָּךְ הוּא מוּקִים בַּר נַשׁ טַב. אַף עַל גַּב לָא קָם אֶלָּא בַּר נַשׁ בִּישׁ. הָדָא הִיא דִכְתִיב וְכֵלַי כֵּלָיו רָעִים. אֲמַר לֵיהּ. לָא לָךְ אֲנָא שְׁמַע. אֵינִי קוֹפֵץ אֶלָּא לְמַה שֶׁאָמַר לִי זְקֵינִי. שֶׁאָמַר לִי. אִם רָאִיתָה חֲלוֹמוֹת קָשִׁים אוֹ חֶזְיוֹנוֹת קָשִׁים קְפוֹץ לִשְׁלוֹשָׁה דְבָרִים וְאַתְּ נִיצּוֹל. וְאֵילּוּ הֵן. לִתְפִילָּה וְלִצְדָקָה וְלִתְשׁוּבָה. וּשְׁלָשְׁתָּן בְּפָסוּק אֶחָד. וְיִכָּנְעוּ עַמִּי אֲשֶׁר נִקְרָא־שְׁמִי עֲלֵיהֶם וְיִתְפַּלְלוּ זֶה תְפִילָּה. וִיבַקְשׁוּ פָנַי זוֹ צְדָקָה. כְּמַה דְתֵימַר אֲנִי בְּצֶדֶק אֶחֱזֶה פָנֶיךָ אֶשְׂבְּעָה בְהָקִיץ תְּמוּנָתֶךָ׃ וְיָשֻׁבוּ מִדַּרְכֵיהֶם הָרָעִים זוֹ תְשׁוּבָה. אִם עָשׂוּ כֵן מַה כְתִיב תַּמָּן. וַאֲנִי אֶשְׁמַע מִן־הַשָּׁמַיִם וְאֶסְלַח לְחַטָּאתָם וְאֶרְפָּא אֶת־אַרְצָם׃ מִיַּד וַיַּסֵּב.

דִּכְתִיב וַיַּסֵּב חִזְקִיָּהוּ פָּנָיו אֶל־הַקִּיר וַיִּתְפַּלֵּל אֶל־יי. לְאֵי זֶה קִיר נָשָׂא עֵינָיו. רִבִּי יְהוֹשֻׁעַ בֶּן לֵוִי אָמַר. לְקִירָהּ שֶׁלְּרָחָב נָשָׂא עֵינָיו. כִּי בֵיתָהּ בְּקִיר הַחוֹמָה וּבַחוֹמָה הִיא יוֹשָׁבֶת׃ אָמַר לְפָנָיו. רִבּוֹן כָּל־הָעוֹלָמִים. רָחָב שְׁתֵּי נְפָשׁוֹת הִצִּילָה לָךְ. רְאֵה כַּמָּה נְפָשׁוֹת הִצַּלְתָּ לָהּ. הָדָא הִיא דִכְתִיב וַיָּבוֹאוּ הַנְּעָרִים הַמְרַגְּלִים וַיּוֹצִיאוּ אֶת־רָחָב וְאֶת בֵּית אָבִיהָ וְאֶת־אִמָּהּ וְאֶת־אַחֶיהָ וְאֶת־כָּל־אֲשֶׁר־לָהּ וְאֵת כָּל־מִשְׁפְּחוֹתֶיהָ הוֹצִיא וַיַּנִּיחוּם מִחוּץ לְמַחֲנֵה יִשְׂרָאֵל. תַּנֵּי רִבִּי שִׁמְעוֹן בֶּן יוֹחַאי. אֲפִילוּ הָיְתָה בְמִשְׁפְּחוֹתֶיהָ מָאתַיִם אֲנָשִׁים וְהָלְכוּ וְנִדְבְּקוּ בְּמָאתַיִם מִשְׁפָּחוֹת כּוּלְּהֶן הָיוּ נִיצָּלִין בִּזְכוּתָהּ. אֲבוֹתַיי שֶׁקֵּרְבוּ לָךְ כָּל־הַגֵּרִים הַלָּלוּ עַל אַחַת כַּמָּה וְכַמָּה שֶׁתִּתֵּן לִי אֶת נַפְשִׁי.

רִבִּי שְׁמוּאֵל בַּר נַחְמָן אָמַר. נָשָׂא עֵינָיו בְּקִירָהּ שֶׁלַּשּׁוּנַמִּית. נַעֲשֶׂה־נָּא עֲלִיַּת קִיר קְטַנָּה וְנָשִׂים לוֹ שָׁם מִיטָּה וְשׁוּלְחָן וְכִסֵּא וּמְנוֹרָה. אָמַר לְפָנָיו. רִבּוֹן כָּל־הָעוֹלָמִים. שׁוּנַמִּית קִיר אֶחָד עָשְׂתָה לֶאֱלִישָׁע וְהֶחֱיֵיתָה אֶת בְּנָהּ. אֲבוֹתַיי שֶׁעָשׂוּ לָךְ אֶת הַשֶּׁבַח הַזֶּה עַל אַחַת כַּמָּה וְכַמָּה שֶׁתִּתֵּן לִי אֶת נַפְשִׁי.

רִבִּי חִינְנָא בַּר פַּפָּא אָמַר. נָתַן עֵינָיו בְּקִירוֹת בֵּית הַמִּקְדָּשׁ. בְּתִתָּם סִפָּם אֶת־סִפִּי וּמְזוּזָתָם אֵצֶל מְזוּזָתִי וְהַקִּיר בֵּינִי וּבֵינֵיהֶן. בְּנֵי אָדָם גְּדוֹלִים הָיוּ וְלֹא הָיוּ יְכוֹלִין לַעֲלוֹת וּלְהִתְפַּלֵּל בְּכָל־שָׁעָה וְהָיוּ מִתְפַּלְּלִין בְּתוֹךְ בָּתֵּיהֶם. וְהַקָּדוֹשׁ בָּרוּךְ הוּא מַעֲלֶה עֲלֵיהֶן כְּאִילוּ נִתְפַּלְּלוּ בְּבֵית הַמִּקְדָּשׁ. אֲבוֹתַיי שֶׁעָשׂוּ לָךְ אֶת כָּל־הַשֶּׁבַח הַזֶּה עַל אַחַת כַּמָּה וְכַמָּה שֶׁתִּתֵּן לִי אֶת נַפְשִׁי.

וְרַבָּנִין אָמְרִין. נָתַן עֵינָיו בְּקִירוֹת לִבּוֹ. שֶׁנֶּאֱמַר מֵעַי | מֵעַי אוֹחִילָה קִירוֹת לִבִּי הוֹמֶה לִּי לִבִּי לֹא אַחֲרִישׁ. אָמַר לְפָנָיו. רִבּוֹן הָעוֹלָמִים. חִיזַּרְתִּי עַל מָאתַיִם וְאַרְבָּעִים וּשְׁמוֹנֶה אֵיבָרִים שֶׁנָּתַתָּה בִּי וְלֹא מָצָאתִי שֶׁהִכְעַסְתִּי אוֹתְךָ בְּאַחַת מֵהֶן. אַחַת כַּמָּה וְכַמָּה תִּינָּתֵן לִי נַפְשִׁי.

כְּתִיב וַיְהִי֙ דְּבַר־יְהֹוָ֔ה אֶל־יְשַׁעְיָ֥הוּ הַנָּבִ֖יא לֵאמֹֽר׃ לֵ֣ךְ וְאָמַרְתָּ֞ אֶל־חִזְקִיָּ֨הוּ נְגִיד עַמִּ֜י כֹּֽה־אָמַ֣ר יי אֱלֹהֵי֙ דָּוִ֣ד אָבִ֔יךָ שָׁמַ֙עְתִּי֙ אֶת־תְּפִלָּתֶ֔ךָ רָאִ֖יתִי אֶת־דִּמְעָתֶ֑ךָ הִנְנִי֙ יוֹסִ֣ף עַל־יָמֶ֔יךָ חֲמֵ֥שׁ עֶשְׂרֵ֖ה שָׁנָֽה׃ אֲמַר לֵיהּ. וּכְדוֹן אֲמְרִית לֵיהּ הָכֵין. וּכְדוֹן אֲנָא מֵימַר לֵיהּ הָכֵין. אֲמַר לֵיהּ. גַּבְרָא רַבָּה הוּא וְלֵית הוּא מְהֵימְנָתִי. אֲמַר לֵיהּ. עִינְוָון סַגִּיי הוּא וְהוּא מְהֵימָן לָךְ. וְלֹא עוֹד אֶלָּא עֲדַיִין לֹא יָצָאת הֲבָרָה בָּעִיר. וַיְהִי יְשַׁעְיָ֫הוּ לֹא יָצָא חָצֵר הַתִּיכֹנָה. הָעִיר כְּתִיב.

What did Manasse do? It is written[165]: *In these days, Hezekias became critically ill,* etc., *for you will die, you will not live. For you will die,* in this world, *you will not live,* in the Future World. He asked him, why? He answered him, because you did not want to have children[166]. He asked him, why do you not want to have children? He answered him, I saw that I will have an evil son; therefore, I do not want to have children. He told him, marry my daughter[167], maybe descending from me and you he will become a good person. Nevertheless the result was only a bad person. That is what is written[168], *but my vessels, his vessels are bad.* He told him, I am not listening to you, I only am jumping on what my ancestor said, who told me[169], if you see bad dreams or bad visions do jump onto three things and you will be saved. These are: prayer, giving alms, and repentance. All three from one verse[170]: *If My people, over whom My Name is called, are subdued and they will pray,* that refers to prayer, *and they will ask before me,* that refers to giving alms, as you say[171], *I, by giving alms, shall see Your Face, I shall be satiated in waking by Your image. They shall repent their evil ways*, that is repentance. If they did this, what is written there? *I shall listen from Heaven, forgive their sins, and heal their land.* Immediately, he turned, as is written.

[172]*Hezekiah turned his face to the wall.* Which wall did he lift his eyes to? Rebbi Joshua ben Levi said, he lifted his eyes to Rahab's wall, *for her house was on the wall of the fortification; she lived on the wall.* He said before Him: Master of all worlds, Rahab saved two souls for You, and see how many souls You saved for her. That is what is written[174]: *The youths, the spies, came and led out Rahab, and her father's house, and her mother, and her brothers, and all of hers, and all her families they brought out and left them outside of Israel's camp.* Rebbi Simeon ben Iohai stated, even if her family was 200 persons strong and they furthermore were related to other families, all of

whom were saved by her merit. My forefathers who brought to You all these proselytes so much more that You should spare my life.

Rebbi Samuel bar Naḥman said, he lifted his eyes to the wall of the woman from Sunem, as it was said[175]: *Let us make a small upper storey on the wall and put there a bed, a table, a chair, and a lamp.* He said before Him: Master of all worlds, the woman from Sunem made one wall for Elisha and You revived her son. My forefathers who built for You all this glory, so much more that You should spare my life.

Rebbi Ḥinena bar Pappus said, he lifted his eyes to the wall of the Temple. [176]*When they put their lintel next to My lintel, their doorposts next to My doorpost, with the wall between Me and them.* They were important people; they could not go and pray in the Temple every time, so they prayed in their house and the Holy One, praise to Him, considers it as if they had prayed in the Temple. My forefathers who built for You all this glory, so much more that You should spare my life.

But the rabbis say, he lifted his eyes to the walls of his heart. [177]*My innards, my innards I make tremble, the walls of my heart are in uproar; my heart is beating inside me, I cannot be silent.* He said before Him: Master of the world, I checked all my 248 limbs[178] that You gave me and I did not find one of them I offended you with; so much more that You should spare my life.

It is written[179]: *The Word of the Eternal was to the prophet Isaiah as follows: Go and tell Hezekias, My people's leader . . . so says the Eternal, your ancestor David's God, I heard your prayer, I saw your tear; now I am adding fifteen years to your days.* He told Him, first I told him one way, now I have to tell him this? He told Him, he is a great personality and will not believe me. He answered him, he is a very meek person and will believe you. Not only that, but the rumor has not yet spread in the city: *Isaiah had not yet left the middle courtyard;* "city" is written[180].

165 *2K.* 20:1, *Is.* 38:1.

166 Babli *Berakhot* 10a.

167 Manasse was born after Hezekias's illness; his mother's name is given without patronymic.

168 *Is.* 32:7.

169 A slightly different version is in *Ta`aniot* 2:1 (65b l.3), *Eccl. rabba* 7(29), *Tanhuma Noah* 8. The Yerushalmi version is the basis of a central piece of the

Ashkenazic service of New Year's day (in the Eastern European version also of the Day of Atonement). The Babli version (*Roš Haššanah* 16b) is quite different.

170 *2Chr.* 7:14.

171 *Ps.* 17:15.

172 *Is.* 38:2.

173 *Jos.* 2:15.

174 *Jos.*6:25.

175 *2K.* 4:10.

176 *Ez.* 43:8.

177 *Jer.* 4:19.

178 Mishnah *Ahilut* 1:8.

179 *2K.* 20:4-5.

180 *Courtyard* is *Qere*, *city* is *Ketib*. The rumor is that Isaiah told the king that he would die. The prophet does not have to fear that his credibility was impaired.

(28c line 44) כַּד דְּקָם מְנַשֶּׁה הֲוָה פרי חוֹרֵי יְשַׁעְיָה. בָּעֵי מִיקְטְלוּנֵיהּ וְהוּא עֲרַק מִן קֳדָמוֹי. עֲרַק לְאַרְזָא וּבְלָעֵי אַרְזָא. חֲסַר צִיצִתָא דְגוּלְתֵיהּ. אֲתוֹן וְאָֽמְרִין קֳדָמוֹי. אֲמַר לוֹן. אַזְלוֹן וְנַסְּרוֹן אַרְזָא. וְנַסְּרוּ לְאַרְזָא וְאִיתְחֲמֵי דָּמָא נְגַד. וְלֹא־אָבָה יְי לִסְלֹחַ. מִיכָּן שֶׁאֵין לוֹ חֵלֶק לְעָתִיד לָבוֹא. וְהָא כְתִיב מִלְּבַד חַטֹּאות מְנַשֶּׁה בֶן־יְחִזְקִיָּהוּ מֶלֶךְ יְהוּדָה. נֵימַר. עַד דְּלֹא יַחֲזוֹר בֵּיהּ. עַל כָּל־הַכְּעָסִים אֲשֶׁר הִכְעִיסוֹ מְנַשֶּׁה. נֵימַר. עַד שֶׁלֹּא עָשָׂה תְשׁוּבָה. וְהָא כְתִיב כִּי הוּא אָמוֹן הִרְבָּה אַשְׁמָה׃ לֹא הוֹסִיף אֶלָּא חִידֵּשׁ. וְהָכְתִיב וְגַם דָּם נָקִי שָׁפַךְ מְנַשֶּׁה הַרְבֵּה מְאֹד עַד אֲשֶׁר־מִלֵּא אֶת־יְרוּשָׁלַםִ פֶּה לָפֶה. וְכִי אֶפְשַׁר לְבָשָׂר וְדָם לְמַלְאוֹת אֶת־יְרוּשָׁלַם דָּם נָקִי פֶּה לָפֶה. אֶלָּא שֶׁהָרַג אֶת יְשַׁעְיָהוּ שֶׁהָיָה שָׁקוּל כְּמֹשֶׁה. דִּכְתִיב בֵּיהּ פֶּה אֶל־פֶּה אֲדַבֶּר־בּוֹ.

When Manasse became king, he was wild[181] after Isaiah; he wanted to kill him, but he fled before him. He fled to a cedar tree, the cedar swallowed him, except to a *sisit* of his coat. They came and reported it before him. He said, go and cut down the cedar. They cut down the cedar and blood was seen flowing[182]. *But the Eternal did not want to pardon*[183]: from here that he has no part in the Future World. And is it not written[184], *in addition to the sins of Manasse ben Hezekias, the king of Jehudah.* Let us say, before he changed his ways. *Because of all the rages by which Manasse enraged him*[185]. Let us say, before he repented. But is it not written[186]: *For he, Amon, increased in criminality.* He did not add, but he found new ways. And is there not written[187]: *Also innocent blood did Manasse spill, a great deal, until he filled Jerusalem from mouth to mouth*? How is it possible for flesh and blood to fill Jerusalem with innocent blood from mouth to mouth? But he slew Isaiah who was equal to Moses, about whom is written[188]: *Mouth to mouth I would speak to him.*

181 This word may be read either as Aramaized פֶּרֶא "wild" or as Latin *ferus* "wild" (E. G.).

182 The story is hinted at in the Babli 103b, *Yebamot* 49b.

183 *2K.* 24:4.

184 A misquote of *Jer.* 15:4.

185 *2K.* 23:26, an almost correct quote.

186 *2Chr.* 33:23.

187 *2K.* 21:16.

188 *Num.* 12:8.

(28c line 55) כָּתוּב וַיְדַבֵּר יי אֶל־מְנַשֶּׁה וְאֶל־עַמּוֹ וְלֹא הִקְשִׁיבוּ׃ וַיָּבֵא עֲלֵיהֶם אֶת־שָׂרֵי הַצָּבָא אֲשֶׁר לְמֶלֶךְ וַיִּלְכְּדוּ אֶת־מְנַשֶּׁה בַּחוֹחִים. מָהוּ בַחוֹחִים. בְּכֵירוֹ־מָנִיקִיָּא. אָמַר רִבִּי לֵוִי. מוּלָא שֶׁלִּנְחוֹשֶׁת עָשׂוּ לוֹ וְנָתְנוּ אוֹתוֹ בְּתוֹכָהּ וְהָיוּ מַסִּיקִין תַּחְתָּיו. כֵּיוָן שֶׁרָאָה שֶׁצָּרָתוֹ צָרָה לֹא הִנִּיחַ עֲבוֹדָה זָרָה בָעוֹלָם שֶׁלֹּא הִזְכִּירָהּ. כֵּיוָן שֶׁלֹּא הוֹאִיל לוֹ כְלוּם אָמַר. זָכוּר אֲנִי שֶׁהָיָה אָבִי מַקְרֶה אוֹתִי אֶת הַפָּסוּק הַזֶּה בְּבֵית הַכְּנֶסֶת בַּצַּר לְךָ וּמְצָאוּךָ כֹּל הַדְּבָרִים הָאֵלֶּה בְּאַחֲרִית הַיָּמִים וְשַׁבְתָּ עַד־יי אֱלֹהֶיךָ וְשָׁמַעְתָּ בְּקוֹלוֹ׃ כִּי אֵל רַחוּם יי אֱלֹהֶיךָ לֹא יַרְפְּךָ וְלֹא יַשְׁחִיתֶךָ וְלֹא יִשְׁכַּח אֶת־בְּרִית אֲבוֹתֶיךָ אֲשֶׁר נִשְׁבַּע לָהֶם׃ הֲרֵי אֲנִי קוֹרֵא אוֹתוֹ. אִם עוֹנֶה אוֹתִי מוּטָּב וְאִם לָאו הָא כָל־אַפַּיָּא שָׁוִין. וְהָיוּ מַלְאֲכֵי הַשָּׁרֵת מְסַתְּמִין אֶת הַחַלּוֹנוֹת שֶׁלֹּא תַעֲלֶה תְפִילָּתוֹ שֶׁלִּמְנַשֶּׁה לִפְנֵי הַקָּדוֹשׁ בָּרוּךְ הוּא. וְהָיוּ מַלְאֲכֵי הַשָּׁרֵת אוֹמְרִים לִפְנֵי הַקָּדוֹשׁ בָּרוּךְ הוּא. רִבּוֹנוֹ שֶׁלְּעוֹלָם. אָדָם שֶׁעָבַד עֲבוֹדָה זָרָה וְהֶעֱמִיד צֶלֶם בַּהֵיכָל אַתָּה מְקַבְּלוֹ בִתְשׁוּבָה. אָמַר לָהֶן. אִם אֵינִי מְקַבְּלוֹ בִתְשׁוּבָה הֲרֵי אֲנִי נוֹעֵל אֶת הַדֶּלֶת בִּפְנֵי כָל־בַּעֲלֵי תְשׁוּבָה. מֶה עָשָׂה לוֹ הַקָּדוֹשׁ בָּרוּךְ הוּא. חָתַר לוֹ חֲתִירָה מִתַּחַת כִּסֵּא הַכָּבוֹד שֶׁלּוֹ וְשָׁמַע תְּחִינָּתוֹ. הָדָא הִיא דִכְתִיב וַיִּתְפַּלֵּל אֵלָיו וַיֵּעָתֶר לוֹ וַיִּשְׁמַע תְּחִנָּתוֹ וַיְשִׁיבֵיהוּ. אָמַר רִבִּי לָעְזָר בֵּירִבִּי שִׁמְעוֹן. בַּעֲרָבְיָיא צְווָחִין לַחֲתִרְתָּה עֲתַרְתָּה. וַיְשִׁיבֵיהוּ יְרוּשָׁלַם לְמַלְכוּתוֹ. בְּמָה הֱשִׁיבוֹ. שְׁמוּאֵל בַּר בִּינָא בְשֵׁם רִבִּי אָחָא. בָּרוּחַ הֱשִׁיבוֹ. כְּמַה דַתְּ מַר מַשִּׁיב הָרוּחַ. וַיֵּדַע מְנַשֶּׁה כִּי יי הוּא הָאֱלֹהִים׃ בְּאוֹתָהּ שָׁעָה אָמַר מְנַשֶּׁה. אִית דִּין וְאִית דַּיָּין.

[189]It is written[190]: *The Eternal spoke to Manasse and to his people but they did not listen. He brought over them the generals of the king [ ]*[191]*; they caught Manasse in ḥoḥîm.* What are *ḥoḥîm*? Handcuffs[192]. Rebbi Levi said, they made a bronze mule[193] for him, put him inside, and started heating it from below. When he realized that he was in real trouble, he did not forget any strange worship but appealed to it. Since this did not help him any, he said, I remember that my father let me read the following verse in the synagogue[194]: *When you are in straits, and all these things will find you in the future, then return to the Eternal, your God, and listen to His voice. For the Eternal, your God, is a merciful power. He will not let you slacken , He will not destroy you, nor will He forget the covenant of your forefathers which He concluded with them.* I shall call to Him. If He hears me, it is good; otherwise all faces

are the same. The angels on duty closed all windows that Manasse's prayer should not ascend before the Holy One, praise to Him. The angels on duty said to the Holy One, praise to Him: Master of the Universe, would You receive in repentance a man who worshipped other powers and put up an idol in the Temple Hall? He told them, If I would not receive his repentance, I would close the door in front of all repenting sinners. What did the Holy One, praise to Him, do for him? He dug out a tunnel under His Seat of Glory and accepted his supplication. That is what is written[195]: *He prayed to Him, He had mercy on him, He accepted his supplication, and He returned him.* Rebbi Eleazar ben Rebbi Simeon said, in Arabia a tunnel is called *`atharta*[196]. *He returned him to Jerusalem, to his kingship*[195]. How did He return him? Samuel bar Bina in the name of Rebbi Aha: He returned him by the wind, as one says, "He returns wind.[197]" At that moment, Manasse said, there is judgment and there is a judge[198].

189 A parallel text is *Pesiqta dR. Cahana, Šuva* (ed. Buber p. 162a, Note 102). Similar texts are in *Deut. rabba* 2, *Ruth rabba ad* 2:14. A quote is in *Pirqe R. Eliezer* 43.

190 *2Chr.* 33:10-11.

191 Both ms. and *editio princeps* lack "of the king of Assyria".

192 Literally "hand-handcuffs"; probably a hybrid from Greek χείρ "hand" and Latin *manicae, -arum* (Byzantine μανίκιον, Soph. 732) "handcuffs". The combined word is not documented in Greek or Latin literature (E.G.).

193 Interpretation of J. Levy, Dictionary vol. 3 p. 48a, confirmed by Targum. The story is inspired by what is told of Phalaris, tyrant of Agrigentum.

194 *Deut.* 4:30-31.

195 *2 Chr.* 33:13.

196 Probably عاثور "a dangerous place". The explanation, quoted in support of the story about the angels, is unnecessary since the word ויעתר also appears in *Gen.* 25:21.

197 From the daily prayer for rain in the rainy season. The identification of נשב and שוב in a sermon is possible only if the duplication of consonants was no longer audible in speech.

198 Therefore Manasse died a believer; in the opinion of the author of Chronicles, he has part in the Future World. The Mishnah follows the opinion of the authors of *Kings* and *Jeremiah.*

(28c line 76) וְכִי מֶה עָשָׂה בִּלְעָם הָרָשָׁע. עַל יְדֵי שֶׁנָּתַן עֵצָה לְבָלָק בֶּן צִפּוֹר לְהַפִּיל אֶת יִשְׂרָאֵל בַּחֶרֶב. אָמַר לוֹ. אֱלוֹהַּ שֶׁלְּאוּמָּה זוֹ הוּא שׂוֹנֵא אֶת זְנוּת. אֶלָּא הֶעֱמִידוּ בְנוֹתֵיכֶם בְּזִימָּה וְאַתֶּם שׁוֹלְטִין בָּהֶן. אֲמַר לֵיהּ. וּמִישְׁמַע לִי אִינּוּן. אֲמַר לֵיהּ. אֲקִים בְּנְתָּךְ קוֹמוֹי וִינּוּן חַמְיָין וְשָׁמְעִין

לָךְ. הָדָא הוּא דִכְתִיב רֹאשׁ אוּמּוֹת בֵּית־אָב בְּמִדְיָן הוּא׃ מֶה עָשׂוּ. בָּנוּ לָהֶן קִינְקְלִין מִבֵּית הַיְשִׁימוֹן עַד הַר הַשֶּׁלֶג וְהוֹשִׁיבוּ בָהֶן נָשִׁים מוֹכְרוֹת מִינֵי כִיסְנִין. הוֹשִׁיבוּ אֶת הַזְּקֵינָה מִבַּחוּץ וְאֶת הַנַּעֲרָה מִבִּפְנִים. וְהָיוּ יִשְׂרָאֵל אוֹכְלִין וְשׁוֹתִין. וְהָיָה אֶחָד מֵהֶן יוֹצֵא לְטַייֵל בַּשּׁוּק וְלִיקַּח לוֹ חֵפֶץ מִן הַחֶנְוָנִי. וְהָיְתָה הַזְּקֵינָה מוֹכֶרֶת לוֹ אֶת הַחֵפֶץ בְּשָׁוְייוֹ וְהַנַּעֲרָה אוֹמֶרֶת לוֹ. בֹּא וְטוֹל לָךְ בְּפָחוֹת. כֵּן בַּיּוֹם הָרִאשׁוֹן וְכֵן יוֹם הַשֵּׁינִי וְכֵן בַּיּוֹם הַשְּׁלִישִׁי. וְהָיְתָה אוֹמֶרֶת לוֹ. מִיכָּן וְהֵילַךְ אַתָּה כְבֶן בַּיִת. הִיכָּנֵס וּבוֹר לָךְ. וְכֵיוָן שֶׁהָיָה נִכְנַס הָיָה שָׁם צַרְצוּר מָלֵא יַיִן מִן הַיַּיִן הָעֲמוֹנִי שֶׁהוּא קָשֶׁה וְהוּא מְפַתֶּה אֶת הַגּוּף לִזְנוּת. וְהָיָה רֵיחוֹ מְפַעְפֵּעַ. וְאַדַּיִין לֹא נֶאֱסַר (יֵינָם שֶׁלְּגוֹיִם) יַיִן נֶסֶךְ עַל יִשְׂרָאֵל. וְהָיְתָה אוֹמֶרֶת לוֹ. רְצוֹנְךָ לִשְׁתּוֹת כּוֹס יַיִן. וְהוּא אוֹמֵר לָהּ. הֵין. וְהִיא נוֹתֶנֶת לוֹ וְהוּא שׁוֹתֶה. וְכֵיוָן שֶׁהוּא שׁוֹתֶה הָיָה הַיַּיִן בּוֹעֵר בּוֹ כִכְרִיסָה שֶׁלַּחֲכִינָה. וְהוּא אוֹמֵר לָהּ. הִישָּׁמְעִי לִי. וְהִיא אוֹמֶרֶת לוֹ. רְצוֹנְךָ שֶׁאֶשְׁמַע לָךְ. וְהוּא אוֹמֵר. הֵין. מִיָּד הָיְתָה מוֹצִיאָה לוֹ טִפּוּס שֶׁלִּפְעוֹר מִתּוֹךְ חֵיקָהּ שֶׁלָּהּ וְהָיְתָה אוֹמֶרֶת לוֹ. הִשְׁתַּחֲוֵה לָזֶה וַאֲנִי נִשְׁמַעַת לָךְ. וְהוּא אוֹמֵר לָהּ. וְכִי לַעֲבוֹדָה זָרָה אֲנִי מִשְׁתַּחֲוֶה. וְהָיְתָה אוֹמֶרֶת לוֹ. אֵין אַתְּ מִשְׁתַּחֲוֶה אֶלָּא בִמְגַלֶּה עַצְמָךְ לוֹ. זוֹ הִיא שֶׁאָמְרוּ חֲכָמִים. הַפּוֹעֵר עַצְמוֹ לְבַעַל פְּעוֹר זוֹ הִיא עֲבוֹדָתוֹ. וְהַזּוֹרֵק אֶבֶן לְמֶרְקוּלִיס זוֹ הִיא עֲבוֹדָתוֹ׃ וְהָיָה שָׁם צַרְצוּר מָלֵא יַיִן מִן הַיַּיִן הָעֲמוֹנִי שֶׁהוּא קָשֶׁה שֶׁהוּא מְפַתֶּה אֶת הַגּוּף לִזְנוּת וְהָיָה רֵיחוֹ מְפַעְפֵּעַ. וְאַדַּיִין לֹא נֶאֱסַר יַיִן נֶסֶךְ עַל יִשְׂרָאֵל. וְהָיְתָה אוֹמֶרֶת לוֹ. רְצוֹנְךָ לִשְׁתּוֹת כּוֹס יַיִן. וְהוּא אוֹמֵר הֵין. וְהִיא נוֹתֶנֶת לוֹ וְהוּא שׁוֹתֶה. כֵּיוָן שֶׁהוּא שׁוֹתֶה הָיָה הַיַּיִן בּוֹעֵר בּוֹ כִכְרִיסָה שֶׁלְּעַכְנָה. וְהוּא אוֹמֵר לָהּ. הִישָּׁמְעִי לִי. וְהָיְתָה אוֹמֶרֶת לוֹ. הִינָּזֵר מִתּוֹרַת מֹשֶׁה וַאֲנִי נִשְׁמַעַת לָךְ. הָדָא הִיא דִכְתִיב הֵמָּה בָּאוּ בַעַל־פְּעוֹר וַיִּנָּזְרוּ לַבֹּשֶׁת וַיִּהְיוּ שִׁיקּוּצִים כְּאָהֳבָם׃ עַד שֶׁנַּעֲשׂוּ שִׁיקּוּצִים לַאֲבִיהֶם שֶׁבַּשָּׁמַיִם.

[199]But what did the evil Bileam do? Because he counseled Balaq ben Sippor to fell Israel by the sword. He told him, the God of this people hates whoring. If you put up your daughters for whoring, you may rule over them. He answered, but will they listen to me? He told him, put your own daughter up, they will see and listen to you. That is what is written[200]: *he is the head of related tribes in Midian.* What did they do? They built dining rooms[201] from Bet Hayyešimon[202] to the Snow Mountain[203] and installed there women selling pastries. They put an old woman outside and a young girl inside. Israel were eating and drinking. If one of them went to stroll around, to buy himself something from the grocer, the old woman would offer to sell to him for the going price, but the girl told him, come and take it for less. This happened that first day, the second day, the third day. After that, she told him, from now on you are like a member of the family; enter and select for yourself. When he entered, there was a pitcher full of wine, of the strong Ammonite

wine which seduces the body to whoring. Its smell was seething and (Gentile wine) [libation wine] was not yet forbidden for Israel[204]. She told him, maybe you want to drink a cup of wine? He answered her, yes. She gave to him and he drank. When he drank, the wine was burning in him like a viper's poison[205]; he told her, consent to me. She told him, do you want me to consent to you? He answered, yes. Immediately she took out a shape of Pe`or from her bosom and told him, bow down before this one and I shall consent to you. But he answered her, should I bow down before foreign worship? She told him, you do not bow down, you only strip for it. This is what the Sages said[206], "one who defecates in front of *Baal Pe`or* follows its worship. One who throws a stone at a statue of Mercury follows its worship."

[207]There was a pitcher full of wine, of the strong Ammonite wine which seduces the body to whoring. Its smell was seething and libation wine was not yet forbidden for Israel. She told him, maybe you want to drink a cup of wine? He answered her, yes. She gave to him and he drank. When he drank, the wine was burning in him like a viper's poison[205]; he told her, consent to me. She told him, do you want me to consent to you? He answered, yes. She told him, make a vow to deny the teachings of Moses and I shall consent to you. That is what is written[208]: *They came to Baal-Pe`or, made vows for the shame, and turned into abominations like their love life.*

199 *Sifry Num.* 131-132 (*Yalqut Hosea* 526). Slightly different formulations in *Tanhuma Balaq* 18, *Num. rabba* 20; Babli 106a. Referred to in *Pirqe R. Eliezer* 47.

200 *Num.* 25:15.

201 Latin *coenaculum* "upper storey room; dining room; garret". Secondary Babli קלעים "partition wall, partition gobelin".

202 In the biblical text בית הישימות.

203 The Hermon.

204 The text in parenthesis is the scribe's original text, the one in brackets his correction. Formally, the original text is the only correct one. Wine used in idolatrous libations is forbidden for all usufruct as חֵרֶם, *Deut.* 13:18. The prohibition of the consumption of other Gentile wine is attributed to Daniel (*Dan.* 1:8); it is not Mosaic. The corrected text and its parallel sequel adopt popular language which calls יֵין נֶסֶךְ what correctly should be called סְתָם יֵינָם "their unspecified wine".

205 Read כריסה.

206 Mishnah 7:12 (Notes 238,239).

207 Duplication of previous text.

208 *Hos.* 9:10.

(28d line 31) אָמַר רִבִּי לָעְזָר. מָה הַמַּסְמֵר הַזֶּה אֵי אֶפְשַׁר לוֹ לִפְרוֹשׁ מִן הַדֶּלֶת בְּלֹא עֵץ כָּךְ אֵי אֶפְשַׁר לִפְרוֹשׁ מִן הַפְּעוֹר בְּלֹא נְפָשׁוֹת. מַעֲשֶׂה בְּסוֹבְתָא מֵאוּלָם שֶׁהִשְׂכִּיר חֲמוֹרוֹ לְגוֹיָה אַחַת לְהִשְׁתַּחֲווֹת לִפְעוֹר. כֵּיוָן שֶׁהִגִּיעוּ לְבֵיתוֹ שֶׁלִּפְעוֹר אָמְרָה לוֹ. הַמְתֵּן לִי כָאן עַד שֶׁאִיכָּנֵס וְאֶשְׁתַּחֲוֶה לִפְעוֹר. כֵּיוָן שֶׁיָּצָאת אָמַר לָהּ. הַמְתִּינִי לִי כָּאן עַד שֶׁאִיכָּנֵס וְאֶעֱשֶׂה כְמוֹת שֶׁעָשִׂית. מֶה עָשָׂה. נִכְנַס וְעָשָׂה אֶת צְרָכָיו וְקִינַּח עַצְמוֹ בְחוֹטְמוֹ שֶׁלִּפְעוֹר. וְהָיוּ הַכֹּל מְקַלְּסִין לְפָנָיו וְאוֹמְרִין. לֹא עָשָׂה אָדָם כְּשֵׁם שֶׁעָשָׂה זֶה. מַעֲשֶׂה בִמְנַחֵם אִישׁ גּוּפְתָּא אֲרִיחַ שֶׁהָיָה מְגַלְגֵּל בְּחָבִיּוֹת וּבָא אֵלָיו שָׂרוֹ שֶׁלִּפְעוֹר בַּלַּיְלָה. מֶה עָשָׂה. נָטַל אֶת הַשְּׁפוּד וְעָמַד עָלָיו וּבָרַח מִמֶּנּוּ. בָּא אֵלָיו בַּלַּיְלָה הַשֵּׁינִי אָמַר לוֹ. מְנַחֵם. מַה אַתָּה מְקַלְלֵנִי. נִתְיָירֵא מִמֶּנּוּ וְאָמַר לוֹ. עוֹד אֵינִי מְקַלְלָךְ. מַעֲשֶׂה בְשִׁלְטוֹן אֶחָד שֶׁבָּא מִמְּדִינַת הַיָּם לְהִשְׁתַּחֲווֹת לִפְעוֹר. אָמַר לָהֶן. הֲבִיאוּ לִי פַּר אֶחָד אַיִל אֶחָד כֶּבֶשׂ אֶחָד לְהִשְׁתַּחֲווֹת לִפְעוֹר. אָמְרוּ לוֹ. אֵין אַתָּה זָקוּק לְכָל־אֵילוּ. אֵין אַתְּ אֶלָּא כְמְגַלֶּה עַצְמָךְ לוֹ. מֶה עָשָׂה. גֵּירָה בָהֶם סניגורים וְהָיוּ מַכִּין אוֹתָן וּמְפַצְּעִין אֶת מוֹחֵיהֶן בְּגִיזִירִין וְאוֹמְרִים לָהֶן. אִי לָכֶם וּלְטָעוּתְכֶם.

Rebbi Eleazar said, just as a nail cannot be taken out of a door without [loss of] wood, so it is impossible to get rid of *Pe`or* without [loss of] life.

It happened that Sabbatai from Ulam leased his donkey to a Gentile woman to bow down before *Pe`or*. When they arrived at *Pe`or's* temple, she told him, wait here for me while I am entering and bowing down before *Pe`or*. After she came out, he told her, wait here for me while I am entering and do what you did. What did he do? He entered, relieved himself, and cleansed himself on *Pe`or*'s nose. All were praising him and said, nobody yet had done what this man did[209].

It happened that Menaḥem from Guvta-Ariaḥ was occupied with amphoras when the spirit of *Pe`or* came to him in the night. What did he do? He took a spit, stood up against him; he fled. He came to him in the second night and asked him, Menaḥem, why do you curse me? He was afraid of him and promised him, I shall not curse you in the future[210].

It happened that a ruler came from overseas to bow down before *Pe`or*. He told them, bring one bull, one ram, and one sheep, to bow down before *Pe`or*. They told him, you have no need for all of these; you only have to strip yourself for him. What did he do? He provoked סניגורים[211] against them; they were hitting them and smashing their brains with bats, saying to them: woe to you and your error.

209 He committed a deadly sin of idol worship while intending to debase the idol.

210 The story is fragmentary. It may be influenced by Christian beliefs that the old gods were turned into demons.

211 Elsewhere, סניגור is συνήγορος "advocate, intercessor". In *Sifry* סנגדודים, in *Yalqut* סנגלרים. According to the context, pretorians must be intended.

(28d line 48) כְּתִיב וַיִּחַר־אַף יי בְּיִשְׂרָאֵל׃ וַיֹּאמֶר יי אֶל־מֹשֶׁה קַח אֶת־כָּל־רָאשֵׁי הָעָם וְהוֹקַע אוֹתָם לַיי נֶגֶד הַשָּׁמֶשׁ. אָמַר לוֹ. הוֹשֵׁב אֶת רָאשֵׁיהֶם דַּייָנִים עֲלֵיהֶם וִיהִיוּ הוֹרְגִים בַּחַטָּאִים נֶגֶד הַשֶּׁמֶשׁ. הָדָא הִיא דִכְתִיב וַיֹּאמֶר מֹשֶׁה אֶל־שׁוֹפְטֵי יִשְׂרָאֵל הִרְגוּ אִישׁ אֲנָשָׁיו הַנִּצְמָדִים לְבַעַל פְּעוֹר׃ כַּמָּה הֵם שׁוֹפְטֵי יִשְׂרָאֵל. שֶׁבַע רִיבּוֹא וּשְׁמוֹנַת אֲלָפִים וְשֵׁשׁ מֵאוֹת. שָׂרֵי אֲלָפִים שֵׁשׁ מֵאוֹת. שָׂרֵי מֵאוֹת שֵׁשֶׁת אֲלָפִים. שָׂרֵי חֲמִשִּׁים שְׁנֵים עָשָׂר אֶלֶף. שָׂרֵי עֲשָׂרוֹת שִׁשִּׁים אֶלֶף. נִמְצְאוּ שׁוֹפְטֵי יִשְׂרָאֵל שֶׁבַע רִיבּוֹא וּשְׁמוֹנַת אֲלָפִים וְשֵׁשׁ מֵאוֹת. אָמַר לוֹן. כָּל־חַד מִינְּכוֹן יִקְטוֹל תְּרֵיי. נִמְצְאוּ הוֹרְגִין חֲמֵשׁ עֶשְׂרֵה רִיבּוֹא וְשִׁבְעַת אֲלָפִים וּמָאתַיִם. וְהִנֵּה אִישׁ מִבְּנֵי יִשְׂרָאֵל בָּא וַיַּקְרֵב אֶל־אֶחָיו אֶת־הַמִּדְיָינִית לְעֵינֵי מֹשֶׁה. מָהוּ לְעֵינֵי מֹשֶׁה. כְּאִינַשׁ דָּמַר. הָא גַו עֵינָךְ מֹשֶׁה. אֲמַר לוֹ. אֵין צִיפּוֹרָה מִדְיָנִית וְאֵין טְלוֹפֶיהָ סְדוּקוֹת. זוֹ טְהוֹרָה וְזוֹ טְמֵיאָה. וְהָיָה שָׁם פִּינְחָס. אָמַר. אֵין כָּאן אָדָם שֶׁיְּהַרְגֶּנּוּ וִיהָרֵג עַל יָדוֹ. אֵיכָן הֵן הָאֲרָיוֹת. גּוּר אַרְיֵה יְהוּדָה. דָּן גּוּר אַרְיֵה. בִּנְיָמִין זְאֵב יִטְרָף. כֵּיוָן שֶׁרָאָה פִינְחָס שֶׁאֵין אָדָם מִיִּשְׂרָאֵל עוֹשֶׂה כְלוּם. מִיָּד עָמַד פִּינְחָס מִתּוֹךְ סַנְהֶדְרִין שֶׁלּוֹ וְלָקַח אֶת הָרוֹמַח בְּיָדוֹ וְנָתַן אֶת הַבַּרְזֶל תַּחַת פַּסִיקִיָּא שֶׁלּוֹ. הִתְחִיל מִסְתַּמֵּךְ עַל עֵץ שֶׁלָּהּ עַד שֶׁהִגִּיעַ לְפִתְחוֹ. כֵּיוָן שֶׁהִגִּיעַ לְפִתְחוֹ אָמְרוּ לוֹ. מֵאַיִין וּלְאַיִין פִּינְחָס. אָמַר לָהֶן. אֵין אַתֶּם מוֹדִין לִי שֶׁשִּׁבְטוֹ שֶׁלְּלֵוִי אֵצֶל שִׁבְטוֹ שֶׁלְּשִׁמְעוֹן בְּכָל־מָקוֹם. אָמְרוּ. הַנִּיחוּ לוֹ שֶׁמָּא הִתִּירוּ פְרוּשִׁים אֶת הַדָּבָר. כֵּיוָן שֶׁנִּכְנַס עָשָׂה לוֹ הַקָּדוֹשׁ בָּרוּךְ הוּא שִׁשָּׁה נִיסִּים. הַנֵּס הָרִאשׁוֹן. דַּרְכָּן לִפְרוֹשׁ זֶה מִזֶּה וְהִדְבִּיקָן הַמַּלְאָךְ זֶה לָזֶה. הַנֵּס הַשֵּׁינִי. כִּיוֵּין אֶת הָרוֹמַח כְּנֶגֶד הַקֵּיבָה שֶׁלָּהּ כְּדֵי שֶׁתְּהֵא זַכְרוּתוֹ נִרְאֵית מִתּוֹךְ קֵיבָהּ שֶׁלָּהּ מִפְּנֵי הַנּוֹקְרָנִין שֶׁלֹּא יְהוּ אוֹמְרִים. אַף הוּא בֵּין כְּתֵיפָיו נִכְנַס עִמָּהֶן וְעָשָׂה אֶת צְרָכָיו. הַנֵּס הַשְּׁלִישִׁי. סָתַם הַמַּלְאָךְ אֶת פִּיהֶן וְלֹא הָיוּ יְכוֹלִין לִצְווֹחַ. הַנֵּס הָרְבִיעִי. לֹא נִשְׁמְטוּ מִן הַזַּיִין אֶלָּא עָמְדוּ בִמְקוֹמָן. הַנֵּס הַחֲמִישִׁי. הִגְבִּיעַ לוֹ הַמַּלְאָךְ אֶת הַשְּׁקוֹף כְּדֵי שֶׁיֵּצְאוּ שְׁנֵיהֶן בֵּין כְּתֵיפָיו. הַנֵּס הַשִּׁישִׁי. כֵּיוָן שֶׁיָּצָא אֶת הַנֶּגֶף שֶׁהוּא מְחַבֵּל בָּעָם מֶה עָשָׂה. הִשְׁלִיכָן לָאָרֶץ וְעָמַד וְנִתְפַּלֵּל. הָדָא הִיא דִכְתִיב וַיַּעֲמוֹד פִּינְחָס וַיְפַלֵּל וַתֵּעָצַר הַמַּגֵּפָה.

It is written[212] *The rage of the Eternal was kindled against Israel. The Eternal said to Moses: Take all the heads of the people and hang them for the Eternal before the sun.* What he told him was, install their heads as judges over them and let them execute the sinners[213] at daytime. That is what is written: *Moses told the judges of Israel: each one should kill his men who cling to the Ba`al Pe`or*[214]. How many were the judges of Israel[215]? 78'600. Heads of thousands, 600. Heads of hundreds, 6'000. Heads of fifties, 12'000.

heads of tens, 60'000. It turns out that the judges of Israel were 78'600. He told them, each of you should execute two. It turns out that the number of the killed was 157'200.

Behold, a man from the Children of Israel came and introduced to his brothers the Midianite woman, to the eyes of Moses[216]. What means *to the eyes of Moses*[217]? Like a man who says, that is in your eyes, Moses. He told him, is not Zippora a Midianite, and are not her hooves split[218]? This one is pure, that one is impure? There, Phineas was present. He said, is there nobody who would kill him or be killed? Where are the lions? *A lion whelp is Jehudah*[219]*; Dan is a lion whelp*[220]*; Benjamin a rapacious wolf*[221]. When Phineas saw that nobody of Israel did anything, he immediately rose from his court, took the spear in his hand, and put its iron under his belt[222]. He was leaning on its wood until he arrived at his door. When he arrived at his[223] door, they[224] asked him, where to, Phineas? He said to them, do you not agree that everywhere the tribe of Levi is with the tribe of Simeon? They said, let him, maybe the Pharisees permitted the matter[225]. When he entered, the Holy One, praise to Him, performed six wonders for him[226]. The first miracle: usually they would separate, but the angel glued the one to the other[227]. The second miracle: He directed the spear into her belly to that his penis should be seen inside her belly because of the fault-finders, lest they say that he muscled himself in with them and satisfied himself[228]. The third miracle: the angel closed their mouths, so they could not cry. The fourth miracle: they did not slip from the weapon but stayed in place. The fifth miracle: The angel lifted the lintel so that both of them were carried out between his shoulders. The sixth miracle: When the plague started to destroy the people, what did he do? He threw them on the ground and prayed. That is what is written: *Phineas stood and prayed; the plague was arrested*[229].

212 *Num.* 25:3-4.

213 Not the heads; cf. the Targumim.

214 *Num.* 25:5.

215 Halakhah 1:7, Note 356.

216 *Num.* 25:6.

217 The text does not say *before his eyes* but *in his eyes*.

218 The sign of a kosher animal.

219 *Gen.* 49:9.

220 *Deut.* 33:22.

221 *Gen.* 49:27.

222 Latin *fascia* "band, girdle".

223 Zimri ben Salu's.

224 The tribe of Simon, protecting their

head.

225 Echoing a popular opinion that the "oral law" can be made to adapt to all circumstances, moral or immoral.

226 Babli 82b, in the name of R. Johanan.

227 If they were not killed in the act, the killing would have been murder.

228 In the Babli: Thus Phineas had direct proof in court that the killing was justified. Phineas's act established a rule of law which could never be used again.

229 *Ps.* 106:30.

(29a line 2) כְּשֶׁבָּאוּ יִשְׂרָאֵל לִנְקוֹם נִקְמַת מִדְיָן מָצְאוּ שָׁם בִּלְעָם בֶּן בְּעוֹר. וְכִי מַה בָא לַעֲשׂוֹת. בָּא לִיטּוֹל שְׂכַר עֶשְׂרִים וְאַרְבָּעָה אֶלֶף שֶׁמֵּתוּ מִיִּשְׂרָאֵל עַל יָדוֹ בַשִּׁיטִּים. אֲמַר לֵיהּ פִּינְחָס. לָא דְבָרְייָךְ עֲבַדְתְּ וְלָא דְבָלָק עֲבַדְתְּ. לָא דְבָרְייָךְ עֲבַדְתְּ. דָּמַר לָךְ. לָא תֵיזִיל עִם שְׁלוּחֵי בָלָק וַאֲזַלְתְּ. וְלָא דְבָלָק עֲבַדְתְּ. דַּאֲמַר לָךְ. אֵיְזִיל לַיֵּיט יִשְׂרָאֵל וּבֵרַכְתְּנוּן. אַף אֲנִי אֵינִי מְקַפְּחָךְ שְׂכָרָךְ. הָדָא הִיא דִכְתִיב וְאֶת־בִּלְעָם בֶּן־בְּעוֹר הַקּוֹסֵם הָרְגוּ בְנֵי־יִשְׂרָאֵל עַל חַלְלֵיהֶם. מָהוּ עַל חַלְלֵיהֶם. שֶׁהָיָה שָׁקוּל כְּנֶגֶד כָּל־חַלְלֵיהֶם. דָּבָר אַחֵר. עַל חַלְלֵיהֶם. מַה חַלְלֵיהֶם אֵין בָּהֶן מַמָּשׁ אַף הוּא אֵין בּוֹ מַמָּשׁ. דָּבָר אַחֵר. עַל חַלְלֵיהֶם. שֶׁהָיָה צָף כְּנֶגֶד כָּל־חַלְלֵיהֶם. וְהָיָה פִּינְחָס מַרְאֶה לוֹ אֶת הַצִּיץ וְהוּא שׁוֹקֵעַ וְיוֹרֵד. דָּבָר אַחֵר. עַל חַלְלֵיהֶם. אֶלָּא מְלַמֵּד שֶׁנָּתְנוּ לוֹ יִשְׂרָאֵל שְׂכָרוֹ מוּשְׁלָם וְלֹא קִיפְּחוּהוּ.

When Israel came to exact vengeance from Midian, they found there Bileam ben Beor. What did he do there? He came to collect his wages for the 24'000 of Israel who died at Shittim. Phineas told him, you followed neither your Creator nor Balaq. You did not follow your Creator, Who told you, do not go with Balaq's emissaries, but you went. You did not follow Balaq who told you to come and curse Israel, but you blessed them. I also will not hold back your wages. That is what is written: *The Children of Israel slew Bileam ben Beor the sorcerer on top of their slain*[230]. What means *on their slain*? That he was as important as all their slain. Another explanation, *on their slain*. Just as their slain were irrelevant, so he was irrelevant. Another explanation, *on their slain*. He was flying over their corpses, but Phineas showed him the [High Priest's] diadem and he fell down. Another explanation, *on their slain*. This teaches that Israel paid him his wages in full and did not hold back.

230 *Jos.* 13:22. The masoretic text, as represented by the Aleppo and Leningrad codices, reads אל־חלליהן, not על־. One finds על־חלליהן in *Num.* 31:8, not referring to Bileam but to the five tribal heads of Midian which in *Num.* are titled "kings" but in *Jos.* "princes of Sihon". *Jos.* describes the situation before the arrival of the Children of

Israel, *Num.* the actual situation after the fall of Sihon. One may read the following explanations as a polemic against opinions like that of M. Noth (*Das Buch Josua, Tübingen* 1938, p. 50) that אל־חלליהן is a gloss, taken from *Num.* 31:8 and inserted in the wrong place.

(29a line 14) דּוֹאֵג אָדָם גָּדוֹל בַּתּוֹרָה הָיָה. בָּאוּ יִשְׂרָאֵל וְשָׁאֲלוּ אֶת דָּוִד. לֶחֶם הַפָּנִים מָהוּ שֶׁיִּדְחֶה אֶת הַשַּׁבָּת. אָמַר לָהֶם. סִידּוּרוֹ דּוֹחֶה אֶת הַשַּׁבָּת לֹא לִישָׁתוֹ וְלֹא עֲרִיכָתוֹ דּוֹחִין אֶת הַשַּׁבָּת. וְהָיָה שָׁם דּוֹאֵג וְאָמַר. מִי הוּא זֶה שֶׁבָּא לְהוֹרוֹת לְפָנַיי. אָמְרוּ לוֹ דָּוִד בֶּן יִשַׁי הוּא. מִיָּד הָלַךְ וְנָתַן עֵצָה לְשָׁאוּל מֶלֶךְ יִשְׂרָאֵל לְהָמִית אֶת נוֹב עִיר הַכֹּהֲנִים. הָדָא הִיא דִכְתִיב וַיֹּאמֶר הַמֶּ֜לֶךְ לָֽרָצִ֣ים הַנִּצָּבִ֣ים עָלָ֗יו ס֣וֹבּוּ וְהָמִ֣יתוּ ׀ כֹּהֲנֵ֣י יי כִּ֤י גַם־יָדָם֙ עִם־דָּוִ֔ד וגו' עַד וְלֹ֥א גָל֖וּ אֶת־אָזְנָ֑יו. מִי הָיוּ. אָמַר רִבִּי שְׁמוּאֵל בַּר רַב יִצְחָק. אַבְנֵר וַעֲמָשָׂא הָיוּ. אָמְרוּ לוֹ. כְּלוּם אִית לָךְ עֲלֵינָן אֶלָּא הָדֵין זוֹנָרָה וְהָדֵין כלינירין. הָא טְרֵיפִין לָךְ. וְלֹֽא־אָב֞וּ עַבְדֵ֤י הַמֶּ֙לֶךְ֙ לִשְׁלֹ֣חַ אֶת־יָדָ֔ם בְּכֹהֲנֵ֖י יי׃ וַיֹּ֨אמֶר הַמֶּ֜לֶךְ לְדוֹיֵ֗ג. אָמַר רִבִּי יְהוּדָה בַּר פָּזִי. לְדוֹיֵג כְּתִיב. אָמְרוּ לוֹ. מִתְפַּשְׂתָּה כְדָג. אַתָּה עֲבַרְתָּה רַבְּתָה. סֹ֣ב אַתָּ֔ה וּפְגַ֖ע בַּכֹּהֲנֵ֣י יי. וַיִּסֹּ֞ב דּוֹאֵ֣ג הָאֲדֹמִ֗י וַיִּפְגַּע֙ בַּכֹּ֣הֲנִ֔ים וגו'. לֹא כֵן תַּנֵּי רִבִּי חִייָה. אֵין מְמַנִּין שְׁנֵי כֹהֲנִים גְּדוֹלִים כְּאַחַת. אֶלָּא מְלַמֵּד שֶׁהָיוּ כוּלָּם רְאוּיִין לִהְיוֹת כֹּהֲנִים גְּדוֹלִים. כֵּיצַד נִתְרָחֵק. רִבִּי חֲנִינָה וְרִבִּי יְהוֹשֻׁעַ בֶּן לֵוִי. חַד אָמַר. אֵשׁ יָצְאָה מִבֵּית קוֹדֶשׁ הַקֳּדָשִׁים וְלִיהֲטָה סְבִיבוֹתָיו. וְחָרָנָה אָמַר. תַּלְמִידִים וַתִּיקִים נִזְדַּוְּוגוּ לוֹ וְהָיוּ לְמֵידִים וְהוּא שָׁכַח. לְקַיֵּים מַה שֶּׁנֶּאֱמַר חַ֣יִל בָּ֭לַע וַיְקִאֶ֑נּוּ מִ֝בִּטְנ֗וֹ יֹרִשֶׁ֥נּוּ אֵֽל׃

Doëg was a man great in Torah. Israel came and asked David, does the showbread supersede the Sabbath[231]? He told them, its arrangement supersedes the Sabbath, but neither its kneading nor its forming supersedes the Sabbath. Doëg was there and said, who is the one who comes to instruct in my presence[232]? They told him, it is David ben Jesse. He went immediately and counseled Saul, the king of Israel, to kill the priests of Nob, the city of priests. This is what is written[233]: *The king said to the runners who stood by him, surround and kill the priests of the Eternal for they also are involved with David,* etc., up to *they did not inform me.* Who were they? Rebbi Samuel bat Rav Isaac said, they were Abner and Amasa. They told him, you have us indebted to you only for this belt[234] and this כלינירין[235]. Here they are torn for you. [233]*The king's servants did not want to kill the priests of the Eternal. The king said to Doyeg.* Rebbi Jehudah bar Pazi said, it is written *to Doyeg*. They told him, you are caught like a fish; you committed a great sin[236]. [237]*Turn you and smite the priests of the Eternal. Doëg the Edomite turned and smote the priests,* etc. But did not Rebbi Hiyya state, "one does not appoint two High Priests together"? But this teaches that all of them were qualified for the High Priesthood. How was he removed[238]? Rebbi Ḥanina and Rebbi Joshua ben Levi: One said, fire came from the Holiest of Holies[239] and burned around him. But the other said, competent students came to him, they were learning but he was forgetting[240], to confirm what is written[241]: *The property swallowed by him he throws up; God removes it from his belly.*

231 The only place where Doëg is mentioned is *IS.* 21-22. Since it is stated in 21:7 that David was given showbread still hot when removed from the Tent of Meeting, it must have been on the Sabbath (*Lev.* 24:8). Since the High Priest earlier had indicated misgivings about giving him holy bread, he must have convinced the High Priest by learned arguments that what he asked for was permitted.

232 It is implied that Doëg claimed status as the generations's teacher. That would make asking anybody else for religious instruction in his presence a deadly sin [*Gittin* 1:2 (Note 94), *Ševi`it* 6:1 (Notes 23-30).]

233 *IS.* 22:17.

234 Greek ζωνάριον, τό "belt".

235 According to *Arukh*, one should read כַּלִינָרִין χαλινάριον "bridle". Levy prefers to read כְּלָנִידִין χλανίδιον "upper garment, blanket." This fits better into the context. They tell the king that they do not need his salary.

236 In Chapter 21, he is called דואג, in Chapter 22 mostly דויג. This must be explained; the second form of the name is derived from דָּג "fish". The episode is an illustration of the maxim that calumny (לָשׁוֹן הָרַע) is a deadly sin.

237 *IS.* 22:18. It is stated that Doeg slew 85 men wearing the *ephod*, a vestment by pentateuchal rules appropriate only for the High Priest.

238 What visible sign was given that he had no part in the Future World.

239 *IS.* 21 makes it clear that there was a Holy Tent at Nob, even though the Ark was still at Qiryat Yearim.

240 Babli 106b.

241 *Job.* 20:15.

(29a line 31) אֲחִיתוֹפֶל אָדָם גִּיבּוֹר בַּתּוֹרָה הָיָה. כָּתוּב וַיֹּסֶף עוֹד דָּוִד אֶת־כָּל־בָּחוּר בְּיִשְׂרָאֵל שְׁלֹשִׁים אָלֶף׃ רִבִּי בֶּרֶכְיָה בְּשֵׁם רִבִּי אַבָּא בַּר כָּהֲנָא. תִּשְׁעִים אֶלֶף זְקֵינִים מִינָּה דָּוִד בְּיוֹם אֶחָד וְלֹא מִינָּה אֲחִיתוֹפֶל עִמָּהֶן. הָדָא הִיא דִכְתִיב וַיֹּסֶף עוֹד דָּוִד אֶת־כָּל־בָּחוּר בְּיִשְׂרָאֵל שְׁלֹשִׁים אָלֶף׃ וַיֹּסֶף תַּלְתִּין. עוֹד תַּלְתִּין. וּפְשׁוּטֵי דִקְרִייָה תַּלְתִּין. הֲרֵי תִשְׁעִין. אַתְּ מוֹצֵא בְשָׁעָה שֶׁבָּא דָוִד לָשֵׂאת אֶת אֲרוֹן בְּרִית יי לֹא נְשָׂאוֹ כַתּוֹרָה. וַיַּרְכִּבוּ אֶת־אֲרוֹן בְּרִית הָאֱלֹהִים עַל עֲגָלָה חֲדָשָׁה וגו'. וַהֲוָה אֲרוֹנָא טָעִין כָּהֲנַיָּא לְרוּמָא וּטְרִיף לוֹן לְאַרְעָא. טָעִין כָּהֲנַיָּא לְרוּמָא וּטְרִיף לוֹן לְאַרְעָא. שְׁלַח דָּוִד וְאַיְיתֵי לַאֲחִיתוֹפֶל. אֲמַר לֵיהּ. לֵית אַתְּ אֲמַר לִי מַה לְדֵין אֲרוֹנָה דוּ טָעִין

כָּהֲנַייָא לְרוּמָא וּטְרִיף לוֹן לְאַרְעָא. טְעִין כָּהֲנַייָא לְרוּמָא וּטְרִיף לוֹן לְאַרְעָא. אֲמַר לֵיהּ. שְׁלַח שְׁאַל לְאִילֵּין חֲכִימַיָּא דִמְנִיתָא. אֲמַר דָּוִד. מָאן דִּיָדַע לְמִקְמְתָא וְלָא מִיקְמָהּ יְהֵא סוֹפֵיהּ מִתְחַנְקָא. אֲמַר דָּבָר קוֹמוֹי וְהוּא קָאִים. הָדָא הִיא דִכְתִיב וַיְהִ֗י כִּ֧י צָֽעֲד֛וּ נֹשְׂאֵ֥י אֲרוֹן־יי שִׁשָּׁ֣ה צְעָדִ֑ים וַיִּזְבַּ֥ח שׁ֖וֹר וּמְרִֽיא׃ רִבִּי חֲנִינָה וְרִבִּי מָנָא. חַד אָמַר. עַל כָּל־צְעִידָה וּצְעִידָה שׁוֹר וּמְרִיא וּבְסוֹף שִׁבְעָה פָרִים וְשִׁבְעָה אֵילִים. וְחָרָנָה אָמַר. עַל כָּל־צְעִידָה וּצְעִידָה שִׁבְעָה פָּרִים וְשִׁבְעָה אֵילִים וּבְסוֹף שׁוֹר וּמְרִיא. אֲמַר הַקָּדוֹשׁ בָּרוּךְ הוּא לַאֲחִיתוֹפֶל. מִילָּא דְּמַיינְקַייָא אָמְרִין בִּכְנִישְׁתָּא בְּכָל־יוֹם לָא אֲמַרְתְּ לֵיהּ. וְלִבְנֵ֥י קְהָ֖ת לֹ֣א נָתָ֑ן כִּֽי־עֲבֹדַ֤ת הַקֹּ֙דֶשׁ֙ עֲלֵהֶ֔ם בַּכָּתֵ֖ף יִשָּֽׂאוּ׃ וְדָא אֲמַרְתְּ לֵיהּ. וְכֵן אַתְּ מוֹצֵא בְּשָׁעָה שֶׁבָּא דָוִד לַחְפּוֹר תֵּימֶלְיוֹסִים שֶׁלְּבֵית הַמִּקְדָּשׁ חָפַר חֲמֵשׁ עֶשֶׂר מָאוּוָן דְּאַמִּין וְלָא אַשְׁכַּח תְּהוֹמָה וּבְסוֹפָא אַשְׁכַּח חַד עֲצִיץ וּבְעָא מִירְמִיתֵיהּ. אֲמַר לֵיהּ. לֵית אַתְּ יְכִיל. אֲמַר לֵיהּ. לָמָּה. אֲמַר לֵיהּ. דְּנָא הָכָא כְּבִישׁ עַל תְּהוֹמָה. אֲמַר לֵיהּ. וּמִן אֵימַת אַתְּ הָכָא. אֲמַר לֵיהּ. מִן שַׁעְתָּא דְּשַׁמַּע רַחֲמָנָא קָלֵיהּ בְּסִינַי אָנֹכִי יי אֱלֹהֶיךָ רְעָדַת אַרְעָא וְשׁוֹקַעַת וַאֲנָא יְהִיב הָכָא כְּבִישׁ עַל תְּהוֹמָא. אַף עַל גַּב כֵּן לָא שְׁמַע לֵיהּ. כֵּיוָן דִּירִימֵיהּ סְלִיק תְּהוֹמָה וּבְעָא מַטְפָּא עַלְמָא. וַהֲוָא אֲחִיתוֹפֶל קָאִים תַּמָּן. אֲמַר. כְּדוֹן דָּוִד מִתְחַנֵּק וַאֲנָא מְלִיךְ. אֲמַר דָּוִד. מָאן דַּחֲכַם דְּיָדַע מְקִימְתֵיהּ וְלָא מֵקִים לֵיהּ יְהֵא סוֹפֵיהּ מִתְחַנְקָא. אֲמַר מַה דַּאֲמַר וְאוּקְמֵיהּ. הִתְחִיל דָּוִד אוֹמֵר שִׁירָה. שִׁיר הַמַּעֲלוֹת. שִׁיר לְמֵאָה עוֹלוֹת. עַל כָּל־מֵאָה אַמָּה הָיָה אוֹמֵר שִׁירָה. אַף עַל גַּב כֵּן הֲוָה סוֹפֵיהּ מִתְחַנְקָה. אָמַר רִבִּי יוֹסֵי. הָדָא הִיא דְמַתְלָא אָמְרָה. צָרִיךְ בַּר נַשׁ חֲשִׁישׁ עַל לְוָטֵיהּ דְּרַבָּה אֲפִילוּ עַל מַגָּן. רִבִּי יִרְמְיָה בְשֵׁם רִבִּי שְׁמוּאֵל בַּר יִצְחָק. מְגִילָּה שֶׁמָּסַר שְׁמוּאֵל לְדָוִד אֲמָרָהּ אֲחִיתוֹפֶל בְּרוּחַ הַקּוֹדֶשׁ. וּמַה הֲוָה אֲחִיתוֹפֶל עֲבִיד. כַּד הֲוָה בַּר נַשׁ אֲזַל מִמְלַךְ בֵּיהּ הֲוָה אֲמַר לֵיהּ. אֵיזִיל עֲבִיד כֵּן וְהָכֵן. וְאִין לֵית אַתְּ מְהֵימָן לִי אֱזַל וּשְׁאִיל בְּאוּרִים וְתוּמִּים. וַהֲוָה אֲזַל שְׁאַל וּמַשְׁכַּח לֵיהּ כֵּן. הָדָא הִיא דִכְתִיב וַעֲצַ֣ת אֲחִיתֹ֗פֶל אֲשֶׁ֣ר יָעָץ֮ בַּיָּמִ֣ים הָהֵ֒ם כַּאֲשֶׁ֥ר יִשְׁאַל וגו' אִישׁ קְרֵי וְלָא כְתִיב. לֹא יָכְלוּ הַכְּתוּבִים לִקְרוֹתוֹ אִישׁ.

Aḥitophel was a man great in Torah. It is written[242]: *David again assembled all young men in Israel, 30'000.* Rebbi Berekhiah in the name of Rebbi Abba bar Cahana[243]: Ninety thousand Elders did David ordain on one day, but he did not ordain Aḥitophel with them[244]. That is what is written: *David again assembled all young men in Israel, 30'000.* He added, 30'000. Again, 30'000, and the simple sense of the verse, 30'000; together 90'000. You find that at the moment when David came to carry the Ark of the Eternal's Covenant, he did not carry it following the Torah[248]. *They moved the Ark of God's Covenant on a new car*[245], etc. The Ark lifted the Cohanim up and tore them down to the ground; lifted the Cohanim up and tore them down to the ground. David sent and brought Aḥitophel. He told him, can you not tell me why the Ark lifted the Cohanim up and tore them down to the ground, lifted the Cohanim up and tore them down to the ground? He answered, send and ask all the wise men whom you ordained. David said, any man who knows how to put this in order but does not put it in order should end up strangled. He said something in front of it and it was steadied. That is what is written[246]: *It was when the carriers of the Eternal's Ark took six steps that he sacrificed a bull and a fattened calf.* Rebbi Ḥanina and Rebbi Mana, one said, for every step a bull and a fattened calf and at the end seven oxen and seven rams; but the other said, for every step seven oxen and seven rams and at the end a bull and a fattened calf[247]. The Holy One, praise to Him, said to Aḥitophel: Something which the schoolchildren say every day in assembly you did not say to him: *to the Bene Qehat he did not give; for the service of the holy [vessels] is on them, they should carry on the shoulder*[248]. But so you told him.

[249]Similarly you find that when David started to excavate the foundations[250] of the Temple, he dug down fifteen hundred cubits and did not find the abyss. At the end he found a clay pot and wanted to lift it. It told him, you cannot lift me. We asked, why? It answered, because I am here suppressing the abyss. He asked it, since when are you here? It answered, from the Moment that the Merciful spoke on Sinai: *I am the Eternal, your God*[251], the earth trembled and sank down, and I was put here to suppress the abyss[252]. Nevertheless, he did not listen to it; when he lifted it the abyss rose and threatened to flood the world. Aḥitophel was standing there. He said, now David will be strangled and I shall rule. David said, any Sage who knows how to put this in order but does not put it in order should end up strangled. He said what he said[253] and it was steady. David started to sing *a song of ascent*, a song for a rise of 100 [cubits]. For each hundred cubits he composed a song. Nevertheless, he ended up strangled. Rebbi Yose said, that is what the proverb says, a person has to worry about the curse of a rabbi, even if it is for nothing[254].

Rebbi Jeremiah in the name of Rebbi Samuel bar Rav Isaac: The scroll which Samuel handed over to David, Aḥitophel composed it by the Holy Spirit[255]. What did Aḥitophel do? If anybody asked for his counsel in anything and he gave his advice, he said go and do such and such, and if you do not believe me ask the Urim and Tummim. He went, asked, and found it correct[256]. That is what is written[257]: *The counsel of Aḥitophel which he gave in those days,* etc. *Man* is read but not written[258]; the verses could not call him "a man.[259]"

242 *2S.* 6:1. The verse is written in military language but does not appear in a military context.

243 *Num. rabba* 4(21),12(25); *Midrash Samuel* 24(5).

244 Justifying Ahitophel's hatred of David. He had enough reason as Batseba's grandfather.

245 *2S.* 6:3.

246 *2S.* 6:13; *2 Chr.* 15:20. The two verses contradict one another.

247 To explain both verses (Note 246). Babli *Sotah* 35b.

248 *Num.* 7:9.

249 Differently Babli *Sukkah* 53a; hinted at *Makkot* 11a.

250 Greek θεμελίωσις; cf. *Sotah* 6:2 Note 17.

251 *Ex.* 20:2.

252 Cf. Babli *`Avodah zarah* 3a, *Midrash Tehillim* 74 #4. The reference is to *Ps.* 76:9: *The earth was fearful and quiet.* The earth was fearful because it was created on condition that Israel accept the Torah; when Israel accepted the Ten Commandments the earth became quiet since its continued existence was assured. The cover on the abyss sits on the waters of the Deluge (*Gen.* 7:11).

253 A magical spell.

254 *Babli* Berakhot 56a, *Makkot* 11a.

255 The blueprint for building the Temple (*1Chr.* 28:11).

256 *Midrash Tehillim* 3(4). (We do not find that the oracle could be used for anything but affairs of state.)

257 *2S.* 16:23.

258 Babli *Nedarim* 37b.

259 In *Midrash Tehillim* 3(4): "but an angel."

(29a line 71) כֵּיצַד נִתְרָחֵק. וַאֲחִיתֹפֶל רָאָה כִּי לֹא־נֶעֶשְׂתָה עֲצָתוֹ וַיַּחֲבוֹשׁ אֶת חֲמוֹרוֹ וגו'. שְׁלֹשָׁה דְבָרִים צִוָּה אֲחִיתוֹפֶל אֶת בָּנָיו. אָמַר לָהֶם. אַל תִּמְרְדוּ בְמַלְכוּת בֵּית דָּוִד. דְּאַשְׁכְּחָן דְּקוּדְשָׁא בְּרִיךְ הוּא נְסִיב לְהוֹן אַפִּין אֲפִילוּ בְּפַרְהֶסְיָא. וְאַל תִּשְׂאוּ וְתִתְּנוּ עִם מִי שֶׁהַשָּׁעָה מְשַׂחֶקֶת לוֹ. וְאִם הָיְתָה הָעֲצֶרֶת בְּרוּרָה זִרְעוּ חִטִּים יָפוֹת. וְלָא יָדְעִין אִם בְּרוּרָה בְטַל וְאִם בְּרוּרָה בְשָׁרָב.

How was he removed[238]? *When Aḥitophel saw that his counsel was not taken, he saddled his donkey*[260], etc.

Three things did Aḥitophel command his sons: Do not rebel against the dynasty of David, since we find that the Holy One, praise to Him, shows them favor even when they acted brazenly[261]. Do not have dealings with anybody who has a lucky streak[262]. And if Pentecost was clear, sow wheat of the best quality[263]. But we do not know whether clear from dew or clear from *šarav*[264].

260 *2S.* 17:23. He committed suicide; therefore his death could not scour off his sins, Note 29. A parallel to this paragraph is in the Babli, *Bava batra* 147a.

261 Greek παρρησία, as in the case of Batseba.

262 Since the other party would win in court or in contract negotiations.

263 The next fall planting season.

265 The dry wind from the East, Arabic *hamsin*.

(29b line 1) גֵּיחֲזִי אָדָם גִּיבּוֹר בַּתּוֹרָה הָיָה. אֶלָּא שֶׁהָיוּ בוֹ שְׁלֹשָׁה דְבָרִים. עַיִן צָרָה וּפָרוּץ בָּעֶרְוָה וְלֹא הָיָה מוֹדֶה בִתְחִיַּית הַמֵּתִים. עַיִן צָרָה. בְּשָׁעָה שֶׁהָיָה אֱלִישָׁע יְתִיב בְּתִינוּיֵיהּ הֲוָה גֵיחֲזִי יְתִיב לֵיהּ עַל תַּרְעָא וְתַלְמִידַיָּא חַמְיִין לֵיהּ וְאָמְרִין. גֵּיחֲזִי לָא אָעַל וַאֲנַן עָלִין. וַהֲוָה תַנָּיו מִתְאֲמַר וּבַר נַשׁ לָא מִתְהֲנֵי כְלוּם. כֵּיוָן שֶׁנִּתְרָחֵק מַה כְתִיב תַּמָּן. וַיֹּאמְרוּ בְנֵי־הַנְּבִיאִים אֶל־אֱלִישָׁע הִנֵּה־נָא (וגו') הַמָּקוֹם אֲשֶׁר אֲנַחְנוּ יוֹשְׁבִים שָׁם לְפָנֶיךָ צַר מִמֶּנּוּ׃ לָא אַסְחִין אוּכְלוּסַיָּא וְתַלְמִידַיָּא דַּהֲווֹן תַּמָּן.

[266]Gehazi was great in Torah, but three things were the matter with him: He was grudging, dissolute in sexual matters, and denied the Resurrection of the Dead.

Grudging. When Elisha sat and formulated his teachings, Gehazi sat outside the door. The students saw him and said, Gehazi did not find room inside, could we find room inside? His[267] statements were said without anybody profiting from them. Once he was removed, what is written there? *The prophecy students said to Elisha* (etc.,) *the place where we are sitting is too narrow for us*[268]. It does not contain the general population[269] and the students who were there.

266 Babli 107b.

267 Elisha's, who had no listeners.

268 *2K.* 6:1, the verse immediately following Gehazi's dismissal.

269 Greek ὄχλος, "multitude".

(29b line 9) וּפָרוּץ בָּעֶרְוָה. שֶׁכֵּן הַשּׁוּנַמִּית אוֹמֶרֶת לְאִישָׁהּ הִנֵּה־נָא יָדַעְתִּי כִּי אִישׁ אֱלֹהִים קָדוֹשׁ הוּא עוֹבֵר עָלֵינוּ תָּמִיד׃ אָמַר רִבִּי יוֹנָה. הוּא קָדוֹשׁ וְאֵין תַּלְמִידוֹ קָדוֹשׁ. אָמַר רִבִּי אָבוּן. שֶׁלֹּא הִבִּיט בָּהּ מִימָיו. וְרַבָּנִין דְּקַיְסָרִין אָמְרִין. שֶׁלֹּא רָאָת טִיפַּת קֶרִי עַל בְּגָדָיו מִיָּמָיו. אַמָּתֵיהּ דְּרִבִּי שְׁמוּאֵל בַּר רַב יִצְחָק אָמְרָה. אֲנָא הֲוֵינָא מְשַׁזְּגָה מָנוֹי דְמָרִי. מִן יוֹמוֹי לָא חֲמִית מִילָּא בִישָׁא בְּמָנוֹי דְמָרִי. כְּתִיב וַיִּגַּשׁ גֵּיחֲזִי לְהָדְפָהּ. מָהוּ לְהָדְפָהּ. אָמַר רִבִּי יוֹסֵי בֶּן חֲנִינָה. שֶׁנָּתַן יָדוֹ בְּהוֹד שֶׁבְּיָפְיָהּ. בֵּין דַּדֶּיהָ.

[270]Dissolute in sexual matters. For the woman of Shunem said to her husband: *Lo, I know that he is a holy man of God*[271]. Rebbi Jonah said, he is holy, but his student is not holy. Rebbi Abun said, because he never looked at her. But the rabbis of Caesarea say, he never had an involuntary emission. The slave girl of Rebbi Samuel ben Rav Isaac said, I was washing my master's garments. I never saw a bad thing on my master's garments. It is written: *Gehazi drew near to push her away*[272]. What is לְהָדְפָהּ? Rebbi Yose ben Hanina said, he put his hand on her beauty spot, between her breasts.

270 *Yebamot* 2:4 (Notes 81-85), *Lev. rabba* 24(6). The text here seems to be original since only here (and *Lev. rabba*) the observation of R. Samuel bar Rav Isaac's maid is given justification.

271 *2K*. 4:9.

272 *2K*. 4:27.

(29b line 16) וְלֹא הָיָה מוֹדֶה בִתְחִיַּית הַמֵּתִים. אַתְּ מוֹצֵא בְשָׁעָה שֶׁבָּא אֱלִישָׁע לְהַחֲיוֹת אֶת בְּנָהּ שֶׁלַּשּׁוּנָמִית אָמַר לוֹ קַח מִשְׁעַנְתִּי בְיָדְךָ וָלֵךְ כִּי תִמְצָא־אִישׁ לֹא תְבָרְכֶנּוּ וְכִי־יְבָרֶכְךָ אִישׁ לֹא תַעֲנֶנּוּ. וְהוּא לָא עֲבַד בֵּן אֶלָּא כַד פְּגַע בַּר נַשׁ וַאֲמַר לֵיהּ. מֵאַיִין וּלְאַיִין גֵּחֲזִי. ווּ אֲמַר לֵיהּ. אֲנָא אֲזִיל מְחַיֶּה מֵתִים. ווּ אֲמַר לֵיהּ. לֵית דִּמְחַיֶּה מֵתִים אֶלָּא הַקָּדוֹשׁ בָּרוּךְ הוּא. דִּכְתִיב בֵּיהּ יְי מֵמִית וּמְחַיֶּה מוֹרִיד שְׁאוֹל וַיָּעַל. אֲזַל לֵיהּ וְלָא עֲבַד כְּלוּם. אֲזַל לְגַבֵּיהּ אֲמַר לֵיהּ. אֲנָא יְדַע אִילוּ הֲוָה דָמִיךְ לָא הֲוָה מִיתְעַר עַל יָדָךְ.

And denied the Resurrection of the Dead. You find that at the time when Elisha came to resurrect the Shunamite's son, he told him[273]: *Take my support staff in your hand and go, and if you meet a man do not greet him, or if a person greets you do not answer him.* But he did not do that, but when a person met him and asked, from where and to where, Gehazi? He told him, I am going to resurrect the dead. This one would tell him, only the Holy One, praise to Him, can resurrect the dead, as it is written[274]: *The Eternal kills and gives life, brings down to the pit and lifts up.* He went there and did not do anything. He returned to him and said to him, I know that if he really were dead, he would not wake up through you.

273 *2K*. 4:29.

274 *1S*. 2:6.

(29b line 24) אַתְּ מוֹצֵא בְשָׁעָה שֶׁבָּא נַעֲמָן שַׂר צְבָא מֶלֶךְ אֲרָם אֵצֶל אֱלִישָׁע בָּא אֵלָיו בְּסוּסוֹ וּבְרִכְבּוֹ. אָמַר רִבִּי יוֹחָנָן. בְּסוּסוֹ כְתִיב. בְּעָא מִיתַּן לֵיהּ דְּהַב וּכְסַף אִסְטָלְוָון וּלְבוּשִׁין אֲבָנִים

טוֹבוֹת וּמַרְגָּלִיּוֹת. וְלֹא קִיבֵּל עָלָיו. הָדָא הִיא דִכְתִיב וַיִּפְצַר־בּוֹ לָקַחַת וַיְמָאֵן׃ אֲתָא גֵיחֲזִי וַאֲמַר חַי־יְי כִּי־אִם־רַצְתִּי אַחֲרָיו וְלָקַחְתִּי מֵאִתּוֹ מְאוּמָה׃ מוּמָה כְּתִיב. אֲזַל וּמָטָה בֵיהּ וּנְסַב מַה דִנְסַב וְאַטְמְרוֹן בְּעִילִיתֵיהּ. אֲתָא גַבֵּהּ אֱלִישָׁע. אֲמַר לֵיהּ. מֵאַיִן וּלְאַיִן גֵּחֲזִי. מֵיאַנְתָּה מַתַּן שְׂכָרָן שֶׁלַּצַּדִּיקִים. אֲמַר לוֹ. לֹא־הָלַךְ עַבְדְּךָ אָנֶה וָאָנָה׃ וַיֹּאמֶר לֹא־לִבִּי הָלַךְ כַּאֲשֶׁר הָפַךְ־אִישׁ מֵעַל מֶרְכַּבְתּוֹ לִקְרָאתֶךָ הַעֵת לָקַחַת כֶּסֶף וְזָהָב הָעֵת לַקַּחַת אֲבָנִים טוֹבוֹת וּמַרְגָּלִיּוֹת. לְפִיכָךְ צָרַעַת נַעֲמָן תִּדְבַּק־בְּךָ. כְּתִיב וְאַרְבָּעָה אֲנָשִׁים הָיוּ מְצוֹרָעִים פֶּתַח הַשָּׁעַר וגו'. וּמִי הָיוּ. רִבִּי יְהוּדָה בְּשֵׁם רַב. גֵּיחֲזִי וּשְׁלֹשֶׁת בָּנָיו הָיוּ.

You find [written] when Na`aman, the army commander of the king of Aram, came to him with his horses and his chariot. Rebbi Johanan said, it is written *with his horse*[275]. He wanted to give him gold and silver, stolas and garments, precious stones and pearls, but he did not accept. That is what is written[276]: *He insisted that he take, but he refused.* Gehazi came and said, *by the living Eternal, if I would run after him and take anything from him*[277]. "A defect" is written[278]. He went, met him, took what he took, and hid it in his upper storey. He came to Elisha, who asked him, *from where* to where, *Gehazi*? You refused the reward of the just[279]! He answered[280], *your servant did not go here or there. But he said, did not my thoughts go when a man turned from his carriage towards you; is it time* to take silver and gold; is it time to take precious stones and pearls? Therefore, *Na`aman's skin disease shall cling to you.* It is written[281]: *Four men afflicted with skin disease were at the door of the gate.* Who were they? Rebbi[282] Jehudah in the name of Rav: They were Gehazi and his three sons.

275 The actual *Ketib* in all sources of *2K.* 5:9.

276 *2K.* 5:16.

277 *2K.*5:20; *Num. rabba* 7(6). The invocation of the Name in a dishonest enterprise is blasphemy.

278 A *Ketib* מומה "its defect" for *Qere* מְאוּמָה "anything" is not in Eastern (Aleppo and Peterburg) codices but it is an old Ashkenazic (Rashi *ad loc.*) and Provençal [*Num. rabba* 7(6)] tradition; cf. Y.S.R. Norzi, מנחת שי *ad loc.*

279 He lost his reward in the Future World.

280 *2K.*5:23-24. In v. 24, Gehazi's skin disease is declared hereditary.

281 *2K.*7:3.

282 Read: *Rav* Jehudah. In the Babli (107b): R. Johanan.

(29b line 36) כְּתִיב וַיָּבֹא אֱלִישָׁע דַּמֶּשֶׂק וּבֶן־הֲדַד מֶלֶךְ־אֲרָם חֹלֶה וגו'. מָה אֲזַל בָּעֵי מֵיעֲבַד תַּמָּן. אֲזַל בָּעֵי מִקְרְבָא לְגֵיחֲזִי וְאַשְׁכְּחֵיהּ מוּחְלָט. מִיכָּן שֶׁדּוֹחִין בִּשְׂמֹאל וּמְקָרְבִין בְּיָמִין. אֲמַר רִבִּי

יוֹחָנָן. בַּחוּץ לֹא־יָלִין גֵּר דְּלָתַיי לָאוֹרַח אֶפְתָּח׃ מִיכָּן שֶׁדּוֹחִין בִּשְׂמֹאל וּמְקָרְבִין בְּיָמִין. לֹא כְשֵׁם שֶׁעָשָׂה אֱלִישָׁע שֶׁדְּחָה אֶת גֵּיחֲזִי בִּשְׁתֵּי יָדָיו. שְׁנֵי חֳלָאִים חָלָה אֱלִישָׁע. אֶחָד כְּדֶרֶךְ כָּל־הָאָרֶץ. וְאֶחָד שֶׁדָּחָה אֶת גֵּיחֲזִי.

It is written[283]: *Elisha came to Damascus when Ben-Hadad the king of Aram was sick.* What did he come to do there? He went to bring back Gehazi but found him absolutely impure[284]. From here that one should push away with one's left hand but bring back close with one's right. Rebbi Johanan said, *the stranger should not stay outside overnight; my doors I opened for the guest*[285]. From here that one should push away with one's left hand but bring back close with one's right. Not as Elisha did who pushed Gehazi away with both hands. Elisha was sick with two sicknesses[286]. One in the ways of the world, and one because he pushed Gehazi away.

283 *2K.* 8:7.

284 Most rules of skin-disease (*Lev.* 13:1-46) define two stages of the diagnosis. In the first one, the sufferer is quarantined (מֻסְגָּר). If he be found pure, a simple immersion in water will make him ritually pure. But if he was found impure after quarantine, he is *absolutely impure* and can regain purity only by the elaborate ceremony described in *Lev.* 14. For an inhabitant of the Northern kingdom, this would present almost insurmountable difficulties. (Na`aman as a Gentile did not need any ceremony.) Elisha is faulted for not helping Gehazi to repent and regain his purity.

285 *Job* 31:32.

286 In the Babli 107b: three sicknesses; the two mentioned here and an additional one for sending the bears against the children. In *2K.* 13:14 it is mentioned that Elisha fell ill "with the sickness which would cause his death". This implies that it was not his only sickness; he must have been sick at least twice.

(29b line 42) רִבִּי חֲנַנְיָה וְרִבִּי יְהוֹשֻׁעַ בֶּן לֵוִי. בְּשָׁעָה שֶׁנִּמְנוּ וְאָמְרוּ. שְׁלֹשָׁה מְלָכִים וְאַרְבָּעָה הֶדְיוֹטוֹת אֵין לָהֶם חֵלֶק לָעוֹלָם הַבָּא. יָצְתָה בַת קוֹל וְאָמְרָה הֲמֵעִמְּךָ יְשַׁלְּמֶנָּה כִּי־מָאַסְתָּ אֶלָּא כִּי־אַתָּה תִבְחַר וְלֹא־אָנִי וּמַה־יָּדַעְתָּ דַבֵּר׃ בִּקְשׁוּ לְצָרֵף אֶת שְׁלֹמֹה עִמָּהֶן. בָּא דָוִד וְנִשְׁתַּטֵּחַ לִפְנֵיהֶן. וְיֵשׁ אוֹמְרִים. אֵשׁ יָצָאת מִבֵּית קָדְשֵׁי הַקֳּדָשִׁים וְלִיהֲטָה סְבִיבוֹתֵיהֶם. הֲדַר עִילָּה. הֲוָה יְלִיף מַצְלֵי וּמִתְעַנֶּה. כֵּיוָן שֶׁנִּמְנָה עִמָּהֶן צְלֵי וְלָא אִיתְעֲנֵי. דּוֹרְשֵׁי רְשׁוּמוֹת אָמְרוּ. כּוּלְּהֶם יֵשׁ לָהֶם חֵלֶק לָעוֹלָם הַבָּא. מַה טַעַם. לִי גִלְעָד | וְלִי מְנַשֶּׁה וְאֶפְרַיִם מָעוֹז רֹאשִׁי יְהוּדָה מְחוֹקְקִי׃ מוֹאָב | סִיר רַחְצִי עַל־אֱדוֹם אַשְׁלִיךְ נַעֲלִי. לִי גִלְעָד זֶה אַחְאָב מֶלֶךְ יִשְׂרָאֵל שֶׁנָּפַל בְּרָמוֹת גִּלְעָד. לִי מְנַשֶּׁה כְּשְׁמוּעוֹ. אֶפְרַיִם מָעוֹז רֹאשִׁי זֶה יָרָבְעָם בֶּן נְבָט אֶפְרָתִי. יְהוּדָה מְחוֹקְקִי זֶה אֲחִיתוֹפֶל. מוֹאָב | סִיר רַחְצִי זֶה גֵיחֲזִי. עַל־אֱדוֹם אַשְׁלִיךְ נַעֲלִי זֶה דוֹאֵג הָאֲדוֹמִי. אָמְרוּ יִשְׂרָאֵל לִפְנֵי

הַקָּדוֹשׁ בָּרוּךְ הוּא. רִבּוֹן כָּל־הָעוֹלָמִים. מַה נַעֲבִיד וְדָוִד מֶלֶךְ יִשְׂרָאֵל מֵיקַל לוֹן. אַנְשֵׁי דָמִים וּמִרְמָה לֹא־יֶחֱצוּ יְמֵיהֶם. אֲמַר לוֹן. עָלַי לַעֲשׂוֹתָן רֵעִים אֵילּוּ לָאֵילּוּ. עָלַי־פְּלֶשֶׁת אֶתְרוֹעָע עָלַי פְּלֶשֶׁת הִתְרֹעָעִי׃ עָלַי לְפַלֵּשׁ לָהֶם מַעֲשִׂים טוֹבִים וְלַעֲשׂוֹתָן רֵיעִים אֵילּוּ לָאֵילּוּ.

[287]Rebbi Hanania and Rebbi Joshua ben Levi: at the time when they voted and said that three kings and four private persons had no part in the Future World, there came a disembodied voice and said[288], *does it pay for you that you oppose, that you choose, not I, and what can you say*[289]? They wanted to include Solomon with them[290]. David came and bowed down before them, but some say that fire came out of the Holiest of Holies and flared around them. Hadar Illa was used to be answered when he prayed. From the time he voted with them he prayed but was not answered. The interpreters of hints say, all of them have part in the Future World. What is the reason? *Mine is Gilead, mine is Manasse, Ephraim my main fortress, Jehudah is my scepter, Moab my washing trough, at Edom I shall throw my shoe*[291]. *Mine is Gilead,* that is Ahab, king of Israel, who fell at Ramot Gilead. *Mine is Manasse*, its plain meaning. *Ephraim my main fortress*, that is Jeroboam ben Nevat the Ephraimite. *Jehudah is my scepter*, that is Ahitophel. *Moab my washing trough*, that is Gehazi[292]. *At Edom I shall throw my shoe*, that is Doëg the Edomite. Israel said before the Holy One, praise to Him: Master of all Worlds, what can we do if David, King of Israel, cursed them? *Men of blood and deceit shall not live to half of their days*[293]! He told them, it is up to Me to make them friends one to the other. *For me Peleshet is friendly; to me Peleshet makes friends*[294]; it is up to Me to lead them to good deeds[295] and to make them friends one to the other.

287 *Num. rabba* 14(1).

288 *Job* 34:33.

289 It is presumptuous for a human theologian to pretend to know God's judgment.

290 Babli 104b.

291 *Ps*. 60:9-10, 108:9-10.

292 Whose sin was connected with Na'aman's washing.

293 *Ps*. 55:24. In the Babli, 69b, 106b, the verse is read as meaning that Doëg and Ahitophel did not live to age 35.

294 The root פלש in addition to "invade" can mean "to clear a path".

(fol. 27b) **משנה ג**: דּוֹר הַמַּבּוּל אֵין לָהֶם חֵלֶק לָעוֹלָם הַבָּא וְאֵין עוֹמְדִין בַּדִּין שֶׁנֶּאֱמַר לֹא יָדוֹן רוּחִי בָאָדָם לְעוֹלָם. אַנְשֵׁי סְדוֹם אֵין לָהֶם חֵלֶק לָעוֹלָם הַבָּא אֲבָל עוֹמְדִין בַּדִּין. רַבִּי נְחֶמְיָה אוֹמֵר, אֵילּוּ וָאֵילּוּ אֵינָן עוֹמְדִין בַּדִּין שֶׁנֶּאֱמַר עַל כֵּן לֹא יָקוּמוּ רְשָׁעִים בַּמִּשְׁפָּט וְחַטָּאִים בַּעֲדַת צַדִּיקִים. עַל כֵּן לֹא יָקוּמוּ רְשָׁעִים בַּמִּשְׁפָּט זֶה דּוֹר הַמַּבּוּל. וְחַטָּאִים בַּעֲדַת צַדִּיקִים אֵלּוּ אַנְשֵׁי סְדוֹם. אָמְרוּ לוֹ בַּעֲדַת צַדִּיקִים אֵינָן עוֹמְדִין אֲבָל עוֹמְדִין הֵן בַּעֲדַת רְשָׁעִים.

Mishnah 3: The generation of the Deluge has no part in the World to Come and they do not stand in judgment, as it is said[296]: *My Spirit shall not judge man forever*. The people of Sodom have no part in the World to Come but they stand in judgment. Rebbi Neḥemiah says, neither of them stands in judgment, as it is said[297]: *Therefore, evildoers shall not rise in judgment, nor sinners in the company of the just. Therefore, evildoers shall not rise in judgment,* that is the generation of the Deluge, *nor sinners in the company of the just,* these are the people of Sodom. They said to him, in the company of the just they will not rise; they will stand in the company of evildoers.

296 *Gen.* 6:3.

297 *Ps.* 1:5.

(29b line 59) **הלכה ג**: דּוֹר הַמַּבּוּל אֵין לָהֶם חֵלֶק לָעוֹלָם הַבָּא. וְאֵינָן רוֹאִין לְעָתִיד לָבוֹא. מַה טַעַם. וַיִּמַח אֶת־כָּל־הַיְקוּם בָּעוֹלָם הַזֶּה. וַיִּמָּחוּ מִן־הָאָרֶץ לְעָתִיד לָבוֹא.

Halakhah 3: "The generation of the Deluge has no part in the World to Come," and will not see the future[298]. What is the reason? [299]*He wiped off all that was standing* in this world; *they were wiped off from the Land*[300], in the future.

298 In contrast to most other sinners whose souls will take part in Eternal Life after having been punished for their sins, these souls will be completely destroyed. Babli 108a.

299 *Gen.* 7:23.

300 The double mention of "wiping off" in one verse implies that each of them must have another object. In Psalms, "the Land" usually refers to the Future Life; the Land of the Living to Paradise, the Land without attribute to the Netherworld.

(29b line 62) תַּנֵּי. רִבִּי נְחֶמְיָה אוֹמֵר. מִמַּשְׁמַע שֶׁנֶּאֱמַר לֹא־יָדוֹן רוּחִי בָאָדָם לְעוֹלָם. רִבִּי יְהוּדָה אוֹמֵר. לֹא יָדוֹן לוֹ רוּחִי. שֶׁאֵינִי נוֹתֵן רוּחִי בָהֶם בְּשָׁעָה שֶׁאֲנִי נוֹתֵן רוּחִי בִּבְנֵי אָדָם. רִבִּי שִׁמְעוֹן אוֹמֵר. לֹא יָדוֹן לוֹ רוּחִי. שֶׁאֵינִי נוֹתֵן רוּחִי בָהֶם בְּשָׁעָה שֶׁאֲנִי נוֹתֵן מַתַּן שְׂכָרָן שֶׁלַּצַּדִּיקִים. אֲחֵרִים אוֹמְרִים. לֹא יָדוֹן לוֹ רוּחִי. שֶׁאֵינִי מַחֲזִירָהּ לִנְדָנָהּ. רִבִּי יְהוֹשֻׁעַ בֶּן לֵוִי אָמַר. עִיקַּר זְרִיבָתָן

לַחוֹלְטָנִית. מַה טַעַם. בְּעֵת יְזוֹרְבוּ נִצְמָתוּ בְּחוּמּוֹ נִדְעֲכוּ מִמְּקוֹמָם: מָהוּ בְּחוּמּוֹ. בְּרִיתוּחָן. אָמַר רִבִּי יוֹחָנָן. כָּל־טִיפָּה וְטִיפָּה שֶׁהָיָה הַקָּדוֹשׁ בָּרוּךְ הוּא מוֹרִיד עֲלֵיהֶן הָיָה מַרְתִּיחָהּ בְּתוֹךְ גֵּיהִנָּם וּמוֹרִידָהּ עֲלֵיהֶן. הָדָא הִיא דִכְתִיב בְּחוּמּוֹ נִדְעֲכוּ מִמְּקוֹמָם: יְהוּדָה בֵּירִבִּי חִזְקִיָּה וְרִבִּי אָמְרִין. הַקָּדוֹשׁ בָּרוּךְ הוּא דָּן אֶת הָרְשָׁעִים בְּגֵיהִנָּם שְׁנֵים עָשָׂר חוֹדֶשׁ. כַּתְּחִילָּה הוּא מַכְנִיס בָּהֶן חֲכָךְ וְאַחַר כָּךְ הוּא מַכְנִיסָן לָאוּר וְהֵן אוֹמְרִים. הוֹי הוֹי. וְאַחַר כָּךְ הוּא מַכְנִיסָן לְשֶׁלֶג וְהֵן אוֹמְרִים. וַוי וַוי. מַה טַעַם. וַיַּעֲלֵנִי | מִבּוֹר שָׁאוֹן מִטִּיט הַיָּוֵן. מָהוּ מִטִּיט הַיָּוֵן. מְקוֹם שֶׁהֵן אוֹמְרִין בּוֹ הוֹי. וִיקַבְּלוּ דִינָם וִיהֵא לָהֶן חֵלֶק לָעוֹלָם הַבָּא. עַל שֵׁם וְלֵץ לֹא־שָׁמַע גְּעָרָה:

[301]It was stated: Rebbi Neḥemiah says, one understands it from what was said[296] *My Spirit shall not judge man forever*. Rebbi Jehudah says, *My Spirit shall not judge him*, for I shall not give My Spirit into them when I shall give My Spirit into people[302]. Rebbi Simeon says, *My Spirit shall not judge him*, for I shall not give My Spirit into them when I shall distribute the rewards of the just. Others say, *My Spirit shall not judge him*, I shall not bring it back into its sheath[303].

Rebbi Joshua ben Levi said, mainly their[304] scalding was parboiling. What is the reason? *At the time when they were scalded they shrank; in its heat they disappear from their place*[305]. What is *in its heat*? In their boiling. Rebbi Joḥanan said, every single drop which the Holy One, praise to Him, rained on them, He brought to a boil in Hell and rained it on them[306]. That is what is written, *in its heat they disappear from their place.*

Jehudah ben Rebbi Ḥizqiah and Rebbi[307] said, the Holy One, praise to Him, judges the evildoers in Hell for twelve months. First He brings the itch on them; then He brings them into fire and they say woe, woe; after that He brings them into snow and they say wai, wai. What is the reason? *He brought me up from the noisy pit, from miry mud*[308]. What is *from* יָוֵן *mud*? From a place where one says woe.

Why could they not receive their punishment[309] and then take part in the World to Come? Because *the scoffer will not hear rebuke*[310].

301 Babli 108a, Tosephta 13:6, *Gen. rabba* 26(6),28(3).

302 At the resurrection. The interpretations differ in formulation, not in meaning.

303 In the container where souls are kept to be born or resurrected.

304 The generation of the flood.

305 *Job* 6:17.

306 *Gen. rabba* 28(9) [M. Sokoloff, *The*

Geniza Fragments of Bereshit Rabba (Jerusalem 1982) p. 120].

307 Probably one should read "Jehudah and Hizqiah, the sons of R. Hiyya", or a name in missing here. In Mishnah *Idiut* 2:10, the Babli, *Šabbat* 33b, and *Thr. rabba* 1(42), the statement is anonymous. In *Gen. rabba* 28(7) it is attributed to R. Johanan, a student of Hizqiah.

The statement is the basis of the rule that prayers for deceased parents may be said only for 11 months, so as not to declare one's parents as evildoers.

308 *Ps.* 40:3.

309 This refers to the statement of the Mishnah that the people of the Deluge have no part in the World to Come, i. e., that their souls were destroyed.

310 Since the goal of punishment is reform, punishment of scoffers is useless. Their souls, instead of being punished, must be destroyed.

(29c line 1) אַנְשֵׁי סְדוֹם אֵין לָהֶם חֵלֶק לָעוֹלָם הַבָּא וְאֵינָן רוֹאִין לְעָתִיד לָבוֹא. מַאי טַעֲמָא. וְאַנְשֵׁי סְדוֹם רָעִים וְחַטָּאִים לַיי מְאֹד׃ רָעִים וְחַטָּאִים בָּעוֹלָם הַזֶּה. לַיי מְאֹד לְעָתִיד לָבוֹא. דָּבָר אַחֵר. רָעִים אֵילּוּ לָאֵילּוּ. וְחַטָּאִים בְּגִילּוּי עֲרָיוֹת. לַיי בַּעֲבוֹדָה זָרָה. מְאֹד בִּשְׁפִיכוּת דָּמִים.

[311]"The people of Sodom have no part in the World to Come," and they will not see the future. What is the reason? *The people of Sodom were very evil and sinful against the Eternal*[312]. *Evil and sinful* in this world, *against the Eternal very much* in the future.

[313]Another explanation. *Evil* against one another, *and sinful* in incest and adultery, *against the Eternal* in foreign worship, *very much* in spilling blood.

311 Babli 109a; Tosephta 13:8. The paragraph also is part of the Mishnah in the Babli and the independent Mishnah mss. not from the Maimonides tradition.

312 *Gen.* 13:13.

313 *Gen. rabba* 41(10).

(fol. 27b) **משנה ד׃** דּוֹר הַמִּדְבָּר אֵין לָהֶן חֵלֶק לָעוֹלָם הַבָּא וְאֵין עוֹמְדִין בַּדִּין שֶׁנֶּאֱמַר בַּמִּדְבָּר הַזֶּה יִתַּמּוּ וְשָׁם יָמֻתוּ דִּבְרֵי רִבִּי עֲקִיבָה. רִבִּי אֱלִיעֶזֶר אוֹמֵר עֲלֵיהֶם הוּא אוֹמֵר אִסְפוּ לִי חֲסִידָי כּוֹרְתֵי בְרִיתִי עֲלֵי זָבַח.

Mishnah 4: The generation of the desert has no part in the World to Come, as it is said[314]: *in this desert they shall be terminated and there they will die*, the words of Rebbi Aqiba. Rebbi Eliezer says, about them it says[315], *assemble for Me My lovely ones, who sealed My Covenant by a sacrifice*[316].

משנה ה: עֲדַת קוֹרַח אֵינָהּ עֲתִידָה לַעֲלוֹת שֶׁנֶּאֱמַר וַתְּכַס עֲלֵיהֶם הָאָרֶץ וַיֹּאבְדוּ מִתּוֹךְ הַקָּהָל דִּבְרֵי רִבִּי עֲקִיבָה. רִבִּי אֱלִיעֶזֶר אוֹמֵר עֲלֵיהֶם הוּא אוֹמֵר יי מֵמִית וּמְחַיֶּה מוֹרִיד שְׁאוֹל וַיָּעַל

Mishnah 5: The band of Korah will not be resurrected in the future, as it is said[317] *the earth covered them; they were lost from among the congregation*, the words of Rebbi Aqiba. Rebbi Eliezer says, about them it says[93], *the Eternal kills and brings to life, He sends down into the pit and raises up.*

314 *Num.* 14:35. The argument in the longer text of the Mishnah in the Babli is reproduced here at the start of the Halakhah. In all these cases, the double emphasis in the verse is interpreted that the first expression refers to this world, the second to the World to Come.

315 *Ps.* 50:5.

316 The ceremony described in *Ex.* 24:1-9 guaranteed their eternal life. Since R. Aqiba war R. Eliezer's student, the inversion of the chronological order clearly indicates that the latter's opinion is accepted as practice.

317 *Num.* 16:33.

(29c line 6) **הלכה ד:** דּוֹר הַמִּדְבָּר אֵין לָהֶן חֵלֶק לָעוֹלָם הַבָּא וְאֵינָן רוֹאִין לֶעָתִיד לָבוֹא. שֶׁנֶּאֱמַר בַּמִּדְבָּר הַזֶּה יִתַּמּוּ וְשָׁם יָמֻתוּ. יִתַּמּוּ בָּעוֹלָם הַזֶּה. וְשָׁם יָמוּתוּ לֶעָתִיד לָבוֹא. וְכֵן הוּא אוֹמֵר. אֲשֶׁר־נִשְׁבַּעְתִּי בְאַפִּי אִם יְבוֹאוּן אֶל־מְנוּחָתִי. דִּבְרֵי רִבִּי עֲקִיבָה. רִבִּי אֱלִיעֶזֶר אוֹמֵר עֲלֵיהֶם הוּא אוֹמֵר אִסְפוּ לִי חֲסִידָי כּוֹרְתֵי בְרִיתִי עֲלֵי זָבַח. רִבִּי יְהוֹשֻׁעַ אוֹמֵר. נִשְׁבַּעְתִּי וָאֲקַיֵּימָה. פְּעָמִים שֶׁאֵינִי מְקַיֵּים. חֲנַנְיָה בֶּן אֲחִי רִבִּי יְהוֹשֻׁעַ אוֹמֵר. כָּתוּב אֲשֶׁר־נִשְׁבַּעְתִּי בְאַפִּי. בְּאַפִּי נִשְׁבַּעְתִּי חוֹזֵר אֲנִי בִי. תַּנֵּי. רִבִּי שִׁמְעוֹן בֶּן מְנַסְיָה אוֹמֵר. עֲלֵיהֶם הוּא אוֹמֵר אִסְפוּ לִי חֲסִידָיי וגו'. חֲסִידָיי שֶׁעָשׂוּ עִמִּי חֶסֶד. כּוֹרְתֵי בְרִיתִי שֶׁנִּכְרְתוּ עַל יָדִי. עֲלֵי זָבַח שֶׁעִילּוּ אוֹתִי וְנִזְבְּחוּ עַל שְׁמִי. תַּנֵּי. רִבִּי יְהוֹשֻׁעַ בֶּן קָרְחָה אוֹמֵר. עַל הַדּוֹרוֹת הַלָּלוּ הוּא אוֹמֵר וּפְדוּיֵי יי יְשׁוּבוּן. רִבִּי אוֹמֵר. אֵילּוּ וָאֵילּוּ יֵשׁ לָהֶן חֵלֶק לָעוֹלָם הַבָּא. וּמַה טַעַם. וְהָיָה | בַּיּוֹם הַהוּא יִתָּקַע בְּשׁוֹפָר גָּדוֹל וּבָאוּ הָאוֹבְדִים בְּאֶרֶץ אַשּׁוּר. אֵילּוּ עֲשֶׂרֶת הַשְּׁבָטִים. וְהַנִּדָּחִים בְּאֶרֶץ מִצְרָיִם זֶה דוֹר הַמִּדְבָּר. אֵילּוּ וָאֵילּוּ וְהִשְׁתַּחֲווּ לַיי בְּהַר הַקּוֹדֶשׁ וּבִירוּשָׁלִָם:

Halakhah 4: [318]"The generation of the desert has no part in the World to Come," and will not see the future, as it is said: *in this desert they shall be terminated and there they will die. In this desert they shall be terminated*, in this world, *and there they will die, in the future*; and so He says[319], *what I swore in My rage, lest they come to My rest*, the words of Rebbi Aqiba. Rebbi Eliezer says, about them it says, *assemble for Me My lovely ones, who sealed My Covenant by a sacrifice.* Rebbi Joshua said, *I swore and I shall keep it*[320]; sometimes I do not keep it. Ḥanania the son of Rebbi Joshua's brother says, it is written: *what I swore in My rage;* I swore in My rage, I am changing My mind.

It was stated: Rebbi Simeon ben Menassia says, about them it says *assemble Me My lovely ones,* who performed acts of love for Me[321]. *The executors of My Covenant*, who were extirpated by Me. *By sacrifice*, they elevated me and were sacrificed for My name.

It was stated: Rebbi Joshua ben Qorha says, about these generations He says[322], *those freed by the Eternal shall return.* Rebbi says, these and those[323] have part in the World to Come. What is the reason? [324]*It shall be on that day, a great ram's horn will be blown, and those lost in the land of Assyria will come*, these are the Ten Tribes, *and those displaced in the land of Egypt,* that is the generation of the desert. These and those *will bow down before the Eternal on the Holy Mountain [and] in Jerusalem.*

318 Babli 110b, Tosephta 13:9-12.

319 *Ps.* 95:11.

320 *Ps.* 119:106; cf. *Eccl. rabba* 10(23) *ad* 10:20. In a more adequate context the verse is quoted in *Hagigah* 1:8.

321 In *Jer.* 2:1, the Exodus is described as an act of love of God.

322 *Is.* 35:10.

323 The generation of the desert and the Ten Tribes (Mishnah 6).

324 *Is.* 27:13; cf. *Eccl. rabba* 1(20).

(29c line 20) עֲדַת קוֹרַח אֵין לָהֶן חֵלֶק לָעוֹלָם הַבָּא וְאֵינָן רוֹאִין לְעָתִיד לָבוֹא. מַה טַעַם. וַתְּכַס עֲלֵיהֶם הַמִּדְבָּר בָּעוֹלָם הַזֶּה. וַיֹּאבְדוּ מִתּוֹךְ הַקָּהָל לְעָתִיד לָבוֹא. תַּנֵּי. רִבִּי יְהוּדָה בֶּן בְּתֵירָה אוֹמֵר. מִמַּשְׁמַע שֶׁנֶּאֱמַר תָּעִיתִי כְּשֶׂה אוֹבֵד בַּקֵּשׁ עַבְדֶּךָ. מָה עֲבֵידָה הָאֲמוּרָה לְהַלָּן סוֹפָהּ לְהִתְבַּקֵּשׁ אַף עֲבֵידָה הָאֲמוּרָה כָּאן סוֹפָהּ לְהִתְבַּקֵּשׁ.

[325]The band of Korah will not have part in the Future World and not be resurrected in the future. What is the reason? [317]*The desert covered them,* in this world; *they were lost from among the congregation*, in the future. It was stated: Rebbi Jehudah ben Bathyra says, one understands from what is said, *I erred like a lost sheep; look after Your servant*[326], that just as the lost object mentioned there at the end will be searched for, so also the lost object mentioned here at the end will be searched for[327].

325 *Babli* 109b, *Tosephta* 13:9.

326 *Ps.* 119:176.

327 By the doctrine of invariability of lexemes.

(29c line 25) מִי נִתְפַּלֵּל עֲלֵיהֶם. רִבִּי שְׁמוּאֵל בַּר נַחְמָן אָמַר. מֹשֶׁה נִתְפַּלֵּל עֲלֵיהֶם. יְחִי רְאוּבֵן וְאַל־יָמוֹת. רִבִּי יְהוֹשֻׁעַ בֶּן לֵוִי אָמַר. חַנָּה נִתְפַּלְלָה עֲלֵיהֶן. הִיא דְּרִבִּי יְהוֹשֻׁעַ בֶּן לֵוִי. דְּאָמַר רִבִּי רִבִּי יְהוֹשֻׁעַ בֶּן לֵוִי. כָּךְ הָיְתָה עֲדָתוֹ שֶׁלְּקֹרַח שׁוֹקַעַת וְיוֹרֶדֶת עַד שֶׁעָמְדָה חַנָּה וְנִתְפַּלְּלָה עֲלֵיהֶן וְאָמְרָה יי מֵמִית וּמְחַיֶּה מוֹרִיד שְׁאוֹל וַיָּעַל:

Who prayed for them? Rebbi Samuel bar Naḥman said, Moses prayed for them, *Reuben shall live and not die*[91]. [92]Rebbi Joshua ben Levi said, Hannah prayed for them. This follows Rebbi Joshua ben Levi, as Rebbi Joshua ben Levi said: Koraḥ's band was continuously sinking until Hannah stood up and said[93], *the Eternal kills and brings to life, He sends down into the pit and lifts up.*

(fol. 27b) **משנה ו**: עֲשֶׂרֶת הַשְּׁבָטִים אֵינָן עֲתִידִין לַחֲזוֹר שֶׁנֶּאֱמַר וַיַּשְׁלִכֵם אֶל אֶרֶץ אַחֶרֶת כַּיּוֹם הַזֶּה. מָה הַיּוֹם הַזֶּה הוֹלֵךְ וְאֵינוֹ חוֹזֵר אַף הֵן הוֹלְכִין וְאֵינָן חוֹזְרִין דִּבְרֵי רִבִּי עֲקִיבָה. רִבִּי אֱלִיעֶזֶר אוֹמֵר, כַּיּוֹם הַזֶּה מָה הַיּוֹם מַאֲפִיל וּמֵאִיר אַף הֵן כְּשֶׁהָיָה אֲפֵלָה לָהֶן עֲתִידָה לֵיאוֹר לָהֶן:

Mishnah 6: The Ten Tribes will not return in the future, as it is said[328], *He threw them into another country like this day*. As this day passes and does never return, so they go, never to return, the words of Rebbi Aqiba. Rebbi Eliezer says, *like this day,* as the day gets dark and then light, so also they for whom there was darkness there will be light in the future.

328 *Deut*. 29:27.

(29c line 29) **הלכה ו**: עֲשֶׂרֶת הַשְּׁבָטִים כול'. עֲשֶׂרֶת הַשְּׁבָטִים אֵין לָהֶן חֵלֶק לָעוֹלָם הַבָּא וְאֵינָן רוֹאִין לֶעָתִיד לָבוֹא. מַה טַעַם. וַיַּשְׁלִכֵם אֶל אֶרֶץ אַחֶרֶת כַּיּוֹם הַזֶּה. מָה הַיּוֹם הוֹלֵךְ וְאֵינוֹ חוֹזֵר אַף הֵן הוֹלְכִין וְאֵינָן חוֹזְרִין דִּבְרֵי רִבִּי עֲקִיבָה. רִבִּי שִׁמְעוֹן בֶּן יְהוּדָה אִישׁ כְּפַר אִכּוֹס אָמַר מִשּׁוּם רִבִּי שִׁמְעוֹן. אִם הָיוּ מַעֲשֵׂיהֶן כַּיּוֹם הַזֶּה אֵינָן חוֹזְרִין וְאִם לָאו חוֹזְרִין הֵן.

Halakhah 6: "The Ten Tribes," etc. [330]The Ten Tribes have no part in the World to Come, and will not see the future. What is the reason? *He threw them into another country like this day*. As the day passes and does never return, so they go, never to return, the words of Rebbi Aqiba. Rebbi Simeon ben Jehudah from Kefar-Ikos said in the name of Rebbi Simeon: If their behavior remains as on this day, they will not return; otherwise, they will return.

330 Babli 110b, Tosephta 13:12.

(29c line 34) רִבִּי חִזְקִיָּה רִבִּי אָבָּהוּ בְשֵׁם רִבִּי לָעְזָר. אִם בָּאִין הֵן גֵּירֵי צֶדֶק לְעָתִיד לָבוֹא אַנְטוֹלִינוּס בָּא בְרֹאשׁ כּוּלָּם. מָה אַתְּ שְׁמַע מִינָּהּ. שֶׁרָאוּ אוֹתוֹ יוֹצֵא בְמִנְעַל פָּחוּת בְּיוֹם הַכִּיפּוּרִים. אַתְּ שְׁמַע מִינָּהּ שֶׁכֵּן אֲפִילוּ יְרֵיאֵי שָׁמַיִם יוֹצְאִין בְּכָךְ. אִית מִילִּין אָמְרִין דְּלָא אִיתְגַּייַר אַנְטוֹלִינוּס. וְאִית מִילִּין אָמְרִין שֶׁנִּתְגַּייַר אַנְטוֹלִינוּס. אַנְטוֹלִינוּס אֲתָא גַבֵּי רִבִּי. אֲמַר לֵיהּ. חֲמִי מֵיכְלָתִי מִן לִוְיָתָן בְּעָלְמָא דַאֲתִי. אֲמַר לֵיהּ. אִין. אֲמַר לֵיהּ. מִן אִימַּר פִּיסְחָא לָא אוֹכְלְתָנִי וּמִן לִוְיָתָן מֵיכְלָתִי בְּעָלְמָא דַאֲתִי. אֲמַר לֵיהּ. וּמַה נַעֲבִיד לָךְ וּבְאִימַּר פִּיסְחָא כְּתִיב וְכָל־עָרֵל לֹא־יֹאכַל בּוֹ׃ הָדָא אָמְרָה דְּלָא אִיתְגַּייַר אַנְטוֹלִינוּס. כֵּיוָן דִּשְׁמַע כֵּן אֲזַל וְגַייַר גַּרְמֵיהּ. אֲתָא גַבֵּי רִבִּי. אֲמַר לֵיהּ. חֲמִי גְזֵירָתִי. אֲמַר לֵיהּ. בְּדִידִי לָא אִיסְתַּכְּלִית מִן יוֹמוֹי וּבְדִידָךְ אֲנָא מִסְתַּכְּלָא. הָדָא אָמְרָה דְּאִיתְגַּייַר אַנְטוֹנִינוּס. וְלָמָּה נִקְרָא רַבֵּינוּ הַקָּדוֹשׁ. שֶׁלֹּא הִבִּיט בְּמִילָתוֹ מִיָּמָיו. וְלָמָּה נִקְרָא שְׁמוֹ נָחוּם אִישׁ קוֹדֶשׁ קָדוֹשִׁים. שֶׁלֹּא הִבִּיט בְּצוּרַת מַטְבֵּעַ מִיָּמָיו. אַנְטוֹלִינוּס אֲתָא גַבֵּי רִבִּי. אֲמַר לֵיהּ. צְלִי עָלַי. אֲמַר לֵיהּ. יְשֵׁיזְבִינָךְ מִן הָדָא צִינְּתָא. דִּכְתִיב לִפְנֵי קָרָתוֹ מִי יַעֲמוֹד. אֲמַר לֵיהּ. רִבִּי. לֵית הָדָא צְלוֹ יַתִּיר. כִּיסִּיתִיךְ תִּכְסֶה וְהָא צִינְּתָא אָזְלָה. אֲמַר לֵיהּ. יְשֵׁיזְבִינָךְ מִן הָדָא שׁוּרְבָא דִנְפַק בָּעָלְמָא. אֲמַר לֵיהּ. הָא צְלוֹ. כְּדוֹן תִּשְׁתַּמַּע צְלוֹתֵיךְ. דִּכְתִיב וְאֵין נִסְתָּר מֵחַמָּתוֹ.

[331]Rebbi Ḥizqiah, Rebbi Abbahu in the name of Rebbi Eleazar: When in the Future World the proselytes come, Antoninus comes at the head of all of them. How do you understand this? Since they saw him walking with a slight shoe on the Day of Atonement[332], what do you infer since even God-fearing people go outside thus. There is information that Antoninus did not become a proselyte, and there is information that Antoninus did become a proselyte. Antoninus came to Rebbi and asked him, can you see me eating from the Leviathan[333] in the World to Come? He said, yes. He told him, from the Passover lamb you would not let me eat, but from Leviathan you make me eat in the World to Come? He answered, what can we do for you since about the Passover lamb it is written that *no uncircumcised man may eat from it*[334]. This implies that Antoninus did not become a proselyte. When he heard this, he went and became a proselyte. He came to Rebbi and said to him, look at my circumcision. He answered him, at mine I never looked[335], and at yours I should look? This implies that Antoninus became a proselyte.

Why is he called our holy teacher? Because he never in his life looked at his circumcision. And why is his name Naḥum the holiest of holies[336]? Because he never in his life looked at the figure on a coin.

Antoninus came to Rebbi; he said to him, pray for me. He said to him, may He save you from the cold, as it is written[337], *who can withstand His cold*? He said, is that not a superfluous prayer? You cover yourself with an outer garment and the cold will go away. He said to him, may He save you from the hot wind that comes into the world. He said, that is a prayer; may your prayer be heard, as it is written[338], *nothing is hidden from His heat.*

331 It is difficult to understand why this digression about a crypto-Jewish Roman emperor was inserted here. It is futile to try to determine to whom one refers; cf. *Kilaim* 9:4, Note 79. It was implied already in Halakhah 1 that Gentiles may have part in the World to Come.

A parallel, in slightly different order, is in *Megillah* 1:13. For the first sentence, cf. *Lev. rabba* 3(20), *Midrash Ps.* 22(29).

332 The wearing of leather shoes is forbidden on the Day of Atonement (except where it is necessary, as when walking on muddy streets.) That Antoninus did not wear leather shoes on the Day of Atonement is no proof that he became a proselyte since many "God-fearing people", Gentiles known as "Friends of the Synagogue", do the same.

333 The just feasting on Leviathan meat in the World to Come are also mentioned in *Lev. rabba* 22(7), Babli *Bava batra* 74b-75a.

334 *Ex.* 12:48.

335 It is indecent to look at sexual organs. References to this insert are *Megillah* 1:13 (72b l.57, 3:3 74a l.39); *Avodah zarah* 3:1 (42c l.5); Babli *Šabbat* 118b, *Pesaḥim* 104a; the text here is copied by Tosaphot *Ketubot* 30a *s.v.* הכל.

336 An otherwise unknown personality.

337 *Ps.* 147:17.

338 *Ps.* 19:7.

(29c line 52) רִבִּי יוֹחָנָן אָמַר. עֲדָתוֹ שֶׁלְּיוֹחָנָן בֶּן קָרֵחַ אֵין לָהֶן חֵלֶק לְעוֹלָם הַבָּא. מַה טַעַם. בַּיי בָּגָדוּ כִּי־בָנִים זָרִים יָלָדוּ עַתָּה יֹאכְלֵם חוֹדֶשׁ אֶת־חֶלְקֵיהֶם.

Rebbi Joḥanan said, the group of Joḥanan ben Qareaḥ[339] has no part in the World to Come. What is the reason? *They were traitors to the Eternal for they produced foreign children. Now a new Moon shall eat their parts*[340].

339 Who flouted Jeremiah's advice and fled to Egypt, *2K.* 42.

340 *Hos.* 5:7.

(29c line 54) רִבִּי לֶעְזָר וְרִבִּי יְהוּדָה. חַד אָמַר. לֹא גָלוּ עַד שֶׁנַּעֲשׂוּ עֲרֵילִים. וְחָרָנָה אָמַר. לֹא גָלוּ עַד שֶׁנַּעֲשׂוּ מַמְזֵירִים. מָאן דְּאָמַר. עֲרֵלִים. לַמִּילָה וּלְמִצְוֹת. וּמָאן דְּאָמַר. מַמְזֵירִים. מֵאֲבוֹתֵיהֶם. אָמַר רִבִּי יוֹחָנָן. לֹא גָלוּ יִשְׂרָאֵל עַד שֶׁנַּעֲשׂוּ עֶשְׂרִים וְאַרְבַּע כִּיתּוֹת שֶׁלְּמִינִים. מַה טַעֲמָא. בֶּן־אָדָם֙ שׁוֹלֵ֨חַ אֲנִ֤י אֽוֹתְךָ֙ אֶל־בְּנֵ֣י יִשְׂרָאֵ֔ל אֶל־גּוֹיִ֥ם הַמּוֹרְדִ֖ים אֲשֶׁ֣ר מָֽרְדוּ־בִ֑י. אֶל גּוֹי הַמּוֹרֵד אֵין כָּתוּב כָּאן אֶלָּא אֶל־גּוֹיִ֥ם הַמּוֹרְדִ֖ים אֲשֶׁ֣ר מָֽרְדוּ־בִ֑י הֵ֤מָּה וַֽאֲבוֹתָם֙ פָּ֣שְׁעוּ בִ֔י עַד־עֶ֖צֶם הַיּ֥וֹם הַזֶּֽה׃

רִבִּי בֶּרֶכְיָה וְרִבִּי חֶלְבּוֹ בְּשֵׁם רִבִּי שְׁמוּאֵל בַּר נַחְמָן. לְשָׁלֹשׁ גָּלִיּוֹת גָּלוּ יִשְׂרָאֵל. אַחַת לִפְנִים מִנְּהַר סַנְבַּטְיוֹן וְאֶחָד לְדַפְנֵי שֶׁלְּאַנְטוֹכְיָא וְאַחַת שֶׁיָּרַד עֲלֵיהֶם הֶעָנָן וְכִסָּה אוֹתָם. כְּשֵׁם שֶׁגָּלוּ לְשָׁלֹשׁ גָּלִיּוֹת כָּךְ גָּלוּ שֵׁבֶט רְאוּבֵן וְגָד וַחֲצִי שֵׁבֶט מְנַשֶּׁה לְשָׁלֹשׁ גָּלִיּוֹת. מַה טַעַם. בְּדֶ֥רֶךְ אֲחוֹתֵ֖ךְ הָלָ֑כְתְּ וְנָתַתִּ֥י כוֹסָ֖הּ בְּיָדֵֽךְ׃ וּכְשֶׁהֵן חוֹזְרִין הֵן חוֹזְרִין מִשָּׁלֹשׁ גָּלִיּוֹת. מַה טַעַם. לֵאמֹ֤ר לַֽאֲסוּרִים֙ צֵ֔אוּ אֵילּוּ שֶׁגָּלוּ לִפְנִים מִנְּהַר סַנְבַּטְיוֹן. לַֽאֲשֶׁ֥ר בַּחֹ֖שֶׁךְ הִגָּל֑וּ אֵילּוּ שֶׁיָּרַד עֲלֵיהֶם הֶעָנָן וְכִסָּה אוֹתָם. עַל־דְּרָכִ֣ים יִרְע֔וּ וּבְכָל־שְׁפָיִ֖ים מַרְעִיתָֽם אֵילּוּ שֶׁגָּלוּ לְדַפְנָא שֶׁלְּאַנְטוֹכְיָא.

Rebbi Eleazar and Rebbi Jehudah. One said, they were exiles only when they were uncircumcised[341]. The other said, they were exiled only when they were bastards. He who says uncircumcised, for circumcision and commandments[342]. But he who says bastards, from their fathers[343]. Rebbi Joḥanan said, Israel was exiled only after they formed 24 heretical sects. What is the reason? *Son of man, I am sending you to the Children of Israel, to rebellious peoples who rebelled against Me*[344]. It is not written "to a rebellious people" but *to rebellious peoples who rebelled against Me; they and their fathers have acted criminally against Me up to this day.*

Rebbi Berekhia and Rebbi Ḥelbo in the name of Rebbi Samuel bar Naḥman. Israel was exiled to three diasporas[345]: one inside the river Sanbation[346], one to Daphne of Antiochia[347], and one on whom the Cloud[348] descended and covered them. Just as they were exiled to three diasporas, so the tribes of Reuben, Gad, and half the tribe of Manasse were exiled into three diasporas. What is the reason? *You went in the way of your sister and I gave her cup into your hand*[349]. So when they return, they will return from three diasporas. What is the reason? [350]*To tell the prisoners, leave,* those who were exiled inside the river Sanbation; *those in darkness, become visible,* those upon whom the Cloud descended and covered them; *on the roads they are grazing and on all plains is their pasturage,* those who were exiled to Daphne of Antiochia.

341 After a digression, one returns to the Ten Tribes.

342 The question is whether people suspected of being descendants of the Ten Tribes, who did not join in the return of Judeans and who clearly will not follow rabbinic rules for marriage and divorce, can be allowed to marry rabbinic Jewish partners. The first opinion states that while they cannot be expected to follow biblical commandments, they are eligible as marriage partners once their Israelite identity is ascertained or they undergo regular conversion (even if this is intrinsically futile for descendants of Jews in the female line.)

343 In this opinion, all descendants of the Ten Tribes are barred from marrying Jewish partners other than bastards or proselytes.

344 *Ez.* 2:3.

345 Since each tribe is called גּוֹי "a people" (*Gen.* 35:11), the plural implies that it counts for at least two, for a total of at least 24. Possibly this is a take-off on the multiplicity of Christian sects.

346 A river which stops flowing on the Sabbath. *Plinius, Hist. nat.* XXXI,2; *Sanhedrin* 65b; *Gen. rabba* 11(6),73(5); *Pesiqta rabbati* 23 [ed. Ish-Shalom Note 79].

347 Site of an Aphrodite shrine of famously ill repute. Cf. Note 343.

348 The Divine Cloud of Exodus (*Ex.* 14:19) and Temple (*1K.* 8:10-11).

349 *Ez.* 23:31.

350 *Is.* 49:9.

(fol. 27b) **משנה ז**: אַנְשֵׁי עִיר הַנִּדַּחַת אֵין לָהֶן חֵלֶק לָעוֹלָם הַבָּא שֶׁנֶּאֱמַר יָֽצְאוּ אֲנָשִׁים בְּנֵי בְלִיַּעַל מִקִּרְבֶּךָ וַיַּדִּיחוּ אֶת יוֹשְׁבֵי עִירָם לֵאמוֹר. הָא אֵינָן נֶהֱרָגִין עַד שֶׁיִּהְיוּ מַדִּיחִים מֵאוֹתָהּ הָעִיר וּמֵאוֹתוֹ הַשֵּׁבֶט וְעַד שֶׁיּוּדַּח רוּבָּהּ וְעַד שֶׁיַּדִּיחוּהָ אֲנָשִׁים. הִדִּיחוּהָ נָשִׁים וּקְטַנִּים אוֹ שֶׁהוּדַּח מִעוּטָהּ אוֹ שֶׁהָיוּ מַדִּיחֶיהָ מֵחוּצָה לָהּ הֲרֵי אֵילוּ כַּיְּחִידִים צְרִיכִים שְׁנֵי עֵדִים וְהַתְרָייָה לְכָל־אֶחָד וְאֶחָד. זֶה חוֹמֶר בַּיְּחִידִים מִבַּמְּרוּבִּים שֶׁהַיְּחִידִים בִּסְקִילָה לְפִיכָךְ מָמוֹנָם פָּלֵט וְהַמְּרוּבִּים בְּסַיִף לְפִיכָךְ מָמוֹנָן אָבֵד:

Mishnah 7: The people of a seduced town[351] have no part in the World to Come, as it is said[352]: *Useless men*[353] *left your midst*[354] *and seduced the inhabitants of their town as follows.* Therefore they cannot be executed unless the seducers be from that town and from that tribe, unless the majority was seduced, unless the seducers were men. If women or minors seduced them, or if a minority were seduced, they are single individuals[355] and need two witnesses and warning for each single one. This is more stringent for individuals than for the multitude since individuals are stoned , therefore their money escapes[356] while the multitude is executed by the sword, therefore their money is lost[357].

351 Who according to Mishnah 9:1 are executed by the sword.

352 *Deut*. 13:14.

353 They left their faith, therefore they cannot receive the reward of the faithful.

354 I. e., from their tribe.

355 They must be prosecuted for idolatry on an individual basis.

356 It is inherited by the heirs.

357 It must be destroyed by fire and is forbidden for all usufruct, *Deut*. 13:17-18.

(29c line 70) **הלכה ז**: אַנְשֵׁי עִיר הַנִּדַּחַת כול'. עִיר וְלֹא כְפָר. עִיר וְלֹא כְרַךְ. וְהִיא שֶׁתְּהֵא מֵחֲמִשָּׁה עַד עֲשָׂרָה. דִּבְרֵי רִבִּי מֵאִיר. רִבִּי יְהוּדָה אוֹמֵר. מִמֵּאָה עַד רוּבּוֹ שֶׁלְּשֵׁבֶט. שְׁנַיִם שֶׁהִדִּיחוּ אֶת שְׁנַיִם. אוֹתָם שְׁנַיִם שֶׁהִדִּיחוּ אֶת שְׁנַיִם מָהוּ לִיתֵּן עֲלֵיהֶם תּוֹרַת הַמַּדִּיחִין תּוֹרַת הַנִּידָּחִים. הָיוּ שָׁם גֵּרִים וְתוֹשָׁבִים מָהוּ שֶׁיַּשְׁלִימוּ לָרוֹב. הָיוּ שָׁם בִּיבָרִים שֶׁלַּחַיָּה וְשֶׁלְּעוֹפוֹת וְשֶׁלְּדָגִים עוֹף שֶׁהוּא טָס לְמַעְלָה מֵעֲשָׂרָה מָהוּ.

Halakhah 7: "The people of a seduced town," etc. A town but not a village, a town but not a fortified place[358]. This means, from five to ten[359], the words of Rebbi Meïr; Rebbi Jehudah says, from one hundred up to a majority of the tribe. If two seduced two, is it possible to try the two who had seduced two both as seducers and as seduced[360]? If there were proselytes and residents[361], are they counted for the majority? If there were menageries[362] for wild animals, birds, or fish[363]; birds flying higher than ten [handbreadths][364], what are the rules[365]?

358 As noted in the dictionaries, both the etymology and the exact meaning of עִיר are unknown. For R. Meïr, עִיר is a village and כְּפָר a hamlet; this is the usual meaning of the words in the Babli. For R. Jehudah, עִיר is any larger settlement. In the Babli, 15b, this is a dispute between authorities of the generation between Tannaïm and Amoraïm. The opinion of R. Jehudah here is adopted there by R. Jonathan while R. Yoshia defines עִיר as a settlement of between 10 and 100 households.

359 Households.

360 Since *men* are mentioned in the verse, the seducers, to be stoned, cannot be less than two. On the other hand, if they did seduce only a few people and the majority was seduced by others, they are not seducers of the עִיר and may be tried as inhabitants, to be decapitated.

361 Resident Gentiles.

362 Latin *vivarium, -ii, n.*

363 These are not domesticated animals; the question is whether they have to be destroyed as property.

364 The airspace above ten handbreadths is

a separate domain. This is important mainly for the rules of the Sabbath but is noted also in property cases.

365 Since (Tosephta 14:1) the case of the seduced city never arose and never will arise, no answers are required.

(29d line 1) רִבִּי שִׁמְעוֹן אוֹמֵר. חֲמוּרָה שְׂרֵיפָה מִסְּקִילָה. וְרַבָּנִין אָמְרִין. חֲמוּרָה סְקִילָה מִשְּׂרֵיפָה. רִבִּי שִׁמְעוֹן אוֹמֵר. חָמוּר חֶנֶק מֵהֶרֶג. וְרַבָּנִין אָמְרִין. חָמוּר הֶרֶג מֵחֶנֶק.

Rebbi Simeon says, burning is worse than stoning, but the rabbis teach that stoning is worse than burning. Rebbi Simeon says, strangulation is worse than decapitation; but the rabbis teach that decapitation is worse than strangulation[366].

366 Chapter 7:1, Note 1 (24b l. 15)

(fol. 27c) **משנה ח**: הַכֵּה תַכֶּה אֶת־יוֹשְׁבֵי הָעִיר הַהִוא לְפִי־חָרֶב. הַחַמֶּרֶת וְהַגַּמֶּלֶת הָעוֹבֶרֶת מִמָּקוֹם לְמָקוֹם הֲרֵי אֵלּוּ מַצִּילִין אוֹתָן. הַחֲרֵם אוֹתָהּ וְאֶת־כָּל־אֲשֶׁר־בָּהּ וְאֶת־בְּהֶמְתָּהּ לְפִי־חָרֶב. מִיכָּאן אָמְרוּ נִכְסֵי צַדִּיקִים שֶׁבְּתוֹכָהּ אוֹבְדִין וְשֶׁבְּחוּצָה לָהּ פְּלֵיטִין וְשֶׁל רְשָׁעִים בֵּין מִתּוֹכָהּ בֵּין מֵחוּצָה לָהּ אוֹבְדִין:

Mishnah 8: *Slaying you shall slay the inhabitants of that town by the sword*[367]. A caravan of donkeys or of camels which passes from place to place saves them[368]. *Destroy it and all which is in it, including its domestic animals*[369], *by the sword.* From here they said, the properties of just people in its midst are lost, what is outside escapes; that of evildoers both inside and outside is lost.

367 *Deut.* 13:16.

368 The Yerushalmi gives no indication as to what this means. The Babli (112a) holds that temporary residents after 30 days become voting citizens of the town; if they do not follow the permanent inhabitants into apostasy, they will deprive the apostates of a majority and the rules of the seduced town cannot be applied. But it might be that the Yerushalmi follows *Sifry Deut.* 94 that if at the moment of judgment there are people in town to whom the judgment does not apply, it cannot be executed since the verse requires that only the inhabitants of *that* town be killed.

369 As property, cf. Note 363.

(29d line 3) **הלכה ח**: הַכֵּה תַכֶּה אֶת־יוֹשְׁבֵי הָעִיר הַהִוא לְפִי־חָרֶב כול'. רִבִּי שִׁמְעוֹן אוֹמֵר. בְּהֶמְתָּהּ וְלֹא בְכוֹרוֹת וְלֹא מַעְשְׂרוֹת שֶׁבְּתוֹכָהּ. שְׁלָלָהּ לֹא כֶסֶף הֶקְדֵּשׁ וּמַעֲשֵׂר שֵׁינִי שֶׁבְּתוֹכָהּ. רִבִּי יוֹסֵי בֶּן חֲנִינָה בָּעֵי. שִׂיעַר צַדְקָנִיּוֹת שֶׁבְּתוֹכָהּ מָהוּ. נִישְׁמְעִינָהּ מֵהָדָא. רִבִּי שִׁמְעוֹן אוֹמֵר. בְּהֶמְתָּהּ וְלֹא בְכוֹרוֹת וּמַעְשְׂרוֹת שֶׁבְּתוֹכָהּ. שְׁלָלָהּ לֹא כֶסֶף הֶקְדֵּשׁ וּמַעֲשֵׂר שֵׁינִי שֶׁבְּתוֹכָהּ. קָדְשֵׁי עִיר הַנִּידַּחַת. רִבִּי יוֹחָנָן אָמַר. אֵין מוֹעֲלִין בָּהֶן. וְרִבִּי שִׁמְעוֹן בֶּן לָקִישׁ אָמַר. מוֹעֲלִין בָּהֶן. מָתִיב רִבִּי יוֹחָנָן לְרֵישׁ לָקִישׁ. עַל דַּעְתָּךְ דַּתְּ מַר. מוֹעֲלִין בָּהֶן. נִיתְנֵי. שֵׁשׁ חַטָּאוֹת מֵתוֹת. אָמַר לֵיהּ. שֶׁכֵּן אֲפִילוּ עוֹלָה בְּדָא מֵתָה. רִבִּי הִילָא בְשֵׁם רִבִּי שִׁמְעוֹן בֶּן לָקִישׁ. מוֹעֲלִין בָּהֶן מִשּׁוּם קָדְשֵׁי מְשׁוּמָּד. וְיִקְרְבוּ. עַל שֵׁם זֶבַח רְשָׁעִים תּוֹעֵיבָה. אָמַר רִבִּי עוּקְבָּה. אוּף בְּהָדָא אִיתְפַּלְגוּן. שׁוֹר שֶׁהוּא יוֹצֵא לִיסָּקֵל וְנִמְצְאוּ עֵידָיו זוֹמְמִין. רִבִּי יוֹחָנָן אָמַר. כָּל־הַקּוֹדֵם בּוֹ זָכָה. רִבִּי שִׁמְעוֹן בֶּן לָקִישׁ אָמַר. יֵיאוּשׁ שֶׁלְּטָעוּת הָיָה. וְכֵן עֶבֶד שֶׁהוּא יוֹצֵא לִיהָרֵג וְנִמְצְאוּ עֵידָיו זוֹמְמִין. רִבִּי יוֹחָנָן אָמַר. זָכָה לְעַצְמוֹ. רִבִּי שִׁמְעוֹן בֶּן לָקִישׁ אָמַר. יֵיאוּשׁ שֶׁלְּטָעוּת הָיָה.

Halakhah 8: *Slaying you shall slay the inhabitants of that town by the sword,* etc. [370]Rebbi Simeon says, *its domesticated animal,* not first born or tithes found there; *its booty*, not Temple money or Second Tithe found there[371]. Rebbi Yose ben Ḥanina asked: What is the status of hair of its just women[372]? Let us hear from the following: Rebbi Simeon says, *its domesticated animal,* not first born or tithes found there; *its booty*, not Temple money or Second Tithe found there.

The *sancta* of a seduced town[373], Rebbi Joḥanan said, one cannot commit larceny with them; Rebbi Simeon ben Laqish said, one can commit larceny with them. Rebbi Joḥanan objected to Rebbi Simeon ben Laqish: According to your opinion that one can commit larceny with them, should one not state that "six purification offerings are left to die"[374]? He answered, because in this case even an elevation offering dies[375]. Rebbi Hila in the name of Rebbi Simeon ben Laqish: One can commit larceny with them because of *sancta* of an apostate. Should they not be sacrificed? Because of *the sacrifice of an evildoer is an abomination*[376].

Rebbi Uqba said, also in the following they disagree: [377]If a bull was led out to be stoned when its witnesses were found to be perjured, Rebbi Joḥanan said, the first to come acquires it; Rebbi Simeon ben Laqish said, it was false despair. Similarly, if a slave was led out to be executed when its witnesses were found to be perjured, Rebbi Joḥanan said, he acquired himself; Rebbi Simeon ben Laqish said, it was false despair.

370 Tosephta 14:5.

371 All the items enumerated are Heaven's property. While the second part of the verse insists that the *town's property* must be destroyed, Heaven's property cannot be destroyed. The disposal of Heaven's property is discussed in Mishnah 9. Babli 112b.

372 Since a woman could cut off her hair and sell it to a wig-maker, it represents value. Should the woman be forced to cut off her hair before she is forced to leave town following the conviction of the town for organized idolatry? Since Temple money must be taken out undamaged, so the just woman must be taken out unhurt. The Babli, 112a, somewhat disagrees.

373 Once an animal has been dedicated as sacrifice, all private use of it is larceny (*Lev.* 5:14-16).

374 Mishnah *Temurah* 4:1 enumerates 5 kinds of purification offerings which can neither be redeemed nor sacrificed. An animal dedicated by an idolator of a seduced town should be added as sixth kind. Babli 112a.

375 Mishnah *Temurah* 4:1 only treats cases particular to purification offerings.

376 *Prov.* 21:27. The Babli, *Hulin* 5a, finds the same result in *Lev.* 1:2.

377 *Bava qamma* 4:9, Notes 122-125

(fol. 27c) **משנה ט**: וְאֶת־כָּל־שְׁלָלָהּ תִּקְבּוֹץ אֶל־תּוֹךְ רְחֹבָהּ. אִם אֵין לָהּ רְחוֹב עוֹשִׂין לָהּ רְחוֹב. הָיָה רְחוֹבָהּ חוּצָה לָהּ כּוֹנְסִין אוֹתוֹ לְתוֹכָהּ שֶׁנֶּאֱמַר אֶל־תּוֹךְ רְחֹבָהּ וְשָׂרַפְתָּ בָאֵשׁ אֶת־הָעִיר וְאֶת־כָּל־שְׁלָלָהּ וְלֹא שְׁלַל שָׁמַיִם. מִכָּאן אָמְרוּ הַהֶקְדֵּישׁוֹת שֶׁבָּהּ יִיפָּדוּ וּתְרוּמוֹת יֵירָקְבוּ מַעֲשֵׂר שֵׁנִי וְכִתְבֵי הַקּוֹדֶשׁ יִגָּנֵזוּ.

Mishnah 9: *All its spoils you shall collect in its public square*[378]. If it has no public square, one creates a public square in it. If its public square was outside, one collects it[379] inside, for it is said: *In its public square you shall burn the town and all its spoils in fire*; its spoils but not Heaven's spoils. From here they said that dedicated objects in it shall be redeemed, heaves shall be left to rot, Second Tithes and Holy Scriptures shall be put away[371].

משנה י: כָּלִיל לַיהֹוָה אֱלֹהֶיךָ אָמַר רַבִּי שִׁמְעוֹן אִם אַתָּה עוֹשֶׂה דִין בְּעִיר הַנִּדַּחַת מַעֲלֶה אֲנִי עָלֶיךָ כְּאִילּוּ אַתָּה מַעֲלֶה עוֹלָה כָלִיל לְפָנָי. וְהָיְתָה תֵּל עוֹלָם לֹא תִבָּנֶה עוֹד. לֹא תֵיעָשֶׂה אֲפִילּוּ גַּנּוֹת וּפַרְדֵּסִים דִּבְרֵי רַבִּי יוֹסֵי הַגָּלִילִי. רַבִּי עֲקִיבָה אוֹמֵר לֹא תִבָּנֶה עוֹד לִכְמוֹ שֶׁהָיְתָה אֵינָהּ נִבְנֵית אֲבָל נַעֲשֵׂית הִיא גַּנּוֹת וּפַרְדֵּסִים.

Mishnah 10: *Totally for the Eternal, your God.* Rebbi Simeon said, if you judge the seduced town, I will credit it for you as if you brought an entire elevation offering before Me. *It shall be an eternal mound, it shall not be* *rebuilt.* It should not even be made into gardens and orchards, the words of Rebbi Yose the Galilean. Rebbi Aqiba says, it shall not be rebuilt as it was but it may be made into gardens and orchards[380].

משנה יא: וְלֹא־יִדְבַּק בְּיָדְךָ מְאוּמָה מִן־הַחֵרֶם לְמַעַן יָשׁוּב ה' מֵחֲרוֹן אַפּוֹ וְנָתַן־לְךָ רַחֲמִים וְרִחַמְךָ וְהִרְבֶּךָ וגו'. שֶׁכָּל זְמַן שֶׁהָרְשָׁעִים בָּעוֹלָם חֲרוֹן אַף בָּעוֹלָם אָבְדוּ רְשָׁעִים מִן הָעוֹלָם נִסְתַּלֵּק חֲרוֹן אַף מִן הָעוֹלָם:

Mishnah 11: *Nothing of what should be destroyed shall stick to your hands, so the Eternal may change from His anger to grant you mercy, have mercy on you and increase you,* etc. Any time evildoers are in the world, anger is in the world; when the evildoers are lost from the world, anger passes away from the world.

378 *Deut.* 13:17-18.

379 One extends the territory of the town to include the public square.

380 R. Yose the Galilean reads תֵּל with the Accadic as *ruin*, R. Aqiba with the Arabic as *mound, butte*.

(29d line 18) **הלכה ט:** וְאֶת־כָּל־שְׁלָלָהּ תִּקְבּוֹץ כול'. אָמַר רַבִּי שִׁמְעוֹן. קַל וָחוֹמֶר בִּדְבָרִים. מָה אִם נְכָסִים שֶׁאֵין בָּהֶן דַּעַת לֹא לְטוֹבָה וְלֹא לְרָעָה וְעַל יְדֵי שֶׁגָּרְמוּ לַצַּדִּיקִים לָדוּר עִם הָרְשָׁעִים אָמְרָה תוֹרָה שֶׁיִּשָּׂרֵפוּ. הַמִּתְכַּוֵּין לְהַטּוֹת אֶת חֲבֵירוֹ וּמַטֵּהוּ מִדֶּרֶךְ טוֹבָה לְדֶרֶךְ רָעָה עַל אַחַת כַּמָּה וְכַמָּה. אָמַר רַבִּי לָעְזָר. מוֹכִיחַ בַּדָּבָר בְּלוֹט שֶׁלֹּא יָשַׁב בִּסְדוֹם אֶלָּא מִפְּנֵי מָמוֹנוֹ אַף הוּא יָצָא וְיָדָיו עַל רֹאשׁוֹ. הָדָא הִיא דִכְתִיב מַהֵר הִמָּלֵט שָׁמָּה. דַּיֶּיךָ שֶׁאַתְּ מְמַלֵּט אֶת נַפְשֶׁךָ.

Halakhah 9: *All its spoils you shall collect,* etc. Rebbi Simeon said, is there not an argument *de minore ad majus* about this? Since properties, which have no knowledge of good or bad, but because they caused the just to dwell with the evildoers the Torah said, should be burned, if somebody has the intention of influencing his neighbor and influences him from good ways to bad ones, not so much more? Rebbi Eleazar said, the matter is demonstrated by Lot who dwelt in Sodom only because of his money but left there with his hands on his head. This is what is written[381]: *Quickly escape to there*; it is enough for you that you escape with your life.

(29d line 25) כָּתוּב בְּיָמָּיו בָּנָה חִיאֵל בֵּית הָאֱלִי אֶת־יְרִיחוֹ. חִיאֵל מִן דִּיהוֹשָׁפָט. יְרִיחוֹ מִן דְּבִנְיָמִין. אֶלָּא מְלַמֵּד שֶׁמְּגַלְגְּלִין אֶת הַחוֹבָה עַל יְדֵי חַייָב. וְכֵן הוּא אוֹמֵר בַּאֲבִירָם בְּכֹרוֹ יִסְּדָהּ וּבִשְׂגוּב צְעִירוֹ. [בַּאֲבִירָם בְּכֹרוֹ לֹא הָיָה מְאַיֵין לְלַמֵּד. וּבִשְׂגוּב] הָרָשָׁע הָיָה לוֹ מְאַיֵין לְלַמֵּד. לְפִי

שֶׁרָצוּ לְרַבּוֹת אֶת מָמוֹנָן נִשְׁלְטָה בָהֶן מְאֵירָה וְהָיוּ מִתְמוֹטְטִין וְהוֹלְכִין. לְקַיֵּים מַה שֶׁנֶּאֱמַר כִּדְבַר יי אֲשֶׁר דִּבֶּר בְּיַד יְהוֹשֻׁעַ בִּן־נוּן.

[382]It is written[143]: *In his days did Ḥiel from Bet-El build Jericho.* Ḥiel is from the descendants of Josaphat, Jericho is in the territory of Benjamin. Only that bad deeds are put in the hands of the unworthy; therefore, it is said, *with his first-born Aviram he set the foundation and with his youngest son Seguv he put in the doors.* [If it was not appropriate for him to learn from his firstborn Aviram, should he not have learned from][383] the wicked Seguv? Because they wanted to make more money, the curse ruled over them and they were continuously weakened to confirm what was said[143], *following the word of the Eternal, the God of Israel, which He had spoken though Joshua ben Nun.*

(29d line 30) כָּלִיל לַיהֹוָה אֱלֹהֶיךָ. וְלֹא־יִדְבַּק בְּיָדְךָ. תַּנֵּי. רִבִּי שִׁמְעוֹן בֶּן אֶלְעָזָר אוֹמֵר. לֹא אוֹתָהּ בָּנוּ אֶלָּא עִיר אַחֶרֶת בָּנוּ. מֵאַחַר שֶׁהִיא נִבְנֵית מוּתָּר אַתְּ לֵישֵׁב בָּהּ. רִבִּי יוֹסֵי וְרִבִּי יְהוֹשֻׁעַ בֶּן קָרְחָה אוֹמְרִים. מַה תַלְמוּד לוֹמַר וּבָנָה אֶת־הָעִיר הַזֹּאת אֶת־יְרִיחוֹ. אֶלָּא שֶׁלֹּא יִבְנֶה עִיר אַחֶרֶת וְיִקְרָא שְׁמָהּ יְרִחוֹ. יְרִחוֹ וְיִקְרָא שְׁמָהּ עִיר אַחֶרֶת. וְכֵן הוּא אוֹמֵר. לֹא תוֹסִפוּן לָשׁוּב בַּדֶּרֶךְ הַזֶּה עוֹד. לִישִׁיבָה אֵין אַתְּ חוֹזֵר. חוֹזֵר אַתְּ לִסְחוֹרָה וְלִפְרַקְמַטְיָא וְלִכְבּוֹשׁ אֶת הָאָרֶץ.

Totally, for the Eternal. your God. Nothing of what should be destroyed shall stick to your hands. It was stated[384]: Rebbi Simeon ben Eleazar says, they did not rebuild it but built another town. After it was built, you are permitted to dwell there[385]. Rebbi Yose[386] and Rebbi Joshua ben Qorḥa say, why does the verse say[143], *who would build this town, Jericho*? That one may not build another town and call it Jericho, or Jericho and call it another town. And so He says[387], *you shall not continue to return on this way*, you may not return for dwelling; you may return for peddling, business[388], or to conquer the land[389].

381 *Gen.* 19:22.

382 Halakhah 2, Notes 143-146.

383 The addition in brackets is only in a Genizah fragment.

384 Tosephta 14:10.

385 As the Tosephta points out, the students of prophecy lived at Jericho, *2K.* 2:5.

386 The Tanna.

387 *Deut.* 17:16.

388 Greek πραγματεία.

389 The verse prohibits return to Egypt to procure war materiel. It seems that the inference is based on a derivation of the word לָשׁוּב not from the root שוב but from ישב.

ואילו הן הנחנקין פרק אחד עשר

(fol. 29b) **משנה א**: וְאֵילוּ הֵן הַנֶּחֱנָקִין הַמַּכֶּה אָבִיו וְאִמּוֹ וְגוֹנֵב נֶפֶשׁ מִיִּשְׂרָאֵל וְזָקֵן מַמְרֵא עַל פִּי בֵית דִּין וּנְבִיא הַשֶּׁקֶר וְהַמִּתְנַבֵּא בְּשֵׁם עֲבוֹדָה זָרָה וְהַבָּא עַל אֵשֶׁת אִישׁ וְזוֹמְמֵי בַת כֹּהֵן וּבוֹעֲלָהּ.

Mishnah 1: But the following are strangled[1]: One who hits his father or his mother[2], and one who kidnaps a person from Israel[3], and the Elder who rebels against the Court[4], and the false prophet[5], and one who prophesies in the name of foreign worship[6], and one who copulates with a married woman[7], and the perjured witness of a Cohen's daughter and her paramour[8].

1 Since no particular form of execution is prescribed for them.

2 *Ex.* 21:15.

3 In order to sell him or her as a slave, *Ex.* 21:16, *Deut.* 24:7.

4 The Supreme Court sitting in the Temple court. *Deut.* 17:12.

5 *Deut.* 18:20-22.

6 *Deut.* 13:6.

7 *Deut.* 22:22. This also applies to the woman.

8 Even though the adulterous daughter of a Cohen is burned, there is no verse to apply the same punishment to the adulterer. Since witnesses to adultery are witnesses simultaneously to both parties, they cannot be punished more than the adulterer would be.

(30a line 13) **הלכה א**: וְאֵילוּ הֵן הַנֶּחֱנָקִין כול'. אַזְהָרָה לַמַּכֶּה אָבִיו וְאִמּוֹ מְנַיִין. אַרְבָּעִים יַכֶּנּוּ לֹא יוֹסִיף. מָה אִם מִי שֶׁהוּא מְצוּוֶּה לְהַכּוֹת הֲרֵי הוּא מְצוּוֶּה שֶׁלֹּא לְהַכּוֹת. מִי שֶׁאֵינוֹ מְצֻוֶּה לְהַכּוֹת אֵינוֹ דִין שֶׁיְּהֵא מְצוּוֶּה שֶׁלֹּא לְהַכּוֹת.

Halakhah 1: But the following are strangled," etc. From where warning[9] for one who hits his father or his mother? *Forty times he shall hit him, he may not add*[10]. Since one who is commanded to hit is commanded not to hit, one who is commanded not to hit *a fortiori* is commanded not to hit[11].

9 Cf. Chapter 7, Note 129.

10 *Deut.* 25:3, speaking of punishment decreed by the court.

11 It is sinful to hit anybody one is not commanded to hit. But only hitting a parent may be a capital crime. *Mekhilta dR. Ismael Mišpatim* 5 (ed. Horovitz-Rabin p. 266). The argument establishes a guide for ethical behavior; it is not one in criminal law for which only explicit verses may form the basis.

(30a line 16) אֵינוֹ חַייָב עַד שֶׁיַּעֲשֶׂה בָהֶן חַבּוּרָה. כְּאֵי זֶה חַבּוּרָה. כְּחַבּוּרַת שַׁבָּת כְּחַבּוּרַת נְזָקִין. אִין תֵּימַר כְּחַבּוּרַת שַׁבָּת. אֲפִילוּ לֹא חִיסֵּר. וְאִין תֵּימַר כְּחַבּוּרַת נְזָקִין. עַד שָׁעָה שֶׁיְּחַסֵּר.

"He is not punishable unless he inflict a wound on them[12]." What kind of wound? A wound for the laws of the Sabbath, a wound for the law of torts? If you say, as a wound for the laws of the Sabbath, even if he did not cause them to miss anything[13]; if you say, as a wound for the laws of torts, only if he caused them to miss something[14].

12 Mishnah 2.

13 It is a desecration of the Sabbath to cause a contusion. Mishnah *Šabbat* 14:1.

14 Some particle of skin or blood. Cf. *Bava qamma* 8:1, Notes 15-17.

(fol. 29d) **משנה ב**: הַמַּכֶּה אָבִיו וְאִמּוֹ אֵינוֹ חַייָב עַד שֶׁיַּעֲשֶׂה בָהֶן חַבּוּרָה. זֶה חוֹמֶר בִּמְקַלֵּל מִבְּמַכֶּה שֶׁהַמְקַלֵּל לְאַחַר מִיתָה חַייָב וְהַמַּכֶּה לְאַחַר מִיתָה פָּטוּר. וְגוֹנֵב נֶפֶשׁ מִיִּשְׂרָאֵל אֵינוֹ חַייָב עַד שֶׁיַּכְנִיסֶנּוּ לִרְשׁוּתוֹ. רִבִּי יְהוּדָה אוֹמֵר עַד שֶׁיַּכְנִיסֶנּוּ לִרְשׁוּתוֹ וְיִשְׁתַּמֵּשׁ בּוֹ שֶׁנֶּאֱמַר וְהִתְעַמֶּר בּוֹ וּמְכָרוֹ. הַגּוֹנֵב אֶת בְּנוֹ רִבִּי יוֹחָנָן בֶּן בְּרוֹקָה מְחַייֵב וַחֲכָמִים פּוֹטְרִין. גָּנַב מִי שֶׁחֶצְיוֹ עֶבֶד וְחֶצְיוֹ בֶּן חוֹרִין רִבִּי יוֹחָנָן בֶּן בְּרוֹקָה מְחַייֵב וַחֲכָמִים פּוֹטְרִין:

Mishnah 2: One who hits his father or his mother is not punishable unless he inflict a wound on them. The following is more aggravating about one who curses[15] than one who hits, in that one who curses is punishable even after death, but one who hits after death cannot be prosecuted. And one who kidnaps a person from Israel is not punishable unless he bring him into his property[16]. Rebbi Jehudah says, unless he bring him into his property and use him, as it is said, *and enslaved him or sold him.* One who kidnaps his own son, Rebbi Joḥanan ben Beroqa[17] declares punishable but the Sages make him not prosecutable. One who kidnapped a person half slave and half free Rebbi Joḥanan ben Beroqa declares punishable but the Sages make him not prosecutable.

15 Father or Mother; Mishnah 7:14.

16 Or sells him as a slave.

17 The Babylonian attributions in the last two cases are different. The Halakhah shows that in the last sentence also here one has to read *R. Jehudah*, not R. Johanan ben Beroqa.

(fol. 29b) **הלכה ב:** הַמַּכֶּה אָבִיו וְאִמּוֹ כול'. אַזְהָרָה לַגְּנֵיבָה הָרִאשׁוֹנָה מְנַיִין. לֹא תִּגְנוֹב. אַזְהָרָה לַגְּנֵיבָה הַשְּׁנִייָה מְנַיִין. וְלֹא תִּגְנוֹבוּ. לֹא תִּגְנוֹב עַל מְנָת לְמַקֵּט. לֹא תִּגְנוֹבוּ עַל מְנָת לְשַׁלֵּם תַּשְׁלוּמֵי כֶפֶל עַל מְנָת לְשַׁלֵּם תַּשְׁלוּמֵי אַרְבָּעָה וַחֲמִשָּׁה. בֶּן בַּגְבַּג אוֹמֵר. לֹא תִגְנֹב אֶת שֶׁלָּךְ מֵאַחַר הַגַּנָּב. שֶׁלֹּא תֵּרָאֶה גוֹנֵב.

רִבִּי בָּא רִבִּי יוֹחָנָן בְּשֵׁם רִבִּי הוֹשַׁעְיָה. אֵינוֹ חַייָב עַד שֶׁיִּגְנוֹב מָעוֹת. רִבִּי זְעִירָא רִבִּי יוֹחָנָן בְּשֵׁם רִבִּי הוֹשַׁעְיָה. אֵינוֹ חַייָב עַד שֶׁיְּזַלְזֵל מָעוֹת. מָהוּ עַד שֶׁיְּזַלְזֵל מָעוֹת. מָה נָן קַייָמִין. אִם בְּאוֹ דְאָמַר. הֵא לָךְ חֲמִשָּׁה וְהַב לִי תְלָתָא. שׁוֹטֶה הוּא. הֵא לָךְ תְּלָתָא וְהַב לִי חֲמִשָּׁה. בַּר נַשׁ הוּא. אֶלָּא כִי נָן קַייָמִין בְּאוֹ דָמַר. הֵא לָךְ חֲמִשָּׁה וְהַב לִי חֲמִשָּׁה.

הֵיידֵינוֹ גַנָּב וְהֵיידֵינוֹ גַזְלָן. אָמַר רִבִּי הִילָא. גָּנַב בִּפְנֵי עֵדִים גַּנָּב. בִּפְנֵי הַבְּעָלִים גּוֹזְלָן הוּא. אָמַר רִבִּי זְעִירָה. מֵעַתָּה אֲפִילוּ נִתְכַּוֵון לְגוּזְלָהּ וְלִבְעִילָה אֲזָלָה אֵין גּוֹזְלָן. וְהֵיי דֵינוֹ גּוֹזְלָן עַל דְּרִבִּי זְעִירָא. רִבִּי שְׁמוּאֵל בַּר סוֹסַרְטָא בְּשֵׁם רִבִּי אַבָּהוּ. עַד שֶׁיִּגְזוֹל בִּפְנֵי עֲשָׂרָה בְנֵי אָדָם. בִּנְייַן אָב שֶׁבְּכוּלָּן וַיִּגְזוֹל אֶת־הַחֲנִית מִיַּד הַמִּצְרִי וגו'.

[18]From where a first warning about stealing: *you shall not steal.* From where a second warning about stealing: *you shall not steal. You shall not steal*, in order to aggravate; *you shall not steal,* in order to pay double restitution, in order to pay quadruple or quintuple restitution. Ben Bagbag says, do not steal your own property back from the thief, lest you be seen stealing.

Rebbi Abba, Rebbi Johanan in the name of Rebbi Hoshaia: he is punishable only if he steals money. Rebbi Ze`ira in the name of Rebbi Hoshaia: he is punishable only if he shows contempt for money. What means showing contempt for money? Where do we hold? If about him who says, here you have five and give me for three, he is an idiot. Here you have three and give me for five, he is a regular person. But we deal with one who says, here you have five and give me for five.

What is a thief and what is a robber? Rebbi Hila said, if he stole in the presence of witnesses, he is a thief, in the presence of the owners he is a robber. Rebbi Ze`ira asked: but if he intended to rob (for copulation)[18], he is not a robber. What is a robber according to Rebbi Ze`ira? Rebbi Samuel ben Sosarta in the name of Rebbi Abbahu: only if he rob in the presence of ten people. The prototype for all these: *He robbed the spear from the hand of the Egyptian,* etc.

17 The entire paragraph is from Halakhah 8:3, Notes 38-43.

18 A copyist's error who wrote לבעילה "for sexual intercourse" instead of לבעליה "in front of its owners" as in Halakhah 8:3.

(30a line 34) מַה טַעֲמָא דְרִבִּי יוֹחָנָן בֶּן בְּרוֹקָה. מִבְּנֵי יִשְׂרָאֵל. מַה טַעֲמוֹן דְּרַבָּנִין. מֵאֶחָיו. לֹא מִבָּנָיו. מַה טַעֲמָא דְרִבִּי יְהוּדָה. מֵאֶחָיו. אֲפִילוּ מִקְצַת אָחִיו. מַה טַעֲמוֹן דְּרַבָּנִין. מֵאֶחָיו. עַד שֶׁיְּהֵא כוּלּוֹ אָחִיו.

What is the reason of Rebbi Johanan ben Beroqa? *Of the Children of Israel*. What is the reason of the rabbis? *Of his brothers,* not his sons[20].

What is the reason of Rebbi Jehudah? *Of his brothers,* even partially his brother. What is the reason of the rabbis? *Of his brothers,* unless he be totally his brother.

20 *Deut*. 24:7 reads: *If a man be found kidnapping one of his brothers, of the Children of Israel, and enslaves him or sells him, the kidnapper shall die; you shall eliminate evil from Israel.* This paragraph speaks of the son, the next (cf. Note 17) of the half-emancipated slave. *Sifry Deut*. 273 parallels the first paragraph but in the case of the semi-emancipated slave treats the rabbis' as unanimous opinion. The Babli 86a finds a reason to exclude the semi-emancipated slave from the partitive *mem* in the verse *of the Children of Israel,* which implies "not all of the Children of Israel."

(fol. 29d) **משנה ג**: זָקֵן מַמְרֵא עַל פִּי בֵית דִּין שֶׁנֶּאֱמַר כִּי יִפָּלֵא מִמְּךָ דָבָר לַמִּשְׁפָּט בֵּין־דָּם | לְדָם בֵּין־דִּין לְדִין'. שְׁלֹשָׁה בָתֵּי דִינִין הָיוּ שָׁם. אֶחָד עַל פֶּתַח הַר הַבַּיִת. וְאֶחָד עַל פֶּתַח הָעֲזָרָה. וְאֶחָד בְּלִשְׁכַּת הַגָּזִית. בָּאִין לָזֶה שֶׁעַל פֶּתַח הַר הַבַּיִת וְאוֹמֵר כָּךְ דָּרַשְׁתִּי וְכָךְ דָּרְשׁוּ חֲבֵרַי כָּךְ לִמַּדְתִּי וְכָךְ לִמְּדוּ חֲבֵרַי. אִם שָׁמְעוּ אָמְרוּ לָהֶם. וְאִם לָאו בָּאִין לָזֶה שֶׁעַל פֶּתַח הָעֲזָרָה וְאוֹמֵר כָּךְ דָּרַשְׁתִּי וְכָךְ דָּרְשׁוּ חֲבֵרַי כָּךְ לִמַּדְתִּי וְכָךְ לִמְּדוּ חֲבֵרָי. אִם שָׁמְעוּ אָמְרוּ לָהֶם. וְאִם לָאו אֵילּוּ וָאֵילּוּ בָּאִין לְבֵית דִּין הַגָּדוֹל שֶׁבְּלִשְׁכַּת הַגָּזִית שֶׁמִּשָּׁם תּוֹרָה יוֹצְאָה לְכָל יִשְׂרָאֵל, שֶׁנֶּאֱמַר מִן הַמָּקוֹם הַהוּא אֲשֶׁר יִבְחַר ה'.

Mishnah 3: The Elder who rebels against the Court, as it is said: *If a law case is too difficult for you, whether blood and blood, or case and case*[21], etc. Three courts were there, one at the entrance of the Temple Mount, one at the entrance of the Temple courtyard, and one in the ashlar hall. They come to the one at the entrance to the Temple Mount and he says, so I argued and so my colleagues argued, so I taught and so my colleague taught. If they had heard it[22], they tell them; otherwise they come to the one at the entrance of the Temple courtyard and he says, so I argued and so my colleagues argued, so I taught and so my colleagues taught. If they had heard it, they tell them; otherwise these and those[23] come to the Supreme Court in the ashlar hall, for from there instruction goes out to all of Israel as it is said[24], *from that place which the Eternal will choose*.

משנה ד: חָזַר לְעִירוֹ וְשָׁנָה וְלִימֵּד כְּדֶרֶךְ שֶׁהָיָה לָמוּד פָּטוּר. הוֹרָה לַעֲשׂוֹת חַייָב שֶׁנֶּאֱמַר וְהָאִישׁ אֲשֶׁר יַעֲשֶׂה בְזָדוֹן וגו'. אֵינוֹ חַייָב עַד שֶׁיּוֹרֶה לַעֲשׂוֹת. תַּלְמִיד שֶׁהוֹרָה לַעֲשׂוֹת פָּטוּר נִמְצָא חוּמְרוֹ קוּלּוֹ:

Mishnah 4: If he returned to his town[25], repeated and taught as was his custom, he cannot be prosecuted. If he instructed to act, he is punishable, as it is said[4], *but the man who would act criminally* etc. He is not punishable unless he instruct to act. A student who instructed to act cannot be prosecuted; it turns out that his severity is his leniency[26].

25 The representative of the lower court who had been told by the Supreme Court that his opinion was wrong.

26 A person unqualified to judge who nevertheless judges commits a grievous sin, worse than the qualified judge who does not obey the rulings of the Supreme Court. But his punishment is reserved for Heaven, not the human court.

(30a line 37) **הלכה ג:** זָקֵן מַמְרֵא כול'. **הלכה ד:** חָזַר לְעִירוֹ וְשָׁנָה וְלִימֵּד כול'. כְּתִיב כִּי יִפָּלֵא מִמְּךָ דָבָר לַמִּשְׁפָּט. מַגִּיד שֶׁבְּמוּפְלָא שֶׁבְּבֵית דִּין הַכָּתוּב מְדַבֵּר. מִמְּךָ זֶה עֵצָה. דָּבָר זוֹ אֲגָדָה. בֵּין־דָּם | לְדָם בֵּין דַּם נִידָּה לְדַם בְּתוּלִים. בֵּין דַּם נִידָּה לְדַם זִיבָה לְדַם צָרַעַת. בֵּין־דִּין לְדִין. בֵּין דִּינֵי מָמוֹנוֹת לְדִינֵי נְפָשׁוֹת. בֵּין־דִּין לְדִין'. בֵּין הַנִּסְקָלִין לַנִּשְׂרָפִין לַנֶּהֱרָגִין וְלַנֶּחֱנָקִין. בֵּין נֶגַע לְנֶגַע. בֵּין מְצוֹרָע מוּסְגָּר לִמְצוֹרָע מוּחְלָט. בֵּין נֶגַע לְנֶגַע. בֵּין נִיגְעֵי אָדָם לְנִגְעֵי בְגָדִים לְנִגְעֵי בָתִּים. דִּבְרֵי זוֹ הַשְׁקָיַית סוֹטָה וַעֲרִיפַת הָעֶגְלָה וְטָהֳרַת הַמְצוֹרָע. רִיבוֹת אֵילּוּ הָעֲרָכִים וְהַחֲרָמִים וְהַתְּמוּרוֹת וְהַהֶקְדֵּישׁוֹת. וְקַמְתָּ. וְקַמְתָּ מִבֵּית דִּין. וְעָלִיתָ זוֹ הָעֲלִייָה.

Halakhah 3: "The Elder who rebels," etc. **Halakhah 4**: "If he returned to his town, repeated and taught as was his custom," etc. [27]It is written[20]: *If something is being distinguished for you in law,* this shows that the verse speaks about the distinguished member of the court[28]. *For you*, this is counsel. *Something* is sermonizing[29]. *Whether blood and blood*, whether menstrual blood or blood of virginity; whether menstrual blood, blood of flux, or blood of skin disease[30]. *Whether case or case*, between those who are stoned, or burned, or decapitated, or strangled[31]. *Whether defect or defect*, between a quarantined sufferer from skin disease or an absolute one[31,32]; *whether defect or defect*, between defects of humans or of garments or of houses[33]. *Words*, that is the drinking of the suspected adulteress, breaking the neck of the calf, and the purification of the sufferer from skin disease[34]. *Quarrels*, these are estimations, bans, and dedications[35]. *You shall get up*, from the court, *and rise*, this is the ascent[36].

27 This *baraita* exists in two other versions, Babli 87a and *Sifry Deut.* 152. It is the subject of a study by E. A. Finkelstein, HUCA XXXII (1961) **א-כה**.

28 The person representing the lower court before the Supreme Court has to be its most distinguished member.

29 In the parallel sources: This is practice. Since the verse defines the areas of competence of the Supreme Court, it is difficult to see what the legal relevance of *aggadah* could be unless one subscribes to Maimonides's opinion that all interpretations of biblical verses by the hermeneutical rules are rabbinic in character, *i. e.*, aggadic.

30 As Finkelstein points out, the plain text of the verse seems to restrict the objects of appeal to purely legal cases; the interpretation given here extends it to all areas of life.

31 This sentence is missing in the parallel sources; it already is contained in the other explanations of the same clause.

32 Cf. Chapter 10, Note 284.

33 *Lev.* 13,14.

34 While the suspected adulteress drinks water with which written words were obliterated (*Num.* 5:23) and the expiation of an unsolved murder case requires the priests to recite words (*Deut.* 21:7-8), the purification of the the sufferer from skin disease is a wordless ceremony. Rashi in the Babli explains that skin disease is punishment for calumniating. One could explain that the first step in the purification is a declaration by a priest that the skin disease was healed and his command to assemble the items necessary for purification (*Lev.* 14:3-4).

35 *Lev.* 27; all of these need dedications by explicit declaration.

36 Climbing up all the way to Jerusalem.

(30a line 46) דָּבָר אַחֵר. וְעָלִיתָ מִיכָּן לְבֵית הַבְּחִירָה שֶׁלֹּא יִבָּנֶה אֶלָּא בְגוּבְהוֹ שֶׁלְּעוֹלָם. מַה טַעַם. כִּי בְּהַר קָדְשִׁי בְּהַר מְרוֹם יִשְׂרָאֵל אֶשְׁתֳּלֶנּוּ וְנָשָׂא עָנָף וְעָשָׂה פֶּרִי וגו'. וּבָאתָ לְרַבּוֹת בֵּית דִּין שֶׁבְּיַבְנֶה. רִבִּי זְעִירָא אוֹמֵר. לִשְׁאֵילָה.

Another explanation: *You shall get up,* from here that the Temple should be built only on the height of the world[37]. What is the reason? *For on* My Holy Mountain, on *the mountain of the height of Israel shall I plant it, that it may sprout branch and carry fruit*[38]. *And you shall come*[39], *to* include the court at Jabneh. Rebbi Ze`ira says, to ask[40].

37 When in fact the Temple Mount is conspicuously lower than the surrounding hills, to indicate that it is not a Canaanite High Place.

38 *Ez.* 17:23. For different approaches to the same statement, cf. Note 27, Babli *Qiddušin* 69a, *Zevahim* 54b, *Sifry Deut.* 37, end.

39 *Deut.* 17:9.

40 As Mishnah 6 shows, disobedience to a court not sitting in the ashlar hall is not a crime punishable by a human court; but nevertheless the obligation to ask the opinion of the Supreme Court in cases of doubt remains as long as such a court exists.

Since Rabban Johanan ben Zakkai asked for "Jabneh and its Sages" from Vespasian, it follows that even during the times of the Temple an important academy existed at Jabneh (and since Miriam the Hasmonean in her will had given Jabneh to Empress Livia, this was the only place in all of Judea which Vespasian could not give away without declaring himself as emperor.)

(30a line 50) זָקֵן מַמְרֵא שֶׁהוֹרָה לַעֲשׂוֹת וְעָשָׂה חַייָב. הוֹרָה וְלֹא עָשָׂה פָּטוּר. הוֹרָה עַל מְנָת שֶׁלֹּא לַעֲשׂוֹת פָּטוּר. הוֹרָה עַל מְנָת לַעֲשׂוֹת אַף עַל פִּי שֶׁלֹּא עָשָׂה חַייָב. אָמַר רִבִּי הִילָא. תַּנֵּי רִבִּי יִשְׁמָעֵאל כֵּן. אֲשֶׁר יַעֲשֶׂה. לֹא הוּא שֶׁיַּעֲשֶׂה. רַב הוּנָא אָמַר. הָיָה מְלַמֵּד הֲלָכָה וּבָא וְאַחַר כָּךְ אִירַע לוֹ בוֹ מַעֲשֶׂה. עוֹשִׂין לוֹ מַעֲשֶׂה. אִם עַד שֶׁלֹּא עָשָׂה לִימֵּד. עוֹשִׂין לַאֲחֵרִים וְלֹא עוֹשִׂין לְעַצְמוֹ.

A rebellious Elder who instructed to act and acted is punishable. If he instructed but did not act, he is not prosecutable. If he instructed not for application, he is not prosecutable. If he instructed for application, even if he himself did not act, he is punishable[41]. Rebbi Hila said, Rebbi Ismael stated thus: *Who would act*[4], even in he did not act himself.

Rav Huna said, if he was instructing for practice and later a case came up, one acts on his instruction. If he taught it on the occasion of a case, one acts on it for others but not for himself[42].

41 Babli 88b. *Sifry Deut.* 155 infers from *Deut.* 17:12 which decrees the death penalty for the person who acts against the judgment which *he* heard from the Supreme Court that any person acting on instructions from a person who *heard* from the Supreme Court

cannot be prosecuted. Therefore, the actions of persons acting on the instructions of a judge are considered actions of the judge, not those of his officers.

42 This is a general legal principle, applicable to civil as well as to criminal law. A legal doctrine formulated before a case arose can be applied to any case. But a doctrine formulated in the discussion of a case cannot be applied if the party formulating it is party to the case; that would be a conflict of interest (Babli *Yebamot* 77a in the name of Rav, Rav Huna's teacher.)

(30a line 55) רִבִּי שִׁמְעוֹן בֶּן מְנַסְיָא אוֹמֵר. הַנּוֹי וְהַכֹּחַ וְהָעוֹשֶׁר וְהַחָכְמָה וְהַשֵּׂיבָה וְהַכָּבוֹד וְהַבָּנִים לַצַּדִּיקִים נָאֶה לָהֶם וְנָאֶה לָעוֹלָם. מַה טַעַם. עֲטֶרֶת תִּפְאֶרֶת שֵׂיבָה בְּדֶרֶךְ צְדָקָה תִּימָּצֵא. עֲטֶרֶת זְקֵינִים בְּנֵי בָנִים וְתִפְאֶרֶת בָּנִים אֲבוֹתָם׃ תִּפְאֶרֶת בַּחוּרִים כּוֹחָם וַהֲדַר זְקֵינִים שֵׂיבָה׃ וְאוֹמֵר וְנֶגֶד זְקֵינָיו כָּבוֹד׃ תַּנֵּי. רַבָּן שִׁמְעוֹן בֶּן גַּמְלִיאֵל אוֹמֵר. אֵילּוּ שֶׁבַע מִידּוֹת שֶׁמָּנוּ חֲכָמִים בַּצַּדִּיקִים כּוּלָּן נִתְקַיְּימוּ בְּרִבִּי וּבָנָיו. רִבִּי יוֹחָנָן אוֹמֵר. כָּל־שֶׁבַע מִידּוֹת שֶׁאָמְרוּ חֲכָמִים בַּצַּדִּיקִים הָיוּ בְרִבִּי. מָאן רִבִּי. הוּא רִבִּי הוּא רִבִּי יְהוּדָה הַנָּשִׂיא. אָמַר רִבִּי אַבָּהוּ. הוּא רִבִּי הוּא רִבִּי יוּדָן הַנָּשִׂיא הוּא רַבֵּינוּ.

[43]Rebbi Simeon ben Menasia says: Beauty, and vigor, and riches, and wisdom, and white hair, and honor, and children, are an adornment for the just. What is the reason? *A crown of glory is white hair; on the way of piety it is found*[44]. *A crown of the elderly are grandchildren; the glory of children are their parents*[45]. *The glory of the young is their force; the splendor of the elderly is white hair*[46]. And it says, *before his Elders in honor*[47]. [48]It was stated: Rabban Simeon ben Gamliel says, these seven qualities which the Sages enumerated for the just were all realized by Rebbi and his sons. Rebbi Johanan said, all seven qualities which the Sages enunciated about the just were in Rebbi. Who was Rebbi? Rebbi is Rebbi Jehudah the Prince. Rebbi Abbahu said, Rebbi is Rebbi Yudan the Prince, is Our Teacher[49].

43 Mishnah *Avot* 6:8, Tosephta *Sanhedrin* 11:8. In these sources, the original author is R. Simeon ben Iohai.

44 *Prov.* 16:31.

45 *Prov.* 17:6.

46 *Prov.* 20.29.

47 *Is.* 24:23.

48 This sentence has to be deleted since Rebbi's father cannot speak about his son and grandsons. Since Rebbi was the last of the Tannaïm, only amoraic statements about him are legitimate.

49 It is not clear whether he refers to R. Jehudah I ben Simeon, mentioned by R. Johanan, or to R. Jehudah II ben Gamliel.

(fol. 29d) **משנה ה**: חוֹמֶר בְּדִבְרֵי סוֹפְרִים מִבְּדִבְרֵי תוֹרָה הָאוֹמֵר אֵין תְּפִילִּין כְּדֵי לַעֲבוֹר עַל דִּבְרֵי תוֹרָה פָּטוּר חָמֵשׁ טוֹטָפוֹת לְהוֹסִיף עַל דִּבְרֵי סוֹפְרִים חַיָּיב:

Mishnah 5: [Denial] about words of the Sopherim is more serious than about words of the Torah. He who says that there are no phylacteries, to transgress the words of the Torah, is not prosecutable. Five compartments to add to the words of the Sopherim is punishable[50].

משנה ו: אֵין מְמִיתִין אוֹתוֹ לֹא בְּבֵית דִּין שֶׁבְּעִירוֹ וְלֹא בְּבֵית דִּין שֶׁבְּיַבְנֶה אֶלָּא מַעֲלִין אוֹתוֹ לְבֵית דִּין הַגָּדוֹל שֶׁבִּירוּשָׁלַם וּמְשַׁמְּרִין אוֹתוֹ עַד הָרֶגֶל וּמְמִיתִין אוֹתוֹ בָּרֶגֶל שֶׁנֶּאֱמַר וְכָל־הָעָם יִשְׁמְעוּ וְיִירָאוּ דִּבְרֵי רַבִּי עֲקִיבָה. רַבִּי יְהוּדָה אוֹמֵר אֵין מְעַנִּין אֶת דִּינוֹ שֶׁל זֶה אֶלָּא מְמִיתִין אוֹתוֹ מִיָּד וְכוֹתְבִין וְשׁוֹלְחִין שְׁלוּחִים בְּכָל־הַמְּקוֹמוֹת אִישׁ פְּלוֹנִי בֶּן אִישׁ פְּלוֹנִי נִתְחַייֵב מִיתָה בְּבֵית דִּין:

Mishnah 6: One executes him not at the court in his town, nor at the court at Jabneh[51] but one transports him to the Supreme Court in Jerusalem, keeps him until a holiday of pilgrimage, and executes him on the holiday[52] as it is said, *the entire people shall see and fear*[53], the words of Rebbi Aqiba. Rebbi Jehudah says, one does not procrastinate in his case but executes him immediately, writes, and sends messengers to all places: Mr. A son of Mr. B was found guilty to be executed by the court.

50 The person who denies a verse in the Torah (in this case *Deut*. 6:8,11:18; *Ex*. 13:16) is harmless since every schoolchild knows better. But the details of the construction of phylacteries are purely traditional , *viz.,* that the phylacteries on the arm have to be put into one box but those of the head into four compartments. As Y. Yadin has noted in his publication on the phylacteries from the Judean desert, they are made in the way of rabbinic phylacteries (at least as they used to be made until 200 years ago, with boxes of 1 cm edge length) but the text contains many more than the authorized verses. These *tefillin* therefore have to be classified as non-rabbinical.

51 The nearby court of appeals.

52 On holiday eve when everybody had arrived.

53 *Deut*. 17:13.

(30a line 64) **הלכה ה**: חוֹמֶר בְּדִבְרֵי סוֹפְרִים כול'. **הלכה ו**: אֵין מְמִיתִין אוֹתוֹ כול'. חֲבֵרַייָא בְשֵׁם רִבִּי יוֹחָנָן. דּוֹדִים דִּבְרֵי סוֹפְרִים לְדִבְרֵי תוֹרָה וַחֲבִיבִים כְּדִבְרֵי תוֹרָה. וְחִכֵּךְ כְּיֵין הַטּוֹב. שִׁמְעוֹן בַּר בָּא בְשֵׁם רִבִּי יוֹחָנָן. דּוֹדִים דִּבְרֵי סוֹפְרִים לְדִבְרֵי תוֹרָה וַחֲבִיבִים יוֹתֵר מִדִּבְרֵי תוֹרָה. כִּי־טוֹבִים דּוֹדֶיךָ מִיָּיִן: רִבִּי בָּא בַּר כֹּהֵן בְּשֵׁם רִבִּי יוּדָה בַּר פָּזִי. תֵּדַע לָךְ שֶׁדִּבְרֵי סוֹפְרִים חֲבִיבִין מִדִּבְרֵי תוֹרָה. שֶׁהֲרֵי רִבִּי טַרְפוֹן אִילּוּ לֹא קָרָא לֹא הָיָה עוֹבֵר אֶלָּא בַּעֲשֵׂה. וְעַל יְדֵי שֶׁעָבַר עַל דִּבְרֵי בֵית הִלֵּל נִתְחַייֵב מִיתָה. עַל שֵׁם וּפֹרֵץ גָּדֵר יִשְּׁכֶנּוּ נָחָשׁ.

2 וחכך | **ת** וחיכך 3 בא | **ת** ווא וחביבים | **ע** ואמונים 4 ר' יודה | **ע** - שדברי סופרים חביבין | **ת** שחביבין דברי סופרים **ע** חביבין יותר

Halakhah 5: "[Denial] about words of the Sopherim is more serious," etc. **Halakhah 6**: "One executes him not," etc. [54]The colleagues in the name of Rebbi Johanan: The words of the Sopherim are related to the words of Scripture and are pleasant like the words of Scripture; *your throat is like good wine*[55]. Simeon bar Abba in the name of Rebbi Johanan: The words of the Sopherim are related to the words of Scripture and are more pleasant than the words of Scripture, *for your friendship is better than wine*[56]. Rebbi Abba bar Cohen in the name of Rebbi Judah bar Pazi: You may know that he words of the Sopherim are more pleasant than the words of Scripture, because if Rebbi Tarphon did not recite at all he would only have transgressed a positive commandment. But because he transgressed the words of the House of Hillel he should have suffered death since it says, *if one breaches a wall he will be bitten by a snake*[56].

54 This and the next paragraphs are from *Berakhot* 1:7 (Notes 182-191) (**ת**). It is copied again in *Avodah zarah* 2:8 41c l. 46 (**ע**).

55 *Cant.* 7:10

56 *Cant.* 1:2.

57 *Eccl.* 10:8.

(30a line 73) תַּנֵּי רִבִּי יִשְׁמָעֵאל דִּבְרֵי תוֹרָה יֵשׁ בָּהֶן אִיסּוּר וְיֵשׁ בָּהֶן הֵיתֵר. יֵשׁ בָּהֶן קוּלִּים וְיֵשׁ בָּהֶן חוּמְרִין. אֲבָל דִּבְרֵי סוֹפְרִים כּוּלָּן חוֹמֶר. תֵּדַע לָךְ שֶׁהוּא כֵן. דְּתַנִּינָן תַּמָּן. הָאוֹמֵר. אֵין תְּפִילִּין כְּדֵי לַעֲבוֹר עַל דִּבְרֵי תוֹרָה פָּטוּר. חָמֵשׁ טוֹטָפוֹת לְהוֹסִיף עַל דִּבְרֵי סוֹפְרִים חַיָּב. אָמַר רִבִּי חִינְנָא בְּרֵיהּ דְּרִבִּי אָדָא בְּשֵׁם רִבִּי תַנְחוּם בַּר חִייָה. חֲמוּרִים דִּבְרֵי זְקֵינִים מִדִּבְרֵי נְבִיאִים. דִּכְתִיב אַל־תַּטִּיפוּ יַטִּיפוּן. וּכְתִיב אַטִּיף לְךָ לַיַּיִן וְלַשֵּׁכָר וגו'. נָבִיא וְזָקֵן לְמָה הֵן דּוֹמִין. לַמֶּלֶךְ שֶׁשָּׁלַח שְׁנֵי פַלְמֶנְטָרִין שֶׁלּוֹ לִמְדִינָה. עַל אֶחָד מֵהֶן כָּתוּב. אִם אֵינוֹ מַרְאֶה חוֹתָם שֶׁלִּי וְסֵמַנְטֵירִין שֶׁלִּי אַל תַּאֲמִינוּ לוֹ. וְעַל אֶחָד כָּתוּב. אַף עַל פִּי שֶׁאֵינוֹ מַרְאֶה חוֹתָם שֶׁלִּי וְסֵמַנְטֵירִין שֶׁלִּי תַּאֲמִינוּ לוֹ. כָּךְ בְּנָבִיא כָתוּב וְנָתַן אֵלֶיךָ אוֹת אוֹ מוֹפֵת. בְּרַם הָכָא. עַל־פִּי הַתּוֹרָה אֲשֶׁר יוֹרוּךָ.

1 קולים | **ת** קולין **ע** קלין 2 סופרים | **ע** סופרין חומר | **ת** חומרין הן תדע לך שהוא כן | **ע** - 4 חיננא | **ת** חנניה **ע** חנינה בריה דר' אדא | **ע** בשם ר' אידי חמורים | **ע** חמודים 5 יטיפון | **ת** יטיפון אל יטיפו לאלה לא יסג כלימות 6 ששלח | **ת** ששולח **ע** ששילח פלממטרין | **ת** פלמטרין **ע** סימנטרין כתוב | **תע** כתב 7 כתוב | **תע** כתב וסימנטרין שלי | **ת** - תאמינו | **ת** האמינוהו בלי חותם וסימנטירין **ע** האמינו

Rebbi Ismael stated: In the Torah there are forbidden matters and permitted matters. There are easy parts and severe parts. But in the words of the Sopherim all are severe. You can realize that this is so since we have stated: "He who says that there are no phylacteries, to transgress the words of the Torah, is not prosecutable. Five compartments to add to the words of the Sopherim is punishable." Rebbi Ḥinena, the son of Rebbi Ada, in the name of Rebbi Tanḥum bar Ḥiyya: The words of the Sages carry more weight than those of the prophets since it is written, *do not preach, they preach*[58]. And it is written, *I shall preach to you for wine and liquor*[59]. The relation of prophet and scholar can be compared to the case of a king who sent two *diplomatarii*[60] to a province. About one of them it was written, if he does not show you my seal and σημαντήριον[61], do not believe him. About the other it was written, even if he does not show you my seal and σημαντήριον, believe him. So about a prophet is written, *he gives you a sign or miracle*[62]. But here it is written, *according to the teachings that they will teach you*[63].

58 *Micha* 2:6.

59 *Micha* 2:11.

60 A person authorized to use the imperial mail; *Berakhot* 1:7 Note 189.

61 "Seal" in Greek; *Berakhot* 1:7 Note 190.

62 *Deut.* 13:2.

63 *Deut.* 17:11.

(30b line 8) הַתּוֹרָה אָֽמְרָה. אַרְבַּע טוֹטָפוֹת שֶׁלְאַרְבַּע פָּרָשִׁיּוֹת. עֲשָׂאָן חָמֵשׁ טוֹטָפוֹת שֶׁלְאַרְבַּע פָּרָשִׁיּוֹת חַייָב. רִבִּי בָּא רִבִּי יוֹחָנָן בְּשֵׁם רִבִּי הוֹשַׁעְיָה. אֵינוֹ חַייָב עַד שֶׁיּוֹרֶה בְדָבָר שֶׁעִיקָּרוֹ מִדִּבְרֵי תוֹרָה וּפֵירוּשׁוֹ מִדִּבְרֵי סוֹפְרִים. כְּגוֹן הַנְּבֵילָה כְּגוֹן הַשֶּׁרֶץ שֶׁעִיקָּרָן מִדִּבְרֵי תוֹרָה וּפֵירוּשָׁן מִדִּבְרֵי סוֹפְרִין. אָמַר רִבִּי זְעִירָא. לְעוֹלָם אֵינוֹ חַיָּיב עַד שֶׁיְּכַפּוּר וְיוֹרֶה בְדָבָר שֶׁעִיקָּרוֹ מִדִּבְרֵי תוֹרָה וּפֵירוּשׁוֹ מִדִּבְרֵי סוֹפְרִין. כְּגוֹן הַנְּבֵילָה וּכְגוֹן שֶׁרֶץ שֶׁעִיקָּרָן מִדִּבְרֵי תוֹרָה וּפֵירוּשָׁן מִדִּבְרֵי סוֹפְרִין. וְהוּא שֶׁיִּגְרַע וְיוֹסִיף בְּדָבָר שֶׁהוּא מְגָרֵעַ וְהוּא מוֹסִיף. זְחֲלִין אַפּוֹי דְּרַב הוֹשַׁעְיָה. אֲמַר לֵיהּ. צְרִיךְ לָךְ שְׁחַק לָךְ. לָא צְרִיךְ לָךְ הַפְלִיג עֲלָךְ. תְּלַת עֶשְׂרֵה שְׁנִין עֲבַד עֲלִיל קוֹמֵי רַבֵּיהּ דְּלָא צְרִיךְ לֵיהּ. רִבִּי שְׁמוּאֵל בְּשֵׁם רִבִּי זְעוּרָא. אִילּוּ לֹא דַיּוֹ אֶלָּא שֶׁהָיָה מְקַבֵּיל פְּנֵי רַבּוֹ. שֶׁכָּל־הַמְקַבֵּיל פְּנֵי רַבּוֹ כְּאִילּוּ מְקַבֵּל פְּנֵי שְׁכִינָה. הָתִיב רִבִּי בֶּרֶכְיָה. וְהָא תַנִּינָן. גּוּפָהּ שֶׁלַּבַּהֶרֶת כִּגְרִיס הַקִּילְקִי מְרוּבָּע. אָמַר רִבִּי אַבָּמָרִי. מָאן דְּאָמַר דְּכֵן. הָתִיב רִבִּי בָּא בַּר מָמָל. וְהָא תַאנֵי. שְׁתֵּי פָרָשִׁיּוֹת שֶׁבַּמְּזוּזָה. אֲמַר לֵיהּ. הִיא תְפִילִין הִיא מְזוּזָה. הָתִיב רַב הַמְנוּנָא. וְהָא תַנֵּי. בַּצִּיצִית אַרְבַּע אֶצְבָּעוֹת שֶׁלְאַרְבַּע חוּטִין. עֲשָׂאָן שָׁלֹשׁ אֶצְבָּעוֹת שֶׁלְאַרְבַּע חוּטִין. אָמַר לֵיהּ. גָּרַע וְלֹא הוֹסִיף. הָתִיב רִבִּי חַגַּיי קוֹמֵי רִבִּי יוֹסֵי. וְהָא תַנֵּי. שְׁלִישׁ לִרְבִיכָה שְׁלִישׁ לַחַלּוֹת שְׁלִישׁ לָרְקִיקִים. שִׁילְּשָׁן שְׁלִישׁ לִרְבִיכָה שְׁלִישׁ לַחַלּוֹת שְׁלִישׁ לָרְקִיקִים. אָמַר לֵיהּ. מִיגְרַע מִן הָֽרְבִיכָה וּמוֹסִיף עַל הַחַלּוֹת וְעַל הָֽרְקִיקִין.

The Torah said, four compartments for four paragraphs[64]. If he made five compartments for four paragraphs, he is punishable. Rebbi Abba, Rebbi Johanan in the name of Rebbi Hoshaia: He is punishable only if he instructs in a matter whose root is from the Torah but whose explanation is from the words of the Sopherim; for example, the carcass; for example, the crawling animal, whose root is from the words of the Torah[65] but whose explanation is from the words of the Sopherim. Rebbi Ze`ira said, he never is punishable unless he deny and instruct in a matter whose root is from the Torah but whose explanation is from the words of the Sopherim; for example, the carcass; for example, the crawling animal, whose root is from the words of the Torah but whose explanation is from the words of the Sopherim, on condition that he simultaneously deduct in a matter which permits subtraction and addition[66].

The face of Rav[67] Hoshaia lit up[68]. He[69] told him, do I need you that you enjoy it? I do not need you, I am adding to your statement. Thirteen years he[69] went and came before his teacher even though he did not need him. Rebbi Samuel in the name of Rebbi Ze`ura: Was it not enough for him to have paid his respects to his teacher since anybody who pays his respects to his teacher is as if he paid his respects to the Divine Presence.

Rebbi Berekhiah objected, did we not state[70], "the body of *baheret* is the square area of a split cilician bean"? Rebbi Abba Mari said, one who said it is pure[71]. Rebbi Abba bar Mamal objected, did we not state[72], "two paragraphs in the *mezuzzah*"? He told him, phylacteries and *mezuzah* are the same[73]. Rav Hamnuna objected, was it not stated[74]: The *sisit* must be four finger lengths for four threads? He told him, in that he diminished but did not add[75]. Rebbi Haggai objected before Rebbi Yose, was it not stated[76], one third for the scalded[77], one third for round cakes, one third for flat cakes. If he used it in thirds, one third for the scalded, one third for round cakes, one third for flat cakes? He told him, he subtracts from the scalded and adds for round cakes and flat cakes[78].

64 The word טטפת (*Ex.*13:16, *Deut.* 6:8,11:18) "head *tefillin*" is confirmed by the Babli's use, *Šabbat* 57a, as "woman's headband". A fancy etymology, which reads the number 4 into the word, to support the statement that head phylacteries must be

made with four compartments (*Sanhedrin* 4b, *Zevahim* 37b, *Menahot* 34b) is rabbinic.

65 The different kinds of impurity of dead animals are described in *Lev.* 11 but the details, in particular the minimal quantities which induce impurity, are rabbinic.

66 R. Ze`ira restricts the original saying of R. Hoshaia, which was extended by R. Johanan to include impurity of dead animals. In the Babli 88b it is asserted that in the interpretation here ascribed to R. Ze`ira the only crime a rebellious Elder could be charged with was to instruct to make head phylacteries not with four but with five compartments. Then he obviously adds to the number of compartments but at the same time, since one of the four texts now has to occupy two compartments, he eliminates the rule which determines the order in which the texts have to be placed into compartments. This is simultaneously adding and subtracting; from the following discussion (Notes 63-71) it follows that this also is the interpretation required for the Yerushalmi. It is clear that *tefillin* of the kind found in the Judean desert (Note 50) are not considered.

67 This should read "Rebbi".

68 He was happy that R. Johanan quoted him even though the extension to include carcasses and dead crawling animals was not his formulation.

69 R. Johanan.

70 Mishnah *Nega`im* 6:1; cf. *Nedarim* 3:2 Note 49, *Ma`serot* 5:7 Notes 122-125.

Baheret is a skin disease in which white spots appear on the skin (*Lev.* 13). The minimum size of such a spot which makes its bearer impure is that of a "square split cilician bean" which is defined as 36 (hairwidths)^2. All questions are directed to R. Ze`ira; one tries to find a law other than that of phylacteries where a ruling by a rebellious Elder could simultaneously add and subtract from the received norm.

It was shown in *Ma`serot*, by a question of R. Berekhiah, that *square* cannot mean that the white spot be an exact square, since nothing in biology exhibits geometrically straight lines and right angles. Therefore, the question can only be whether the spot must contain a square of minimal size or only have surface area of 36 (hairwidths)^2.

71 For ms. דכן "pure" (Mishnah *Idiut* 8:4) *editio princeps* has הכן "so", which made the clause incomprehensible. In *Ma`serot* and *Nedarim*, it was determined that the Mishnah has to be read as referring to surface area. An elder who would read the Mishnah as requiring a white spot containing a square of minimal size would actually declare most impure spots as pure. This is diminution; nothing is added.

72 Mishnah *Menahot* 3:7. Again the obligation to write words of the Torah on one's doorposts is biblical (*Deut.* 6:9,11:19) while the selection of the texts and the details are rabbinic. If one put the two texts into two cases instead of writing them on one sheet of parchment, it would be simultaneously adding and subtracting.

73 It is agreed that instead of "only *tefillin*" one should accept "only *tefillin* and *mezuzzot*" as possible objects of the Elder's misdeeds since both are mentioned together in the biblical texts.

74 *Menahot* 41b, *Bekhorot* 39b, determining the minimal length of the

unknotted part of the *ṣisit*, the threads to be attached to the corners of one's rectangular garment.

75 This is pure diminution; nothing is added.

76 Mishnah *Menahot* 7:1, *Menaḥot* 89a, *Sifra Saw Pereq* 11(6). The rules of a thanksgiving sacrifice (*Lev*. 7:12-14) require three kinds of unleavened oiled breads in addition to a set of leavened bread. The rabbinic interpretation requires that the flour be divided into three equal parts but that half of the oil be used on the unleavened bread scalded in hot water like a bagel, the rest being used for the other two kinds. If instead somebody instructed also to distribute the oil evenly, would he not subtract from one kind and add to the others?

77 Explanation of Rashi in *Menaḥot*.

78 The questioner considered all three kinds of *mazzah* as one commandment when in fact they are three different obligations; there is no simultaneity for one obligation.

(fol. 29d) **משנה ז**: וּנְבִיא הַשֶּׁקֶר וְהַמִּתְנַבֵּא עַל מַה שֶׁלֹּא שָׁמַע וּמַה שֶׁלֹּא נֶאֱמַר לוֹ. אֲבָל הַכּוֹבֵשׁ אֶת נְבוּאָתוֹ וְהַמְּוַותֵּר עַל דִּבְרֵי נָבִיא וְנָבִיא שֶׁעָבַר עַל דִּבְרֵי עַצְמוֹ מִיתָתוֹ בִּידֵי שָׁמַיִם שֶׁנֶּאֱמַר אָנֹכִי אֶדְרוֹשׁ מֵעִמּוֹ:

Mishnah 7: And the false prophet and one who prophesies what he did not hear and what was not said to him[79]. But as to one who suppresses his vision, and one who disregards the prophet's words, and a prophet who transgressed his own word, their death is by the Hand of Heaven as it is said, *I shall ask it from him*[80].

79 These are cases for the human court.

80 *Deut*. 18:19, cf. *Sifry Deut.* 177.

(30b line 29) **הלכה ז**: וּנְבִיא הַשֶּׁקֶר כול'. הַמִּתְנַבֵּא עַל מַה שֶׁלֹּא שָׁמַע. כְּצִדְקִיָּה בֶּן כְּנַעֲנָה. וּמַה שֶׁלֹּא נֶאֱמַר לוֹ. כַּחֲנַנְיָה בֶּן עַזּוּר. רִבִּי יְהוֹשֻׁעַ בֶּן לֵוִי אָמַר. חֲנַנְיָה בֶּן עַזּוּר נְבִיא אֱמֶת הָיָה אֶלָּא שֶׁהָיָה לוֹ קִיבּוּסֶת וְהָיָה שׁוֹמֵעַ מַה שֶׁיִּרְמְיָה מִתְנַבֵּא בַשּׁוּק הָעֶלְיוֹן וְיוֹרֵד וּמִתְנַבֵּא בַשּׁוּק הַתַּחְתּוֹן. אֲמַר לֵיהּ חֲנַנְיָה בֶּן עַזּוּר. כָּל־סֵמָּא דְמִילְּתָא לָא דָא הִיא אֶלָּא לְפִי מְלֹאת לְבָבֶל שִׁבְעִים שָׁנָה אֶפְקוֹד אֶתְכֶם. כָּל־יָמָיו שֶׁלִּמְנַשֶּׁה אֵינָן אֶלָּא חֲמִשִּׁים וְחָמֵשׁ שָׁנָה. צֵא מֵהֶן עֶשְׂרִים שֶׁאֵין בֵּית דִּין שֶׁלְּמַעֲלָה עוֹנְשִׁין וְכוֹרְתִים. וּשְׁתַּיִם שֶׁלְּאָמוֹן וּשְׁלֹשִׁים וְאַחַת שֶׁלְּיֹאשִׁיָּהוּ. הָדָא הִיא דִכְתִיב וַיְהִי | הַשָּׁנָה הַהִיא בְּרֵאשִׁית מַמְלֶכֶת צִדְקִיָּהוּ מֶלֶךְ־יְהוּדָה בַּשָּׁנָה הַחֲמִשִׁית בַּחוֹדֶשׁ הַחֲמִישִׁי אָמַר אֵלַי חֲנַנְיָה בֶן־עַזּוּר הַנָּבִיא אֲשֶׁר מִגִּבְעוֹן בֵּית יי לְעֵינֵי הַכֹּהֲנִים וְכָל־הָעָם לֵאמֹר: כֹּה־אָמַר יי צְבָאוֹת אֱלֹהֵי יִשְׂרָאֵל לֵאמֹר שָׁבַרְתִּי אֶת עוֹל מֶלֶךְ בָּבֶל בְּעוֹד | שְׁנָתַיִם יָמִים אֲנִי מֵשִׁיב אֶל־הַמָּקוֹם הַזֶּה אֶת־כָּל־כְּלֵי בֵּית יי אֲשֶׁר לָקַח נְבוּכַדנֶאצַּר מֶלֶךְ־בָּבֶל מִן־הָעִיר הַזֹּאת

וַיְבִיאֵם בָּבֶל׃ אָמַר לוֹ יִרְמְיָה. אַתָּה אוֹמֵר. בְּעוֹד | שְׁנָתַיִם יָמִים אֲנִי מֵשִׁיב וגו'. וַאֲנִי אוֹמֵר שֶׁנְּבוּכַדְנֶאצַּר בָּא וְנוֹטֵל אֶת הַשְּׁאָר. בָּבֶלָה יוּבָאוּ וְשָׁמָּה יִהְיוּ וגו'. אָמַר לוֹ. תֵּן סֵימָן לִדְבָרֶיךָ. אָמַר לֵיהּ. אֲנִי מִתְנַבֵּא לְרָעָה וְאֵינִי יָכוֹל לִיתֵּן סֵימָן לִדְבָרַיי. שֶׁהַקָּדוֹשׁ בָּרוּךְ הוּא אוֹמֵר לְהָבִיא רָעָה וּמִתְנָחֵם. וְאַתָּה מִתְנַבֵּא לְטוֹבָה. אַתְּ הוּא שֶׁאַתְּ הוּא צָרִיךְ לִיתֵּן סֵימָן לִדְבָרֶיךָ. אָמַר לוֹ. לָאו. אַתְּ הוּא שֶׁאַתְּ צָרִיךְ לִיתֵּן סֵימָן לִדְבָרֶיךָ. אָמַר לוֹ. אִין כֵּינִי הֲרֵי אֲנִי נוֹתֵן אוֹת וּמוֹפֵת בְּאוֹתוֹ הָאִישׁ. הַשָּׁנָה הַהִיא הוּא מֵת. כִּי סָרָה דִבֵּר עַל יי. וַהֲוָת לֵיהּ כֵּן וַיָּמָת חֲנַנְיָה הַנָּבִיא בַּשָּׁנָה הַהִיא בַּחוֹדֶשׁ הַשְּׁבִיעִי׃ שָׁנָה אַחֶרֶת הָיְתָה וַתְּ מַר הָכֵין. אֶלָּא מְלַמֵּד שֶׁמֵּת בְּעֶרֶב רֹאשׁ הַשָּׁנָה וְצִוָּה אֶת בָּנָיו וְאֶת בְּנֵי בֵיתוֹ לְהַסְתִּיר אֶת הַדָּבָר שֶׁיּוֹצִיאוּהוּ אַחַר רֹאשׁ הַשָּׁנָה בִּשְׁבִיל לַעֲשׂוֹת נְבוּאָתוֹ שֶׁל יִרְמְיָה שֶׁקֶר.

Halakhah 7: "And the false prophet," etc. "And one who prophesies what he did not hear," like Ṣedekias ben Kenaana[81]. "And what was not said to him," like Ḥanania ben Azzur. Rebbi Joshua ben Levi said, Ḥanania ben Azzur was a true prophet;[82] only he took instruction[83] and heard what Jeremiah prophesied in the upper market; he went and prophesied in the lower market. Ḥanania ben Azzur told him, is not the essence[84] of the matter *only once seventy years will be fullfilled for Babylon, I shall remember you*[85]. In all, the days of Manasse were 55 years. Deduct from them 20 years for which the Heavenly Court does not punish or extirpate, add the two of Amon and 31 of Josia[86]. That is what is written[87]: *At the beginning of the reign of Ṣedekias the king of Jehudah, in the fifth*[88] *year, in the fifth month, Ḥanania ben Azzur, the prophet from Gibeon, said to me in the House of the Eternal, before the priests and all the people, as follows: So said the Eternal of Hosts, the God of Israel, as follows. I broke the yoke of the king of Babylon; in another two years I shall return to this place all the Temple vessels which Nebuchadnezzar, the king of Babylon, took from this city and brought to Babylon.* Jeremiah told him, you are saying that *in another two years I shall return*, etc. But I say that Nebuchadnezzar will come and take the remainder. *To Babylon they will be brought and stay there*[89], etc. He[90] said to him, give a sign. He[91] answered, I am prophesying bad things and cannot give a sign for my words since the Holy One, praise to Him, said to bring evil and might refrain from it[92]. But you prophesy good things; you are obligated to give a sign. He[90] said to him, no, it is you who has to give a sign for your words. He[91] answered, if it is so, I shall give a sign and miracle in the person of that man; this year he dies, for he spoke obstinately about the Eternal. This happened to him; *Hanania the prophet died in this year, in the Seventh month*[93]. This was another year and you are saying so? But it teaches that he died on the Eve of New Year's Day and ordered his sons and wife to hide the matter, that they should bury him after the new Year in order to falsify Jeremiah's prophecy.

81 *1K.* 22:11, Babli 89a.

82 Since Jeremiah called him a prophet.

83 Deriving the unexplained word קיבוסת from Arabic قنس which among other meanings also signifies "to take instructions from somebody." The background is explained in the Babli, 89a: Since Hanania had heard Jeremiah predict the downfall of Elam, which the talmudic authors take as an ally, not an adversary, of Babylonia, and concluded that if the ally fell, the principal would fall with him.

84 Explaining סמא either from Arabic سما "to be high" or from Latin *summa.*

85 *Jer.* 29:10.

86 This follows the author of Kings who puts all blame for the Babylonian exile on Manasse. While the numbers add up to 68, they make no sense. Manasse became king at age 12, therefore he was responsible during 47 years of kingship. (For the doctrine that people become responsible adults in the eyes of Heaven at age 20, cf. *Bikkurim* 2:1, Note 13, Babli *Šabbat* 89b.) Josia became king at age 8; his 31 years therefore should be reduced to 23 but, since he was the only good king following Manasse, he should not be counted at all. Adding then 2 for Amon, 11 for Joyakim, and 5 for Sedekias, one only obtains 65 years (or 66 if a full year is counted for Joyachin.)

87 *Jer.*28:1-3.

88 In the verse: fourth.

89 *Jer.* 27:22.

90 Hananiah.

91 Jeremiah.

92 This is generally accepted; repentance always may avert evil.

93 *Jer.* 28:17. While the Talmud assumes that the "Day of Remembrance," the first of the seventh month, always was New Year's Day, it is clear that *Jer.* follows the Judean calendar which starts the year in Spring.

(30b line 56) הַכּוֹבֵשׁ עַל נְבוּאָתוֹ. כְּיוֹנָה בֶּן אֲמִיתַּיי. אָמַר רִבִּי יוֹנָה. יוֹנָה בֶּן אֲמִיתַּיי נְבִיא אֱמֶת הָיָה. אַתְּ מוֹצֵא בְּשָׁעָה שֶׁאָמַר לוֹ הַקָּדוֹשׁ בָּרוּךְ הוּא קוּם לֵךְ אֶל־נִינְוֵה הָעִיר הַגְּדוֹלָה וּקְרָא עָלֶיהָ כִּי־עָלְתָה רָעָתָם לְפָנָיי: אָמַר יוֹנָה. יוֹדֵעַ אֲנִי שֶׁהַגּוֹיִים קְרוֹבֵי תְשׁוּבָה הֵן. וַהֲרֵינִי הוֹלֵךְ וּמִתְנַבֵּא עֲלֵיהֶם וְהֵם עוֹשִׂים תְּשׁוּבָה וְהַקָּדוֹשׁ בָּרוּךְ הוּא בָּא וּפוֹרֵעַ מִשּׂוֹנְאֵיהֶן שֶׁלְּיִשְׂרָאֵל. וּמֶה עָלַי לַעֲשׂוֹת. לִבְרוֹחַ. וַיָּקָם יוֹנָה֙ לִבְרֹחַ תַּרְשִׁישָׁה מִלִּפְנֵי יי וַיֵּרֶד יָפוֹ וַיִּמְצָא אֳנִיָּה | בָּאָה תַרְשִׁישׁ וַיִּתֵּן שְׂכָרָהּ וַיֵּרֶד בָּהּ֙ וגו'.

"And one who suppresses his prophecy," like Jonah ben Amitai[94]. Rebbi Jonah said, Jonah ben Amitai was a true prophet. You find that when the Holy One, praise to Him, told him, *get up and go to the great city of Nineveh and call out over it that their evil came before Me*[95], Jonah said, I know that Gentiles are close to repentance; if I would go and prophesy for them and they repented, the Holy One, praise to Him, would make himself paid from the haters of Israel[96]. What can I do? I must flee! *Jonah got up to flee to Tarshish from before the Eternal; he descended to Jaffa, found a ship destined for Tarshish, paid his fare and entered it,*[97]" etc.

94 Babli 89a; Tosephta 14:15.

95 *Jonah* 1:2.

96 I. e., punish Israel for not repenting.

97 *Jonah* 1:3.

(30b line 63) וְהַמְוותֵּר עַל דִּבְרֵי הַנָּבִיא. כְּעִידוֹ הַחוֹזֶה. אָמַר רִבִּי שְׁמוּאֵל בַּר רַב יִצְחָק. זֶה אֲמַצְיָה כֹהֵן בֵּיתאֵל. אָמַר רִבִּי יוֹסֵי. פִּיתְפּוּתֵי בֵצִים הָיוּ שָׁם. וְאֵי זֶה זֶה. זֶה יְהוֹנָתָן בֶּן גֵּרְשׁוֹם בֶּן מְנַשֶּׁה.

"And one who disregards the prophet's words." Like the seer Ido[98]. Rebbi Samuel bar Rav Isaac said, this is Amaṣiah the priest of Bethel. Rebbi Yose said, this is breaking of eggs[99]; who is it? He is Jonathan ben Gershom ben Manasse[100].

98 The text is lacunary. One must read with the Tosephta (14:15) and the Babli (89b): One who disregards the prophet's words, like the companion of Micha (*1K.* 20:35) and the prophet who disregards his own words like the seer Ido (mentioned in *2Chr.* 12:15 who in all talmudic sources is identified as the anonymous "prophet from Jehudah" in *1K.* 13). R. Samuel bar Rav Isaac said, the old prophet living in Bethel (*1K.* 13:11) is Amasiah the priest of Bethel (*Am.* 7:12).

99 R. Samuel bar Rav Isaac spoke in error; the old prophet at the time of Jeroboam I cannot be the priest at the time of Jeroboam II.

100 Jonathan ben Gershom ben Moses, as asserted in an anonymous note (*Berakhot* 9:3, Note 135). To support this assertion, the next paragraph is a rearrangement of a text in *Berakhot* 9:3 (Notes 128-135); it lacks the punch line that Jonathan was the old prophet.

(30b line 65) אַתְּ מוֹצֵא בְּשָׁעָה שֶׁבָּא דָוִד וּמְצָאוֹ שֶׁהוּא עוֹבֵד עֲבוֹדָה זָרָה אָמַר לוֹ. אַתָּה בֶּן בְּנוֹ שֶׁלְאוֹתוֹ צַדִּיק וְאַתְּ עוֹבֵד עֲבוֹדָה זָרָה. אָמַר לוֹ. מְסוֹרֶת בְּיָדִי מֵאֲבִי אַבָּא. מְכוֹר עַצְמְךָ לַעֲבוֹדָה

זָרָה וְאַל תִּצְטָרֵךְ לַבְּרִיּוֹת. אָמַר לוֹ. חַס וְשָׁלוֹם לֹא אָמַר לָךְ כֵּן אֶלָּא מְכוֹר עַצְמְךָ לַעֲבוֹדָה שֶׁהִיא זָרָה לָךְ וְאַל תִּצְטָרֵךְ לַבְּרִיּוֹת. כֵּיוָן שֶׁרָאָה דָוִד שֶׁהָיָה הַמָּמוֹן חָבִיב עָלָיו מִינֵיהוּ קוֹמֵס תֵּיסַוְורִין עַל בֵּית הַמִּקְדָּשׁ. הָדָא הִיא דִכְתִיב וּשְׁבוּאֵל בֶּן־גֵּרְשׁוֹם בֶּן־מנשה נָגִיד עַל־הָאוֹצָרוֹת׃ שְׁבוּאֵל שֶׁשָּׁב אֶל אֵל בְּכָל־כּוֹחוֹ. נָגִיד עַל־הָאוֹצָרוֹת. שֶׁמִּינֵיהוּ קוֹמֵס תֵּיסַוְורִין עַל־הָאוֹצָרוֹת.

חֲבֵרַייָא בְּעוֹן קוֹמֵי רִבִּי שְׁמוּאֵל בַּר נַחְמָן. כּוֹמֶר לַעֲבוֹדָה זָרָה וְהֶאֱרִיךְ יָמִים. אֲמַר לוֹן. עַל שֶׁהָיְתָה עֵינוֹ צָרָה בַּעֲבוֹדָה זָרָה שֶׁלּוֹ. וּמָה הָיְתָה עֵינוֹ צָרָה בַּעֲבוֹדָה זָרָה שֶׁלּוֹ. הֲוָה בַּר נַשׁ מַייְתֵי לֵיהּ תּוֹר אוֹ אִימֵּר אוֹ גְדִי לַעֲבוֹדָה זָרָה וַאֲמַר לֵיהּ. פַּייְסֵיהּ עָלַי. וְהוּא אֲמַר לֵיהּ. לָמָּה. וְכִי מַה מוֹעִילָה לָךְ. אֵינָהּ אוֹכֶלֶת וְאֵינָהּ שׁוֹתָה וְלֹא מֵטִיבָה וְלֹא מְרֵיעָה. וְהוּא אֲמַר לֵיהּ. הֵיךְ נַעֲבִיד. וְהוּא אֲמַר לֵיהּ. אֵיזִל וְאַייְתִי לִי חַד פִּינַךְ דְּסוֹלֶת וְעֶשֶׂר בֵּיעִין עֲלוֹי וַנָּא מְפַייֵס לֵיהּ עֲלָךְ. כֵּיוָן דַּהֲוָה אֲזַל הֲוָה אֲכִיל לוֹן. אֲתָא חַד בַּר פַּחִין וַאֲמַר לֵיהּ כֵּן. אָמַר לֵיהּ. אִם אֵינָהּ מוֹעִילָה כְלוּם מָה אַתְּ עֲבִיד הָכָא. אֲמַר לֵיהּ. בְּגִין חַיַּי.

מְתִיבִין לְרִבִּי שְׁמוּאֵל בַּר נַחְמָן. וְהָא כְתִיב עַד־יוֹם גְּלוֹת הָאָרֶץ. אֲמַר לוֹן כֵּיוָן שֶׁמֵּת דָּוִד וְעָמַד שְׁלֹמֹה וְהֶחֱלִיף כָּל־סֵנְקְלֵיטִין שֶׁלּוֹ חָזַר לְקִילְקוּלוֹ.

You find that when David came and found him serving foreign worship, he asked him: You are the grandson of that righteous man and you worship idols? *He*[100a] said to him, *I* have a tradition from my grandfather, sell yourself to foreign worship rather than need other people. He said to *him*: Heaven forbid! He did not say so, but rather sell yourself to work that is strange to you rather than need other people. When David saw that *he* loved money, he made *him* Count[100b] of the Temple treasuries. That is what is written, *Shabuel ben Gershom ben Moshe, overseer of the treasuries.* "Shabuel" because he returned to God with all his might; "overseer of the treasuries" that he made him Count of the treasuries.

The colleagues asked before Rebbi Samuel ben Naḥman: *He* was a priest of idol worship and lived so long? He said to them, because *he* was grudging to his idol. How was *he* grudging to his idol? If a man came to sacrifice an ox, a sheep, or a goat to the idol and told him: Make it favorably inclined towards me, *he* would say, what use does it have for you? It never eats, nor drinks, nor does good or evil. He said to *him*, what should we do? *He* said to him, go, make, and bring me a wooden vessel full of fine flour and put on it ten eggs, then *I* shall make it favorably inclined towards you. After he left, *he* would eat it. One day, a son of pashas came and *he* said that to him. He said to *him*, if it is of no use, what are *you* doing here? *He* answered him, because of my livelihood.

They objected to Rebbi Samuel bar Nahman: *Until the day the Land went into exile.* He said to them, when David died, Solomon rose and exchanged all his counselors[100c]. *He* returned to his former bad ways.

100a *Italics* show that Jonathan is the speaker.

100b Latin *comes* "associate, partner", a Byzantine title for a high-level bureaucrat.

The combination תֵּיסוּוְרִין עַל־הָאוֹצָרוֹת is a Greek-Hebrew double expression.

100c A description of Byzantine practices.

(30c line 9) וְנָבִיא שֶׁעָבַר עַל דִּבְרֵי עַצְמוֹ. כַּחֲבֵירוֹ שֶׁלְּמִיכָה. הָדָא הִיא דִכְתִיב וְנָבִ֤יא אֶחָד֙ זָקֵ֔ן יֹשֵׁ֖ב בְּבֵֽית־אֵ֑ל וַיָּב֣וֹא בְנ֡וֹ וַיְסַפֶּר־ל֣וֹ אֶת־כָּל־הַמַּעֲשֶׂ֣ה אֲשֶׁר־עָשָׂה֩ אִישׁ־הָאֱלֹהִ֨ים וגו'. וַיְדַבֵּ֧ר אֲלֵהֶ֛ם אֲבִיהֶ֖ם אֵי־זֶ֥ה הַדֶּ֖רֶךְ הָלָ֑ךְ וגו'. וַיֹּ֙אמֶר֙ אֶל־בָּנָ֔יו חִבְשׁוּ־לִ֖י אֶת הַחֲמ֑וֹר וגו'. וַיֵּ֗לֶךְ אַחֲרֵי֙ אִ֣ישׁ הָאֱלֹהִ֔ים וַֽיִּמְצָאֵ֔הוּ יוֹשֵׁ֖ב תַּ֣חַת הָאֵלָ֑ה וגו'. וַיֹּ֣אמֶר לֵ֔ךְ אִתִּ֖י הַבָּ֑יְתָה וֶאֱכֹ֖ל לָֽחֶם׃ וַיֹּ֗אמֶר לֹ֥א אוּכַ֛ל לָשׁ֥וּב וגו' עד וַיֹּ֣אמֶר ל֗וֹ גַּם־אֲנִ֣י נָבִיא֮ כָּמ֒וֹךָ֒ וּמַלְאָ֗ךְ דִּבֶּ֨ר אֵלַ֜י בִּדְבַ֤ר יי לֵאמֹר וגו' עַד וַיֹּ֥אכַל לֶ֛חֶם בְּבֵית֖וֹ וַיֵּ֥שְׁתְּ מָֽיִם כִּחֵ֖שׁ לֽוֹ׃ מָה הוּא כִּיחֵשׁ לוֹ. שִׁיקֵּר בֵּיהּ. וַיְהִ֕י הֵ֥ם יוֹשְׁבִ֖ים עַל הַשֻּׁלְחָ֑ן וַֽיְהִי֙ דְּבַר יי אֶל־הַנָּבִ֖יא אֲשֶׁ֥ר הֱשִׁיבֽוֹ׃ אֲשֶׁר הוֹשַׁב אֵין כָּתוּב כָּאן אֶלָּא אֲשֶׁר הֱשִׁיבוֹ. וַהֲרֵי הַדְּבָרִים קַל וָחוֹמֶר. וּמַה אִם מִי שֶׁהֶאֱכִיל אֶת חֲבֵירוֹ לֶחֶם שֶׁקֶר זָכָה שֶׁנִּתְיַיחֵד עָלָיו הַדִּיבֵּר. הַמַּאֲכִיל אֶת חֲבֵירוֹ לֶחֶם אֱמֶת עַל אַחַת כַּמָּה וְכַמָּה.

"And a prophet who transgressed his own word," like the companion of Micha[101]. That is what is written[102]: *An old prophet was dwelling at Bethel; his son came and told him all the actions which the man of God had wrought*, etc. *Their father asked them, which way did he go*, etc. *He told his sons, saddle the donkey for me*, etc. *He followed the man of God and found him sitting under the terebinth*, etc. *He said to him, come with me to my house and eat. He told him, I cannot return*, etc., up to *he said to him, I also am a prophet like you and an angel spoke to me the words of the Eternal as follows*, etc., up to *he should eat food and drink water; he tricked him.* What means "tricked him"? He lied to him. *While they were sitting at table, the word of the Eternal came to the prophet who had turned him back.* It is not written "who had returned," but "who had turned him back." Is that not an argument *de minore ad majus*? Since one who fed his neighbor food in falsehood was worthy of the Word to be addressed to him, one who feeds his neighbor food in truth, so much more.

101 This should read: "the prophet Ido" (Note 91).

102 *1K.* 13:11-20. The verses obviously are quoted from memory.

(30c line 21) כָּתוּב וְאִישׁ אֶחָד מִבְּנֵי הַנְּבִיאִים אָמַר אֶל־רֵעֵהוּ בִּדְבַר יְי וגו'. וַיֹּאמֶר לוֹ יַעַן אֲשֶׁר לֹא־שָׁמַעְתָּ֙ בְּקוֹל יְי הִנְּךָ הוֹלֵךְ֙ מֵאִתִּי וְהִכְּךָ הָאַרְיֵה וַיֵּלֶךְ֙ מֵאִתּוֹ וַיִּמְצָאֵהוּ הָאַרְיֵה וַיַּכֵּהוּ׃ וַיִּמְצָא֙ אִישׁ אַחֵר וַיֹּאמֶר הַכֵּינִי נָא וַיַּכֵּהוּ וגו'. וַיֵּלֶךְ֙ הַנָּבִיא וַיַּעֲמֹד לַמֶּלֶךְ עַל־הַדָּרֶךְ וַיִּתְחַפֵּשׂ בָּאֲפֵר עַל־עֵינָיו׃ וַיְהִי הַמֶּלֶךְ֙ עוֹבֵר וְהוּא צָעַק אֶל־הַמֶּלֶךְ וגו'. וַיְהִי עַבְדְּךָ עֹשֶׂה הֵנָּה וָהֵנָּה וגו'. וַיְמַהֵר וַיָּסַר֙ אֶת־הָאֲפֵר מֵעַל עֵינָיו וגו'. וַיֹּאמֶר לוֹ כֹּה אָמַר יְי יַעַן אֲשֶׁר שִׁלַּחְתָּ אֶת־אִישׁ־חֶרְמִי מִיָּד וְהָיְתָה נַפְשְׁךָ֙ תַּחַת נַפְשׁוֹ וְעַמְּךָ תַּחַת עַמּוֹ׃ וְכָתוּב וַיִּגַּשׁ אִישׁ הָאֱלֹהִים וַיֹּאמֶר כֹּה־אָמַר יְי. וְלָמָּה וַיֹּאמֶר וַיֹּאמֶר שְׁנֵי פְעָמִים. אֶלָּא בָאֲמִירָה רִאשׁוֹנָה אָמַר לוֹ. אִם בָּא בֶּן הֲדַד מֶלֶךְ אֲרָם תַּחַת יָדֶךָ אַל תָּחוּס עָלָיו וְאַל תַּחְמוֹל עָלָיו. וּבָאֲמִירָה הַשְּׁנִייָה אָמַר לוֹ יַעַן אֲשֶׁר שִׁלַּחְתָּ אֶת־אִישׁ־חֶרְמִי וגו'. כַּמָּה מְצוּדוֹת וַחֲרָמִים עָשִׂיתִי לוֹ עַד שֶׁמְּסַרְתִּיו תַּחַת יָדֶךָ וְשִׁלַּחְתּוֹ וְהָלַךְ בְּשָׁלוֹם. לְפִיכָךְ וְהָיְתָה נַפְשְׁךָ֙ תַּחַת נַפְשׁוֹ וְעַמְּךָ תַּחַת עַמּוֹ׃ אַתְּ מוֹצֵא בְשָׁעָה שֶׁיָּצְאוּ יִשְׂרָאֵל לַמִּלְחָמָה לֹא מֵת מִכּוּלָּם אֶלָּא אַחְאָב מֶלֶךְ יִשְׂרָאֵל בִּלְבַד. וְהָדָא הִיא דִכְתִיב וְאִישׁ מָשַׁךְ בַּקֶּשֶׁת֙ לְתוּמּוֹ וַיַּךְ אֶת־מֶלֶךְ יִשְׂרָאֵל בֵּין הַדְּבָקִים וּבֵין הַשִּׁרְיָן וַיֹּאמֶר לְרַכָּבוֹ הֲפוֹךְ יָדְךָ וְהוֹצִיאֵנִי מִן־הַמַּחֲנֶה כִּי הָחֳלֵיתִי׃ מָה אֲנִי מְקַיֵּים וְעַמְּךָ תַּחַת עַמּוֹ׃ רִבִּי יוֹחָנָן בְּשֵׁם רִבִּי שִׁמְעוֹן בֶּן יוֹחַי. אוֹתָהּ הַטִּיפָּה שֶׁיָּצָאת מֵאוֹתוֹ צַדִּיק כִּיפְּרָה עַל כָּל־יִשְׂרָאֵל.

It is written[103]: *One of the young prophets said to his neighbor by the Word of the Eternal*, etc. *He told him, since you did not listen to the Word of the Eternal, when you depart from me the lion will hit you; he departed from him, the lion found him and hit him. He found another man, said to him, hit me, and he hit him*[104] etc. *The prophet went, stood in the king's way, and had disguised himself by a band over his eyes. When the king passed by, he cried to the king*, etc. *Your servant went to and fro*, etc. *He told him, so says the Eternal: Because you sent away from your hand the man whom I had banned, your life will be for his life, and your people for his people.* And it is written[105]: *The man of God approached and said, so says the Eternal.* Why two times "and said"? But in the first address he told him, if Ben Hadad falls into you hand, do not have mercy on him and do not spare him. In the second address he told him, *because you sent away from your hand the man whom I had banned,* how many traps and hunting nets[106] I made for him until I delivered him into your hand, and you sent him away and he went in peace. Therefore, *your life will be for his life, and your people for his people*.

You find that when Israel went to war, nobody of them died but Ahab, the king of Israel. That is what is written[107]: *A man shot from his bow without aiming and hit the king of Israel between the joints of his armor; he told the driver, take me out of the camp because I became sick.* How can I confirm *your people for his people*? Rebbi Joḥanan in the name of Rebbi Simeon ben Ioḥai: That drop of blood which was drawn from the just man[108] did atone for all of Israel.

103 *1K.* 20:35-42.

104 The quote stops short of *he injured him* which later (Note 101) will be shown to be essential.

105 *Threni rabbati* 1(43). The full verse reads: *The man of God approached and said to the king of Israel and said, . . .*

106 Identifying חרם حرم "ban" with חרם خرم "netting".

107 *1K.* 22:34.

108 The prophet who was injured (Note 103). The suffering of the Just as atonement for the entire people is an idea found in apocryphal literature such as IV Maccabees; in rabbinic texts otherwise only in Midrash literature [*Tanhuma Wayyaqhel* 9 = *Ex. rabba* 35(4), *Lev. rabba* 2(1).]

(fol. 30a) **משנה ח**: הַמִּתְנַבֵּא בְשֵׁם עֲבוֹדָה זָרָה וְאוֹמֵר כָּךְ אָמְרָה עֲבוֹדָה זָרָה אֲפִלּוּ כִּוֵּן אֶת הַהֲלָכָה לְטַמֵּא אֶת הַטָּמֵא וּלְטַהֵר אֶת הַטָּהוֹר. הַבָּא עַל אֵשֶׁת אִישׁ כֵּיוָן שֶׁנִּכְנְסָה לִרְשׁוּת הַבַּעַל מִן הַנִּישׂוּאִין אַף עַל פִּי שֶׁלֹּא נִבְעֲלָה הַבָּא עָלֶיהָ הֲרֵי זֶה בְּחֶנֶק. וְזוֹמְמֵי בַת כֹּהֵן וּבוֹעֲלָהּ. הָא כָּל־הַזּוֹמְמִין מַקְדִּימִין לְאוֹתָהּ מִיתָה חוּץ מִזּוֹמְמֵי בַת כֹּהֵן וּבוֹעֲלָהּ:

Mishnah 8: One who prophesies in the name of foreign worship[109] and says, so speaks the foreign worship, even if he stated practice correctly to declare the impure impure and the pure pure. One who copulates with a married woman, from the moment she is in the husband's domain for definitive marriage even if she did not have intercourse[110], one who copulates with her is strangled. And the false witnesses of a Cohen's daughter and her paramour. Therefore all false witnesses are executed by that death except for the false witnesses of a Cohen's daughter and her paramour[111].

109 Who is strangled, Mishnah 11:1.

110 The preliminarily married virgin and her paramour are stoned. But once she entered the place where the definitive marriage is scheduled to take place, even though she still is a virgin, her adultery is punished by strangulation. This presupposes that the definitive marriage is celebrated on the husband's property.

111 The whoring daughter of a Cohen is burned only if she committed adultery while married (Chapter 7, Notes 8-12). But the adulterer with a married woman is strangled. The perjured witnesses have to be executed in the way the adulterer would have been executed had their testimony stood up in court since (*Deut.* 19:19) *you shall do to him what he intended to do to his brother*. Therefore, it is impossible to punish the perjured witnesses of a Cohen's daughter by exactly the death they intended to bring her to. This is the introduction to the next Chapter (*Makkot* 1 - *Sanhedrin* 12) which starts by exploring the punishment of perjured witnesses accusing a Cohen of breaking priestly rules.

(30c line 41) **הלכה ח**: וְהַמִּתְנַבֵּא בְשֵׁם עֲבוֹדָה זָרָה עול׳. אָמַר רִבִּי יוֹסֵי בֶּן חֲנִינָה. הַכֹּל הָיָה בִכְלָל לֹא־תַעֲנֶה בְרֵעֲךָ עֵד שָׁקֶר. יָצָא לִידוֹן בֵּין בְּאוֹת בֵּין בְּמוֹפֵת בֵּין בַּעֲבוֹדָה זָרָה בֵּין בִּשְׁאָר כָּל־הַמִּצְוֹת. אֶלָּא שֶׁעֲבוֹדָה זָרָה בֵּין שֶׁנִּתְכַּוֵּן לַעֲקוֹר אֶת כָּל־הַגּוּף בֵּין שֶׁלֹּא נִתְכַּוֵּן לַעֲקוֹר אֶת כָּל־הַגּוּף דִּבְרֵי רִבִּי שִׁמְעוֹן פּוֹטְרִין אוֹתוֹ. וְדִבְרֵי חֲכָמִים סוֹקְלִין אוֹתוֹ. אֲבָל בִּשְׁאָר כָּל־הַמִּצְוֹת דִּבְרֵי חֲכָמִים סוֹקְלִין אוֹתוֹ וּדִבְרֵי רִבִּי שִׁמְעוֹן יָבִין לֵיהּ פיונטייה.

Halakhah 8: "One who prophesies in the name of foreign worship," etc. [112]Rebbi Yose ben Ḥanina said, everything was included in *do not testify against your neighbor as a false witness*. It came to judge whether by sign, or by miracle, whether about foreign worship or any other commandment. But about foreign worship, whether he intended to uproot the entire body or did not intend to uproot the entire body, by the words of Rebbi Simeon one does not prosecute him, but by the words of the Sages one stones him. For any other commandment by the words of the Sages one stones him, by the words of Rebbi Simeon he should understand his *pywnṭ*.

112 This paragraph is thoroughly corrupt; the meaning can be understood approximately by reference to Tosephta 14:13: "He who prophesies to uproot one of the words of the Torah is punishable. Rebbi Simeon says, if he prophesies to uproot one of the words of the Torah but affirms others he cannot be prosecuted; but about foreign worship, even if he endorses it today but reneges tomorrow he is punishable."

With *Qorban Ha`edah* it seems that the quote from the Ten Commandments (*Ex.* 20:16) was induced by the parallel text at the beginning of the next Halakhah and should be replaced by *Deut.* 18:22. The argument would go as follows: In *Deut.*

18:20-22, the court is commanded to punish the false prophet by a death sentence. The manner of execution is not specified; this implies that it must be by strangling. But in 13:2-12 the punishment of strange worship (idolatry) is stoning.

A person can be punished as a false prophet only if first he had established his credentials as a prophet by a sign or a miracle (*Deut.* 13:2, 18:22; Note 106). Then if the prophet argues for idolatry, even if he does not abolish any commandment of the Torah, he has to be punished (even if he propagates foreign worship in the name of the Eternal; Babli 89b). If he tells others not to obey some of the precepts of the Torah, for the Sages he is punishable, but not for R. Simeon. The prophet can be prosecuted only if he induces others to neglect Torah precepts, not if he himself seemingly violates them by Divine Command, as Elijah did on Mount Carmel, sacrificing on an altar which was authorized only for him.

Qorban Ha`edah gives a reconstruction of the paragraph which is not impossible but not supported by any parallel evidence.

In the word פיונטייה the ending ־יה is the possessive suffix "his". For the remaining פיונטי the best available conjecture is Kohut's, Latin *punitio*, *-onis* "punishment" [or *poenaria* (*actiones*), punishable (actions) (E. G.)].

(30c line 46) וְהַנָּבִיא שֶׁנִּתְנַבֵּא בַּתְּחִילָּה. אִם נָתַן אוֹת וּמוֹפֵת שׁוֹמְעִין לוֹ וְאִם לָאו אֵין שׁוֹמְעִין לוֹ. שְׁנֵי נְבִיאִים שֶׁנִּתְנַבְּאוּ כְאַחַת. שְׁנֵי נְבִיאִים שֶׁנִּתְנַבְּאוּ בְּכֶרֶךְ אֶחָד. רִבִּי יִצְחָק וְרִבִּי הוֹשַׁעְיָה. חַד אָמַר. צָרִיךְ לִיתֵּן אוֹת וּמוֹפֵת. וְחָרָנָה אָמַר. אֵינוֹ צָרִיךְ לִיתֵּן אוֹת וּמוֹפֵת. מְתִיב מָאן דְּאָמַר צָרִיךְ לְמָאן דְּאָמַר אֵינוֹ צָרִיךְ. וְהָא כְתִיב וַיֹּאמֶר חִזְקִיָּהוּ אֶל־יְשַׁעְיָהוּ מָה אוֹת. אָמַר לֵיהּ. שַׁנְיָיא הִיא תַמָּן דּוּ עָסֵק בִּתְחִיַּית הַמֵּתִים. יְחַיֵּינוּ מִיּוֹמָיִים בַּיּוֹם הַשְּׁלִישִׁי יְקִמֵנוּ וְנִחְיֶה לְפָנָיו׃

If a prophet starts to prophesy, one listens to him if he gives a sign or miracle; otherwise one does not listen to him[113]. Two prophets who prophesied indentically, two prophets who prophesied in the same sense[114]? Rebbi Isaac and Rebbi Hoshaia: One said, each one has to provide a sign or a miracle; the other said, not each one has to provide a sign or a miracle[115]. The one who said he did objected to the one who said he did not: Is it not written[116], *Ezekias said to Isaias, what is the sign*? He told him, that is different since he was occupied in reviving the dead. *He shall revive us after two days; on the third day He will lift us up and we shall live before Him*[117].

113 *Deut.* 13:2. It is no disrespect to Heaven if one disregards the sayings of an unqualified prophet.

114 This reading (*Pene Moshe*) is preferable to reading בְּכֶרֶךְ אֶחָד "in the same fortified place" (*Qorban Ha`edah*).

115 But the accredited prophet can legitimate his companion.

116 *2K.* 20:8.

117 *Hos.* 6:2. The verse is the basic source for the belief that the resurrection has to be on the third day, or that souls have to suffer punishment for their misdeeds while alive for two days and on the third day are admitted to Paradise (*Berakhot* 5:2 Note 64; *Ta`aniot* 1:1 63d l.52). Ezekias was declared ready to die (*2K.* 20:1) and was well enough to go to the Temple on the third day; this shows that his recovery was indeed a resurrection.

(30c line 54) אָמַר רִבִּי יְהוּדָה בֶּן פָּזִי. לֹא סוֹף דָּבָר לַחוּפָּה אֶלָּא אֲפִילוּ לַבַּיִת שֶׁיֵּשׁ בּוֹ חוּפָּה. בְּעָיָא הָדָא מִילְּתָא. טְרִיקְלִין וְקָיְטוֹן. חוּפָּה וְקָיְטוֹן. נִכְנְסָה לִטְרִיקְלִין. לְיֵי דָא מִילָּא. לְיוֹרְשָׁהּ. רִבִּי יוֹחָנָן אָמַר. לְיוֹרְשָׁהּ. רֵישׁ לָקִישׁ אָמַר. לְהָפֵר נְדָרֶיהָ. אָמַר רִבִּי זְעִירָא. אַף עַל גַּב דְּרִבִּי שִׁמְעוֹן בֶּן לָקִישׁ אָמַר לְהָפֵר נְדָרֶיהָ. מוֹדֶה שֶׁאֵינוֹ מֵיפֵר לָהּ עַד שֶׁתִּיכָּנֵס לַחוּפָּה. אָמַר רִבִּי הוּנָא. קְרָיָא מְסַייֵעַ לְרִבִּי שִׁמְעוֹן בֶּן לָקִישׁ. לִזְנוֹת בֵּית אָבִיהָ. פְּרָט שֶׁמְּסָרוּהָ שְׁלוּחֵי הָאָב לִשְׁלוּחֵי הַבַּעַל. שֶׁלֹּא תְהֵא בִסְקִילָה אֶלָּא בְחֶנֶק.

[118]Rebbi Jehudah ben Pazi said. not only to the bridal chamber but also to a house containing the bridal chamber[119]. The following is problematic: Dining room[120] and bedroom[121], bridal chamber and bedroom; if she entered the dining room, for which consequence[122]? Rebbi Johanan said, to inherit from her[123]. Rebbi Simeon ben Laqish said, to dissolve her vows[124]. Rebbi Ze`ira said, even though Rebbi Simeon ben Laqish said, to dissolve her vows, he agrees that he cannot actually dissolve them before she enters the bridal chamber[125]. Rebbi Huna[126] said, a verse supports Rebbi Simeon ben Laqish: *to whore in her father's house*[127]. This excludes the case where the father's agents handed her over to the husband's agents, that she could not be stoned, but is strangled[128].

118 This now refers to the adulterous definitively married woman. A closely related text is *Ketubot* 4:7, Notes 154-160.

119 Where the definitive marriage is contracted. This חוּפָּה is not the wedding canopy used today, but a room where the newlyweds will consummate the marriage and spend the following week.

From here to the end of *Sanhedrin-Makkot* (except *Makkot* 1:13-2:7) there exists a Genizah fragment (G) edited (with readings compared to the Krotoschin Yerushalmi) by S. Wieder, *Tarbiz* 17 (1946) 130-135.

120 Greek τρικλίνιον, τό, Latin *triclinium*.

121 Cf. Chapter 7:19, Note 363.

122 Before the definitive marriage ceremony.

123 As definitive husband, if the woman died before entering the bridal chamber. Since this idea is not followed up, it does not represent practice. In *Ketubot*, the name

is R. Eleazar. Therefore, the illegible name in G cannot be emended to "R. Johanan" as given in *Tarbiz* 17.

124 *Nedarim*, Chapters 10,11.

125 If the time allotted to the husband to dissolve his wife's vows elapses between the arrival of his bride at his home when she stated the fact of her vows and the definitive marriage ceremony, he lost his right of dissolution.

126 In G, "Huna" is corrected to "Jonah".

127 *Deut.* 22:21.

128 A preliminarily married virgin who no longer is in her father's charge is treated in criminal law as if she already were definitively married. Babli *Ketubot* 49a.

(30c line 61) כְּיוֹצֵא בָהֶם בִּשְׂרֵיפָה הִיא וָהֵן בִּשְׂרֵיפָה. כְּיוֹצֵא בָהֶן בִּסְקִילָה הִיא וָהֵן בִּסְקִילָה. כְּיוֹצֵא בָהֶן בְּחֶנֶק הִיא וָהֵן בְּחֶנֶק.

Similarly by burning, she and they by burning. Similarly by stoning, she and they by stoning. Similarly by strangulation, she and they by strangulation[129].

129 This refers to the perjured witnesses. The text is a copy from Halakhah 7:1, Note 17; Tosephta 14:17. If no man is involved, the perjured witnesses are punished by what the woman would have suffered had their testimony been truthful.

מסכת מכות
כיצד העדים פרק ראשון

(fol. 30d) **משנה א**: כֵּיצַד הָעֵדִים נַעֲשִׂים זוֹמְמִין מְעִידִים אָנוּ בְאִישׁ פְּלוֹנִי שֶׁהוּא בֶן גְּרוּשָׁה אוֹ בֶן חֲלוּצָה אֵין אוֹמְרִין יֵיעָשֶׂה זֶה בֶּן גְּרוּשָׁה אוֹ בֶן חֲלוּצָה תַחְתָּיו אֶלָּא לוֹקֶה אַרְבָּעִים. מְעִידִים אָנוּ בְאִישׁ פְּלוֹנִי שֶׁהוּא חַייָב גָּלוּת. אֵין אוֹמְרִים יִגְלֶה זֶה תַחְתָּיו אֶלָּא לוֹקֶה אַרְבָּעִים. מְעִידִין אָנוּ בְאִישׁ פְּלוֹנִי שֶׁגֵּירַשׁ אֶת אִשְׁתּוֹ וְלֹא נָתַן לָהּ כְּתוּבָּתָהּ וַהֲלֹא בֵּין הַיּוֹם וּבֵין לְמָחָר סוֹפוֹ לִתֵּן לָהּ כְּתוּבָּתָהּ. אֶלָּא אוֹמְדִים כַּמָּה אָדָם רוֹצֶה לִיתֵּן בִּכְתוּבָּתָהּ שֶׁל זוֹ שֶׁאִם נִתְאַלְמְנָה אוֹ נִתְגָּרְשָׁה וְאִם מֵתָה יִירָשֶׁנָּה בַעְלָהּ.

Mishnah 1: How are plotting witnesses treated[1]? "We testify about this man that he is the son of a divorcee or a woman who had received *ḥalîṣah*.[2]" One does not say that he should be decreed to be the son of a divorcee or a woman who had received *ḥalîṣah* in his stead, but he is flogged 40 [lashes][3].

"We testify about this man that he is obligated to go into exile[4]." One does not say, this one should go into exile in his stead but he is flogged 40 [lashes][5].

"We testify about this man that he divorced his wife but did not pay her *ketubah*.[6]" Would he not finally have to pay her *ketubah* today or tomorrow? But one estimates how much would a man be willing to pay for the *ketubah* of this woman in case she would be widowed or divorced, but if she died her husband would inherit from her.

1 It is one of the Ten Commandments not to testify falsely. In addition, *Deut*. 19:16-20 prescribes that a "plotting" false witness has to be punished by the penalty which would have been imposed on his victim had his testimony been found true. By rabbinic definition, a "plotting" witness is one whose testimony not only is false but shown to be impossible, in that there are witnesses to the fact that he testified to be eye witness of a fact which he could not have seen since at the time it was supposed to have happened he was at another place (*Sanhedrin* Chapter 5, Note 3). There are cases when plotting perjury is proven but the penalty cannot be imposed. Then the false witness must be punished for breaking the Eighth Commandment, which is the standard punishment decreed for breaking any prohibition for which the penalty was not specified, fixed in *Deut*. 25:3 as at most 40 lashes (which, because the court marshal might err in his count, is limited to 39 lashes).

The Babli (2b) disagrees with this explanation; it classifies simple perjury as "actionless crime" for which no penalty is possible; this clearly is not the Yerushalmi's position (cf. *Ketubot* 4:4 Note 196.)

2 The son of a Cohen from a woman he is prohibited from marrying (*Lev.* 21:7,14) is desecrated; he cannot function as a priest and the priestly revenues are forbidden to him. The divorcee is biblically forbidden to the Cohen. The widow receiving *halîsah* from the former husband's brother is forbidden rabbinically; her son is rabbinically desecrated, which for practical consequences does not make any difference.

3 If the witness is not a Cohen, declaring him as son of a divorcee would not change his status at all. If he is a Cohen, declaring him as son of a divorcee would punish not only him but also his descendants, against the biblical text as explained in the Halakhah.

4 The unintentional homicide (*Num.* 35:9-34).

5 As explained in the Halakhah, the perjurer is barred from fleeing to a city of refuge.

6 When in fact the woman is still married to her husband. Then the witness could be fined only if in the future the *ketubah* would not be paid, i. e., if the woman stayed married to her husband and predeceased him. He can be fined the current discounted expected value of such a *ketubah*.

(31a line) **הלכה א**: כֵּיצַד הָעֵדִים נַעֲשִׂים זוֹמְמִין כול'. אָמַר רִבִּי יוֹסֵי בֶּן חֲנִינָה. הַכֹּל הָיָה בִכְלָל לֹא־תַעֲנֶה בְרֵעֲךָ עֵד שָׁקֶר. יָצָא וַעֲשִׂיתֶם לוֹ כַּאֲשֶׁר זָמַם לַעֲשׂוֹת לְאָחִיו. אֶת שֶׁאַתְּ יָכוֹל לְקַיֵּם בּוֹ וַעֲשִׂיתֶם לוֹ כַּאֲשֶׁר זָמַם וגו' אַתְּ מְקַיֵּים בּוֹ (לֹא־תַעֲנֶה) [וַעֲשִׂיתֶם לוֹ כַּאֲשֶׁר זָמַם לַעֲשׂוֹת]. וְאֶת שֶׁאֵין אַתְּ יָכוֹל לְקַיֵּם בּוֹ וַעֲשִׂיתֶם לוֹ כַּאֲשֶׁר זָמַם לַעֲשׂוֹת לְאָחִיו (אֵין) אַתְּ מְקַיֵּים בּוֹ לֹא־תַעֲנֶה בְרֵעֲךָ. דָּבָר אַחֵר. וַעֲשִׂיתֶם לוֹ. לֹא לְזַרְעוֹ.

Halakhah 1: "How are plotting witnesses treated," etc. Rebbi Yose ben Ḥanina said, everything was included in *do not testify against your neighbor as a false witness*. As an exception, *do to him as he plotted to do to his neighbor*. If you can satisfy *do to him as he plotted* then fulfill (*do not testify*)[7] [*do to him as he plotted to do*][8]. But if you cannot satisfy *do to him as he plotted to do to his neighbor* then (do not)[7] satisfy *do not testify against your neighbor*[1].

Another explanation: *Do to him*, not to his descendants[3].

7 Text of the Leiden ms., to be deleted.

8 Text of G, to be accepted.

(31a line 13) רִבִּי יְהוֹשֻׁעַ בֶּן לֵוִי אָמַר. וַעֲשִׂיתֶם לוֹ. שְׁנֵי דְבָרִים מְסוּרִין לְבֵית דִּין אַתְּ תּוֹפֵס אֶחָד מֵהֶן. יָצָא דָבָר שֶׁהוּא מָסוּר לַשָּׁמַיִם.

Rebbi Joshua ben Levi said, if two alternatives are presented to the court, one chooses one of them[9]. This excludes matters in the Power of Heaven[10].

9 As a general principle, no crime can be punished by more than one punishment. There never can be separate penalties for testifying falsely (*Ex.*20:13) and plotting (*Deut*. 19:19). This justifies the alternative presented in the preceding paragraph.

The text is copied from *Terumot* 7:1 Note 14; also *Bava qamma* 7:2, Note 30.

10 This sentence refers to the topic in *Terumot*; it is irrelevant here.

(31a line 14) כָּתוּב וְלֹא־יְחַלֵּל זַרְעוֹ בְּעַמָּיו. אֵין לִי אֶלָּא זֶרַע שֶׁהוּא מִתְחַלֵּל. הִיא עַצְמָהּ מְנַיִין. וְדִין הוּא. מָה אִם הַזֶּרַע שֶׁלֹּא עָבַר עֲבֵירָה הֲרֵי הוּא מִתְחַלֵּל. הִיא שֶׁעָבְרָה עֲבֵירָה אֵינוֹ דִין שֶׁתִּתְחַלֵּל. הוּא עַצְמוֹ יוֹכִיחַ. שֶׁעָבַר עֲבֵירָה וְאֵינוֹ מִתְחַלֵּל. לֹא. אִם אָמַרְתָּה בְאִישׁ שֶׁאֵינוֹ מִתְחַלֵּל בְּכָל־מָקוֹם תֹּאמַר בְּאִשָּׁה שֶׁהִיא מִתְחַלֶּלֶת בְּכָל־מָקוֹם. הוֹאִיל וְהִיא מִתְחַלֶּלֶת בְּכָל־מָקוֹם דִּין הוּא שֶׁתִּתְחַלֵּל. וְאִם נַפְשָׁךְ לוֹמַר. לֹא יָחוֹל וְלֹא־יְחַלֵּל. אַף מִי שֶׁהָיָה כָשֵׁר וְנִתְחַלֵּל.

בַּר פְּדָיָה אָמַר. הַמְחַלֵּל לֹא נִתְחַלֵּל הֵיאַךְ זֶה מִתְחַלֵּל.

[11]It is written[12]: *He shall not desecrate his issue in his people*. Not only his issue will be desecrated; from where also she[13]? Is this not a logical inference? Since the issue, which did not sin, is desecrated, should she, who committed a sin[14], not logically be desecrated? He himself is a counter example, since he committed a sin but was not desecrated[15]. No. If you argue about a man who is not desecrated in any circumstance, what can you say about a woman who is desecrated in many circumstances[16]? Since she is desecrated in many circumstances, it is logical that she should be desecrated. If you wish you can say "not to desecrate", *not to desecrate*, about somebody who was qualified and became desecrated[17].

Bar Pedaya said, the desecrator was not desecrated: how can this one be desecrated[18]?

11 Babli *Qiddušin* 77a, *Sifra Emor Pereq* 2(7-8).

12 *Lev.* 21:15. This verse is written for the High Priest, but it is applied to all priests who marry women forbidden to them.

13 In *Lev.* 21:7,14 the "desecrated woman" is mentioned in the list of women forbidden to the Cohen. The verse implies that the daughter of a Cohen from an illicit union is conceived desecrated. There is no verse which spells out the conditions under which a woman otherwise may become desecrated. There is a verse which specifies that the daughter of a Cohen married to a

non-Cohen or mother of a non-Cohen child is disqualified from priestly revenues (*Lev.* 22:12-13), but not desecrated. Since the "desecrated woman" is always mentioned together with the prostitute, it is inferred that sexual offenses of a woman desecrate her.

14 On the face of it, the verses only imply that the male Cohen who marries an unsuitable woman commits a sin. Since both *Lev.* 21:7, addressed to the common priest, repeat the verb "do not marry", this is read to mean that the first mention is the prohibition for the male to marry, the second the prohibition for the female to agree to be married (*Yebamot* 9:1 Note 13, *Qiddušin* 3:14 Note 243; *Sifra Emor Pereq* 1(12), Babli *Yebamot* 84b).

15 Since the verse emphasizes that his children will be desecrated, it implies that the father himself is not desecrated (even if he consorts with a Gentile or a slave); *Sifra Emor Pereq* 2(8). The son of a Cohen from an illicit union is desecrated from conception; he does not *become* desecrated. This implies that no male Cohen may *become* desecrated; he may, however, become unfit for his office.

16 In order to avoid circular reasoning it is necessary to classify "disqualified" with "desecrated". Then it follows that there exist classes of females desecrated for the priesthood without equivalent among males.

17 The text of this sentence is in doubt. There is no biblical verb חול "to profane" as required by the reading here and in the Babli. In *Sifra*, most texts read יחלל both times; but from Ravad's commentary one sees that the first time he read יַחֵל (*Num.* 30:3), identical in meaning with יְחַלֵּל.

As explained in Note 16, actively "to desecrate" implies the existence of an object which is not yet desecrated. Since any child of the illicit union of a Cohen is intrinsically desecrated, it cannot be *made* desecrated. Since the male is not desecrated, the use of the active יְחַלֵּל therefore implies that the female is desecrated.

18 This refers back to the Mishnah. Since the male is not desecrated by marrying a divorcee, the Cohen who is a perjured witness cannot be declared desecrated.

(31a line 22) עֵדִים שֶׁנִּזְדַּמְּמוּ. רִבִּי יוֹחָנָן אָמַר. שֶׁקֶר שֶׁקֶר. עֵדִים שֶׁנִּזְדַּמְּמוּ וְחָזְרוּ וְנִשְׁתַּקְּרוּ. רִבִּי יוֹחָנָן אָמַר. שֶׁקֶר שֶׁקֶר. רִבִּי לָעְזָר אָמַר. רָשָׁע רָשָׁע. נֶאֱמַר רָשָׁע בִּמְחוּייָבֵי מִיתוֹת וְנֶאֱמַר רָשָׁע בִּמְחוּייָבֵי מַכּוֹת. מַה רָשָׁע שֶׁנֶּאֱמַר בִּמְחוּייָבֵי מִיתוֹת אֵין מָמוֹן אֶצֶל מִיתָה. אַף רָשָׁע שֶׁנֶּאֱמַר בִּמְחוּייָבֵי מַכּוֹת אֵין מָמוֹן אֶצֶל מַכּוֹת.

Witnesses found guilty of plotting. Rebbi Johanan said, *falsehood, falsehood*[19]. Witnesses found guilty of plotting and then found guilty of lying[20]. Rebbi Johanan said, *falsehood, falsehood.* Rebbi Eleazar said, *evildoer, evildoer.* [21]It is said *evildoer* for death penalty cases, and it is said *evildoer* for cases of whipping. Since for the *evildoer* subject to the death penalty there is no fine accompanying the death penalty, so for the *evildoer* subject to whipping there is no fine accompanying whipping.

19 *Deut.* 21:18: *Behold, a witness of falsehood is the witness, falsehood he spoke about his brother.* The repetition of the term indicates that every single falsehood in testimony subjects the witness to a separate penalty.

20 In the same testimony, the witnesses were found guilty of "plotting", of rendering impossible testimony, and then of false (but possible) testimony. If this is a civil case, where the witnesses have to pay for "plotting", can they still be flogged for false testimony? R. Johanan says yes, R. Eleazar and R. Simeon ben Laqish say no, as discussed at length in *Terumot* 7:1 Notes 7-29, in particular Note 19 (*Ketubot* 3:1 Note 29).

21 The text is from *Terumot* 7:1 Notes 21-23. The murderer is called *evildoer* in *Num.* 35:31, the person subject to flogging in *Deut.* 25.

(31a line 27) בַּר פְּדָיָה אָמַר. הוּא יָנוּס לֹא זוֹמְמָיו.

וְאֵין מְשַׁלְּמִין כָּל־הַכְּתוּבָּה אֲבָל מְשַׁלְּמִין טוֹבַת הֲנָיַית כְּתוּבָּה. כֵּיצַד. אוֹמְרִים כַּמָּה אָדָם רוֹצֶה לִיתֵּן בִּכְתוּבָּתָהּ שֶׁלָּזוֹ שֶׁמָּה תָמוּת בְּחַיֵּי בַעֲלָהּ וְיִירָשֶׁנָּה בַעֲלָהּ אוֹ שֶׁמָּא יָמוּת בַּעֲלָהּ בְּחַיֶּיהָ וְיִרַשׁ הַלָּה אֶת כְּתוּבָּתָהּ. לְפִיכָךְ הוּא מְשַׁלֵּם.

Bar Pedaia said, *he shall flee*[22], not his plotters.

[6]They do not pay the entire *ketubah*, but they pay the personal benefit of the *ketubah*. How? One asks, how much would a person pay for the *ketubah* of this [woman], maybe she would die during her husband's lifetime and her husband would inherit from her, or maybe her husband would die during her lifetime and this one would inherit her *ketubah*. Accordingly[23] he has to pay.

22 *Deut.* 19:5, speaking of the homicide. Cf. Notes 4,5.

23 For לפיכך read לפי כך.

(fol. 30d) **משנה ב**: מְעִידִים אָנוּ בְאִישׁ פְּלוֹנִי שֶׁהוּא חַייָב לַחֲבֵרוֹ אֶלֶף זוּז עַל מְנָת לִיתְּנָם מִכָּן וְעַד שְׁלֹשִׁים יוֹם וְהוּא אוֹמֵר מִכָּן וְעַד עֶשֶׂר שָׁנִים אוֹמֵד כַּמָּה אָדָם רוֹצֶה לִיתֵּן וְיִהְיוּ אֶלֶף זוּז בְּיָדוֹ בֵּין לִיתְּנָהּ מִכָּן וְעַד שְׁלֹשִׁים יוֹם בֵּין לִיתְּנָם מִכָּן וְעַד עֶשֶׂר שָׁנִים:

Mishnah 2: "We testify against this man that he owes another 1'000 denars payable within 30 days" but he says, within ten years[24]. One estimates how much a person would be willing to pay to have 1'000 denars at his disposal to return them after ten years instead of returning them after thirty days.

משנה ג: מְעִידִין אָנוּ בְאִישׁ פְּלוֹנִי שֶׁהוּא חַיָּב לַחֲבֵרוֹ מָאתַיִם זוּז וְנִמְצְאוּ זוֹמְמִין לוֹקִין וּמְשַׁלְּמִין שֶׁלֹּא הַשֵּׁם הַמְּבִיאוֹ לִידֵי מַכּוֹת מְבִיאוֹ לִידֵי תַשְׁלוּמִין דִּבְרֵי רַבִּי מֵאִיר. וַחֲכָמִים אוֹמְרִים כָּל הַמְשַׁלֵּם אֵינוֹ לוֹקֶה:

Mishnah 3: "We testify against this man that he owes another 200 denars" and they are found to be plotting, they are flogged and have to pay since the title which brings him to flogging is not the one which brings him to restitution[25], the words of Rebbi Meïr. But the Sages say, anybody who pays is not flogged[9].

משנה ד: מְעִידִין אָנוּ בְאִישׁ פְּלוֹנִי שֶׁהוּא חַיָּב מַלְקוּת אַרְבָּעִים וְנִמְצְאוּ זוֹמְמִין לוֹקִים שְׁמוֹנִים מִשּׁוּם לֹא תַעֲנֶה בְרֵעֲךָ עֵד שָׁקֶר וּמִשּׁוּם וַעֲשִׂיתֶם לוֹ כַּאֲשֶׁר זָמַם לַעֲשׂוֹת לְאָחִיו דִּבְרֵי רַבִּי מֵאִיר. וַחֲכָמִים אוֹמְרִים אֵינָן לוֹקִין אֶלָּא אַרְבָּעִים.

Mishnah 4: "We testify against this man that he is liable to be flogged 40 lashes" and they are found plotting, they are whipped 80 because of *do not testify against your neighbor as a false witness* and because of *do to him as he plotted to do to his neighbor*, the words of Rebbi Meïr. But the Sages say, they only are flogged 40 times[9].

משנה ה: מְשַׁלְּשִׁים בְּמָמוֹן וְאֵין מְשַׁלְּשִׁים בְּמַכּוֹת. כֵּיצַד הֵעִידוּהוּ שֶׁהוּא חַיָּב לַחֲבֵרוֹ מָאתַיִם זוּז וְנִמְצְאוּ זוֹמְמִין מְשַׁלְּשִׁין בֵּינֵיהֶם. הֵעִידוּהוּ שֶׁהוּא חַיָּב מַלְקוּת אַרְבָּעִים וְנִמְצְאוּ זוֹמְמִין כָּל אֶחָד וְאֶחָד לוֹקֶה אַרְבָּעִים:

Mishnah 5: One distributes money but one does not distribute floggings. How? If they testified that he owes another person 200 denars and were found plotting, one distributes between them[26]. If they testified that he is liable to be flogged 40 lashes and were found plotting, each one of them is flogged 40 lashes.

24 The witnesses found to be plotting wanted to deprive their victim of the use of 1'000 denars for almost ten years.

25 They are flogged for false testimony and have to pay restitution as plotters.

26 There must be at least 2 witnesses for their testimony to be heard. If there were *n* witnesses, each one has to pay 200/*n* denars.

(31a line 31) **הלכה ב:** מְעִידִין אָנוּ בְאִישׁ פְּלוֹנִי כול׳. **הלכה ג:** מְעִידִין אָנוּ בְאִישׁ פְּלוֹנִי כול׳. **הלכה ד:** מְעִידִין אָנוּ כול׳. **הלכה ה:** מְשַׁלְּשִׁין בַּמָּמוֹן כול׳. רִבִּי בָּא בַּר מָמָל רַב עַמְרָם רַב מַתָּנָה בְשֵׁם רַב. הַמַּלְוֶה אֶת חֲבֵירוֹ עַל מְנָת שֶׁלֹּא לְתוֹבְעוֹ הַשְּׁבִיעִית מְשַׁמְּטָתוֹ. וְהָא תַנִּינָן הַשּׁוֹחֵט אֶת הַפָּרָה וְחִילְּקָהּ בְּרֹאשׁ הַשָּׁנָה. וָמַר רִבִּי לָעְזָר. רִבִּי יְהוּדָה הִיא. וְרָאוּי הוּא לְתוֹבְעוֹ בְּרֹאשׁ הַשָּׁנָה. כַּיי דָמַר רִבִּי בָּא בְשֵׁם רִבִּי זְעִירָא. מִכֵּיוָן שֶׁאֵינוֹ רָאוּי לְתוֹבְעוֹ כְּמִי שֶׁאֵינוֹ רָאוּי לְהַאֲמִינוֹ. וְכֵיוָן שֶׁאֵינוֹ רָאוּי לְהַאֲמִינוֹ כְּמִי שֶׁאֵינוֹ רָאוּי לִיתֵּן לוֹ מָעוֹת. וְכָאן הוֹאִיל וְהוּא רָאוּי לִיתֵּן לוֹ מָעוֹת וְלֹא נָתַן נַעֲשִׂית הָרִאשׁוֹנָה מִלְוָה.

2 רב עמרם | **7G** עמרם מתנה | **7** מתני 3 השביעית | **7** שביעית והא תנינן | **7** והתני 4 ומר | **7** ואמ׳ יהודה | **7** יודה השנה | **G** שנה 5 דמר | **7** דאמ׳ זעירא | **G** זעורה שאינו { **7** שהוא (twice) **G** שאת (first time only) 6 שאינו { **7** שהוא (twice) וכאן | **G** וכן מעות | **7** - 7 הראשונה | **7** ראשונה

רִבִּי יוֹסֵי בֵּירִבִּי בּוּן בְּשֵׁם רַב. הַמַּלְוֶה אֶת חֲבֵירוֹ עַל מְנָת שֶׁלֹּא תַשְׁמִיטֶינּוּ שְׁמִיטָּה אֵין הַשְּׁבִיעִית מְשַׁמְּטָתוֹ. וְהָא תַנִּינָן. בֵּין נוֹתְנָן מִיכָּן וְעַד שְׁלֹשִׁים יוֹם בֵּין נוֹתְנָן מִיכָּן וְעַד עֶשֶׂר שָׁנִים: וְיֵשׁ עֶשֶׂר שָׁנִים בְּלֹא שְׁמִיטָּה. רִבִּי הוּנָא אָמַר. אִתְפַּלְּגוֹן רַב נַחְמָן וְרַב שֵׁשֶׁת. חַד אָמַר. בְּמַלְוֶה עַל הַמַּשְׁכּוֹן. וְחָרָנָה אָמַר. בְּכוֹתֵב לוֹ פְּרוֹזְבּוֹל.

1 תשמיטינו | **7** תשמטינו **G** תשמיטנו שמיטה | **7** שביעית [תיקון המגיה] 2 נותנן | **7** נותנין **G** נותן בין נותנן | **7** ובין נותנין **G** בין נותן 3 עשר | **7** י׳ ר׳ הונא אמ׳ | **7** אמ׳ ר׳ הונא **G** רב הונה אמ׳ נחמן | **G7** נחמן בר יעקב

תַּנֵּי. שְׁלֹשִׁים יוֹם לֹא אִיתִי. מָהוּ שְׁלֹשִׁים יוֹם לֹא אִיתִי. שְׁמוּאֵל אָמַר. הַמַּלְוֶה אֶת חֲבֵירוֹ סְתָם אֵינוֹ רַשַּׁאי לְתוֹבְעוֹ עַד שְׁלֹשִׁים יוֹם. עָאַל רִבִּי יְהוּדָה וָמַר טַעֲמָא. קָֽרְבָ֣ה שְׁנַֽת־הַשֶּׁ֘בַע֮ שְׁנַ֣ת הַשְּׁמִיטָּה. לֹא הִיא שְׁנַת־הַשֶּׁבַע הִיא שְׁנַת הַשְּׁמִיטָּה. וּמַה תַלְמוּד לוֹמַר קָֽרְבָ֣ה שְׁנַֽת־הַשֶּׁ֘בַע֮ שְׁנַ֣ת הַשְּׁמִיטָּה. שֶׁלֹּא תֹאמַר. כָּל־שְׁלֹשִׁים יוֹם אֵין רַשַּׁאי לְתוֹבְעוֹ. לְאַחַר ל׳ יוֹם כְּהַשְׁמֵט כְּסָפִים הוּא לֹא יִגְבֶּנּוּ. לָפוּם כָּךְ צָרַךְ מֵימַר קָֽרְבָ֣ה שְׁנַֽת־הַשֶּׁ֘בַע֮ שְׁנַ֣ת הַשְּׁמִיטָּה. וְלֹא כֵן אָמַר רִבִּי בָּא בַּר מָמָל רַב עַמְרָם רַב מַתָּנָה בְּשֵׁם רַב. הַמַּלְוֶה אֶת חֲבֵירוֹ עַל מְנָת שֶׁלֹּא לְתוֹבְעוֹ הַשְּׁבִיעִית מְשַׁמְּטָתוֹ. אַשְׁכָּח תַּנֵּי רִבִּי יִשְׁמָעֵאל. קָֽרְבָ֣ה שְׁנַֽת־הַשֶּׁ֘בַע֮ שְׁנַ֣ת הַשְּׁמִיטָּה. לֹא הִיא שְׁנַת־הַשֶּׁבַע הִיא שְׁנַת הַשְּׁמִיטָּה. וּמַה תַלְמוּד לוֹמַר קָֽרְבָ֣ה שְׁנַֽת־הַשֶּׁ֘בַע֮ שְׁנַ֣ת הַשְּׁמִיטָּה. שֶׁלֹּא תֹאמַר. כָּל־שֵׁשׁ שָׁנִים כַּרְמוֹ לְפָנָיו שָׂדֵהוּ לְפָנָיו וּלְאַחַר שֵׁשׁ שָׁנִים בְּהַשְׁמֵט כְּסָפִים הוּא לֹא יִגְבֶּנּוּ. לָפוּם כָּךְ צָרַךְ מֵימַר קָֽרְבָ֣ה שְׁנַֽת־הַשֶּׁ֘בַע֮ שְׁנַ֣ת הַשְּׁמִיטָּה.

1 איתי | **G7** איתיי (twice) מהו | **G** מהוא המלוה | **G** המלווה 2 אינו | **7** שאינו רשאי | **G** רשיי ר׳ יהודה | **G** רב יהודה 3 היא שנת השמיטה | **7** ולא היא שנת השמיטה ומה | **7** מה 4 תאמר | **G** תומר אין | **G7** אינו רשאי | **G** רשיי כהשמט | **7** בהשמט 5 יגבנו | **G7** יגבינו לפום | **G** לפם 6 רב עמרם | **7G** עמרם 8 היא | **7** - תאמר | **G** תומר 9 כרמו לפניו שדהו לפניו | **7** שדהו לפניי כרמו לפניי יגבנו | **G7** יגבינו לפום | **G** לפם

[27]Rebbi Abba bar Mamal, Rav[28] Amram, Rab Mattanah in the name of Rav: If somebody makes a loan to another person stipulating that he won't press for repayment, the Sabbatical will remit it. Did we not state: "If somebody slaughters a cow and divides it up on New Year's Day"? And Rebbi Eleazar said, this follows Rebbi Jehudah. But can he require payment

on New Year's Day? As Rebbi Abba said in the name of Rebbi Ze`ira: Since he could not ask him for payment, it is as if he could not believe him. And since he could not believe him, it is as if he could not pay him. And here, because he could have given him but did not give, the first [debt] is turned into a loan.

Rebbi Yose ben Rebbi Abun in the name of Rav: If somebody gives a loan to a person on condition that the Sabbatical not remit it, the Sabbatical does not remit it, as we have stated: "to return them after ten years instead of returning them after thirty days". Are there ten years without a Sabbatical? Rebbi[29] Huna said, Rav Nahman and Rav Sheshet disagreed. One of them said, if the loan was given on a pledge; but the other said, if he writes him a *prozbul*.

It was stated: "For thirty days he will not come." What means "for thirty days he will not come"? Samuel said, if somebody gives a loan to a person without specifying details, he has no right to ask for payment until after 30 days. Rebbi[29] Jehudah came and explained: *The Sabbatical year, the remitting year, is close.* Is not the Sabbatical year the remitting year? Why does the verse say, *the Sabbatical year, the remitting year, is close*? Lest you say, I am not permitted to ask for payment until after 30 days; after 30 days the debt will be remitted and I will not collect. Therefore, it must say, *the Sabbatical year, the remitting year, is close.* Did not Rebbi Abba bar Mamal, Rav Amram, Rav Mattanah say in the name of Rav: If somebody makes a loan to another person stipulating that he will not press for repayment, the Sabbatical will remit it? It was found stated by Rebbi Ismael: *The Sabbatical year, the remitting year, is close.* Is not the Sabbatical year the remitting year? Why does the verse say, *the Sabbatical year, the remitting year, is close*? Lest you say, the entire six years his vineyard is available, his field is available but after six years the debt is remitted and I cannot collect. Therefore, it must say, *the Sabbatical year, the remitting year, is close.*

27 This Halakhah also is Halakhah *Ševi`it* 10:2 (7), explained there in Notes 57-68. In G, the first paragraph is Halakhah 2, the remainder Halakhah 3.

28 This is his Babylonian title; in the Yerushalmi he seems not to carry a title; cf. the variant readings.

29 Read: "Rav", cf. the variant readings.

(fol. 30d) **משנה ו**: אֵין הָעֵדִים נַעֲשִׂים זוֹמְמִים עַד שֶׁיָּזוֹמּוּ אֶת עַצְמָן. כֵּיצַד אָמְרוּ מְעִידִין אָנוּ בְּאִישׁ פְּלוֹנִי שֶׁהָרַג אֶת הַנֶּפֶשׁ אָמְרוּ לָהֶן הֵיאַךְ אַתֶּם מְעִידִים שֶׁהֲרֵי הַנֶּהֱרָג הַזֶּה אוֹ הַהוֹרֵג הַזֶּה עִמָּנוּ אוֹתוֹ הַיּוֹם בְּמָקוֹם פְּלוֹנִי אֵין אֵילוּ זוֹמְמִין. אֲבָל אָמְרוּ לָהֶן הֵיאַךְ אַתֶּם מְעִידִין שֶׁהֲרֵי אַתֶּם הֱיִיתֶם עִמָּנוּ אוֹתוֹ הַיּוֹם בְּמָקוֹם פְּלוֹנִי הֲרֵי אֵלוּ זוֹמְמִין וְנֶהֱרָגִין עַל פִּיהֶן:

Mishnah 6: Witnesses become plotters only by their own testimony. How is this? If they said, we testify against this man that he killed a person; [others] told them, how can you testify, for this murder victim or this murderer was with us at such place on that day; they are not plotters[30]. But if they told them, how can you testify, for you were with us at such place on that day; they are plotters and are executed on their testimony[31].

משנה ז: בָּאוּ אֲחֵרִים וְהִזִּימוּם בָּאוּ אֲחֵרִים וְהִזִּימוּם אֲפִילוּ מֵאָה כּוּלָּם יֵיהָרֵגוּ. רִבִּי יְהוּדָה אוֹמֵר, איסטיסית הִיא זוֹ אֵינָהּ נֶהֱרֶגֶת אֶלָּא כַּת הָרִאשׁוֹנָה בִּלְבַד:

Mishnah 7: If others came and they showed them to be plotters, if others came and they showed them to be plotters, even a hundred, all should be executed[32]. Rebbi Jehudah says, this is איסטיסית[33]; only the first group is executed.

30 The testimony may be implausible but it is not impossible. The court may reject the testimony but it cannot be sanctioned.

31 If the witnesses were shown to have been far from the place of the crime at the date of the crime, the testimony is impossible; they are plotters and must be punished according to the law of plotters. But this must be based on the testimony of the witnesses in the required investigations (Mishnah *Sanhedrin* 5:1), not by circumstantial evidence.

32 The first group of witnesses accuses A to have murdered B at a certain place at a certain time. A second group testifies that the first witnesses were with them at another place, more than a day's trip away, at that time. Groups 3-99 support group 1, and group 2 shows all of them to be plotters. (Explanation of Alfasi and Maimonides.)

33 Alfasi and Maimonides read the word as *isatis* "indigo", that the second group which taints the others' testimony "tints" them. This is rejected by *Arukh*, based on a Gaonic responsum which identifies איסטיסית with קוביוסטית "gambling". R. Hananel and Maimonides read the word as אסטסיס, the Syriac form of Greek στάσις "conspiracy", or possibly ἀστασία "uncertainty" (Levy, who also considers the forms ἀσταθής, ἄστατος). Rashi considers the word as Semitic, עדות סטיא "incredible testimony" that the second group should be able to testify against all others. In Tosephta 1:10, Zuckermandel notes the readings איסטיטית, איצטניסית. Brüll proposes *astutia*.

(31a line 59) **הלכה ו**: אֵין הָעֵדִים נַעֲשִׂין זוֹמְמִין כול'. רִבִּי בָּא בַּר מָמָל. וְהוּא שֶׁנֶּהֱרַג. אֲבָל אִם לֹא נֶהֱרַג לֹא. הָדָא הִיא דְתַנִּינָן. אֵינָהּ נֶהֱרֶגֶת אֶלָּא כַת הָרִאשׁוֹנָה בִלְבַד: רִבִּי בּוּן בַּר חִיָּה בְעָא קוֹמֵי רִבִּי זְעִירָא. הָיוּ עוֹמְדִין וּמְעִידִין עָלָיו שֶׁהָרַג אֶת הַנֶּפֶשׁ בְּלוֹד. בָּאוּ אֲחֵרִים וְאָמְרוּ לָהֶן. הֵיאַךְ אַתֶּם מְעִידִין שֶׁהֲרֵי אַתֶּם הֱיִיתֶם עִמָּנוּ בַּחֲמִשָּׁה בחוֹדֶשׁ בְּקֵיסָרִי. וּבָאוּ בָאוּ אֲחֵרִים וְאָמְרוּ לָהֶן. הֵיאַךְ אַתֶּם מְעִידִין שֶׁהֲרֵי אַתֶּם הֱיִיתֶם עִמָּנוּ בַּעֲשָׂרָה בחוֹדֶשׁ בְּצִיפּוֹרִי. הַהוֹרֵג אֵינוֹ נֶהֱרַג שֶׁמָּא עֵדִים זוֹמְמִין הֵן. וְהָעֵדִים אֵינָן נֶהֱרָגִין שֶׁמָּא אֱמֶת אָמְרוּ.

Halakhah 6: "Witnesses become plotters," etc. Rebbi Abba bar Mamal: Only if he was killed. But not if he was not killed. That is what we have stated: "Only the first group is executed.[34]"

Rebbi Abun bar Ḥiyya asked before Rebbi Ze`ira: If they were standing, testifying that he killed a person in Lydda[35]. Others came and told them, how can you testify since you were with us in Caesarea[36] on the fifth of the month? Then others came and told them, how can you testify since you were with us in Sepphoris on the tenth of the month[37]? The murderer cannot be executed since possibly they are plotting witnesses. The witnesses cannot be executed since possibly they are telling the truth.

34 This refers to Mishnah 7. Since R. Jehudah holds that wholesale disqualifications are not believable, why should the first group of witnesses be condemned when all others, testifying to the same facts, are not? The answer is that if the third group comes before the first is condemned and executed, nobody is condemned. Babli 5b in the name of R. Abbahu.

35 Presumably on the first of the month.

36 In G: קיסרין, Caesarea Philippi, more than a five days' walk from Lydda. Caesarea Maritima is less than two days from Lydda.

37 This is difficult to understand since Sepphoris is reachable from both Caesareas in two to three days. One has to assume that round numbers were chosen to make memorization easy.

The third group of witnesses testifies to undercut the credibility of the second.

(fol. 30d) **משנה ח**: אֵין הָעֵדִים זוֹמְמִים נֶהֱרָגִין עַד שֶׁיִּגָּמֵר הַדִּין שֶׁהֲרֵי הַצְּדוּקִין אוֹמְרִים עַד שֶׁיֵּיהָרֵג שֶׁנֶּאֱמַר נֶפֶשׁ תַּחַת נָפֶשׁ. אָמְרוּ לָהֶן חֲכָמִים וַהֲלֹא כְבָר נֶאֱמַר וַעֲשִׂיתֶם לוֹ כַּאֲשֶׁר זָמַם לַעֲשׂוֹת לְאָחִיו וַהֲרֵי אָחִיו קַיָּים. אִם כֵּן לָמָּה נֶאֱמַר נֶפֶשׁ תַּחַת נָפֶשׁ. יָכוֹל מִשֶּׁקִּבְּלוּ עֵדוּתָן יֵיהָרְגוּ תַּלְמוּד לוֹמַר נֶפֶשׁ תַּחַת נָפֶשׁ הָא אֵינָן נֶהֱרָגִין עַד שֶׁיִּיגָּמֵר הַדִּין:

Mishnah 8: Plotting witnesses cannot be executed unless judgment was rendered, for the Sadducees say, unless he was executed, for it says, *a life for a life*[38]. The Sages told them, was it not already said, *do to him as he plotted to do to his brother*[39], does this not imply that his brother is alive? Then why does it say, *a life for a life*? I could think that they would be executed once they had testified, but the verse says, *a life for a life*; i. e., they cannot be executed unless judgment was passed[40].

משנה ט: עַל פִּי שְׁנַיִם עֵדִים אוֹ שְׁלֹשָׁה עֵדִים יוּמַת הַמֵּת אִם מִתְקַיֶּימֶת הָעֵדוּת בִּשְׁנַיִם לָמָּה פָּרַט הַכָּתוּב בִּשְׁלֹשָׁה אֶלָּא לְהַקִּישׁ שְׁלֹשָׁה לִשְׁנַיִם. מַה שְּׁלֹשָׁה מַזִּימִין אֶת הַשְּׁנַיִם אַף הַשְּׁנַיִם יָזֹמּוּ הַשְּׁלֹשָׁה. וּמְנַיִין אֲפִילוּ מֵאָה תַּלְמוּד לוֹמַר עֵדִים.

Mishnah 9: *By the words of two witnesses or three witnesses shall a death sentence be imposed*[41]. If testimony is confirmed by two, why did the verse mention three? Only to compare three to two. Since three may prove that two are plotters, two also may prove that three are plotters. And from where even a hundred? The verse says "witnesses"[42].

משנה י: רִבִּי שִׁמְעוֹן אוֹמֵר מַה שְּׁנַיִם אֵינָן נֶהֱרָגִין עַד שֶׁיְּהוּ שְׁנֵיהֶן זוֹמְמִין אַף שְׁלֹשָׁה אֵינָן נֶהֱרָגִין עַד שֶׁיְּהוּ שְׁלָשְׁתָּן זוֹמְמִין. וּמְנַיִין אֲפִילוּ מֵאָה תַּלְמוּד לוֹמַר עֵדִים.

Mishnah 10: Rebbi Simeon says, since two are executed only if both are plotters, so three are executed only if all three are plotters. And from where even a hundred? The verse says "witnesses"[42].

משנה יא: רִבִּי עֲקִיבָה אוֹמֵר לֹא בָא הַשְּׁלִישִׁי אֶלָּא לְהַחְמִיר עָלָיו וְלַעֲשׂוֹת דִּינוֹ כַּיּוֹצֵא בָאֵילּוּ. אִם כֵּן עָנַשׁ הַכָּתוּב לַנִּיטְפָּל לְעוֹבְרֵי עֲבֵירָה כְּעוֹבְרֵי עֲבֵירָה עַל אַחַת כַּמָּה וְכַמָּה יְשַׁלֵּם שָׂכָר לַנִּיטְפָּל לְעוֹשֶׂה מִצְוָה כְּעוֹשֶׂה מִצְוָה:

Mishnah 11: Rebbi Aqiba says, the third is only mentioned to punish him harshly and to identify his judgment with that of the others. If the verse in this way punished the accessory of criminals like criminals[43], so much more it will reward the accessory to one who keeps the commandments as one who keeps the commandments.

38 This is a misquote. It should be נֶפֶשׁ בְּנֶפֶשׁ (*Deut*. 19:21), not נֶפֶשׁ תַּחַת נֶפֶשׁ (*Lev*. 24:18) which applies to an animal.

39 *Deut*. 19:19. It says "he plotted", not "he did". This implies that the plot was discovered before it succeeded.

40 The court might not believe the witnesses even if no formal perjury was proved. Then the testimony becomes irrelevant and cannot be sanctioned. If no

sentence had been passed on the accused, it is impossible to sentence the witnesses to the same penalty.

41 *Deut.* 19:15. Criminal sentences can be imposed only on the basis of oral testimony, not of circumstantial evidence.

42 The repetition, *two witnesses or three witnesses*, when it could have been "two or three witnesses", implies that any number of witnesses have the same status as do two.

43 Since the third witness is not essential for proof in court.

(31a line 67) **הלכה ח**: אֵין הָעֵדִים הַזּוֹמְמִין. אָמַר רִבִּי זְעִירָה. הָדָא אָמְרָה. עֵד זוֹמֵם אֵינוֹ נִפְסָל בְּבֵית דִּין אֶלָּא מֵעַצְמוֹ הוּא נִפְסָל. פָּתַר לָהּ בְּהַתְרָייָה. וְתַנֵּי כֵן. אָמַר רִבִּי יוֹסֵי. בַּמֶּה דְבָרִים אֲמוּרִים. בִּשְׁתֵּי כִיתֵּי עֵידִיּוֹת וּבִשְׁתֵּי הַתְרָיוֹת. אֲבָל בְּעֵדוּת אַחַת וּבְהַתְרָייָה אַחַת כָּל־עֵדוּת שֶׁבָּטְלָה מִקְצָתָהּ בָּטְלָה כוּלָּהּ. מָהוּ כָּל־עֵדוּת שֶׁבָּטְלָה מִקְצָתָהּ בָּטְלָה כוּלָּהּ. הָיוּ עוֹמְדִין וּמְעִידִין עָלָיו בַּעֲשָׂרָה בְנִיסָן שֶׁגָּנַב אֶת הַשּׁוֹר בְּאֶחָד בְּנִיסָן וְטָבַח וּמָכַר בַּחֲמִשָּׁה בְנִיסָן וְהוּזְמוּ בְּאַחַד עָשָׂר בְּנִיסָן. כָּל־עֵדוּת שֶׁהֵעִידוּ מִב' בְּנִיסָן עַד חֲמִשָּׁה בְנִיסָן לְמַפְרֵעַ הֲרֵי אֵילוּ פְסוּלִין. אָמַר רִבִּי בָּא בַּר מָמָל. תִּיפְתָּר בִּמְעִידִין עָלָיו בְּכֶרֶךְ אֶחָד וְלֵית שְׁמַע מִינָּהּ כְּלוּם. וְתַנֵּי כֵן. הָיוּ הֵן הָרִאשׁוֹנִים וְהֵן הָאַחֲרוֹנִים. הוּזְמוּ בָרִאשׁוֹנָה אֵין בְּכָךְ כְּלוּם. בַּשְּׁנִייָה הֲרֵי הִיא לוֹ עֵדוּת אַחַת. בַּשְּׁלִישִׁית הֲרֵי הִיא לוֹ כִשְׁתֵּי עֵדִיּוֹת. וְהֵיכֵי. אִמ[44] בִּמְעִידִין עָלָיו בְּכֶרֶךְ אֶחָד לֵית שְׁמַע מִינָּהּ כְּלוּם. לֹא אַתְיָיא אֶלָּא עַל יְדֵי עֵדִיּוֹת סַגִּין. אָמַר רִבִּי זְעִירָא. הָדָא אָמְרָה. עֵד זוֹמֵם אֵינוֹ נִפְסָל בְּבֵית דִּין אֶלָּא מֵעַצְמוֹ הוּא נִפְסָל.

Halakhah 8: "Plotting witnesses cannot be". [45]Rebbi Ze`ira said, this implies that a plotting witness is not disqualified by the court but is disqualified by himself. Explain it by warning, as it was stated: "Rebbi Yose said, when has this been said? For two testimonies with two warnings. But for one testimony and one warning[46] any testimony which is partially disqualified is totally disqualified." What does it mean, "if it is partially disqualified it is totally disqualified"? If they were standing and testifying against him on the tenth of Nisan that he had stolen an ox on the first of Nisan, and slaughtered or sold it on the fifth of Nisan. They were shown to be plotting on the eleventh of Nisan. Any testimony which they delivered between the second and the fifth of Nisan[47] is retroactively disqualified. Rebbi Abba bar Mamal said, explain it if they deliver their testimony in one group and you cannot infer anything, as we have stated[48]: "They were the first and they were the later [witnesses]. If they were shown to be plotting at first, there is nothing. At the second time, there is one testimony[49]. At the third time, there are two testimonies. How? If they testify on one occasion, you could not infer anything. It only comes based on multiple testimonies. [50]Rebbi Ze`ira said, this implies that a plotting witness is not disqualified by the court but is disqualified by himself.

44 Scribal error for אם, correct in G and *Bava qamma*.

45 The entire Halakhah is copied from *Bava qamma* 7:4, explained there in Notes 45-51. (Babli *Bava qamma* 72b/73a).

46 Warnings given to the witnesses that perjury is a crime and punishable.

47 In G and *Bava qamma*: between the tenth and the fifteenth of Nisan. This is the correct reading. Testimony of perjured witnesses must be struck from court records from the date of the testimony, not the date of the discovery of the fact of perjury. Babli *Sanhedrin* 27a.

48 Tosephta *Bava batra* 2:9; testimony to affirm title to real estate by proving three years of undisturbed possession.

49 Here ends the first sheet of G.

50 This sentence, which affirms the correctness of R. Ze`ira's statement, against R. Abba bar Mamal, is found only here. In contrast to the disqualifications listed in Mishnah *Sanhedrin* 3:6, perjured witnesses are automatically disqualified from the moment of perjury, without any action by the court.

(fol. 30d) **משנה יב**: מַה שְׁנַיִם נִמְצָא אֶחָד מֵהֶן קָרוֹב אוֹ פָסוּל עֵדוּתָן בְּטֵילָה אַף שְׁלֹשָׁה נִמְצָא אֶחָד מֵהֶן קָרוֹב אוֹ פָסוּל עֵדוּתָן בְּטֵילָה. וּמְנַיִין אֲפִילוּ מֵאָה תַּלְמוּד לוֹמַר עֵדִים.

Mishnah 12: Since the testimony of two [witnesses] is invalid if one of them is found to be a relative or a disqualified person[51], the same holds for three if one of them is found to be a relative or a disqualified person. From where even for a hundred? The verse says[42], *witnesses*.

משנה יג: אָמַר רִבִּי יוֹסֵי בַּמֶּה דְבָרִים אֲמוּרִים בְּדִינֵי נְפָשׁוֹת אֲבָל בְּדִינֵי מָמוֹנוֹת תִּתְקַיֵּים הָעֵדוּת בַּשְּׁאָר. רִבִּי אוֹמֵר אֶחָד דִּינֵי מָמוֹנוֹת וְאֶחָד דִּינֵי נְפָשׁוֹת בִּזְמַן שֶׁהִיתְרוּ בָהֶן. אֲבָל בִּזְמַן שֶׁלֹּא הִתְרוּ בָהֶן מַה יַּעֲשׂוּ שְׁנֵי אַחִין שֶׁרָאוּ בְאֶחָד שֶׁהָרַג אֶת הַנֶּפֶשׁ:

Mishnah 13: Rebbi Yose said, when has this been said? In criminal trials, but in civil trials the testimony should be upheld by the remaining [witnesses][52]. Rebbi says, both in criminal and in civil trials, if they warned them[53]. But if they did not warn them, what should two brothers do who were eye-witnesses to a murder?

51 If one witness is disqualified by the rules of Mishnah *Sanhedrin* either 3:6 or 3:7, there is only one testimony, insufficient by biblical standards.

52 Since *Deut*. 19:19 is formulated for criminal trials, the argument that any number of witnesses have the same status as two witnesses is not necessarily true for civil trials. In money matters, any two qualified witnesses can testify. For example, it is admissible that marriage contracts be signed first by two qualified witnesses and after them by any number of family members of both sides (cf. *Gittin* 8:12, Note 105).

53 If in a criminal case a disqualified person or two related persons both warned the perpetrator not to engage in criminal behavior, their action makes them witnesses and all witnesses have to be disqualified under the argument of Mishnah 12. But if they were eye witnesses but not those who delivered the warning, they are not forced to testify; the trial may proceed without them.

(31b line 5) **הלכה יג**: אָמַר רִבִּי יוֹסֵי בַּמֶּה דְבָרִים אֲמוּרִים כול'. יֵאָמֵר דִּינֵי מָמוֹנוֹת וְאַל יֵאָמֵר דִּינֵי נְפָשׁוֹת. שֶׁאִילּוּ נֶאֱמַר דִּינֵי מָמוֹנוֹת וְלֹא נֶאֱמַר דִּינֵי נְפָשׁוֹת הָיִיתִי אוֹמֵר. דִּינֵי מָמוֹנוֹת הַקַּלִּים שְׁלֹשָׁה מְזַמְּמִין אֶת הַשְּׁנַיִם וּשְׁנַיִם אֵין מְזַמִּין אֶת הַשְּׁלֹשָׁה. מְנַיִין אֲפִילוּ מֵאָה. תַּלְמוּד לוֹמַר עֵדִים. אוֹ אִילּוּ נֶאֱמַר דִּינֵי נְפָשׁוֹת וְלֹא נֶאֱמַר דִּינֵי מָמוֹנוֹת הָיִיתִי אוֹמֵר. דִּינֵי נְפָשׁוֹת הַחֲמוּרִין שְׁנַיִם מְזַמִּין אֶת הַשְּׁלֹשָׁה שְׁלֹשָׁה אֵינָן מְזִימִין אֶת הַשְּׁנַיִם. מְנַיִין אֲפִילוּ הַמֵּאָה. תַּלְמוּד לוֹמַר עֵדִים.

Halakhah 13: "Rebbi Yose said, when has this been said?" [54]It should have been said for civil trials and would not have been needed for criminal trials. If it had been said for civil trials, not for criminal trials, I would have said that in the relaxed standards of civil trials three [witnesses] may prove two [witnesses] to be plotting but two may not prove three to be plotting. From where even a hundred? The verse says, *witnesses*[42]. Or if it had been said for criminal trials, not for civil trials, I would have said that according to the stringent standards of criminal trials two [witnesses] may prove three [witnesses] to be plotting; three may not prove two to be plotting[55]. From where even a hundred? The verse says, *witnesses*[42].

54 The argument refers to all Mishnaiot 9-13. The requirement of "two witnesses or three witnesses" for criminal convictions is written in *Deut*. 17:6, 19:15. (In addition, rendering judgment in a criminal trial on the basis of a single testimony is forbidden in *Num*. 35:30.) While in both verses of *Deut*. the background clearly is that of criminal trials, the redundancy is taken as a sign that in civil trials (not on arbitration panels) the biblical rules of evidence of criminal trials have to be followed. The Babli disagrees in the name of Rav Nahman (6b).

55 It seems to be clear that in this

sentence the positions of "two" and "three" have to be switched, resulting in a sentence completely parallel to the preceding one.

(fol. 30d) **משנה יד**: הָיוּ שְׁנַיִם רוֹאִין אוֹתוֹ מֵחַלּוֹן זֶה וּשְׁנַיִם רוֹאִין אוֹתוֹ מֵחַלּוֹן זֶה וְאֶחָד מַתְרֶה בוֹ בָּאֶמְצַע בִּזְמַן שֶׁמִּקְצָתָן רוֹאִין אֵילּוּ אֶת אֵילּוּ הֲרֵי אֵילּוּ עֵדוּת אֶחָת. וְאִם לָאו הֲרֵי אֵילּוּ שְׁתֵּי עֵדִיּוֹת. לְפִיכָךְ אִם נִמְצֵאת אַחַת מֵהֶן זוֹמֶמֶת הוּא וָהֵן נֶהֱרָגִין וְהַשְּׁנִייָה פְטוּרָה.

Mishnah 14: If two [witnesses] saw him from one window, two from another window, and a person in the middle gives the warning[56], if partially they can see one another[57] then this is one testimony. Otherwise, these are two testimonies. Therefore, if one [group] of them is found plotting, he[58] and they are executed; the second [group] is not prosecutable[59].

56 To a potential criminal not to engage in criminal activity.

57 If one of each group of witnesses sees the other or the person in the middle sees one of each group.

58 The criminal, convicted on basis of the testimony of the witnesses not found to be perjured.

59 If after the convicted person was executed the second group also was found plotting, they cannot be executed (Mishnah 8).

(31b line 12) **הלכה יד**: הָיוּ שְׁנַיִם רוֹאִין אוֹתוֹ כול'. אָמַר רִבִּי יִרְמְיָה. חֲמִי אֵיךְ תַּנִּינָן הָכָא. הָיוּ שְׁנַיִם רוֹאִין אוֹתוֹ מֵחַלּוֹן זֶה וּשְׁנַיִם רוֹאִין אוֹתוֹ מֵחַלּוֹן זֶה וְאֶחָד מַתְרֶה בוֹ בָּאֶמְצַע. בִּזְמַן שֶׁמִּקְצָתָן רוֹאִין אֵילּוּ אֶת אֵילּוּ הֲרֵי אֵילּוּ עֵדוּת אַחַת וְאִם לָאו הֲרֵי אֵילּוּ שְׁתֵּי עֵדִיּוֹת. הָא אִם הָיוּ שְׁלֹשָׁה שְׁלֹשָׁה לֹא בְדָא. אָמַר רִבִּי יוֹסֵי. תַּנִּינָן שְׁלֹשָׁה שְׁלֹשָׁה לֹא בְדָא. תַּנִּינָן הָכָא מַה דְלֹא תַנִּינָן בְּכָל סַנְהֶדְרִין. הוּא וָהֵן נֶהֱרָגִין וְהַשְּׁנִייָה פְטוּרָה.

Halakhah 14: "If two [witnesses] saw him," etc. Rebbi Jeremiah said, look how we are stating here: "If two [witnesses] saw him from one window, two from another window, and a person in the middle gives the warning, if partially they can see one another then this is one testimony. Otherwise, these are two testimonies."[60] Therefore, if they were three each, this does not apply. Rebbi Yose said, we stated "three each not so. [61]"

We state here what was not stated in all of *Sanhedrin*: "he and they are executed; the second [group] is not prosecutable.[62]"

60 It is not clear what the argument is; there are at least two very different explanations. In the opinion of *Pene Moshe*, R. Jeremiah points out that if the single person in the middle sees each group of witnesses, then the testimony is one of "three and three", i. e., the person in the middle with each one of the groups of two witnesses. It is a single testimony; if one group is found plotting, the entire testimony becomes invalid and nobody can be executed. The criminal cannot be convicted since there is no testimony; the witnesses cannot be executed because not all of them have been shown to be plotting.

Others explain that if in each window there are three witnesses and the person in the middle only sees one in each, the two groups of two witnesses that are not seen by the person in the middle form two independent groups of witnesses; the person in the middle does not connect them. In any case, the Babli will not agree (6b).

61 A *baraita* confirms the interpretation, whatever it may be.

62 To contemplate that the rules require a clear miscarriage of justice.

(fol. 30d) **משנה טו:** רִבִּי יוֹסֵי בֵּי רִבִּי יְהוּדָה אוֹמֵר לְעוֹלָם אֵינוֹ נֶהֱרָג עַד שֶׁיְּהוּ שְׁנֵי עֵדָיו מַתְרִין בּוֹ שֶׁנֶּאֱמַר עַל פִּי שְׁנַיִם עֵדִים. דָּבָר אַחֵר עַל פִּי שְׁנַיִם עֵדִים שֶׁלֹּא תְהֵא סַנְהֶדְרִין שׁוֹמַעַת מִפִּי הַתּוּרְגְּמָן:

Mishnah 15: Rebbi Yose ben Rebbi Jehudah[63] says, nobody can be executed unless his two witnesses warned him[64], as it is said: *By the mouth of two witnesses*[54]. Another explanation: *By the mouth of two witnesses*, that the court may not hear from the mouth of an interpreter[65].

63 In the Babli and most independent Mishnah mss: "R. Yose" (i. e., ben Halaphta). The reading of the Yerushalmi in Mishnah and Halakhah contradicts Mishnah 2:6. Since the statement of R. Yose ben R. Jehudah is not discussed in Halakhah 2:6, the correct attribution there cannot be determined. Since his statement is not accepted as practice in the Babli, it seems that "R. Yose ben R. Jehudah" is the correct attribution here.

64 Warning by a single person is invalid, even if witnessed by two persons.

65 Testimony and cross examinations are possible only if all judges understand the witnesses without translator. The Babli (6b) permits cross-examination using a translator if the witnesses' answers are directly understood by the judges.

(31b line 18) **הלכה טו:** רִבִּי יוֹסֵי בֵּי רִבִּי יְהוּדָה אוֹמֵר כול'. תַּנֵּי רִבִּי הוֹשַׁעְיָה. הַפָּסוּק הַזֶּה אָמוּר בִּשְׁתֵּי כִיתֵּי עֵדִים. כִּֽי־יָק֥וּם עֵד־חָמָ֖ס בְּאִ֑ישׁ. עֵד זוֹמֵם שֶׁהוּא עוֹנֶה בְאִישׁ. לַעֲנ֥וֹת בּ֖וֹ. לֹא בְעֵידוּתוֹ. עֵדִים זוֹמְמִין מָהוּ שֶׁיְּהוּ צְרִיכִין לְקַבֵּל הַתְרָייָה. רִבִּי יִצְחָק בַּר טֶבְלַיי בְּשֵׁם רִבִּי לָעְזָר. עֵדִים זוֹמְמִין אֵינָן צְרִיכִין לְקַבֵּל הַתְרָייָה. אָמַר רִבִּי אַבָּהוּ. לֹא חַיישׁוּן לוֹן. אָמַר רִבִּי יַעֲקֹב בַּר דַּסַּי. וְאִית נְכוּלִין סַגִּין מָאן אִילֵּין חַמְיָין חֲבֵרֵיהוֹן נַפְקִין מִיקְטְלָא וְלָא אָמְרִין כְּלוּם.

Halakhah 15: "Rebbi Yose ben Rebbi Jehudah says," etc. Rebbi Hoshaia stated: The following verse is said about two groups of witnesses. *If an oppressive witness arises against a man*, a plotting witness who answers to a man. *Answering him*, not his testimony[66].

Do plotting witnesses have to be warned? Rebbi Isaac bar Tevlai in the name of Rebbi Eleazar: Plotting witnesses do not have to accept warning[67]. Rebbi Abbahu said, we do not take notice of this. Rebbi Jacob bar Dassai said, and there are very cunning people who even if they see their comrades being led out to be killed do not say anything[68].

66 While testimony may not stand up under cross-examination, the worst that can happen to a witness in that case is that the court does not believe him. A criminal conviction can only follow if the new group of witnesses *answer him,* the plotting witness, by showing that he could not have been present at the place of the alleged crime or transaction. This paragraph belongs to Mishnah 6.

67 In the Babli, *Ketubot* 32a, this is an anonymous statement accepted without discussion.

68 It is not clear whether this statement supports R. Eleazar or R. Abbahu. In the first case, he argues that a special warning about penalties of plotting perjury is unnecessary since the bad guys automatically will stay away as far as possible from the court. In the second case he wants to point out that good people will not be kept away from being witnesses by being admonished by the court about penalties of plotting perjury, and it is a good thing that bad people will be frightened away.

(fol. 30d) **משנה יו:** מִי שֶׁנִּגְמַר דִּינוֹ וּבָרַח וּבָא לִפְנֵי אוֹתוֹ בֵית דִּין אֵין סוֹתְרִין אֶת דִּינוֹ. כָּל מָקוֹם שֶׁיַּעַמְדוּ שְׁנַיִם וְיֹאמְרוּ מְעִידִין אָנוּ בְאִישׁ פְּלוֹנִי שֶׁנִּגְמַר דִּינוֹ בְּבֵית דִּינוֹ שֶׁל פְּלוֹנִי וּפְלוֹנִי וּפְלוֹנִי עֵידָיו הֲרֵי זֶה יֵיהָרֵג.

Mishnah 16: If somebody escaped after sentence was passed, if he is returned to the same court, his case is not reopened. Anywhere two [people] will come forward and say, we testify against this man that he was condemned in court X on the testimony of Y and Z, he shall be executed.

(31b line 25) **הלכה יו:** מִי שֶׁנִּגְמַר דִּינוֹ כול'. כָּתַב כָּל־נְכָסָיו לִשְׁנֵי בְנֵי אָדָם כְּאַחַת הָיוּ הָעֵדִים כְּשֵׁירִין לָזֶה וּפְסוּלִין לָזֶה. רִבִּי הִילָא אָמַר. אִתְפַּלְּגוֹן רִבִּי יוֹחָנָן וְרִבִּי שִׁמְעוֹן בֶּן לָקִישׁ. חַד אָמַר. מֵאַחַר שֶׁהֵן פְּסוּלִין לָזֶה פְּסוּלִין לָזֶה. וְחָרָנָה אָמַר. כְּשֵׁירִין לָזֶה וּפְסוּלִין לָזֶה. רִבִּי מָנָא לֹא מְפָרֵשׁ. רִבִּי אָבוּן מְפָרֵשׁ. רִבִּי יוֹחָנָן אָמַר. מֵאַחַר שֶׁהֵן פְּסוּלִין לָזֶה פְּסוּלִין לָזֶה. רִבִּי שִׁמְעוֹן בֶּן לָקִישׁ אָמַר. כְּשֵׁירִין לָזֶה וּפְסוּלִין לָזֶה. אָמַר רִבִּי לָעְזָר. מַתְנִיתָא מְסַיְּיעָה לְרִבִּי יוֹחָנָן. מַה הַשְּׁנַיִם נִמְצָא אֶחָד מֵהֶן קָרוֹב אוֹ פָּסוּל עֵדוּתָן בְּטֵילָה אַף הַשְּׁלֹשָׁה נִמְצָא אֶחָד מֵהֶן קָרוֹב אוֹ פָּסוּל עֵדוּתָן בְּטֵילָה. מְנַיִין אֲפִילוּ מֵאָה תַּלְמוּד לוֹמַר עֵדִים. רִבִּי יַעֲקֹב בַּר אָחָא אָמַר. אִתְפַּלְּגוֹן רִבִּי חֲנִינָה חֲבֵרוֹן דְּרַבָּנִין וְרַבָּנִין. חַד אָמַר. יֵאוּת אָמַר רִבִּי לָעְזָר. וְחָרָנָה אָמַר. לֹא אָמַר רִבִּי לָעְזָר יֵאוּת. מָאן דְּאָמַר. יֵאוּת אָמַר רִבִּי לָעְזָר. נַעֲשִׂית כְּעֵידוּת אַחַת וּכְהַתְרָייָה אַחַת. וְכָל־עֵדוּת שֶׁבָּטְלָה מִקְצָתָהּ בָּטְלָה כוּלָּהּ. מָאן דְּאָמַר. לֹא אָמַר רִבִּי לָעְזָר יֵאוּת. נַעֲשִׂית כִּשְׁתֵּי כִיתֵּי עֵדִים כְּשֵׁירִין לָזֶה וּפְסוּלִין לָזֶה.

Halakhah 16: "Whose sentence was passed," etc. [69]If somebody wrote all his property over to two persons in one document and the testimony of the witnesses was valid for one but invalid for the other. Rebbi Hila said, Rebbi Johanan and Rebbi Simeon ben Laqish disagreed; one said, since it is invalid for one it is invalid for the other, but the other said, it is valid for one and invalid for the other. Rebbi Mana did not specify; Rebbi Abun specified: Rebbi Johanan said, since it is invalid for one it is invalid for the other; but Rebbi Simeon ben Laqish said, it is valid for one and invalid for the other. Rebbi Eleazar said, the Mishnah supports Rebbi Johanan: "Since the testimony of two [witnesses] is invalid if one of them is found to be a relative or a disqualified person[51], the same holds for three if one of them is found to be a relative or a disqualified person. From where even for a hundred? The verse says[42], *witnesses.*" Rebbi Jacob bar Aha said, Rebbi Ḥanina the colleague of the rabbis and the rabbis disagree. One says, the argument of Rebbi Eleazar is correct, but the other says, the argument of Rebbi Eleazar is not correct. For him who says, the argument of Rebbi Eleazar is correct, it is a single testimony and a single warning, and any testimony which is partially disqualified is totally disqualified[70]. For him who says, the argument of Rebbi Eleazar is not correct, it is as if two groups of witnesses came, valid for one and invalid for the other.

69 This paragraph refers to Mishnah 12, not 16. It is also found in *Ketubot* 11:6, explained there in Notes 94-102, and *Gittin* 1:1 (Notes 20-21).

70 Tosephta *Bava qamma* 6:23.

(fol. 30d) **משנה יז**: סַנְהֶדְרִין נוֹהֶגֶת בָּאָרֶץ וּבְחוּצָה לָאָרֶץ. סַנְהֶדְרִין הַהוֹרֶגֶת אֶחָד בַּשָּׁבוּעַ נִקְרֵאת חַבְלָנִית. רַבִּי לָעְזָר בֶּן עֲזַרְיָה אוֹמֵר אֶחָד לְשִׁבְעִים שָׁנָה. רִבִּי טַרְפוֹן וְרִבִּי עֲקִיבָה אוֹמְרִים אִילּוּ הָיִינוּ בְסַנְהֶדְרִין לֹא נֶהֱרַג בָּהּ אָדָם מֵעוֹלָם. רַבָּן שִׁמְעוֹן בֶּן גַּמְלִיאֵל אוֹמֵר אַף הֵן מַרְבִּין שׁוֹפְכֵי דָמִים בְּיִשְׂרָאֵל:

Mishnah 17: Criminal courts apply in the Land and outside the Land. A criminal court which hands out a death sentence once in a Sabbatical period is called terrorist. Rebbi Eleazar ben Azariah said, once in seventy years. Rebbi Tarphon and Rebbi Aqiba say, if we had been members of a criminal court, nobody ever would have been condemned to death there. Rabban Simeon ben Gamliel said, they would have increased the number of murderers in Israel.

(31b line 39) **הלכה יז**: סַנְהֶדְרִין נוֹהֶגֶת בָּאָרֶץ כול'. סַנְהֶדְרִין נוֹהֶגֶת בָּאָרֶץ וּבְחוּצָה לָאָרֶץ. דִּכְתִיב וְהָיוּ אֵלֶּה לָכֶם לְחוּקַּת מִשְׁפָּט לְדֹרֹתֵיכֶם בְּכֹל מוֹשְׁבוֹתֵיכֶם: וּמַה תַלְמוּד לוֹמַר שׁוֹפְטִים וְשֹׁטְרִים תִּתֶּן־לְךָ בְּכָל־שְׁעָרֶיךָ. בְּעָרֵי אֶרֶץ יִשְׂרָאֵל. אֶלָּא שֶׁבְּעָרֵי אֶרֶץ יִשְׂרָאֵל מוֹשִׁיבִין דַּייָנִים בְּכָל־עִיר וָעִיר וּבְחוּצָה לָאָרֶץ מוֹשִׁיבִין אוֹתָן פְּלָכִים פְּלָכִים. תַּנֵּי. רִבִּי דוֹסְתַי בֵּירִבִּי יַנַּאי אוֹמֵר. מִצְוָה לְכָל־שֵׁבֶט שֶׁיְּהֵא דָן אֶת שִׁבְטוֹ. דִּכְתִיב שֹׁפְטִים וְשֹׁטְרִים תִּתֶּן־לְךָ בְּכָל־שְׁעָרֶיךָ אֲשֶׁר יי אֱלֹהֶיךָ נֹתֵן לְךָ לִשְׁבָטֶיךָ.

Halakhah 17: "Criminal courts apply in the Land," etc. [71]"Criminal courts apply in the Land and outside the Land, as it is written[72]: *This shall be for you a law statute for your generations, in all your dwellings.* And why does the verse say[73], *judges and marshals you shall appoint for yourself in all your gates*, in the towns of the Land of Israel. Only that in the Land of Israel one installs judges in every town and outside the Land one appoints them by circuits." It was stated: [74]"Rebbi Dositheos ben Rebbi Yannai says, there is an obligation for every tribe to judge his own tribe, as it is written[73]: *Judges and marshals you shall appoint for yourself in all your gates which the Eternal, your God, gives you for your tribes."*

71 Tosephta *Sanhedrin* 3:10, Babli 7a.

72 *Num.* 35:29.

73 *Deut.* 16:18.

74 *Sifry Deut.* 144, Babli *Sanhedrin* 16b. There and in the sources given in Note 71 the author is Rabban Simeon ben Gamliel.

The difference between the anonymous Tanna of the first Tosephta and R. Dositheos b. Yannai / Rabban Simeon ben Gamliel is that according to the first Tanna the claimant in a civil suit has the choice of the jurisdiction to file his suit whereas the dissenters restrict him to courts of his own tribe (L. Finkelstein, Commentary to *Sifry*).

(31b line 46) תַּנֵּי רַבָּן שִׁמְעוֹן בֶּן גַּמְלִיאֵל. מְחוּיְּבֵי מִיתוֹת שֶׁבָּֽרְחוּ מִן הָאָרֶץ לְחוּצָה לָאָרֶץ מְמִיתִין אוֹתָן מִיַּד. בָּֽרְחוּ מֵחוּצָה לָאָרֶץ לָאָרֶץ אֵין מְמִיתִין אוֹתוֹ מִיַּד אֶלָּא דָנִין אוֹתָן כַּתְּחִילָּה.

[75]Rabban Simeon ben Gamliel stated: People sentenced to death who fled from the Land to outside the Land one executes immediately. People sentenced to death who fled from outside the Land to the Land one does not execute immediately but gives them a new trial.

75 Tosephta *Sanhedrin* 3:11 in the name of R. Dositheos ben Jehudah. Babli 7a in the name of R. Jehudah b. Dositheos in the name of R. Simeon ben Shetah (*editio princeps*) but R. Dositheos ben Jehudah in the name of R. Simeon (Munich ms.).

אילו הן הגולין פרק שני

(fol. 31b) **משנה א**: אֵילּוּ הֵן הַגּוֹלִין הַהוֹרֵג נֶפֶשׁ בִּשְׁגָגָה. הָיָה מְעַגֵּל בַּמְּעְגֵּילָה וְנָפְלָה עָלָיו וַהֲרָגַתּוּ הָיָה מְשַׁלְשֵׁל בֶּחָבִית וְנָפְלָה עָלָיו וַהֲרָגַתּוּ הָיָה יוֹרֵד בַּסּוּלָּם וְנָפַל עָלָיו וַהֲרָגוֹ הֲרֵי זֶה גּוֹלֶה. אֲבָל אִם הָיָה מוֹשֵׁךְ בַּמְּעְגֵּילָה וְנָפְלָה עָלָיו וַהֲרָגַתּוּ הָיָה דוֹלֶה בֶחָבִית וְנִפְסַק הַחֶבֶל וְנָפְלָה עָלָיו וַהֲרָגַתּוּ הָיָה עוֹלֶה בַּסּוּלָּם וְנָפַל עָלָיו וַהֲרָגוֹ הֲרֵי זֶה אֵינוֹ גוֹלֶה. זֶה הַכְּלָל כָּל שֶׁבְּדֶרֶךְ הוֹרָדָתוֹ גּוֹלֶה וְשֶׁלֹּא בְדֶרֶךְ הוֹרָדָתוֹ אֵינוֹ גוֹלֶה.

Mishnah 1: The following are exiled: the unintentional homicide[1]. If he was rolling with the roller[2] when it fell on somebody and killed him, or lowering an amphora when it fell on somebody and killed him, or was descending on a ladder when he fell on somebody and killed him, he is exiled. But if he was drawing the roller when it fell on somebody and killed him, or lifting an amphora when it fell on somebody and killed him, or was climbing a ladder when he fell on somebody and killed him, he is not exiled. This is the principle, by anything lowered, he is exiled, if it is not lowered, he is not exiled[3].

1 The rules of exile of the unintentional homicide are detailed in *Num*. 35, *Deut*. 19:1-10.

2 The roller is used to smoothe the surface of a roof after waterproofing.

3 The rules of *Num*. 35 essentially absolve the homicide from exile if there was a freak accident, where nobody could have expected a deadly outcome. Then when the theme is taken up again in *Deut*., v. 19:5 gives as example that two people go to cut down a tree, one swings his axe to cut the tree when the blade comes off the handle (or jumps off the tree to be cut) while the axe is lowered and kills the other person. The verse ends with an emphatic statement, this one *has to flee to a city of asylum to stay alive.* This is read to mean that exile is appropriate only if the impetus given to the deadly object is reinforced by gravity, not if it is attenuated by it.

(31c line 43) **הלכה א**: אֵילּוּ הֵן הַגּוֹלִין כול'. רִבִּי יְהוּדָה פּוֹטֵר עַד שֶׁיַּפִּיל אֶת כָּל־הַחֶבֶל. רִבִּי שִׁמְעוֹן פּוֹטֵר עַד שֶׁיַּתִּיר אֶת כָּל־הַמַּחֲלָצוֹן. מַאי דָּמַר רִבִּי שִׁמְעוֹן בִּפְסִיקַת הַחֶבֶל. מַה דָּמַר רִבִּי יְהוּדָה בִּשְׁמִיטַּת הַמַּחֲלָצוֹן.

רִבִּי יִרְמְיָה בְּעָא קוֹמֵי רִבִּי אַבָּהוּ. הָיָה מְעַגֵּל בַּמְּעְגֵּילָה כְּדֶרֶךְ הֲלִיכָתָהּ וְהוֹצִיא הֲלָה אֶת רֹאשׁוֹ וְהִטִּיחָה לוֹ. אָמַר לֵיהּ. הִיא עֲלִייָה הִיא יְרִידָה. רִבִּי יִרְמְיָה בְּעָא קוֹמֵי רִבִּי אַבָּהוּ. הָיָה מְעַגֵּיל בַּמַּעְגֵּילָה כְּדֶרֶךְ הֲלִיכָתָהּ וְהוֹשִׁיט הַתִּינוֹק אֶת יָדוֹ וּרְצָצָהּ. אָמַר לֵיהּ. אַטְרַחְתְּ בָּהּ. הִיא עֲלִייָה הִיא יְרִידָה.

Halakhah 1[4]: "The following are exiled," etc. Rebbi Jehudah declares him not liable unless the entire rope falls from his hand[5]. Rebbi Simeon declares him not liable unless he let go the trowel completely[6]. What Rebbi Simeon said refers to breaking of the rope. What Rebbi Jehudah said, was about letting the trowel go[7].

Rebbi Jeremiah asked before Rebbi Abbahu: If one was using a roller going forward when another person stuck out his head and the roller hit him. He told him, there is no difference between upward and downward movement[8].

Rebbi Jeremiah asked before Rebbi Abbahu: If one was using a roller going forward when a child stuck out his hand and it was smothered. He told him, you are bothering me about this; there is no difference between upward and downward movement[9].

4 This note is found only in the *editio princeps*; it is missing in the ms.

5 This refers to the case of a person lowering a load by means of a rope when the load comes crashing down and kills somebody. If he loosens his grip, the homicide is due to his negligence and he is exiled. If the rope breaks (assuming he was not negligent in using a rope not suitable for its task by common engineering standards), it is an act of God and he is not liable.

6 Both Rashi (French *truelle*) and the `Arukh (Italian *cazzuola*) define this as builder's trowel (Babli 9b). If the builder is standing on a roof and lets go of the trowel which falls down and kills, he is negligent. But if the tool breaks (assuming it was well maintained), it is an act of God and he is not liable.

7 Meaning that the argument of R. Jehudah applied to R. Simeon's case would have resulted in R. Simeon's statement and vice-versa.

8 This is a personal injury case, not one of homicide. The particular distinction derived from *Deut.* 19:5 is not applicable.

9 If there is no negligence on the part of the operator, he is not liable and the distinction becomes meaningless.

(fol. 31b) **משנה ב**: נִשְׁמַט הַבַּרְזֶל מִקַּתּוֹ וְהָרַג רִבִּי אוֹמֵר אֵינוֹ גוֹלֶה. וַחֲכָמִים אוֹמְרִים גּוֹלֶה. מִן הָעֵץ הַמִּתְבַּקֵּעַ רִבִּי אוֹמֵר גּוֹלֶה. וַחֲכָמִים אוֹמְרִים אֵינוֹ גוֹלֶה׃

Mishnah 2: If the iron slipped off the handle and killed, Rebbi said he does not go into exile, but the Sages say he does go. From the wood to split, Rebbi says he goes into exile, but the Sages say, he does not go[10].

10 This is a matter of interpretation of *Deut.* 19:5 as explained in the Halakhah (Babli 7b/8a, *Sifry Deut.* 183.) The Babli points out that for the Sages indirect causation is not punishable as negligence, while for Rebbi it is.

(31c line 50) **הלכה ב**: נִשְׁמַט הַבַּרְזֶל מִקַּתּוֹ כול'. מַה טַעֲמָא דְרִבִּי. נֶאֱמַר כָּאן נְשִׁילָה וְנֶאֱמַר לְהַלָּן כִּי יִשַּׁל זֵיתֶךָ. מַה נְשִׁילָה שֶׁנֶּאֶמְרָה לְהַלָּן נְשִׁירָה אַף כָּאן נְשִׁירָה. מַה טַעֲמוֹן דְּרַבָּנִין. נֶאֱמַר כָּאן נְשִׁילָה וְנֶאֱמַר לְהַלָּן וְנָשַׁל יי אֱלֹהֶיךָ אֶת־הַגּוֹיִם הָאֵל מִפָּנֶיךָ וגו'. מַה נְשִׁילָה שֶׁנֶּאֶמְרָה לְהַלָּן מַכָּה אַף כָּאן מַכָּה.

Halakhah 2: "If the iron slipped off the handle," etc. What is Rebbi's reason? It is said here[11] getting lost and it says there[12], *for your olives will fall off.* Since getting lost there means falling off, here also it means falling off. What is the rabbis' reason? It is said here getting lost and it says there[13], *the Eternal, your God, will eliminate these peoples before you.* Since getting lost there means taking a hit, here also taking a hit.

11 In *Deut.* 19:5: וְנָשַׁל הַבַּרְזֶל מִן־הָעֵץ *the iron was lost from the wood.* The *wood* might either be the handle or the tree to be felled. Cf. Arabic نسل "to beget, procreate; to pluck; to unravel, untwist, fray; to molt; to fall out" (1st conjugation).

12 *Deut.* 17:40. נשר is Mishnaic Hebrew for all material shed by a plant.

13 *Deut.* 7:22.

(fol. 31b) **משנה ג**: זָרַק אֶת הָאֶבֶן לִרְשׁוּת הָרַבִּים וְהָרַג הֲרֵי זֶה גוֹלֶה. רִבִּי אֱלִיעֶזֶר בֶּן יַעֲקֹב אוֹמֵר אִם מִשֶּׁיָּצָאת הָאֶבֶן מִיָּדוֹ וְהוֹצִיא הַלָּה אֶת רֹאשׁוֹ וְקִיבְּלָהּ הֲרֵי זֶה פָּטוּר.

Mishnah 3: If one threw a stone into the public domain and it killed someone, he is exiled[14]. Rebbi Eliezer ben Jacob says, if after the stone left his[15] hand, the other one stuck out his head and received it, he[15] is not liable.

14 As negligent homicide.

15 The thrower's.

(31c line 55) **הלכה ג׃** זָרַק אֶת הָאֶבֶן כול׳. תַּנֵּי רִבִּי אֱלִיעֶזֶר בֶּן יַעֲקֹב וּמָצָא. שֶׁיְּהֵא מָצוּי לוֹ בְשָׁעָה שֶׁהוּא הוֹרְגוֹ. וְיֵשׁ רְשׁוּת לִזְרוֹק אֶת הָאֶבֶן לִרְשׁוּת הָרַבִּים. אָמַר רִבִּי יוֹסֵי בֵּירִבִּי בּוּן. תִּפְתָּר שֶׁהָיָה כוֹתְלוֹ גוֹהָא.

Halakhah 3: "If one threw a stone," etc. Rebbi Eliezer ben Jacob stated, *it found.* That he should have been there at the moment he killed him[16]. But is there permission to throw the stone into the public domain? Rebbi Yose ben Abun said, explain it if his wall was inclined[17].

16 *Deut.* 19:5 reads: *If somebody goes with another to a forest to cut down trees; his hand was coming down with the axe to cut the tree, the iron was lost from the wood,* *found the other, and he died; this one has to flee to one of these towns and live.* If the person killed was not in the trajectory of the flying object at the start, the thrower is not guilty of negligent homicide. (Babli 8a; *Sifry Deut.* 183).

17 The wall of his property tilted towards the outside and threatens to fall into the public domain. The owner of the wall throws stones into the overhang to support the wall to remove the danger to the public. The anonymous Tanna assumes that the stones will have to be carried there, not thrown. (Babli 8a, in the name of R. Samuel bar Rav Isaac).

(fol. 31b) **משנה ד׃** זָרַק אֶת הָאֶבֶן לַחֲצֵירוֹ וְהָרַג אִם יֵשׁ רְשׁוּת לַנִּיזָּק לִיכָּנֵס לְשָׁם גּוֹלֶה. וְאִם לָאו אֵינוֹ גוֹלֶה. שֶׁנֶּאֱמַר וַאֲשֶׁר יָבֹא אֶת רֵעֵהוּ בַיַּעַר. מָה הַיַּעַר רְשׁוּת לַנִּיזָּק וְלַמַּזִּיק לִיכָּנֵס לְשָׁם. יָצָא חֲצַר בַּעַל הַבַּיִת שֶׁאֵין רְשׁוּת לַנִּיזָּק וְלַמַּזִּיק לִיכָּנֵס לְשָׁם. אַבָּא שָׁאוּל אוֹמֵר מַה חֲטָבַת עֵצִים רְשׁוּת. יָצָא הָאָב הַמַּכֶּה אֶת בְּנוֹ וְהָרַב הָרוֹדֶה אֶת תַּלְמִידוֹ וּשְׁלִיחַ בֵּית דִּין׃

Mishnah 4: If he threw the stone into his own courtyard and it killed, if the person damaged had the right to enter there, he is exiled, but if not, he is not exiled, as it is said, *if somebody goes with another to a forest*[16]. Since the forest is a place where the person injured and the one causing the injury both may enter, this excludes a private courtyard where the person injured and the one causing the injury may not enter together. Abba Shaul says, since cutting down trees is a voluntary act, this excludes a father who hits his son[18], a teacher who disciplines his student, and the court bailiff[19].

18 In the course of his duty as educator.

19 Acting on the orders of the court in flogging people.

(31c line 58) **הלכה ד:** זָרַק אֶת הָאֶבֶן לַחֲבֵירוֹ כול'. אָמַר רִבִּי יַנַּאי. טַבָּח שֶׁהוּא מְקַצֵּב וְהִיכָּה בֵּין מִלְּמַעֲלָה בֵּין מִלְּמַטָּה גוֹלֶה. וְאַתְיָיא כַּיי דָמַר רִבִּי הוּנָא. טַבָּח שֶׁהוּא מְקַצֵּב וְהִכָּה לְפָנָיו לְמַטָּן גוֹלֶה לְמַעֲלָן אֵינוֹ גוֹלֶה. לְאַחֲרָיו לְמַעֲלָן גוֹלֶה לְמַטָּן אֵינוֹ גוֹלֶה. אָמַר רִבִּי יִצְחָק. כָּל־מִילָּה וּמִילָּה לְדַעְתֵּיהּ. יָשַׁב לוֹ עַל גַּבֵּי מִיטָּה בַּיּוֹם וְאֵין דֶּרֶךְ הַתִּינוֹק לִינָּתֵן עַל גַּבֵּי מִיטָּה בַּיּוֹם גוֹלֶה. בַּלַּיְלָה וְדֶרֶךְ הַתִּינוֹק הַנָּתוּן עַל גַּבֵּי מִיטָּה בַּלַּיְלָה אֵינוֹ גוֹלֶה. יָשַׁב לוֹ עַל גַּבֵּי עֲרִיסָה בַּיּוֹם וְדֶרֶךְ הַתִּינוֹק לִינָּתֵן עַל גַּבֵּי עֲרִיסָה בַּיּוֹם אֵינוֹ גוֹלֶה. בַּלַּיְלָה וְאֵין דֶּרֶךְ הַתִּינוֹק לִינָּתֵן עַל גַּבֵּי עֲרִיסָה בַּלַּיְלָה גוֹלֶה.

אָמַר רִבִּי יוֹסֵי בַּר חֲנִינָה. הָיָה עוֹמֵד וּמְבַקֵּעַ עֵצִים בַּחֲצֵירוֹ וְנִכְנַס הַפּוֹעֵל לִיטּוֹל שְׂכָרוֹ נִתְּזָה הַבִּקַּעַת עָלָיו וְהִזִּיקַתּוּ חַייָב. וְאִם מֵת אֵינוֹ גוֹלֶה. שֶׁאֵינוֹ כְיַעַר. תַּנֵּי רִבִּי חֲנִינָה פָּטוּר. וְלָא פְלִיגִין. מַה דָמַר רִבִּי יוֹסֵי בֶּן חֲנִינָה. בְּשֶׁלֹּא רָאוּ אוֹתוֹ. וּמַה דְתַנֵּי רִבִּי חִייָה. בְּשֶׁרָאוּ אוֹתוֹ. אִם בְּשֶׁלֹּא רָאוּ אוֹתוֹ כֵּיוָן שֶׁאָמַר לוֹ הִיכָּנֵס חַייָב. תַּנֵּי רִבִּי חִייָה. פָּטוּר. כֵּיוָן שֶׁאָמַר לוֹ הִיכָּנֵס צָרִיךְ לְשַׁמֵּר אֶת עַצְמוֹ. וְאִית דְּבָעֵי מֵימַר. כֵּיוָן שֶׁאָמַר לוֹ הִיכָּנֵס נַעֲשִׂית כַּחֲצַר שׁוּתָפִין. רִבִּי חִייָה בְשֵׁם רִבִּי יוֹחָנָן. הַשּׁוּתָפִין קוֹנִין זֶה מִזֶּה בְחָצֵר. וּמַמְחִין זֶה עַל יְדֵי זֶה בְחָצֵר. וְחַייָבִין זֶה בְנִזְקֵי זֶה. (וְלֹא כֵן אָמַר רַב. מְמַלֵּא אֶת כָּל־רְשׁוּת הָרַבִּים. וְזוֹ אֵינָהּ מְמַלְּאָה אֶת כָּל־רְשׁוּת הָרַבִּים. מִכֵּיוָן שֶׁדַּרְכָּן לְהַלֵּךְ בְּחָצֵר כְּמִי שֶׁהִיא מְמַלֵּא אֶת כָּל־הֶחָצֵר.

1 בר | **ק** בן ליטול | **ק** לתבוע נתזה | **ק** ונתזה 2 עליו | **ק** - שאינו כיער | **ק** - תני | **ק** והתני חנינה | **ק** חייה פליגין | **ק** פליגי 3 בן חנינה | **ק** - בשלא ראו אותו | **ק** בשראהו דתני | **ק** דמר בשראו אותו | **ק** בשלא ראהו 4 ראו אותו | **ק** ראהו תני | **ק** והתני היכנס | **ק** הכנס לשמר את | **ק** לשמור 6 שותפין | **ק** השותפין ר' חייה בשם ר' יוחנן | **ק** דמר ר' יוחנן בשם ר' חייה 6 וממחין זה על ידי זה | **ק** - זה | **ק** וזה 7 ממלא | **ק** בממלא את | **ק** - (twice) אינה ממלאה { **ק** ממלא מכיון | **ק** אמ'. מכיון 8 שדרכן | **ק** שדרכן את | **ק** -

Halakhah 4: If he threw the stone into his (comrade)[20]," etc. Rebbi Yannai said, a butcher who was cutting up [a carcass] and hit somebody whether raising or descending has to go into exile. This follows what Rebbi Huna said: A butcher who was cutting up [a carcass] and hit somebody in front of him in a descending motion goes into exile, in an ascending motion does not go into exile. In his back, in an ascending motion he goes into exile, in a descending motion he does not go into exile[21]. Rebbi Isaac said, each case goes by its circumstances. If somebody sat on a bed during the day, and it is not usual to find a baby in a bed during the day, he goes into exile. During the night, when it is usual to find a baby in a bed during the night, he does not go into exile. If somebody sat on a crib during the day, and it is usual to find a baby in a crib during the day, he does not go into exile. During the night, when it is not usual to find a baby in a crib during the night, he goes into exile[22].

[23]Rebbi Yose ben Ḥanina said, if he was splitting wood in his courtyard, when a worker entered to collect his wages, and a splinter ricocheted and injured him, he is liable. If he died, he does not go into exile, for it is not like a forest. Rebbi Ḥanina[24] stated, he is not liable. They do not disagree. What Rebbi Yose ben Ḥanina said, when they did not see him. But what Rebbi Ḥiyya stated, when they saw him[25]. When they did not see him, from the moment he told him: enter, should he not be liable? Rebbi Ḥiyya stated, he is not liable. Since he told him: enter, he has to take precautions. Some would say, since he told him to enter, it becomes like the courtyard of partners. Rebbi Ḥiyya[26] in the name of Rebbi Joḥanan: Partners acquire from one another in a courtyard; they object to one another in a courtyard[27], and are mutually liable for damages. But did not Rav say, if he filled the entire public domain? This did not fill the entire public domain! Since they usually walk in the entire domain, it is as if he had filled the entire domain[28].

20 A scribal error, חבירו "his comrade" for חצירו "his courtyard.

21 (Babli 7b). A butcher is cutting up a cattle carcass into quarters using a meat cleaver. He holds the cleaver behind his back, raises it over his head, and brings it down in front to split the animal. Therefore, the ascending motion behind his back is a necessary prelude to the descending motion in front, and is part of a descending motion in the sense of Mishnah 1. An ascending motion in front and the following descending motion in his back are both classified as ascending; an accident during this motion does not qualify to send the perpetrator into exile.

22 A person sits on a bed or a crib without looking whether a baby is lying there and by his action kills the baby. If he could reasonably have expected to find a baby there, his action is murder; otherwise it is involuntary homicide which qualifies for exile. During the day, the baby is put in a movable crib, so the mother can have him close by at all times. During the night, the baby is in his mother's bed (*1K.* 3:19).

23 This is from *Baba qamma* 3:8 (ק, Notes 112-117). While the origin of the text clearly is in *Bava qamma*, neither text is a copy of the other; they are derived from a common source. "Liable" and "not liable" refer to the payments due for personal injury claims.

24 Read with ק "R. Ḥiyya" (the Elder).

25 The occurrences of "liable" and "not liable" should be exchanged, following ק.

26 R. Ḥiyya bar Abba.

27 In a condominium courtyard, only outdoor activities (other than access to the

houses built around the courtyard) agreeable to all parties can be performed. Cf. *Nedarim* 5:1 (Note 4).

28 This refers to Halakhah *Bava qamma* 3:6 (Note 104). Would the right of access given to the worker be restricted to a narrow path of shortest access? The answer is negative; also in this aspect the property owner is liable.

(fol. 31b) **משנה ה**: הָאָב גּוֹלֶה עַל יְדֵי בְּנוֹ וְהַבֵּן עַל יְדֵי הָאָב. הַכֹּל גּוֹלִים עַל יְדֵי יִשְׂרָאֵל וְיִשְׂרָאֵל גּוֹלִים עַל יְדֵיהֶם חוּץ מֵעַל יְדֵי גֵּר תּוֹשָׁב. וְגֵר תּוֹשָׁב גּוֹלֶה עַל יְדֵי גֵּר תּוֹשָׁב.

Mishnah 5: The father is exiled for his son, and the son for the father[29]. Everybody[30] is exiled for an Israel, and an Israel for everybody except a sojourner. A sojourner is exiled for a sojourner[31].

משנה ו: הַסּוּמָא אֵינוֹ גוֹלֶה דִּבְרֵי רִבִּי יְהוּדָה. רִבִּי מֵאִיר אוֹמֵר גּוֹלֶה. הַשּׂוֹנֵא אֵינוֹ גוֹלֶה. רַבִּי יוֹסֵי בֵּי רִבִּי יְהוּדָה אוֹמֵר הַשּׂוֹנֵא נֶהֱרָג מִפְּנֵי שֶׁהוּא כְמוּעָד. רִבִּי שִׁמְעוֹן אוֹמֵר יֵשׁ שׂוֹנֵא גוֹלֶה וְיֵשׁ שֶׁאֵינוֹ גוֹלֶה. כֹּל שֶׁהוּא יָכוֹל לוֹמַר לָדַעַת הָרַג אֵינוֹ גוֹלֶה. וְשֶׁלֹּא לָדַעַת הָרַג הֲרֵי זֶה גוֹלֶה:

Mishnah 6: A blind person is not exiled, the words of Rebbi Jehudah; Rebbi Meïr says, he is exiled[32]. Rebbi Yose ben Rebbi Jehudah[33] says, the hater is executed for he is as if notorious[34]. Rebbi Simeon says, there is a hater who is exiled and one who is not exiled. In any case where one can say that he killed intentionally, he is not exiled; unintentionally, he is exiled.

29 If the father kills his son unintentionally. If he kills him during a punishment for educational reasons he is not liable for any penalty (Note 18); if he kills him otherwise intentionally he must be prosecuted for murder and the perpetrator is barred from the cities of refuge even if no conviction is possible, e.g., for lack of eye witnesses or warning. Similarly, a son is exiled for the unintentional killing of his father.

30 Adult Israel, Samaritan, or circumcised slave of a Jewish master.

31 A Gentile observing the Noahide commandments.

32 They disagree about the interpretation of *Num*. 35:23.

33 In the later editions of the Babli: R. Yose, by actions of editors who held that R. Simeon, contemporary of R. Jehudah, could not react to an opinion of the latter's son.

34 He does not need warning and in his opinion cannot claim that he did it unintentionally.

(31d line 1) **הלכה ה**: הָאָב גּוֹלֶה עַל יְדֵי הַבֵּן כול׳. אָמַר רִבִּי זְעוּרָא. תַּנָּא רִבִּי שִׁילָא בַּר בִּינָה. כִּלְפִּי שֶׁנֶּאֱמַר גּוֹאֵל הַדָּם הוּא יָמִית אֶת־הָרֹצֵחַ. הֲרֵי מִי שֶׁהִכָּה אֶת בְּנוֹ אֵין בְּנוֹ הַשֵּׁינִי נַעֲשֶׂה גוֹאֵל הַדָּם לְהָמִית אֶת אָבִיו. אֲבָל אָח שֶׁהִכָּה אֶת אָחִיו אָחִיו הַשֵּׁינִי נַעֲשֶׂה גוֹאֵל הַדָּם לְהָמִית אֶת אָחִיו. תַּנֵּי רִבִּי לִיעֶזֶר בֶּן יַעֲקֹב. כִּלְפִּי שֶׁנֶּאֱמַר גּוֹאֵל הַדָּם הוּא יָמִית אֶת־הָרֹצֵחַ. הֲרֵי מִי שֶׁהִכָּה אֶת בְּנוֹ בְּנוֹ הַשֵּׁינִי נַעֲשֶׂה גוֹאֵל הַדָּם לְהָמִית אֶת אָבִיו. אֲבָל אָח שֶׁהִכָּה אָחִיו אֵין אָחִיו הַשֵּׁינִי נַעֲשֶׂה גוֹאֵל הַדָּם לְהָמִית אֶת אָחִיו. וּמְנַיִין אֲפִילוּ אָמַר. שֶׁאֵינִי יָכוֹל לְהַקְבִּילוֹ. תַּלְמוּד לוֹמַר בְּפִגְעוֹ־בוֹ הוּא יְמִיתֶנּוּ׃

Halakhah 5: "The father is exiled for the son," etc. Rebbi Ze`ira said that Rebbi Shila bar Binah stated: Even though it be written[35], *the redeemer of the blood*[36] *himself shall kill the murderer,* nevertheless if somebody smote his son, his second son does not become the redeemer of the blood to kill his father. But if a brother smote his brother, the second brother becomes the redeemer of the blood to kill his brother. Rebbi Eliezer ben Jacob stated: Even though it be written, *the redeemer of the blood himself shall kill the murderer,* nevertheless if somebody smote his son, his second son becomes the redeemer of the blood to kill his father. But if a brother smote his brother, the second brother does not become the redeemer of the blood to kill his brother[37].

And from where even if he said, I cannot face him[38], the verse says[35], *when he comes upon him he shall kill him*[36].

35 *Num*. 35:19.

36 The closest family member of the murder victim is required to lead the execution of the duly convicted murderer. *Num*. 35:30 requires that the killing of the murderer be in the presence of witnesses; this implies that the killing be in execution of a court order (*Sifry Num*. 161).

37 The Babli 12a simply notes the existence of contradictory interpretations, without attaching names to the traditions. R. Eliezer ben Jacob probably is the second of this name, of the fourth generation of Tannaïm. R. Shila bar Binah (Avinna) belongs to the generation of transition from Tannaïm and Amoraïm.

38 That he is forced to witness the execution, *Sifry Num*. 160.

(31d line 10) וְהַסּוּמָא. אָמַר רִבִּי בָּא. מָאן תַּנָּא סוּמָא. רִבִּי יוּדָה. דְּרִבִּי יוּדָה פּוֹטְרוֹ מִכָּל־מִצְוֹת הָאֲמוּרוֹת בַּתּוֹרָה. דְּתַנִּינָן תַּמָּן. רַבִּי יוּדָה אוֹמֵר. כֹּל שֶׁלֹּא רָאָה מְאוֹרוֹת מִיָּמָיו לֹא יִפְרוֹשׂ אֶת שְׁמַע׃ הָא אִם רָאָה פּוֹרֵשׂ. וּשְׁנֵיהֶן מִקְּרָא אֶחָד דָּרְשׁוּ. בְּלֹא רְאוֹת. רִבִּי מֵאִיר אוֹמֵר. לְרַבּוֹת אֶת הַסּוּמָא. רִבִּי יוּדָה אוֹמֵר. פְּרָט לַסּוּמָא. מִחְלְפָה שִׁיטָּתֵיהּ דְּרִבִּי מֵאִיר. תַּמָּן הוּא

אָמַר פְּרָט וְכָא הוּא אָמַר לְרַבּוֹת. אָמַר רִבִּי חֲנִינָה בְּרֵיהּ דְּרִבִּי הִלֵּל. בְּיוֹשֵׁב בְּבַיִת אָפֵל הִיא מַתְנִיתָא. כָּךְ אָנוּ אוֹמְרִים. הַיּוֹשֵׁב בְּבַיִת אָפֵל לֹא יִפְרוֹשׂ אֶת שְׁמַע׃ בְּרַם הָכָא בְּלֹא רְאוֹת לְרַבּוֹת אֶת הַסּוּמָא. מַה מְקַיְּימִין רַבָּנִין בְּלֹא רְאוֹת. לְהָבִיא אֶת הַמַּכֶּה בַלַּיְלָה.

"And the blind person." Rebbi Abba said, who stated "the blind person"? Rebbi Jehudah, for Rebbi Jehudah frees him from all obligations of the Torah[39], as we have stated there[40]: "Rebbi Jehudah said, anyone who never saw light in his life may not cover the *Shema*`.[41]" Therefore, if he saw once he may cover. And both of them explained the same verse, *without seeing*[42]. Rebbi Meïr says, to include the blind person. Rebbi Jehudah says, excluding the blind person.

[43]The argument of Rebbi Meïr seems inverted. There he says, excluding, but here he says, to include. Rebbi Ḥanina the son of Rebbi Hillel said, the Mishnah is about one sitting in a dark house. So we are saying, "one sitting in a dark house may not cover the *Shema*`.[44]" But here, *without seeing*, to include the blind person. How do the rabbis read *without seeing*? To include one who smites in the night[45].

39 *Sotah* 2:6 (Note 201), Babli *Bava qamma* 87a.

40 *Megillah* Mishnah 4:7.

41 He cannot lead the congregation in the recital of the benedictions before and after the recitation of the *Shema*` since they start with a praise of God for the creation of the celestial shining bodies. The majority opinion holds that while a blind person cannot see the sun's light, he profits from it since other people who can see can help him during daylight.

42 *Num*. 35:23, part of the definition of involuntary homicide. Babli 9b, *Sifry Num*. 160. As the Babli explains, the double restriction mentioned by the verse, *unintentional, without seeing*, has to be read as an inclusion.

43 A parallel to this paragraph is in *Megillah* 4:7. One has to read "Jehudah" for Meïr, as in *Megillah*, since only for R. Jehudah are two opinions recorded. Also "there" means *Makkot*, "here" *Megillah*.

44 In his explanation, R. Jehudah does not exclude the blind person but one born and raised in a cave who never saw daylight.

45 He is included in the list of the exiled together with the blind person.

(fol. 31c) **משנה ז**: לְאֵיכָן גּוֹלִין לְעָרֵי מִקְלָט. לְשָׁלֹשׁ שֶׁבְּעֵבֶר הַיַּרְדֵּן וּלְשָׁלֹשׁ שֶׁבְּאֶרֶץ כְּנַעַן שֶׁנֶּאֱמַר אֵת שְׁלֹשׁ הֶעָרִים תִּתְּנוּ מֵעֵבֶר לַיַּרְדֵּן וְגוֹ'. עַד שֶׁלֹּא נִבְחֲרוּ שָׁלֹשׁ שֶׁבְּאֶרֶץ יִשְׂרָאֵל לֹא הָיוּ שָׁלֹשׁ שֶׁבְּעֵבֶר הַיַּרְדֵּן קוֹלְטוֹת שֶׁנֶּאֱמַר שֵׁשׁ עָרֵי מִקְלָט תִּהְיֶינָה. עַד שֶׁיִּהְיוּ שִׁשְׁתָּן קוֹלְטוֹת כְּאַחַת:

Mishnah 7: Where are they exiled to? To the cities of refuge. To the three in Transjordan and the three in the Land of Canaan, as it is said[46]: *Three cities you shall designate in Transjordan,* etc. As long as those in the Land of Israel had not been selected[47], those in Transjordan were not receiving, as it is said[48], *there shall be six cities of refuge,* not until all six were receiving together[49].

משנה ח: וּמְכוּוָּנוֹת לָהֶן דְּרָכִים מִזּוֹ לָזוֹ שֶׁנֶּאֱמַר תָּכִין לְךָ הַדֶּרֶךְ וְשִׁלַּשְׁתָּ אֶת־גְּבוּל אַרְצְךָ. וּמוֹסְרִין לָהֶן שְׁנֵי תַלְמִידֵי חֲכָמִים שֶׁמָּא יַהַרְגֶנּוּ בַדֶּרֶךְ וִידַבְּרוּ אֵלָיו. רַבִּי מֵאִיר אוֹמֵר אַף הוּא מְדַבֵּר עַל יְדֵי עַצְמוֹ שֶׁנֶּאֱמַר וְזֶה דְּבַר הָרוֹצֵחַ:

Mishnah 8: Roads were maintained from one to the other, as it is said[50]: *Maintain the road for yourselves, and divide the domain of your Land into three parts*[51]. One sends with them[52] two scholars lest he[53] kill him[52] on the road, to argue with him. Rebbi Meïr says, he[53] may argue for himself as it is said[54], *this is the word of the homicide.*

משנה ט: רַבִּי יוֹסֵי בֵּי רַבִּי יְהוּדָה אוֹמֵר בַּתְּחִלָּה אֶחָד שׁוֹגֵג וְאֶחָד מֵזִיד מַקְדִּימִין לְעָרֵי מִקְלָט וּבֵית דִּין שׁוֹלְחִין וּמְבִיאִין אוֹתוֹ מִשָּׁם. מִי שֶׁנִּתְחַיֵּב מִיתָה הֲרָגוּהוּ וְשֶׁלֹּא נִתְחַיֵּב מִיתָה פְּטָרוּהוּ וְשֶׁנִּתְחַיֵּב גָּלוּת מַחֲזִירִין אוֹתוֹ לִמְקוֹמוֹ שֶׁנֶּאֱמַר וְהֵשִׁיבוּ אֹתוֹ הָעֵדָה אֶל עִיר מִקְלָטוֹ. אֶחָד מָשׁוּחַ בְּשֶׁמֶן הַמִּשְׁחָה וְאֶחָד הַמְרוּבֶּה בִּבְגָדִים וְאֶחָד שֶׁעָבַר מִמְּשִׁיחָתוֹ. רַבִּי יְהוּדָה אוֹמֵר אַף מְשׁוּחַ מִלְחָמָה מַחֲזִיר אֶת הָרוֹצֵחַ. לְפִיכָךְ אִימּוֹתֵיהֶן שֶׁל כֹּהֲנִים מְסַפְּקוֹת לָהֶן מִחְיָה וּכְסוּת כְּדֵי שֶׁלֹּא יִתְפַּלְלוּ עַל בְּנֵיהֶן שֶׁיָּמוּתוּ.

Mishnah 9: Rebbi Yose ben Rebbi Jehudah says, at the start both the involuntary and the voluntary [homicide] go to the city of refuge; the court sends and brings them back from there. If one is found guilty by a death sentence, they execute him. If he is found not guilty in a capital case, he is freed. If he is found guilty to be exiled they return him to his place as it is said[55], *the community shall return him to his city of refuge.*

Not only[56] a [High Priest] anointed with the anointing oil[57], but also one wearing the many vestments[58], and one deposed from his office[59]. Rebbi Jehudah says, also the one anointed for war[60] returns the homicide. Therefore, the mothers of the [High] Priests support them with food and clothing, so they should not pray for the death of their sons.

משנה י: נִגְמַר דִּינוֹ וּמֵת כֹּהֵן גָּדוֹל הֲרֵי זֶה אֵינוֹ גוֹלֶה. אִם עַד שֶׁלֹּא נִגְמַר דִּינוֹ מֵת כֹּהֵן גָּדוֹל וּמִינּוּ אַחֵר תַּחְתָּיו וּלְאַחַר מִיכֵּן נִגְמַר דִּינוֹ חוֹזֵר בְּמִיתָתוֹ שֶׁל שֵׁנִי:

Mishnah 10: If sentence had been passed when the High Priest died, he is not exiled. If sentence had not yet been passed when the High Priest died, and sentence was passed after a successor had been appointed, he returns after the death of the second.

משנה יא: נִגְמַר דִּינוֹ בְּלֹא כֹהֵן גָּדוֹל הַהוֹרֵג כֹּהֵן גָּדוֹל וְכֹהֵן גָּדוֹל שֶׁהָרַג אֵינוֹ יוֹצֵא מִשָּׁם לְעוֹלָם. וְאֵינוֹ יוֹצֵא לֹא לְעֵדוּת מִצְוָה וְלֹא לְעֵדוּת מָמוֹן וְלֹא לְעֵדוּת נְפָשׁוֹת וַאֲפִילוּ יִשְׂרָאֵל צְרִיכִין לוֹ וַאֲפִילוּ שַׂר צְבָא יִשְׂרָאֵל כְּיוֹאָב בֶּן צְרוּיָה אֵינוֹ יוֹצֵא מִשָּׁם לְעוֹלָם שֶׁנֶּאֱמַר שָׁמָּה. שָׁם תְּהֵא דִירָתוֹ וְשָׁם תְּהֵא מִיתָתוֹ וְשָׁם תְּהֵא קְבוּרָתוֹ

Mishnah 11: If sentence was passed when there was no High Priest, or one who killed a High Priest, or a High Priest who killed, can never leave from there.

He[52] cannot leave from there, neither for a testimony of obligation,[61] nor a testimony in a civil suit, nor a testimony in a criminal suit, not even if Israel needs him like Joab ben Ṣeruya[62], he cannot ever leave from there, as it is said *there*[55]. There shall be his dwelling, there he shall die, there he shall be buried.

משנה יב: כְּשֵׁם שֶׁהָעִיר קוֹלֶטֶת כָּךְ תְּחוּמָהּ קוֹלֵט. רוֹצֵחַ שֶׁיָּצָא חוּץ לַתְּחוּם וּמְצָאוֹ גוֹאֵל הַדָּם רִבִּי יוֹסֵי הַגְּלִילִי אוֹמֵר מִצְוָה בְּיַד גּוֹאֵל הַדָּם וּרְשׁוּת בְּיַד כָּל־אָדָם. רִבִּי עֲקִיבָה אוֹמֵר רְשׁוּת בְּיַד גּוֹאֵל הַדָּם וְכָל אָדָם אֵין חַיָּבִין עָלָיו.

Mishnah 12: Just as the city grants asylum, so does its domain grant asylum[63]. If a murderer left the domain and was found by the avenger of the blood, Rebbi Yose the Galilean says, it is the obligation of the avenger of the blood and the right of everybody[64]. Rebbi Aqiba says, it is the right of the avenger of the blood and nobody would be liable because of him.

משנה יג: אִילָן שֶׁהוּא עוֹמֵד בְּתוֹךְ הַתְּחוּם וְנוֹפוֹ נוֹטֶה חוּץ לַתְּחוּם אוֹ עוֹמֵד חוּץ לַתְּחוּם וְנוֹפוֹ נוֹטֶה בְתוֹךְ הַתְּחוּם הַכֹּל הוֹלֵךְ אַחַר הַנּוֹף. הָרַג בְּאוֹתָהּ הָעִיר גּוֹלֶה מִשְּׁכוּנָה לִשְׁכוּנָה. וּבֶן לֵוִי גּוֹלֶה מֵעִיר לְעִיר:

Mishnah 13: If a tree stands inside the domain but its crown is outside the domain, or the tree stands outside the domain but its crown is inside the domain, everything follows the crown[65].

If somebody killed in one of these cities, he is exiled from quarter to quarter; but a Levite[66] who killed is exiled from one city to another.

משנה יד: כַּיּוֹצֵא בוֹ רוֹצֵחַ שֶׁגָּלָה לְעִיר מִקְלָט וְרָצוּ אַנְשֵׁי הָעִיר לְכַבְּדוֹ יֹאמַר לָהֶם רוֹצֵחַ אָנִי. אָמְרוּ לוֹ אַף עַל פִּי כֵן יְקַבֵּל מֵהֶן שֶׁנֶּאֱמַר וְזֶה דְּבַר הָרֹצֵחַ.

Mishnah 14: Similarly[67], a homicide exiled to a city of refuge whom the citizens of the town wanted to honor, should say to them, I am a homicide. If they tell him, anyway, he should accept, for it is said[54], *this is the word of a homicide.*

משנה טו: וּמַעֲלוֹת הָיוּ שָׂכָר לַלְוִיִּם דִּבְרֵי רִבִּי יְהוּדָה. רִבִּי מֵאִיר אוֹמֵר לֹא הָיוּ מַעֲלוֹת לָהֶן שָׂכָר. וְחוֹזֵר לִשְׂרָרָה שֶׁהָיָה בָהּ דִּבְרֵי רִבִּי מֵאִיר. רִבִּי יְהוּדָה אוֹמֵר לֹא הָיָה חוֹזֵר לִשְׂרָרָה שֶׁהָיָה בָהּ:

Mishnah 15: They[68] were paying rent to the Levites, the words of Rebbi Jehudah. Rebbi Meïr said, they were not paying rent. He returns to the office he held earlier[69], the words of Rebbi Meïr; Rebbi Jehudah says, he does not return to the office he held earlier.

46 *Num*. 35:14.

47 *Jos*. 20:7. *Sifry Num*. 160.

48 *Num*. 35:13.

49 Giving asylum to the involuntary homicide.

50 *Deut*. 19:3.

51 Divide both the Land of Israel and Transjordan into three Voronoi domains each so that the nearest city of refuge always was indicated on the sign posts.

52 The homicide.

53 The avenger of the blood.

54 *Deut*. 19:4.

55 *Num*. 35:25.

56 The homicide may return to his home town upon the death of the High Priest (*Num*. 35:28).

57 A High Priest of the period of Judges or Kings, anointed from the vial prepared by Moses (*Ex*. 30:22-33).

58 A High Priest of Second Temple times, wearing an imitation of the High Priest's robes.

59 A High Priest of Herodian times or later, when High Priests usually were appointed annually.

60 To exhort the army, *Deut*. 20:2.

61 A religious act, neither civil nor criminal; e. g., to testify to the appearance of the New Moon.

62 David's general.

63 Every city of refuge also is a Levitic city (*Num*. 35:6). Each Levitic city was surrounded by a greenbelt of 2'000 cubits,

having the same status as the city itself (*Lev.* 35:4-5; *Sotah* 5:4 Notes 107-111.) The avenger of the blood has no right to pursue the homicide into the city's domain.

64 To kill the homicide who left the city of refuge (in the Babli: intentionally).

65 If most of the crown is outside (inside), the entire tree is considered outside (inside). In the Babli, the crown is only taken as an extension of the tree.

66 Whose city it is. Only a Levite can be a permanent resident of a city of refuge.

67 This makes no sense here; it is copied from the identical Mishnah *Ševi`it* 10:8.

68 The feminine form of the verb is confirmed by the readings of Maimonides and Rashi, as well as the Munich ms. of the Babli. In the Babli, the question is raised whether the homicide (reading מעלים) pays rent or his hometown (reading מעלות) pays indemnity to the Levites in either the city of refuge or the 42 additional Levitic cities which also serve as cities of asylum. Since neither *Sifry* nor the Yerushalmi mention this, it seems that the Yerushalmi recognizes only the six cities of refuge as proper places of asylum.

69 The public office held by the homicide before his exile. The question is whether the homicide is barred from holding public office upon his return.

(31d line 18) **הלכה ז:** לְאֵיכָן גּוֹלִין כול'. שָׁלֹשׁ עֲיָירוֹת הִפְרִישׁ מֹשֶׁה בְּעֵבֶר הַיַּרְדֵּן. וּמִשֶּׁבָּאוּ לָאָרֶץ הִפְרִישׁוּ עוֹד שָׁלֹשׁ. אֵילּוּ וְאֵילּוּ לֹא הָיוּ קוֹלְטוֹת עַד שֶׁכִּיבְּשׁוּ וְחִילְּקוּ. כֵּיוָן שֶׁכִּיבְּשׁוּ וְחִילְּקוּ נִתְחַיְּיבָה הָאָרֶץ בַּשְּׁמִיטִּין וּבַיּוֹבֵילוֹת וְהָיוּ אֵילּוּ וְאֵילּוּ קוֹלְטוֹת. שָׁלֹשׁ עָרִים שֶׁהִפְרִישׁוּ בְּאֶרֶץ יִשְׂרָאֵל הָיוּ מְכוּוָּנוֹת כְּנֶגֶד שָׁלֹשׁ עָרִים שֶׁהִפְרִישׁ מֹשֶׁה בְּעֵבֶר הַיַּרְדֵּן כִּשְׁתֵּי שׁוּרוֹת שֶׁלְּכֶרֶם. אֶת חֶבְרוֹן בִּיהוּדָה כְּנֶגֶד בֶּצֶר בַּמִּדְבָּר. וְאֶת שְׁכֶם בְּהַר אֶפְרַיִם כְּנֶגֶד רָאמוֹת בַּגִּלְעָד. אֶת קֶדֶשׁ בַּגָּלִיל כְּנֶגֶד גּוֹלָן בַּבָּשָׁן. עַד שֶׁלֹּא הִפְרִישׁוּ שְׁכֶם בְּהַר אֶפְרַיִם לֹא הָיְתָה קוֹלֶטֶת. הִפְרִישׁוּ קִרְיַת יְעָרִים תַּחְתֶּיהָ עַד שֶׁכִּיבְּשׁוּ אֶת שְׁכֶם. עַד שֶׁלֹּא הִפְרִישׁוּ קֶדֶשׁ בַּגָּלִיל לֹא הָיְתָה קוֹלֶטֶת. הִפְרִישׁ גַּמְלָה תַּחְתֶּיהָ עַד שֶׁכִּיבְּשׁוּ אֶת קֶדֶשׁ.

וְשִׁלַּשְׁתָּ֒. שֶׁיְּהוּ מְשׁוּלָּשׁוֹת. כְּדֵי שֶׁתְּהֵא מֵחֶבְרוֹן לִיהוּדָה כְּמֵחֶבְרוֹן לִשְׁכֶם וּמֵחֶבְרוֹן לִשְׁכֶם כְּמִשְּׁכֶם לְקֶדֶשׁ.

נָפְלָה אַחַת מֵהֶן בּוֹנִין אוֹתָהּ מֵאוֹתוֹ הַשֵּׁבֶט. וּמְנַיִין אַף בִּשְׁאָר כָּל־הַשְּׁבָטִים. תַּלְמוּד לוֹמַר שֵׁשׁ. שֶׁיְּהוּ מְכוּוָּנוֹת וְקוֹלְטוֹת כָּרִאשׁוֹנוֹת.

הֶעָרִים הַלָּלוּ אֵין בּוֹנִין אוֹתָן לֹא כְּרָכִים גְּדוֹלִים וְלֹא עֲיָירוֹת קְטַנּוֹת אֶלָּא בֵּינוֹנִיּוֹת. אֵין בּוֹנִין אוֹתָהּ אֶלָּא עַל הַשּׁוּק. אִם אֵין שָׁם שׁוּק עוֹשִׂין לְשָׁם שׁוּק. אֵין בּוֹנִין אוֹתָם אֶלָּא עַל הַמַּיִם. אִם אֵין שָׁם מַיִם מְבִיאִין לְשָׁם מַיִם. נִתְמָעֲטוּ דִּיּוּרֵיהֶן מְבִיאִין אֲחֵרִים תַּחְתֵּיהֶן. אִם אֵין שָׁם אוֹכְלוּסִין מְבִיאִין לְשָׁם כֹּהֲנִים לְוִיִּים וְיִשְׂרְאֵלִים.

אֵין עוֹשִׂין בְּתוֹכָן לֹא בֵּית הַבַּד וְלֹא בֵּית הַבְּצִירָה. דִּבְרֵי רִבִּי נְחֶמְיָה. וַחֲכָמִים מַתִּירִין. אֵין מַפְשִׁילִין בְּתוֹכָן חֲבָלִים. וְאֵין עוֹשִׂין בְּתוֹכָן כְּלֵי זְכוּכִית בִּשְׁבִיל לְהַרְגִּיל אֶת הָרֶגֶל לְשָׁם.

Halakhah 7: "Where are they exiled to," etc. [70]"Three cities did Moses designate in Transjordan[71]. When they came to the Land they designated another three[72]. Neither of them were giving asylum until after they conquered and divided[73]. After they conquered and divided, the Land became obligated for Sabbaticals and Jubilees and these and those[74] were giving asylum. The three cities which they designated in the Land of Israel were parallel to the three cities which Moses had designated in Transjordan like two rows in a vineyard. Hebron in Judea parallels Beṣer in the desert. Sichem on Mount Ephraim parallels Ramot Gilead. Qedesh in Galilee parallels Golan in Bashan. (Before) [even though][75] they had designated Sichem on Mount Ephraim it could not give asylum; they designated Qiryat-Yearim in its place until they conquered Sichem[76]. (Before) [even though][75] they had designated Qedesh in Galilee it could not give asylum; they designated Gamla in its place until they conquered Qedesh.[77]"

"*Divide into three parts*[51]. That it should be from Hebron to (Jehudah)[78] as from Hebron to Sichem and from Hebron to Sichem as from Sichem to Qedesh."

"If any of them collapsed, one rebuilds it from the same tribe. And from where also from other tribes? The verse says, *six*[79]. That they should be parallel and receiving like the earlier ones."

"One builds these cities not as great fortified places or small villages but in average sizes. One only builds them around a market place. If they have no market place one creates a market place for them. One only builds them near water. If they have no water one brings water to them[80]. If the number of households declined, one brings others there. If the number of inhabitants declined, one brings there Cohanim, Levites, and Israel[81]."

"One builds in them neither an olive press nor a wine press[82], the words of Rebbi Nehemiah, but the Sages permit it. One does not braid ropes there, nor does one manufacture glass, in order not to attract visitors.[83]"

70 Tosephta 3:1-4, 8-9. Babli 9b-10a.

71 *Deut.* 4:41.

72 *Jos.* 20:7.

73 Since the Transjordan towns are rededicated by Josua, *Jos.* 20:8. *Sifry Num.* 160.

74 The towns dedicated by Moes and Joshua.

75 The text in parentheses, to be deleted, is from the ms., the one in brackets from the Tosephta.

76 The king of Sichem is not listed among the kings vanquished by Josua (*Jos.* 12).

77 This is difficult to understand since the king of Qedesh is listed in *Jos.* 12. Gamla is not a biblical name; it was situated on the Eastern shore of the sea of Galilee.

78 Read with the Tosephta and the Babli: From the Southern border to Hebron.

79 *Num.* 35:15.

80 By aquaeduct.

81 Even though they are Levitic cities. Levitic cities were not renewed in the Second Commonwealth; in talmudic times we only hear of priestly villages in Galilee, quite different from the biblical towns enumerated in *Jos.* The parallel mention of דיורין "apartment dwellers" (Hebrew) and ὄχλος "multitude" expresses the same idea twice in different languages.

82 Presses for hire to be used by the surrounding agricultural population. The idea is that one does not want to attract too much traffic. A small number of people can be controlled; an "avenger of the blood" going after one of the homicides can be evicted or at least be warned that any killing within the asylum domain is murder. Greater traffic makes this impossible. The Sages hold that local traffic is acceptable; only manufactures that attract exporters have to be discouraged.

83 Here the Sages agree.

(31d line 40) רִבִּי יוֹחָנָן שָׁלַח לְרַבָּנִין דְּתַמָּן. תַּרְתֵּין מִילִּין אַתּוֹן אָמְרִין בְּשֵׁם רַב וְלֵית אִינּוּן כֵּן. אַתּוֹן אָמְרִין בְּשֵׁם רַב. יְפַת תּוֹאַר לֹא הִתִּירוּ בָהּ אֶלָּא בְעִילָה רִאשׁוֹנָה בִּלְבַד. וַאֲנִי אוֹמֵר. לֹא בְעִילָה רִאשׁוֹנָה וְלֹא בְעִילָה אַחֲרוֹנָה אֶלָּא לְאַחַר כָּל־הַמַּעֲשִׂים. וְאַחַר כֵּן תָּבוֹא אֵלֶיהָ וּבְעַלְתָּהּ. אַחַר כָּל־הַמַּעֲשִׂים.

וְאַתּוֹן אָמְרִין בְּשֵׁם רַב. סָבוּר הָיָה יוֹאָב שֶׁקַּרְנוֹת הַמִּזְבֵּחַ קוֹלְטוֹת וְאֵינוֹ קוֹלֵט אֶלָּא גַגּוֹ. שֶׁל שִׁילוֹ קוֹלֵט. וְשֶׁלְּבֵית הָעוֹלָמִים אֵינוֹ קוֹלֵט. וַאֲנִי אוֹמֵר. לֹא מִזְבֵּחַ קוֹלֵט וְלֹא גַגּוֹ קוֹלֵט לֹא שֶׁל שִׁילוֹ קוֹלֵט וְלֹא שֶׁלְּבֵית הָעוֹלָמִים קוֹלֵט. אֵין לְךָ קוֹלֵט אֶלָּא שֵׁשׁ עָרֵי מִקְלָט בִּלְבַד. וְאֶיפְשַׁר יוֹאָב דִּכְתִיב בֵּיהּ תַּחְכְּמוֹנִי רֹאשׁ הַשָּׁלִישִׁי הָיָה טוֹעֶה בְדָבָר זֶה. אָמַר רִבִּי תַנְחוּמָא. לְסַנְהֶדְרִין בָּרַח. כְּהָדָא דְתַנֵּי. הֲרוּגֵי בֵית דִּין נִכְסֵיהֶן לַיּוֹרְשִׁין. הֲרוּגֵי מַלְכוּת נִכְסֵיהֶן לַמַּלְכוּת. אָמַר יוֹאָב. מוּטָּב שֶׁאֵיהָרֵג בְּבֵית דִּין וְיִירָשׁוּנִי בָנַיי וְאַל יַהַרְגֵינִי הַמֶּלֶךְ וְיִירָשֵׁינִי. כַּד שְׁמַע שְׁלֹמֹה כֵּן אָמַר. לְמָמוֹנוֹ אֲנִי צָרִיךְ. מִיָּד וַהֲסִירוֹתִי דְּמֵי חִנָּם. אֵין מָמוֹנוֹ חִנָּם. וַיִּשְׁלַח בְּיַד בְּנָיָהוּ וַיִּפְגַּע־בּוֹ וַיְמִיתֵיהוּ וַיִּקָּבְרוּהוּ בְּבֵיתוֹ בַּמִּדְבָּר׃ וְכִי מִדְבָּר הָיָה בֵיתוֹ. אֶלָּא לְלַמְּדָךְ שֶׁכֵּיוָן שֶׁמֵּת יוֹאָב שַׂר צְבָא יִשְׂרָאֵל נַעֲשׂוּ יִשְׂרָאֵל כַּמִּדְבָּר. אִין תֵּימַר. שֶׁהָיָה בוֹזֵז וּבוֹנֶה לָהֶן דֵּימוֹסִיּוֹת וּמֶרְחֲצָאוֹת. שְׁבָח. וְאִין תֵּימַר. שֶׁהָיָה בוֹזֵז וּמַאֲכִיל חֲכָמִים וְתַלְמִידֵיהֶם. שְׁבַח שְׁבָחִים. וּמְנַיִין שֶׁהָיְתָה סַנְהֶדְרִין גְּדוֹלָה אֵצֶל הַמִּזְבֵּחַ. וְלֹא־תַעֲלֶה בְמַעֲלוֹת עַל־מִזְבְּחִי. וּמַה כְתִיב תַּמָּן. וְאֵלֶּה הַמִּשְׁפָּטִים אֲשֶׁר תָּשִׂים לִפְנֵיהֶם.

Rebbi Joḥanan sent to the rabbis there[84]: Two things you say in the name of Rav which are not so. You say in the name of Rav that only the first copulation with the beautiful woman[85] is permitted. But I am saying, the first or the later copulations are permitted only after all ceremonies; *after that you may come to her and copulate with her*[86], after all ceremonies.

Also you say that Joab was of the opinion that the horns of an altar give asylum[87] but only its top gives asylum; in fact only the top of the one in Shilo gives asylum, but that of the Temple does not give asylum. But I am saying that neither the altar gives asylum, nor does its top give asylum, nor the one in Shilo gives asylum, nor that of the Temple gives asylum. Nothing except the six cities of refuge give asylum. Is it possible that Joab, about whom it is written, *the most wise, head of the third*[88] should err in this matter? Rebbi Tanḥuma said, he fled to the Sanhedrin, because it is stated: The property of people executed by the court goes to their heirs; the property of people executed by the government goes to the government[89]. Joab said, it is better that I should be executed by the court and my sons will inherit from me than that the king should execute me and inherit from me. When Solomon heard this he said, do I need his money? Immediately, *I shall remove the blood for free*[90], but his money is not free. *He sent through Benaiahu who smote him and killed him; they buried him in his house in the wilderness*[91]. Was his house a wilderness? But to tell you that when Joab the commander of Israel's army died[92], Israel was turned into a wilderness. If you say that he collected booty to build public baths and baths[93], this is worthy of praise. But if you say that he collected booty to support Sages and their students, it is worthy of the highest praise[94]. And from where that the Supreme Sanhedrin is near the altar? *Do not ascend on my altar by stairs.* What is written next? *These are the rules of law you shall put before them*[95].

84 Babylonia.

85 The female prisoner of war whom her captor desires, *Deut.* 21:10-14. The Babli *Qiddušin* 21b (*Tosaphot* 22a *s. v.* שלא) seems to permit a first copulation before the woman undergoes formal conversion even for a Cohen to whom the convert will be forbidden.

86 *Deut.* 21:13, after full conversion. The Babli (*Qiddušin* 68a) reads the verse as: *after that you may copulate with her as her husband*, meaning that valid marriage is possible only after conversion.

87 *1K.* 2:28, Babli 12a.

88 *2S.* 23:8. Joab himself is not mentioned in the Chapter. Targum Jonathan and the Babli (*Mo`ed qatan* 16b) read the expression as referring to David.

89 This projects Roman practice into Jewish law.

90 *1K.* 2:31. In the MT, confirmed by LXX, וַהֲסִירֹתָ. The blood is the innocent blood of Abner and Amasa.

91 A combination of *1K.* 2:29,34.

92 Here starts the second sheet of the Genizah fragment (G).

93 A double expression of Greek (*Sanhedrin* 7:19, Note 357) and Hebrew terms for public baths.

94 Babli *Sanhedrin* 49a refers to *1Chr.* 11:8 as proof that Joab used his riches to support scholars.

95 *Ex.* 20:23, 21:1.

(31d line 60) [נִגְמַר דִּינוֹ וּמֵת כֹּהֵן גָּדוֹל הֲרֵי זֶה אֵינוֹ גוֹלֶה.] תַּנֵּי רִבִּי לִיעֶזֶר בֶּן יַעֲקֹב אוֹמֵר. מִקְלָט מִקְלָט כָּתוּב בְּפָרָשַׁת דְּרָכִים. כְּדֵי שֶׁיְּהֵא הָרוֹצֵחַ רוֹאֶה אֶת הַכָּתוּב וְהוֹלֵךְ. אָמַר רִבִּי אָבוּן. כְּמִין יָד הָיְתָה מַרְאָה לָהֶן אֶת הַדֶּרֶךְ. אָמַר רִבִּי פִּינְחָס. טוֹב וְיָשָׁר. לָמָּה הוּא טוֹב. שֶׁהוּא יָשָׁר. וְלָמָּה הוּא יָשָׁר. שֶׁהוּא טוֹב. עַל־כֵּן יוֹרֶה חַטָּאִים בַּדָּרֶךְ. שֶׁמּוֹרֶה דֶּרֶךְ תְּשׁוּבָה. שָׁאֲלוּ לַחָכְמָה. חוֹטֵא מָהוּ עוֹנְשׁוֹ. אָמְרָה לָהֶם. חַטָּאִים תְּרַדֵּף רָעָה. שָׁאֲלוּ לַנְּבוּאָה. חוֹטֵא מָהוּ עוֹנְשׁוֹ. אָמְרָה לָהֶן. הַנֶּפֶשׁ הַחֹטֵאת הִיא תָמוּת׃ שָׁאֲלוּ לְקוּדְשָׁא בְּרִיךְ הוּא. חוֹטֵא מָהוּ עוֹנְשׁוֹ. אָמַר לָהֶן. יַעֲשֶׂה תְשׁוּבָה וְיִתְכַּפֵּר לוֹ. הַיְינוּ דִכְתִיב. עַל־כֵּן יוֹרֶה חַטָּאִים בַּדָּרֶךְ. יוֹרֶה לַחַטָּאִים דֶּרֶךְ לַעֲשׂוֹת תְּשׁוּבָה. כְּתִיב כַּצִּפּוֹר לָנוּד כַּדְּרוֹר לָעוּף כֵּן אִישׁ נוֹדֵד מִמְּקוֹמוֹ.

["If sentence had been passed when the High Priest died, he is not exiled."][96] It was stated[97]: "Rebbi Eliezer ben Jacob says, 'refuge, refuge' was written at crossroads, so that the homicide might see what was written and continue." Rebbi Abun said, a sign-post was directing them[98].

[99]Rebbi Phineas said, *good and straightforward*[100]. Why is He good? Because He is straightforward. And why is He straightforward? Because He is good. *Therefore, He teaches the way to the sinners.* He instructs in the way of repentance.

[101]They asked Wisdom, what is the punishment of the sinner? She told them, *evil will pursue sinners*[102]. They asked Prophecy, what is the punishment of the sinner? She told them, *the sinning soul is the one which will die*[103]. They asked the Holy One, praise to Him, what is the punishment of the sinner? He said to them, let him repent and it will be atoned for him. That is what is written, *therefore, He teaches the way to the sinners*[100], the way to repentance.

[104]It is written: *Like a bird to move, like a swallow to fly,* so is a man moving from his place.

96 Added from G; referring to Mishnah 10 even though the Halakhah refers to Mishnah 8.

97 Babli 10b, Tosephta 3:5.

98 He does not assume that everybody be literate.

99 This paragraph is shortened in G, it is only hinted at in the Babli, 10b (in the name of Rav Ḥama bar Ḥanina), extended in *Midrash Tehillim* 25[10].

100 *Ps.* 25:8.

101 There exist various versions of this homily. In G, the text reads:
שְׁאֲלוּ לַתּוֹרָה. הַחוֹטֵא בְּמָהוּא עוֹנְשׁוֹ. אָמְרָה לָהֶן יָבִיא קָרְבָּן וְיִתְכַּפֵּר לוֹ. שְׁאֲלוּ לַנְּבוּאָה. הַחוֹטֵא מָהוּ עוֹנְשׁוֹ. אָמְרָה. הַנֶּפֶשׁ הַחֹטֵאת הִיא תָמוּת׃ שְׁאֲלוּ לְדָוִיד הַחוֹטֵא בְמָה עוֹנְשׁוֹ. אָמַר לָהֶן יִתַּמּוּ חַטָּאִים | מִן־הָאָרֶץ וגו׳. שְׁאֲלוּ לַחָכְמָה. חוֹטֵא מָהוּ עוֹנְשׁוֹ. אָמְרָה לָהֶן. חַטָּאִים תְּרַדֵּף רָעָה וג׳. שְׁאֲלוּ לְקוּדְשָׁא בְּרִיךְ הוּא. חוֹטֵא מָהוּ עוֹנְשׁוֹ. אָמַר לָהֶן. יַעֲשֶׂה תְשׁוּבָה וַאֲנִי מְקַבֵּל דִּכְתִיב. טוֹב וְיָשָׁר יי. לָמָּה הוּא טוֹב.

They asked the Torah, what is the punishment of the sinner? She told them, he shall bring a sacrifice and it will be atoned for him. They asked Prophecy, what is the punishment of the sinner? She told them, *the sinning soul is the one which will die.* They asked David, what is the punishment of the sinner? He told them, *may sins vanish from the earth* etc. They asked Wisdom, what is the punishment of the sinner? She told them, *evil will pursue sinners.* . They asked the Holy One, praise to Him, what is the punishment of the sinner? He said to them, let him repent and I will accept.. That is what is written, *good and straightforward is the Eternal.* (Why is he good?)

A slightly different version of G's text is in *Pesiqta dR. Cahana Shuva* (ed. Buber p. 158b), quoted in *Yalqut Shimony* (Psalms 702, Ezechiel 358).

102 *Prov.* 13:21.

103 *Ez.* 18:4.

104 The continuation of the quote is not a verse; it seems to be the invention of a copyist who did not understand it. In G, the quote "*Like a bird to move, like a swallow to fly,* etc.", is a paragraph by itself. In the Babli 11a, the quote *like a bird to move, like a swallow to fly, so undeserved curse will not happen* (*Prov.* 26:2) is quoted in reference to Mishnah 9. Why do the mothers of the High Priests have to support the exiled homicides if their prayers would be ineffective?

(31d line 69) [נִגְמַר דִּינוֹ בְּלֹא כֹהֵן גָּדוֹל]. וְתֵימַר אָכֵן. תִּפְתָּר שֶׁהָיָה עֵת וְעוֹנָה. כַּיי דָּמַר רִבִּי יוֹסֵי בֶּן חֲלַפְתָּא. עִיתִּים הֵן לַתְּפִילָּה. אָמַר דָּוִד לִפְנֵי הַקָּדוֹשׁ בָּרוּךְ הוּא. רִבּוֹן הָעוֹלָמִים. בְּשָׁעָה שֶׁאֲנִי מִתְפַּלֵּל אֵלֶיךָ תְּהֵא עֵת רָצוֹן. דִּכְתִיב וַאֲנִי תְפִלָּתִי־לְךָ | יי עֵת רָצוֹן.

[If sentence was passed when there was no High Priest.][105] And you say so [106]? Explain it that it was time and period [107]. As Rebbi Yose ben Ḥalaphta says, there are times for prayer. David said before the Holy One, praise to Him: Master of Universes, at the moment when I am praying to You it should be a moment of goodwill. As is it written [108]: *But I, my prayer is to You at a time of goodwill.*

105 Added from G, referring to Mishnah 11, even though the discussion continuous about Mishnah 9.

106 This continues from Note 104. Why are the priests' mothers worried?

107 The prayers of the exiles might be heard even if it was not their special merit that made the prayers effective. The Babli 11a holds that the prayers of the exiles may be effective if the High Priests fail to uphold very high standards of conduct.

108 *Ps.* 69:14.

(31d line 73) רִבִּי שְׁמוּאֵל בַּר נַחְמָן בְּשֵׁם רִבִּי יוֹנָתָן. כָּל־מָקוֹם שֶׁנֶּאֱמַר דִּיבּוּר חִידּוּשׁ מִקְרָא [יֵשׁ] שָׁם. וְהָא כְתִיב וַיְדַבֵּר אֱלֹהִים (כול' גרשה) [אֶל־נֹחַ וְאֶל־בָּנָיו אִתּוֹ לֵאמֹר. מַה חִידּוּשׁ מִקְרָא יֵשׁ שָׁם. חִידֵּשׁ בּוֹ אֵבֶר מִן הַחַי. וְהָא כְתִיב וַיִּפֹּל אַבְרָם עַל־פָּנָיו וַיְדַבֵּר אִתּוֹ אֱלֹהִים לֵאמֹר׃ מַה חִידּוּשׁ מִקְרָא יֵשׁ שָׁם חִידֵּשׁ בּוֹ אֶת הַמִּילָה. וְהָא כְתִיב דָּבָר שָׁלַח יי בְּיַעֲקֹב וג' מַה חִידּוּשׁ מִקְרָא יֵשׁ שָׁם חִידֵּשׁ בּוֹ אֶת הַ. . לה. וְהָא כְתִיב וַיְדַבֵּר אֱלֹהִים אֶל־מֹשֶׁה וַיֹּאמֶר אֵלָיו אֲנִי יי. מַה חִידּוּשׁ מִקְרָא יֵשׁ שָׁם חִידֵּשׁ בּוֹ קִידּוּשׁ הַשֵּׁם. וְהָא כְתִיב וַיְדַבֵּר יְהֹוָה אֶל־יְהוֹשֻׁעַ לֵאמֹר׃ מַה חִידּוּשׁ מִקְרָא יֵשׁ שָׁם. אִין תֵּימַר שֵׁשׁ עָרֵי מִקְלָט. כְּבָר נִתְּנוּ לְמֹשֶׁה מִסִּינַי. אֶלָּא אַף הוּא נֶאֱמַר לוֹ דָּבָר שֶׁלֹּא נֶאֱמַר לְמֹשֶׁה וְנָס אֶל־אַחַת | מֵהֶעָרִים הָאֵלֶּה וְעָמַד פֶּתַח וג' וְנָתְנוּ־לוֹ מָקוֹם וְיָשַׁב עִמָּם׃] מָהוּ וְיָשַׁב עִמָּם׃ רַבָּנִין דְּקֵיסָרִין בְּשֵׁם רִבִּי שִׁילֹה. שֶׁאִם הָיָה תַלְמִיד חָכָם עוֹשִׂין לוֹ בֵית וַעַד.

[109]Rebbi Samuel bar Nahman in the name of Rebbi Jonathan: At every occasion where *dibbur*[110] is said, there is a new biblical commandment. But is it not written, *God spoke* (etc., repetition) [*to Noah* (*and his sons with him as follows*)[111]? What new biblical commandment is there? He newly introduced limb of a living animal. But is it not written, *Abram fell on his face and God spoke to him as follows*[112]? What new biblical commandment is there? He newly introduced circumcision. But is it not written, *a word the Eternal sent to Jacob*[113]? What new biblical commandment is there? He newly introduced . . .[114] But is it not written[115], *God spoke to Moses and said to him, I am the Eternal*? What new biblical commandment is there? He newly introduced Sanctification of the Name. But is it not written[116], *the Eternal spoke to Joshua as follows*? What new biblical commandment is there? If you want to say the six cities of refuge, were they not already given to Moses at Sinai?

But even to him was spoken what was not said to Moses: *He shall flee to one of these cities and stand at the gate* etc., *and they shall give him a place that he stay with them.*[117]] What means *that he stay with them*? The rabbis of Caesarea in the name of Rebbi Shila[118]: If he is a scholar, they make him a house of assembly[119].

109 This paragraph is very much truncated in the Leiden ms.; after the introduction is noted "repetition", i. e., it is found elsewhere and needs no repetition here. But the paragraph is not known from any other place in the Yerushalmi; it is preserved almost completely in the Genizah fragment [G]. Already in 1934 S. Lieberman discovered the full text in *Yalqut Makhiri Isaiah* (*Tarbiz* 5, p. 109.) The Genizah text is given here in brackets; at one place where it is illegible it is completed from *Yalqut Makhiri* in the Notes.

110 If God addresses a human using the root דבר instead of אמר, נאם it is a sign that a new commandment is contained in the following paragraph.

111 *Gen.* 8:15. The scribe, quoting from memory, erroneously added the end of v. 9:8.

112 *Gen.* 17:3.

113 *Is.* 9:7.

114 As the editor of G noted, the illegible word here seems to be מילה, belonging to the preceding sentence. Following *Yalqut Makhiri* one has to read: The ischiatic tendon. The verse is also quoted in the Babli, *Hulin* 91a, to prove that the ischiatic tendon remains forbidden in Israel even though its prohibition was not repeated in the Torah after the epiphany of Sinai (in contrast to circumcision, which is mentioned in *Lev.* 12:3.) As S. Lieberman noted, the argument is correctly explained by Maharsha (R. Samuel Eliezer Idels) in his Notes to *Hulin*: The prohibition of the ischiatic tendon is the only commandment (דבר) which the Eternal sent through Jacob. The Babli is completely intelligible only on the basis of the Yerushalmi here.

115 *Ex.* 6:2, the only case of דבר to Moses not in connection with a commandment.

116 *Jos.* 20:1, introduction to the designation of cities of refuge; the reason for placing the paragraph in this Halakhah.

117 *Jos.* 20:4.

118 A student of R. Simeon ben Laqish.

119 Where others can come and profit from his knowledge (Babli 10a).

(31d line 76) [כְּשֵׁם שֶׁהָעִיר קוֹלֶטֶת כָּךְ הָיָה תְּחוּמָהּ קוֹלֵט.] שָׁלֹשׁ עָרִים הִפְרִישׁ מֹשֶׁה בְּעֵבֶר הַיַּרְדֵּן. מִשֶּׁבָּאוּ לָאָרֶץ הִפְרִישׁוּ עוֹד שָׁלֹשׁ. וּלְעָתִיד לָבוֹא מַפְרִישִׁין עוֹד שָׁלֹשׁ. שֶׁנֶּאֱמַר שָׁלֹשׁ שָׁלֹשׁ שָׁלֹשׁ. הֲרֵי ט'. אַבָּא שָׁאוּל אוֹמֵר. שָׁלֹשׁ. שָׁלֹשׁ שֶׁלְּשָׁלֹשׁ שָׁלֹשׁ הֲרֵי ט'. וְעוֹד הֲרֵי י"ב. רִבִּי נְהוֹרַאי אוֹמֵר. שָׁלֹשׁ שָׁלֹשׁ שָׁלֹשׁ הֲרֵי ט'. וְעוֹד הֲרֵי י"ב. עַל הַשָּׁלֹשׁ הֲרֵי ט"ו. כָּתוּב שֵׁשׁ־עָרֵי מִקְלָט תִּהְיֶינָה לָכֶם׃ שֶׁיְּהוּ שִׁשָּׁתָן קוֹלְטוֹת כְּאַחַת. וְתֵימַר אָכֵן. וַתְיָיא כַּיי דָמַר רִבִּי שְׁמוּאֵל [בַּר

יַיְנָא] בְּשֵׁם רִבִּי אָחָא. חֲמִשָּׁה דְבָרִים חָסֵר מִקְדָּשׁ אַחֲרוֹן מִמִּקְדָּשׁ רִאשׁוֹן. דִּכְתִיב עֲלוּ הָהָר וַהֲבֵאתֶם עֵץ וגו' עַד וְאֶכָּבְדָה. וְאֶכָּבְדְ כָּתוּב חָסֵר ה"א. אֵילוּ ה' דְבָרִים שֶׁחָסֵר מִקְדָּשׁ אַחֲרוֹן מִמִּקְדָּשׁ רִאשׁוֹן. וְאֵילוּ הֵן. אֵשׁ. אָרוֹן. אוּרִים וְתוּמִּים. שֶׁמֶן הַמִּשְׁחָה וְרוּחַ הַקּוֹדֶשׁ.

[120][Just as the city grants asylum, so does its domain grants asylum.] [121]"Three cities did Moses designate in Transjordan. When they came to the Land they designated another three. In the future there will be another three, as it is said *three, three, three*[122]. This makes nine. Abba Shaul says, *three*. Three of three times three makes nine. *Additional* makes twelve. Rebbi Nehorai says, *three, three, three* make nine. *Additional* makes twelve. *To these three* makes fifteen." It is written[123]: *Six cities of refuge there shall be for you*, that all six of them give asylum simultaneously. And you say so[124]? It follows what Rebbi Samuel [ben Aina][125] said in the name of Rebbi Aḥa: Five things was the last Temple missing which were in the first Temple, as it is written[126]: *Go to the mountain, bring wood,* etc., up to *I may be honored.* It is written *I shall be honored*, without the letter *he*[127]. These are the five things which the last Temple was missing which were in the first Temple. They are: The fire[128], the Ark[124], Urim and Tummim[129], anointing oil[124], and the Holy Spirit[130].

120 Reference to Mishnah 12, found only in G.

121 Tosephta 3:10, *Sifry Deut.* 185. The Tosephta credits Abba Shaul with the statement quoted here for R. Nehorai. *Sifry* quotes R. Nehorai and (Rebbi) Shaul, in inverse order.

122 *Deut.* 19:9. It is written there in v. 7, "three cities you shall designate". Since it is already reported in *Deut.* 4:41-43 that Moses designated three cities in Transjordan, v. 19:7 must refer to the three cities which Joshua designated. Therefore 19:9 must refer to another three cities situated in the Northern part of the Land of Promise (*Num.* 34:1-15) that never was part of the historical Land of Israel. In the opinion of Abba Shaul this Northern part, promised only if the *entire* people keep *all* biblical commandments, was as wide as the Cis- and Transjordan parts of the Land of Israel, and therefore needed not three but six additional cities of refuge. It is difficult to make sense of R. Nehorai's statement.

In the text probably one should read *three* (*Deut.* 19:7), *three, the three* (*Deut.* 19:9). The words עוֹד "additional", עַל אֵלֶּה "to these" are in *Deut.* 19:9. In the Constantinople edition, the argument of Abba Shaul for the first 9 is identical to that of the anonymous Tanna; this might be *lectio facilior.*

123 *Num.* 35:13.

124 If this refers to the previous statement,

then it is pointed out that *Num.* 35:13, which limits the number to six, cannot be squared with *Deut.* 19:9 which suggests nine. The question can be directed only at the anonymous Tanna who requires 9, and R. Nehorai who requires 15 cities, but not at Abba Shaul who envisages two pairs of six cities each.

Another interpretation (*Pene Moshe*) has this sentence starting a new paragraph, referring to Mishnah 9, and wonders why a High Priest of Second Temple times, who was not anointed with the holy oil compounded by Moses (*Ex.* 30:22-33) should have the power to free the exiled homicide. It is stated there in v. 23 that only Moses himself could compound this oil and in v. 31 that it should be used for all subsequent generations. By tradition, Josia buried the oil flask together with the Ark of the Covenant in the Temple Mount (*2Chr.* 35:3) after the prophetess Hulda informed him of the imminent destruction of the Temple.

125 Added from G (and the parallels, *Ta`aniot* 2:1, *Horaiot* 3:2, as well as the Babli, *Yoma* 21b). Only R. Samuel bar Aina is known as student of R. Aha.

126 *Hag.* 1:8.

127 *Ketib* וְאֶכָּבֵד, *Qere* וְאֶכָּבְדָה . Both spellings make sense. The missing ה is interpreted in the Alexandrian system of numeration as "5".

128 The Heavenly fire (*2Chr.* 7:1).

129 Which are mentioned as worn by the High Priest (*Ex.* 28:30) but for which no description or instructions are given.

130 The spirit of prophecy.

(32a line 10) [אִילָן שֶׁהוּא עוֹמֵד בְּתוֹךְ הַתְּחוּם וְנוֹפוֹ נוֹטֶה חוּץ לַתְּחוּם.] אָמַר [רִבִּי] אַבַּיי. תַּלְמִיד חָכָם צָרִיךְ לְפַרְסֵם אֶת עַצְמוֹ. הֵיךְ בַּר נַשׁ דַּחֲכַם חָדָא מֵיכְלָה וְאֲזִיל לַאֲתַר וְאִינּוּן מְיַיקְרִין לֵיהּ כַּד הֲוָה חֲכַם תְּרֵין מֵיכְלָה צָרִיךְ מֵימַר לוֹן חָדָא מֵיכְלָה אֲנָא חֲכַם. רַב הוּנָא אָמַר. אוֹמֵר בְּשָׂפָה רָפָה וְהַיָּמִין פְּשׁוּטָה לְקַבֵּל.

[131][If a tree stands inside the domain but its crown is outside the domain.] [Rebbi][132] Abbai said, a scholar has to make his qualifications known. [133]If he knows one collection and he comes to a place where they honor him as if he knew two, he has to tell them, I know one collection. [134](Rav Huna said, he says it in a soft voice and his right hand is stretched out to receive.)

131 From G, a quote from Mishnah 13. The discussion refers to Mishnah 14 which also is Mishnah *Ševi`it* 10:8 (Note 67), *viz.,* the case that a homicide is honored.

132 From G. In *Ševi`it* 10:8 the speaker is R. Yose (the Amora).

133 Halakhah *Ševi`it* 10:8, Note 123. He has memorized and completely mastered one collection of Tannaitic statements.

134 This does not belong here; it has been copied from *Ševi`it* 10:7. If a lender is offered repayment of a loan in a Sabbatical, when it should be forgiven, he may say softly that he observes the Sabbatical,

implying that he will not urge repayment while at the same time accepting the voluntary liquidation of the debt.

(32a line 14) מַה טַעֲמָא דְרִבִּי יוּדָה. כִּי יֵחַם לְבָבוֹ.
אָמַר רִבִּי אַבָּהוּ. וְחוֹזֵר בְּמִיתָתוֹ שֶׁלַּשְּׁלִישִׁי. אָמַר רִבִּי אַבָּהוּ. צָרְכוּ לַדָּבָר שׁוֹלְחִין וּמְבִיאִין אוֹתוֹ מִשָּׁם. אָמַר רִבִּי יוֹסֵי. מַתְנִיתִין לֹא אָמְרָה כֵן. אֶלָּא אֲפִילוּ יִשְׂרָאֵל צְרִיכִין לוֹ. אֲפִילוּ שַׂר צָבָא כְּיוֹאָב בֶּן צְרוּיָה אֵין יוֹצֵא מִשָּׁם לְעוֹלָם. שֶׁנֶּאֱמַר שָׁמָּה. שָׁם תְּהֵא דִירָתוֹ כול'.

What is Rebbi Jehudah's[135] reason? *For his blood is hot*[136].

Rebbi Abbahu said, but he returns upon the death of the third[137]. Rebbi Abbahu said, if they need it[138], they send and bring him from there. Rebbi Yose said, our Mishnah does not say so, but "even if Israel needs him like Joab ben Ṣeruya[62], he cannot ever leave from there, as it is said *there*[55]. There shall be his dwelling, etc."

135 In G: R. Huna. If the reference is to Mishnah 12, it should be "R. Yose the Galilean." If the reference is to the anonymous statement in Mishnah 8, the attribution to R. Jehudah might be correct.

136 *Deut*. 19:6.

137 In G: "the second." This reading has to be rejected since it is that of Mishnah 10. It rather seems to refer to Mishnah 11, about one who killed a High Priest, or a homicidal High Priest.

138 In G: If they (the High Court or the government) need *him* (the homicide.)

(32a line 18) [מַעֲלוֹת הָיוּ שָׂכָר לַלְוִיִּם.] תַּנֵּי רִבִּי יוּדָה אוֹמֵר. לְמַחְלוֹקֶת נִיתְּנוּ. רִבִּי יוֹסֵי אוֹמֵר. לְבֵית דִּירָה נִיתְּנוּ. וַתְייָא דְרִבִּי יוֹסֵי כְרִבִּי יוּדָה. וּדְרִבִּי מֵאִיר כְּדַעְתֵּיהּ. דְּתַנִּינָן. מַעֲלוֹת הָיוּ שָׂכָר לַלְוִיִּם דִּבְרֵי רִבִּי (מֵאִיר) [יְהוּדָה]. רִבִּי (יְהוּדָה) [מֵאִיר] אוֹמֵר לֹא הָיוּ מַעֲלוֹת שָׂכָר לַלְוִיִּם.

[139][They[68] were paying rent to the Levites.] [140]It was stated: Rebbi Jehudah says, they were given to be distributed. Rebbi Yose said, they were given as dwellings. It turns out that Rebbi Yose holds with Rebbi Jehudah, and Rebbi Meïr follows his own opinion as we have stated: "They[68] were paying rent to the Levites, the words of Rebbi (Meïr) [Jehudah]. Rebbi (Jehudah) [Meïr] said, they were not paying rent to the Levites."

139 The text in brackets is from G. Here starts the discussion of Mishnah 15. The text in parentheses is from the Leiden ms. The correct quote of the Mishnah is in G.

140 *Ma`aser Šeni* 5:8, Notes 165-167. The question is whether individual houses in Levitic cities were private or tribal property, as explained there. Even though three

sources (the Leiden ms. here and in *Ma`aser Šeni* and G here) confirm the text "R. Yose said, they were given as dwellings" one must read "R. Meïr", as shown. R. Yose holds with R. Jehudah in Mishnah *Ma`aser Šeni* 5:9. In the Babli (13a) it is held that the six cities of refuge were tribal property; for the other 42 Levitic cities the dispute is not resolved.

(32a line 22) רַבָּא בְּשֵׁם רִבִּי יוּדָה רִבִּי זְעִירָא בְשֵׁם מַר עוּקְבָא. אֵין מְקַדְּדִין אֶלָּא בְחֶבֶל שֶׁלְּחֲמִשִּׁים אַמָּה. רִבִּי זְעִירָא בְשֵׁם רַב חִסְדָּא אוֹמֵר. אֵין מְקַדְּדִין לֹא בְעָרֵי הַלְּוִיִּם וְלֹא בִמְקוֹם עֶגְלָה עֲרוּפָה. וַתְיָיא כְמָאן דְּאָמַר. אֶלֶף אַמָּה מִגְרָשׁ וְאַלְפַּיִים תְּחוּם שַׁבָּת. בְּרַם כְּמָאן דָּמַר. אֶלֶף מִגְרָשׁ וְאַלְפַּיִם שָׂדוֹת וּכְרָמִים. כְּלוּם לָמְדוּ לִתְחוּם שַׁבָּת לֹא מִתְּחוּם עָרֵי לְוִיִּם. לְעִיקָּר אֵין מְקַדְּדִין לַטְּפֵילָה מְקַדְּדִין.

וּמְנַיִין שֶׁלֹּא יְהוּ קוֹבְרִין בְּעָרֵי הַלְּוִיִּם. רִבִּי אַבָּהוּ בְשֵׁם רִבִּי יוֹסֵי בַּר חֲנִינָה. וּמִגְרְשֵׁיהֶם יִהְיוּ לִבְהֶמְתָּם וְלִרְכוּשָׁם וּלְכֹל חַיָּתָם׃ לַחַיִּים נִיתְּנוּ וְלֹא לִקְבוּרָה נִיתְּנוּ.

[141]Rebbi Abba in the name of Rebbi Jehudah, Rebbi Ze`ira in the name of Mar Uqba: One strip-measures only with a rope of 50 cubits. Rebbi Ze`ira in the name of Rav Ḥisda: One strip-measures neither for the Levitic cities nor for the place of breaking the calf's neck. This would be acceptable for him who says, 1000 cubits of open space and 2000 cubits of Sabbath domain. But for him who says, 1000 cubits of open space and 2000 cubits of fields and vineyards, did they not learn the Sabbath domain from the Levitic cities? For the main thing one does not strip-measure; does one strip-measure for the derivative?

From where that one does not bury in Levitic cities? Rebbi Abbahu in the name of Rebbi Yose bar Ḥanina: *And their open spaces shall be for their animals, and their property, and all their lives*[142]. They were given for living; they were not given for burial.

141 This text is also in *Sotah* 5:5, explained in detail in Notes 120-123 and *Eruvin* 5 (22d l. 26). In these sources, the deviations from the text here and the inclusion of the remark about burial, irrelevant for the topics of the other quotes, make it clear that the text here is the source.

The problem is whether the 1000 or 2000 cubits of surrounding territory given to Levitic cities (*Num.* 35:4,5) have to be measured with a measuring rope hugging the terrain or with ropes following the terrain being held horizontally each time. This second way, called "strip-measuring" amounts to measuring the distances on a map onto which the geographic features have been orthogonally projected. The Babli (*Eruvin* 58b) and also the Yerushalmi *Eruvin* (5, 22d l. 9) more reasonably require that strip-measuring be done by ropes four cubits long.

142 *Num.* 35:3. The Babli, 12a, exempts homicides from burial outside the town limits on the basis of Mishnah 11.

אילו הן הלוקין פרק שלישי

(fol. 32a) **משנה א**: וְאֵילוּ הֵן הַלּוֹקִין הַבָּא עַל אֲחוֹתוֹ וְעַל אֲחוֹת אָבִיו וְעַל אֲחוֹת אִמּוֹ וְעַל אֲחוֹת אִשְׁתּוֹ וְעַל אֵשֶׁת אָחִיו וְעַל אֵשֶׁת אֲחִי אָבִיו וְעַל הַנִּדָּה. אַלְמָנָה לְכֹהֵן גָּדוֹל גְּרוּשָׁה וַחֲלוּצָה לְכֹהֵן הֶדְיוֹט. אַלְמָנָה וּגְרוּשָׁה חַייָבִין עָלֶיהָ מִשּׁוּם שְׁנֵי שֵׁמוֹת. גְּרוּשָׁה וַחֲלוּצָה אֵינוֹ חַייָב אֶלָּא מִשּׁוּם שֵׁם אֶחָד בִּלְבָד:

Mishnah 1: The following are flogged[1]: He who copulates with his sister[2], or his father's sister, or his mother's sister[3], or his wife's sister[4], or his brother's wife[5], or his father's brother's wife[6], or a menstruating woman[7]. A widow for the High Priest[8], or a divorcee[9] or one having received *ḥalîṣah* for a common priest. For a widow and divorcee one is liable because of two categories[10]. For a divorcee having received *ḥalîṣah* one is only liable for one category[11].

משנה ב: הַטָּמֵא שֶׁאָכַל אֶת הַקּוֹדֶשׁ וְהַבָּא אֶל הַמִּקְדָּשׁ טָמֵא הָאוֹכֵל חֵלֶב וְדָם וְנוֹתָר וּפִגּוּל וְטָמֵא הַשּׁוֹחֵט וְהַמַּעֲלֶה בַחוּץ וְהָאוֹכֵל חָמֵץ בַּפֶּסַח. וְהָאוֹכֵל וְהָעוֹשֶׂה מְלָאכָה בְּיוֹם הַכִּיפּוּרִים וְהַמְּפַטֵּם אֶת הַשֶּׁמֶן וְהַמְּפַטֵּם אֶת הַקְּטוֹרֶת וְהַסָּךְ בְּשֶׁמֶן הַמִּשְׁחָה וְהָאוֹכֵל נְבֵילוֹת וּטְרֵיפוֹת שְׁקָצִים וּרְמָשִׂים. אָכַל טֶבֶל וּמַעֲשֵׂר רִאשׁוֹן שֶׁלֹּא נִיטְלוּ תְרוּמָתוֹ וּמַעֲשֵׂר שֵׁנִי וְהֶקְדֵּשׁ שֶׁלֹּא נִפְדּוּ. כַּמָּה יֹאכַל מִן הַטֶּבֶל וִיהֵא חַייָב. רִבִּי שִׁמְעוֹן אוֹמֵר כָּל שֶׁהוּא וַחֲכָמִים אוֹמְרִים כַּזַּיִת. אָמַר לָהֶן רִבִּי שִׁמְעוֹן אֵין אַתֶּם מוֹדִין לִי בָּאוֹכֵל (נְבֵילָה) [נְמָלָה] כָּל־שֶׁהוּא שֶׁהוּא חַייָב. אָמְרוּ לוֹ מִפְּנֵי שֶׁהִיא כִבְרִייָתָהּ. אָמַר לָהֶן אַף חִיטָּה אַחַת כִּבְרִיָּתָהּ:

Mishnah 2: An impure person who ate holy food[12], or who came into the Temple when impure[13]. One who eats fat[14], or blood[15], or leftover, or *piggul*[16], or impure[17] [sacrificial meat]. One who sacrifices outside[19], or one who eats leavened matter on Passover[20]. One who eats or does work on the Day of Atonement[21], and one who compounds the oil[22], or compounds the incense[23], and who rubs with the anointing oil[22], and one who eats carcass[24] or torn meat[25], abominations and crawling things[26]. If one ate *ṭevel*[27] or first tithe from which heave was not taken[28], or second tithe[29] or dedicated food[30] which was not redeemed. How much does he have to eat from *ṭevel* to be liable? Rebbi Simeon says, anything; but the Sages say, the volume of an olive. Rebbi Simeon told them, do you not agree that one who eats (carcass meat) [an ant][31] is liable? They told him, because it is a creature. He answered them, also a grain of wheat[32] is a creature.

משנה ג: הָאוֹכֵל בִּיכּוּרִים עַד שֶׁלֹּא קָרָא עֲלֵיהֶן. קָדְשֵׁי קֳדָשִׁים חוּץ לַקְּלָעִים. קֳדָשִׁים קַלִּין וּמַעֲשֵׂר שֵׁנִי חוּץ לַחוֹמָה. הַשּׁוֹבֵר אֶת הָעֶצֶם בַּפֶּסַח טָהוֹר הֲרֵי זֶה לוֹקֶה אַרְבָּעִים. אֲבָל הַמּוֹתִיר בַּטָּהוֹר וְהַשּׁוֹבֵר בַּטָּמֵא אֵינוֹ לוֹקֶה אַרְבָּעִים:

Mishnah 3: One who eats First Fruits before he recited over them[33], or most holy sacrifices outside the Temple enclosure[34], or simple sacrifices or Second Tithe outside of the wall[35]. One who breaks a bone of a pure Passover sacrifice is flogged 40 [lashes][36]. But one who leaves over of the pure[37] or breaks a bone of the impure[38] is not flogged 40 [lashes].

משנה ד: הַנּוֹטֵל אֵם עַל הַבָּנִים רִבִּי יְהוּדָה אוֹמֵר לוֹקֶה וְאֵינוֹ מְשַׁלֵּחַ. וַחֲכָמִים אוֹמְרִים מְשַׁלֵּחַ וְאֵינוֹ לוֹקֶה. זֶה הַכְּלָל כָּל מִצְוָה בְלֹא תַעֲשֶׂה שֶׁיֵּשׁ בָּהּ קוּם וַעֲשֵׂה אֵין חַיָּבִין עָלֶיהָ:

Mishnah 4: He who takes the mother with the young, Rebbi Jehudah says he is flogged but does not have to send away. But the Sages say, he sends away and is not flogged[39]. This is the principle: One is not liable for any prohibition coupled with a positive commandment.

משנה ה: הַקּוֹרֵחַ קָרְחָה בְּרֹאשׁוֹ וְהַמַּקִּיף פְּאַת רֹאשׁוֹ וְהַמַּשְׁחִית פְּאַת זְקָנוֹ וְהַשּׂוֹרֵט שְׂרִיטָה אַחַת עַל הַמֵּת חַיָּב. שָׂרַט שְׂרִיטָה אַחַת עַל חֲמִשָּׁה מֵתִים אוֹ חָמֵשׁ שְׂרִיטוֹת עַל מֵת אֶחָד חַיָּב עַל כָּל אַחַת וְאַחַת. עַל הָרֹאשׁ שְׁתַּיִם אַחַת מִכָּאן וְאַחַת מִכָּאן וְעַל הַזָּקָן שְׁתַּיִם מִכָּאן וּשְׁתַּיִם מִכָּאן וְאַחַת מִלְּמַטָּה. רִבִּי אֱלִעֶזֶר אוֹמֵר אִם נְטָלָן כּוּלָּן כְּאַחַת אֵינוֹ חַיָּב אֶלָּא אַחַת. וְאֵינוֹ חַיָּב עַד שֶׁיִּטְּלֶנּוּ בְתַעַר. רִבִּי לָעְזָר אוֹמֵר אֲפִלּוּ לִקְּטוֹ בְּמַלְקֵט אוֹ בְרַהִיטְנִי חַיָּב:

Mishnah 5: One who shaves a bald spot on his head[40], and who shaves off his sideburns, and who shaves off the corners of his beard,[41] and one who scratches one scratch for a deceased is liable. If he scratched one scratch for five deceased, or five scratches for one deceased, he is liable for each single one[42]; for the head two, one for each side; for the beard two on each side and one for the chin[43]. Rebbi Eleazar[44] says, if he removed all at once he is liable only once. He is liable only if he took them off with a razor; Rebbi Eleazar says, even if he took them off with pincers or a plane.

משנה ו: הַכּוֹתֵב כְּתוֹבֶת קַעֲקַע כָּתַב וְלֹא קִיעֲקַע קִיעֲקַע וְלֹא כָתַב אֵינוֹ חַיָּב עַד שֶׁיִּכְתּוֹב וִיקַעֲקַע בַּדְּיוֹ וּבְכָחוֹל וּבְכָל־דָּבָר שֶׁהוּא רוֹשֵׁם. רִבִּי שִׁמְעוֹן בֶּן יְהוּדָה אוֹמֵר, אֵינוֹ חַיָּב עַד שֶׁיִּכְתּוֹב שָׁם הַשֵּׁם שֶׁנֶּאֱמַר וּכְתוֹבֶת קַעֲקַע לֹא תִתְּנוּ בָּכֶם אֲנִי ה':

Mishnah 6: One who writes a tattoo. If he designed but did not tattoo, or tattooed but did not design, he is not liable until he design and permanently color with ink of *kohl* or anything that leaves a mark. Rebbi Simeon ben Jehudah says, only if the writes the Name, as it is said[45], *a tattoo design you shall not put on yourselves, I am the Eternal.*

משנה ז: נָזִיר שֶׁהָיָה שׁוֹתֶה בַּיַּיִן כָּל הַיּוֹם אֵינוֹ חַייָב אֶלָּא אַחַת. אָֽמְרוּ לוֹ אַל תִּשְׁתֶּה אַל תִּשְׁתֶּה וְהוּא שׁוֹתֶה חַייָב עַל כָּל אַחַת וְאַחַת:

Mishnah 7: [46]If a *nazir* was drinking wine a whole day long, he is liable only once. If one told him, do not drink, do not drink, if then he drinks he is liable for every single occasion.

משנה ח: הָיָה מִיטַּמֵּא לַמֵּתִים כָּל־הַיּוֹם אֵינוֹ חַייָב אֶלָּא אַחַת. אָֽמְרוּ לוֹ אַל תִּיטַּמֵּא אַל תִּיטַּמֵּא וְהוּא מִיטַּמֵּא חַייָב עַל כָּל אַחַת וְאַחַת

Mishnah 8: [47]If he was defiling himself with corpses a whole day long, he is liable only once. If one told him, do not defile yourself, do not defile yourself, if then he defiles himself he is liable for every single occasion.

משנה ט: הָיָה מְגַלֵּחַ כָּל הַיּוֹם אֵינוֹ חַייָב אֶלָּא אַחַת. אָֽמְרוּ לוֹ אַל תְּגַלַּח אַל תְּגַלַּח וְהוּא מְגַלֵּחַ חַייָב עַל כָּל אַחַת וְאַחַת.

Mishnah 9: [48]If he was shaving a whole day long, he is liable only once. If one told him, do not shave, do not shave, if then he shaves he is liable for every single occasion.

משנה י: הָיָה לָבוּשׁ בְּכִלְאַיִם כָּל הַיּוֹם אֵינוֹ חַייָב אֶלָּא אַחַת. אָֽמְרוּ לוֹ אַל תִּלְבַּשׁ אַל תִּלְבַּשׁ וְהוּא פּוֹשֵׁט וְלוֹבֵשׁ חַייָב עַל כָּל אַחַת וְאַחַת:

Mishnah 10: If he was dressed in *kilaim* a whole day long, he is liable only once[49]. If one told him, do not dress, do not dress, and he took off and put on, he is liable for every single occasion.

משנה יא: יֵשׁ חוֹרֵשׁ תֶּלֶם אֶחָד וְחַייָב עָלָיו מִשּׁוּם שְׁמוֹנָה לָאוִין. הַחוֹרֵשׁ בְּשׁוֹר וַחֲמוֹר וְהֵן מוּקְדָּשִׁים בְּכִלְאַיִם בַּכֶּרֶם וּשְׁבִיעִית וְיוֹם טוֹב וְכֹהֵן וְנָזִיר וְאַף בֵּית הַטּוּמְאָה. חוֹנִיָּה בֶּן חֲכִינַאי אוֹמֵר אַף הַלּוֹבֵשׁ כִּלְאָיִם. אָֽמְרוּ לוֹ אֵינוֹ הַשֵּׁם. אָמַר לָהֶן אַף לֹא הַנָּזִיר הוּא הַשֵּׁם:

Mishnah 11: One might plough a single furrow and be liable because of it for eight prohibitions. If one ploughs with an ox and a donkey which had been sanctified for *kilaim* in a vineyard, in a Sabbatical year, on a holiday, he is a Cohen and a *nazir* at an impure place[50]. Onias ben Ḥakhinai said, also if he wore *kilaim*. They told him, this is not of the same category. He told them, neither is the *nazir* of the same category.

משנה יב: כַּמָּה מַלְקִין אוֹתוֹ, אַרְבָּעִים חָסֵר אַחַת. שֶׁנֶּאֱמַר בְּמִסְפָּר אַרְבָּעִים. מִנְיָין שֶׁהוּא סָמוּךְ לְאַרְבָּעִים. רִבִּי יְהוּדָה אוֹמֵר אַרְבָּעִים שְׁלֵמוֹת. וְאֵיכָן הוּא לוֹקֶה אֶת הַיְתֵרָה בֵּין כְּתֵיפָיו:

Mishnah 12: How much is he flogged? Forty minus one, as it is said: *in number: forty*[51], a number close to forty. Rebbi Jehudah says, he is flogged a full forty. Where is he flogged the extra one[2]? Between his shoulders.

משנה יג: אֵין אוֹמְדִין אוֹתוֹ אֶלָּא בְמַכּוֹת הָרְאוּיוֹת לְהִשְׁתַּלֵּשׁ. אֲמָדוּהוּ לְקַבֵּל אַרְבָּעִים. לָקָה מִקְצָת וְאָמְרוּ שֶׁאֵינוֹ יָכוֹל לְקַבֵּל אַרְבָּעִים פָּטוּר. אֲמָדוּהוּ לְקַבֵּל שְׁמוֹנֶה עֶשְׂרֵה מִשֶּׁלָּקָה אָמְרוּ יָכוֹל הוּא לְקַבֵּל אַרְבָּעִים פָּטוּר. עָבַר עֲבֵירָה שֶׁיֶּשׁ בָּהּ שְׁנֵי לָאוִין אֲמָדוּהוּ אוֹמֶד אֶחָד לוֹקֶה וּפָטוּר. וְאִם לָאו לוֹקֶה וּמִתְרַפֵּא וְחוֹזֵר וְלוֹקֶה:

Mishnah 13: One estimates him only for floggings divisible by three[52]. If they estimated that he could receive forty; after he was flogged some, they[53] said that he could not withstand forty, he is not liable. If they had estimated him for eighteen; after he was flogged they said that he could withstand forty, he is not liable[54]. If he committed a transgression which involved two prohibitions, if they estimated him in one estimation he is flogged and then is no longer liable; otherwise[55] he is flogged, recovers, and is flogged a second time.

משנה יד: כֵּיצַד מַלְקִין אוֹתוֹ כּוֹפֵת שְׁתֵּי יָדָיו עַל הָעַמּוּד הֵילָךְ וְהֵילָךְ וְחַזַּן הַכְּנֶסֶת אוֹחֵז בִּבְגָדָיו אִם נִקְרְעוּ נִקְרְעוּ וְאִם נִפְרְמוּ נִפְרְמוּ. עַד שֶׁהוּא מְגַלֶּה אֶת לִבּוֹ וְהָאֶבֶן נְתוּנָה מֵאַחוֹרָיו. חַזַּן הַכְּנֶסֶת עוֹמֵד עָלֶיהָ וּרְצוּעָה שֶׁל עֵגֶל בְּיָדוֹ כְּפוּלָה אֶחָד לִשְׁנַיִם וּשְׁנַיִם לְאַרְבָּעָה וּשְׁתֵּי רְצוּעוֹת עוֹלוֹת וְיוֹרְדוֹת בָּהּ:

Mishnah 14: How does one flog him? One binds both his hands on both sides of a pillar. The beadle grabs his clothing. If it tore, it tore; if it unravelled, it unravelled, until he uncovers his heart. A stone is put behind him on which the beadle stands with a strip of calf's leather in his hand, folded one into two and two into four, and two strips[56] go up and down in it.

משנה טו: יָדָהּ טֶפַח וְרָחְבָּהּ טֶפַח וּמַגַּעַת עַל פִּי כְרֵיסוֹ. וּמַכֶּה שְׁלִישׁ מִלְּפָנָיו וּשְׁתֵּי יָדוֹת מֵאַחוֹרָיו. וְאֵינוֹ מַכֶּה אוֹתוֹ לֹא עוֹמֵד וְלֹא יוֹשֵׁב אֶלָּא מוּטֶּה, שֶׁנֶּאֱמַר וְהִפִּילוֹ הַשּׁוֹפֵט וְהִכָּהוּ לְפָנָיו וגו'. וְהַמַּכֶּה מַכֶּה בְיָדוֹ אַחַת בְּכָל כֹּחוֹ:

Mishnah 15: The handle is one hand-breadth long; its width is one hand-breadth, and it reaches to his belly. He flogs him one third on his front and two thirds on his back. He flogs him neither standing nor sitting but bending down as it is written[51], *the judge shall make him fall and flog him on his front* etc. The person who flogs, flogs with one hand with full force.

משנה יו: וְהַקּוֹרֵא קוֹרֵא אִם־לֹא תִשְׁמֹר לַעֲשׂוֹת אֶת־כָּל־דִּבְרֵי הַתּוֹרָה וגומ'. וְהִפְלָא יי אֶת־מַכּוֹתְךָ וְגוֹ', וְחוֹזֵר לִתְחִלַּת הַמִּקְרָא. וְאִם מֵת תַּחַת יָדוֹ פָּטוּר. הוֹסִיף לוֹ רְצוּעָה אַחַת וָמֵת הֲרֵי זֶה גוֹלֶה עַל יָדוֹ. נִתְקַלְקֵל בֵּין בְּרֵיעִי בֵּין בְּמַיִם פָּטוּר. רַבִּי יְהוּדָה אוֹמֵר הָאִישׁ בְּרֵיעִי וְהָאִשָּׁה בְּמַיִם:

Mishnah 16: The reader reads[57] *if you will not observe to fulfill all the words of this Torah* etc.; *the Eternal will your flogging exemplary,* etc. and returns to the beginning of the verse. If he[58] died under his hand, he[59] is not liable. If he[59] added a single strip and he[58] died, he[59] is exiled because of him[58]. If he[58] dirtied himself whether by feces or by urine, he is no longer liable[60]. Rebbi Jehudah says, a man by feces, a woman by urine.

משנה יז: כָּל חַיָּיבֵי כְרִיתוֹת שֶׁלָּקוּ נִפְטְרוּ יְדֵי כְרִיתָתָן שֶׁנֶּאֱמַר וְנִקְלָה אָחִיךָ לְעֵינֶיךָ. מִשֶּׁלָּקָה הֲרֵי הוּא כְאָחִיךָ דִּבְרֵי רַבִּי חֲנַנְיָה בֶּן גַּמְלִיאֵל. וּמָה אִם הָעוֹבֵר עֲבֵירָה אַחַת נַפְשׁוֹ נִיטְלָה עָלֶיהָ. הָעוֹשֶׂה מִצְוָה אַחַת עַל אַחַת כַּמָּה וְכַמָּה שֶׁתִּינָּתֵן לוֹ נַפְשׁוֹ. רַבִּי שִׁמְעוֹן אוֹמֵר מִמְּקוֹמוֹ הוּא לָמֵד שֶׁנֶּאֱמַר וְנִכְרְתוּ הַנְּפָשׁוֹת הָעוֹשֹׂת מִקֶּרֶב עַמָּם. וְאוֹמֵר אֲשֶׁר יַעֲשֶׂה אוֹתָם הָאָדָם וָחַי בָּהֶם. הָא כָּל־הַיּוֹשֵׁב וְלֹא עָבַר עֲבֵירָה נוֹתְנִין לוֹ שָׂכָר כְּעוֹשֶׂה מִצְוָה.

Mishnah 17: All those subject to extirpation are no longer liable to extirpation once they were flogged, as it is said, *your brother would be despicable in your eyes*[60]. After he was flogged, he is your brother[61], the words of Rebbi Ḥanania ben Gamliel. And since one who commits a transgression may lose his soul because of it, if one fulfills a commandment certainly his soul shall be given to him. Rebbi Simeon says, from its place[62] it can be inferred as it is written, *the souls of the perpetrators will be extirpated*, and it says, *that a human shall do and live in them.* Therefore, to anybody who quietly does not transgress a prohibition is given reward like somebody keeping the Commandments.

משנה יח: רַבִּי שִׁמְעוֹן בְּרַבִּי אוֹמֵר הֲרֵי הוּא אוֹמֵר רַק חֲזַק לְבִלְתִּי אֲכֹל הַדָּם כִּי הַדָּם הוּא הַנֶּפֶשׁ. וּמָה אִם הַדָּם שֶׁנַּפְשׁוֹ שֶׁל אָדָם חָתָה מִמֶּנּוּ הַפּוֹרֵשׁ מִמֶּנּוּ מְקַבֵּל שָׂכָר. גָּזֵל וַעֲרָיוֹת שֶׁנַּפְשׁוֹ שֶׁל אָדָם מִתְאַוָּה לָהֶן וּמְחַמְדָתָן הַפּוֹרֵשׁ מֵהֶן עַל אַחַת כַּמָּה וְכַמָּה שֶׁיִּזְכֶּה לוֹ וּלְדוֹרוֹתָיו וּלְדוֹרוֹת דּוֹרוֹתָיו עַד סוֹף כָּל הַדּוֹרוֹת:

Mishnah 18: Rebbi Simeon ben Rebbi says, does it not say[63], *only be strong not to eat blood, for blood is the life?* Since one who desists from blood, from which a person recoils, receives reward, if one desists of robbery and sexual offenses, which a person desires and cherishes, certainly he should acquire the merit for himself, his descendants, and his descendants' descendants to the end of all generations.

משנה יט: רַבִּי חֲנִינָה בֶּן עֲקַשְׁיָה אוֹמֵר רָצָה הַקָּדוֹשׁ בָּרוּךְ הוּא לְזַכּוֹת יִשְׂרָאֵל לְפִיכָךְ הִרְבָּה לָהֶם תּוֹרָה וּמִצְוֹת שֶׁנֶּאֱמַר יְיָ חָפֵץ לְמַעַן צִדְקוֹ יַגְדִּיל תּוֹרָה וְיַאְדִּיר:

Mishnah 19: Rebbi Haninah ben Aqashiah says: The Holy One, praise to Him, wanted to increase the merit of Israel; therefore He multiplied for them teaching and commandments, as it is written[64], *the Eternal desires for the sake of His justice to make His instruction great and prodigious.*

1 As a matter of principle, all transgressions of biblical prohibitions are punishable by flogging unless specifically exempted. The rules are spelled out by Maimonides in his Commentary to this Mishnah. It is understood that a sentence of flogging can be passed only after a trial based on the testimony of two witnesses both to the fact of the crime and the necessary warning given to the perpetrator.

A crime punishable by the death penalty can never lead to a sentence of flogging, even if the death penalty cannot be imposed because of a material or technical obstacle. Crimes punishable by extirpation or Death by the Hand of Heaven are subject to flogging, since in this case the earthly punishment guarantees the sinner his part in the World to Come (Mishnah 17).

A crime punishable by a fine cannot lead to punishment by flogging. Crimes done by speech without accompanying action are not punishable by flogging, except swearing falsely, substituting sacrifices (*Lev.* 27:10), and cursing using the Name which is a potential capital crime.

A crime connected to a positive commandment cannot lead to punishment by flogging as long as the positive commandment still can be executed (Mishnah 4).

The infraction of a positive commandment cannot be punished. For example, the High Priest is commanded to marry a virgin. He is prohibited of marrying a widow, divorcee, or desecrated woman (*Lev.* 21:13-14). If he marries a woman who is not forbidden but not a virgin, he cannot be punished.

A prohibition understood by inference, not written explicitly, cannot be punished.

2 *Lev.* 20:17. The list starts with sexual transgressions punishable by Heaven.

3 *Lev.* 20:19.

4 *Lev.* 18:18. This is a simple prohibition.

5 *Lev.* 20:21.

6 *Lev.* 20:20.

7 *Lev.* 20:18.

8 *Lev.* 21:14, a simple prohibition.

9 *Lev.* 21:7. The clause about *haliṣah*, the freeing of the widow of a childless man from levirate marriage, is in dispute; the majority holds that the prohibition of the widow after *halîsah* is rabbinic.

10 If the High Priest marries a widow who had been a divorcee.

11 Since *haliṣah* is forbidden only as a kind of divorce.

12 *Lev.* 7:20,21; transgressions punishable by extirpation.

13 *Num.* 19:13.

14 *Lev.* 7:25.

15 *Lev.* 7:27.

16 *Lev.* 19:8.

17 "Leftover" refers to meat from acceptable sacrifices which was not eaten during the statutory time limit. *Piggul* is a sacrifice which was offered with the idea in mind (of the offerer or the officiating priest) that it should be eaten out of its allotted time (or place); *Lev.* 7:18,19:8. The root of *piggul* probably is فجل "to be soft".

18 *Lev.* 7:19.

19 *Lev.* 17:4.

20 *Ex.* 12:19.

21 *Lev.* 23:29-30.

22 *Ex.* 30:33. The anointing oil in the proportions spelled out there.

23 For profane purposes, *Ex.* 30:38. Incense had to be compounded fresh every year.

24 *Deut.* 14:21, a simple prohibition.

25 *Ex.* 22:30, a simple prohibition.

26 *Lev.* 11:11,44.

27 Fully harvested produce of which the priests' heave was not taken; *Lev.* 22:10.

28 The obligation is *Num.* 18:28, the penalty *Num.* 18:32.

29 Outside the place of the Sanctuary it needs redemption, *Deut.* 14:24.

30 Donated to the Temple to be sold for its value, not dedicated to the altar; *Lev.* 27:11.

31 In *editio princeps* and ms., נבילה "carcass meat". In all other sources נמלה "ant". The latter reading is the only one which makes sense since it both is forbidden (*Lev.* 11:42) and much less than the size of an olive.

32 Given as heave (biblically restricted to grain, wine, and olive oil).

33 First Fruits have to be eaten by the priest (*Deut.* 12:17) after the Temple ceremony. This point is in dispute between R. Aqiba and others.

34 They are restricted to priests (*Lev.* 10:15).

35 *Lev.* 10:14 for priests, *Deut.* 12:17 for others.

36 *Ex.* 12:46.

37 Example of a prohibition subordinated to a positive commandment; cf. Note 1.

38 It lost its holiness.

39 *Deut.* 22:6-7.

40 *Lev.* 21:5, *Deut.* 14:1.

41 *Lev.* 19:27.

42 Since *Lev.* 19:28 forbids a single scratch for a single deceased.

43 The five corners of a beard are: near the ear on each side, the cheekbone on each side, and the chin.

44 Most sources read: R. Eliezer.

45 *Lev.* 19:28. Tattooing has two parts: making a scratch and coloring it with permanent color. It is not too clear which

name is intended.

46 Mishnah *Nazir* 6:4.

47 Mishnah *Nazir* 6:6.

48 Mishnah *Nazir* 6:5.

49 *Lev.* 19:19. Cf. Introduction to Tractate *Kilaim*.

50 Ploughing with ox and donkey, *Deut.* 22:10. Growing *kilaim* in a vineyard, *Deut.* 22:9; it makes growth and vines forbidden for all use. Sabbatical year *Lev.* 25:4 (the verse only forbids sowing). Holiday, *Ex.* 12:16. Cohen in an impure place, *Lev.* 21:1.

51 *Deut.* 25:2-3. Since "40" is the only number in the text, it is read as standard punishment subject to medical evaluation. (Also in *2Cor.* 11:24 it is not clear whether 40-1 is the real number or simply is the standard expression for flogging.)

52 As described later, for one stripe in the front one hits two in the back, for a total number divisible by 3. Therefore, the 40th can be neither in front nor in back.

53 The medical experts.

54 For further flogging.

55 If he is tried for only one transgression, he later can be tried for another transgression based on the same facts.

56 Two double strips of calf hide and two single strips (of donkey hide).

57 *Deut.* 28:58-59 contain a total of 34 words. One adds the first 5 words of 28:58 a second time for a total of 39 words, one word for each stroke.

58 The culprit.

59 The beadle.

60 Since *Deut.* 25:3 prohibits to degrade the criminal, the flogging must stop immediately.

61 As your brother, he has part in the World to Come; Mishnah *Sanhedrin* 10:1. Since extirpation implies denial of the World to Come, it is eliminated.

62 *Lev.* 18 ends (v. 29) with extirpation for transgressors but starts with assurances of Eternal Life for those who live by the Torah (v. 5).

63 *Deut.* 12:23.

64 *Is.* 42:21.

[רִבִּי חֲנַנְיָה בֶּן עֲקַשְׁיָה אוֹמֵר רָצָה הַקָּדוֹשׁ בָּרוּךְ הוּא וגו'. מִפְּנֵי מַה מְכַנִּים שְׁמוֹ שֶׁל הַקָּדוֹשׁ בָּרוּךְ הוּא וְקוֹרִין אוֹתוֹ מָקוֹם לוֹמַר שֶׁהוּא מְקוֹמוֹ שֶׁל עוֹלָמוֹ וְאֵין עוֹלָמוֹ מְקוֹמוֹ. רִבִּי חוּנָה בְּשֵׁם רִבִּי אִימִּי כָּתוּב מְעוֹנָה אֱלֹהֵי קֶדֶם לוֹמַר שֶׁהוּא מְעוֹנוֹ שֶׁל עוֹלָמוֹ וְאֵין עוֹלָמוֹ מְעוֹנוֹ. רִבִּי יוֹסֵה בֶּן חֲלַפְתָּה אָמַר כָּתוּב וַיֹּאמֶר יי הִנֵּה מָקוֹם אִתִּי לוֹמַר שֶׁהוּא מְקוֹמוֹ שֶׁל עוֹלָמוֹ וְאֵין עוֹלָמוֹ מְקוֹמוֹ. אָמַר רִבִּי יִצְחָק כְּתִיב יי בָּם סִינַי בַּקֹּדֶשׁ: לָא מִסְתַּבְּרָה אֶלָּא קוֹדֶשׁ בְּסִינַי. לוֹמַר שֶׁהוּא מְקוֹמוֹ שֶׁל עוֹלָמוֹ וְאֵין עוֹלָמוֹ מְקוֹמוֹ. אָמַר רִבִּי יוּדָן לְגִיבּוֹר שֶׁהוּא רוֹכֵב עַל הַסּוּס וְכֵילָיו מְשׁוּפָּעִים הֵלַךְ הֵלַךְ לֹא שֶׁהַסּוּס סוֹבֵל אֶת הַגִּיבּוֹר אֶלָּא שֶׁהַגִּיבּוֹר הוּא סוֹבֵל אֶת הַסּוּס.

אָמַר רִבִּי אָחָא כְּתִיב יי חָפֵץ לְמַעַן צִדְקוֹ לְמַעַן צִדְקוֹ לְמַעַן צַדֶּקְךָ בִּשְׁבִיל לְזַכּוֹתָךְ אֲמַרְתִּיהָ לָךְ.

זבינו להשלים בשלום נזכה ונחיה להשלים ללמד וללמד את כל ש' סדרי משנה בשלום אמן

ברוך יי לעולם אמן ואמן ברוך שם כבוד מלכותו לעולם ועד]

[65]["Rebbi Ḥananiah ben Aqashiah says: *The Holy One, praise to Him, wanted* etc." Why does one use a substitute name for the Name of the Holy One, praise to Him, and calls Him Place? To say that He is the Place of the world but the world is not His place.

[66]Rebbi Ḥuna in the name of Rebbi Immi: It is written[67], *dwelling is the Primordial God*, to say that He is the dwelling of the world but the world is not His dwelling.

Rebbi Yose ben Ḥalaphta said, it is written: [68]*The Eternal said, there is a place with Me;* to say that He is the Place of the world but the world is not His place.

Rebbi Isaac said, it is written[69]: *The Eternal is there, Sinai in the Holy.* Would "the Holy in Sinai" not have been more reasonable? To say that He is the Place of the world but the world is not His place.

[70]Rebbi Yudan said, [a parable of] a hero riding on a horse with his weapons hanging down at both sides. It is not that the horse puts up with the hero, but the hero puts up with the horse.

Rebbi Aḥa said[64], *the Eternal desires for the sake of His justice*. For His justice? In order to justify you! In order to give merit to you I told it to you[71].

[72]We had the merit to finish in peace. May we be worthy and live to finish studying and teaching all six orders of the Mishnah in peace, Amen.
Praise to the Eternal forever, Amen and Amen[73]. Praise to the Name of the glory of His Kingdom forever and ever[74].]

65 This Halakhah is preserved only in G, but it is quoted in the name of the Yerushalmi in the book האמונה והבטחון "Faith and Trust" from the cabbalistic circle of Nachmanides [Chapter 15; in H. D. Chavel's edition of *The Works of Nachmanides*, vol. 2 (Jerusalem 1964) p.399.] Parallel texts are in *Gen. rabba* 68(10), copied in *Yalqut Shimony* 117, and *Pesiqta rabbati Ten Commandments* (ed. Ish-Shalom p. 104b). It is of great theological significance in that it proclaims not only God's Omnipresence but also His Existence outside of space and time and the possibility of the simultaneous existence of an infinity of different worlds.

66 In *Gen. rabba* and *Pesiqta*, they are credited with the statement of the preceding paragraph. "Faith and Trust" quotes the text here.

67 *Deut.* 33:27. In *Gen. rabba* and *Pesiqta* quoted by R. Isaac.

68 *Ex.* 33:21. In *Gen. rabba* and *Pesiqta* quoted by R. Huna, R. Immi but *Yalqut* R. Yose ben Halafta.

69 *Ps.* 68:18. In *Gen. rabba* quoted by R. Isaac; anonymous in *Pesiqta*, missing in *Yalqut*. In *Emunah weBittahon* R. [ ] in the name of R. Jacob.

70 In *Gen. rabba* in the name of R. Abba bar Yudan, in *Pesiqta* more elaborated, in the name of R. Yudan, anonymous in *Yalqut*.

71 The context in *Is.* makes it clear that צִדְקוֹ should not be translated as in the homiletic use of the verse "His justice" but "his justification" referring to God's servant.

72 The Colophon of the scribe, not part of the Talmud text.

73 *Ps.* 89:53.

74 The required eulogy after the recitation of *Deut.* 6:4.

Introduction to Tractate Horaiot

Tractate Horaiot is an appendix to the Order *Neziqin*; its arguments mostly are more appropriate for the Fifth Order, *Qodashim*. In the introductory part of *Leviticus*, containing the rules of private sacrifices, the rules for private purification offerings (*Lev*. 4:27-35), discussed at length in Tractate *Zevaḥim*, are preceded by rules for the official purification offerings of the anointed High Priest (4:1-12), the Synhedrion as representatives of the people (4:13-21), and the Prince (4:22-26). They are followed by the rules of public or private purification offerings for compromising Temple purity (5:1-13); the same rules apply to private offerings for unintended breaches of obligations affirmed by oaths. The detailed explanation of the rules preceding and following those for private purification offerings are the topic of *Horaiot*. The discussion of the rules for the High Court which became aware that it had ruled wrongly in a practical case can qualify as appendix to *Sanhedrin*, those of atonement for breaches of oaths as appendix to *Ševuot*.

The conditions which trigger the obligations for these sacrifices and their consequences are treated in the first two Chapters, with special emphasis on the implications of erroneous High Court rulings on individuals in the first and breaches of Temple purity in the second Chapters. The third Chapter starts by noting that in *Lev*. 4:1-12 the High Priest is called the Anointed Priest. It is inferred from *Ex*. 30:34 that the only person empowered to compound the anointing oil was Moses. The High Priests of the Second Temple were invested, not anointed; the rules of *Lev*. 4:1-12 did not apply to them. Similarly, the rules for the Prince did apply only those who were kings with divine (prophetic) sanction. The rules for the *Sanhedrin* apply only to the High Court sitting in the Temple compound. Therefore, it is likely that the only part of the discussion of the first two Chapters which refers to practices in force during the Second Temple period were the rules developed in interpretation of *Lev*. 5:1-13.

Most of the third Chapter is devoted to the rules of precedence in religious ceremonies. These rules are of practical importance. The Tractate closes with a homily in praise of the study of Torah.

In addition to the Leiden ms., the text of the Tractate was printed, from a different source, in the original Venice edition of the Babli. This is treated as a separate source and its (sometimes superior) readings are noted in the text. The text is much shorter than the Leiden text since as a rule it does not copy passages which appear elsewhere in the Yerushalmi; it only contains remarks which direct the reader to the parallel occurrences, and also is lacunary at other places. In later editions the text was completed (and otherwise changed) following the Venice print of the Yerushalmi; these texts cannot be used as independent sources. For a small part of Chapter Three there also exists a Genizah fragment. The text from the Babli is noted B if there are other texts to be considered; otherwise its readings are noted following the quotes from the Leiden text without indication of the source.

הורו בית דין פרק ראשון

(fol. 45c) **משנה א:** הוֹרוּ בֵית דִּין לַעֲבוֹר עַל אַחַת מִכָּל־מִצְוֹת הָאֲמוּרוֹת בַּתּוֹרָה וְהָלַךְ הַיָּחִיד וְעָשָׂה שׁוֹגֵג עַל פִּיהֶם בֵּין שֶׁעָשׂוּ וְעָשָׂה עִמָּהֶן בֵּין שֶׁעָשׂוּ וְעָשָׂה אַחֲרֵיהֶן בֵּין שֶׁלֹּא עָשׂוּ וְעָשָׂה פָּטוּר מִפְּנֵי שֶׁתָּלָה בְבֵית דִּין. הוֹרוּ בֵית דִּין וְיָדַע אֶחָד מֵהֶן שֶׁטָּעוּ אוֹ תַלְמִיד שֶׁהוּא רָאוּי לְהוֹרָיָה וְהָלַךְ וְעָשָׂה עַל פִּיהֶם בֵּין שֶׁעָשׂוּ וְעָשָׂה עִמָּהֶם בֵּין שֶׁעָשׂוּ וְעָשָׂה אַחֲרֵיהֶם בֵּין שֶׁלֹּא עָשׂוּ וְעָשָׂה הֲרֵי זֶה חַיָּיב מִפְּנֵי שֶׁלֹּא תָלָה בְבֵית דִּין. זֶה הַכְּלָל הַתּוֹלֶה בְעַצְמוֹ חַיָּיב וְהַתּוֹלֶה בְבֵית דִּין פָּטוּר:

Mishnah 1: If the Court[1] ruled to violate one of the commandments spelled out in the Torah[2] and a single person went and acted inadvertently[3] following their pronouncement, whether they acted and he acted simultaneously with them, or they acted and he followed their example, or they did not act but he did, he is not liable[4] since he depended on the Court. If the Court ruled but one of them knew that they erred, or a student worthy of ordination[5] went and acted following their pronouncement, whether they acted and he acted simultaneously with them, or they acted and he followed their example, or they did not act but he did, he is liable[4] since he did not depend on the Court. This is the principle: The person depending on himself is liable[6], but one depending on the Court is not liable.

1 The High Court.

2 A commandment clearly spelled out, like the prohibition of eating blood, where the biblical text does not imply an authorization of the rabbinical authorities to define the parameters of the obligation.

3 When the Court realized its error and changed its ruling, the person acting in good faith on their prior ruling is now faced with the fact that his act violated a biblical commandment, against his intention.

4 For a purification sacrifice (*Lev.* 4:27-35) or, in the absence of a Temple, repentance and an expiatory action.

5 He knows how to answer when asked any question of religious law.

6 This rule, which declares that no instruction of the High Court supersedes one's own certain knowledge, does not contradict the law of the rebellious Elder (*Sanhedrin* Chapter 8) since by definition the rebellious Elder came to ask the High Court; in the matter he came to ask, his knowledge is not independent of the Court.

(45c line 59) **הלכה א**: הורו בֵית דִין כול'. נֶפֶשׁ כִּי־תֶחֱטָא. אַחַת תֶּחֱטָא. בַּעֲשׂוֹתָהּ תֶּחֱטָא. הֲרֵי אֵילּוּ מִיעוּטִין. הַתּוֹלֶה בְעַצְמוֹ חַייָב וְהַתּוֹלֶה בְבֵית דִּין פָּטוּר: בְּכָל־אַתַר אַתְּ מַר. מִיעוּט אַחַר מִיעוּט לְרַבּוֹת. וְכָא אַתְּ מַר. מִיעוּט אַחַר מִיעוּט לְמָעֵט. אָמַר רִבִּי מַתַּנְיָה. שַׁנְייָא הִיא. דִּכְתִיב מִיעוּט אַחַר מִיעוּט אַחַר מִיעוּט.

1 כי | - 2 והתולה | - את מר | איתמר 3 את מר | איתמר שנייא | שניה 4 אחר } לאחר (2 times)

Halakhah 1: [7]"If the Court ruled." etc. *A person who would transgress; one would transgress; acting he would transgress*; these are restrictions[8]: the person depending on himself is liable, but one dependent on the Court is not liable. Everywhere it is said that a restriction after a restriction is an addition, but here it is said, a restriction after a restriction is to reduce? Rebbi Mattaniah said, it is different here since there is written a restriction after a restriction after a restriction[9].

7 The text is that of the Leiden ms., the readings are those of the Yerushalmi text in the Bomberg Babli of 1520.

8 The quotes are correct in the Yerushalmi text of the Babli *editio princeps*, but the first of the quotes in the Leiden ms. is a misquote, referring to *Lev.* 4:2 instead of 4:27. The basic text is in *Sifra Wayyiqra Parašah* 7(1), referred to in Babli 2b, discussed in detail *Šabbat* 93a.

Chapter 4 in *Lev.* treats the purification sacrifices for unintentional sin first by the High Priest (vv. 1-12), then the High Court (13-21), then a chief, identified in Mishnah 3:3 as a king (22-26), and finally by a commoner (27-35). V. 27 reads: *If one person of the populace transgresses inadvertently, by acting on one prohibitions of the Eternal, and feels guilt.* It is noted that the sentence seems to be unnecessarily wordy. Why does it not say simply, "if somebody inadvertently transgresses a prohibition of the Eternal"? The additional words must have a meaning; they describe restrictions. In Babli *Šabbat* 93a one derives from the insistence that *one* person commit the sin that a violation of a commandment cannot be prosecuted if committed by two persons acting in common, so that no single person commits a punishable act but the combined result is a clear violation,. Such a violation cannot be atoned for by a purification sacrifice. It also is clear that only *acts* are punishable.

In the context here the additional terms are interpreted to mean that only a person acting on his own is required to offer a purification sacrifice; this excludes one who is told by a religious authority that his act is permitted.

9 It is a generally recognized principle that a double restriction is an addition and a double addition a restriction (*Peah* 6:9 Note 154, *Yebamot* 12:1 Note 10, *Sotah* 9:2 Note 63, *Roš Haššanah* 1:1 56a l.58, *Megillah* 4:4 75b l.14; Babli *Megillah* 23b, *Yoma* 43a, *Bava qamma* 15b, *Bava*

batra 15a, *Sanhedrin* 15a,44b,66a, *Makkot* 9b, *Ševuot* 7b, *Menahot* 9b,67a, *Hulin* 132a.) The principle is extended here to read that any even number of restrictions (additions) is an addition (restriction) while any odd number of restrictions (additions) is a restriction (addition); cf. Rashi in *Sanhedrin* 15a *s. v.* חמשה.

(45c line 63) רִבִּי חַגַּיי שָׁאַל לַחֲבֵרַייָה. מְנַיִין לָאוֹכֵל בִּרְשׁוּת שֶׁהוּא פָטוּר. מַה בֵּין סָבוּר שֶׁהוּא חוּלִין וְנִמְצֵאת תְּרוּמָה שֶׁהוּא חַייָב. מַה בֵּין הַמַּחֲזִיק בְּעַצְמוֹ שֶׁהוּא כֹהֵן וְנִמְצָא יִשְׂרָאֵל שֶׁהוּא פָּטוּר. אָֽמְרִין לֵיהּ. מִן הוֹרָיוֹת בֵּית דִּין. אָמַר לוֹן. אוּף אֲנָא צְרִיכָה לִי. מַה בֵּין סָבוּר שֶׁהוּא חוֹל וְנִמְצֵאת שַׁבָּת שֶׁהוּא חַייָב. מַה בֵּין סָבוּר שֶׁהוּא פֶסַח וְנִמְצָא שְׁלָמִים שֶׁהוּא פָטוּר. אָֽמְרִין לֵיהּ. מִן הַשּׁוֹחֵט בִּרְשׁוּת. אָמַר לוֹן. אוּף אֲנָא צְרִיכָה לִי. מַה בֵּין סָבוּר שֶׁהוּא מוּתָּר וְנִמְצָא אָסוּר שֶׁהוּא חַייָב. מַה בֵּין סָבוּר שֶׁהוּא חֵלֶב וְנִמְצָא שׁוּמָּן שֶׁהוּא פָטוּר. לֹא אָֽמְרוּ לֵיהּ כְּלוּם. אָמַר לוֹן. נֵימָא לְכוֹן מִינָּן. אוֹ הוֹדַע אֵלָיו חַטָּאתוֹ וְהֵבִיא. אָעַל רִבִּי יוֹסֵי. אָֽמְרִין לֵיהּ. קַשְׁי לוֹן הָדָא מִילְּתָא. אָמַר לוֹן. וְלָמָּה לָא אַגִּיבְתּוֹנֵיהּ מִן הָדָא אוֹ הוֹדַע אֵלָיו חַטָּאתוֹ וְהֵבִיא. אָֽמְרִין לֵיהּ. חַגַּיי קַשְׁיתָהּ חַגַּיי קַייְמָתָהּ.

1 חגיי | חגי לחברייא | לחבריא מניין | מנין 3 אמרין | אמרון הוריות | הורית אוף | אף 4 אמרין | אמרון 6 אמרו | אמרון 7 נימא לכון מינן | נמר לכון אנן אעל | על דעתיה ר' | דר' אמרין | אמרון 8 הדא | הא אגיבתוניה | אגבתוני 9 קיימתה | קיימה

[10]Rebbi Ḥaggai asked the colleagues: From where that he who eats with permission be not liable[11]? What is the difference between him[12] who thought that it was profane but it turned out to be heave, who is liable, and him who thought that he was a Cohen but it turned out that he was an Israel, who is not liable[13]? They said to him, by the instruction of the court. He said to them, still I am having a problem. What is the difference between him who thought that it was weekday but it turned out that it was Sabbath[14], who is liable, and him who thought that it was a Passover sacrifice but it turned out to be a well-being offering, who is not liable[15]. They said to him, because he slaughtered with permission. He said to them, still I am having a problem. What is the difference between him who thought that it was permitted but it turned out to be forbidden[15], who is liable, and him who thought that it was forbidden fat[16] and it turned out to be permitted fat, who is not liable. They did not answer at all. He told them, let me tell you from myself[17]: *Or his transgression in which he sinned was made known to him; he has to bring*[18]. Rebbi Yossi came to visit them; they told him, that problem is hard for us. He asked them, why did you not answer him, *or his transgression in which he*

sinned was made known to him; he has to bring? They told him, Ḥaggai asked the question, Ḥaggai gave the answer.

10 This paragraph has a parallel in *Terumot* 8:1, Notes 14-22. As explained there, the background of the paragraph in *Terumot* is different from the one presumed here; therefore at a place where the readings there and here seem to be opposite to one another, both are correct in their settings.

11 Referring to Mishnah *Terumot* 8:1; a childless woman of non-priestly birth, married to a Cohen, was eating heave in purity, as is her right and duty, when she was informed of her husband's death. By this death she returns to her non-priestly status and heave is forbidden to her. Nevertheless, she is not liable for a reparation sacrifice nor to pay for the heave eaten in error. This is the topic of *Terumot* 8:1, it is not followed up here.

12 An Israel to whom heave is forbidden, Mishnah *Terumot* 6:1.

13 He had been told from childhood that he was a Cohen; he was stripped of his priesthood by a court on the testimony of two witnesses that one of his female ancestors had been forbidden to her Cohen husband. His case is not different from that of the woman in Note 12.

14 This is a paradigm of an inadvertent sin as mentioned in *Lev*. 4:27.

15 Cf. *Terumot* 8:1, Note 18. The Passover sacrifice must be slaughtered in the afternoon of the 14th of Nisan, whether Sabbath or weekday. A festival well-being offering may not be slaughtered on the Sabbath. If the 14th was a Sabbath and somebody slaughtered a sheep in the Temple courtyard thinking that it was a designated Passover sacrifice when in fact it had been designated as a well-being offering, R. Joshua, an overriding authority, declares him not liable (Mishnah *Pesaḥim* 6:4).

16 Fat of animals which would be burned on the altar if these animals were sacrifices, and the fat into which ischiatic tendons are embedded, is forbidden for human consumption. All other fat is permitted. If a person intended to commit a sin but, unknown to him at the time, failed to commit the sin, he is not liable for a purification sacrifice.

17 Translated using the Bomberg Babli text.

18 *Lev*. 4:28. Since he was informed that he failed to commit the sin, he cannot bring a purification sacrifice. His repentance for his sinful intent will be a private matter between him and God.

(45c line 75) עַל דַּעְתֵּיהּ דְּרִבִּי יִשְׁמָעֵאל דְּלָא מַפְנֶה אָהֵן קִרְייָה בִּמְחוּייָבֵי חַטָּאוֹת וַאֲשָׁמוֹת וַדָּאִין שֶׁעָבַר עֲלֵיהֶן יוֹם הַכִּיפּוּרִים נִיחָא. עַל דַּעְתֵּיהּ דְּרִבִּי עֲקִיבָה דְּמַפְנֶה אָהֵן קִרְייָה בִּמְחוּייָבֵי חַטָּאוֹת וַאֲשָׁמוֹת וַדָּאִין שֶׁעָבַר עֲלֵיהֶן יוֹם הַכִּיפּוּרִים. דְּתַנֵּי. מְנַיִין לִמְחוּייָבֵי חַטָּאוֹת וַאֲשָׁמוֹת וַדָּאִין שֶׁעָבַר עֲלֵיהֶן יוֹם הַכִּיפּוּרִים שֶׁהֵן חַייָבִין לְהָבִיא לְאַחַר יוֹם הַכִּיפּוּרִים וְחַייָבֵי אֲשָׁמוֹת

תְּלוּיִין פְּטוּרִין. תַּלְמוּד לוֹמַר אוֹ הוֹדַע אֵלָיו חַטָּאתוֹ וְהֵבִיא. אַף לְאַחַר יוֹם הַכִּיפּוּרִים. מִן הָדָא. נֶפֶשׁ כִּי־תֶחֱטָא. אַחַת תֶּחֱטָא. בַּעֲשׂוֹתָהּ. הֲרֵי אֵילּוּ מִיעוּטִין. הַתּוֹלֶה בְעַצְמוֹ חַיָּב. הַתּוֹלֶה בְבֵית דִּין פָּטוּר:

1 קרייה | קריה במחוייבי | במחויבי חטאות ואשמות וודאין | אשמות וחטאות ודיין 2 דמפנה | דו מפנה אהן קרייה במחוייבי חטאות ואשמות וודאין | קריה במחויבי אשמות וחטאות ודיין 3 למחוייבי חטאות ואשמות וודאין | למחויבי אשמות וחטאות ודיין 5 תלויין | תלוין 6 כי | - אחת תחטא | - אילו מיעוטין | אלו מעוטין

In the opinion of Rebbi Ismael, who does not refer this verse to those obligated for purification sacrifices and certain reparation sacrifices for whom the Day of Atonement had passed, it is understandable[19]. But what is the opinion of Rebbi Aqiba, who refers this verse to those obligated for purification sacrifices and certain reparation sacrifices for whom the Day of Atonement had passed, as we have stated[20]: From where that those obligated for purification sacrifices and certain reparation sacrifices for whom the Day of Atonement had passed, are obligated to bring them after the Day of Atonement, but those obligated for suspended reparation offerings are no longer liable? The verse says[18], *or his transgression in which he sinned was made known to him; he has to bring*, even after the Day of Atonement. [21]From the following: *A person who would transgress; one would transgress; acting he would transgress*; these are restrictions[8]: the person depending on himself is liable, {but one dependent}[9] on the Court is not liable.

19 This paragraph has no direct connection with the theme of the Mishnah, but is added here to elucidate *Lev.* 4:27. Since our halakhic Midrashim are all from the school of R. Aqiba, we have to accept the occasional indications of the Yerushalmi on the interpretations of the school of R. Ismael. For him, the verses 4:27-28 detail the conditions on which a private person is permitted and obligated to bring a purification offering.

20 Mishnah *Keritut* 6:4; *Sifra Wayyiqra 2 Paršetah* 3(1), 6(1), *Ahare Mot Parašah* 4(8).

Reparation sacrifices are required (1) for sins against a fellow man after restitution (*Lev.* 5:20-26; *Num.* 5:5-10), (2) misappropriation of *sancta* (*Lev.* 5:14-16), (3) to regain sanctified status after skin disease (*Lev.* 14). A *suspended* reparation sacrifice is due if a person suspects that he may have committed an inadvertent sin, without having proof either way. Since the sin is forgiven on the Day of Atonement (with due repentance), such a sacrifice cannot be offered after that day since the scapegoat carries away *all* iniquities (*Lev.* 16:21).

21 This copy from the first paragraph has no discernible meaning here.

אֵין חַייָבִין אֶלָּא עַל דָּבָר שֶׁהָיָה גָלוּי לָהֶן וְנִכְסֶה מֵהֶן. וּמַה טַעַם. וְנֶעְלַם דָּבָר. דָּבָר שֶׁהָיָה גָלוּי לָהֶן וְנִכְסֶה מֵהֶן. עַל דַּעְתֵּיהּ דְּרִבִּי יִשְׁמָעֵאל דּוּ אָמַר. וְנֶעְלַם מִמֶּנּוּ. מִכְּלָל שֶׁהָיָה יוֹדֵעַ. וְהוּא יָדַע. הֲרֵי שְׁתֵּי יְדִיעוֹת. עַל דַּעְתֵּיהּ דְּרִבִּי עֲקִיבָה דּוּ אָמַר. וְנֶעְלַם מִמֶּנּוּ וְנֶעְלַם מִמֶּנּוּ שְׁנֵי פְעָמִים. מִכְּלָל שֶׁבָּאת לוֹ יְדִיעָה בַּתְּחִילָּה וִידִיעָה בְסוֹף וְהֶעֱלֵם בֵּינְתַיִים. תַּלְמוּד לוֹמַר וְנֶעְלַם מִמֶּנּוּ. דָּבָר שֶׁהָיָה גָלוּי לָהֶן וְנִכְסֶה מֵהֶן.

1 ונכסה | ומכוסה ומה טעם. ונעלם דבר. דבר שהיה גלוי להן ונכסה מהן | - 4 שבאת לו | שהיתה 5 מהן | מהם

[22]They only are liable[23] for something[24] that was clear to them and then covered from them[25]. What is the reason? *something was hidden*[26], something that was clear to them and then hidden from them. [27]In the opinion of Rebbi Ismael who said, *it became hidden from him*, therefore he had known, *and he knew*[28], these are two knowledges[29]. In the opinion of Rebbi Aqiba who said, *it became hidden*, *it became hidden*, two times[30], therefore he had knowledge at the beginning and knowledge at the end and oblivion in between, [31]something that was clear to them and then hidden from them.

22 Here one returns to a discussion of the theme of the Tractate, *viz.*, the obligation of the High Court, as representatives of the people, to offer a purification sacrifice for a wrong ruling as described in *Lev*. 4:13-21.

It is sinful to bring an animal into the Temple precinct which is not dedicated as a sacrifice. For voluntary offerings this presents no problem; one simply has to dedicate them when bringing. But for obligatory offerings it implies that a sacrifice may be presented only if all conditions which make it obligatory are actually fulfilled.

23 To bring the sacrifice.

24 An official ruling by the Court.

25 They forgot either a precedent or their own ruling.

26 *Lev*. 4:13. An erring High Priest (*Lev*. 4:1-12) or ruler (22-26) have to offer a sacrifice if they err inadvertently; the condition that a ruling must have been forgotten is introduced only for the Court.

27 There is no problem with the explanation just given. One tries to connect the statement with a discussion about similar rules regarding sacrifices due for violations of either Temple purity or oaths (*Lev*. 5:1-13), where the same condition in mentioned in *Lev*. 5:2,3,4. R. Ismael and R. Aqiba differ in *Ševuot* 1:2 about the interpretation of the verses, but not about the actual rules.

28 *Lev*. 5:4: . . . *an oath which a man would utter without thinking, it became hidden from him, and he knew and realized his guilt* . . .

29 One when he uttered the oath and one when he remembered it, separated by a period of oblivion.

30 R. Aqiba and R. Ismael actually are not differing in their interpretations; only R. Aqiba argues about violations of

Temple purity (*Lev.* 5:2-3) where in both verses oblivion is mentioned but not remembering. However, in Babylonian sources [*Ševuot* 14b, *Keritut* 19a, *Sifra Wayyiqra 2, Pereq* 12(7)], R. Ismael is reported to read one about oblivion the impurity and the second oblivion about being in the Temple.

31 Returning to our topic, Note 22.

(45d line 19) אֵין חַייָבִין עַד שֶׁיּוֹרוּ לְבַטֵּל מִקְצָת וּלְקַייֵם מִקְצָת. שְׁמוּאֵל אָמַר. וְהֵן שֶׁהוֹרוּ מוּתָּר. אֲבָל אִם הוֹרוּ פָּטוּר לֹא בְדָא. אֵין חַייָבִין עַד שֶׁתְּהֵא הוֹרָייָה מִלִּשְׁכַּת הַגָּזִית. אָמַר רִבִּי יוֹחָנָן. טַעֲמֵיהּ דְּהַדְּ תַּנָּייָא מִן־הַמָּקוֹם הַהוּא אֲשֶׁר יִבְחַר יְי. אָמַר רִבִּי מָנָא בַּר תַּנְחוּם. נִכְנְסוּ מֵאָה. עַד שֶׁיּוֹרוּ כוּלָּן. תַּמָּן אָמַר רִבִּי זְעִירָא. וְהוּא שֶׁיְּהוּא כוּלָּן מוֹרִין מִצַּד אֶחָד. וָכָא מַה.

1 שהורו | שהן 2 שתהא הורייה | שתבוא הוריה 3 דהך תנייא | דההן תנייה מנא | מונא 4 שיהוא | שהיו וכא מה | והכא אמר כן

They are not liable unless they void part and confirm part[32]. Samuel said, only if they ruled that it was permitted; but not if they ruled that it was not prosecutable[33]. They are not liable unless instruction was given from the ashlar hall[34]. Rebbi Johanan said, the reason of this Tanna: *From that place which the Eternal will choose*[35]. Rebbi Mana bar Tanhum said, if a hundred came together, only if they ruled unanimously[36]. There[37], Rebbi Ze`ira said, only if they all rule for the same reason. And here, what[38]?

32 If they declared a biblical prohibition as void, nobody would follow them since even schoolchildren would know that this is wrong. But if they were to abolish traditional restrictions, they would be followed. This is explicit in Mishnah 3; cf. Babli 4a, Tosephta 1:7, *Sifra Wayyiqra 2, Parašah* 4(7).

33 This is a commentary on the preceding sentence. Abolishing a biblical commandment entirely means declaring the prohibition as void; declaring it valid but unenforceable means partly confirming it.

34 The seat of the High Court; *Sanhedrin* Chapter 1, Note 345.

35 *Deut.* 17:10.

36 The ruling triggers the obligation of a purification sacrifice only if it was unanimous, including the opinions of the law students sitting before the 72 members of the Court. Mishnah 4 requires in addition that the president of the court be present and voting [Babli 4b, *Sifra Wayyiqra 2, Parašah* 4(4).]

37 *Sanhedrin* 1:2, Note 166. He holds that a ruling of the High Court to intercalate a month based on the testimony of laymen is valid only if it not only is unanimous in fact but also in reason. Concurrent opinions, reaching the same conclusion for different reasons, invalidate the judgment. Why is this not mentioned here? The text confirms the reading of the ms. in *Roš Haššanah* (2:6 58b l.25) against the one in Sanhedrin.

38 B has the usual formula, "and here he says so?"

(45d line 19) הָלַךְ הַיָּחִיד וְעָשָׂה שׁוֹגֵג עַל פִּיהֶן. וְכִי יֵשׁ זְדוֹן שְׁגָגָה לְיָחִיד אֶצֶל הוֹרָיַית בֵּית דִּין. רִבִּי אִימִּי בְשֵׁם רִבִּי שִׁמְעוֹן בֶּן לָקִישׁ. מַתְנִיתָא כְּגוֹן שִׁמְעוֹן בֶּן עַזַּאי יוֹשֵׁב לִפְנֵיהֶן. מָה אֲנָן קַייָמִין. אִם בְּיוֹדֵעַ כָּל־הַתּוֹרָה וְאֵינוֹ יוֹדֵעַ אוֹתוֹ דָּבָר אֵין זֶה שִׁמְעוֹן בֶּן עַזַּאי. וְאִם בְּיוֹדֵעַ אוֹתוֹ דָּבָר וְאֵינוֹ יוֹדֵעַ כָּל־הַתּוֹרָה שִׁמְעוֹן בֶּן עַזַּאי הוּא אֶצֶל אוֹתוֹ דָּבָר. אֶלָּא כִּי נָן קַייָמִין בְּיוֹדֵעַ כָּל־הַתּוֹרָה וּבְיוֹדֵעַ אוֹתוֹ דָּבָר. אֶלָּא שֶׁהוּא כְטוֹעֶה לוֹמַר. הַתּוֹרָה אָמְרָה אַחֲרֵיהֶם אַחֲרֵיהֶם. וְאִם בְּטוֹעֶה לוֹמַר הַתּוֹרָה אָמְרָה אַחֲרֵיהֶם אַחֲרֵיהֶם. אֵין זֶה שִׁמְעוֹן בֶּן עַזַּאי. כְּהָדָא דְתַנֵּי. יָכוֹל אִם יֹאמְרוּ לָךְ עַל יְמִין שֶׁהִיא שְׂמֹאל וְעַל שְׂמֹאל שֶׁהִיא יְמִין תִּשְׁמַע לָהֶם. תַּלְמוּד לוֹמַר לָלֶכֶת יָמִין וּשְׂמֹאל. שֶׁיֹּאמְרוּ לָךְ עַל יָמִין שֶׁהוּא יָמִין וְעַל שְׂמֹאל שֶׁהִיא שְׂמֹאל. מַאי כְדוֹן. רִבִּי יוֹסֵי בְשֵׁם רִבִּי הִילָא. לְפִי שֶׁבְּכָל־מָקוֹם שׁוֹגֵג פָּטוּר וּמֵזִיד חַייָב. וְכָא אֲפִילוּ מֵזִיד פָּטוּר. מִפְּנֵי שֶׁתָּלָה בְּבֵית דִּין.

1 הוריית | הורית 2 אימי | אמי מתני' | מתניא 3 התורה | התורה כולה 4 אלא | ואלא 5 וביודע | ויודע כטועה | טועה 5-6 אחריהם | אחריהן (x 4) 7 תשמע | שתשמע 8 שיאמרו | עד שיאמרו שהוא | שהיא 9 הילא | לא

"And a single person went and acted inadvertently[3] following their pronouncement." Is there an intentional inadvertent action concerning an instruction by the Court[39]? Rebbi Immi in the name of Rebbi Simeon ben Laqish: Our Mishnah, for example, if Simeon ben Azzai[40] was sitting before them. Where do we hold? If he knows the entire Torah but does not know this detail, he is not Simeon ben Azzai. If he knows this particular subject but not the entire Torah, he is Simeon ben Azzai for this particular subject. But we must hold that he knows the entire Torah and knows the particular subject, but he errs to believe that the Torah said, after them, after them[41]. If he errs to believe that the Torah said, after them, after them, he is not Simeon ben Azzai. As we have stated, I could think that if they tell you about right that it is left, and about left that it is right, you should listen to them? The verse says, "to go to the right or to the left;[42]" that they should tell you about the right that it is right, and about the left that it is left [43]. What about it[44]? Rebbi Yose in the name of Rebbi Hila: Because everywhere for an inadvertent sin one is not liable but for an intentional one is liable, and here even intentionally he is not liable[45].

39 The formulation of the Mishnah does not make any sense. The person who follows the instructions of the Court does

this intentionally; how can he be inadvertent?

40 The paradigm of the know-all; he was ready to answer any question about religious law on the spot. The Babli knows of a number of famous rabbis who tried to imitate him but quickly were confronted with a question they could not answer. He never was ordained; therefore he could not have been part of the Court, but as an outsider he could have pointed out the Court's error.

41 This is the expression which R. Jehudah ben Bathyra used to convince Hanania ben Hanania, the foremost authority in Babylonia, to accept the overriding authority of the patriarch's court in Palestine (*Nazir* 6:13, Note 128; *Sanhedrin* 1:2, p. 36).

42 A misquote of *Deut.* 17:11.

43 This is the opposite of the teachings of *Sifry Deut.* 154, *Cant. rabba* 1(18), which require one to follow the instructions of the rabbis even if they tell him to believe that left is right. Sound methodology would require one to follow the Talmud in preference to Midrashim. The *Sifry* text seems to be formulated as a polemic against the Yerushalmi.

44 Since the first explanation of the Mishnah was found to be untenable, what would be a reasonable explanation?

45 *Any* action following the wrong teachings of the High Court has the status of unintended action even if it was intended. "Liable" and "not liable" here refer to criminal responsibility, not to obligations to offer sacrifices.

(45d line 31) חֲבֵרַייָא בְשֵׁם שְׁמוּאֵל. יָחִיד מַשְׁלִים לְרוֹב הַצִּיבּוּר הִיא מַתְנִיתָא. אֲבָל כָּל־יָחִיד וְיָחִיד שֶׁעָשָׂה בִפְנֵי עַצְמוֹ פָּטוּר. אָמַר רִבִּי יוֹחָנָן אֲפִילוּ כָּל־יָחִיד וְיָחִיד שֶׁעָשָׂה בִפְנֵי עַצְמוֹ מֵבִיא כִשְׂבָּה וּשְׂעִירָה. וְקַשְׁיָא עַל דַּעְתֵּיהּ דִּשְׁמוּאֵל לֹא נִמְצָא כָּל־יָחִיד וְיָחִיד מִתְכַּפֵּר לוֹ בִשְׁנֵי חַטָּאוֹת. רִבִּי זְעִירָא בְשֵׁם שְׁמוּאֵל. הַיָּחִיד תָלוּי. אָכְלוּ רוֹב. בֵּית דִּין מְבִיאִין. אָכְלוּ מִיעוּט. הַיָּחִיד מֵבִיא. כָּל־הַהוֹרָייָה שֶׁבֵּית דִּין פָּר אֵין הַיָּחִיד מֵבִיא כִשְׂבָּה וּשְׂעִירָה.

1 חברייא | חבריא יחיד | ויחיד 2 ויחיד | - 3 בשני | בשתי 5 ההורייה | הוריה פר | מביאין פר ושעירה | וכל הוריה שב"ד אין מביאין פר היחיד מביא כשבה או שעירה שמואל פתר מתניתא ברוב ומיעוט אכלו רוב הואיל ואין ב"ד מביאי' פר היחיד מביא כשב' או שעיר'

The colleagues in the name of Samuel. The Mishnah deals with an individual who complements the multitude[46]. But any individual who acted on his own is not liable[47]. Rebbi Joḥanan said, even any single individual who acted on his own brings a female sheep or goat[48]. It is difficult. In Samuel's opinion, would any single individual be atoned by two sacrifices[49]? Rebbi Ze`ira in the name of Samuel: The individual is suspended[50]. If a majority ate, the court brings. If a minority ate, each individual brings. For any ruling for which the court [bring] a bull, the individual does not bring a female sheep or goat[51].

[52]For any ruling for which the court bring a bull, the individual does not bring a female sheep; for any ruling for which the court does not bring a bull, the individual brings a female sheep or goat. Samuel explains the Mishnah by majority and minority. If a majority ate[53], since the court does not bring a bull, an individual brings a female sheep or goat.

46 As explained at the end of the paragraph (Babli 2b in the name of R. Jehudah). His problem with the prior explanation is that it does not fit the setting of the Mishnah. Since we are referring to sacrifices, the inadvertent sinner, while he is immune to prosecution, is obligated to bring a purification sacrifice; the intentional sinner, who can be punished, is barred from bringing a sacrifice. Therefore, if one compares the intentional to the unintentional sinner, the opposite of the argument of R. Hila should be formulated. (In contrast to the Babli, the Yerushalmi does not care for chronological consistency; Samuel of the first generation opposes R. Hila of the third.)

47 Tosephta 1:2. If somebody acted in parallel with the ruling of the court but following his own interpretation of the biblical law, he is not liable for a purification sacrifice since in fact he is barred from offering one, and since he happened to act in parallel with the Court's ruling neither is he prosecutable. Both interpretations of פטור are possible here. There is no reason to change the text which is confirmed by the two Yerushalmi texts and the Tosephta.

48 Since acting on a faulty interpretation is qualified as acting in error, which for an individual requires the offering of a female sheep or goat (Note 51).

49 Since, as is explained next, Samuel makes the Court's offering dependent on whether a majority of the people acted on their instructions or not, it could be that after a number of individuals brought their own sacrifices it turns out that in the end a majority forces the Court to bring its own. But there cannot be more than one sacrifice for one infraction. Since the purification offering is eaten by the priests, it cannot be retroactively nullified.

50 The problem raised in the previous Note cannot occur. The individuals are prevented from bringing their own sacrifices until the situation is cleared.

51 *Lev.* 27:35.

52 Translation of the text of B, expanding the last sentence of the Leiden ms.

53 Referring to the standard example, that the Court allowed some forbidden fat (Note 14) to be eaten.

(45d line 42) רִבִּי יוֹחָנָן פָּתַר מַתְנִיתָא בְּהוֹרָיַית בֵּית דִּין. הוֹרוּ בֵית דִּין לַעֲקוֹר אֶת כָּל־הַגּוּף. הוֹאִיל וּבֵית דִּין מְבִיאִין פָּר אֵין הַיָּחִיד מֵבִיא כִשְׂבָּה וּשְׂעִירָה. הוֹרוּ לְבַטֵּל מִקְצָת וּלְקַייֵם מִקְצָת. הוֹאִיל וְאֵין בֵּית דִּין מְבִיאִין פָּר הַיָּחִיד מֵבִיא כִשְׂבָּה וּשְׂעִירָה.

שְׁמוּאֵל אָמַר מַתְנִיתָא. אַדַּיִין אֲנִי אוֹמֵר. מִיעוּט הַקָּהָל שֶׁעָשׂוּ חַייָבִין שֶׁאֵין בֵּית דִּין מְבִיאִין עֲלֵיהֶן פָּר. תַּלְמוּד לוֹמַר עַם הָאָרֶץ. אֲפִילוּ כּוּלּוֹ. אֲפִילוּ רוּבּוֹ. רִבִּי יוֹחָנָן פָּתַר מַתְנִיתָא. אַדַּיִין אֲנִי אוֹמֵר. מִיעוּט הַקָּהָל שֶׁעָשׂוּ בְלֹא הוֹרָייָה חַייָבִין. שֶׁכֵּן בְּהוֹרָייָה אֵין בֵּית דִּין מְבִיאִין פָּר. שְׁמוּאֵל אָמַר. אֲבָל הֵן מְבִיאִין כִּשְׂבָּה וּשְׂעִירָה. רִבִּי יוֹחָנָן אָמַר. לֹא הֵן מְבִיאִין כִּשְׂבָּה וּשְׂעִירָה. עַל דַּעְתֵּיהּ דִּשְׁמוּאֵל דּוּ יְלִיף לָהּ חַייָב מֵחַייָב נִיחָא. עַל דַּעְתֵּיהּ דְּרִבִּי יוֹחָנָן דּוּ יְלִיף לָהּ חִיּוּב מִפְּטוֹר. מַתְנִיתָא אָמְרָה פְלִיגָא עַל שְׁמוּאֵל. אוֹ הוֹדַע אֵלָיו חַטָּאתוֹ אֲשֶׁר חָטָא וְהֵבִיא. יָצָא הַמְשׁוּמָּר. מַתְנִיתָא פְלִיגָא עַל שְׁמוּאֵל. נֶפֶשׁ כִּי־תֶחֱטָא. אַחַת תֶּחֱטָא. בַּעֲשׂוֹתָהּא. הֲרֵי אֵילּוּ מִיעוּטִין. הַתּוֹלֶה בְעַצְמוֹ חַייָב. הַתּוֹלֶה בְבֵית דִּין פָּטוּר׃ הָדָא פְלִיגָא עַל שְׁמוּאֵל וְלֵית לָהּ קִיּוּם.

1 בהוריית | בהורית 2 ושעירה | או שעירה 3 ושעירה | או שעירה 4 אמ' | פתר אדיין | אדין מיעוט | משם מיעוט 5 עליהן פר | פר עליהן כולו | מקצתו אפי' | ואפילו אדיין | אדין 6 הורייה | הוריה בית דין | - 7 הן | היו ושעירה | - 8 חייב מחייב | חיוב מחיוב על | אלא על 9 אמרה | - 10 משומר | משומד כי | -

Rebbi Joḥanan explains the Mishnah by instruction from the Court. If the Court ruled to eliminate the entire body, since the Court has to bring a bull a private person does not have to bring a female sheep or goat. If they ruled to confirm part and to eliminate part, since the Court does not bring a bull a private person has to bring a female sheep or goat[54].

Samuel spoke about the Mishnah: "I still am saying, if a minority acted they are liable because the Court will not bring a bull for them. The verse says[55], *[from] the people of the Land*. Even [all of them] (part of them)[56], even most of them." Rebbi Joḥanan explains the Mishnah: I still am saying, if a minority acted without ruling they are liable because with instruction the Court will not bring a bull[57]. Samuel said, but they bring a female sheep or goat. Rebbi Joḥanan said, they do not bring a female sheep or goat[58]. According to Samuel, who infers liability from liability, it is understandable. According to Rebbi Joḥanan, who infers liability from exemption[59]? The statement of a *baraita*[60] disagrees with Samuel. *Or his transgression in which he sinned was made known to him*[18]*;* this excludes the apostate. A *baraita* disagrees with Samuel, "*A person who would transgress; one would transgress; acting he would transgress*; these are restrictions[8]: the person depending on himself is liable, but one dependent on the Court is not liable." This disagrees with Samuel and cannot be confirmed[61].

54 Even though the text is confirmed by B, it cannot be accepted since Mishnah 3 explicitly states the opposite (Note 32), and R. Johanan does not disagree with an anonymous Mishnah. Therefore, one has to switch the place of the statements "bring" and "do not bring". He disagrees with Samuel in that he does not require that a majority of the people act upon the instructions of the Court. If a single person consciously commits a sin by acting upon their instruction, the individual is barred from bringing a sheep and the Court is required to bring a bull.

55 *Lev.* 4:27.

56 The text is a *baraita* in *Sifra Wayyiqra 2, Parašah* 7(5), quoted in the Babli, 2b. Usually, a prefix מ "from" is interpreted to mean "not all". This is behind the reading of B. The reading of the ms., in brackets, is that of *Sifra* and the Babli; it means that without instruction from the Court, any number of the people, maybe all except the members of the Court, may be required to bring private purification offerings simultaneously. This would not be a case that *all of the congregation of Israel err* (*Lev.* 4:13); this expression is reserved for pronouncements of the Court.

57 A person acting on the instructions of the Court can never bring a purification offering since his action is not inadvertent. If the conditions for such an offering by the Court are not satisfied, no sacrifice at all is due or possible for the action.

58 This is a repetition of their prior positions. For Samuel, a private offering is due if and only if there is no Court offering. For R. Johanan, no offering is possible for action on the instruction of the Court, independent of what the Court has or does not have to do.

59 Samuel is understandable; either the rules of the Court sacrifice or those of the private one do apply; never both together nor none of them. But might R. Johanan, who accepts a situation where both the individual and the Court are exempted from bringing an offering, have a situation where both apply simultaneously? The question is not answered.

60 *Sifra Sifra Wayyiqra 2, Parašah* 7(7), quoted in the Babli, 2a. The apostate wants to forget; even if he really forgot it was desired by him; he never qualifies for a purification offering, even if his transgression happens to be in a situation for which the Court would have to bring an offering if its conditions were fulfilled.

61 If the Court permitted certain intrinsically forbidden things and an individual acted on his own but did what they had allowed, then both the Court and the individual have to bring sacrifices for the same kind of action.

(fol. 45c) **משנה ב**: הוֹרוּ בֵית דִּין וְיָֽדְעוּ שֶׁטָּעוּ וְחָֽזְרוּ בָהֶן בֵּין שֶׁהֵבִיאוּ כַפָּרָתָן וּבֵין שֶׁלֹּא הֵבִיאוּ כַפָּרָתָן וְהָלַךְ וְעָשָׂה עַל פִּיהֶן רִבִּי שִׁמְעוֹן פּוֹטֵר וְרִבִּי לְעֶזֶר אוֹמֵר סָפֵק. אֵיזֶהוּ סָפֵק יָשַׁב לוֹ בְתוֹךְ בֵּיתוֹ חַיָּב. הָלַךְ לוֹ לִמְדִינַת הַיָּם פָּטוּר. אָמַר רִבִּי עֲקִיבָה מוֹדֶה אֲנִי בָזֶה שֶׁהוּא קָרוֹב לִפְטוֹר מִן הַחוֹבָה. אָמַר לוֹ בֶן עַזַּאי מַה שָּׁנָה זֶה מִן הַיּוֹשֵׁב בְּבֵיתוֹ שֶׁהַיּוֹשֵׁב בְּבֵיתוֹ אֶיפְשַׁר הָיָה לוֹ שֶׁיִּשְׁמַע וְזֶה לֹא הָיָה אֶיפְשַׁר לוֹ שֶׁיִּשְׁמַע:

Mishnah 2: If the Court gave an instruction; then they realized that they erred and reversed themselves[62]; whether they brought their atonement or they did not bring their atonement[63], another person went and acted on their instructions[64], Rebbi Simeon declares him not liable, but Rebbi Eliezer[65] says, it is in doubt. What is the doubt? If he remained at home, he is liable; if he went overseas he is not liable. Rebbi Aqiba said, I agree in this case that he is closer to not being liable than being liable. Ben Azzai asked him, what is the difference between him and the one staying at home? For one who stays at home might be informed[66] but the other one could not be informed.

62 Publicly.

63 The sacrifice prescribed in *Lev.* 4:13-21.

64 He followed the original instructions after the Court had reversed itself. R. Simeon holds that the responsibility remains the Court's as long as not all of Israel were duly informed of the new ruling.

65 One should read with the Babli and many independent Mishnah mss. "R. Eleazar" (ben Shamua`), since the third generation R. Simeon cannot be quoted preceding the first generation R. Eliezer.

66 It would be his duty to stay informed. The one who is far away is still depending on the earlier ruling of the Court; he is not liable for a sacrifice according to everybody. The difference between R. Aqiba and ben Azzai is that the latter requires a sacrifice from anyone who could have known of the reversal whereas the former requires it only from one who should have known.

(45c line 51) **הלכה ב**: הוֹרוּ בֵית דִּין וְיָֽדְעוּ שֶׁטָּעוּ כול'. רִבִּי אִימִּי בְשֵׁם רִבִּי שִׁמְעוֹן בֶּן לָקִישׁ. מַתְנִיתָא כְּגוֹן שִׁמְעוֹן בֶּן עַזַּאי יוֹשֵׁב לִפְנֵיהֶן. מָה נָן קַיָּמִין. אִם בְּשֶׁסִּילְּקָן תְּבַטְּלוּ הוֹרָיָיתָן. אִם בְּשֶׁסִּילְּקוּ אוֹתוֹ תְּבַטֵּל הוֹרָיָיתוֹ. אֶלָּא כִי נָן קַיָּמִין בְּשֶׁזֶּה עוֹמֵד בִּתְשׁוּבָתוֹ וָזֶה עוֹמֵד בִּתְשׁוּבָתוֹ. הוֹרָיָיתָן אֶצְלוֹ אֵינָהּ הוֹרָאָה. שֶׁלֹּא סִילְּקוּ אוֹתוֹ. אֶצֶל אֲחֵרִים הוֹרָיָיה. שֶׁלֹּא סִילְּקָן. לֵית הָדָא פְלִיגָא עַל רִבִּי מָנָא בַּר תַּנְחוּם. דְּרִבִּי מָנָא בַּר תַּנְחוּם אָמַר. נִכְנְסוּ מֵאָה. עַד שֶׁיּוֹרוּ כוּלָּן. פָּתַר לָהּ בְּשֶׁלֹּא נִכְנַס. אִם בְּשֶׁלֹּא נִכְנַס. מְעַכֵּב. פָּתַר לָהּ כְּרִבִּי. דְּרִבִּי אָמַר. אֵין לָךְ מְעַכֵּב אֶלָּא מוּפְלָא שֶׁלְּבֵית דִּין (בלוד). וְהָא רִבִּי מָנָא בַּר תַּנְחוּם אָמַר. נִכְנְסוּ מֵאָה. עַד שֶׁיּוֹרוּ כוּלָּן. אַף בַּחֲזִירָה כֵן אוֹ רוֹב. כת פְּשִׁיטָא לָךְ רוֹב. מָה רוֹב. רוֹב הַהוֹרָיָיה רוֹב הַמִּשְׁתַּיֵּיר. הֵיךְ עֲבִידָא.

נִכְנְסוּ מֵאָה וּמֵתוּ מֵהֶן עֲשָׂרָה. אִין תֹּאמַר. רוֹב הַהוֹרָיָיה. חֲמִשִּׁים וְאֶחָד. וְאִין תֹּאמַר. רוֹב הַמִּשְׁתַּייֵר. אַרְבָּעִים וְשִׁשָּׁה.

1 אימי | אמי 2 לפניהן | ועוסק לפניהם בשסילקן תבטלו | בשסלקו תבטל אם | ואם 3 בשסילקו | בשסלקו הורייתו | הוריתו 4 סילקו | סלקו סילקן | סלקן 7 בלוד | בלבד 8 או | - כת | צייתי רוב ההורייה | רובו הוריה רוב | או רוב 9 אין תאמ' | אי תימ' ההורייה | הוריה ואין תאמ' | ואי תימר

Halakhah 2: "If the Court gave an instruction; then they realized that they erred," etc. Rebbi Immi in the name of Rebbi Simeon ben Laqish: Our Mishnah, for example, if Simeon ben Azzai[40] was sitting before them. Where do we hold? If he removed[67] them, their instruction would be invalid. If they removed him, his instruction would be invalid. But we hold in the case that each side stands by its answer. For him, their instruction is no instruction, for they did not remove him[68]. For others it is an instruction, for he did not remove them. Does this not disagree with Rebbi Mana bar Tanḥum, since Rebbi Mana bar Tanḥum said, if a hundred came together, only if they instructed unanimously[36]? One explains it, that he was not present[69]. Does this invalidate[70]? He explains it following Rebbi, since Rebbi said, no one invalidates but the distinguished member of the Court (at Lydda) [only][71]. Since Rebbi Mana bar Tanḥum said, if a hundred came together, only if they instructed unanimously; is it the same in retraction or by majority? If it is obvious for you[72] by majority, what kind of majority? The majority of those who instructed or the majority of those remaining? How is this? If there were a hundred but ten of them had died. If you say, a majority of those who instructed, 51. If you say, a majority of those remaining, 46.

67 In general, the *Piel* form סִלֵּק, from the root סלק "to raise, lift", means "to remove (from office)", comparable to German *entheben*. Here it must mean, "to silence the opposing party" either by a convincing argument of the single opponent, or by a formal judgment of the High Court.

68 Since they could not convince him, he does not have to follow them against his better knowledge; cf. Note 43.

69 At the vote.

70 The text of B is more intelligible: If he was not present, does this invalidate the vote?

71 The ms. text, בלוד, "at Lydda" makes no sense since the High Court must sit in the ashlar hall on the Temple Mount. One has to read with B בלבד "only". The president of the Court is the only one for whom no substitute can be found.

72 Read כַּד "if it is" for כַּת "group" in the text. The reading of B, צַיְיתֵי "they obey" might be acceptable; since

everywhere a majority opinion of religious authorities is to be followed, it is obvious that a retraction by a majority has to be followed. The original instruction also would have had to be followed if rendered by a majority of the Court; it is only the obligation of a sacrifice which is triggered by a unanimous vote.

(45d line 64) הִפְרִישׁ חַטָּאתוֹ. נִתְחָרֵשׁ אוֹ נִשְׁטָה אוֹ נִשְׁתַּמֵּד אוֹ שֶׁהוֹרוּ בֵּית דִּין מוּתָּר לֶאֱכוֹל חֵלֶב. רִבִּי יוֹחָנָן אָמַר. נִדְחֵית חַטָּאתוֹ. רִבִּי שִׁמְעוֹן בֶּן לָקִישׁ אָמַר. לֹא נִדְחֵית חַטָּאתוֹ. רִבִּי יוֹסֵי בֵּירִבִּי בּוּן אָמַר. רִבִּי אָחָא מַחְלֵף שְׁמוּעָתָא דְלָא אֲתִי מִילְּתֵיהּ דְּרִבִּי יוֹחָנָן פְּלִיגָא עַל מִילְּתֵיהּ. דָּמַר רִבִּי שִׁמְעוֹן בַּר בָּא בְשֵׁם רִבִּי יוֹחָנָן. כּוּס זוֹרְקִין עָלָיו מִדַּם חַטָּאתוֹ וּמִדַּם אֲשָׁמוֹ. רַבָּנִין דְּקַיְסָרִין אָמְרִין. רִבִּי חִיָּיה אִמִּי מַחְלֵף. וחַד אָמַר כָּאן תַּנָּייָה.

1 נשטה | נשתטה 2 נדחית | נדחת (2) יוסי | יוסה 3 ביר' | בר' אתי | תהא מילתיה | מילתא 4 דמר | דאמר כוס | הגוסס 5 אמי | ור' אמי חד כאן | כהן

[73]If somebody had selected his purification sacrifice when he became a deaf-mute, or insane, or an apostate, or the Court rules that fat may be eaten, Rebbi Joḥanan said, his sacrifice of purification is pushed aside[74], Rebbi Simeon ben Laqish said, his sacrifice of purification is not pushed aside. Rebbi Yose ben Rebbi Abun said, Rebbi Aḥa switches traditions, to avoid that a word of Rebbi Joḥanan contradict his own word. For Rebbi Simeon bar Abba said in the name of Rebbi Joḥanan: One sprinkles the blood of a purification sacrifice or a reparation sacrifice for a person [terminally ill][75]. The Rebbi of Caesarea said, Rebbi Ḥiyya and [Rebbi] Immi, [one] switches and one says like [this] Tanna.

73 This paragraph also is in *Gittin* 7:1, explained there in Notes 10-21. In the translation, the words in brackets follow the text of B. The ms. text here has quite a number of scribal errors. A parallel is in the Babli, *Zebahim* 12b.

74 This version is confirmed in the Babli, 11a.

75 In the ms: "a cup".

(45d line 70) מָאן דְּמַחְלֵף לֵית לֵיהּ בְּאִילֵּין קִישׁוּאַייָה. כְּמָאן דָּמַר. לֹא נִדְחֵית חַטָּאתוֹ. מִי מְקַבְּלָהּ הֵימֶינּוּ. יַמְתִּין עַד שֶׁיַּחְזְרוּ בָהֶן בֵּית דִּין. אֶלָּא כְשֶׁהָיָה כֹהֵן עָבֵד וְהִקְרִיב וְכִיפֵּר. הָיָה שִׁמְעוֹן בֶּן עַזַּאי. מִי מְקַבְּלָהּ הֵימֶינּוּ. יַמְתִּין עַד שֶׁיַּחְזְרוּ בָהֶן בֵּית דִּין. כְּמָאן דָּמַר. לֹא נִדְחֵית חַטָּאתוֹ.

1 מאן | מן קישואייה | קשואייה כמאן | כמן 2 הימינו | ממנו וכיפר | וכפר 3 כמאן | כמן

He who switches has none of these difficulties[76]. For him who says, his sacrifice of purification is not pushed aside[77], who would accept it from him?

He has to wait until the Court retracts, or if he was a Cohen who served, sacrificed, and atoned[78]. If he was Simeon ben Azzai[79], who would accept it from him? He has to wait until the Court retracts, for him who says, his sacrifice of purification is not pushed aside.

76 The one difficulty pointed out in the previous paragraph that R. Johanan accepts the sacrifice on behalf of a dying person even though the sacrifice of a dead person is impossible. The second difficulty is that R. Johanan permits the writing and delivery of a divorce document to a wife whose husband became insane after he had ordered the document to be written.

77 If the sacrifice becomes invalid, there is no problem. But since a purification sacrifice cannot be offered voluntarily, even according to him who said that the sacrifice remains valid, are the officiating priests not required to refuse the sacrifice after the Court ruled that the action for which it is offered was not forbidden?

78 A layman can do nothing but wait whether the Court change its mind. But a Cohen can bring his own sacrifice and eat its meat for atonement if at the moment of the action it would have been sinful for anybody. Since he does not have to explain his reasons to a priest, he is not dependent on the Court.

79 A layman who knows that the Court erred is not freed from an obligation to bring a sacrifice by the Court's ruling; nevertheless he cannot find a priest who would accept it before the Court changes its mind.

(45d line 74) תּוֹלְדוֹת הוֹרַייָה כְהוֹרַייָה. הוֹרַייָה בְהוֹרַייָה מָה הֵן שֶׁיִּצְטָרְפוּ. הֵיךְ עֲבִידָא. אָכְלוּ צִיבּוּר חֲלָבִים וְהִפְרִישׁוּ קָרְבְּנוֹתֵיהֶן. אִין תֵּימַר. תּוֹלְדוֹת הוֹרַייָה כְהוֹרַייָה. בֵּית דִּין חַייָבִין. אִין תֵּימַר. אֵין תּוֹלְדוֹת הוֹרַייָה כְהוֹרַייָה. בֵּית דִּין פְּטוּרִין. כתי פְּשִׁיטָא לָךְ. תּוֹלְדוֹת הוֹרַייָה כְהוֹרַייָה. הוֹרַייָה בְהוֹרַייָה מָה הֵן שֶׁיִּצְטָרְפוּ. הֵיךְ עֲבִידָא. הוֹרוּ בֵית דִּין. חֵלֶב כּוּלְיָיא שֶׁלְּיָמִין מוּתָּר וְשֶׁלִּשְׂמֹאל וּלוֹ מִכְסֶה אָסוּר. חָזְרוּ וְהֶחֱלִיפוּ. אָכְלוּ רוֹב בָּרִאשׁוֹנָה וָרוֹב בַּשְּׁנִייָה. אִין תֵּימַר. מִצְטָרְפִין. חַייָבִין אַחַת. וְאִין תֵּימַר. אֵין מִצְטָרְפִין. חַייָבִין שְׁתַּיִם. שְׁתֵּי הוֹרָיוֹת בָּעֲבוֹדָה אַחַת מָה הֵן שֶׁיִּצְטָרְפוּ. הֵיךְ עֲבִידָא. אָכְלוּ רוֹב וְשָׁחֲטוּ רוֹב. עַל דַּעְתֵּיהּ דְּרִבִּי מֵאִיר חַייָבִין אַחַת. עַל דַּעְתֵּיהּ דְּרִבִּי שִׁמְעוֹן חַייָבִין שְׁתַּיִם. אָכְלוּ מִיעוּט בָּרִאשׁוֹנָה וּמִיעוּט בַּשְּׁנִייָה. עַל דַּעְתֵּיהּ דְּרִבִּי מֵאִיר חַייָבִין. וְעַל דַּעְתֵּיהּ דְּרִבִּי שִׁמְעוֹן פְּטוּרִין.

1 הורייה | הוריה (all occasions) מה הן | מהו (all occasions) 2 קרבנותיהן | קרבנותיהם אין | אי (all occasions) 3 פטורין | פטרין כתי | כיני 4 חלב | - 5 ולו | ושל אכלו | ואכלו 7 בעבודה | בעבירה

Are consequences of a ruling like the ruling? Do ruling within ruling combine[80]? How is that? If the public ate forbidden fat and designated their sacrifices. If you say that consequences of a ruling are like the ruling, the

Court is liable[81]. If you say that consequences of a ruling are not like the ruling, the Court is not liable. The following should be obvious to you: the consequences of a ruling are like the ruling[82]. Do ruling within ruling combine with each other? How is that? If the Court ruled that the fat in the right side kidney was permitted but that of the left side and its cover[83] was forbidden; then they reversed themselves and said the opposite. Most ate the first time, and most the second time. If you say that they combine, they are liable for one. But if you say that they do not combine, they are liable for two[84]. Do two instructions about one kind of work[85] combine? How is that? If a majority ate and a majority slaughtered[86]. In Rebbi Meïr's opinion they are once liable; in Rebbi Simeon's opinion they are twice liable[87]. If a minority ate the first time and a minority the second time. In Rebbi Meïr's opinion they are liable; in Rebbi Simeon's opinion they are not liable[88].

80 The meaning of these expressions will be explained by examples in the text.

81 Most of the people ate forbidden fat (which makes the sinner subject to extirpation and therefore requires a sacrifice if inadvertent, Mishnah 3:7) without a ruling of the Court, and they already had dedicated their sacrifices when the Court ruled that eating fat is permitted. When it rescinded its ruling, it turned out that in the meantime nobody had acted on their instruction. According to the opinion that the ruling of the Court pushed aside the dedicated sacrifices, the Court certainly has to bring their own sacrifice since they invalidated the private sacrifices. But if one holds that the private sacrifices were re-installed upon recission, then if the rule is that consequences of instructions are like instructions, the Court still is liable for a sacrifice for preventing the purification offerings to be brought in the meantime, even though this was not included or intended in the original ruling. Otherwise, the private offerings will now be brought and the Court's ruling is eliminated without further consequences.

82 This should not be so obvious since it implies that a purification sacrifice which for outside reasons could not be offered is reinstated when the outside reason disappears.

83 The fat in lumps outside the kidney which is forbidden together with the fat embedded in the kidney lobes.

84 If the Court followed one wrong decision with another wrong one on the same subject, it is an unresolved question whether they have to offer one or two sacrifices when they finally see their errors.

85 In B: "Two instructions about one kind of *sin*." While the text as it stands is difficult, the text of B is impossible since, as explained in *Makkot* 3:11, while

committing one sin one may commit any number of others at the same time.

The following example makes it clear that instead of "two instructions about one kind of work" one has to read "one instruction about two kinds of work."

86 It seems that one contemplates the case that the Court decided that one does not have to keep the Day of Atonement. This one instruction implicitly allows both work (slaughter) and eating on that day; both are sins punishable by extirpation.

87 The difference between R. Meïr, the presumed author of the anonymous statement in Mishnah 3:3, and R. Simeon is that R. Meïr holds that the sin determines the sacrifice whereas R. Simeon holds that the status of the sinner at the moment he becomes aware of his sin is determining. Since the Court issued one statement, they have to bring one sacrifice. Since the people became aware of two kinds of sins, two sacrifices are due. This shows that R. Simeon does not hold that the consequences of an instruction have the status of the instruction.

88 If the two majorities together form a majority, the conditions for the Court to be liable are satisfied; for R. Simeon the two minorities cannot be combined.

(46a line 10) אָמַר רִבִּי זְעִירָא וְשָׁהוּת בֵּינֵיהוֹן. רִבִּי מֵאִיר אָמַר. נוֹתְנִין לוֹ שָׁהוּת עַד שֶׁיִּשְׁמַע. רִבִּי שִׁמְעוֹן אוֹמֵר. עַד שֶׁיִּשְׁפַּע. וְתַנֵּי כֵן. הוֹרוּ בֵית דִּין בְּשׁוּק הָעֶלְיוֹן וְיָחִיד בְּשׁוּק הַתַּחְתּוֹן. בֵּית דִּין בַּבַּיִת וְיָחִיד בָּעֲלִייָה. פָּטוּר עַד שֶׁיִּשְׁמַע מַמָּשׁ.

1 ביניהון | ביניהן מאיר | - אמ' | אומר 2 שישפע | שישמע ממש

Rebbi Ze`ira said, the time span is between them[89]. Rebbi Meïr said, one gives him time until he may hear. Rebbi Simeon said, until he must have heard, and we have stated so: If the Court instructed in the upper market and a single person was in the lower market, or the Court on the ground floor and a single person on the upper floor, he is not liable until he actually heard.

89 This refers back to the Mishnah, about a person who acted on the Court's instruction after the Court reversed itself. It is stated in *Sifra Wayyiqra 2, Paršetah* 7(3) that R. Simeon does not hold him liable (for a sacrifice) but R. Meïr does. It is explained that neither does R. Simeon free him forever nor R. Meïr hold him liable immediately, but R. Meïr holds him liable if he could have heard, and R. Simeon only if he had ample time to be informed. The reading of the ms., עַד שֶׁיִּשְׁפַּע, i. e., "until he had ample (time to be informed)" is preferable over that of B, "until he actually was informed."

(46a line 13) עַל דַּעְתֵּיהּ דְּרִבִּי עֲקִיבָה אַדַּיִין הוּא סָפֵק. אָמַר רִבִּי בּוּן בַּר חִייָה. בָּעוֹמֵד בֵּין שְׁנֵי תְחוּמִין. בֵּין שְׁנֵי תְחוּמֵי אֶרֶץ יִשְׂרָאֵל לִתְחוּמֵי אֶרֶץ יִשְׂרָאֵל.

רִבִּי אִמִּי בְשֵׁם רִבִּי שִׁמְעוֹן בֶּן לָקִישׁ. לַהוֹרָייָה הִילְכוּ אַחַר יְשִׁיבַת אֶרֶץ יִשְׂרָאֵל. לַטּוּמְאָה הִילְכוּ אַחַר רוֹב נִכְנָסִין לָעֲזָרָה. מַה. כָּל־כַּת וָכַת מְשַׁעֲרִין אֶלָּא כַת הָרִאשׁוֹנָה בִלְבַד. אָמַר רִבִּי יוֹסֵי בֵּירִבִּי בּוּן. עַד שֶׁהֵן מִבַּחוּץ הֵן מְשַׁעֲרִין עַצְמָן. רִבִּי יְהוֹשֻׁעַ בֶּן לֵוִי. לִירְאִייָה הִילְכוּ מִלְּבוֹא חֲמַת עַד נַחַל מִצְרַיִם. רִבִּי תַנְחוּמָא בְשֵׁם רִבִּי הוּנָא. טַעֲמָא דְּרִבִּי יְהוֹשֻׁעַ בֶּן לֵוִי וַיַּעַשׂ שְׁלֹמֹה בָעֵת־הַהִיא | אֶת־הֶחָג וְכָל־יִשְׂרָאֵל עִמּוֹ וגו'.

1 עקיבה | עקיבא אדיין | אדין חייה | חייא שני | - 2 ארץ ישראל (2nd) | חוצה לארץ 3 - | אמר להורייה | להוריה הילכו | הלכו 4 לעזרה | בעזרה אלא | או אין משערין אלא 5 יוסי ביר' | יוסה בר הן | היו לוי | לוי אמר לראייה | לראיה הילכו | הלכו מלבוא | מלבא 6 וכל ישראל עמו וגו' | בחדש

In Rebbi Aqiba's opinion it remains a doubt[90]. Rebbi Abun bar Ḥiyya said, if he stands between two domains, between two domains of the Land of Israel and domains of the Land of Israel[91].

[92]Rebbi Immi in the name of Rebbi Simeon ben Laqish. For instructions they considered the settlement of the Land of Israel[93]. For impurity they considered the majority of those coming to the Temple precinct[94]. How? Do they estimate every group or only the first group? Rebbi Yose ben Rebbi Abun said, when they are still outside they estimate themselves[95]. Rebbi Joshua ben Levi: For appearance[96] they consider from Levo-Ḥamat to the brook of Egypt. Rebbi Tanḥuma in the name of Rebbi Ḥuna: The reason of Rebbi Joshua ben Levi is, *at that time Solomon celebrated the holiday, and all of Israel,* [97]etc.

90 This refers to R. Aqiba's statement in the Mishnah. Even though the position of one who could have known but did not inform himself looks as if he should not be liable, a doubt remains and in fact he has to bring a suspended reparation offering (cf. Note 19).

91 The reading in B is: Between domains of the Land of Israel and domains outside the Land. In this version, "overseas" mentioned in the Mishnah is interpreted to mean, "outside the Land." The text of the ms. is to be read to mean that a person living outside of urban centers in the Land of Israel has the same status as a city dweller on an overseas trip, since he is far from sources of information.

92 This paragraph is also in *Pesahim* 7:6 (34c line 66), following the wording of B.

93 The definition of "majority" which would trigger the liability of the Court for a sacrifice for issuing false instruction counts only the Jewish population of the Land of Israel. Since the verse from *1Kings* is not quoted here (in contrast to the Babli, 3a), the definition of the Land of Israel is that given in *Ševi`it* 6:1, Notes 31-51.

94 *Babli Pesahim* 94b. A private sacrifice may be presented in the Temple only by a person ritually pure. But the

Passover lamb has the status of a public sacrifice; if most of the public are impure (of a kind which cannot be remedied by simple immersion in water), the sacrifice is slaughtered and eaten in impurity (cf. *Nazir* 9:2 Note 66.)

95 Since the Temple courtyard was rather small, the Passover lambs were slaughtered in three groups. Making the count depending on the composition of the groups would lead to the paradoxical situation that a first group might be permitted to slaughter and eat the lamb in impurity while from a second group only the pure members are admitted and have to follow the rules of purity. Also, it is impossible to make the decision depending on "those in the Temple court" since only pure persons could enter the Temple precinct in the absence of a *prior* finding that most of Israel were impure.

96 The assembly of all of Israel in a Sabbatical year (*Deut.* 31:10-13) could proceed in impurity if most of Israel in the domain of Solomon's empire were impure.

97 *1K.* 8:65 (misquoted in B.)

(fol. 45c) **משנה ג**: הוֹרוּ בֵית דִּין לַעֲקוֹר אֶת כָּל הַגּוּף אָמְרוּ אֵין נִידָּה בַתּוֹרָה אֵין שַׁבָּת בַּתּוֹרָה. אֵין עֲבוֹדָה זָרָה בַתּוֹרָה הֲרֵי אֵילּוּ פְטוּרִין. הוֹרוּ לְבַטֵּל מִקְצָת וּלְקַיֵּים מִקְצָת הֲרֵי אֵילּוּ חַייָבִין. כֵּיצַד אָמְרוּ יֵשׁ נִידָּה בַתּוֹרָה אֲבָל הַבָּא עַל שׁוֹמֶרֶת יוֹם כְּנֶגֶד יוֹם פָּטוּר. יֵשׁ שַׁבָּת בַּתּוֹרָה אֲבָל הַמּוֹצִיא מֵרְשׁוּת הַיָּחִיד לִרְשׁוּת הָרַבִּים פָּטוּר. יֵשׁ עֲבוֹדָה זָרָה בַתּוֹרָה אֲבָל הַמִּשְׁתַּחֲוֶה פָּטוּר הֲרֵי אֵילּוּ חַייָבִין שֶׁנֶּאֱמַר וְנֶעְלַם דָּבָר. דָּבָר וְלֹא כָל־הַגּוּף:

Mishnah 3: If the Court ruled to uproot an entire subject; if they said, the menstruating woman is not mentioned in the Torah, Sabbath is not mentioned in the Torah, idolatry is not mentioned in the Torah, they are not liable[98]. If they ruled to eliminate part and to confirm part, they are liable. How is that? If they said, the menstruating woman is mentioned in the Torah but one who copulates with one who is watching a day to the next day is not liable[99]; Sabbath is mentioned in the Torah but one who brings from a private domain to a public domain is not liable[100]; idolatry is mentioned in the Torah but one who prostrates himself is not liable[101]; these are liable for it is said[102] *something was hidden*, something but not an entire subject.

98 Since anything written in the Torah is public knowledge and nobody would listen to them.

99 In rabbinic medical theory, the minimum time which must elapse between one menstrual period and the

next is the seven days of the *niddah* (*Lev.* 15:19) followed by another 11 days. If a woman has a discharge on one of these 11 days, she is not classified as *niddah* but as *zavah*, whose rules are spelled out in *Lev.* 15:25-30. Since the verse speaks of a discharge of *many days*, it is concluded that the full rules of *zavah* only apply after 3 days. For the first and second discharges in that 11 day period, the woman is called "watching one day to the next day". For a day she is under the rules of *niddah* (*Lev.* 15:25) and therefore forbidden to her husband. But since the verse uses the expression *all the days of the flow of her impurity shall be like the days of her menstruation*, one could think that she is impure only during the day and not during the following night, or that a discharge during the night does not make her impure. This is clearly a matter of rabbinic interpretation.

100 The pentateuchal root of the prohibition to carry from a private to the public domain is *Ex.* 16:29, *nobody should go out from his place*, which is explained in *Jer.* 17:22 by *do not move a load from your houses.* Since as a matter of principle prophetic utterances should not be used as legal texts, the ruling of the Court could not be dismissed out of hand.

101 This is more difficult to understand since *Deut.* 17:3 clearly defines prostrating oneself in idolatry as a capital crime. Therefore, one has to agree with Maimonides's Commentary that the Court changed the definition of "prostration", e. g., ruling that kneeling down, bowing the head to the ground, is not punishable as long as one does not lie on the ground with outstretched hands and feet.

102 *Lev.* 4:13. *Sifra Wayyiqra 2, Parašah* 4(7-8).

(46a line 22) **הלכה ג**: הוֹרוּ בֵית דִּין לַעֲקוֹר אֶת כָּל הַגּוּף כול'. רִבִּי חִזְקִיָּה אָמַר. מִדָּבָר. לֹא כָל־דָּבָר. אָמַר רִבִּי הִילָא. מִמִּצְוֹת. לֹא כָל־מִצְוֹת. וְכָתוּב כֵּן. כַּיי דָמַר רִבִּי אִמִּי בְשֵׁם רִבִּי יוֹחָנָן. גּוֹרְעִין לִדְרוֹשׁ מִתְּחִילַּת הַפָּרָשָׁה עַד סוֹפָהּ. רִבִּי חֲנַנְיָה בְשֵׁם רִבִּי יִרְמְיָה. וַאֲפִילוּ בְאֶמְצַע תֵּיבָה. וְיָצַקְתָּ עָלֶיהָ שֶׁמֶן מִנְחָה הִיא: לְרַבּוֹת כָּל־הַמְּנָחוֹת לִיצִיקָה.

1 את כל הגוף | - ר' חזקיה אמ'. מדבר. לא כל דבר | - 2 ר' | - לא | ולא כן. כיי דמר | ה' אמר 3 מתחילת | מתחלת ר' חנניה בשם ר' ירמיה. ואפי' | ר' יוסה בו חנינה אמ' אפי' 4 מנחה היא | ויצקת שמן מנחה

Halakhah 3: "If the Court ruled to uproot an entire subject," etc. Rebbi Ḥizqiah said, "of a subject," not the entire subject. Rebbi Hila said, "of the commandments", not entire commandments[103]. [104]Is that written? As Rebbi Immi said in the name of Rebbi Joḥanan: For interpretation, one removes from the beginning of the paragraph to its end. Rebbi Ḥananiah in the name of Rebbi Jeremiah: Even a middle word. *You have to pour oil on it, it is a flour offering*, to include all flour offerings for pouring[105].

103 In *Lev.* 4:13, R. Hizqiah reads וְנֶעֱלַם דָּבָר as וְנֶעֱלַם מִדָּבָר, presupposing a script which does not differentiate between regular and final *mem*. R. Hila's comment is really unnecessary since מִכָּל־מִצְוֹת already means "of any commandments" but not entire commandments. In all situations, prefix *mem* is read as partitive, some but not all; cf. *Nazir* 5:4 Note 105.

104 The following text also is found in *Sotah* 5:1, explained in Notes 8-10, *Nazir* 5:1 Note 56.

105 *Sifra Wayyiqra 1 Pereq* 12 on *Lev.* 2:6. The ms. text follows the argument of *Sifra* while B reproduces the text of *Sotah* and *Nazir*. The argument of *Sifra* has no connection with the theories of RR. Johanan and Jeremiah; it is a straightforward reading of the verse. Since it is stated that one has to pour oil on the bread crumbs *because it is a flour-offering*, it follows that a flour-offering requires pouring oil over it unless it be explicitly excluded as in the purification offering of v. 5:11.

(46a line 27) וְלֹא נִמְצֵאתָ עוֹקֵר כָּל־שֵׁם שׁוֹמֶרֶת יוֹם כְּנֶגֶד יוֹם. בְּשֶׁאָמְרוּ. הַלַּיְלָה מוּתָּר וְהַיּוֹם אָסוּר. וְלֹא נִמְצֵאתָ עוֹקֵר כָּל־שְׁחִיחָה. שְׁמוּאֵל בַּר אַבָּא אָמַר. בְּשֶׁאָמְרוּ. אַמָּה מוּתֶּרֶת וּשְׁתֵּי אַמּוֹת אֲסוּרוֹת. וְלֹא נִמְצֵאתָ עוֹקֵר כָּל־שֵׁם הִשְׁתַּחֲוָיָה. בְּשֶׁאָמְרוּ. מוּתָּר לְהִשְׁתַּחֲוֹת וְאָסוּר לָשׁוּחַ. וְלֹא נִמְצֵאתָ עוֹקֵר כָּל־שֵׁם הוֹצָאָה. אָמַר רִבִּי שְׁמוּאֵל בַּר רַב יִצְחָק. בְּשֶׁאָמְרוּ. גְּרוֹגֶרֶת מוּתֶּרֶת וּשְׁתֵּי גְרוֹגְרוֹת אֲסוּרוֹת. וְאַתְיָיא כְּמָאן דָּמַר. הַכְנָסָה וְהוֹצָאָה אַחַת הִיא. בְּרַם כְּמָאן דָּמַר. הַכְנָסָה וְהוֹצָאָה שְׁתַּיִם הֵן. וְלֹא נִמְצֵאתָ עוֹקֵר כָּל־שֵׁם הַכְנָסָה. אָמַר רִבִּי יוֹסֵי. לֹא שֶׁהוֹרוּ מוּתָּר לֶאֱכוֹל חֵלֶב. יוֹדְעִין הָיוּ שֶׁאָסוּר לוֹכַל חֵלֶב. וְהַתּוֹרָה נָתְנָה רְשׁוּת לְבֵית דִּין לְהוֹרוֹת. רִבִּי בּוּן בַּר חִיָּה בָּעֵי. כְּזַיִת הַיּוֹם וְכִשְׁנֵי זֵיתִים לְמָחָר. הֵיךְ עֲבִידָא נָבִיא וּמֵדִיחַ. יָכוֹל אִם יֹאמְרוּ לָךְ. אַל תִּתֵּן תְּפִילִין הַיּוֹם תֵּן לְמָחָר. תִּשְׁמַע לָהֶם. תַּלְמוּד לוֹמַר לָלֶכֶת בָּהֶם. בְּכוּלָּן וְלֹא בְמִקְצָתָן. הֲרֵי עָקַרְתָּ שֵׁם כָּל־אוֹתוֹ הַיּוֹם. וַתֵּ מַר אֵין כָּאן עֲקִירַת גּוּף. וְכָא אֵין כָּאן עֲקִירַת גּוּף. רִבִּי מָנָא שָׁמַע לָהּ מִן דְּבַתְרָהּ. שְׁמוּאֵל בַּר בָּא אָמַר. בְּשֶׁאָמְרוּ. אַמָּה מוּתֶּרֶת וּשְׁתֵּי אַמּוֹת אֲסוּרוֹת. הֲרֵי עָקַרְתָּ שֵׁם כָּל כָּל־אוֹתָהּ הָאַמָּה. וְתֵי מַר אֵין כָּאן עֲקִירַת גּוּף. וָכָא אֵין כָּאן עֲקִירַת גּוּף.

1 בשאמרו | כשאמרו (all occurrences) 2 כל | כל שם אבא | בא 3 השתחוייה | השתחויה 4 גרוגרת | כגרוגרת 5 אסורות | אסורה ואתייא כמאן | ותייא כמן כמאן | כמן 6 יוסי | יוסה 8 חייה | חייא וכשני | ושתי יאמרו | יאמר 9 למחר | תפילין 10 עקרת | עקרתה ות מר | ותימר גוף | הגוף 11 עקרת | עקרתה 12 גוף | הגוף (twice)

But would you not have eliminated the entire notion of one who watches a day for the next day[106]? If they said, the night is permitted but the day is forbidden. Would you not have eliminated the entire notion of bending? Samuel bar Abba said, if they said, one cubit is permitted but two are forbidden[107]. Would you not have eliminated the entire notion of prostrating? If they said, it is permitted to prostrate oneself but forbidden to sink down[108].

Would you not have eliminated the entire notion of taking out? Rebbi Samuel ben Rav Isaac said, if they said, one dried fig is permitted but two dried figs are forbidden[109]. This follows him who said that bringing in and taking out are the same[110]. But for him who said that bringing in and taking out are two notions, would you not have eliminated the entire notion of bringing in? Rebbi Yose said, not that they said that it was permitted to eat fat; they knew that it is forbidden to eat fat, but the Torah gave permission to the Court to instruct[111]. Rebbi Abun bar Ḥiyya asked, the [amount of] an olive today and of two olives tomorrow[112]? What about a prophet and seducer[113]? I could think that if they said to you, do not put on phylacteries today, put them on tomorrow[114], that you should listen to them. The verse says[115], *to walk in them,* in all of them, not only in part of them; you would have eliminated the notion of that entire day. You can say that this is not elimination of the entire subject. And here it is not elimination of the entire subject[116]. Rebbi Mana understood it from the following[107]; Samuel bar Abba said, if they said, one cubit is permitted but two are forbidden. You can say that this is not elimination of the entire subject. And here it is not elimination of the entire subject.

106 The literal text of the Mishnah could be read as a hypothetical ruling that there be no restriction on relations between a man and a temporary *zavah.* But since the verse declares the one who watches a day for the next day as being under the rules of *niddah* for whom such relations are forbidden (*Lev.* 18:19), such a ruling would in effect eliminate all rules for the one who watches a day for the next day. Cf. Note 99. Babli 4a.

107 It is not at all clear to what the *hapax* שחיות refers. Since in the Mishnah the Sabbath is mentioned in second place, a reasonable reference would be to Mishnah *Šabbat* 1:1 which describes forbidden transactions on the Sabbath as, e. g., a person standing behind a window handing a parcel to another who is standing outside. While the distance by which the parcel is moved is irrelevant in practice since only the fact counts that it is transported across the border line between public and private domains, a ruling that a minimum distance be required for the transfer to be a violation of Sabbath law is thinkable.

108 While prostrating oneself before an idol is certainly subject to a biblical prohibition, there is no biblical definition of what constitutes prostrating. Since *1K.* 19:18 shows that going down on one's knees is forbidden worship, it is possible to imagine a ruling that going down on

one's knees is prosecutable but other forms of prostration are not.

109 This refers to the prohibitions of the Sabbath. While the prohibition of moving things from one place to another is only one of the 49 categories of forbidden actions, its rules in effect cover half of Tractate *Šabbat* and all of Tractate *'Eruvin*. Moving minute quantities from domain to domain is not punishable. For example, transporting vegetable seeds in a volume less that of a dried fig is not punishable (Mishnah *Šabbat* 9:7). The long list of minimal quantities is traditional, not biblical. A wrong ruling in these matters does not abolish the principle that some minimal quantity is defined for everything.

110 Everybody agrees that "transporting" for the rules of the Sabbath comprises taking up, moving, and putting down. There is a discussion at the start of Tractate *Šabbat* (1:1, 2b l.11 ff.) whether the inclusion of putting down is scriptural or is a matter of indirect inference. If one accepts that "taking up" implies "putting down", then the formulation of the Mishnah covers rulings both about taking up and putting down; but if the biblical status of "putting down" is different from "taking up", the latter should have been mentioned. An answer is unnecessary since the consensus is that "taking up" implies "putting down".

111 While fat is not mentioned in the Mishnah, R. Yose explains how the Court might be liable for a false ruling concerning fat. The only fat (חֵלֶב) forbidden for consumption is (a) fat of domestic animals which for any sacrifice would be burned on the altar and (b) the fat in which the hip tendons are embedded. All other fat is permitted (שׁוּמָן). The exact definition of each category is a matter of rabbinic tradition and as such within the purview of the Court.

112 He asks whether the entire discussion about abolishing an entire commandment or only a detail makes any sense. If they would permit eating one olive-sized piece of *ḥelev* today, two tomorrow, etc., they might come to disestablish the entire commandment by a succession of steps, none of which can be classified as total negation of the commandment.

113 To whom the distinction between abolishing a commandment and modifying it also applies, Babli 4b, *Sanhedrin* 11:8, Note 112 (Tosephta *Sanhedrin* 14:13).

114 This would be a situation in which the accredited prophet could eliminate a commandment in steps, similar to the Court ruling on fat. Since phylacteries are mentioned in connection with the study of Torah (*Deut*. 6:8,11:18), wearing them is a daily biblical commandment.

115 There is no such verse. The reference is to *Deut*. 13:6 where the reading is לָלֶכֶת בָּהּ.

116 Since R. Bun bar Hiyya's question could have been asked about any example in the Mishnah, but the Mishnah makes a distinction between eliminating and modifying a commandment. It is true that a modification is only a modification even if its open-ended iteration could result in eliminating the commandment.

(fol. 45c) **משנה ד**: הוֹרוּ בֵית דִּין וְיָדַע אֶחָד מֵהֶן שֶׁטָּעוּ וְאָמַר לָהֶן טוֹעִין אַתֶּם אוֹ שֶׁלֹּא הָיָה מוּפְלָא שֶׁל בֵּית דִּין שָׁם אוֹ שֶׁהָיָה אֶחָד מֵהֶן גֵּר אוֹ מַמְזֵר אוֹ נָתִין אוֹ זָקֵן שֶׁלֹּא רָאָה לוֹ בָנִים הֲרֵי זוֹ פָּטוּר שֶׁנֶּאֱמַר כָּאן עֵדָה וְנֶאֱמַר לְהַלָּן עֵדָה. מָה עֵדָה הָאֲמוּרָה לְהַלָּן כּוּלָּן רְאוּיִין לְהוֹרָיָה. אַף עֵדָה הָאֲמוּרָה כָּאן כּוּלָּן רְאוּיִין לְהוֹרָיָה.

Mishnah 4: If the Court ruled but one of them knew that it was in error and he told them, you are erring[117], or that the distinguished member of the Court was not there[118], or that one of them was a proselyte, or a bastard, or a Gibeonite[119], or a childless old man[120], it is not liable since it is said here "congregation" and it is said there "congregation"[121]. Since in the congregation mentioned there, all of them were worthy of ordination, also the congregation here all have to be worthy of ordination.

117 Then the ruling of the Court is not unanimous; no sacrifice is due; Note 36.

118 The ruling is not *ex cathedra*, Note 71.

119 While they can be civil judges, they are not eligible for the High Court as explained in the Halakhah.

120 He should not be member of a criminal court since he never raised children and as a consequence never learned to have a positive attitude towards misbehaving people.

121 "Here" is *Lev*. 4:13; "there" is *Num*. 35:12,24,25 containing the rules of criminal courts.

(46a line 43) **הלכה ד**: הוֹרוּ בֵית דִּין וְיָדַע אֶחָד מֵהֶן שֶׁטָּעוּ כול'. מַתְנִיתָא דְרִבִּי. דְּרִבִּי אָמַר. אֵין לְךָ מְעַכֵּב אֶלָּא מוּפְלָא שֶׁלְּבֵית דִּין (בלוד). כְּתִיב וְהָיָה אִם מֵעֵינֵי הָעֵדָה. מִי שֶׁהוּא עָשׂוּי עֵינַיִם לָעֵדָה. כְּתִיב וְהִתְיַצְּבוּ שָׁם עִמָּךְ. מָה אַתְּ לא גֵר וְלֹא נָתִין וְלֹא מַמְזֵר. אַף הֵן לֹא גֵרִים וְלֹא נְתִינִים וְלֹא מַמְזֵרִים וְלֹא עֲבָדִים. נִיחָא גֵר. מַמְזֵר. בֵּית דִּין מְמַנִּין מַמְזֵירִין. רַב חוּנָא אָמַר. בְּשֶׁעֲבָרוּ וּמִינּוּ. רִבִּי חֲנַנְיָה רִבִּי מָנָא. חַד אָמַר. בְּתוֹךְ שִׁבְעִים. וְחָרָנָה אָמַר. חוּץ לְשִׁבְעִים. מָאן דָּמַר. חוּץ לְשִׁבְעִים. נִיחָא. וּמָאן דָּמַר. בְּתוֹךְ שִׁבְעִים. הָא חוּץ לְשִׁבְעִים לֹא. מִכֵּיוָן שֶׁאֵינוֹ רָאוּי לְהוֹרָיָה נַעֲשֶׂה כָּאֶבֶן.

1 דר' | כר' 2 בלוד | בלבד כת' | וכתיב 3 כת' | וכתיב את | אתה הן | הם 4 ממזירין | ממזרים חונא | הונא 5 חנניה | חנינא ר' | ור' וחרנה | וחרנא מאן | מן 6 דמר | דאמר ומאן דמר | ומן דאמר 7 להורייה | להוריה

Halakha 4: "If the Court ruled but one of them knew that it was in error," etc. The Mishnah is Rebbi's, since Rebbi said, no one invalidates but the distinguished member of the Court (at Lydda) [only][71]. It is written[122]: *If from the eyes of the congregation*, from him who is appointed as eyes of the congregation. It is written[123], *they shall stand there with you.* Just as you are neither proselyte, nor Gibeonite, nor a bastard[124], so they should be neither proselytes, nor Gibeonites, nor slaves, nor bastards. Rav Ḥuna said, when they breached the rules and appointed[125]. Rebbi Ḥanania, Rebbi Mana. One said, as part of the Seventy; the other said, apart from the Seventy[126]. He who said, apart from the Seventy, is understandable. But he who said, as part of the Seventy, therefore not apart from the Seventy? Since he is not suitable for ordination, he is considered like a stone[127].

122 *Num.* 15:24, detailing the rules governing the sacrifice of a goat if the Court unintentionally permitted idolatry. This is taken as biblical proof that the Court cannot rule in the absence of its president.

123 *Num.* 11:16, the appointment of the 70 Elders, the paradigm for the High Court. Babli 4b

124 As son of a man and his aunt, Moses would have been a bastard if his parents had married after the promulgation of Torah laws.

125 The exclusion of proselytes, Gibeonites, and bastards is strongly recommended but a breach does not invalidate the appointment.

126 He holds that the exclusion is prescriptive; an appointment would be invalid.

127 If their vote cannot be counted, then automatically not all who are present are voting; therefore the false ruling will never trigger the obligation of a sacrifice.

(fol. 45c) **משנה ה׃** הוֹרוּ בֵית דִּין שׁוֹגְגִין וְעָשׂוּ כָּל הַקָּהָל שׁוֹגְגִין מְבִיאִין פָּר. מְזִידִין וְעָשׂוּ שׁוֹגְגִין מְבִיאִין כִּשְׂבָּה אוֹ שְׂעִירָה. שׁוֹגְגִין וְעָשׂוּ מְזִידִין הֲרֵי אֵילּוּ פְטוּרִין׃

Mishnah 5: If the Court ruled in error and the public acted in error, they have to bring a bull; intentionally but they acted in error, they bring a female sheep or goat; in error but they acted intentionally, they are not liable[128].

128 All purification sacrifices have a stated prerequisite, *viz.*, that the sin to be expiated was committed unintentionally (*Lev.* 4:2,13,22,27). If both Court and public acted in error, the conditions for a sacrifice by the Court are satisfied. If the Court intentionally gave a false ruling, their sin cannot be atoned by a sacrifice; the public are forced to bring individual sacrifices. If the Court ruled in error but the public, although realizing the error, intentionally followed the false ruling, the Court cannot bring a sacrifice since the public did not follow their intent, and the public is barred from any sacrifice since they did not act in error.

(46a line 52) **הלכה ה:** הוֹרוּ בֵית דִּין שׁוֹגְגִין כול'. לֵית הָדָא פְלִיגָא עַל רִבִּי שִׁמְעוֹן בֶּן לָקִישׁ. דָּמַר רִבִּי אִמִּי בְשֵׁם רִבִּי שִׁמְעוֹן בֶּן לָקִישׁ. מַתְנִיתָא כְּגוֹן שִׁמְעוֹן בֶּן עַזַּאי יוֹשֵׁב לִפְנֵיהֶן. **וּמְזִידִין** וְעָשׂוּ שׁוֹגְגִין. וְכִי יֵשׁ זָדוֹן לִשְׁגָגָה לְיָחִיד אֶצֶל הוֹרָיַית בֵּית דִּין. חֲבֵרַייָא בְשֵׁם רִבִּי שִׁמְעוֹן בֶּן לָקִישׁ. בְּשֶׁלֹּא קִיבְּלוּ רוֹב הַצִּיבּוּר עֲלֵיהֶן. רִבִּי זְעִירָא בְשֵׁם רִבִּי שִׁמְעוֹן בֶּן לָקִישׁ. בְּשֶׁבָּעֲטוּ בְהוֹרָיָיתָן. מַה מַפְקָה מִבֵּינֵיהוֹן. קִיבְּלוּ עֲלֵיהֶן וְחָזְרוּ וּבָעֲטוּ. עַל דַּעְתּוֹן דַּחֲבֵרַייָא כֵּיוָן שֶׁבָּעֲטוּ פְטוּרִין. עַל דַּעְתֵּיהּ דְּרִבִּי זְעִירָא מִכֵּיוָן שֶׁקִּיבְּלוּ עֲלֵיהֶן מִשָּׁעָה רִאשׁוֹנָה הֲרֵי אִילּוּ חַיָּבִין.

2 דמר | דאמר 3 לשגגה | שגגה הוריית | הורית חברייא | חבריא 4 קיבלו | קבעו עליהן | עליהם
5 בהורייתן | בהוריתן קיבלו | קבלו דחברייא | דחבריא 6 שקיבלו עליהן | שקבלו עליהם

Halakhah 5: "If the Court ruled in error," etc. Does this not disagree with Rebbi Simeon ben Laqish? Since Rebbi Immi said in the name of Rebbi Simeon ben Laqish: Our Mishnah, for example, if Simeon ben Azzai[40] was sitting before them[129]. "Intentionally but they acted in error." Is there intentional misdeed or error with respect of an instruction by the Court[130]? The colleagues in the name of Rebbi Simeon ben Laqish: If not most of the public accepted it[131]. Rebbi Ze`ira in the name of Rebbi Simeon ben Laqish, if they rebelled against their instruction[132]. What is the difference between them? If they first accepted and then rebelled. In the opinions of the colleagues, since they rebelled, they are not liable[133]. In the opinion of Rebbi Ze`ira, since at the first moment they accepted it, those are liable[134].

129 He would immediately have pointed out the error; then one would be back at the situation of Mishnah 4; the case of Mishnah 5 never could arise.

130 It already was stated in Mishnah 1 that a person acting upon the instructions of the Court is never liable for a purification offering, irrespective of the quality of the Court's ruling. Why should the individual be held liable?

131 Then the main condition for a sacrifice of the Court is not fulfilled; automatically there is no valid ruling of the Court, only actions of individuals.

132 A High Court without authority is no High Court; it cannot claim to be the subject of *Lev.* 4:13.

133 Since at the moment a sacrifice would be due the conditions are not met, the Court is no longer liable.

134 Since the authority of the Court is acknowledged, a later rejection does not change the fact of the Court's false ruling, and the Court is liable.

(fol. 45c) **משנה ו**: הוֹרוּ בֵית דִּין וְעָשׂוּ כָל־הַקָּהָל אוֹ רוּבָּן עַל פִּיהֶן מְבִיאִין פָּר. וּבַעֲבוֹדָה זָרָה מְבִיאִין פַּר וְשָׂעִיר דִּבְרֵי רִבִּי מֵאִיר. רִבִּי יְהוּדָה אוֹמֵר שְׁנֵים עָשָׂר שְׁבָטִים מְבִיאִין שְׁנֵים עָשָׂר פָּרִים וּבַעֲבוֹדָה זָרָה שְׁנֵים עָשָׂר שְׁבָטִים מְבִיאִין שְׁנֵים עָשָׂר פָּרִים וּשְׁנֵים עָשָׂר שְׂעִירִים. רִבִּי שִׁמְעוֹן אוֹמֵר שְׁלֹשָׁה עָשָׂר פָּרִים. וּבַעֲבוֹדָה זָרָה שְׁלֹשָׁה עָשָׂר פָּרִים וּשְׁלֹשָׁה עָשָׂר שְׂעִירִים פַּר וְשָׂעִיר לְכָל־שֵׁבֶט פַּר וְשָׂעִיר לְבֵית דִּין.

Mishnah 6: If the Court ruled and all the public or a majority acted on their instruction, they bring a bull; or in a matter of idolatry a bull and a goat[135], the words of Rebbi Meïr. Rebbi Jehudah says, the Twelve Tribes bring twelve bulls and in a matter of idolatry the Twelve Tribes bring twelve bulls and twelve goats[136]. Rebbi Simeon says, thirteen oxen, and in a matter of idolatry thirteen bulls and thirteen goats; a bull and a goat for each tribe; a bull and a goat for the Court.

135 Sacrifices for unintended sins committed by the entire community are prescribed both in *Lev*. 4:13-31 (a bull) and *Num*. 15:22-26 (a bull as elevation offering and a goat as purification offering). The verses in *Num*. are interpreted to refer to the sin of idolatry since that is the only sin by which in one action one violates *all* commandments (*Num*. 15:22). Since the sacrifice for violating all commandments cannot be less than that for violating one commandment, it is logical that the sacrifice for idolatry must be more than the regular sacrifice *Lev*. 4:13-31. (*Sifry Num*. 111)

136 As discussed in the Halakhah, this is a problem of definition of עֵדָה and קָהָל.

(46a line 60) **הלכה ו**: הוֹרוּ בֵית דִּין וְעָשׂוּ כָל־הַקָּהָל כול'. מָאן תַּנָּא רוֹב. רִבִּי מֵאִיר. דְּתַנֵּי. הִיא מַחֲצִית כָּל־הַשְּׁבָטִים הִיא מַחֲצִית כָּל־שֵׁבֶט וָשֵׁבֶט וּבִלְבַד רוֹב. רִבִּי יוּדָה אוֹמֵר. חֲצִי כָל־שֵׁבֶט וָשֵׁבֶט וּבִלְבַד רוּבֵי שְׁבָטִים שְׁלֵימִים. שֵׁבֶט אֶחָד גּוֹרֵר כָּל־הַשְּׁבָטִים. רִבִּי מֵאִיר אוֹמֵר. כָּל־הַשְּׁבָטִים קְרוּיִין קָהָל. רִבִּי יוּדָה אוֹמֵר. כָּל־שֵׁבֶט וָשֵׁבֶט קָרוּי קָהָל. וְאַתְיָיא דְּרִבִּי שִׁמְעוֹן כְּרִבִּי יוּדָה. כְּמַה דְּרִבִּי יוּדָה אָמַר. כָּל־שֵׁבֶט וָשֵׁבֶט קָרוּי קָהָל. כֵּן רִבִּי שִׁמְעוֹן אוֹמֵר. כָּל־שֵׁבֶט וָשֵׁבֶט קָרוּי קָהָל. מַה בֵּינֵיהוֹן. גְּרִירָה. רִבִּי יוּדָה אוֹמֵר. שֵׁבֶט אֶחָד גּוֹרֵר כָּל־הַשְּׁבָטִים. רִבִּי שִׁמְעוֹן אוֹמֵר. אֵין שֵׁבֶט אֶחָד גּוֹרֵר אֶת כָּל־הַשְּׁבָטִים. מוֹדֶה וְהוּא שֶׁתְּהֵא הוֹרָייָה מִלִּשְׁכַּת הַגָּזִית. אָמַר רִבִּי יוֹסֵי. טַעֲמֵיהּ דְּהֵין תַּנַּיָּא מִן־הַמָּקוֹם הַהוּא אֲשֶׁר יִבְחַר יי. רִבִּי אַבּוּן בְּשֵׁם רִבִּי בִּנְיָמִין בַּר לֵוִי. קִרְיָיא מְסַייֵעַ לְמָאן דָּמַר. כָּל־שֵׁבֶט וָשֵׁבֶט קָרוּי קָהָל. דִּכְתִיב גּוֹי וּקְהַל גּוֹיִם יִהְיֶה מִמֶּךָּ. וְאַדַּיִין לֹא נוֹלַד בִּנְיָמִין. אָמַר רִבִּי חִיָּיה בַּר בָּא. כְּשֵׁם שֶׁהֵן חֲלוּקִין כָּאן כָּךְ הֵן חֲלוּקִין בְּטוּמְאָה. דְּתַנֵּי. הָיָה צִיבּוּר חֶצְיָין טְהוֹרִין וְחֶצְיָין טְמֵאִין. הַטְּהוֹרִין עוֹשִׂין אֶת הָרִאשׁוֹן וְהַטְּמֵאִין עוֹשִׂין אֶת הַשֵּׁינִי. רִבִּי יוּדָה אוֹמֵר. הַטְּהוֹרִין עוֹשִׂין לְעַצְמָן וְהַטְּמֵאִין עוֹשִׂין לְעַצְמָן.

אֲמְרוּ לוֹ. אֵין הַפֶּסַח לַחֲצָאִין אוֹ כוּלָּן יַעֲשׂוּ בְטוּמְאָה אוּ כוּלָּן יַעֲשׂוּ בְטַהֲרָה. מִינוּ אֲמְרוּ לוֹ. כְּרִבִּי יוּדָה. דְּתַנֵּי. נִיטְמֵאת אַחַת מִן הַחַלּוֹת אוֹ אֶחָד מִן שְׁיָרִים רִבִּי יוּדָה אוֹמֵר שְׁנֵיהֶן יֵצְאוּ לְבֵית הַשְּׂרֵיפָה. שֶׁאֵין קָרְבַּן צִבּוּר חָלוּק. וַחֲכָמִים אוֹמְרִים. הַטָּמֵא בְטוּמְאָתוֹ וְהַטָּהוֹר יֵאָכֵל׃ רִבִּי יוֹסֵי בֵּרִבִּי בּוּן בְּשֵׁם רִבִּי יוֹחָנָן אָמַר. מִינוּ אֲמְרוּ לוֹ. חֲכָמִים שֶׁהֵן כְּשִׁיטַּת רִבִּי יְהוּדָה.

1 מאן | מן 2 יודה | יהודה 3 רובי | רוב שלימין | שלמין 4 יודה | יהודה ואתייא | ותיא גר' | ר' 5 כר' | ר' יודה | יהודה אמ' | אומר 6 ביניהון | ביניהם גרירה | גרירא יודה | יהודה ר' | ור' 7 את | - | אע"ג דרבי יהודה אומר שבט אחד גורר כל השבטים שתהא | שתיהיה הורייה | הוריה 8 יוסי | יוסה דהין | דההין 9 קרייא | קרא מסייע | מסייעא 10 ואדיין | ואדין חייה | חייא חלוקין כאן | כן 11 טהורין | טמאין טמאין | טהורין את | אותו את 12 שיני | שני יודה | יהודה 13 לחצאין | בא לחצאין כולן | כולו (2 times) מינו | מנו 14 יודה | יהודה (2 times) ניטמאת | נטצית אחד מן ישריים | אחת מן הסדרים שניהן | שניהם 16 יוסי | יוסה בר' | בר אמ' | - מינו | מנו שהן | שהן עושין

Halakhah 6: "If the Court ruled and all the public acted," etc. [137]Who stated "a majority"? Rebbi Meïr, as it was stated: Either half of the tribes or half of each tribe, if only it be a majority[138]. Rebbi Jehudah says, half of each tribe, but only a majority of entire tribes[139]. One tribe drags all tribes[140].

Rebbi Meïr says, all tribes are called "the public"[141]. Rebbi Jehudah says, each single tribe is called "public". And Rebbi Simeon follows Rebbi Jehudah. Just as Rebbi Jehudah said, each single tribe is called "public", so Rebbi Simeon says, each single tribe is called "public". What is between them? Dragging. Rebbi Jehudah says, one tribe drags all tribes[140]. Rebbi Simeon says, one tribe does not drag all tribes[142]. [Even though Rebbi Jehudah says, one tribe drags all tribes,][143] he agrees that only if the ruling came from the ashlar hall[144]. Rebbi Yose said, the reason of that Tanna: *From this place which the Eternal will choose*[145]. Rebbi Abun in the name of Rebbi Bejamin ben Levi: The verse supports him who said that each tribe is called "public", as it is written[146]: *A people and a public of peoples will come from you,* and Benjamin was not yet born.

Rebbi Ḥiyya bar Abba said, just as they differ here, so they differ about impurity[137], as we have stated: If the public was half pure and half impure; pure [people] celebrate the first [Passover] and impure the second. Rebbi Jehudah said, the pure ones celebrate for themselves, and the impure ones celebrate for themselves[147]. They told him, there is no split Passover; either all celebrate in impurity or all celebrate in purity. Who is "they told him"? Following Rebbi Jehudah? As it was stated[148]: "If one of the loaves or one of the (leftovers) [orders][149] became impure, Rebbi Jehudah said, both have to be brought to be burned[150] for a public offering cannot be split. But the Sages say, the impure in its impurity, and the pure shall be eaten.[151]" Rebbi Yose ben Rebbi Abun said in the name of Rebbi Johanan, who is "they told him"? The Sages[152] who argue like Rebbi Jehudah.

137 The entire Halakhah is shortened from *Pesahim* 7:6. *Num.* 9:9-14 prescribes that individuals who were impure on Passover have to bring their Passover sacrifice a month later, on the Second Passover celebrated on the 14th of the Second Month. It is concluded that if the entire people are impure, the Second Passover is impossible and everybody celebrates the (First) Passover in impurity in the Temple. The problem then arises which percentage of the people have to be impure so that they represent the entire people; just as here the question is, how many people do have to follow the erroneous ruling of the Court so that "all of Israel were in error" (*Lev.* 4:13).

138 He holds that everywhere 50%+1 represent "all"; Babli 5b.

139 The language is somewhat self-contradictory. He also requires that a majority of Israel follow the erroneous ruling but in addition he demands that in a majority of tribes a majority follow the ruling. Babli 5b.

140 If one tribe has more members than all the others together, the action of one tribe triggers the obligation of all of them. He does not hold that the law about erroneous rulings of the High Court became moot with the exile of the Ten Tribes. Even later, when the tribe of Jehudah represented the overwhelming majority of Israel, a majority of the people can be considered a majority of all twelve tribes and the majority of Judeans triggers the obligation for all tribes.

141 The purification sacrifice for an erroneous ruling by the Court has to be brought by "the public" (*Lev.* 4:14). The difference of opinions in the Mishnah is traced to different interpretations of this notion. R. Meïr holds that only the entire people of Israel qualify as "public"; RR. Jehudah and Simeon consider each tribe as a separate public. (Babli 5b, *Pesahim* 80a, *Menahot* 15a).

142 Therefore he requires a separate sacrifice for the people of Israel in their entirety.

143 Missing in the ms., from B and the *Pesahim* text; required by the context.

144 Even though each tribe has to bring its own sacrifice, the ruling of a tribal High Court cannot trigger an obligation of any other tribe; only the Court sitting at the central sanctuary has this power.

145 *Deut.* 17:10.

146 *Gen.* 35:11, said to Jacob after the birth of 11 sons. Babli 5b.

147 Both offer their sacrifices in the Temple, in separate groups. For this to happen, the number of pure people in Jerusalem on the 14th of Nisan must be *exactly* equal to the number of impure ones.

148 Mishnah *Menahot* 2:2.

149 The text in parentheses is from the

ms.; the text in brackets is from B, the text in *Pesahim,* and all sources of the Mishnah; it is the only one which makes sense.

The Mishnah speaks of the two public cereal offerings which have to be baked, *viz.*, the weekly show-bread and the two leavened loaves presented at Pentecost. The 12 show-breads were presented in two rows, here called "orders" (*Lev.* 24:6).

150 Outside the Temple precinct.

151 By the officiating priests.

152 Since the opinions of R. Jehudah and his opponents in *Pesaḥim* are the opinions of his opponents and R. Jehudah in *Menahot*, both seem to contradict themselves. One has to conclude that they agree in principle and they only differ about the practical applications of their theory. In this sense, B reads: The Sages *acting* in the sense of R. Jehudah.

(fol. 45c) **משנה ז**: הוֹרוּ בֵית דִּין וְעָשׂוּ שִׁבְעָה שְׁבָטִים אוֹ רוּבָּן עַל פִּיהֶן מְבִיאִין פָּר וּבַעֲבוֹדָה זָרָה מְבִיאִין פַּר וְשָׂעִיר דִּבְרֵי רִבִּי מֵאִיר. רִבִּי יְהוּדָה אוֹמֵר שִׁבְעָה שְׁבָטִים שֶׁחָטְאוּ מְבִיאִין שִׁבְעָה פָּרִים. וּשְׁאָר שְׁבָטִים שֶׁלֹּא חָטְאוּ מְבִיאִין עַל יְדֵיהֶן פַּר פַּר שֶׁאַף אֵילוּ שֶׁלֹּא חָטְאוּ מְבִיאִין עַל יְדֵיהֶן פַּר פַּר עַל יְדֵי הַחוֹטְאִים. רִבִּי שִׁמְעוֹן אוֹמֵר שְׁמוֹנָה פָּרִים. וּבַעֲבוֹדָה זָרָה שְׁמוֹנָה פָּרִים וּשְׁמוֹנָה שְׂעִירִים פַּר וְשָׂעִיר לְכָל שֵׁבֶט וּפַר וְשָׂעִיר לְבֵית דִּין.

Mishnah 7: If the Court ruled and seven tribes or a majority[153] acted on their saying they bring a bull and for idolatry they bring a bull and a goat, the words of Rebbi Meïr. Rebbi Jehudah says, the seven tribes who sinned bring seven bulls, and the remaining tribes who did not sin bring because of them a bull each, for also those who did not sin each bring a bull because of the sinners. Rebbi Simeon says eight bulls[154], and for idolatry eight oxen and eight goats, a bull and a goat for each tribe and a bull and a goat for the Court.

153 Either seven tribes who form a majority of the tribes or a majority of the people of Israel irrespective of tribes.

154 As stated in the preceding Halakhah, he disputes that innocent tribes should be dragged with the sinners into offering sacrifice.

(46b line 7) **הלכה ז**: הוֹרוּ בֵית דִּין וְעָשׂוּ שִׁבְעָה שְׁבָטִים כול'. תַּנֵּי. רִבִּי שִׁמְעוֹן בֶּן אֶלְעָזָר אוֹמֵר מִשְּׁמוֹ. חָטְאוּ שִׁשָּׁה וְהֵן רוּבּוֹ. הָא שִׁבְעָה אַף עַל פִּי שֶׁאֵין רוּבּוֹ הֲרֵי אֵילוּ חַיָּבִין. אָמַר רִבִּי לְעָזָר. לֹא מַר אֶלָּא שִׁשָּׁה וְהֵן רוּבּוֹ. הָא חֲמִשָּׁה אַף עַל פִּי שֶׁהֵן רוּבּוֹ הֲרֵי אֵילוּ פְטוּרִין. אָמַר רִבִּי יוֹסֵי בֵּרִבִּי בּוּן. מַתְנִיתָא אָמְרָה כֵן. מַחֲצִית שְׁבָטִים וּבִלְבַד רוֹב אוֹכְלוֹסִין. וְדִכְווָתָהּ. מַחֲצִית

אוֹכְלוּסִין וּבִלְבַד רוֹב שְׁבָטִים. רִבִּי יוֹסֵי בֵּרִבִּי בּוּן אָמַר. שְׁאִילְתָא דְכֹהֵן הַמָּשִׁיחַ מִן. הָדָא הוֹרָיַית בֵּית דִּין הַגָּדוֹל הוֹרָיַית בֵּית דִּין קָטָן.

2 הא | או אילו | אלו 3 לעזר | אלעזר מר | אמרו אילו | אלו 4 יוסי | יוסה בר' בון | בר רבי ודכוותה | ודכותה 5 יוסי | יוסה 6 הוריית | הורית (twice)

Halakhah 7: "If the Court ruled and seven tribes acted," etc. It was stated: Rebbi Simeon ben Eleazar says in his[155] name, if six sinned and they are a majority. Therefore seven even though they do not form a majority are liable[156]. Rebbi Eleazar said, he only said "six and they are a majority". Therefore for five, even though they are a majority, they are not liable. Rebbi Yose ben Rebbi Abun said, a *baraita* said so: Half of the tribes on condition that they be most of the population. And similarly, half of the population on condition that they be most of the tribes.

[157]Rebbi Yose ben Rebbi Abun said, the question of the Anointed Priest, is it as from the High Court or a lower court?

155 In the name of R. Meïr, Tosephta 1:7; *Sifra Wayyiqra 2, Parašah* 4(17); Babli 3a, 5b.

156 In the Babli, *Menahot* 45a, this is the conclusion of R. Johanan. Since in the next sentence R. Eleazar disagrees, one has to assume that the name originally was stated here also.

157 This does not belong here but at the end of Halakhah 2:1, speaking of rulings by the High Priest.

(fol. 45c) **הלכה ח**: הוֹרוּ בֵּית דִּין שֶׁל אֶחָד מִן הַשְּׁבָטִים וְעָשָׂה אוֹתוֹ הַשֵּׁבֶט עַל פִּיהֶם אוֹתוֹ הַשֵּׁבֶט הוּא חַייָב וּשְׁאָר כָּל הַשְּׁבָטִים פְּטוּרִין דִּבְרֵי רִבִּי יְהוּדָה. וַחֲכָמִים אוֹמְרִין אֵין חַייָבִין אֶלָּא עַל הוֹרָיַית בֵּית דִּין הַגָּדוֹל בִּלְבַד שֶׁנֶּאֱמַר וְאִם כָּל־עֲדַת יִשְׂרָאֵל יִשְׁגּוּ וְנֶעְלַם דָּבָר מֵעֵינֵי הָעֵדָה. וְלֹא עֲדַת אוֹתוֹ הַשֵּׁבֶט:

Halakhah 8: If the Court of one of the tribes[158] ruled and that tribe acted on their pronouncement, that tribe is liable but any other tribes are not liable, the words of Rebbi Jehudah[159]. But the Sages say, they are only liable for a ruling by the High Court, as it is said, *if the entire congregation of Israel be in error, and something was hidden from the eyes of the congregation*[160], not the congregation of that tribe.

158 The tribal High Court.
159 Since he holds that the expression קָהָל refers to each of the tribes.
160 *Lev*. 4:13. The verse is misquoted; the masoretic text reads הַקָּהָל "the public" instead of הָעֵדָה "the congregation", supporting R. Jehudah. In most Mishnah sources, only the first clause of the verse is copied.

(46b line 14) **הלכה ח:** הורוּ בֵּית דִּין שֶׁלְּאֶחָד מִן הַשְּׁבָטִים כול'. רִבִּי מֵאִיר אוֹמֵר. חוֹבַת בֵּית דִּין הִיא. רִבִּי יוּדָה אוֹמֵר. חוֹבַת צִיבּוּרָא. אָמַר רִבִּי שִׁמְעוֹן. חוֹבַת בֵּית דִּין וְחוֹבַת צִיבּוּרָא הִיא. מַה טַעֲמֵיהּ דְּרִבִּי מֵאִיר. נֶאֱמַר כָּאן מֵעֵינֵי וְנֶאֱמַר לְהַלָּן מֵעֵינֵי. מַה מֵעֵינֵי שֶׁנֶּאֱמַר לְהַלָּן בֵּית דִּין אַף כָּאן בֵּית דִּין. מַה טַעַם דְּרִבִּי יוּדָה. נֶאֱמַר כָּאן מֵעֵינֵי וְנֶאֱמַר לְהַלָּן מֵעֵינֵי. מַה מֵעֵינֵי שֶׁנֶּאֱמַר לְהַלָּן צִיבּוּר אַף כָּאן צִיבּוּר. מַה טַעֲמָא דְּרִבִּי שִׁמְעוֹן. נֶאֱמַר כָּאן מֵעֵינֵי וְנֶאֱמַר לְהַלָּן מֵעֵינֵי. מַה מֵעֵינֵי שֶׁנֶּאֱמַר לְהַלָּן בֵּית דִּין אַף מֵעֵינֵי שֶׁנֶּאֱמַר כָּאן בֵּית דִּין. וּמַה מֵעֵינֵי שֶׁנֶּאֱמַר לְהַלָּן צִיבּוּר אַף כָּאן צִיבּוּר. מָאן דָּמַר. חוֹבַת בֵּית דִּין הִיא. בֵּית דִּין מְבִיאִין. מָאן דְּאָמַר. חוֹבַת צִיבּוּר הִיא. מִי מֵבִיא. דְּתַנֵּי. מַטִּילִין הָיוּ עֲלֵיהֶן וּבָאִין. דִּבְרֵי רִבִּי מֵאִיר. רִבִּי יוּדָה אוֹמֵר. מִתְּרוּמַת הַלִּשְׁכָּה הָיוּ בָאִין. מָאן דָּמַר. חוֹבַת בֵּית דִּין הִיא. בֵּית דִּין סוֹמְכִין. מָאן דָּמַר. חוֹבַת צִיבּוּר הִיא. מִי סוֹמֵךְ. דְּתַנֵּי. שְׁלֹשָׁה מִכָּל־שֵׁבֶט וָשֵׁבֶט וְרֹאשׁ בֵּית דִּין עַל גַּבֵּיהֶן סוֹמְכִין יְדֵיהֶן עַל רֹאשׁ הַפָּר. יְדֵיהֶם. יְדֵי כָל־יָחִיד וְיָחִיד. יְדֵיהֶם עַל רֹאשׁ הַפָּר. פַּר טָעוּן סְמִיכָה אֵין שְׂעִירֵי עֲבוֹדָה זָרָה טְעוּנִין סְמִיכָה. דִּבְרֵי רִבִּי יוּדָה. רִבִּי שִׁמְעוֹן אוֹמֵר. פַּר טָעוּן סְמִיכָה בִזְקֵינִים אֵין שְׂעִירֵי עֲבוֹדָה זָרָה טְעוּנִין סְמִיכָה בִזְקֵינִים. שֶׁרִבִּי שִׁמְעוֹן אוֹמֵר. כָּל־חַטַּאת צִיבּוּר שֶׁדָּמָהּ נִכְנַס לִפְנִים טְעוּנָה סְמִיכָה. מְתִיבִין לְרִבִּי יוּדָה. וְהָכְתִיב וַיַּגִּשׁוּ אֶת־שְׂעִירֵי הַחַטָּאת. רִבִּי חִייָה בְשֵׁם רִבִּי יוֹחָנָן. הוֹרָאַת שָׁעָה הָיְתָה.

1 או' | אומר אין[161] 2 יודה | יהודה ציבורא | צבור היא אמ' | - ציבורא | צבור 3 מה | מאי 4 יודה | יהודה מעיני | אם מעיני העדה שנאמר | האמור 5 להלן | שם ציבור | ציבורא (2X) מה | ומאי 6 מעיני שנ' | - ציבור | צבור (2X) 7 מאן | מן (2X) דאמר | דמר ציבור | צבור 8 יודה | יהודה 9 היא. בית דין | - מאן | מן מאן | ומאן ציבור | צבור 10 ידיהם | ידיהם על ראש הפרים[162] 11 אין | ואין 12 יודה | יהודה בזקינים | בזקנים אין | ואין 13 בזקינים | בזקנים 14 יודה | יהודה חייה | חייא 15הוראת | הורית

רִבִּי יוֹחָנָן בָּעֵי. צִיבּוּר שֶׁמֵּת אֶחָד מָהוּ שֶׁיָּבִיא תַחְתָּיו. הָתִיבוֹן. וְהָכְתִיב הַבָּאִים מֵהַשְּׁבִי וגו'. אֶיפְשַׁר חַטָּאת עוֹלָה. אֶלָּא מַה עוֹלָה לֹא נֶאֱכְלָה אַף חַטָּאת לֹא נֶאֱכְלָה. רִבִּי יוּדָה אוֹמֵר. עַל עֲבוֹדָה זָרָה הֵבִיאוּם. רִבִּי חִזְקִיָּה רִבִּי יִרְמְיָה רִבִּי חִייָה בְשֵׁם רִבִּי יוֹחָנָן. הוֹרַיִית שָׁעָה הָיְתָה. רִבִּי יִרְמְיָה לָמַד[163] כֵּן. אֶלָּא פַּר טָעוּן סְמִיכָה בִזְקֵנִים. אֵין שְׂעִירֵי עֲבוֹדָה זָרָה טְעוּנִין סְמִיכָה בִזְקֵינִים. אֶלָּא בְמִי. רִבִּי יִרְמְיָה סָבַר מֵימַר. בְּאַהֲרֹן וּבָנָיו. אָמַר לֵיהּ רִבִּי יוֹסֵי. וְהָתַנֵּי רִבִּי חִייָה. וְסָמַךְ וְסָמְכוּ. לְרַבּוֹת שְׂעִירֵי עֲבוֹדָה זָרָה בִסְמִיכָה וְלֹא בִזְקֵנִים. רִבִּי יוֹסֵי לָמַד[163] כֵּן. אֶלָּא חַי טָעוּן סְמִיכָה בְאַהֲרֹן אֵין שְׂעִירֵי עֲבוֹדָה זָרָה טְעוּנִין סְמִיכָה בְאַהֲרֹן. וּכְתִיב וְסָמַךְ אַהֲרֹן אֶת־שְׁתֵּי יָדָיו עַל־רֹאשׁ הַשָּׂעִיר הַחַי. חַי טָעוּן סְמִיכָה בְאַהֲרֹן. אֵין שְׂעִירֵי עֲבוֹדָה זָרָה טְעוּנִין סְמִיכָה בְאַהֲרֹן. מָה עָבְדִין לָהּ רִבִּי יִרְמְיָה. פָּתַר לָהּ בְּכֹהֵן הֶדְיוֹט.

1 ציבור | צבור אחד | אחד מהן שיביא | שיביאו מהשבי | על[161] מהשבי הגולה הביאו עולות 2 איפשר | אפשר יודה | יהודה 3 חייה | חייא 4 הוריית | הורית הייתה | היתה 4 למד | לא אמר בזקינים | בזקנים אין | ואין 5 בזקינים | בזקנים יוסי | יוסה חייה | חייא 6 ולא | אלא יוסי למד | יוסה לא אמר חי | הוא 7 אין | ואין וכת' | דכת' 8 אין | ואין 9 לה | ליה

Halakhah 8: "If the Court of one of the tribes ruled," etc. [164]Rebbi Meïr says, it is the Court's obligation. Rebbi Jehudah says, it is the public's obligation. Rebbi Simeon said, it is an obligation of the Court and an obligation of the public. What is Rebbi Meïr's reason? It is said here *from the eyes*[165], and it is said there *from the eyes*[166]. Since *from the eyes* said there refers to the Court, here it also refers to the Court[167]. What is Rebbi Jehudah's reason? It is said here *from the eyes*, and it is said there *from the eyes*. Since *from the eyes* said there refers to the public, here it also refers to the public[168]. What is Rebbi Simeon's reason? It is said here *from the eyes*, and it is said there *from the eyes*. Since *from the eyes* said there refers to the Court, also *from the eyes* here refers to the Court. Since *from the eyes* said there refers to the public, here it also refers to the public[169]. For him who says, it is the Court's obligation, the Court has to bring[170]. For him who says, it is the public's obligation, who brings[171]? As we have stated[172], "one imposes and collects, the words of Rebbi Meïr; Rebbi Jehudah says, they are brought from the Temple tax". For him who says, it is the Court's obligation, the Court has to lay their hands on. For him who says, it is the public's obligation, who lays their hands on[173]? As we have stated, three from every tribe,[174] led by the president of the Court, lay their hands on the head of the bull. "*Their hands*, the hands of each single one. *Their hands on the head of the bull*; the bull needs laying on of hands but the goats of idolatry do not need laying on of hands, the words of Rebbi Jehudah. Rebbi Simeon said, the bull needs laying on of hands by the Elders but the goats of idolatry do not need laying on of hands by the Elders; for Rebbi Simeon says, every public purification offering whose blood is brought inside[175] needs laying on of hands.[176]" One objected to Rebbi Jehudah, is it not written, *they presented the goats of the purification offering*[177]? Rebbi Ḥiyya in the name of Rebbi Joḥanan, it was a temporary ruling[178].

Rebbi Joḥanan asked: If one of the public died, can it be brought in his stead[179]? They answered, is it not written, *those who came from captivity*[180]?

Is a purification offering an elevation offering? But just as an elevation offering is not eaten, this purification offering was not eaten[181]. Rebbi Jehudah says, they brought it for idolatry; Rebbi Ḥizqiah, Rebbi Jeremiah, Rebbi Ḥiyya in the name of Rebbi Joḥanan, it was a temporary ruling[178]. Rebbi Jeremiah (learned) [did not say][163] so but the bull needs laying on of hands by the Elders while the goats of idolatry do not need laying on of hands by the Elders. By whom? Rebbi Jeremiah wanted to say, by Aaron and his sons. Rebbi Yose told him, Rebbi Ḥiyya also stated, *he shall put his hands on, they shall put their hands on*[182], to include the goats of idolatry for laying on hands but not by the Elders. Rebbi Yose (learned) [did not say][163] so but the living [goat] needs laying on of hands by Aaron, but the goats of idolatry do not need laying on of hands by Aaron. It is written so, "*Aaron shall lean with both his hands on the living goat's head*; the living [goat] needs laying on of hands by Aaron, but he goats of idolatry do not need laying on of hands by Aaron.[183]" What does Rebbi Jeremiah do with this? He explains it, for a common priest[184].

161 To delete.

162 This is a quote from *Num.* 8:12, not fitting for the context.

163 The text in the Babli shows that one has to read למר i. e. לֹא אָמַר.

164 The Halakhah does not refer to Mishnah 8 but to Mishnaiot 6-7, to explain why R. Meïr requires only one bull, R. Jehudah 12, and R. Simeon 13.

165 *Lev.* 4:13.

166 *Num.* 15:24.

167 This argument is difficult to explain. In *Sifra Wayyiqra 2 Parašah* 4(2), the expression עֲדַת יִשְׂרָאֵל used in *Lev.* 4:13 is explained as referring to the High Court, the selected group from Israel, based on v. 15 which makes it clear that the bull has to be presented by the Elders, the members of the High Court. Then R. Meïr's argument is to infer from *Lev.* 4:13 to *Num.* 15:24: Since the bull is the responsibility of the Court, the goat for idolatry also must be the responsibility of the Court.

168 His argument is straightforward. Since the entire paragraph *Num.* 15:22-26 speaks only about עֵדָה, without any mention of the Elders, it is addressed to the public. Then the use of parallel terms is taken to transfer the setting to *Lev.* 4:13.

169 He accepts arguing both from *Lev.* 4:13 to *Num.* 15:24 and vice versa.

170 They have to pay for the bull from their own money and present it in the Temple.

171 Who has to pay and who has to officiate?

172 One imposes a tax and collects from everybody. In all other sources, Babli 3b, *Menahot* 52a; Tosephta *Šeqalim* 2:6, the

argument is between R. Jehudah and R. Simeon. This is the reasonable reading since for R. Meïr the Court pays from their own means.

173 Since obviously not every single Israelite can be called to lay his hands on the bull.

174 This follows R. Simeon in *Sifra Wayyiqra 2 Pereq* 6(2); R. Jehudah requires five.

175 The only sacrifices whose blood is brought inside the sanctuary to be sprinkled on the incense altar are the purification offerings of the High Priest and the Community as well as the offerings of the Day of Atonement. The body of any such sacrifice must be burned outside the holy precinct (*Lev.* 6:23,16:27).

176 *Sifra Wayyiqra 2 Pereq* 6(3); Tosephta *Menahot* 10:9; Babli *Menahot* 92a.

177 *2Chr.* 29:23. As usual, the argument is from the part of the verse which was not quoted: *they presented the goats of the purification offering before the king and the public; they laid their hands on them.* The goats were offered by Josiah to atone for the idolatry of his father Ahas.

178 A temporary deviation from Torah norms acceptable by prophetic instruction as long as it does not violate prohibitions. The absence of a bull and the presence of multiple goats both deviate from Torah prescriptions.

179 This is a question for RR. Jehudah and Simeon. If a person dedicated an animal as a purification offering but died before it was sacrificed, the animal cannot be sacrificed without its owner nor can it be redeemed or used for any profane or holy purpose whatsoever. If the bull really is the obligation of the public and paid by the public's money, it should become unusable if anybody who gave money for the sacrifice (Note 172) died before the ceremony was held. Practically, this would make the ceremony impossible.

180 *Ezra* 8:35: *Those who came from captivity, from the diaspora, sacrificed elevation offerings to the God of Israel, twelve bulls for all of Israel, 96 goats, 77 sheep, purification goats twelve, all of it an elevation offering for the Eternal.* An elevation offering is completely burned; the meat of a purification offering is eaten by the priests. To call a purification offering an elevation offering is a contradiction in terms.

181 Babli 6a. Since they brought 12 goats, R. Jehudah has Ezra's authority for his position. This interpretation justifies the reading of *Num.* 15:24 by the Mishnah. That verse requires the congregation to bring *a bull as elevation offering and a goat as purification offering.* If a purification offering which may not be eaten can be called an elevation offering, it is possible to identify this bull with the one prescribed in *Lev.* 4:13. V. 24 requires the congregation (i. e., its Elders) to proffer the sacrifices but v. 25 requires the Cohen to conduct the entire ceremony. Both the opinions that the Elders do the laying on of their hands as also that the Cohen has to do it have biblical support.

182 *Lev.* 16:21 prescribes that Aaron has to lay his hand on the live goat. Since the

entire service of the Day of Atonement is by the unaided High Priest, the mention of the name seems to be superfluous; it could as well have said "he has to lay his hands on." It is concluded (next Note) that this is the only case in which the High Priest is required to lay his hands on. In parallel, one may read *Lev*. 4:15 where the Elders of the congregation are required to lay their hands on the bull, that they are not required to lay their hands on the goat.

183 *Sifra Ahare Mot Parašah* 4(4).

184 Since neither the High Priest nor the Elders are empowered but *Num*. 15:25 requires the participation of a common priest, all biblical requirements are satisfied by having the common priest do the entire ceremony.

(46b line 46) רִבִּי זְעִירָא בְּשֵׁם רַב הַמְנוּנָא כְּרִבִּי מֵאִיר. תַּנֵּי תַמָּן. הוֹרוּ בֵית דִּין וְעָשׂוּ קָהָל. מֵת אֶחָד מִבֵּית דִּין פְּטוּרִין. מֵת אֶחָד מִן הַצִּיבּוּר חַייָבִין. אָמַר לָהֶן רִבִּי מֵאִיר. אִם לַאֲחֵרִים הוּא פוֹטֵר לֹא כָל־שֶׁכֵּן עַל עַצְמוֹ. אָמְרוּ לוֹ. יִפְטוֹר לַאֲחֵרִים שֶׁיֵּשׁ לָהֶן בַּמֶּה לִתְלוֹת וְאַל יִפְטוֹר לְעַצְמוֹ שֶׁאֵין לוֹ בַּמֶּה לִתְלוֹת.

1 המנונא כר' מאיר | אדא ברבי מאיר תני | תניי מת | ומת 2 להן | להם הוא | יהא 3 להן | להם לתלות | להתלות 4 לתלות | להתלות

רִבִּי זְעִירָא בְּשֵׁם רַב חִסְדַּאי. תַּנֵּיי תַמָּן. הוֹרוּ בֵית דִּין וְעָשׂוּ הֵן וְיָדְעוּ מָה הוֹרוּ. טָעוּ מָה הוֹרוּ שָׁגוּ מָה הוֹרוּ יָכוֹל יְהוּ חַייָבִין. תַּלְמוּד לוֹמַר וְנוֹדְעָה֙ הַחַטָּאת וְלֹא שֶׁיִּוָּדְעוּ הַחוֹטְאִין. מַה נַפְשָׁךְ. חֵלֶב כְּרִבִּי יְהוֹשֻׁעַ אַתְיָא הִיא בְּשֶׁהוֹרוּ וְלֹא יָדְעוּ מָה הוֹרוּ אִם עֲבוֹדָה זָרָה אִם שְׁאָר כָּל־הַמִּצְוֹת. אִם עֲבוֹדָה זָרָה בְּפָר אִם שְׁאָר כָּל־הַמִּצְוֹת בְּשָׂעִיר. סָפֵק פַּר וְשָׂעִיר שִׁינּוּי קָרְבָּן הוּא וְהוּא פָטוּר.

1 חסדאי | חסדי תניי | תני טעו | וטעו 2 שגו | ושגגו שיודעו | שיוודעו החוטאין | החוטאים 3 חלב | חלב הורו חייבין שבת הורו חייבין. אמר רבי בון בר חייא ותיא כר' אליעזר ברם כר' יהושע לא אתיא אמר רבי יוסה ברם 4 ושעיר | ספק פר ושעיר

Rebbi Ze`ira in the name of Rav Hamnuna: Following Rebbi Meïr[185]. There, it was stated: If the Court ruled and the public acted[186]. If a member of the Court died, they are not liable. If a member of the public died, they are liable[187]. Rebbi Meïr told them, if he[188] relieves others of their liability, not so much more for himself? They told him, he can relieve others from their liability since they have where to hang on; he cannot relieve himself of liability since he has nothing to hang on.

Rebbi Ze`ira in the name of Rav Ḥisdai. There, it was stated[189]: "If the Court ruled, and they themselves acted, and they realized what they ruled about. If they erred in what they ruled, would they be liable? The verse says, *if the sin became known*[190], not that the sinners became known." Anyway you take it[191], if about fat [[192]they ruled they are liable, if about Sabbath they ruled they are liable. Rebbi Abun bar Ḥiyya said, this follows Rebbi Eliezer[193]; it does not follow Rebbi Joshua. Rebbi Yose said, but] it follows Rebbi Joshua if they ruled and they did not know whether about idolatry or about any other commandment[194]. If about idolatry by a bull, if about any other commandment a goat[195]. Since it is in doubt whether a bull or [a bull and[196]] a goat, it is a difference in sacrifice and he[197] is not liable.

185 The following *baraita* can be understood only following R. Meïr who declares the bull to be the exclusive responsibility of the Court.

186 *Sifra Wayyiqra 2 Paršetah* 4(10). The Court is not liable as long as the public did not act on their instructions.

187 If a member of the Court died, the bull becomes a purification sacrifice whose part-owner had died; it cannot be brought nor sacrificed. While the sacrifice is brought for the benefit of the public, the public has no monetary interest in the bull following Rebbi Meïr. For him, all the public does is trigger the obligation.

188 If a member of the Court acted on his own faulty ruling, the bull cannot relieve him of the obligation for a private purification sacrifice since the bull only is intended to shield those who acted on instructions of the Court. He himself does not depend on the Court and still is liable (Mishnah 1; Note 191).

189 Babli 5a, *Sifra Wayyiqra 2 Paršetah* 4(12).

190 *Lev.* 4:14. V. 13 makes it clear that the actions of the people trigger the obligation of the bull, not the actions of the court when it is not followed by the people.

191 This refers to another situation which is described at the end. The court ruled, they were followed by the people, they realized their error but know they cannot decide which paragraph of the law they misinterpreted. In the Babli 5a, *Ševuot* 18b, *Keritut* 19a, R. Eliezer is quoted to hold that if one is not sure of the exact category of the sin committed it does not matter as long as all of them require a sacrifice. R. Joshua holds that a purification sacrifice is possible only if the legal definition of the transgression is known, as in all cases the verse requires that the sin be known (*Lev.* 4:14 for the court, v. 23 for the prince, v. 28 for a private person; cf. Note 22.) From the text here it seems that the Yerushalmi tradition switches the names.

192 Text of B, missing in the ms. The text must be supposed also for the ms. since otherwise the reference to R. Joshua is unmotivated.

193 Who in the Yerushalmi version prohibits the Court from offering the bull if they cannot define exactly which commandment had been breached.

194 The argument in Note 191 is valid only if the different infractions all carry the same penalty. But if there is a question about which sacrifice to offer, no sacrifice is possible. Purification (and reparation) offerings cannot be brought as

voluntary offerings since in contrast to these all voluntary offerings need gifts of flour and wine. Therefore one could not bring both kinds of sacrifice stipulating that the inappropriate one should be considered as voluntary.

195 Clearly, one has to switch the positions of "bull" and "goat".

196 Text of B, more correct since the bull for unspecified sins is a purification offering and that for idolatry an elevation offering.

197 The Court.

הורה כהן משיח פרק שני

(fol. 46b) **משנה א**: הוֹרָה כֹּהֵן מָשִׁיחַ לְעַצְמוֹ שׁוֹגֵג וְעָשָׂה שׁוֹגֵג מֵבִיא פָּר. שׁוֹגֵג וְעָשָׂה מֵזִיד מֵזִיד וְעָשָׂה שׁוֹגֵג פָּטוּר שֶׁהוֹרָיַית כֹּהֵן מָשִׁיחַ לְעַצְמוֹ כְּהוֹרָיַית בֵּית דִּין לַצִּיבּוּר׃

Mishnah 1: If the Anointed Priest[1] ruled for himself in error and acted in error, he brings a bull[2]. If in error but he acted intentionally, or intentionally and he acted in error, he is not liable[3] since the ruling of the Anointed Priest for himself is like the ruling of the Court for the public.

1 This is the expression used in *Lev*. 4:1-12 for the High Priest. Since the verse refers here to "the Anointed Priest" while in *Lev*. 21:10 he is called "the High Priest", it is inferred (Mishnah 3:4, *Megillah* 1:9) that High Priests of the Second Temple who were not anointed were not entitled to this ceremony. The Anointed has to confess his sin while leaning with his hands on the bull's head. The remainder of the ceremony, as also that of the Court's bull, may be performed by a common priest. *Sifra Wayyiqra 2 Parashah* 3(6).

2 As described in *Lev*. 4:1-12, his private purification offering.

3 He cannot bring a purification offering unless it was an unintentional act. If he ruled wrongly but then did not act on his ruling because he did not trust his judgment, no sacrifice is due or possible.

(46c line 15) **הלכה א**: הוֹרָה כֹּהֵן מָשִׁיחַ כול׳. נֶפֶשׁ אִם הַכֹּהֵן הַמָּשִׁיחַ. הֲרֵי מָשִׁיחַ כְּיָחִיד. מַה יָחִיד אִם אָכַל בְּהוֹרָיַית בֵּית דִּין פָּטוּר. אַף זֶה אִם אָכַל בְּהוֹרָיַית בֵּית דִּין פָּטוּר. מַה יָחִיד אִם אָכַל בְּלֹא הוֹרָייָה חַייָב. אַף זֶה אִם אָכַל בְּלֹא הוֹרָייָה חַייָב. תַּלְמוּד לוֹמַר לְאַשְׁמַת הָעָם. הֲרֵי אַשְׁמָתוֹ כְּאַשְׁמַת הָעָם. מָה הָעָם אֵינָן חַייָבִין אֶלָּא אִם כֵּן הוֹרוּ. אַף זֶה אֵינוֹ חַייָב אֶלָּא אִם כֵּן הוֹרָה. אִית תַּנָּיֵי תַנֵּי. הָעָם בֵּית דִּין. מָה הָעָם הוֹרוּ הֵן וְעָשׂוּ אֲחֵרִים חַייָבִין אַף זֶה הוֹרָה הוּא וְעָשׂוּ אֲחֵרִים יְהֵא חַייָב. תַּלְמוּד לוֹמַר אֲשֶׁר חָטָא. עַל מַה שֶׁחָטָא הוּא מֵבִיא וְאֵינוֹ מֵבִיא עַל מַה שֶׁחָטְאוּ אֲחֵרִים. אִית תַּנָּיֵי תַנֵּי. הָעָם צִיבּוּר. מָה הָעָם הוֹרוּ אֲחֵרִים וְעָשׂוּ הֵן חַייָבִין אַף זֶה הוֹרוּ אֲחֵרִים וְעָשָׂה הוּא יְהֵא חַייָב. תַּלְמוּד לוֹמַר אֲשֶׁר חָטָא. עַל מַה שֶׁחָטָא הוּא מֵבִיא. אֵינוֹ מֵבִיא עַל מַה שֶׁחָטְאוּ אֲחֵרִים. רִבִּי יַעֲקֹב בְּשֵׁם רִבִּי לָעְזָר. וְהוּא שֶׁיְּהֵא יוֹדֵעַ לִישָּׂא וְלִיתֵּן בַּהֲלָכָה. דְּלֹא כֵן מָה נָן אָמְרִין. וְיֵשׁ שׁוֹטִים מוֹרִין. מָשִׁיחַ שֶׁאָכַל בְּהוֹרָיַית בֵּית דִּין פָּטוּר. בְּהוֹרָיַית מָשִׁיחַ אַחֵר חַייָב. בְּהוֹרָיַית בֵּית דִּין פָּטוּר. שֶׁאֵין הוֹרָיַית אֲחֵרִים אֵצֶל הוֹרָייָתָן כולן. בְּהוֹרָיַית מָשִׁיחַ אַחֵר חַייָב. וְהוּא שֶׁהוֹרָה כְּיוֹצֵא בוֹ.

1 כול' | וכו' הרי | - 2 בהוריית | בהורית בהוריית | בהוראת מה | או מה 3 בלא הורייה | בלי הוראה (2)
5 הן | - הוא | - 7 ציבור | צבור 8 אינו | ואינו 9 יעקב | יעקב בר אחא לעזר | אלעזר 10 אמרין |
קיימין בהוריית | בהוראת בהוריית | בהורית 11 בהוריית | בהורית הוריית אחרים | הוריתו הוריית כולן
} הוריתן כלום בהוריית | בהורית

Halakhah 1: "If the Anointed Priest ruled," etc. *A person*; *if the Anointed Priest.*[4]" This makes the Anointed like a private person[5]. Since the private person is not liable if he ate[6] on the Court's ruling, also neither is this one liable if he ate on the Court's ruling. Since the private person is liable if he ate without a ruling, this one also should be liable if he ate without a ruling[7]; the verse says, *for the fault of the people*. As the people[8] are liable only if they issued a ruling, this one also is liable only if he issued a ruling. There are Tannaïm who state that *the people* are the Court. Since the people[8] are liable if they instructed and others acted, this one also should be liable if he ruled and others acted. The verse says, *as he sinned*. He brings for what he sinned but he does not bring for what others sinned. There are Tannaïm[9] who state that *the people* are the public. Since the people are liable if others ruled and they acted, this one also should be liable if others ruled and he acted. The verse says, *as he sinned*. He brings for what he sinned but he does not bring for what others sinned[10]. Rebbi Jacob[11] in the name of Rebbi Eleazar. Only if he is competent to argue about practice[12]. Otherwise, would we say the incompetents give instructions?

The anointed who ate following the Court's prescript is not liable; following another Anointed's prescript he is liable. Following the Court's prescript he is not liable, since the prescript of others is nothing[13] compared to their prescripts[14]. Following another Anointed's prescript he is liable, on condition that he instructed similarly[15].

4 *Lev*. 4:2,3.

5 In v. 2, the High Priest is mentioned as "a person"; only in v. 3 as Anointed. It is concluded that the Anointed Priest follows the rules of private persons unless there is an indication to the contrary. Babli 7b, *Sifra Wayyiqra 2 Paršeta* 2(1).

6 Taking eating forbidden fat as standard example of a forbidden action.

7 The question is raised why does the Mishnah require a sacrifice only if the Anointed Priest first gives an inadvertent wrong instruction and then acts on it without realizing his error? This mixes required features of the purification offerings both of the Court (only after issuing a prescript, not acting on it themselves) and the private person (not

instructing anybody but acting).

8 This argument identifies "the people" as the Court.

9 Babli 7a, *Sifra Wayyiqra 2 Pereq* 2(1,4).

10 Including the Court. Since the High Priest is mentioned before the Court, his purification offering cannot be dependent on the Court's ruling.

11 In B: R. Jacob bar Aha. It is impossible to decide which reading is preferable or whether the same person is meant in both sources.

12 This shows that the rules are applicable to the High Priests of the Second Temple, who were invested but not anointed. The High Priests of the First Temple were supposed to be the guardians of the Law. The Hasmonean kings and the later High Priests mostly had no claim to learning.

13 The translation follows B. The text of the ms., "since the prescript of others is by all their prescripts" does not make any sense.

14 As explained in Note 10, the High Priests cannot be made dependent on the prescripts of others. The High Priest is "not dependent on the Court" *ex officio*. But as explained earlier, he cannot bring his purification offering unless his action was based on his own ruling.

15 It is not required that the High Priest have original thoughts when acting; he is presumed to follow (correct) precedent.

(fol. 46c) **משנה ב**: הוֹרָה בִפְנֵי עַצְמוֹ וְעָשָׂה בִפְנֵי עַצְמוֹ מִתְכַּפֵּר לוֹ בִפְנֵי עַצְמוֹ. הוֹרָה עִם הַצִּיבּוּר וְעָשָׂה עִם הַצִּיבּוּר מִתְכַּפֵּר לוֹ עִם הַצִּיבּוּר. שֶׁאֵין בֵּית דִּין חַייָבִין עַד שֶׁיּוֹרוּ לְבַטֵּל מִקְצָת וּלְקַייֵם מִקְצָת. וְכֵן הַמָּשִׁיחַ. וְלֹא בַעֲבוֹדָה זָרָה עַד שֶׁיּוֹרוּ לְבַטֵּל מִקְצָת וּלְקַייֵם מִקְצָת:

Mishnah 2: If he ruled for himself and acted for himself, it is atoned for himself. If he ruled with the public and acted with the public, it is atoned for him with the public[16]. As the Court is not liable unless they instruct to void part and confirm part, so is the Anointed[17]. Also for idolatry they are not liable unless they instruct to void part and confirm part[18].

16 As shown in the preceding paragraph, his sacrifice is reserved for inadvertent sins peculiar to himself. Even if he concurred with an erroneous ruling by the Court, a separate offering would be inappropriate. This differs from the ritual of the Day of Atonement where the High Priest has to atone for himself (*Lev.* 16:6) before he can officiate for the other priests (v. 11) and the people (v. 15). But here he is not acting on behalf of others.

17 All rules established in Chapter 1 for the Court's bull apply to the High Priest's bull. In the verse (*Lev.* 4:20) it is formulated the other way: All rules of the High Priest's bull apply to the Court's.

18 The rules concerning general infractions are transferred to idolatry by an argument similar to Chapter 1, Note 167.

(46c line 31) **הלכה ב**: הוֹרָה בִפְנֵי עַצְמוֹ כול'. הוֹרוּ בֵית דִּין וְהוֹרָה אַחֲרֵיהֶן וְהֶחֱלִיף. פְּשִׁיטָא נַעֲשִׂית אֶצְלוֹ כַעֲקִירַת גּוּף. אֶלָּא הוֹרָה הוּא תְחִילָּה וְהוֹרוּ בֵית דִּין אַחֲרֵיהֶן וְהֶחֱלִיפוּ. אֲפִילוּ כֵן נַעֲשִׂית אֶצְלוֹ כַעֲקִירַת גּוּף. אוֹ מֵאַחַר שֶׁהוֹרָה הוּא תְחִילָּה וְנִדְחָה הוֹרָייָתוֹ בְהוֹרָייָתָן וְאֵינָהּ נַעֲשִׂית אֶצְלוֹ כַעֲקִירַת גּוּף. הוֹרוּ בֵית דִּין וְהוֹרָה אַחֲרֵיהֶן. פְּשִׁיטָא אָכַל בְּהוֹרָיַית בֵּית דִּין פָּטוּר. אֲבָל מִשֶּׁחָזְרוּ בָהֶן בֵּית דִּין חַייָב. אָמַר רִבִּי יוֹסֵי. וְלֹא מַתְנִיתָא הִיא. הוֹרָה בִפְנֵי עַצְמוֹ מִתְכַּפֵּר לוֹ בִפְנֵי עַצְמוֹ. מִפְּנֵי שֶׁהוֹרָה בִפְנֵי עַצְמוֹ וְעָשָׂה בִפְנֵי עַצְמוֹ. אֲבָל אִם הוֹרָה עִם הַצִּיבּוּר וְעָשָׂה עִם הַצִּיבּוּר מִתְכַּפֵּר לוֹ עִם הַצִּיבּוּר. מִפְּנֵי שֶׁהוֹרָה עִם הַצִּיבּוּר וְעָשָׂה עִם הַצִּיבּוּר. אֲבָל הוֹרָה בִפְנֵי עַצְמוֹ מִתְכַּפֵּר לוֹ בִפְנֵי עַצְמוֹ.

1 הלכה ב. הוֹרָה בִפְנֵי עַצְמוֹ כול'. | - 2 אחריהן | אחריו 3 נעשית | נעשת ונדחה הורייתו בהורייתן | תדחה הוריתו להוריתן 4 נעשית | נעשת 5 משחזרו | משהורו חייב | - יוסי | יוסה היא | - - | ועשה בפני עצמו 6 הורה | היה 7 מפני | אמר רבי מנא דשלחת קודמין היא ואמור דבתרא הורה עם הצבור ועשה עם הצבור מתכפר לו עם הצבור. מפני אבל | אבל אם 8 - | ועשה בפני עצמו

Halakhah 2: "If he ruled for himself," etc. The Court ruled, he ruled following them, and then changed. It is obvious that for him it is the equivalent of uprooting the whole[19]. But if he ruled first, the Court then ruled following him, and afterwards they reversed themselves. Nevertheless is it for him the equivalent of uprooting the whole[20], or because he ruled first, but his ruling was overturned by their ruling, for him it should not be the equivalent of uprooting the whole[21]? If the Court ruled and he ruled following them, it is obvious that he is not liable if he ate[22] according to the ruling of the Court[23]. But after the Court reversed itself, he is liable[24]. Rebbi Yose said, is that not the Mishnah? "If he ruled for himself [and acted for himself][25], it is atoned for himself." Because he ruled for himself and acted for himself. "But if he ruled with the public and acted with the public, it is atoned for him with the public."[26] Because he ruled with the public and acted with the public, but "if he ruled for himself [and acted for himself][25], it is atoned for himself."

19 R. Moses Margolis (*Pene Moshe* and *Mar'eh Happanim*), the author of the only complete Commentary to *Horaiot*, explains that the Court and the High Priest originally issued consistent rulings. Then the High Priest changed his mind, and issued a new ruling on the same subject so that the two inconsistent prohibitions together amount to a complete removal of a biblical prohibition which according to Mishnah 1:3 prevents atonement by a sacrifice. It is difficult to find this in the

language of the paragraph since it says clearly that the High Priest changed his mind, i. e., he permits what the Court forbade and the Court forbids what the High Priest forbade; neither of the parties uproots the entire commandment.

Therefore, it seems that at first the High Priest followed the High Court's ruling, as stated in the text, but then reversed himself and opposed the High Court's ruling. Then irrespective of the topic of the dispute, the High Court uprooted *Deut*. 17:8-13. If the Court stays with its pronouncement, the High Priest is barred from rehabilitating himself by a sacrifice.

20 If he continues to adhere to his own ruling after the Court reversed itself.

21 Since he first ruled by scriptural authorization. The question remains unanswered.

22 Forbidden fat which the Court had permitted; the standard example of a sin atonable by a sacrifice.

23 Since he follows the public, his action in performing the rites for the Court's offering also atones for him as noted in the Mishnah.

24 Since the Temple is adjacent to the Court's seat, he will know immediately of the Court's decision and, therefore, his later actions are not covered by the Court's offering (Halakhah 1:2). The text in the Babli lacks the last word; this text has to be read as a question: "But after the Court reversed itself? Rebbi Yose said, is that not the Mishnah? . . .", i. e., the answer to the question is obvious. There is no material difference in the meaning of the two texts.

25 Addition from B.

26 B here has an additional text:

Rebbi Mana said, what you want to prove from the first part [of the Mishnah] is stated in the later part, "if he ruled with the public and acted with the public, it is atoned for him with the public."

In this text, the quote of the same statement preceding the statement of R. Mana (II, student of R. Yose and R. Jonah) should be omitted.

(fol. 46b) **משנה ג**: אֵין חַייָבִין אֶלָּא עַל הֶעֱלֵם דָּבָר עִם שִׁגְגַת הַמַּעֲשֶׂה וְכֵן הַמָּשִׁיחַ. וְלֹא בַעֲבוֹדָה זָרָה אֶלָּא עַל הֶעֱלֵם דָּבָר עִם שִׁגְגַת הַמַּעֲשֶׂה.

Mishnah 3: They[27] are liable only for forgetting a topic[28] with action in error; the same applies to the Anointed. Also for idolatry[29] only for forgetting a topic with action in error.

27 The High Court.

28 There must be an element of oblivion in their ruling; either forgetting a certain law or that it applies in the given situation.

29 Since it was stated in Halakhah 1:8

that the special offerings required for the sin of idolatry follow the rules of the bull required for all other infractions.

(46c line 41) **הלכה ג:** אֵין חַייָבִין אֶלָּא עַל הֶעֱלֵם דָּבָר כול'. רִבִּי זְעִירָא בְשֵׁם רַב יִרְמְיָה. מַתְנִיתָא רִבִּי מֵאִיר אוֹ דִייֵק רִבִּי מֵאִיר. אָמַר רִבִּי יוֹסֵי. רִבִּי מֵאִיר דוּ אָמַר. חוֹבַת בֵּית דִּין הִיא. אָמַר רִבִּי מָנָא כְּרִבִּי מֵאִיר. תַּנֵּי תַמָּן. הוֹרוּ בֵית דִּין וְעָשׂוּ קָהָל. מֵת אֶחָד מִבֵּית דִּין פְּטוּרִין. מֵת אֶחָד מִן הַצִּיבּוּר חַייָבִין. אָמַר לָהֶן רִבִּי מֵאִיר. אִם לַאֲחֵרִים הוּא פוֹטֵר לֹא כָל־שֶׁכֵּן עַל עַצְמוֹ. אָמְרוּ לוֹ. יִפְטוֹר לַאֲחֵרִים שֶׁיֵּשׁ לָהֶן בַּמֶּה לִתְלוֹת. וְאַל יִפְטוֹר לְעַצְמוֹ שֶׁאֵין לוֹ בַּמֶּה לִתְלוֹת.

רִבִּי יִרְמְיָה בְעָא קוֹמֵי רִבִּי זְעִירָא. מַה כְרִבִּי. אִין. מָשִׁיחַ בִּשְׁיגְגַת מַעֲשֶׂה הוּא. וְאִין כְּרַבָּנָן. בְּהֶעֱלֵם דָּבָר הוּא. אָמַר רִבִּי הוּנָא. עַל רַבָּנָן נִצְרְכָה. שֶׁלֹּא תֹאמַר. מָשִׁיחַ וַעֲבוֹדָה זָרָה. רִבִּי אָמַר. בִּשְׁיגְגַת מַעֲשֶׂה. וְרַבָּנִן אָמְרִין. בְּהֶעֱלֵם דָּבָר. אָמַר מה לקל מה בְגִין דְּלֹא תַנִּינָן מָשִׁיחַ. וְהָא קַדְמִיתָא לֹא תַנִּינָן מָשִׁיחַ וּמָשִׁיחַ בִּכְלָל. וְכָא אַף עַל גַּב דְּלֹא תַנִּינָן מָשִׁיחַ מָשִׁיחַ בִּכְלָל.

1 רב | רבי 2 מתניתא | מתנית' או דייק | היי הך יוסי | יוסה 3 תני | תניי 4 הציבור | הצבור להן | להם פוטר | פטור על עצמו | לעצמו 5 לתלות | להתלות 6 אין. משיח בשיגגת | דרבי אמר משוח בשגגת 7 הונא | חייא תאמר | תימר 7 ורבנן | הרבנין מי לקל מה | לון 8 קדמיתא | קדמייתא וכא | והא תנינתה לא תנינן משיח ומשיח בכלל ובא

Halakhah 3: "They are liable only for forgetting," etc. Rebbi Ze`ira in the name of Rav Jeremiah. The Mishnah[30] is Rebbi Meïr's or has inferences like Rebbi Meïr[31]. Rebbi Yose said, Rebbi Meïr who said, it is an obligation of the Court. [32]Rebbi Mana said, following Rebbi Meïr. There, it was stated: If the Court ruled and the public acted. If a member of the Court died, they are not liable. If a member of the public died, they are liable. Rebbi Meïr told them, if he relieves others of their liability, not so much more for himself? They told him, he can relieve others of their liability since they have where to hang on; he cannot relieve himself of liability since he has nothing to hang on.

Rebbi Jeremiah asked before Rebbi Ze`ira: Maybe following Rebbi? If[33] the Anointed, error in action it is. But if the rabbis, oblivion of a topic it is. Rebbi Huna[34] said, it was needed for the rabbis. That you should not say, the Anointed and idolatry: Rebbi said, in acting in error; the rabbis said, in forgetting a topic. He said [ ][35], because we did not state about the Anointed. But in the former[36], we did not state about the Anointed but the Anointed is included, and here, even though we did not state about the Anointed, the Anointed is included.

30 The spelling in B is a scribal error.

31 It is difficult to make sense of this statement. The version of B is straightforward: "Which R. Meïr?" Meaning, which statement of R. Meïr fits the Mishnah? The answer to this question is given by R. Yose. Since the Mishnah refers to the Court's, not to the public's monetary responsibility, it must accept R. Meïr's position which, being formulated as anonymous doctrine, becomes practice.

32 This text is from Halakhah 1:8, Notes 185-188. (There, R. Ze`ira reports in the name of a Sage whose identity is not clear.)

33 There is a lacuna in the text which must be filled by the text of B:

[Does it follow Rebbi, for Rebbi said,] the Anointed refers to the case of action in error, but for the rabbis, it refers to forgetting a topic.

In contrast to the Mishnah, which for the High Priest as for the Court requires both an element of oblivion and acting in error, Rebbi points out that for the Court, the forgetting is the Court's but the action in error is the public's. Rebbi compares the status of the High Priest to that of the Court. Since for general errors the Mishnah states that the same rules apply to the High Priest as to the Court, the argument must be about the sin of idolatry where the High Priest is not mentioned. The rabbis note that the High Priest does not have the status of the Court vis-a-vis the public; his rulings are private, not public actions. Therefore, he cannot be held responsible unless he act. They do not deny that an element of oblivion is required to trigger the obligation of the purification sacrifice.

34 The reading "R. Huna", a student of R. Jeremiah, is preferable to the reading of B: "R. Hiyya", the teacher of R. Ze`ira.

35 The text of the ms., "what for easy what" seems corrupt. It is better to follow the reading of B: "He said to them, why? Because ... ". The Anointed is not mentioned in the last sentence of the Mishnah, but this does not mean that the rule given there does not apply to him.

36 In Mishnah 2, in the last sentence about idolatry the High Priest is not mentioned but everybody agrees that it also applies to him; so the parallel sentence in Mishnah 3 also must apply to him. The Mishnah strictly follows the rabbis, not Rebbi.

(fol. 46b) **משנה ד:** אֵין חַייָבִין אֶלָּא עַל דָּבָר שֶׁזְּדוֹנוֹ כָּרֵת וְשִׁגְגָתוֹ חַטָּאת וְכֵן הַמָּשִׁיחַ. וְלֹא בַעֲבוֹדָה זָרָה אֶלָּא עַל דָּבָר שֶׁזְּדוֹנוֹ כָּרֵת וְשִׁגְגָתוֹ חַטָּאת׃

Mishnah 4. They[27] are liable only for something which when intentional is punishable by extirpation[37] and when unintentional by a purification sacrifice[38]. The same applies to the Anointed. Also for idolatry[29] only for something which when intentional is punishable by extirpation and when unintentional by a purification sacrifice[35].

37 These are enumerated in the first Chapter of Tractate *Keritut*.

38 This excludes violations of *sancta* which require a different kind of sacrifice as described in *Lev.* 5. Cf. Mishnah 5. There remain 31 topics for which High Priest or Court may be required to sacrifice a bull.

(46c line 52) **הלכה ד**: אֵין חַייָבִין אֶלָּא עַל דָּבָר שֶׁזְּדוֹנוֹ כָרֵת כול'. מִצְוֹת יי. הָיִיתִי אוֹמֵר. אַף אוֹכְלֵי שְׁקָצִים וּרְמָשִׂים בְּמַשְׁמַע. נֶאֱמַר כָּאן מֵעֵינֵי וְנֶאֱמַר לְהַלָּן מֵעֵינֵי. מַה מֵעֵינֵי שֶׁנֶּאֱמַר לְהַלָּן דָּבָר שֶׁחַייָבִין עַל זְדוֹנוֹ כָרֵת וְעַל שִׁגְגָתוֹ חַטָּאת. אַף מֵעֵינֵי שֶׁנֶּאֱמַר כָּאן דָּבָר שֶׁחַייָבִין עַל זְדוֹנוֹ כָרֵת וְעַל שִׁגְגָתוֹ חַטָּאת. אוֹ מַה מֵעֵינֵי שֶׁנֶּאֱמַר לְהַלָּן דָּבָר שֶׁיֵּשׁ בּוֹ מִיתַת בֵּית דִּין. אַף מֵעֵינֵי שֶׁנֶּאֱמַר כָּאן דָּבָר שֶׁיֵּשׁ בּוֹ מִיתַת בֵּית דִּין. אָמַר רִבִּי יוֹסֵי בַּר חֲנִינָה. מָקוֹם שֶׁנִּכְלְלוּ כָל־הָעֲרָיוֹת לְהִיכָּרֵת. יָצָא אֵשֶׁת אִישׁ אֲבָל לְלַמֵּד עַל הַמַּמְזֵר. רִבִּי אוֹמֵר. עָלֶיהָ עָלֶיהָ. מַה עָלֶיהָ שֶׁנֶּאֱמַר לְהַלָּן דָּבָר שֶׁחַייָבִין עַל זְדוֹנוֹ כָרֵת וְעַל שִׁגְגָתוֹ חַטָּאת. אַף עָלֶיהָ שֶׁנֶּאֱמַר כָּאן דָּבָר שֶׁחַייָבִין עַל זְדוֹנוֹ כָרֵת וְעַל שִׁגְגָתוֹ חַטָּאת. וְלָמָּה לֹא דָרַשׁ רִבִּי מֵעֵינֵי מֵעֵינֵי. אָמַר רִבִּי יוֹסֵי. אִין יִדְרוֹשׁ רִבִּי מֵעֵינֵי מֵעֵינֵי. מַה מֵעֵינֵי שֶׁנֶּאֱמַר לְהַלָּן דָּבָר שֶׁיֵּשׁ בּוֹ מִיתַת בֵּית דִּין. אַף מֵעֵינֵי שֶׁנֶּאֱמַר כָּאן דָּבָר שֶׁיֵּשׁ בּוֹ מִיתַת בֵּית דִּין. לְפוּם כֵּן לֹא דָרַשׁ רִבִּי מֵעֵינֵי מֵעֵינֵי. וְלֵית לֵיהּ סִפְרָא דְרִבִּי מִידְרוֹשׁ מֵעֵינֵי מֵעֵינֵי. דְּלֹא כֵן מְנָן לֵיהּ הַיָּחִיד וְהַנָּשִׂיא וְהַמָּשִׁיחַ. לֹא מֵעֵינֵי מֵעֵינֵי. דְּלֹא כֵן מְנָן לֵיהּ הוֹרַייַת בֵּית דִּין גָּדוֹל הוֹרַייַת בֵּית דִּין קָטָן לֹא מֵעֵינֵי מֵעֵינֵי. אָמַר רִבִּי חֲנַנְיָה קוֹמֵי רִבִּי מָנָא. עַד שֶׁיּוֹרוּ לְבַטֵּל מִקְצָת וּלְקַייֵם מִקְצָת לֹא מֵעֵינֵי מֵעֵינֵי. דְּלֹא כֵן מְנָן לֵיהּ הוֹרַייַת בֵּית דִּין קָטָן לֹא מֵעֵינֵי מֵעֵינֵי. אָמַר רִבִּי חֲנַנְיָה קוֹמֵי רִבִּי מָנָא. וְלֵית סוֹפֵיהּ דְּרִבִּי מִדְרוֹשׁ מֵעֵינֵי מֵעֵינֵי. מָה אַתְּ בָּעֵי מֵרִבִּי. רִבִּי כְדַעְתֵּיהּ. דְּרִבִּי אָמַר. מָשִׁיחַ בְּשִׁיגְגַת הַמַּעֲשֶׂה הוּא. וְאֵין כְּתִיב זָדוֹן שְׁגָגָה לְיָחִיד אֶלָּא בְּבֵית דִּין וּבִלְבַד. אוֹתוֹ. מִיעֵט קָרְבָּנוֹ לְמִצְוָה יְחִידִית שֶׁלֹּא יִכָּנֵס דָּמוֹ לִפְנִים. מָה כְרִבִּי. דְּרִבִּי אָמַר. מָשִׁיחַ בְּשִׁיגְגַת הַמַּעֲשֶׂה הוּא. וְאִין כְּתַבְנָן בְּהֶעֱלֵם דָּבָר הוּא. אָמַר רַב הוּנָא. עַל דְּרַבָּנִן נִצְרְכָה. שֶׁלֹּא תֹאמַר. הוֹאִיל וְהוּא בְהִיכָּרֵת יִכָּנֵס דָּמוֹ לִפְנַיי לִפְנִים. לְפוּם כֵּן צָרִיךְ מֵימַר. אוֹתוֹ. מִיעֵט קָרְבָּנוֹ לְמִצְוָה יְחִידִית שֶׁלֹּא יִכָּנֵס דָּמוֹ לִפְנִים.

Text of B

הלכה. אֵין חַיָּבִין אֶלָּא עַל דָּבָר שֶׁזְּדוֹנוֹ כָרֵת וכו'. מִצְוֹת יי. הָיִיתִי אוֹמֵר אַף אוֹכְלֵי שְׁקָצִים וּרְמָשִׂים בְּמַשְׁמָעוֹ. נֶאֱמַר כָּאן מֵעֵינֵי וְנֶאֱמַר לְהַלָּן מֵעֵינֵי מַה מֵעֵינֵי שֶׁנֶּאֱמַר לְהַלָּן דָּבָר שֶׁחַייָבִין עַל זְדוֹנוֹ כָרֵת וְעַל שִׁגְגָתוֹ חַטָּאת אַף מֵעֵינֵי שֶׁנֶּאֱמַר כָּאן דָּבָר יֵשׁ עַל זְדוֹנוֹ כָרֵת וְעַל שִׁגְגָתוֹ חַטָּאת אוֹ מַה מֵעֵינֵי שֶׁנֶּאֱמַר לְהַלָּן דָּבָר שֶׁיֵּשׁ בּוֹ מִיתַת בֵּית דִּין אַף מֵעֵינֵי שֶׁנֶּאֱמַר כָּאן דָּבָר שֶׁיֵּשׁ בּוֹ מִיתַת בֵּית דִּין אָמַר רִבִּי יוֹסֵה בְּרִבִּי חֲנִינָא. מָקוֹם שֶׁנִּכְלְלוּ כָל־הָעֲרָיוֹת בְּהִכָּרֵת יָצְאת אֵשֶׁת אָב לְלַמֵּד עַל הַמַּמְזֵר רִבִּי אוֹמֵר עָלֶיהָ עָלֶיהָ מָה עָלֶיהָ שֶׁנֶּאֱמַר לְהַלָּן דָּבָר שֶׁחַייָבִין עַל זְדוֹנוֹ כָרֵת וְעַל שִׁגְגָתוֹ חַטָּאת אַף עָלֶיהָ שֶׁנֶּאֱמַר כָּאן דָּבָר שֶׁחַייָבִין עַל זְדוֹנוֹ כָרֵת וְעַל שִׁגְגָתוֹ חַטָּאת וְלָמָּה לֹא דָרַשׁ רִבִּי מֵעֵינֵי מֵעֵינֵי אָמַר ר' זְעִירָא אִם דָּרִישׁ רִבִּי

מֵעֵינֵי מֵעֵינֵי מַה מֵעֵינֵי שֶׁנֶּאֱמַר לְהַלָּן מָשִׁיחַ בְּשִׁגְגַת הַמַּעֲשֶׂה הוּא אַף מֵעֵינֵי שֶׁנֶּאֱמַר כָּאן בְּשִׁגְגַת הַמַּעֲשֶׂה הוּא לְפוּם כֵּן לֹא דָרִישׁ רִבִּי מֵעֵינֵי מֵעֵינֵי אָמַר רִבִּי יוֹסֵה אִין יִדְרוֹשׁ רִבִּי מֵעֵינֵי מֵעֵינֵי מַה מֵעֵינֵי שֶׁנֶּאֱמַר לְהַלָּן דָּבָר שֶׁיֵּשׁ בּוֹ מִיתַת בֵּית דִּין אַף מֵעֵינֵי שֶׁנֶּאֱמַר כָּאן דָּבָר שֶׁיֵּשׁ בּוֹ מִיתַת בֵּית דִּין לְפוּם כֵּן לֹא דָרִישׁ רִבִּי מֵעֵינֵי מֵעֵינֵי וְלֵית סוֹפֵיהּ רִבִּי מִדְרוֹשׁ מֵעֵינֵי מֵעֵינֵי דִּלְכֵן מְנָן לֵיהּ הַיָּחִיד וְהַנָּשִׂיא וְהַמָּשִׁיחַ לֹא מֵעֵינֵי מֵעֵינֵי אָמַר ר׳ חֲנִינָא דִּלְכֵן מְנָן לֵיהּ עַד שֶׁיּוֹרוּ לְבַטֵּל מִקְצָת וּלְקַיֵּים מִקְצָת לֹא מֵעֵינֵי דִּל׳ כֵן מְנָן לֵיהּ הוֹרָיַת בֵּית דִּין גָּדוֹל הוֹרָיַת בֵּית דִּין קָטָן לָאו מֵעֵינֵי מֵעֵינֵי אָמַר רִבִּי חֲנִינָא קוֹמֵי רִבִּי מָנָא. וְלֵית סוֹפֵיהּ דְּרִבִּי מִדְרוֹשׁ מֵעֵינֵי מֵעֵינֵי אָמַר לֵיהּ מָה אַתְּ בָּעֵי מֵרִבִּי רִבִּי כְּדַעְתֵּיהּ דְּרִבִּי אָמַר מָשִׁיחַ בְּשִׁגְגַת מַעֲשֶׂה הוּא. וְאֵין כְּתִיב זָדוֹן שְׁגָגָה לְיָחִיד אֶלָּא בֵּית דִּין בִּלְבַד אוֹתוֹ מִיעֵט קָרְבָּנוֹ לְמִצְוָה יְחִידִית שֶׁלֹּא יִכָּנֵס מִדָּמוֹ לִפְנִים מָה כְרִבִּי דְּרִבִּי אָמַר מָשִׁיחַ בְּשִׁגְגַת מַעֲשֶׂה הוּא וְאֵין כָּרְבָּנוֹ הֶעְלֵם דָּבָר הוּא אָמַר ר׳ הוּנָא עַל רַבָּנִין נִצְרְכָה שֶׁלֹּא תֵימַר הוֹאִיל וְהוּא בְּהִכָּרֵת יִכָּנֵס דָּמוֹ לִפְנַי לִפְנִים לְפוּם כֵּן צָרִיךְ מֵימַר אוֹתוֹ מִיעֵט קָרְבָּנוֹ לְמִצְוָה יְחִידִית שֶׁלֹּא יִכָּנֵס דָּמוֹ לִפְנִים.

Halakhah 4: "They are only liable for something which when intentional is punishable by extirpation," etc. [39]*The commandments of the Eternal*[40]. I could think that this also includes those who eat abominations and crawling things. [41]It says here *from the eyes* and it says there *from the eyes*. Just as *from the eyes* mentioned there means something which is punished by extirpation in case of intentional sin[42] and needs a purification sacrifice for an inadvertent sin, so *from the eyes* mentioned here means something which is punished by extirpation in case of intentional sin and needs a purification sacrifice for an inadvertent sin. Or since *from the eyes* mentioned there means something that can lead to the death penalty, so *from the eyes* mentioned here should mean something that can lead to the death penalty[43]?

[44]Rebbi Yose ben Ḥanina said, from a place where all incest prohibitions were taken as one set [of sins] causing extirpation, the (married woman) [father's wife] came out to tell you about the bastard.

[45]Rebbi said *over which, over her*. Since *over her* mentioned there refers to something which is punished by extirpation in case of intentional sin and needs a purification sacrifice for an inadvertent sin, so *over which* mentioned here means something for which one is punished by extirpation in case of intentional sin and needs a purification sacrifice for an inadvertent sin. Why does Rebbi not infer from *from the eyes, from the eyes*?

[46][Rebbi Ze`ira said: If Rebbi would infer from *from the eyes, from the eyes*, then *from the eyes* mentioned there for the Anointed refers to action

in error; also *from the eyes* mentioned here would have to refer to action in error. Therefore, Rebbi will not infer from *from the eyes, from the eyes*.]

Rebbi Yose said: If Rebbi would infer from *from the eyes, from the eyes*, then since *from the eyes* mentioned there means something that can lead to the death penalty, so *from the eyes* mentioned here means something that can lead to the death penalty[47]. Therefore, Rebbi does not infer from *from the eyes, from the eyes*. (Does Rebbi not have a book) [Will Rebbi not in the end have][48] to infer *from the eyes, from the eyes*?

[49]For if it is not so, from where would we have the rules for the individual, the chief, and the Anointed? Not from *from the eyes, from the eyes*?

[50]For if it is not so, from where would we have "unless they ruled to eliminate part and to confirm part"? Not from *from the eyes, from the eyes*?

For if it is not so, from where would we have [the difference between] a ruling of the High Court and a ruling of a lower court[51]? Rebbi Ḥanania[52] said before Rebbi Mana: Would not Rebbi in the end have to infer from *from the eyes, from the eyes*? He told him, what do you want from Rebbi? Rebbi follows his own opinion, since Rebbi said, the Anointed refers to action in error. Intentional error is only written for the Court[46].

[53]*It*. It specifies about his sacrifice that for the singular commandment its blood should not be brought into the Sanctuary. Does this follow Rebbi, as Rebbi said, the Anointed refers to action in error; if it would follow the rabbis, there must be an instance of forgetting. (Rav) [Rebbi][54] Huna said, it was needed for the rabbis. Lest you say, because there is extirpation[55] its blood should be brought into the Sanctuary. Therefore, it was necessary to say *it*, it specifies his sacrifice that for the singular commandment its blood should not be brought into the Sanctuary.

39 Cf. *Yebamot* 4:15, Notes 219-227.

40 Since the introduction to the rules of purification sacrifices, *Lev*. 4:2, seems to prescribe such a sacrifice for *all the Commandments of the Eternal*, it needs an argument why in all four cases (the High Priest, the High Court, Prince, and commoner) simple transgressions are excluded.

41 Cf. Halakhah 1:8, Notes 145 ff. Here also one compares the transgressions for which the Court has to bring a bull to the

sin of idolatry for which a bull and a goat are required.

42 The punishment for idolatry in the absence of witnesses or warning.

43 The punishment for idolatry if there are witnesses for warning and deed.

44 This is a wrong quote from *Yebamot* (Note 220). The father's wife who is not the mother is forbidden in *Deut.* 23:1 (in addition to *Lev.* 18:8, 20:11). The bastard is mentioned in *Deut.* 23:3; it is inferred that the bastard is a child from a forbidden union exemplified by the father's wife.

One may assume that the intended quote from *Yebamot* was the answer given there to the question: "R. Yose ben Hanina said, from the place from which idolatry was singled out to teach about all who are subject to extirpation (*Num.* 15:31), there was no mention of anything but extirpation (*Num.* 15:30-31). But the death penalty is written elsewhere (*Lev.* 20:2, *Deut.* 17:5)." (Note 226).

45 Babli 8a, *Yebamot* 9a. In *Lev.* 4:14, speaking of the Court's sacrifice, it is said, *and the sin became known concerning which (עָלֶיהָ) they had sinned.* In *Lev.* 18:18 one reads: *Do not marry a woman in addition to her sister, to make them co-wives, to uncover her nakedness over her (עָלֶיהָ) during her lifetime. Lev.* 18:29 is a blanket warning that all sexual crimes mentioned in the Chapter are punishable by extirpation. The wife's sister is not mentioned in the list of punishments in *Lev.* 20. Therefore this is a reference only to divine extirpation; even with witnesses and due warnings no death penalty is involved (*Sanhedrin* 7:5, Note 78).

46 Text found only in B. Since the argument of R. Ze`ira is identical to that of R. Mana (student of R. Ze`ira's student), the text is suspect. In Halakhah 3 it was established that Rebbi requires the High Priest to bring a sacrifice for an erroneous action even without an element of oblivion. If Rebbi would accept transfer of the argument of Halakhah 1:8, Notes 165ff. to the problem here, he would have to hold that the same applies to the Court. But since forgetting is mentioned in the verse speaking of the Court, this would disprove his thesis. Therefore, Rebbi cannot accept the application of the argument of Halakhah 1:8 to the problem of Mishnah 2:4.

47 He accepts the question (Note 43) as valid.

48 The text in parentheses is from the ms., the one in brackets from B. It seems that the ms. text is a scribal error.

49 Text of the ms. Since Rebbi only denies that for the High Priest's offering an element of oblivion is necessary, for all others he accepts the reasoning of *Sifra Wayyiqra 2 Parašah* 4(6) that from a comparison with the rules for unintentional idolatry it is established that both oblivion and unintentional action are needed. The connection is established by *from the eyes, from the eyes.*

50 Text of B. But in Halakhah 3, there is no reference to inferences from idolatry.

51 The fact that the court mentioned in *Lev.* 4 is the High Court is proven from *Num.* 15:24. The connection is established by *from the eyes, from the eyes.*

52 This is the correct attribution, not R. Hanina as in B.

53 *Sifra Wayyiqra 2 Parašah* 3(7). The reference is to *Lev*. 4:5: *The Anointed Priest shall take of the bull's blood and bring it to the Tent of Meeting.* "To bring it" could have been expressed as וְהֱבִיאוֹ, but it is given as וְהֵבִיא אֹתוֹ. The choice of a separate word for "it" is read as emphasizing that precisely *this* blood is brought into the sanctuary, not blood of similar sacrifices. The one sacrifice similar to the bull of the High Priest and the one of the Court which follows the same rule (*Lev*. 4:16, where the language is: *of the bull's blood*) is the bull offered for inadvertent idolatry. The latter is called "the singular commandment" both because it requires a rite of atonement different from all other commandments as also it is the only sin which in one act violates all commandments (cf. Halakhah 1:6, Note 135).

54 The text in parentheses is from the ms., the (correct) one in brackets from B. Cf. Note 34.

55 For idolatry which cannot be prosecuted in court for lack of eye witnesses or due warning.

(fol. 46b) **משנה ה**: אֵין חַייָבִין עַל עֲשֵׂה וְעַל לֹא תַעֲשֶׂה שֶׁבַּמִּקְדָּשׁ וְאֵין מְבִיאִין אָשָׁם תָּלוּי עַל עֲשֵׂה וְעַל לֹא תַעֲשֶׂה שֶׁבַּמִּקְדָּשׁ. אֲבָל חַייָבִין עַל עֲשֵׂה וְעַל לֹא תַעֲשֶׂה שֶׁבַּנִּדָּה וּמְבִיאִין אָשָׁם תָּלוּי עַל עֲשֵׂה וְעַל לֹא תַעֲשֶׂה שֶׁבַּנִּידָּה. וְאֵי זוֹ הִיא מִצְוַת עֲשֵׂה שֶׁבַּנִּדָּה פְּרוֹשׁ מִן הַנִּדָּה. וּמִצְוַת לֹא תַעֲשֶׂה לֹא תָבוֹא אֶל הַנִּידָּה:

Mishnah 5: They are not liable for a positive commandment or a prohibition in the Temple[56]; one does not bring a suspended reparation sacrifice for a positive commandment or a prohibition in the Temple. But they are liable for a positive commandment or a prohibition about the menstruating woman[57]; one brings a suspended reparation sacrifice for a positive commandment or a prohibition about the menstruating woman. What is the positive commandment about the menstruating woman? Separate from the menstruating woman[58]. The prohibition, do not copulate with a menstruating woman[59].

56 At least not for any incorrect ruling regarding impurity in the Temple or of sacrifices. A private person who unintentionally violates any of those rules is required to offer a sacrifice, as described in *Lev*. 5, whose value depends on the wealth of the offerer. The sacrifices prescribed in *Lev*. 4 for the High Priest, the Court, the Prince, and private persons, all are of fixed value. It will be

argued that both the sacrifice of the Court as also "suspended" sacrifices, those offered for suspected sins, are possible only under circumstances in which the certainly sinning individual would be liable for a fixed-value offering.

57 That means any sin which if committed unintentionally requires a fixed-value offering. The Mishnah does not refer to the standard example, eating prohibited fat, since there no positive commandment is involved.

58 As will be explained in the Halakhah.

59 A rather weaker statement than *Lev.* 18:19.

(46d line 3) **הלכה ה:** וְאֵין חַייָבִין עַל עֲשֵׂה וְעַל לֹא תַעֲשֶׂה שֶׁבַּמִּקְדָּשׁ כול'. כָּהֲנָא אָמַר. אֵיפְשַׁר שֶׁלֹּא הָיָה בָהּ יְדִיעָה בַּתְּחִילָּה וִידִיעָה בַסּוֹף וְהֶעֱלֵם בֵּינְתַיִים. הָתִיב רִבִּי שְׁמוּאֵל בַּר אֶבְדַּיְמִי קוֹמֵי רִבִּי מָנָא. וִיהֵא כֵן בַּמּוֹרִים. אָמַר לֵיהּ. אֲנַן בָּעֵי נִבְנָסִין וְאַתְּ מַייְתֵי לָן מוֹרִים. מַאי כְדוֹן. אָמַר רִבִּי שְׁמוּאֵל בַּר רַב יִצְחָק. מִצְוֹת מִצְוֹת. מַה מִצְוֹת שֶׁנֶּאֱמַר לְהַלָּן בִּקְבוּעָה אַף כָּאן בִּקְבוּעָה.

1 כהנא | B כהנה אמ' | B - איפשר | B אפשר **ש** אי איפשר 2 היה | **ש** היתה בינתיים | B בינתים התיב | B אותיב אבדימי | B אבודמי **ש** אבודימי 3 מנא | B מונא ויהא | **ש** ויהיו במורים | **ש** המורים בעי | B בעיין **ש** בעיי נכנסין | B לכנסיה מורים | **ש** מורין מאי | B מי 4 מצוות מצוות | B**ש** מצות מצות מצוות | B**ש** מצות בקבועה | **ש** בקבוע 5 בקבועה | **ש** בקבוע

Halakhah 5: "They are not liable for a positive commandment or a prohibition in the Temple," etc. [60]Cahana said, is it impossible that there was knowledge at the beginning and knowledge at the end and oblivion in between[61]? Rebbi Samuel ben Eudaimon objected before Rebbi Mana: Could that be for the teachers[62]? He told him, we have a problem with those entering and you bring us teachers? What about it? Rebbi Samuel bar Rav Isaac said, *commandments, commandments*. Since *commandments* mentioned there are about fixed-value [offerings], here also about fixed-value [offerings][63].

60 This paragraph also is Halakhah 2:4 in *Ševuot* (ש).

61 He questions why it should be impossible to bring a suspended sacrifice for violating the Temple's sanctity by impurity. In the introduction to the rules of the variable-value reparation offering (*Lev.* 5:3), one of the cases for such an offering is described as *or if he touch a human's impurity, any impurity that make him impure, and it was hidden from him, and then he knew and was guilty.* It is clear that causing damage by impurity is subject to a sacrifice only if there was knowledge of the impurity interrupted by a period of unawareness. Why should it be impossible that this condition be satisfied for one entering the Temple while impure?

62 Since the Mishnah is formulated for the Court, why can it not be read as addressing only the teachers of the law

but not all impure individuals? But for issuing a ruling a suspended reparation sacrifice is impossible; therefore, the Mishnah refers not only to the Court but to everybody.

63 The introduction to the rules of the suspended reparation sacrifice (*Lev.* 5:17) reads: *But if a person sin, violating one of the commandments of the Eternal that are prohibitions; if he is unsure whether he be guilty and have to carry his sin.* The introduction to the rules of the fixed-rate purification sacrifices of an individual reads: *But if a person of the people of the Land sin inadvertently, violating one of the commandments of the Eternal that are prohibitions, and is guilty.* The parallel language implies parallel rules; suspended sacrifices are possible only for suspected sins whose atonement would be covered by the rules of *Lev.* 4, not *Lev.* 5. A different argument with identical result is in *Sifra Wayyiqra 2, Parašah* 12(10).

(46d line 8) וְאֵין חַייָבִין עַל כָּל־מִצְוַת עֲשֵׂה שֶׁבַּתּוֹרָה. אָמַר רִבִּי מַתַּנְיָה. לָא אֲתִינָן מַתְנֵי אֶלָּא מִילָּה דַמְיָיא לְמִילָּה. הֵיךְ עֲבִידָא. נִכְנַס לַמִּקְדָּשׁ טָמֵא חַייָב. נִכְנַס טָהוֹר וְנִטְמָא. בָּא לוֹ בָּאֲרוּכָה חַייָב וּבִקְצָרָה פָּטוּר. וְדִכְוָותָהּ. הָיָה מְשַׁמֵּשׁ עִם הַטְּמֵאָה חַייָב. הָיָה מְשַׁמֵּשׁ עִם הַטְּהוֹרָה וְאָמְרָה לוֹ. נִטְמֵאתִי. בָּא לוֹ בָּאֲרוּכָה חַייָב וּבִקְצָרָה פָּטוּר. אֵי זוֹ הִיא קְצָרָה שֶׁלּוֹ. יִצֵּן.

1 כל | - מתני | - 2 מילה דמייא למילה | מלה דמיא למלה 3 ובקצרה | בקצרה ודכוות' | ודכותה 4 ובקצרה | בקצרה זו | זה שלו | שלא

But one never is liable for any positive commandment in the Torah[64]! Rebbi Mattaniah said, we only came to state matters similar to the matter[65]. How is that? If he entered the Temple impure, he is liable[66]. If he entered pure but became impure, if he leaves on a long path he is liable, on a short one not liable[67]. Similarly, if he was having sex with an impure woman, he is liable. If he was having sex with a pure one and she said to him, I became impure, if he leaves on a long path he is liable, on a short one not liable[68]. What is his shortcut? He shall cool down[69].

64 Since the rules for purification sacrifices clearly say that they are for inadvertent violations of prohibitions. *Sifra Wayyiqra 2 Paršeta* 1(6).

65 The only positive commandments which can lead to the liability for a purification sacrifice are special obligations to take steps to avoid certain prohibitions. The only examples are impurity in the Temple and relations with a menstruating woman; cf. Note 70.

66 There are many verses forbidding entry into the holy precinct to impure people, each one for a specific impurity. For impurity of the dead, the sufferer from skin disease, and the sufferer from gonorrhea *Num.* 5:2 (taking together *Num.* 19:20, *Lev.* 13:46, 15:15); for the woman after childbirth *Lev.* 12:4. The general prohibition covering all impurities is *Lev.*

15:31 as noted in the next paragraph.

67 Babli *Ševuot* 14b. There and in *Nazir* 3:5 (Note 68) it is stated that the person noticing his impurity must leave in less time than is needed to prostrate himself.

68 The Babli, *Ševuot* 18a, last line in the Wilna ed., objects to a time limit in this case while agreeing with the practice as explained in the next paragraph.

69 He must remain immobilized until his erection has disappeared.

(46d line 14) אֵי זוֹ הִיא מִצְוַת עֲשֵׂה שֶׁבְּנִדָּה. אָמַר רִבִּי אָבִין. וְהִזַּרְתֶּם אֶת־בְּנֵי־יִשְׂרָאֵל מִטּוּמְאָתָם. רִבִּי יוֹנָתָן שָׁלַח שָׁאַל לְרִבִּי שִׁמְעוֹן בֵּירִבִּי יוֹסֵי בֶּן לַקּוֹנִיָּא. אַזְהָרָה לַמְשַׁמֵּשׁ עִם הַטְּמֵאָה מְנַיִין. וּבְעָא כֵּיפָה מִזְרוֹק בַּתְרֵיהּ. אֲמַר לֵיהּ. מִילָּא דְמַיינוּקַיָּא אָמְרִין בִּכְנִישְׁתָּא בְּכָל־יוֹם אַתְּ שְׁאִיל לִי. וְאֶל־אִשָּׁה בְּנִידַּת טוּמְאָתָהּ לֹא תִקְרַב לְגַלּוֹת עֶרְוָתָהּ. אֲמַר לֵיהּ. לָא צְרִיכָה לֵיהּ הָדָא. וְלֵית צוֹרְכָא דְלָא. הָיָה מְשַׁמֵּשׁ עִם הַטְּמֵאָה חַייָב. הָיָה מְשַׁמֵּשׁ עִם הַטְּהוֹרָה וְאָמְרָה לוֹ. נִטְמֵאתִי. פֵּירַשׁ מִיָּד. מָהוּ שֶׁיְּהֵא חַייָב. אֲמַר לֵיהּ. אֲנָא וְאַתְּ צְרִיכָא לָן. נֵצֵא לַחוּץ וְנִלְמַד. נָפְקִין וְשָׁמְעוּן קָלֵיהּ דְּתַנָּייָא תַנֵּי כְּהָדָא דְחִזְקִיָּה. וְאִם שָׁכֹב יִשְׁכַּב אִישׁ אוֹתָהּ. אֵין לִי אֶלָּא מְשַׁמֵּשׁ עִם הַטְּמֵאָה חַייָב. הָיָה מְשַׁמֵּשׁ עִם הַטְּהוֹרָה וְאָמְרָה לוֹ. נִטְמֵאתִי. פֵּירֵשׁ מִיָּד. מָהוּ שֶׁיְּהֵא חַייָב. תַּלְמוּד לוֹמַר. וּתְהִי נִדָּתָהּ. וַאֲפִילוּ פִירְשָׁה עָלָיו נִדָּתָהּ. מַה יַּעֲשֶׂה. רַב הוֹשַׁעְיָה רַב יְהוּדָה בְּשֵׁם שְׁמוּאֵל. יָצֵן. לֹא הִיצֵּן. אָמַר רִבִּי יוֹסֵי. קוֹרֵא אֲנִי עָלָיו אַל תִּקְרַב. אַל תִּפְרוֹשׁ. קְרִיבָה פְּרִישָׁה. רַב הוּנָא בְשֵׁם רַב אַבָּא. כְּהָדָא הָאוֹמְרִים קְרַב אֵלֶיךָ אַל־תִּגַּע בִּי כִּי קִידַּשְׁתִּיךָ. אָמַר רִבִּי זְעִירָא. יְהֵא רוֹאֶה אֶת הַחֶרֶב כִּילּוּ מְחַתֶּכֶת בִּבְשָׂרוֹ. וְכָל־עַמָּא רִבִּי זְעִירָא. רִבִּי תַנְחוּמָא בְשֵׁם רַב חוּנָה. יִטּוֹחַ רָאשֵׁי עֶצְבְּעוֹתָיו בַּכּוֹתֶל וִיהֵא מֵיצֵן.

כְּתִיב וַתֵּשֶׁב בְּאֵיתָן קַשְׁתּוֹ. רִבִּי שְׁמוּאֵל בַּר נַחְמָן. נִמְתְּחָה הַקֶּשֶׁת וְחָזְרָה. אָמַר רִבִּי אָבוּן. נִתְפַּזֵּר זַרְעוֹ וְיָצָא לוֹ בְצִיפָּרְנֵי יָדָיו. וַיָּפֹזּוּ זְרֹעֵי יָדָיו. רַב חוּנָה בְשֵׁם רַב מַתָּנָה. תָּלָה עֵינָיו וְרָאָה אֵיקוֹנִין שֶׁלְּאָבִיו. מִיָּד הֵיצֵן. מִידֵי אֲבִיר יַעֲקֹב. אָמַר רִבִּי אָבִין. אַף אֵיקוֹנִין שֶׁלְּרָחֵל רָאָה. מִשָּׁם רֹעֶה אֶבֶן יִשְׂרָאֵל.

1 אבין | אבון 2 מטומאתם | מטומאותם יוסי | יוסה לקונייא | לקוניה 3 הטמאה מניין | הנדה מנין ובעא | וטען מילא דמיינוקייא | מלה דמינוקייה בכנשתא בכל יום | בכל יום בכנשתא 5 צריכה | נצרבא ולית | לית 6 מהו | הוא 7 נפקין | נפקון קליה | קריה דתנייא | תניי שכב | שכוב איש | - אותה | אותה ותהי נדתה עליו וטמא וגו' 9 מהו | מניין נדתה | נדתה עליו פירשה | פירסה עליו נדתה | נדתה עליו 10 בשם | - היצן | הצן יוסי | איסי 11 תפרוש | תפרש פרישה | פריסה 12 קידשתיך | קדשתיך זעירא | זעורא 13 ר' | רב יטוח | יטיח ויהא מיצן | והוא מצן 14אבון | יצחק 16 שלאביו | של אבינו יעקב אבין | בון

"What is the positive commandment about the menstruating woman?" Rebbi Abin said, *Keep the Children of Israel away from their impurities*[70]. Rebbi Jonathan sent to ask Rebbi Simeon ben Rebbi Yose bar Lakonia, from where a warning for one having sex with an impure woman? He wanted to throw a stone after him; he told him, you are asking me something that children recite every day in the synagogue[71]: *To a woman in the separation of her impurity you shall not come near to uncover her nakedness*[72]. He answered him, that is not my problem. My only problem is rather "if he was having sex with an impure woman, he is liable. If he was having sex with a pure one and she said to him, I became impure," if he separates immediately, is he liable[73]? He told him, I and you have the same problem. Let us go out and learn. They went out and heard the voice of a Tanna who stated following Ḥiskiah: *If lying a man will lie with her*[74]. Not only that if he was having sex with an impure woman, he is liable. If he was having sex with a pure one and she said to him, I became impure, if he separates immediately, is he liable? The verse says, *her secretion shall be*[74], even if her secretion starts[75] with him. What should he do? Rav Hoshaia, Rav Jehudah in the name of Samuel, he shall cool down. If he did not cool down? Rebbi Yose said, for him I am reading *do not come near*[72] as "do not separate". Closeness is separation. Rav Ḥuna in the name of Rav Abba: *Those who say, be close to yourself, do not touch me for I sanctified you*[76]. Rebbi Ze`ira said, he should imagine that a sword is cutting into his flesh. Is everybody Rebbi Ze`ira? Rebbi Tanḥuma in the name of Rav Ḥuna: He shall press his fingertips on the wall, then he will cool down[77].

[78]It is written: *His bow was sitting immobile.* Rebbi Samuel bar Naḥman: his bow was spanned and relaxed. Rebbi Abun said, his semen spread out and came out from under his fingernails, *the arms of his hands were excited.* Rav Ḥuna in the name of Rav Mattanah, he lifted his eyes, saw the picture[79] of his father, and cooled down immediately, *from the hands of the noble Jacob.* Rebbi Abin said, he also saw the picture of Rachel, *from there the shepherd, the rock of Israel.*

70 *Lev.* 15:31. The verse continues: *Lest they die in their impurities when they defile My abode which is in their midst.* This is the positive commandment not to defile the Temple. The verse concludes the chapters on impurities created by the human body (childbirth, skin diseases, male and female venereal diseases, menstruation, and sexual relations with a menstruating woman). Therefore it also is the positive commandment regarding the menstruating woman and is interpreted to forbid sexual relations with a woman close to the expected onset of her menses. The question about the woman experiencing a discharge during sex must refer to an unexpected event. Babli *Ševuot* 18b, most of the paragraph.

71 Serving as elementary school under the system of compulsory elementary education instituted by Joshua ben Gamla.

72 *Lev.* 18:19.

73 As the Babli explains, interrupting the coition during an erection is pleasurable for the male and therefore forbidden under the circumstances. The end of the erection must precede the separation.

74 *Lev.* 15:24.

75 The rabbinic expression for the onset on the menses is פְּרֶס נִידָּה, "breaking through".

76 *Is.* 65:5. Also in the Babli the verse is quoted in support of the interpretation of the root קרב as "to separate".

77 Babli *Ševuot* 18a.

78 An explanation of the difficult verse *Gen.* 49:24 as describing Joseph's reaction to the advances of Potiphar's wife, as appendix on the difficulties of eliminating an unwanted erection. *Gen. rabba* 98(24).

79 Greek εἰκόνιον. It would not be impossible to vocalize אֵיקוֹנִין. In B: "The picture of our father Jacob; immediately he cooled down."

(fol. 46b) **משנה ו**: אֵין חַייָבִין עַל שְׁמִיעַת הַקּוֹל וְעַל בִּיטּוּי שְׂפָתַיִם וְעַל טוּמְאַת מִקְדָּשׁ וְקֳדָשָׁיו. וְהַנָּשִׂיא כַּיּוֹצֵא בָהֶם דִּבְרֵי רִבִּי יוֹסֵי הַגָּלִילִי. רִבִּי עֲקִיבָה אוֹמֵר הַנָּשִׂיא חַייָב בְּכוּלָּן חוּץ מִשְּׁמִיעַת קוֹל שֶׁהַמֶּלֶךְ לֹא דָן וְלֹא דָנִין אוֹתוֹ לֹא מֵעִיד וְלֹא מְעִידִין אוֹתוֹ:

Mishnah 6: They are not liable for hearing a sound, or expression of the lips, or the impurity of the Temple and its *sancta*[80]. The same applies to the Prince[81], the words of Rebbi Yose the Galilean. Rebbi Aqiba says, the Prince is liable for all of them except the hearing of a sound since the king does not judge, nor may one judge him; he does not testify, nor may one testify against him[82].

80 As explained in the preceding Halakhah, the Court does not bring a sacrifice for a false ruling in a case subject to a sacrifice which depends on the wealth of the person. These are enumerated in *Lev.* 5:1-4; the Mishnah uses the biblical expressions to characterize the different categories.

"Hearing of a voice" refers to *Lev.* 5:1: *If a person sin, for he heard the sound of an imprecation when he is a witness, or saw, or knew; if he does not tell he has to bear his iniquity.* If a person is asked by another to testify in his case before the court; he refuses and assents to an oath to the effect that he does not know about the case, if that was a lie he is subject to the variable reparation offering for swearing falsely.

"Expression of the lips" (v.4) refers to an oath made by a person on his own initiative but not kept since he forgot about his own oath. This also subjects the maker to the same obligation.

Improper handling of impurity because of oblivion is mentioned in vv. 2-3.

81 He is identified with the king.

82 Mishnah *Sanhedrin* 2:3. He extends the rules created for the non-Davidic kings to all kings.

(46d line 37) **הלכה ו**: אֵין חַייָבִין עַל שְׁמִיעַת קוֹל אָלָה כול'. אָמַר רִבִּי יוֹחָנָן. טַעֲמָא דְרִבִּי יוֹסֵי הַגָּלִילִי. וְאִם־דַּ֣ל ה֗וּא וְאֵ֣ין יָדוֹ֮ מַשֶּׂגֶת֒. אֵת שֶׁהוּא רָאוּי לָבוֹא לִידֵי דַלּוּת. יָצָא מָשִׁיחַ שֶׁאֵינוֹ רָאוּי לָבוֹא לִידֵי דַלּוּת. רִבִּי שִׁמְעוֹן בֶּן לָקִישׁ אָמַר. וְהָיָ֥ה כִֽי־יֶאְשַׁ֖ם לְאַחַ֣ת מֵאֵ֑לֶּה. אֵת שֶׁהוּא חַייָב עַל כּוּלָּן חַייָב עַל מִקְצָתָן. וְאֵת שֶׁאֵינוֹ חַייָב עַל כּוּלָּן אֵינוֹ חַייָב עַל מִקְצָתָן. רִבִּי יִצְחָק שָׁאַל. מֵעַתָּה לֹא יִטָּמֵא בְצָרַעַת. שֶׁאֵינוֹ רָאוּי בְקַלּוֹת וְכֵן דַּלּוּת וְכֵן דַּלֵּי דַלּוּת. רַב הוֹשַׁעְיָה בָעֵי. מֵעַתָּה אִשָּׁה לֹא תְהֵא חַייֶבֶת עַל בִּיאַת הַמִּקְדָּשׁ. אֵין הָאִשָּׁה מְבִיאָה. רִבִּי יוֹסֵי בְשֵׁם רִבִּי יוֹחָנָן. טַעֲמָא דְרִבִּי עֲקִיבָה. זֶ֞ה קָרְבַּ֨ן אַהֲרֹ֜ן וּבָנָ֗יו. זֶה הוּא מֵבִיא. אֵינוֹ מֵבִיא עֲשִׂירִית הָאֵיפָה אַחֶרֶת. רִבִּי זְעִירָא בְעָא קוֹמֵי רִבִּי יָסָא. וְאֵינוֹ מֵבִיא נְדָבָה. אָמַר לֵיהּ. אִין. חוֹבָה אֵינוֹ מֵבִיא נְדָבָה הוּא מֵבִיא.

בֵּינִי מַתְנִיתָא שֶׁהַמֶּלֶךְ לֹא מֵעִיד וְלֹא מְעִידִין אוֹתוֹ:

2 לבוא | לבא שאינו | שאין 3 דלות | דלות התיבו' והרי נשיא הרי אינו ראוי לבא לידי דלות 5 בקלות וכן | לבא 6 אין | שאין יוסי | יוסה 7 עקיבה | עקיבא האיפה | איפה 8 יסא | יוסה

Halakhah 6: "They are not liable for hearing the sound of an imprecation," etc. Rebbi Joḥanan said, the reason of Rebbi Yose the Galilean is, *if he is poor and cannot afford it*[83]. Somebody who is apt to fall into poverty; this excludes the Anointed[84] who is not apt to fall into poverty. [[85]They objected: There is the prince who is not apt to fall into poverty.] Rebbi Simeon ben Laqish said, *it shall be if he becomes guilty of any of these*[86]. He who can be liable for all of them is liable for part of them; but one who cannot be liable for all of them is not liable for part of them[87]. Rebbi Isaac asked: Then he should not become impure by skin disease since he is not apt (easily and then) [to fall][88] into poverty or the deepest of poverty[89]. Rav Hoshaia asked: Then a woman should not be liable for entering the Temple. Does the woman not bring[90]?

Rebbi Yose in the name of Rebbi Joḥanan: The reason of Rebbi Aqiba, <u>this</u> *is the offering of Aaron and his sons*[91]. This one he brings; he does not bring another tenth of an *ephah*. Rebbi Ze`ira asked before Rebbi Yasa[92] may he not bring a voluntary offering? He told him, yes. He does not bring an obligatory one; he may bring a voluntary one.

So is the Mishnah, [93]"since the king does not testify, nor may one testify against him."

83 *Lev*. 14:21. This is a wrong quote since it refers to the sacrifice of the healed sufferer from skin disease. The expression used in *Lev*. 5 is וְאִם־לֹא תַגִּיעַ יָדוֹ "if it is out of his reach" for the poor person and וְאִם־לֹא תַשִּׂיג יָדוֹ "if he cannot afford" for the poorest.

84 He is not mentioned in our Mishnah text, but Mishnah 8 states that the High Priest is exempt according to everybody; only for the king does R. Aqiba disagree; Babli 9a. According to Tosephta 1:10, the king is exempted only for disregarding a request for testimony and the High Priest for violations of impurity (since his diadem is a permanent atonement for imperfect sacrifices, *Ex*. 28:38.)

The High Priest is required (*Lev*. 21:10) to be the richest priest; if he is not, the other priests have to make him so. R. Joseph David Sinzheim (*Yad David* on *Horaiot*) notes that the High Priest had the choice always to officiate at the burning of incense. Any other priest was given only a once in a lifetime occasion for this (Mishnah *Yoma* 2:4) since presenting the incense made the presenter rich (explicit in the Babli, implicit in the Yerushalmi, *Yoma* Halakhah 2:4, 40a 12). The king natu- rally has taxing powers.

Since king and High Priest are never able to bring a sacrifice according to the rules of the poor (*Lev*. 5:7-10) or the very poor (vv. 11-13), they are prohibited from ever bringing a sacrifice depending on the offerer's wealth.

85 Text of B. It seems that this text presupposes a Mishnah mentioning only the Anointed; no such Mishnah is known.

86 *Lev*. 5:5.

87 Since the king is exempt from testimony and the High Priest for violations of impurity (Note 84), neither of them is qualified to bring a sacrifice for all cases enumerated in vv. 1-4; they are not under the rules of vv. 6-7.

88 The text in brackets, from B, is the only one making sense; the text of the ms., in parentheses, seems to be a scribal error.

89 Since the verse quoted at the start of the Halakhah refers to the poor sufferer healed from skin disease. But there is no verse requiring that the sufferer from skin disease be able to bring all possible sacrifices; the question does not deserve an answer.

90 Since a woman cannot be a formal witness in court, she cannot be the subject of an imprecation forcing here to testify. But the question is moot since women after childbirth are ordered in *Lev*. 12:6-8 to bring a sacrifice after being impure.

91 *Lev*. 6:13, the daily flour offering of the High Priest, identical in quantity to the variable sacrifice of the very poor. Babli 9a.

92 This is the correct attribution, against the text of B.

93 The fact that he does not judge is irrelevant for our topic (and certainly not true for Davidic kings.)

(fol. 46c) **משנה ז**: כָּל מִצְוֹת שֶׁבַּתּוֹרָה שֶׁחַייָבִין עַל זְדוֹנָן כָּרֵת וְעַל שִׁגְגָתָן חַטָּאת הַיָּחִיד מֵבִיא כִשְׂבָּה וּשְׂעִירָה וְהַנָּשִׂיא שָׂעִיר וּמָשִׁיחַ וּבֵית דִּין מְבִיאִין פָּר. וּבַעֲבוֹדָה זָרָה הַיָּחִיד וְהַנָּשִׂיא וְהַמָּשִׁיחַ מְבִיאִין שְׂעִירָה. וּבֵית דִּין פַּר וְשָׂעִיר פַּר לָעוֹלָה וְשָׂעִיר לַחַטָּאת:

Mishnah 7: For all commandments of the Torah where one is liable to extirpation for willful infraction and a purification sacrifice for unintentional infraction, the individual brings a sheep or a she-goat[94], the Prince a he-goat[95], and the Anointed or the Court bring a bull[96]. For idolatry the individual, the Prince, and the Anointed bring a she-goat, the Court bring a bull as elevation offering and a goat as purification sacrifice[97].

משנה ח: אָשָׁם תָּלוּי הַיָּחִיד וְהַנָּשִׂיא חַייָבִין וּמָשִׁיחַ וּבֵית דִּין פְּטוּרִין. אָשָׁם וַדַּאי הַיָּחִיד וְהַנָּשִׂיא וְהַמָּשִׁיחַ חַייָבִין וּבֵית דִּין פְּטוּרִין. עַל שְׁמִיעַת הַקּוֹל וּבִיטּוּי שְׂפָתַיִם וְטוּמְאַת מִקְדָּשׁ וְקֳדָשָׁיו בֵּית דִּין פְּטוּרִין הַיָּחִיד וְהַנָּשִׂיא וְהַמָּשִׁיחַ חַייָבִין אֶלָּא שֶׁאֵין כֹּהֵן גָּדוֹל חַייָב עַל טוּמְאַת מִקְדָּשׁ וְקֳדָשָׁיו דִּבְרֵי רִבִּי שִׁמְעוֹן. וּמָה הֵן מְבִיאִין קָרְבָּן עוֹלֶה וְיוֹרֵד. רִבִּי אֱלִיעֶזֶר אוֹמֵר הַנָּשִׂיא מֵבִיא שָׂעִיר:

Mishnah 8: For a suspended reparation sacrifice the individual and the Prince are liable but the Anointed and the Court are not liable[98]. For a certain reparation sacrifice the individual, and the Prince, and the Anointed are liable but the Court is not liable[99]. For hearing a sound, or expression of the lips, or the impurity of the Temple and its *sancta*, the Court is not liable, the individual, and the Prince, and the Anointed are liable[100] but the Anointed is not liable for the impurity of the Temple and its *sancta*, the words of Rebbi Simeon[84]. What do they bring? A variable sacrifice. Rebbi Eliezer says, the Prince brings a goat[101].

94 *Lev*. 4:28,32.

95 *Lev*. 4:23

96 Cf. Mishnaiot 1:6, 2:1.

97 *Num*. 15:22-25.

98 Mishnah 5.

99 The reparation sacrifices for robberies or defrauding (*Lev*. 5:20-26), larceny of *sancta* (*Lev*. 5:14-16), the semi-manumitted slave girl (*Lev*. 19:20-22), the *nazir* (*Num*. 6:12), and the healed sufferer from skin disease (*Lev*. 14:1-32). Since no extirpation is involved, the Court is not liable for a sacrifice in case they rule wrongly in one of these matters.

100 Mishnah 6.

101 This is qualified in the Halakhah.

(46d line 48) **הלכה ז**: כָּל מִצְוֹת שֶׁבַּתּוֹרָה כול'. **הלכה ח**: אָשָׁם תָּלוּי הַיָּחִיד וְהַנָּשִׂיא חַייָבִין כול'.
נֶפֶשׁ. לְרַבּוֹת הַנָּשִׂיא. יַרְבֶּה הַמָּשִׁיחַ. בְּחֶטְאָה בִּשְׁגָגָה. אֵת שֶׁהוּא בְשִׁגְגַת מַעֲשֶׂה. יָצָא מָשִׁיחַ

שֶׁאֵינוֹ בְשִׁגְגַת מַעֲשֶׂה. וּכְרִבִּי דוּ אָמַר מָשִׁיחַ בְּשִׁגְגַת מַעֲשֶׂה הוּא. אֵת שֶׁהוּא בְשִׁגְגַת מַעֲשֶׂה לְכָל־הַדְּבָרִים. יָצָא מָשִׁיחַ שֶׁאֵינוֹ בְשִׁגְגַת מַעֲשֶׂה לְכָל־הַדְּבָרִים. נֶפֶשׁ. לְרַבּוֹת הַנָּשִׂיא וְהַמָּשִׁיחַ. הָכָא אַתְּ מַר. לְרַבּוֹת הַנָּשִׂיא. וְכָא אַתְּ מַר. לְרַבּוֹת מָשִׁיחַ. כַּחַטָּאת אָשָׁם. מַה חַטָּאת מְכַפֶּרֶת וּמְמָרֶקֶת. אַף אָשָׁם מְכַפֵּר וּמְמָרֵק. יָצָא אָשָׁם תָּלוּי שֶׁהוּא מְכַפֵּר וּמְשַׁייֵר.

2 הנשיא | את הנשיא ירבה | וריבה 3 הוא | - את | או 5 אשם | ואשם

Halakhah 7: "For all commandments of the Torah," etc. **Halakhah 8**: "For a suspended sacrifice the individual and the Prince are liable," etc. *A person*, to include the Prince[102]. Should it include the Anointed? "*And sinned inadvertently.*[103]" Any depending on acting inadvertently. This excludes the Anointed who is not depending on acting inadvertently[104]. But following Rebbi who said, the Anointed is depending on acting inadvertently[105]? One dependent on acting inadvertently in any situation. This excludes the Anointed who is not dependent on acting inadvertently in any situation. *A person*, to include the Prince and the Anointed[106]. Here you say, to include the prince, and there you say, to include the Anointed? *Like the purification sacrifices is the reparation sacrifice*[107]. Just as the purification sacrifice atones and wipes clean, also the reparation sacrifice atones and wipes clean. This excludes the suspended reparation sacrifice which atones but leaves a residue[108].

102 *Lev.* 5:17, the introduction to the rules for the suspended reparation sacrifice.

103 *Lev.* 5:15. There are two problems with this quote: The first that it is a misquote, it reads וְחָטְאָה בִּשְׁגָגָה not בְּחָטְאָה בִּשְׁגָגָה. This is easily explainable since in talmudic times under the influence of Greek every ב sounded like *v*. The serious problem is that the quote is from the paragraph detailing the rules of the fixed reparation sacrifice for larceny committed with *sancta*. It seems that the quote from *Lev.* 5:17 refers to the full text וְאִם־נֶפֶשׁ *in addition, if a person* . . which in *Sifra Wayyiqra 2 Parašah* 12(1) is explained as meaning that the rules of the suspended reparation sacrifice, vv. 17-19 are an appendix to the rules of the reparation sacrifice for larceny involving *sancta*, vv. 14-16.

104 He is liable for a sacrifice only if there is an element of ruling falsely, Mishnah 3.

105 Halakhah 3. Rebbi declares him liable for a bull and a goat without an element of ruling falsely in case the subject was idolatry, not in any other case. This permits to formulate the preceding argument so it remains valid even for Rebbi.

106 *Lev.* 5:20, the introduction to the

rules for the reparation sacrifice for monetary offenses.

107 *Lev*. 7:7.

108 If at the end it becomes clear that a sin had be committed which qualifies for a purification offering, the suspended offering did not take its place, and a second sacrifice is due. Therefore the rules for the suspended sacrifice are separate from those of other reparation sacrifices.

(46d line 55) כֵּינִי מַתְנִיתָא. אֶלָּא שֶׁאֵין כֹּהֵן גָּדוֹל חַייָב עַל טוּמְאַת מִקְדָּשׁ וְקֳדָשָׁיו. דִּבְרֵי הַכֹּל. וְהַנָּשִׂיא עַל שְׁמִיעַת קוֹל. דִּבְרֵי רִבִּי שִׁמְעוֹן. אָמַר רִבִּי יוֹחָנָן. וּמִן־הַמִּקְדָּשׁ֙ לֹ֣א יֵצֵ֔א וְלֹ֣א יְחַלֵּ֔ל. הָא אִם יָצָא אֵינוֹ מְחַלֵּל. רִבִּי אַשְׁיָאן רִבִּי יוֹנָה רִבִּי בּוּן בַּר כַּהֲנָא מַקְשֵׁי. וְהָכְתִיב אַלְמָנָ֤ה וּגְרוּשָׁה֙ וַחֲלָלָ֣ה זֹנָ֔ה אֶת־אֵ֖לֶּה לֹ֣א יִקָּ֑ח. הָא אִם לָקַח אֵינוֹ מְחַלֵּל. מַאי כְדוֹן. אָמַר חִזְקִיָּה. וְנִכְרְתָ֛ה הַנֶּ֥פֶשׁ הַהִ֖וא מִתּ֣וֹךְ הַקָּהָ֑ל. אֵת שֶׁקָּרְבָּנוֹ שָׁוֶה לַקָּהָל. יָצָא מָשִׁיחַ שֶׁלֹּא שָׁוֶה קָרְבָּנוֹ לַקָּהָל. הָתִיבוֹן. הֲרֵי נָשִׂיא לֹא שָׁוֶה קָרְבָּנוֹ לַקָּהָל. שָׁוֶוה בְּיוֹם הַכִּיפּוּרִים. הֲרֵי אֶחָיו הַכֹּהֲנִים לֹא שָׁווּ בְּיוֹם הַכִּיפּוּרִים. שָׁווּ בִשְׁאָר יְמוֹת הַשָּׁנָה. אָמַר רִבִּי יוּדָן בַּר שָׁלוֹם. שָׁווּ בְּמַתָּן דָּמִים בַּחוּץ.

2 קול | הקול 3 אש׳יאן | יאשיא 4 מאי | מיי אמר | תני 6 הרי | והרי שווה | שוה הרי | והרי 7 בר | בר׳

So is the Mishnah: "but the Anointed is not liable for the impurity of the Temple and its *sancta*, *everybody's opinion, and neither is the Prince for hearing a sound,* the words of Rebbi Simeon.[109]" Rebbi Johanan said, *and the Sanctuary he shall not leave, nor desecrate*. Therefore, if he left, he would not desecrate[110]. Rebbi Ashian[111], Rebbi Jonah: Rebbi Abun bar Cahana found a difficulty. Is it not written, *a widow, or a divorcee, or a desecrated, a harlot, these he shall not marry,* therefore if he married he would not desecrate[112]? What about it? [113]Hizqiah said, *this person would be extirpated from the community*[114]. One whose sacrifice is identical to that of the community. This excludes the Anointed whose sacrifice is not equal to that of the community[115]. They objected, is not also the Prince's sacrifice not equal to that of the community[116]? It is equal on the day of Atonement[117]. But his brothers the priests are not equal on the day of Atonement! They are equal on the other days of the year[118]. Rebbi Yudan bar Shalom said, they are equal in that the blood is given outside[119].

109 Babli 9a; Tosephta 1:10. The Babli 9b points out that there are three levels of variable sacrifices and the argument of Note 84 excludes only the sacrifice of the very poor for the High Priest. In R. Simeon's opinion, the High Priest is still liable at least for a poor man's sacrifice for disregarding a summons to testify.

110 *Lev.* 21:12. The argument seems to be: If the High Priest does not leave the Sanctuary, he has no occasion to desecrate it. Therefore the verse is read as: *and the Sanctuary he shall not leave; he will not desecrate.* The implication would be that the High Priest not only is exempt from bringing a sacrifice (which is a dubious distinction since it denies him a means of atonement) but his infraction of the Sanctuary's purity does not need atonement.

111 A student of R. Jonah's. The reading of B, R. Joshia, referring to an Amora preceding R. Jonah by two generations, is impossible.

112 *Lev.* 21:13. The next verse gives the reason for the prohibition: So he may not desecrate his descendants. Since the child of a Cohen from a woman forbidden to him by the special rules of the priesthood is desecrated, R. Johanan's interpretation of v. 12 is shown to be unacceptable.

113 A slightly different version of the following is in the Babli, 9b.

114 *Num.* 19:19. The entire Chapter deals with the preservation of the purity of the Sanctuary (*Sifry Num.* 129).

115 By his office he is excluded from being one of the community. His sacrifice is either a bull or nothing; the sacrifice of a member of the community is the variable offering (a female sheep or goat, or two pigeons, or flour.)

116 It always is a goat.

117 On that day, the High Priest brings three sacrifices (*Lev.* 16) cf. Note 16. The first one for himself and his family; the second for his fellow priests and their families, and the third a double offering for the people. There the king (unless he is a usurping High Priest and king) is included with the people.

118 The lesser priests are subject to the rules of the variable value sacrifice.

119 On the Day of Atonement, only the blood of the first and third sacrifices are brought inside the Temple to purify the incense altar; the blood of the second sacrifice, the atonement of the priests, is sprinkled on the large outside alter like any other sacrifice. Similarly, the blood of the prince's purification sacrifice is treated like that of a commoner, to be sprinkled on the outside altar.

(46d line 65) אָמַר רִבִּי יוֹחָנָן. לֹא אָמַר רִבִּי לִיעֶזֶר אֶלָּא מִפְּנֵי כְרִיתוֹ. רַב הוֹשַׁעְיָה בָעֵי. מֵעַתָּה אֲפִילוּ בִקְבוּעָה. אָמַר רִבִּי יוֹנָה. מִיסְבּוֹר סָבַר רִבִּי הוֹשַׁעְיָה שֶׁנֶּעֱקַר מִכָּל־הַפָּרָשָׁה. אֶלָּא כְהֶדְיוֹט עָשִׁיר עֲבִיד לֵיהּ רִבִּי לִיעֶזֶר. אָמַר רִבִּי מָנָא. אִין כְּהֶדְיוֹט עָשִׁיר עֲבִיד לֵיהּ רִבִּי לִיעֶזֶר אֲפִילוּ עַל שְׁמִיעַת קוֹל וְעַל בִּיטּוּי שְׂפָתַיִם. דְּתַנֵּי. לֹא נֶחְלְקוּ רִבִּי אֶלְעָזָר וַחֲכָמִים עַל עַל שְׁמִיעַת קוֹל וְעַל בִּיטּוּי שְׂפָתַיִם שֶׁאֵינוֹ מֵבִיא שָׂעִיר אֶלָּא שְׂעִירָה. וְעַל מַה נֶחְלְקוּ. עַל טוּמְאַת מִקְדָּשׁ וְקֳדָשָׁיו. שֶׁרִבִּי לִיעֶזֶר אוֹמֵר. הוֹאִיל וְהוּא בְהִיכָּרֵת לָמָּה אֵינוֹ מֵבִיא שָׂעִיר אֶלָּא שְׂעִירָה. הָתִיבוֹן. הֲרֵי מָשִׁיחַ וַעֲבוֹדָה זָרָה הֲרֵי אֵינוֹ מֵבִיא שָׂעִיר אֶלָּא שְׂעִירָה.

1ליעזר | אליעזר הושעיה | הושעיא 2 בקבועה | כן בקבועה הושעיה | הושעיא 3 ליעזר | אליעזר (2X) 4 קול | הקול ביטוי | בטוי אלעזר | אליעזר 5 קול | הקול ביטוי | בטוי 6 ליעזר | אלעזר בהיכרת | בהכרת למה | ולמה

Rebbi Johanan said, Rebbi Eliezer said this only because of his extirpation[120]. Rebbi Hoshaia asked: If so, then even for a fixed [sacrifice][121]? Rebbi Jonah said, Rebbi Hoshaia is of the opinion that he is uprooted from the entire paragraph; but Rebbi Eliezer treats him like a rich commoner[122]. Rebbi Mana said, if Rebbi Eliezer treats him like a rich commoner, then also for hearing a sound, or expression of the lips[80], as it was stated: Rebbi (Eleazar) [Eliezer] and the Sages did not differ about hearing a sound, or expression of the lips, that he does not bring a male goat but a she-goat[123]. About what did they differ? About impurity of the Sanctuary and its *sancta*, where Rebbi Eliezer says since he is subject to extirpation why should he not bring a male goat instead of a she-goat[124]? They objected: Is there not the Anointed in the case of idolatry where he does not bring a male goat but a she-goat[125].

120 Of all the sins calling for a variable sacrifice, only infractions of the purity of the sanctuary or of sacrifices are punished by extirpation. Therefore R. Eliezer lets him bring the fixed-value sacrifice prescribed for the Prince for all other cases of possible extirpation.

The entire paragraph has an inconclusive parallel in the Babli 9b.

121 If the argument of R. Johanan were correct, R. Eliezer also should require that the prince bring a he-goat, not a she-goat, as the fixed-value sacrifice required for inadvertent idolatry, against Mishnah 7.

122 R. Hoshaia's argument is unacceptable since only R. Yose the Galilean denies the Prince any variable-value sacrifice; we follow R. Aqiba who is granting him a sacrifice for any sin but freeing him from any obligation regarding a summons to testify.

123 In fact only for expression of the lips.

124 Since the king cannot become poor, he should not be under the rules of variable-value sacrifices.

125 Not only the Anointed but also the Prince are included in the rules for the individual inadvertently committing idolatry. Since there are no exceptions for the rules of *Num.* 15, the argument made for R. Eliezer does not hold. In addition,; the she-goat of *Lev.* 5 is a reparation sacrifice but his he-goat of *Lev.* 43 a purification sacrifice.

כהן משיח שחטא פרק שלישי

(fol. 47a) **משנה א**: כֹּהֵן מָשִׁיחַ שֶׁחָטָא וְאַחַר כָּךְ עָבַר מִמְּשִׁיחוּתוֹ. וְכֵן נָשִׂיא שֶׁחָטָא וְאַחַר כָּךְ עָבַר מִגְּדוּלָּתוֹ. כֹּהֵן מָשִׁיחַ מֵבִיא פָּר. וְהַנָּשִׂיא מֵבִיא שָׂעִיר:

Mishnah 1: An Anointed Priest who sinned and then was removed from his anointed status, or a Prince who sinned and then was removed from his exalted status. The Anointed Priest brings a bull and the Prince brings a goat[1].

משנה ב: כֹּהֵן מָשִׁיחַ שֶׁעָבַר מִמְּשִׁיחוּתוֹ וְאַחַר כָּךְ חָטָא וְכֵן הַנָּשִׂיא שֶׁעָבַר מִגְּדֻלָּתוֹ וְאַחַר כָּךְ חָטָא כֹּהֵן מָשִׁיחַ מֵבִיא פָּר וְהַנָּשִׂיא כַּהֶדְיוֹט:

Mishnah 2: An Anointed Priest who was removed from his anointed status and then sinned, or a Prince who was removed from his exalted status and then sinned: The Anointed Priest brings a bull and the Prince is like a commoner[2].

1 Since at the moment of the sin they became obligated for the sacrifices, a later change of status has no influence. The difference between ecclesiastical and political offices will become clear in Mishnah 2.

2 Again the moment of the sin determines the kind of sacrifice. Priestly offices follow the rule that "one rises in holiness; one does not descend;" the former Anointed Priest remains in his status. He cannot officiate as Anointed Priest since another one holds the office; neither can he officiate as common priest since he may not descend in rank. The same is true for an unanointed High Priest. But a politician who loses his rank is free to run for any other office; his sacrifice is a female goat or sheep like everybody else's.

(47a) **הלכה א**: כֹּהֵן מָשִׁיחַ שֶׁחָטָא כול'. **הלכה ב**: כֹּהֵן מָשִׁיחַ שֶׁעָבַר מִמְּשִׁיחוּתוֹ כול'. אָמַר רִבִּי לָעְזָר. כֹּהֵן גָּדוֹל שֶׁחָטָא מַלְקִין אוֹתוֹ וְאֵין מַעֲבִירִין אוֹתוֹ מִגְּדוּלָּתוֹ. אָמַר רִבִּי מָנָא. כְּתִיב כִּ֠י נֵ֣זֶר שֶׁ֣מֶן מִשְׁחַ֧ת אֱלֹהָ֛יו עָלָ֖יו אֲנִ֥י יי. כִּבְיָכוֹל מָה אֲנִי בִגְדוּלָּתִי אַף אַהֲרוֹן בִּגְדוּלָּתוֹ. אָמַר רִבִּי אָבוּן. קָדוֹשׁ יִֽהְיֶה־לָּ֑ךְ. כִּבְיָכוֹל אֲנִי בִקְדוּשָּׁתִי אַף אַהֲרוֹן בִּקְדוּשָּׁתוֹ. רִבִּי חֲנִינָה כְּתוּבָא רִבִּי אָחָא בְשֵׁם רִבִּי שִׁמְעוֹן בֶּן לָקִישׁ. כֹּהֵן מָשִׁיחַ שֶׁחָטָא מַלְקִין אוֹתוֹ בְּבֵית דִּין שֶׁלִּשְׁלֹשָׁה. אִין תֵּימַר בְּבֵית דִּין שֶׁלְּכ"ג. נִמְצָא עֲלִייָתוֹ יְרִידָה לוֹ. רִבִּי שִׁמְעוֹן בֶּן לָקִישׁ אָמַר. נָשִׂיא שֶׁחָטָא מַלְקִין אוֹתוֹ בְּבֵית דִּין שֶׁלִּשְׁלֹשָׁה. מַה מַחֲזִרִין לֵיהּ. אָמַר רִבִּי חַגַּיי. מוּטָּב דִּינוֹן מַחֲזִרִין לֵיהּ דּוּ קְטַלּוֹן לֵיהּ. שָׁמַע רִבִּי יוּדָה נְשִׂיאָה וְכָעַס. שָׁלַח גּוּתִּיִין לְמִיתְפַּשׂ יַת רִבִּי שִׁמְעוֹן בֶּן לָקִישׁ. וַעֲרַק בְּדָא דְמוּגְדָּלָא.

וְאִית דְּאָמְרִין בְּרָה דִכְפַר חִיטַּיָּא. סְלִיק רִבִּי יוֹחָנָן לְבֵית וַועֲדָא. סְלַק רִבִּי יוּדָה נְסִיָּא לְבֵית וַועֲדָא. אֲמַר לֵיהּ. לָמָּה לֵית מָרִי אֲמַר לוֹן מִילָּה דְאוֹרַיְיָא. שְׁרֵי טְפַח בְּחָדָא יָדֵיהּ. אֲמַר לֵיהּ. וּבְחָדָא יָדָא טַפְּחִין. אֲמַר לֵיהּ. לָאו. אִין לֹא בֶּן לָקִישׁ לֹא. אֲמַר לֵיהּ. לֹא. אֲמַר לֵיהּ. וְאָנוּ מְפַתְּחָא. אֲמַר לֵיהּ. בְּרָא דְמוּגְדָּלָא. אֲמַר לֵיהּ. אֲנָא וְאַתְּ נְפִיק לְקַדְמֵיהּ. שְׁלַח רִבִּי יוֹחָנָן גַּבֵּי רִבִּי שִׁמְעוֹן בֶּן לָקִישׁ. עֲתֵיר לָךְ מִילָּה דְאוֹרַיְיָא דִּנְשִׂיָּא נְפִיק לְקַדְמָךְ. נְפַק לְקַדְמוֹן. מַר. דֵּיגְמַא דִידְכוֹן דָּמֵי לְבָרֵייכוֹן. כַּד אֲתַא רַחֲמָנָא לְמִפְרַק יַת יִשְׂרָאֵל מִמִּצְרַיִם לֹא שָׁלַח לֹא שָׁלִיחַ וְלֹא מַלְאָךְ. אֶלָּא הַקָּדוֹשׁ בָּרוּךְ הוּא בְעַצְמוֹ. דִּכְתִיב וְעָבַרְתִּי בְאֶרֶץ־מִצְרַיִם בַּלַּיְלָה הַזֶּה. וְלֹא עוֹד אֶלָּא הוּא וְכָל־דּוֹרְגוֹן דִּידֵיהּ. אֲשֶׁר הָלַךְ אֱלֹהִים אֵין כָּתוּב כָּאן אֶלָּא אֲשֶׁר הָלְכוּ־אֱלֹהִים. אָמְרִין לֵיהּ. מַה חֲמִיתָהּ מֵימוֹר לָן הָדָא מִילְּתָא. אֲמַר לוֹן. מָה אַתּוּן סָבְרִין. מַה דְחִיל מִינְּכוֹן הֲוִינָא מְנַע אוּלְפָּנֵיהּ דְּרַחֲמָנָא. אָמַר רִבִּי שְׁמוּאֵל בַּר רַב יִצְחָק אַל בָּנָיי כִּי לֹא טוֹבָה הַשְּׁמוּעָה וגו'. מַעֲבִרִים עַם־יי. מַעֲבִירִין אוֹתוֹ.

Halakhah 1: "An Anointed Priest who sinned," etc. **Halakhah 2**: "An Anointed Priest who was removed from his anointed status," etc.

[3]Rebbi Eleazar said, if a High Priest sinned, one whips him but does not remove him from his elevated status. Rebbi Mana said, it is written: *For the crown of his God's ointment is on him, I am the Eternal*; if one could compare it, just as I am in My Greatness, so Aaron is in his greatness. Rebbi Abun said, it is written[4]: *Holy shall he be for you*; if one could compare it, I am in My Sanctity, so Aaron is in his sanctity. Rebbi Ḥanina the scribe, Rebbi Aḥa in the name of Rebbi Simeon ben Laqish: if an Anointed Priest sinned, one whips him in a court of three [judges]. If you would say in a court of 23, his elevation would be his degradation. Rebbi Simeon ben Laqish said, if a patriarch sinned, one whips him in a court of three [judges]. Does one return him? Rebbi Ḥaggai said, better if one did return him, he would kill them. Rebbi Jehudah the Prince heard this and became angry. He sent Goths to catch Rebbi Simeon ben Laqish. He fled to Magdala, some say to Kefar Ḥiṭṭim. Rebbi Joḥanan went to the assembly hall; Rebbi Jehudah the Prince also went to the assembly hall. He said to him, why is the master not telling us words of instruction? He started clapping with one hand. He asked, does one clap with one? He answered him, no, but without ben Laqish there is nothing. He said, no. He told him, I shall free him. He said to him, in Magdala. He told him, I and you will go out to meet him. Rebbi Joḥanan sent to Rebbi Simeon ben Laqish, prepare for yourself some words of instruction

since the Patriarch will go out to meet you. He went out to meet them and said, your example is similar to that of your Creator. For when the Merciful went to liberate Israel from Egypt, He sent neither messenger nor angel but He went Himself, as is written: *I shall pass through the Land of Egypt in that night, not only* He but all His Court. It is not written in this context "when Power went" but *when Powers went*[5]. They asked him, why did you say these things? He told them, what are you thinking? That for fear of you I would refrain from the teachings of the Merciful? As Rebbi Samuel ben Rav Isaac said, *No my sons, because the reputation is not good*, etc., *you remove the Eternal's people*[6], one removes him.

3 A slightly enlarged version of a paragraph in *Sanhedrin* 2:1, Notes 14 ff. The paragraph is missing in B, as in all similar cases it was added by later editors of the Babli from the Yerushalmi. Only the few added verses are indicated here. The additions are printed in a different typeface. In a few places, the text here is slightly shortened.

4 *Lev.* 21:8.

5 *2S.* 7:23.

6 *1S.* 2:24. This quote is the gist of the entire sermon, missing in *Sanhedrin*.

(fol. 47a) **משנה ג**: חָטְאוּ עַד שֶׁלֹּא נִתְמַנּוּ וְאַחַר כָּךְ נִתְמַנּוּ הֲרֵי אֵילּוּ כַהֶדְיוֹט. רִבִּי שִׁמְעוֹן אוֹמֵר אִם נוֹדַע לָהֶם עַד שֶׁלֹּא נִתְמַנּוּ חַייָבִין וּמִשֶּׁנִּתְמַנּוּ פְּטוּרִין. וְאֵי זֶה הוּא הַנָּשִׂיא זֶה הַמֶּלֶךְ שֶׁנֶּאֱמַר וְעָשָׂה אַחַת מִכָּל־מִצְוֹת יי אֱלֹהָיו נָשִׂיא שֶׁאֵין עַל גַּבָּיו אֶלָּא ה' אֱלֹהָיו. וְאֵי זֶה הוּא הַמָּשִׁיחַ זֶה הַמָּשׁוּחַ בְּשֶׁמֶן הַמִּשְׁחָה וְלֹא הַמְרוּבֶּה בִבְגָדִים.

Mishnah 3: If they sinned before being appointed; when afterwards they were appointed, they remain commoners[1,7]. Rebbi Simeon says, if it became known to them before they were appointed, they are obligated; if after they were appointed they are not liable.

Who is the Prince? This is the king, as it is said[8], *if he transgressed one of the commandments of the Eternal, his God*; a Prince who has none above him but the Eternal, his God.

And who is the Anointed? This is one anointed with the anointing oil, not one clothed in multiple garb[9].

משנה ד׳: אֵין בֵּין כֹּהֵן הַמָּשׁוּחַ בְּשֶׁמֶן הַמִּשְׁחָה לִמְרוּבֵּה בְגָדִים אֶלָּא פַּר הַבָּא עַל כָּל הַמִּצְוֹת. וְאֵין בֵּין כֹּהֵן מְשַׁמֵּשׁ לְכֹהֵן שֶׁעָבַר אֶלָּא פַּר יוֹם הַכִּיפּוּרִים וַעֲשִׂירִית הָאֵיפָה.

Mishnah 4: The only difference between the priest anointed with the anointing oil and the one clothed in multiple garb is the bull brought for all commandments[10]. And the only difference between an officiating High Priest and a deposed one is the bull of the Day of Atonement[11] and the tenth of an *ephah*[12].

משנה ה׳: זֶה וָזֶה שָׁוִין בַּעֲבוֹדַת יוֹם הַכִּיפּוּרִים וּמְצוּוִּין עַל הַבְּתוּלָה וַאֲסוּרִין עַל הָאַלְמָנָה וְאֵינָן מִיטַּמְּאִין בִּקְרוֹבֵיהֶן וְלֹא פוֹרְעִין וְלֹא פוֹרְמִין וּמַחֲזִירִין אֶת הָרוֹצֵחַ׃

Mishnah 5: Both are equal in the office of the day of Atonement[13], commanded about the virgin[14], and prohibited for a widow[15], and do not defile themselves for close relatives[16], and may not let their hair grow[17] or rend their garments[18], and let the homicide return[19].

7 For the purposes of this sacrifice.

8 *Lev.* 4:22.

9 Making the anointing oil was commanded personally to Moses (*Ex.* 30:25). All High Priests up to the time of king Josiah were anointed with it. Since that time, the oil was no longer available; it cannot be reconstituted. The later High Priests were inducted into their office by investiture with the High Priest's garments.

10 The rules about the High Priest's purification sacrifice explained in Chapter 2 became obsolete with the destruction of the First Temple and could be restored to validity only if a dig on the Temple Mount would recover the flask containing the original oil. The High Priests of the Second Temple had the status of commoners in this respect.

11 Which has to be acquired by the High Priest with his own money together with a goat (*Lev.* 16:3).

12 The personal daily offering of the High Priest, *Lev.* 6:12-16, of about 3.84 l of fine flour.

13 If the acting High Priest becomes impure or otherwise incapacitated, a former High Priest can replace him without special dedication. No common priest can perform any of the prescribed acts of the Day of Atonement.

14 *Lev.* 21:13. This applies only if the High Priest marries while High Priest. If he married a widow while a common priest, he still may be elevated to High Priest.

15 *Lev.* 21:14.

16 *Lev.* 21:11.

17 *Lev.* 21:10.

18 *Lev.* 21:10. These are forbidden as mourning rites.

19 *Num.* 35:25 (where anointing is mentioned), 32 (where anointing is not mentioned).

(47a line 56) **הלכה ג׃** חָטְאוּ עַד שֶׁלֹּא נִתְמַנּוּ כול'. חֲבֵרַייָא אָֽמְרִין טַעֲמָא דְרִבִּי שִׁמְעוֹן. מִשֵּׁם שֶׁהַגְּדוּלָּה מְכַפֶּרֶת. אָמַר רִבִּי יוֹסֵי. שֶׁאֵין חֵטְאוֹ וִידִיעָתוֹ שָׁוִין. מַה מַפְקָה מִבֵּינֵיהוֹן. רֵישָׁא דְפִירְקָא. כֹּהֵן מָשִׁיחַ שֶׁחָטָא וְאַחַר כָּךְ עָבַר מִמְּשִׁיחוּתוֹ. וְכֵן נָשִׂיא שֶׁחָטָא וְאַחַר כָּךְ עָבַר מִגְּדוּלָּתוֹ. כֹּהֵן מָשִׁיחַ מֵבִיא פָר וְהַנָּשִׂיא מֵבִיא שָׂעִיר׃ חָטְאוּ בְסָפֵק. מָאן דָּמַר. מִשֵּׁם שֶׁהַגְּדוּלָּה מְכַפֶּרֶת. כְּשֵׁם שֶׁהִיא מְכַפֶּרֶת עַל הַוַּדַּאי כָּךְ הִיא מְכַפֶּרֶת עַל הַסָּפֵק. מָאן דָּמַר. אֵין חֵטְאוֹ וִידִיעָתוֹ שָׁוִין. אֵין חֵטְאוֹ וִידִיעָתוֹ שָׁוִין. חָטְאוּ עַד שֶׁלֹּא נִתְמַנּוּ מִשֶּׁנִּתְמַנּוּ עָבְרוּ. מָאן דָּמַר. מִשֵּׁם שֶׁהַגְּדוּלָּה מְכַפֶּרֶת. כִּיפְּרָה הַגְּדוּלָּה עַל הָרִאשׁוֹן וְחַייָב עַל הַשֵּׁינִי וְעַל הַשְּׁלִישִׁי. מָאן דָּמַר. אֵין חֵטְאוֹ וִידִיעָתוֹ שָׁוִין. חָטְאוּ עַל שְׁמִיעַת קוֹל וְעַל בִּיטּוּי שְׂפָתַיִם וְעַל טוּמְאַת מִקְדָּשׁ וְקֳדָשָׁיו. מָאן דָּמַר. אֵין חֵטְאוֹ וִידִיעָתוֹ שָׁוִין. הֲרֵי חֵטְאוֹ וִידִיעָתוֹ שָׁוִין. מָאן דָּמַר. מִשֵּׁם שֶׁהַגְּדוּלָּה מְכַפֶּרֶת. אֲפִילוּ כֵן הַגְּדוּלָּה מְכַפֶּרֶת.

1 משם | כשם 2 יוסי | יוסה רישא | רישיה 3 ממשיחותו | ממשיחתו 4 מאן | מן משם | כשם 5 מאן | ומן 6 משנתמנו | ומשנתמנו מאן | מן 7 משם | כשם השיני | השני מאן | מן 8 קול | הקול 9 מאן | מן (2) משם | כשם

Halakhah 3 "If they sinned before being appointed," etc. The colleagues say that the reason of Rebbi Simeon is because greatness atones[20]. Rebbi Yose said, because his sin and his knowledge are not equal[21]. What is the difference[22] between them? Referring to the beginning of the Chapter: "An Anointed Priest who sinned and then was removed from his anointed status, or a Prince who sinned and then was removed from his exalted status. The Anointed Priest brings a bull and the Prince brings a goat;" if there is any doubt whether they sinned. He who said, because greatness atones; just as it atones for the certain [sin] so it atones for the doubt. He who said. because his sin and his knowledge are not equal; his sin and his knowledge are not equal[23]. If they sinned before they were appointed and after they were appointed they breached, for him who said, because greatness atones, greatness atoned for the first, but he is liable for the second and the third[24]. For him who said, because his sin and his knowledge are not equal[25]. If they sinned regarding hearing a sound, or expression of the lips, or the impurity of the Temple and its *sancta*, for him who said, because his sin and his knowledge are not equal, here his sin and his knowledge are equal[26]. For him who said, because greatness atones, even in this case greatness atones[27].

20 As will become clear later (Note 29), it is not the high office which atones but the appointment to high office. This is the Babli's interpretation of *IS*. 13:1, that Saul was 1 year old when he became king; his sins were remitted and he was

innocent like a one year old baby (*Yoma* 22b).

The colleagues are Rav Hanania and Rav Oshia, two Babylonians of the third generation of Amoraim who lived in Galilee but never held office there.

21 This is the only opinion mentioned in the Babli, 3a. Since the status of the individual at the moment of the sin determines the appropriate sacrifice, if later his status changes he is prevented from sacrificing.

22 Are there practical differences depending on which doctrine one chooses? Since only R. Simeon's opinion is discussed, it seems that the Yerushalmi accepts his as practice, as far as these rules have practical applications.

23 There is no practical difference between rulings based on the colleagues' or R. Yose's opinions.

24 The first case occurred before he was appointed, the second while he was in office, the third after he was removed from office. According to the colleagues, the induction into exalted office cancels the previous sins; once he entered office no further benefits accrue; cf. Note 29.

25 No detail is given since the answer is complicated; the problem is taken up again in Note 64. There is no sacrifice possible if the status of the sinner has changed between the date of the sin and the realization that it happened. The only problem is that of a sin committed in stage 1 which becomes known in stage 3; whether or not a sacrifice is possible depends on the difference between R. Johanan and R. Simeon ben Laqish in 1:2, cf. there Note 74; cf. also the following Note 61.

26 A sacrifice of variable value is required in all three cases; for R. Simeon under the restrictions of Chapter 2, Note 84.

27 The complications discussed in Chapter 2 regarding the variable sacrifice become irrelevant by the elevation of a person to exalted status.

(47a line 68) אָמַר רִבִּי מַתַּנְיָה. לְעוֹלָם אֵין הַגְּדוּלָּה מְכַפֶּרֶת עַד שֶׁתִּיוָּדַע לוֹ גְדוּלָּתוֹ. אָכַל חֲצִי זַיִת עַד שֶׁלֹּא נִתְמַנֶּה וַחֲצִי זַיִת מִשֶּׁנִּתְמַנֶּה. אֲפִילוּ בְעֶלֶם אֶחָד פָּטוּר. סָפֵק חֲצִי זַיִת עַד שֶׁלֹּא נִתְמַנֶּה וְסָפֵק חֲצִי זַיִת מִשֶּׁנִּתְמַנֶּה. מֵבִיא אָשָׁם תָּלוּי. מָצִינוּ דָבָר עִיקָּרוֹ פָטוּר סְפֵיקוֹ חַייָב. וְלֹא אַשְׁכַּחְנָן כֵּן. אָכַל שְׁנֵי זֵיתִים וְנִתְוַודַּע לָךְ בְּוַודַּייו שֶׁלְּאֶחָד מֵהֶן. שֵׁינִי עָמַד לוֹ בִסְפֵיקוֹ. רִבִּי יַעֲקֹב דְּרוֹמִייָא בְעָא קוֹמֵי רִבִּי יוֹסֵי. מַה נַפְשָׁךְ. חֵלֶב אָכַל כִּיפֵּר. אָמַר רִבִּי יוֹסֵי. כָּל־דָּבָר שֶׁנִּרְאֶה עָלָיו לְהָבִיא אָשָׁם תָּלוּי יְדִיעַת סְפֵיקָהּ קוֹבְעָתוֹ לְחַטָּאו. הֲרֵי מָצִינוּ דָבָר עִיקָּרוֹ פָטוּר וּסְפֵיקוֹ חַייָב. וְכָא עִיקָּרוֹ פָטוּר וּסְפֵיקוֹ חַייָב.

1 מתניה | מתניא 2 גדולתו | שגגתו אפילו בעלם אחד פטור. ספק חצי זית עד שלא נתמנה וספק חצי זית משנתמנה | -[28] 3 עיקרו | שעיקרו ספיקו | וספיקו 4 אשכחנן | אשכחן אכל | אלא אכל ומתוודע לך בוודייו | ונודע לו בודאי שיני | את השני ספיקו | ספקו 5 דרומייא | דרומיא יוסי | יוסה (2X) כיפר | כפר שומן אכל כפר 6 ספיקה | ספקו ספיקו | ספקו 7 ספיקו | ספקו

Rebbi Mattania said: Greatness cannot atone (until his greatness becomes known to him) [unless his error became known to him.][29] If he ate half the volume of an olive before he was appointed and half the volume of an olive after he was appointed, even in one oblivion he is not liable[30]. A doubt of half the volume of an olive before he was appointed and a doubt of half the volume of an olive after he was appointed: he brings a suspended reparation offering[31]. Do we find anything where for the actual offense he is not liable but for a doubt he is liable? We do not find this! If he ate the volume of two olives, the true nature of one of them became known to him, the other remained for him in doubt[32]. Rebbi Jacob the Southerner asked before Rebbi Yose: As you take it, if he ate forbidden fat, it atoned. [If he ate permitted fat, it atoned.][33] Rebbi Yose said, anything which convinced him to bring a suspended reparation offering, the knowledge of the doubt establishes his transgression[34]. So we find a case where for the actual offense he is not liable but for a doubt he is liable[35].

28 Omission because of homeoteleuton.

29 The text in parentheses is from L, the one in brackets is from B. It seems that the latter is the correct one. Since it was established in the preceding paragraph that in the opinion of the colleagues it is the act of elevation which wipes off earlier guilt, only those transgressions which are known to the person being elevated are being atoned for. The argument is also acceptable to R. Yose since once the transgression became known to the person, it determines the sacrifice which he is obligated to bring. If then his status changes, he might be prevented from ever bringing this sacrifice.

30 While the consumption of any forbidden food is sinful, the transgression is prosecutable, or if committed inadvertently requires a sacrifice, only if the amount consumed was at least the volume of an olive (except it one ate a complete being, such as an ant.) All transgressions committed during one period of oblivion are added together, on condition that their accumulation result in one and the same sacrifice. But if his appointment changes the nature of the sacrifice, the partial transgressions cannot be added.

31 Since the appointment does not change the nature of the required suspended reparation sacrifice (except that the Anointed Priest is not liable for possible infractions relating to the purity of the Temple and its *sancta*.)

32 This now refers to anybody and is not subject to varying purification sacrifices. If he ate two different foods, for one it became known to him that it was forbidden, the other is only suspected of not being kosher. Then for the forbidden food he is liable to bring a purification sacrifice, for the suspected one a suspended reparation sacrifice. Bringing

a suspended reparation sacrifice implies an obligation to bring a purification sacrifice if it should become clear that a sin had actually been committed.

33 The text in brackets is from B; it makes for a smoother reading but one could argue that it is redundant.

R. Jacob's argument is that a second purification sacrifice (and possibly the suspended reparation sacrifice) should be unnecessary (and therefore impossible) since if the two kinds of food were both known to be not kosher and they were eaten in one period of oblivion, one purification sacrifice would be prescribed. If the second food turned out to be kosher, no sacrifice would be needed.

34 The previous argument is rejected. The obligation of sacrifices is fixed at the moment the person realizes the sinfulness of his actions. Since at that moment, the status of the second food remained in doubt, it required a suspended reparation sacrifice. But a suspended reparation sacrifice carries with it the implicit obligation of a purification sacrifice in case the situation could be cleared up.

35 In case of a certain violation, one sacrifice would have been due. Because of the doubt, two or three are due now. The previous statement is disproved.

(47b line 1) אָכַל כְּזַיִת עַד שֶׁלֹּא נִתְמַנֶּה וּכְזַיִת מִשֶּׁנִּתְמַנֶּה. בְּהֶעֱלֵם אֶחָד אֵינוֹ חַייָב אֶלָּא אַחַת. סָפֵק כְּזַיִת עַד שֶׁלֹּא נִתְמַנֶּה וְסָפֵק כְּזַיִת מִשֶּׁנִּתְמַנֶּה. בְּהֶעֱלֵם אֶחָד אֵינוֹ חַייָב אֶלָּא אַחַת. בִּשְׁנֵי הֶעֱלֵימוֹת חַייָב שְׁתַּיִם.

3 העלימות | העלמות

אָכַל שְׁלֹשָׁה זֵיתִים וְסָבוּר שֶׁהֵן שְׁנַיִם. הִפְרִישׁ חַטָּאת כְּדְרַבִּי יוֹחָנָן. דְּרַבִּי יוֹחָנָן אָמַר. נִתְכַּפֵּר מִקְצַת הַחֵט נִתְכַּפֵּר כּוּלּוֹ. רִבִּי שִׁמְעוֹן בֶּן לָקִישׁ אָמַר. נִתְכַּפֵּר מִקְצַת הַחֵט לֹא נִתְכַּפֵּר כּוּלּוֹ.

1 וסבור | סבור כר' יוחנן | אחת כפר דר' | ר' 2 החט | החטא (2X)

אָכַל חֲמִשָּׁה זֵיתִים וְנִתְוַודַּע לוֹ בְסָפֵק כָּל־אֶחָד וְאֶחָד. וְאַחַר כָּךְ נִתְוַודַּע לוֹ בֵית דִּין. רִבִּי שִׁמְעוֹן בֶּן לָקִישׁ אָמַר. יְדִיעַת סְפֵיקוֹ קוֹבְעָתוֹ לְחַטָּאוֹ. רִבִּי יוֹחָנָן אָמַר. אֵין יְדִיעַת סְפֵיקוֹ קוֹבְעָתוֹ לְחַטָּאוֹ. רִבִּי יוֹסֵי בֵּירִבִּי בּוּן בְּשֵׁם רִבִּי שְׁמוּאֵל בַּר רַב יִצְחָק. מוֹדֶה רִבִּי שִׁמְעוֹן בֶּן לָקִישׁ בְּכֹהֵן מָשִׁיחַ שֶׁאֵין יְדִיעַת סְפֵיקוֹ קוֹבְעָתוֹ לְחַטָּאוֹ. וּמַה טַעַם. כְּחַטָּאת כְּאָשָׁם. אֵת שֶׁהוּא מֵבִיא אָשָׁם תָּלוּי סְפֵיקוֹ קוֹבְעָתוֹ לְחַטָּאוֹ. וְאֵת שֶׁאֵינוֹ מֵבִיא אָשָׁם תָּלוּי אֵין סְפֵיקוֹ קוֹבְעָתוֹ לְחַטָּאוֹ.

1 ונתוודע | ונתודע נתוודע | נתודע בית דין | בודאי 2 קובעתו | קובעת 3 קובעתו | קובעת יוסי | יוסה בשם | אמ' ר' שמעון בן לקיש | ריש לקיש 4 קובעתו | קובעת ומה | מה שהוא מביא | שמביא 5 קובעתו | קובעת

מִחְלְפָה שִׁיטָּתֵיהּ דְּרִבִּי שִׁמְעוֹן בֶּן לָקִישׁ. תַּמָּן הוּא אָמַר. יְדִיעַת סְפֵיקוֹ קוֹבְעָתוֹ לְחַטָּאוֹ. וְכָא אָמַר. אֵין יְדִיעַת סְפֵיקוֹ קוֹבְעָתוֹ לְחַטָּאוֹ. תַּמָּן אֲשָׁמוֹ קוֹבְעוֹ. וְכָא מָה אִית לָךְ.

1 אמר | אומר 2 וכא אמ' | והא הוא אומר קובעו | קובעתו

מְחָלְפָה שִׁיטָתֵיהּ דְּרִבִּי יוֹחָנָן. תַּמָּן הוּא אָמַר. נִתְכַּפֵּר מִקְצַת הַחֵט נִתְכַּפֵּר כּוּלּוֹ. וְכָא הוּא אָמַר אָכֵן. לֹא אָמַר רִבִּי יוֹחָנָן אֶלָּא בִידִיעָה אַחֲרוֹנָה שֶׁאֵין בָּהּ שׁוּם קָרְבָּן.

1 אמ' | אומר החט | החטא וכא | והא 2 אמ' אכן | אומר הכן אחרונה | האחרונה שום | חיוב

One ate the volume of an olive before he was appointed and the volume of an olive after he was appointed. If it was in one oblivion, he is liable only for one [sacrifice][36]. If the volume of an olive was in doubt before he was appointed, and the volume of an olive was in doubt after he was appointed, in one oblivion he is liable only for one, in two forgettings he is liable for two [sacrifices.[37]]

One ate the volume of three olives but was of the opinion that he ate only two. {He selected a sacrifice following Rebbi Joḥanan.[38]} [If he selected one sacrifice, this atones.[39]] For Rebbi Joḥanan said, if part of the sin was atoned for, all of the sin was atoned for. Rebbi Simeon ben Laqish said, if part of the sin was atoned for, not all of the sin was atoned for.

One ate five times the volume of an olive; he separately realized a doubt about each one. Afterwards it became known to him (in court) [as a certainty.[40]] Rebbi Simeon ben Laqish said, the knowledge about his doubt determines his kind of transgression. Rebbi Joḥanan said, the knowledge about his doubt does not determine his kind of transgression[41]. Rebbi Yose bar Abun in the name of Rebbi Samuel bar Rav Isaac: Rebbi Simeon ben Laqish agrees that for the Anointed Priest the knowledge about his doubt does not determine his kind of transgression[42]. What is the reason? *Like purification offering, like reparation offering*[43]. The knowledge about his doubt determines his kind of transgression for one who brings a suspended reparation offering. The knowledge about his doubt does not determine his kind of transgression for one who does not bring a suspended reparation offering.

The argument of Rebbi Simeon ben Laqish seems to be inverted. There he says, the knowledge about his doubt determines his kind of transgression. But here he says, the knowledge about his doubt does not determine his kind of transgression. There, his reparation offering determines it. Here what do you have[44]?

The argument of Rebbi Johanan seems to be inverted. There, he said, if part of the sin was atoned, all of the sin was atoned. And here he says so? Rebbi Johanan said this only for the last realization which does not require any sacrifice[45].

36 The moment of realization of the transgression determines the kind of sacrifice required. Since the Anointed and the king are forbidden to offer the sacrifice of a commoner and vice-versa, only one sacrifice is possible.

37 Since a suspended reparation sacrifice is authorized for everybody, it can be offered both by a commoner and by an Anointed Priest or a king. But it was established earlier that elevation starts new obligations of sacrifices. Therefore, obligations of suspended reparation sacrifices before and after elevation cannot be combined.

38 Text of L.

39 Text of B. The two texts have the same meaning; B's is more easily understood. The Babli, *Šabbat* 71b, switches the attributions between RR. Johanan and Simeon ben Laqish.

For R. Simeon ben Laqish, the dedication of the sacrifice to atone for two infractions requires a new sacrifice for the third. For R. Johanan, the one sacrifice automatically is valid for the third also.

40 The text in parentheses is from L, the one in brackets from B. Since the testimony as to the occurrence of a sinful act by a single witness in court is sufficient to obligate the perpetrator for a sacrifice (even though a single witness is not admissible in any criminal procedure and may be contradicted by an oath in civil proceedings) the text in parentheses has to be preferred as *lectio difficilior* while the meaning for the English reader is more easily understood from the text of B.

41 The problem discussed here has no direct connection with change of status; it applies as well to a commoner who progressively becomes aware of multiple transgressions of the same kind; *Ševuot* 2:1 (33d l. 10) Babli *Keritut* 18b, *Ševuot* 19b. The Babli finds here a tannaitic controversy. It was stated that the awareness of a transgression determines the obligation of a purification sacrifice, but the obligation of a suspended reparation sacrifice may cover separate incidents. The question then arises what are the obligations if the doubts about a single suspended reparation sacrifice are resolved on different occasions? (In the Babli, R. Simeon ben Laqish's opinion is attributed to Rebbi, that of R. Johanan to Rebbi's teachers R. Yose ben R. Jehudah and R. Eleazar ben R. Simeon.)

In the example, the doubt is whether he ate permitted or prohibited fat.

42 The paragraph is referred to in *Ševuot* 2:1.

Since the Anointed Priest is barred from bringing a reparation sacrifice, the knowledge of the doubt has no influence on his status.

43 *Lev.* 7:7. The verse appears in a

different context, i. e., that the technicalities of purification and reparation sacrifices are identical [*Sifra Ṣaw Pereq* 9(1)]. In Maimonides's opinion, the quote here is an allusion, not a proof.

43 The origin of this paragraph is in *Ševuot* 2:1; therefore "there" means here, "here" means *Ševuot* 2:1. As explained in Note 42, information which does not imply any obligation for a sacrifice cannot influence any further such obligation. The problem discussed in *Ševuot* 2:1 refers to impurity of the Sanctuary, violations of which category are atoned for by a variable sacrifice (*Lev.* 5:1-13) and do not call for a suspended reparation sacrifice in case of doubt. Therefore, information of a doubt in this case does not imply any obligation for a sacrifice.

44 R. Simeon ben Laqish is not inconsistent. Here, he holds that the moment which determines one's obligation for a reparation offering also determines the conditions for a future purification offering. But in *Ševuot* 2:1, the doubt arises about impurity of the Sanctuary which is not subject to a suspended reparation offering. There is no sacrifice which could define future obligations.

45 This paragraph also appears in *Ševuot* 2:1; its original place is here. In the case of three olives he holds that the supplementary in- formation about the third olive is irrelevant since the purification sacrifice for the first two also covers the third. In the case of the volume of five olives, the supplementary information that he ate forbidden fat triggers the obligation of a purification sacrifice which did not exist before; it is relevant.

(47b line 19) הַכֹּל מוֹדִין שֶׁאִם הָיְתָה רִאשׁוֹנָה קַייֶמֶת שֶׁהִיא נִדְחֵית. מַה יֵעָשֶׂה בָהּ. רִבִּי יוֹסֵי אָמַר. תְּלוּיָה בְכַפָּרָה. אָמַר רִבִּי זְעִירָא. כָּל־שֶׁלֹּא נִרְאִית לֹא הִיא וְלֹא דָמֶיהָ מֵתָה מִיָּד.

1 מודין | מודים נדחית | נדחת יוסי | יוסה 2 אמ' | אומר מתה | מיתה

Everybody agrees that if the first one was still in existence it is pushed aside[46]. What should be done with it? Rebbi Yose said, it is suspended for atonement[47]. Rebbi Ze`ira said, where neither itself nor its blood are usable it dies immediately[48].

46 In the case of three volumes of olive size R. Johanan asserts that if a sacrifice was brought for the first two before the person was informed of the third, no additional sacrifice is needed. But if the animal was only dedicated to atone for two and before it was slaughtered its owner was informed of the third, it is asserted that the dedication becomes invalid and a new animal is needed even according to R. Johanan. (Therefore, a careful person will formally dedicate his animal at the last possible moment, just before entering the Temple precinct. An intention to use the animal, short of formal dedication, is no obstacle to using it for another purpose.)

47 It should be left to graze until it

develops a bodily defect or becomes too old to serve as sacrifice, then be sold and its proceeds used to buy the new purification sacrifice.

While both sources here read "R. Yose", the only acceptable reading is that of L in the next paragraph, "R. Yasa", of the generation of R. Ze`ira's teachers. R. Yose was the student of R. Ze`ira's student R. Jeremiah.

48 He objects that the animal now has the status of a purification sacrifice whose owner's sin was atoned for by another animal, which has to be left to die (Mishnah *Temurah* 2:2) since it can neither be redeemed, nor used, nor allowed to produce young which would perpetuate its impossible situation.

(47b line 21) אָכַל חֲמִשָּׁה זֵיתִים וְנוֹדַע לוֹ בִסְפֵיקוֹ מִשֶּׁנִּתְמַנֶּה וּבְבֵית דִּין מֵעָבַר. עַל דַּעְתֵּיהּ דְּרִבִּי שִׁמְעוֹן בֶּן לָקִישׁ פָּטוּר. עַל דַּעְתֵּיהּ דְּרִבִּי יוֹחָנָן חַייָב. כֵּן אָמַר רִבִּי שִׁמְעוֹן בֶּן לָקִישׁ לִפְטוֹר וְלֹא לְחִיּוּב. אֶלָּא כֵינִי. אָכַל חֲמִשָּׁה זֵיתִים וְנִתְוַדַּע לוֹ בִסְפֵיקוֹ עַד שֶׁלֹּא נִתְמַנֶּה וְוַדָּייו מִשֶּׁנִּתְמַנֶּה. עַל דַּעְתֵּיהּ דְּרִבִּי שִׁמְעוֹן בֶּן לָקִישׁ דּוּ אָמַר. יְדִיעַת סְפֵיקוֹ קוֹבְעָתוֹ לְחַטָּאוֹ. דּוּ אָמַר. חַייָב. עַל דַּעְתֵּיהּ דְּרִבִּי יוֹחָנָן דּוּ אָמַר. אֵין יְדִיעַת סְפֵיקוֹ קוֹבְעָתוֹ לְחַטָּאוֹ. דּוּ אָמַר. פָּטוּר. הַכֹּל מוֹדִין שֶׁאִם הָיְתָה רִאשׁוֹנָה קַייֶמֶת שֶׁהִיא נִדְחֵית. מַה יֵעָשֶׂה בָהּ. רִבִּי יָסָא אָמַר. תְּלוּיָה בְכַפָּרָה. אָמַר רִבִּי זְעִירָא. כָּל־שֶׁלֹּא נִרְאִית לֹא הִיא וְלֹא דָמֶיהָ מֵתָה מִיָּד.

1 ונודע | ונתודע בספיקו | בספקן ובבית דין מעבר | ובודיין משעבר 2 שמעון בן לקיש פטור | יוחנן חייב יוחנן חייב | שמעון בן לקיש פטור ולא | לא 3 לחיוב | ליחייב כיני | כי ונתוודע | ונתודע בספיקו | בספקן וודייו | ובודיין 4 דו אמ' | דאמר ספיקו קובעתו | ספקו קובעת דו | כן 5 ספיקו | ספקו דו | כן מודין | מודים 6 נדחית | נדחת יסא | יוסה

If he ate five times the volume of an olive; the doubt became known to him before he was appointed (and in court) [as the certainty][40] after he was removed[49]. In the opinion of Rebbi Simeon ben Laqish he is not liable; in the opinion of Rebbi Joḥanan he is liable[50]. Did Rebbi Simeon ben Laqish state to free from liability, not rather to insist on liability[51]? But it must be as follows: He ate five times the volume of an olive. The doubt became known to him before he was appointed; the certainty after he was appointed. Following the opinion of Rebbi Simeon ben Laqish who said, the knowledge about his doubt determines his kind of transgression, he must say[52] that one is liable[53]. Following the opinion of Rebbi Joḥanan who said, the knowledge about his doubt does not determine his kind of transgression, he must say that one is not liable[54].

Everybody agrees that if the first one was still in existence it is pushed aside[46]. What should be done with it? Rebbi Yasa said, it is suspended for atonement[47]. Rebbi Ze`ira said, if neither itself not its blood are usable, it dies immediately[48].

49 One now applies the preceding discussion to the Mishnah, following R. Simeon who insists that the status of the person at the moment at which he receives the information determines his liability.

50 In this interpretation, since according to R. Simeon ben Laqish the obligation of a suspended sacrifice implies that of the corresponding purification sacrifice, the prior obligation which was eliminated by the appointment is not re-instituted by removal from office. For R. Johanan the status of the suspended sacrifice is irrelevant for the purification offering. Since after removal the person is again under the rules of a commoner, his obligation is not changed.

51 Since the original statement of R. Simeon ben Laqish referred to a case where he is more restrictive than R. Johanan, it is inadmissible to quote him in support of a more lenient position. In the case considered there is unanimity that for a transgression committed as a commoner, which could not have been atoned for while one was elevated, the original obligation of a purification sacrifice of a female sheep or goat is re-instituted.

52 The construction in L is rather awkward; that of B is more smooth, but this probably indicate that the text of B is babylonized.

53 Since the obligation preceded the elevation it cannot be removed following R. Simeon.

54 Since the obligation of a purification sacrifice became known when the person was prohibited from offering a commoner's sacrifice, following R. Simeon the person is prevented from offering any sacrifice.

(47b line 31) אָכַל חֲצִי זַיִת עַד שֶׁלֹּא נִתְמַנֶּה וַחֲצִי זַיִת עַד מִשֶּׁנִּתְמַנֶּה חֲצִי זַיִת שֶׁעָבַר. הוֹאִיל וּבָא חִיּוּב קָרְבָּן בֵּינְתַיִים מִצְטָרְפִין. נִישְׁמְעִינָהּ מִן הָדָא. הָיוּ לְפָנָיו שְׁלֹשָׁה. אָכַל אֶת הָרִאשׁוֹן וְלֹא נִתְווַדַּע לוֹ. שֵׁינִי וּשְׁלִישִׁי הֶעֱלִימוֹ שֶׁלְּרִאשׁוֹן. נִתְוַדַּע לוֹ עַל הָרִאשׁוֹן וְלֹא נִתְווַדַּע לוֹ עַל הַשֵּׁינִי. שְׁלִישִׁי בְּהֶעֱלֵימוֹ שֶׁלְּשֵׁינִי. וְאַחַר כָּךְ נִתְווַדַּע לוֹ עַל כּוּלְּהֶם. רִבִּי יוֹחָנָן אָמַר. חַייָב עַל הָרִאשׁוֹן וְעַל הַשֵּׁינִי וּפָטוּר עַל הַשְּׁלִישִׁי. אָמַר רִבִּי יוֹסֵי. שֵׁינִי לְדַעְתּוֹ הַדָּבָר תָּלוּי. רָצָה מִתְכַּפֵּר לוֹ עַל הָרִאשׁוֹן. רָצָה מִתְכַּפֵּר לוֹ עַל הַשְּׁלִישִׁי. חֲבֵרַייָא מְדַמְייָא לָהּ לְאַרְבָּעָה חֲצָיֵי זֵיתִים. אִם הָיָה פִיקֵּחַ מֵבִיא קָרְבָּן אֶחָד. וְאִם לָאו מֵבִיא שְׁנֵי קָרְבָּנוֹת. הֵיךְ עֲבִידָא. מֵבִיא עַל הָרִאשׁוֹן וְעַל הַשֵּׁינִי אֶחָד. עַל הַשְּׁלִישִׁי וְעַל הָרְבִיעִי אֶחָד. רִבִּי יוֹסֵי מְדַמֶּה לָהּ לְזֵיתִים שְׁלֵימִים. אִם הָיָה פִיקֵּחַ מֵבִיא שְׁנֵי קָרְבָּנוֹת. וְאִם לָאו מֵבִיא שְׁלֹשָׁה קָרְבָּנוֹת. הֵיךְ עֲבִידָא. מֵבִיא עַל הָרִאשׁוֹן וְעַל הַשֵּׁינִי אֶחָד וְעַל הַשְּׁלִישִׁי וְעַל הָרְבִיעִי אֶחָד. אִם הֵבִיא עַל הָאֶמְצָעִיִים פָּטוּר עַל הָרִאשׁוֹן וְעַל הָרְבִיעִי. רִבִּי יוֹסֵי מְדַמֵּי לָהּ לְזֵיתִים שְׁלֵימִים. אִם הָיָה פִיקֵּחַ מֵבִיא שְׁנֵי קָרְבָּנוֹת וְאִם לָאו מֵבִיא

שְׁלֹשָׁה קָרְבָּנוֹת. הֵיךְ עֲבִידָא. מֵבִיא עַל הָרִאשׁוֹן וְעַל הַשֵּׁינִי אֶחָד וְעַל הַשְּׁלִישִׁי וְעַל הָרְבִיעִי אֶחָד. אִם הֵבִיא עַל הָאֶמְצָעִיִּים חַייָב עַל הָרִאשׁוֹן בִּפְנֵי עַצְמוֹ וְעַל הָרְבִיעִי בִּפְנֵי עַצְמוֹ.

1 חצי זית שעבר | וחצי זית משעבר ובא | ולא בא 2 בינתיים | בינתים נישמעינה | נשמע הדא | הדה שלשה | שלשה זיתים 3 נתוודע | נתודע (X2) שיני ושלישי העלימו שלראשון | שני בהעלמו של ראשון השיני | השני 4 בהעלימו שלשיני | בהעלמו של שני נתוודע | נתודע 5 השיני | השני יוסי | יוסה לדעתו | לדעת זה הדבר | דבר 6 חברייא מדמייא | חברייה מדמיי חציי | חצי זיתים | זתים 7 פיקח | פקח שני | שתי 8 על | ועל ר' יוסי מדמה לה לזיתים שלימים. אם היה 9 פיקח מביא שני קרבנות. ואם לאו מביא שלשה קרבנות. היך עבידא. מביא על הראשון ועל 10 השיני אחד ועל השלישי ועל הרביעי אחד | - 11 שלימים | שלמים פיקח | פקח שני קרבנות | קרבן אחד 12 שלשה | ב' אחד | -

[55]If one ate half the volume of an olive before he was appointed, half the volume of an olive after he was appointed, half the volume of an olive after he was removed from office. Since [no][56] obligation of a sacrifice came in between, do they combine? Let us hear from the following[57]: Before him were three [olive sized pieces][58]. He ate the first but did not realize it; the second (and the third)[59] while he was oblivious of the first. He was informed of the first but was not informed of the second. [He ate] the third while oblivious of the second. Afterwards he was informed about all of them. Rebbi Joḥanan said, he is liable for the first and the second but not liable for the third[60]. Rebbi Yose said, the second depends on his intention. If he wishes, he atones for it with the first; if he wishes, he atones for it with the third[61]. The colleagues compare it to four half-olives[62]. If he was intelligent, he brings one sacrifice; otherwise, he brings two sacrifices. How is that? He brings one for the first and the second together; one for the third and fourth together. (Rebbi Yose compares it to full olive sizes. If he was intelligent, he brings two sacrifices; otherwise, he brings three sacrifices. How is that? He brings one for the first and the second together, and one for the third and fourth together.)[63] If he brought for the middle ones, he is not liable for the first and the fourth[64]. Rebbi Yose compares it to full olive sizes. If he was intelligent, he brings two sacrifices; otherwise, he brings three sacrifices. How is that? He brings one for the first and the second together, and one for the third and fourth together. If he brought for the middle ones, he is liable for the first separately and for the fourth separately[65].

55 A similar problem is treated in the Babli, 11a.

56 Text of B, necessary in the text. Since no full olive-sized piece of forbidden food was eaten while the person was in his privileged appointed status, the

previous argument that the new obligation of sacrifices invalidates the old one does not apply. The question is raised whether the two unrelated episodes of a commoner's obligation can be added. In the Babli, the question remains undecided in principle.

57 Cf. Babli *Šabbat* 71b.

58 Text of B.

59 Text of L. It is preferable to delete it since if the second and third olives are eaten under similar circumstances, the remaining text of the statement becomes redundant.

60 When he became obligated for a purification sacrifice for the first piece, he did not know of his obligation for the second. Following R. Simeon, the obligation for the first piece and the future one for the second are incompatible. But if the information about the second and the third reaches him after the third had been eaten, one sacrifice covers both of them.

61 He disputes R. Johanan's interpretation of R. Simeon's position. Since the first and second pieces were eaten in ignorance, even if the information reached the perpetrator piecemeal, one sacrifice still may cover both. The argument for using one and the same sacrifice for the second and third pieces is the same as that given by R. Johanan.

62 He ate pieces 1,2,3,4 in a situation when while eating piece i he was informed about the forbidden character of piece i-2 but not yet about piece i-1. (If one of these numbers be 0 or negative, the relative information is void.) Then one sacrifice covers pieces 1 and 2 which were eaten in ignorance. But since at the time he was eating piece 3 he already was informed about piece 1, the sacrifice for 1 and 2 cannot be applied to 3. Since he was informed about 2 but not 3 when he ate 4, the last two pieces can be atoned for by one sacrifice.

63 This text, missing in B, is an intrusion of the later text into the current discussion; it should be disregarded.

64 The intelligent person will dedicate his sacrifice for pieces 2 and 3. Then 1 is a single half-olive which does not qualify for a sacrifice. The same holds true for 4. Since the information about 1 was available when 4 was consumed, 1 and 4 do not combine.

65 The situation contemplated by R. Yose is parallel to that considered by the colleagues but this time each of the pieces has the full volume of an olive. Then each piece itself qualifies for a sacrifice. The second best solution of the colleagues now becomes the best for R. Yose; their best now is the second best.

(47b line 49) רִבִּי יִצְחָק שָׁאַל. אַף בַּאֲכִילַת פְּרָסִים כֵּן. אָמַר רִבִּי יוֹסֵי. כָּל־זֶה שְׁאִילְתָּה דְרִבִּי יִצְחָק לֵית הִיא כְלוּם. וכתיב בַּאֲכִילַת פְּרָסִים הַדָּבָר תָּלוּי. אִילּוּ אָכַל חֲצִי זַיִת בְּתוֹךְ כְּדֵי פְרַס זֶה וַחֲצִי זַיִת בְּתוֹךְ כְּדֵי פְרַס זֶה שֶׁמָּא כְלוּם הוּא. אָכַל כַּמָּה זֵיתִים וְכַמָּה פְרָסִים בְּהֶיעְלֵם אֶחָד אֵינוֹ חַייָב אֶלָּא אַחַת. רַבָּנִין דְּקֵיסָרִין אָמְרֵי. עַד דֵּין מְדַמֶּה לָהּ לַחֲלָבִים וּדְמִינָהּ לַשַּׁבָּת. אִילּוּ אָרַג חוּט אֶחָד בְּתוֹךְ כְּדֵי בֶגֶד זֶה וְחוּט אֶחָד בְּתוֹךְ כְּדֵי בֶגֶד זֶה שֶׁמָּא כְלוּם הוּא. אָרַג כַּמָּה

חוּטִין בְּכַמָּה בְגָדִים בְּהֶיעָלֵם אֶחָד אֵינוֹ חַייָב אֶלָּא אַחַת. הֲרֵי בָּא חִיּוּב בְּקָרְבָּן בֵּינְתַיִים וְתֵימַר מִצְטָרְפִין. אָמַר רִבִּי אָבוּן. תַּמָּן חִייוּב בְּקָרְבָּן. בְּרַם הָכָא קָרְבָּן.

1 פרסים | פרסיים יוסי | יוסה כל זה שאילתה | בלדה שאילתיה 2 לית | ולית וכתיב | וכי פרסים | פרסיים פרס | אכילת פרס 3 פרס | אכילת פרס וכמה | בכמה 4 קיסרין | קסרין אמרי | אמרין דין מדמה | דמדמה ודמינה | ידמינה 6 בהיעלם | בהעלם בינתיים | בינתים 7 אבון | בון חייוב בקרבן | חיוב קרבן קרבן | שינוי קרבן

Rebbi Isaac asked: Is it the same with the eating of half loaves[66]? Rebbi Yose said, this question of Rebbi Isaac is nothing. (Is it written) [Does][67] the matter depend on eating half loaves? If one ate the volume of half an olive during the time allotted for this half loaf and another volume of half an olive during the time allotted for that half loaf, is that anything[68]? If one ate the volume of several olives during times allotted for several half-loaves in one oblivion, he is liable only for one [sacrifice][69]. The rabbis of Caesarea say, instead of comparing it to kinds of fat, why not compare it to [the laws of] Sabbath[70]? If he wove a single thread for one cloth and a single thread for another cloth, is that anything? If he wove several threads for several pieces of cloth in one oblivion, he is liable only for one [sacrifice]. Was there not an obligation for a sacrifice in the meantime, and you say that they are counted together[71]? Rebbi Abun said, there it is about the obligation of a sacrifice; but here [a change][72] of sacrifice.

66 פְּרָס is the technical term for half a loaf of bread. (The punctuation פְּרָסִים is the ms.'s. The term is derived either from Hebrew פרס "to break bread" or Latin *pars* "part, share, portion" of food). The time needed to eat half a loaf serves as definition of the time needed for a minimal meal. For example, any person entering an infected house becomes impure (*Lev*. 14:46) but his garments also become a source of original impurity only if he stays there for a meal, i. e., the time needed to eat half a loaf (v. 47). Tosephta *Nega`im* 7:10 (Mishnah *Eruvin* 8:2) defines the loaf in question as baked from wheat flour in the volume of a third of a *qab*. Halakhah *Terumot* 5:3 (Note 44) estimates a *modius*, 4 *qab*, as the volume of 96 eggs. This makes a פְּרָס a piece of bread baked from the volume of 4 eggs of wheat flour. The sources give no indication of a translation of this definition into terms of time.

Snacks eaten at times separated by more that the time needed to eat a *peras* must be counted as separate meals. Therefore, eating forbidden food triggers the obligation of a purification sacrifice only if the volume of an entire olive was eaten in the time needed to eat a *peras* (Mishnah *Keritut* 3:3).

67 The text in parentheses is from L, the

one in brackets from B. It seems that the scribe of L read 'וכ instead of וכי and unthinkingly interpreted 'כ as the common abbreviation of כְּתִיב.

68 As explained in Note 56, no atonable sin was committed.

69 As explained before, if an atonable sin was committed, any number of sins corresponding to the same definition committed during one spell of oblivion are atoned for by one sacrifice.

70 This remark does not fit in here; it shows that the text was taken from *Šabbat* 1:1 (2b line 32 ff.) where R. Yose's (the Amora's) remark here is put in the mouth of R. Yudan (the Amora) to explain the opinion of R. Yose (the Tanna) about violations of Sabbath prohibitions. It is forbidden to transport goods from one place to another on the Sabbath. "Transporting" means taking up the goods, moving them from one domain to another, and unloading. If any of the three actions be missing, no prosecutable sin was committed. In addition, for each kind of goods the Mishnah specifies minimal amounts. If less than the amount specified was transported while the person was oblivious of the Sabbath, no purification offering is required. On the other hand, if any number of transports were executed within one period of oblivion, only one sacrifice is needed. R. Yose the Tanna then specifies that repeated transports of less than a minimal amount add up to an atonable sin only if the different pieces were transported between the same domains [*Šabbat* 1:1 (2b line 22), Babli *Šabbat* 80a, *Bava batra* 55b, *Keritut* 17a.] This is compared to the rules specifying purification sacrifices for eating pieces of forbidden fat. The rabbis of Caesarea object that there is no proof that the rules of the Sabbath be identical to the rules for other biblical prohibitions, but the rules detailed for transporting are paralleled by rules for other kinds of activities on the Sabbath. Mishnah *Šabbat* 13:1 states that weaving is forbidden and the threshold for an action requiring a purification sacrifice is weaving two threads. For the majority, weaving two threads in one oblivion triggers the obligation of a sacrifice, for R. Yose only if the two rows were added to the same piece of cloth.

71 Now one returns to the problem posed in the preceding paragraph, of the person who ate three half-olive sized pieces of forbidden fat while he was in different states for possible purification sacrifices. Is it possible to decide between R. Johanan on one side and R. Yose (the Amora) and the colleagues on the other? For the latter, it should make sense to combine the two pieces eaten while the person was a commoner. This is rejected, since the two states of commoner are separated by an interval in which the purification offering had to be different, everybody will agree that the three half sized pieces do not add up to one full sized piece.

72 Text of B, forgotten by the scribe of L.

(47b line 59) אָכַל כְּזַיִת עַד שֶׁלֹּא נִתְמַנֶּה וּכְזַיִת מִשֶּׁנִּתְמַנֶּה וּכְזַיִת מִשֶּׁעָבַר. עַל דַּעְתּוֹן דַּחֲבֵרַיָּא דִּינוּן אָמְרִין. מִשֵּׁם שֶׁהַגְּדוּלָּה מְכַפֶּרֶת. כִּיפְּרָה הַגְּדוּלָּה עַל הָרִאשׁוֹן וְחַיָּיב עַל הַשֵּׁינִי וְעַל הַשְּׁלִישִׁי. עַל דַּעְתֵּיהּ דְּרִבִּי יוֹסֵי דּוּ אָמַר. אֵין חֶטְאוֹ וִידִיעָתוֹ שָׁוִין. חַיָּיב עַל הָרִאשׁוֹן וְעַל הַשֵּׁינִי וּפָטוּר עַל הַשְּׁלִישִׁי. אָכַל כְּזַיִת. סָפֵק עַד שֶׁלֹּא נִתְמַנֶּה סָפֵק מִשֶּׁנִּתְמַנֶּה. סָפֵק עַד שֶׁלֹּא נִתְגַּייֵר סָפֵק מִשֶּׁנִּתְגַּייֵר. סָפֵק עַד שֶׁלֹּא הֵבִיא שְׁתֵּי שְׂעָרוֹת סָפֵק מִשֶּׁהֵבִיא שְׁתֵּי שְׂעָרוֹת. מֵבִיא אָשָׁם תָּלוּי.

1 דעתון | דעתין דחברייא | דחבריא 2 הגדולה | גדולה 3 יוסי | יוסה

From the start of line 4 to the end of the discussion, the text is missing in B. There is a Note: חסרון יש כאן "here is a lacuna".

If one ate the volume of an olive before he was appointed, the volume of an olive after he was appointed, and the volume of an olive after he was removed from office. In the opinion of the colleagues who say, because high office atones[20], the office atoned for the first and he is liable for the second and the third[73]. In the opinion of Rebbi Yose who said, because his sin and his knowledge are not equal[21], he is liable for the first and the second, but not liable for the third[74].

He ate the size of an olive. If it is in doubt whether he ate before he was appointed or after he was appointed[75], or whether it was before he converted or after he converted[76], or whether it was before he had grown two pubic hairs or after he had grown two pubic hairs[67], he brings a suspended reparation sacrifice[78].

73 As explained at the start of the chapter, it is not the high office but the appointment to high office which atones; the occupant of a high office is responsible for his actions like everybody else.

74 It is difficult to make sense of this statement. If the information became known in stage three, which seems to be the hypothesis, there can be no sacrifice for unresolved sins committed in stage 2. The only problem would be a sin committed in stage 1, for which a sacrifice in stage 3 was ruled out by R. Abun in the preceding paragraph. The author of this paragraph seems to disagree with R. Abun.

75 In the first case, a purification sacrifice is needed but not in the second, both for the colleagues and R. Yose.

76 The Gentile is not required to observe biblical commandments except the Seven Noahide commandments. In no case is a purification sacrifice possible for an unconverted Gentile.

77 The child before puberty is not obligated for any commandment. It is his parents' duty to educate him in the observation of commandments, but a parent cannot bring a purification sacrifice

for any action of his child.

78 This means that a reparation sacrifice is required not only in case the criminality of the act is in question but even if the possibility of a purification sacrifice is in doubt.

(47b line 66) אָכַל סָפֵק כְּזַיִת וְאֵין יָדוּעַ אִם בְּיוֹם הַכִּיפּוּרִים אֲכָלוֹ אִם קוֹדֶם יוֹם הַכִּיפּוּרִים אֲכָלוֹ. סְפֵק כַּפָּרָה כִיפֵּר. אִם אִם בְּיוֹם הַכִּיפּוּרִים אֲכָלוֹ אִם לְאַחַר יוֹם הַכִּיפּוּרִים אֲכָלוֹ. חֲבֵרַייָא אָמְרִין. סְפֵק כַּפָּרָה כִיפֵּר. אָמַר רִבִּי מַתַּנְייָה. לְעוֹלָם אֵין סְפֵק כַּפָּרָה מְכַפֵּר אֶלָּא עַל מִינֵי דָמִים. מַתְנִיתָא מְסַייְעָא לַחֲבֵרַייָה. שַׁבָּת וְיוֹם הַכִּיפּוּרִים וְעָשָׂה מְלָאכָה בֵּין הַשְּׁמָשׁוֹת. מַה נַפְשָׁךְ. יוֹם הַכִּיפּוּרִים הוּא כִיפֵּר. חוֹל הוּא מוּתָּר. וְהָתַנֵּי וְאָכַל. אָמַר רִבִּי יוֹסֵי בֵּירִבִּי בּוּן. בַּאֲכִילַת הֵיתֵר.

If he ate a full olive sized piece[80] but there is doubt whether he ate it on the Day of Atonement or before the Day of Atonement. The atonement atones for the doubt[81]. Whether he ate it on the Day of Atonement or after the Day of Atonement. The colleagues say, atonement atones for the doubt[82]. Rebbi Mattaniah said, the atonement atones only for doubt of the kinds of blood[83]. A Mishnah supports the colleagues: "Sabbath and the Day of Atonement and he worked in twilight.[84]" As you take it, if it was the Day of Atonement, it atoned. If it was weekday, it is permitted. But did we not state "he ate"[85]? Rebbi Yose ben Rebbi Abun said, eating permitted [food].

80 Kosher food, which only is forbidden on the Day of Atonement.

81 Cf. Chapter 1, Note 19.

82 If the food was eaten in the twilight at the end of the Day of Atonement and the next day already had started, no sin was committed (*Lev.* 23:32). If it still was the day of Atonement, doctrine is that in the absence of a scapegoat the end of the day provides the Atonement [*Yoma* 8:8 45c l. 15; *Ševuot* 1:9 33c l. 3, lacunary *Sanhedrin* 10:1 Note 34; Tosefta *Kippurim* 4:17].

83 R. Mattaniah holds that the Day of Atonement only eliminates a suspended reparation sacrifice which certainly was due. But in the case where the doubt arises whether it was the Day of Atonement or not, there is no prior obligation and, therefore, it cannot be eliminated.

84 Mishnah *Keritut* 4:2. The Mishnah deals with a case which is impossible in our computed calendar, where the Day of Atonement was either Friday or Sunday and somebody was doing some forbidden work during the twilight between the days. R. Joshua, the overriding authority, holds that in this case no suspended sacrifice is due since one may assume that part of the work was done on the day of Atonement; this part of an unintended sin then is eliminated, leaving an incomplete work for the Sabbath which needs no

sacrifice (Note 60). This shows that the colleagues are correct in extending the power of the Day of Atonement.

85 The questioner thinks that the food in question was forbidden fat. In that case, the Day of Atonement cannot eliminate the obligation of a suspended sacrifice for the following night. The answer is that in contrast to the cases considered earlier, one supposes that kosher food was eaten.

(47b line 74) אָכַל חֲמִשָּׁה זֵיתִים וְנִתְוַדַּע לוֹ בִסְפֵיקָן עַד שֶׁלֹּא נִתְמַנֶּה וּבְבֵית דִּין מִשֶּׁמִּתְמַנֶּה. עַל דַּעְתֵּיהּ דְּרִבִּי שִׁמְעוֹן בֶּן לָקִישׁ חַייָב. עַל דַּעְתֵּיהּ דְּרִבִּי יוֹחָנָן פָּטוּר. כֵּן אָמַר רִבִּי שִׁמְעוֹן בֶּן לָקִישׁ לְחִיּוּב וְלֹא לִפְטוֹר. אֶלָּא כֵינִי. אָכַל חֲמִשָּׁה זֵיתִים וְנִתְוַדַּע לוֹ בִסְפֵיקָן מִשֶּׁנִּתְמַנֶּה וּבְבֵית דִּין מִשֶּׁעָבַר. עַל דַּעְתֵּיהּ דְּרִבִּי שִׁמְעוֹן בֶּן לָקִישׁ דּוּ אָמַר. נִתְכַּפֵּר מִקְצָת הַחֵט לֹא נִתְכַּפֵּר כּוּלּוֹ. דּוּ אָמַר. פָּטוּר. עַל דַּעְתֵּיהּ דְּרִבִּי יוֹחָנָן דּוּ אָמַר. נִתְכַּפֵּר מִקְצָת הַחֵט נִתְכַּפֵּר כּוּלּוֹ. דּוּ אָמַר. חַייָב. הַכֹּל מוֹדִין שֶׁאִם הָיְתָה רִאשׁוֹנָה קַייֶמֶת שֶׁהִיא נִדְחֵית. מַה יֵּעָשֶׂה בָהּ. רִבִּי יָסָא אָמַר. תְּלוּיָה בְכַפָּרָה. אָמַר רִבִּי זְעִירָא. כָּל־שֶׁלֹּא נִרְאֵית לֹא הִיא וְלֹא דָמֶיהָ מֵתָה מִיָּד.

If he ate five times the volume of an olive; the doubt became known to him before he was appointed, and (in court)[86] after he was appointed. In the opinion of Rebbi Simeon ben Laqish he is liable; in the opinion of Rebbi Johanan he is not liable[87]. Did Rebbi Simeon ben Laqish state to insist on liability, not rather to free from liability[88]? But it must be as follows: He ate five times the volume of an olive[89]. The doubt became known to him after he was appointed; (in court)[86] after he was removed. Following the opinion of Rebbi Simeon ben Laqish who said, if the sin was partially atoned for it was not totally atoned, he must say[42] that he is not liable[90]. Following the opinion of Rebbi Johanan who said, if the sin was partially atoned for it was totally atoned, he must say that one is liable[94].

Everybody agrees that if the first one was still in existence it is pushed aside[46]. What should be done with it? Rebbi Yasa said, it is suspended for atonement[47]. Rebbi Ze`ira said, if neither it nor its blood are usable it dies immediately[48].

86 Cf. Note 30. It seems that one should read "its certainty".

87 Since R. Simeon ben Laqish holds that his status at the moment of the first notification determines his obligation for sacrifices (Note 43), he became obligated for a purification offering. If now he is not a commoner, he is obligated for an exalted person's purification offering. For R. Johanan who disagrees (Note 44), the knowledge of the doubt does not determine the obligation when he is informed

of the certainty. Following R. Simeon, action and information referred to different status; no sacrifice is possible.

88 This is the reverse of the question asked in Note 41; in any case the argument is inconclusive since the exact position of R. Simeon ben Laqish is unknown.

89 Before he was appointed.

90 One does not argue directly from R. Simeon ben Laqiah's statement but from his argument, based on the principle stated, in the case of three pieces when he realized only that he had eaten two (Note 19). R. Simeon ben Laqish holds that the moment of first information determines his status for sacrifices. Since he was informed of a transgression as a commoner when he was exalted and therefore prevented of bringing a sacrifice, had he then been informed of the certainty, the additional information reaching him after he reverted to commoner status cannot change the situation. R. Johanan, who in the situation of Note 29 extends the validity of the sacrifice, will allow the information reaching him as a commoner to determine the sacrifice due for an act committed as a commoner.

(47c line 9) מוֹדֶה רִבִּי יוֹחָנָן שֶׁאִם הָיְתָה רִאשׁוֹנָה קַייֶמֶת שֶׁהִיא נִדְחֵית. מַה יֵעָשֶׂה בָהּ. רִבִּי יָסָא אָמַר. תְּלוּיָה בְכַפָּרָה. אָמַר רִבִּי זְעִירָא. כָּל־שֶׁלֹּא נִרְאֵית לֹא הִיא וְלֹא דָמֶיהָ מֵתָה מִיָּד.

מוֹדֶה רִבִּי יוֹחָנָן שֶׁאִם הָיְתָה רִאשׁוֹנָה קַייֶמֶת שֶׁהִיא נִדְחֵית. מַה יֵעָשֶׂה בָהּ. רִבִּי יָסָא אָמַר. תְּלוּיָה בְכַפָּרָה. לְפוּם כֵּן רִבִּי יוֹסֵי בֵּירִבִּי בּוּן הֲוֵי עָלֶיהָ. אָכַל חֲמִשָּׁה זֵיתִים וְנִתְוַדַּע לוֹ בָּרִאשׁוֹן וּמֵבִיא קָרְבָּן. בַּשֵּׁינִי וּמֵבִיא קָרְבָּן. בַּשְּׁלִישִׁי וּמַקְרִיב קָרְבָּן. בָּרְבִיעִי וּמַקְרִיב קָרְבָּן. בַּחֲמִשִׁי וּמַקְרִיב קָרְבָּן. רִבִּי יוֹחָנָן אָמַר. נִתְכַּפֵּר לוֹ בָּרִאשׁוֹן שֶׁהוּא לִפְנֵי אֲכִילַת כּוּלְּהֶם וְהַשְּׁאָר יִפְּלוּ לִנְדָבָה. רִבִּי שִׁמְעוֹן בֶּן לָקִישׁ אָמַר. נִתְכַּפֵּר לוֹ בָּאַחֲרוֹן שֶׁהוּא לְאַחַר אֲכִילַת כּוּלְּהֶם וְהַשְּׁאָר יִדָּחוּ. רַב חִסְדָּא וְרַב הַמְנוּנָא. רַב חִסְדָּא כְּרִבִּי יוֹחָנָן. רַב הַמְנוּנָא כְּרִבִּי שִׁמְעוֹן בֶּן לָקִישׁ. מְתִיב רַב חִסְדָּא לְרַב הַמְנוּנָא. וְהָא מַתְנִיתָא מְסַייְעָה לָךְ וּפְלִיגָא עֲלַי. אִם הָיְתָה יְדִיעָה בֵּינְתַיִים. כְּשֵׁם שֶׁהוּא מֵבִיא חַטָּאת עַל כָּל־אַחַת וְאַחַת כָּךְ יוּא מֵבִיא אָשָׁם תָּלוּי עַל כָּל־אַחַת וְאַחַת. אִילּוּ תַנָּא אָשָׁם וְקָם לֵיהּ. יְאוּת. אָמַר רִבִּי חִינְנָה. אֲפִילוּ כֵן לִצְדָדִין דְּתֵימַר כֵּן.

Rebbi Joḥanan agrees that if the first one was still in existence it is pushed aside. What should be done with it? Rebbi Yasa said, it is suspended for atonement. Rebbi Ze`ira said, if neither it nor its blood are usable it dies immediately[91].

Does Rebbi Joḥanan agree that if the first one was still in existence it is pushed aside[92]? What should be done with it? Rebbi Yasa said, it is suspended for atonement[93]. Therefore Rebbi Yose ben Rebbi Abun discussed it. If he ate five times the volume of an olive[94]; the first became known to him and he brought a sacrifice. The second, and he brought a sacrifice. The third, and he offered a sacrifice. The fourth, and he offered a sacrifice. The fifth, and he offered a sacrifice. Rebbi Joḥanan said, his sin is atoned for by the first which precedes the eating of all of them; the remainder shall fall to voluntary offerings[95]. Rebbi Simeon ben Laqish said, his sin is atoned for by the last which follows the eating of all of them; the others shall be set aside[96]. Rav Ḥisda and Rav Hamnuna. Rav Ḥisda like Rebbi Joḥanan; Rav Hamnuna like Rebbi Simeon ben Laqish. Rav Ḥisda remarked to Rav Hamnuna, there is a Mishnah which seems to support you and disagrees with me[97]: "If there was awareness in between, just as he brings a purification sacrifice for each single one, so he brings a suspended reparation sacrifice for each single one[98]." If he had stated the reparation sacrifice and stopped[99]! Rebbi Ḥinena said, even so, for all eventualities you may say so[100].

91 It seems that this paragraph is superfluous text. The scribe copied the preceding text with the wrong start and then copied again the (almost) correct text in the next paragraph.

92 R. Yose ben R. Abun will show that the often repeated statement that "everybody agrees" is false; R. Johanan disagrees; the explanation given in Note 36 has to be amended.

93 These two sentences are copied from the previous statement; they are copied to point out that R. Ze`ira's statement is disregarded since it would lead to a complication in R. Simeon ben Laqish's statement.

94 While he ate the five pieces, he was oblivious either of the fact that these were forbidden fat or of the law that certain kinds of fat are forbidden. Then he was informed of the forbidden character of these pieces one by one and immediately after each information dedicated an animal but did not sacrifice yet.

95 The argument is the same as in the case of three pieces discussed earlier; one constructs a case for five only because for R. Joḥanan in the case of three only one animal was needed. One could have done with four pieces.

For R. Joḥanan, the validity of the dedication of the first animal can be extended to cover all five pieces. The other four animals cannot be used, but dedicated animals cannot become undedicated. They are sent to graze until they either develop a defect which makes them unfit for the altar or they exceed the age limit for sacrificial animals (Mishnah *Parah* 1:1) when they can be sold and the money used for voluntary elevation offerings.

96 Since for him dedications cannot be extended, only the last animal can legitimately be sacrificed. The others have to be sent to graze.

97 Mishnah *Keritut* 4:2.

98 Since temporary oblivion is a prere-

quisite for the possibility of a purification sacrifice, sins committed when there was an interval of awareness between them cannot be atoned for by one and the same sacrifice. This rule is extended to suspended sacrifices. Since in the case in question the selection of new sacrifices was in response to information, one should read the Mishnah as forbidding the extension of the meaning of dedications.

99 The formulation of the Mishnah and the explanation given in the preceding Note are all wrong. The verses introducing purification sacrifices emphasize that these atone only for *unintentional* sins. The requirement of *oblivion* is only mentioned for the suspended reparation sacrifice (*Lev.* 5:17). The Mishnah should have mentioned suspended sacrifices first. Since purification sacrifices were mentioned first, the Mishnah cannot be read as referring to the effect of information after the fact, only to information reaching the person between two intrinsically forbidden acts.

100 Rav Hisda's objection is well taken. The formulation of the Mishnah is elliptic. One should read it as follows: "Just as he brings a purification sacrifice for each single one if there was awareness *of certainty* in between, so he brings a suspended reparation sacrifice for each single one if there was awareness *of doubt* in between."

(47c line 21) אֲשֶׁר נָשִׂיא יֶחֱטָא. אָמַר רַבָּן יוֹחָנָן בֶּן זַכַּאי. אַשְׁרֵי שֶׁהַנָּשִׂיא שֶׁלּוֹ מֵבִיא חַטָּאת. עַל שִׁיגְגָתוֹ הוּא מֵבִיא לֹא כָּל־שֶׁכֵּן עַל זְדוֹנוֹ. נָשִׂיא שֶׁלּוֹ מֵבִיא חַטָּאת. לֹא כָּל־שֶׁכֵּן הַהֶדְיוֹט.

1 אשר | כתוב אשר אשרי | אשרי הדור שלו | - 2 ההדיוט | הדיוט

נָשִׂיא. יָכוֹל נְשִׂיא שְׁבָטִים כְּנַחְשׁוֹן. תַּלְמוּד לוֹמַר וְעָשָׂה אַחַת מִכָּל־מִצְוֹת יי אֱלֹהָיו. וּלְהַלָּן הוּא אוֹמֵר לְמַעַן יִלְמַד לְיִרְאָה אֶת־יי אֱלֹהָיו. אֱלֹהָיו לִגְזֵירָה שָׁוָה. מָה אֱלֹהָיו שֶׁנֶּאֱמַר לְהַלָּן נָשִׂיא שֶׁאֵין עַל גַּבָּיו אֶלָּא אֱלֹהָיו. אַף אֱלֹהָיו שֶׁנֶּאֱמַר כָּאן נָשִׂיא שֶׁאֵין עַל גַּבָּיו אֶלָּא אֱלֹהָיו.

1 נשיא | - 2 אלהיו | אלהיו אלהיו 3 אלהיו | יי אלהיו (2x)

אֲשֶׁר | יֵשׁ צַדִּיקִים וגו'. אַשְׁרֵיהֶם הַצַּדִּיקִים שֶׁמַּגִּיעַ אֲלֵיהֶם כְּמַעֲשֵׂה הָרְשָׁעִים בָּעוֹלָם הַזֶּה. וַוי לָרְשָׁעִים שֶׁמַּגִּיעַ אֲלֵיהֶם כְּמַעֲשֵׂה הַצַּדִּיקִים בָּעוֹלָם הַזֶּה.

1 אשר | כתי' אשר וגו' | אשר מגיע אליהם כמעשה הרשעים ויש רשעים שמגיע אליהם כמעשה הצדיקים הזה | הזה כן 2 ווי | ואללי

מֶלֶךְ יִשְׂרָאֵל וּמֶלֶךְ יְהוּדָה שְׁנֵיהֶן שָׁוִין. לֹא זֶה גָּדוֹל מִזֶּה וְלֹא זֶה גָּדוֹל מִזֶּה. וּמַה טַעַם. וּמֶלֶךְ יִשְׂרָאֵל וּמֶלֶךְ יְהוּדָה וגו' בְּגוֹרֶן. כִּבְגוֹרֶן. אָמַר רִבִּי יוֹסֵי בֵּירִבִּי בּוּן. וּבִלְחוּד עַד דְּיֵהוּא בֶּן נִמְשִׁי. וּמַה טַעַם. בְּנֵי רְבִיעִים יֵשְׁבוּ לְךָ עַל־כִּסֵּא יִשְׂרָאֵל. מִכָּן וְאֵילָךְ בְּלִיסְטַיָּא הָיוּ נוֹטְלִין אוֹתָהּ.

1 שניהן | שניהם ומה טעם | מאי טעמא 2 ומלך יהודה וגו' | ויהושפט מלך יהודה יושבים יוסי ביר' בון | יוסה ברבי דיהוא | יהוא 3 בני | בנים ואילך | והלן בליסטייא | בליסטיא

[It is written][101]: *If the Prince sin.*[102] Rabban Joḥanan ben Zakkai said, fortunate [is the generation][101] whose Prince brings a purification sacrifice.

He brings it for his inadvertent sin, not so much more for his intentional one[103]? If its Prince brings, not so much more the commoner?

"The Prince." I could think a tribal chieftain like Nahshon; the verse says, "*if he transgressed one of the commandments of the Eternal, his God*[8]; and further it says, *that he may learn to fear the Eternal, his God*[104]. "His God, [his God]" for an equal cut. Since "his God" mentioned there refers to a Prince over whom there is only [the Eternal][101] his God, so also "his God" mentioned here refers to a Prince over whom there is only [the Eternal][101] his God[95].

[It is written:][101] *There are just people*[106] *[to whom happens what should happen to evildoers and there are evildoers to whom happens what should happen to just people.]*[101] It is fortunate for just people if to them happens in this world what should happen to evildoers; woe to evildoers if to them happens in this world what should happen to just people[107].

A king of Israel and a king of Jehudah are both equal, neither of them is greater than the other. What is the reason? *The king of Israel and [Josaphat]*[101] *the king of Jehudah [were sitting]*[101] *in the threshing floor*[108]. As in a threshing floor[109]. Rebbi Yose ben Rebbi Abun said, but only up to Jehu ben Nimshi. What is the reason? *Your descendants in the fourth generation will sit on the throne of Israel*[110]. After that they were taking it by robbery.

101 From B, missing in L.

102 *Lev.* 4:22. The sermon is mentioned in the Babli 10, Tosephta *Bava qamma* 7:5, *Sifra Hova (Wayyiqra II) Parašah* 5(1). It is standard homiletics to derive the conjunction אֲשֶׁר from the root אשר "to be fortunate."

103 There is no formal atonement for intentional sin. If the Prince is aware of his unintentional missteps, he will be careful to avoid intentional ones.

104 *Deut.* 17:19. This is justification for the short statement in the Mishnah. Babli 11a/b, *Sifra Hova (Wayyiqra II) Parašah* 5(1).

105 Since the paragraph in *Deut.* refers to the king, not the Prince.

106 *Eccl.* 8:14. Since the parallel in the Babli, 10b, also has only a short quote, it seems that the extensive quote of the verse in B is secondary. *Eccl. rabbati* 8(15), wording of B.

107 This is a continuation of Rabban Johanan ben Zakkai's homily about אשר, אשרי. The Just who are poor and unhappy in this world have already been punished for their sins and will go to the World to Come for unlimited eternal bliss. (The Babli somewhat disagrees.) The evildoers who have received the reward of their

good deeds in this world will go to the World to Come for unmitigated pain.

108 *1K.* 22:10.

109 They sat together in a circle (Mishnah *Sanhedrin* 4:9) so that none had any advantage over the other. Babli *Hulin* 5a (*Lev. rabba* 11(8); *Eccl. rabbati* 1(30)).

110 *2K.* 15:12. Jeroboam became king with prophetic sanction; Ba`sha at least had prophetic acknowledgment; Omri was appointed by popular acclaim, and Jehu by prophetic anointment. All permanent kings of Israel from Jeroboam I to Jeroboam II's son had religious sanction. After that the kings of Israel with only one exception murdered their precedessors.

(47c line 33) וְאֵי זֶה הוּא מָשִׁיחַ. הַמָּשׁוּחַ בְּשֶׁמֶן הַמִּשְׁחָה כול'. אָמַר רַב חוּנָה. כָּל־אוֹתָן שִׁשָּׁה חֳדָשִׁים שֶׁהָיָה דָוִד בּוֹרֵחַ מִפְּנֵי אַבְשָׁלוֹם שְׂעוֹרָה הֲוַות מִתְכַּפֵּר לוֹ כְהֶדְיוֹט.

1 ואי | אי משיח | משוח חונה | הונא אותן | - 2 אבשלום | אבשלום בנו שעורה הוות מתכפר לו | היה מתכפר בשעירה

תַּנֵּי. רִבִּי יוּדָה בֵּירִבִּי אִלְעַאי אוֹמֵר. שֶׁמֶן הַמִּשְׁחָה שֶׁעָשָׂה מֹשֶׁה בָּהָר מַעֲשֶׂה נִיסִּים נַעֲשׂוּ בָהּ מִתְּחִילָּה וְעַד סוֹף. שֶׁמִּתְּחִילָּה לֹא הָיָה בוֹ אֶלָּא שְׁנֵים עָשָׂר לוֹג. שֶׁנֶּאֱמַר וְשֶׁמֶן זַיִת הִין׃ אִם לָסוּךְ בּוֹ אֶת הָעֵצִים לֹא הָיָה סָפֵק. עַל אַחַת כַּמָּה וְכַמָּה שֶׁהָאוֹר בּוֹלֵעַ וְהַיּוֹרָה בוֹלַעַת וְהָעֵצִים בּוֹלְעִין. מִמֶּנּוּ נִמְשְׁחוּ הַמִּשְׁכָּן וְכָל־כֵּילָיו. הַמִּזְבֵּחַ וְכָל־כֵּילָיו. מְנוֹרָה וְכָל־כֵּילֶיהָ. כִּיּוֹר וְכַנּוֹ. מִמֶּנּוּ נִמְשְׁחוּ אַהֲרֹן כֹּהֵן גָּדוֹל וּבָנָיו כָּל־שִׁבְעַת יְמֵי הַמִּילּוּאִים. מִמֶּנּוּ נִמְשְׁחוּ כֹּהֲנִים גְּדוֹלִים וּמְלָכִים. מֶלֶךְ בַּתְּחִילָּה טָעוּן מְשִׁיחָה. מֶלֶךְ בֶּן מֶלֶךְ אֵין טָעוּן מְשִׁיחָה. שֶׁנֶּאֱמַר קֻם מְשָׁחֵהוּ כִּי־זֶה הוּא. זֶה טָעוּן מְשִׁיחָה וְאֵין בָּנָיו טְעוּנִין מְשִׁיחָה. אֲבָל כֹּהֵן גָּדוֹל בֶּן כֹּהֵן גָּדוֹל אֲפִילוּ עַד עֲשָׂרָה דוֹרוֹת טָעוּן מְשִׁיחָה. וְכוּלּוֹ קַיָּם לֶעָתִיד לָבוֹא. שֶׁנֶּאֱמַר שֶׁמֶן מִשְׁחַת־קוֹדֶשׁ יִהְיֶה זֶה לִי לְדֹרוֹתֵיכֶם׃

1 יודה | יהודה בהר | - מעשה | - 2 מתחילה | מתחלה שמתחילה | שמתחלה היה | היו 3 ספק | מספיק 4 ממנו | וממנו (X2) מנורה | המנורה 5 כהן גדול | - ממנו | וממנו כהנים גדולים ומלכים | מלכים וכהנים גדולים 6 אין | אינו שנ' | דכתי' קום | ויאמר ה' קום משיחהו | משחהו 7 ואין | אין בניו | בנו כהן גדול | כהני' גדולי' 8 טעון | טעונין לדרותיכם | לדורותיכם

אֵין מוֹשְׁחִין אֶת הַמְּלָכִים אֶלָּא עַל גַּבֵּי הַמַּעְייָן. שֶׁנֶּאֱמַר וְהִרְכַּבְתֶּם אֶת־שְׁלֹמֹה בְנִי וגו' וּמָשַׁח אֹתוֹ שָׁם צָדוֹק הַכֹּהֵן וְנָתָן הַנָּבִיא לְמֶלֶךְ עַל־יִשְׂרָאֵל. אֵין מוֹשְׁחִין אֶת הַמְּלָכִים אֶלָּא מִפְּנֵי הַמַּחֲלוֹקֶת. מִפְּנֵי מַה נִמְשַׁח שְׁלֹמֹה. מִפְּנֵי מַחֲלוֹקְתּוֹ שֶׁלַּאֲדוֹנִיָּהוּ. וְיוֹאָשׁ מִפְּנֵי עֲתַלְיָה. וְיֵהוּא מִפְּנֵי יוֹרָם. לֹא כֵן כָּתוּב קֻם מְשָׁחֵהוּ כִּי־זֶה הוּא. זֶה טָעוּן מְשִׁיחָה וְאֵין מַלְכֵי יִשְׂרָאֵל טְעוּנִין מְשִׁיחָה. וְלֹא יֹאשִׁיָּהוּ גְּנָזוֹ. הָדָא אָמְרָה. בְּאַפֵּי־בַּלְסָמוֹן נִמְשְׁחוּ. יוֹאָחָז מִפְּנֵי יְהוֹיָקִים אָחִיו שֶׁהָיָה גָדוֹל מִמֶּנּוּ שְׁתֵּי שָׁנִים. אֵין מוֹשְׁחִין מְלָכִים אֶלָּא מִן הַקֶּרֶן. שָׁאוּל וְיֵהוּא נִמְשְׁחוּ מִן הַפָּךְ הָיְתָה מַלְכוּתָן מַלְכוּת עוֹבֶרֶת. דָּוִד וּשְׁלֹמֹה נִמְשְׁחוּ מִן הַקֶּרֶן הָיְתָה מַלְכוּתָן מַלְכוּת קַיֶּמֶת. אֵין מוֹשְׁחִין מְלָכִים כֹּהֲנִים. רִבִּי יוּדָה עַנְתּוֹדְרַייָא. עַל שֵׁם לֹא־יָסוּר שֵׁבֶט מִיהוּדָה. אָמַר רִבִּי חִייָה בַּר בָּא. לְמַעַן יַאֲרִיךְ יָמִים עַל־מַמְלַכְתּוֹ הוּא וּבָנָיו בְּקֶרֶב כָּל־ יִשְׂרָאֵל׃ מַה כְתִיב בַּתְרֵיהּ. לֹא־יִהְיֶה לַכֹּהֲנִים הַלְוִיִּם.

1 את המלכים | מלכים המעיין | מעין וגו' | על הפרדה אשר לי והורדתם אותו אל גיחון 2 ונתן הנביא למלך על ישראל | וגו' 3 שלאדוניהו | של אדוניה ויואש | יואש ויהוא | יהוא ואין | ואין בנו טעון משיחה.

זה טעון משיחה ואין 5 באפלסמון | באפי בלסמון 7 מלכות | - 8 יודה ענתודרייא | יודן ענתריה 9 בא | אבא

וְהָכְתִיב הַבְּכוֹר֙ יוֹחָנָ֔ן. הַבְּכוֹר לַמַּלְכוּת. וְהָכְתִיב הַשְּׁלִישִׁי צִדְקִיָּ֔הוּ הָרְבִיעִ֖י שַׁלּֽוּם׃ שְׁלִישִׁי לַמַּלְכוּת. רְבִיעִי לְתוֹלֶדֶת. צִדְקִיָּהוּ שֶׁצִּידֵּק עָלָיו אֶת הַדִּין. שַׁלּוּם שֶׁבְּיָמָיו שָׁלְמָה מַלְכוּת בֵּית דָּוִד. לָא שַׁלּוּם הֲוָה שְׁמֵיהּ וְלָא צִדְקִיָּה הֲוָה שְׁמֵיהּ אֶלָּא מַתַּנְיָיה. הָדָא הִיא דִכְתִיב וַיַּמְלֵ֧ךְ מֶֽלֶךְ־בָּבֶ֛ל אֶת־מַתַּנְיָ֥ה דֹד֖וֹ תַּחְתָּ֑יו וגו'.

1 והכת' | אמר ר' יוחנן הוא יהואחז הוא יוחנן והכתי' השלישי | והשלישי הרביעי | והרביעי 2 לתולדת | לתולדות 3 הוה שמיה | היה שמו הוה שמיה | - 4 תחתיו | -

"And who is the Anointed? This is one anointed with the anointing oil," etc. Rav Huna said, the entire six months during which David was in flight before his son Absalom, his sins would have been atoned for by a female goat for a commoner[111].

[112]It was stated: Rebbi Jehudah bar Ilai says: The anointing oil made by Moses on the Mountain[113] was from beginning to end a series of miracles since there were only twelve *log* to start with, as it was said: *and olive oil one hin*[114]. It would not have been enough to rub the wooden planks with it; so much more since the fire swallows, the kettle swallows, wood absorbs! From it the Tabernacle and all its vessels were anointed, the altar and all its vessels, the candelabra and all its vessels, the wash basin and its base. From it Aaron the High Priest and his sons were anointed all of the seven days of induction; from it all high priests and kings were anointed. A king who is first needs anointing; a king who is a king's son does not need anointing, for it is said: *Do anoint him, for this one is it*[115], this one needs anointing, but his son does not need anointing. But a High Priest who is the son of a High Priest needs anointing even for ten generations. Nevertheless, it is there for the future, as it was said: *a holy anointing oil will this be for Me, for all your generations*[116].

One anoints kings only at a spring, as it was said: *Let Solomon, my son, ride on my mule and take him down to the Giḥon; there Ṣadoq the priest and Nathan the prophet shall anoint him as king over Israel*[117]. One anoints kings only because of disputes. Why was Solomon anointed? Because of the dispute of Adoniahu, Joash because of Athaliah, Jehu because of Joram. Is it not written, *do anoint him, for this one is it,* this one needs anointing, but the kings of Israel do not need anointing? [118]But did not Josiah hide it? That means that they anointed with balsamum. Joaḥaz because of his brother

Joakin who was two years his elder. One anoints kings only from a horn. Saul and Jehu were anointed from a can because their kingdom was temporary; David and Solomon were anointed from a horn because their kingdom was permanent. One does not anoint priests as kings. Rebbi Jehudah Antordiya said, because of *the scepter shall not be removed from Jehudah*[119]. Rebbi Ḥiyya bar Abba said, because of *he shall have many days of his kingdom, he and his sons in the midst of Israel*[120]. What is written after that? *The levitic Cohanim should not*[121].

Rebbi Joḥanan said, Joḥanan is Joaḥaz. But is it not written: *The first born Joḥanan*[122], the first in kingdom. [123]*The third Sedekiah, the fourth Shallum*? *Sedekiah*, because he accepted the judgment on himself, *Shallum*, because in his days the dynasty of David was completed. [124]His name was neither Shallum nor Sedekiah but Mattaniah. That is what is written: *The king of Babylon made his uncle Mattaniah king in his stead*[125] etc.

111 The same statement also is found in *Roš Haššanah* 1:1 (56b l. 49). A king who is not in control of his government does not have the status of king [Cf. *Sanhedrin* 2:4 (Note 108)].

112 This text is part of a longer text found in *Soṭah* 8:3, Notes 69-92 (L. Ginzberg, *Yerushalmi Fragments from the Genizah*, New York 1909, p. 214), and, what seems to be the original source, *Šeqalim* 6:1, 49c l. 52 ff., Babli *editio princeps* 9d l. 21. Only the biblical quotes and major deviations from the *Sotah* text are noted here.

113 In *Sotah* and *Šeqalim*: "in the desert." The place is not mentioned in B.

114 *Ex*. 30:24.

115 *1S*. 16:12.

116 *Ex*. 30:31.

117 *1K*. 1:33-34.

118 In all other sources, this follows the quote about the sons of Josiah. If Josiah had buried the holy oil together with the ark, how could his son have been anointed?

119 *Gen*. 49:10.

120 *Deut*. 17:20.

121 *Deut*. 18:1.

122 *1Chr*. 3:15.

123 There the introduction is missing, that R. Joḥanan identified Sedekiah and Shallum as one and the same person. In the Babli 11b this and the following are a tannaitic statement.

124 In the *Šeqalim* text of the Babli *editio princeps* the statement is attributed to R. Simeon ben Laqish.

125 *2K*. 24:17.

(47c line 63) הַמָּשׁוּחַ בַּשֶּׁמֶן הַמִּשְׁחָה. בַּבִּנְייָן הָרִאשׁוֹן. לְמְרוּבֶּה בִבְגָדִים. בַּבִּנְייָן הָאַחֲרוֹן. וַאֲתַאי כַּיי דָמַר רִבִּי אִינָא בְשֵׁם רִבִּי אָחָא. חֲמִשָּׁה דְבָרִים הָיָה בְבֵית הַמִּקְדָּשׁ הָאַחֲרוֹן חָסֵר מִן

הָרִאשׁוֹן. מַאי טַעֲמָא. עֲלוּ הָהָר וַהֲבֵאתֶם עֵץ וגו' אֶכָּבְדָ֗ חָסֵר ה'. אֵלּוּ ה' דְבָרִים שֶׁהָיוּ בֵּית הַמִּקְדָּשׁ הָאַחֲרוֹן חָסֵר מִן הָרִאשׁוֹן. וְאֵילּוּ הֵן. אֵשׁ וְאָרוֹן וְאוּרִים וְתוּמִּים וְשֶׁמֶן הַקּוֹדֶשׁ.

1 בבניין | בבנין (X2) למרובה | מרובה 2 ואתאי כיי | ואתי כי ר' אינא | ר' שמעו' בר יינא בבית | בית 3 מ"ט | דכתי' וגו' | ובנו את הבית וארצה בו אכבד | ואכבד חסר ה' | כתיב חסר אלו | הרי אלו שהיו | שהיה 4 ואילו | ואלו הקודש | המשחה ורוח הקדש

[126]"The anointed with the anointing oil," in the first Temple. "The one clothed in multiple garb," in the later Temple. It follows what Rebbi Ina[127] said in the name of Rebbi Aḥa: In five things was the later Temple deficient compared with the first. What is the reason? *Go to the mountain, bring wood,* etc. *I should be honored* is missing a [128]ה. These are the five things in which the later Temple was deficient compared with the first. And these are it: The fire[129], the ark, Urim and Tummim[130], the (holy) oil [of anointing and the holy spirit.][131]

126 Here starts the discussion of the last sentence of the Mishnah, which continues with discussion of Mishnah 4 (= Mishnah *Megillah* 1:12).

127 In the Babli (*Yoma* 21b) and the Horaiot text in the Babli, as well as the parallels in *Makkot* 2:7 (explained in Notes 125-130), *Ta`aniot* 2:1 (65a l. 60): R. Samuel bar Ainia. Since the latter name appears as that of a student of R. Aḥa several times in different Tractates but "R. Ina" only here, the reading of B is preferable.

128 *Hag.* 1:8. אכבד is the *Ketib*, אכבדה the *Qere*. In the Alexandrian system of numeration by letters, 'ה is 5.

129 The fire on the outer altar in the first Temple was of divine origin (*2Chr.* 7:1), but not that of the second Temple.

130 The oracle whose nature was unknown in later times.

131 Text of B; a necessary addition since the text of L mentions only 4 items. The list in the Babli is slightly different. The holy spirit is that of prophecy.

(47b line 68) תַּנֵּי. כֹּהֵן הַמָּשִׁיחַ מֵבִיא פָּר. אֵין מְרוּבֶּה בְגָדִים מֵבִיא פָּר. וּדְלָא כְרִבִּי מֵאִיר. מַה טַעֲמֵיהּ דְּרִבִּי מֵאִיר. מָשִׁיחַ. וּמַה תַלְמוּד לוֹמַר כֹּהֵן. לְהוֹצִיא לִמְרוּבֶּה בְגָדִים. מַה טַעֲמוֹן דְּרַבָּנִן. מָשִׁיחַ. יָכוֹל זֶה הַמֶּלֶךְ. וּמַה תַלְמוּד לוֹמַר כֹּהֵן. לְרַבּוֹת מְרוּבֶּה בְגָדִים. הָכָא אַתְּ מַר. לְהוֹצִיא לִמְרוּבֶּה בְגָדִים. וְכָא אַתְּ מַר. לְרַבּוֹת מְרוּבֶּה בְגָדִים. אָמַר רִבִּי הִילָא. כָּל־מִדְרַשׁ וּמִדְרַשׁ לְעִנְיָינוֹ. אִילּוּ נֶאֱמַר מָשִׁיחַ וְלֹא נֶאֱמַר כֹּהֵן. הָיִיתִי אוֹמֵר. עַל הֶעֱלֵם דָּבָר מֵבִיא פָר וְעַל שִׁגְגַת הַמַּעֲשֶׂה מֵבִיא שָׂעִיר. הֲוֵי צוֹרֶךְ הוּא שֶׁיֵּאָמֵר כֹּהֵן. אוֹ אִילּוּ כֹּהֵן וְלֹא מָשִׁיחַ. הָיִיתִי אוֹמֵר. זֶה הַמֶּלֶךְ. אִם תֹּאמַר. בְּפָר קָדְמָה פָּרָשַׁת הַמֶּלֶךְ שֶׁיּוּטַל עַל הֶעֱלֵם דָּבָר מֵבִיא פָר וְעַל שִׁגְגַת הַמַּעֲשֶׂה מֵבִיא שָׂעִיר. הֲוֵי צוֹרֶךְ הוּא שֶׁיֵּאָמֵר מָשִׁיחַ וְצוֹרֶךְ הוּא שֶׁיֵּאָמֵר כֹּהֵן.

גרסינן במגלה מן ריש הלכה ועד סופה ועוד היא בכפורים[132]

[133]It was stated: The Anointed Priest brings a bull, the one clothed in multiple garb does not bring a bull. This disagrees with Rebbi Meïr. What is Rebbi Meïr's reason? *The Anointed.* Why does the verse say *priest*? To exclude the one clothed in multiple garb. What is the rabbis' reason? *The anointed.* I could think that this is the king. Why does the verse say, *priest*? To include the one clothed in multiple garb. Here you say, to exclude the one clothed in multiple garb. But there you say, to include the one clothed in multiple garb. Rebbi Hila said, each inference refers to its meaning. If it had said *the Anointed* but not *priest*, I would have said, he brings a bull for forgetting a topic, but for acting in error he brings a goat. Therefore it is necessary that it mention *priest*. But if it had mentioned *priest* but not *the Anointed*, I would have said, this refers to the king. If you would say by a bull, preceding the paragraph about the king, assuming that for forgetting a topic he brings a bull but for acting in error he brings a goat. Therefore it is necessary that it mention *the Anointed* and that it mention *priest*.

132 Note of B: "One studies all this in *Megillah* (Halakhah 1:12) from beginning of the Halakhah to its end; in addition it (partially) is in *Kippurim*." The text of B continues with the quote later of Mishnah *Yoma* 1:1.

133 The text and the following paragraphs up to the quote from *Idiut* 5:6 is from *Megillah* 1:12. The secondary character of the text here is shown by the thorough corruption of the present paragraph compared to the parallel text in *Megillah* and partially *Sifra Ḥovah (Wayyiqra 2) Paršeta* 2(6). One might conjecture that the editor of B neither did want to rearrange the text nor print it in disorder. The text of *Megillah* is readily understandable; it also explains the mutilated text here. The additional text is given in a different typeface.

תַּנֵּי. כֹּהֵן הַמָּשִׁיחַ מֵבִיא פָּר. אֵין הַמְרוּבֶּה בְגָדִים מֵבִיא פָּר. וּדְלָא כְרִבִּי מֵאִיר. דְּרִבִּי מֵאִיר אָמַר. הַמְרוּבֶּה בְגָדִים מֵבִיא פָּר. מַה טַעֲמֵיהּ דְּרִבִּי מֵאִיר. מָשִׁיחַ. וּמַה תַלְמוּד לוֹמַר כֹּהֵן. לְרַבּוֹת אֶת הַמְרוּבֶּה בְגָדִים. מַה טַעֲמוֹן דְּרַבָּנָן. מָשִׁיחַ. יָכוֹל זֶה הַמֶּלֶךְ. תַּלְמוּד לוֹמַר כֹּהֵן. אִי כֹהֵן יָכוֹל אַף מְרוּבֶּה בְגָדִים. תַּלְמוּד לוֹמַר מָשִׁיחַ. אוֹ יָכוֹל שֶׁאֲנִי מַרְבֶּה אַף מְשׁוּחַ מִלְחָמָה. תַּלְמוּד לוֹמַר מָשִׁיחַ. שֶׁאֵין עַל גַּבָּיו מָשִׁיחַ. מִחְלְפָה שִׁיטָּתוֹן דְּרַבָּנִן. הָכָא כְתִיב מָשִׁיחַ וְהָכָא כְתִיב מָשִׁיחַ. הָכָא אִינּוּן אָמְרִין. לְרַבּוֹת מְרוּבֶּה בְגָדִים. וְהָכָא אִינּוּן אָמְרִין. לְהוֹצִיא אֶת הַמְּרוּבֶּה בְגָדִים. אָמַר רִבִּי אִילָא. כָּל־מִדְרָשׁ וּמִדְרָשׁ בְּעִנְייָנוֹ. תַּמָּן כָּל־הַפָּרָשָׁה אֲמוּרָה בְאַהֲרֹן. לְאֵי־זֶה דָבָר נֶאֱמַר כֹּהֵן. לְרַבּוֹת אֶת הַמְרוּבֶּה בְגָדִים. בְּרַם הָכָא אֵין הַפָּרָשָׁה אֲמוּרָה בְאַהֲרֹן. אִילּוּ נֶאֱמַר מָשִׁיחַ וְלֹא נֶאֱמַר כֹּהֵן. הָיִיתִי אוֹמֵר. לְעוֹלָם עַל הֶעֱלֵם דָּבָר מֵבִיא פָר וְעַל שִׁגְגַת מַעֲשֶׂה מֵבִיא שָׂעִיר. הֲוֵי צוֹרֶךְ הוּא שֶׁיֹּאמַר כֹּהֵן. אוֹ אִלּוּ נֶאֱמַר כֹּהֵן וְלֹא נֶאֱמַר מָשִׁיחַ. הָיִיתִי אוֹמֵר. זֶה הַמֶּלֶךְ. אֵין תֹּאמַר. כְּבָר קָדְמָה פָרָשַׁת הַמֶּלֶךְ. הָיִיתִי אוֹמֵר. עַל הֶעֱלֵם דָּבָר מֵבִיא פָר וְעַל שִׁגְגַת מַעֲשֶׂה מֵבִיא שָׂעִיר. הֲוֵי צוֹרֶךְ הוּא שֶׁיֹּאמַר מָשִׁיחַ וְצוֹרֶךְ הוּא שֶׁיֹּאמַר כֹּהֵן.

It was stated: The Anointed Priest brings a bull, the one clothed in multiple garb does not bring a bull. This disagrees with Rebbi Meïr, for Rebbi Meïr said, the one clothed in multiple garb brings a bull[134]. What is Rebbi Meïr's reason? *The Anointed.* Why does the verse say *priest*? To add the one clothed in multiple garb[135]. What is the rabbis' reason? *The anointed.* I could think that this is the king. The verse says, *priest*. If priest, I could think the one clothed in multiple garb. The verse says, *anointed*[136]. Then I could think that I am adding also the one anointed for war[137]. The verse says, *Anointed*; one who has no anointed person over him. The argument of the rabbis seems inverted. Here[138] is written *anointed* and there is written *anointed.* Here they say, to include the one clothed in multiple garb[139]. But here[140] they say, to exclude the one clothed in multiple garb. Rebbi Hila said, each inference refers to its meaning. There the entire paragraph is said for Aaron. Why is said *priest*? To include the one clothed in multiple garb[141]. But here the paragraph does not mention Aaron. If it had said *the Anointed* but not *priest*, I would have said, he brings a bull for forgetting a topic, but for acting in error he brings a goat[142]. Therefore it is necessary that it would mention *priest.* But if it had mentioned *priest* but not *the Anointed*, I would have said, this refers to the king[143]. If you would say already this[144] precedes the paragraph about the king[145], I would have said that for forgetting a topic he brings a bull but for acting in error he brings a goat. Therefore it is necessary that it mention *the Anointed* and that it mention *priest.*

134 The definite article used in *Lev.* 4:3, *the* priest, would alone have sufficed to characterize the High Priest, biblically distinguished from all others.

135 Tosephta 2:3.

136 The double restriction, *the* priest (the High Priest), *anointed,* makes it clear that only an anointed high priest is meant. The rabbinic disagreement implies that no High Priest of Second Temple times ever brought a purification sacrifice for himself.

137 The one mentioned in *Deut.* 20:3 charged with addressing the army. He also is called *the* priest (*Sotah* Chapter 8) and bound by all restrictions imposed on the High Priest in *Lev.* 21:10-15 (Tosephta 2:1).

138 *Lev.* 6:15, on the daily flour sacrifice of the High Priest.

139 Mishnah 4 mentions the daily offering of a tenth of a *ephah* as duty of the High Priest clothed in multiple garb [*Sifra Saw Pereq* 5(1)].

140 In the Chapter on purification sacrifices.

141 Aaron and his successors are mentioned in v. 13. In v. 15, the mention of "the priest, anointed from his descendants in his stead" does not seem to require a mention of anointing as a definition.

142 As explained in Chapter 2:3, The High Priest may offer a bull only for his forgetting a topic in religious law. One could argue that for simple acting in error, he should bring a commoner's sacrifice (or, since a male is mentioned, the goat

characterized earlier as sacrifice for inadvertent idolatry.) The specific mention of *priest* bars him from a commoner's sacrifice.

143 Since *Cohen* may simply mean "public servant" (*2S*. 8:18).

144 The unintelligible בפר in the text here is a plausible misreading for כבר .

145 Which is only the third in the Chapter. The argument is parallel to that mentioned in Note 131.

(47d line 2) אָמַר רִבִּי יוֹחָנָן עָבַר וְהֵבִיא עֲשִׂירַת הָאֵיפָה שֶׁלּוֹ כָּשֵׁר.

Rebbi Johanan said, if he transgressed and offered his tenth of an *ephah* it is valid[145].

145 This refers to the statement in Mishnah 4 that the only difference between acting and emeritus High Priests are the High Priest's bull on the Day of Atonement and the daily flour offering of a tenth of an *ephah*. It is now stated that if the ex-High Priest, who, as will be explained later in the Halakhah, should be unfit to serve as High Priest and is barred from serving as common priest, nevertheless acts as High Priest, the offering is legitimate.

(47c line 3) מַתְקִינִין לוֹ כֹּהֵן אַחֵר תַּחְתָּיו שֶׁמָּא יֶאֱרַע בּוֹ פְסוּל. מַה. מְיַיחֲדִין לֵיהּ עִימֵּיהּ. אָמַר רִבִּי חַגַּי. מֹשֶׁה. דִּינוּן מְיַיחֲדִין לֵיהּ עִימֵּיהּ דּוּ קְטִיל לֵיהּ. אוֹתוֹ. אֶחָד מוֹשְׁחִין וְאֵין מוֹשְׁחִין שְׁנַיִם. אָמַר רִבִּי יוֹחָנָן. מִפְּנֵי הָאֵיבָה.

1 מתקיניו | מתקנין מייחדין { מיחדין 2 חגי | חגיי דינון | אין מייחדין | מיחדין דו | דהוא ליה | לו עימיה

[146]"One arranges for another Cohen as his replacement, maybe a disqualification of his will happen.[147]" How? Does one leave them alone together? Rebbi Haggai said, by Moses[148]! If one would leave them alone together, he would kill him! *Him*[149]. One anoints one, one does not anoint two. Rebbi Johanan said, because of rivalry[150].

146 From here on there is a parallel in *Yoma* 1:1 (38c l. 72 ff.).

147 Mishnah *Yoma* 1:1. Since the entire service of the Day of Atonement is valid only if conducted by the High Priest, a replacement must be available in case the High Priest becomes impure or otherwise incapacitated. The High Priest undergoes a week of preparation for the service, to train for a very crowded program. The question then arises whether the designated backup also has to undergo the same training, possibly at the same place.

148 In *Yoma* "because of", a scribal error. "By Moses" was a preferred expression of R. Haggai's.

149 *Lev*. 6:12; the offering of the High Priest starting with the day he is anointed

for his office. *Sifra Saw Parašah* 3(3). The singular indicates that only one High Priest can be appointed at one time. This implies that the reserve appointee for the day of Atonement cannot have the status of High Priest unless he actually is needed.

150 He disagrees and holds that while the two could not have been anointed on the same day, they could have been anointed on different days. The rule that the back-up Cohen has lower status is practical, not biblical, as is the entire institution of the back-up.

(47d line 6) עָבַר זֶה וְשִׁימֵּשׁ זֶה. הָרִאשׁוֹן כָּל־קְדוּשַּׁת כְּהוּנָּה עָלָיו. הַשֵּׁינִי אֵינוֹ כָשֵׁר לֹא לְכֹהֵן גָּדוֹל וְלֹא לְכֹהֵן הֶדְיוֹט. אָמַר רִבִּי יוֹחָנָן. עָבַר וְעָבַד עֲבוֹדָתוֹ פְסוּלָה. עֲבוֹדָתוֹ מִשֶּׁל מִי. נִשְׁמְעִינָהּ מִן הָדָא. מַעֲשֶׂה בְּבֶן אִלֵּם בְּצִיפֹּרִים שֶׁאִירַע קֶרִי בְכֹהֵן גָּדוֹל בְּיוֹם הַכִּיפּוּרִים וְנִכְנַס בֶּן אִלֵּם וְשִׁימֵּשׁ תַּחְתָּיו. יָצָא וְאָמַר לַמֶּלֶךְ. פָּר וְאַיִל הַקְּרֵיבִים הַיּוֹם מִשֶּׁלְּמִי הֵן קְרֵיבִין. מִשֶּׁלּוֹ אוֹ מִשֶּׁלְּכֹהֵן גָּדוֹל. וְיָדַע הַמֶּלֶךְ מָהוּ שׁוֹאֲלוֹ. אָמַר לוֹ. לֹא דַיֶּיךָ שֶׁשִּׁימַּשְׁתָּ שָׁעָה אַחַת לִפְנֵי מִי שֶׁאָמַר וְהָיָה הָעוֹלָם. וְיָדַע בֶּן אִלֵּם שֶׁהוּסַּע מִכְּהוּנָּה גְּדוֹלָה.

1 זה | אחר זה קדושת | מצות השיני | השני כשר | ראוי 2 פסולה | כשרה עבודתו | עבודה משל | של 3 הדא | הדה אלם | אילם בציפורים | מציפורי גדול | - בן | - 4 אלם | - תחתיו | תחתיו בכהונה יצא | - הקריבים | הקרבים קריבין | - משלו | משלי 5 שעה אחת לפני מי שאמר והיה העולם | - לפני מי שאמר והיה העולם שעה אחת 6 אלם | אילם מכהונה הגדולה | מן הכהונה

If one was incapacitated and the other officiated. The first has all the sanctity of the High Priesthood on him; the second one is qualified neither as High Priest nor as common priest[151]. Rebbi Johanan said, if he transgressed and officiated, his officiating is (invalid) [valid][152]. Whose officiating? [153]Let us hear from the following: It happened to Ben Illem from Sepphoris[154] that the High Priest experienced an emission of semen on the Day of Atonement[155]; Ben Illem entered and officiated in his stead. He went out and asked the king: "The bull and the ram which are brought today, from whose property are they offered? From his or from the High Priest's?[156]" The king understood what he was asking and answered him, "is it not enough for you that you served once before Him Who spoke and the world was created?" Ben Illem understood that he was removed from the High Priesthood.

151 As the Babli explains (*Yoma* 12b), "one increases in sanctity but never decreases" (cf. *Bikkurim* 3:3, Note 57; *Yoma* 3:8 41a l. 10, *Megillah* 1:12 72a l. 47, *Ševuot* 1:8, 33b l.13). Since the service of the Day of Atonement is valid only if performed by the High Priest, the substitute becomes a temporary High Priest. He cannot act as a High Priest if the actual High Priest's temporary disability is removed and he is permanently barred from acting as a

common priest. As the Babli points out, if the High Priest dies, the substitute automatically becomes his successor.

152 The text in parentheses is that of L, the one in brackets that of B as well as the parallels in *Megillah* and *Yoma* and the Babli (*Yoma* 13a). The text of L cannot be correct since it is held in general that a doubt about the legitimacy of officiating in the Temple does not invalidate the offering (*Terumot* 8:1, Note 26).

153 The case is told not only in the two parallels in *Megillah* and *Yoma*, but also in abbreviated form in the Babli, *Yoma* 12b where, however, the ruling is not the king's (necessarily of the Herodian dynasty) but "the rabbis'." There is no reason to doubt the historicity of the Yerushalmi version.

154 This translation follows B and the parallels. The text of L, "in Sepphoris", is impossible.

155 The High Priest is taken to live in the Temple, and therefore deprived of sexual activity, for seven days preceding the Day of Atonement. In the night of the Day of Atonement he is deprived of sleep (*Yoma* Mishnah 1:7) to avoid the danger of him having an involuntary emission. If he has one anyhow, he is disqualified for the entire day even if he immediately purifies himself in a *miqweh* since the disqualification by temporary impurity is not removed by the removal of the impurity until the following sundown (*Lev.* 22:7; cf. *Ma`aser Šeni* 3:2, Notes 21-22.)

(47d line 14) מַעֲשֶׂה בְשִׁמְעוֹן בֶּן קִמְחִית שֶׁיָּצָא לְטַייֵל עִם הַמֶּלֶךְ עֶרֶב יוֹם הַכִּיפּוּרִים עִם חֲשֵׁיכָה. וְנִתְּזָה צִינּוֹרָה שֶׁלְּרוֹק מִפִּיו עַל בְּגָדָיו וְטִמְּאַתּוּ. וְנִכְנַס יְהוּדָה אָחִיו וְשִׁימֵּשׁ תַּחְתָּיו. אוֹתוֹ הַיּוֹם רָאֲת אִימָּן שְׁנֵי בָנֶיהָ כֹּהֲנִים גְּדוֹלִים. שִׁבְעָה בָנִים הָיוּ לָהּ לְקִמְחִית וְכוּלָּן שִׁימְּשׁוּ בִּכְהוּנָּה גְדוֹלָה. שָׁלְחוּ וְאָמְרוּ לְקִמְחִית. מַה מַּעֲשִׂים טוֹבִים יֵשׁ בְּיָדֵיךְ. אָמְרָה לָהֶן. יָבוֹא עָלַי אִם רָאוּ קוֹרוֹת בֵּיתִי שְׂעָרוֹת רֹאשִׁי וְאִימְרַת חָלוּקִי מִיָּמַיי. אָמְרִין. כָּל־קִמְחַיָּא קִימְחִין וְקִמְחָא דְקִימְחִית סוֹלֶת. קָרְאוּ עָלֶיהָ הַפָּסוּק הַזֶּה כָּל־כְּבוּדָּה בַת־מֶלֶךְ פְּנִימָה מִמִּשְׁבְּצוֹת זָהָב לְבוּשָׁהּ׃

1 המלך | מלך הערבי 2 צינורה | צינורא יהודה | יודה ושימש | - 3 אימן | אמן

The remainder of the text (to line three of the next paragraph) is missing in B without indication of a lacuna.

[156]It happened that Simeon ben Qimḥit went out for a walk with the [157]king on the Day of Atonement at sundown and a drop of spittle squirted on his garment and defiled him. His brother Jehudah entered and officiated in his stead. On that day their mother saw two of her sons as High Priests. Qimḥit had seven sons; all of them served as High Priests[158]. They sent and asked Qimḥit, what good deeds are in your hand? She told them, there should come over me if the beams of the roof of my house ever saw the hair on my head or the seam of my undershirt[159]. They said, all flours are flour but Qimḥit's flour

is fine flour[159a]. They recited about her the verse[160]: *All the honor of the king's daughter is inside; gold settings her garments*[161].

156 In addition to the two parallels there is a short version in the Babli, *Yoma* 47a. There, the names are Ismael and Joseph. The passages are discussed in detail by Grätz, *Geschichte der Juden* vol. 3/2[4] Note 19/II. Josephus transscribes בֶּן קִמְחִית as τοῦ Καμύδου.

157 The text is not clear here. The text of L is also found in the parallel in *Yoma*. The text of B, "with the Arab (Nabatean) king" is also the text of *Megillah*. In the Babli, "with an Arab on the Day of Atonement". (For some reason, the Russian censor of the Wilna Babli changed "Arab" into "a nobleman".) The confusion comes from the similarity if ערב "evening" and ערבי "Arab." The explicit reference to sundown should argue for the version of L. If the Arab was not converted to Judaism, the High Priest would have had to leave the holy precinct on the Day of Atonement, a most unlikely happening before he had finished all his duties.

The version of the text presupposes that the king had immersed himself in a *miqweh* so he could enter the restricted area on the Temple Mount. Nevertheless, (Mishnah *Hagigah* 2:7) "The garments of the vulgar are severely impure for Pharisees; the garments of Pharisees are severely impure for those eating heave; the garments of those eating heave are severely impure for those sacrificing." The severe impurity of מִדְרָס referred to here is the impurity of seats or beds used by a sufferer from gonorrhea or a menstruating woman, which makes anyone touching it impure and requires immersion in water and waiting until sundown. Since the king could not sacrifice on the Day of Atonement, he could not have immersed himself with the intention which would make him co-pure with the High Priest. Since the incident happened at sundown, the High Priest was automatically disqualified for the next 24 hours.

While a living Gentile is not under the rules of biblical impurity, rabbinically every Gentile is impure and this impurity cannot be removed by immersion in water (Babli *Avodah zarah* 36b).

158 Under the Herodian kings, when the High Priesthood was conferred and removed at the whim of the king.

159 It is indecent for a married woman to be seen in public with uncovered hair. She was clothed at home as she was for the street and never undressed except in the dark. The Babli notes that many women follow this custom.

159a A pun on the name of *Qimhit* "flour lady".

160 *Ps*. 45:14.

161 According to Rashi's commentary in *Yoma*, the argument means that the reward of a woman who behaves with dignity in her home is that her son will be High Priest whose garment is adorned with golden settings for precious stones. (Cf. *Tanḥuma Wayyišlaḥ* 6, *Bemidbar* 3.)

(47d line 22) יָכוֹל לֹא יְהֵא מְשׁוּחַ מִלְחָמָה מִפְּנֵי עֲשִׂירִית הָאֵיפָה שֶׁלּוֹ. תַּלְמוּד לוֹמַר תַּחְתָּיו מִבָּנָיו. אֵת שֶׁבְּנוֹ עוֹמֵד תַּחְתָּיו מֵבִיא עֲשִׂירִית הָאֵיפָה. וְאֵת שֶׁאֵין בְּנוֹ עוֹמֵד תַּחְתָּיו אֵינוֹ מֵבִיא עֲשִׂירִית הָאֵיפָה. וּמְנַיִין לִמְשׁוּחַ מִלְחָמָה שֶׁאֵין בְּנוֹ עוֹמֵד תַּחְתָּיו. תַּלְמוּד לוֹמַר שִׁבְעַת יָמִים יִלְבָּשָׁם הַכֹּהֵן וגו'. אֵת שֶׁהוּא בָא אֶל אוֹהֶל מוֹעֵד לְשָׁרֵת בַּקּוֹדֶשׁ בְּנוֹ עוֹמֵד תַּחְתָּיו. וְאֵת שֶׁאֵינוֹ בָא אֶל אוֹהֶל מוֹעֵד לְשָׁרֵת בַּקּוֹדֶשׁ אֵין בְּנוֹ עוֹמֵד תַּחְתָּיו. וּמְנַיִין שֶׁהוּא מִתְמַנֶּה לִהְיוֹת כֹּהֵן גָּדוֹל. פִּינְחָס בֶּן־אֶלְעָזָר נָגִיד הָיָה עֲלֵיהֶם לְפָנִים יי עִמּוֹ׃ רִבִּי יוֹסֵי כַּד הֲוָה בָעֵי מְקַנְתְּרֵהּ לְרִבִּי לָעְזָר בֵּירִבִּי יוֹסֵי הֲוָה אֲמַר לֵיהּ. לְפָנִים עִמּוֹ׃ בִּימֵי זִמְרִי מִיחָה. וּבִימֵי פִּילֶגֶשׁ בְּגִבְעָה לֹא מִיחָה.

3 ומניין | מנין 4 וגו' | תחתיו מבניו וגו' ואת שאינו | ושאינו 5 ומניין | ומנין 6 פינחס | דכתי' פנחס עליהם | - יי | ה' מקנתרה | מקנתרא 7 עמו | ה' עמו

I could think that the one anointed for war[137] should (not)[162] bring his tenth of an *ephah*[139]. The verse says[138], *in his stead, of his sons.* One whose son will stand in his stead brings a tenth of an *ephah.* But one whose sons will not stand in his stead does not bring a tenth of an *ephah.* From where the anointed's for war son will not stand in his stead? The verse says[163], *seven days shall the priest wear them,* etc. If one officiates in the Tent of Meeting, his son will stand in his stead. But one who does not officiate in the Tent of Meeting, his son will not stand in his stead. From where that he can be appointed as High Priest[164]? [As is written,] [165]*Phineas the son of Eleazar was leader over them; in earlier times the Eternal was with him.* When Rebbi Yose wanted to needle[166] Rebbi Eleazar ben Rebbi Yose[167], he said to him, "before, he was with him." In the days of Zimri[168], he protested. In the days of the concubine at Gibea[169], he did not protest.

162 Text of L, missing in the two parallels and contradicted by the following text.

163 *Ex.* 29:30. As often, the proof is from the part of the verse not quoted: *Seven days the priest shall wear them who of his sons will stand in his stead to officiate in the Sanctuary.* The only hereditary office in Divine Service is that of the High Priest. Babli *Yoma* 72b/73a.

164 Since the Anointed for War is under the restrictions valid for the High Priest one has to ascertain that his office be subordinate, not coordinate, to the High Priesthood and that an appointment to High Priesthood does not violate the rule that one may not reduce the holiness of one's position (Note 151).

165 *1Chr.* 9:20. The leader of the priests is the High Priest. Phineas was appointed Anointed for War by Moses, *Num.* 31:6.

166 Hebrew verb built on a Greek root; cf. *Berakhot* 3, Note 96.

167 R. Yose seems to have complained about a lack of leadership on the part of his son.

168 *Num.* 27:1-15.

169 *Jud.* 19-21. In the opinion of *Seder Olam,* based on the teachings of R. Yose the Tanna (who is meant here), the affair at Gibea happened at the start of the period of the Judges, when Phineas was High Priest. Cf. the author's edition of *Seder Olam* (Northvale NJ 1998), pp. 122-123.

(47d line 31) וּמְנַיִין שֶׁהָיָה עוֹבֵד בִּשְׁמוֹנָה. רִבִּי בָּא בַּר חִייָה בְּשֵׁם רִבִּי יוֹחָנָן. וּבִגְדֵי הַקּוֹדֶשׁ
אֲשֶׁר לְאַהֲרֹן יִהְיוּ לְבָנָיו אַחֲרָיו. וּמַה תַלְמוּד לוֹמַר אַחֲרָיו. לִגְדוּלָּה שֶׁלְּאַחֲרָיו. וּמְנַיִין שֶׁהוּא
נִשְׁאַל בִּשְׁמוֹנָה. רִבִּי יִרְמְיָה רִבִּי אִימִּי בְּשֵׁם רִבִּי יוֹחָנָן. וּבִגְדֵי הַקּוֹדֶשׁ אֲשֶׁר לְאַהֲרֹן יִהְיוּ לְבָנָיו.
וּמַה תַלְמוּד לוֹמַר אַחֲרָיו. לִקְדוּשָּׁה שֶׁלְּאַחֲרָיו. בְּכַמָּה הוּא נִשְׁאַל. אַייְתִיהוּ רבבהו שֶׁעָלָה
מַתְנִיתָא דְבַר קַפָּרָא מִדְּרוֹמָא וְתַנָּא. אֵינוֹ עוֹבֵד לֹא בְאַרְבָּעָה שֶׁלְּכֹהֵן הֶדְיוֹט וְלֹא בִשְׁמוֹנָה
שֶׁלְּכֹהֵן גָּדוֹל. אָמַר רִבִּי בָּא. בְּדִין הָיָה שֶׁיְּהֵא עוֹבֵד בְּאַרְבָּעָה. וְלָמָּה אָמְרוּ אֵינוֹ עוֹבֵד. שֶׁלֹּא יְהוּ
אוֹמְרִין. רָאִינוּ כֹהֵן הֶדְיוֹט פְּעָמִים שֶׁהוּא עוֹבֵד בִּשְׁמוֹנָה כְּכֹהֵן גָּדוֹל. אָמַר רִבִּי יוֹנָה. וְלֹא בִפְנִים
הוּא עוֹבֵד. וַהֲלֹא בַחוּץ הוּא נִשְׁאַל וטוֹעִין דָּבָר מִבִּפְנִים לְבַחוּץ. וְכִי רִבִּי טַרְפוֹן רַבָּן
שֶׁלְּכָל־יִשְׂרָאֵל לֹא טָעָה בֵין תְּקִיעַת הַקָּהֵל לִתְקִיעַת קָרְבָּן. דִּכְתִיב וּבְנֵי אַהֲרֹן הַכֹּהֲנִים יִתְקְעוּ
בַּחֲצוֹצְרוֹת. תְּמִימִם לֹא בַעֲלֵי מוּמִין. דִּבְרֵי רִבִּי עֲקִיבָה. אָמַר לוֹ רִבִּי טַרְפוֹן. אֶקְפַּח אֶת בָּנַיי
אִם לֹא רָאִיתִי שִׁמְעוֹן אֲחִי אִימָּה חִיגֵּר בְּאַחַת מֵרַגְלָיו וְעוֹמֵד בָּעֲזָרָה וַחֲצוֹצַרְתּוֹ בְיָדוֹ וְתוֹקֵעַ.
אָמַר לוֹ רִבִּי עֲקִיבָה. שֶׁמָּא לֹא רָאִיתוֹ אֶלָּא בִשְׁעַת הַקָּהֵל. וַאֲנִי אוֹמֵר. בִּשְׁעַת קָרְבָּן. אָמַר לוֹ
רִבִּי טַרְפוֹן. אֶקְפַּח אֶת בָּנַיי שֶׁלֹּא הִיטִּיתָה יָמִין וּשְׂמֹאל. אֲנִי הוּא שֶׁשָּׁמַעְתִּי וְלֹא הָיָה לִי לְפָרֵשׁ.
וְאַתָּה דוֹרֵשׁ וּמַסְכִּים שְׁמוּעָה. הָא כָל־הַפּוֹרֵשׁ מִמְּךָ כְּפוֹרֵשׁ מֵחַיָּיו.

1 ומניין | מנין חייה | חייא 2 ומה | מה ומניין | ומנין 3 אימי | חייא 4 ומה | מה 5 lines missing
10 עקיבה | עקיבא בניי | בני 11 אימה | אמא 12 עקיבה | עקיבא 13 בניי | בני היטיתה | היטית
14 שמועה | על השמועה

[170]And from where that he officiated in eight? Rebbi Abba bar Ḥiyya in the name of Rebbi Joḥanan: *And Aaron's holy garments shall be for his descendants in his stead*[163]. Why does the verse say, *in his stead*? For greatness after him. And from where that he was asked in eight? Rebbi Jeremiah, Rebbi Immi in the name of Rebbi Joḥanan: *And Aaron's holy garments shall be for his descendants in his stead.* Why does the verse say, *in his stead*? For holiness after him. In what was he asked? They brought it, רבבהו , a Mishnah of Bar Qappara came from the South which stated: He officiates neither in the four of a common priest nor in the eight of a High Priest. Rebbi Abba said, it would be logical that he officiate in four[176]. Why did they say that he did not officiate? Lest people say, we saw a simple priest who sometimes officiated in eight like a High Priest[177]. Rebbi Jonah said, would he not officiate inside and would he not be asked outside? Does one

err between inside and outside? But did Rebbi Tarphon, the teacher of all of Israel, not err between blowing for assembly and the blowing for a sacrifice? As it is written: *The descendants of Aaron, the priests, shall blow the trumpets*[178], blameless ones, not with bodily defects, the words of Rebbi Aqiba. Rebbi Tarphon said to him, I would hit my sons[179] if I did not see Simeon, my mother's brother, lame in one of his legs, standing in the Temple court with his trumpet in his hand and blowing! Rebbi Aqiba answered him, maybe you saw him only at the time of assembly[180]; but I was saying, at the time of sacrifices[181]. Rebbi Tarphon said to him, I would hit my sons but you did not deviate right or left. I am the one who heard but I could not explain. You derive it and agree with tradition. Therefore, anybody who separates from you is as if he separated himself from his life[182].

170 The text here up to the quote from Bar Qappara's Mishnah is corrupt, contradictory in itself and mostly missing in B. Since it is a careless copy of the text in *Yoma* (1:1 38b l. 26) *and Megillah* (2:12 71a l. 75), an explanation must be based on that text. The paragraph discusses the rules for the priest Anointed for War. It starts with an assertion that the Anointed for War officiates in the Temple in the High Priest's garb while later it is asserted without dissent that he be barred from any service in the Sanctuary. The entire topic is a reconstruction of the environment in which one has to place David's inquiries to God as recorded in the books of Samuel.

A consistent whole is found in the *Yoma/Megillah* text. In the following, standard font is used for the *Yoma* text; where the *Megillah* text deviates, it is given in different typeface.

מְנַיִין שֶׁהָיָה (שֶׁהוּא) נִשְׁאַל בִּשְׁמוֹנָה. ר׳ בָּא רִבִּי חִיָּיה בְשֵׁם רִבִּי יוֹחָנָן. וּבִגְדֵי הַקּוֹדֶשׁ אֲשֶׁר לְאַהֲרֹן יִהְיוּ לְבָנָיו אַחֲרָיו. מַה תַלְמוּד לוֹמַר אַחֲרָיו. אֶלָּא לִגְדוּלָּה שֶׁלְּאַחֲרָיו. וּמְנַיִין (מְנַיִין) שֶׁהוּא עוֹבֵד בִּשְׁמוֹנָה. רִבִּי יִרְמְיָה ר׳ אִימִּי בְשֵׁם רִבִּי יוֹחָנָן. וּבִגְדֵי הַקּוֹדֶשׁ אֲשֶׁר לְאַהֲרֹן יִהְיוּ לְבָנָיו. מַה תַלְמוּד לוֹמַר אַחֲרָיו. אֶלָּא לִקְדוּשָּׁה (לִגְדוּלָּה) שֶׁלְּאַחֲרָיו. אָמַר לֵיהּ רִבִּי יוֹנָה. עִמָּךְ הָיִיתִי. לֹא אָמַר עוֹבֵד אֶלָּא נִשְׁאַל. וּבַמֶּה (בַּמֶּה הוּא) נִשְׁאַל. אַייתֵי רַב הוֹשַׁעְיָה מַתְנִיתָא דְבַר קַפָּרָא מִן דָּרוֹמָא (דְּרוֹמָה) וְתַנָּא. וַחֲכָמִים אוֹמְרִים. אֵינוֹ עוֹבֵד לֹא בִשְׁמוֹנָה שֶׁל כֹּהֵן גָּדוֹל וְלֹא בְאַרְבָּעָה שֶׁל כֹּהֵן הֶדְיוֹט.

And from where that he was asked in eight[171]? Rebbi Abba Rebbi Hiyya in the name of Rebbi Johanan: *And Aaron's holy garments shall be for his descendants in his stead*[163]. Why does the verse say, *in his stead*? For greatness after him[172]. And from where that he officiated in eight[173]? Rebbi Jeremiah, Rebbi Immi in the name of Rebbi Johanan: *And Aaron's holy garments shall be for his descendants.* Why does the verse say, *in his stead*? For holiness after him. In what was he asked[174]? Rebbi Jonah said to him[175], I was with you; he did not say "officiated" but "was asked". Rav Hoshaia brought a Mishnah of Bar Qappara from the South which stated: He officiates neither in the four of a common priest nor in the eight of a High Priest.

171 The Anointed for War has two jobs. One is to address the army as described in *Deut.* 20:1-9, the other to ask the Urim and Tummim oracle on behalf of the army commander. Since this oracle is mentioned only in connection with the High Priest's garments (*Ex.* 28:30) it is obvious that the Anointed for War must wear one of these garments for the oracle. But since all eight garments of the High Priest form an indivisible unit, he must wear all of them.

172 *Ex.* 29:30 continues: *To be anointed in them and inducted into office.* Since the one Anointed for War is anointed, he seems to qualify.

173 This seems logical. Since the Anointed for War is required to wear the High Priest's garb, "one increases in sanctity but does not decrease" (cf. Note 151). Otherwise one will have to disqualify the Anointed for War from all office in the Sanctuary.

174 If R. Jeremiah, in opposition to R. Abba bar Hiyya, speaks about officiating, what is his opinion about inquiring from the Urim and Tummim?

175 The name of R. Jonah's interlocutor is not given. It must be another student of R. Jeremiah (R. Yose?) since he points out that the words of his teacher were incorrectly transmitted and that R. Jeremiah's statement was identical with that of R. Abba bar Hiyya, the companion of R. Jeremiah's teacher R. Ze`ira. In the Babli, *Yoma* 73a, the students of R. Johanan already point out that R. Johanan only gave his opinion on interrogation of the oracle, not of officiating.

176 He holds that as a matter of principle, the Anointed for War could use the eight garments of the High Priest strictly for his duties outside the sanctuary and still be a common priest inside without violating the principle of Note 151. The Babli disagrees (*Yoma* 73a) and bases the rule strictly on that principle.

177 In contrast to the Babli, this would be strictly a rabbinic rule, not based on biblical principles, and therefore not a historical reconstruction by a new rule for the days of the Messiah.

178 *Num.* 10:8.

179 His oath formula, cursing himself if his statement should be found false. Babli *Šabbat* 17a.

180 The command to call all the community in the desert by the sound of trumpets (*Num.* 10:3) is extended to use trumpets to introduce the public Torah reading in the Temple at Tabernacles in the Sabbatical Year (*Deut.* 31:10-13).

181 *Num.* 10:10; cf. *Sanhedrin* 3:3 Note 155.

182 A similar text in *Sifry Num.* 75 (a better text *Yalqut* 725).

(47d line 49) וְכִפֶּר הַכֹּהֵן אֲשֶׁר־יִמְשַׁח אוֹתוֹ. מַה תַלְמוּד לוֹמַר. לְפִי שֶׁכָּל־הַפָּרָשָׁה נֶאֶמְרָה בְּאַהֲרֹן. אֵין לִי אֶלָּא מְשׁוּחַ בְּשֶׁמֶן הַמִּשְׁחָה. מְרוּבֶּה בְגָדִים מְנַיִין. תַּלְמוּד לוֹמַר וַאֲשֶׁר יְמַלֵּא אֶת־יָדוֹ. וּמְנַיִין לְרַבּוֹת אַחֵר הַמִּתְמַנֶּה. תַּלְמוּד לוֹמַר וְכִפֶּר הַכֹּהֵן. בַּמֶּה הוּא מִתְמַנֶּה. רַבָּנִין דְּקֵיסָרִין בְּשֵׁם רִבִּי חִייָה בַּר יוֹסֵף. בְּפֶה. אָמַר רִבִּי זְעִירָא. הָדָא אָמְרָה שֶׁמְּמַנִּין זְקֵינִים בַּפֶּה. אָמַר רִבִּי חִייָה בַּר אָדָא. מַתְנִיתָא אָמְרָה כֵן. חֲזוֹר בָּךְ בְּאַרְבָּעָה דְבָרִים שֶׁהָיִיתָ אוֹמֵר וְנַעַשְׂךָ אַב בֵּית דִּין לְיִשְׂרָאֵל.

1 נאמרה |B כולה אמורה **ו** אמורה 2 B**ומ** משוח | אהרן עצמו מניין לרבות כהן אחר ת"ל אשר ימשח אותו אין לו אלא משוח מניין | B מנין 3 ומניין | B ומנין כהן המתמנה | **ו** המתכפר מתמנה | **ו** מתכפר 4 חייה | **ו** חייא זעירא | מתמנה | **ו** המתכפר זוירה זקינים | **מו** זקן 5 חייה | B חייא בך | B - 8 לישראל | **ו** עלך ישראל **מ** -

The priest shall atone who was anointed[183]. Since the entire chapter is said about Aaron, from where [to include another priest? The verse says, *who was anointed*;][184] not only the anointed with the anointing oil; from where the one clothed in multiple garb? The verse says, *who was inducted into office*. And from where another who was appointed[185]? The verse says, *the priest shall atone*[186]. How is he being appointed? The rabbis of Caesarea in the name of Rebbi Ḥiyya bar Joseph, by mouth[187]. Rebbi Ze`ira said, this implies that one may ordain Elders by word of mouth. Rebbi Ḥiyya bar Ada said, a Mishnah says so: "Recant the four things that you are used to say and we shall make you president of the Court for Israel.[188]"

183 *Lev*. 16:32. The problem is the legitimacy of a priest appointed *ad hoc* as High Priest to conduct the service of the Day of Atonement for which common priests are disqualified.

184 From B and the parallels in *Yoma* (**ו**) and *Megillah* (**מ**) (Note 170). The first 30 verses of the Chapter mention Aaron exclusively.

185 In an emergency of the Day of Atonement where no formal session of a court can be held. Even when anointing oils was available, simple investiture ws enough.

186 Since it does not stress "the High Priest", it follows that any priest can be appointed to fill the office.

187 It does not need the laying on of hands nor a document of appointment. (Tosaphot *Yoma* 12b *s, v.* כהן).

188 Mishnah *Idiut* 5:6. The oral promise was irrevocable.

Here end the parallels in *Yoma* and *Megillah*.

(47d line 56) הוּא. לֹא הַמֶּלֶךְ. הוּא. לֹא הַנָּשִׂיא. הוּא. לְרַבּוֹת כֹּהֵן מְשׁוּחַ מִלְחָמָה. אִשָּׁה בִבְתוּלֶיהָ יִקָּח. פְּרָט לְבוֹגֶרֶת שֶׁכָּלוּ בְתוּלֶיהָ. רִבִּי לָעְזָר וְרִבִּי שִׁמְעוֹן מַכְשִׁירִין בְּבוֹגֶרֶת. רִבִּי

יִצְחָק שָׁאַל. אַף בִּשְׁאָר כָּל־הַדְּבָרִים כֵּן. קוֹמֵץ וְאַחֵר מַקְטִיר. וּמְקַבֵּל וְאַחֵר זוֹרֵק. שׂוֹרֵף וְאַחֵר יַזֶּה. רִבִּי יַעֲקֹב בַּר אִידִי בְּשֵׁם רִבִּי יִצְחָק. עָשׂוּ אוֹתָהּ חַטָּאת גְּדוֹלָה שֶׁלֹּא נוֹדְעָה לָרַבִּים. הָדָא אָמְרָה. קוֹמֵץ וְאַחֵר מָקְטִיר. מְקַבֵּל וְאַחֵר זוֹרֵק. שׂוֹרֵף וְאַחֵר יַזֶּה. רִבִּי בֶּרֶכְיָה רִבִּי יַעֲקֹב בַּר אִידִי רִבִּי יִצְחָק שָׁאַל. הָיָה עוֹמֵד וּמַקְרִיב עַל גַּבֵּי הַמִּזְבֵּחַ וְנוֹדַע שֶׁהוּא בֶּן גְּרוּשָׁה אוֹ בֶן חֲלוּצָה. מֵת עֲבַד לָהּ. שֶׁמֵּת וְיַחֲזוֹר הָרוֹצֵחַ לִמְקוֹמוֹ אוֹ יֵעָשֶׂה כְמוֹ שֶׁנִּגְמַר דִּינוֹ בְלֹא כֹהֵן גָּדוֹל. וְאַל יֵצֵא מִשָּׁם לְעוֹלָם.

1 - | הלכה זה וזה שוין בעבודת יום הכיפורים וכו'. המלך | על המלך 2 לעזר | אלעזר 3 ואחר | ואחר כך (3) 4 יזה | מזה בשם | - חטאת | כחטאת גדולה | גזולה הדא | הכא 5 אמרה | אמרינן ואחר | אחר כך (3X) יזה | מזה ר' יעקב | ור' יעקב 6 מת | מה את שמת | כמי שמת 7 ויחזור | ומחזי'

[**Halakhah**: "Both are equal in the office of the day of Atonement," etc.][189] [190]*He*, not the king. *He*, not the chieftain[191]. *He*, to include the priest Anointed for War[192]. *A woman in her virginity he shall marry*; this excludes an adult whose hymen has atrophied. Rebbi Eleazar and Rebbi Simeon qualify the adult[193].

[194]Rebbi Isaac asked, are these things so in all other things? He takes the fist full and the other burns it; he receives and the other throws, he burns and the other sprinkles? Rebbi Jacob bar Idi in the name of Rebbi Isaac: They made it like a (great) [robbed][195] purification sacrifice which was not publicly known. This implies that he takes the fistful and the other burns it, he receives and the other throws, he burns and the other sprinkles.

[196]Rebbi Berekhiah, Rebbi Jacob bar Idi: Rebbi Isaac asked. If he was standing sacrificing on the altar when it became known that he was the son of a divorcee or the son of a woman having received *ḥaliṣah*, how do you treat him? [As if][197] he had died and the homicide might return to his home town or should he be treated as one whose trial had been concluded without a High Priest and he never can leave from there?

189 The beginning of the discussion of Mishnah 5 is noted only in B.

190 *Sifra Emor Parašah* 2(7), on *Lev*. 21:13. Since the High Priest was mentioned in the preceding verses, the pronoun is unnecessary by the rules of grammar. It is added for emphasis; only the High Priest is restricted to marrying a virgin.

191 Since the king was mentioned separately, נָשִׂיא here cannot be identified as the king; it must be a tribal chieftain.

192 Since the rules of the High Priest were tied in *Lev*. 21:10 to wearing the High Priest's garments and the Anointed for War is required to wear these when asking the oracle, he is bound by all rules enumerated in vv. 10-15.

193 *Lev.* 21:14. The parallels in the Babli, *Yebamot* 59a, *Ketubot* 97b, identify the first opinion as R. Meïr's. It is agreed that if a girl is fully grown, the breaking of her hymen may not be noticed by the man.

194 The interpretation of this paragraph depends on whether one considers the texts of L and B as two different texts or that the correct text is that of B, except for the name tradition identical with *Terumot* 8:2, Notes 29-31, with the text of L badly corrupted. Since in the characterization of the sacrifice, the text of L is certainly corrupt, the second alternative has much to commend itself. In the text itself, the crucial point is whether to read אחר as אַחֵר "another" or אַחַר "after". Since the text of L, but not that of B, refers to the High Priest, in the absence of a clear solution both texts are presented and explained.

In the text of L one refers to the statement in the Mishnah that an acting High Priest and a deposed one are equal in all but the service of the Day of Atonement. The question is whether the acting High Priest may take the required fist full of incense and the deposed one then may bring the incense to the inner altar and burn it there; or the acting High Priest receive the blood of his sacrifices and the deposed one sprinkle of the blood on the walls of the altar. The question is not asked anywhere else and the positive answer is difficult to accept. Therefore, it is better to accept the text of B, even though it does not refer to the High Priest, as necessary introduction to the following paragraph which does.

That text reads:

Rebbi Isaac asked, does this apply to the remaining actions? He took the fist full and afterwards burned it; he received and afterwards threw it, he burned and afterwards sprinkled? Rebbi Jacob bar Idi in the name of Rebbi Isaac: They made it like a robbed purification sacrifice which was not publicly known. This implies that if he took the fistful afterwards he burns it, if he received [the blood] afterwards he throws [it on the walls of the altar], he burned [the red cow] he afterwards sprinkles [water with its ashes to purify others].

As explained in *Terumot*, the question is asked about a Cohen who is informed that he is disbarred from the priesthood because of his birth from a woman forbidden to priests when he had completed one sacral action which by necessity must be followed by a different one. The answer is that the desecrated son of a Cohen who innocently started officiating may officiate to the end even though in the future he will be barred from officiating.

196 The reference is to Mishnah *Gittin* 5:5, as explained in *Terumot*. The text of L is in parentheses, the correct text in brackets is from B. The point of the

argument is missing here in both texts, that the purification offering is acceptable (i., e., that the Temple authorities are prohibited from inquiring into the way the offerer acquired his animal.)

197 *Terumot* 8:2, Notes 32-33,40. If the High Priest after his elevation was found to be desecrated by his birth and thereby is removed, is this considered to be his death as far as the Sanctuary is concerned and releases any homicide sentenced during his tenure of office from the city of refuge or is his tenure as High Priest erased from the annals of the Sanctuary (*Makkot* 2:10-11)? No answer is given here; the first eventuality is chosen in *Terumot*.

(fol. 47a) **משנה ו**: כֹּהֵן גָּדוֹל פּוֹרֵם מִלְּמַטָּן וְהַהֶדְיוֹט מִלְמַעְלָן. כֹּהֵן גָּדוֹל מַקְרִיב אוֹנֵן וְלֹא אוֹכֵל וְהַהֶדְיוֹט לֹא מַקְרִיב וְלֹא אוֹכֵל:

Mishnah 6: The High Priest rends his garment below, the common priest above[198]. The High Priest sacrifices while in deep mourning but does not eat; the common priest neither sacrifices nor eats[199].

198 Rending one's garment is a required mourning rite for a close relative (as defined in *Lev.* 21:2-3). The High Priest is forbidden any mourning rites, including rending his garment (Mishnah 5). One allows him to make a tear at the bottom of his robe where nobody will notice it.

199 "Deep mourning" is the time between the death of a close relative and his burial (on the same day or the following night). Since the High Priest is forbidden to leave the Sanctuary (*Lev.* 21:12) he must be permitted to officiate. But eating *sancta* while in deep mourning is forbidden to everybody (*Deut.* 26:14), including the High Priest (*Lev.* 10:19-20). The common priest is required to defile himself for the burial of a close relative (*Lev.* 21:1-2); automatically he is excluded from the Sanctuary and all its service.

(47d line 66) **הלכה ו**: כֹּהֵן גָּדוֹל פּוֹרֵם מִלְּמַטָּן כול'. רִבִּי לָעְזָר בְּשֵׁם כַּהֲנָא. לְמַעְלָן. לְמַעְלָן מִקָּנֶה שָׂפָה. לְמַטָּן. לְמַטָּן מִקָּנֶה שָׂפָה. רִבִּי יוֹחָנָן אָמַר. לְמַטָּן מַמָּשׁ. רִבִּי יוֹחָנָן סְלִיק לִמְבַקְּרָה לְרִבִּי חֲנִינָה. כַּד הֲוָה גַּו אִיסְטְרָטָה שְׁמַע דִּדְמָךְ. שְׁלַח וְאַייתִי מָנוֹי טַבְיָיא דְשׁוּבְתָא וּבְזָעָן. רִבִּי יוֹחָנָן פְּלִיג עַל דְּרִבִּי יְהוּדָה תַּרְתֵּין. וְאַתְיָיא רִבִּי לָעְזָר בְּשֵׁם כַּהֲנָא כְּרִבִּי יוּדָה. אִין כְּרִבִּי יוּדָה לֹא יִפְרוֹם כָּל־עִיקָּר. לָא אַתְיָיא דָא אֶלָּא עַל אָבִיו וְעַל אִמּוֹ כְּדִבְרֵי רִבִּי מֵאִיר. דְּתַנֵּי. עַל כָּל־הַמֵּתִים אֵינוֹ מַבְדִּיל קָנֶה שָׂפָה אֶלָּא עַל אָבִיו וְעַל אִמּוֹ. כְּדִבְרֵי רִבִּי מֵאִיר. רִבִּי יוּדָה אוֹמֵר. כָּל־קֶרַע שֶׁאֵינוֹ מַבְדִּיל קָנֶה שָׂפָה הֲרֵי זֶה קֶרַע שֶׁלְּתִפְלוּת. מַאי כְדוֹן. אוֹמֵר הוּא בְכֹהֵן גָּדוֹל שֶׁיְּהֵא מַבְדִּיל קָנֶה שָׂפָה.

1 לעזר | אליעזר למעלן למעלן מקנה שפה | למעלה למעלה מקמי שפה[201] 2 למטן למטן מקני שפה | למטה למטה מקמי שפה למטן | למטה למטה סליק | סלק 3 כד הוה | - איסטרטא | אוסטירטא דשובתא | דשבתא The remainder of the Halakhah is missing.

[200]Rebbi Eleazar in the name of Cahana: On top, high starting with the seam, below, low starting with the seam. Rebbi Johanan said, really low. Rebbi Johanan was going up to visit Rebbi Ḥanina; on the road he heard that he had died. He sent, brought his good Sabbath garment, and tore it. Rebbi Johanan disagrees with Rebbi Jehudah in two things, but Rebbi Eleazar in the name of Cahana follows Rebbi Jehudah. If following Rebbi Jehudah, he should not tear at all! This refers only to his father or mother, following Rebbi Meïr, as it was stated: One tears the seam for nobody who died except for father and mother, the words of Rebbi Meïr. Rebbi Jehudah says, any tear which does not completely sever the seam is a frivolous tear. How is that? It is said[202] for the High Priest that he shall sever the seam completely.

200 The entire Halakhah is from *Sanhedrin* 3:1, Notes 33-56.

201 Cf. Sanhedrin 3:1, Note 34.

202 This is a simple copyist's error for חוֹמֶר "a stringency".

(47d line 75) כֹּהֵן גָּדוֹל מַקְרִיב אוֹנֵן וְלֹא אוֹכֵל. דִּבְרֵי רִבִּי מֵאִיר. רִבִּי יוּדָה אוֹמֵר. כָּל־אוֹתוֹ הַיּוֹם. רִבִּי שִׁמְעוֹן אוֹמֵר. גּוֹמֵר כָּל־הָעֲבוֹדָה שֶׁבְּיָדוֹ וּבָא לוֹ. בֵּין רִבִּי מֵאִיר לְרִבִּי שִׁמְעוֹן חָדָא בֵּין רִבִּי יוּדָה לְרִבִּי שִׁמְעוֹן חָדָא. בֵּין רִבִּי מֵאִיר לְרִבִּי יוּדָה הַכְנָסָה. רִבִּי יַעֲקֹב בַּר דּוֹסַיי. מְפַסֵּק בֵּינֵיהוֹן. רִבִּי מֵאִיר אוֹמֵר. הָיָה בִפְנִים הָיָה יוֹצֵא. הָיָה בַחוּץ לֹא הָיָה נִכְנָס. רִבִּי יוּדָה אוֹמֵר. הָיָה בִפְנִים הָיָה יֹצֵא. הָיָה בַחוּץ לֹא הָיָה נִכְנָס. רִבִּי שִׁמְעוֹן אוֹמֵר. גּוֹמֵר כָּל־הָעֲבוֹדָה שֶׁבְּיָדוֹ וּבָא לוֹ. רִבִּי יוֹסֵי בֵּירִבִּי בּוּן בְּשֵׁם רַב חוּנָא. מַתְנִיתָא דְּרִבִּי שִׁמְעוֹן. וּמִן הַמִּקְדָּשׁ לֹא יֵצֵא. עִמָּהֶן אֵינוֹ יֵצֵא. יוֹצֵא הוּא אַחֲרֵיהֶן. אֶלָּא הֵן נִכְנָסִין וְהוּא יוֹצֵא. הֵן ניכְסִין וְהוּא נִגְלֶה וְיוֹצֵא אַחֲרֵיהֶן עַד פֶּתַח הָעִיר. דִּבְרֵי רַבִּי מֵאִיר. רַבִּי יוּדָה אוֹמֵר. אֵינוֹ יוֹצֵא מִן הַמִּקְדָּשׁ. כְּתִיב וּמִן הַמִּקְדָּשׁ לֹא יֵצֵא. לָמֵד אֶלָּא לֹא יֵצֵא. יָצָא לֹא הָיָה חוֹזֵר.

"The High Priest sacrifices while in deep sorrow but does not eat, the words of Rebbi Meïr; Rebbi Jehudah says, the entire day. Rebbi Simeon says, he completely finishes the service he is engaged in and then leaves." Between Rebbi Meïr and Rebbi Simeon there is one [difference], between Rebbi Jehudah and Rebbi Simeon there is one [difference]. Between Rebbi Meïr and Rebbi Jehudah is entering. Rebbi Jacob ben Dositheos: interruption is between them. Rebbi Meïr says, if he was inside, he leaves; if he was outside, he does not enter. Rebbi Jehudah says, if he was inside, he (leaves); if he was outside, he does not enter. Rebbi Simeon says, he completely finishes the service he is engaged in and then leaves. Rebbi Yose ben Rebbi Abun in the name of Rav Huna: a *baraita* is from Rebbi Simeon: "*The Sanctuary he shall not leave,* he may not leave with them, but he may leave after them. (But they enter and he leaves). If they are unseen he can be seen; he leaves with them up to the city gate, the words of Rebbi Meïr; Rebbi Jehudah said, he does not leave the Temple since it is said: *The Sanctuary he shall not leave*. If he left, he may not return."

(48a line 11) רִבִּי אַבָּהוּ בְשֵׁם רִבִּי לָעְזָר. אֵין אֲנִינָה אֶלָּא לְמֵת בִּלְבַד. דִּכְתִיב וְאָנוּ וְאָבְלוּ פְּתָחֶיהָ. הָתִיב רִבִּי חִייָה בַּר אָדָא. וְהֶכְתִיב וְאָנוּ הַדַּייָגִים וְאָבְלוּ כָּל־מַשְׁלִיכֵי בַיְאוֹר חַכָּה. אָמַר רִבִּי חֲנִינָה. מַתְנִיתָא אֵין אֲנִינָה טֻמְאָה אֶלָּא לְמֵת בִּלְבַד. אֵי זוֹ הִיא אֲנִינָה. מִשְּׁעַת מִיתָה וְעַד שְׁעַת קְבוּרָה. דִּבְרֵי רִבִּי. וַחֲכָמִים אוֹמְרִים. כָּל־אוֹתוֹ הַיּוֹם. אַשְׁכָּחַת אָמַר קוּלּוֹת וְחוּמְרוֹת עַל דְּרִבִּי. קוּלּוֹת וְחוּמְרוֹת עַל דְּרַבָּנִן. מַה מַפְקָה מִבֵּינֵיהוֹן. מֵת וְנִקְבַּר בְּשַׁעְתּוֹ. עַל דַּעְתְּהוֹן דְּרַבָּנִן אָסוּר כָּל־אוֹתוֹ הַיּוֹם. עַל דַּעְתֵּיהּ דְּרִבִּי אֵינוֹ אָסוּר אֶלָּא אוֹתָהּ הַשָּׁעָה בִּלְבַד. מֵת וְנִקְבַּר לְאַחַר שְׁלֹשָׁה יָמִים. עַל דַּעְתְּהוֹן דְּרַבָּנִן אָסוּר כָּל־אוֹתוֹ הַיּוֹם. עַל דַּעְתֵּיהּ דְּרִבִּי אָסוּר עַד ג' יָמִים. אֲתָא רִבִּי אַבָּהוּ בְשֵׁם רִבִּי יוֹחָנָן רַב חִסְדָּא תְּרֵיהוֹן אָמְרִין. מוֹדֶה רִבִּי לַחֲכָמִים שֶׁאֵין אָסוּר אֶלָּא אוֹתוֹ הַיּוֹם בִּלְבַד. כְּהָדָא דְתַנֵּי. רִבִּי אוֹמֵר. תֵּדַע לָךְ שֶׁאֵין אֲנִינוּת לַיְלָה תוֹרָה. שֶׁהֲרֵי אָמְרוּ. אוֹנֵן טוֹבֵל וְאוֹכֵל פִּסְחוֹ לָעֶרֶב. וַהֲרֵי אָמְרוּ. אֲנִינַת יוֹם תּוֹרָה. רִבִּי יוֹסֵי בֵּירִבִּי בּוּן בְּשֵׁם רַב הוּנָא. תִּיפְתָּר שֶׁנִּקְבַּר בְּדִמְדוּמֵי חַמָּה. וְלֵית שְׁמַע מִינָּהּ כְּלוּם.

Rebbi Abbahu in the name of Rebbi Eleazar: "Deep sorrow" is only for the dead, for it is written: *Its gates are in deep sorrow and mourning.* Rebbi Ḥiyya bar Ada objected: Is it not written[51]: *the fishermen are in deep sorrow, mourning are all who throw a fish-hook into the Nile*? Rebbi Ḥanina said, so is the *baraita*: there is no deep sorrow in impurity except for the dead. It was stated: "What is deep sorrow? From the moment of death until the moment of burial, the word of Rebbi. Bur the Sages say, the entire day." It turns out that one describes leniencies and stringencies following Rebbi, leniencies and stringencies following the rabbis. What is the difference between them? If someone died and was buried within the hour. Following the rabbis, he is forbidden the entire day; following Rebbi he is forbidden only that hour. If the person died and was buried after three days. Following the rabbis, he is forbidden the entire day; following Rebbi he is forbidden up to three days. There came Rebbi Abbahu in the name of Rebbi Johanan, and Rav Ḥisda, both of whom said that Rebbi agrees with the Sages that he is forbidden only during the first day, as it was stated: Rebbi said, you know that deep mourning in the night is not biblical, since they said, "the deep mourner immerses himself and eats his Passover sacrifice in the evening." But they said, deep mourning during daytime is biblical. Rebbi Yose ben Rebbi Abun in the name of Rebbi Huna: Explain it that the person was buried close to sundown and one cannot infer anything.

(fol. 47a) **משנה ז׃** כָּל הַתָּדִיר מֵחֲבֵירוֹ קוֹדֵם אֶת חֲבֵירוֹ. וְכָל הַמְקוּדָּשׁ מֵחֲבֵירוֹ קוֹדֵם אֶת חֲבֵירוֹ. פַּר הַמָּשִׁיחַ וּפַר הָעֵדָה עוֹמְדִין פַּר הַמָּשִׁיחַ קוֹדֵם לְפַר הָעֵדָה בְּכָל מַעֲשָׂיו׃

Mishnah 7: Anything which is more frequent than another precedes the other[203]. Anything more holy than another precedes the other[204]. If the bull of the Anointed and the bull of the community are standing, the Anointed's bull precedes the community's bull in all its ceremonies[205].

משנה ח׃ הָאִישׁ קוֹדֵם לָאִשָּׁה לְהַחֲיוֹת וּלְהָשִׁיב אֲבֵדָה וְהָאִשָּׁה קוֹדֶמֶת לָאִישׁ לִכְסוּת וּלְהוֹצִיאָהּ מִבֵּית הַשֶּׁבִי. בִּזְמַן שֶׁשְּׁנֵיהֶם עוֹמְדִים לְקַלְקָלָה הָאִישׁ קוֹדֵם לָאִשָּׁה׃

Mishnah 8: The man precedes the woman to be kept alive[206] and to regain his lost property[207]. But the woman precedes the man for clothing[208] and to be freed from captivity[209]. At a time when both are used for immorality[210], the man precedes the woman.

משנה ט׃ כֹּהֵן קוֹדֵם לְלֵוִי לֵוִי לְיִשְׂרָאֵל יִשְׂרָאֵל לְמַמְזֵר וּמַמְזֵר לְנָתִין וְנָתִין לְגֵר וְגֵר לְעֶבֶד מְשׁוּחְרָר. אֵימָתַי בִּזְמַן שֶׁכּוּלָּן שָׁוִין. אֲבָל אִם הָיָה מַמְזֵר תַּלְמִיד חָכָם וְכֹהֵן גָּדוֹל עַם הָאָרֶץ מַמְזֵר תַּלְמִיד חָכָם קוֹדֵם לְכֹהֵן גָּדוֹל עַם הָאָרֶץ׃

Mishnah 9: A priest precedes a Levite, a Levite an Israel, an Israel a bastard, a bastard a Gibeonite[211], a Gibeonite a proselyte[212], a proselyte a manumitted slave. When? If they are all equal[213]. But if the bastard was learned and the High Priest ignorant, the learned bastard precedes[214] the ignorant High Priest.

203 Anything which is done more frequently is executed before anything less frequent is done. The statement of the Mishnah is repeated in *Zebahim* 10:1, where the implications for the Temple service are detailed. For example, if New Year's Day falls on a Sabbath, the first sacrifices are the daily offerings (offered 365 days a year), followed by the Sabbath sacrifice (52 times), then the New Moon sacrifice (12 times), and last the New Year's Day sacrifice (1). Synagogue practice imitates this rule.

204 For example, if a person brings animals for a purification sacrifice, an elevation sacrifice, and a well-being sacrifice to the Temple, they have to be offered in this order (Mishnah *Zebahim* 10:2).

205 The rules for the Court's (the community's) purification sacrifice (*Lev.* 4:13-21) are dependent on the Anointed's sacrifice (*Lev.* 4:1-12). If they are offered simultaneously then the Anointed's has precedence.

206 This usually is interpreted to mean that if a man and a woman are simultaneously in mortal danger, the man has to be saved first. But it also could mean that if a man and a woman are looking for a livelihood, the man has to be considered first.

207 Cf. Mishnah *Bava Mesia`* 2:13.

208 A poor man will not be hurt by appearing in rags. A woman cannot possibly be seen in rags.

209 A woman is more likely to be raped in captivity than a man.

210 If they are forced into prostitution, the man is in addition forced into homosexuality.

211 The bastard has (in general) genuinely Jewish parents; the Gibeonites became Jewish by deceit.

212 The Gibeonite's parents were Jewish, the proselyte's not.

213 In religious learning.

214 In honor due to him.

(48a line 25) **הלכה ז:** כָּל הַתָּדִיר מֵחֲבֵירוֹ כול׳. לְפִי שֶׁזֶּה מְכַפֵּר וְזֶה מִכַּפֵּר. מוּטָּב שֶׁיִּקְדּוֹם הַמְכַפֵּר לַמִּתְכַּפֵּר. כְּמָה דִכְתִיב וְכִפֶּר בַּעֲדוֹ וּבְעַד בֵּיתוֹ וּבְעַד כָּל־קְהַל יִשְׂרָאֵל׃ נִדְבַת מָשִׁיחַ וְנִדְבַת נָשִׂיא. נִדְבַת מָשִׁיחַ קוֹדֶמֶת. נִדְבַת צִיבּוּר וְנִדְבַת נָשִׂיא. נִדְבַת נָשִׂיא. קוֹדֶמֶת. נִדְבַת מָשִׁיחַ וְנִדְבַת צִיבּוּר מִי קוֹדֵם. נִישְׁמְעִינָהּ מִן הָדָא. נִדְבַת מָשִׁיחַ וּשְׂעִירֵי עֲבוֹדָה זָרָה עוֹמְדִין. שְׂעִירֵי עֲבוֹדָה זָרָה קוֹדְמִין מִפְּנֵי שֶׁדָּמָן נִכְנַס לִפְנִים. לֹא מַר אֶלָּא שֶׁדָּמָן נִכְנַס לִפְנִים. הָדָא אָמְרָה. נִדְבַת מָשִׁיחַ וְנִדְבַת צִיבּוּר נִדְבַת מָשִׁיחַ קוֹדֶמֶת. הָיָה שָׁם פַּר עֲבוֹדָה זָרָה וְשָׂעִיר הַבָּא עִמּוֹ וְחַטָּאת אַחֶרֶת. פָּר קוֹדֵם לְשָׂעִיר. וְשָׂעִיר קוֹדֵם לַחַטָּאת אַחֶרֶת. וְחַטָּאת אַחֶרֶת קוֹדֶמֶת לַפָּר. הֵיךְ עֲבִידָה. אָמַר רִבִּי יוֹסֵי. מִכֵּיוָן שֶׁהַשָּׂעִיר מְחוּסָּר זְמַן לַפָּר כְּמִי שֶׁקְּדָמוֹ פָּר. וְחַטָּאת אַחֶרֶת קוֹדֶמֶת לַפָּר. פַּר שֶׁלַּעֲבוֹדָה זָרָה קוֹדֵם לַשָּׂעִיר הַבָּא עִמּוֹ מִפְּנֵי שֶׁקְּדָמוֹ בַּמִּקְרָא. רִבִּי שְׁמוּאֵל אֲחוֹי דְרִבִּי בֶּרֶכְיָה בָּעֵי. מֵעַתָּה שֶׁלְּרֹאשׁ חוֹדֶשׁ יִקְדּוֹם לְשָׂעִיר הַבָּא עִמּוֹ מִפְּנֵי שֶׁקְּדָמוֹ. אָמַר רִבִּי בָּא מָרִי. לֵית יְכִיל. חַטָּאת דִּידֵיהּ חָסֵר. עַל־עֹלַת הַתָּמִיד יֵעָשֶׂה וְנִסְכּוֹ׃ סְמָכוֹ לְעוֹלַת הַתָּמִיד. קָרְבַּן אִישׁ וְקָרְבַּן אִשָּׁה. קָרְבַּן אִישׁ קוֹדֵם. הָדָא דְתֵימַר בְּשֶׁהָיוּ שְׁנֵיהֶן שָׁוִין. אֲבָל אִם

הָיָה זֶה פָר וְזֶה גְדִי כָּהִיא דָּמַר רִבִּי פִינְחָס בְּשֵׁם רִבִּי הוֹשַׁעְיָה. עֶבֶד מֵבִיא פָּר וְרַבּוֹ מֵבִיא פָּר. עֶבֶד קוֹדֵם לְרַבּוֹ. דְּתַנִּינָן תַּמָּן. פַּר מָשִׁיחַ וּפַר עֵדָה עוֹמְדִים. פַּר מָשִׁיחַ קוֹדֵם לְפַר עֵדָה לְכָל מַעֲשָׂיו:

1 לפי | פר המשיח ופר העדה עומדים פר המשיח קודם לפר העדה בכל מעשיו לפי שזה מכפר וזה מכפר | שהדי' מכפר ודין מתכפר 3 קודמת | קודמת לנדבת נשיא נדבת ציבור ונדבת נשיא | נדבת נשיא ונדבת צבור 4 קודם | קודמת נדבת | פר עומדין | עומדים 5 מר | אמרו 6 ע"ז | של ע"ז 7 פר | הפר ושעיר | והשעיר 8 עבידה | עבידא 10 יקדום | יקדים שקדמו | שקדמו במקרא 11 אמ' ר' בא מרי | אמר ר' שמואל אמר ר' אבא מרי יכיל | את יכיל חטאת דידיה חסר | דחטאת דידה אחיר 12 שניהן | שניהם 13 כהיא | הדא היא ר' | - 14 עבד | העבד תמן | - עדה עומדים. פר משיח קודם לפר עדה לכל מעשיו | וכו'

Halakhah 7: "Anything which is more frequent than another," etc. ["If the bull of the Anointed and the bull of the community are standing, the Anointed's bull precedes the community's bull",][215] for one is atoning, the other is being atoned for[216]. It is preferable that the atoner precede the atoned for, as it is written, *he shall atone for himself, and for his house, and for all the congregation of Israel*[217].

Between a voluntary gift of the Anointed and a voluntary gift of the prince, the voluntary gift of the Anointed has precedence[218]. Between a voluntary gift of the community and a voluntary gift of the prince, the voluntary gift of the prince has precedence[219]. Between a voluntary gift of the Anointed and a voluntary gift of the community, which one has precedence? Let us hear from the following: A voluntary gift of the Anointed and rams of idolatry[220] were standing. The rams of idolatry have precedence since their blood enters inside[221]. He only said "since their blood enters inside;" this implies that between a voluntary gift of the Anointed and a voluntary gift of the community, the voluntary gift of the Anointed has precedence.

If there were standing the bull of idolatry, the ram which accompanies it, and another purification sacrifice. The bull precedes the ram[222], the ram precedes the other purification sacrifice, and the other purification sacrifice precedes the bull[223]. How is this done? Rebbi Yose said, since the ram is dependent in time on the bull, it is as if the bull preceded it, and the other purification sacrifice precedes the bull. The bull of idolatry precedes the ram because it precedes in Scripture[224]. Rebbi Samuel the brother of Rebbi Berekhiah asked: But then that of the New Moon should precede the ram which comes with it because it precedes [in Scripture.[225]][226] Rebbi Abba Mari said, you cannot do this; its *purification sacrifice* is defective[227]: *After the permanent elevation offering it shall be made, with its libation*; it made it lean on the permanent elevation offering.

Between the sacrifice of a man and the sacrifice of a woman, the man's sacrifice has precedence[228]. That is, if both were equal. But if one was a bull and the other a lamb, it is what Rebbi Phineas said in the name of Rebbi Hoshaia: A slave brings a bull and his master brings a bull, the slave's precedes the master's, as we have stated there: "If the bull of the Anointed and the bull of the community are standing, the Anointed's bull precedes the community's bull in all its ceremonies.[229]"

215 From B; a necessary introduction to the following text.

216 This also is the reason given in the Babli (13a) for the precedence of a purification offering over a simultaneously presented elevation offering, both being most holy sacrifices.

217 *Lev.* 16:17. The argument really refers to the service of the Day of Atonement in its entirety, where the High Priest performs three acts of atonement, the first for himself and his family, the second for himself and the priests, and then the third for himself, the priests, and all of Israel. The priest performing the rite of atonement has to be purified himself before being able to serve others. (Tosephta *Horaiot* 2:4, *Zevahim* 10:1).

218 Again because the priest has to act to present the king's gift.

219 Since he is the representative of the community.

220 Cf. Chapter 1, Notes 122,135. For the number of rams, cf. Mishnah 1:6.

221 While this is not indicated elsewhere, if the bull is identified as the bull prescribed in *Lev.* 4, the ram is attached to a sacrifice whose blood is brought inside the Sanctuary and which, therefore, has precedence as the more holy sacrifice.

222 As will be explained later in this paragraph.

223 The bull of idolatry is defined as an elevation sacrifice which takes second place after a purification sacrifice (Note 216). The rules lead to an infinite loop.

224 The bull is prescribed in the first half of *Num.* 15:24, the ram in the second half.

225 The sacrifices for the Day of the New Moon are prescribed in *Num.* 28:11 (elevation sacrifices) and 28:15 (the purification sacrifice). This contradicts our rule from Note 216.

226 Added from B, not absolutely necessary.

227 The argument is very elliptic. The ram of idolatry follows the bull not really because it is mentioned later in the verse, but mainly because it is spelled defective, not as חטאת but only as חטת (Babli 13a, *Zevaḥim* 90b). But the purification offering of the special days is directly connected with the daily offerings which start the day in the sanctuary (*Num.*

28:15.)

228 If both are voluntary offerings of equal value. But an obligatory offering always has precedence over a voluntary one (*Tosephta* Zevahim 10:4).

229 The argument is a *non sequitur*. Some commentators want to emend the text, in that the slave brings a bull but his master a goat. While this connects to the preceding, it severs the connection to the statement of R. Phineas. As a matter of principle, an emendation is totally inadmissible since the text is confirmed not only by the two independent sources here but also by *Lev. rabba* 5(4) where the case of slave and master both bringing a bull follows a story about the merit of contributing to the support of scholars. As the text is presented here, one wonders why the following stories are placed here and what connection they could have with the topic of the Mishnah. But *Lev. rabba*, an old text, shows that the case of slave and master is not a legal but a homiletic statement. There the argument is that the High Priest is the servant of the people; the Sanctuary is run only on behalf of the people. After the destruction of the Temple, the rabbinic establishment became the servant of the people, looking after their needs. Therefore, the rules of preference should be transferred from Temple service to the rabbinic establishment.

(48a line 44) מַעֲשֶׂה בְּירִבִּי אֱלִיעֶזֶר וְרִבִּי יְהוֹשֻׁעַ וְרִבִּי עֲקִיבָה שֶׁעָלוּ לְחוּלַת אַנְטוֹכִיָּא עַל עֵסֶק מִגְבַּת חֲכָמִים. וַהֲוָה תַמָּן חַד אַבָּא יְהוּדָה עֲבִיד מִצְוָה בְעַיִן טוֹבָה. פַּעַם אַחַת יָרַד מִנְּכָסָיו וְרָאָה רַבּוֹתֵינוּ וְנִתְיָיאַשׁ מֵהֶן. עָלָה לוֹ לְבֵיתוֹ וּפָנָיו חוֹלָנִיּוֹת. אָמְרָה לוֹ אִשְׁתּוֹ. מִפְּנֵי מַה פָּנֶיךָ חוֹלָנִיּוֹת. אָמַר לָהּ. רַבּוֹתֵינוּ כָאן וְאֵינִי יוֹדֵעַ מָה אֶעֱשֶׂה. אִשְׁתּוֹ שֶׁהָיְתָה צַדֶּקֶת מִמֶּנּוּ אָמְרָה לוֹ. נִשְׁתַּיְּירָה לָךְ שָׂדֶה אַחַת. לֵךְ וּמְכוֹר חֶצְיָהּ וְתֵן לָהֶן. הָלַךְ וְעָשָׂה כֵן. וּבָא לוֹ אֶצֶל רַבּוֹתֵינוּ וְנָתַן לָהֶן. וְנִתְפַּלְּלוּ עָלָיו רַבּוֹתֵינוּ. אָמְרוּ לוֹ. אַבָּא יְהוּדָה. הַקָּדוֹשׁ בָּרוּךְ הוּא יְמַלֵּא חֶסְרוֹנוֹתֶיךָ. עִם כְּשֶׁהָלְכוּ לָהֶם יָרַד לַחֲרוֹשׁ בְּתוֹךְ חֲצִי שָׂדֵהוּ. עִם כְּשֶׁהוּא חוֹרֵשׁ בְּתוֹךְ חֲצִי שָׂדֵהוּ שָׁקְעָה פָּרָתוֹ וְנִשְׁבְּרָה. יָרַד לְהַעֲלוֹתָהּ וְהֵאִיר הַקָּדוֹשׁ בָּרוּךְ הוּא עֵינָיו וּמָצָא סִימָא. אָמַר. לְטוֹבָתִי נִשְׁתַּבְּרָה רֶגֶל פָּרָתִי. וּבַהֲדוֹרַת רַבּוֹתֵינוּ שָׁאֲלוּן עָלוֹי. אָמְרִין. מָה אַבָּא יְהוּדָה עֲבִיד. אָמְרִין. מָאן יְכִיל חָמֵי אַפּוֹי דְּאַבָּא יְהוּדָה. אַבָּא יְהוּדָה דְתוֹרוֹי אַבָּא יְהוּדָה דִגְמָלוֹי אַבָּא יְהוּדָה דַחֲמוֹרוֹי. חָזַר אַבָּא יְהוּדָה לִכְמוֹת שֶׁהָיָה וּבָא אֶצֶל רַבּוֹתֵינוּ וְשָׁאַל בִּשְׁלוֹמָן. אָמְרִין לֵיהּ. אַבָּא יְהוּדָה עֲבִיד. אָמַר לָהֶן. עָשְׂתָה תְפִילַּתְכֶם פֵּירוֹת וּפֵירֵי פֵירוֹת. אָמְרוּ לוֹ. אַף עַל פִּי שֶׁנָּתְנוּ אֲחֵרִים יוֹתֵר מִמְּךָ בָּרִאשׁוֹנָה אוֹתְךָ כָתַבְנוּ רֹאשׁ טִימוּס. נְטָלוּהוּ וְהוֹשִׁיבוּהוּ אֶצְלָם וְקָרְאוּ עָלָיו הַפָּסוּק הַזֶּה מַתָּ֣ן אָ֭דָם יַרְחִ֣יב ל֑וֹ וְלִפְנֵ֖י גְדֹלִ֣ים יַנְחֶֽנּוּ׃

1 ביר' | בר' עקיבה | עקיבא 2 יהודה | יודן עביד | עבד וראה | וראה את 3 מהן | מהם 4 נשתיירה | נשתייר 5 לך | - להן | להם ועשה כן. ובא אצל רבותינו | הלך ומכר חציה להן | להם 6 עליו רבותינו. אמרו לו | ואמרו יהודה | יודן 7 חצי | - פרתו | רגל פרתו 8 לטובתי | לטובתו 9 פרתי | פרתו 9 ובהדורת | ובחזירת יהודה עביד | יודן עבד מאן | מי 10 יהודה | יודן (4X) 11 ובא | בא יהודה עביד | יודן עבד 13 עליו הפסוק | את המקרא

[230]It happened that Rebbi Eliezer, Rebbi Joshua, and Rebbi Aqiba went to the dunes of Antiochia on the occasion of fundraising for the rabbis[231]. There was there a certain Abba Jehudah who gave alms generously. Once he lost his property, he saw our teachers and gave up hope about them. He went home looking sickly. His wife asked him, why are you looking sickly? He told her, our teachers are here and I do not know what I could do. His wife, who was even more pious than he, told him: You have a field left; go, sell half of it, and give to them. He went and did so, came to our teachers and gave them. Our teachers prayed for him and said to him, Abba Jehudah, the Holy One, praise to Him, may fill your want. After they left, he went to plough his half of the field. When he was ploughing in his half of the field, his cow sank down and broke [its leg][232]. He went to lift her up when the Holy One, praise to Him, enlightened his eyes and he found a treasure. He said, my cow's leg broke for my benefit. When our teachers returned, they inquired about him. They asked, how is Abba Jehudah doing? They answered, who can appear before Abba Jehudah? Abba Jehudah of his cattle, Abba Jehudah of his camels, Abba Jehudah of his donkeys! Abba Jehudah had returned to his former self; he came to our teachers to greet them. They asked him, how is Abba Jehudah doing? He told them, your prayer brought result and compound results. They told him, even though others had given more than you the last time, we wrote you on top of the honor list[233]. They took him, made him sit with them, and recited for him this verse[234]: *The gifts of a man put him at ease; in front of great ones they will make him rest.*

רִבִּי חִיָּה בַּר בָּא עֲבִיד פְּסִיקָא בָּהֵין בֵּית מִדְרָשָׁא דְטִיבֵּרְיָא. וַהֲוֹון תַּמָּן מִן אִילֵּין דְּבַר סִילְנֵי. וּפְסַק חָדָא לִיטְרָא דְהַב. נְטָלוֹ רִבִּי חִיָּה רַבָּה וְהוֹשִׁיבוֹ אֶצְלוֹ וְקָרָא עָלָיו הַפָּסוּק הַזֶּה מַתָּן אָדָם יַרְחִיב לוֹ וגו'.

1 חייה | B חייא בההין | B בההן מן | B חד מן 2 חייה רבה | BG חייא בר בא

Rebbi Ḥiyya bar Abba held a pledging for a certain house of study at Tiberias. There was one there of the family of Bar Silene, who pledged a pound of gold. (The Elder Rebbi Ḥiyya) [Rebbi Ḥiyya bar Abba][235] took him, made him sit with him, and recited for him this verse: *The gifts of a man put him at ease*, etc.

רִבִּי שִׁמְעוֹן בֶּן לָקִישׁ עָאַל לְבוֹצְרָה וַהֲוָה תַמָּן חַד רַמַּייָא. חַס לֵיהּ דְּלָא הֲוָה רַמַּאי אֶלָּא שֶׁהָיָה מְרַמֶּה בְמִצְוֹות. וַהֲוָה חֲמִי כְּמָה דְצִיבּוּרָא פְסַק וְהוּא פְסִיק לְקָבְלֵיהּ. נְטָלוֹ רִבִּי שִׁמְעוֹן בֶּן לָקִישׁ וְהוֹשִׁיבוֹ אֶצְלוֹ. וְקָרָא עָלָיו הַפָּסוּק הַזֶּה מַתָּן אָדָם יַרְחִיב לוֹ וגו'.

1 רמייא | B רב בון דמייחס ליה   חס ליה דלא | B לא   רמאי | B רמיי G רבון רמייה   רמאי | G רמיי   2 מרמה } GB מרמי   כמה | GB מה   3 וגו' | B ולפני גדולים ינחנו

[236]Rebbi Simeon ben Laqish went up to Bostra. Over there was a cheater. God forbid that he was a cheater, but he cheated in charity. He looked how much the community pledged, and he pledged the same amount[237]. Rebbi Simeon ben Laqish took him, made him sit with him, and recited for him this verse: *The gifts of a man put him at ease*, etc.

230 These texts are also in *Lev. rabba* 5(4); the first one only also in *Deut. rabba* 4(8). Here also starts a Genizah fragment of half-lines (G) edited by L. Ginzberg (*Yerushalmi Fragments from the Genizah*, New York 1909, pp. 281-286.)

231 Projecting third and fourth Cent. fundraising into a story dated at the first. It is a typically oriental story where people do not get rich by commercial success but by finding a treasure.

232 Added from B.

233 Greek τῖμος, an old poetic form of τιμή "esteem, value, honor" appearing also in late prose texts. The talmudic form supports late classical Greek lexicography; cf. also E. and H. Guggenheimer, *Talmudic Evidence for Greek Spelling,* Studi Classici in Onore di Quintino Cataudela, vol. 4, Catania 1972, pp. 71-72.`

234 *Prov.* 18:16.

235 The impossible text in parentheses is from L; the correct text in brackets is from B.

236 In B, the last two paragraphs are in the inverse order. This is the chronologically correct order, teacher followed by student. Chronological consistency is one of the hallmarks of the Babli.

237 His cheating was that he gave the minimum amount necessary to maintain his standing as the richest man around.

(48a line 69) הָאִישׁ קוֹדֵם לָאִשָּׁה כול'. עַד כְּדוֹן בְּשֶׁהָיָה זֶה לְהַחֲיוֹת וְזֶה לְהַחֲיוֹת זֶה לִכְסוּת וְזֶה לִכְסוּת. הֲרֵי שֶׁהָיָה זֶה לְהַחֲיוֹת וְזֶה לִכְסוּת. נִישְׁמְעִינָהּ מִן הָדָא דָּמַר רִבִּי יְהוֹשֻׁעַ בֶּן לֵוִי בְשֵׁם רִבִּי אַנְטִיגְנָס. כְּסוּת אֵשֶׁת חָבֵר וְחַיֵּי עַם הָאָרֶץ. כְּסוּת אֵשֶׁת חָבֵר קוֹדֶמֶת לְחַיֵּי עַם הָאָרֶץ מִפְּנֵי כְבוֹדוֹ שֶׁלְּחָבֵר. לֹא מַר אֶלָּא כְסוּת אֵשֶׁת חָבֵר כְּחַיֵּי חָבֵר. אֲבָל אִם הָיָה זֶה לְהַחֲיוֹת וְזֶה לִכְסוּת אוֹתוֹ שֶׁלְּהַחֲיוֹת קוֹדֵם.

1 האיש קודם לאשה כול' | G הל'   כול' | B להחיות וכו'   להחיות | B לכסות   2 הרי שהיה | B - G היה   הדא | B הדה   3 אמטיגנס | B חנינא בן אנטיגנוס (supported by G)   4 מר | B אמרו   כחיי חבר | B וחיי עם הארץ G בחיי חביר

"The man precedes the woman," etc. So far if each one was to be kept alive or each one was for clothing. If one was to be kept alive and the other for clothing[238]? Let us hear from the following, as Rebbi Joshua ben Levi said in the name of Rebbi [Ḥanina ben][239] Antigonos, the clothing of the wife of a fellow[240] and the life of a vulgar; the clothing of the wife of a fellow has precedence over the life of a vulgar because of the dignity of the fellow. He only said that the clothing of the wife of a fellow was like the life of the fellow[241]. But if there was one to be kept alive and one for clothing, the one to be kept alive has precedence.

238 The question really is raised about the livelihood of a woman and the clothing of a man.

239 From B; no R. Antigonos is known from other sources. G is defective here but the length of the lacuna supports the reading of B.

240 Here "fellow" and "vulgar" are the technical terms defined in the Introduction to Tractate Demai, respectively of a person strictly keeping all rules of levitic purity (long after the destruction of the Temple) and tithes, and one disregarding the rules of purity and lax in the observance of the rules of tithes.

241 B has a different text: "He only said between the clothing of the wife of a fellow and the livelihood of a vulgar." The best is the reading of G: "The clothing of the wife of a fellow during the lifetime of the fellow."

(48a line 75) אֲבֵידָתוֹ וַאֲבֵידַת אָבִיו שֶׁלּוֹ קוֹדֶמֶת. אֲבֵידָתוֹ וַאֲבֵיידַת רַבּוֹ שֶׁלּוֹ קוֹדֶמֶת. אֲבֵידַת אָבִיו וַאֲבֵידַת רַבּוֹ שֶׁלְּרַבּוֹ קוֹדֶמֶת. שֶׁאָבִיו הֵבִיאוֹ לְחַיֵּי הָעוֹלָם הַזֶּה. וְרַבּוֹ שֶׁלִּימְּדוֹ חָכְמָה הֵבִיאוֹ לְחַיֵּי הָעוֹלָם הַבָּא. וְרַבּוֹ שְׁלִּימְּדוֹ מִשְׁנָה לֹא רַבּוֹ שְׁלִּימְּדוֹ מִקְרָא. אִם הָיָה אָבִיו שָׁקוּל כְּרַבּוֹ אָבִיו קוֹדֵם.

1 אבידתו | B אבדתו ואבידת | B ואבדת אבידתו | B אבדתו ואבידת | B ואבדת אבידת | B אבדת 2 אבידת | B אבדת קודמת | GB קודמת לשל אביו העולם | B - שלימדו | B שלמדו 3 שלימדו | B שלמדו משנה | B חכמה אם | B ואם כרבו | B כנגד רבו [242]

מָה הוֹעִיל. אָמַר רִבִּי יוֹסֵי בֵּירִבִּי בּוּן. כְּשֶׁהָיָה חֲצִי תַלְמוּדוֹ מִזֶּה וַחֲצִי תַלְמוּדוֹ מִזֶּה. אֲבֵידַת אָבִיו שֶׁחֲצִי תַלְמוּדוֹ מִמֶּנּוּ וַאֲבֵידַת אִמּוֹ גְּרוּשָׁה מֵאָבִיו מִי קוֹדֵם. אָבִיו הוּא שֶׁיִּקְדּוֹם אוֹ עַד שֶׁיְּהֵא כָל־תַּלְמוּדוֹ מִמֶּנּוּ. אֲבֵידַת רַבּוֹ שֶׁחֲצִי תַלְמוּדוֹ הֵימֶינּוּ וַאֲבֵידַת אִמּוֹ גְּרוּשָׁה מֵאָבִיו מִי קוֹדֵם. רַבּוֹ הוּא שֶׁיִּקְדּוֹם אוֹ עַד שֶׁיְּהֵא כָל־תַּלְמוּדוֹ הֵימֶינּוּ. אֲבֵידָתוֹ וַאֲבֵידַת אָבִיו וַאֲבֵידַת אִמּוֹ וַאֲבֵידַת רַבּוֹ. שֶׁלּוֹ קוֹדֵם לְאָבִיו וְאָבִיו לְאִמּוֹ וְאִמּוֹ לְרַבּוֹ. וְלֹא מַתְנִיתָה הִיא. הָאִישׁ קוֹדֵם לָאִשָּׁה לְהַחֲיוֹת וּלְהָשִׁיב אֲבֵדָה. סָבְרִין מֵימַר. בְּשֶׁאֵין רַבּוֹ שָׁם. אֲתָא מֵימַר לָךְ. וַאֲפִילוּ רַבּוֹ שָׁם. הוּא וְאִמּוֹ וְרַבּוֹ וְאָבִיו עוֹמְדִיח בַּשֶּׁבִי. הוּא קוֹדֵם לְאִמּוֹ וְאִמּוֹ לְרַבּוֹ וְרַבּוֹ לְאָבִיו. וְלֹא מַתְנִיתָה הִיא.

הָאִשָּׁה קוֹדֶמֶת לָאִישׁ לִכְסוּת וּלְהוֹצִיאָהּ מִבֵּית הַשֶּׁבִי. סָבְרִין מֵימַר. בְּשֶׁאֵין רַבּוֹ שָׁם. אֲתָא מֵימַר לָךְ. וַאֲפִילוּ רַבּוֹ שָׁם.

5 קודם | G קודמת 6 בשאין | G כשאין מימר | G מימור 7 בשבי | G בשיבי 8 השבי | G [ה]שיבי

"Between his lost property and his father's lost property, his own has precedence. Between his lost property and his teacher's lost property, his own has precedence. Between his father's lost property and his teacher's lost property, his teacher's lost property has precedence, for his father brought him to the life of this world, but his teacher who taught him wisdom brought him to the life of the future world.[243]" The teacher who taught him (Mishnah) [wisdom][244], not the teacher who taught him Scripture[245]. "But if his father was his teacher's equal, his father's lost property has precedence."

What does it help[246]? Rebbi Yose ben Rebbi Abun said, if half of his learning was from one and half of his learning from the other. His father's lost property if half of his learning was from him and his mother's lost property if she was divorced from his father, which has precedence[247]? Does his father's have precedence or only if all his learning was from him? His teacher's lost property if half of his learning was from him and his mother's lost property if she was divorced from his father, which has precedence[248]? Does his teacher's have precedence or only if all his learning was from him? His lost property, and his father's lost property, and his mother's lost property, and his teacher's lost property. His own precedes his father's, his father's his mother's, and his mother's his teacher's. Is that not a Mishnah, "the man precedes the woman to be kept alive and to return his lost property"? They wanted to say, if his teacher was not there[249]. He comes to tell you, even if his teacher was there. He, and his mother, and his teacher, and his father, were in captivity. He precedes his mother, his mother his teacher, and his teacher his father[250]. Is that not a Mishnah, "but the woman precedes the man for clothing and to be freed from captivity"? They wanted to say, if his teacher was not there. He comes to tell you, even if his teacher was there.

242 The remainder of the discussion of this part of Mishnah 8 is missing in B.

243 Mishnah *Bava Mesi`a* 2:13, Note 135.

244 The text in parentheses is from L, the one in brackets from B. The text of B is the one from the Mishnah, the one of L can be justified as text of the Tanna R.

Yose in the following paragraph.

245 How does the fact that his father was as learned as his teacher change the argument of the Mishnah?

246 As long as his mother was married to his father, his father has precedence since his wife also is bound to honor him (Mishnah *Keritut* 6:9). But the divorced mother in all respects is equal to the father (Babli *Qiddušin* 31a). If the father was also the teacher then he had precedence as teacher. But if he was only a partial teacher, is his claim strong enough or does the son still have the choice whom to help first?

248 Is the teacher who taught him half his learning the teacher in the sense of the Mishnah or not?

249 The language implies that the statements in question are tannaitic, similar to the first part of Tosephta *Horaiot* 2:5.

250 Babli 13a.

(48b line 15) אֵי זֶהוּ רַבּוֹ שֶׁלִּימְּדוֹ חָכְמָה. כָּל־שֶׁפָּתַח לוֹ תְחִילָּה. דִּבְרֵי רִבִּי מֵאִיר. רִבִּי יוּדָה אוֹמֵר. כָּל־שֶׁרוֹב תַּלְמוּדוֹ מִמֶּנּוּ. רִבִּי יוֹסֵי אוֹמֵר. כָּל־שֶׁהֵאִיר עֵינָיו בְּמִשְׁנָתוֹ. אָתָא רִבִּי אַבָּהוּ בְּשֵׁם רִבִּי יוֹחָנָן. הֲלָכָה כְמִי שֶׁהוּא אוֹמֵר. כָּל־שֶׁרוֹב תַּלְמוּדוֹ הֵימֶינּוּ. וְלָמָּה לֹא פָּתַר לָהּ כְּרִבִּי יוּדָה. אִית תַּנָּיֵי תַנֵּי וּמַחֲלִיף. רִבִּי לְעָזָר קָרַע עַל שֶׁפָּתַח לוֹ תְחִילָּה. שְׁמוּאֵל חָלַץ עַל שֶׁהֵאִיר עֵינָיו בְּמִשְׁנָתוֹ. וּמַה הֵאִיר עֵינָיו בְּמִשְׁנָתוֹ. אָמַר רִבִּי יוֹסֵי בֵּירִבִּי בּוּן. מַפְתֵּחַ אֶחָד יוֹרֵד לְאַמַּת בֵּית הַשֶּׁיחִי וְאֶחָד פּוֹתֵחַ כֵּיוָן׃ וּמַה אֶחָד יוֹרֵד לְאַמַּת בֵּית הַשֶּׁיחִי. שֶׁהָיָה שׁוֹחֵחַ אַמָּה עַד שֶׁלֹּא יִפָּתֵחַ. רִבִּי חֲנַנְיָה הֲוָה מִיסְתַּמֵּיךְ בְּרִבִּי חִיָּיה בַּר בָּא דְצִיפּוֹרִין. חֲמָא כָּל־עַמָּא פָּרְיֵי. אֲמַר לֵיהּ. לָמָּה כָּל־עַמָּא פָּרְיֵי. אֲמַר לֵיהּ. רִבִּי יוֹחָנָן יְתִיב דְּרִישׁ בְּבֵית מִדְרְשָׁא דְרִבִּי בְנַיָּיה וְכָל־עַמָּא פָּרְיֵי מִישְׁמְעִינֵיהּ. אֲמַר. בְּרִיךְ רַחֲמָנָא דַחֲמִי לִי פֵירִין עַד דַּאֲנָא בְחַיִּים. וְכָל־אֲגַדְתָּא פְּשַׁטִית לֵיהּ חוּץ מִמִּשְׁלֵי וְקוֹהֶלֶת.

1 שלימדו | G שילמדו   יודה | G יהודה   2 אבהו | G אבהוא   3 שרוב | G שירוב   הימינו | G ממ[נו]   5
האיר | G היאיר   במשנתו | G במישנתו   6 כיון | G כיוון   ומה | G מהוא   השיחי | G השיחי ואחד פותיח
כיוון   7 חנניה | G חנינה   בר' | G על ר'   בר בא | G ברווה   חמא | G חמה   ליה | G -   8 פריי | G פרייה
מדרשא | G מדרשה   בנייה | G בניה   9 דאנא בחיים | G דאנה בחיין   וכל אגדתא | G כל אגדתה

[251]"Who is the teacher who taught him wisdom? The one who taught him first, the words of Rebbi Meïr. Rebbi Jehudah said, the one from whom he received most of his instruction. Rebbi Yose said, anyone who explained a Mishnah to him.[252]" Rebbi Abbahu came in the name of Rebbi Joḥanan: Practice follows him who said, the one from whom he received most of his instruction. Why did he not explain that this follows Rebbi Jehudah? There are Tannaïm who state it switched[253]. Rebbi Eleazar tore his garment for his first teacher. Samuel took off [his phylacteries] for one who had explained a Mishnah to him[254]. What Mishnah did he explain to him? Rebbi Yose ben

Rebbi Abun said, "for one key he has to go down to his arm-pit and one opens straight.[255]" What means "for one he has to gown to his arm-pit," he had to lower his hand under his arm-pit until it could be opened[256].

Rebbi Ḥanania[257] was leaning on Rebbi Ḥiyya bar Abba in Sepphoris, when he saw everybody running. He asked him, why is everybody running? He answered, Rebbi Joḥanan is sitting preaching in Rebbi Banaia's house of study and everybody is running to hear him. He said, praised be the Merciful Who showed me fruits while I am alive. In *Agadah* I explained him everything except Proverbs and Ecclesiastes[258].

251 For the following, cf. *Bava mesia`* 3:13, Notes 136-145; *Mo`ed qatan* 3:7.

252 Tosephta 2:5, *Bava mesia`* 2:30.

253 The name tradition in the Tosephta is not certain.

254 As a sign of mourning. The phylacteries are identified as the "splendor" which Ezechiel had to remove in mourning, *Ez.* 24:17. The text in *Bava mesia`* parallels the Babli (*Bava mesia`* 33a) in reporting that he tore his garment.

255 Mishnah *Tamid* 3:6.

256 The doors of the Temple Hall could be opened only from the inside. When the door was locked, a Cohen entered from a small side door which led to a guard room. The lock of this side door was hidden; the Cohen had to take the key, lower his entire arm to the arm-pit behind the partition wall and only then could insert the key. *Tamid* 30b.

257 With G read "Hanina".

258 This proves that even a teacher of homiletics has the rank of teacher.

(48b line 28) שְׁנֵיהֶם עוֹמְדִין בְּקָלוֹן הָאִישׁ קוֹדֵם לָאִשָּׁה׃ לָמָּה. שֶׁהָאִשָּׁה דַּרְכָּהּ לָכֵן וְהָאִישׁ אֵין דַּרְכּוֹ לָכֵן. מַעֲשֶׂה בְּיִרְבִּי יְהוֹשֻׁעַ שֶׁעָלָה לְרוֹמִי. אָמְרוּ עָלָיו עַל תִּינוֹק אֶחָד יְרוּשַׁלְמִי שֶׁהָיָה אַדְמוֹנִי עִם יְפֵה עֵינַיִם וְטוֹב רוֹאִי וּקְווּצוֹתָיו מְסוּדָּרוֹת לוֹ תַּלְתַּלִּים. וְהוּא עוֹמֵד בְּקָלוֹן. וְהָלַךְ רִבִּי יְהוֹשֻׁעַ לְבוֹדְקוֹ. כֵּיוָן שֶׁהִגִּיעַ לְפִתְחוֹ נַעֲנֶה רִבִּי יְהוֹשֻׁעַ וְאָמַר לוֹ. מִי־נָתַן לִמְשִׁיסָּה יַעֲקֹב וְיִשְׂרָאֵל לְבוֹזְזִים הֲלוֹא יי. נַעֲנֶה הַתִּינוֹק וְאָמַר לוֹ. זוּ חָטָאנוּ לוֹ וְלֹא־אָבוּ בִדְרָכָיו הָלוֹךְ וְלֹא שָׁמְעוּ בְּתוֹרָתוֹ׃ מִיָּד זָלְגוּ עֵינָיו דְּמָעוֹת וְאָמַר. מֵעִיד אֲנִי עָלַי אֶת הַשָּׁמַיִם וְאֶת הָאָרֶץ שֶׁאֵינִי זָז מִכָּאן עַד שֶׁאֶפְדֶּנּוּ. וּפְדָאוֹ בְּמָמוֹן הַרְבֵּה וְשִׁילְּחוֹ לְאֶרֶץ יִשְׂרָאֵל. וְקָרָא עָלָיו הַפָּדוּק הַזֶּה בְּנֵי צִיּוֹן הַיְקָרִים וגו'.

1 שניהם | G בזמן ששניהם שהאשה | G האשה 2 ביר' | G בר' 4 לבודקו | G לבדקו כיון | G כייון לפתחו | G לפיתחו למשיסה | G למשסה 5 נענה | G ניענה 6 מיד | G מייד עלי | G עליי

"If both of them stand in [a house of] ill repute, the man precedes the woman." Why? For a woman it is natural, for a man it is not natural[210].

[259]It happened that Rebbi Joshua went to Rome. They informed him about a child from Jerusalem who was reddish with beautiful eyes, good to look at, and his locks ordered in curls[260], standing in [a house of] ill repute. Rebbi Joshua went to check him out. When he came to the door, Rebbi Joshua started and said, *who gave Jacob to be booty and Israel to plunderers, is that not the Eternal*[261]? The child answered him and told him, *it is because we sinned against Him; they did not want to walk in His ways and did not listen to His teaching*[261]. Immediately his eyes were flowing with tears and he said, I take as my witnesses heaven and earth that I shall not move from here until I buy his freedom. He bought his freedom for much money, sent him to the Land of Israel, and quoted for him this verse, *the dear children of Zion*[262]etc.

259 Tosephta 2:5,6; *Thr. rabbati* 4(4); Babli *Gittin* 58a.

260 A combination of biblical adjectives, *1S.* 17:42, *Cant.* 5:11.

261 *Is.* 42:24.

262 *Thr.* 4:2.

(48b line 37) כֹּהֵן קוֹדֵם לְלֵוִי לֵוִי לְיִשְׂרָאֵל יִשְׂרָאֵל לְמַמְזֵר כול׳. חָכָם קוֹדֵם לַמֶּלֶךְ. מֶלֶךְ קוֹדֵם לְכֹהֵן גָּדוֹל. כֹּהֵן גָּדוֹל קוֹדֵם לְנָבִיא. נָבִיא קוֹדֵם לִמְשׁוּחַ מִלְחָמָה. מְשׁוּחַ מִלְחָמָה קוֹדֵם לְרֹאשׁ מִשְׁמָר. רֹאשׁ מִשְׁמָר קוֹדֵם לְבֵית אָב. בֵּית אָב קוֹדֵם לְמַרְכֹּל. וְהַמַּרְכֹּל קוֹדֵם לְגִיזְבָּר. גִּיזְבָּר קוֹדֵם לְכֹהֵן הֶדְיוֹט. כֹּהֵן הֶדְיוֹט קוֹדֵם לְלֵוִי. לֵוִי לְיִשְׂרָאֵל. יִשְׂרָאֵל לְמַמְזֵר. מַמְזֵר לְנָתִין. נָתִין לְגֵר. גֵּר לְעֶבֶד מְשׁוּחְרָר. אֵימָתַי. בִּזְמַן שֶׁכּוּלָּן שָׁוִין. אֲבָל אִם הָיָה מַמְזֵר תַּלְמִיד חָכָם וְכֹהֵן גָּדוֹל עַם הָאָרֶץ. מַמְזֵר תַּלְמִיד חָכָם קוֹדֵם לְכֹהֵן גָּדוֹל עַם הָאָרֶץ:

1 כהן | B הלכה כהן[263] לוי לישראל ישראל לממזר כול׳ | B וכו׳ The rest is missing in B 2 לכהן | G לכוהן כהן | G וכוהן 3 לבית | G לראש בית בית | G ראש בית למרכל | G למרכיל והמרכל | G מרכיל 5 אימתי | G אמתי שכולן שוין | G [ש]כולם שווים חכם | G חכמין וכהן | G וכוהן 6 חכם | G חכמין לכהן | G לכוהן

"A priest precedes a Levite, a Levite an Israel, an Israel a bastard," etc. [264]"A Sage has precedence over the king, the king has precedence over the High Priest, the High Priest has precedence over a prophet, a prophet has precedence over the Anointed for War, the Anointed for war has precedence over the head of the watch[265], the head of the watch has precedence over the [head of a] clan[266], the [head of a] clan has precedence over the executive officer[267], the executive officer has precedence over the treasurer[268], the treasurer has precedence over a common priest, a common priest has precedence over a Levite, a Levite over an Israel, an Israel over a bastard, a bastard over a Gibeonite, a Gibeonite over a proselyte, a proselyte over a manumitted slave. When? If they are all equal. But if the bastard was learned and the High Priest ignorant, the learned bastard precedes the ignorant High Priest."

263 A Note that here starts the discussion of Mishnah 9.

264 Cf. Tosephta 2:10.

265 Of one of the 24 watches into which the Cohanim were organized (*1Chr.* 24), each of which served for one week in the Temple.

266 A clan of priests belonging to one of the watches. The correct reading here is that of G, confirmed later also by L (lines 61ff.)

267 The permanent member of the Temple staff who organizes the daily routine. As a paid official he comes after the volunteers who do the actual officiating. In Babylonian sources, his title is spelled אמרכל.

268 The Temple treasurer.

(48b line 45) חָכָם קוֹדֵם לַמֶּלֶךְ. חָכָם שֶׁמֵּת אֵין לָנוּ כְיוֹצֵא בוֹ. מֶלֶךְ שֶׁמֵּת כָּל־יִשְׂרָאֵל רְאוּיִין לַמַּלְכוּת.

1 חכם | G וכן חכם ראויין | G [ר]אויים

"A Sage has precedence over the king." If a Sage dies, we do not have a replacement[269]. If a king dies, all of Israel are qualified for the kingdom[270].

269 This restricts the statement to a truly outstanding Sage. In G, this is not a reference to the text of the Mishnah but a continuation of the statement that a learned bastard has precedence over the boorish High Priest, "and similarly, a Sage has precedence over a king." The text of L is that of Tosephta 2:8.

270 This legitimizes non-Davidic kings. The Babli (13a) agrees. The current printed Babli editions were adulterated by a censor who inserted "king of Israel", to preserve the superiority of the ruler by the grace of God. Already Maimonides in his Commentary to the Mishnah notes that all the precedences enumerated in this Mishnah are ethical only, rather than practical.

(48b line 46) אָמַר רִבִּי יוֹחָנָן. כָּל־אוֹתָן אַרְבָּעִים יוֹם שֶׁעָשָׂה מֹשֶׁה בָהָר לָמַד תּוֹרָה וּמְשַׁכְּחָהּ. וּבְסוֹף נִיתְּנָה לוֹ בְמַתָּנָה. כָּל־כָּךְ לָמָּה. בִּשְׁבִיל לְהַחֲזִיר אֶת הַטִּיפְּשִׁים.

1 אותן | B אותם למד | B היה למד G היה למיד 2 ניתנה | B נתנו בשביל | G בישביל הטיפשים | B הטפשים

Rebbi Joḥanan said, all these 40 days which Moses spent on the Mountain, he studied Torah and forgot it. At the end it was given to him as a gift. Why so much? To return the stupid ones[271].

271 To encourage people who do not understand a subject to return to study; they can always hope that at the end the understanding will be given to them in their sleep. The argument would be better if addressed to scientists who fail to solve a problem; if they persevere they have the hope to finally receive the answer from Heaven in their sleep.

(48b line 49) כַּד דְּמַךְ רִבִּי סִימוֹן בַּר זְבִיד אָעַל רִבִּי הִילַי וְאַפְטַר עֲלוֹי. כִּ֣י יֵ֣שׁ לַכֶּ֣סֶף מוֹצָ֑א וגו' בַּ֭רְזֶל מֵעָפָ֣ר יֻקָּ֑ח וגו'. אֵילוּ אִם אָבְדוּ יֵשׁ לָנוּ חֲלִיפִין. אֲבָל תַּלְמִיד חָכָם שֶׁמֵּת מִי מֵבִיא לָנוּ כְּיוֹצֵא בוֹ. וְ֭הַחָכְמָה מֵאַיִן תִּימָּצֵא וגו'. וְֽ֭נֶעֶלְמָה מֵעֵינֵ֣י כָל־חָ֑י וגו'. אָמַר רִבִּי לֵוִי. מָה אִם אֲחֵי יוֹסֵף עַל שֶׁמָּצְאוּ מְצִיאָה יָצָא לִיבָּם. דִּכְתִיב וַיֵּ֣צֵא לִבָּ֔ם. אָנוּ שֶׁאָבַדְנוּ רִבִּי סִימוֹן בַּר זְבִיד עַל אַחַת כַּמָּה וְכַמָּה.

1 בר | G בר' הילי | B - עלוי | B עלוי לגוי וגו' | G [ז]הב יזיקו 2 וגו' | B - G [ואבו י]צוק נחושה אילו | B אלו חליפין | G חליפים שמת | B - כיוצא בו | B חליפתו מי יביא לנו תמורתו מי יביא לנו כיוצא בו G מיביא 3 וגו' | B ואי זה מקום בינה וגו' | GB ומעוף השמים נסתרה על | B על ידי 4 ליבם | B לבם ויחרדו 5 וכמה | G ואחת כמה

[272]When Rebbi Simeon ben Zevid died, Rebbi Illai rose and eulogized him. *But silver has a source*[273], etc. *Iron is taken from dust*[274], etc. Those, if they are lost, have replacement. But a scholar who died, who can bring us one similar to him? *Wisdom, where can it be found*[275], etc. *It is hidden from the eyes of all living*[276], etc. Rebbi Levi said, if the brothers of Joseph lost their spirit because they found a find, as it is written, *they lost their spirit*[277], we, who lost Rebbi Simeon bar Zevid, so much more[278]!

272 The homily here is a considerably shortened version of one in *Berakhot* 1:8 (5c l. 29; Notes 322-324) where R. Illai (La) notes that 4 useful things mentioned in *Job* can be replaced when lost. Text B has the full quotes but still lacks the necessary introduction. The homily of R. Levi is unchanged.

273 *Job* 28:1.

274 *Job* 28:2.

275 *Job* 28:20.

276 *Job* 28:21.

277 *Gen.* 42:28.

278 Note in G the unusual form עַל אַחַת כַּמָּה וְאַחַת כַּמָּה for the common עַל אַחַת כַּמָּה וְכַמָּה "so much more".

(48d line 54) מֶלֶךְ קוֹדֵם לְכֹהֵן גָּדוֹל. דִּכְתִיב וְהִרְכַּבְתֶּם֙ אֶת־שְׁלֹמֹ֣ה בְנִ֔י וגו'. כֹּהֵן גָּדוֹל לְנָבִיא. דִּכְתִיב וּמָשַׁ֣ח אֹת֣וֹ ֠שָׁם צָד֨וֹק הַכֹּהֵ֜ן וְנָתָ֧ן הַנָּבִ֛יא לְמֶ֖לֶךְ. הִקְדִּים צָדוֹק לְנָתָן. רִבִּי יוֹנָה בְשֵׁם רִבִּי חָמָא בַּר חֲנִינָה. נָבִיא מְכַפֵּת יָדָיו וְרַגְלָיו וְיוֹשֵׁב לוֹ בִפְנֵי כֹהֵן גָּדוֹל. וּמַה טַעֲמֵיהּ. שְֽׁמַֽע־נָ֞א יְהוֹשֻׁ֣עַ ׀ הַכֹּהֵ֣ן הַגָּד֗וֹל אַתָּה֙ וְרֵעֶ֨יךָ֙ הַיֹּשְׁבִ֣ים לְפָנֶ֔יךָ. יָכוֹל יְהוּ הֶדְיוֹטוֹת. תַּלְמוּד לוֹמַר כִּ֥י־אַנְשֵׁ֛י מוֹפֵ֖ת הֵ֑מָּה. וְאֵין מוֹפֵת אֶלָּא נְבוּאָה. הֵיךְ מַה דְתֵימַר וְנָתַ֥ן אֵלֶ֛יךָ א֖וֹת א֥וֹ מוֹפֵֽת׃

1 לכהן | G לכוהן דכת' | B שנאמר וגו' כהן גדול לנביא דכת' | B על הפרדה אשר לי 2 למלך | B - יונה | B הונא 3 חמא | G חמה חנינה | B חנינא מכפת | B מכפר G מכפית כהן | G כוהן טעמ' | B טעם 4 וריעיך | GB ורעיך יהו הדיוטית | B הדיוטות היו 5 היך מה | GB כמה דתימר | G דתמר

[279]The king has precedence over the High Priest, as it is written: *You shall let my son Solomon ride*[280], etc. The High Priest over the prophet, as it is written: *There, Ṣadoq the Priest and Nathan the Prophet shall anoint him as king*[281], etc. He mentioned Ṣadoq before Nathan. Rebbi Jonah in the name of Rebbi Ḥama bar Ḥanina: The prophet folds his hands and feet and sits before the High Priest[282]. What is his reason? *Listen, Joshua the High Priest, you and your friends who are sitting before you*[283]. I could think that they were common people; the verse says, *because they are men of miracle*, and "miracle" only means prophecy, as you say, *and he gave you a sign or a miracle*[284].

279 Tosephta 2:9, Babli 13a.

280 *1K.* 1:33.

281 *1K.* 1:34.

282 He sits on the floor or the carpet with his feet folded under him.

283 *Zach.* 3:8.

284 *Deut.* 13:2.

(48b line 61) נָבִיא קוֹדֵם לִמְשׁוּחַ מִלְחָמָה. מְשׁוּחַ מִלְחָמָה קוֹדֵם לְרֹאשׁ מִשְׁמָר. רֹאשׁ מִשְׁמָר קוֹדֵם לְרֹאשׁ בֵּית אָב. רֹאשׁ בֵּית אָב קוֹדֵם לְמַרְכֹּל. וְהַמַּרְכֹּל קוֹדֵם לְגִיזְבָּר. גִּיזְבָּר קוֹדֵם לְכֹהֵן הֶדְיוֹט. כֹּהֵן קוֹדֵם לְלֵוִי. לֵוִי לְיִשְׂרָאֵל. (וְיִשְׂרָאֵל לְמַמְזֵר.) לֹא הוּא לֵוִי הוּא. אָמַר רִבִּי אָבוּן. בִּשְׁעַת הַדּוּכָן שָׁנוּ. אָמַר רִבִּי אָבוּן. גֵּר וּמְשׁוּמָּד מְשׁוּמָּד קוֹדֵם מִפְּנֵי מַעֲשֶׂה שֶׁאֵירַע. מִפְּנֵי מַה הַכֹּל רָצִין אַחַר הַגִּיוֹרֶת וְאֵין הַכֹּל רָצִין אַחַר מְשׁוּחְרֶרֶת. שֶׁהַגִּיוֹרֶת בְּחֶזְקַת מִשְׁתַּמֶּרֶת וּמְשׁוּחְרֶרֶת בְּחֶזְקַת הֶבְקֵר. וּמִפְּנֵי מַה הַכֹּל רָצִין אַחַר חֲעַכְבָּר. מִפְּנֵי שֶׁעִסְקוֹ רַע עִם הַבְּרִיּוֹת. אָמַר רִבִּי יוֹחָנָן. אַל תַּאֲמִין בְּעֶבֶד עַד שִׁשָּׁה עָשָׂר דּוֹר. בָּ֣א יִשְׁמָעֵ֣אל בֶּן־נְ֠תַנְיָה בֶּן־אֱלִֽישָׁמָ֨ע מִזֶּ֤רַע הַמְּלוּכָה֙ וַיַּכֶּ֖ה אֶת־גְּדַלְיָ֑הוּ בַּמִּצְפָּֽה.

2 למרכל | G למרכיל לגיזבר | GB לגזבר גיזבר | GB גזבר 3 כהן | B כהן הדיוט לממזר | B קודם לממזר הוא. | B לא הוא ישראל G הוא ישראל אבון | B אבין 4 שנו | B שנינו אבון | B בון ומשומד | B משומד שאירע G שארע 5 רצין | G רצים (2X) משוחררת | המשחררת ומשוחררת | G ומשחררת 6

ומפני | B מפני רצין אחא העכבר | GB שואלין על העבד עם | G בין מפני | B - אמ' | B ואמר 7
תאמין | B תאמן ששה | G שישה נתניה | G נתנייה 8 גדליהו | B גדליה

[285]"A prophet has precedence over the Anointed for War, the Anointed for War has precedence over the head of the watch, the head of the watch has precedence over the head of a clan, the head of a clan has precedence over the executive officer, the executive officer has precedence over the treasurer, the treasurer has precedence over a common priest, a common priest has precedence over a Levite, a Levite over an Israel (an Israel over a bastard[286])." Is not the Levite equal [to an Israel][287]? Rebbi Abun said, this was taught in the days of the podium[288]. Rebbi Abun said, a proselyte and an apostate, the apostate has preference because of what had happened[289]. "Why does everybody run after a proselyte woman, but not after a freedwoman? For the proselyte is presumed to have been guarding herself but the freedwoman[290] is presumed to be irresponsible." And why does everybody (run after a rat)[291] [inquire after a slave][292]? Because his dealings are bad for people. Rebbi Johanan said, do not believe a slave up to sixteen generations. *Ismael ben Netaniah ben Elishama of royal descent came and slew Gedaliahu at Mispah*[293].

285 Tosephta 2:10, Babli 13a (cf. Notes 264-268).

286 This clause was erased by the scribe of L, it is not in B or G.

287 Added from B and G; must be understood in L.

288 When the Levites had a role in Temple worship, either as singers on the podium or as watchmen. The statement that Levites are no different from Israel shows that the custom that Levites have to pour water of the Cohen's hands before he goes to pronounce the priestly blessing is not talmudic. (The source is *Zohar* III, 146b; the custom is not followed by Yemenites and some other Oriental groups.)

289 If a Gentile comes to a rabbi asking to become a proselyte and a Jewish apostate comes at the same time asking to be readmitted to the Jewish community, the rabbi has to deal with the apostate's case first, not to turn him away permanently as in the case of Joshua ben Perahia (or Jehudah ben Tabbai) (*Sanhedrin* 6:6, Note 79) and similar stories about Elisha and Gehazi (*Sanhedrin* 10:3, Notes 284,286).

290 As long as the freedwoman (Latin: *libertina*) was a slave, she could not marry and, therefore, was free to have guiltless sex with any man she pleased (except Jews.) She cannot be supposed to have changed her ways radically upon manumission. The proselyte as a free woman is supposed to be married as a virgin (Babli 13a).

291 To kill them. This is the text of L, taken from the Babli 13a, but it seems that one should accept the text of B and G in brackets.

292 Since the slave has no *persona* in law, he is irresponsible, and cannot be sued for damages. Therefore, a prospective buyer is well advised to inquire whether this slave may in the future expose him to suits for damages caused by his slave.

292 *2K.* 25:25. On *1Chr.* 2:35, about a man who had no sons, only daughters, and gave a daughter to his slave who produced a male grandson, Pseudo-Rashi explains: "From here the Sages said in Yerushalmi (Yebamot) [Horaiot] do not trust a (proselyte) [slave] up to 15 generations for there were 15 generations from Athai to Ismael and some say 16 generations with Yarha (the slave). In the explanation of our rabbis is is possible that (it does not mean) *of royal descent* since Ismael was from Yerahmeel but not from Ram (David's ancestor), but that he gave of his descendants to the Moloch." This explanation identifies Elishama, the grandfather of Ismael,, with Elishama mentioned in *1Chr.* 2:41. According to David Qimhi on *1Chr.* 2:26, *Atarah* "crown", the wife of Yerahmeel, was a converted Gentile from a royal family and from her there were 24 generations to Ismael.

(48b line 71) רִבִּי יְהוֹשֻׁעַ בֶּן לֵוִי אָמַר. רֹאשׁ וְזָקֵן זָקֵן קוֹדֵם. שֶׁאֵינוֹ רֹאשׁ אִם אֵינוֹ זָקֵן. מַה טַעֲמֵהּ. אַתֶּ֨ם נִצָּבִ֤ים הַיּוֹם֙ כּוּלְּכֶם וגו'. וַיֶּאֱסֹ֧ף יְהוֹשֻׁ֛עַ אֶת־כָּל־זִקְנֵ֥י יִשְׂרָאֵ֖ל שְׁכֶ֑מָה. מֹשֶׁה הִקְדִּים רָאשִׁים לִזְקֵינִים. יְהוֹשֻׁעַ הִקְדִּים זְקֵינִים לְרָאשִׁים. מֹשֶׁה עַל יְדֵי שֶׁהָיוּ הַכֹּל תַּלְמִידָיו הִקְדִּים רָאשִׁים לִזְקֵינִים. יְהוֹשֻׁעַ עַל יְדֵי שֶׁלֹּא הָיוּ הַכֹּל תַּלְמִידָיו הִקְדִּים זְקֵינִים לְרָאשִׁים. מֹשֶׁה עַל שֶׁלֹּא צָרַךְ לָהֶם בְּכִיבּוּשׁ הָאָרֶץ הִקְדִּים רָאשִׁים לִזְקֵינִים. יְהוֹשֻׁעַ עַל יְדֵי שֶׁצָּרַךְ לָהֶם בְּכִיבּוּשׁ הָאָרֶץ הִקְדִּים זְקֵינִים לְרָאשִׁים. מֹשֶׁה עַל יְדֵי שֶׁלֹּא נִתְייַגֵּעַ בְּתַלְמוּד תּוֹרָה הִקְדִּים רָאשִׁים לִזְקֵנִים. יְהוֹשֻׁעַ עַל יְדֵי שֶׁנִּתְייַגֵּעַ בְּתַלְמוּד תּוֹרָה הִקְדִּים זְקֵנִים לְרָאשִׁים. רִבִּי יְהוֹשֻׁעַ דְּסִיכְנִין בְּשֵׁם רִבִּי לֵוִי. מֹשֶׁה עַל יְדֵי שֶׁצָּפָה בְרוּחַ הַקּוֹדֶשׁ שֶׁעֲתִידִין יִשְׂרָאֵל לְהִסְתַּבֵּר בַּמַּלְכִיּוֹת וְרָאשֵׁיהֶן עוֹמְדִין עַל גַּבֵּיהֶן הִקְדִּים רָאשִׁים לִזְקֵינִים.

1 זקן | B ראש G ר[אש] לזקן שאינו ראש | G - אם אינו זקן | GB - 2 טעמ' | B טעם ויאסוף | GB וכתיב ויאסוף את כל זקני ישראל שכמה | B את זקני ישראל - | G וגו' הקדים | G היקדים 3 יהושע | G יהושוע לזקינים | B לזקנים זקינים | B זקנים (and so at all occurrences) 4-3 B the order of the sentences is switched, Joshua precedes Moses 5 בכיבוש | B לכבוש (2X) 6 הקדים | G היקדים (all occurences) נתייגע |B נתיגע G ניתייגע 7 שמתייגע | B שנתיגע 8 הקודש | B הקדש שעתידין ישראל | B שישראל עתידין להסתבר | GB להסתבך[293] 9 על גביהן | B עליהם

Rebbi Joshua ben Levi said: A head[294] and an Elder[295], the (Elder) [head][296] has precedence, for nobody is a head if he is not an Elder. What is his reason? *All of you are standing today*[297], etc. *Joshua assembled all Elders of Israel at Sichem*[298]. Moses preferred heads over Elders; Joshua preferred Elders over heads. Moses preferred heads over Elders because all were his students. Joshua preferred Elders over heads because not all were his students. Moses preferred heads over Elders because he did not need them in conquering the Land; Joshua preferred Elders over heads because be needed them in conquering the Land[299]. Moses preferred heads over Elders because he needed no exertion in the study of Torah, Joshua preferred Elders over heads because he had to exert himself in the study of Torah. Rebbi Joshua of Sikhnin in the name of Rebbi Levi: Moses preferred heads over Elders because he saw by the Holy Ghost that in the future Israel will be (reasonable) [in trouble][293,296] with governments and their heads will stand up for them[300].

293 Here ends the fragment G.
294 The learned in the law, i. e., the rabbinic authorities.
295 The tribal heads, paradigms for later political office holders.
296 The text in parentheses is that of L, the one in brackets that of B,G. The reason given shows that the latter text was intended by all sources.
297 *Deut*. 29:9; later in the verse the tribal heads are mentioned before the Elders.
298 *Jos*. 24:1 (misquoted); Elders are mentioned before tribal heads. Similarly in 23:2.
299 While he did not need them for military decisions, they prepared the maps for the distribution of the Land (Chapter 18).
300 A clear declaration of the priority of the political leadership over the religious.

(48c line 7) תַּנֵּי. הַסּוֹדְרָן קוֹדֵם לְפִילְפְּלָן. רִבִּי שְׁמוּאֵל אֲחוֹי דְרִבִּי בֶּרֶכְיָה בָּעֵי. אֲפִילוּ כְּרִבִּי אִמִּי. אֲמַר לֵיהּ. מִיתְבָּעֵי מֵרִבִּי אִימִּי. הוּא הַפִּילְפְּלָן. הָדָא אָמְרָה. מִשְׁנָה קוֹדֶם לְמִקְרָא. וְדָא מְסַייְעָא לֵיהּ. דְּתַנֵּי רִבִּי שִׁמְעוֹן בֶּן יוֹחַי. הָעוֹסֵק בַּמִּקְרָא מִידָּה שֶׁאֵינָהּ מִידָּה. וְרַבָּנָן עָבְדִין מִקְרָא כְּמִשְׁנָה. רִבִּי שְׁמוּאֵל בַּר נַחְמָן אָמַר. מִשְׁנָה קוֹדֶם לְתַלְמוּד. וּמַה טַעֲמָא. קְנֵה֙ חָכְמָה קְנֵ֣ה בִינָ֑ה וגו'. רִבִּי יוֹחָנָן אָמַר. תַּלְמוּד קוֹדֵם לְמִשְׁנָה. וּמַה טַעֲמָא. קְנֹה־חָכְמָה מַה־טּ֖וֹב מֵחָר֑וּץ. מַה מְקַייֵם רִבִּי יוֹחָנָן טַעֲמֵיהּ דְּרִבִּי שְׁמוּאֵל בַּר נַחְמָן. מַיִם בְּזוֹל וְיַיִן בְּיוֹקֶר. אֶיפְשַׁר לְעוֹלָם לִחְיוֹת בְּלֹא יַיִן. אֵי אֶיפְשַׁר לְעוֹלָם לִחְיוֹת בְּלֹא מַיִם. וּמַה מְקַייֵם שְׁמוּאֵל בַּר נַחְמָן טַעֲמֵיהּ דְּרִבִּי יוֹחָנָן. מֶלַח בְּזוֹל פִּילְפְּלִין בְּיוֹקֶר. אֶיפְשַׁר לְעוֹלָם לִחְיוֹת בְּלֹא פִּילְפְּלִין. אֵי אֶיפְשַׁר לְעוֹלָם לִחְיוֹת בְּלֹא מֶלַח. לְעוֹלָם הֱוֵי רָץ אַחַר הַמִּשְׁנָה יוֹתֵר מִן הַתַּלְמוּד. הָדָא דְתֵימַר עַד שֶׁלֹּא שִׁיקַּע בּוֹ רִבִּי רוֹב מִשְׁנָיוֹת. אֲבָל מִשֶּׁשִּׁיקַּע בּוֹ רִבִּי רוֹב מִשְׁנָיוֹת לְעוֹלָם הֱוֵי רָץ אַחַר הַתַּלְמוּד יוֹתֵר מִן הַמִּשְׁנָה.

1 הסודרן | הסדרן קודם | קודמת הוא הפילפלן | דהוא סדרן והוא פלפלן 2 אמי | אימי מיתבעי מר' | מאי את בעי מן ר' ודא | והדא 3 ליה | להיא שאינה | ואינה[301] ורבנן | ורבני'. The rest is missing.

It was stated: The systematizer has precedence over the dialectician[302]. Rebbi Samuel, Rebbi Berekhia's brother, asked: Even like Rebbi Immi? He told him, what do you want from Rebbi Immi? He is a dialectician[303]. This means, the Mishnah has precedence over Scripture[304]. The following supports this, as Rebbi Simeon ben Iohai stated, one who studies Scripture is a qualification which is not a qualification. But the rabbis consider Scripture equally with the Mishnah[305].

Rebbi Samuel bar Nahman said, the Mishnah has precedence over the Talmud. What is the reason? *Acquire wisdom, acquire understanding*[306], etc. Rebbi Johanan said, the Talmud has precedence over the Mishnah. What is the reason? *Is acquiring wisdom not better than pure gold*[307]*?* How does Rebbi Johanan explain Rebbi Samuel bar Nahman's reason? Water is cheap, wine is expensive. It is possible for the world to exist without wine; it is impossible for the world to exist without water[308]. How does Rebbi Samuel bar Nahman explain Rebbi Johanan's reason? Salt is cheap, pepper is expensive. It is possible for the world to exist without pepper; it is impossible for the world to exist without salt[309]. Always pursue the Mishnah more than the Talmud. That is, before Rebbi incorporated most Mishnaiot into it[310]. But since Rebbi incorporated most Mishnaiot into it, pursue the Talmud more than the Mishnah.

301 This is typically the Babli's language in quoting the *baraita* (*Bava meṣia*` 33a). The version of L is found also in *Berakhot* 1:5 (Note 175), *Šabbat* 1:2 (3c l. 19), 16:1 (15c l. 27).

302 The scholar who can bring order into the vast amount of rabbinic traditions is on a higher level than the one who finds apparent contradictions between traditional statements and explains them by finding the underlying principles. In the Babli (14a) the question is between "Sinai" and "one who uproots mountains" (and grinds them down), i. e., between a living encyclopedia and a practitioner of dialectics, and it is reported that in Galilee Sinai was preferred. There is no mention there about an effort at systematizing and in fact it is in general impossible to derive a valid rule of practice by basing oneself on one talmudic discussion alone, but all Tractates of the Babli have simultaneously to be considered.

303 In B: "He is both a systematizer and a dialectician." In both Talmudim, the teachings of R. Immi and his companion R. Yasa are too sporadic to allow a judgment between the two versions.

304 Since the Mishnah is a first attempt at systematizing Jewish teaching, its study, while presupposing a prior study of Scripture, is on a higher level since it is less anecdotal or self-contradictory.

305 They agree to the value of analysis

and explanation of Scripture also independent of traditional interpretations.

306 *Prov.* 4:5. "Wisdom" is identified here as the Mishnah, the encyclopedia of traditional knowledge. "Understanding" is the explanation of the formulaic statements of the Mishnah, the Talmud, whether formulated in one of the Talmudim or in a prior state of oral explanation. Wisdom precedes understanding.

307 *Prov.* 16:16. The verse reads: *Is acquiring wisdom not better than pure gold, acquisition of understanding more select than silver*? Here also wisdom precedes understanding, but silver is everyday coin; gold is used only for major transactions and by the very rich.

308 In both verses, the less valuable but more essential is mentioned in second place. This does not make the second less essential.

309 He agrees that without interpretation and explanation ("the Talmud") the Mishnah cannot be applied; the salt of the Talmud, the silver, is absolutely necessary. This does not diminish the value of the gold.

A different version of the preceding arguments is in *Massekhet Sopherim* 15:7, 8.

310 Here it is intimated that Rebbi's edition of the Mishnah from the start was intended as providing the skeleton around which a systematic exposition of the Talmud, the oral tradition, could be organized. In this way, the Mishnah automatically is studied in a privileged way if the Talmud is studied. Cf. *Lev. rabba* 21(4) which declares the study of the Mishnah as prerequisite for everything else.

(48c line 21) דָּרַשׁ רִבִּי שְׁמוּאֵל בְּרֵיהּ דְּרִבִּי יוֹסֵי בֵּירִבִּי בּוּן. חָכָם בְּעֵינָיו אִישׁ עָשִׁיר וְדַל מֵבִין יַחְקְרֶנּוּ׃ חָכָם בְּעֵינָיו אִישׁ עָשִׁיר זֶה בַּעַל הַתַּלְמוּד. וְדַל מֵבִין יַחְקְרֶנּוּ זֶה בַּעַל אֲגָדָה. לִשְׁנַיִם שֶׁנִּכְנְסוּ לָעִיר. בְּיַד זֶה עֲשָׁתוֹת שֶׁלְּזָהָב וּבְיַד זֶה פְּרוּטְרוֹט. זֶה שֶׁבְּיָדוֹ עֲשָׁתוֹת שֶׁלְּזָהָב אֵינוֹ מוֹצִיא וְחָיָה. וְזֶה שֶׁבְּיָדוֹ פְּרוּטְרוֹט מוֹצִיא וְחָיָה.

Rebbi Samuel, son of Rebbi Yose ben Rebbi Abun[311], preached: *A rich man is wise in his own eyes, but an understanding poor man will think little of him.* [312]*A rich man is wise in his own eyes,* this is the master of Talmud. *But an understanding poor man will think little of him*[313], that is the master of homiletics. A parable of two people who entered a city, in the hand of one are gold bars, in the other's hand small change. The holder of the gold bars cannot spend them and survive; the holder of small change can spend it to survive[314].

311 One of the very last Amoraim mentioned in the Yerushalmi. He explains why his generation turned from work on a Talmud to work on Midrashim.

312 *Prov.* 28:11. *Eccl. rabba* 6:2, end.
313 Cf. Arabic حقر "to despise somebody or something, think little of him."
314 Nobody comes to hear lectures on Talmud, everybody comes to hear a preacher. Cf. Babli *Bava batra* 145b. For a negative view of homiletics three generations earlier cf. *Ma`serot* 3:10 Note 161 (Sopherim Chapter 15).

(48c line 25) דָּרַשׁ רִבִּי אָחָא. פֶּלֶס | וּמֹאזְנֵי מִשְׁפָּט לַיי מַעֲשֵׂהוּ כָּל־אַבְנֵי־כִיס׃ פֶּלֶס זֶה הַמִּקְרָא. מֹאזְנֵי זֶה הַמִּשְׁנָה. מִשְׁפָּט זֶה הַתַּלְמוּד. לַיי זֶה תַתּוֹסֶפֶת. מַעֲשֵׂהוּ כָּל־אַבְנֵי־כִיס. כּוּלְּהֶם נוֹטְלִין שְׂכָרָן מִכִּיס אֶחָד.

Rebbi Aḥa preached: *Scales and balances of justice are the Eternal's; His work are all stones in the purse*[315]. "Scales" is Scripture. "Balances" are the Mishnah. "Justice" is the Talmud. "The Eternal's" are the additions[316]. *His work are all stones in the purse*; they all take their wages from the same purse.

315 *Prov.* 16:11. The purse is the container in which weight stones are kept (*Deut.* 25:13, *Mi.* 6:11). It may also mean the wallet where money is kept, *Prov.* 1:14, *Is.* 46:6. The sermon identifies the two and declares all religious studies of equal value.
316 The extra-talmudic texts; not only Tosephta collections but also Midrashim and similar compositions.

(48c line 28) רִבִּי אַבָּא בַּר כַּהֲנָא אֲזַל לְחַד אֲתַר. אַשְׁכַּח רִבִּי לֵוִי יָתִיב דָּרַשׁ. אִישׁ אֲשֶׁר יִתֶּן־לוֹ הָאֱלֹהִים עוֹשֶׁר וּנְכָסִים וְכָבוֹד וְאֵינֶנּוּ חָסֵר לְנַפְשׁוֹ | מִכֹּל אֲשֶׁר־יִתְאַוֶּה וְלֹא־יַשְׁלִיטֶנּוּ הָאֱלֹהִים לֶאֱכוֹל מִמֶּנּוּ כִּי אִישׁ נָכְרִי יֹאכְלֶנּוּ. עוֹשֶׁר זֶה הַמִּקְרָא. נְכָסִים אֵילּוּ הֲלָכוֹת. וְכָבוֹד זֶה הַתּוֹסֶפֶת. וְאֵינֶנּוּ חָסֵר לְנַפְשׁוֹ | מִכֹּל אֲשֶׁר־יִתְאַוֶּה. אֵילּוּ מִשְׁנָיוֹת גְּדוֹלוֹת כְּגוֹן מִשְׁנָתוֹ שֶׁלְּרִבִּי חוּנָה מִשְׁנָתוֹ שֶׁלְּרִבִּי הוֹשַׁעְיָה וּמִשְׁנָתוֹ שֶׁלְּבַר קַפָּרָא. וְלֹא־יַשְׁלִיטֶנּוּ הָאֱלֹהִים לֶאֱכוֹל מִמֶּנּוּ. זֶה בַּעַל אֲגָדָה שֶׁאֵינוֹ לֹא אוֹסֵר וְלֹא מַתִּיר לֹא מְטַמֵּא וְלֹא מְטַהֵר. כִּי אִישׁ נָכְרִי יֹאכְלֶנּוּ. זֶה בַּעַל הַתַּלְמוּד. קָם רִבִּי אַבָּא בַּר כַּהֲנָא וְנַשְׁקֵיהּ בְּרֵישֵׁיהּ. אֲמַר. זָכִיתָה מֵימְרִינָהּ יְקִים תִּזְכֵּי מֵימְרִינָהּ מֵיתִיב.

[317]Rebbi Abba bar Cahana went to a certain place where he found Rebbi Levi installed and preaching: *A man to whom God gives riches, and properties, and honor, and nothing is missing of anything he might desire, but God does not let him take possession to eat from it, for a stranger will eat from it*[318]. *Riches*, that is Scripture. *Properties*, these are practices[319]. *And honor*, these are the additions[316]. *And nothing is missing of anything he might desire,* these are the great Mishnah collections[320], such as the Mishnah of

Rebbi Huna[321], the Mishnah of Rebbi Hoshaia, or the Mishnah of Bar Qappara. *But God does not let him take possession to eat from it,* that is the master of Aggadah who neither prohibits nor permits, neither declares impure nor pure. *For a stranger will eat from it*, that is the master of Talmud[322]. Rebbi Abba bar Cahana got up and kissed him on his head, saying, just as you were worthy to preach this standing, may you be worthy preaching this sitting[323].

317 *Eccl. rabba* 6:2.

318 *Eccl.* 6:2.

319 A code of practices in a culture of oral transmission was a very valuable property.

320 *Baraita* collections such as underlying the later Tosephta, or Mishnah collections preceding or competing with Rebbi's Mishnah. *Eccl. rabba* adds R. Aqiba's Mishnah.

321 No collection of Rebbi Huna is known; also he would be an Amora of a later generation, unable to collect an independent collection. In *Eccl. rabba*, the reference is correctly to R. Hiyya (the Elder.)

322 Who has to master all the preceding topics and has the right to decide between forbidden and permitted acts.

323 R. Levi, who became the foremost preacher of his time, at this moment was rabbi of a small congregation who delivered his sermons in person standing in front of his congregation. R. Abba blessed him that he should become the head of a school who would deliver the concept of his speech to an Amora, a professional speaker, who would elaborate on the topics given to him by the head who remained seated.

(48c line 38) בִּיקְשׁוּ לְמְנוֹת זְקֵינִים מֵאֵכָן הֵן מְמַנִּין. מִטִּיבֵּרְיָּה אִמִּדְּרוּמָה. אָמַר רִבִּי סִימוֹן. יְהוּדָה יַעֲלֶה. אָמַר לֵיהּ רִבִּי מָנָא. הָדָא דְתֵימַר לַמִּלְחָמָה. אֲבָל לְמִנּוּיֵי רוֹאֵי פְּנֵי הַמֶּלֶךְ הַיּוֹשְׁבִים רִאשׁוֹנָה בַּמַּלְכוּת.

רִבִּי יַעֲקֹב בַּר אִידִי בְּשֵׁם רִבִּי יְהוֹשֻׁעַ בֶּן לֵוִי. מַעֲשֶׂה שֶׁנִּכְנְסוּ זְקֵינִים לַעֲלִיַּית בֵּית גַּדְיָיא בִּירִיחוֹ וְיָצְתָה בַּת קוֹל וְאָמְרָה לָהֶן. יֵשׁ בֵּינֵיכֶם שְׁנַיִם רְאוּיִין לְרוּחַ הַקּוֹדֶשׁ וְהִלֵּל הַזָּקֵן אֶחָד מֵהֶן. נָתְנוּ עֵינֵיהֶן בִּשְׁמוּאֵל הַקָּטָן. שׁוּב נִכְנְסוּ זְקֵינִים לַעֲלִייָה בְּיַבְנֶה וְיָצְתָה בַּת קוֹל וְאָמְרָה לָהֶן. יֵשׁ בֵּינֵיכֶם שְׁנַיִם רְאוּיִין לְרוּחַ הַקּוֹדֶשׁ וּשְׁמוּאֵל הַקָּטָן אֶחָד מֵהֶן. נָתְנוּ עֵינֵיהֶן בֶּאֱלִיעֶזֶר בֶּן הוּרְקָנוֹס. וְהָיוּ שְׂמֵיחִין עַל שֶׁהִסְכִּימָה דַּעְתָּן לְדַעַת רוּחַ הַקּוֹדֶשׁ.

If they intended to appoint Elders, from where do they appoint? From Tiberias or from the South[324]? Rebbi Simon said, *Jehudah shall go first*[325]. Rebbi Mana said to him, this refers to war. But for ordination, *those who see the face of the king, sitting first in government*[326].

[327]Rebbi Jacob bar Idi in the name of Rebbi Joshua ben Levi: It happened that the Elders assembled in the upper story of the House Gadya at Jericho when there came a disembodied voice and told them, there are two among you worthy of the Holy Spirit and one of them is Hillel the Elder. They looked at Samuel Minor. Then the Elders assembled in the upper story at Jabneh when there came a disembodied voice and told them, there are two among you worthy of the Holy Spirit and one of them is Samuel Minor. They looked at Eliezer ben Hyrcanos. They were happy that their opinion coincided with that of the Holy Spirit[327].

324 The main Academy was at Tiberias in Galilee. There were minor centers of learning in the South, at Lydda and at Kefar Darom, in the plain which in Second Temple times was part of Judea. The question was which center of learning should be the first to propose candidates for ordination by the Patriarch.

325 *Jud.* 1:2. R. Simon came from the South.

326 *Esther* 1:14. The preeminent rabbis at this time were in Tiberias.

327 The same text in *Sotah* 9:17 Note 265; most of the story in greater detail *Sotah* 9:13-14, Notes 212-218, and the parallels given there in Note 212.

(48c line 48) אִילֵין דְּבַר פָּזִי וּדְבַר הוֹשַׁעְיָה הֲווּ עָלִין וּשְׁאֵלִין בִּשְׁלָמֵיהּ דִּנְשִׂיָּא בְּכָל־יוֹם. וַהֲווֹן אִילֵין דְּרִבִּי הוֹשַׁעְיָה עָלִין קַדְמַאי. אָזְלוֹן אִילֵין דְּבַר פָּזִי וְאִיתְחַתְּנוּן בִּנְשִׂיאוּתָא. אֲתוֹן בְּעוֹן מֵיעוֹל קַדְמַאי. אֲתוֹן וּשְׁאָלוֹן לְרִבִּי אִימִּי. וַהֲקֵמוֹתָ אֶת־הַמִּשְׁכָּן כְּמִשְׁפָּטוֹ. וְכִי יֵשׁ מִשְׁפָּט לָעֵצִים. אֶלָּא אֵי זֶה קֶרֶשׁ זָכָה לִינָּתֵן בַּצָּפוֹן יִינָּתֵן בַּצָּפוֹן. בַּדָּרוֹם יִינָּתֵן בַּדָּרוֹם.

1 ודבר | ודר' הושעיה | יהושעי' ושאלין | שאלון דנשייא | דנשיא 2 הושעיה | יהושעיא קדמאי | קדמיי ונפקין קדמיי אזלון | - ואיתחתנון | ואיתחתננון אתון בעון | ובעון 3 מיעול קדמאי | למיפק קדמיי ושאלון | ובעון אימי | אמי 4 לינתן | להנתן ייתנן בצפון בדרום ייתנן בדרום | ואי זה קרקש זבה להנתן בדרום

תַּרְתֵּין זַרְעִין בְּצִיפּוֹרִין בּוּלֶווּטַיָּא וּפַגָּנַיָּא הֲווּ עָלִין וּשְׁאֵלִין בִּשְׁלָמֵיהּ דִּנְשִׂיָּא בְּכָל־יוֹם. וַהֲווֹן בּוּלֶווּטַיָּא עָלִין קַדְמַאי וְנָפְקִין קַדְמַיי. אָזְלוֹן פַּגָּנַיָּא וְזָכוֹן לְאוֹרַיְיתָא. אֲתוֹן בְּעוֹן מֵיעוֹל קַדְמַאי. אִישְׁתָּאֲלַת לְרִבִּי שִׁמְעוֹן בֶּן לָקִישׁ. שָׁאֲלָהּ רִבִּי שִׁמְעוֹן בֶּן לָקִישׁ לְרִבִּי יוֹחָנָן. אָעַל רִבִּי יוֹחָנָן וּדְרָשָׁהּ בְּבֵית מִדְרָשָׁא דְּרִבִּי בְנָיָה. אֲפִילוּ מַמְזֵר תַּלְמִיד חָכָם וְכֹהֵן גָּדוֹל עַם הָאָרֶץ מַמְזֵר תַּלְמִיד חָכָם קוֹדֵם לְכֹהֵן גָּדוֹל עַם הָאָרֶץ׃ סָבְרִין מֵימַר. לִיפָּדוֹת וּלְהַחֲיוֹת וְלִכְסוּת. הָא לִישִׁיבָה לֹא. אָמַר רִבִּי אָבוּן. אַף לִישִׁיבָה. וּמַה טַעַם׃ יְקָרָה הִיא מִפְּנִינִים. וַאֲפִילוּ מִזֶּה שֶׁהוּא נִכְנָס לִפְנַיי לְפָנִים.

1 זרעין | B זרעייא הוון ש זרעיין הוון בציפורין | Bש בצפרין בולווטייא | B בוולבטיה ש בולווטיא ופגנייא | B ופגנייה ש ופגניא הוו | Bש הוון עלין | ש - ושאלין | B ושאלון ש שאלין דנשייא | B דנשיא 2

בולווטייא | B בולוטייא ש בולווטיא קדמאי | Bש קדמיי (2X) פגנייא | B פגנייה לאורייתא | B לאוריתא ש באוריתא 3 קדמאי | B - ש קדמיי אישתאלת | B אשתאלת שאלה | B שאל אעל | B על 4 בבית | B בי ש בבי דר' בנייה | B דטבריא 5 ליפדות | Bש לפדות ולהחיות ולכסות | ש ולכסות ולהחיות 6 ומה | Bש מה מפניינים | B מפנינם 7 לפניי | B לפני

Those of Bar Pazi and (Bar) [Rebbi][328] Hoshaia went and greeted the Patriarch every day. Those of Rebbi Hoshaia went in first [and left first][329]. Those of Bar Pazi went and became related by marriage to the patriarchate. They came and wanted to enter first. They went and asked Rebbi Immi. *You shall erect the tabernacle according to its ruling*[330]. Does there exist a ruling for wood? But the log which merited to be put in the North should be put in the North, in the South should be put in the South.

[331]Two families were in Sepphoris, one of city councillors[332] and one rural[333], who were greeting the Patriarch every day. The councillors went in first and left first. The rural ones went and acquired [knowledge in] Torah. They came and wanted to have precedence. It was asked before Rebbi Simeon ben Laqish. Rebbi Simeon ben Laqish asked it from Rebbi Johanan. Rebbi Johanan went up and preached in Rebbi Benaiah's house of study[334]: "But if the bastard was learned and the High Priest ignorant, the learned bastard precedes the ignorant High Priest[335]." They wanted to say, to be redeemed, for livelihood, and for clothing, but not for the Academy. Rebbi Abun said, even for the Academy. What is the reason? *It is more precious than pearls*[336], even than he who enters into the Most Holy [of the Sanctuary.]

328 The text of L is in parentheses, the one from B in bracketrs. Since the second family is also called "R. Hoshaia's" later in L, and the entire story makes sense only if this family was distinguished in learning, the reading from B has to be accepted.

329 *Ex.* 26:30. This argument is a legal argument of R. Immi's in *Šabbat* 12:3 (13c l. 60). The Mishnah states that it is a prosecutable sin to write two letters on the Sabbath. Since the Sabbath prohibition is repeated after the instructions for building the Tabernacle (*Ex.* 31:12-17; 35:1-3) it is concluded that the forbidden actions on the Sabbath are exactly those which were necessary for the construction of the Tabernacle. R. Immi explains that all logs which formed the walls of the Tabernacle carried two letters and that sides bearing the same letters were put together when the Tabernacle was re-assembled after being transported. This is taken here as a sign that nothing should be changed; marrying into the family of the patriarch cannot erase the advantage conferred by

learning.

330 *Ex.* 26:30.

331 A parallel text (ש) is in *Šabbat* 12:3 (13c l. 62 ff.) The text here is primary; there the story is told as an appendix to the argument of R. Immi which, however, responds not to the question asked about precedence but about Sabbath prohibitions as explained in Note 329.

332 Greek βουλευταί.

333 Latin *pagani.*

334 The text of B, "of Tiberias" has to be rejected. Not only is the text of L confirmed by the text in *Šabbat*, but also the remark that he "went up" refers to going from Tiberias below Sea level to Sepphoris high in the mountains but also the entire story is placed at Sepphoris and only there a public ruling was needed.

335 Mishnah 3:9.

336 *Prov..* 3:15.

Indices

Sigla

Parallel Texts from Yerushalmi Tractates

Chapter 11	א	Avodah zarah	ע
Beṣah	ב	Pesahim	פ
Horaiot	ה	Bava qamma	ק
Yoma	ו	Roš Haššanah	ר
Chapter 8	ח	Ševuot	ש
Yebamot	י	Šabbat	שׂ
Ketubot	כ	Berakhot	ת
Megillah	מ	Kilaim	ך
Soṭah	ס	Ševi`it	7

Manuscript texts and early prints

Yerushalmi Horaiot in Bomberg Babli	B	Leiden Manuscript	L
Genizah Texts	G		

Index of Biblical Quotations

Index of Talmudical Quotations

Babylonian Talmud

Jerusalem Talmud

Mishnah

Tosephta

Midrashim and Minor Tractates

Rabbinic Literature

Index of Greek, Latin, and Hebrew Words

Author Index

Subject Index